Transactions of the Association for Computational Linguistics

(TACL 2014)

TACL Volume 2, Issue 1

ISBN: 978-1-63439-612-7

Printed from e-media with permission by:

Curran Associates, Inc.
57 Morehouse Lane
Red Hook, NY 12571

proceedings.com

Some format issues inherent in the e-media version may also appear in this print version.

Printed by Curran Associates, Inc. (2014)

Association for Computational Linguistics
209 N. Eighth Street
Stroudsburg, Pennsylvania 18360

Phone: 1-570-476-8006
Fax: 1-570-476-0860

acl@aclweb.org

Additional copies of this publication are available from:

Curran Associates, Inc.
57 Morehouse Lane
Red Hook, NY 12571 USA
Phone: 845-758-0400
Fax: 845-758-2634
Email: curran@proceedings.com
Web: www.proceedings.com

TABLE OF CONTENTS

Heterogeneous Networks and Their Applications: Scientometrics, Name Disambiguation, and Topic Modeling

Ben King, Rahul Jha
Department of EECS
University of Michigan
Ann Arbor, MI
{benking,rahuljha}@umich.edu

Dragomir R. Radev
Department of EECS
School of Information
University of Michigan
Ann Arbor, MI
radev@umich.edu

Abstract

We present heterogeneous networks as a way to unify lexical networks with relational data. We build a unified ACL Anthology network, tying together the citation, author collaboration, and term-cooccurence networks with affiliation and venue relations. This representation proves to be convenient and allows problems such as name disambiguation, topic modeling, and the measurement of scientific impact to be easily solved using only this network and off-the-shelf graph algorithms.

1 Introduction

Graph-based methods have been used to great effect in NLP, on problems such as word sense disambiguation (Mihalcea, 2005), summarization (Erkan and Radev, 2004), and dependency parsing (McDonald et al., 2005). Most previous studies of networks consider networks with only a single type of node, and in some cases using a network with a single type of node can be an oversimplified view if it ignores other types of relationships.

In this paper we will demonstrate *heterogeneous networks*, networks with multiple different types of nodes and edges, along with several applications of them. The applications in this paper are not presented so much as robust attempts to out-perform the current state-of-the-art, but rather attempts at being competitive against top methods with little effort beyond the construction of the heterogeneous network.

Throughout this paper, we will use the data from the ACL Anthology Network (AAN) (Bird et al., 2008; Radev et al., 2013), which contains additional metadata relationships not found in the ACL Anthology, as a typical heterogeneous network. The results in this paper should be generally applicable to other heterogeneous networks.

1.1 Heterogeneous AAN schema

We build a heterogeneous graph $G(V, E)$ from AAN, where V is the set of vertices and E is the set of edges connecting vertices. A vertex can be one of five semantic types: {paper, author, venue, institution, term}. An edge can also be one of five types, each connecting different types of vertices:

- author — [writes] — paper
- paper — [cites] — paper
- paper — [published in] — venue[1]
- author — [affiliated with] — institution[2]
- paper — [contains] — term

All of this data, except for the terms, is available for all papers in the 2009 release of AAN. Terms are extracted from titles by running TextRank (Mihalcea and Tarau, 2004) on NP-chunks from titles and manually filtering out bad terms.

We show the usefulness of this representation in several applications: the measurement of scientific impact (Section 2), name disambiguation (Section 3), and topic modeling (Section 4). The heterogeneous network representation provides a simple framework for combining lexical networks (like the term co-occurence network) with metadata relations from a source like AAN and allows us to begin to develop NLP-aware methods for problems like scientometrics and name disambiguation, which are not usually framed in an NLP perspective.

[1] For a joint meeting of venues A and B publishing a paper x, two edges (x, A) and (x, B) are created.

[2] Author-affiliation edges are weighted according to the number of papers an author has published from an institution.

Transactions of the Association for Computational Linguistics, 2 (2014) 1–14. Action Editor: Lillian Lee.
Submitted 3/2013; Revised 6/2013; Published 2/2014.

2 Scientific Impact Measurement

The study of scientometrics, which attempts to quantify the scientific impact of papers, authors, etc. has received much attention recently, even within the NLP community. In the past few years, there have been many proposed measures of scientific impact based on relationships between entities. Intuitively, a model that can take into account many different types of relationships between entities should be able to measure scientific impact more accurately than simpler measures like citation counts or h-index.

We propose using *Pagerank on the heterogeneous AAN* (Page et al., 1999) to measure scientific impact. Since changes in the network schema can affect the relative rankings between different types of entities, this method is probably not appropriate for comparing entities of two different types against each other. But between nodes of the same type, this measure is an appropriate (and as we will show, accurate) way to compare impacts.

We see this method as a first logical step in the direction of heterogeneous network-based scientometrics. This method could easily be extended to use a directed schema (Kurland and Lee, 2005) or a schema that is aware of the lexical content of citation sentences, such as sentiment-based signed networks (Hassan et al., 2012).

Determining the intrinsic quality of scientific impact measures can be difficult since there is no way to collect gold standard measurements for real-world entities. Previous studies have attempted to show that their measures give high scores to a few known high-impact entities, *e.g.* Nobel prize winners (Hirsch, 2005), or have performed a statistical component analysis to find the most important measures in a group of related statistics (Bollen et al., 2009). Our approach, instead, is to generate *realistic* data from *synthetic* entities whose impacts are known.

We had considered alternative formulations that did not rely on synthetic data, but each of them presented problems. When we attempted manual prominence annotation for AAN data, the inter-judge agreement (measured by Spearman correlation) in our experiments ranged from decent (0.9 in the case of institutions) to poor (0.3 for authors) to nearly random (0.03 for terms), far too low to use in most cases. We also considered evaluating prominence measures by their ability to predict future citations to an entity. Citations are often used as a proxy for impact, but our measurements have found that correlation between past citations and future citations is too high for citation prediction to be a meaningful evaluation[3].

2.1 Creating a synthetic AAN

In network theory, a common technique for testing network algorithms when judgments of real-world data are expensive or impossible to obtain is to test the algorithm on a synthetic network. To create such a synthetic network, the authors define a simple, but realistic generative process by which the real-world networks of interest may arise. The properties of the network are measured to ensure that it replicates certain observable behaviors of the real-world network. They can then test network algorithms to see how well they are able to recover the hidden parameters that generated the synthetic network. (Pastor-Satorras and Vespignani, 2001; Clauset et al., 2009; Karrer and Newman, 2011)

We take a two-step approach to generating this synthetic data, first generating entities with known impacts, and second, linking these entities together according to their latent impacts. Our heuristic is that high impact entities should be linked to other high impact entities and vice-versa. As in the network theory literature, we must show that this data reflects important properties observed in the true AAN.

One such property is that the number of citations per paper follows a power law distribution (Redner, 1998). We observe this behavior in AAN along with several other small-world behaviors, such as a small diameter, a small average shortest path length, and a high clustering coefficient in the coauthorship graph. We strive to replicate these properties in our synthetic data.

[3]Most existing impact measurements require access to at least one year's worth of citation information. The Spearman correlation between the number of citations received after one year and after five years is 0.79 with correlation between successive years as high as 0.99. Practically this means that the measures that best correlate with citations after five years are exactly those that best correlate with citations after one year.

Since scientific impact measures attempt to quantify the true impact of entities, we can use these measures to help understand how the true impact measures are distributed across different entities. In fact, citation counts, being a good estimate of impact, can be used to generate these latent impact variables for each entity. For each type of entity (papers, authors, institutions, venues, and terms), we create a latent impact by sampling from the appropriate citation count distribution. After sampling, all the impacts are normalized to fall in the $[0, 1]$ interval, with the highest-impact entity of each type having a latent impact of 1. Additive smoothing is used to avoid having an impact of 0.

Once we have created the entities, our method for placing edges is most similar to the Erdős-Réyni method for creating random graphs (Erdős and Rényi, 1960), in which edges are distributed uniformly at random between pairs of vertices. Instead of distributing links uniformly, links between entities are sampled proportionally to $I(a)I(b)(1 - (I(a) - I(b))^2)$, where $I(x)$ is the latent impact of entity x.

We tried several other formulae that failed to replicate the properties of the real AAN. The $I(a)I(b)$ part of the formula above reflects a preference for nodes of any type to connect with high-impact entities (*e.g.*, major conferences receive many submissions even though most submissions will be rejected), but the $1 - (I(a) - I(b))^2$ part also reflects the reality that entities of similar prominence are most likely to attach to each other (*e.g.*, well-known authors publish in major conferences, while less well-known authors may publish mostly in lesser-known workshops).

Using this distribution, we randomly sample links between papers and authors; authors and institutions; papers and venues; and papers and terms. The only exception to this was paper-to-paper citation links, for which we did not expect this same behavior to apply, as low-impact papers regularly cite high-impact papers, but not *vice-versa*. To model citations, we selected citing papers uniformly at random and cited papers in proportion to their impacts. (Albert and Barabási, 2002)

Finally, we generated a network equal in size to AAN, that is, with the exact same numbers of papers, authors, etc. and the exact same number of paper-author links, paper-venue links, etc. Table 1 compares the observed properties of the true AAN with the observed properties of this synthetic version of AAN. None of the statistics are exact matches, but when building random graphs, it is not uncommon for measures to differ by many orders of magnitude, so a model that has measures that are on the same order of magnitude as the observed data is generally considered to be a decent model (Newman and Park, 2003).

Relationship	True value	Synth. value
Paper-citations power law coeff.	1.82	2.12
Diameter	9	8
Avg. shortest path	4.27	4.05
Collaboration network clustering coeff.	0.34	0.26

Table 1: Network properties of the synthetic AAN compared with the true AAN.

2.2 Measuring impact on the synthetic AAN

This random network is, of course, still imperfect in some regards. First of all, it has no time aspect, so it is not possible for impact to change over time, which means we cannot test against some impact measures that have a time component like CiteRank (Maslov and Redner, 2008). Second, there are some constraints present in the real world that are not enforced here. Because the edges are randomly selected, some papers have no venues, while others have multiple venues. There is also nothing to enforce certain consistencies, such as authors publishing many papers from relatively few institutions, or repeatedly collaborating with the same authors.

We had also considered using existing random graph models such as the Barabási-Albert model (Barabási and Albert, 1999), which are known to produce graphs that exhibit power law behavior. These models, however, do not provide a way to respect the latent impacts of the entities, as they add links in proportion only to the number of existing links a node has.

We measure the quality of impact measures by comparing ranked lists: the ordering of the entities

Paper measure	Agreement
Heterogeneous network Pagerank	**0.773**
Citation network Pagerank	0.558
Citation count	0.642
Author measure	**Agreement**
Heterogeneous network Pagerank	**0.461**
Coauthorship network Pagerank	0.244
h-index (Hirsch, 2005)	0.292
Aggregated citation count	0.236
i10-index	0.235
Institution measure	**Agreement**
Heterogeneous network Pagerank	**0.373**
h-index (Mitra, 2006)	0.334
Aggregated citation count	0.327
Venue measure	**Agreement**
Heterogeneous network Pagerank	**0.449**
h-index (Braun et al., 2006)	0.425
Aggregated citation count	0.370
Impact factor	0.092
Venue citation network Pagerank (Bollen et al., 2006)	0.366

Table 2: Agreement of various impact measures with the true latent impact.

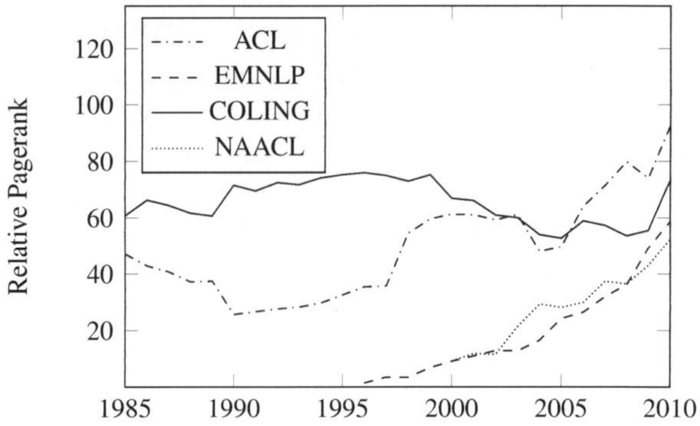

Figure 1: Evolution of conference impacts. The y-axis measures relative Pagerank, the entity's Pagerank relative to the average Pagerank in that year.

by their true (but hidden) impact against their ordering according to the impact measure. The agreement between these lists is measured by Kendall's Tau. Table 2 compares several well-known impact measures with our impact measure, Pagerank centrality on the heterogeneous AAN network. We find that some popular methods, such as h-index (Hirsch, 2005) are too coarse to accurately capture much of the underlying variation. There is a version of Kendall's Tau that accounts for ties, and while this metric slightly helps the coarser measures, Pagerank on the heterogeneous network is still the clear winner.

When comparing different ordering methods, it is natural to wonder which of entities the orderings disagree on. In general, non-heterogeneous measures like h-index or collaboration network Pagerank, which only focus on one type of relationship can suffer when the entity in question has an important relationship of another type. For example, if an author is highly cited, but mostly works alone, his contribution would be undervalued in the collaboration network, but would be more accurate in the heterogeneous network.

The majority of the differences between the impact measures, though, tend to be in how they handle entities of low prominence. It seems that, for the most part, there is relatively little disagreement in the orderings of high-impact entities between different impact measures. That is, most highly prominent entities tend to be highly rated by most measures. But when an author or a paper, for example, only has one or two citations, it can be advantageous to look at more types of relationships than just citations. The paper may be written by an otherwise prominent author, or published at a well-known venue, and having many types of relations at its disposal can help a method like heterogeneous network Pagerank better distinguish between two low-prominence entities.

2.3 Top-ranked entities according to heterogeneous network PageRank

Table 3 shows the papers, authors, institutions, venues, and terms that received the highest Pagerank in the heterogeneous AAN. It is obvious that the top-ranked entities in this network are not simply the most highly cited entities.

This ranking also does not have any time bias toward the entities that are currently prominent, as some of the top authors were more prolific in previous decades than at the current time. We also see this effect with COLING, which for many of the early years, is the only venue in the ACL Anthology.

	Top Papers		Top Authors		Top Institutions		Top Venues		Top Terms
–	Building A Large Annotated Corpus Of English: The Penn Treebank	△ 15	Jun'ichi Tsujii	△ 8	Carnegie Mellon University	△ 1	COLING	–	translation
–	The Mathematics Of Statistical Machine Translation: Parameter Estimation	△ 7	Aravind K. Joshi	△ 1	University of Edinburgh	▽ 1	ACL	△ 3	speech
–	Attention, Intentions, And The Structure Of Discourse	△ 18	Ralph Grishman	▽ 2	University of Pennsylvania	△ 2	HLT	▽ 1	parsing
–	A Maximum Entropy Approach To Natural Language Processing	△ 75	Hitoshi Isahara	▽ 2	Massachusetts Institute of Technology	△ 4	EACL	▽ 1	machine translation
–	BLEU: a Method for Automatic Evaluation of Machine Translation	△ 20	Yuji Matsumoto	△ 12	Saarland University	△ 7	LREC	△ 3	generation
–	A Maximum-Entropy-Inspired Parser	△ 7	Kathleen R. McKeown	▽ 2	IBM T.J. Watson Research Center	–	NAACL	△ 3	evaluation
△ 2	A Stochastic Parts Program And Noun Phrase Parser For Unrestricted Text	△ 13	Eduard Hovy	△ 39	CNRS	▽ 3	EMNLP	△ 6	grammar
▽ 1	A Systematic Comparison of Various Statistical Alignment Models	△ 10	Christopher D. Manning	△ 26	University of Tokyo	▽ 5	Computational Linguistics	△ 16	dialogue
△ 4	Transformation-Based Error-Driven Learning and Natural Language Processing: a Case Study in Part-of-Speech Tagging	△ 93	Yorick Wilks	▽ 4	Stanford University	△ 4	IJCNLP	△ 10	knowl-edge
△ 1	A Maximum Entropy Model for Part-of-Speech Tagging	▽ 9	Hermann Ney	△ 3	BBN Technologies	△ 1	Workshop on Speech and Natural Language	△ 1	discourse

Table 3: The entities of each type receiving the highest scores from the heterogeneous network Pagerank impact measure along with their respective changes in ranking when compared to a simple citation count measure.

One possible way to address this is to use a narrower time window when creating the graph, such as only including edges from the previous five years. We apply this technique in the following section.

2.4 Entity impact evolution

The heterogeneous graph formalism also provides a natural way to study the *evolution of impact* over time, as in (Hall et al., 2008), but at a much finer granularity. Hall et al. measured the year-by-year prominence of statistical topics, but we can measure year-by-year prominence for any entity in the graph.

To measure the evolution of impacts over the years, we iteratively create year-by-year versions of the heterogeneous AAN. Each of these graphs contains all entities along with all edges occurring in a five year window. Due to space, we cannot comprehensively exhibit this technique and the data it produces, but as a brief example, in Figure 1, we show how the impacts of some major NLP conferences changes over time.

The graph shows that NAACL and EMNLP have been steadily gaining prominence since their introductions, but also shows that ACL has had to make up a lot of ground since 1990 to surpass COLING. We also notice that all the major conferences have grown in impact since 2005, and believe that as the field continues to grow, the major conferences will continue to become more and more important.

3 Name Disambiguation

We frame network name disambiguation in a link prediction setting (Taskar et al., 2003; Liben-Nowell and Kleinberg, 2007). The problems of name disambiguation and link prediction share many characteristics, and we have found that if two ambiguous name nodes are close enough to be selected by a link-prediction method, then they likely correspond to the same real-world author.

We intend to show that the heterogeneous bibliographic network can be used to better disambiguate author names than the author collaboration network. The heterogeneous network for this problem contains papers, authors, terms, venues, and institutions. We compare several well-known network similarity measures from link prediction by transforming the

Network	Distance Measure	Precision	Recall	F1-score	Rand index	Purity	NMI
Heterogeneous	Truncated Commute Time	0.59	0.78	0.63	0.63	0.71	0.43
Heterogeneous	Shortest Path	**0.90**	0.79	0.83	**0.87**	**0.94**	0.76
Heterogeneous	PropFlow	0.89	**0.83**	**0.84**	**0.87**	0.93	**0.77**
Coauthorship	Truncated Commute Time	0.47	0.80	0.54	0.47	0.60	0.18
Coauthorship	Shortest Path	0.54	0.73	0.60	0.61	0.67	0.31
Coauthorship	PropFlow	0.57	0.76	0.64	0.66	0.71	0.43
Coauthorship	GHOST	0.89	0.60	0.69	0.81	**0.94**	0.63

Table 4: Performance of different networks and distance measures on the author name disambiguation task. The performance measures are averaged over the sets of two, three, and four authors. Rand index is from (Rand, 1971) and NMI is an abbreviation for normalized mutual information (Strehl and Ghosh, 2003)

similarities to distances and inducing clusters of authors based on these distances.

We compare three distance measures: shortest path, truncated commute time (Sarkar et al., 2008), and PropFlow (Lichtenwalter et al., 2010). *Shortest path distance* can be a useful metric for author disambiguation because it is small when two ambiguous nodes are neighbors in the graph or share a neighbor. Its downside is that it only considers one path between nodes, the shortest, and cannot take advantage of the fact that there may be many short paths between two nodes.

Truncated commute time is a variant of commute time where all paths longer than some threshold are truncated. The truncation threshold l should be set such that no semantically meaningful path is truncated. We use a value of ten for l in the heterogeneous graph and three in the coauthorship graph[4]. The advantage of truncated commute time over ordinary commute time is simpler calculation, as no paths longer than l need be considered. The downside of this method is that large branching factors tend to lead to less agreement between commute time and truncated commute time.

PropFlow is a quantity that measures the probability that a non-intersecting random walk starting at node a reaches node b in l steps or fewer, where l is again a threshold. As before, l should be a bound on the length of semantically meaningful paths, so we use the same values for l as with truncated commute time. Of course, PropFlow is not a metric, which is required for some clustering methods. We use the following equation to transform PropFlow to a metric: $d(a, b) = \frac{1}{PropFlow(a,b)} - 1$.

With each of the distance measures, we apply the same clustering method: partitioning around medoids, with the number of clusters automatically determined using the gap statistic method (Tibshirani et al., 2001). We create the null distribution needed for the gap statistic method by many iterations of randomly sampling distances from the complete distance matrix between all nodes in the graph. The gap statistic method automatically selects the number of clusters from two, three, or four author clusters.

We compare our methods against GHOST (Fan et al., 2011), a high-performance author disambiguation method based on the coauthorship graph.

3.1 Data

To generate name disambiguation data, we use the *pseudoword method* of (Gale et al., 1992). Specifically, we choose two or more completely random authors and conflate them by giving all instances of both authors the same name. We let each paper written by this pseudoauthor be an instance to be clustered. The clusters produced by any author disambiguation method can then be compared against the papers actually written by each of the two authors. This method, of course, relies on having all of the underlying authors completely disambiguated, which AAN provides.

This method is used to create 100 distambiguation sets with two authors, 100 for three authors, and 100 for four authors.

[4]This is a standard coauthorship graph with the edge weights equal to the number of publications shared between authors. The heterogeneous network does not have author-to-author links, as authors are linked by paper nodes.

3.2 Results

Table 4 shows the performance of author name disambiguation with different networks and distance metrics. F1-score is the measure that is most often used to compare author disambiguation methods. Both PropFlow and shortest path similarity on the heterogeneous network perform quite well according this measure, as well as the other reported measures. While comparable recall can be achieved using only the coauthorship graph, the heterogeneous graph allows for much higher precision.

4 Random walk topic model

Here we present a topic model based entirely on graph random walks. This method is not truly a statistical model as there are no statistical parameters being learned, but rather a topic-discovery and -assignment method, attempting to solve the same problem as statistical topic models such as probabilistic latent semantic analysis (pLSA) (Hofmann, 1999) or latent Dirichlet allocation (LDA) (Blei et al., 2003). In the absence of better terminology, we use the name *random walk topic model.*

While this method does not have the robust mathematical foundation that statistical topic models possess, in its favor it has modularity, simplicity, and interpretability. This language model is *modular* as it completely separates the discovery of topics from the association of topics with entities. It is *simple* because it requires only a clustering algorithm and random walk algorithms, instead of complex inference algorithms. The method also does not require any modification if the topology of the network changes, whereas statistical models may need an entirely different inference procedure if, *e.g.*, author topics are desired in addition to paper topics. Thirdly this method is easily *interpretable* with topics provided by clustering in the word-relatedness graph and topic association based on random walks from entities to topics.

4.1 Topics from word graph clustering

From the set of ACL anthology titles, we create two graphs: (1) a *word relatedness graph* by creating a weighted link between each pair of words corresponding to the PropFlow (Lichtenwalter et al., 2010) measure between them on the full heterogeneous graph and (2) a *word co-occurence graph* by creating a weighted link between each pair of words corresponding to the number of titles in which both words occur.

Both of these graphs are then clustered using Graph Factorization Clustering (GFC). GFC is a soft clustering algorithm for graphs that models graph edges as a mixture of latent node-cluster association variables. (Yu et al., 2006)

Given a word graph G with vertices V and adjacency matrix $[w]_{ij}$, GFC attempts to fit a bipartite graph $K(V, U)$ with adjacency matrix $[b]_{ij}$ onto this data, with the m nodes of U representing the clusters. Whereas in G, similarity between two words i and j can be measured with w_{ij}, we can similarly measure their similarity in K with $w'_{ij} = \sum_{p=1}^{m} \frac{b_{ip}b_{jp}}{\lambda_p}$ where $\lambda_p = \sum_{i=1}^{n} b_{ip}$ is the degree of vertex $p \in U$.

Essentially the bipartite graph attempts to approximate the transition probability between i and j in G with the sum of transition probabilities from i to j through any of the m nodes in U. Yu, et al. (2006) present an algorithm for minimizing the divergence distance $\ell(\mathbf{X}, \mathbf{Y}) = \sum_{ij}(x_{ij} log \frac{x_{ij}}{yij} - x_{ij} + y_{ij})$ between $[w]_{ij}$ and $[w']_{ij}$.

We run GFC with this distance metric and $m = 100$ clusters on the word graph until convergence (change in log-likelihood $< 0.1\%$). After convergence, the nodes in U become the clusters and the weights b_{ip} (constrained to sum to 1 for each cluster) become the topic-word association scores.

Examples of some topics found by this method are shown in Table 5. From manual inspection of these topics, we found them to be very much like topics created by statistical topic models. We find instances of all the types of topics listed in (Mimno et al., 2011): chained, intruded, random, and unbalanced. For an evaluation of these topics see Section 4.3.1.

4.2 Entity-topic association

To associate entities with topics, we first create the heterogeneous network as in previous sections, adding links between papers and their title words, along with links between words and the topics that were discovered in the previous section. Word-topic links are also weighted according to the weights

Word sense induction	sense disambiguation word induction unsupervised clustering senses based similarity chinese
CRFs + their applications	entity named recognition random conditional fields chinese entities biomedical segmentation
Dependency parsing	parsing dependency projective probabilistic incremental deterministic algorithm data syntactic trees
Tagging	models tagging model latent markov conditional random parsing unsupervised segmentation
Multi-doc summarization	summarization multi document text topic based query extractive focused summaries
Chinese word segmentation	word segmentation chinese based alignment character tagging bakeoff model crf
Lexical semantics	lexical semantic distributional similarity wordnet resources lexicon acquistion semantics representation
Cross-lingual IR	cross lingual retrieval document language linguistic multi person multilingual coreference
Generation for summar.	sentence based compression text summarization ordering approach ranking generation
Spoken language	speech recognition automatic prosodic tagging spontaneous news broadcast understanding conversational
French function words	de la du des le automatique analyse une en pour
Question answering	question answering system answer domain retrieval web based open systems
Unsupervised learning	unsupervised discovery learning induction knowledge graph acquisition concept clustering pattern
SVMs for NLP	support vector machines errors space classification correcting word parsing detecting
MaxEnt models	entropy maximum approach based attachment model models phrase prepositional disambiguation
Dialogue systems	dialogue spoken systems human conversational multi interaction dialogues utterances multimodal
Semantic role-labeling	semantic role labeling parsing syntactic features ill dependency formed framenet
SMT	based translation machine statistical phrase english approach learning reordering model
Coreference resolution	resolution coreference anaphora reference pronoun ellipsis ambiguity resolving approach pronominal
Semi- and weak-supervision	learning supervised semi classification active data clustering approach graph weakly
Information retrieval	based retrieval similarity models semantic space model distance measures document
Discourse	discourse relations structure rhetorical coherence temporal representation text connectives theory
CFG parsing	context free grammars parsing linear probabilistic rewriting grammar systems optimal
Min. risk train. and decod.	minimum efficient training error rate translation risk bayes decoding statistical
Phonology	phoneme conversion letter phonological grapheme rules applying transliteration syllable sound
Sentiment	sentiment opinion reviews classification mining polarity analysis predicting product features
Neural net speech recog.	speech robust recognition real network time neural networks language environments
Finite state methods	state finite transducers automata weighted translation parsing incremental minimal construction
Mechanical Turk	mechanical turk automatic evaluation amazon techniques data articles image scientific

Table 5: Top 10 words for several topics created by the co-occurence random walk topic model. The left column is a manual label.

Topic 59		Topic 82	
translation	0.1953	parsing	0.1715
machine	0.1802	dependency	0.1192
statistical	0.0784	projective	0.0138
Machine Translation	0.0018	K-best Spanning Tree Parsing	0.0025
Better Hypothesis Testing for Statistical Machine Translation: Controlling for Optimizer Instability	0.0016	Pseudo-Projective Dependency Parsing	0.0024
Filtering Antonymous, Trend- Contrasting, and Polarity-Dissimilar Distributional Paraphrases for Improving Statistical Machine Translation	0.0015	Shift-Reduce Dependency DAG Parsing	0.0017
Knight, Kevin	0.0083	Nivre, Joakim	0.0120
Koehn, Philipp	0.0074	Johnson, Mark	0.0085
Ney, Hermann	0.0072	Nederhof, Mark-Jan	0.0064
RWTH Aachen University	0.0212	Vaxjo University	0.0113
Carnegie Mellon University	0.0183	Brown University	0.0107
University of Southern California	0.0177	University of Amsterdam	0.0094
Workshop on Statistical Machine Translation	0.0590	ACL	0.0512
EMNLP	0.0270	EMNLP	0.0259
COLING	0.0173	CoNLL	0.0223

Table 6: Examples of entities associated with selected topics.

determined by GCF. We then simply take random walks from topics to entities and measure the proportion at which the random walk arrives at each entity of interest. These proportions become the entity-topic association scores.

For example, if we wanted to find the authors most associated with topic 12, we would take a number of random walks (say 50,000) starting at topic 12 and terminating as soon as the random walk first reaches an author node. Measuring the proportion at which random walks arrive at each allows us to compute an association score between topic 12 and each author.

A common problem in random walks on large graphs is that the walk can easily get "lost" between two nodes that should be very near by taking a just a few steps in the wrong direction. To keep the random walks from taking these wrong steps, we adjust the topology of the network using directed links to keep the random walks moving in the "right" direction. We design the graph such that if we desire a random walk from nodes of type s to nodes of type t, the random walk will never be able to follow an outgoing link that does not decrease its distance from the nodes of t.

As shown in section 2.3, there are certain nodes at which a random walk (like Pagerank) arrives at more often than others simply because of their positions in the graph. This suggests that there may be stationary random walk distributions over entities, which we would need to adjust for in order to find the most *significant* entities for a topic.

Indeed this is what we do find. As an example, if we sample topics uniformly and take random walks to author nodes, by chance we end up at Jun'ichi Tsujii on 0.3% of random walks, Eduard Hovy on 0.2% of walks, etc. These values are about 1000 times greater than would be expected at random.

To adjust for this effect, when we take a random walk from a topic x to an entity type t, we subtract out this stationary distribution for t, which corresponds to the proportion of random walks that end at any particular entity of type t by chance, and not by virtue of the fact that the walk started at topic x. The resulting distribution yields the entities of t that are most significantly associated with topic x. Table 6 gives examples of the most significant entities for a couple of topics.

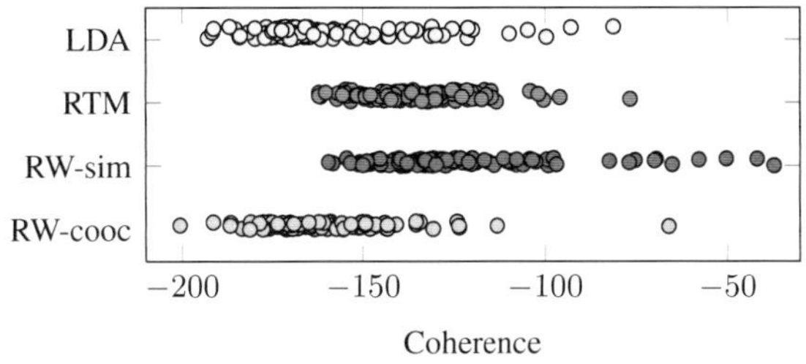

Figure 2: Distribution of topic coherences for the four topic models.

4.3 Topic Model Evaluation

We provide two separate evaluations in this section, one of the topics alone, and one extrinstic evaluation of the entire paper-topic model. The variants of random walk topic models are compared against LDA and the relational topic model (RTM), each with 100 topics (Chang and Blei, 2010). As RTM allows only a single type of relationship between documents, we use citations as the inter-document relationships.

4.3.1 Topic Coherence

The *coherence* of a topic is evaluated using the coherence metric introduced in (Mimno et al., 2011). Given the top M words $V^{(t)} = (v_1^{(t)}, ..., v_M^{(t)})$ for a topic t, the coherence of that topic can be calculated with the following formula:

$$C(t; V^{(t)}) = \sum_{m=2}^{M} \sum_{l=1}^{m-1} log \left(\frac{D(v_m^{(t)}, v_l^{(t)}) + 1}{D(v_l^{(t)})} \right),$$

where $D(v)$ is the number of documents containing v and $D(v, v')$ is the number of documents containing both v and v'.

This measure of coherence is highly correlated with manual annotations of topic quality, with a higher coherence score corresponding to a more coherent, higher quality topic. After calculating the coherence for each of the 100 topics for RTM and the random-walk topic model, the average coherence for RTM topics was -135.2 and the average coherence for word-similarity random walk topics was -122.2, with statistical significance at $p < 0.01$. Figure 2 demonstrates this, showing that the word similarity-based random walk method generates several highly coherent topics. The average coherence for the LDA and the co-occurence random walk model were significantly lower.

4.3.2 Extrinsic Evaluation

One difficulty in evaluating this random-walk topic model intrinsically against a statistical topic model like RTM is that existing evaluation measures assume certain statistical properties of the topic, for example, that the topics are generated according to a Dirichlet prior. Because of this, we choose instead to evaluate this topic model extrinsically with a downstream application. We choose an information retrieval application, returning a ranked list of similar documents, given a reference document.

We evaluate five different methods: citation-RTM, LDA, the two versions of the random-walk topic model, and a simple word vector similarity baseline. Similarity between documents with the topic models are determined by cosine similarity between the topic vectors of the two documents. Word vector similarity determines the similarity between documents by taking the cosine similarity of their word vectors. From these similarity scores, a ranked list is produced.

The document set for this task is the set of all papers appearing at ACL between 2000 and 2011. The top 10 results returned by each method are pooled and manually evaluated with a relevance score between 1 and 10. Thirty such result sets were manually annotated. We then evaluate each method according to its discounted cumulative gain (DCG) (Järvelin and Kekäläinen, 2000).

Performance of these methods is summarized in Table 7. The co-occurence-based random walk topic model performed comparably with the best performer at this task, LDA, and there was no significant difference between the two at $p < 0.05$.

Going forward, an important problem is to reconcile the co-occurence- and word-similarity-based formulations of this topic model, as the two formulations perform very differently in our two evaluations. Heuristically, the co-occurence model seems to create good human-readable topics, while the word-similarity model creates topics that are more mathematically-coherent, but less human-readable.

Method	DCG
Word vector	1.345 ± 0.007
LDA	3.302 ± 0.008
RTM	3.058 ± 0.011
Random-walk (cooc)	3.295 ± 0.006
Random-walk (sim)	2.761 ± 0.007

Table 7: DCG Performance of the various topic models and baselines on the related document finding task. A 95% confidence interval is provided.

5 Related Work

Heterogeneous networks have been studied in a number of different fields, such as biology (Sioson, 2005), transportation networks (Lozano and Storchi, 2002), social networks (Lambiotte and Ausloos, 2006), and bibliographic networks (Sun et al., 2011). These networks are also sometimes known by the name complex networks or multimodal networks, but both these terms have other connotations. We prefer "heterogeneous networks" as used by Sun et al. (2009).

There has also been some study of these networks in general, in community detection (Murata, 2010), clustering (Long et al., 2008; Sun et al., 2012), and data mining (Muthukrishnan et al., 2010), but there has not yet been any comprehensive study. Recently, NLP has seen several uses of heterogeneous networks (though not by that name) for use with label propagation algorithms (Das and Petrov, 2011; Speriosu et al., 2011) and random walks (Toutanova et al., 2004; Kok and Brockett, 2010).

Several authors have proposed the idea of using network centrality measures to rank the impacts of journals, authors, papers, etc. (Bollen et al., 2006; Bergstrom et al., 2008; Chen et al., 2007; Liu et al., 2005), and it has even been proposed that centrality can be applicable in bipartite networks (Zhou et al., 2007). We propose that Pagerank on any general heterogeneous network is appropriate for creating ranked lists for each type of entity. Most previous papers also lack a robust evaluation, demonstrating agreement with previous methods or with some external awards or recognitions. We use a random graph that replicates the properties of the real-world network to show that Pagerank on the heterogeneous network outperforms other methods.

Name disambiguation has been studied in a number of different settings, including graph-based settings. It is common to use the coauthorship graph (Kang et al., 2009; Fan et al., 2011), but authors have also used lexical similarity graphs (On and Lee, 2007), citation graphs (McRae-Spencer and Shadbolt, 2006), or social networks (Malin, 2005). Almost all graph methods are unsupervised.

There have been some topic models developed specifically for relational data (Wang et al., 2006; Airoldi et al., 2008), but both of these models have limitations in the types of relational data they are able to model. The group topic model described in (Wang et al., 2006) is able to create stronger topics by considering associations between words, events, and entities, but is very coarse in the way it handles the behavior of entities, and does not generalize to multiple different types of entities. The stochastic blockmodel of (Airoldi et al., 2008) can create blocks of similar entities in a graph and is general in the types of graphs it can handle, but produces less meaningful results on graphs that have specific schemas.

6 Conclusion and Future Directions

In this paper, we present a heterogeneous network treatment of the ACL Anthology Network and demonstrate several applications of it. Using only off-the-shelf graph algorithms with a single data representation, the heterogeneous AAN, we are able to very easily build a scientific impact measure that is more accurate than existing measures, an author disambiguation system better than existing graph-based author disambiguation systems, and a random-walk-based topic model that is competitive with statistical topic models.

While there are many other tasks, such as citation-based summarization, that could likely be approached using this framework with the appropriate addition of new types of nodes into the heterogeneous AAN network, there are even some potential synergies between the tasks described in this paper that have yet to be explored. For example, we may consider that the methods of the author disambiguation or topic modeling tasks could be to find the highest-impact papers associated with a term (for survey generation, perhaps) or high-impact authors associated with a workshop's topic (to select good reviewers for it). We believe that heterogeneous graphs are a flexible framework that will allow researchers to find simple, flexible solutions for a variety of problems.

Acknowledgments

This research is supported by the Intelligence Advanced Research Projects Activity (IARPA) via Department of Interior National Business Center (DoI/NBC) contract number D11PC20153. The U.S. Government is authorized to reproduce and distribute reprints for Governmental purposes notwithstanding any copyright annotation thereon. Disclaimer: The views and conclusions contained herein are those of the authors and should not be interpreted as necessarily representing the official policies or endorsements, either expressed or implied, of IARPA, DoI/NBC, or the U.S. Government.

References

Edoardo M. Airoldi, David M. Blei, Stephen E. Fienberg, and Eric P. Xing. 2008. Mixed membership stochastic blockmodels. *The Journal of Machine Learning Research*, 9:1981–2014.

Réka Albert and Albert-László Barabási. 2002. Statistical mechanics of complex networks. *Reviews of modern physics*, 74(1):47.

A.L. Barabási and R. Albert. 1999. Emergence of scaling in random networks. *Science*, 286(5439):509–512.

Carl T. Bergstrom, Jevin D. West, and Marc A. Wiseman. 2008. The eigenfactor metrics. *The Journal of Neuroscience*, 28(45):11433–11434.

Steven Bird, Robert Dale, Bonnie J Dorr, Bryan Gibson, Mark Joseph, Min-Yen Kan, Dongwon Lee, Brett Powley, Dragomir R Radev, and Yee Fan Tan. 2008. The ACL anthology reference corpus: A reference dataset for bibliographic research in computational linguistics. In *Proc. of the 6th International Conference on Language Resources and Evaluation Conference (LREC08)*, pages 1755–1759.

D.M. Blei, A.Y. Ng, and M.I. Jordan. 2003. Latent dirichlet allocation. *the Journal of machine Learning research*, 3:993–1022.

Johan Bollen, Marko A. Rodriguez, and Herbert Van de Sompel. 2006. Journal status. *CoRR*, abs/cs/0601030.

Johan Bollen, Herbert Van de Sompel, Aric Hagberg, and Ryan Chute. 2009. A principal component analysis of 39 scientific impact measures. *PloS one*, 4(6):e6022.

Tibor Braun, Wolfgang Glänzel, and András Schubert. 2006. A hirsch-type index for journals. *Scientometrics*, 69(1):169–173.

Jonathan Chang and David M Blei. 2010. Hierarchical relational models for document networks. *The Annals of Applied Statistics*, 4(1):124–150.

Peng Chen, Huafeng Xie, Sergei Maslov, and Sid Redner. 2007. Finding scientific gems with googles pagerank algorithm. *Journal of Informetrics*, 1(1):8–15.

Aaron Clauset, Cosma Rohilla Shalizi, and Mark EJ Newman. 2009. Power-law distributions in empirical data. *SIAM review*, 51(4):661–703.

Dipanjan Das and Slav Petrov. 2011. Unsupervised part-of-speech tagging with bilingual graph-based projections. In *Proceedings of the 49th Annual Meeting of the Association for Computational Linguistics: Human Language Technologies*, pages 600–609.

Paul Erdős and Alfréd Rényi. 1960. On the evolution of random graphs. *Magyar Tud. Akad. Mat. Kutató Int. Közl*, 5:17–61.

Günes Erkan and Dragomir R. Radev. 2004. Lexrank: Graph-based lexical centrality as salience in text summarization. *J. Artif. Intell. Res. (JAIR)*, 22:457–479.

Xiaoming Fan, Jianyong Wang, Xu Pu, Lizhu Zhou, and Bing Lv. 2011. On graph-based name disambiguation. *J. Data and Information Quality*, 2(2):10:1–10:23, February.

William A. Gale, Kenneth W. Church, and David Yarowsky. 1992. Work on statistical methods for word sense disambiguation. In *Working Notes of the AAAI Fall Symposium on Probabilistic Approaches to Natural Language*, volume 54, page 60.

David Hall, Daniel Jurafsky, and Christopher D. Manning. 2008. Studying the history of ideas using topic models. In *Proceedings of the Conference on Empirical Methods in Natural Language Processing*, pages 363–371. ACL.

Ahmed Hassan, Amjad Abu-Jbara, and Dragomir Radev. 2012. Extracting signed social networks from text. *TextGraphs-7*, page 6.

Jorge E. Hirsch. 2005. An index to quantify an individual's scientific research output. *Proceedings of the National Academy of Sciences of the United states of America*, 102(46):16569.

Thomas Hofmann. 1999. Probabilistic latent semantic indexing. In *Proceedings of the 22nd annual international ACM SIGIR conference on Research and development in information retrieval*, pages 50–57. ACM.

Kalervo Järvelin and Jaana Kekäläinen. 2000. IR evaluation methods for retrieving highly relevant documents. In *Proceedings of the 23rd annual international ACM SIGIR conference on Research and development in information retrieval*, pages 41–48. ACM.

In-Su Kang, Seung-Hoon Na, Seungwoo Lee, Hanmin Jung, Pyung Kim, Won-Kyung Sung, and Jong-Hyeok Lee. 2009. On co-authorship for author disambiguation. *Information Processing & Management*, 45(1):84–97.

Brian Karrer and Mark EJ Newman. 2011. Stochastic blockmodels and community structure in networks. *Physical Review E*, 83(1):016107.

Stanley Kok and Chris Brockett. 2010. Hitting the right paraphrases in good time. In *Human Language Technologies: The 2010 Annual Conference of the North American Chapter of the Association for Computational Linguistics*, pages 145–153. ACL.

Oren Kurland and Lillian Lee. 2005. Pagerank without hyperlinks: Structural reranking using links induced by language models. In *SIGIR '05*.

Renaud Lambiotte and Marcel Ausloos. 2006. Collaborative tagging as a tripartite network. *Computational Science–ICCS 2006*, pages 1114–1117.

David Liben-Nowell and Jon Kleinberg. 2007. The link-prediction problem for social networks. *Journal of the American society for information science and technology*, 58(7):1019–1031.

R.N. Lichtenwalter, J.T. Lussier, and N.V. Chawla. 2010. New perspectives and methods in link prediction. In *Proceedings of the 16th ACM SIGKDD international conference on Knowledge discovery and data mining*, pages 243–252. ACM.

Xiaoming Liu, Johan Bollen, Michael L. Nelson, and Herbert Van de Sompel. 2005. Co-authorship networks in the digital library research community. *Information processing & management*, 41(6):1462–1480.

Bo Long, Zhongfei Zhang, and Tianbing Xu. 2008. Clustering on complex graphs. In *Proc. the 23rd Conf. AAAI 2008*.

Angelica Lozano and Giovanni Storchi. 2002. Shortest viable hyperpath in multimodal networks. *Transportation Research Part B: Methodological*, 36(10):853–874.

Bradley Malin. 2005. Unsupervised name disambiguation via social network similarity. In *Workshop on Link Analysis, Counterterrorism, and Security*, volume 1401, pages 93–102.

Sergei Maslov and Sidney Redner. 2008. Promise and pitfalls of extending google's pagerank algorithm to citation networks. *The Journal of Neuroscience*, 28(44):11103–11105.

Ryan McDonald, Fernando Pereira, Kiril Ribarov, and Jan Hajič. 2005. Non-projective dependency parsing using spanning tree algorithms. In *Proceedings of the conference on Human Language Technology and Empirical Methods in Natural Language Processing*, pages 523–530. ACL.

Duncan M. McRae-Spencer and Nigel R. Shadbolt. 2006. Also by the same author: Aktiveauthor, a citation graph approach to name disambiguation. In *Proceedings of the 6th ACM/IEEE-CS joint conference on Digital libraries*, pages 53–54. ACM.

Rada Mihalcea and Paul Tarau. 2004. Textrank: Bringing order into texts. In *Proceedings of EMNLP*, volume 4, pages 404–411. Barcelona, Spain.

Rada Mihalcea. 2005. Unsupervised large-vocabulary word sense disambiguation with graph-based algorithms for sequence data labeling. In *Proceedings of HLT-EMNLP*, pages 411–418. ACL.

David Mimno, Hanna M. Wallach, Edmund Talley, Miriam Leenders, and Andrew McCallum. 2011. Optimizing semantic coherence in topic models. In *Proceedings of the Conference on Empirical Methods in Natural Language Processing*, pages 262–272. ACL.

Panchanan Mitra. 2006. Hirsch-type indices for ranking institutions scientific research output. *Current Science*, 91(11):1439.

Tsuyoshi Murata. 2010. Detecting communities from tripartite networks. In *Proceedings of the 19th international conference on World wide web*, pages 1159–1160. ACM.

Pradeep Muthukrishnan, Dragomir Radev, and Qiaozhu Mei. 2010. Edge weight regularization over multiple graphs for similarity learning. In *Data Mining (ICDM), 2010 IEEE 10th International Conference on*, pages 374–383. IEEE.

Mark E.J. Newman and Juyong Park. 2003. Why social networks are different from other types of networks. *Physical Review E*, 68(3):036122.

Byung-Won On and Dongwon Lee. 2007. Scalable name disambiguation using multi-level graph partition. In *Proceedings of the 7th SIAM international conference on data mining*, pages 575–580.

Lawrence Page, Sergey Brin, Rajeev Motwani, and Terry Winograd. 1999. The pagerank citation ranking: bringing order to the web.

Romualdo Pastor-Satorras and Alessandro Vespignani. 2001. Epidemic spreading in scale-free networks. *Physical review letters*, 86(14):3200–3203.

Dragomir R. Radev, Pradeep Muthukrishnan, Vahed Qazvinian, and Amjad Abu-Jbara. 2013. The ACL anthology network corpus. *Language Resources and Evaluation*, pages 1–26.

William M. Rand. 1971. Objective criteria for the evaluation of clustering methods. *Journal of the American Statistical association*, 66(336):846–850.

S. Redner. 1998. How popular is your paper? an empirical study of the citation distribution. *The European Physical Journal B-Condensed Matter and Complex Systems*, 4(2):131–134.

P. Sarkar, A.W. Moore, and A. Prakash. 2008. Fast incremental proximity search in large graphs. In *Proceedings of the 25th international conference on Machine learning*, pages 896–903. ACM.

Allan A. Sioson. 2005. *Multimodal networks in biology*. Ph.D. thesis, Virginia Polytechnic Institute and State University.

Michael Speriosu, Nikita Sudan, Sid Upadhyay, and Jason Baldridge. 2011. Twitter polarity classification with label propagation over lexical links and the follower graph. In *Proceedings of the First workshop on Unsupervised Learning in NLP*, pages 53–63, Edinburgh, Scotland, July. ACL.

Alexander Strehl and Joydeep Ghosh. 2003. Cluster ensembles—a knowledge reuse framework for combining multiple partitions. *The Journal of Machine Learning Research*, 3:583–617.

Yizhou Sun, Jiawei Han, Peixiang Zhao, Zhijun Yin, Hong Cheng, and Tianyi Wu. 2009. Rankclus: integrating clustering with ranking for heterogeneous information network analysis. In *Proceedings of the 12th International Conference on Extending Database Technology: Advances in Database Technology*, pages 565–576. ACM.

Yizhou Sun, Rick Barber, Manish Gupta, and Jiawei Han. 2011. Co-author relationship prediction in heterogeneous bibliographic networks.

Yizhou Sun, Charu C. Aggarwal, and Jiawei Han. 2012. Relation strength-aware clustering of heterogeneous information networks with incomplete attributes. *Proceedings of the VLDB Endowment*, 5(5):394–405.

Ben Taskar, Ming-Fai Wong, Pieter Abbeel, and Daphne Koller. 2003. Link prediction in relational data. In *Neural Information Processing Systems*, volume 15.

Robert Tibshirani, Guenther Walther, and Trevor Hastie. 2001. Estimating the number of clusters in a data set via the gap statistic. *Journal of the Royal Statistical Society: Series B (Statistical Methodology)*, 63(2):411–423.

Kristina Toutanova, Christopher D Manning, and Andrew Y Ng. 2004. Learning random walk models for inducing word dependency distributions. In *Proceedings of the twenty-first international conference on Machine learning*, page 103. ACM.

Xuerui Wang, Natasha Mohanty, and Andrew McCallum. 2006. Group and topic discovery from relations and their attributes. Technical report, DTIC Document.

Kai Yu, Shipeng Yu, and Volker Tresp. 2006. Soft clustering on graphs. *Advances in Neural Information Processing Systems*, 18:1553.

Ding Zhou, Sergey A. Orshanskiy, Hongyuan Zha, and C. Lee Giles. 2007. Co-ranking authors and documents in a heterogeneous network. In *Data Mining, 2007. ICDM 2007. Seventh IEEE International Conference on*, pages 739–744. IEEE.

FLORS: Fast and Simple Domain Adaptation for Part-of-Speech Tagging

Tobias Schnabel
Department of Computer Science
Cornell University
tbs49@cornell.edu

Hinrich Schütze
Center for Information & Language Processing
University of Munich
inquiries@cislmu.org

Abstract

We present FLORS, a new part-of-speech tagger for domain adaptation. FLORS uses robust representations that work especially well for unknown words and for known words with unseen tags. FLORS is simpler and faster than previous domain adaptation methods, yet it has significantly better accuracy than several baselines.

1 Introduction

In this paper we describe FLORS, a part-of-speech (POS) tagger that is Fast in training and tagging, uses LOcal context only (as opposed to finding the optimal tag sequence for the entire sentence), performs Robustly on target domains (TDs) in unsupervised domain adaptation (DA) and is Simple in architecture and feature representation.

FLORS constructs a robust representation of the local context of the word v that is to be tagged. This representation consists of distributional features, suffixes and word shapes of v and its local neighbors. We show that it has two advantages.

First, since the main predictors used by FLORS are distributional features (not the word's identity), FLORS *predicts unseen tags of known words better* than prior work on DA for POS. Second, since FLORS uses representations computed from unlabeled text, representations of unknown words are in principle of the same type as representations of known words; this property of FLORS results in *better performance on unknown words* compared to prior work. These two advantages are especially beneficial for TDs that contain high rates of unseen tags of known words and high rates of unknown words. We show that FLORS achieves excellent DA tagging results on the five domains of the SANCL 2012 shared task (Petrov and McDonald, 2012) and outperforms three state-of-the-art taggers on Blitzer et al.'s (2006) biomedical data.

FLORS is also simpler and faster than other POS DA methods. It is simple in that the input representation consists of three simple types of features: distributional count features and two types of binary features, suffix and shape features. Many other word representations that are used for improving generalization (e.g., (Brown et al., 1992; Collobert et al., 2011)) are costly to train or have difficulty handling unknown words. Our representations are fast to build and can be created on-the-fly for unknown words that occur during testing.

The learning architecture is simple and fast as well. We train k binary one-vs-all classifiers that use local context only and no sequence information (where k is the number of tags). Thus, tagging complexity is $O(k)$. Many other learning setups for DA are more complex; e.g., they *learn* representations (as opposed to just counting), they learn *several classifiers* for different subclasses of words (e.g., known vs. unknown) or they combine *left-to-right and right-to-left* taggings.

The next two sections describe experimental data, setup and results. Results are discussed in Section 4. We compare FLORS to alternative word representations in Section 5 and to related work in Section 6. Section 7 presents our conclusions.

2 Experimental data and setup

Data. Our source domain is the Penn Treebank (Marcus et al., 1993) of Wall Street Journal (WSJ)

Transactions of the Association for Computational Linguistics, 2 (2014) 15–26. Action Editor: Sharon Goldwater.
Submitted 9/2013; Revised 11/2013; Published 2/2014.

text. Following Blitzer et al. (2006), we use sections 2-21 for training and 100,000 WSJ sentences from 1988 as unlabeled data in training.

We evaluate on six different TDs. The first five TDs (newsgroups, weblogs, reviews, answers, emails) are from the SANCL shared task (Petrov and McDonald, 2012). Additionally, the SANCL dataset contains sections 22 and 23 of the WSJ for in-domain development and testing, respectively. Each SANCL TD has an unlabeled training set of 100,000 sentences and development and test sets of about 1000 labeled sentences each. The sixth TD is BIO, the Penn BioTreebank data set distributed by Blitzer. It consists of dev and test sets of 500 sentences each and 100,000 unlabeled sentences.

Classification setup. Similar to SVMTool (Giménez and Màrquez, 2004) and Choi and Palmer (2012) (henceforth: C&P), we use *local context only* for tagging instead of performing sequence classification. For a word w occurring as token v_i in a sentence, we build a feature vector for a local window of size $2l + 1$ around v_i. The representation of the object to be classified is this feature vector and the target class is the POS tag of v_i.

We use the linear L2-regularized L2-loss SVM implementation provided by LIBLINEAR (Fan et al., 2008) to train k one-vs-all classifiers on the training set where k is the number of POS tags in the training set (in our case $k = 45$). We train with untuned default parameters; in particular, $C = 1$. In the special case of linear SVMs, the value of C does not need to be tuned exhaustively as the solution remains constant after C has reached a certain threshold value C^* (Keerthi and Lin, 2003). Training can easily be parallelized by giving each binary SVM its own thread.

Windows. The local context for tagging token v_i is a window of size $2l + 1$ centered around v_i: $(v_{i-l}, \ldots, v_i, \ldots, v_{i+l})$. We pad sentences on either side with $\langle$BOUNDARY$\rangle$ to ensure sufficient context for all words. Given a mapping f from words to feature vectors (see below), the representation F of a token v_i is the concatenation of the $2l + 1$ word vectors in its window

$$F(v_i) = f(v_{i-l}) \oplus \ldots \oplus f(v_{i+l})$$

where $\oplus$ is vector concatenation.

Word features. We represent each word w by four components: (i) counts of left neighbors, (ii) counts of right neighbors, (iii) binary suffix features and (iv) binary shape features. These four components are concatenated:

$$f(w) = f_{\text{left}}(w) \oplus f_{\text{right}}(w) \oplus f_{\text{suffix}}(w) \oplus f_{\text{shape}}(w)$$

We consider these sources of information equally important and normalize each of the four component vectors to unit length. Normalization also has a beneficial effect on SVM training time because it alleviates numerical problems (Fan et al., 2008).

Distributional features. We follow a long tradition of older (Finch and Chater, 1992; Schütze, 1993; Schütze, 1995) and newer (Huang and Yates, 2009) work on creating distributional features for POS tagging based on local left and right neighbors.

Specifically, the ith entry x_i of $f_{\text{left}}(w)$ is the weighted number of times that the *indicator word* c_i occurs immediately to the left of w:

$$x_i = \text{tf}\left(\text{freq}\left(\text{bigram}(c_i, w)\right)\right)$$

where c_i is the word with frequency rank i in the corpus, $\text{freq}\left(\text{bigram}(c_i, w)\right)$ is the number of times the bigram "c_i w" occurs in the corpus and we weight the non-zero frequencies logarithmically: $\text{tf}(x) = 1 + \log(x)$. tf-weighting has been used by other researchers (Huang and Yates, 2009) and showed good performance in our own previous work.

$f_{\text{right}}(w)$ is defined analogously. We restrict the set of indicator words to the $n = 500$ most frequent words in the corpus. To avoid zero vectors, we add an entry x_{n+1} to each vector that counts omitted contexts:

$$x_{n+1} = \text{tf}\left(\sum_{j:j>n} \text{freq}\left(\text{bigram}(c_j, w)\right)\right)$$

We compute distributional vectors on the joint corpus $\mathcal{D}_{\text{ALL}}$ of all labeled and unlabeled text of source domain and TD. The text is preprocessed by lowercasing everything – which is often done when computing word representations, e.g., by Turian et al. (2010) – and by padding sentences with $\langle$BOUNDARY$\rangle$ tokens.

Suffix features. Suffixes are promising for DA because basic morphology rules are the same in different domains. In contrast to other work on tagging

	model	classifier	features
1	TnT	HMM	$p_{-\{0,1,2\}}$, v_0, suffixes (for OOVs)
2	Stanford	bidir. MEMM	$p_{\pm\{0,1,2\}}$, $v_{\pm\{0,1\}}$, affixes, orthography
3	SVMTool	SVM	$p_{\pm\{0,1,2,3\}}$, $v_{\pm\{0,1,2,3\}}$, affixes, orthography, word length
4	C&P	SVM	$p_{\pm\{0,1,2,3\}}$, $v_{\pm\{0,1,2,3\}}$, affixes, orthography
5	FLORS	SVM	distributions of $v_{\pm\{0,1,2\}}$, suffixes, orthography

Table 1: Overview of baseline taggers and FLORS. v_i: token, p_i: POS tag. Positions included in the sets of token indices are relative to the position i of the word v_0 to be tagged; e.g., $p_{\pm\{0,1,2\}}$ is short for $\{p_{-0}, p_{-1}, p_{-2}, p_0, p_1, p_2\}$. To represent tokens v_i, models 1–4 use vocabulary indices and FLORS uses distributional representations. Models 2–4 use combinations of features (e.g., tag-word) as well.

(e.g., Ratnaparkhi (1996), Toutanova et al. (2003), Miller et al. (2007)) we simply use *all (lowercase) suffixes* to avoid the need for selecting a subset of suffixes; and we treat *all words* equally as opposed to using suffix features for only a subset of words. For suffix s, we set the dimension corresponding to s in $f_{\text{suffix}}(w)$ to 1 if lowercased w ends in s and to 0 otherwise. Note that w is a suffix of itself.[1]

Shape features. We use the Berkeley parser word signatures (Petrov and Klein, 2007). Each word is mapped to a bit string encompassing 16 binary indicators that correspond to different orthographic (e.g., does the word contain a digit, hyphen, uppercase character) and morphological (e.g., does the word end in -ed or -ing) features. There are 50 unique signatures in WSJ. We set the dimension of $f_{\text{shape}}(w)$ that corresponds to the signature of w to 1 and all other dimensions to 0. We note that the shape features we use were designed for English and probably would have to be adjusted for other languages.

Baselines. We address the problem of unsupervised domain adaptation for POS tagging. For this problem, we consider three types of baselines: (i) high-performing publicly available systems, (ii) the taggers used at SANCL and (iii) POS DA results published for BIO.

Most of our experiments use taggers from category (i) because we can ensure that experimental conditions are directly comparable. The four baselines in category (i) are shown in Table 1. Three have near state-of-the-art performance on WSJ: SVMTool (Giménez and Màrquez, 2004), Stanford (Toutanova et al., 2003) (a birectional MEMM) and C&P. TnT (Brants, 2000) is included as a representative of fast and simple HMM taggers. In addition, C&P is a tagger that has been extensively tested in DA scenarios with excellent results. Unless otherwise stated, we train all models using their default configuration files. We use the optimized parameter configuration published by C&P for the C&P model.

Test set results will be compared with the SANCL taggers (category (ii)) at the end of Section 3.

As far as category (iii) is concerned, most work on POS DA has been evaluated on BIO. We discuss our concerns about the BIO evaluation sets in Section 4, but also show that FLORS beats previously published results on BIO as well (see Table 6).

3 Experimental results

We train k binary SVM classifiers on the training set. A token in the test set is classified by building its feature vector, running the classifiers on it and then assigning it to the POS class whose one-vs-all LIBLINEAR classifier returns the largest score.

Results for ALL accuracy (accuracy for all tokens) and OOV accuracy (accuracy for tokens not occurring in the labeled WSJ data) are reported in Table 2. Results with an asterisk are significantly worse than a column's best result using McNemar's test ($p < .001$). We use the same test and p-value throughout this paper.

The basic FLORS model (Table 2, line 5) uses window size 5 ($l = 2$). Each word in the window has 1002 distributional features (501 left and right), 91,161 suffix features and 50 shape features. The final feature vector for a token has a dimensionality of about 500,000, but is very sparse.

FLORS outperforms all baselines on the five TDs

[1] One could also compute these suffixes for _w (w prefixed by underscore) instead of for w to include words as distinguishable special suffixes. We test this alternative in Table 2, line 15.

			newsgroups		reviews		weblogs		answers		emails		wsj	
			ALL	OOV	ALL	OOV	ALL	OOV	ALL	OOV	ALL	OOV	ALL	OOV
1	TnT		88.66*	54.73*	90.40*	56.75*	93.33*	74.17*	88.55*	48.32*	88.14*	58.09*	95.75*	88.30
2	Stanford		89.11*	56.02*	91.43*	58.66*	94.15*	77.13*	88.92*	49.30*	88.68*	58.42*	**96.83**	90.25
3	SVMTool		89.14*	53.82*	91.30*	54.20*	94.21*	76.44*	88.96*	47.25*	88.64*	56.37*	96.63	87.96
4	C&P		89.51*	57.23*	91.58*	59.67*	94.41*	78.46*	89.08*	48.46*	88.74*	58.62*	96.78	88.65
5	FLORS	basic	90.86	66.42	92.95	75.29	94.71	83.64	90.30	62.15	89.44*	62.61	96.59	90.37
6	FLORS	$n = 250$	**90.93**	**67.03**	92.93	75.45	94.69	83.69	90.29	62.20	**89.63**	63.43	96.56*	89.45
7	FLORS, $v_{\pm\{0,1,2\}}$	$n = 0$	89.14*	55.59*	91.80*	66.31*	93.40*	72.55*	89.47*	55.82*	88.21*	57.83*	96.29*	85.55*
8	FLORS, $v_{\pm\{0,1,2\}}$	no suffixes	90.60	65.17	92.74	71.94*	94.77	**84.92**	89.77*	58.71*	89.30*	62.09	96.28*	88.88
9	FLORS, $v_{\pm\{0,1,2\}}$	no shapes	89.70*	63.10*	92.24*	68.70*	92.60*	74.72*	89.55*	59.08*	**89.63**	**64.17**	95.52*	83.94*
10	FLORS, $v_{\pm\{1,2\}}$	$n = 0$	90.61*	65.95	92.76*	75.56	94.62	84.62	90.23	61.87	89.40*	63.82	96.51*	90.02
11	FLORS, $v_{\pm\{1,2\}}$	no suffixes	90.66	64.78*	92.88	75.08	**94.83**	84.52	90.36	61.92	89.42	62.74	96.64	89.45
12	FLORS, $v_{\pm\{1,2\}}$	no shapes	90.74	**67.03**	**93.02**	**75.88**	94.57	83.83	90.23	61.73	89.41*	63.49	96.57	90.25
13	FLORS	$l = 1$	90.44*	63.62*	92.69*	75.72	94.48*	84.03	90.02*	62.66	89.17*	62.71	96.44*	88.65
14	FLORS	L-to-R	90.56*	66.08	92.97	75.40	94.57	83.79	**90.43**	**62.80**	89.43	63.13	96.53*	**90.94**
15	FLORS	voc. indices	**90.93**	66.64	92.91	75.03	94.71	84.08	90.27	61.92	89.37*	62.26	96.63	90.60

Table 2: Tagging accuracy of four baselines and FLORS on the dev sets. The table is structured as follows: baselines (lines 1–4), basic FLORS setup (lines 5–6), effect of omitting one of the three feature types if the word to be tagged is changed compared to the basic FLORS setup (lines 7–9) and if the word to be tagged is not changed compared to basic FLORS (lines 10–12), effect of three important configuration choices on tagging accuracy: window size (line 13), inclusion of prior tagging decision (line 14) and vocabulary index (line 15). n: number of indicator words. $2l + 1$: size of the local context window. Lines 10–12: Only the neighbors of v_0 are modified compared to basic (line 5). Lines 7–9: All five token representations (including v_0) are modified. A column's best result is bold.

(line 5 vs. lines 1–4). Only in-domain on WSJ, three baselines are slightly superior. The baselines are slightly better on ALL accuracy because they were designed for tagging in-domain data and use feature sets that have been found to work well on the source domain. Generally, C&P performs best for DA among the baselines. On answers and WSJ, however, Stanford has better overall accuracies. These results are in line with C&P.

On lines 6–15, we investigate how different modifications of the basic FLORS model affect performance. First, we examine the effect of leaving out components of the representation: distributional features ($f_{\text{left}}(w)$, $f_{\text{right}}(w)$), suffixes ($f_{\text{suffix}}(w)$) and shape features ($f_{\text{shape}}(w)$).

Distributional features boost performance in all domains: ALL and OOV accuracies are consistently worse for $n = 0$ (line 7) than for $n \in \{250, 500\}$ (lines 6&5). FLORS with $n = 250$ has better OOV accuracies in 5 of 6 domains. However, ALL accuracy for FLORS with $n = 500$ is better in the majority of domains. The main result of this comparison is that FLORS does not seem to be very sensitive to the value of n if n is large enough.

Shape features also improve results in all domains, with one exception: emails (lines 9 vs 5). For emails, shape features decrease ALL accuracy by .19 and OOV accuracy by 1.56. This may be due to the fact that many OOVs are NNP/NN and that tagging conventions for NNP/NN vary between domains. See Section 4 for discussion.

Performance benefits from suffixes in all domains but weblogs (lines 8 vs 5). Weblogs contain many foreign names such as *Abdul* and *Yasim*. For these words, shapes apparently provide better information for classification than suffixes. ALL accuracies suffer little when leaving out suffixes, but the feature space is much smaller: about 3000 dimensions. Thus, for domains where we expect few OOVs, omitting suffix features could be considered.

Lines 7–9 omit one of the components of $f(v_i)$ for all five words in the local context: $i \in \{-2, -1, 0, 1, 2\}$. Lines 10–12 omit the same components for the neighbor words only – i.e., $i \in \{-2, -1, 1, 2\}$ – and leave $f(v_0)$ unchanged. 14 of the 6×3 ALL accuracies on lines 10–12 are worse than FLORS basic, 4 are better. The largest differences are .25 for newsgroups and .19 for reviews (lines 5 vs 10), but differences for the other domains are negligible. This shows that the most important feature representation is that of v_0 (not surprisingly) and that the distributional features of the other words can be omitted at the cost of some loss in accuracy if a small average number of active features is desired.

Another FLORS parameter is the size of the local context. Surprisingly, OOV accuracies benefit a bit in four domains if we reduce l from 2 to 1 (lines 13 vs 5). However, ALL accuracy consistently drops in all six domains. This argues for using $l = 2$, i.e., a window size of 5.

Results for left-to-right (L-to-R) tagging are given on line 14. Similar to SVMTool and C&P, each sentence is tagged from left to right and previous tagging decisions are used for the current classification. In this setting, we use the previous tag p_{i-1} as one additional feature in the feature vector of v_i.

The effect of left-to-right is similar to the effect of omitting suffixes: OOV accuracies go up in some domains, but ALL accuracies decrease (except for an increase of .02 for reviews). This is in line with the experiments in (Schnabel and Schütze, 2013) where sequential information in a CRF was not robust across domains. OOV tagging may benefit from correct previous tags because the larger left context that is indirectly made available by left-to-right tagging compensates partially for the lack of information about the OOV word.

In contrast to standard approaches to POS tagging, the FLORS basic representation does not contain vocabulary indices. Line 15 shows what happens if we add them; the dimensionality of the feature vector is increased by $5|V|$ – where V is the training set vocabulary – and in training one binary feature is set to one for each of the five local context words. Performance is almost indistinguishable from FLORS basic, suggesting that only using suffixes – which can be viewed as "ambiguous" vocabulary indices, e.g., "at" is on for "at", "mat", "hat", "laundromat" etc – is sufficient.

In summary, we find that distributional features, word signatures and suffixes all contribute to successful POS DA. Factors with only minor impact on performance are the number of indicator words used for the distributional representations, the window size l and the tagging scheme (L-to-R vs. non-L-to-R). Unknown words and known words behave differently with respect to certain feature choices.

The different behavior of unknown and known words suggests that training and optimizing two separate models – an approach used by SVMTool – would further increase tagging accuracy. Note that there has been at least one publication (Schnabel and Schütze, 2013) on optimizing a separate model for unknown words that has in some cases better performance on OOV accuracy than what we publish here.[2] However, this would complicate the architecture of FLORS. We opted for a maximally simple model in this paper, potentially at the cost of some performance.

Test set results. Table 3 reports results on the test sets. FLORS again performs significantly better on all five TDs, both on ALL and OOV. Only in-domain on WSJ, ALL performance is worse.

Finally, we compare our results to the POS taggers for which performance was reported at SANCL 2012 (Petrov and McDonald, 2012, Table 4). Constituency-based parsers – which also tag words as a by-product of deriving complete parse trees – are excluded from the comparison because they are trained on a richer representation, the syntactic structure of sentences.[3] FLORS' results are better than the best non-parsing-based results at SANCL 2012, which were accuracies of 92.32 on newsgroups (HIT), 90.65 on reviews (HIT) and 91.07 on answers (IMS-1).

4 Discussion

Advantages of FLORS representation. As we can see in Table 1, the main representational difference between FLORS and the other taggers is that the FLORS representation does not include vocabulary indices of the word to be tagged or its neighbors – the FLORS vector only consists of distributional, suffix and shape features.

This is an obvious advantage for OOVs. In other representational schemes, OOVs have representations that are fundamentally different from known

[2] Schnabel and Schütze (2013) report OOV accuracies of 56.62 (newsgroups), 64.61 (reviews), 71.86 (weblogs), 54.28 (answers), 61.05 (emails) and 64.64 (BIO) for their basic model and even higher OOV accuracies if parameters are optimized on a per-domain basis.

[3] DCU-Paris13 is listed in the dependency parser tables, but DCU-Paris13 results are derived from a constituency parser. DCU also developed sophisticated preprocessing rules for the different domains, which can be viewed as a kind of manual domain adaptation.

		newsgroups		reviews		weblogs		answers		emails		wsj	
		ALL	OOV	ALL	OOV	ALL	OOV	ALL	OOV	ALL	OOV	ALL	OOV
1	TnT	90.85*	56.60*	89.67*	50.98*	91.37*	62.65*	89.36*	51.82*	87.38*	55.12*	96.57*	86.27
2	Stanford	91.25*	57.96*	90.30*	51.87*	92.32*	67.85*	89.74*	53.41*	87.77*	57.10*	97.43	**88.71**
3	SVMTool	91.21*	54.40*	90.01*	45.05*	92.05*	63.59*	89.90*	51.07*	87.74*	53.23*	97.26	86.47
4	C&P	91.68*	60.58*	90.42*	51.12*	92.22*	66.91*	89.90*	53.31*	87.91*	54.47*	**97.44**	88.20
5	FLORS basic	**92.41**	**66.91**	**92.25**	**70.87**	**93.14**	**75.32**	**91.17**	**67.93**	**88.67**	**61.09**	97.11*	87.79

Table 3: Tagging accuracy of four baselines and FLORS on the test sets.

		newsgroups	reviews	weblogs	answers	emails	wsj	bio
pct tokens	unknown tag	0.31	0.06	0.00	0.25	0.80	0.00	0.98
	OOV	10.34	6.84	8.45	8.53	10.56	2.72	19.86
	unseen word+tag	2.44	2.22	1.46	2.91	3.47	0.61	2.50
accuracy on unseen word+tag	TnT	0.00	0.00	0.00	0.00	0.00	0.00	0.00
	Stanford	3.66	5.74	9.40	5.46	2.77	15.23	4.64
	SVMTool	0.00	0.16	0.00	0.00	0.10	0.00	0.00
	C&P	14.47	14.75	20.51	13.37	10.29	38.07	8.98
	FLORS basic	**21.06**	**21.97**	**21.65**	**17.19**	**15.13**	**41.12**	**12.69**

Table 4: Top: Percentage of unknown tags, OOVs and unseen word+tag combinations (i.e., known words tagged with unseen tags) in the dev sets. Bottom: Tagging accuracy on unseen word+tag.

words – since their vocabulary index does not occur in the training set and cannot be used for prediction. In contrast, given enough unlabeled TD data, FLORS represents known and unknown words in essentially the same way and prediction of the correct tag is easier. This explanation is supported by the experiments in Table 2: FLORS beats all other systems on OOVs – even in-domain on WSJ.

In our analysis we found that apart from better handling of OOVs there is a second beneficial effect of distributional representations: they facilitate the correct tagging of *known words occurring with tags unseen in the training set*, which we call *unseen word+tags*. Table 4 gives statistics on this case and shows that unseen word+tags occur at least two times as often out-of-domain (e.g., 1.46% for weblogs) than in-domain (.61% for WSJ). The bottom part of the table shows performance of the five taggers on unseen word+tags. FLORS is the top performer on all seven domains, with large differences of more than 5% in some domains.

The explanation is similar to the OOV case: FLORS does not restrict the set of possible POS's of a word. The other taggers in Table 2 use the vocabulary index of the word to be tagged and will therefore give a strong preference to seen tags. Since FLORS uses distributional features, it can more easily assign an unseen tag as long as it is compatible with the overall pattern of distribution, suffixes and shapes typical of the tag. C&P also perform relatively well on unseen word+tag due to the ambiguity classes in their model, but FLORS representations are better for every domain. We take these results to mean that constraints on a word's possible POS tags may well be helpful for in-domain data, but for out-of-domain data an overly strong bias for a word's observed tags is harmful.

It is important to stress that representations similar to FLORS representations have been used for a long time; we would expect many of them to have similar advantages for unseen word+tags. E.g., Brown clusters (Brown et al., 1992) and word embeddings (Collobert et al., 2011) are similar to FLORS in this respect. However, FLORS representations are extracted by simple counting whereas the computation of Brown clusters or word embeddings is much more expensive. The speed with which FLORS representations can be computed is particularly beneficial when taggers need to be adapted to new domains. FLORS can easily adapt its representations on the fly – as each new occurrence of a word is encountered, the counts that are the basis for the x_i can simply be incremented. We present a direct comparison of FLORS representations with other representations in Section 5.

"Local context" vs. sequence classification. The most common approach to POS tagging is to tag a sentence with its most likely sequence; in contrast, independent tagging of local context is not guaranteed to find the best sequence. Recent work on English suggests that window-based tagging can perform as well as sequence-based methods (Liang et al., 2008; Collobert et al., 2011). Toutanova et al. (2003) report similar results. In our experiments, we also did not find consistent improvements when we incorporated sequence constraints (Table 2, line 14). However, there may be languages and applications involving long-distance relationships where local-context classification is suboptimal.

Local-context classification has two advantages compared to sequence classification. (i) It simplifies the classification and tagging setup: we can use any existing statistical classifier. Sequence classification limits the range of methods that can be applied; e.g., it is difficult to find a good CRF implementation that can handle real-valued features – which are of critical importance for our representation.

(ii) The time complexity of FLORS in tagging is $O(skf)$ where s is the length of the sentence, k is the number of tags and f is the number of non-zero features per local-context representation. In contrast, sequence decoding complexity is $O(sk^2f)$. This difference is not of practical importance for standard English POS sets, but it could be an argument against sequence classification for tagging problems with much larger tag sets.

In summary, replacing sequence classification with local-context classification is attractive for large-scale, practical tagging.

What DA can and cannot do. Despite the superior DA tagging results we report for FLORS in this paper, there is still a gap of 2%–7% (depending on the domain) between in-domain WSJ accuracy and DA accuracy on SANCL. In our analysis of this gap, we found some evidence that DA performance can be further improved – especially as more unlabeled TD data becomes available. But we also found two reasons for low performance that unsupervised DA cannot do anything about: differences in tag sets – or unknown tags – and differences in annotation guidelines.

Table 4 shows that *unknown tags* occur in five of the seven TDs at rates between 0% (weblogs) and 1% (BIO). Each token that is tagged with an unknown tag is necessarily an error in unsupervised DA. Furthermore, the unknown tag can also impact tagging accuracy in the local context[4] – so the unknown tag rates in Table 4 are probably lower bounds for the error that is due to unknown tags. Based on these considerations, it is not surprising that tagging accuracy (e.g., of FLORS basic) and unknown tag rate are correlated as we can see in Tables 2, 4 and 6; e.g., we get the highest accuracies in the two domains that do not have unknown tags (weblogs and WSJ) and the lowest accuracy in the domain with the highest rate (BIO).

Since unknown tags cannot be predicted correctly, one could simply report accuracy on known tags. However, given the negative effect of unknown tags on tagging accuracy of the local context in which they occur, excluding unknown tags does not fully address the problem. For this reason, it is probably best to keep the common practice of simply reporting accuracy on all tokens, including unknown tags. But the percentages of unknown tags should also be reported for each dataset as a basis for a more accurate interpretation of results.

Another type of error that cannot be avoided in unsupervised DA is due to differences in *annotation guidelines*. There are a few such problems in SANCL; e.g., file names like "Services.doc" are annotated as NN in the email domain. But their distributional and grammatical behavior is more similar to NNPs; as a consequence, most file names are incorrectly tagged. In general, it is difficult to discriminate NNs from NNPs. The Penn Treebank annotation guidelines (Santorini, 1990) are compatible with either tag in many cases and it may simply be impossible to write annotation guidelines that avoid these problems (cf. Manning (2011)). NN-NNP inconsistencies are especially problematic for OOV tagging since most OOVs are NNs or NNPs.

[4]For example, there is a special tag ADD in the web domain for web addresses. The last two words of the sentence "I would like to host my upcoming website to/IN Liquidweb.com/ADD" are mistagged by Stanford tagger as "... to/TO Liquidweb.com/VB". So the missing tag in this case also affects the tagging of surrounding words.

	bio dev		wsj train
	OOV	ALL	ALL
NN	62.4	25.4	14.4
JJ	15.9	8.9	6.2
NNS	10.2	7.5	6.3
NNP	0.5	0.2	9.5
NNPS	0.0	0.0	0.3

Table 5: Frequency of some tags (percent of tokens) for bio dev and wsj train.

While the amount of inconsistent annotation is limited for SANCL, it is a serious problem for BIO. Table 5 shows that the proportion of NNPs in BIO is less than a tenth of that in WSJ (.2 in BIO vs. 9.5 in WSJ). This is due to the fact that many bio-specific names, in particular genes, are annotated as NN. In contrast, the distributionally and orthographically most similar names in WSJ are tagged as NNP. For example, we find "One cell was teased out, and its DNA/NNP extracted" in WSJ vs. "DNA/NN was isolated" in BIO.

		standard setup		NNP→NN	
		ALL	OOV	ALL	OOV
	TnT	87.49*	59.08*	91.75*	78.33*
	Stanford	88.46*	62.55*	92.36*	79.19*
	SVMTool	88.33*	61.30*	92.47	79.46*
	C&P	87.82*	60.60*	92.06*	79.30*
FLORS	basic	88.90	64.74	92.91	82.58
FLORS	$n = 250$	88.90	64.51	92.93	82.47
FLORS	$n = 0$	87.27*	57.75*	90.91*	73.57*
FLORS	no suffixes	88.09*	62.20*	91.98*	79.27*
FLORS	no shapes	87.78*	59.82*	91.81*	77.31*
FLORS	$l = 1$	**89.12**	**65.52**	**92.99**	**82.90**

Table 6: Tagging accuracy on bio dev. NNP→NN results were obtained by replacing NNPs with NNs.

Given this large discrepancy in the frequency of the tag NNP – which arguably is due to different annotation guidelines, not due to underlying differences between the two genres – BIO should probably not be used for evaluating DA. This is why we did not include it in our comparison in Table 2.

For sake of completeness, we provide tagging accuracies for BIO in Table 6, "standard setup". The results are in line with SANCL results: FLORS beats the baselines on ALL and OOV accuracies. However, if we build the NN bias into our model by simply replacing all NNP tags with NN tags, then accuracy goes up by 4% on ALL and by almost 20% on OOV. Even TnT, the most basic tagger, achieves ALL/OOV accuracy of 91.75/78.33, better than any method in the standard setup. These accuracies are well above those in (Blitzer et al., 2006) and (Huang and Yates, 2010).

Since simply replacing NNPs with NNs has such a large effect, BIO cannot be used sensibly for evaluating DA methods. In practice, it is not possible to separate "true" improvements due to generic better DA from elements of the proposed method that simply introduce a negative bias for NNP.

In summary, when comparing different DA methods caution should be exercised in the choice of domains. In particular, the effect of unknown tags should be made transparent and the gold standards should be analyzed to determine whether the task addressed in the TD differs significantly in some aspects from that addressed in the source domain.

5 Comparison of word representations

Our approach to DA is an instance of representation learning: we aim to find representations that are robust across domains. In this section, we compare FLORS with two other widely used representation learning methods: (i) Brown clusters (Brown et al., 1992) and (ii) C&W embeddings, the word embeddings of Collobert et al. (2011). We use $f_{\text{dist}}(w) = f_{\text{left}}(w) \oplus f_{\text{right}}(w)$ to refer to our own distributional word representations (see Section 2).

The perhaps oldest and most frequently used low-dimensional representation of words is based on Brown clusters. Typically, prefixes of Brown clusters (Brown et al., 1992) are added to increase the robustness of POS taggers (e.g., Toutanova et al. (2003)). Computational costs are high (quadratic in the vocabulary size) although the computation can be parallelized (Uszkoreit and Brants, 2008).

More recently, general word representations (Collobert et al., 2011; Turian et al., 2010) have been used for robust POS tagging. These word representations are typically trained on a large amount of unlabeled text and fine-tuned for specific NLP tasks. Similar to Brown clusters, they are low-dimensional and can be used as features in many NLP tasks, either alone or in combination with other features.

To compare $f_{\text{dist}}(w)$ (our distributional representations) with Brown clusters, we induced 1000 Brown clusters on the joint corpus data $\mathcal{D}_{\text{ALL}}$ (see Section 2) using the publicly available implementation of Liang (2005). We padded sentences with $\langle$BOUNDARY$\rangle$ tokens on each side and used path prefixes of length 4, 6, 10 and 20 as features for each word (cf. Ratinov and Roth (2009), Turian et al. (2010)).

C&W embeddings are provided by Collobert et al. (2011): 50-dimensional vectors for 130,000 words from WSJ, trained on Wikipedia. Similar to our distributional representations $f_{\text{dist}}(w)$, the embeddings also contain a $\langle$BOUNDARY$\rangle$ token (which they call PADDING). Moreover, they have a special embedding for unknown words (called UNKNOWN) which we use whenever we encounter a word that is not in their lookup table. We preprocess our raw tokens the same way they do (lowercase and replace sequences of digits by "0") before we look up a representation during training and testing.

We replaced the distributional features in our basic setup by either Brown cluster features or C&W embeddings. Table 7 repeats lines 5 and 7 of Table 2 and gives results of the modified FLORS setup.

All three representations improve both ALL and OOV accuracies in all domains. f_{dist} outperforms Brown in all cases except for OOV on emails. Brown may suffer from noisy data; cleaning methods have been used in the literature (Liang, 2005; Turian et al., 2010), but they are not unproblematic since a large part of the data available is lost, which results in more unknown words.

Brown and f_{dist} can be directly compared since they were trained on exactly the same data. f_{dist} and C&W are harder to compare directly because there are many differences. (i) C&W is trained on a much larger dataset. One consequence of this is that OOV accuracy on WSJ may be higher because some words that are unknown for other methods are actually known to C&W. (ii) C&W vectors are not trained on the SANCL TD data sets – this gives f_{dist} an advantage. (iii) C&W vectors are not trained on the WSJ. Again, this could give f_{dist} an advantage. (iv) C&W and f_{dist} are fundamentally different in the way they handle unknown words. C&W has a limited vocabulary and must replace all words not in this vocabulary by the token UNKNOWN. In contrast, f_{dist} can create a meaningful individual representation for any OOV word it encounters.

Our FLORS tagger provides best ALL accuracies in all domains but WSJ, where C&W has best results. The good performance of C&W is rather unsurprising since the embeddings were created for the 130,000 most frequent words of the WSJ and thus cover the WSJ domain much better. Also, WSJ was used to tune parameters during development. As with our previous experiments, OOV results on emails seem slightly more sensitive to parameter choices than on other domains (recall the discussion of this issue in Section 4).

In summary, we have shown that f_{dist} representations work better for POS DA than Brown clusters. Furthermore, the evidence we have presented suggests that f_{dist} are comparable in performance to C&W embeddings if not better for POS DA.

The most important difference between f_{dist} and Brown / C&W is that f_{dist} are much simpler and much faster to compute. They are simpler because they are just slightly transformed counts in contrast to the other two approaches, which solve complex optimization problems. f_{dist} can be computed efficiently through simple incrementation in one pass through the corpus. In contrast, the other two approaches are an order of magnitude slower.

6 Related work

Unsupervised DA methods can be broadly put into four categories: representation learning and constraint-based frameworks – which require some tailoring to a task – and instance weighting and bootstrapping – which can be more generally applied to a wide range of problems. Since many approaches are application-specific, we focus on the ones that have been applied to POS tagging.

Representation learning. We already discussed two important approaches to representation learning in Section 5: C&W embeddings and Brown clusters.

Blitzer et al.'s (2006) structural correspondence learning (SCL) supports DA by creating similar representations for correlated features in the *pivot feature space*. This is a potentially powerful method. FLORS is simpler in that correlations are made directly accessible to the supervised learner.

		newsgroups		reviews		weblogs		answers		emails		wsj	
		ALL	OOV	ALL	OOV	ALL	OOV	ALL	OOV	ALL	OOV	ALL	OOV
1	FLORS $f_{dist}(w)$, n=500	**90.86**	**66.42**	**92.95**	**75.29**	**94.71**	**83.64**	**90.30**	**62.15**	**89.44**	62.61	96.59	90.37
2	FLORS $f_{dist}(w)$, n=0	89.14*	55.59*	91.80*	66.31*	93.40*	72.55*	89.47*	55.82*	88.21*	57.83*	96.29*	85.55*
3	FLORS C&W for $f_{dist}(w)$	90.57	64.57	92.54*	72.48*	94.51	80.58*	90.23	60.99	**89.44**	63.13	**96.72**	**90.48**
4	Brown for $f_{dist}(w)$	90.34*	62.41*	92.23*	71.47*	94.45	81.76	89.71*	56.28*	89.02*	**63.20**	96.48*	87.50

Table 7: Tagging accuracy of different word representations on the dev sets. Line 1 corresponds to FLORS basic. n: number of indicator words. A column's best result is bold.

Moreover, FLORS representations consist of simple counts whereas SCL solves a separate optimization problem for each pivot feature.

Umansky-Pesin et al. (2010) derive distributional information for OOVs by running web queries. This approach is slow since it depends on a search engine.

Ganchev et al. (2012) successfully use search logs. This is a promising enhancement for FLORS.

Huang and Yates (2009) evaluate CRFs with distributional features. They examine lower dimensional feature representations using SVD or the latent states of an unsupervised HMM. They find better accuracies for their HMM method than Blitzer et al. (2006); however, they do not compare them against a CRF baseline using distributional features.

In later work, Huang and Yates (2010) add the latent states of multiple, differently trained HMMs as features to their CRF. Huang and Yates (2012) argue that finding an optimal feature representation is computationally intractable and propose a new framework that allows prior knowledge to be integrated into representation learning.

Latent sequence states are a form of word representation. Thus, it would be interesting to compare them to the non-sequence-based distributional representation that FLORS uses.

Constraint-based methods. Rush et al. (2012) use global constraints on OOVs to improve out-of-domain tagging. Although constraints ensure consistency, they require careful manual engineering. Distributional features can also be seen as a form of constraint since feature weights will be shared among all words.

Subramanya et al. (2010) construct a graph to encourage similar n-grams to be tagged similarly, resulting in moderate gains in one domain, but no gains on BIO when compared to self-training. The reason could be an insufficient amount of unsupervised data for BIO (100,000 sentences). Our approach does not seem to suffer from this problem.

Bootstrapping. Both self-training (McClosky et al., 2006) – which uses one classification model – and co-training (Blum and Mitchell, 1998) – which uses $\geq$2 models – have been applied to POS tagging.

Self-training usually improves a POS baseline only slightly if at all (Huang et al., 2009; Huang and Yates, 2010). Devising features based on labeled instances (instead of training on them) has been more successful (Florian et al., 2004; Søgaard, 2011).

Chen et al. (2011) use co-training for DA. In each round of their algorithm, both new training instances from the unlabeled data and new features are added. Their model is limited to binary classification. The co-training method of Kübler and Baucom (2011) trains several taggers and adds sentences from the TD to the training set on which they agree. They report slight, but statistically significant increases in accuracy for POS tagging of dialogue data.

Instance weighting. Instance weighting formalizes DA as the problem of having data from different probability distributions in each domain. The goal is to make these two distributions align by using instance-specific weights during training. Jiang and Zhai (2007) propose a framework that integrates prior knowledge from different data sets into the learning objective by weights.

In related work, C&P train *generalized* and *domain-specific* models. An input sentence is tagged by the model that is most similar to the sentence. FLORS could be easily extended along these lines, an experiment we plan for the future.

In terms of the basic classification setup, our POS tagger is most similar to the SVM-based approaches of Giménez and Màrquez (2004) and C&P. However, we do not use a left-to-right approach when tagging sentences. Moreover, SVMTool trains two separate models, one for OOVs and one for known words. FLORS only has a single model. In addition, we do not make use of ambiguity classes, token-tag dictionaries and rare feature thresholds. Instead, we rely only on three types of features: distributional representations, suffixes and word shapes.

The local-context-only approach of SVMTool, C&P and FLORS is different from standard sequence classification such as MEMMs (e.g., Ratnaparkhi (1996), Toutanova et al. (2003), Tsuruoka and Tsujii (2005)) and CRFs (e.g., Collins (2002)). Sequence models are more powerful in theory, but this may not be an advantage in DA because the subtle dependencies they exploit may not hold across domains.

7 Conclusion

We have presented FLORS, a new POS tagger for DA. FLORS uses robust representations that work especially well for unknown words and for known words with unseen tags. FLORS is simpler and faster than previous DA methods, yet we were able to demonstrate that it has significantly better accuracy than several baselines.

Acknowledgments. This work was supported by DFG (Deutsche Forschungsgemeinschaft).

References

John Blitzer, Ryan McDonald, and Fernando Pereira. 2006. Domain adaptation with structural correspondence learning. In *EMNLP*, pages 120–128.

Avrim Blum and Tom Mitchell. 1998. Combining labeled and unlabeled data with co-training. In *COLT*, pages 92–100.

Thorsten Brants. 2000. TnT: A statistical part-of-speech tagger. In *ANLP*, pages 224–231.

Peter F. Brown, Peter V. deSouza, Robert L. Mercer, Vincent J. Della Pietra, and Jenifer C. Lai. 1992. Class-based n-gram models of natural language. *Computational Linguistics*, 18:467–479.

Minmin Chen, Kilian Q. Weinberger, and John Blitzer. 2011. Co-training for domain adaptation. In *NIPS*, pages 1–9.

Jinho D. Choi and Martha Palmer. 2012. Fast and robust part-of-speech tagging using dynamic model selection. In *ACL: Short Papers*, pages 363–367.

Michael Collins. 2002. Discriminative training methods for hidden Markov models: Theory and experiments with perceptron algorithms. In *EMNLP*, pages 1–8.

Ronan Collobert, Jason Weston, Léon Bottou, Michael Karlen, Koray Kavukcuoglu, and Pavel Kuksa. 2011. Natural language processing (almost) from scratch. *The Journal of Machine Learning Research*, 12:2493–2537.

Rong-En Fan, Kai-Wei Chang, Cho-Jui Hsieh, Xiang-Rui Wang, and Chih-Jen Lin. 2008. LIBLINEAR: A library for large linear classification. *The Journal of Machine Learning Research*, 9:1871–1874.

Steven Finch and Nick Chater. 1992. Bootstrapping syntactic categories using statistical methods. In *Background and Experiments in Machine Learning of Natural Language*, pages 229–235.

Radu Florian, Hany Hassan, Abraham Ittycheriah, Hongyan Jing, Nanda Kambhatla, Xiaoqiang Luo, Nicolas Nicolov, and Salim Roukos. 2004. A statistical model for multilingual entity detection and tracking. In *HLT-NAACL*, pages 1–8.

Kuzman Ganchev, Keith Hall, Ryan McDonald, and Slav Petrov. 2012. Using search-logs to improve query tagging. In *ACL: Short Papers*, pages 238–242.

Jesús Giménez and Lluís Màrquez. 2004. SVMTool: A general pos tagger generator based on support vector machines. In *LREC*, pages 43–46.

Fei Huang and Alexander Yates. 2009. Distributional representations for handling sparsity in supervised sequence-labeling. In *ACL-IJCNLP*, pages 495–503.

Fei Huang and Alexander Yates. 2010. Exploring representation-learning approaches to domain adaptation. In *DANLP*, pages 23–30.

Fei Huang and Alexander Yates. 2012. Biased representation learning for domain adaptation. In *EMNLP-CoNLL*, pages 1313–1323.

Zhongqiang Huang, Vladimir Eidelman, and Mary Harper. 2009. Improving a simple bigram HMM part-of-speech tagger by latent annotation and self-training. In *NAACL-HLT: Short Papers*, pages 213–216.

Jing Jiang and ChengXiang Zhai. 2007. Instance weighting for domain adaptation in NLP. In *ACL*, pages 264–271.

S. Sathiya Keerthi and Chih-Jen Lin. 2003. Asymptotic behaviors of support vector machines with Gaussian kernel. *Neural computation*, 15(7):1667–1689.

Sandra Kübler and Eric Baucom. 2011. Fast domain adaptation for part of speech tagging for dialogues. In *RANLP*, pages 41–48.

Percy Liang, Hal Daumé III, and Dan Klein. 2008. Structure compilation: trading structure for features. In *ICML*, pages 592–599.

Percy Liang. 2005. Semi-supervised learning for natural language processing. Master's thesis, Massachusetts Institute of Technology.

Christopher D. Manning. 2011. Part-of-speech tagging from 97% to 100%: Is it time for some linguistics? In *CICLing*, pages 171–189.

Mitchell P. Marcus, Mary Ann Marcinkiewicz, and Beatrice Santorini. 1993. Building a large annotated corpus of English: The Penn treebank. *Computational Linguistics*, 19(2):313–330.

David McClosky, Eugene Charniak, and Mark Johnson. 2006. Reranking and self-training for parser adaptation. In *ACL*, pages 337–344.

John Miller, Manabu Torii, and Vijay K. Shanker. 2007. Building domain-specific taggers without annotated (domain) data. In *EMNLP-CoNLL*, pages 1103–1111.

Slav Petrov and Dan Klein. 2007. Improved inference for unlexicalized parsing. In *HLT-NAACL*, pages 404–411.

Slav Petrov and Ryan McDonald. 2012. Overview of the 2012 Shared Task on Parsing the Web. Notes of the 1st SANCL Workshop.

Lev Ratinov and Dan Roth. 2009. Design challenges and misconceptions in named entity recognition. In *CoNLL*, pages 147–155.

Adwait Ratnaparkhi. 1996. A maximum entropy model for part-of-speech tagging. In *EMNLP*, pages 133–142.

Alexander M. Rush, Roi Reichart, Michael Collins, and Amir Globerson. 2012. Improved parsing and POS tagging using inter-sentence consistency constraints. In *EMNLP-CoNLL*, pages 1434–1444.

Beatrice Santorini. 1990. Part-of-speech tagging guidelines for the Penn Treebank project (3rd revision, 2nd printing). Technical report, Department of Linguistics, University of Pennsylvania.

Tobias Schnabel and Hinrich Schütze. 2013. Towards robust cross-domain domain adaptation for part-of-speech tagging. In *IJCNLP*, pages 198–206.

Hinrich Schütze. 1993. Part-of-speech induction from scratch. In *ACL*, pages 251–258.

Hinrich Schütze. 1995. Distributional part-of-speech tagging. In *EACL*, pages 141–148.

Anders Søgaard. 2011. Semisupervised condensed nearest neighbor for part-of-speech tagging. In *ACL: Short papers*, pages 48–52.

Amarnag Subramanya, Slav Petrov, and Fernando Pereira. 2010. Efficient graph-based semi-supervised learning of structured tagging models. In *EMNLP*, pages 167–176.

Kristina Toutanova, Dan Klein, Christopher D. Manning, and Yoram Singer. 2003. Feature-rich part-of-speech tagging with a cyclic dependency network. In *NAACL-HLT*, pages 173–180.

Yoshimasa Tsuruoka and Jun'ichi Tsujii. 2005. Bidirectional inference with the easiest-first strategy for tagging sequence data. In *EMNLP-HLT*, pages 467–474.

Joseph Turian, Lev Ratinov, and Yoshua Bengio. 2010. Word representations: A simple and general method for semi-supervised learning. In *ACL*, pages 384–394.

Shulamit Umansky-Pesin, Roi Reichart, and Ari Rappoport. 2010. A multi-domain web-based algorithm for POS tagging of unknown words. In *COLING*, pages 1274–1282.

Jakob Uszkoreit and Thorsten Brants. 2008. Distributed word clustering for large scale class-based language modeling in machine translation. In *ACL*, pages 755–762.

Automatic Detection and Language Identification of Multilingual Documents

Marco Lui[♡♣]**, Jey Han Lau**[♠] **and Timothy Baldwin**[♡♣]
[♡] Department of Computing and Information Systems
The University of Melbourne
[♣] NICTA Victoria Research Laboratory
[♠] Department of Philosophy
King's College London
mhlui@unimelb.edu.au, jeyhan.lau@gmail.com, tb@ldwin.net

Abstract

Language identification is the task of automatically detecting the language(s) present in a document based on the content of the document. In this work, we address the problem of detecting documents that contain text from more than one language (*multilingual* documents). We introduce a method that is able to detect that a document is multilingual, identify the languages present, and estimate their relative proportions. We demonstrate the effectiveness of our method over synthetic data, as well as real-world multilingual documents collected from the web.

1 Introduction

Language identification is the task of automatically detecting the language(s) present in a document based on the content of the document. Language identification techniques commonly assume that every document is written in one of a closed set of known languages for which there is training data, and is thus formulated as the task of selecting the most likely language from the set of training languages. In this work, we remove this monolingual assumption, and address the problem of language identification in documents that may contain text from more than one language from the candidate set. We propose a method that concurrently detects that a document is multilingual, and estimates the proportion of the document that is written in each language.

Detecting multilingual documents has a variety of applications. Most natural language processing techniques presuppose monolingual input data, so inclusion of data in foreign languages introduces noise, and can degrade the performance of NLP systems (Alex et al., 2007; Cook and Lui, 2012). Automatic detection of multilingual documents can be used as a pre-filtering step to improve the quality of input data. Detecting multilingual documents is also important for acquiring linguistic data from the web (Scannell, 2007; Abney and Bird, 2010), and has applications in mining bilingual texts for statistical machine translation from online resources (Resnik, 1999; Nie et al., 1999; Ling et al., 2013). There has been particular interest in extracting text resources for low-density languages from multilingual web pages containing both the low-density language and another language such as English (Yamaguchi and Tanaka-Ishii, 2012; King and Abney, 2013). King and Abney (2013, p1118) specifically mention the need for an automatic method "to examine a multilingual document, and with high accuracy, list the languages that are present in the document".

We introduce a method that is able to detect multilingual documents, and simultaneously identify each language present as well as estimate the proportion of the document written in that language. We achieve this with a probabilistic mixture model, using a document representation developed for monolingual language identification (Lui and Baldwin, 2011). The model posits that each document is generated as samples from an unknown mixture of languages from the training set. We introduce a Gibbs sampler to map samples to languages for any given set of languages, and use this to select the set of languages that maximizes the posterior probability of the document.

Transactions of the Association for Computational Linguistics, 2 (2014) 27–40. Action Editor: Kristina Toutanova.
Submitted 1/2013; Revised 7/2013; Published 2/2014.

Our method is able to learn a language identifier for multilingual documents from monolingual training data. This is an important property as there are no standard corpora of multilingual documents available, whereas corpora of monolingual documents are readily available for a reasonably large number of languages (Lui and Baldwin, 2011). We demonstrate the effectiveness of our method empirically, firstly by evaluating it on synthetic datasets drawn from Wikipedia data, and then by applying it to real-world data, showing that we are able to identify multilingual documents in targeted web crawls of minority languages (King and Abney, 2013).

Our main contributions are: (1) we present a method for identifying multilingual documents, the languages contained therein and the relative proportion of the document in each language; (2) we show that our method outperforms state-of-the-art methods for language identification in multilingual documents; (3) we show that our method is able to estimate the proportion of the document in each language to a high degree of accuracy; and (4) we show that our method is able to identify multilingual documents in real-world data.

2 Background

Most language identification research focuses on language identification for *monolingual* documents (Hughes et al., 2006). In monolingual LangID, the task is to assign each document D a unique language $L_i \in L$. Some work has reported near-perfect accuracy for language identification of large documents in a small number of languages (Cavnar and Trenkle, 1994; McNamee, 2005). However, in order to attain such accuracy, a large number of simplifying assumptions have to be made (Hughes et al., 2006; Baldwin and Lui, 2010a). In this work, we tackle the assumption that each document is monolingual, i.e. it contains text from a single language.

In language identification, documents are modeled as a stream of characters (Cavnar and Trenkle, 1994; Kikui, 1996), often approximated by the corresponding stream of bytes (Kruengkrai et al., 2005; Baldwin and Lui, 2010a) for robustness over variable character encodings. In this work, we follow Baldwin and Lui (2010a) in training a single model for languages that naturally use multiple encodings (e.g. UTF8, Big5 and GB encodings for Chinese), as issues of encoding are not the focus of this research.

The document representation used for language identification generally involves estimating the relative distributions of particular byte sequences, selected such that their distributions differ between languages. In some cases the relevant sequences may be externally specified, such as function words and common suffixes (Giguet, 1995) or grammatical word classes (Dueire Lins and Gonçalves, 2004), though they are more frequently learned from labeled data (Cavnar and Trenkle, 1994; Grefenstette, 1995; Prager, 1999a; Lui and Baldwin, 2011).

Learning algorithms applied to language identification fall into two general categories: Bayesian classifiers and nearest-prototype (Rocchio-style) classifiers. Bayesian approaches include Markov processes (Dunning, 1994), naive Bayes methods (Grefenstette, 1995; Lui and Baldwin, 2011; Tiedemann and Ljubešić, 2012), and compressive models (Teahan, 2000). The nearest-prototype methods vary primarily in the distance measure used, including measures based on rank order statistics (Cavnar and Trenkle, 1994), information theory (Baldwin and Lui, 2010a), string kernels (Kruengkrai et al., 2005) and vector space models (Prager, 1999a; McNamee, 2005).

Language identification has been applied in domains such as USENET messages (Cavnar and Trenkle, 1994), web pages (Kikui, 1996; Martins and Silva, 2005; Liu and Liang, 2008), web search queries (Ceylan and Kim, 2009; Bosca and Dini, 2010), mining the web for bilingual text (Resnik, 1999; Nie et al., 1999), building minority language corpora (Ghani et al., 2004; Scannell, 2007; Bergsma et al., 2012) as well as a large-scale database of Interlinear Glossed Text (Xia et al., 2010), and the construction of a large-scale multilingual web crawl (Callan and Hoy, 2009).

2.1 Multilingual Documents

Language identification over documents that contain text from more than one language has been identified as an open research question (Hughes et al., 2006). Common examples of multilingual documents are web pages that contain excerpts from another language, and documents from multilingual organizations such as the European Union.

	English	French	Italian	German	Dutch	Japanese
character	`the␣`	`pour`	`␣di␣`	`␣auf`	`voo`	は
byte	`74 68 65 20`	`70 6F 75 7`	`20 64 69 20`	`20 61 75 66`	`76 6F 6`	`E3 81 AF`

Table 1: Examples of per-language byte sequences selected by information gain.

The Australiasian Language Technology Workshop 2010 hosted a shared task where participants were required to predict the language(s) present in a held-out test set containing monolingual and bilingual documents (Baldwin and Lui, 2010b). The dataset was prepared using data from Wikipedia, and bilingual documents were produced using a segment from a page in one language, and a segment from the same page in another language. We use the dataset from this shared task for our initial experiments.

To the authors' knowledge, the only other work to directly tackle identification of multiple languages and their relative proportions in a single document is the LINGUINI system (Prager, 1999a). The system is based on a vector space model, and cosine similarity between a feature vector for the test document and a feature vector for each language L_i, computed as the sum of feature vectors for all the documents for language L_i in the training data. The elements in the feature vectors are frequency counts over byte n-grams ($2 \leq n \leq 5$) and words. Language identification for multilingual documents is performed through the use of *virtual mixed languages*. Prager (1999a) shows how to construct vectors representative of particular combinations of languages independent of the relative proportions, and proposes a method for choosing combinations of languages to consider for any given document.

Language identification in multilingual documents could also be performed by application of supervised language segmentation algorithms. Given a system that can segment a document into labeled monolingual segments, we can then extract the languages present as well as the relative proportion of text in each language. Several methods for supervised language segmentation have been proposed. Teahan (2000) proposed a system based on text compression that identifies multilingual documents by first segmenting the text into monolingual blocks. Rehurek and Kolkus (2009) perform language segmentation by computing a relevance score between terms and languages, smoothing across adjoining terms and finally identifying points of transition between high and low relevance, which are interpreted as boundaries between languages. Yamaguchi and Tanaka-Ishii (2012) use a minimum description length approach, embedding a compressive model to compute the description length of text segments in each language. They present a linear-time dynamic programming solution to optimize the location of segment boundaries and language labels.

3 Methodology

Language identification for multilingual documents is a multi-label classification task, in which a document can be mapped onto any number of labels from a closed set. In the remainder of this paper, we denote the set of all languages by L. We denote a document D which contains languages L_x and L_y as $D \rightarrow \{L_x, L_y\}$, where $L_x, L_y \in L$. We denote a document that does not contain a language L_x by $D \rightarrow \{\overline{L_x}\}$, though we generally omit all the languages not contained in the document for brevity. We denote classifier output using $\rhd$; e.g. $D \rhd \{L_a, L_b\}$ indicates that document D has been predicted to contain text in languages L_a and L_b.

3.1 Document Representation and Feature Selection

We represent each document D as a frequency distribution over byte n-gram sequences such as those in Table 1. Each document is converted into a vector where each entry counts the number of times a particular byte n-gram is present in the document. This is analogous to a bag-of-words model, where the vocabulary of "words" is a set of byte sequences that has been selected to distinguish between languages.

The exact set of features is selected from the training data using Information Gain (IG), an information-theoretic metric developed as a splitting criterion for decision trees (Quinlan, 1993). IG-based feature selection combined with a naive Bayes classifier has been shown to be particularly effective for language identification (Lui and Baldwin, 2011).

3.2 Generative Mixture Models

Generative mixture models are popular for text modeling tasks where a mixture of influences governs the content of a document, such as in multi-label document classification (McCallum, 1999; Ramage et al., 2009), and topic modeling (Blei et al., 2003). Such models normally assume full exchangeability between tokens (i.e. the bag-of-words assumption), and label each token with a single discrete label.

Multi-label text classification, topic modeling and our model for language identification in multilingual documents share the same fundamental representation of the latent structure of a document. Each label is modeled with a probability distribution over tokens, and each document is modeled as a probabilistic mixture of labels. As presented in Griffiths and Steyvers (2004), the probability of the ith token (w_i) given a set of T labels $z_1 \cdots z_T$ is modeled as:

$$P(w_i) = \sum_{j=1}^{T} P(w_i|z_i = j)P(z_i = j) \quad (1)$$

The set of tokens w is the document itself, which in all cases is observed. In the case of topic modeling, the tokens are words and the labels are topics, and z is latent. Whereas topic modeling is generally unsupervised, multi-label text classification is a supervised text modeling task, where the labels are a set of pre-defined categories (such as RUBBER, IRON-STEEL, TRADE, etc. in the popular Reuters-21578 data set (Lewis, 1997)), and the tokens are individual words in documents. z is still latent, but constrained in the training data (i.e. documents are labeled but the individual words are not). Some approaches to labeling unseen documents require that z for the training data be inferred, and methods for doing this include an application of the Expectation-Maximization (EM) algorithm (McCallum, 1999) and Labeled LDA (Ramage et al., 2009).

The model that we propose for language identification in multilingual documents is similar to multi-label text classification. In the framework of Equation 1, each per-token label z_i is a language and the vocabulary of tokens is not given by words but rather by specific byte sequences (Section 3.1). The key difference with multi-label text classification is that we use monolingual (i.e. mono-label) training data. Hence, z is effectively observed for the training data (since all tokens must share the same label). To infer z for unlabeled documents, we utilize a Gibbs sampler, closely related to that proposed by Griffiths and Steyvers (2004) for LDA. The sampling probability for a label z_i for token w in a document d is:

$$\begin{aligned} P(z_i = j|z_{-i}, w) &\propto \phi_j^{(w)} \cdot \theta_j^{(d)} \\ \phi_j^{(w)} &= P(w_i|z_i = j, z_{-i}, w_{-i}) \\ \theta_j^{(d)} &= P(z_i = j|z_{-i}) \end{aligned} \quad (2)$$

In the LDA model, $\theta_j^{(d)}$ is assumed to have a Dirichlet distribution with hyperparameter α, and the word distribution for each topic $\phi_j^{(w)}$ is also assumed to have a Dirichlet distribution with hyperparameter β. Griffiths (2002) describes a generative model for LDA where both $\phi_j^{(w)}$ and $\theta_j^{(d)}$ are inferred from the output of a Gibbs sampler. In our method, we estimate $\phi_j^{(w)}$ using maximum likelihood estimation (MLE) from the training data. Estimating $\phi_j^{(w)}$ through MLE is equivalent to a multinomial Naive Bayes model (McCallum and Nigam, 1998):

$$\hat{\phi}_j^{(w)} = \frac{n_j^{(w)} + \beta}{n_j^{(\cdot)} + W\beta} \quad (3)$$

where $n_j^{(w)}$ is the number of times word w occurs with label j, and $n_j^{(\cdot)}$ is the total number of words that occur with label j. By setting β to 1, we obtain standard Laplacian smoothing. Hence, only $\hat{\theta}_j^{(d)}$ is updated at each step in the Gibbs sampler:

$$\hat{\theta}_j^{(d)} = \frac{n_{-i,j}^{(d)} + \alpha}{n_{-i}^{(d)} + T\alpha} \quad (4)$$

where $n_{-i,j}^{(d)}$ is the number of tokens in document d that are currently mapped to language j, and $n_{-i}^{(d)}$ is the total number of tokens in document d. In both cases, the current assignment of z_i is excluded from the count. T is the number of languages (i.e. the size of the label set). For simplicity, we set α to 0. We note that in the LDA model, α and β influence the sparsity of the solution, and so it may be possible to tune these parameters for our model as well. We leave this as an avenue for further research.

3.3 Language Identification in Multilingual Documents

The model described in Section 3.2 can be used to compute the most likely distribution to have generated an unlabeled document over a given set of languages for which we have monolingual training data, by letting the set of terms w be the byte n-gram sequences we selected using per-language information gain (Section 3.1), and allowing the labels z to range over the set of all languages L. Using training data, we compute $\hat{\phi}_j^{(w)}$ (Equation 3), and then we infer $P(L_j|D)$ for each $L_j \in L$ for the unlabeled document, by running the Gibbs sampler until the samples for z_i converge and then tabulating z_i over the whole d and normalizing by $|d|$. Naively, we could identify the languages present in the document by $D \triangleright \{L_x \text{ if } \exists(z_i = L_x|D)\}$, but closely-related languages tend to have similar frequency distributions over byte n-gram features, and hence it is likely that some tokens will be incorrectly mapped to a language that is similar to the "correct" language.

We address this issue by finding the subset of languages λ from the training set L that maximizes $P(\lambda|D)$ (a similar approach is taken in McCallum (1999)). Through an application of Bayes' theorem, $P(\lambda|D) \propto P(D|\lambda) \cdot P(\lambda)$, noting that $P(D)$ is a normalizing constant and can be dropped. We assume that $P(\lambda)$ is constant (i.e. any subset of languages is equally likely, a reasonable assumption in the absence of other evidence), and hence maximize $P(D|\lambda)$. For any given $D = w_1 \cdots w_n$ and λ, we infer $P(D|\lambda)$ from the output of the Gibbs sampler:

$$P(D|\lambda) = \prod_{i=1}^{N} P(w_i|\lambda) \quad (5)$$

$$= \prod_{i=1}^{N} \sum_{j \in \lambda} P(w_i|z_i = j) P(z_i = j) \quad (6)$$

where both $P(w_i|z_i = j)$ and $P(z_i = j)$ are estimated by their maximum likelihood estimates.

In practice, exhaustive evaluation of the powerset of L is prohibitively expensive, and so we greedily approximate the optimal λ using Algorithm 1. In essence, we initially rank all the candidate languages by computing the most likely distribution over the full set of candidate languages. Then, for each of the top-N languages in turn, we consider whether

Algorithm 1 $DetectLang(L, D)$

```
L_N ← top-N z ∈ L by P(z|D)
λ ← {L_u}
for each L_t ∈ L_N do
    λ' ← λ ∪ L_t
    if P(D|λ) + t < P(D|λ') then
        λ ← λ'
    end if
end for
λ ← λ \ {L_u}
return D ▷ λ
```

to add it to λ. λ is initialized with L_u, a dummy language with a uniform distribution over terms (i.e. $P(w|L_u) = \frac{1}{|w|}$). A language is added if it improves $P(D|\lambda)$ by at least t. The threshold t is required to suppress the addition of spurious classes. Adding languages gives the model additional freedom to fit parameters, and so will generally increase $P(D|\lambda)$. In the limit case, adding a completely irrelevant language will result in no tokens being mapped to the a language, and so the model will be no worse than without the language. The threshold t is thus used to control "how much" improvement is required before including the new language in λ.

3.4 Benchmark Approaches

We compare our approach to two methods for language identification in multilingual documents: (1) the *virtual mixed languages* approach (Prager, 1999a); and (2) the text segmentation approach (Yamaguchi and Tanaka-Ishii, 2012).

Prager (1999a) describes LINGUINI, a language identifier based on the vector-space model commonly used in text classification and information retrieval. The document representation used by Prager (1999a) is a vector of counts across a set of character sequences. Prager (1999a) selects the feature set based on a TFIDF-like approach. Terms with occurrence count $m < n \times k$ are rejected, where m is the number of times the term occurs in the training data (the TF component), n is the number of languages in which the term occurred (the IDF component, where "document" is replaced with "language"), and k is a parameter to control the overall number of terms selected. In Prager (1999a), the value of k is reported to be optimal in the region 0.3 to 0.5. In practice, the value of k indirectly controls the number of features selected. Values of k are not comparable across datasets as m is not normalized for the size of the training data, so in this work we do not report the values of k and instead directly select the top-N features, weighted by $\frac{m}{n}$. In LINGUINI, each language is modeled as a single pseudo-document, obtained by concatenating all the training data for the given language. A document is then classified according to the vector with which it has the smallest angle; this is implemented by finding the language vector with the highest cosine with the document vector.

Prager (1999a) also proposes an extension to the approach to allow identification of bilingual documents, and suggests how this may be generalized to any number of languages in a document. The gist of the method is simple: for any given pair of languages, the projection of a document vector onto the hyperplane containing the language vectors of the two languages gives the mixture proportions of the two languages that minimizes the angle with the document vector. Prager (1999a) terms this projection a *virtual mixed language* (VML), and shows how to find the angle between the document vector and the VML. If this angle is less than that between the document vector and any individual language vector, the document is labeled as bilingual in the two languages from which the mixed vector was derived. The practical difficulty presented by this approach is that exhaustively evaluating all possible combinations of languages is prohibitively expensive. Prager (1999a) addresses this by arguing that in multilingual documents, "the individual component languages will be close to d (the document vector) – probably closer than most or all other languages". Hence, language mixtures are only considered for combinations of the top m languages.

Prager (1999a) shows how to obtain the mixture coefficients for bilingual VMLs, arguing that the process generalizes. Prager (1999b) includes the coefficients for 3-language VMLs, which are much more complex than the 2-language variants. Using a computer algebra system, we verified the analytic forms of the coefficients in the 3-language VML. We also attempted to obtain an analytic form for the coefficients in a 4-language VML, but these were too complex for the computer algebra system to compute. Thus, our evaluation of the VML approach proposed by Prager (1999a) is limited to 3-language VMLs. Neither Prager (1999a) nor Prager (1999b) include an empirical evaluation over multilingual documents, so to the best of our knowledge this paper is the first empirical evaluation of the method on multilingual documents. As no reference implementation of this method is available, we have produced our own implementation, which we have made freely available.[1]

The other benchmark we consider in this paper is the method for text segmentation by language proposed by Yamaguchi and Tanaka-Ishii (2012) (hereafter referred to as SEGLANG). The actual task addressed by Yamaguchi and Tanaka-Ishii (2012) is to divide a document into monolingual segments. This is formulated as the task of segmenting a document $D = x_1, \cdots, x_{|D|}$ (where x_i denotes the ith character of D and $|D|$ is the length of the document) by finding a list of boundaries $B = [B_1, \cdots, B_{|B|}]$ where each B_i indicates the location of a language boundary as an offset from the start of the document, resulting in a list of segments $X = [X_0, \cdots, X_{|B|}]$. For each segment X_i, the system predicts L_i, the language associated with the segment, producing a list of labellings $L = [L_0, \cdots, L_{|B|}]$, with the constraint that adjacent elements in L must differ. Yamaguchi and Tanaka-Ishii (2012) solve the problem of determining X and L for an unlabeled text using a method based on minimum description length. They present a dynamic programming solution to this problem, and analyze a number of parameters that affect the overall accuracy of the system. Given this method to determine X and L, it is then trivial to label an unlabeled document according to $D \triangleright \{L_x \text{ if } \exists L_x \in L\}$, and the length of each segment in X can then be used to determine the proportions of the document that are in each language. In this work, we use a reference implementation of SEGLANG kindly provided to us by the authors.

Using the text segmentation approach of SEGLANG to detect multilingual documents differs from LINGUINI and our method primarily in that LINGUINI and our method fragment the document into small sequences of bytes, and discard information about the relative order of the fragments. This is in contrast to SEGLANG, where this information

[1] `https://github.com/saffsd/linguini.py`

System	$\mathcal{P}_M$	$\mathcal{R}_M$	$\mathcal{F}_M$	$\mathcal{P}_\mu$	$\mathcal{R}_\mu$	$\mathcal{F}_\mu$
Benchmark	.497	.467	.464	.833	.826	.829
Winner	.718	.703	.699	.932	.931	.932
SEGLANG	.801	.810	.784	.866	.946	.905
LINGUINI	.616	.535	.513	.713	.688	.700
Our method	.753	.771	.748	.945	.922	.933

Table 2: Results on the ALTW2010 dataset. "Benchmark" is the benchmark system proposed by the shared task organizers. "Winner" is the highest-$\mathcal{F}_\mu$ system submitted to the shared task.

is utilized in the sequential prediction of labels for consecutive segments of text, and is thus able to make better use of the locality of text (since there are likely to be monolingual blocks of text in any given multilingual document). The disadvantage of this is that the underlying model becomes more complex and hence more computationally expensive, as we observe in Section 5.

3.5 Evaluation

We seek to evaluate the ability of each method: (1) to correctly identify the language(s) present in each test document; and (2) for multilingual documents, to estimate the relative proportion of the document written in each language. In the first instance, this is a classification problem, and the standard notions of precision ($\mathcal{P}$), recall ($\mathcal{R}$) and F-score ($\mathcal{F}$) apply. Consistent with previous work in language identification, we report both the document-level *micro-average*, as well as the language-level *macro-average*. For consistency with Baldwin and Lui (2010a), the macro-averaged F-score we report is the average of the per-class F-scores, rather than the harmonic mean of the macro-averaged precision and recall; as such, it is possible for the F-score to not fall between the precision and recall values. As is common practice, we compute the F-score for $\beta = 1$, giving equal importance to precision and recall.[2] We tested the difference in performance for statistical significance using an approximate randomization procedure (Yeh, 2000) with 10000 iterations. Within each table of results (Tables 2, 3 and 4), all differences between systems are statistically significant at a $p < 0.05$ level.

To evaluate the predictions of the relative proportions of a document D written in each detected language L_i, we compare the topic proportion predicted by our model to the gold-standard proportion, measured as a byte ratio as follows:

$$gs(L_i|D) = \frac{\text{length of } L_i \text{ part of } D \text{ in bytes}}{\text{length of } D \text{ in bytes}} \quad (7)$$

We report the correlation between predicted and actual proportions in terms of Pearson's r coefficient. We also report the mean absolute error (MAE) over all document–language pairs.

4 Experiments on ALTW2010

Our first experiment utilizes the ALTW2010 shared task dataset (Baldwin and Lui, 2010b), a synthetic dataset of 10000 bilingual documents[3] generated from Wikipedia data, introduced in the ALTW2010 shared task,[4] The dataset is organized into training, development and test partitions. Following standard machine learning practice, we train each system using the training partition, and tune parameters using the development partition. We then report macro and micro-averaged precision, recall and F-score on the test partition, using the tuned parameters.

The results on the ALTW2010 shared task dataset are summarized in Table 2. Each of the three systems we compare was re-trained using the training data provided for the shared task, with a slight difference: in the shared task, participants were provided with multilingual training documents, but the systems targeted in this research require monolingual training data. We thus split the training documents into monolingual segments using the metadata provided with the dataset. The metadata was only published after completion of the task and was not available to task participants. For comparison, we have included the benchmark results published by the shared task organizers, as well as the score attained by the winning entry (Tran et al., 2010).

[2] Intuitively, it may seem that the maximal precision and recall should be achieved when precision and recall are balanced. However, because of the multi-label nature of the task and variable number of labels assigned to a given document by our models, it is theoretically possible and indeed common in our results for the maximal macro-averaged F-score to be achieved when macro-averaged precision and recall are not balanced.

[3] With a small number of monolingual documents, formed by randomly selecting the two languages for a given document independently, leaving the possibility of the same two languages being selected.

[4] http://comp.mq.edu.au/programming/task_description/

We tune the parameters for each system using the development partition of the dataset, and report results on the test partition. For LINGUINI, there is a single parameter k to be tuned: the number of features per language. We tested values between 10000 and 50000, and selected 46000 features as the optimal value. For our method, there are two parameters to be tuned: (1) the number of features selected for each language, and (2) the threshold t for including a language. We tested features-per-language counts between 30 and 150, and found that adding features beyond 70 per language had minimal effect. We tested values of the threshold t from 0.01 to 0.15, and found the best value was 0.14. For SEGLANG, we introduce a threshold t on the minimum proportion of a document (measured in bytes) that must be labeled by a language before that language is included in the output set. This was done because our initial experiments indicate that SEGLANG tends to over-produce labels. Using the development data, we found the best value of t was 0.10.

We find that of the three systems tested, two outperform the winning entry to the shared task. This is more evident in the macro-averaged results than in the micro-averaged results. In micro-averaged terms, our method is the best performer, whereas on the macro-average, SEGLANG has the highest F-score. This suggests that our method does well on higher-density languages (relative to the ALTW2010 dataset), and poorly on lower-density languages. This also accounts for the higher micro-averaged precision but lower micro-averaged recall for our method as compared to SEGLANG. The improved macro-average F-score of SEGLANG comes at a much higher computational cost, which increases dramatically as the number of languages is increased. In our testing on a 16-core workstation, SEGLANG took almost 24 hours to process the ALTW2010 shared task test data, compared to 2 minutes for our method and 40 seconds for LINGUINI. As such, SEGLANG is poorly suited to detecting multilingual documents where a large number of candidate languages is considered.

The ALTW2010 dataset is an excellent starting point for this research, but it predominantly contains bilingual documents, making it difficult to assess the ability of systems to distinguish multilingual documents from monolingual ones. Furthermore, we are unable to use it to assess the ability of systems to detect more than 2 languages in a document. To address these shortcomings, we construct a new dataset in a similar vein. The dataset and experiments performed on it are described in the next section.

5 Experiments on WIKIPEDIAMULTI

To fully test the capabilities of our model, we generated WIKIPEDIAMULTI, a dataset that contains a mixture of monolingual and multilingual documents. To allow for replicability of our results and to facilitate research in language identification, we have made the dataset publicly available.[5] WIKIPEDIAMULTI is generated using excerpts from the mediawiki sources of Wikipedia pages downloaded from the Wikimedia foundation.[6] The dumps we used are from July–August 2010.

To generate WIKIPEDIAMULTI, we first normalized the raw mediawiki documents. Mediawiki documents typically contain one paragraph per line, interspersed with structural elements. We filtered each document to remove all structural elements, and only kept documents that exceeded 2500 bytes after normalization. This yielded a collection of around 500,000 documents in 156 languages. From this initial document set (hereafter referred to as WIKICONTENT), we only retained languages that had more than 1000 documents (44 languages), and generated documents for WIKIPEDIAMULTI as follows:

1. randomly select the number of languages K ($1 \leq K \leq 5$)
2. randomly select a set of K languages $S = \{L_i \in L \text{ for } i = 1 \cdots K\}$ without replacement
3. randomly select a document for each $L_i \in S$ from WIKICONTENT without replacement
4. take the top $\frac{1}{K}$ lines of the document
5. join the K sections into a single document.

As a result of the procedure, the relative proportion of each language in a multilingual document tends not to be uniform, as it is conditioned on the length of the original document from which it was sourced, independent of the other $K-1$ for the other languages that it was combined with. Overall, the average document length is 5500 bytes (standard deviation = 3800 bytes). Due to rounding up in taking

[5] http://www.csse.unimelb.edu.au/~tim/
[6] http://dumps.wikimedia.org

System	$\mathcal{P}_M$	$\mathcal{R}_M$	$\mathcal{F}_M$	$\mathcal{P}_\mu$	$\mathcal{R}_\mu$	$\mathcal{F}_\mu$
SEGLANG	.809	.975	.875	.771	.975	.861
LINGUINI	.853	.772	.802	.838	.774	.805
Our method	.962	.954	.957	.963	.955	.959

Table 3: Results on the WIKIPEDIAMULTI dataset.

the top $\frac{1}{k}$ lines (step 4), documents with higher K tend to be longer (6200 bytes for $K = 5$ vs 5100 bytes for $K = 1$).

The WIKIPEDIAMULTI dataset contains training, development and test partitions. The training partition consists of 5000 monolingual (i.e. $K = 1$) documents. The development partition consists of 5000 documents, 1000 documents for each value of K where $1 \leq K \leq 5$. The test partition contains 200 documents for each K, for a total of 1000 documents. There is no overlap between any of the partitions.

5.1 Results over WIKIPEDIAMULTI

We trained each system using the monolingual training partition, and tuned parameters using the development partition. For LINGUINI, we tested feature counts between 10000 and 50000, and found that the effect was relatively small. We thus use 10000 features as the optimum value. For SEGLANG, we tested values for threshold t between 0.01 and 0.20, and found that the maximal macro-averaged F-score is attained when $t = 0.06$. Finally, for our method we tested features-per-language counts between 30 and 130 and found the best performance with 120 features per language, although the actual effect of varying this value is rather small. We tested values of the threshold t for adding an extra language to λ from 0.01 to 0.15, and found that the best results were attained when $t = 0.02$.

The results of evaluating each system on the test partition are summarized in Table 3. In this evaluation, our method clearly outperforms both SEGLANG and LINGUINI. The results on WIKIPEDIAMULTI and ALTW2010 are difficult to compare directly due to the different compositions of the two datasets. ALTW2010 is predominantly bilingual, whereas WIKIPEDIAMULTI contains documents with text in 1–5 languages. Furthermore, the average document in ALTW2010 is half the length of that in WIKIPEDIAMULTI. Overall, we observe that SEGLANG has a tendency to over-label (despite the introduction of the t parameter to reduce this effect), evidenced by high recall but lower precision. LINGUINI is inherently limited in that it is only able to detect up to 3 languages per document, causing recall to suffer on WIKIPEDIAMULTI. However, it also tends to always output 3 languages, regardless of the actual number of languages in the document, hurting precision. Furthermore, even on ALTW2010 it has lower recall than the other two systems.

6 Estimating Language Proportions

In addition to detecting multiple languages within a document, our method also estimates the relative proportions of the document that are written in each language. This information may be useful for detecting documents that are candidate bitexts for training machine translation systems, since we may expect languages in the document to be present in equal proportions. It also allows us to identify the predominant language of a document.

A core element of our model of a document is a distribution over a set of labels. Since each label corresponds to a language, as a first approximation, we take the probability mass associated with each label as a direct estimate of the proportion of the document written in that language. We examine the results for predicting the language proportions in the test partition of WIKIPEDIAMULTI. Mapping label distributions directly to language proportions produces excellent results, with a Pearson's r value of 0.863 and an MAE of 0.108.

Although labels have a one-to-one correspondence with languages, the label distribution does not actually correspond directly to the language proportion, because the distribution estimates the proportion of byte n-gram sequences associated with a label and not the proportion of bytes directly. The same number of bytes in different languages can produce different numbers of n-gram sequences, because after feature selection not all n-gram sequences are retained in the feature set. Hereafter, we refer to each n-gram sequence as a *token*, and the average number of tokens produced per byte of text as the *token emission rate*.

We estimate the per-language token emission rate (Figure 1) using the training partition of WIKIPEDIAMULTI. To improve our estimate of the language proportions, we correct our label distribution

Original text	`the_cat_in_the_hat`
n-gram features	{ `he_` : 2, `the_` : 2, `_hat` : 1, `_in_` : 1, `_th` : 1, `_the` : 1, `hat` : 1, `he_c` : 1, `in_t` : 1, `n_th` : 1 }
Emission rate	$\frac{\#\text{bytes}}{\#\text{tokens}} = \frac{18}{12} = 1.5$ bytes/token

Figure 1: Example of calculating n-gram emission rate for a text string.

using estimates of the per-language token emission rate R_{L_i} in bytes per token for $L_i \in L$. Assume that a document D of length $|D|$ is estimated to contain K languages in proportions P_i for $i = 1 \cdots K$. The corrected estimate for the proportion of L_i is:

$$Prop(L_i) = \frac{P_i \times R_{L_i}}{\sum_{j=1}^{K} (P_j \times R_{L_j})} \tag{8}$$

Note that the $|D|$ term is common to the numerator and denominator and has thus been eliminated.

This correction improves our estimates of language proportions. After correction, the Pearson's r rises to 0.981, and the MAE is reduced to 0.024. The improvement is most noticeable for language–document pairs where the proportion of the document in the given language is about 0.5 (Figure 2).

7 Real-world Multilingual Documents

So far, we have demonstrated the effectiveness of our proposed approach using synthetic data. The results have been excellent, and in this section we validate the approach by applying it to a real-world task that has recently been discussed in the literature. Yamaguchi and Tanaka-Ishii (2012) and King and Abney (2013) both observe that in trying to gather linguistic data for "non-major" languages from the web, one challenge faced is that documents retrieved often contain sections in another language. SEGLANG (the solution of Yamaguchi and Tanaka-Ishii (2012)) concurrently detects multilingual documents and segments them by language, but the approach is computationally expensive and has a tendency to over-label (Section 5). On the other hand, the solution of King and Abney (2013) is incomplete, and they specifically mention the need for an automatic method "to examine a multilingual document, and with high accuracy, list the languages that are present in the document". In this section, we show that our method is able to fill this need. We make use of manually-annotated data kindly provided to us by Ben King, which consists of 149 documents containing 42 languages retrieved from the web using a set of targeted queries for low-density languages. Note that the dataset described in King and Abney (2013) was based on manual confirmation of the presence of English in addition to the low-density language of primary interest; our dataset contains these bilingual documents as well as monolingual documents in the low-density language of interest. Our purpose in this section is to investigate the ability of automatic systems to select this subset of bilingual documents. Specifically, given a collection of documents retrieved for a target language, the task is to identify the documents that contain text in English in addition to the target language. Thus, we re-train each system for each target language, using only training data for English and the target language. We reserve the data provided by Ben King for evaluation, and train our methods using data separately obtained from the Universal Declaration of Human Rights (UDHR). Where UDHR translations for a particular language were not available, we used data from Wikipedia or from a bible translation. Approximately 20–80 kB of data were used for each language. As we do not have suitable development data, we made use of the best parameters for each system from the experiments on WIKIPEDIAMULTI.

System	$\mathcal{P}$	$\mathcal{R}$	$\mathcal{F}$
Baseline	0.719	1.00	0.837
SEGLANG	0.779	0.991	0.872
LINGUINI	0.729	0.981	0.837
Our method	0.907	0.916	0.912

Table 4: Detection accuracy for English-language inclusion in web documents from targeted web crawls for low-density languages.

We find that all 3 systems are able to detect that each document contains the target language with 100% accuracy. However, systems vary in their ability to detect if a document also contains English in addition to the target language. The detection accuracy for English-language inclusion is summarized in Table 4.[7] For comparison, we include a heuristic baseline based on labeling all documents as contain-

[7]Note that Table 2 and Table 3 both report macro and micro-averaged results across a number of languages. In contrast Table 4 only reports results for English, and the values are not directly comparable to our earlier evaluation.

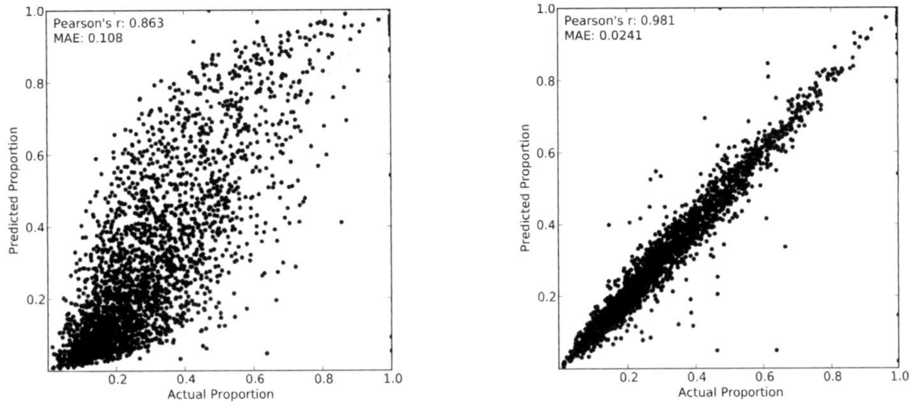

(a) without emission rate correction

(b) with emission rate correction

Figure 2: Scatterplot of the predicted vs. actual language proportions in a document for the test partition of WIKIPEDIAMULTI (predictions are from our method; each point corresponds to a document-language pair).

ing English. We find that, like the heuristic baseline, SEGLANG and LINGUINI both tend to over-label documents, producing false positive labels of English, resulting in increased recall at the expense of precision. Our method produces less false positives (but slightly more false negatives). Overall, our method attains the best $\mathcal{F}$ for detecting English inclusions. Manual error analysis suggests that the false negatives for our method generally occur where a relatively small proportion of the document is written in English.

8 Future Work

Document segmentation by language could be accomplished by a combination of our method and the method of King and Abney (2013), which could be compared to the method of Yamaguchi and Tanaka-Ishii (2012) in the context of constructing corpora for low-density languages using the web. Another area we have identified in this paper is the tuning of the parameters α and β in our model (currently $\alpha = 0$ and $\beta = 1$), which may have some effect on the sparsity of the model.

Further work is required in dealing with cross-domain effects, to allow for "off-the-shelf" language identification in multilingual documents. Previous work has shown that it is possible to generate a document representation that is robust to variation across domains (Lui and Baldwin, 2011), and we intend to investigate if these results are also applicable to language identification in multilingual documents. Another open question is the extension of the generative mixture models to "unknown" language identification (i.e. eliminating the closed-world assumption (Hughes et al., 2006)), which may be possible through the use of non-parametric mixture models such as Hierarchical Dirichlet Processes (Teh et al., 2006).

9 Conclusion

We have presented a system for language identification in multilingual documents using a generative mixture model inspired by supervised topic modeling algorithms, combined with a document representation based on previous research in language identification for monolingual documents. We showed that the system outperforms alternative approaches from the literature on synthetic data, as well as on real-world data from related research on linguistic corpus creation for low-density languages using the web as a resource. We also showed that our system is able to accurately estimate the proportion of the document written in each of the languages identified. We have made a full reference implementation of our system freely available,[8] as well as the synthetic dataset prepared for this paper (Section 5), in order to facilitate the adoption of this technology and further research in this area.

[8] https://github.com/saffsd/polyglot

Acknowledgments

We thank Hiroshi Yamaguchi for making a reference implementation of SEGLANG available to us, and Ben King for providing us with a collection of real-world multilingual web documents. This work was substantially improved as a result of the insightful feedback received from the reviewers.

NICTA is funded by the Australian Government as represented by the Department of Broadband, Communications and the Digital Economy and the Australian Research Council through the ICT Centre of Excellence program.

References

Steven Abney and Steven Bird. 2010. The human language project: building a universal corpus of the world's languages. In *Proceedings of the 48th Annual Meeting of the Association for Computational Linguistics*, pages 88–97. Association for Computational Linguistics.

Beatrice Alex, Amit Dubey, and Frank Keller. 2007. Using foreign inclusion detection to improve parsing performance. In *Proceedings of the Joint Conference on Empirical Methods in Natural Language Processing and Computational Natural Language Learning 2007 (EMNLP-CoNLL 2007)*, pages 151–160, Prague, Czech Republic.

Timothy Baldwin and Marco Lui. 2010a. Language identification: The long and the short of the matter. In *Proceedings of Human Language Technologies: The 11th Annual Conference of the North American Chapter of the Association for Computational Linguistics (NAACL HLT 2010)*, pages 229–237, Los Angeles, USA.

Timothy Baldwin and Marco Lui. 2010b. Multilingual language identification: ALTW 2010 shared task dataset. In *Proceedings of the Australasian Language Technology Workshop 2010 (ALTW 2010)*, pages 5–7, Melbourne, Australia.

Shane Bergsma, Paul McNamee, Mossaab Bagdouri, Clayton Fink, and Theresa Wilson. 2012. Language identification for creating language-specific Twitter collections. In *Proceedings the Second Workshop on Language in Social Media (LSM2012)*, pages 65–74, Montréal, Canada.

David M. Blei, Andrew Y. Ng, and Michael I. Jordan. 2003. Latent Dirichlet allocation. *Journal of Machine Learning Research*, 3:993–1022.

Alessio Bosca and Luca Dini. 2010. Language identification strategies for cross language information retrieval. In *Working Notes of the Cross Language Evaluation Forum (CLEF)*.

Jamie Callan and Mark Hoy. 2009. *ClueWeb09 Dataset*. Available at `http://boston.lti.cs.cmu.edu/Data/clueweb09/`.

William B. Cavnar and John M. Trenkle. 1994. N-gram-based text categorization. In *Proceedings of the Third Symposium on Document Analysis and Information Retrieval*, pages 161–175, Las Vegas, USA.

Hakan Ceylan and Yookyung Kim. 2009. Language identification of search engine queries. In *Proceedings of the Joint Conference of the 47th Annual Meeting of the ACL and the 4th International Joint Conference on Natural Language Processing of the AFNLP*, pages 1066–1074, Singapore.

Paul Cook and Marco Lui. 2012. langid.py for better language modelling. In *Proceedings of the Australasian Language Technology Association Workshop 2012*, pages 107–112, Dunedin, New Zealand.

Rafael Dueire Lins and Paulo Gonçalves. 2004. Automatic language identification of written texts. In *Proceedings of the 2004 ACM Symposium on Applied Computing (SAC 2004)*, pages 1128–1133, Nicosia, Cyprus.

Ted Dunning. 1994. Statistical identification of language. Technical Report MCCS 940-273, Computing Research Laboratory, New Mexico State University.

Rayid Ghani, Rosie Jones, and Dunja Mladenic. 2004. Building minority language corpora by learning to generate web search queries. *Knowledge and Information Systems*, 7(1):56–83.

Emmanuel Giguet. 1995. Categorisation according to language: A step toward combining linguistic knowledge and statistical learning. In *Proceedings of the 4th International Workshop on Parsing Technologies (IWPT-1995)*, Prague, Czech Republic.

Gregory Grefenstette. 1995. Comparing two language identification schemes. In *Proceedings of Analisi Statistica dei Dati Testuali (JADT)*, pages 263–268, Rome, Italy.

Thomas L. Griffiths and Mark Steyvers. 2004. Finding scientific topics. *Proceedings of the National Academy of Sciences*, 101:5228–5235.

Thomas Griffiths. 2002. Gibbs sampling in the generative model of latent Dirichlet allocation. *Technical Report, Stanford University*.

Baden Hughes, Timothy Baldwin, Steven Bird, Jeremy Nicholson, and Andrew MacKinlay. 2006. Reconsidering language identification for written language resources. In *Proceedings of the 5th International Conference on Language Resources and Evaluation (LREC 2006)*, pages 485–488, Genoa, Italy.

Genitiro Kikui. 1996. Identifying the coding system and language of on-line documents on the internet. In *Proceedings of the 16th International Conference on Computational Linguistics (COLING '96)*, pages 652–657, Kyoto, Japan.

Ben King and Steven Abney. 2013. Labeling the languages of words in mixed-language documents using weakly supervised methods. In *Proceedings of the 2013 Conference of the North American Chapter of the Association for Computational Linguistics: Human Language Technologies*, pages 1110–1119, Atlanta, Georgia.

Canasai Kruengkrai, Prapass Srichaivattana, Virach Sornlertlamvanich, and Hitoshi Isahara. 2005. Language identification based on string kernels. In *Proceedings of the 5th International Symposium on Communications and Information Technologies (ISCIT-2005)*, pages 896–899, Beijing, China.

David D. Lewis. 1997. The Reuters-21578 data set. available at `http://www.daviddlewis.com/resources/testcollections/reuters21578/`.

Wang Ling, Guang Xiang, Chris Dyer, Alan Black, and Isabel Trancoso. 2013. Microblogs as parallel corpora. In *Proceedings of the 51st Annual Meeting of the Association for Computational Linguistics (Volume 1: Long Papers)*, pages 176–186, Sofia, Bulgaria, August. Association for Computational Linguistics.

Jicheng Liu and Chunyan Liang. 2008. Text Categorization of Multilingual Web Pages in Specific Domain. In *Proceedings of the 12th Pacific-Asia Conference on Advances in Knowledge Discovery and Data Mining*, PAKDD'08, pages 938–944, Osaka, Japan.

Marco Lui and Timothy Baldwin. 2011. Cross-domain feature selection for language identification. In *Proceedings of the 5th International Joint Conference on Natural Language Processing (IJCNLP 2011)*, pages 553–561, Chiang Mai, Thailand.

Bruno Martins and Mário J. Silva. 2005. Language identification in web pages. In *Proceedings of the 2005 ACM symposium on Applied computing*, pages 764–768, Santa Fe, USA.

Andrew McCallum and Kamal Nigam. 1998. A comparison of event models for Naive Bayes text classification. In *Proceedings of the AAAI-98 Workshop on Learning for Text Categorization*, pages Available as Technical Report WS-98-05, AAAI Press., Madison, USA.

Andrew Kachites McCallum. 1999. Multi-label text classification with a mixture model trained by EM. In *Proceedings of AAAI 99 Workshop on Text Learning*.

Paul McNamee. 2005. Language identification: a solved problem suitable for undergraduate instruction. *Journal of Computing Sciences in Colleges*, 20(3):94–101.

Jian-Yun Nie, Michel Simard, Pierre Isabelle, and Richard Durand. 1999. Cross-language information retrieval based on parallel texts and automatic mining of parallel texts from the web. In *Proceedings of 22nd International ACM-SIGIR Conference on Research and Development in Information Retrieval (SIGIR'99)*, pages 74–81, Berkeley, USA.

John M. Prager. 1999a. Linguini: language identification for multilingual documents. In *Proceedings the 32nd Annual Hawaii International Conference on Systems Sciences (HICSS-32)*, Maui, Hawaii.

John M. Prager. 1999b. Linguini: Language identification for multilingual documents. *Journal of Management Information Systems*, 16(3):71–101.

John Ross Quinlan. 1993. *C4.5: Programs for Machine Learning*. Morgan Kaufmann, San Mateo, USA.

Daniel Ramage, David Hall, Ramesh Nallapati, and Christopher D. Manning. 2009. Labeled LDA: A supervised topic model for credit attribution in multi-labeled corpora. In *Proceedings of the 2009 Conference on Empirical Methods in Natural Language Processing (EMNLP 2009)*, pages 248–256, Singapore.

Radim Rehurek and Milan Kolkus. 2009. Language Identification on the Web: Extending the Dictionary Method. In *Proceedings of Computational Linguistics and Intelligent Text Processing, 10th International Conference (CICLing 2009)*, pages 357–368, Mexico City, Mexico.

Philip Resnik. 1999. Mining the Web for bilingual text. In *Proceedings of the 37th Annual Meeting of the Association for Computational Linguistics*, pages 527–534, College Park, USA.

Kevin P Scannell. 2007. The Crúbadán Project: Corpus building for under-resourced languages. In *Building and Exploring Web Corpora: Proceedings of the 3rd Web as Corpus Workshop*, pages 5–15, Louvain-la-Neuve, Belgium.

W. J. Teahan. 2000. Text Classification and Segmentation Using Minimum Cross-Entropy. In *Proceedings the 6th International Conference "Recherche d'Information Assistee par Ordinateur" (RIAO'00)*, pages 943–961, Paris, France.

Yee Whye Teh, Michael I. Jordan, Matthew J. Beal, and David M. Blei. 2006. Hierarchical Dirichlet processes. *Journal of the American Statistical Association*, 101:1566–1581.

Jörg Tiedemann and Nikola Ljubešić. 2012. Efficient discrimination between closely related languages. In *Proceedings of the 24th International Conference on Computational Linguistics (COLING 2012)*, pages 2619–2634, Mumbai, India.

Giang Binh Tran, Dat Ba Nguyen, and Bin Thanh Kieu. 2010. N-gram based approach for multilingual language identification. poster. available at http://comp.mq.edu.au/programming/task_description/VILangTek.pdf.

Fei Xia, Carrie Lewis, and William D. Lewis. 2010. Language ID for a thousand languages. In *LSA Annual Meeting Extended Abstracts*, Baltimore,USA.

Hiroshi Yamaguchi and Kumiko Tanaka-Ishii. 2012. Text segmentation by language using minimum description length. In *Proceedings the 50th Annual Meeting of the Association for Computational Linguistics (Volume 1: Long Papers)*, pages 969–978, Jeju Island, Korea.

Alexander Yeh. 2000. More accurate tests for the statistical significance of result differences. In *Proceedings of the 18th International Conference on Computational Linguistics (COLING 2000)*, pages 947–953, Saarbrücken, Germany.

A Crossing-Sensitive Third-Order Factorization for Dependency Parsing

Emily Pitler*
Google Research
76 9th Avenue
New York, NY 10011
epitler@google.com

Abstract

Parsers that parametrize over wider scopes are generally more accurate than edge-factored models. For graph-based non-projective parsers, wider factorizations have so far implied large increases in the computational complexity of the parsing problem. This paper introduces a "crossing-sensitive" generalization of a third-order factorization that trades off complexity in the *model* structure (i.e., scoring with features over multiple edges) with complexity in the *output* structure (i.e., producing crossing edges). Under this model, the optimal 1-Endpoint-Crossing tree can be found in $O(n^4)$ time, matching the asymptotic run-time of *both* the third-order *projective* parser and the *edge-factored* 1-Endpoint-Crossing parser. The crossing-sensitive third-order parser is significantly more accurate than the third-order projective parser under many experimental settings and significantly less accurate on none.

1 Introduction

Conditioning on wider syntactic contexts than simply individual head-modifier relationships improves parsing accuracy in a wide variety of parsers and frameworks (Charniak and Johnson, 2005; McDonald and Pereira, 2006; Hall, 2007; Carreras, 2007; Martins et al., 2009; Koo and Collins, 2010; Zhang and Nivre, 2011; Bohnet and Kuhn, 2012; Martins et al., 2013). This paper proposes a new graph-based dependency parser that efficiently produces the globally optimal dependency tree according to a third-order model (that includes features over grandparents and siblings in the tree) in the class of 1-Endpoint-Crossing trees (that includes all projective trees and the vast majority of *non-projective* structures seen in dependency treebanks).

*The majority of this work was done while at the University of Pennsylvania.

Within graph-based *projective* parsing, the *third-order* parser of Koo and Collins (2010) has a runtime of $O(n^4)$, just one factor of n more expensive than the edge-factored model of Eisner (2000). Incorporating richer features *and* producing trees with crossing edges has traditionally been a challenge, however, for graph-based dependency parsers. If parsing is posed as the problem of finding the optimal scoring directed spanning tree, then the problem becomes NP-hard when trees are scored with a grandparent and/or sibling factorization (McDonald and Pereira, 2006; McDonald and Satta, 2007). For various definitions of mildly non-projective trees, even edge-factored versions are expensive, with *edge-factored* running times between $O(n^4)$ and $O(n^7)$ (Gómez-Rodríguez et al., 2011; Pitler et al., 2012; Pitler et al., 2013; Satta and Kuhlmann, 2013).

The third-order projective parser of Koo and Collins (2010) and the edge-factored 1-Endpoint-Crossing parser described in Pitler et al. (2013) have some similarities: both use $O(n^4)$ time and $O(n^3)$ space, using sub-problems over intervals with one exterior vertex, which are constructed using one free split point. The two parsers differ in *how the exterior vertex is used*: Koo and Collins (2010) use the exterior vertex to store a grandparent index, while Pitler et al. (2013) use the exterior vertex to introduce crossed edges between the point and

Transactions of the Association for Computational Linguistics, 2 (2014) 41–54. Action Editor: Joakim Nivre.
Submitted 9/2013; Revised 11/2013; Published 2/2014.

	Projective	1-Endpoint-Crossing
Edge	$O(n^3)$ Eisner (2000)	$O(n^4)$ Pitler et al. (2013)
CS-GSib	$O(n^4)$ Koo and Collins (2010)	$\mathbf{O(n^4)}$ This paper

Table 1: Parsing time for various output spaces and model factorizations. CS-GSib refers to the (crossing-sensitive) grand-sibling factorization described in this paper.

the interval. This paper proposes *merging* the two parsers to achieve the best of both worlds – producing the best tree in the wider range of 1-Endpoint-Crossing trees while incorporating the identity of the grandparent and/or sibling of the child in the score of an edge whenever the local neighborhood of the edge does not contain crossing edges. The crossing-sensitive grandparent-sibling 1-Endpoint-Crossing parser proposed here takes $O(n^4)$ time, matching the runtime of both the third-order projective parser and of the edge-factored 1-Endpoint-Crossing parser (see Table 1).

The parsing algorithms of Koo and Collins (2010) and Pitler et al. (2013) are reviewed in Section 2. The proposed crossing-sensitive factorization is defined in Section 3. The parsing algorithm that finds the optimal 1-Endpoint-Crossing tree according to this factorization is described in Section 4. The implemented parser is significantly more accurate than the third-order projective parser in a variety of languages and treebank representations (Section 5). Section 6 discusses the proposed approach in the context of prior work on non-projective parsing.

2 Preliminaries

In a *projective* dependency tree, each subtree forms one consecutive interval in the sequence of input words; equivalently (assuming an artificial root node placed as either the first or last token), when all edges are drawn in the half-plane above the sentence, no two edges *cross* (Kübler et al., 2009). Two vertex-disjoint edges *cross* if their endpoints interleave. A *1-Endpoint-Crossing* tree is a dependency tree such that for each edge, all edges that cross it share a common vertex (Pitler et al., 2013). Note that the class of projective trees is properly included within the class of 1-Endpoint-Crossing trees.

To avoid confusion between intervals and edges,

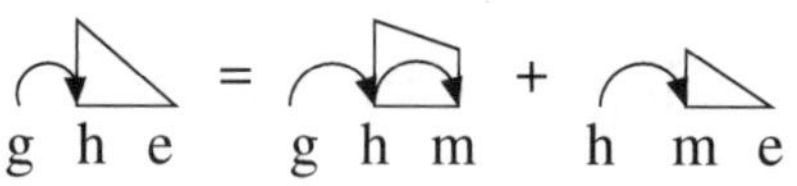

(a) m is the child of h that e is descended from

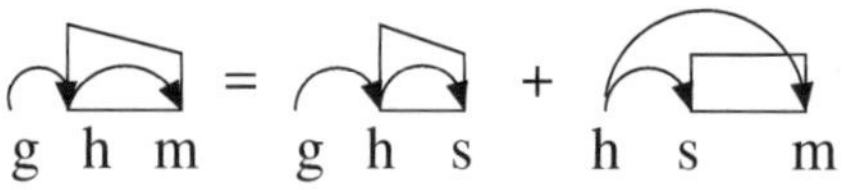

(b) The edge $\vec{e}_{hm}$ is added to the tree; s is m's adjacent inner sibling

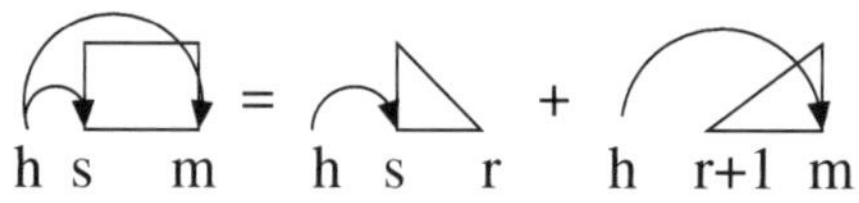

(c) r is s's outermost descendant; $r+1$ is m's innermost descendant

Figure 1: Algorithm for grand-sibling projective parsing; the figures replicate Figure 6 in Koo and Collins (2010).

$\vec{e}_{ij}$ denotes the *directed edge* from i to j (i.e., i is the parent of j). Interval notation ((i,j), $[i,j]$, $(i,j]$, or $[i,j)$) is used to denote *sets of vertices* between i and j, with square brackets indicating closed intervals and round brackets indicating open intervals.

2.1 Grand-Sibling Projective Parsing

A grand-sibling factorization allows features over 4-tuples of (g,h,m,s), where h is the parent of m, g is m's grandparent, and s is m's adjacent inner sibling. Features over these grand-sibling 4-tuples are referred to as "third-order" because they scope over three *edges* simultaneously ($\vec{e}_{gh}$, $\vec{e}_{hs}$, and $\vec{e}_{hm}$). The parser of Koo and Collins (2010) produces the highest-scoring projective tree according to this grand-sibling model by adding an external grandparent index to each of the sub-problems used in the sibling factorization (McDonald and Pereira, 2006). Figure 6 in Koo and Collins (2010) provided a pictorial view of the algorithm; for convenience, it is replicated in Figure 1. An edge $\vec{e}_{hm}$ is added to the tree in the "trapezoid" step (Figure 1b); this allows the edge to be scored conditioned on m's grandparent (g) and its adjacent inner sibling (s), as all four relevant indices are accessible.

2.2 Edge-factored 1-Endpoint-Crossing Parsing

The edge-factored 1-Endpoint-Crossing parser of Pitler et al. (2013) produces the highest scoring 1-

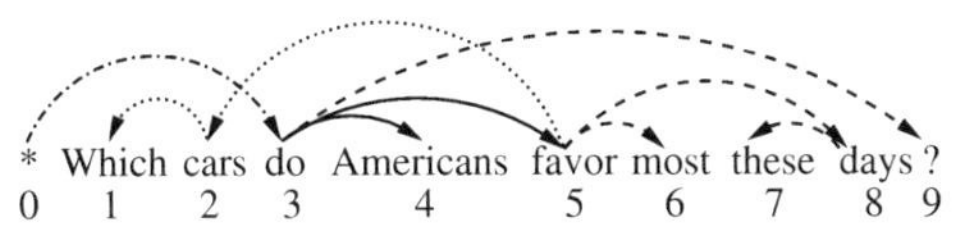

Figure 2: A 1-Endpoint-Crossing non-projective English sentence from the WSJ Penn Treebank (Marcus et al., 1993), converted to dependencies with PennConverter (Johansson and Nugues, 2007).

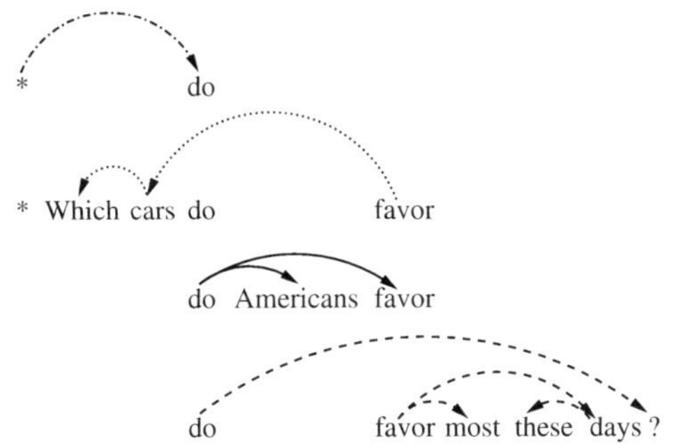

Figure 3: Constructing a 1-Endpoint-Crossing tree with intervals with one exterior vertex (Pitler et al., 2013).

Endpoint-Crossing tree with each edge $\vec{e}_{hm}$ scored according to $\mathrm{Score(Edge(h, m))}$. The 1-Endpoint-Crossing property allows the tree to be built up in edge-disjoint pieces each consisting of intervals with one exterior point that has edges into the interval. For example, the tree in Figure 2 would be built up with the sub-problems shown in Figure 3.

To ensure that crossings *within* a sub-problem are consistent with the crossings that happen as a result of combination steps, the algorithm uses four different "types" of sub-problems, indicating whether the edges incident to the exterior point may be internally crossed by edges incident to the left boundary point (L), the right (R), either (LR), or neither (N). In Figure 3, the sub-problem over $[*, do] \cup \{favor\}$ would be of type R, and $[favor, ?] \cup \{do\}$ of type L.

2.2.1 Naïve Approach to Including Grandparent Features

The example in Figure 3 illustrates the difficulty of incorporating grandparents into the scoring of all edges in 1-Endpoint-Crossing parsing. The vertex *favor* has a parent or child in *all three* of the sub-problems. In order to use grandparent scoring for the edges from *favor* to *favor*'s children in the other two sub-problems, we would need to augment the problems with the grandparent index *do*. We also must add the parent index *do* to the middle sub-problem to ensure consistency (i.e., that *do* is in fact the parent assigned). Thus, a first attempt to score all edges with grandparent features within 1-Endpoint-Crossing trees raises the runtime from $O(n^4)$ to $O(n^7)$ (all of the four indices need a "predicted parent" index; at least one edge is always implied so one of these additional indices can be dropped).

3 Crossing-Sensitive Factorization

Factorizations for projective dependency parsing have often been designed to allow efficient parsing. For example, the algorithms in Eisner (2000) and McDonald and Pereira (2006) achieve their efficiency by assuming that children to the left of the parent and to the right of the parent are independent of each other. The algorithms of Carreras (2007) and Model 2 in Koo and Collins (2010) include grandparents for only the outermost grand-children of each parent for efficiency reasons. In a similar spirit, this paper introduces a variant of the Grand-Sib factorization that scores crossed edges independently (as a $\mathrm{CrossedEdge}$ part) and uncrossed edges under either a grandparent-sibling, grandparent, sibling, or edge-factored model depending on whether relevant edges in its local neighborhood are crossed.

A few auxiliary definitions are required. For any parent h and grandparent g, h's children are partitioned into *interior* children (those between g and h) and *exterior children* (the complementary set of children).[1] Interior children are numbered from closest to h through furthest from h; exterior children are first numbered on the side closer to h from closest to h through furthest, then the enumeration wraps around to include the vertices on the side closer to g. Figure 4 shows a parent h, its grandparent g, and a possible sequence of three interior and four exterior children. Note that for a projective tree, there would not be any children on the far side of g.

Definition 1. *Let h be m's parent.* $\mathbf{Outer}(m)$ *is the set of siblings of m that are in the same subset of h's children and are later in the enumeration than m is.*

For example, in the tree in Figure 2,

[1] Because dependency trees are directed trees, each node except for the artificial root has a unique parent. To ensure that *grandparent* is defined for the root's children, assume an artificial parent of the root for notational convenience.

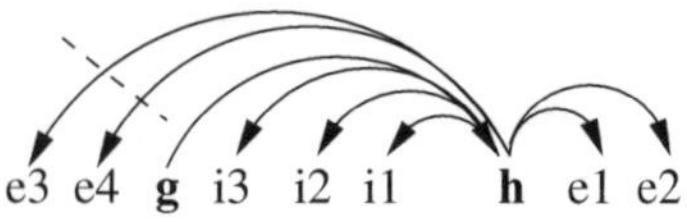

Figure 4: The exterior children are numbered first beginning on the side closest to the parent, then the side closest to the grandparent. There must be a path from the root to g, so the edges from h to its exterior children on the far side of g are guaranteed to be crossed.

	$Crossed(\vec{e}_{hs})$	$\neg Crossed(\vec{e}_{hs})$
$\neg GProj(\vec{e}_{hm})$	Edge(h, m)	Sib(h, m, s)
$GProj(\vec{e}_{hm})$	Grand(g, h, m)	GrandSib(g, h, m, s)

Table 2: Part type for an uncrossed edge $\vec{e}_{hm}$ for the crossing-sensitive third-order factorization (g is m's grandparent; s is m's inner sibling).

$Outer(most) = \{days, cars\}$.

Definition 2. *An uncrossed edge $\vec{e}_{hm}$ is GProj if both of the following hold:*

1. *The edge $\vec{e}_{gh}$ from h's parent to h is not crossed*
2. *None of the edges from h to $Outer(m)$ (m's outer siblings) are crossed*

Uncrossed *GProj* edges include the grandparent in the part. The part includes the sibling if the edge $\vec{e}_{hs}$ from the parent to the sibling is not crossed. Table 2 gives the factorization for uncrossed edges.

The parser in this paper finds the optimal 1-Endpoint-Crossing tree according to this factorized form. A fully projective tree would decompose into *exclusively* GrandSib parts (as all edges would be uncrossed and *GProj*). As all projective trees are within the 1-Endpoint-Crossing search space, the optimization problem that the parser solves includes all projective trees scored with grand-sibling features everywhere. Projective parsing with grand-sibling scores can be seen as a special case, as the crossing-sensitive 1-Endpoint-Crossing parser can simulate a grand-sibling projective parser by setting all Crossed(h, m) scores to $-\infty$.

In Figure 2, the edge from *do* to *Americans* is not *GProj* because Condition (1) is violated, while the edge from *favor* to *most* is not *GProj* because Condition (2) is violated. Under this definition, the vertices *do* and *favor* (which have children in multiple sub-problems) do not need external grandparent indices in *any* of their sub-problems. Table 3 lists the parts in the tree in Figure 2 according to this crossing-sensitive third-order factorization.

CrossedEdge(**,do*)	Sib(*cars, Which, -*)
CrossedEdge(*favor,cars*)	Sib(*do, Americans, -*)
Sib(*do, favor, Americans*)	CrossedEdge(*do,?*)
Sib(*favor, most, -*)	Sib(*favor, days, most*)
GSib(*favor, days, these, -*)	

Table 3: Decomposing Figure 2 according to the crossing-sensitive third-order factorization described in Section 3. Null inner siblings are indicated with -.

4 Parsing Algorithm

The parser finds the maximum scoring 1-Endpoint-Crossing tree according to the factorization in Section 3 with a dynamic programming procedure reminiscent of Koo and Collins (2010) (for scoring uncrossed edges with grandparent and/or sibling features) and of Pitler et al. (2013) (for including crossed edges). The parser also uses novel sub-problems for transitioning between portions of the tree with and without crossed edges. This formulation of the parsing problem presents two difficulties:

1. The parser must know whether an edge is crossed when it is added.
2. For *uncrossed* edges, the parser must use the appropriate part for scoring according to whether *other* edges are crossed (Table 2).

Difficulty 1 is solved by adding crossed and uncrossed edges to the tree in distinct sub-problems (Section 4.1). Difficulty 2 is solved by producing different versions of subtrees over the same sets of vertices, both with and without a grandparent index, which differ in their assumptions about the tree *outside* of that set (Section 4.2). The list of all sub-problems with their invariants and the full dynamic program are provided in the supplementary material.

4.1 Enforcing Crossing Edges

The parser adds crossed and uncrossed edges in distinct portions of the dynamic program. Uncrossed edges are added *only* through trapezoid sub-problems (that may or may not have a grandparent index), while crossed edges are added in *non*-trapezoid sub-problems. To add *all* uncrossed edges in trapezoid sub-problems, the parser (a) enforces that any edge added anywhere else must be crossed, and (b) includes transitional sub-problems to build trapezoids when the edge $\vec{e}_{hm}$ is not crossed, but the edge to its inner sibling $\vec{e}_{hs}$ is (and so the construction step shown in Figure 1b cannot be used).

4.1.1 Crossing Conditions

Pitler et al. (2013) included crossing edges by using "crossing region" sub-problems over intervals with an external vertex that *optionally* contained edges between the interval and the external vertex. An uncrossed edge could then be included either by a derivation that prohibited it from being crossed or a derivation which allowed (but did not force) it to be crossed. This ambiguity is removed by enforcing that (1) each crossing region contains at least one edge incident to the exterior vertex, and (2) all such edges are crossed by edges in another sub-problem. For example, by requiring at least one edge between *do* and (*favor*, *?*] and also between *favor* and (*, *do*), the edges in the two sets are guaranteed to cross.

4.1.2 Trapezoids with Edge to Inner Sibling Crossed

To add *all* uncrossed edges in trapezoid-style sub-problems, we must be able to construct a trapezoid over vertices $[h, m]$ whenever the edge $\vec{e}_{hm}$ is not crossed. The construction used in Koo and Collins (2010), repeated graphically in Figure 5a, *cannot* be used if the edge $\vec{e}_{hs}$ is crossed, as there would then exist edges between (h, s) and (s, m), making s an invalid split point. The parser therefore includes some "transitional glue" to allow alternative ways to construct the trapezoid over $[h, m]$ when $\vec{e}_{hm}$ is not crossed but the edge $\vec{e}_{hs}$ to m's inner sibling is.

The two additional ways of building trapezoids are shown graphically in Figures 5b and 5c. Consider the "chain of crossing edges" that includes the edge $\vec{e}_{hs}$. If none of these edges are in the subtree rooted at m, then we can build the tree involving m and its inner descendants separately (Figure 5b) from the rest of the tree rooted at h. Within the interval $[h, e-1]$ the furthest edge incident to h ($\vec{e}_{hs}$) must be crossed: these intervals are parsed choosing s and the crossing point of $\vec{e}_{hs}$ simultaneously (as in Figure 4 in Pitler et al. (2013)).

Otherwise, the sub-tree rooted at m is involved in

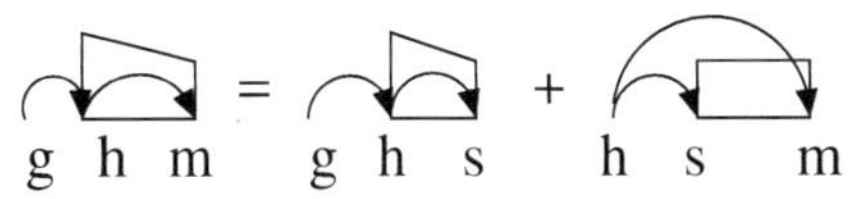

(a) Edge from h to inner sibling s is *not* crossed (repeats Figure 1b)

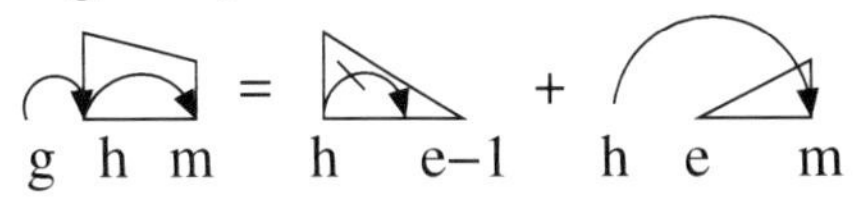

(b) $\vec{e}_{hs}$ is crossed, but the chain of crossing edges involving $\vec{e}_{hs}$ does not include any descendants of m. e is m's descendant furthest from m within (h, m). $s \in (h, e-1)$.

(c) $\vec{e}_{hs}$ is crossed, and the chain of crossing edges involving $\vec{e}_{hs}$ includes descendants of m. Of m's descendants that are incident to edges in the chain, d is the one closest to m (d can be m itself). $s \in (h, d)$.

Figure 5: Ways to build a trapezoid when the edge $\vec{e}_{hs}$ to m's inner sibling may be crossed.

the chain of crossing edges (Figure 5c). The chain of crossing edges between h and d (m's descendant, which may be m itself) is built up first then concatenated with the triangle rooted at m containing m's inner descendants not involved in the chain.

Chains of crossing edges are constructed by repeatedly applying two specialized types of L items that alternate between adding an edge from the interval to the exterior point (right-to-left) or from the exterior point to the interval (left-to-right) (Figure 6). The boundary edges of the chain can be crossed more times without violating the 1-Endpoint-Crossing property, and so the beginning and end of the chain can be unrestricted crossing regions. These specialized chain sub-problems are also used to construct *boxes* (Figure 1c) over $[s, m]$ with shared parent h when neither edge $\vec{e}_{hs}$ nor $\vec{e}_{hm}$ is crossed, but the subtrees rooted at m and at s cross each other (Figure 7).

Lemma 1. *The GrandSib-Crossing parser adds all uncrossed edges and only uncrossed edges in a tree in a "trapezoid" sub-problem.*

Proof. The *only* part is easy: when a trapezoid is built over an interval $[h, m]$, all edges are internal to the interval, so no earlier edges could cross $\vec{e}_{hm}$. Af-

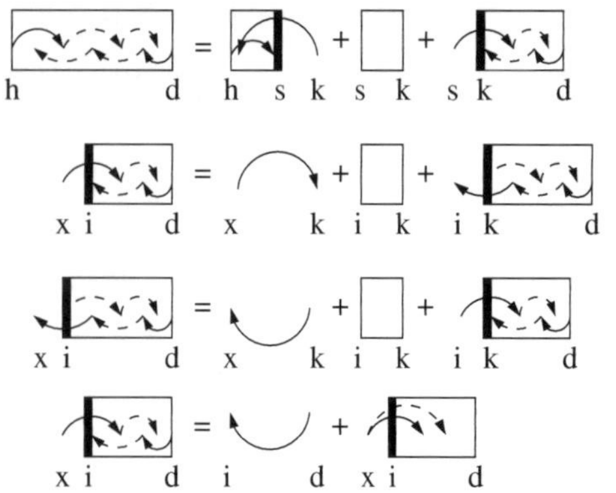

Figure 6: Constructing a chain of crossing edges

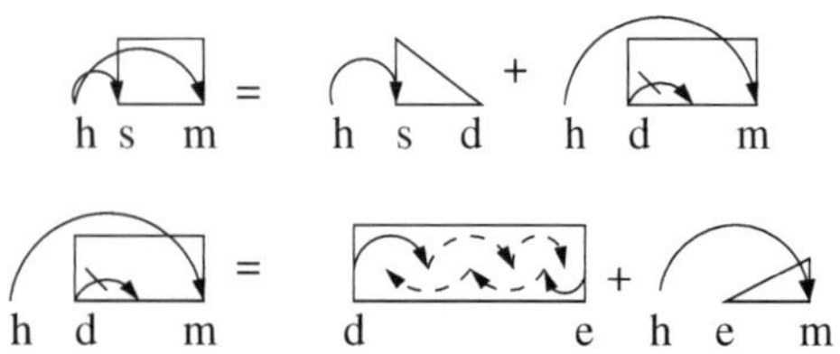

Figure 7: Constructing a box when edges in m and s's subtrees cross each other.

ter the trapezoid is built, only the interval endpoints h and m are accessible for the rest of the dynamic program, and so an edge between a vertex in (h, m) and a vertex $\notin [h, m]$ can never be added. The Crossing Conditions ensure that every edge added in a non-trapezoid sub-problem is crossed. □

Lemma 2. *The GrandSib-Crossing parser considers* all *1-Endpoint-Crossing trees and* only *1-Endpoint-Crossing trees.*

Proof. All trees that could have been built in Pitler et al. (2013) are still possible. It can be verified that the additional sub-problems added all obey the 1-Endpoint-Crossing property. □

4.2 Reduced Context in Presence of Crossings

A crossed edge (added in a non-trapezoid sub-problem) is scored as a CrossedEdge part. An uncrossed edge added in a trapezoid sub-problem, however, may need to be scored according to a GrandSib, Grand, Sib, or Edge part, depending on whether the relevant *other* edges are crossed. In this section we show that sibling and grandparent features are included in the GrandSib-Crossing parser as specified by Table 2.

(a) For good contexts (b) For bad contexts

Figure 8: For each of the interval sub-problems in Koo and Collins (2010), the parser constructs versions with and without the additional grandparent index. Figure 8b is used if the edge from *do* to *favor* is crossed, or if there are any crossed edges from *favor* to children to the left of *do* or to the right of *days*. Otherwise, Figure 8a is used.

4.2.1 Sibling Features

Lemma 3. *The GrandSib-Crossing parser scores an uncrossed edge $\vec{e}_{hm}$ with a* Sib *or* GrandSib *part if and only if $\vec{e}_{hs}$ is not crossed.*

Proof. Whether the edge to an uncrossed edge's inner sibling is crossed is known bottom-up through how the trapezoid is constructed, since the inner sibling is *internal* to the sub-problem. When $\vec{e}_{hs}$ is not crossed, the trapezoid is constructed as in Figure 5a, using the inner sibling as the split point. When the edge $\vec{e}_{hs}$ is crossed, the trapezoid is constructed as in Figure 5b or 5c; note that both ways force the edge to the inner sibling to be crossed. □

4.2.2 Grandparent Features for *GProj* Edges

Koo and Collins (2010) include an external grandparent index for each of the sub-problems that the edges within use for scoring. We want to avoid adding such an external grandparent index to *any* of the crossing region sub-problems (to stay within the desired time and space constraints) or to interval sub-problems when the external context would make all internal edges $\neg$*GProj*.

For each interval sub-problem, the parser constructs versions both with and without a grandparent index (Figure 8). Which version is used depends on the external context. In a *bad context*, all edges to children within an interval are guaranteed to be $\neg$*GProj*. This section shows that all boundary points in crossing regions are placed in bad contexts, and then that edges are scored with grandparent features if and only if they are *GProj*.

Bad Contexts for Interval Boundary Points For *exterior vertex* boundary points, all edges from it to its children will be crossed (Section 4.1.1), so it does not need a grandparent index.

Lemma 4. *If a boundary point i's parent (call it g) is within a sub-problem over vertices $[i,j]$ or $[i,j] \cup \{x\}$, then for all uncrossed edges $\vec{e}_{im}$ with m in the sub-problem, the tree outside of the sub-problem is irrelevant to whether $\vec{e}_{im}$ is GProj.*

Proof. The sub-problem contains the edge $\vec{e}_{gi}$, so Condition (1) is checked internally. m cannot be x, since $\vec{e}_{im}$ is uncrossed. If g is x, then $\vec{e}_{im}$ is $\neg GProj$ regardless of the outer context. If both g and $m \in (i,j]$, then $Outer(m) \subseteq (i,j]$: If m is an interior child of i ($m \in (i,g)$) then $Outer(m) \subseteq (m,g) \subseteq (i,j]$. Otherwise, if m is an exterior child ($m \in (g,j]$), by the "wrapping around" definition of $Outer$, $Outer(m) \subseteq (g,m) \subseteq (i,j]$. Thus Condition (2) is also checked internally. □

We can therefore focus on interval boundary points with their parent outside of the sub-problem.

Definition 3. *The left boundary vertex of an interval $[i,j]$ is in a* bad context *($BadContext_L(i,j)$) if i receives its parent (call it g) from outside of the sub-problem and either of the following hold:*

1. **Grand-Edge Crossed**: *$\vec{e}_{gi}$ is crossed*
2. **Outer-Child-Edge Crossed**: *An edge from i to a child of i outside of $[i,j]$ and Outer to j will be crossed (recall this includes children on the far side of g if g is to the left of i)*

$BadContext_R(i,j)$ is defined symmetrically regarding j and j's parent and children.

Corollary 1. *If $BadContext_L(i,j)$, then for all $\vec{e}_{im}$ with $m \in (i,j]$, $\vec{e}_{im}$ is $\neg GProj$. Similarly, if $BadContext_R(i,j)$, for all $\vec{e}_{jm}$ with $m \in [i,j)$, $\vec{e}_{jm}$ is $\neg GProj$.*

No Grandparent Indices for Crossing Regions We would exceed the desired $O(n^4)$ run-time if *any* crossing region sub-problems needed *any* grandparent indices. In Pitler et al. (2013), LR sub-problems with edges from the exterior point crossed by both the left and the right boundary points were constructed by concatenating an L and an R sub-problem. Since the split point was not necessarily incident to a crossed edge, the split point might have $GProj$ edges to children on the side other than where it gets its parent; accommodating this would add another factor of n to the running time and space

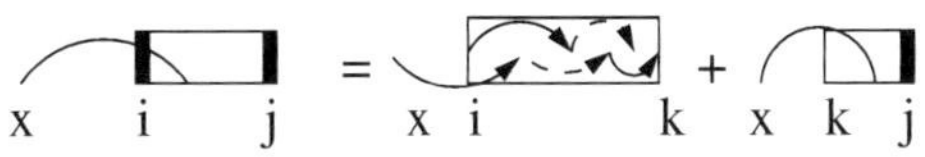

Figure 9: For all split points k, the edge from k's parent to k is crossed, so all edges from k to children on either side were $\neg GProj$. The case when the split point's parent is from the right is symmetric.

(a) x is Outer to all children of k in $(k,j]$.

(b) x is Outer to all children of k in $[i,k)$.

Figure 10: The edge $\vec{e}_{kx}$ is guaranteed to be crossed, so k is in a BadContext for whichever side it does not get its parent from.

to store the split point's parent. To avoid this increase in running time, they are instead built up as in Figure 9, which chooses the split point so that the edge from the parent of the split point to it is crossed.

Lemma 5. *For all crossing region sub-problems $[i,j] \cup \{x\}$ with i's parent $\notin [i,j] \cup \{x\}$, $BadContext_L(i,j)$. Similarly, when j's parent $\notin [i,j] \cup \{x\}$, $BadContext_R(i,j)$.*

Proof. Crossing region sub-problems either combine to form intervals or larger crossing regions. When they combine to form intervals as in Figure 3, it can be verified that all boundary points are in a bad context. LR sub-problems were discussed above. Split points for the *L/R/N* sub-problems by construction are incident to a crossed edge to a further vertex. If that edge is from the split point's parent to the split point, then the grand-edge is crossed and so both sides are in a bad context. If the crossed edge is from the split point to a child, then that child is Outer to all other children on the side in which it does not get its parent (see Figure 10). □

Corollary 2. *No grandparent indices are needed for any crossing region sub-problem.*

Triangles and Trapezoids with and without Grandparent Indices The presentation that follows assumes left-headed versions. Uncrossed edges are added in two distinct types of trapezoids: (1) TrapG[h, m, g, L] with an external grandparent index g, scores the edge $\vec{e}_{hm}$ with grandparent features, and (2) Trap$[h, m, L]$ *without* a grandparent index, scores the edge $\vec{e}_{hm}$ without grandparent features. Triangles also have versions with (TriG[h, e, g, L] and without (Tri[h, e, L]) a grandparent index. What follows shows that all *GProj* edges are added in TrapG sub-problems, and all $\neg$*GProj* uncrossed edges are added in Trap sub-problems.

Lemma 6. *For all* $k \in (i, j)$, *if* $BadContext_L(i, j)$, *then* $BadContext_L(i, k)$. *Similarly, if* $BadContext_R(i, j)$, *then* $BadContext_R(k, j)$.

Proof. $BadContext_L(i, j)$ implies either the edge from i's parent to i is crossed and/or an edge from i to a child of i outer to j is crossed. If the edge from i's parent to i is crossed, then $BadContext_L(i, k)$. If a child of i is outer to j, then since $k \in (i, j)$, such a child is also outer to k. □

Lemma 7. *All left-rooted triangle sub-problems* Tri[i, j, L] *without a grandparent index are in a* $BadContext_L(i, j)$. *Similarly for all* Tri[i, j, R], $BadContext_R(i, j)$.

Proof. All triangles without grandparent indices are either placed immediately into a bad context (by adding a crossed edge to the triangle's root from its parent, or a crossed edge from the root to an outer child) or are combined with other sub-trees to form larger crossing regions (and therefore the triangle is in a bad context, using Lemmas 5 and 6). □

Lemma 8. *All triangle sub-problems with a grandparent index* TriG[h, e, g, L] *are placed in a* $\neg BadContext_L(h, e)$. *Similarly,* TriG[e, h, g, R] *are only placed in* $\neg BadContext_R(h, e)$.

Proof. Consider where a non-empty triangle ($h \neq e$) with a grandparent index TriG[h, e, g, L] can be placed in the full dynamic program and what each step would imply about the rest of the tree.

If the triangle contains exterior children of h (e and g are on opposite sides of h), then it can either combine with a trapezoid to form another larger triangle (as in Figure 1a) or it can combine with another sub-problem to form a box with a grandparent index (Figure 1c or 7). Boxes with a grandparent index can only combine with another trapezoid to form a larger trapezoid (Figure 1b). Both cases force $\vec{e}_{gh}$ to not be crossed and prevent h from having any outer crossed children, as h becomes an internal node within the larger sub-problem.

If the triangle contains interior children of h (e lies between g and h), then it can either form a trapezoid from g to h by combining with a triangle (Figure 5b) or a chain of crossing edges (Figure 5c), or it can be used to build a box with a grandparent index (Figures 1c and 7), which then can only be used to form a trapezoid from g to h. In either case, a trapezoid is constructed from g to h, enforcing that $\vec{e}_{gh}$ cannot be crossed. These steps prevent h from having any additional children between g and e (since h does not appear in the adjacent sub-problems at all whenever $h \neq e$), so again the children of h in (e, h) have no outer siblings. □

Lemma 9. *In a* TriG[h, e, g, L] *sub-problem, if an edge* $\vec{e}_{hm}$ *is not crossed and no edges from i to siblings of m in* $(m, e]$ *are crossed, then* $\vec{e}_{hm}$ *is GProj.*

Proof. This follows from (1) the edge $\vec{e}_{hm}$ is not crossed, (2) the edge $\vec{e}_{gh}$ is not crossed by Lemma 8, and (3) no outer siblings are crossed (outer siblings in $(m, e]$ are not crossed by assumption and siblings outer to e are not crossed by Lemma 8). □

Lemma 10. *An edge* $\vec{e}_{hm}$ *scored with a* GrandSib *or* Grand *part (added through a* TrapG$[h, m, g, L]$ *or* TrapG$[m, h, g, R]$ *sub-problem) is GProj.*

Proof. A TrapG can either (1) combine with descendants of m to form a triangle with a grandparent index rooted at h (indicating that m is the outermost inner child of h) or (2) combine with descendants of m and of m's adjacent outer sibling (call it o), forming a trapezoid from h to o (indicating that $\vec{e}_{ho}$ is not crossed). Such a trapezoid could again only combine with further uncrossed outer siblings until eventually the final triangle rooted at h with grandparent index g is built. As $\vec{e}_{hm}$ was not crossed, no edges from h to outer siblings within the triangle are crossed, and $\vec{e}_{hm}$ is within a TriG sub-problem, $\vec{e}_{hm}$ is *GProj* by Lemma 9. □

Lemma 11. *An uncrossed edge* $\vec{e}_{hm}$ *scored with a* Sib *or* Edge *part (added through a* Trap[h, m, L] *or* Trap[m, h, R] *sub-problem) is* $\neg$*GProj.*

Proof. A Trap can only (1) form a triangle without a grandparent index, or (2) form a trapezoid to an outer sibling of m, until eventually a final triangle rooted at h without a grandparent index is built. This triangle without a grandparent index is then placed in a bad context (Lemma 7) and so $\vec{e}_{hm}$ is $\neg GProj$ (Corollary 1). □

4.3 Main Results

Lemma 12. *The crossing-sensitive third-order parser runs in $O(n^4)$ time and $O(n^3)$ space when the input is an unpruned graph. When the input to the parser is a pruned graph with at most k incoming edges per node, the crossing-sensitive third-order parser runs in $O(kn^3)$ time and $O(n^3)$ space.*

Proof. All sub-problems are either over intervals (two indices), intervals with a grandparent index (three indices), or crossing regions (three indices). No crossing regions require any grandparent indices (Corollary 2). The only sub-problems that require a maximization over two internal split points are over intervals and need no grandparent indices (as the furthest edges from each root are guaranteed to be crossed within the sub-problem). All steps either contain an edge in their construction step or in the invariant of the sub-problem, so with a pruned graph as input, the running time is the number of edges ($O(kn)$) times the number of possibilities for the other two free indices ($O(n^2)$). The space is not reduced as there is not necessarily an edge relationship between the three stored vertices. □

Theorem 1. *The GrandSib-Crossing parser correctly finds the maximum scoring 1-Endpoint-Crossing tree according to the crossing-sensitive third-order factorization (Section 3) in $O(n^4)$ time and $O(n^3)$ space. When the input to the parser is a pruned graph with at most k incoming edges per node, the GrandSib-Crossing parser correctly finds the maximum scoring 1-Endpoint-Crossing tree that uses only unpruned edges in $O(kn^3)$ time and $O(n^3)$ space.*

Proof. The correctness of scoring follows from Lemmas 3, 10, and 11. The search space of 1-Endpoint-Crossing trees was in Lemma 2 and the time and space complexity in Lemma 12. □

The parser produces the optimal tree in a well-defined output space. Pruning edges restricts the output space the same way that constraints enforcing projectivity or the 1-Endpoint-Crossing property also restrict the output space. Note that if the optimal unconstrained 1-Endpoint-Crossing tree does not include any pruned edges, then whether the parser uses pruning or not is irrelevant; both the pruned and unpruned parsers will produce the exact same tree.

5 Experiments

The crossing-sensitive third-order parser was implemented as an alternative parsing algorithm within *dpo3* (Koo and Collins, 2010).[2] To ensure a fair comparison, all code relating to input/output, features, learning, etc. was re-used from the original projective implementation, and so the only substantive differences between the projective and 1-Endpoint-Crossing parsers are the dynamic programming charts, the parsing algorithms, and the routines that extract the maximum scoring tree from the completed chart.

The treebanks used to prepare the CoNLL shared task data (Buchholz and Marsi, 2006; Nivre et al., 2007) vary widely in their conventions for representing conjunctions, modal verbs, determiners, and other decisions (Zeman et al., 2012). The experiments use the newly released HamleDT software (Zeman et al., 2012) that normalizes these treebanks into one standard format and also provides built-in transformations to other conjunction styles. The unnormalized treebanks input to HamleDT were from the CoNLL 2006 Shared Task (Buchholz and Marsi, 2006) for Danish, Dutch, Portuguese, and Swedish and from the CoNLL 2007 Shared Task (Nivre et al., 2007) for Czech.

The experiments include the default Prague style (Böhmová et al., 2001), Mel'čukian style (Mel'čuk, 1988), and Stanford style (De Marneffe and Manning, 2008) for conjunctions. Under the grandparent-sibling factorization, the two words being conjoined would never appear in the same scope for the Prague style (as they are siblings on different sides of the conjunct head). In the Mel'čukian style, the two conjuncts are in a grandparent relationship and in the Stanford style the two conjuncts

[2] http://groups.csail.mit.edu/nlp/dpo3/

are in a sibling relationship, and so we would expect to see larger gains for including grandparents and siblings under the latter two representations. The experiments also include a nearly projective dataset, the English Penn Treebank (Marcus et al., 1993), converted to dependencies with PennConverter (Johansson and Nugues, 2007).

The experiments use marginal-based pruning based on an edge-factored directed spanning tree model (McDonald et al., 2005). Each word's set of potential parents is limited to those with a marginal probability of at least .1 times the probability of the most probable parent, and cut off this list at a maximum of 20 potential parents per word. To ensure that there is always at least one projective and/or 1-Endpoint-Crossing tree achievable, the artificial root is always included as an option. The pruning parameters were chosen to keep 99.9% of the true edges on the English development set.

Following Carreras (2007) and Koo and Collins (2010), before training the training set trees are transformed to be the best achievable within the model class (i.e., the closest projective tree or 1-Endpoint-Crossing tree). All models are trained for five iterations of averaged structured perceptron training. For English, the model after the iteration that performs best on the development set is used; for all other languages, the model after the fifth iteration is used.

Model	Du	Cz	Pt	Da	Sw
			Prague		
Proj GSib	80.45	85.12	88.85	**88.17**	85.50
Proj Edge	80.38	84.04	88.14	**88.29**	**86.09**
1-EC CS-GSib	**82.78**	**85.90**	**89.74**	**88.64**	85.70
1-EC Edge	**83.33**	84.97	**89.21**	**88.19**	**86.46**
			Mel'čukian		
Proj GSib	82.26	**87.96**	89.19	**90.23**	**89.59**
Proj Edge	82.09	86.18	88.73	89.29	**89.00**
1-EC CS-GSib	**86.03**	**87.89**	**90.34**	**90.50**	**89.34**
1-EC Edge	85.28	**87.57**	**89.96**	**90.14**	88.97
			Stanford		
Proj GSib	81.16	86.83	88.80	**88.84**	87.27
Proj Edge	80.56	86.18	88.61	**88.69**	**87.92**
1-EC CS-GSib	**84.67**	**88.34**	**90.20**	**89.22**	**88.15**
1-EC Edge	83.62	87.13	89.43	**88.74**	87.36

Table 4: Overall Unlabeled Attachment Scores (UAS) for all words.[3] CS-GSib is the proposed crossing-sensitive grandparent-sibling factorization. For each data set, we bold the most accurate model and those not significantly different from the most accurate (sign test, $p < .05$). Languages are sorted in increasing order of projectivity.

Model	UAS
Proj GSib	**93.10**
Proj Edge	92.63
1-EC CS-GSib	**93.22**
1-EC Edge	92.80

Table 5: English results

5.1 Results

Results for edge-factored and (crossing-sensitive) grandparent-sibling factored models for both projective and 1-Endpoint-Crossing parsing are in Tables 4 and 5. In 14 out of the 16 experimental set-ups, the third-order 1-Endpoint-Crossing parser is more accurate than the third-order projective parser. It is significantly better than the projective parser in 9 of the set-ups and significantly worse in none.

Table 6 shows how often the 1-EC CS-GSib parser used each of the GrandSib, Grand, Sib, Edge, and CrossedEdge parts for the Mel'čukian and Stanford style test sets. In both representations, the parser is able to score with a sibling context more often than it is able to score with a grandparent, perhaps explaining why the datasets using the Stanford conjunction representation saw the largest gains from including the higher order factors into the 1-Endpoint-Crossing parser.

Across languages, the third-order 1-Endpoint-Crossing parser runs 2.1-2.7 times slower than the third-order projective parser (71-104 words per second, compared with 183-268 words per second). Parsing speed is correlated with the amount of pruning. The level of pruning mentioned earlier is relatively permissive, retaining 39.0-60.7% of the edges in the complete graph; a higher level of pruning could likely achieve much faster parsing times with the same underlying parsing algorithms.

[3]Following prior work in graph-based dependency parsing (for example, Rush and Petrov (2012)), English results use automatically produced part-of-speech tags and results exclude punctuation, while the results for all other languages use gold part-of-speech tags and include punctuation.

Part Used	Du	Cz	Pt	Da	Sw
			Mel'čukian		
CrossedEdge	8.5	4.5	3.2	1.4	1.2
GrandSib	81.2	89.1	90.7	95.7	96.2
Grand	1.1	0.5	0.8	0.3	0.2
Sib	9.0	5.8	5.2	2.6	2.3
Edge	< 0.1	< 0.1	0	< 0.1	0
			Stanford		
CrossedEdge	8.4	5.1	3.3	2.0	1.8
GrandSib	81.4	87.8	90.5	94.2	95.2
Grand	1.1	0.5	0.7	0.3	0.3
Sib	8.9	6.5	5.2	3.5	2.6
Edge	< 0.1	0.1	0	< 0.1	0

Table 6: The proportion of edges in the predicted output trees from the CS-GSib 1-Endpoint-Crossing parser that would have used each of the five part types for scoring.

6 Discussion

There have been many other notable approaches to non-projective parsing with larger scopes than single edges, including transition-based parsers, directed spanning tree graph-based parsers, and mildly non-projective graph-based parsers.

Transition-based parsers score actions that the parser may take to transition between different configurations. These parsers typically use either greedy or beam search, and can condition on any tree context that is in the history of the parser's actions so far. Zhang and Nivre (2011) significantly improved the accuracy of an arc-eager transition system (Nivre, 2003) by adding several additional classes of features, including some third-order features. Basic arc-eager and arc-standard (Nivre, 2004) models that parse left-to-right using a stack produce projective trees, but transition-based parsers can be modified to produce crossing edges. Such modifications include pseudo-projective parsing in which the dependency labels encode transformations to be applied to the tree (Nivre and Nilsson, 2005), adding actions that add edges to words in the stack that are not the topmost item (Attardi, 2006), adding actions that swap the positions of words (Nivre, 2009), and adding a second stack (Gómez-Rodríguez and Nivre, 2010).

Graph-based approaches to non-projective parsing either consider all directed spanning trees or restricted classes of mildly non-projective trees. Directed spanning tree approaches with higher order features either use approximate learning techniques, such as loopy belief propagation (Smith and Eisner, 2008), or use dual decomposition to solve relaxations of the problem (Koo et al., 2010; Martins et al., 2013). While not guaranteed to produce optimal trees within a fixed number of iterations, these dual decomposition techniques do give certificates of optimality on the instances in which the relaxation is tight and the algorithm converges quickly.

This paper described a mildly non-projective graph-based parser. Other parsers in this class find the optimal tree in the class of well-nested, block degree two trees (Gómez-Rodríguez et al., 2011), or in a class of trees further restricted based on gap inheritance (Pitler et al., 2012) or the head-split property (Satta and Kuhlmann, 2013), with edge-factored running times of $O(n^5) - O(n^7)$. The factorization used in this paper is not immediately compatible with these parsers: the complex cases in these parsers are due to *gaps*, not *crossings*. However, there may be analogous "gap-sensitive" factorizations that could allow these parsers to be extended without large increases in running times.

7 Conclusion

This paper proposed an exact, graph-based algorithm for non-projective parsing with higher order features. The resulting parser has the same asymptotic run time as a third-order projective parser, and is significantly more accurate for many experimental settings. An exploration of other factorizations that facilitate non-projective parsing (for example, an analogous "gap-sensitive" variant) may be an interesting avenue for future work. Recent work has investigated faster variants for third-order graph-based projective parsing (Rush and Petrov, 2012; Zhang and McDonald, 2012) using structured prediction cascades (Weiss and Taskar, 2010) and cube pruning (Chiang, 2007). It would be interesting to extend these lines of work to the crossing-sensitive third-order parser as well.

Acknowledgments

I would like to thank Sampath Kannan, Mitch Marcus, Chris Callison-Burch, Michael Collins, Mark Liberman, Ben Taskar, Joakim Nivre, and the three anonymous reviewers for valuable comments on earlier versions of this material.

References

G. Attardi. 2006. Experiments with a multilanguage non-projective dependency parser. In *Proceedings of CoNLL*, pages 166–170.

A. Böhmová, J. Hajič, E. Hajičová, and B. Hladká. 2001. The Prague Dependency Treebank: Three-level annotation scenario. In Anne Abeillé, editor, *Treebanks: Building and Using Syntactically Annotated Corpora*, pages 103–127. Kluwer Academic Publishers.

B. Bohnet and J. Kuhn. 2012. The best of both worlds – a graph-based completion model for transition-based parsers. In *Proceedings of EACL*, pages 77–87.

S. Buchholz and E. Marsi. 2006. CoNLL-X shared task on multilingual dependency parsing. In *Proceedings of CoNLL*, pages 149–164.

X. Carreras. 2007. Experiments with a higher-order projective dependency parser. In *Proceedings of the CoNLL Shared Task Session of EMNLP-CoNLL*, pages 957–961.

E. Charniak and M. Johnson. 2005. Coarse-to-fine n-best parsing and maxent discriminative reranking. In *Proceedings of ACL*, pages 173–180.

D. Chiang. 2007. Hierarchical phrase-based translation. *Computational Linguistics*, 33(2):201–228.

M. De Marneffe and C. Manning. 2008. Stanford typed dependencies manual.

J. Eisner. 2000. Bilexical grammars and their cubic-time parsing algorithms. In Harry Bunt and Anton Nijholt, editors, *Advances in Probabilistic and Other Parsing Technologies*, pages 29–62. Kluwer Academic Publishers.

C. Gómez-Rodríguez and J. Nivre. 2010. A transition-based parser for 2-planar dependency structures. In *Proceedings of ACL*, pages 1492–1501.

C. Gómez-Rodríguez, J. Carroll, and D. Weir. 2011. Dependency parsing schemata and mildly non-projective dependency parsing. *Computational Linguistics*, 37(3):541–586.

K. Hall. 2007. K-best spanning tree parsing. In *Proceedings of ACL*, pages 392–399.

R. Johansson and P. Nugues. 2007. Extended constituent-to-dependency conversion for English. In *Proceedings of the 16th Nordic Conference on Computational Linguistics (NODALIDA)*, pages 105–112.

T. Koo and M. Collins. 2010. Efficient third-order dependency parsers. In *Proceedings of ACL*, pages 1–11.

T. Koo, A. M. Rush, M. Collins, T. Jaakkola, and D. Sontag. 2010. Dual decomposition for parsing with non-projective head automata. In *Proceedings of EMNLP*, pages 1288–1298.

T. Koo. 2010. *Advances in discriminative dependency parsing*. Ph.D. thesis, Massachusetts Institute of Technology.

S. Kübler, R. McDonald, and J. Nivre. 2009. Dependency parsing. *Synthesis Lectures on Human Language Technologies*, 2(1):1–127.

M. P. Marcus, M. A. Marcinkiewicz, and B. Santorini. 1993. Building a large annotated corpus of English: The Penn Treebank. *Computational Linguistics*, 19(2):313–330.

A. F. T. Martins, N. A. Smith, and E. P. Xing. 2009. Concise integer linear programming formulations for dependency parsing. In *Proceedings of ACL*, pages 342–350.

A. Martins, M. Almeida, and N. A. Smith. 2013. Turning on the turbo: Fast third-order non-projective turbo parsers. In *Proceedings of ACL (Short Papers)*, pages 617–622.

R. McDonald and F. Pereira. 2006. Online learning of approximate dependency parsing algorithms. In *Proceedings of EACL*, pages 81–88.

R. McDonald and G. Satta. 2007. On the complexity of non-projective data-driven dependency parsing. In *Proceedings of the 10th International Conference on Parsing Technologies*, pages 121–132.

R. McDonald, F. Pereira, K. Ribarov, and J. Hajič. 2005. Non-projective dependency parsing using spanning tree algorithms. In *Proceedings of HLT/EMNLP*, pages 523–530.

I. Mel'čuk. 1988. *Dependency Syntax: Theory and Practice*. State University of New York Press.

J. Nivre and J. Nilsson. 2005. Pseudo-projective dependency parsing. In *Proceedings of ACL*, pages 99–106.

J. Nivre, J. Hall, S. Kübler, R. McDonald, J. Nilsson, S. Riedel, and D. Yuret. 2007. The CoNLL 2007 shared task on dependency parsing. In *Proceedings of the CoNLL Shared Task Session of EMNLP-CoNLL*, pages 915–932.

J. Nivre. 2003. An efficient algorithm for projective dependency parsing. In *Proceedings of the 8th International Workshop on Parsing Technologies*, pages 149–160.

J. Nivre. 2004. Incrementality in deterministic dependency parsing. In *Proceedings of the Workshop on Incremental Parsing: Bringing Engineering and Cognition Together*, pages 50–57.

J. Nivre. 2009. Non-projective dependency parsing in expected linear time. In *Proceedings of ACL*, pages 351–359.

E. Pitler, S. Kannan, and M. Marcus. 2012. Dynamic programming for higher order parsing of gap-minding trees. In *Proceedings of EMNLP*, pages 478–488.

E. Pitler, S. Kannan, and M. Marcus. 2013. Finding optimal 1-Endpoint-Crossing trees. *Transactions of the Association for Computational Linguistics*, 1(Mar):13–24.

A. Rush and S. Petrov. 2012. Vine pruning for efficient multi-pass dependency parsing. In *Proceedings of NAACL*, pages 498–507.

G. Satta and M. Kuhlmann. 2013. Efficient parsing for head-split dependency trees. *Transactions of the Association for Computational Linguistics*, 1(July):267–278.

D. A. Smith and J. Eisner. 2008. Dependency parsing by belief propagation. In *Proceedings of EMNLP*, pages 145–156.

D. Weiss and B. Taskar. 2010. Structured Prediction Cascades. In *AISTATS*, pages 916–923.

D. Zeman, D. Mareček, M. Popel, L. Ramasamy, J. Štěpánek, Z. Žabokrtský, and J. Hajič. 2012. HamleDT: To parse or not to parse? In *Proceedings of the Eight International Conference on Language Resources and Evaluation (LREC'12)*, pages 2735–2741.

H. Zhang and R. McDonald. 2012. Generalized higher-order dependency parsing with cube pruning. In *Proceedings of EMNLP*, pages 320–331.

Y. Zhang and J. Nivre. 2011. Transition-based dependency parsing with rich non-local features. In *Proceedings of ACL (Short Papers)*, pages 188–193.

Cross-lingual Projected Expectation Regularization for Weakly Supervised Learning

Mengqiu Wang and **Christopher D. Manning**
Computer Science Department
Stanford University
Stanford, CA 94305 USA
{mengqiu,manning}@cs.stanford.edu

Abstract

We consider a multilingual weakly supervised learning scenario where knowledge from annotated corpora in a resource-rich language is transferred via bitext to guide the learning in other languages. Past approaches project labels across bitext and use them as features or gold labels for training. We propose a new method that projects model expectations rather than labels, which facilities transfer of model uncertainty across language boundaries. We encode expectations as constraints and train a discriminative CRF model using Generalized Expectation Criteria (Mann and McCallum, 2010). Evaluated on standard Chinese-English and German-English NER datasets, our method demonstrates F_1 scores of 64% and 60% when no labeled data is used. Attaining the same accuracy with supervised CRFs requires 12k and 1.5k labeled sentences. Furthermore, when combined with labeled examples, our method yields significant improvements over state-of-the-art supervised methods, achieving best reported numbers to date on Chinese OntoNotes and German CoNLL-03 datasets.

1 Introduction

Supervised statistical learning methods have enjoyed great popularity in Natural Language Processing (NLP) over the past decade. The success of supervised methods depends heavily upon the availability of large amounts of annotated training data. Manual curation of annotated corpora is a costly and time consuming process. To date, most annotated resources resides within the English language, which hinders the adoption of supervised learning methods in many multilingual environments.

To minimize the need for annotation, significant progress has been made in developing unsupervised and semi-supervised approaches to NLP (Collins and Singer 1999; Klein 2005; Liang 2005; Smith 2006; Goldberg 2010; *inter alia*) . More recent paradigms for semi-supervised learning allow modelers to directly encode knowledge about the task and the domain as constraints to guide learning (Chang et al., 2007; Mann and McCallum, 2010; Ganchev et al., 2010). However, in a multilingual setting, coming up with effective constraints require extensive knowledge of the foreign[1] language.

Bilingual parallel text (bitext) lends itself as a medium to transfer knowledge from a resource-rich language to a foreign languages. Yarowsky and Ngai (2001) project labels produced by an English tagger to the foreign side of bitext, then use the projected labels to learn a HMM model. More recent work applied the projection-based approach to more language-pairs, and further improved performance through the use of type-level constraints from tag dictionary and feature-rich generative or discriminative models (Das and Petrov, 2011; Täckström et al., 2013).

In our work, we propose a new projection-based method that differs in two important ways. First, we never explicitly project the labels. Instead, we project expectations over the labels. This projection

[1]For experimental purposes, we designate English as the resource-rich language, and other languages of interest as "foreign". In our experiments, we simulate the resource-poor scenario using Chinese and German, even though in reality these two languages are quite rich in resources.

Transactions of the Association for Computational Linguistics, 2 (2014) 55–66. Action Editor: Lillian Lee.
Submitted 9/2013; Revised 12/2013; Published 2/2014.

acts as a soft constraint over the labels, which allows us to transfer more information and uncertainty across language boundaries. Secondly, we encode the expectations as constraints and train a model by minimizing divergence between model expectations and projected expectations in a Generalized Expectation (GE) Criteria (Mann and McCallum, 2010) framework.

We evaluate our approach on Named Entity Recognition (NER) tasks for English-Chinese and English-German language pairs on standard public datasets. We report results in two settings: a weakly supervised setting where no labeled data or a small amount of labeled data is available, and a semi-supervised settings where labeled data is available, but we can gain predictive power by learning from unlabeled bitext.

2 Related Work

Most semi-supervised learning approaches embody the principle of learning from constraints. There are two broad categories of constraints: multi-view constraints, and external knowledge constraints.

Examples of methods that explore multi-view constraints include self-training (Yarowsky, 1995; McClosky et al., 2006),[2] co-training (Blum and Mitchell, 1998; Sindhwani et al., 2005), multi-view learning (Ando and Zhang, 2005; Carlson et al., 2010), and discriminative and generative model combination (Suzuki and Isozaki, 2008; Druck and McCallum, 2010).

An early example of using knowledge as constraints in weakly-supervised learning is the work by Collins and Singer (1999). They showed that the addition of a small set of "seed" rules greatly improve a co-training style unsupervised tagger. Chang et al. (2007) proposed a constraint-driven learning (CODL) framework where constraints are used to guide the selection of best self-labeled examples to be included as additional training data in an iterative EM-style procedure. The kind of constraints used in applications such as NER are the ones like "the words CA, Australia, NY are LOCATION" (Chang et al., 2007). Notice the similarity of this particular constraint to the kinds of features one would expect to see in a discriminative MaxEnt model. The difference is that instead of learning the validity (or weight) of this feature from labeled examples — since we do not have them — we can constrain the model using our knowledge of the domain. Druck et al. (2009) also demonstrated that in an active learning setting where annotation budget is limited, it is more efficient to label features than examples. Other sources of knowledge include lexicons and gazetteers (Druck et al., 2007; Chang et al., 2007).

While it is straight-forward to see how resources such as a list of city names can give a lot of mileage in recognizing locations, we are also exposed to the danger of over-committing to hard constraints. For example, it becomes problematic with city names that are ambiguous, such as Augusta, Georgia.[3] To soften these constraints, Mann and McCallum (2010) proposed the Generalized Expectation (GE) Criteria framework, which encodes constraints as a regularization term over some score function that measures the divergence between the model's expectation and the target expectation. The connection between GE and CODL is analogous to the relationship between hard (Viterbi) EM and soft EM, as illustrated by Samdani et al. (2012).

Another closely related work is the Posterior Regularization (PR) framework by Ganchev et al. (2010). In fact, as Bellare et al. (2009) have shown, in a discriminative model these two methods optimize exactly the same objective.[4] The two differ in optimization details: PR uses a EM algorithm to approximate the gradients which avoids the expensive computation of a covariance matrix between features and constraints, whereas GE directly calculates the gradient. However, later results (Druck, 2011) have shown that using the Expectation Semiring techniques of Li and Eisner (2009), one can compute the exact gradients of GE in a Conditional Random Fields (CRF) (Lafferty et al., 2001) at costs

[2] A multi-view interpretation of self-training is that the self-tagged additional data offers new views to learners trained on existing labeled data.

[3] This is a city in the state of Georgia in USA, famous for its golf courses. It is ambiguous since both Augusta and Georgia can also be used as person names.

[4] The different terminology employed by GE and PR may be confusing to discerning readers, but the "expectation" in the context of GE means the same thing as "marginal posterior" as in PR.

no greater than computing the gradients of ordinary CRF. And empirically, GE tends to perform more accurately than PR (Bellare et al., 2009; Druck, 2011).

Obtaining appropriate knowledge resources for constructing constraints remain as a bottleneck in applying GE and PR to new languages. However, a number of past work recognizes parallel bitext as a rich source of linguistic constraints, naturally captured in the translations. As a result, bitext has been effectively utilized for unsupervised multilingual grammar induction (Alshawi et al., 2000; Snyder et al., 2009), parsing (Burkett and Klein, 2008), and sequence labeling (Naseem et al., 2009).

A number of recent work also explored bilingual constraints in the context of simultaneous bilingual tagging, and showed that enforcing agreements between language pairs give superior results than monolingual tagging (Burkett et al., 2010; Che et al., 2013; Wang et al., 2013a). Burkett et al. (2010) also demonstrated a *uptraining* (Petrov et al., 2010) setting where tag-induced bitext can be used as additional monolingual training data to improve monolingual taggers. A major drawback of this approach is that it requires a readily-trained tagging models in each languages, which makes a weakly supervised setting infeasible. Another intricacy of this approach is that it only works when the two models have comparable strength, since mutual agreements are enforced between them.

Projection-based methods can be very effective in weakly-supervised scenarios, as demonstrated by Yarowsky and Ngai (2001), and Xi and Hwa (2005). One problem with projected labels is that they are often too noisy to be directly used as training signals. To mitigate this problem, Das and Petrov (2011) designed a label propagation method to automatically induce a tag lexicon for the foreign language to smooth the projected labels. Fossum and Abney (2005) filter out projection noise by combining projections from from multiple source languages. However, this approach is not always viable since it relies on having parallel bitext from multiple source languages. Li et al. (2012) proposed the use of crowd-sourced Wiktionary as additional resources for inducing tag lexicons. More recently, Täckström et al. (2013) combined token-level and type-level constraints to constrain legitimate label sequences and and recalibrate the probability distribution in a CRF. The tag dictionary used for POS tagging are analogous to the gazetteers and name lexicons used for NER by Chang et al. (2007).

Our work is also closely related to Ganchev et al. (2009). They used a two-step projection method similar to Das and Petrov (2011) for dependency parsing. Instead of using the projected linguistic structures as ground truth (Yarowsky and Ngai, 2001), or as features in a generative model (Das and Petrov, 2011), they used them as constraints in a PR framework. Our work differs by projecting expectations rather than Viterbi one-best labels. We also choose the GE framework over PR. Experiments in Bellare et al. (2009) and Druck (2011) suggest that in a discriminative model (like ours), GE is more accurate than PR. More recently, Ganchev and Das (2013) further extended this line of work to directly train discriminative sequence models using cross lingual projection with PR. The types of constraints applied in this new work are similar to the ones in the monolingual PR setting proposed by Ganchev et al. (2010), where the total counts of labels of a particular kind are expected to match some fraction of the projected total counts. Our work differ in that we enforce expectation constraints at token level, which gives tighter guidance to learning the model.

3 Approach

Given bitext between English and a foreign language, our goal is to learn a CRF model in the foreign language from little or no labeled data. Our method performs **C**ross-**Li**ngual **P**rojected **E**xpectation **R**egularization (**CLiPER**).

For every aligned sentence pair in the bitext, we first compute the posterior marginal at each word position on the English side using a pre-trained English CRF tagger; then for each aligned English word, we project its posterior marginal as expectations to the aligned word position on the foreign side. Figure 1 shows a snippet of a sentence from real corpus. Notice that if we were to directly project the Viterbi best assignment from English to Chinese, all three Chinese words that are named entities would have gotten the wrong tags. But projecting the English CRF model expectations preserves some uncertainties, informing the Chinese model that there is a 40%

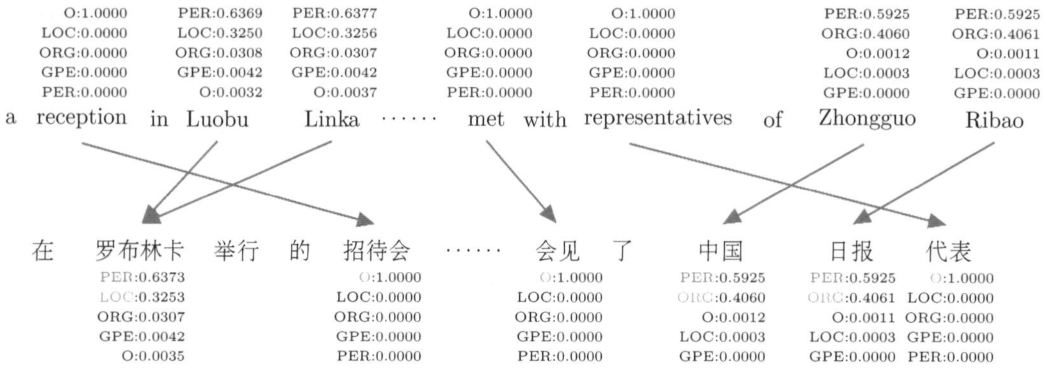

Figure 1: Diagram illustrating the projection of model expectation from English to Chinese. The posterior probabilities assigned by the English CRF model is shown above each English word; automatically induced word alignments are shown in red; the correct projected labels for Chinese words are shown in green, and incorrect labels are shown in red.

chance that "中国日报" (*China Daily*) is an organization in this context.

We would like to learn a CRF model in the foreign language that has similar expectations as the projected expectations from English. To this end, we adopt the Generalized Expectation (GE) Criteria framework introduced by Mann and McCallum (2010). In the remainder of this section, we follow the notation used in (Druck, 2011) to explain our approach.

3.1 CLiPER

The general idea of GE is that we can express our preferences over models through constraint functions. A desired model should satisfy the imposed constraints by matching the expectations on these constraint functions with some target expectations (attained by external knowledge like lexicons or in our case transferred knowledge from English). We define a constraint function ϕ_{i,l_j} for each word position i and output label assignment l_j. $\phi_{i,l_j} = 0$ is a constraint in that position i cannot take label l_j.

The set $\{l_1, \cdots, l_m\}$ denotes all possible label assignment for each y_i, and m is number of label values. A_i is the set of English words aligned to Chinese word i. ϕ_{i,l_j} are defined for all position i such that $A_i \neq \emptyset$. In other words, the constraint function applies only to Chinese word positions that have at least one aligned English word. Each $\phi_{i,l_j}(\mathbf{y})$ can be treated as a Bernoulli random variable, and we concatenate the set of all ϕ_{i,l_j} into a *random vector* $\boldsymbol{\phi}(\mathbf{y})$, where $\boldsymbol{\phi}_k = \phi_{i,l_j}$ if $k = i * m + j$. We drop the $(\mathbf{y})$ in $\boldsymbol{\phi}$ for simplicity.

The target expectation over ϕ_{i,l_j}, denoted as $\tilde{\phi}_{i,l_j}$, is the expectation of assigning label l_j to English word A_i under the English conditional probability model. When multiple English words are aligned to the same foreign word, we average the expectations.

The expectation over $\boldsymbol{\phi}$ under a conditional probability model $P(\mathbf{y}|\mathbf{x};\boldsymbol{\theta})$ is denoted as $E_{P(\mathbf{y}|\mathbf{x};\boldsymbol{\theta})}[\boldsymbol{\phi}]$, and simplified as $E_{\boldsymbol{\theta}}[\boldsymbol{\phi}]$ whenever it is unambiguous.

The conditional probability model $P(\mathbf{y}|\mathbf{x};\boldsymbol{\theta})$ in our case is defined as a standard linear-chain CRF:[5]

$$P(\mathbf{y}|\mathbf{x};\boldsymbol{\theta}) = \frac{1}{Z(\mathbf{x};\boldsymbol{\theta})}\exp\left(\sum_{i}^{n}\boldsymbol{\theta}\mathbf{f}(\mathbf{x}, y_i, y_{i-1})\right)$$

where $\mathbf{f}$ is a set of feature functions; $\boldsymbol{\theta}$ are the matching parameters to learn; $n = |\mathbf{x}|$.

The objective function to maximize in a standard CRF is the log probability over a collection of labeled documents:

$$L_{CRF}(\boldsymbol{\theta}) = \sum_{a=1}^{a'} \log P(\mathbf{y}_a^*|\mathbf{x}_a;\boldsymbol{\theta}) \qquad (1)$$

a' is the number of labeled sentences. $\mathbf{y}^*$ is an observed label sequence.

The objective function to maximize in GE is defined as the sum over all unlabeled examples on the

[5]We simplify notation by dropping the L_2 regularizer in the CRF definition, but apply it in our experiments.

foreign side of bitext, denoted as $\mathbf{x}_b$, over some cost function S between the model expectation over ϕ ($E_{\boldsymbol{\theta}}[\phi]$) and the target expectation ($\tilde{\phi}$).

We choose S to be the negative L_2^2 squared error sum[6] defined as:

$$L_{GE}(\boldsymbol{\theta}) = \sum_{b=1}^{n'} S\left(E_{P(\mathbf{y}_b|\mathbf{x}_b;\boldsymbol{\theta})}[\phi(\mathbf{y}_b)], \tilde{\phi}_b\right)$$
$$= \sum_{b=1}^{n'} -\|\tilde{\phi}_b - E_{\boldsymbol{\theta}}[\phi(\mathbf{y}_b)]\|_2^2 \quad (2)$$

n' is the total number of unlabeled bitext sentence pairs.

When both labeled and bitext training data are available, the joint objective is the sum of Eqn. 1 and 2. Each is computed over the labeled training data and foreign half in the bitext, respectively.

We can optimize this joint objective by computing the gradients and use a gradient-based optimization method such as L-BFGS. Gradients of L_{CRF} decomposes down to the gradients over each labeled training example $(\mathbf{x}, \mathbf{y}^*)$. Computing the gradient of L_{GE} decomposes down to the gradients of $S(E_{P(\mathbf{y}|\mathbf{x}_b;\boldsymbol{\theta}}[\phi])$ for each unlabeled foreign sentence $\mathbf{x}$ and the constraints over this example ϕ . The gradients can be calculated as:

$$\frac{\partial}{\partial \boldsymbol{\theta}} S(E_{\boldsymbol{\theta}}[\phi]) = -\frac{\partial}{\partial \boldsymbol{\theta}}\left(\tilde{\phi} - E_{\boldsymbol{\theta}}[\phi]\right)^T \left(\tilde{\phi} - E_{\boldsymbol{\theta}}[\phi]\right)$$
$$= 2\left(\tilde{\phi} - E_{\boldsymbol{\theta}}[\phi]\right)^T \left(\frac{\partial}{\partial \boldsymbol{\theta}} E_{\boldsymbol{\theta}}[\phi]\right)$$

We redefine the penalty vector $\mathbf{u} = 2\left(\tilde{\phi} - E_{\boldsymbol{\theta}}[\phi]\right)$ to be u. $\frac{\partial}{\partial \boldsymbol{\theta}} E_{\boldsymbol{\theta}}[\phi]$ is a matrix where each column contains the gradients for a particular model feature θ with respect to all constraint functions ϕ. It can be computed as:

$$\frac{\partial}{\partial \boldsymbol{\theta}} E_{\boldsymbol{\theta}}[\phi] = \sum_{\mathbf{y}} \phi(\mathbf{y}) \frac{\partial}{\partial \boldsymbol{\theta}} P(\mathbf{y}|\mathbf{x};\boldsymbol{\theta})$$
$$= \sum_{\mathbf{y}} \phi(\mathbf{y}) \frac{\partial}{\partial \boldsymbol{\theta}} \left(\frac{1}{Z(\mathbf{x};\boldsymbol{\theta})} \exp(\boldsymbol{\theta}^T \mathbf{f}(\mathbf{x},\mathbf{y}))\right)$$
$$= \sum_{\mathbf{y}} \phi(\mathbf{y}) \left(\frac{1}{Z(\mathbf{x};\boldsymbol{\theta})} \left(\frac{\partial}{\partial \boldsymbol{\theta}} \exp(\boldsymbol{\theta}^T \mathbf{f}(\mathbf{x},\mathbf{y}))\right) + \exp(\boldsymbol{\theta}^T \mathbf{f}(\mathbf{x},\mathbf{y})) \left(\frac{\partial}{\partial \boldsymbol{\theta}} \frac{1}{Z(\mathbf{x};\boldsymbol{\theta})}\right)\right)$$

$$= \sum_{\mathbf{y}} \phi(\mathbf{y}) \Big(P(\mathbf{y}|\mathbf{x};\boldsymbol{\theta}) \mathbf{f}(\mathbf{x},\mathbf{y})^T - P(\mathbf{y}|\mathbf{x};\boldsymbol{\theta}) \sum_{\mathbf{y}'} P(\mathbf{y}'|\mathbf{x};\boldsymbol{\theta}) \mathbf{f}(\mathbf{x},\mathbf{y}')^T \Big)$$
$$= \sum_{\mathbf{y}} P(\mathbf{y}|\mathbf{x};\boldsymbol{\theta}) \sum_{\mathbf{y}} \phi(\mathbf{y}) \mathbf{f}(\mathbf{x},\mathbf{y})^T - \Big(\sum_{\mathbf{y}} P(\mathbf{y}|\mathbf{x};\boldsymbol{\theta}) \phi(\mathbf{y})\Big)\Big(\sum_{\mathbf{y}} P(\mathbf{y}|\mathbf{x};\boldsymbol{\theta}) \mathbf{f}(\mathbf{x},\mathbf{y})^T\Big)$$
$$= \mathrm{COV}_{P(\mathbf{y}|\mathbf{x};\boldsymbol{\theta})}(\phi(\mathbf{y}), \mathbf{f}(\mathbf{x},\mathbf{y})) \quad (3)$$
$$= E_{\boldsymbol{\theta}}[\phi \mathbf{f}^T] - E_{\boldsymbol{\theta}}[\phi] E_{\boldsymbol{\theta}}[\mathbf{f}^T] \quad (4)$$

Eqn. 3 gives the intuition of how optimization works in GE. In each iteration of L-BFGS, the model parameters are updated according to their covariance with the constraint features, scaled by the difference between current expectation and target expectation. The term $E_{\boldsymbol{\theta}}[\phi \mathbf{f}^T]$ in Eqn. 4 can be computed using a dynamic programming (DP) algorithm, but solving it directly requires us to store a matrix of the same dimension as $\mathbf{f}^T$ in each step of the DP. We can reduce the complexity by using the same trick as in (Li and Eisner, 2009) for computing Expectation Semiring. The resulting algorithm has complexity $O(nm^2)$, which is the same as the standard forward-backward inference algorithm for CRF. (Druck, 2011, 93) gives full details of this derivation.

3.2 Hard vs. soft Projection

Projecting expectations instead of one-best label assignments from English to foreign language can be thought of as a soft version of the method described in (Das and Petrov, 2011) and (Ganchev et

[6]In general, other loss functions such as KL-divergence can also be used for S. We found L_2^2 to work well in practice.

al., 2009). Soft projection has its advantage: when the English model is not certain about its predictions, we do not have to commit to the current best prediction. The foreign model has more freedom to form its own belief since any marginal distribution it produces would deviates from a flat distribution by just about the same amount. In general, preserving uncertainties till later is a strategy that has benefited many NLP tasks (Finkel et al., 2006). Hard projection can also be treated as a special case in our framework. We can simply recalibrate posterior marginal of English by assigning probability mass 1 to the most likely outcome, and zero everything else out, effectively taking the argmax of the marginal at each word position. We refer to this version of expectation as the "hard" expectation. In the hard projection setting, GE training resembles a "project-then-train" style semi-supervised CRF training scheme (Yarowsky and Ngai, 2001; Täckström et al., 2013). In such a training scheme, we project the one-best predictions of English CRF to the foreign side through word alignments, then include the newly "tagged" foreign data as additional training data to a standard CRF in the foreign language. Rather than projecting labels on a per-word basis, Yarowsky and Ngai (2001) also explored an alternative method for noun-phrase (NP) bracketing task that amounts to projecting the spans of NPs based on the observation that individual NPs tend to retain their sequential spans across translations. We experimented with the same method for NER, but found that this method of projecting the NE spans does not help in reducing noise and actually lowers model performance.

Besides the difference in projecting expectations rather than hard labels, our method and the "project-then-train" scheme also differ by optimizing different objectives: CRF optimizes maximum conditional likelihood of the observed label sequence, whereas GE minimizes squared error between model's expectation and "hard" expectation based on the observed label sequence. In the case where squared error loss is replaced with a KL-divergence loss, GE has the same effect as marginalizing out all positions with unknown projected labels, allowing more robust learning of uncertainties in the model. As we will show in the experimental results in Section 4.2, soft projection in combination of the GE objective significantly outperforms the project-then-train style CRF training scheme.

	O	PER	LOC	ORG	GPE
O	291339	391	141	1281	221
PER	1263	6721	5	56	73
LOC	409	23	546	123	133
ORG	2423	143	52	8387	196
GPE	566	239	69	668	6604

	O	PER	LOC	ORG	MISC
O	81209	24	38	155	103
PER	77	5725	41	69	10
LOC	49	40	3743	127	60
ORG	178	102	142	4075	91
MISC	175	41	30	114	1826

Table 1: Raw counts in the error confusion matrix of English CRF models. Top table contains the counts on OntoNotes test data, and bottom table contains CoNLL-03 test data counts. Rows are the true labels and columns are the observed labels. For example, item at row 2, column 3 of the top table reads: we observed 5 times where the true label should be PERSON, but English CRF model output label LOCATION.

3.3 Source-side noise

An additional source of noise comes from errors generated by the source-side English CRF models. We know that the English CRF models gives F_1 score of 81.68% on the OntoNotes dataset for English-Chinese experiment, and 90.45% on the CoNLL-03 dataset for English-German experiment. We present a simple way of modeling English-side noise by picturing the following process: the labels assigned by the English CRF model (denoted as $\mathbf{y}$) are some noised version of the true labels (denoted as $\mathbf{y}^*$). We can recover the probability of the true labels by marginalizing over the observed labels: $P(\mathbf{y}^*|\mathbf{x}) = \sum_{\mathbf{y}} P(\mathbf{y}^*|\mathbf{y}) * P(\mathbf{y}|\mathbf{x})$. $P(\mathbf{y}|\mathbf{x})$ is the posterior probabilities given by the CRF model, and we can approximate $P(\mathbf{y}^*|\mathbf{y})$ by the column-normalized error confusion matrix shown in Table 1. This source-side noise model is likely to be overly simplistic. Generally speaking, we could build much more sophisticated noising model for the source-side, possibly conditioning on context, or capturing higher-order label sequences.

4 Experiments

We conduct experiments on Chinese and German NER. We evaluate CLiPER in two learning settings: weakly supervised and semi-supervised. In the weakly supervised setting, we simulate the condition of having no labeled training data, and evaluate the model learned from bitext alone. We then vary the amount of labeled data available to the model, and examine the model's learning curve. In the semi-supervised setting, we assume our model has access to the full labeled data; our goal is to improve performance of the supervised method by learning from additional bitext.

4.1 Dataset and setup

We used the latest version of Stanford NER Toolkit[7] as our base CRF model in all experiments. Features for English, Chinese and German CRFs are documented extensively in (Che et al., 2013) and (Faruqui and Padó, 2010) and omitted here for brevity. It it worth noting that the current Stanford NER models include recent improvements from semi-supervise learning approaches that induces distributional similarity features from large word clusters. These models represent the current state-of-the-art in supervised methods, and serve as a very strong baseline.

For Chinese NER experiments, we follow the same setup as Che et al. (2013) to evaluate on the latest OntoNotes (v4.0) corpus (Hovy et al., 2006).[8] A total of 8,249 sentences from the parallel Chinese and English Penn Treebank portion [9] are reserved for evaluation. Odd-numbered documents are used as development set, and even-numbered documents are held out as blind test set. The rest of OntoNotes annotated with NER tags are used to train the English and Chinese CRF base taggers. There are about 16k and 39k labeled sentences for Chinese and English training, respectively. The English CRF tagger trained on this training corpus gives F_1 score of 81.68% on the OntoNotes test set. Four entities types[10] are used for both Chinese and English with a IO tagging scheme.[11] The English-Chinese bitext comes from the Foreign Broadcast Information Service corpus (FBIS).[12] We randomly sampled 80k parallel sentence pairs to use as bitext in our experiments. It is first sentence aligned using the Champollion Tool Kit,[13] then word aligned with the BerkeleyAligner.[14]

For German NER experiments, we evaluate using the standard CoNLL-03 NER corpus (Sang and Meulder, 2003). The labeled training set has 12k and 15k sentences, containing four entity types.[15] An English CRF model is also trained on the CoNLL-03 English data with the same entity types. For bitext, we used a randomly sampled set of 40k parallel sentences from the de-en portion of the *News Commentary* dataset.[16] The English CRF tagger trained on CoNLL-03 English training corpus gives F_1 score of 90.4% on the CoNLL-03 test set.

We report typed entity precision (P), recall (R) and F_1 score. Statistical significance tests are done using a paired bootstrap resampling method with 1000 iterations, averaged over 5 runs. We compare against three recently approaches that were introduced in Section 2. They are: semi-supervised learning method using factored bilingual models with Gibbs sampling (Wang et al., 2013a); bilingual NER using Integer Linear Programming (ILP) with bilingual constraints, by (Che et al., 2013); and constraint-driven bilingual-reranking approach (Burkett et al., 2010). The code from (Che et al., 2013) and (Wang et al., 2013a) are publicly available.[17] Code from (Burkett et al., 2010) is obtained through personal communications.

Since the objective function in Eqn. 2 is non-convex, we adopted the early stopping training scheme from (Turian et al., 2010) as the following: after each iteration in L-BFGS training, the model

[7] `http://www-nlp.stanford.edu/ner`

[8] LDC catalogue No.: LDC2011T03

[9] File numbers: chtb_0001-0325, ectb_1001-1078

[10] PERSON, LOCATION, ORGANIZATION and GPE.

[11] We did not adopt the commonly seen BIO tagging scheme (Ramshaw and Marcus, 1999), because when projected across swapping word alignments, the "B-" and "I-" tag distinction may not be well-preserved and may introduce additional noise.

[12] The FBIS corpus is a collection of radio news casts and contains translations of openly available news and information from media sources outside the United States. The LDC catalogue No. is LDC2003E14.

[13] `champollion.sourceforge.net`

[14] `code.google.com/p/berkeleyaligner`

[15] PERSON, LOCATION, ORGANIZATION and MISCELLANEOUS.

[16] `http://www.statmt.org/wmt13/training-parallel-nc-v8.tgz`

[17] `https://github.com/stanfordnlp/CoreNLP`

is evaluated against the development set; the training procedure is terminated if no improvements have been made in 20 iterations.

4.2 Weakly supervised results

Figure 2a and 2b show results of weakly supervised learning experiments. Quite remarkably, on Chinese test set, our proposed method (CLiPER) achieves a F_1 score of 64.4% with 80k bitext, when no labeled training data is used. In contrast, the supervised CRF baseline would require as much as 12k labeled sentences to attain the same accuracy. Results on the German test set is less striking. With no labeled data and 40k of bitext, CLiPER performs at F_1 of 60.0%, the equivalent of using 1.5k labeled examples in the supervised setting. When combined with 1k labeled examples, performance of CLiPER reaches 69%, a gain of over 5% absolute over supervised CRF. We also notice that supervised CRF model learns much faster in German than Chinese. This result is not too surprising, since it is well recognized that Chinese NER is more challenging than German or English. The best supervised results for Chinese is 10-20% (F_1 score) behind best German and English supervised results. Chinese NER relies more on lexicalized features, and therefore needs more labeled data to achieve good coverage. The results suggest that CLiPER seems to be very effective at transferring lexical knowledge from English to Chinese.

Figure 2c and 2d compares soft GE projection with hard GE projection and the "project-then-train" style CRF training scheme (*cf.* Section 3.2). We observe that both soft and hard GE projection significantly outperform the "project-then-train" style training scheme. The difference is especially pronounced on the Chinese results when fewer labeled examples are available. Soft projection gives better accuracy than hard projection when no labeled data is available, and also has a faster learning rate.

Incorporating source-side noise using the method described in Section 3.3 gives a small improvement on Chinese with supervised data, increasing F_1 score from 64.40% to 65.50%. This improvement is statistically significant at 92% confidence interval. However, on the German data, we observe a tiny decrease with no statistical significance in F_1 score, dropping from 59.88% to 59.66%. A likely explanation of the difference is that the English CRF model in the English-Chinese experiment, which is trained on OntoNotes data, has a much higher error rate (18.32%) than the English CRF model in the English-German experiment trained on CoNLL-03 (9.55%). Therefore, modeling noise in the English-Chinese case is likely to have a greater effect than the English-German case.

4.3 Semi-supervised results

In the semi-supervised experiments, we let the CRF model use the full set of labeled examples in addition to the unlabeled bitext. Results on the test set are shown in Table 2. All semi-supervised baselines are tested with the same number of unlabeled bitext as CLiPER in each language. The "project-then-train" semi-supervised training scheme severely hurts performance on Chinese, but gives a small improvement on German. Moreover, on Chinese it learns to achieve high precision but at a significant loss in recall. On German its behavior is the opposite. Such drastic and erratic imbalance suggest that this method is not robust or reliable. The other three semi-supervised baselines (row 3-5) all show improvements over the CRF baseline, consistent with their reported results. CLIPER_s gives the best results on both Chinese and German, yielding statistically significant improvements over all baselines except for CWD13 on German. The hard projection version of CLiPER also gives sizable gain over CRF. However, in comparison, CLIPER_s is superior.

The improvements of CLIPER_s over CRF on Chinese test set is over 2.8% in absolute F_1. The improvement over CRF on German is almost a percent. To our knowledge, these are the best reported numbers on the OntoNotes Chinese and CoNLL-03 German datasets.

4.4 Efficiency

Another advantage of our proposed approach is efficiency. Because we eliminated the previous multi-stage "uptraining" paradigm, but instead integrating the semi-supervised and supervised objective into one joint objective, we are able to attain significant speed improvements over all methods except CRF_{ptt}. Table 3 shows the required training time.

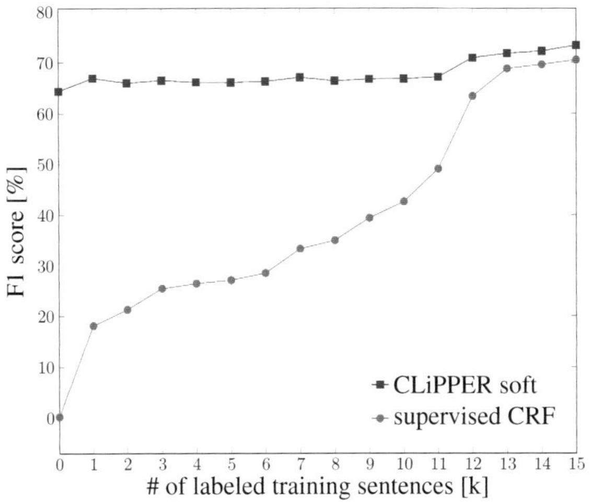

(a) Chinese Test

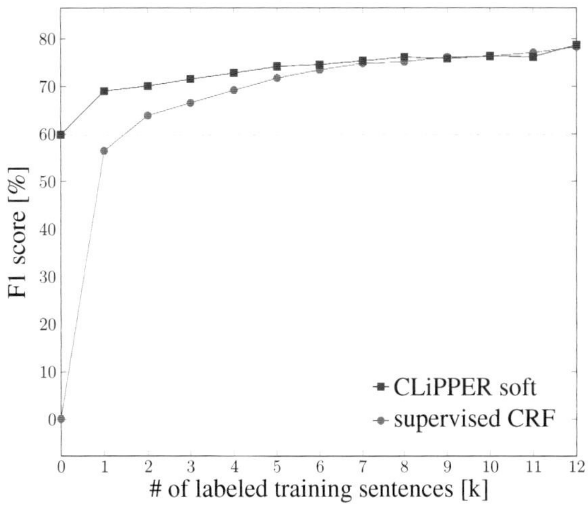

(b) German Test

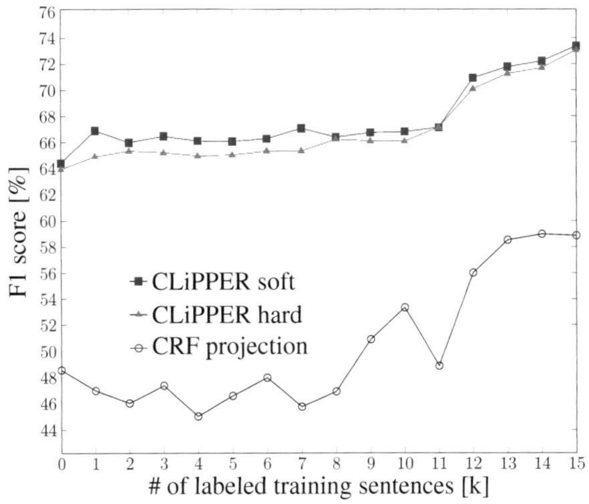

(c) Soft vs. Hard on Chinese Test

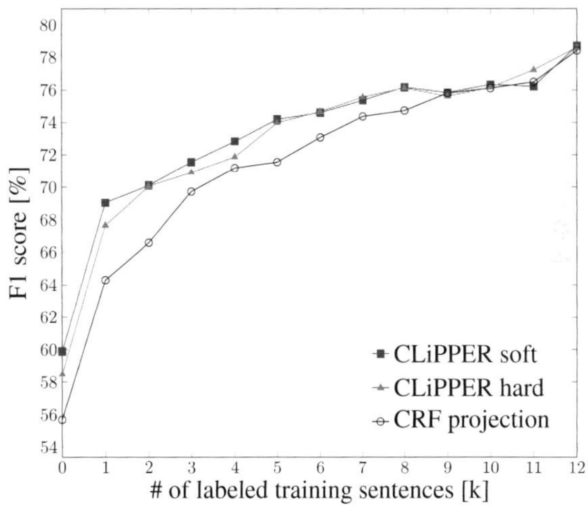

(d) Soft vs. Hard on German Test

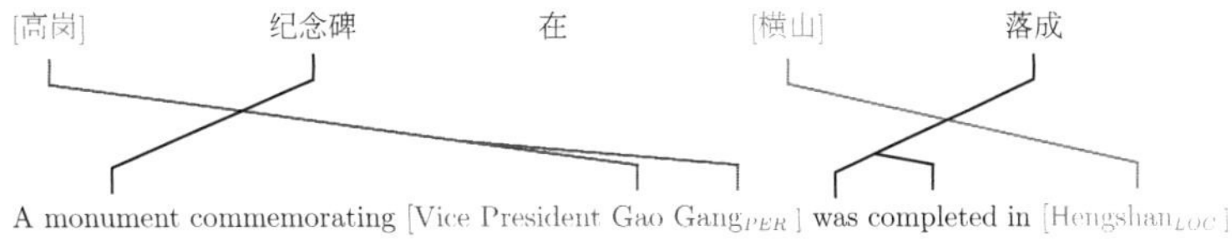

(e) Word proceeding "monument" is PERSON

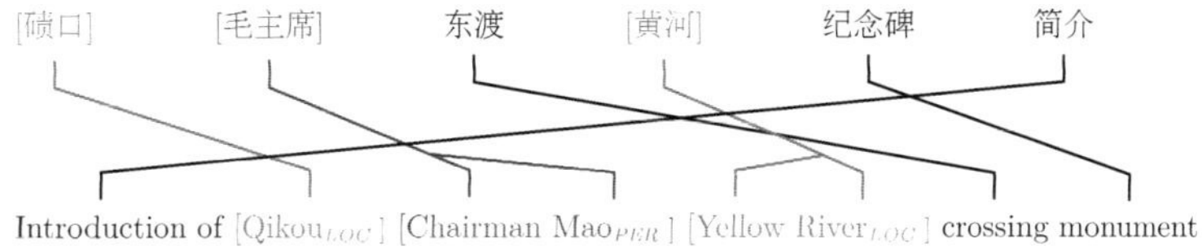

(f) Word proceeding "monument" is LOCATION

Figure 2: Top four figures show performance curves of CLiPER with varying amounts of available labeled training data in a weakly supervised setting. Vertical axes show the F_1 score on the test set. Performance curves of supervised CRF and "project-then-train" CRF are plotted for comparison. Bottom two figures are examples of aligned sentence pairs in Chinese and English.

	Chinese			German		
	P	R	F_1	P	R	F_1
CRF	79.09	63.59	70.50	86.69	71.30	78.25
CRF_{ptt}	**84.01**	45.29	58.85	81.50	**75.56**	78.41
BPBK10	79.25	65.67	71.83	84.00	72.17	77.64
CWD13	81.31	65.50	72.55	85.99	72.98	78.95
WCD13a	80.31	65.78	72.33	85.98	72.37	78.59
WCD13b	78.55	66.54	72.05	85.19	72.98	78.62
$CLiPER_h$	83.67	64.80	$73.04^{\S\ddagger}$	86.52	72.02	78.61^{*}
$CLiPER_s$	82.57	**65.99**	$\mathbf{73.35}^{\S\dagger\star}_{\diamond *}$	**87.11**	72.56	$\mathbf{79.17}^{\ddagger\star}_{*\S}$

Table 2: Test set Chinese, German NER results. Best number of each column is highlighted in bold. CRF is the supervised baseline. CRF_{ptt} is the "project-then-train" semi-supervised scheme for CRF. BPBK10 is (Burkett et al., 2010), WCD13 is (Wang et al., 2013a), CWD13A is (Che et al., 2013), and WCD13B is (Wang et al., 2013b) . $CLIPER_s$ and $CLIPER_h$ are the soft and hard projections. § indicates F_1 scores that are statistically significantly better than CRF baseline at 99.5% confidence level; ⋆ marks significance over CRF_{ptt} with 99.5% confidence; † and ‡ marks significance over WCD13 with 99.9% and 94% confidence; and ⋄ marks significance over CWD13 with 99.7% confidence; ∗ marks significance over BPBK10 with 99.9% confidence.

	Chinese	German
CRF	19m30s	7m15s
CRF_{ptt}	34m2s	12m45s
WCD13	3h17m	1h1m
CWD13a	16h42m	4h49m
CWD13b	16h42m	4h49m
BPBK10	6h16m	2h42m
$CLiPER_h$	1h28m	16m30s
$CLiPER_s$	1h40m	18m51s

Table 3: Timing stats during model training.

5 Discussions

Figure 2e and 2f give two examples of cross-lingual projection methods in action. Both examples have a named entity that immediately proceeds the word "纪念碑" (monument) in the Chinese sentence. In Figure 2e, the word "高岗" has literal meaning of *a hillock located at a high position*, which also happens to be the name of a former vice president of China. Without having previously observed this word as a person name in the labeled training data, the CRF model does not have enough evidence to believe that this is a PERSON, instead of LOCATION. But the aligned words in English ("Gao Gang") are clearly part of a person name as they were preceded by a title ("Vice President"). The English model has high expectation that the aligned Chinese word of "Gao Gang" is also a PERSON. Therefore, projecting the English expectations to Chinese provides a strong clue to help disambiguating this word. Figure 2f gives another example: the word "黄河"(Huang He, the Yellow River of China) can be confused with a person name since "黄"(Huang or Hwang) is also a common Chinese last name.[18]. Again, knowing the translation in English, which has the indicative word "River" in it, helps disambiguation.

The CRF_{ptt} and $CLIPER_h$ methods successfully labeled these two examples correctly, but failed to produce the correct label for the example in Figure 1. On the other hand, a model trained with the $CLIPER_s$ method does correctly label both entities in Figure 1, demonstrating the merits of the soft projection method.

6 Conclusion

We introduced a domain and language independent semi-supervised method for training discriminative models by projecting expectations across bitext. Experiments on Chinese and German NER show that our method, learned over bitext alone, can rival performance of supervised models trained with thousands of labeled examples. Furthermore, applying our method in a setting where all labeled examples are available also shows improvements over state-of-the-art supervised methods. Our experiments also showed that soft expectation projection is more favorable to hard projection. This technique can be generalized to all sequence labeling tasks, and can be extended to include more complex constraints. For future work, we plan to apply this method to more language pairs and also explore data selection strategies and modeling alignment uncertainties.

[18] In fact, a people search of the name 黄河 on the most popular Chinese social network (renren.com) returns over 13,000 matches.

Acknowledgments

The authors would like to thank Jennifer Gillenwater for a discussion that inspired this work, Behrang Mohit and Nathan Schneider for their help with the Arabic NER data, and David Burkett for providing the source code of their work for comparison. We would also like to thank editor Lillian Lee and the three anonymous reviewers for their valuable comments and suggestions. We gratefully acknowledge the support of the U.S. Defense Advanced Research Projects Agency (DARPA) Broad Operational Language Translation (BOLT) program through IBM. Any opinions, findings, and conclusion or recommendations expressed in this material are those of the authors and do not necessarily reflect the view of DARPA, or the US government.

References

Hiyan Alshawi, Srinivas Bangalore, and Shona Douglas. 2000. Head-transducer models for speech translation and their automatic acquisition from bilingual data. *Machine Translation*, 15.

Rie Kubota Ando and Tong Zhang. 2005. A high-performance semi-supervised learning method for text chunking. In *Proceedings of ACL*.

Kedar Bellare, Gregory Druck, and Andrew McCallum. 2009. Alternating projections for learning with expectation constraints. In *Proceedings of UAI*.

Avrim Blum and Tom Mitchell. 1998. Combining labeled and unlabeled data with co-training. In *Proceedings of COLT*.

David Burkett and Dan Klein. 2008. Two languages are better than one (for syntactic parsing). In *Proceedings of EMNLP*.

David Burkett, Slav Petrov, John Blitzer, and Dan Klein. 2010. Learning better monolingual models with unannotated bilingual text. In *Proceedings of CoNLL*.

Andrew Carlson, Justin Betteridge, Richard C. Wang, Estevam R. Hruschka Jr., and Tom M. Mitchell. 2010. Coupled semi-supervised learning for information extraction. In *Proceedings of WSDM*.

Ming-Wei Chang, Lev Ratinov, and Dan Roth. 2007. Guiding semi-supervision with constraint-driven learning. In *Proceedings of ACL*.

Wanxiang Che, Mengqiu Wang, and Christopher D. Manning. 2013. Named entity recognition with bilingual constraints. In *Proceedings of NAACL*.

Michael Collins and Yoram Singer. 1999. Unsupervised models for named entity classification. In *Proceedings of EMNLP*.

Dipanjan Das and Slav Petrov. 2011. Unsupervised part-of-speech tagging with bilingual graph-based projections. In *Proceedings of ACL*.

Gregory Druck and Andrew McCallum. 2010. High-performance semi-supervised learning using discriminatively constrained generative models. In *Proceedings of ICML*.

Gregory Druck, Gideon Mann, and Andrew McCallum. 2007. Leveraging existing resources using generalized expectation criteria. In *Proceedings of NIPS Workshop on Learning Problem Design*.

Gregory Druck, Burr Settles, and Andrew McCallum. 2009. Active learning by labeling features. In *Proceedings of EMNLP*.

Gregory Druck. 2011. *Generalized Expectation Criteria for Lightly Supervised Learning*. Ph.D. thesis, University of Massachusetts Amherst.

Manaal Faruqui and Sebastian Padó. 2010. Training and evaluating a German named entity recognizer with semantic generalization. In *Proceedings of KONVENS*.

Jenny Rose Finkel, Christopher D. Manning, and Andrew Y. Ng. 2006. Solving the problem of cascading errors: Approximate bayesian inference for linguistic annotation pipelines. In *Proceedings of EMNLP*.

Victoria Fossum and Steven Abney. 2005. Automatically inducing a part-of-speech tagger by projecting from multiple source languages across aligned corpora. In *Proceedings of IJCNLP*.

Kuzman Ganchev and Dipanjan Das. 2013. Cross-lingual discriminative learning of sequence models with posterior regularization. In *Proceedings of EMNLP*.

Kuzman Ganchev, Jennifer Gillenwater, and Ben Taskar. 2009. Dependency grammar induction via bitext projection constraints. In *Proceedings of ACL*.

Kuzman Ganchev, Jo ao Graça, Jennifer Gillenwater, and Ben Taskar. 2010. Posterior regularization for structured latent variable models. *JMLR*, 10:2001–2049.

Andrew B. Goldberg. 2010. *New Directions in Semi-supervised Learning*. Ph.D. thesis, University of Wisconsin-Madison.

Eduard Hovy, Mitchell Marcus, Martha Palmer, Lance Ramshaw, and Ralph Weischedel. 2006. OntoNotes: the 90% solution. In *Proceedings of NAACL-HLT*.

Dan Klein. 2005. *The Unsupervised Learning of Natural Language Structure*. Ph.D. thesis, Stanford University.

John D. Lafferty, Andrew McCallum, and Fernando C. N. Pereira. 2001. Conditional random fields: Probabilistic models for segmenting and labeling sequence data. In *Proceedings of ICML*.

Zhifei Li and Jason Eisner. 2009. First- and second-order expectation semirings with applications to minimum-risk training on translation forests. In *Proceedings of EMNLP*.

Shen Li, Jo ao Graça, and Ben Taskar. 2012. Wiki-ly supervised part-of-speech tagging. In *Proceedings of EMNLP-CoNLL*.

Percy Liang. 2005. Semi-supervised learning for natural language. Master's thesis, Massachusetts Institute of Technology.

Gideon Mann and Andrew McCallum. 2010. Generalized expectation criteria for semi-supervised learning with weakly labeled data. *JMLR*, 11:955–984.

David McClosky, Eugene Charniak, and Mark Johnson. 2006. Effective self-training for parsing. In *Proceedings of NAACL-HLT*.

Tahira Naseem, Benjamin Snyder, Jacob Eisenstein, and Regina Barzilay. 2009. Multilingual part-of-speech tagging: Two unsupervised approaches. *JAIR*, 36:1076–9757.

Slav Petrov, Pi-Chuan Chang, Michael Ringgaard, and Hiyan Alshawi. 2010. Uptraining for accurate deterministic question parsing. In *Proceedings of EMNLP*.

Lance A. Ramshaw and Mitchell P. Marcus. 1999. Text chunking using transformation-based learning. *Natural Language Processing Using Very Large Corpora*, 11:157–176.

Rajhans Samdani, Ming-Wei Chang, and Dan Roth. 2012. Unified expectation maximization. In *Proceedings of NAACL*.

Erik F. Tjong Kim Sang and Fien De Meulder. 2003. Introduction to the CoNLL-2003 shared task: language-independent named entity recognition. In *Proceedings of CoNLL*.

Vikas Sindhwani, Partha Niyogi, and Mikhail Belkin. 2005. A co-regularization approach to semi-supervised learning with multiple views. In *Proceedings of ICML Workshop on Learning with Multiple Views, International Conference on Machine Learning*.

Noah A. Smith. 2006. *Novel Estimation Methods for Unsupervised Discovery of Latent Structure in Natural Language Text*. Ph.D. thesis, Johns Hopkins University.

Benjamin Snyder, Tahira Naseem, and Regina Barzilay. 2009. Unsupervised multilingual grammar induction. In *Proceedings of ACL*.

Jun Suzuki and Hideki Isozaki. 2008. Semi-supervised sequential labeling and segmentation using giga-word scale unlabeled data. In *Proceedings of ACL*.

Oscar Täckström, Dipanjan Das, Slav Petrov, Ryan McDonald, and Joakim Nivre. 2013. Token and type constraints for cross-lingual part-of-speech tagging. In *Proceedings of ACL*.

Joseph Turian, Lev Ratinov, and Yoshua Bengio. 2010. Word representations: A simple and general method for semi-supervised learning. In *Proceedings of ACL*.

Mengqiu Wang, Wanxiang Che, and Christopher D. Manning. 2013a. Effective bilingual constraints for semi-supervised learning of named entity recognizers. In *Proceedings of AAAI*.

Mengqiu Wang, Wanxiang Che, and Christopher D. Manning. 2013b. Joint word alignment and bilingual named entity recognition using dual decomposition. In *Proceedings of ACL*.

Chenhai Xi and Rebecca Hwa. 2005. A backoff model for bootstrapping resources for non-english languages. In *Proceedings of HLT-EMNLP*.

David Yarowsky and Grace Ngai. 2001. Inducing multilingual POS taggers and NP bracketers via robust projection across aligned corpora. In *Proceedings of NAACL*.

David Yarowsky. 1995. Unsupervised word sense disambiguation rivaling supervised methods. In *Proceedings of ACL*.

From image descriptions to visual denotations: New similarity metrics for semantic inference over event descriptions

Peter Young Alice Lai Micah Hodosh Julia Hockenmaier
Department of Computer Science
University of Illinois at Urbana-Champaign
{pyoung2, aylai2, mhodosh2, juliahmr}@illinois.edu

Abstract

We propose to use the *visual denotations* of linguistic expressions (i.e. the set of images they describe) to define novel *denotational similarity metrics*, which we show to be at least as beneficial as distributional similarities for two tasks that require semantic inference. To compute these denotational similarities, we construct a *denotation graph*, i.e. a subsumption hierarchy over constituents and their denotations, based on a large corpus of 30K images and 150K descriptive captions.

1 Introduction

The ability to draw inferences from text is a prerequisite for language understanding. These inferences are what makes it possible for even brief descriptions of everyday scenes to evoke rich mental images. For example, we would expect an image of *people shopping in a supermarket* to depict aisles of produce or other goods, and we would expect most of these people to be customers who are either standing or walking around. But such inferences require a great deal of commonsense world knowledge. Standard *distributional* approaches to lexical similarity (Section 2.1) are very effective at identifying which words are related to the same topic, and can provide useful features for systems that perform semantic inferences (Mirkin et al., 2009), but are not suited to capture precise entailments between complex expressions. In this paper, we propose a novel approach for the automatic acquisition of *denotational* similarities between descriptions of everyday situations (Section 2). We define the *(visual) denotation* of a linguistic expression as the set of images it describes. We create a corpus of images of everyday activities (each paired with multiple captions; Section 3) to construct a large scale *visual denotation graph* which associates image descriptions with their denotations (Section 4). The algorithm that constructs the denotation graph uses purely syntactic and lexical rules to produce simpler captions (which have a larger denotation). But since each image is originally associated with several captions, the graph can also capture similarities between syntactically and lexically unrelated descriptions. We apply these similarities to two different tasks (Sections 6 and 7): an approximate entailment recognition task for our domain, where the goal is to decide whether the hypothesis (a brief image caption) refers to the same image as the premises (four longer captions), and the recently introduced Semantic Textual Similarity task (Agirre et al., 2012), which can be viewed as a graded (rather than binary) version of paraphrase detection. Both tasks require semantic inference, and our results indicate that denotational similarities are at least as effective as standard approaches to similarity. Our code and data set, as well as the denotation graph itself and the lexical similarities we define over it are available for research purposes at http://nlp.cs.illinois.edu/Denotation.html.

2 Towards Denotational Similarities

2.1 Distributional Similarities

The distributional hypothesis posits that linguistic expressions that appear in similar contexts have a

Transactions of the Association for Computational Linguistics, 2 (2014) 67–78. Action Editor: Lillian Lee.
Submitted 6/2013; Revised 10/2013; Published 2/2014.

Gray haired man in black suit and yellow tie working in a financial environment.
A graying man in a suit is perplexed at a business meeting.
A businessman in a yellow tie gives a frustrated look.
A man in a yellow tie is rubbing the back of his neck.
A man with a yellow tie looks concerned.

A butcher cutting an animal to sell.
A green-shirted man with a butcher's apron uses a knife to carve out the hanging carcass of a cow.
A man at work, butchering a cow.
A man in a green t-shirt and long tan apron hacks apart the carcass of a cow while another man hoses away the blood.
Two men work in a butcher shop; one cuts the meat from a butchered cow, while the other hoses the floor.

Figure 1: Two images from our data set and their five captions

similar meaning (Harris, 1954). This has led to the definition of vector-based distributional similarities, which represent each word w as a vector $\mathbf{w}$ derived from counts of w's co-occurrence with other words. These vectors can be used directly to compute the *lexical similarities* of words, either via the cosine of the angle between them, or via other, more complex metrics (Lin, 1998). More recently, asymmetric similarities have been proposed as more suitable for semantic inference tasks such as entailment (Weeds and Weir, 2003; Szpektor and Dagan, 2008; Clarke, 2009; Kotlerman et al., 2010). Distributional word vectors can also be used to define the *compositional similarity* of longer strings (Mitchell and Lapata, 2010). To compute the similarity of two strings, the lexical vectors of the words in each string are first combined into a single vector (e.g. by element-wise addition or multiplication), and then an appropriate vector similarity (e.g. cosine) is applied to the resulting pair of vectors.

2.2 Visual Denotations

Our approach is inspired by truth-conditional semantic theories in which the *denotation* of a declarative sentence is assumed to be the set of all situations or possible worlds in which the sentence is true (Montague, 1974; Dowty et al., 1981; Barwise and Perry, 1980). Restricting our attention to visually descriptive sentences, i.e. non-negative, episodic (Carlson, 2005) sentences that can be used to describe an image (Figure 1), we propose to instantiate the abstract notions of possible worlds or situations with concrete sets of images. The interpretation function $[\![\cdot]\!]$ maps sentences to their **visual denotations** $[\![\mathrm{s}]\!]$, which is the set of images $\mathbf{i} \in U_{\mathrm{s}} \subseteq U$ in a 'universe' of images U that s describes:

$$[\![\mathrm{s}]\!] = \{\mathbf{i} \in U \mid \text{s is a truthful description of } \mathbf{i}\} \quad (1)$$

Similarly, we map nouns and noun phrases to the set of images that depict the objects they describe, and verbs and verb phrases to the set of images that depict the events they describe.

2.3 Denotation Graphs

Denotations induce a partial ordering over descriptions: if s (e.g. *"a poodle runs on the beach"*) entails a description s′ (e.g. *"a dog runs"*), its denotation is a subset of the denotation of s′ ($[\![\mathrm{s}]\!] \subseteq [\![\mathrm{s}']\!]$), and we say that s′ *subsumes* the more specific s ($\mathrm{s}' \sqsubseteq \mathrm{s}$). In our domain of descriptive sentences, we can obtain more generic descriptions by simple **syntactic and lexical operations** $\omega \in O \subset S \times S$ that preserve upward entailment, so that if $\omega(\mathrm{s}) = \mathrm{s}'$, $[\![\mathrm{s}]\!] \subseteq [\![\mathrm{s}']\!]$. We consider three types of operations: the removal of optional material (e.g PPs like *on the beach*), the extraction of simpler constituents (NPs, VPs, or simple Ss), and lexical substitutions of nouns by their hypernyms (*poodle* $\rightarrow$ *dog*). These operations are akin to the *atomic edits* of MacCartney and Manning (2008)'s NatLog system, and allow us to construct large subsumption hierarchies over image descriptions, which we call **denotation graphs**. Given a set of (upward entailment-preserving) operations $O \subset S \times S$, the denotation graph $DG = \langle E, V \rangle$ of a set of images I and a set of strings S represents a subsumption hierarchy in which each node $V = \langle \mathrm{s}, [\![\mathrm{s}]\!] \rangle$ corresponds to a string $\mathrm{s} \in S$ and its denotation $[\![\mathrm{s}]\!] \subseteq I$. Directed edges $e = (\mathrm{s}, \mathrm{s}') \in E \subseteq V \times V$ indicate a subsumption relation $\mathrm{s} \sqsubseteq \mathrm{s}'$ between a more generic expression s and its child s′. An edge from s to s′

exists if there is an operation $\omega \in O$ that *reduces* the string s' to s (i.e. $\omega(s') = s$) and its inverse ω^{-1} *expands* the string s to s' (i.e. $\omega^{-1}(s) = s'$).

2.4 Denotational Similarities

Given a denotation graph over N images, we estimate the denotational probability of an expression s with a denotation of size $|[\![s]\!]|$ as $P_{[\![]\!]}(s) = |[\![s]\!]|/N$, and the joint probability of two expressions analogously as $P_{[\![]\!]}(s, s') = |[\![s]\!] \cap [\![s']\!]|/N$. The conditional probability $P_{[\![]\!]}(s \mid s')$ indicates how likely s is to be true when s' holds, and yields a simple directed denotational similarity. The (normalized) pointwise mutual information (PMI) (Church and Hanks, 1990) defines a symmetric similarity:

$$nPMI_{[\![]\!]}(s, s') = \frac{\log\left(\frac{P_{[\![]\!]}(s,s')}{P_{[\![]\!]}(s)P_{[\![]\!]}(s')}\right)}{-\log(P_{[\![]\!]}(s, s'))}$$

We set $P_{[\![]\!]}(s|s) = nPMI_{[\![]\!]}(s, s) = 1$, and, if s or s' are not in the denotation graph, $nPMI_{[\![]\!]}(s, s') = P_{[\![]\!]}(s, s') = 0$.

3 Our Data Set

Our data set (Figure 1) consists of 31,783 photographs of everyday activities, events and scenes (all harvested from Flickr) and 158,915 captions (obtained via crowdsourcing). It contains and extends Hodosh et al. (2013)'s corpus of 8,092 images. We followed Hodosh et al. (2013)'s approach to collect images. We also use their annotation guidelines, and use similar quality controls to correct spelling mistakes, eliminate ungrammatical or non-descriptive sentences. Almost all of the images that we add to those collected by Hodosh et al. (2013) have been made available under a Creative Commons license. Each image is described independently by five annotators who are not familiar with the specific entities and circumstances depicted in them, resulting in captions such as *"Three people setting up a tent"*, rather than the kind of captions people provide for their own images (*"Our trip to the Olympic Peninsula"*). Moreover, different annotators use different levels of specificity, from describing the overall situation (*performing a musical piece*) to specific actions (*bowing on a violin*). This variety of descriptions associated with the same image is what allows us to induce denotational similarities between expressions that are not trivially related by syntactic rewrite rules.

4 Constructing the Denotation Graph

The construction of the denotation graph consists of the following steps: preprocessing and linguistic analysis of the captions, identification of applicable transformations, and generation of the graph itself.

Preprocessing and Linguistic Analysis We use the Linux spell checker, the OpenNLP tokenizer, POS tagger and chunker (`http://opennlp.apache.org`), and the Malt parser (Nivre et al., 2006) to analyze the captions. Since the vocabulary of our corpus differs significantly from the data these tools are trained on, we resort to a number of heuristics to improve the analyses they provide. Since some heuristics require us to identify different entity types, we developed a lexicon of the most common entity types in our domain (people, clothing, bodily appearance (e.g. hair or body parts), containers of liquids, food items and vehicles).

After spell-checking, we normalize certain words and compounds with several spelling variations, e.g. *barbecue (barbeque, BBQ)*, *gray (grey)*, *waterski (water ski)*, *brown-haired (brown haired)*, and tokenize the captions using the OpenNLP tokenizer. The OpenNLP POS tagger makes a number of systematic errors on our corpus (e.g. mistagging main verbs as nouns). Since these errors are highly systematic, we are able to correct them automatically by applying deterministic rules (e.g. *climbs* is never a noun in our corpus, *stand* is a noun if it is preceded by *vegetable* but a verb when preceded by a noun that refers to people). These fixes apply to 27,784 (17% of the 158,915 image captions). Next, we use the OpenNLP chunker to create a shallow parse. Fixing its (systematic) errors affects 28,587 captions. We then analyze the structure of each NP chunk to identify heads, determiners and prenominal modifiers. The head may include more than a single token if WordNet (or our hypernym lexicon, described below) contains a corresponding entry (e.g. *little girl*). Determiners include phrases such as *a couple* or *a few*. Although we use the Malt parser (Nivre et al., 2006) to identify subject-verb-object dependencies, we have found it more accurate to develop deterministic heuristics and lexical rules to identify the boundaries of complex (e.g. conjoined) NPs, allowing us to treat *"a man with red shoes and a white hat"* as an NP followed by a single PP, but *"a man with red shoes and a white-haired woman"* as two NPs, and to transform e.g. *"standing by a man and a woman"* into *"standing"* and not *"standing and a woman"* when dropping the PP.

Hypernym Lexicon We use our corpus and WordNet to construct a hypernym lexicon that allows us to replace head nouns with more generic terms. We only consider hypernyms that occur themselves with sufficient frequency in the original captions (replacing *"adult"* with *"person"*, but not with *"organism"*). Since the language in our corpus is very concrete, each noun tends to have a single sense, allowing us to always replace it with the same hypernyms.[1] But since WordNet provides us with multiple senses for most nouns, we first have to identify which sense is used in our corpus. To do this, we use the heuristic cross-caption coreference algorithm of Hodosh et al. (2010) to identify coreferent NP chunks among the original five captions of each image.[2] For each ambiguous head noun, we consider every non-singleton coreference chains it appears in, and reduce its synsets to those that stand in a hypernym-hyponym relation with at least one other head noun in the chain. Finally, we apply a greedy majority voting algorithm to iteratively narrow down each term's senses to a single synset that is compatible with the largest number of coreference chains it occurs in.

Caption Normalization In order to increase the recall of the denotations we capture, we drop all punctuation marks, and lemmatize nouns, verbs, and adjectives that end in *"-ed"* or *"-ing"* before generating the denotation graph. In order to distinguish between frequently occurring homonyms where the noun is unrelated to the verb, we change all forms of the verb *dress* to *dressed*, all forms of the verb *stand* to *standing* and all forms of the verb *park* to *parking*. Finally, we drop sentence-initial *there/here/this is/are* (as in *there is a dog splashing in the water*), and normalize the expressions *in X* and *dressed (up) in X* (where *X* is an article of clothing or a color) to *wear X*. We reduce plural determiners to {*two, three, some*}, and drop singular determiners except for *no*.

4.1 Rule Templates

The denotation graph contains a directed edge from s to s′ if there is a rule ω that reduces s′ to s, with an inverse ω^{-1} that expands s to s′. Reduction rules can drop optional material, extract simpler constituents, or perform lexical substitutions.

Drop Pre-Nominal Modifiers: *"red shirt"* $\rightarrow$ *"shirt"* In an NP of the form "X Y Z", where X and Y both modify the head Z, we only allow X and Y to be dropped separately if "X Z" and "Y Z" both occur elsewhere in the corpus. Since *"white building"* and *"stone building"* occur elsewhere in the corpus, we generate both *"white building"* and *"stone building"* from the NP *"white stone building"*. But since *"ice player"* is not used, we replace *"ice hockey player"* only with *"hockey player"* (which does occur) and then *"player"*.

Drop Other Modifiers *"run quickly"* $\rightarrow$ *"run"* We drop ADVP chunks and adverbs in VP chunks. We also allow a prepositional phrase (a preposition followed by a possibly conjoined NP chunk) to be dropped if the preposition is locational (*"in"*, *"on"*, *"above"*, etc.), directional (*"towards"*, *"through"*, *"across"*, etc.), or instrumental (*"by"*, *"for"*, *"with"*). Similarly, we also allow the dropping of all *"wear* NP*"* constructions. Since the distinction between particles and prepositions is often difficult, we also use a predefined list of phrasal verbs that commonly occur in our corpus to identify constructions such as *"climb up a mountain"*, which is transformed into *"climb a mountain"* or *"walk down a street"*, which is transformed into *"walk"*.

Replace Nouns by Hypernyms: *"red shirt"* $\rightarrow$ *"red clothing"* We iteratively use our hypernym

[1] Descriptions of people that refer to both age and gender (e.g. *"man"*) can have multiple distinct hypernyms (*"adult"*/*"male"*). Because our annotators never describe young children or babies as *"persons"*, we only allow terms that are likely to describe adults or teenagers (including occupations) to be replaced by the term *"person"*. This means that the term *"girl"* has two senses: a female child (the default) or a younger woman. We distinguish the two senses in a preprocessing step: if the other captions of the same image do not mention children, but refer to teenaged or adult women, we assign *girl* the *woman*-sense. Some nouns that end in *-er* (e.g. *"diner"*, *"pitcher"* also violate our monosemy assumption.

[2] Coreference resolution has also been used for word sense disambiguation by Preiss (2001) and Hu and Liu (2011).

```
GenerateGraph():
Q, Captions, Rules ← ∅
for all c ∈ ImageCorpus do
    Rules(c) ← GenerateRules(s_c)
    pushAll(Q, {c} × RootNodes(s_c, Rules(c)))
while ¬empty(Q) do
    (c, s) ← pop(Q)
    Captions(s) ← Captions(s) ∪ {c}
    if |Captions(s)| = 2 then
        for all c′ ∈ Captions(s) do
            pushAll(Q, {c′} × Children(s, Rules(c′)))
    else if |Captions(s)| > 2 then
        pushAll(Q, {c} × Children(s, Rules(c)))
```

Figure 2: Generating the graph

lexicon to make head nouns more generic. We only allow head nouns to be replaced by their hypernyms if any age based modifiers have already been removed: *"toddler"* can be replaced with *"child"*, but not *"older toddler"* with *"older child"*.

Handle Partitive NPs: *cup of tea* → *"cup", "tea"* In most partitive NP_1-of-NP_2 constructions (*"cup of tea"*, *"a team of football players"*) the corresponding entity can be referred to by both the first or the second NP. Exceptions include the phrase *"body of water"*, and expressions such as *"a kind/type/sort of"*, which we treat similar to determiners.

Handle *VP_1-to-VP_2* Cases Depending on the first verb, we replace VPs of the form **X to Y** with both **X** and **Y** if **X** is a movement or posture (*jump to catch*, etc.). Otherwise we distinguish between cases we can only replace with **X** (*wait to jump*) and those we can only replace with **Y** (*seem to jump*).

Extract Simpler Constituents Any noun phrase or verb phrase can also be used as a node in the graph and simplified further. We use the Malt dependencies (and the person terms in the entity type lexicon) to identify and extract subject-verb-object chunks which correspond to simpler sentences that we would otherwise not be able to obtain: from *"man laugh(s) while drink(ing)"*, we extract *"man laugh"* and *"man drink"*, and then further split those into *"man"*, *"laugh(s)"*, and *"drink"*.

4.2 Graph Generation

The naive approach to graph generation would be to generate all possible strings for each caption. However, this would produce far more strings than can be processed in a reasonable amount of time, and most of these strings would have uninformative denotations, consisting of only a single image. To make graph generation tractable, we use a top-down algorithm which generates the graph from the most generic (root) nodes, and stops at nodes that have a singleton denotation (Figure 2). We first identify the set of rules that can apply to each original caption (*GenerateRules*). These rules are then used to reduce each caption as much as possible. The resulting (maximally generic) strings are added as root nodes to the graph (*RootNodes*), and added to the queue Q. Q keeps track of all currently possible node expansions. It contains items $\langle c, \mathbf{s}\rangle$, which pair the ID of an original caption and its image (c) with a string (s) that corresponds to an existing node in the graph and can be derived from c's caption. When $\langle c, \mathbf{s}\rangle$ is processed, we check how many captions have generated s so far (Captions(s)). If s has more than a single caption, we use each of the applicable rewrite rules of c's caption to create new strings s′ that correspond to the children of s in the graph, and push all resulting $\langle c, \mathbf{s}'\rangle$ onto Q. If **c** is the second caption of s, we also use all of the applicable rewrite rules from the first caption c' to create its children.

A post-processing step (not shown in Figure 2) attaches each original caption to all leaf nodes of the graph to which it can be reduced. Finally, we obtain the denotation of each node s from the set of images whose captions are in Captions(s).

5 The Denotation Graph

Size and Coverage On our corpus of 158,439 unique captions and 31,783 images, the denotation graph contains 1,749,097 captions, out of which 230,811 describe more than a single image. Table 1 provides the distribution of the size of denotations. It is perhaps surprising that the 161 captions which describe each over 1,000 images do not just consist of nouns such as *person*, but also contain simple sentences such as *woman standing*, *adult work*, *person walk street*, or *person play instrument*. Since the graph is derived from the original captions by very simple syntactic operations, the denotations it captures are most likely incomplete: $[\![soccer\ player]\!]$ contains 251 images, $[\![play\ soccer]\!]$ contains 234 images, and $[\![soccer\ game]\!]$ contains

Size of denotations	$\lvert[\![s]\!]\rvert \geq 1$	$\lvert[\![s]\!]\rvert \geq 2$	$\lvert[\![s]\!]\rvert \geq 5$	$\lvert[\![s]\!]\rvert \geq 10$	$\lvert[\![s]\!]\rvert \geq 100$	$\lvert[\![s]\!]\rvert \geq 1000$
Nr. of captions	1,749,096	230,811	53,341	22,683	1,921	161

Table 1: Distribution of the size of denotations in our graph

119 images. We have not yet attempted to identify variants in word order (*"stick tongue out"* vs. *"stick out tongue"*) or equivalent choices of preposition (*"look into mirror"* vs. *"look in mirror"*). Despite this brittleness, the current graph already gives us a large number of semantic associations.

Denotational Similarities The following examples of the similarities found by $nPMI_{[\![]\!]}$ and $P_{[\![]\!]}$ show that denotational similarities do not simply find topically related events, but instead find events that are related by entailment:

$P_{[\![]\!]}(x\|y)$	x	y
0.962	*sit*	*eat lunch*
0.846	*play guitar*	*strum*
0.811	*surf*	*catch wave*
0.800	*ride horse*	*rope calf*
0.700	*listen*	*sit in classroom*

If someone is *eating lunch*, it is likely that they are *sitting*, and people who *sit in a classroom* are likely to be *listening* to somebody. These entailments can be very precise: *"walk up stair"* entails *"ascend"*, but not *"descend"*; the reverse is true for *"walk down stair"*:

$P_{[\![]\!]}(x\|y)$	x =*ascend*	x =*descend*
y =*walk up stair*	32.0	0.0
y =*walk down stair*	0.0	30.8

$nPMI_{[\![]\!]}$ captures paraphrases as well as closely related events: people *look in a mirror* when *shaving their face*, and baseball players may *try to tag* someone who is *sliding into base*:

$nPMI_{[\![]\!]}$	x	y
0.835	*open present*	*unwrap*
0.826	*lasso*	*try to rope*
0.791	*get ready to kick*	*run towards ball*
0.785	*try to tag*	*slide into base*
0.777	*shave face*	*look in mirror*

Comparing the expressions that are most similar to *"play baseball"* or *"play football"* according to the denotational $nPMI_{[\![]\!]}$ and the compositional Σ similarities reveals that the denotational similarity finds a number of actions that are part of the particular sport, while the compositional similarity finds events that are similar to *playing baseball* (*football*):

play baseball

$nPMI_{[\![]\!]}$		Σ	
0.674	*tag him*	0.859	*play softball*
0.637	*hold bat*	0.782	*play game*
0.616	*try to tag*	0.768	*play ball*
0.569	*slide into base*	0.741	*play catch*
0.516	*pitch ball*	0.739	*play cricket*

play football

$nPMI_{[\![]\!]}$		Σ	
0.623	*tackle person*	0.826	*play game*
0.597	*hold football*	0.817	*play rugby*
0.545	*run down field*	0.811	*play soccer*
0.519	*wear white jersey*	0.796	*play on field*
0.487	*avoid*	0.773	*play ball*

6 Task 1: Approximate Entailment

A caption never provides a complete description of the depicted scene, but commonsense knowledge often allows us to draw implicit inferences: when somebody mentions a *bride*, it is quite likely that the picture shows a woman in a *wedding dress*; a picture of a *parent* most likely also has a *child* or *baby*, etc. In order to compare the utility of denotational and distributional similarities for drawing these inferences, we apply them to an *approximate entailment task*, which is loosely modeled after the Recognizing Textual Entailment problem (Dagan et al., 2006), and consists of deciding whether a brief caption $\mathbf{h}$ (the hypothesis) can describe the same image as a set of captions $\mathbf{P} = \{\mathbf{p}_1, ..., \mathbf{p}_N\}$ known to describe the same image (the premises).

Data We generate positive and negative items $\langle \mathbf{P}, \mathbf{h}, \pm \rangle$ (Figure 3) as follows: Given an image, any subset of four of its captions form a set of premises. A hypothesis is either a short verb phrase or sentence that corresponds to a node in the denotation graph. By focusing on short hypotheses, we minimize the possibility that they contain extraneous details that cannot be inferred from the premises. Positive examples are generated by choosing a node $\mathbf{h}$ as hypothesis and an image $i \in [\![\mathbf{h}]\!]$ such that exactly one caption of i generates $\mathbf{h}$ and the other four captions of i are not descendants of $\mathbf{h}$ and hence do not trivially entail $\mathbf{h}$, giving an unfair advantage to denotational approaches. Negative examples are generated by choosing a node $\mathbf{h}$ as hypothesis and selecting four of the captions of an image $i \notin [\![\mathbf{h}]\!]$.

Premises:	A woman with dark hair in bending, open mouthed, towards the back of a dark headed toddler's head. A dark-haired woman has her mouth open and is hugging a little girl while sitting on a red blanket. A grown lady is snuggling on the couch with a young girl and the lady has a frightened look. A mom holding her child on a red sofa while they are both having fun.
VP Hypothesis:	make face
Premises:	A man editing a black and white photo at a computer with a pencil in his ear. A man in a white shirt is working at a computer. A guy in white t-shirt on a mac computer. A young main is using an Apple computer.
S Hypothesis:	man sit

Figure 3: Positive examples from the Approximate Entailment tasks.

Since our items are created automatically, a positive hypothesis is not necessarily logically entailed by its premises. We have performed a small-scale human evaluation on 300 items (200 positive, 100 negative), each judged independently by the same three judges (inter-annotator agreement: Fleiss-κ = 0.74). Our results indicate that over half (55%) of the positive hypotheses can be inferred from their premises alone without looking at the original image, while almost none of the negative hypotheses (100% for sentences, 96% for verb phrases) can be inferred from their premises. The training items are generated from the captions of 25,000 images, and the test items are generated from a disjoint set of 3,000 images. The VP data set consists of 290,000 training items and 16,000 test items, while the S data set consists of 400,000 training items and 22,000 test items. Half of the items in each set are positive, and the other half are negative.

Models All of our models are binary MaxEnt classifiers, trained using MALLET (McCallum, 2002). We have two baseline models: a plain bag-of-words model (BoW) and a bag-of-words model where we add all hypernyms in our lexicon to the captions before computing their overlap (BoW-H). This is intended to minimize the advantage the denotational features obtain from the hypernym lexicon used to construct the denotation graph. In both cases, a global BoW feature captures the fraction of tokens in the hypothesis that are contained in the premises. Word-specific BoW features capture the product of the frequencies of each word in $\mathbf{h}$ and $\mathbf{P}$. All other models extend the BoW-H model.

Denotational Similarity Features We compute denotational similarities $nPMI_{[\![]\!]}$ and $P_{[\![]\!]}$ (Section 2.4) over the pairs of nodes in a denotation graph that is restricted to the training images. We only consider pairs of nodes $\mathbf{n}, \mathbf{n}'$ if their denotations contain at least 10 images and their intersection contains at least 2 images.

To map an item $\langle \mathbf{P}, \mathbf{h} \rangle$ to denotational similarity features, we represent the premises as the set of all nodes P that are ancestors of its captions. A sentential hypothesis is represented as the set of nodes $H = \{h_S, h_{sbj}, h_{VP}, h_v, h_{dobj}\}$ that correspond to the sentence ($\mathbf{h}$ itself), its subject, its VP and its direct object. A VP hypothesis has only the nodes $H = \{h_{VP}, hv, h_{dobj}\}$. In both cases, h_{dobj} may be empty. Both of the denotational similarities $nPMI_{[\![]\!]}(h,p)$ and $P_{[\![]\!]}(h|p)$ for $h \in H$, $p \in P$ lead to two constituent-specific features, sum_x and $\max_x$, (e.g. $\mathrm{sum}_{sbj} = \sum_p \mathrm{sim}(h_{sbj}, p)$, $\max_{dobj} = \max_p \mathrm{sim}(h_{dobj}, p)$) and two global features $\mathrm{sum}_{p,h} = \sum_{p,h} \mathrm{sim}(h,p)$ and $\max_{p,h} = \max_{p,h} \mathrm{sim}(h,p)$. Each constituent type also has a set of node-specific $\mathrm{sum}_{x,\mathbf{s}}$ and $\max_{x,\mathbf{s}}$ features that are on when constituent x in $\mathbf{h}$ is equal to the string $\mathbf{s}$ and whose value is equal to the constituent-based feature. For $P_{[\![]\!]}$, each constituent (and each constituent-node pair) has an additional feature $P(h|P) = 1 - \prod_n (1 - P_{[\![]\!]}(h|p_n))$ that estimates the probability that h is generated by some node in the premise.

Lexical Similarity Features We use two symmetric lexical similarities: standard cosine distance (cos), and Lin (1998)'s similarity (Lin):

$$\cos(\mathbf{w}, \mathbf{w}') = \frac{\mathbf{w} \cdot \mathbf{w}'}{\|\mathbf{w}\| \|\mathbf{w}'\|}$$

$$\mathrm{Lin}(\mathbf{w}, \mathbf{w}') = \frac{\sum_{i:\mathbf{w}(i)>0 \wedge \mathbf{w}'(i)>0} \mathbf{w}(i) + \mathbf{w}'(i)}{\sum_i \mathbf{w}(i) + \sum_i \mathbf{w}'(i)}$$

We use two directed lexical similarities: Clarke (2009)'s similarity (Clk), and Szpektor and Dagan (2008)'s balanced precision (Bal), which builds on Lin and on Weeds and Weir (2003)'s similarity ($\mathbf{W}$):

$$\begin{aligned}\mathrm{Clk}(\mathbf{w} \mid \mathbf{w}') &= \frac{\sum_{i:\mathbf{w}(i)>0 \wedge \mathbf{w}'(i)>0} \min(\mathbf{w}(i), \mathbf{w}'(i))}{\sum_i \mathbf{w}(i)} \\ \mathrm{Bal}(\mathbf{w} \mid \mathbf{w}') &= \sqrt{\mathbf{W}(\mathbf{w} \mid \mathbf{w}') \times \mathrm{Lin}(\mathbf{w}, \mathbf{w}')} \\ \mathbf{W}(\mathbf{w} \mid \mathbf{w}') &= \frac{\sum_{i:\mathbf{w}(i)>0 \wedge \mathbf{w}'(i)>0} \mathbf{w}(i)}{\sum_i \mathbf{w}(i)}\end{aligned}$$

We also use two publicly available resources that provide precomputed similarities, Kotlerman et al. (2010)'s DIRECT noun and verb rules and Chklovski and Pantel (2004)'s VERBOCEAN rules. Both are motivated by the need for numerically quantifiable semantic inferences between predicates. We only use entries that correspond to single tokens (ignoring e.g. phrasal verbs).

Each lexical similarity results in the following features: words in the output are represented by a max-sim$_w$ feature which captures its maximum similarity with any word in the premises (max-sim$_w$ = $\max_{w' \in P} \mathrm{sim}(w, w')$) and by a sum-sim$_w$ feature which captures the sum of its similarities to the words in the premises (sum-sim$_w$ = $\sum_{w' \in P} \mathrm{sim}(w, w')$). Global max sim and sum sim features capture the maximal (resp. total) similarity of any word in the hypothesis to the premise.

We compute distributional and compositional similarities (cos, Lin, Bal, Clk, Σ, Π) on our image captions ("cap"), the BNC and Gigaword. For each corpus C, we map each word w that appears at least 10 times in C to a vector $\mathbf{w}_C$ of the non-negative normalized pointwise mutual information scores (Section 2.4) of w and the 1,000 words (excluding stop words) that occur in the most sentences of C. We generally define $P(w)$ (and $P(w, w')$) as the fraction of sentences in C in which w (and w') occur. To allow a direct comparison between distributional and denotational similarities, we first define $P(w)$ (and $P(w, w')$) over individual captions ("cap"), and then, to level the playing field, we redefine $P(w)$ (and $P(w, w')$) as the fraction of images in whose captions w (and w') occur ("img"), and then we use our lexicon to augment captions with all hypernyms ("+hyp"). Finally, we include BNC and Gigaword similarity features ("all").

	VP task		S task	
Baseline 1: BoW	58.7		71.2	
Baseline 2: BoW-H	59.0		73.6	
External 1: DIRECT	59.2		73.5	
External 2: VerbOcean	60.8		74.0	
	Cap	**All**	**Cap**	**All**
Distributional cos	67.5	**71.9**	76.1	**78.9**
Distributional Lin	62.6	70.2	75.4	77.8
Distributional Bal	62.3	69.6	74.7	75.3
Distributional Clk	62.4	69.2	75.4	77.5
Compositional Π	68.4	70.3	75.3	77.3
Compositional Σ	67.8	71.4	76.9	79.2
Compositional Π, Σ	69.8	**72.7**	77.0	**79.6**
Denotational $nPMI_{[\![]\!]}$	74.9		80.2	
Denotational $P_{[\![]\!]}$	73.8		79.5	
$nPMI_{[\![]\!]}, P_{[\![]\!]}$	**75.5**		**81.2**	
Combined cos, Π, Σ	71.1	72.6	77.4	79.2
$nPMI_{[\![]\!]}, P_{[\![]\!]}, \Pi, \Sigma$	75.6	**75.9**	80.2	80.7
$nPMI_{[\![]\!]}, P_{[\![]\!]}$, cos	75.6	75.7	80.2	**81.2**
$nPMI_{[\![]\!]}, P_{[\![]\!]}$, cos, Π, Σ	75.8	**75.9**	**81.2**	80.5

Table 2: Test accuracy on Approximate Entailment.

Compositional Similarity Features We use two standard compositional baselines to combine the word vectors of a sentence into a single vector: addition ($\mathbf{s}_{\sum} = \mathbf{w}_1 + ... + \mathbf{w}_n$, which can be interpreted as a disjunctive operation), and element-wise (Hadamard) multiplication ($\mathbf{s}_{\prod} = \mathbf{w}_1 \odot ... \odot \mathbf{w}_n$, which can be seen as a conjunctive operation). In both cases, we represent the premises (which consist of four captions) as a the sum of each caption's vector $\mathbf{p} = \mathbf{p}_1 + ...\mathbf{p}_4$. This gives two compositional similarity features: $\Sigma = \cos(\mathbf{p}_\Sigma, \mathbf{h}_\Sigma)$, and $\Pi = \cos(\mathbf{p}_\Pi, \mathbf{h}_\Pi)$.

6.1 Experimental Results

Table 2 provides the test accuracy of our models on the VP and S tasks. Adding hypernyms (BOW-H) yields a slight improvement over the basic BOW model. Among the external resources, VERBOCEAN is more beneficial than DIRECT, but neither help as much as in-domain distributional similarities (this may be due to sparsity).

Table 2 shows only the simplest ("Cap") and the most complex ("all") distributional and compositional models, but Table 3 provides accuracies of these models as we go from standard sentence-based co-occurrence counts towards more denotation graph-like co-occurrence counts that are based on all captions describing the same image ("Img"),

	VP task				S task			
	Cap	**Img**	**+Hyp**	**All**	**Cap**	**Img**	**+Hyp**	**All**
cos	67.5	69.3	69.8	**71.9**	76.1	76.8	77.5	**78.9**
Lin	62.6	63.4	61.3	**70.0**	75.4	74.8	75.2	**77.8**
Bal	62.3	61.9	62.8	**69.6**	74.7	75.5	75.1	**75.3**
Clk	62.4	67.3	68.0	**69.2**	75.4	75.5	76.0	**77.5**
Π	68.4	**70.5**	**70.5**	70.3	75.3	76.6	77.1	**77.3**
Σ	67.8	71.4	**71.6**	71.4	76.9	78.1	79.1	**79.2**
Π, Σ	69.8	72.7	**72.9**	72.7	77.0	78.6	79.3	**79.6**
$nPMI_{[\![]\!]}$			74.9				80.2	
$P_{[\![]\!]}$			73.8				79.5	
$nPMI_{[\![]\!]}, P_{[\![]\!]}$			**75.5**				**81.2**	

Table 3: Accuracy on hypotheses as various additions are made to the vector corpora. **Cap** is the image corpus with caption co-occurrence. **Img** is the image corpus with image co-occurrence. **+Hyp** augments the image corpus with hypernyms and uses image co-occurrence. **All** adds the BNC and Gigaword corpora to **+Hyp**.

	VP task			S task		
Words in h	**1**	**2**	**3+**	**2**	**3**	**4+**
% of items	**72.8**	**13.9**	**13.3**	**65.3**	**22.8**	**11.9**
BoW-H	52.0	75.0	80.1	69.1	80.8	84.4
cos (All)	68.8	79.4	81.1	75.9	83.9	85.7
$\sum$ (All)	68.1	80.8	79.5	76.5	83.9	85.1
$nPMI_{[\![]\!]}$	**72.0**	**82.9**	**82.2**	**77.3**	**85.4**	**86.2**

Table 4: Accuracy on hypotheses of varying length.

include hypernyms ("+Hyp"), and add information from other corpora ("All"). The "+Hyp" column in Table 3 shows that the denotational metrics clearly outperform any distributional metric when both have access to the same information. Although the distributional models benefit from the BNC and Gigaword-based similarities ("All"), their performance is still below that of the denotational models. Among the distributional model, the simple cos performs better than Lin, or the directed Clk and Bal similarities. In all cases, giving models access to different similarity features improves performance.

Table 4 shows the results by hypothesis length. As the length of **h** increases, classifiers that use similarities between pairs of words (BOW-H and cos) continue to improve in performance relative to the classifiers that use similarities between phrases and sentences (Σ and $nPMI_{[\![]\!]}$). Most likely, this is due to the lexical similarities having a larger set of features to work with for longer **h**. $nPMI_{[\![]\!]}$ does especially well on shorter **h**, likely due to the shorter **h** having larger denotations.

7 Task 2: Semantic Textual Similarity

To assess how the denotational similarities perform on a more established task and domain, we apply them to the 1500 sentence pairs from the MSR Video Description Corpus (Chen and Dolan, 2011) that were annotated for the SemEval 2012 Semantic Textual Similarity (STS) task (Agirre et al., 2012). The goal of this task is to assign scores between 0 and 5 to a pair of sentences, where 5 indicates equivalence, and 0 unrelatedness. Since this is a symmetric task, we do not consider directed similarities. And because the goal of this experiment is not to achieve the best possible performance on this task, but to compare the effectiveness of denotational and more established similarities, we only compare the impact of denotational similarities with compositional similarities computed on our own corpus. Since the MSR Video corpus associates each video with multiple sentences, it is in principle also amenable to a denotational treatment, but the STS task description explicitly forbids its use.

7.1 Models

Baseline and Compositional Features Our starting point is Bär et al. (2013)'s DKPro Similarity, one of the top-performing models from the 2012 STS shared task, which is available and easily modified. It consists of a log-linear regression model trained on multiple text features (word and character n-grams, longest common substring and longest common subsequence, Gabrilovich and Markovitch (2007)'s Explicit Semantic Analysis, and Resnik (1995)'s WordNet-based similarity). We investigate the effects of adding compositional (computed on the vectors obtained from the image-caption training data) and denotational similarity features to this state-of-the-art system.

Denotational Features Since the STS task is symmetric, we only consider $nPMI_{[\![]\!]}$ similarities. We again represent each sentence s by features based on 5 types of constituents: $S = \{s_S, s_{sbj}, s_{VP}, s_v, s_{dobj}\}$. Since sentences might be complex, they might contain multiple constituents of the same type, and we therefore think of each feature as a feature over sets of nodes. For each constituent C we consider two sets of nodes in the denotation graph: C itself (typically leaf nodes),

	DKPro	$+\Sigma, \Pi$ (img)	$+nPMI_{[\![]\!]}$	*+both*
Pearson r	0.868	0.880	0.888	0.890

Table 5: Performance on the STS MSRvid task: DKPro (Bär et al., 2013) plus compositional (Σ, Π) and/or denotational similarities ($nPMI_{[\![]\!]}$) from our corpus

and C^{anc}, their parents and grandparents. For each pair of sentences, C-C similarities compute the similarity of the constituents of the same type, while C-all similarities compute the similarity of a C constituent in one sentence against all constituents in the other sentence. For each pair of constituents we consider three similarity features: $\mathrm{sim}(C_1, C_2)$, $\max(\mathrm{sim}(C_1 C_2^{anc}), \mathrm{sim}(C_1^{anc}, C_2))$, $\mathrm{sim}(C_1^{anc}, C_2^{anc})$. The similarity of two sets of nodes is determined by the maximal similarity of any pair of their elements: $\mathrm{sim}(C_1, C_2) = \max_{c_1 \in C_1, c_2 \in C_2} nPMI_{[\![]\!]}(c_1, c_2)$. This gives us 15 C-C features and 15 C-all features.

7.2 Experiments

We use the STS 2012 train/test data, normalized in the same way as the image captions for the denotation graph (i.e. we re-tokenize, lemmatize, and remove determiners). Table 5 shows experimental results for four models: *DKPro* is the off-the-shelf DKProSimilarity model (Bär et al., 2013). From our corpus, we either add additive and multiplicative *compositional* features (Σ, Π) from Section 6 (img), the C-C and C-All *denotational* features based on $nPMI_{[\![]\!]}$, or *both* compositional and denotational features. Systems are evaluated by the Pearson correlation (r) of their predicted similarity scores to the human-annotated ones. We see that the denotational similarities outperform the compositional similarities, and that including compositional similarity features in addition to denotational similarity features has little effect. For additional comparison, the published numbers for the TakeLab Semantic Text Similarity System (Šarić et al., 2012), another top-performing model from the 2012 shared task, are $r = 0.880$ on this dataset.

8 Conclusion

Summary of Contributions We have defined novel *denotational* metrics of linguistic similarity (Section 2), and have shown them to be at least competitive with, if not superior to, distributional similarities for two tasks that require simple semantic inferences (Sections 6, 7), even though our current method of computing them is somewhat brittle (Section 5). We have also introduced two new resources: a large data set of images paired with descriptive captions, and a *denotation graph* that pairs generalized versions of these captions with their *visual denotations*, i.e. the sets of images they describe. Both of these resources are freely available (`http://nlp.cs.illinois.edu/Denotation.html`) Although the aim of this paper is to show their utility for a purely linguistic task, we believe that they should also be of great interest for people who aim to build systems that automatically associate image with sentences that describe them (Farhadi et al., 2010; Kulkarni et al., 2011; Li et al., 2011; Yang et al., 2011; Mitchell et al., 2012; Kuznetsova et al., 2012; Gupta et al., 2012; Hodosh et al., 2013).

Related Work and Resources We believe that the work reported in this paper has the potential to open up promising new research directions. There are other data sets that pair images or video with descriptive language, but we have not yet applied our approach to them. Chen and Dolan (2011)'s MSR Video Description Corpus (of which the STS data is a subset) is most similar to ours, but its curated part is significantly smaller. Instead of several independent captions, Grubinger et al. (2006)'s IAPR TC-12 data set contains longer descriptions. Ordonez et al. (2011) harvested 1 million images and their user-generated captions from Flickr to create the SBU Captioned Photo Dataset. These captions tend to be less descriptive of the image. The denotation graph is similar to Berant et al. (2012)'s 'entailment graph', but differs from it in two ways: first, entailment relations in the denotation graph are defined extensionally in terms of the images described by the expressions at each node, and second, nodes in Berant et al.'s entailment graph correspond to generic propositional templates (*X treats Y*), whereas nodes in our denotation graph correspond to complete propositions (*a dog runs*).

Acknowledgements

We gratefully acknowledge the support of the National Science Foundation under NSF awards 0803603 *"INT2-Medium: Understanding the meaning of images"*, 1053856 *"CAREER: Bayesian Models for Lexicalized Grammars"*, and 1205627 *"CI-P:Collaborative Research: Visual entailment data set and challenge for the Language and Vision Community"*, as well as via an NSF Graduate Research Fellowship to Alice Lai.

References

Eneko Agirre, Mona Diab, Daniel Cer, and Aitor Gonzalez-Agirre. 2012. SemEval-2012 task 6: a pilot on semantic textual similarity. In *Proceedings of the First Joint Conference on Lexical and Computational Semantics - Volume 1: Proceedings of the main conference and the shared task, and Volume 2: Proceedings of the Sixth International Workshop on Semantic Evaluation*, SemEval '12, pages 385–393.

Daniel Bär, Torsten Zesch, and Iryna Gurevych. 2013. DKPro Similarity: An Open Source Framework for Text Similarity. In *Proceedings of the 51st Annual Meeting of the Association for Computational Linguistics: System Demonstrations*, pages 121–126, Sofia, Bulgaria, August.

Jon Barwise and John Perry. 1980. Situations and attitudes. *Journal of Philosophy*, 78:668–691.

Jonathan Berant, Ido Dagan, and Jacob Goldberger. 2012. Learning entailment relations by global graph structure optimization. *Computational Linguistics*, 38(1):73–111.

Greg Carlson, 2005. *The Encyclopedia of Language and Linguistics*, chapter Generics, Habituals and Iteratives. Elsevier, 2nd edition.

David Chen and William Dolan. 2011. Collecting highly parallel data for paraphrase evaluation. In *Proceedings of the 49th Annual Meeting of the Association for Computational Linguistics: Human Language Technologies*, pages 190–200, Portland, Oregon, USA, June.

Timothy Chklovski and Patrick Pantel. 2004. Verbocean: Mining the web for fine-grained semantic verb relations. In *Proceedings of the 2004 Conference on Empirical Methods in Natural Language Processing (EMNLP)*, pages 33–40, Barcelona, Spain, July.

Kenneth Ward Church and Patrick Hanks. 1990. Word association norms, mutual information, and lexicography. *Computational Linguistics*, 16(1):22–29.

Daoud Clarke. 2009. Context-theoretic semantics for natural language: an overview. In *Proceedings of the Workshop on Geometrical Models of Natural Language Semantics*, pages 112–119, Athens, Greece, March.

Ido Dagan, Oren Glickman, and Bernardo Magnini. 2006. The PASCAL Recognising Textual Entailment challenge. In *Machine Learning Challenges*, volume 3944 of *Lecture Notes in Computer Science*, pages 177–190. Springer.

David Dowty, Robert Wall, and Stanley Peters. 1981. *Introduction to Montague Semantics*. Reidel, Dordrecht.

Ali Farhadi, Mohsen Hejrati, Mohammad Amin Sadeghi, Peter Young, Cyrus Rashtchian, Julia Hockenmaier, and David Forsyth. 2010. Every picture tells a story: Generating sentences from images. In *Proceedings of the European Conference on Computer Vision (ECCV), Part IV*, pages 15–29, Heraklion, Greece, September.

Evgeniy Gabrilovich and Shaul Markovitch. 2007. Computing semantic relatedness using wikipedia-based explicit semantic analysis. In *Proceedings of the 20th international joint conference on Artifical intelligence*, IJCAI'07, pages 1606–1611.

Michael Grubinger, Paul Clough, Henning Müller, and Thomas Deselaers. 2006. The IAPR benchmark: A new evaluation resource for visual information systems. In *OntoImage 2006, Workshop on Language Resources for Content-based Image Retrieval during LREC 2006*, pages 13–23, Genoa, Italy, May.

Ankush Gupta, Yashaswi Verma, and C. Jawahar. 2012. Choosing linguistics over vision to describe images. In *Proceedings of the Twenty-Sixth AAAI Conference on Artificial Intelligence*, Toronto, Ontario, Canada, July.

Zellig S Harris. 1954. Distributional structure. *Word*, 10:146–162.

Micah Hodosh, Peter Young, Cyrus Rashtchian, and Julia Hockenmaier. 2010. Cross-caption coreference resolution for automatic image understanding. In *Proceedings of the Fourteenth Conference on Computational Natural Language Learning*, pages 162–171, Uppsala, Sweden, July.

Micah Hodosh, Peter Young, and Julia Hockenmaier. 2013. Framing image description as a ranking task: Data, models and evaluation metrics. *Journal of Artificial Intelligence Research (JAIR)*, 47:853–899.

Shangfeng Hu and Chengfei Liu. 2011. Incorporating coreference resolution into word sense disambiguation. In Alexander F. Gelbukh, editor, *Computational Linguistics and Intelligent Text Processing*, volume 6608 of *Lecture Notes in Computer Science*, pages 265–276. Springer Berlin Heidelberg.

Lili Kotlerman, Ido Dagan, Idan Szpektor, and Maayan Zhitomirsky-Geffet. 2010. Directional distributional similarity for lexical inference. *Natural Language Engineering*, 16(4):359–389.

Girish Kulkarni, Visruth Premraj, Sagnik Dhar, Siming Li, Yejin Choi, Alexander C. Berg, and Tamara L. Berg. 2011. Baby talk: Understanding and generating simple image descriptions. In *Proceedings of the 2011 IEEE Conference on Computer Vision and Pattern Recognition (CVPR)*, pages 1601–1608.

Polina Kuznetsova, Vicente Ordonez, Alexander Berg, Tamara Berg, and Yejin Choi. 2012. Collective generation of natural image descriptions. In *Proceedings of the 50th Annual Meeting of the Association for Computational Linguistics (Volume 1: Long Papers)*, pages 359–368, Jeju Island, Korea, July.

Siming Li, Girish Kulkarni, Tamara L. Berg, Alexander C. Berg, and Yejin Choi. 2011. Composing simple image descriptions using web-scale n-grams. In *Proceedings of the Fifteenth Conference on Computational Natural Language Learning (CoNLL)*, pages 220–228, Portland, OR, USA, June.

Dekang Lin. 1998. An information-theoretic definition of similarity. In *Proceedings of the Fifteenth International Conference on Machine Learning (ICML)*, pages 296–304, Madison, WI, USA, July.

Bill MacCartney and Christopher D. Manning. 2008. Modeling semantic containment and exclusion in natural language inference. In *Proceedings of the 22nd International Conference on Computational Linguistics (Coling 2008)*, pages 521–528, Manchester, UK, August.

Andrew Kachites McCallum. 2002. Mallet: A machine learning for language toolkit. http://www.cs.umass.edu/ mccallum/mallet.

Shachar Mirkin, Ido Dagan, and Eyal Shnarch. 2009. Evaluating the inferential utility of lexical-semantic resources. In *Proceedings of the 12th Conference of the European Chapter of the ACL (EACL 2009)*, pages 558–566, Athens, Greece, March.

Jeff Mitchell and Mirella Lapata. 2010. Composition in distributional models of semantics. *Cognitive Science*, 34(8):1388–1429.

Margaret Mitchell, Jesse Dodge, Amit Goyal, Kota Yamaguchi, Karl Stratos, Xufeng Han, Alyssa Mensch, Alex Berg, Tamara Berg, and Hal Daume III. 2012. Midge: Generating image descriptions from computer vision detections. In *Proceedings of the 13th Conference of the European Chapter of the Association for Computational Linguistics (EACL)*, pages 747–756, Avignon, France, April.

Richard Montague. 1974. *Formal philosophy: papers of Richard Montague*. Yale University Press, New Haven. Edited by Richmond H. Thomason.

Joakim Nivre, Johan Hall, and Jens Nilsson. 2006. Maltparser: A data-driven parser-generator for dependency parsing. In *Proceedings of the International Conference on Language Resources and Evaluation (LREC)*, pages 2216–2219.

Vicente Ordonez, Girish Kulkarni, and Tamara L. Berg. 2011. Im2text: Describing images using 1 million captioned photographs. In *Advances in Neural Information Processing Systems 24*, pages 1143–1151.

Judita Preiss. 2001. Anaphora resolution with word sense disambiguation. In *Proceedings of SENSEVAL-2 Second International Workshop on Evaluating Word Sense Disambiguation Systems*, pages 143–146, Toulouse, France, July.

Philip Resnik. 1995. Using information content to evaluate semantic similarity in a taxonomy. In *Proceedings of the 14th international joint conference on Artificial intelligence - Volume 1*, IJCAI'95, pages 448–453.

Idan Szpektor and Ido Dagan. 2008. Learning entailment rules for unary templates. In *Proceedings of the 22nd International Conference on Computational Linguistics (Coling 2008)*, pages 849–856, Manchester, UK, August. Coling 2008 Organizing Committee.

Frane Šarić, Goran Glavaš, Mladen Karan, Jan Šnajder, and Bojana Dalbelo Bašić. 2012. Takelab: Systems for measuring semantic text similarity. In *Proceedings of the Sixth International Workshop on Semantic Evaluation (SemEval 2012)*, pages 441–448, Montréal, Canada, 7-8 June.

Julie Weeds and David Weir. 2003. A general framework for distributional similarity. In *Proceedings of the 2003 Conference on Empirical Methods in Natural Language Processing (EMNLP)*, pages 81–88.

Yezhou Yang, Ching Teo, Hal Daume III, and Yiannis Aloimonos. 2011. Corpus-guided sentence generation of natural images. In *Proceedings of the 2011 Conference on Empirical Methods in Natural Language Processing (EMNLP)*, pages 444–454, Edinburgh, UK, July.

The Language Demographics of Amazon Mechanical Turk

Ellie Pavlick[1] **Matt Post**[2] **Ann Irvine**[2] **Dmitry Kachaev**[2] **Chris Callison-Burch**[1,2]
[1]Computer and Information Science Department, University of Pennsylvania
[2]Human Language Technology Center of Excellence, Johns Hopkins University

Abstract

We present a large scale study of the languages spoken by bilingual workers on Mechanical Turk (MTurk). We establish a methodology for determining the language skills of anonymous crowd workers that is more robust than simple surveying. We validate workers' self-reported language skill claims by measuring their ability to correctly translate words, and by geolocating workers to see if they reside in countries where the languages are likely to be spoken. Rather than posting a one-off survey, we posted paid tasks consisting of 1,000 assignments to translate a total of 10,000 words in each of 100 languages. Our study ran for several months, and was highly visible on the MTurk crowdsourcing platform, increasing the chances that bilingual workers would complete it. Our study was useful both to create bilingual dictionaries and to act as census of the bilingual speakers on MTurk. We use this data to recommend languages with the largest speaker populations as good candidates for other researchers who want to develop crowdsourced, multilingual technologies. To further demonstrate the value of creating data via crowdsourcing, we hire workers to create bilingual parallel corpora in six Indian languages, and use them to train statistical machine translation systems.

1 Overview

Crowdsourcing is a promising new mechanism for collecting data for natural language processing research. Access to a fast, cheap, and flexible workforce allows us to collect new types of data, potentially enabling new language technologies. Because crowdsourcing platforms like Amazon Mechanical Turk (MTurk) give researchers access to a worldwide workforce, one obvious application of crowdsourcing is the creation of multilingual technologies. With an increasing number of active crowd workers located outside of the United States, there is even the potential to reach fluent speakers of lower resource languages. In this paper, we investigate the feasibility of hiring language informants on MTurk by conducting the first large-scale demographic study of the languages spoken by workers on the platform.

There are several complicating factors when trying to take a census of workers on MTurk. The workers' identities are anonymized, and Amazon provides no information about their countries of origin or their language abilities. Posting a simple survey to have workers report this information may be inadequate, since (a) many workers may never see the survey, (b) many opt not to do one-off surveys since potential payment is low, and (c) validating the answers of respondents is not straightforward.

Our study establishes a methodology for determining the language demographics of anonymous crowd workers that is more robust than simple surveying. We ask workers what languages they speak and what country they live in, and validate their claims by measuring their ability to correctly translate words and by recording their geolocation. To increase the visibility and the desirability of our tasks, we post 1,000 assignments in each of 100 languages. These tasks each consist of translating 10 foreign words into English. Two of the 10 words have known translations, allowing us to validate that the workers' translations are accurate. We construct bilingual dictionaries with up to 10,000 entries, with the majority of entries being new.

Surveying thousands of workers allows us to analyze current speaker populations for 100 languages.

Transactions of the Association for Computational Linguistics, 2 (2014) 79–92. Action Editor: Mirella Lapata.
Submitted 12/2013; Published 2/2014.

Figure 1: The number of workers per country. This map was generated based on geolocating the IP address of 4,983 workers in our study. Omitted are 60 workers who were located in more than one country during the study, and 238 workers who could not be geolocated. The size of the circles represents the number of workers from each country. The two largest are India (1,998 workers) and the United States (866). To calibrate the sizes: the Philippines has 142 workers, Egypt has 25, Russia has 10, and Sri Lanka has 4.

The data also allows us to answer questions like: How quickly is work completed in a given language? Are crowdsourced translations reliably good? How often do workers misrepresent their language abilities to obtain financial rewards?

2 Background and Related Work

Amazon's Mechanical Turk (MTurk) is an online marketplace for work that gives employers and researchers access to a large, low-cost workforce. MTurk allows employers to provide micropayments in return for workers completing microtasks. The basic units of work on MTurk are called 'Human Intelligence Tasks' (HITs). MTurk was designed to accommodate tasks that are difficult for computers, but simple for people. This facilitates research into human computation, where people can be treated as a function call (von Ahn, 2005; Little et al., 2009; Quinn and Bederson, 2011). It has application to research areas like human-computer interaction (Bigham et al., 2010; Bernstein et al., 2010), computer vision (Sorokin and Forsyth, 2008; Deng et al., 2010; Rashtchian et al., 2010), speech processing (Marge et al., 2010; Lane et al., 2010; Parent and Eskenazi, 2011; Eskenazi et al., 2013), and natural language processing (Snow et al., 2008; Callison-Burch and Dredze, 2010; Laws et al., 2011).

On MTurk, researchers who need work completed are called 'Requesters', and workers are often referred to as 'Turkers'. MTurk is a true market, meaning that Turkers are free to choose to complete the HITs which interest them, and Requesters can price their tasks competitively to try to attract workers and have their tasks done quickly (Faridani et al., 2011; Singer and Mittal, 2011). Turkers remain anonymous to Requesters, and all payment occurs through Amazon. Requesters are able to accept submitted work or reject work that does not meet their standards. Turkers are only paid if a Requester accepts their work.

Several reports examine Mechanical Turk as an economic market (Ipeirotis, 2010a; Lehdonvirta and Ernkvist, 2011). When Amazon introduced MTurk, it first offered payment only in Amazon credits, and later offered direct payment in US dollars. More recently, it has expanded to include one foreign currency, the Indian rupee. Despite its payments being limited to two currencies or Amazon credits, MTurk claims over half a million workers from 190 countries (Amazon, 2013). This suggests that its worker population should represent a diverse set of languages.

A demographic study by Ipeirotis (2010b) focused on age, gender, martial status, income levels, motivation for working on MTurk, and whether workers used it as a primary or supplemental form of income. The study contrasted Indian and US workers. Ross et al. (2010) completed a longitudinal follow-on study. A number of other studies have informally investigated Turkers' language abilities. Munro and Tily (2011) compiled survey responses of 2,000 Turkers, revealing that four of the six most represented languages come from India (the top six being Hindi, Malayalam, Tamil, Spanish, French, and Telugu). Irvine and Klementiev (2010) had Turkers evaluate the accuracy of translations that had been automatically inducted from monolingual texts. They examined translations of 100 words in 42 low-resource languages, and reported geolocated countries for their workers (India, the US, Romania, Pakistan, Macedonia, Latvia, Bangladesh and the Philippines). Irvine and Klementiev discussed the difficulty of quality control and assessing the plausibility of workers' language skills for rare languages, which we address in this paper.

Several researchers have investigated using MTurk to build bilingual parallel corpora for machine translation, a task which stands to benefit low cost, high volume translation on demand (Germann, 2001). Ambati et al. (2010) conducted a pilot study by posting 25 sentences to MTurk for Spanish, Chinese, Hindi, Telugu, Urdu, and Haitian Creole. In a study of 2000 Urdu sentences, Zaidan and Callison-Burch (2011) presented methods for achieving professional-level translation quality from Turkers by soliciting multiple English translations of each foreign sentence. Zbib et al. (2012) used crowdsourcing to construct a 1.5 million word parallel corpus of dialect Arabic and English, training a statistical machine translation system that produced higher quality translations of dialect Arabic than a system a trained on 100 times more Modern Standard Arabic-English parallel data. Zbib et al. (2013) conducted a systematic study that showed that training an MT system on crowdsourced translations resulted in the same performance as training on professional translations, at $\frac{1}{5}$ the cost. Hu et al. (2010; Hu et al. (2011) performed crowdsourced translation by having monolingual speakers collaborate and iteratively improve MT output.

English	689	Tamil	253	Malayalam	219
Hindi	149	Spanish	131	Telugu	87
Chinese	86	Romanian	85	Portuguese	82
Arabic	74	Kannada	72	German	66
French	63	Polish	61	Urdu	56
Tagalog	54	Marathi	48	Russian	44
Italian	43	Bengali	41	Gujarati	39
Hebrew	38	Dutch	37	Turkish	35
Vietnamese	34	Macedonian	31	Cebuano	29
Swedish	26	Bulgarian	25	Swahili	23
Hungarian	23	Catalan	22	Thai	22
Lithuanian	21	Punjabi	21	Others	≤ 20

Table 1: Self-reported native language of 3,216 bilingual Turkers. Not shown are 49 languages with $\leq$20 speakers. We omit 1,801 Turkers who did not report their native language, 243 who reported 2 native languages, and 83 with $\geq$3 native languages.

Several researchers have examined cost optimization using active learning techniques to select the most useful sentences or fragments to translate (Ambati and Vogel, 2010; Bloodgood and Callison-Burch, 2010; Ambati, 2012).

To contrast our research with previous work, the main contributions of this paper are: (1) a robust methodology for assessing the bilingual skills of anonymous workers, (2) the largest-scale census to date of language skills of workers on MTurk, and (3) a detailed analysis of the data gathered in our study.

3 Experimental Design

The central task in this study was to investigate Mechanical Turk's bilingual population. We accomplished this through self-reported surveys combined with a HIT to translate individual words for 100 languages. We evaluate the accuracy of the workers' translations against known translations. In cases where these were not exact matches, we used a second pass monolingual HIT, which asked English speakers to evaluate if a worker-provided translation was a synonym of the known translation.

Demographic questionnaire At the start of each HIT, Turkers were asked to complete a brief survey about their language abilities. The survey asked the following questions:

- Is [language] your native language?
- How many years have you spoken [language]?

- Is English your native language?
- How many years have you spoken English?
- What country do you live in?

We automatically collected each worker's current location by geolocating their IP address. A total of 5,281 unique workers completed our HITs. Of these, 3,625 provided answers to our survey questions, and we were able to geolocate 5,043. Figure 1 plots the location of workers across 106 countries. Table 1 gives the most common self-reported native languages.

Selection of languages We drew our data from the different language versions of Wikipedia. We selected the 100 languages with the largest number of articles [1] (Table 2). For each language, we chose the 1,000 most viewed articles over a 1 year period,[2] and extracted the 10,000 most frequent words from them. The resulting vocabularies served as the input to our translation HIT.

Translation HIT For the translation task, we asked Turkers to translate individual words. We showed each word in the context of three sentences that were drawn from Wikipedia. Turkers were allowed to mark that they were unable to translate a word. Each task contained 10 words, 8 of which were words with unknown translations, and 2 of which were quality control words with known translations. We gave special instruction for translating names of people and places, giving examples of how to handle 'Barack Obama' and 'Australia' using their interlanguage links. For languages with non-Latin alphabets, names were transliterated.

The task paid $0.15 for the translation of 10 words. Each set of 10 words was independently translated by three separate workers. 5,281 workers completed 256,604 translation assignments, totaling more than 3 million words, over a period of three and a half months.

Gold standard translations A set of gold standard translations were automatically harvested from Wikipedia for every language to use as embedded controls. We used Wikipedia's inter-language links to pair titles of English articles with their corresponding foreign article's title. To get a more translatable set of pairs, we excluded any pairs where: (1) the English word was not present in the WordNet ontology (Miller, 1995), (2) either article title was longer than a single word, (3) the English Wikipedia page was a subcategory of person or place, or (4) the English and the foreign titles were identical or a substring of the other.

Manual evaluation of non-identical translations We counted all translations that exactly matched the gold standard translation as correct. For non-exact matches we created a second-pass quality assurance HIT. Turkers were shown a pair of English words, one of which was a Turker's translation of the foreign word used for quality control, and the other of which was the gold-standard translation of the foreign word. Evaluators were asked whether the two words had the same meaning, and chose between three answers: 'Yes', 'No', or 'Re-

500K+ ARTICLES: German (de), English (en), Spanish (es), French (fr), Italian (it), Japanese (ja), Dutch (nl), Polish (pl), Portuguese (pt), Russian (ru)
100K-500K ARTICLES: Arabic (ar), Bulgarian (bg), Catalan (ca), Czech (cs), Danish (da), Esperanto (eo), Basque (eu), Persian (fa), Finnish (fi), Hebrew (he), Hindi (hi), Croatian (hr), Hungarian (hu), Indonesian (id), Korean (ko), Lithuanian (lt), Malay (ms), Norwegian (Bokmal) (no), Romanian (ro), Slovak (sk), Slovenian (sl), Serbian (sr), Swedish (sv), Turkish (tr), UKrainian (UK), Vietnamese (vi), Waray-Waray (war), Chinese (zh)
10K-100K ARTICLES: Afrikaans (af) Amharic (am) Asturian (ast) Azerbaijani (az) Belarusian (be) Bengali (bn) Bishnupriya Manipuri (bpy) Breton (br) Bosnian (bs) Cebuano (ceb) Welsh (cy) Zazaki (diq) Greek (el) West Frisian (fy) Irish (ga) Galician (gl) Gujarati (gu) Haitian (ht) Armenian (hy) Icelandic (is) Javanese (jv) Georgian (ka) Kannada (kn) Kurdish (ku) Luxembourgish (lb) Latvian (lv) Malagasy (mg) Macedonian (mk) Malayalam (ml) Marathi (mr) Neapolitan (nap) Low Saxon (nds) Nepali (ne) Newar / Nepal Bhasa (new) Norwegian (Nynorsk) (nn) Piedmontese (pms) Sicilian (scn) Serbo-Croatian (sh) Albanian (sq) Sundanese (su) Swahili (sw) Tamil (ta) Telugu (te) Thai (th) Tagalog (tl) Urdu (ur) Yoruba (yo)
<10K ARTICLES: Central Bicolano (bcl) Tibetan (bo) Ilokano (ilo) Punjabi (pa) Kapampangan (pam) Pashto (ps) Sindhi (sd) Somali (so) Uzbek (uz) Wolof (wo)

Table 2: A list of the languages that were used in our study, grouped by the number of Wikipedia articles in the language. Each language's code is given in parentheses. These language codes are used in other figures throughout this paper.

[1] http://meta.wikimedia.org/wiki/List_of_Wikipedias

[2] http://dumps.wikimedia.org/other/pagecounts-raw/

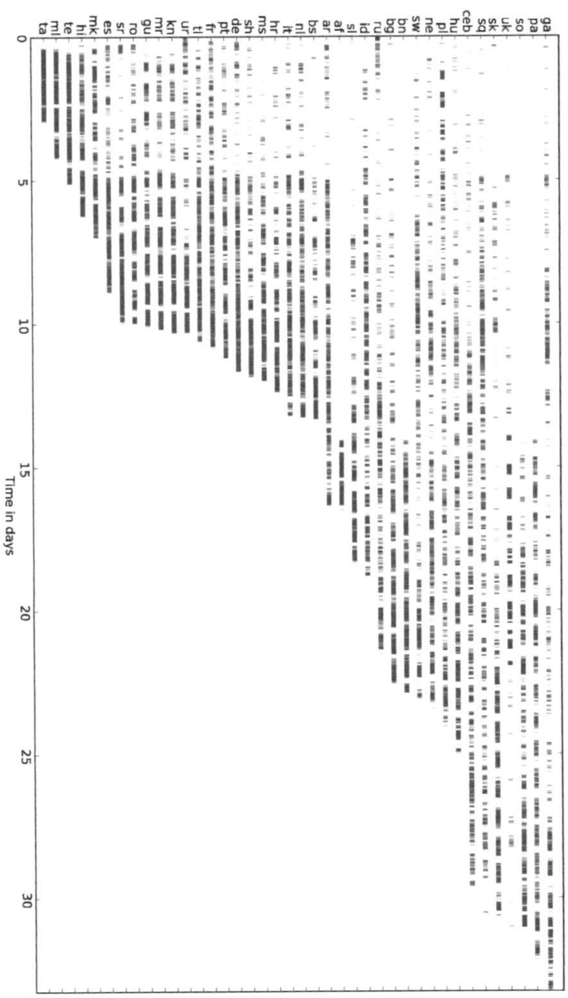

Figure 2: Days to complete the translation HITs for 40 of the languages. Tick marks represent the completion of individual assignments.

lated but not synonymous.' Examples of meaning equivalent pairs include: <*petroglyphs, rock paintings*>, <*demo, show*> and <*loam, loam: soil rich in decaying matter*>. Non-meaning equivalents included: <*assorted, minutes*>, and <*major,* URL of image>. Related items were things like <*sky, clouds*>. Misspellings like <*lactation, lactiation* > were judged to have same meaning, and were marked as misspelled. Three separate Turkers judged each pair, allowing majority votes for difficult cases.

We checked Turkers who were working on this task by embedding pairs of words which were either known to be synonyms (drawn from WordNet) or unrelated (randomly chosen from a corpus). Automating approval/rejections for the second-pass evaluation allowed the whole pipeline to be run automatically. Caching judgments meant that we ultimately needed only 20,952 synonym tasks to judge all of the submitted translations (a total of 74,572 non-matching word pairs). These were completed by an additional 1,005 workers. Each of these assignments included 10 word pairs and paid $0.10.

पाकिस्तान ने भी प्रतिकार स्वरूप २८ मई १९९८ में छह परमाणु परीक्षण कर डाले।

In retribution pakistan also did six nuclear tests on 28 may 1998.
On 28 May Pakistan also conducted six nuclear tests as an act of redressal.
Retaliating on this 'Pakistan' conducted Six(6) Nuclear Tests on 28 May, 1998.
pakistan also did 6 nuclear test in retribution on 28 may, 1998

Figure 3: An example of the Turkers' translations of a Hindi sentence. The translations are unedited and contain fixable spelling, capitalization and grammatical errors.

Full sentence translations To demonstrate the feasibility of using crowdsourcing to create multilingual technologies, we hire Turkers to construct bilingual parallel corpora from scratch for six Indian languages. Germann (2001) attempted to build a Tamil-English translation system from scratch by hiring professional translators, but found the cost prohibitive. We created parallel corpora by translating the 100 most viewed Wikipedia pages in Bengali, Malyalam, Hindi, Tamil, Telugu, and Urdu into English. We collected four translations from different Turkers for each source sentence.

Workers were paid $0.70 per HIT to translate 10 sentences. We accepted or rejected translations based on a manual review of each worker's submissions, which included a comparison of the translations to a monotonic gloss (produced with a dictionary), and metadata such as the amount of time the worker took to complete the HIT and their geographic location.

Figure 3 shows an example of the translations we obtained. The lack of a professionally translated reference sentences prevented us from doing a systematic comparison between the quality of profes-

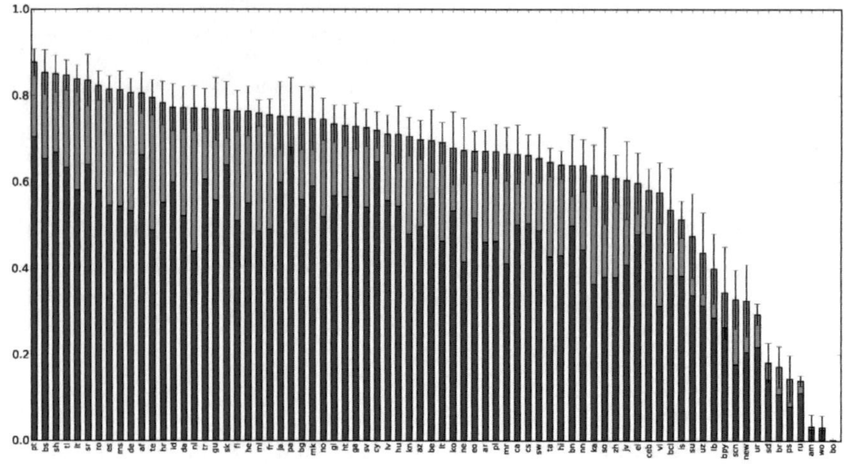

Figure 4: Translation quality for languages with at least 50 Turkers. The dark blue bars indicate the proportion of translations which exactly matched gold standard translations, and light blue indicate translations which were judged to be correct synonyms. Error bars show the 95% confidence intervals for each language.

sion and non-professional translations as Zaidan and Callison-Burch (2011) did. Instead we evaluate the quality of the data by using it to train SMT systems. We present results in section 5.

4 Measuring Translation Quality

For single word translations, we calculate the quality of translations on the level of individual assignments and aggregated over workers and languages. We define an assignment's quality as the proportion of controls that are correct in a given assignment, where correct means exactly correct or judged to be synonymous.

$$\text{Quality}(a_i) = \frac{1}{k_i}\sum_{j=1}^{k_i}\delta(tr_{ij} \in \texttt{syns}\,[g_j]) \quad (1)$$

where a_i is the ith assignment, k_i is the number of controls in a_i, tr_{ij} is the Turker's provided translation of control word j in assignment i, g_j is the gold standard translation of control word j, $\texttt{syns}\,[g_j]$ is the set of words judged to be synonymous with g_j and includes g_j, and $\delta(x)$ is Kronecker's delta and takes value 1 when x is true. Most assignments had two known words embedded, so most assignments had scores of either 0, 0.5, or 1.

Since computing overall quality for a language as the average assignment quality score is biased towards a small number of highly active Turkers, we instead report language quality scores as the average per-Turker quality, where a Turker's quality is the average quality of all the assignments that she completed:

$$\text{Quality}(t_i) = \frac{\sum_{a_j \in \texttt{assigns}\,[i]} \text{Quality}(a_j)}{|\,\texttt{assigns}\,[i]\,|} \quad (2)$$

where $\texttt{assigns}\,[i]$ is the assignments completed by Turker i, and Quality(a) is as above.

Quality for a language is then given by

$$\text{Quality}(l_i) = \frac{\sum_{t_j \in \texttt{turkers}\,[i]} \text{Quality}(t_j)}{|\,\texttt{turkers}\,[i]\,|} \quad (3)$$

When a Turker completed assignments in more than one language, their quality was computed separately for each language. Figure 4 shows the translation quality for languages with contributions from at least 50 workers.

Cheating using machine translation One obvious way for workers to cheat is to use available online translation tools. Although we followed best practices to deter copying-and-pasting into online MT systems by rendering words and sentences as images (Zaidan and Callison-Burch, 2011), this strategy does not prevent workers from typing the words into an MT system if they are able to type in the language's script.

To identify and remove workers who appeared to be cheating by using Google Translate, we calculated each worker's overlap with the Google translations. We used Google to translate all 10,000 words for the 51 foreign languages that Google Translate covered at the time of the study. We measured the percent of workers' translations that exactly matched the translation returned from Google.

Figure 5a shows overlap between Turkers's translations and Google Translate. When overlap is high, it seems likely that those Turkers are cheating. It is also reasonable to assume that honest workers will overlap with Google some amount of the time as Google's translations are usually accurate. We divide the workers into three groups: those with very high overlap with Google (likely cheating by using Google to translate words), those with reasonable overlap, and those with no overlap (likely cheating by other means, for instance, by submitting random text).

Our gold-standard controls are designed to identify workers that fall into the third group (those who are spamming or providing useless translations), but they will not effectively flag workers who are cheating with Google Translate. We therefore remove the 500 Turkers with the highest overlap with Google. This equates to removing all workers with greater than 70% overlap. Figure 5b shows that removing workers at or above the 70% threshold retains 90% of the collected translations and over 90% of the workers.

Quality scores reported throughout the paper reflect only translations from Turkers whose overlap with Google falls below this 70% threshold.

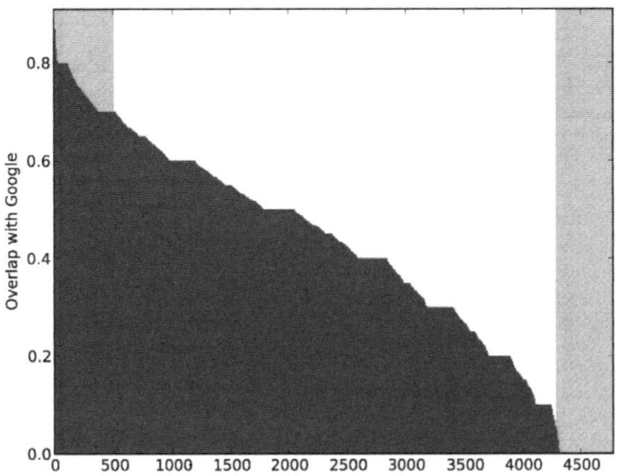

(a) Individual workers' overlap with Google Translate. We removed the 500 workers with the highest overlap (shaded region on the left) from our analyses, as it is reasonable to assume these workers are cheating by submitting translations from Google. Workers with no overlap (shaded region on the right) are also likely to be cheating, e.g. by submitting random text.

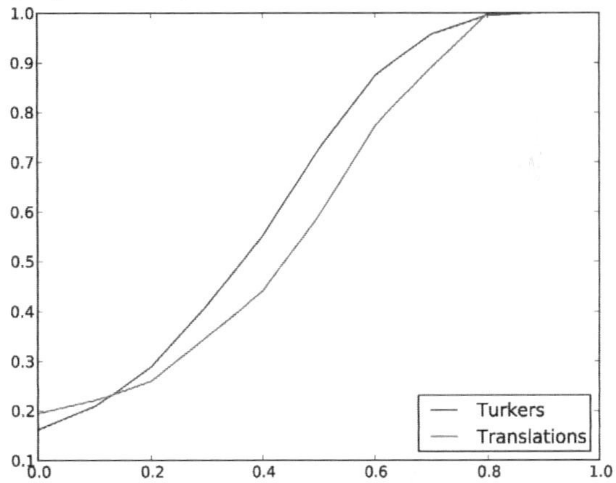

(b) Cumulative distribution of overlap with Google translate for workers and translations. We see that eliminating all workers with >70% overlap with google translate still preserves 90% of translations and >90% of workers.

Figure 5

5 Data Analysis

We performed an analysis of our data to address the following questions:

- Do workers accurately represent their language abilities? Should we constrain tasks by region?
- How quickly can we expect work to be completed in a particular language?
- Can Turkers' translations be used to train MT systems?
- Do our dictionaries improve MT quality?

Language skills and location We measured the average quality of workers who were in countries that plausibly speak a language, versus workers from countries that did not have large speaker populations of that language. We used the Ethnologue (Lewis

	Avg. Turker quality (# Ts)		Primary locations	Primary locations
	In region	Out of region	of Turkers in region	of Turkers out of region
Hindi	0.63 (296)	**0.69** (7)	India (284) UAE (5) UK (3)	Saudi Arabia (2) Russia (1) Oman (1)
Tamil	**0.65** (273) **	0.25 (2)	India (266) US (3) Canada (2)	Tunisia (1) Egypt (1)
Malayalam	0.76 (234)	**0.83** (2)	India (223) UAE (6) US (3)	Saudi Arabia (1) Maldives (1)
Spanish	0.81 (191)	**0.84** (18)	US (122) Mexico (16) Spain (14)	India (15) New Zealand (1) Brazil (1)
French	0.75 (170)	**0.82** (11)	India (62) US (45) France (23)	Greece (2) Netherlands (1) Japan (1)
Chinese	**0.60** (116)	0.55 (21)	US (75) Singapore (13) China (9)	Hong Kong (6) Australia (3) Germany (2)
German	**0.82** (91)	0.77 (41)	Germany (48) US (25) Austria (7)	India (34) Netherlands (1) Greece (1)
Italian	**0.86** (90) *	0.80 (42)	Italy (42) US (29) Romania (7)	India (33) Ireland (2) Spain (2)
Amharic	**0.14** (16) **	0.01 (99)	US (14) Ethiopia (2)	India (70) Georgia (9) Macedonia (5)
Kannada	0.70 (105)	NA (0)	India (105)	
Arabic	**0.74** (60) **	0.60 (45)	Egypt (19) Jordan (16) Morocco (9)	US (19) India (11) Canada (3)
Sindhi	**0.19** (96)	0.06 (9)	India (58) Pakistan (37) US (1)	Macedonia (4) Georgia (2) Indonesia (2)
Portuguese	0.87 (101)	**0.96** (3)	Brazil (44) Portugal (31) US (15)	Romania (1) Japan (1) Israel (1)
Turkish	0.76 (76)	**0.80** (27)	Turkey (38) US (18) Macedonia (8)	India (19) Pakistan (4) Taiwan (1)
Telugu	**0.80** (102)	0.50 (1)	India (98) US (3) UAE (1)	Saudi Arabia (1)
Irish	**0.74** (54)	0.71 (47)	US (39) Ireland (13) UK (2)	India (36) Romania (5) Macedonia (2)
Swedish	**0.73** (54)	0.71 (45)	US (25) Sweden (22) Finland (3)	India (23) Macedonia (6) Croatia (2)
Czech	**0.71** (45) *	0.61 (50)	US (17) Czech Republic (14) Serbia (5)	Macedonia (22) India (10) UK (5)
Russian	**0.15** (67) *	0.12 (27)	US (36) Moldova (7) Russia (6)	India (14) Macedonia (4) UK (3)
Breton	0.17 (3)	**0.18** (89)	US (3)	India (83) Macedonia (2) China (1)

Table 3: Translation quality when partitioning the translations into two groups, one containing translations submitted by Turkers whose location is within regions that plausibly speak the foreign language, and the other containing translations from Turkers outside those regions. In general, in-region Turkers provide higher quality translations. (**) indicates differences significant at p=0.05, (*) at p=0.10.

et al., 2013) to compile the list of countries where each language is spoken. Table 3 compares the average translation quality of assignments completed within the region of each language, and compares it to the quality of assignments completed outside that region.

Our workers reported speaking 95 languages natively. US workers alone reported 61 native languages. Overall, 4,297 workers were located in a region likely to speak the language from which they were translating, and 2,778 workers were located in countries considered out of region (meaning that about a third of our 5,281 Turkers completed HITs in multiple languages).

Table 3 shows the differences in translation quality when computed using in-region versus out-of-region Turkers, for the languages with the greatest number of workers. Within region workers typically produced higher quality translations. Given the number of Indian workers on Mechanical Turk, it is unsurprising that they represent majority of out-of-region workers. For the languages that had more than 75 out of region workers (Malay, Amharic, Icelandic, Sicilian, Wolof, and Breton), Indian workers represented at least 70% of the out of region workers in each language.

A few languages stand out for having suspiciously strong performance by out of region workers, notably Irish and Swedish, for which out of region workers account for a near equivalent volume and quality of translations to the in region workers. This is admittedly implausible, considering the relatively small number of Irish speakers worldwide, and the very low number living in the countries in which our Turkers were based (primarily India). Such results highlight the fact that cheating using online translation resources is a real problem, and despite our best efforts to remove workers using Google Translate, some cheating is still evident. Restricting to within region workers is an effective way to reduce the prevalence of cheating. We discuss the languages which are best supported by true native speakers in section 6.

Speed of translation Figure 2 gives the completion times for 40 languages. The 10 languages to finish in the shortest amount of time were: Tamil, Malayalam, Telugu, Hindi, Macedonian, Spanish, Serbian, Romanian, Gujarati, and Marathi. Seven of the ten fastest languages are from India, which is un-

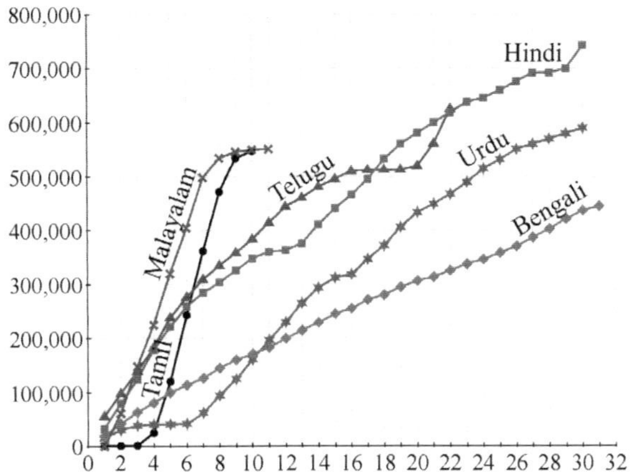

Figure 6: The total volume of translations (measured in English words) as a function of elapsed days.

language	sentence pairs	English + foreign words	dictionary entries
Bengali	22k	732k	22k
Hindi	40k	1,488k	22k
Malayalam	32k	863k	23k
Tamil	38k	916k	25k
Telugu	46k	1,097k	21k
Urdu	35k	1,356k	20k

Table 4: Size of parallel corpora and bilingual dictionaries collected for each language.

surprising given the geographic distribution of workers. Some languages follow the pattern of having a smattering of assignments completed early, with the rate picking up later.

Figure 6 gives the throughput of the full-sentence translation task for the six Indian languages. The fastest language was Malayalam, for which we collected half a million words of translations in just under a week. Table 4 gives the size of the data set that we created for each of these languages.

Training SMT systems We trained statistical translation models from the parallel corpora that we created for the six Indian languages using the Joshua machine translation system (Post et al., 2012). Table 5 shows the translation performance when trained on the bitexts alone, and when incorporating the bilingual dictionaries created in our earlier HIT. The scores reflect the performance when tested on held out sentences from the training data. Adding the dictionaries to the training set produces consistent performance gains, ranging from 1 to 5 BLEU points. This represents a substantial improvement. It is worth noting, however, that while the source documents for the full sentences used for testing were kept disjoint from those used for training, there is overlap between the source materials for the dictionaries and those from the test set, since both the dictionaries and the bitext source sentences were drawn from Wikipedia.

language	trained on bitexts alone	bitext + dictionaries	BLEU Δ
Bengali	12.03	17.29	5.26
Hindi	16.19	18.10	1.91
Malayalam	6.65	9.72	3.07
Tamil	8.08	9.66	1.58
Telugu	11.94	13.70	1.76
Urdu	19.22	21.98	2.76

Table 5: BLEU scores for translating into English using bilingual parallel corpora by themselves, and with the addition of single-word dictionaries. Scores are calculated using four reference translations and represent the mean of three MERT runs.

6 Discussion

Crowdsourcing platforms like Mechanical Turk give researchers instant access to a diverse set of bilingual workers. This opens up exciting new avenues for researchers to develop new multilingual systems. The demographics reported in this study are likely to shift over time. Amazon may expand its payments to new currencies. Posting long-running HITs in other languages may recruit more speakers of those languages. New crowdsourcing platforms may emerge. The data presented here provides a valuable snapshot of the current state of MTurk, and the methods used can be applied generally in future research.

Based on our study, we can confidently recommend 13 languages as good candidates for research now: Dutch, French, German, Gujarati, Italian, Kannada, Malayalam, Portuguese, Romanian, Serbian, Spanish, Tagalog, and Telugu. These languages have large Turker populations who complete tasks quickly and accurately. Table 6 summarizes the strengths and weaknesses of all 100 languages covered in our study. Several other languages are viable

workers	quality	speed	
many	high	fast	Dutch, French, German, Gujarati, Italian, Kannada, Malayalam, Portuguese, Romanian, Serbian, Spanish, Tagalog, Telugu
		slow	Arabic, Hebrew, Irish, Punjabi, Swedish, Turkish
	low or medium	fast	Hindi, Marathi, Tamil, Urdu
		slow	Bengali, Bishnupriya Manipuri, Cebuano, Chinese, Nepali, Newar, Polish, Russian, Sindhi, Tibetan
few	high	fast	Bosnia, Croatian, Macedonian, Malay, Serbo-Croatian
		slow	Afrikaans, Albanian, Aragonese, Asturian, Basque, Belarusian, Bulgarian, Central Bicolano, Czech, Danish, Finnish, Galacian, Greek, Haitian, Hungarian, Icelandic, Ilokano, Indonesian, Japanese, Javanese, Kapampangan, Kazakh, Korean, Lithuanian, Low Saxon, Malagasy, Norwegian (Bokmal), Sicilian, Slovak, Slovenian, Thai, UKranian, Uzbek, Waray-Waray, West Frisian, Yoruba
	low or medium	fast	–
		slow	Amharic, Armenian, Azerbaijani, Breton, Catalan, Georgian, Latvian, Luxembourgish, Neapolitian, Norwegian (Nynorsk), Pashto, Piedmontese, Somali, Sudanese, Swahili, Tatar, Vietnamese, Walloon, Welsh
none	low or medium	slow	Esperanto, Ido, Kurdish, Persian, Quechua, Wolof, Zazaki

Table 6: The green box shows the best languages to target on MTurk. These languages have many workers who generate high quality results quickly. We defined *many* workers as 50 or more active in-region workers, *high* quality as $\geq$70% accuracy on the gold standard controls, and *fast* if all of the 10,000 words were completed within two weeks.

candidates provided adequate quality control mechanisms are used to select good workers.

Since Mechanical Turk provides financial incentives for participation, many workers attempt to complete tasks even if they do not have the language skills necessary to do so. Since MTurk does not provide any information about workers demographics, including their language competencies, it can be hard to exclude such workers. As a result naive data collection on MTurk may result in noisy data. A variety of techniques should be incorporated into crowdsourcing pipelines to ensure high quality data. As a best practice, we suggest: (1) restricting workers to countries that plausibly speak the foreign language of interest, (2) embedding gold standard controls or administering language pretests, rather than relying solely on self-reported language skills, and (3) excluding workers whose translations have high overlap with online machine translation systems like Google translate. If cheating using external resources is likely, then also consider (4) recording information like time spent on a HIT (cumulative and on individual items), patterns in keystroke logs, tab/window focus, etc.

Although our study targeted bilingual workers on Mechanical Turk, and neglected monolingual workers, we believe our results reliably represent the current speaker populations, since the vast majority of the work available on the crowdsourced platform is currently English-only. We therefore assume the number of non-English speakers is small. In the future, it may be desirable to recruit monolingual foreign workers. In such cases, we recommend other tests to validate their language abilities in place of our translation test. These could include performing narrative cloze, or listening to audio files containing speech in different language and identifying their language.

7 Data release

With the publication of this paper, we are releasing all data and code used in this study. Our data release includes the raw data, along with bilingual dictionaries that are filtered to be high quality. It will include 256,604 translation assignments from 5,281 Turkers and 20,952 synonym assignments from 1,005 Turkers, along with meta information like geolocation and time submitted, plus external dictionaries used for validation. The dictionaries will contain 1.5M total translated words in 100 languages, along with code to filter the dictionaries based on different criteria. The data also includes parallel corpora for six Indian languages, ranging in size between 700,000 to 1.5 million words.

8 Acknowledgements

This material is based on research sponsored by a DARPA Computer Science Study Panel phase 3 award entitled "Crowdsourcing Translation" (contract D12PC00368). The views and conclusions contained in this publication are those of the authors and should not be interpreted as representing official policies or endorsements by DARPA or the U.S. Government. This research was supported by the Johns Hopkins University Human Language Technology Center of Excellence and through gifts from Microsoft and Google.

The authors would like to thank the anonymous reviewers for their thoughtful comments, which substantially improved this paper.

References

Amazon. 2013. Service summary tour for requesters on Amazon Mechanical Turk. https://requester.mturk.com/tour.

Vamshi Ambati and Stephan Vogel. 2010. Can crowds build parallel corpora for machine translation systems? In *Proceedings of the NAACL HLT 2010 Workshop on Creating Speech and Language Data with Amazon's Mechanical Turk*. Association for Computational Linguistics.

Vamshi Ambati, Stephan Vogel, and Jaime Carbonell. 2010. Active learning and crowd-sourcing for machine translation. In *Proceedings of the 7th International Conference on Language Resources and Evaluation (LREC)*.

Vamshi Ambati. 2012. *Active Learning and Crowdsourcing for Machine Translation in Low Resource Scenarios*. Ph.D. thesis, Language Technologies Institute, School of Computer Science, Carnegie Mellon University, Pittsburgh, PA.

Michael S. Bernstein, Greg Little, Robert C. Miller, Bjrn Hartmann, Mark S. Ackerman, David R. Karger, David Crowell, and Katrina Panovich. 2010. Soylent: a word processor with a crowd inside. In *Proceedings of the ACM Symposium on User Interface Software and Technology (UIST)*.

Jeffrey P. Bigham, Chandrika Jayant, Hanjie Ji, Greg Little, Andrew Miller, Robert C. Miller, Robin Miller, Aubrey Tatarowicz, Brandyn White, Samual White, and Tom Yeh. 2010. VizWiz: nearly real-time answers to visual questions. In *Proceedings of the ACM Symposium on User Interface Software and Technology (UIST)*.

Michael Bloodgood and Chris Callison-Burch. 2010. Large-scale cost-focused active learning for statistical machine translation. In *Proceedings of the 48th Annual Meeting of the Association for Computational Linguistics*.

Chris Callison-Burch and Mark Dredze. 2010. Creating speech and language data with Amazon's Mechanical Turk. In *Proceedings of the NAACL HLT 2010 Workshop on Creating Speech and Language Data with Amazon's Mechanical Turk*, pages 1–12, Los Angeles, June. Association for Computational Linguistics.

Jia Deng, Alexander Berg, Kai Li, and Li Fei-Fei. 2010. What does classifying more than 10,000 image categories tell us? In *Proceedings of the 12th European Conference of Computer Vision (ECCV*, pages 71–84.

Maxine Eskenazi, Gina-Anne Levow, Helen Meng, Gabriel Parent, and David Suendermann. 2013. *Crowdsourcing for Speech Processing, Applications to Data Collection, Transcription and Assessment*. Wiley.

Siamak Faridani, Björn Hartmann, and Panagiotis G. Ipeirotis. 2011. What's the right price? pricing tasks for finishing on time. In *Third AAAI Human Computation Workshop (HCOMP'11)*.

Ulrich Germann. 2001. Building a statistical machine translation system from scratch: How much bang for the buck can we expect? In *ACL 2001 Workshop on Data-Driven Machine Translation*, Toulouse, France.

Chang Hu, Benjamin B. Bederson, and Philip Resnik. 2010. Translation by iterative collaboration between monolingual users. In *Proceedings of ACM SIGKDD Workshop on Human Computation (HCOMP)*.

Chang Hu, Philip Resnik, Yakov Kronrod, Vladimir Eidelman, Olivia Buzek, and Benjamin B. Bederson. 2011. The value of monolingual crowdsourcing in a real-world translation scenario: Simulation using haitian creole emergency sms messages. In *Proceedings of the Sixth Workshop on Statistical Machine Translation*, pages 399–404, Edinburgh, Scotland, July. Association for Computational Linguistics.

Panagiotis G. Ipeirotis. 2010a. Analyzing the mechanical turk marketplace. In *ACM XRDS*, December.

Panagiotis G. Ipeirotis. 2010b. Demographics of Mechanical Turk. Technical Report Working paper

CeDER-10-01, New York University, Stern School of Business.

Ann Irvine and Alexandre Klementiev. 2010. Using Mechanical Turk to annotate lexicons for less commonly used languages. In *Workshop on Creating Speech and Language Data with MTurk*.

Ian Lane, Matthias Eck, Kay Rottmann, and Alex Waibel. 2010. Tools for collecting speech corpora via mechanical-turk. In *Proceedings of the NAACL HLT 2010 Workshop on Creating Speech and Language Data with Amazon's Mechanical Turk*, Los Angeles.

Florian Laws, Christian Scheible, and Hinrich Schütze. 2011. Active learning with amazon mechanical turk. In *Proceedings of the 2011 Conference on Empirical Methods in Natural Language Processing*, Edinburgh, Scotland.

Matthew Lease, Jessica Hullman, Jeffrey P. Bigham, Juho Kim Michael S. Bernstein and, Walter Lasecki, Saeideh Bakhshi, Tanushree Mitra, and Robert C. Miller. 2013. Mechanical Turk is not anonymous. `http://dx.doi.org/10.2139/ssrn.2228728`.

Vili Lehdonvirta and Mirko Ernkvist. 2011. Knowledge map of the virtual economy: Converting the virtual economy into development potential. `http://www.infodev.org/en/Document.1056.pdf`, April. An InfoDev Publication.

M. Paul Lewis, Gary F. Simons, and Charles D. Fennig (eds.). 2013. Ethnologue: Languages of the world, seventeenth edition. `http://www.ethnologue.com`.

Greg Little, Lydia B. Chilton, Rob Miller, and Max Goldman. 2009. Turkit: Tools for iterative tasks on mechanical turk. In *Proceedings of the Workshop on Human Computation at the International Conference on Knowledge Discovery and Data Mining (KDD-HCOMP '09)*, Paris.

Matthew Marge, Satanjeev Banerjee, and Alexander Rudnicky. 2010. Using the Amazon Mechanical Turk to transcribe and annotate meeting speech for extractive summarization. In *Workshop on Creating Speech and Language Data with MTurk*.

George A. Miller. 1995. WordNet: a lexical database for english. *Communications of the ACM*, 38(11):39–41.

Robert Munro and Hal Tily. 2011. The start of the art: Introduction to the workshop on crowdsourcing technologies for language and cognition studies. In *Crowdsourcing Technologies for Language and Cognition Studies*, Boulder.

Scott Novotney and Chris Callison-Burch. 2010. Cheap, fast and good enough: Automatic speech recognition with non-expert transcription. In *Human Language Technologies: The 2010 Annual Conference of the North American Chapter of the Association for Computational Linguistics*, pages 207–215. Association for Computational Linguistics.

Gabriel Parent and Maxine Eskenazi. 2011. Speaking to the crowd: looking at past achievements in using crowdsourcing for speech and predicting future challenges. In *Proceedings Interspeech 2011, Special Session on Crowdsourcing*.

Matt Post, Chris Callison-Burch, and Miles Osborne. 2012. Constructing parallel corpora for six indian languages via crowdsourcing. In *Proceedings of the Seventh Workshop on Statistical Machine Translation*, pages 401–409, Montréal, Canada, June. Association for Computational Linguistics.

Alexander J. Quinn and Benjamin B. Bederson. 2011. Human computation: A survey and taxonomy of a growing field. In *Computer Human Interaction (CHI)*.

Cyrus Rashtchian, Peter Young, Micah Hodosh, and Julia Hockenmaier. 2010. Collecting image annotations using Amazon's Mechanical Turk. In *Workshop on Creating Speech and Language Data with MTurk*.

Joel Ross, Lilly Irani, M. Six Silberman, Andrew Zaldivar, and Bill Tomlinson. 2010. Who are the crowdworkers?: Shifting demographics in Amazon Mechanical Turk. In *alt.CHI session of CHI 2010 extended abstracts on human factors in computing systems*, Atlanta, Georgia.

Yaron Singer and Manas Mittal. 2011. Pricing mechanisms for online labor markets. In *Third AAAI Human Computation Workshop (HCOMP'11)*.

Rion Snow, Brendan O'Connor, Daniel Jurafsky, and Andrew Y. Ng. 2008. Cheap and fast - but is it good? Evaluating non-expert annotations for natural language tasks. In *Proceedings of EMNLP*.

Alexander Sorokin and David Forsyth. 2008. Utility data annotation with amazon mechanical turk. In *First IEEE Workshop on Internet Vision at CVPR*.

Luis von Ahn. 2005. *Human Computation*. Ph.D. thesis, School of Computer Science, Carnegie Mellon University, Pittsburgh, PA.

Omar F. Zaidan and Chris Callison-Burch. 2011. Crowdsourcing translation: Professional quality from non-professionals. In *Proceedings of the 49th Annual Meeting of the Association for Computational Linguistics: Human Language Technologies*, pages 1220–1229. Association for Computational Linguistics.

Rabih Zbib, Erika Malchiodi, Jacob Devlin, David Stallard, Spyros Matsoukas, Richard Schwartz, John Makhoul, Omar F. Zaidan, and Chris Callison-Burch. 2012. Machine translation of Arabic dialects. In *The 2012 Conference of the North American Chapter of the Association for Computational Linguistics*. Association for Computational Linguistics.

Rabih Zbib, Gretchen Markiewicz, Spyros Matsoukas, Richard Schwartz, and John Makhoul. 2013. Systematic comparison of professional and crowdsourced reference translations for machine translation. In *Proceedings of the 2013 Conference of the North American Chapter of the Association for Computational Linguistics: Human Language Technologies*, Atlanta, Georgia.

Exploring the Role of Stress in Bayesian Word Segmentation using Adaptor Grammars

Benjamin Börschinger[1,2] **Mark Johnson**[1,3]

[1]Department of Computing, Macquarie University, Sydney, Australia
[2]Department of Computational Linguistics, Heidelberg University, Heidelberg, Germany
[3]Santa Fe Institute, Santa Fe, USA
{benjamin.borschinger|mark.johnson}@mq.edu.au

Abstract

Stress has long been established as a major cue in word segmentation for English infants. We show that enabling a current state-of-the-art Bayesian word segmentation model to take advantage of stress cues noticeably improves its performance. We find that the improvements range from 10 to 4%, depending on both the use of phonotactic cues and, to a lesser extent, the amount of evidence available to the learner. We also find that in particular early on, stress cues are much more useful for our model than phonotactic cues by themselves, consistent with the finding that children do seem to use stress cues before they use phonotactic cues. Finally, we study how the model's knowledge about stress patterns evolves over time. We not only find that our model correctly acquires the most frequent patterns relatively quickly but also that the Unique Stress Constraint that is at the heart of a previously proposed model does not need to be built in but can be acquired jointly with word segmentation.

1 Introduction

Among the first tasks a child language learner has to solve is picking out words from the fluent speech that constitutes its linguistic input.[1] For English, stress has long been claimed to be a useful cue in infant word segmentation (Jusczyk et al., 1993; Jusczyk et al., 1999b), following the demonstration of its effectiveness in adult speech processing (Cutler et al., 1986). Several studies have investigated the role of stress in word segmentation using computational models, using both neural network and "algebraic" (as opposed to "statistical") approaches (Christiansen et al., 1998; Yang, 2004; Lignos and Yang, 2010; Lignos, 2011; Lignos, 2012). Bayesian models of word segmentation (Brent, 1999; Goldwater, 2007), however, have until recently completely ignored stress. The sole exception in this respect is Doyle and Levy (2013) who added stress cues to the Bigram model (Goldwater et al., 2009), demonstrating that this leads to an improvement in segmentation performance. In this paper, we extend their work and show how to integrate stress cues into the flexible Adaptor Grammar framework (Johnson et al., 2007). This allows us to both start from a stronger baseline model and to investigate how the role of stress cues interacts with other aspects of the model. In particular, we find that phonotactic cues to word-boundaries interact with stress cues, indicating synergistic effects for small inputs and partial redundancy for larger inputs. Overall, we find that stress cues add roughly 6% token f-score to a model that does not account for phonotactics and 4% to a model that already incorporates phonotactics. Relatedly and in line with the finding that stress cues are used by infants before phonotactic cues (Jusczyk et al., 1999a), we observe that phonotactic cues require more input than stress cues to be used efficiently. A closer look at the knowledge acquired by our models shows that the Unique Stress Constraint of Yang (2004) can be acquired jointly with segmenting the input instead

[1]The datasets and software to replicate our experiments are available from http://web.science.mq.edu.au/~bborschi/

Transactions of the Association for Computational Linguistics, 2 (2014) 93–104. Action Editor: Stefan Riezler.
Submitted 12/2013; Published 2/2014.

of having to be pre-specified; and that our models correctly identify the predominant stress pattern of the input but underestimate the frequency of iambic words, which have been found to be missegmented by infant learners.

The outline of the paper is as follows. In Section 2 we review prior work. In Section 3 we introduce our own models. In Section 4 we explain our experimental evaluation and its results. Section 5 discusses our findings, and Section 6 concludes and provides some suggestions for future research.

2 Background and related work

Lexical stress is the "accentuation of syllables within words" (Cutler, 2005) and has long been argued to play an important role in adult word recognition. Following Cutler and Carter (1987)'s observation that stressed syllables tend to occur at the beginnings of words in English, Jusczyk et al. (1993) investigated whether infants acquiring English take advantage of this fact. Their study demonstrated that this is indeed the case for 9 month olds, although they found no indication of using stressed syllables as cues for word boundaries in 6 month olds. Their findings have been replicated and extended in subsequent work (Jusczyk et al., 1999b; Thiessen and Saffran, 2003; Curtin et al., 2005; Thiessen and Saffran, 2007). A brief summary of the key findings is as follows: English infants treat stressed syllables as cues for the beginnings of words from roughly 7 months of age, suggesting that the role played by stress needs to be acquired, and that this requires antecedent segmentation by non-stress-based means (Thiessen and Saffran, 2007). They also exhibit a preference for low-pass filtered stress-initial words from this age, suggesting that it is indeed stress and not other phonetic or phonotactic properties that are treated as a cue for word-beginnings (Jusczyk et al., 1993). In fact, phontactic cues seem to be used later than stress cues (Jusczyk et al., 1999a) and seem to be outweighed by stress cues (Mattys and Jusczyk, 2000).

The earliest computational model for word segmentation incorporating stress cues we are aware of is the recurrent network model of Christiansen et al. (1998) and Christiansen and Curtin (1999). They only reported a word-token f-score of 44% (roughly, segmentation accuracy: see Section 4), which is considerably below the performance of subsequent models, making a direct comparison complicated. Yang (2004) introduced a simple incremental algorithm that relies on stress by embodying a Unique Stress Constraint (USC) that allows at most a single stressed syllable per word. On pre-syllabified child directed speech, he reported a word token f-score of 85.6% for a non-statistical algorithm that exploits the USC. While the USC has been argued to be near-to-universal and follows from the "culminative function of stress" (Fromkin, 2001; Cutler, 2005), the high score Yang reported crucially depends on every word token carrying stress, including function words. More recently, Lignos (2010, 2011, 2012) further explored Yang's original algorithm, taking into account that function words should not be assumed to possess lexical stress cues. While his scores are in line with those reported by Yang, the importance of stress for this learner were more modest, providing a gain of around 2.5% (Lignos, 2011). Also, the Yang/Lignos learner is unable to acquire knowledge about the role stress plays in the language, e.g. that stress tends to fall on particular positions within words.

Doyle and Levy (2013) extend the Bigram model of Goldwater et al. (2009) by adding stress-templates to the lexical generator. A stress-template indicates how many syllables the word has, and which of these syllables (if any) are stressed. This allows the model to acquire knowledge about the stress patterns of its input by assigning different probabilities to the different stress-templates. However, Doyle and Levy (2013) do not directly examine the probabilities assigned to the stress-templates; they only report that their model does slightly prefer stress-initial words over the baseline model by calculating the fraction of stress-initial word types in the output segmentations of their models. They also demonstrate that stress cues do indeed aid segmentation, although their reported gain of 1% in token f-score is even smaller than that reported by Lignos (2011). Our own approach differs from theirs in assuming phonemic rather than pre-syllabified input (although our model could, trivially, be run on syllabified input as well) and makes use of Adaptor Grammars instead of the Goldwater et al. (2009) Bigram model, providing us with a flexible framework for exploring the usefulness of stress in different models.

Adaptor Grammar (Johnson et al., 2007) is a grammar-based formalism for specifying non-parametric hierarchical models. Previous work explored the usefulness of, for example, syllable-structure (Johnson, 2008b; Johnson and Goldwater, 2009) or morphology (Johnson, 2008b; Johnson, 2008a) in word segmentation. The closest work to our own is Johnson and Demuth (2010) who investigate the usefulness of tones for Mandarin phonemic segmentation. Their way of adding tones to a model of word segmentation is very similar to our way of incorporating stress.

3 Models

We give an intuitive description of the mathematical background of Adaptor Grammars in 3.1, referring the reader to Johnson et al. (2007) for technical details. The models we examine are derived from the collocational model of Johnson and Goldwater (2009) by varying three parameters, resulting in 6 models: two baselines that do not take advantage of stress cues and either do or do not use phonotactics, as described in Section 3.2; and four stress models that differ with respect to the use of phonotactics, and as to whether they embody the Unique Stress Constraint introduced by Yang (2004). We describe these models in section 3.3.

3.1 Adaptor Grammars

Briefly, an Adaptor Grammar (AG) can be seen as a probabilistic context-free grammar (PCFG) with a special set of *adapted* non-terminals. We use underlining to distinguish adapted non-terminals ($\underline{\mathrm{X}}$) from non-adapted non-terminals (Y). The distribution for each adapted non-terminal $\underline{\mathrm{X}}$ is drawn from a Pitman-Yor Process which takes as its base-distribution the tree-distribution over trees rooted in $\underline{\mathrm{X}}$ as defined by the PCFG. As an effect, each adapted non-terminal can be seen as having associated with it a cache of previously-generated subtrees that can be reused without having to be regenerated using the individual PCFG rules. This allows AGs to learn reusable sub-trees such as words, sequences of words, or smaller units such as Onsets and Codas. Thus, while ordinary PCFGs have a finite number of parameters (one probability for each rule), Adaptor Grammars in addition have a parameter for every possible complete tree rooted in any of its adapted non-terminals, leading to a potentially infinite number of such parameters. The Pitman-Yor Process induces a rich-get-richer dynamics, biasing the model towards identifying a small set of units that can be reused as often as possible. In the case of word segmentation, the model will try to identify as compact a lexicon as possible to segment the unsegmented input.

3.2 Baseline models

Our starting point is the state-of-the-art AG model for word segmentation, Johnson and Goldwater (2009)'s colloc3-syll model, reproduced in Figure 1.[2] The model assumes that words are grouped into larger collocational units that themselves can be grouped into even larger collocational units. This accounts for the fact that in natural language, there are strong word-to-word dependencies that need to be accounted for if severe undersegmentations of the form "is in the" are to be avoided (Goldwater, 2007; Johnson and Goldwater, 2009; Börschinger et al., 2012). It also uses a language-independent form of syllable structure to constrain the space of possible words. Finally, this model can learn word-initial onsets and word-final codas. In a language like English, this ability provides additional cues to word-boundaries as certain onsets are much more likely to occur word-initially than medially (e.g. "bl" in "black"), and analogously for certain codas (e.g. "dth" in "width" or "ngth" in "strength").

We define an additional baseline model by replacing rules (5) and (6) by (17), and deleting rules (7) to (12). This removes the model's ability to use phonotactic cues to word-boundaries.

$$\underline{\mathrm{Word}} \rightarrow \mathrm{Syll}\,(\,\mathrm{Syll}\,)\,(\,\mathrm{Syll}\,)\,(\,\mathrm{Syll}\,) \qquad (17)$$

We refer to the model in Figure 1 as the colloc3-phon model, and the model that results from substituting and removing rules as described as the colloc3-nophon model. Alternatively, one could limit the models ability to capture word-to-word dependencies by removing rules (1) to (3). This results

[2]We follow Johnson and Goldwater (2009) in limiting the length of possible words to four syllables to speed up runtime. In pilot experiments, this choice did not have a noticeable effect on segmentation performance.

$$\text{Collocations3} \rightarrow \underline{\text{Collocation3}}^{+} \tag{1}$$
$$\underline{\text{Collocation3}} \rightarrow \underline{\text{Collocation2}}^{+} \tag{2}$$
$$\underline{\text{Collocation2}} \rightarrow \underline{\text{Collocation}}^{+} \tag{3}$$
$$\underline{\text{Collocation}} \rightarrow \underline{\text{Word}}^{+} \tag{4}$$
$$\underline{\text{Word}} \rightarrow \text{SyllIF} \tag{5}$$
$$\underline{\text{Word}} \rightarrow \text{SyllI}\,(\,\text{Syll}\,)\,(\,\text{Syll}\,)\,\text{SyllF} \tag{6}$$
$$\text{SyllIF} \rightarrow (\,\underline{\text{OnsetI}}\,)\,\text{RhymeF} \tag{7}$$
$$\text{SyllI} \rightarrow (\,\underline{\text{OnsetI}}\,)\,\text{Rhyme} \tag{8}$$
$$\text{SyllF} \rightarrow (\,\underline{\text{Onset}}\,)\,\text{RhymeF} \tag{9}$$
$$\underline{\text{CodaF}} \rightarrow \text{Consonant}^{+} \tag{10}$$
$$\text{RhymeF} \rightarrow \text{Vowel}\,(\,\underline{\text{CodaF}}\,) \tag{11}$$
$$\underline{\text{OnsetI}} \rightarrow \text{Consonant}^{+} \tag{12}$$
$$\text{Syll} \rightarrow (\,\underline{\text{Onset}}\,)\,\text{Rhyme} \tag{13}$$
$$\text{Rhyme} \rightarrow \text{Vowel}\,(\,\underline{\text{Coda}}\,) \tag{14}$$
$$\underline{\text{Onset}} \rightarrow \text{Consonant}^{+} \tag{15}$$
$$\underline{\text{Coda}} \rightarrow \text{Consonant}^{+} \tag{16}$$

Figure 1: The baseline model. We use regular-expression notation to abbreviate multiple rules. $\text{X}^{\{n\}}$ stands for up to n repetitions of X, brackets indicate optionality, and X^{+} stands for one or more repetitions of X. $\underline{\text{X}}$ indicates an adapted non-terminal. Rules that introduce terminals for the pre-terminals Vowel, Consonant are omitted. Refer to the main text for an explanation of the grammar.

in the colloc-model (Johnson, 2008b) that has previously been found to behave similarly to the Bigram model used in Doyle and Levy (2013) (Johnson, 2008b; Börschinger et al., 2012). We performed experiments with the colloc-model as well and found similar results to Doyle and Levy (2013) which are, while overall worse, similar in trend to the results obtained for the colloc3-models. For the rest of the paper, therefore, we will focus on variants of the colloc3-model.

3.3 Stress-based models

In order for stress cues to be helpful, the model must have some way of associating the position of stress with word-boundaries. Intuitively, the reason stress helps infants in segmenting English is that a stressed syllable is a reliable indicator of the beginning of a word (Jusczyk et al., 1993). More generally, if there is a (reasonably) reliable relationship between the position of stressed syllables and beginnings (or

$$\underline{\text{Word}} \rightarrow \{\,\text{SSyll} \mid \text{USyll}\,\}^{\{1,4\}} \tag{18}$$
$$\text{SSyll} \rightarrow (\,\underline{\text{Onset}}\,)\,\text{RhymeS} \tag{19}$$
$$\text{USyll} \rightarrow (\,\underline{\text{Onset}}\,)\,\text{RhymeU} \tag{20}$$
$$\text{RhymeS} \rightarrow \text{Vowel} * (\,\underline{\text{Coda}}\,) \tag{21}$$
$$\text{RhymeU} \rightarrow \text{Vowel}\,(\,\underline{\text{Coda}}\,) \tag{22}$$
$$\underline{\text{Onset}} \rightarrow \text{Consonant}^{+} \tag{23}$$
$$\underline{\text{Coda}} \rightarrow \text{Consonant}^{+} \tag{24}$$

Figure 2: Description of the all-stress-patterns model. We use $\text{X}^{\{m,n\}}$ for "at least m and at most n repetitions of X" and $\{\,\text{X} \mid \text{Y}\,\}$ for "either X or Y". Stress is associated with a vowel by suffixing it with the special terminal symbol $*$, leading to a distinction between stressed (SSyll) and unstressed (USyll) syllables. A word can consist of any possible sequence of up to four syllables, as indicated by the regular-expression notation. By additionally adding initial and final variants of SSyll and USyll as in Figure 1, phonotactics can be combined with stress cues.

endings) of words, a learner might exploit this relationship. In a Bayesian model, this intuition can be captured by modifying the lexical generator, that is, the distribution that generates $\underline{\text{Word}}$s.

Here, changing the lexical generator corresponds to modifying the rules expanding $\underline{\text{Word}}$. A straightforward way to modify it accordingly is to enumerate all possible sequences of stressed and unstressed syllables.[3] A lexical generator like this is given in Figure 2. In the data, stress cues are represented using a special terminal "$*$" that follows a stressed vowel, as illustrated in Figure 3. In the grammar, "$*$" is constrained to only surface following a Vowel, rendering a syllable in which it occurs stressed (SSyll). Syllables that do not contain a "$*$" are considered unstressed (USyll). By performing inference for the probabilities assigned to the different expansions of rule (18), our models can, for example, learn that a bi-syllabic word that is stress-initial (a trochee) is more probable than one that puts stress on the second syllable (an iamb). This (partly) captures the tendency of English for stress-initial words and thus provide an additional cue for identifying words; and it is exactly the kind of preference infant learners of English seem to acquire (Jusczyk

[3]This is, in essence, also the strategy chosen by Doyle and Levy (2013).

grammar	phon	stress	USC
colloc3-nophon			
colloc3-phon	•		
colloc3-nophon-stress		•	
colloc3-phon-stress	•	•	
colloc3-nophon-stress-usc		•	•
colloc3-phon-stress-usc	•	•	•

Table 1: The different models used in our experiments. "phon" indicates whether phonotactics are used, "stress" whether stress cues are used and "usc" whether the Unique Stress Constraint is assumed.

orthographic	the **do**-gie
no-stress	dh ah d ao g iy
stress	dh ah d ao * g iy

Figure 3: Illustration of the input-representation we choose. We indicate primary stress according to the dictionary with bold-face in the orthography. The phonemic transcription uses ARPABET and is produced using an extended version of CMUDict. Primary stress is indicated by inserting the special symbol "*" after the vowel of a stressed syllable.

et al., 1993).

We can combine this lexical generator with the colloc3-nophon baseline, resulting in the colloc3-nophon-stress model. We can also add phonotactics to the lexical generator in Figure 2 by adding initial and final variants of SSyll and USyll, analogous to rules (5) to (12) in Figure 1. This yields the colloc3-phon-stress model. We can also add the Unique Stress Constraint (USC) (Yang, 2004) by excluding all variants of rule (18) that generate two or more stressed syllables. For example, while the lexical generator for the colloc3-nophon-stress model will include the rule Word → SSyll SSyll, the lexical generator embodying the USC lacks this rule. We refer to the models that include the USC as colloc3-nophon-stress-usc and colloc3-phon-stress-usc models. A compact overview of the six different models is given in Table 1.

4 Experiments

We evaluate our models on several corpora of child directed speech. We first describe the corpora we used, then the experimental methodology employed and finally the experimental results. As the trend is comparable across all corpora, we only discuss in detail results obtained on the Alex corpus. For completeness, however, Table 3 reports the "standard" evaluation of performing inference over all of the three corpora.

4.1 Corpora and corpus creation

Following Christiansen et al. (1998) and Doyle and Levy (2013), we use the Korman corpus (Korman, 1984) as one of our corpora. It comprises child-directed speech for very young infants, aged between 6 and 16 weeks and, like all other corpora used in this paper, is available through the CHILDES database (MacWhinney, 2000). We derive a phonemicized version of the corpus using an extended version of CMUDict (Carnegie Mellon University, 2008)[4], as we were unable to obtain the stress-annotated version of this corpus used in previous experiments. The phonemicized version is produced by replacing each orthographic word in the transcript with the first pronunciation given by the dictionary. CMUDict also annotates lexical stress, and we use this information to add stress cues to the corpus. We only code primary lexical stresses in the input, ignoring secondary stresses in line with experimental work that indicates that human listeners are capable of reliably distinguishing primary and secondary stress (Mattys, 2000). Due to the very low frequency of words with 3 or more syllables in these corpora, this choice has very little effect on the number of stress cues available in the input. Our version of the Korman corpus contains, in total, 11413 utterances. Unlike Christiansen et al. (1998), Yang (2004), and Doyle and Levy (2013), we follow Lignos and Yang (2010) in making the more realistic assumption that the 94 mono-syllabic function words listed by Selkirk (1984) never surface with lexical stress. As function words account for roughly 50% of the tokens but only roughly 5% of the types in our corpora, this means that the type and token distribution of stress patterns differs dramatically in all our corpora, as can be seen from Table 2.

We also added stress information to the Brent-Bernstein-Ratner corpus (Bernstein-Ratner, 1987; Brent, 1999), following the procedure just outlined. This corpus is a de-facto standard for evaluat-

[4] http://svn.code.sf.net/p/cmusphinx/code/trunk/cmudict/cmudict.0.7a

Pattern	brent		korman		alex	
	Tok	Typ	Tok	Typ	Tok	Typ
W^+	.48	.07	.47	.08	.44	.05
SW^*	.49	.86	.49	.86	.52	.87
WSW^*	.03	.07	.03	.06	.04	.07
Other	.00	.00	.00	.00	.00	.00

Table 2: Relative frequencies for stress patterns for the corpora used in our study. X^* stands for 0 or more, X^+ for one or more repetitions of X, and S for a stressed and W for an unstressed syllable. Note the stark asymmetry between type and token frequencies for unstressed words. Up to two-decimal places, patterns other than the ones given have relative frequency 0.00 (frequencies might not sum to 1 as an artefact of rounding to 2 decimal places).

ing models of Bayesian word segmentation (Brent, 1999; Goldwater, 2007; Goldwater et al., 2009; Johnson and Goldwater, 2009), comprising in total 9790 utterances.

As our third corpus, we use the Alex portion of the Providence corpus (Demuth et al., 2006; Börschinger et al., 2012). A major benefit of the Providence corpus is that the video-recordings from which the transcripts were produced are available through CHILDES alongside the transcripts. This will allow future work to rely on even more realistic stress cues that can be derived directly from the acoustic signal. While beyond the scope of this paper, we believe choosing a corpus that makes richer information available will be important for future work on stress (and other acoustic) cues. Another major benefit of the Alex corpus is that it provides longitudinal data for a single infant, rather than being a concatenation of transcripts collected from multiple children, such as the Korman and the Brent-Bernstein-Ratner corpus. In total, the Alex corpus comprises 17948 utterances.

Note that despite the differences in age of the infants and overall make-up of the corpora, the distribution of stress patterns across the corpora is roughly the same, as shown by Table 2 for the first 10,000 utterances of each of the corpora. This suggests that the distribution of stress patterns both at a token and type level is a robust property of English child-directed speech.

4.2 Evaluation procedure

The aim of our experiments is to understand the contribution of stress cues to the Bayesian word segmentation models described in Section 3. To get an idea of how input size interacts with this, we look at prefixes of the corpora with increasing sizes (100, 200, 500, 1000, 2000, 5000, and 10,000 utterances). In addition, we are interested in understanding what kind of stress pattern preferences our models acquire. For this, we also collect samples of the probabilities assigned to the different expansions of rule (18), allowing us to examine this directly. The standard evaluation of segmentation models involves having them segment their input in an unsupervised manner and evaluating performance on how well they segmented that input. We additionally evaluate the models on a test set for each corpus. Use of a separate test set has previously been suggested as a means of testing how well the knowledge a learner acquired generalizes to novel utterances (Pearl et al., 2011), and is required for the kind of comparison across different sizes of input we are interested in to determine whether there the role of stress cues interacts with the input size.

We create the test-sets by taking the final 1000 utterances for each corpus. These 1000 utterances will be segmented by the model after it has performed inference on its input, without making any further changes to the lexicon that the model has induced. In other words, the model will have to segment each of the test utterances using only the lexicon (and any additional knowledge about co-occurrences, phonotactics, and stress) it has acquired from the training portion of the corpus during inference.

We measure segmentation performance using the standard metric of token f-score (Brent, 1999) which is the harmonic mean of token precision and recall. Token f-score provides an overall impression of how accurate individual word tokens were identified. To illustrate, if the gold segmentation is "the dog", the segmentation "th e dog" has a token precision of $\frac{1}{3}$ (one out of three predicted words is correct); a token recall of $\frac{1}{2}$ (one of the two gold words was correctly identified); and a token f-score of 0.4.

4.3 Inference

For inference, we closely follow Johnson and Goldwater (2009): we put vague priors on all the hyper-

p	s	usc	alex		korman		brent	
			train	test	train	test	train	test
			.81	.81	.85	.83	.82	.82
•			.85	.84	.86	.84	.86	.86
	•		.86	.87	.87	.86	.86	.87
•	•		**.88**	**.88**	**.88**	.87	**.87**	.87
	•	•	.87	**.88**	.87	**.88**	.86	.87
•	•	•	**.88**	**.88**	**.88**	.87	**.87**	**.88**

Table 3: Token f-scores on both train and test portions for all three corpora when inference is performed over the full corpus. Note that the benefit of stress is clearer when evaluating on the test set, and that overall, performance of the different models is comparable across all three corpora. Models are coded according to the key in Table 1.

parameters of our models and run 4 chains for 1000 iterations, collecting 20 samples from each chain with a lag of 10 iterations between each sample after a burn-in of 800 iterations, using both batch-initialization and table-label resampling to ensure good convergence of the sampler. We construct a single segmentation from the posterior samples using their minimum Bayes risk decoding, providing a single score for each condition.

4.4 Experimental conditions

Each of our six models is evaluated on inputs of increasing size, starting at 100 and ending at 10,000 utterances, allowing us to investigate both how performance and "knowledge" of the learner varies as a function of input size. For completeness, we also report the "standard" evaluation, i.e. performance of our models on all corpora when trained on the entire input in Table 3. We will focus our discussion on the results obtained on the Alex corpus, which are depicted in Figure 4, where the input size is depicted on the x-axis, and the segmentation f-score for the test-set on the y-axis.

5 Discussion

We find a clear improvement for the stress-models over both the colloc3-nophon and the colloc3-phon models. As can be seen in Table 3, the overall trend is the same for all three corpora, both when evaluating on the input and the separate test-set.[5] Note how the relative gain for stress is roughly 1% higher when evaluating on the test-set; this might have to do with Jusczyk (1997)'s observation that the advantage of stress "might be more evident for relatively unexpected or unfamiliarized strings" (Jusczyk, 1997). A closer look at Figure 4 indicates further interesting differences between the colloc3-nophon and the colloc3-phon models that only become evident when considering different input sizes.

5.1 Stress cues without phonotactics

For the colloc3-nophon models, we observe a relatively stable improvement by adding stress cues of 6-7%, irrespective of input size and whether or not the Unique Stress Constraint (USC) is assumed. The sole exception to this occurs when the learner only gets to see 100 utterances: in this case, the colloc-nophon-stress model only shows a 3% improvement, whereas the colloc3-nophon-stress-usc model obtains a boost of roughly 8%. Noticeable consistent differences between the colloc3-nophon-stress and colloc3-nophon-stress-usc model, however, all but disappear starting from around 500 utterances. This is somewhat surprising, considering that it is the USC that was argued by Yang (2004) to be key for taking advantage of stress.[6]

We take this behaviour to indicate that even with as little evidence as 200 to 500 utterances, a Bayesian ideal learner can effectively infer that something like the USC is true of English. This also becomes clear when examining how the learners' preferences for different stress patterns evolve over time, as we do in Section 5.3 below.

5.2 Stress cues and phonotactics

Overall, the models including phonotactic cues perform better than those that do not rely on phonotactics. However, the overall gain contributed by stress to the colloc3-phon baseline is smaller, al-

[5] We performed Wilcox rank sum tests on the individual scores of the 4 independent chains for each model on the full training data sets and found that the stress-models were always significantly more accurate ($p < 0.05$) than the baseline models except when evaluating on the training data for the Korman and Brent corpora.

[6] On data in which function words are marked for stress (as in Yang (2004) and Doyle and Levy (2013)), the USC yields extremely high scores across all models, simply because roughly every second word is a function word. Given that this assumption is extremely unnatural, we do not take this as an argument for the USC.

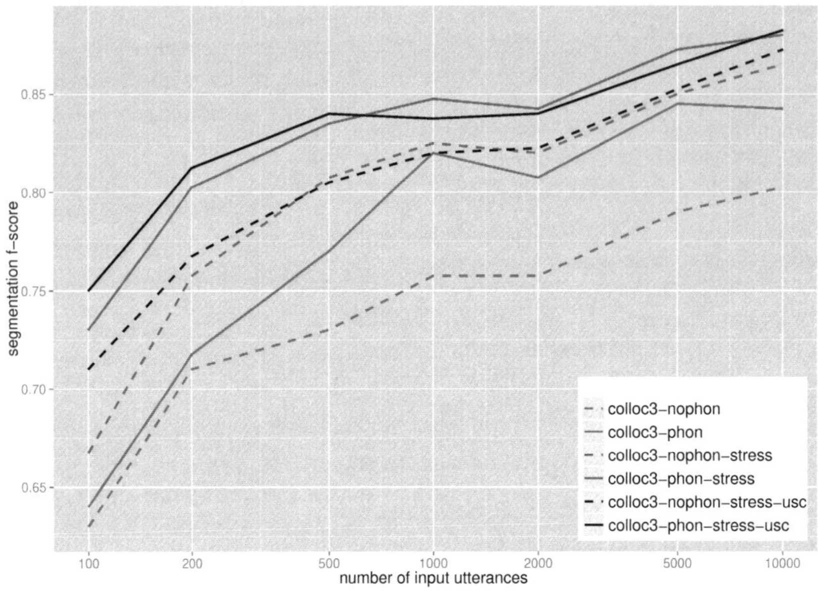

Figure 4: Segmentation performance of the different models, across different input sizes and as evaluated on the test-set for the Alex corpus. The no-stress baselines are given in red, the stress-models without the Unique Stress Constraint (USC) in green and the ones including the USC in black. Solid lines indicate models that use, dashed lines models that do not use phonotactics. Refer to the text for discussion.

though this seems to depend on the size of the input. While phonotactics by itself appears to be a powerful cue, yielding a noticeable 4-5% improvement over the colloc3-nophon baseline, the learner seems to require at least around 500 utterances before the colloc3-phon model becomes clearly more accurate than the colloc3-nophon model. In contrast, even for only 100 utterances stress cues by themselves provide a 3% improvement to the colloc3-nophon model, indicating that they can be taken advantage of earlier. While the number of utterances processed by a Bayesian ideal learner is not directly related to developmental stages, this observation is consistent with the psycholinguists' claim that phonotactics are used by infants for word segmentation after they have begun to use stress for segmentation (Jusczyk et al., 1999a).

Turning to the interaction between stress and phonotactics, we see that there is no consistent advantage of including the USC in the model. This is, in fact, even clearer than for the colloc3-nophon model where at least for small inputs of size 100, the USC added almost 5% in performance. For the colloc3-phon models, we only observe a 1-2% improvement by adding the USC up until 500 utterances. This further strengthens the point that even in the absence of such an innate constraint, a statistical learner can take advantage of stress cues and, as we show below, actually acquire something like the USC from the input.

The 4% difference between the colloc3-phon-stress / colloc3-phon-stress-usc models to the colloc3-phon baseline is smaller than the 7% difference between the colloc3-nophon and colloc3-nophon-stress models. This shows that there is a redundancy between phonotactic and stress cues in large amounts of data, as their joint contribution to the colloc3-nophon baseline is less than the sum of their individual contributions at 10,000 utterances, of 4% (for phonotactics) and 7% (for stress).

Unlike for the colloc3-nophon models, we also see a clear impact of input size. In particular, at 100 utterances the addition of stress cues leads to an 8 – 10% improvement, depending on whether or not the USC is assumed, whereas for the colloc3-nophon model we only observed a 3 – 8% improvement. This is particularly striking when we consider that by themselves, the phonotactic cues only contribute a 1% improvement to the colloc3-nophon baseline when trained on the 100 utterance corpus, indicating a synergistic interaction (rather than redundancy) between phonotactics and stress for small inputs. This effect disappears starting from around 1000 utterances; for inputs of size 1000 and larger, the net-gain of stress drops from roughly 10% to a 3–4% improvement. That is, while we did not notice any relationship between input size and impact of stress cues for the colloc3-nophon model, we do see such an interaction for the combination of phonotactics and stress cues which, taken together, lead to a larger relative gain in performance on smaller inputs than on large ones.

5.3 Acquisition of stress patterns

In addition to acquiring a lexicon, the Bayesian learner acquires knowledge about the possible stress patterns of English words. The fact that this knowledge is explicitly represented through the PCFG rules and their probabilities that define the lexical generator allows us to study the generalisations about stress the model actually acquires. While Doyle and Levy (2013) suggest carrying out such an analysis, they restrict themselves to estimating the fraction of stress patterns in the segmented output. As shown in Table 2, however, the type and token distributions of stress patterns can differ substantially. We therefore investigate the stress preferences acquired by our learner by examining the probabilities assigned to the different expansions of rule (18), aggregating the probabilities of the individual rules into patterns. For example, the rules $\underline{\text{Word}} \rightarrow \text{SSyll}\,(\,\text{USyll}\,)^{\{0,3\}}$ correspond to the pattern "Stress on the first syllable", whereas the rules $\underline{\text{Word}} \rightarrow \text{USyll}^{\,\{1,4\}}$ correspond to the pattern "Unstressed word". By computing the respective probabilities, we get the overall probability assigned by a learner to the pattern.

Figure 5 provides this information for several different rule patterns. Additionally, these plots include the empirical type (red dotted) and token proportions (red double-dashed) for the input corpus. Note how for the two major patterns, all models successfully track the type, rather than the token frequency, correctly developing a preference for stress-initial over unstressed words, despite the comparable token frequency of these two patterns. This is compatible with a recent proposal by Thiessen and Saffran (2007), who argue that infants infer the stress pattern over their lexicon. For a Bayesian model such as ours or Goldwater et al. (2009)'s, there is no need to pre-specify that the distribution ought to be learned over types rather than tokens, as the models automatically interpolate between type and token statistics according to the properties of their input (Goldwater et al., 2006). In addition, a Bayesian framework provides a simple answer to the question of how a learner might identify the role of stress in its language without already having acquired at least some words. By combining different kinds of cues, e.g. distributional, phonotactic and prosodic, in a principled manner a Bayesian learner can jointly segment its input and learn the appropriate role of each cue, without having to prespecify specific preferences that might differ across languages.

The iambic rule pattern that puts stress on the second syllable is much more infrequent on a token level. All models track this low token frequency, underestimating the type frequency of this pattern by a fair amount. This suggests that learning this pattern correctly requires considerably more input than for the other patterns. Indeed, the iambic pattern is known to pose problems for infants when they start using stress as an effective cue. It is only from roughly 10 months of age that infants successfully segment iambic words (Jusczyk et al., 1999b). Not surprisingly, the USC doesn't aid in learning about this pattern because it is completely silent on where stress might fall (and does not noticeably improve segmentation performance to begin with).

Finally, we can also investigate whether the models that lack the USC nevertheless learn that words contain at most one lexically stressed syllable. The bottom-right graph in Figure 5 plots the probability assigned by the models to patterns that violate the USC. This includes, for example, the rules $\underline{\text{Word}} \rightarrow \text{SyllS SyllS}$ and $\underline{\text{Word}} \rightarrow \text{SyllS SyllU SyllS}$. Note how the probabilities assigned to these rules approaches zero, indicating that the learner becomes more certain that there are no words that contain more than one syllable with lexical stress. As we argued above, this suggests that a Bayesian learner can acquire the USC from a modest amount of data — it will properly infer that the unnatural patterns are simply not supported by the input. To summarize, by examining the internal

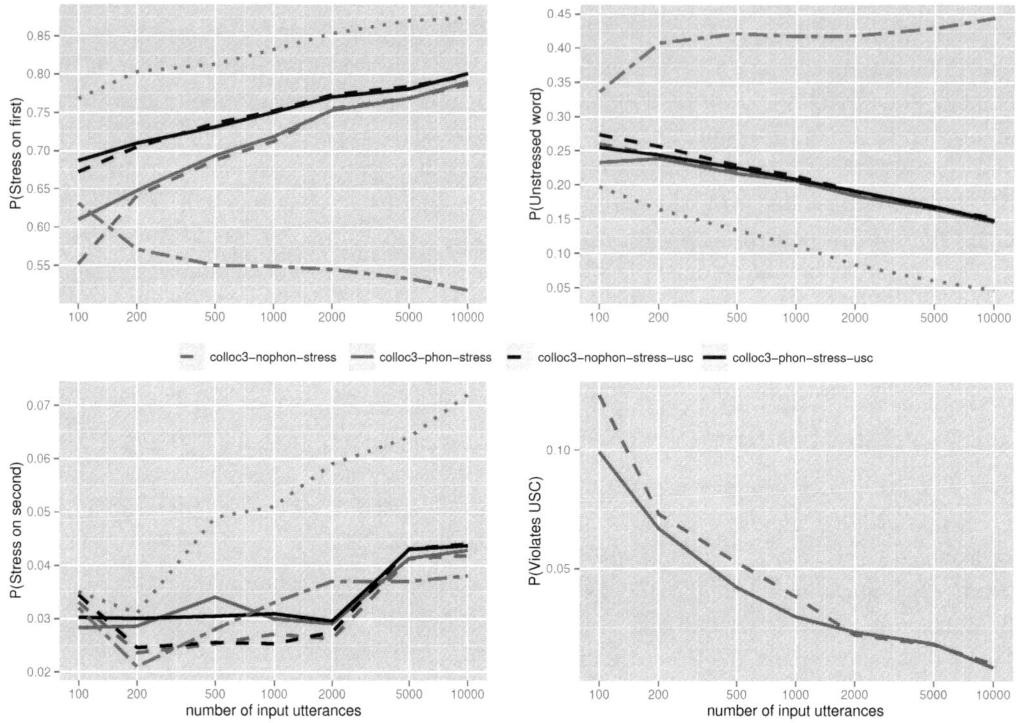

Figure 5: Evolution of the knowledge the learner acquires on the Alex corpus. The red dotted line indicates the empirical type distribution of a specific pattern, and the double-dashed line the empirical token distribution. Top-Left: Stress-initial pattern, Top-Right: Unstressed Words, Bottom-Left: Stress-second pattern, Bottom-Right: Patterns that violate the USC.

state of the Bayesian learners we can characterise how their knowledge about the stress preferences of their languages develops, rather than merely measuring how well they perform word segmentation. We find that the iambic pattern that has been observed to pose problems for infant learners also is harder for the Bayesian learner to acquire, arguably due to its extremely low token-frequency.

6 Conclusion and Future Work

We have presented Adaptor Grammar models of word segmentation that are able to take advantage of stress cues and are able to learn from phonemic input. We find that phonotactics and stress interact in interesting ways, and that stress cues makes a stable contribution to existing word segmentation models, improving their performance by 4-6% token f-score. We also find that the USC introduced by Yang (2004) need not be prebuilt into a model but can be acquired by a Bayesian learner from the data. Similarly, we directly investigate the stress preferences acquired by our models and find that for stress-initial and unstressed words, they track type rather than token frequencies. The rare stress-second pattern seems to require more input to be properly acquired, which is compatible with infant development data.

An important goal for future research is to evaluate segmentation models on typologically different languages and to study the relative usefulness of different cues cross-lingually. For example, languages such as French lack lexical stress; it would be interesting to know whether in such a case, phonotactic (or other) cues are more important. Relatedly, recent work such as Börschinger et al. (2013) has found that artificially created data often masks the complexity exhibited by real speech. This suggests that future work should use data directly derived from the acoustic signal to account for contextual effects, rather than using dictionary look-up or other heuristics. In using the Alex corpus, for which good quality audio is available, we have taken a first step in this direction.

Acknowledgements

This research was supported by the Australian Research Council's Discovery Projects funding scheme (project numbers DP110102506 and DP110102593). We'd like to thank Professor Dupoux and our other colleagues at the Laboratoire de Sciences Cognitives et Psycholinguistique in Paris for hosting us while this research was performed, as well as the Mairie de Paris, the fondation Pierre Gilles de Gennes, the Ecole des Hautes Etudes en Sciences Sociales, the Ecole Normale Supérieure, The Region Ile de France, the European Research Council (ERC-2011-AdG-295810 BOOTPHON), the Agence Nationale pour la Recherche (ANR-2010-BLAN-1901-1 BOOTLANG, ANR-10-IDEX-0001-02 and ANR-10-LABX-0087) and the Fondation de France. We'd also like to thank three anonymous reviewers for helpful comments and suggestions.

References

N. Bernstein-Ratner. 1987. The phonology of parent-child speech. In K. Nelson and A. van Kleeck, editors, *Children's Language*, volume 6. Erlbaum, Hillsdale, NJ.

Benjamin Börschinger, Katherine Demuth, and Mark Johnson. 2012. Studying the effect of input size for Bayesian word segmentation on the Providence corpus. In *Proceedings of the 24th International Conference on Computational Linguistics (Coling 2012)*, pages 325–340. Coling 2012 Organizing Committee.

Benjamin Börschinger, Mark Johnson, and Katherine Demuth. 2013. A joint model of word segmentation and phonological variation for English word-final /t/-deletion. In *Proceedings of the 51st Annual Meeting of the Association for Computational Linguistics (Volume 1: Long Papers)*, pages 1508–1516. Association for Computational Linguistics.

M. Brent. 1999. An efficient, probabilistically sound algorithm for segmentation and word discovery. *Machine Learning*, 34:71–105.

M. Christiansen and S. Curtin. 1999. The power of statistical learning: No need for algebraic rules. In *Proceedings of the 21st Annual Conference of the Cognitive Science Society.*

Morten H Christiansen, Joseph Allen, and Mark S Seidenberg. 1998. Learning to segment speech using multiple cues: A connectionist model. *Language and Cognitive Processes*, 13(2-3):221–268.

Suzanne Curtin, Toben H Mintz, and Morten H Christiansen. 2005. Stress changes the representational landscape: Evidence from word segmentation. *Cognition*, 96(3):233–262.

Anne Cutler and David M Carter. 1987. The predominance of strong initial syllables in the English vocabulary. *Computer Speech and Language*, 2(3):133–142.

Anne Cutler, Jacques Mehler, Dennis Norris, and Juan Segui. 1986. The syllable's differing role in the segmentation of French and English. *Journal of Memory and Language*, 25(4):385 – 400.

Anne Cutler. 2005. Lexical stress. In David B. Pisoni and Robert E. Remez, editors, *The Handbook of Speech Perception*, pages 264–289. Blackwell Publishing.

K. Demuth, J. Culbertson, and J. Alter. 2006. Word-minimality, epenthesis, and coda licensing in the acquisition of English. *Language and Speech*, 49:137–174.

Gabriel Doyle and Roger Levy. 2013. Combining multiple information types in Bayesian word segmentation. In *Proceedings of the 2013 Conference of the North American Chapter of the Association for Computational Linguistics: Human Language Technologies*, pages 117–126. Association for Computational Linguistics.

Victoria Fromkin, editor. 2001. *Linguistics: An Introduction to Linguistic Theory.* Blackwell, Oxford, UK.

Sharon Goldwater, Tom Griffiths, and Mark Johnson. 2006. Interpolating between types and tokens by estimating power-law generators. In Y. Weiss, B. Schölkopf, and J. Platt, editors, *Advances in Neural Information Processing Systems 18*, pages 459–466. MIT Press.

Sharon Goldwater, Thomas L. Griffiths, and Mark Johnson. 2009. A Bayesian framework for word segmentation: Exploring the effects of context. *Cognition*, 112(1):21–54.

Sharon Goldwater. 2007. *Nonparametric Bayesian Models of Lexical Acquisition.* Ph.D. thesis, Brown University.

Mark Johnson and Katherine Demuth. 2010. Unsupervised phonemic Chinese word segmentation using Adaptor Grammars. In *Proceedings of the 23rd International Conference on Computational Linguistics (Coling 2010)*, pages 528–536. Coling 2010 Organizing Committee.

Mark Johnson and Sharon Goldwater. 2009. Improving nonparameteric Bayesian inference: experiments on unsupervised word segmentation with adaptor grammars. In *Proceedings of Human Language Technologies: The 2009 Annual Conference of the North American Chapter of the Association for Computational*

Linguistics, pages 317–325. Association for Computational Linguistics.

Mark Johnson, Thomas L. Griffiths, and Sharon Goldwater. 2007. Adaptor Grammars: A framework for specifying compositional nonparametric Bayesian models. In B. Schölkopf, J. Platt, and T. Hoffman, editors, *Advances in Neural Information Processing Systems 19*, pages 641–648. MIT Press, Cambridge, MA.

Mark Johnson. 2008a. Unsupervised word segmentation for Sesotho using Adaptor Grammars. In *Proceedings of the Tenth Meeting of ACL Special Interest Group on Computational Morphology and Phonology*, pages 20–27. Association for Computational Linguistics.

Mark Johnson. 2008b. Using Adaptor Grammars to identify synergies in the unsupervised acquisition of linguistic structure. In *Proceedings of the 46th Annual Meeting of the Association of Computational Linguistics*, pages 398–406. Association for Computational Linguistics.

Peter W Jusczyk, Anne Cutler, and Nancy J Redanz. 1993. Infants' preference for the predominant stress patterns of English words. *Child Development*, 64(3):675–687.

Peter W. Jusczyk, E. A. Hohne, and A. Bauman. 1999a. Infants' sensitivity to allophonic cues for word segmentation. *Perception and Psychophysics*, 61:1465–1476.

Peter W. Jusczyk, Derek M. Houston, and Mary Newsome. 1999b. The beginnings of word segmentation in English-learning infants. *Cognitive Psychology*, 39(3-4):159–207.

Peter Jusczyk. 1997. *The discovery of spoken language*. MIT Press, Cambridge, MA.

Myron Korman. 1984. Adaptive aspects of maternal vocalizations in differing contexts at ten weeks. *First Language*, 5:44–45.

Constantine Lignos and Charles Yang. 2010. Recession segmentation: simpler online word segmentation using limited resources. In *Proceedings of the Fourteenth Conference on Computational Natural Language Learning*, pages 88–97. Association for Computational Linguistics.

Constantine Lignos. 2011. Modeling infant word segmentation. In *Proceedings of the Fifteenth Conference on Computational Natural Language Learning*, pages 29–38. Association for Computational Linguistics.

Constantine Lignos. 2012. Infant word segmentation: An incremental, integrated model. In *Proceedings of the West Coast Conference on Formal Linguistics 30*.

Brian MacWhinney. 2000. The CHILDES project: Tools for analyzing talk: Volume I: Transcription format and programs, volume II: The database. *Computational Linguistics*, 26(4):657–657.

Sven L Mattys and Peter W Jusczyk. 2000. Phonotactic cues for segmentation of fluent speech by infants. *Cognition*, 78(2):91–121.

Sven L Mattys. 2000. The perception of primary and secondary stress in English. *Perception and Psychophysics*, 62(2):253–265.

Lisa Pearl, Sharon Goldwater, and Mark Steyvers. 2011. Online learning mechanisms for Bayesian models of word segmentation. *Research on Language and Computation*, 8(2):107–132.

Elisabeth O. Selkirk. 1984. *Phonology and Syntax: The Relation Between Sound and Structure*. MIT Press.

Erik D Thiessen and Jenny R Saffran. 2003. When cues collide: use of stress and statistical cues to word boundaries by 7-to 9-month-old infants. *Developmental Psychology*, 39(4):706.

Erik D Thiessen and Jenny R Saffran. 2007. Learning to learn: Infants acquisition of stress-based strategies for word segmentation. *Language Learning and Development*, 3(1):73–100.

Carnegie Mellon University. 2008. The CMU pronouncing dictionary, v.0.7a.

Charles Yang. 2004. Universal grammar, statistics or both? *Trends in Cognitive Sciences*, 8(10):451–456.

Parallel Algorithms for Unsupervised Tagging

Sujith Ravi
Google
Mountain View, CA 94043
sravi@google.com

Sergei Vassilivitskii
Google
Mountain View, CA 94043
sergeiv@google.com

Vibhor Rastogi*
Twitter
San Francisco, CA
vibhor.rastogi@gmail.com

Abstract

We propose a new method for unsupervised tagging that finds minimal models which are then further improved by Expectation Maximization training. In contrast to previous approaches that rely on manually specified and multi-step heuristics for model minimization, our approach is a simple greedy approximation algorithm DMLC (DISTRIBUTED-MINIMUM-LABEL-COVER) that solves this objective in a single step.

We extend the method and show how to efficiently parallelize the algorithm on modern parallel computing platforms while preserving approximation guarantees. The new method easily scales to large data and grammar sizes, overcoming the memory bottleneck in previous approaches. We demonstrate the power of the new algorithm by evaluating on various sequence labeling tasks: Part-of-Speech tagging for multiple languages (including low-resource languages), with complete and incomplete dictionaries, and supertagging, a complex sequence labeling task, where the grammar size alone can grow to millions of entries. Our results show that for all of these settings, our method achieves state-of-the-art scalable performance that yields high quality tagging outputs.

1 Introduction

Supervised sequence labeling with large labeled training datasets is considered a solved problem. For instance, state of the art systems obtain tagging accuracies over 97% for part-of-speech (POS) tagging on the English Penn Treebank. However, learning accurate taggers without labeled data remains a challenge. The accuracies quickly drop when faced with data from a different domain, language, or when there is very little labeled information available for training (Banko and Moore, 2004).

Recently, there has been an increasing amount of research tackling this problem using unsupervised methods. A popular approach is to learn from POS-tag dictionaries (Merialdo, 1994), where we are given a raw word sequence and a dictionary of legal tags for each word type. Learning from POS-tag dictionaries is still challenging. Complete word-tag dictionaries may not always be available for use and in every setting. When they are available, the dictionaries are often noisy, resulting in high tagging ambiguity. Furthermore, when applying taggers in new domains or different datasets, we may encounter new words that are missing from the dictionary. There have been some efforts to learn POS taggers from incomplete dictionaries by extending the dictionary to include these words using some heuristics (Toutanova and Johnson, 2008) or using other methods such as type-supervision (Garrette and Baldridge, 2012).

In this work, we tackle the problem of unsupervised sequence labeling using tag dictionaries. The first reported work on this problem was on POS tagging from Merialdo (1994). The approach involved training a standard Hidden Markov Model (HMM) using the Expectation Maximization (EM) algorithm (Dempster et al., 1977), though EM does not

*The research described herein was conducted while the author was working at Google.

Transactions of the Association for Computational Linguistics, 2 (2014) 105–118. Action Editor: Sharon Goldwater.
Submitted 11/2013; Revised 2/2014; Published 4/2014.

perform well on this task (Johnson, 2007). More recent methods have yielded better performance than EM (see (Ravi and Knight, 2009) for an overview).

One interesting line of research introduced by Ravi and Knight (2009) explores the idea of performing model minimization followed by EM training to learn taggers. Their idea is closely related to the classic Minimum Description Length principle for model selection (Barron et al., 1998). They (1) formulate an objective function to find the smallest model that explains the text (model minimization step), and then, (2) fit the minimized model to the data (EM step). For POS tagging, this method (Ravi and Knight, 2009) yields the best performance to date; 91.6% tagging accuracy on a standard test dataset from the English Penn Treebank. The original work from (Ravi and Knight, 2009) uses an integer linear programming (ILP) formulation to find minimal models, an approach which does not scale to large datasets. Ravi et al. (2010b) introduced a two-step greedy approximation to the original objective function (called the MIN-GREEDY algorithm) that runs much faster while maintaining the high tagging performance. Garrette and Baldridge (2012) showed how to use several heuristics to further improve this algorithm (for instance, better choice of tag bigrams when breaking ties) and stack other techniques on top, such as careful initialization of HMM emission models which results in further performance gains. Their method also works under incomplete dictionary scenarios and can be applied to certain low-resource scenarios (Garrette and Baldridge, 2013) by combining model minimization with supervised training.

In this work, we propose a new scalable algorithm for performing model minimization for this task. By making an assumption on the structure of the solution, we prove that a variant of the greedy set cover algorithm always finds an approximately optimal label set. This is in contrast to previous methods that employ heuristic approaches with no guarantee on the quality of the solution. In addition, we do not have to rely on ad hoc tie-breaking procedures or careful initializations for unknown words. Finally, not only is the proposed method approximately optimal, it is also easy to distribute, allowing it to easily scale to very large datasets. We show empirically that our method, combined with an EM training step outperforms existing state of the art systems.

1.1 Our Contributions

- We present a new method, DISTRIBUTED MINIMUM LABEL COVER, DMLC, for model minimization that uses a fast, greedy algorithm with formal approximation guarantees to the quality of the solution.

- We show how to efficiently parallelize the algorithm while preserving approximation guarantees. In contrast, existing minimization approaches cannot match the new distributed algorithm when scaling from thousands to millions or even billions of tokens.

- We show that our method easily scales to both large data and grammar sizes, and does not require the corpus or label set to fit into memory. This allows us to tackle complex tagging tasks, where the tagset consists of several thousand labels, which results in more than one million entries in the grammar.

- We demonstrate the power of the new method by evaluating under several different scenarios—POS tagging for multiple languages (including low-resource languages), with complete and incomplete dictionaries, as well as a complex sequence labeling task of supertagging. Our results show that for all these settings, our method achieves state-of-the-art performance yielding high quality taggings.

2 Related Work

Recently, there has been an increasing amount of research tackling this problem from multiple directions. Some efforts have focused on inducing POS tag clusters without any tags (Christodoulopoulos et al., 2010; Reichart et al., 2010; Moon et al., 2010), but evaluating such systems proves difficult since it is not straightforward to map the cluster labels onto gold standard tags. A more popular approach is to learn from POS-tag dictionaries (Merialdo, 1994; Ravi and Knight, 2009), incomplete dictionaries (Hasan and Ng, 2009; Garrette and Baldridge, 2012) and human-constructed dictionaries (Goldberg et al., 2008).

Another direction that has been explored in the past includes bootstrapping taggers for a new language based on information acquired from other languages (Das and Petrov, 2011) or limited annotation resources (Garrette and Baldridge, 2013). Additional work focused on building supervised taggers for noisy domains such as Twitter (Gimpel et al., 2011). While most of the relevant work in this area centers on POS tagging, there has been some work done for building taggers for more complex sequence labeling tasks such as supertagging (Ravi et al., 2010a).

Other related work include alternative methods for learning sparse models via priors in Bayesian inference (Goldwater and Griffiths, 2007) and posterior regularization (Ganchev et al., 2010). But these methods only encourage sparsity and do not explicitly seek to minimize the model size, which is the objective function used in this work. Moreover, taggers learned using model minimization have been shown to produce state-of-the-art results for the problems discussed here.

3 Model

Following Ravi and Knight (2009), we formulate the problem as that of label selection on the sentence graph. Formally, we are given a set of sequences, $\mathcal{S} = \{S_1, S_2, \ldots, S_n\}$ where each S_i is a sequence of words, $S_i = w_{i1}, w_{i2}, \ldots, w_{i,|S_i|}$. With each word w_{ij} we associate a set of possible tags T_{ij}. We will denote by m the total number of (possibly duplicate) words (tokens) in the corpus.

Additionally, we define two special words w_0 and w_∞ with special tags *start* and *end*, and consider the modified sequences $S'_i = w_0, S_i, w_\infty$. To simplify notation, we will refer to $w_\infty = w_{|S_i|+1}$. The sequence label problem asks us to select a valid tag $t_{ij} \in T_{ij}$ for each word w_{ij} in the input to minimize a specific objective function.

We will refer to a tag pair $(t_{i,j-1}, t_{ij})$ as a *label*. Our aim is to minimize the number of distinct labels used to cover the full input. Formally, given a sequence S'_i and a tag t_{ij} for each word w_{ij} in S'_i, let the induced set of labels for sequence S'_i be

$$L_i = \bigcup_{j=1}^{|S'_i|} \{(t_{i,j-1}, t_{ij})\}.$$

The total number of distinct labels used over all sequences is then

$$\phi = |\cup_i L_i| = |\bigcup_i \bigcup_{j=1}^{|S_i|+1} \{(t_{i,j-1}, t_{ij})\}|.$$

Note that the order of the tokens in the label makes a difference as {(NN, VP)} and {(VP, NN)} are two distinct labels.

Now we can define the problem formally, following (Ravi and Knight, 2009).

Problem 1 (Minimum Label Cover). *Given a set $\mathcal{S}$ of sequences of words, where each word w_{ij} has a set of valid tags T_{ij}, the problem is to find a valid tag assignment $t_{ij} \in T_{ij}$ for each word that minimizes the number of distinct labels or tag pairs over all sequences,* $\phi = \left|\bigcup_i \bigcup_{j=1}^{|S_i|+1} \{(t_{i,j-1}, t_{ij})\}\right|$.

The problem is closely related to the classical Set Cover problem and is also NP-complete. To reduce Set Cover to the label selection problem, map each element i of the Set Cover instance to a single word sentence $S_i = w_{i1}$, and let the valid tags T_{i1} contain the names of the sets that contain element i. Consider a solution to the label selection problem; every sentence S_i is covered by two labels (w_0, k_i) and (k_i, w_∞), for some $k_i \in T_{i1}$, which corresponds to an element i being covered by set k_i in the Set Cover instance. Thus any valid solution to the label selection problem leads to a feasible solution to the Set Cover problem ($\{k_1, k_2, \ldots\}$) of exactly half the size.

Finally, we will use $\{\{\ldots\}\}$ notation to denote a multiset of elements, i.e. a set where an element may appear multiple times.

4 Algorithm

In this Section, we describe the DISTRIBUTED-MINIMUM-LABEL-COVER, DMLC, algorithm for approximately solving the minimum label cover problem. We describe the algorithm in a centralized setting, and defer the distributed implementation to Section 5. Before describing the algorithm, we briefly explain the relationship of the minimum label cover problem to set cover.

4.1 Modification of Set Cover

As we pointed out earlier, the minimum label cover problem is at least as hard as the Set Cover prob-

1: **Input:** A set of sequences $\mathcal{S}$ with each words w_{ij} having possible tags T_{ij}.

2: **Output:** A tag assignment $t_{ij} \in T_{ij}$ for each word w_{ij} approximately minimizing labels.

3: Let $\mathcal{M}$ be the multi set of all possible labels generated by choosing each possible tag $t \in T_{ij}$.

$$\mathcal{M} = \bigcup_{i} \left(\bigcup_{j=1}^{|S_i|+1} \bigcup_{\substack{t' \in T_{i,j-1} \\ t \in T_{ij}}} \{\{(t', t)\}\} \right) \quad (1)$$

4: Let $\mathcal{L} = \emptyset$ be the set of selected labels.

5: **repeat**

6: Select the most frequent label not yet selected: $(t', t) = \arg\max_{(s',s) \notin \mathcal{L}} |\mathcal{M} \cap (s', s)|$.

7: For each bigram $(w_{i,j-1}, w_{ij})$ where $t' \in T_{i,j-1}$ and $t \in T_{ij}$ tentatively assign t' to $w_{i,j-1}$ and t to w_{ij}. Add (t', t) to $\mathcal{L}$.

8: If a word gets two assignments, select one at random with equal probability.

9: If a bigram $(w_{i,j-1}, w_{ij})$ is consistent with assignments in (t', t), fix the tentative assignments, and set $T_{i,j-1} = \{t'\}$ and $T_{ij} = \{t\}$. Recompute $\mathcal{M}$, the multiset of possible labels, with the updated $T_{i,j-1}$ and T_{ij}.

10: **until** there are no unassigned words

Algorithm 1: MLC Algorithm

1: **Input:** A set of sequences $\mathcal{S}$ with each words w_{ij} having possible tags T_{ij}.

2: **Output:** A tag assignment $t_{ij} \in T_{ij}$ for each word w_{ij} approximately minimizing labels.

3: (Graph Creation) Initialize each vertex v_{ij} with the set of possible tags T_{ij} and its neighbors $v_{i,j+1}$ and $v_{i,j-1}$.

4: **repeat**

5: (Message Passing) Each vertex v_{ij} sends its possibly tags T_{ij} to its forward neighbor v_{ij+1}.

6: (Counter Update) Each vertex receives the the tags $T_{i,j-1}$ and adds all possible labels $\{(s, s') | s \in T_{i,j-1}, s' \in T_{ij}\}$ to a global counter (M).

7: (MaxLabel Selection) Each vertex queries the global counter $\mathcal{M}$ to find the maximum label (t, t').

8: (Tentative Assignment) Each vertex v_{ij} selects a tag tentatively as follows: If one of the tags t, t' is in the feasible set T_{ij}, it tentatively selects the tag.

9: (Random Assignment) If both are feasible it selects one at random. The vertex communicates its assignment to its neighbors.

10: (Confirmed Assignment) Each vertex receives the tentative assignment from its neighbors. If together with its neighbors it can match the selected label, the assignment is finalized. If the assigned tag is T, then the vertex v_{ij} sets the valid tag set T_{ij} to $\{t\}$.

11: **until** no unassigned vertices exist.

Algorithm 2: DMLC Implementation

lem. An additional challenge comes from the fact that labels are tags for a pair of words, and hence are related. For example, if we label a word pair $(w_{i,j-1}, w_{ij})$ as (NN, VP), then the label for the next word pair $(w_{ij}, w_{i,j+1})$ has to be of the form (VP, *), i.e., it has to start with VP.

Previous work (Ravi et al., 2010a; Ravi et al., 2010b) recognized this challenge and employed two phase heuristic approaches. Eschewing heuristics, we will show that with one natural assumption, even with this extra set of constraints, the standard greedy algorithm for this problem results in a solution with a provable approximation ratio of $O(\log m)$. In practice, however, the algorithm performs far better than the worst case ratio, and similar to the work of (Gomes et al., 2006), we find that the greedy approach selects a cover approximately 11% worse than the optimum solution.

4.2 MLC Algorithm

We present in Algorithm 1 our MINIMUM LABEL COVER algorithm to approximately solve the minimum label cover problem. The algorithm is simple, efficient, and easy to distribute.

The algorithm chooses labels one at a time, selecting a label that covers as many words as possible in every iteration. For this, it generates and maintains a multi-set of all possible labels $\mathcal{M}$ (Step 3). The multi-set contains an occurrence of each valid label, for example, if $w_{i,j-1}$ has two possible valid tags NN and VP, and w_{ij} has one possible valid tag VP, then $\mathcal{M}$ will contain two labels, namely (NN, VP) and (VP, VP). Since M is a multi-set it will contain duplicates, e.g. the label (NN, VP) will appear for each adjacent pair of words that have NN and VP as valid tags, respectively.

In each iteration, the algorithm picks a label with the most number of occurrences in $\mathcal{M}$ and adds it to the set of chosen labels (Step 6). Intuitively, this is a greedy step to select a label that covers the most number of word pairs.

Once the algorithm picks a label (t', t), it tries to assign as many words to tags t or t' as possible (Step 7). A word can be assigned t' if t' is a valid tag for it, and t a valid tag for the next word in sequence. Similarly, a word can be assigned t, if t is a valid tag for it, and t' a valid tag for the previous word. Some words can get both assignments, in which case we choose one tentatively at random (Step 8). If a word's tentative random tag, say t, is consistent with the choices of its adjacent words (say t' from the previous word), then the tentative choice is fixed as a permanent one. Whenever a tag is selected, the set of valid tags T_{ij} for the word is reduced to a singleton $\{t\}$. Once the set of valid tags T_{ij} changes, the multi-set $\mathcal{M}$ of all possible labels also changes, as seen from Eq 1. The multi-set is then recomputed (Step 9) and the iterations repeated until all of words have been tagged.

We can show that under a natural assumption this simple algorithm is approximately optimal.

Assumption 1 (c-feasibility). *Let $c \geq 1$ be any number, and k be the size of the optimal solution to the original problem. In each iteration, the* MLC *algorithm fixes the tags for some words. We say that the algorithm is c-feasible, if after each iteration there exists some solution to the remaining problem, consistent with the chosen tags, with size at most ck .*

The assumption encodes the fact that a single bad greedy choice is not going to destroy the overall structure of the solution, and a nearly optimal solution remains. We note that this assumption of c-feasibility is not only sufficient, as we will formally show, but is also necessary. Indeed, without any assumptions, once the algorithm fixes the tag for some words, an optimal label may no longer be consistent with the chosen tags, and it is not hard to find contrived examples where the size of the optimal solution doubles after each iteration of MLC.

Since the underlying problem is NP-complete, it is computationally hard to give direct evidence verifying the assumption on natural language inputs. However, on small examples we are able to show that the greedy algorithm is within a small constant factor of the optimum, specifically it is within 11% of the optimum model size for the POS tagging problem using the standard 24k dataset (Ravi and Knight, 2009). Combined with the fact that the final method outperforms state of the art approaches, this leads us to conclude that the structural assumption is well justified.

Lemma 1. *Under the assumption of c-feasibility, the* MLC *algorithm achieves a $O(c \log m)$ approximation to the minimum label cover problem, where $m = \sum_i |S_i|$ is the total number of tokens.*

Proof. To prove the Lemma we will define an objective function $\bar{\phi}$, counting the number of unlabeled word pairs, as a function of possible labels, and show that $\bar{\phi}$ decreases by a factor of $(1 - O(1/ck))$ at every iteration.

To define $\bar{\phi}$, we first define ϕ, the number of labeled word pairs. Consider a particular set of labels, $\mathcal{L} = \{L_1, L_2, \ldots, L_k\}$ where each label is a pair (t_i, t_j). Call $\{t_{ij}\}$ a valid assignment of tokens if for each w_{ij}, we have $t_{ij} \in T_{ij}$. Then the score of $\mathcal{L}$ under an assignment t, which we denote by ϕ_t, is the number of bigram labels that appear in $\mathcal{L}$. Formally, $\phi_t(\mathcal{L}) = | \cup_{i,j} \{\{(t_{i,j-1}, t_{ij}) \cap \mathcal{L}\}\}|$. Finally, we define $\phi(\mathcal{L})$ to be the best such assignment, $\phi(\mathcal{L}) = \max_t \phi_t(\mathcal{L})$, and $\bar{\phi}(\mathcal{L}) = m - \phi(\mathcal{L})$ the number of uncovered labels.

Consider the label selected by the algorithm in every step. By the c-feasibility assumption, there exists some solution having ck labels. Thus, some label from that solution covers at least a $1/ck$ fraction of the remaining words. The selected label (t, t') maximizes the intersection with the remaining feasible labels. The conflict resolution step ensures that in expectation the realized benefit is at least a half of the maximum, thereby reducing $\bar{\phi}$ by at least a

$(1 - 1/2ck)$ fraction. Therefore, after $O(kc \log m)$ operations all of the labels are covered. □

4.3 Fitting the Model Using EM

Once the greedy algorithm terminates and returns a minimized grammar of tag bigrams, we follow the approach of Ravi and Knight (2009) and fit the minimized model to the data using the alternating EM strategy.

In this step, we run an alternating optimization procedure iteratively in phases. In each phase, we initialize (and prune away) parameters within the two HMM components (transition or emission model) using the output from the previous phase. We initialize this procedure by restricting the transition parameters to only those tag bigrams selected in the model minimization step. We train in conjunction with the original emission model using EM algorithm which prunes away some of the emission parameters. In the next phase, we alternate the initialization by choosing the pruned emission model along with the original transition model (with full set of tag bigrams) and retrain using EM. The alternating EM iterations are terminated when the change in the size of the observed grammar (i.e., the number of unique bigrams in the tagging output) is $\leq 5\%$.[1] We refer to our entire approach using greedy minimization followed by EM training as DMLC + EM.

5 Distributed Implementation

The DMLC algorithm is directly suited towards parallelization across many machines. We turn to Pregel (Malewicz et al., 2010), and its open source version Giraph (Apa, 2013). In these systems the computation proceeds in rounds. In every round, every machine does some local processing and then sends arbitrary messages to other machines. Semantically, we think of the communication graph as fixed, and in each round each vertex performs some local computation and then sends messages to its neighbors. This mode of parallel programming directs the programmers to "Think like a vertex."

The specific systems like Pregel and Giraph build infrastructure that ensures that the overall system is fault tolerant, efficient, and fast. In addition, they provide implementation of commonly used distributed data structures, such as, for example global counters. The programmer's job is simply to specify the code that each vertex will run at every round.

We implemented the DMLC algorithm in Pregel. The implementation is straightforward and given in Algorithm 2. The multi-set $\mathcal{M}$ of Algorithm 1 is represented as a global counter in Algorithm 2. The message passing (Step 3) and counter update (Step 4) steps update this global counter and hence perform the role of Step 3 of Algorithm 1. Step 5 selects the label with largest count, which is equivalent to the greedy label picking step 6 of Algorithm 1. Finally steps 6, 7, and 8 update the tag assignment of each vertex performing the roles of steps 7, 8, and 9, respectively, of Algorithm 1.

5.1 Speeding up the Algorithm

The implementation described above directly copies the sequential algorithm. Here we describe additional steps we took to further improve the parallel running times.

Singleton Sets: As the parallel algorithm proceeds, the set of feasible sets associated with a node slowly decreases. At some point there is only one tag that a node can take on, however this tag is rare, and so it takes a while for it to be selected using the greedy strategy. Nevertheless, if a node and one of its neighbors have only a single tag left, then it is safe to assign the unique label [2].

Modifying the Graph: As is often the case, the bottleneck in parallel computations is the communication. To reduce the amount of communication we reduce the graph on the fly, removing nodes and edges once they no longer play a role in the computation. This simple modification decreases the communication time in later rounds as the total size of the problem shrinks.

6 Experiments and Results

In this Section, we describe the experimental setup for various tasks, settings and compare empirical performance of our method against several existing

[1] For more details on the alternating EM strategy and how initialization with minimized models improve EM performance in alternating iterations, refer to (Ravi and Knight, 2009).

[2] We must judiciously initialize the global counter to take care of this assignment, but this is easily accomplished.

baselines. The performance results for all systems (on all tasks) are measured in terms of tagging accuracy, i.e. % of tokens from the test corpus that were labeled correctly by the system.

6.1 Part-of-Speech Tagging Task

6.1.1 Tagging Using a Complete Dictionary

Data: We use a standard test set (consisting of 24,115 word tokens from the Penn Treebank) for the POS tagging task. The tagset consists of 45 distinct tag labels and the dictionary contains 57,388 word/tag pairs derived from the entire Penn Treebank. Per-token ambiguity for the test data is about 1.5 tags/token. In addition to the standard 24k dataset, we also train and test on larger data sets—973k tokens from the Penn Treebank, 3M tokens from PTB+Europarl (Koehn, 2005) data.

Methods: We evaluate and compare performance for POS tagging using four different methods that employ the model minimization idea combined with EM training:

- EM: Training a bigram HMM model using EM algorithm (Merialdo, 1994).
- ILP + EM: Minimizing grammar size using integer linear programming, followed by EM training (Ravi and Knight, 2009).
- MIN-GREEDY + EM: Minimizing grammar size using the two-step greedy method (Ravi et al., 2010b).
- DMLC + EM: This work.

Results: Table 1 shows the results for POS tagging on English Penn Treebank data. On the smaller test datasets, all of the model minimization strategies (methods 2, 3, 4) tend to perform equally well, yielding state-of-the-art results and large improvement over standard EM. When training (and testing) on larger corpora sizes, DMLC yields the best reported performance on this task to date. A major advantage of the new method is that it can easily scale to large corpora sizes and the distributed nature of the algorithm still permits fast, efficient optimization of the global objective function. So, unlike the earlier methods (such as MIN-GREEDY) it is fast enough to run on several millions of tokens to yield additional performance gains (shown in last column).

Speedups: We also observe a significant speedup when using the parallelized version of the DMLC algorithm. Performing model minimization on the 24k tokens dataset takes 55 seconds on a single machine, whereas parallelization permits model minimization to be feasible even on large datasets. Fig 1 shows the running time for DMLC when run on a cluster of 100 machines. We vary the input data size from 1M word tokens to about 8M word tokens, while holding the resources constant. Both the algorithm and its distributed implementation in DMLC are linear time operations as evident by the plot. In fact, for comparison, we also plot a straight line passing through the first two runtimes. The straight line essentially plots runtimes corresponding to a linear speedup. DMLC clearly achieves better runtimes showing even better than linear speedup. The reason for this is that distributed version has a constant overhead for initialization, independent of the data size. While the running time for rest of the implementation is linear in data size. Thus, as the data size becomes larger, the constant overhead becomes less significant, and the distributed implementation appears to complete slightly faster as data size increases.

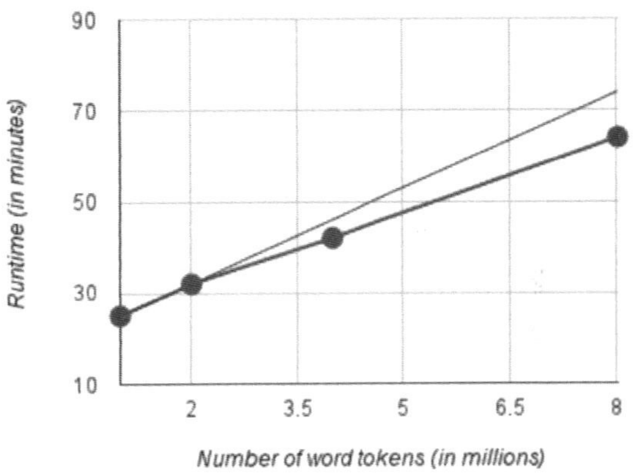

Figure 1: Runtime vs. data size (measured in # of word tokens) on 100 machines. For comparison, we also plot a straight line passing through the first two runtimes. The straight line essentially plots runtimes corresponding to a linear speedup. DMLC clearly achieves better runtimes showing a better than linear speedup.

6.1.2 Tagging Using Incomplete Dictionaries

We also evaluate our approach for POS tagging under other resource-constrained scenarios. Obtain-

Method	Tagging accuracy (%)		
	te=24k	*te*=973k	
	tr=24k	*tr*=973k	*tr*=3.7M
1. EM	81.7	82.3	
2. ILP + EM (Ravi and Knight, 2009)	91.6	-	
3. MIN-GREEDY + EM (Ravi et al., 2010b)	91.6	87.1	
4. DMLC + EM (this work)	91.4	87.5	87.8

Table 1: Results for unsupervised part-of-speech tagging on English Penn Treebank dataset. Tagging accuracies for different methods are shown on multiple datasets. *te* shows the size (number of tokens) in the test data, *tr* represents the size of the raw text used to perform model minimization.

ing a complete dictionary is often difficult, especially for new domains. To verify the utility of our method when the input dictionary is incomplete, we evaluate against standard datasets used in previous work (Garrette and Baldridge, 2012) and compare against the previous best reported performance for the same task. In all the experiments (described here and in subsequent sections), we use the following terminology—*raw* data refers to unlabeled text used by different methods (for model minimization or other unsupervised training procedures such as EM), *dictionary* consists of word/tag entries that are legal, and *test* refers to data over which tagging evaluation is performed.

English Data: For English POS tagging with incomplete dictionary, we evaluate on the Penn Treebank (Marcus et al., 1993) data. Following (Garrette and Baldridge, 2012), we extracted a word-tag dictionary from sections 00-15 (751,059 tokens) consisting of 39,087 word types, 45,331 word/tag entries, a per-type ambiguity of 1.16 yielding a per-token ambiguity of 2.21 on the raw corpus (treating unknown words as having all 45 possible tags). As in their setup, we then use the first 47,996 tokens of section 16 as raw data and perform final evaluation on the sections 22-24. We use the raw corpus along with the unlabeled test data to perform model minimization and EM training. Unknown words are allowed to have all possible tags in both these procedures.

Italian Data: The minimization strategy presented here is a general-purpose method that does not require any specific tuning and works for other languages as well. To demonstrate this, we also perform evaluation on a different language (Italian) using the TUT corpus (Bosco et al., 2000). Following (Garrette and Baldridge, 2012), we use the same data splits as their setting. We take the first half of each of the five sections to build the word-tag dictionary, the next quarter as raw data and the last quarter as test data. The dictionary was constructed from 41,000 tokens comprised of 7,814 word types, 8,370 word/tag pairs, per-type ambiguity of 1.07 and a per-token ambiguity of 1.41 on the raw data. The raw data consisted of 18,574 tokens and the test contained 18,763 tokens. We use the unlabeled corpus from the raw and test data to perform model minimization followed by unsupervised EM training.

Other Languages: In order to test the effectiveness of our method in other non-English settings, we also report the performance of our method on several other Indo-European languages using treebank data from CoNLL-X and CoNLL-2007 shared tasks on dependency parsing (Buchholz and Marsi, 2006; Nivre et al., 2007). The corpus statistics for the five languages (Danish, Greek, Italian, Portuguese and Spanish) are listed below. For each language, we construct a dictionary from the raw training data. The unlabeled corpus from the raw training and test data is used to perform model minimization followed by unsupervised EM training. As before, unknown words are allowed to have all possible tags. We report the final tagging performance on the test data and compare it to baseline EM.

Garrette and Baldridge (2012) treat unknown words (words that appear in the raw text but are missing from the dictionary) in a special manner and use several heuristics to perform better initialization for such words (for example, the probability that an unknown word is associated with a particular tag is conditioned on the openness of the tag). They also use an auto-supervision technique to smooth counts learnt from EM onto new words encountered during testing. In contrast, we do not apply any such technique for unknown words and allow them to be mapped uniformly to all possible tags in the dictionary. For this particular set of experiments, the only difference from the Garrette and Baldridge (2012) setup is that we include unlabeled text from the test data (but without any dictionary tag labels or special heuristics) to our existing word tokens from raw text for performing model minimization. This is a standard practice used in unsupervised training scenarios (for example, Bayesian inference methods) and in general for scalable techniques where the goal is to perform inference on the same data for which one wishes to produce some structured prediction.

Language	**Train** (tokens)	**Dict** (entries)	**Test** (tokens)
DANISH	94386	18797	5852
GREEK	65419	12894	4804
ITALIAN	71199	14934	5096
PORTUGUESE	206678	30053	5867
SPANISH	89334	17176	5694

Results: Table 2 (column 2) compares previously reported results against our approach for English. We observe that our method obtains a huge improvement over standard EM and gets comparable results to the previous best reported scores for the same task from (Garrette and Baldridge, 2012). It is encouraging to note that the new system achieves this performance without using any of the carefully-chosen heuristics employed by the previous method. However, we do note that some of these techniques can be easily combined with our method to produce further improvements.

Table 2 (column 3) also shows results on Italian POS tagging. We observe that our method achieves significant improvements in tagging accuracy over all the baseline systems including the previous best system (+2.9%). This demonstrates that the method generalizes well to other languages and produces consistent tagging improvements over existing methods for the same task.

Results for POS tagging on CoNLL data in five different languages are displayed in Figure 2. Note that the proportion of raw data in test versus train

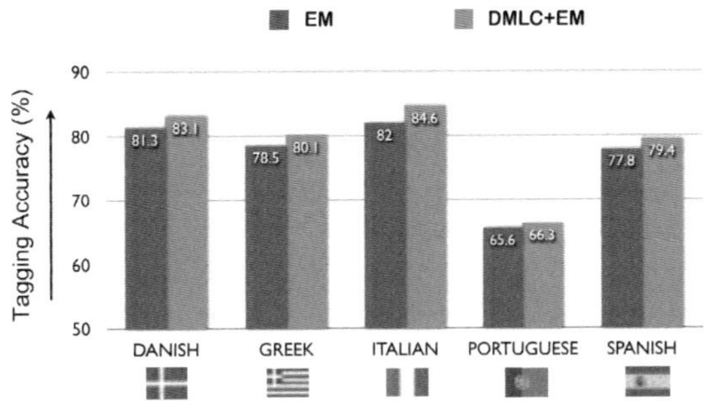

Figure 2: Part-of-Speech tagging accuracy for different languages on CoNLL data using incomplete dictionaries.

(from the standard CoNLL shared tasks) is much smaller compared to the earlier experimental settings. In general, we observe that adding more raw data for EM training improves the tagging quality (same trend observed earlier in Table 1: column 2 versus column 3). Despite this, DMLC + EM still achieves significant improvements over the baseline EM system on multiple languages (as shown in Figure 2). An additional advantage of the new method is that it can easily scale to larger corpora and it produces a much more compact grammar that can be efficiently incorporated for EM training.

6.1.3 Tagging for Low-Resource Languages

Learning part-of-speech taggers for severely low-resource languages (e.g., Malagasy) is very challenging. In addition to scarce (token-supervised) labeled resources, the tag dictionaries available for training taggers are tiny compared to other languages such as English. Garrette and Baldridge (2013) combine various supervised and semi-supervised learning algorithms into a common POS tagger training pipeline to address some of these challenges. They also report tagging accuracy improvements on low-resource languages when using the combined system over any single algorithm. Their system has four main parts, in order: (1) Tag dictionary expansion using label propagation algorithm, (2) Weighted model minimization, (3) Expectation maximization (EM) training of HMMs using auto-supervision, (4) MaxEnt Markov Model (MEMM) training. The entire procedure results in a trained tagger model that can then be applied to tag any raw data.[3] Step 2 in this procedure involves

[3]For more details, refer (Garrette and Baldridge, 2013).

Method	Tagging accuracy (%)	
	English (PTB 00-15)	Italian (TUT)
1. Random	63.53	62.81
2. EM	69.20	60.70
3. Type-supervision + HMM initialization (Garrette and Baldridge, 2012)	88.52	72.86
4. DMLC + EM (this work)	88.11	75.79

Table 2: Part-of-Speech tagging accuracy using PTB sections 00-15 and TUT to build the tag dictionary. For comparison, we also include the results for the previously reported state-of-the-art system (method 3) for the same task.

Method	Tagging accuracy (%)		
	Total	Known	Unknown
Low-resource tagging using (Garrette and Baldridge, 2013)	80.7 (70.2)	87.6 (90.3)	66.1 (45.1)
Low-resource tagging using DMLC + EM (this work)	81.1 (70.8)	87.9 (90.3)	66.7 (46.5)

Table 3: Part-of-Speech tagging accuracy for a low-resource language (Malagasy) on *All/Known/Unknown* tokens in the test data. Tagging performance is shown for multiple experiments using different (incomplete) dictionary sizes: (a) *small*, (b) *tiny* (shown in parentheses). The new method (row 2) significantly outperforms the existing method with $p < 0.01$ for *small* dictionary and $p < 0.05$ for *tiny* dictionary.

a weighted version of model minimization which uses the multi-step greedy approach from Ravi et al. (2010b) enhanced with additional heuristics that uses tag weights learnt via label propagation (in Step 1) within the minimization process.

We replace the model minimization procedure in their Step 2 with our method (DMLC + EM) and directly compare this new system with their approach in terms of tagging accuracy. Note for all other steps in the pipeline we follow the same procedure (and run the same code) as Garrette and Baldridge (2013), including the same smoothing procedure for EM initialization in Step 3.

Data: We use the exact same setup as Garrette and Baldridge (2013) and run experiments on Malagasy, an Austronesian language spoken in Madagascar. We use the publicly available data[4]: 100k raw tokens for training, a word-tag dictionary acquired with 4 hours of human annotation effort (used for type-supervision), and a held-out test dataset (5341 tokens). We provide the unlabeled corpus from the raw training data along with the word-tag dictionary as input to model minimization and evaluate on the test corpus. We run multiple experiments for different (incomplete) dictionary scenarios: (a) *small* = 2773 word/tag pairs, (b) *tiny* = 329 word/tag pairs.

Results: Table 3 shows results on Malagasy data comparing a system that employs (unweighted) DMLC against the existing state-of-the-art system that incorporates a multi-step weighted model minimization combined with additional heuristics. We observe that switching to the new model minimization procedure alone yields significant improvement in tagging accuracy under both dictionary scenarios. It is encouraging that a better minimization procedure also leads to higher tagging quality on the unknown word tokens (column 4 in the table), even when the input dictionary is tiny.

[4] github.com/ dhgarrette/low-resource-pos-tagging-2013

6.2 Supertagging

Compared to POS tagging, a more challenging task is learning supertaggers for lexicalized grammar formalisms such as Combinatory Categorial Grammar (CCG) (Steedman, 2000). For example, CCG-bank (Hockenmaier and Steedman, 2007) contains 1241 distinct supertags (lexical categories) and the most ambiguous word has 126 supertags. This provides a much more challenging starting point for the semi-supervised methods typically applied to the task. Yet, this is an important task since creating grammars and resources for CCG parsers for new domains and languages is highly labor- and knowledge-intensive.

As described earlier, our approach scales easily to large datasets as well as label sizes. To evaluate it on the supertagging task, we use the same dataset from (Ravi et al., 2010a) and compare against their baseline method that uses an modified (two-step) version

Method	Supertagging accuracy (%)	
	Ambiguous	Total
1. EM	38.7	45.6
2. ILP* + EM (Ravi et al., 2010a)	52.1	57.3
3. DMLC + EM (this work)	55.9	59.3

Table 4: Results for unsupervised supertagging with a dictionary. Here, we report the total accuracy as well as accuracy on just the ambiguous tokens (i.e., tokens which have more than one tagging possibility). *The baseline method 2 requires several pre-processing steps in order to run feasibly for this task (described in Section 6.2). In contrast, the new approach (DMLC) runs fast and also permits efficient parallelization.

of the ILP formulation for model minimization.

Data: We use the CCGbank data for this experiment. This data was created by semi- automatically converting the Penn Treebank to CCG derivations (Hockenmaier and Steedman, 2007). We use the standard splits of the data used in semi-supervised tagging experiments (Banko and Moore, 2004)—sections 0-18 for training (i.e., to construct the word-tag dictionary), and sections 22-24 for test.

Results: Table 4 compares the results for two baseline systems—standard EM (method 1), and a previously reported system using model minimization (method 2) for the same task. We observe that DMLC produces better taggings than either of these and yields significant improvement in accuracy (+2% overall, +3.8% on ambiguous tokens).

Note that it is not feasible to run the ILP-based baseline (method 2 in the table) directly since it is very slow in practice, so Ravi et al. (2010a) use a set of pre-processing steps to prune the original grammar size (unique tag pairs) from >1M to several thousand entries followed by a modified two-step ILP minimization strategy. This is required to permit their model minimization step to be run in a feasible manner. On the other hand, the new approach DMLC (method 3) scales better even when the data/label sizes are large, hence it can be run with the full data using the original model minimization formulation (rather than a two-step heuristic).

Ravi et al. (2010a) also report further improvements using an alternative approach involving an ILP-based weighted minimization procedure. In Section 7 we briefly discuss how the DMLC method can be extended to this setting and combined with other similar methods.

7 Discussion and Conclusion

We present a fast, efficient model minimization algorithm for unsupervised tagging that improves upon previous two-step heuristics. We show that under a fairly natural assumption of c-feasibility the solution obtained by our minimization algorithm is $O(c \log m)$-approximate to the optimal. Although in the case of two-step heuristics, the first step guarantees an $O(\log m)$-approximation, the second step, which is required to get a consistent solution, can introduce many additional labels resulting in a solution arbitrarily away from the optimal. Our one step approach ensures consistency at each step of the algorithm, while the c-feasibility assumption means that the solution does not diverge too much from the optimal in each iteration.

In addition to proving approximation guarantees for the new algorithm, we show that it is parallelizable, allowing us to easily scale to larger datasets than previously explored. Our results show that the algorithm achieves state-of-the-art performance, outperforming existing methods on several different tasks (both POS tagging and supertagging) and works well even with incomplete dictionaries and extremely low-resource languages like Malagasy.

For future work, it would be interesting to apply a weighted version of the DMLC algorithm where labels (i.e., tag pairs) can have different weight distributions instead of uniform weights. Our algorithm can be extended to allow an input weight distribution to be specified for minimization. In order to initialize the weights we could use existing strategies such as grammar-informed initialization (Ravi et al., 2010a) or output distributions learnt via other methods such as label propagation (Garrette and Baldridge, 2013).

References

2013. Apache giraph. http://giraph.apache.org/.

Michele Banko and Robert C. Moore. 2004. Part-of-speech tagging in context. In *Proceedings of COLING*, pages 556–561.

Andrew R Barron, Jorma Rissanen, and Bin Yu. 1998. The Minimum Description Length Principle in Coding and Modeling. *IEEE Transactions of Information Theory*, 44(6):2743–2760.

Cristina Bosco, Vincenzo Lombardo, Daniela Vassallo, and Leonardo Lesmo. 2000. Building a Treebank for Italian: a data-driven annotation schema. In *Proceedings of the Second International Conference on Language Resources and Evaluation LREC-2000*, pages 99–105.

Sabine Buchholz and Erwin Marsi. 2006. Conll-x shared task on multilingual dependency parsing. In *Proceedings of CoNLL*, pages 149–164.

Christos Christodoulopoulos, Sharon Goldwater, and Mark Steedman. 2010. Two decades of unsupervised POS induction: How far have we come? In *Proceedings of the Conference on Empirical Methods in Natural Language Processing (EMNLP)*, pages 575–584.

Dipanjan Das and Slav Petrov. 2011. Unsupervised part-of-speech tagging with bilingual graph-based projections. In *Proceedings of the 49th Annual Meeting of the Association for Computational Linguistics: Human Language Technologies - Volume 1*, pages 600–609.

A. P. Dempster, N. M. Laird, and D. B. Rubin. 1977. Maximum likelihood from incomplete data via the EM algorithm. *Journal of the Royal Statistical Society, Series B*, 39(1):1–38.

Kuzman Ganchev, João Graça, Jennifer Gillenwater, and Ben Taskar. 2010. Posterior regularization for structured latent variable models. *Journal of Machine Learning Research*, 11:2001–2049.

Dan Garrette and Jason Baldridge. 2012. Type-supervised Hidden Markov Models for part-of-speech tagging with incomplete tag dictionaries. In *Proceedings of the Conference on Empirical Methods in Natural Language Processing and Computational Natural Language Learning (EMNLP-CoNLL)*, pages 821–831.

Dan Garrette and Jason Baldridge. 2013. Learning a part-of-speech tagger from two hours of annotation. In *Proceedings of the Conference of the North American Chapter of the Association for Computational Linguistics: Human Language Technologies*, pages 138–147.

Kevin Gimpel, Nathan Schneider, Brendan O'Connor, Dipanjan Das, Daniel Mills, Jacob Eisenstein, Michael Heilman, Dani Yogatama, Jeffrey Flanigan, and Noah A. Smith. 2011. Part-of-speech tagging for Twitter: annotation, features, and experiments. In *Proceedings of the 49th Annual Meeting of the Association for Computational Linguistics: Human Language Technologies: short papers - Volume 2*, pages 42–47.

Yoav Goldberg, Meni Adler, and Michael Elhadad. 2008. EM can find pretty good HMM POS-taggers (when given a good start). In *Proceedings of ACL*, pages 746–754.

Sharon Goldwater and Thomas L. Griffiths. 2007. A fully Bayesian approach to unsupervised part-of-speech tagging. In *ACL*.

Fernando C. Gomes, Cludio N. Meneses, Panos M. Pardalos, and Gerardo Valdisio R. Viana. 2006. Experimental analysis of approximation algorithms for the vertex cover and set covering problems.

Kazi Saidul Hasan and Vincent Ng. 2009. Weakly supervised part-of-speech tagging for morphologically-rich, resource-scarce languages. In *Proceedings of the 12th Conference on the European Chapter of the Association for Computational Linguistics*, pages 363–371.

Julia Hockenmaier and Mark Steedman. 2007. CCGbank: A corpus of CCG derivations and dependency structures extracted from the Penn Treebank. *Computational Linguistics*, 33(3):355–396.

Mark Johnson. 2007. Why doesn't EM find good HMM POS-taggers? In *Proceedings of the Joint Conference on Empirical Methods in Natural Language Processing and Computational Natural Language Learning (EMNLP-CoNLL)*, pages 296–305.

Philipp Koehn. 2005. Europarl: A Parallel Corpus for Statistical Machine Translation. In *Machine Translation Summit X*, pages 79–86.

Grzegorz Malewicz, Matthew H. Austern, Aart J.C Bik, James C. Dehnert, Ilan Horn, Naty Leiser, and Grzegorz Czajkowski. 2010. Pregel: a system for large-scale graph processing. In *Proceedings of the 2010 ACM SIGMOD International Conference on Management of data*, pages 135–146.

Mitchell P. Marcus, Beatrice Santorini, and Mary Ann Marcinkiewicz. 1993. Building a large annotated corpus of English: The Penn Treebank. *Computational Linguistics*, 19(2):313–330.

Bernard Merialdo. 1994. Tagging English text with a probabilistic model. *Computational Linguistics*, 20(2):155–171.

Taesun Moon, Katrin Erk, and Jason Baldridge. 2010. Crouching Dirichlet, Hidden Markov Model: Unsupervised POS tagging with context local tag generation. In *Proceedings of the Conference on Empirical Methods in Natural Language Processing*, pages 196–206.

Joakim Nivre, Johan Hall, Sandra Kübler, Ryan McDonald, Jens Nilsson, Sebastian Riedel, and Deniz Yuret. 2007. The CoNLL 2007 shared task on dependency parsing. In *Proceedings of the CoNLL Shared Task Session of EMNLP-CoNLL*, pages 915–932.

Sujith Ravi and Kevin Knight. 2009. Minimized models for unsupervised part-of-speech tagging. In *Proceedings of the Joint Conferenceof the 47th Annual Meeting of the Association for Computational Linguistics and the 4th International Joint Conference on Natural Language Processing of the Asian Federation of Natural Language Processing (ACL-IJCNLP)*, pages 504–512.

Sujith Ravi, Jason Baldridge, and Kevin Knight. 2010a. Minimized models and grammar-informed initialization for supertagging with highly ambiguous lexicons. In *Proceedings of the 48th Annual Meeting of the Association for Computational Linguistics (ACL)*, pages 495–503.

Sujith Ravi, Ashish Vaswani, Kevin Knight, and David Chiang. 2010b. Fast, greedy model minimization for unsupervised tagging. In *Proceedings of the 23rd International Conference on Computational Linguistics (COLING)*, pages 940–948.

Roi Reichart, Raanan Fattal, and Ari Rappoport. 2010. Improved unsupervised POS induction using intrinsic clustering quality and a Zipfian constraint. In *Proceedings of the Fourteenth Conference on Computational Natural Language Learning*, pages 57–66.

Mark Steedman. 2000. *The Syntactic Process*. MIT Press, Cambridge, MA, USA.

Kristina Toutanova and Mark Johnson. 2008. A Bayesian LDA-based model for semi-supervised part-of-speech tagging. In *Advances in Neural Information Processing Systems (NIPS)*, pages 1521–1528.

A Tabular Method for Dynamic Oracles in Transition-Based Parsing

Yoav Goldberg
Department of
Computer Science
Bar Ilan University, Israel
yoav.goldberg@gmail.com

Francesco Sartorio
Department of
Information Engineering
University of Padua, Italy
sartorio@dei.unipd.it

Giorgio Satta
Department of
Information Engineering
University of Padua, Italy
satta@dei.unipd.it

Abstract

We develop parsing oracles for two transition-based dependency parsers, including the arc-standard parser, solving a problem that was left open in (Goldberg and Nivre, 2013). We experimentally show that using these oracles during training yields superior parsing accuracies on many languages.

1 Introduction

Greedy transition-based dependency parsers (Nivre, 2008) incrementally process an input sentence from left to right. These parsers are very fast and provide competitive parsing accuracies (Nivre et al., 2007). However, greedy transition-based parsers still fall behind search-based parsers (Zhang and Clark, 2008; Huang and Sagae, 2010) with respect to accuracy.

The training of transition-based parsers relies on a component called the parsing **oracle**, which maps parser configurations to optimal transitions with respect to a gold tree. A discriminative model is then trained to simulate the oracle's behavior. A parsing oracle is deterministic if it returns a single canonical transition. Furthermore, an oracle is partial if it is defined only for configurations that can reach the gold tree, that is, configurations representing parsing histories with no mistake. Oracles that are both deterministic and partial are called **static**. Traditionally, only static oracles have been exploited in training of transition-based parsers.

Recently, Goldberg and Nivre (2012; 2013) showed that the accuracy of greedy parsers can be substantially improved without affecting their parsing speed. This improvement relies on the introduction of novel oracles that are nondeterministic and complete. An oracle is nondeterministic if it returns the set of all transitions that are optimal with respect to the gold tree, and it is complete if it is well-defined and correct for every configuration that is reachable by the parser. Oracles that are both nondeterministic and complete are called **dynamic**.

Goldberg and Nivre (2013) develop dynamic oracles for several transition-based parsers. The construction of these oracles is based on a property of transition-based parsers that they call arc decomposition. They also prove that the popular arc-standard system (Nivre, 2004) is not arc-decomposable, and they leave as an open research question the construction of a dynamic oracle for the arc-standard system. In this article, we develop one such oracle (§4) and prove its correctness (§5).

An extension to the arc-standard parser was presented by Sartorio et al. (2013), which relaxes the bottom-up construction order and allows mixing of bottom-up and top-down strategies. This parser, called here the LR-spine parser, achieves state-of-the-art results for greedy parsing. Like the arc-standard system, the LR-spine parser is not arc-decomposable, and a dynamic oracle for this system was not known. We extend our oracle for the arc-standard system to work for the LR-spine system as well (§6).

The dynamic oracles developed by Goldberg and Nivre (2013) for arc-decomposable systems are based on local properties of computations. In contrast, our novel dynamic oracle algorithms rely on arguably more complex structural properties of computations, which are computed through dynamic programming. This leaves open the question of whether a machine-learning model can learn to effectively simulate such complex processes: will the

Transactions of the Association for Computational Linguistics, 2 (2014) 119–130. Action Editor: Ryan McDonald.
Submitted 11/2013; Revised 2/2014; Published 4/2014.

benefit of training with the dynamic oracle carry over to the arc-standard and LR-spine systems? We show experimentally that this is indeed the case (§8), and that using the training-with-exploration method of (Goldberg and Nivre, 2013) with our dynamic programming based oracles yields superior parsing accuracies on many languages.

2 Arc-Standard Parser

In this section we introduce the arc-standard parser of Nivre (2004), which is the model that we use in this article. To keep the notation at a simple level, we only discuss the unlabeled version of the parser; however, a labeled extension is used in §8 for our experiments.

2.1 Preliminaries and Notation

The set of non-negative integers is denoted as $\mathbb{N}_0$. For $i, j \in \mathbb{N}_0$ with $i \leq j$, we write $[i, j]$ to denote the set $\{i, i+1, \ldots, j\}$. When $i > j$, $[i, j]$ denotes the empty set.

We represent an input sentence as a string $w = w_0 \cdots w_n$, $n \in \mathbb{N}_0$, where token w_0 is a special root symbol, and each w_i with $i \in [1, n]$ is a lexical token. For $i, j \in [0, n]$ with $i \leq j$, we write $w[i, j]$ to denote the substring $w_i w_{i+1} \cdots w_j$ of w.

We write $i \rightarrow j$ to denote a grammatical **dependency** of some unspecified type between lexical tokens w_i and w_j, where w_i is the head and w_j is the dependent. A **dependency tree** for w is a directed, ordered tree $t = (V_w, A)$, such that $V_w = [0, n]$ is the set of nodes, $A \subseteq V_w \times V_w$ is the set of arcs, and node 0 is the root. Arc (i, j) encodes a dependency $i \rightarrow j$, and we will often use the latter notation to denote arcs.

2.2 Transition-Based Dependency Parsing

We assume the reader is familiar with the formal framework of transition-based dependency parsing originally introduced by Nivre (2003); see Nivre (2008) for an introduction. We only summarize here our notation.

Transition-based dependency parsers use a stack data structure, where each stack element is associated with a tree spanning (generating) some substring of the input w. The parser processes the input string incrementally, from left to right, applying at each step a transition that updates the stack and/or consumes one token from the input. Transitions may also construct new dependencies, which are added to the current configuration of the parser.

We represent the **stack** data structure as an ordered sequence $\sigma = [\sigma_d, \ldots, \sigma_1]$, $d \in \mathbb{N}_0$, of nodes $\sigma_i \in V_w$, with the topmost element placed at the right. When $d = 0$, we have the empty stack $\sigma = []$. Sometimes we use the vertical bar to denote the append operator for σ, and write $\sigma = \sigma'|\sigma_1$ to indicate that σ_1 is the topmost element of σ.

The parser also uses a **buffer** to store the portion of the input string still to be processed. We represent the buffer as an ordered sequence $\beta = [i, \ldots, n]$ of nodes from V_w, with i the first element of the buffer. In this way β always encodes a (non-necessarily proper) suffix of w. We denote the empty buffer as $\beta = []$. Sometimes we use the vertical bar to denote the append operator for β, and write $\beta = i|\beta'$ to indicate that i is the first token of β; consequently, we have $\beta' = [i+1, \ldots, n]$.

When processing w, the parser reaches several states, technically called configurations. A **configuration** of the parser relative to w is a triple $c = (\sigma, \beta, A)$, where σ and β are a stack and a buffer, respectively, and $A \subseteq V_w \times V_w$ is a set of arcs. The **initial** configuration for w is $([], [0, \ldots, n], \emptyset)$. For the purpose of this article, a configuration is **final** if it has the form $([0], [], A)$, and in a final configuration arc set A always defines a dependency tree for w.

The core of a transition-based parser is the set of its transitions, which are specific to each family of parsers. A **transition** is a binary relation defined over the set of configurations of the parser. We use symbol $\vdash$ to denote the union of all transition relations of a parser.

A **computation** of the parser on w is a sequence $c_0, \ldots, c_m$, $m \in \mathbb{N}_0$, of configurations (defined relative to w) such that $c_{i-1} \vdash c_i$ for each $i \in [1, m]$. We also use the reflexive and transitive closure relation $\vdash^*$ to represent computations. A computation is called **complete** whenever c_0 is initial and c_m is final. In this way, a complete computation is uniquely associated with a dependency tree for w.

2.3 Arc-Standard Parser

The arc-standard model uses the three types of transitions formally specified in Figure 1

$$(\sigma, i|\beta, A) \vdash_{\mathsf{sh}} (\sigma|i, \beta, A)$$
$$(\sigma|i|j, \beta, A) \vdash_{\mathsf{la}} (\sigma|j, \beta, A \cup \{j \rightarrow i\})$$
$$(\sigma|i|j, \beta, A) \vdash_{\mathsf{ra}} (\sigma|i, \beta, A \cup \{i \rightarrow j\})$$

Figure 1: Transitions in the arc-standard model.

- Shift (sh) removes the first node in the buffer and pushes it into the stack;
- Left-Arc (la) creates a new arc with the topmost node on the stack as the head and the second-topmost node as the dependent, and removes the second-topmost node from the stack;
- Right-Arc (ra) is symmetric to la in that it creates an arc with the second-topmost node as the head and the topmost node as the dependent, and removes the topmost node.

Notation We sometimes use the functional notation for a transition $\tau \in \{\mathsf{sh}, \mathsf{la}, \mathsf{ra}\}$, and write $\tau(c) = c'$ in place of $c \vdash_\tau c'$. Naturally, sh applies only when the buffer is not empty, and la,ra require two elements on the stack. We denote by $\mathsf{valid}(c)$ the set of valid transitions in a given configuration.

2.4 Arc Decomposition

Goldberg and Nivre (2013) show how to derive dynamic oracles for any transition-based parser which has the arc decomposition property, defined below. They also show that the arc-standard parser is not arc-decomposable.

For a configuration c, we write A_c to denote the associated set of arcs. A transition-based parser is **arc-decomposable** if, for every configuration c and for every set of arcs A that can be extended to a projective tree, we have

$$\forall(i \rightarrow j) \in A, \exists c'[c \vdash^* c' \wedge (i \rightarrow j) \in A_{c'}] \Rightarrow \exists c''[c \vdash^* c'' \wedge A \subseteq A_{c''}] \,.$$

In words, if each arc in A is individually derivable from c, then the set A in its entirety can be derived from c as well. The arc decomposition property is useful for deriving dynamic oracles because it is relatively easy to investigate derivability for single arcs and then, using this property, draw conclusions about the number of gold-arcs that are simultaneously derivable from the given configuration.

Unfortunately, the arc-standard parser is not arc-decomposable. To see why, consider a configuration with stack $\sigma = [i, j, k]$. Consider also arc set $A = \{(i, j), (i, k)\}$. The arc (i, j) can be derived through the transition sequence ra, ra, and the arc (i, k) can be derived through the alternative transition sequence la, ra. Yet, it is easy to see that a configuration containing both arcs cannot be reached.

As we cannot rely on the arc decomposition property, in order to derive a dynamic oracle for the arc-standard model we need to develop more sophisticated techniques which take into account the interaction among the applied transitions.

3 Configuration Loss and Dynamic Oracles

We aim to derive a dynamic oracle for the arc-standard (and related) system. This is a function that takes a configuration c and a gold tree t_G and returns a set of transitions that are "optimal" for c with respect to t_G. As already mentioned in the introduction, a dynamic oracle can be used to improve training of greedy transition-based parsers. In this section we provide a formal definition for a dynamic oracle.

Let t_1 and t_2 be two dependency trees over the same string w, with arc sets A_1 and A_2, respectively. We define the **loss** of t_1 with respect to t_2 as

$$\mathcal{L}(t_1, t_2) = |A_1 \setminus A_2| \,. \tag{1}$$

Note that $\mathcal{L}(t_1, t_2) = \mathcal{L}(t_2, t_1)$, since $|A_1| = |A_2|$. Furthermore $\mathcal{L}(t_1, t_2) = 0$ if and only if t_1 and t_2 are the same tree.

Let c be a configuration of our parser relative to input string w. We write $\mathcal{D}(c)$ to denote the set of all dependency trees that can be obtained in a computation of the form $c \vdash^* c_f$, where c_f is some final configuration. We extend the loss function in (1) to configurations by letting

$$\mathcal{L}(c, t_2) = \min_{t_1 \in \mathcal{D}(c)} \mathcal{L}(t_1, t_2) \,. \tag{2}$$

Assume some reference (desired) dependency tree t_G for w, which we call the **gold** tree. Quantity $\mathcal{L}(c, t_G)$ can be used to compute a dynamic oracle relating a parser configuration c to a set of optimal actions by setting

$$\mathsf{oracle}(c, t_G) = \{\tau \mid \mathcal{L}(\tau(c), t_G) - \mathcal{L}(c, t_G) = 0\} \,. \tag{3}$$

We therefore need to develop an algorithm for computing (2). We will do this first for the arc-standard parser, and then for an extension of this model.

Notation We also apply the loss function $\mathcal{L}(t, t_G)$ in (1) when t is a dependency tree for a substring of w. In this case the nodes of t are a subset of the nodes of t_G, and $\mathcal{L}(t, t_G)$ provides a count of the nodes of t that are assigned a wrong head node, when t_G is considered as the reference tree.

4 Main Algorithm

Throughout this section we assume an arc-standard parser. Our algorithm takes as input a projective gold tree t_G and a configuration $c = (\sigma_L, \beta, A)$. We call σ_L the **left stack**, in contrast with a right stack whose construction is specified below.

4.1 Basic Idea

The algorithm consists of two steps. Informally, in the first step we compute the largest subtrees, called here tree fragments, of the gold tree t_G that have their span entirely included in the buffer β. The root nodes of these tree fragments are then arranged into a stack data structure, according to the order in which they appear in β and with the leftmost root in β being the topmost element of the stack. We call this structure the right stack σ_R. Intuitively, σ_R can be viewed as the result of pre-computing β by applying all sequences of transitions that match t_G and that can be performed independently of the stack in the input configuration c, that is, σ_L.

In the second step of the algorithm we use dynamic programming techniques to simulate all computations of the arc-standard parser starting in a configuration with stack σ_L and with a buffer consisting of σ_R, with the topmost token of σ_R being the first token of the buffer. As we will see later, the search space defined by these computations includes the dependency trees for w that are reachable from the input configuration c and that have minimum loss. We then perform a Viterbi search to pick up such value.

The second step is very similar to standard implementations of the CKY parser for context-free grammars (Hopcroft and Ullman, 1979), running on an input string obtained as the concatenation of σ_L and σ_R. The main difference is that we restrict ourselves to parse only those constituents in $\sigma_L\sigma_R$ that dominate the topmost element of σ_L (the rightmost element, if σ_L is viewed as a string). In this way, we account for the additional constraint that we visit only those configurations of the arc-standard parser that can be reached from the input configuration c. For instance, this excludes the reduction of two nodes in σ_L that are not at the two topmost positions. This would also exclude the reduction of two nodes in σ_R: this is correct, since the associated tree fragments have been chosen as the largest such fragments in β.

The above intuitive explanation will be made mathematically precise in §5, where the notion of linear dependency tree is introduced.

4.2 Construction of the Right Stack

In the first step we process β and construct a stack σ_R, which we call the **right stack** associated with c and t_G. Each node of σ_R is the root of a tree t which satisfies the following properties

- t is a tree fragment of the gold tree t_G having span entirely included in the buffer β;
- t is **bottom-up complete** for t_G, meaning that for each node i of t different from t's root, the dependents of i in t_G cannot be in σ_L;
- t is **maximal** for t_G, meaning that every supertree of t in t_G violates the above conditions.

The stack σ_R is incrementally constructed by processig β from left to right. Each node i is copied into σ_R if it satisfies any of the following conditions

- the parent node of i in t_G is not in β;
- some dependent of i in t_G is in σ_L or has already been inserted in σ_R.

It is not difficult to see that the nodes in σ_R are the roots of tree fragments of t_G that satisfy the condition of bottom-up completeness and the condition of maximality defined above.

4.3 Computation of Configuration Loss

We start with some notation. Let $\ell_L = |\sigma_L|$ and $\ell_R = |\sigma_R|$. We write $\sigma_L[i]$ to denote the i-th element of σ_L and $t(\sigma_L[i])$ to denote the corresponding tree fragment; $\sigma_R[i]$ and $t(\sigma_R[i])$ have a similar meaning. In order to simplify the specification of the algorithm, we assume below that $\sigma_L[1] = \sigma_R[1]$.

Algorithm 1 Computation of the loss function for the arc-standard parser

1: $\mathcal{T}[1,1](\sigma_L[1]) \leftarrow \mathcal{L}(t(\sigma_L[1]), t_G)$
2: **for** $d \leftarrow 1$ **to** $\ell_L + \ell_R - 1$ **do** ▷ d is the index of a sub-anti-diagonal
3:   **for** $j \leftarrow \max\{1, d - \ell_L + 1\}$ **to** $\min\{d, \ell_R\}$ **do** ▷ j is the column index
4:     $i \leftarrow d - j + 1$ ▷ i is the row index
5:     **if** $i < \ell_L$ **then** ▷ expand to the left
6:       **for each** $h \in \Delta_{i,j}$ **do**
7:         $\mathcal{T}[i+1,j](h) \leftarrow \min\{\mathcal{T}[i+1,j](h),\ \mathcal{T}[i,j](h) + \delta_G(h \rightarrow \sigma_L[i+1])\}$
8:         $\mathcal{T}[i+1,j](\sigma_L[i+1]) \leftarrow \min\{\mathcal{T}[i+1,j](\sigma_L[i+1]),\ \mathcal{T}[i,j](h) + \delta_G(\sigma_L[i+1] \rightarrow h)\}$
9:     **if** $j < \ell_R$ **then** ▷ expand to the right
10:       **for each** $h \in \Delta_{i,j}$ **do**
11:         $\mathcal{T}[i,j+1](h) \leftarrow \min\{\mathcal{T}[i,j+1](h),\ \mathcal{T}[i,j](h) + \delta_G(h \rightarrow \sigma_R[j+1])\}$
12:         $\mathcal{T}[i,j+1](\sigma_R[j+1]) \leftarrow \min\{\mathcal{T}[i,j+1](\sigma_R[j+1]), \mathcal{T}[i,j](h) + \delta_G(\sigma_R[j+1] \rightarrow h)\}$
13: **return** $\mathcal{T}[\ell_L, \ell_R](0) + \sum_{i \in [1,\ell_L]} \mathcal{L}(t(\sigma_L[i]), t_G)$

Therefore the elements of σ_R which have been constructed in §4.2 are $\sigma_R[i]$, $i \in [2, \ell_R]$.

Algorithm 1 uses a two-dimensional array $\mathcal{T}$ of size $\ell_L \times \ell_R$, where each entry $\mathcal{T}[i,j]$ is an association list from integers to integers. An entry $\mathcal{T}[i,j](h)$ stores the minimum loss among dependency trees rooted at h that can be obtained by running the parser on the first i elements of stack σ_L and the first j elements of buffer σ_R. More precisely, let

$$\Delta_{i,j} = \{\sigma_L[k] \mid k \in [1,i]\} \cup \{\sigma_R[k] \mid k \in [1,j]\}\ . \quad (4)$$

For each $h \in \Delta_{i,j}$, the entry $\mathcal{T}[i,j](h)$ is the minimum loss among all dependency trees defined as above and with root h. We also assume that $\mathcal{T}[i,j](h)$ is initialized to $+\infty$ (not reported in the algorithm).

Algorithm 1 starts at the top-left corner of $\mathcal{T}$, visiting each individual sub-anti-diagonal of $\mathcal{T}$ in ascending order, and eventually reaching the bottom-right corner of the array. For each entry $\mathcal{T}[i,j]$, the left expansion is considered (lines 5 to 8) by combining with tree fragment $\sigma_L[i+1]$, through a left or a right arc reduction. This results in the update of $\mathcal{T}[i+1,j](h)$, for each $h \in \Delta_{i+1,j}$, whenever a smaller value of the loss is achieved for a tree with root h. The Kronecker-like function used at line 8 provides the contribution of each single arc to the loss of the current tree. Denoting with A_G the set of arcs of t_G, such a function is defined as

$$\delta_G(i \rightarrow j) = \begin{cases} 0, & \text{if } (i \rightarrow j) \in A_G; \\ 1, & \text{otherwise.} \end{cases} \quad (5)$$

A symmetrical process is implemented for the right expansion of $\mathcal{T}[i,j]$ through tree fragment $\sigma_R[j+1]$ (lines 9 to 12).

As we will see in the next section, quantity $\mathcal{T}[\ell_L, \ell_R](0)$ is the minimal loss of a tree composed only by arcs that connect nodes in σ_L and σ_R. By summing the loss of all tree fragments $t(\sigma_L[i])$ to the loss in $\mathcal{T}[\ell_L, \ell_R](0)$, at line 13, we obtain the desired result, since the loss of each tree fragment $t(\sigma_R[j])$ is zero.

5 Formal Properties

Throughout this section we let w, t_G, σ_L, σ_R and $c = (\sigma_L, \beta, A)$ be defined as in §4, but we no longer assume that $\sigma_L[1] = \sigma_R[1]$. To simplify the presentation, we sometimes identify the tokens in w with the associated nodes in a dependency tree for w.

5.1 Linear Trees

Algorithm 1 explores all dependency trees that can be reached by an arc-standard parser from configuration c, under the condition that (i) the nodes in the buffer β are pre-computed into tree fragments and collapsed into their root nodes in the right stack σ_R, and (ii) nodes in σ_R cannot be combined together prior to their combination with other nodes in the left stack σ_L. This set of dependency trees is char-

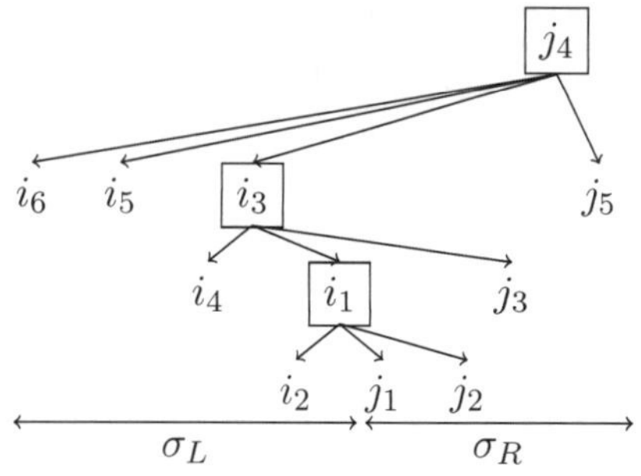

Figure 2: A possible linear tree for string pair (σ_L, σ_R), where $\sigma_L = i_6 i_5 i_4 i_3 i_2 i_1$ and $\sigma_R = j_1 j_2 j_3 j_4 j_5$. The spine of the tree consists of nodes j_4, i_3 and i_1.

acterized here using the notion of linear tree, to be used later in the correctness proof.

Consider two nodes $\sigma_L[i]$ and $\sigma_L[j]$ with $j > i > 1$. An arc-standard parser can construct an arc between $\sigma_L[i]$ and $\sigma_L[j]$, in any direction, only after reaching a configuration in which $\sigma_L[i]$ is at the top of the stack and $\sigma_L[j]$ is at the second topmost position. In such configuration we have that $\sigma_L[i]$ dominates $\sigma_L[1]$. Furthermore, consider nodes $\sigma_R[i]$ and $\sigma_R[j]$ with $j > i \geq 1$. Since we are assuming that tree fragments $t(\sigma_R[i])$ and $t(\sigma_R[j])$ are bottom-up complete and maximal, as defined in §4.2, we allow the construction of an arc between $\sigma_R[i]$ and $\sigma_R[j]$, in any direction, only after reaching a configuration in which $\sigma_R[i]$ dominates node $\sigma_L[1]$.

The dependency trees satisfying the restrictions above are captured by the following definition. A **linear tree** over (σ_L, σ_R) is a projective dependency tree t for string $\sigma_L\sigma_R$ satisfying both of the additional conditions reported below. The path from t's root to node $\sigma_L[1]$ is called the **spine** of t.

- Every node of t not in the spine is a dependent of some node in the spine.
- For each arc $i \rightarrow j$ in t with j in the spine, no dependent of i can be placed in between i and j within string $\sigma_L\sigma_R$.

An example of a linear tree is depicted in Figure 2. Observe that the second condition above forbids the reduction of two nodes i and j, in case none of these dominates node $\sigma_L[1]$. For instance, the ra reduction of nodes i_3 and i_2 would result in arc $i_3 \rightarrow i_2$ replacing arc $i_1 \rightarrow i_2$ in Figure 2. The new dependency tree is not linear, because of a violation of the second condition above. Similarly, the la reduction of nodes j_3 and j_4 would result in arc $j_4 \rightarrow j_3$ replacing arc $i_3 \rightarrow j_3$ in Figure 2, again a violation of the second condition above.

Lemma 1 *Any tree $t \in \mathcal{D}(c)$ can be decomposed into trees $t(\sigma_L[i])$, $i \in [1, \ell_L]$, trees t_j, $j \in [1, q]$ and $q \geq 1$, and a linear tree t_l over $(\sigma_L, \sigma_{R,t})$, where $\sigma_{R,t} = r_1 \cdots r_q$ and each r_j is the root node of t_j.* □

PROOF (SKETCH) Trees $t(\sigma_L[i])$ are common to every tree in $\mathcal{D}(c)$, since the arc-standard model can not undo the arcs already built in the current configuration c. Similar to the construction in §4.2 of the right stack σ_R from t_G, we let t_j, $j \in [1, q]$, be tree fragments of t that cover only nodes associated with the tokens in the buffer β and that are bottom-up complete and maximal for t. These trees are indexed according to their left to right order in β. Finally, t_l is implicitly defined by all arcs of t that are not in trees $t(\sigma_L[i])$ and t_j. It is not difficult to see that t_l has a spine ending with node $\sigma_L[1]$ and is a linear tree over $(\sigma_L, \sigma_{R,t})$. ■

5.2 Correctness

Our proof of correctness for Algorithm 1 is based on a specific dependency tree t^* for w, which we define below. Let $S_L = \{\sigma_L[i] \mid i \in [1, \ell_L]\}$ and let D_L be the set of nodes that are descendants of some node in S_L. Similarly, let $S_R = \{\sigma_R[i] \mid i \in [1, \ell_R]\}$ and let D_R be the set of descendants of nodes in S_R. Note that sets S_L, S_R, D_L and D_R provide a partition of V_w.

We choose any linear tree t_l^* over (σ_L, σ_R) having root 0, such that $\mathcal{L}(t_l^*, t_G) = \min_t \mathcal{L}(t, t_G)$, where t ranges over all possible linear trees over (σ_L, σ_R) with root 0. Tree t^* consists of the set of nodes V_w and the set of arcs obtained as the union of the set of arcs of t_l^* and the set of arcs of all trees $t(\sigma_L[i])$, $i \in [1, \ell_L]$, and $t(\sigma_R[j])$, $j \in [1, \ell_R]$.

Lemma 2 $t^* \in \mathcal{D}(c)$. □

PROOF (SKETCH) All tree fragments $t(\sigma_L[i])$ have already been parsed and are available in the stack associated with c. Each tree fragment $t(\sigma_R[j])$ can later be constructed in the computation, when a configuration c' is reached with the relevant segment of w at the start of the buffer. Note also that parsing of $t(\sigma_R[j])$ can be done in a way that does not depend on the content of the stack in c'.

Finally, the parsing of the tree fragments $t(\sigma_R[j])$ is interleaved with the construction of the arcs from the linear tree t_l^*, which are all of the form $(i \to j)$ with $i, j \in (S_L \cup S_R)$. More precisely, if $(i \to j)$ is an arc from t_l^*, at some point in the computation nodes i and j will become available at the two topmost positions in the stack. This follows from the second condition in the definition of linear tree. ■

We now show that tree t^* is "optimal" within the set $\mathcal{D}(c)$ and with respect to t_G.

Lemma 3 $\mathcal{L}(t^*, t_G) = \mathcal{L}(c, t_G)$. □

PROOF Consider an arbitrary tree $t \in \mathcal{D}(c)$. Assume the decomposition of t defined in the proof of Lemma 1, through trees $t(\sigma_L[i])$, $i \in [1, \ell_L]$, trees t_j, $j \in [1, q]$, and linear tree t_l over $(\sigma_L, \sigma_{R,t})$.

Recall that an arc $i \to j$ denotes an ordered pair (i, j). Let us consider the following partition for the set of arcs of any dependency tree for w

$$\begin{aligned} A_1 &= (S_L \cup D_L) \times D_L \,, \\ A_2 &= (S_R \cup D_R) \times D_R \,, \\ A_3 &= (V_w \times V_w) \setminus (A_1 \cup A_2) \,. \end{aligned}$$

In what follows, we compare the losses $\mathcal{L}(t, t_G)$ and $\mathcal{L}(t^*, t_G)$ by separately looking into the contribution to such quantities due to the arcs in A_1, A_2 and A_3.

Note that the arcs of trees $t(\sigma_L[i])$ are all in A_1, the arcs of trees $t(\sigma_R[j])$ are all in A_2, and the arcs of tree t_l^* are all in A_3. Since t and t^* share trees $t(\sigma_L[i])$, when restricted to arcs in A_1 quantities $\mathcal{L}(t, t_G)$ and $\mathcal{L}(t^*, t_G)$ are the same. When restricted to arcs in A_2, quantity $\mathcal{L}(t^*, t_G)$ is zero, by construction of the trees $t(\sigma_R[j])$. Thus $\mathcal{L}(t, t_G)$ can not be smaller than $\mathcal{L}(t^*, t_G)$ for these arcs. The difficult part is the comparison of the contribution to $\mathcal{L}(t, t_G)$ and $\mathcal{L}(t^*, t_G)$ due to the arcs in A_3. We deal with this below.

Let $A_{S,G}$ be the set of all arcs from t_G that are also in set $(S_L \times S_R) \cup (S_R \times S_L)$. In words, $A_{S,G}$ represents gold arcs connecting nodes in S_L and nodes in S_R, in any direction. Within tree t, these arcs can only be found in the t_l component, since nodes in S_L are all placed within the spine of t_l, or else at the left of that spine.

Let us consider an arc $(j \to i) \in A_{S,G}$ with $j \in S_L$ and $i \in S_R$, and let us assume that $(j \to i)$ is in t_l^*. If token a_i does not occur in $\sigma_{R,t}$, node i is not in t_l and $(j \to i)$ can not be an arc of t. We then have that $(j \to i)$ contributes one unit to $\mathcal{L}(t, t_G)$ but does not contribute to $\mathcal{L}(t^*, t_G)$. Similarly, let $(i \to j) \in A_{S,G}$ be such that $i \in S_R$ and $j \in S_L$, and assume that $(i \to j)$ is in t_l^*. If token a_i does not occur in $\sigma_{R,t}$, arc $(i \to j)$ can not be in t. We then have that $(i \to j)$ contributes one unit to $\mathcal{L}(t, t_G)$ but does not contribute to $\mathcal{L}(t^*, t_G)$.

Intuitively, the above observations mean that the winning strategy for trees in $\mathcal{D}(c)$ is to move nodes from S_R as much as possible into the linear tree component t_l, in order to make it possible for these nodes to connect to nodes in S_L, in any direction. In this case, arcs from A_3 will also move into the linear tree component of a tree in $\mathcal{D}(c)$, as it happens in the case of t^*. We thus conclude that, when restricted to the set of arcs in A_3, quantity $\mathcal{L}(t, t_G)$ is not smaller than $\mathcal{L}(t^*, t_G)$, because stack σ_R has at least as many tokens corresponding to nodes in S_R as stack $\sigma_{R,t}$, and because t_l^* has the minimum loss among all the linear trees over (σ_L, σ_R).

Putting all of the above observations together, we conclude that $\mathcal{L}(t, t_G)$ can not be smaller than $\mathcal{L}(t^*, t_G)$. This concludes the proof, since t has been arbitrarily chosen in $\mathcal{D}(c)$. ■

Theorem 1 *Algorithm 1 computes* $\mathcal{L}(c, t_G)$. □

PROOF (SKETCH) Algorithm 1 implements a Viterbi search for trees with smallest loss among all linear trees over (σ_L, σ_R). Thus $\mathcal{T}[\ell_L, \ell_R](0) = \mathcal{L}(t_l^*, t_G)$. The loss of the tree fragments $t(\sigma_R[j])$ is 0 and the loss of the tree fragments $t(\sigma_L[i])$ is added at line 13 in the algorithm. Thus the algorithm returns $\mathcal{L}(t^*, t_G)$, and the statement follows from Lemma 2 and Lemma 3. ■

5.3 Computational Analysis

Following §4.2, the right stack σ_R can be easily constructed in time $\mathcal{O}(n)$, n the length of the input string. We now analyze Algorithm 1. For each entry $\mathcal{T}[i, j]$ and for each $h \in \Delta_{i,j}$, we update $\mathcal{T}[i, j](h)$ a number of times bounded by a constant which does not depend on the input. Each updating can be computed in constant time as well. We thus conclude that Algorithm 1 runs in time $\mathcal{O}(\ell_L \cdot \ell_R \cdot (\ell_L + \ell_R))$. Quantity $\ell_L + \ell_R$ is bounded by n, but in practice the former is significantly smaller. When measured over the sentences in the Penn

Treebank, the average value of $\frac{\ell_L+\ell_R}{n}$ is 0.29. In terms of runtime, training is 2.3 times slower when using our oracle instead of a static oracle.

6 Extension to the LR-Spine Parser

In this section we consider the transition-based parser proposed by Sartorio et al. (2013), called here the LR-spine parser. This parser is not arc-decomposable: the same example reported in §2.4 can be used to show this fact. We therefore extend to the LR-spine parser the algorithm developed in §4.

6.1 The LR-Spine Parser

Let t be a dependency tree. The **left spine** of t is an ordered sequence $\langle i_1, \ldots, i_p \rangle$, $p \geq 1$, consisting of all nodes in a descending path from the root of t taking the leftmost child node at each step. The **right spine** of t is defined symmetrically. We use $\oplus$ to denote sequence concatenation.

In the LR-spine parser each stack element $\sigma[i]$ denotes a partially built subtree $t(\sigma[i])$ and is represented by a pair (ls_i, rs_i), with ls_i and rs_i the left and the right spine, respectively, of $t(\sigma[i])$. We write $ls_i[k]$ ($rs_i[k]$) to represent the k-th element of ls_i (rs_i, respectively). We also write $r(\sigma[i])$ to denote the root of $t(\sigma[i])$, so that $r(\sigma[i]) = ls_i[1] = rs_i[1]$.

Informally, the LR-spine parser uses the same transition typologies as the arc-standard parser. However, an arc $(h \rightarrow d)$ can now be created with the head node h chosen from any node in the spine of the involved tree. The transition types of the LR-spine parser are defined as follows.

- Shift (sh) removes the first node from the buffer and pushes into the stack a new element, consisting of the left and right spines of the associated tree

$$(\sigma, i|\beta, A) \vdash_{\mathsf{sh}} (\sigma|(\langle i \rangle, \langle i \rangle), \beta, A) .$$

- Left-Arc k (la_k) creates a new arc $h \rightarrow d$ from the k-th node in the left spine of the topmost tree in the stack to the head of the second element in the stack. Furthermore, the two topmost stack elements are replaced by a new element associated with the resulting tree

$$(\sigma'|\sigma[2]|\sigma[1], \beta, A) \vdash_{\mathsf{la}_k} (\sigma'|\sigma_{\mathsf{la}_k}, \beta, A \cup \{h \rightarrow d\})$$

where we have set $h = ls_1[k]$, $d = r(\sigma[2])$ and $\sigma_{\mathsf{la}_k} = (\langle ls_1[1], \ldots, ls_1[k] \rangle \oplus ls_2, rs_1)$.

- Right-Arc k (ra_k for short) is defined symmetrically with respect to la_k

$$(\sigma'|\sigma[2]|\sigma[1], \beta, A) \vdash_{\mathsf{ra}_k} (\sigma'|\sigma_{\mathsf{ra}_k}, \beta, A \cup \{h \rightarrow d\})$$

where we have set $h = rs_2[k]$, $d = r(\sigma[1])$ and $\sigma_{\mathsf{ra}_k} = (ls_2, \langle rs_2[1], \ldots, rs_2[k] \rangle \oplus rs_1)$.

Note that, at each configuration in the LR-spine parser, there are $|ls_1|$ possible la_k transitions, one for each choice of a node in the left spine of $t(\sigma[1])$; similarly, there are $|rs_2|$ possible ra_k transitions, one for each choice of a node in the right spine of $t(\sigma[2])$.

6.2 Configuration Loss

We only provide an informal description of the extended algorithm here, since it is very similar to the algorithm in §4.

In the first phase we use the procedure of §4.2 for the construction of the right stack σ_R, considering only the roots of elements in σ_L and ignoring the rest of the spines. The only difference is that each element $\sigma_R[j]$ is now a pair of spines $(ls_{R,j}, rs_{R,j})$. Since tree fragment $t(\sigma_R[j])$ is bottom-up complete (see §4.1), we now restrict the search space in such a way that only the root node $r(\sigma_R[j])$ can take dependents. This is done by setting $ls_{R,j} = rs_{R,j} = \langle r(\sigma_R[j]) \rangle$ for each $j \in [1, \ell_R]$. In order to simplify the presentation we also assume $\sigma_R[1] = \sigma_L[1]$, as done in §4.3.

In the second phase we compute the loss of an input configuration using a two-dimensional array $\mathcal{T}$, defined as in §4.3. However, because of the way transitions are defined in the LR-spine parser, we now need to distinguish tree fragments not only on the basis of their roots, but also on the basis of their left and right spines. Accordingly, we define each entry $\mathcal{T}[i, j]$ as an association list with keys of the form (ls, rs). More specifically, $\mathcal{T}[i, j](ls, rs)$ is the minimum loss of a tree with left and right spines ls and rs, respectively, that can be obtained by running the parser on the first i elements of stack σ_L and the first j elements of buffer σ_R.

We follow the main idea of Algorithm 1 and expand each tree in $\mathcal{T}[i, j]$ at its left side, by combining with tree fragment $t(\sigma_L[i+1])$, and at its right side, by combining with tree fragment $t(\sigma_R[j+1])$.

Tree combination deserves some more detailed discussion, reported below.

We consider the combination of a tree t_a from $\mathcal{T}[i,j]$ and tree $t(\sigma_L[i+1])$ by means of a left-arc transition. All other cases are treated symmetrically. Let (ls_a, rs_a) be the spine pair of t_a, so that the loss of t_a is stored in $\mathcal{T}[i,j](ls_a, rs_a)$. Let also (ls_b, rs_b) be the spine pair of $t(\sigma_L[i+1])$. In case there exists a gold arc in t_G connecting a node from ls_a to $r(\sigma_L[i+1])$, we choose the transition la_k, $k \in [1, |ls_a|]$, that creates such arc. In case such gold arc does not exists, we choose the transition la_k with the maximum possible value of k, that is, $k = |ls_a|$. We therefore explore only one of the several possible ways of combining these two trees by means of a left-arc transition.

We remark that the above strategy is safe. In fact, in case the gold arc exists, no other gold arc can ever involve the nodes of ls_a eliminated by la_k (see the definition in §6.1), because arcs can not cross each other. In case the gold arc does not exist, our choice of $k = |ls_a|$ guarantees that we do not eliminate any element from ls_a.

Once a transition la_k is chosen, as described above, the reduction is performed and the spine pair (ls, rs) for the resulting tree is computed from (ls_a, rs_a) and (ls_b, rs_b), as defined in §6.1. At the same time, the loss of the resulting tree is computed, on the basis of the loss $\mathcal{T}[i,j](ls_a, rs_a)$, the loss of tree $t(\sigma_L[i+1])$, and a Kronecker-like function defined below. This loss is then used to update $\mathcal{T}[i+1,j](ls, rs)$.

Let t_a and t_b be two trees that must be combined in such a way that t_b becomes the dependent of some node in one of the two spines of t_a. Let also $p_a = (ls_a, rs_a)$ and $p_b = (ls_b, rs_b)$ be spine pairs for t_a and t_b, respectively. Recall that A_G is the set of arcs of t_G. The new Kronecker-like function for the computation of the loss is defined as

$$\delta_G(p_a, p_b) = \begin{cases} 0, & \text{if } r(t_a) < r(t_b) \wedge \\ & \quad \exists k[(rs_a^k \rightarrow r(t_b)) \in A_G]; \\ 0, & \text{if } r(t_a) > r(t_b) \wedge \\ & \quad \exists k[(ls_a^k \rightarrow r(t_b)) \in A_G]; \\ 1, & \text{otherwise.} \end{cases}$$

6.3 Efficiency Improvement

The algorithm in §6.2 has an exponential behaviour. To see why, consider trees in $\mathcal{T}[i,j]$. These trees are produced by the combination of trees in $\mathcal{T}[i-1,j]$ with tree $t(\sigma_L[i])$, or by the combination of trees in $\mathcal{T}[i,j-1]$ with tree $t(\sigma_R[j])$. Since each combination involves either a left-arc or a right-arc transition, we obtain a recursive relation that resolves into a number of trees in $\mathcal{T}[i,j]$ bounded by 4^{i+j-2}.

We introduce now two restrictions to the search space of our extended algorithm that result in a huge computational saving. For a spine s, we write $\mathcal{N}(s)$ to denote the set of all nodes in s. We also let $\Delta_{i,j}$ be the set of all pairs (ls, rs) such that $\mathcal{T}[i,j](ls, rs) \neq +\infty$.

- Every time a new pair (ls, rs) is created in $\Delta[i,j]$, we remove from ls all nodes different from the root that do not have gold dependents in $\{r(\sigma_L[k]) \mid k < i\}$, and we remove from rs all nodes different from the root that do not have gold dependents in $\{r(\sigma_R[k]) \mid k > j\}$.
- A pair $p_a = (ls_a, rs_a)$ is removed from $\Delta[i,j]$ if there exists a pair $p_b = (ls_b, rs_b)$ in $\Delta[i,j]$ with the same root node as p_a and with $(ls_a, rs_a) \neq (ls_b, rs_b)$, such that $\mathcal{N}(ls_a) \subseteq \mathcal{N}(ls_b)$, $\mathcal{N}(rs_a) \subseteq \mathcal{N}(rs_b)$, and $\mathcal{T}[i,j](p_a) \geq \mathcal{T}[i,j](p_b)$.

The first restriction above reduces the size of a spine by eliminating a node if it is irrelevant for the computation of the loss of the associated tree. The second restriction eliminates a tree t_a if there is a tree t_b with smaller loss than t_a, such that in the computations of the parser t_b provides exactly the same context as t_a. It is not difficult to see that the above restrictions do not affect the correctness of the algorithm, since they always leave in our search space some tree that has optimal loss.

A mathematical analysis of the computational complexity of the extended algorithm is quite involved. In Figure 3, we plot the worst case size of $\mathcal{T}[i,j]$ for each value of $j+i-1$, computed over all configurations visited in the training phase (see §7). We see that $|\mathcal{T}[i,j]|$ grows linearly with $j+i-1$, leading to the same space requirements of Algorithm 1. Empirically, training with the dynamic

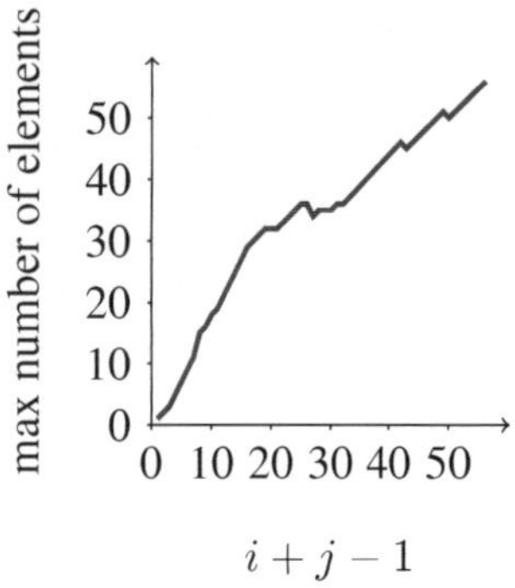

Figure 3: Empirical worst case size of $\mathcal{T}[i, j]$ for each value of $i + j - 1$ as measured on the Penn Treebank corpus.

Algorithm 2 Online training for greedy transition-based parsers

---

$\mathbf{w} \leftarrow 0$
for k iterations **do**
  shuffle(corpus)
  for sentence w and gold tree t_G in corpus **do**
    $c \leftarrow \textsc{Initial}(w)$
    while not $\textsc{Final}(c)$ **do**
      $\tau_p \leftarrow \text{argmax}_{\tau \in \mathsf{valid}(c)} \mathbf{w} \cdot \phi(c, \tau)$
      $\tau_o \leftarrow \text{argmax}_{\tau \in \mathsf{oracle}(c, t_G)} \mathbf{w} \cdot \phi(c, \tau)$
      if $\tau_p \notin \mathsf{oracle}(c, t_G)$ **then**
        $\mathbf{w} \leftarrow \mathbf{w} + \phi(c, \tau_o) - \phi(c, \tau_p)$
      $\tau \leftarrow \begin{cases} \tau_p & \text{if } \textsc{Explore} \\ \tau_o & \text{otherwise} \end{cases}$
      $c \leftarrow \tau(c)$
return *averaged*($\mathbf{w}$)

---

oracle is only about 8 times slower than training with the oracle of Sartorio et al. (2013) without exploring incorrect configurations.

7 Training

We follow the training procedure suggested by Goldberg and Nivre (2013), as described in Algorithm 2. The algorithm performs online learning using the averaged perceptron algorithm. A weight vector **w** (initialized to 0) is used to score the valid transitions in each configuration based on a feature representation ϕ, and the highest scoring transition τ_p is predicted. If the predicted transition is not optimal according to the oracle, the weights **w** are updated away from the predicted transition and towards the highest scoring oracle transition τ_o. The parser then moves to the next configuration, by taking either the predicted or the oracle transition. In the "error exploration" mode (EXPLORE is true), the parser follows the predicted transition, and otherwise the parser follows the oracle transition. Note that the error exploration mode requires the completeness property of a dynamic oracle.

We consider three training conditions: *static*, in which the oracle is deterministic (returning a single canonical transition for each configuration) and no error exploration is performed; *nondet*, in which we use a nondeterministic partial oracle (Sartorio et al., 2013), but do not perform error exploration; and *explore* in which we use the dynamic oracle and perform error exploration. The *static* setup mirrors the way greedy parsers are traditionally trained. The *nondet* setup allows the training procedure to choose which transition to take in case of spurious ambiguities. The *explore* setup increases the configuration space explored by the parser during training, by exposing the training procedure to non-optimal configurations that are likely to occur during parsing, together with the optimal transitions to take in these configurations. It was shown by Goldberg and Nivre (2012; 2013) that the *nondet* setup outperforms the *static* setup, and that the *explore* setup outperforms the *nondet* setup.

8 Experimental Evaluation

Datasets Performance evaluation is carried out on CoNLL 2007 multilingual dataset, as well as on the Penn Treebank (PTB) (Marcus et al., 1993) converted to Stanford basic dependencies (De Marneffe et al., 2006). For the CoNLL datasets we use gold part-of-speech tags, while for the PTB we use automatically assigned tags. As usual, the PTB parser is trained on sections 2-21 and tested on section 23.

Setup We train labeled versions of the arc-standard (std) and LR-spine (lrs) parsers under the *static*, *nondet* and *explore* setups, as defined in §7. In the *nondet* setup we use a nondeterministic partial oracle and in the *explore* setup we use the nondeterministic complete oracles we present in this paper. In the *static* setup we resolve oracle ambiguities and choose a canonic transition sequence by attaching arcs as soon as possible. In the *explore* setup,

parser:train	Arabic	Basque	Catalan	Chinese	Czech	English	Greek	Hungarian	Italian	Turkish	PTB
						UAS					
std:static	81.39	75.37	90.32	85.17	78.90	85.69	79.90	77.67	82.98	77.04	89.86
std:nondet	81.33	74.82	90.75	84.80	79.92	86.89	81.19	77.51	84.15	76.85	90.56
std:explore	82.56	74.39	90.95	85.65	81.01	87.70	81.85	78.72	84.37	77.21	90.92
lrs:static	81.67	76.07	91.47	84.24	77.93	86.36	79.43	76.56	84.64	77.00	90.33
lrs:nondet	83.14	75.53	91.31	84.98	80.03	88.38	81.12	76.98	85.29	77.63	91.18
lrs:explore	84.54	75.82	91.92	86.72	81.19	89.37	81.78	77.48	85.38	78.61	91.77
						LAS					
std:static	71.93	65.64	84.90	80.35	71.39	84.60	72.25	67.66	78.77	65.90	87.56
std:nondet	71.09	65.28	85.36	80.06	71.47	85.91	73.40	67.77	80.06	65.81	88.30
std:explore	72.89	65.27	85.82	81.28	72.92	86.79	74.22	69.57	80.25	66.71	88.72
lrs:static	72.24	66.21	86.02	79.36	70.48	85.38	72.36	66.79	80.38	66.02	88.07
lrs:nondet	72.94	65.66	86.03	80.47	71.32	87.45	73.09	67.70	81.32	67.02	88.96
lrs:explore	74.54	66.91	86.83	82.38	72.72	88.44	74.04	68.76	81.50	68.06	89.53

Table 1: Scores on the CoNLL 2007 dataset (including punctuation, gold parts of speech) and on Penn Tree Bank (excluding punctuation, predicted parts of speech). Label 'std' refers to the arc-standard parser, and 'lrs' refers to the LR-spine parser. Each number is an average over 5 runs with different randomization seeds.

from the first round of training onward, we always follow the predicted transition (EXPLORE is true). For all languages, we deal with non-projectivity by skipping the non-projective sentences during training but not during test. For each parsing system, we use the same feature templates across all languages.[1] The arc-standard models are trained for 15 iterations and the LR-spine models for 30 iterations, after which all the models seem to have converged.

Results In Table 1 we report the labeled (LAS) and unlabeled (UAS) attachment scores. As expected, the LR-spine parsers outperform the arc-standard parsers trained under the same setup. Training with the dynamic oracles is also beneficial: despite the arguable complexity of our proposed oracles, the trends are consistent with those reported by Goldberg and Nivre (2012; 2013). For the arc-standard model we observe that the move from a static to a nondeterministic oracle during training improves the accuracy for most of languages. Making use of the completeness of the dynamic oracle and moving to the error exploring setup further improve results. The only exceptions are Basque, that has a small dataset with more than 20% of non-projective sentences, and Chinese. For Chinese we observe a reduction of accuracy in the *nondet* setup, but an increase in the *explore* setup.

For the LR-spine parser we observe a practically constant increase of performance by moving from the static to the nondeterministic and then to the error exploring setups.

[1]Our complete code, together with the description of the feature templates, is available on the second author's homepage.

9 Conclusions

We presented dynamic oracles, based on dynamic programming, for the arc-standard and the LR-spine parsers. Empirical evaluation on 10 languages showed that, despite the apparent complexity of the oracle calculation procedure, the oracles are still learnable, in the sense that using these oracles in the error exploration training algorithm presented in (Goldberg and Nivre, 2012) considerably improves the accuracy of the trained parsers.

Our algorithm computes a dynamic oracle using dynamic programming to explore a forest of dependency trees that can be reached from a given parser configuration. For the arc-standard parser, the computation takes cubic time in the size of the largest of the left and right input stacks. Dynamic programming for the simulation of arc-standard parsers have been proposed by Kuhlmann et al. (2011). That algorithm could be adapted to compute minimum loss for a given configuration, but the running time is $\mathcal{O}(n^4)$, n the size of the input string: besides being asymptotically slower by one order of magnitude, in practice n is also larger than the stack size above.

Acknowledgments We wish to thank the anonymous reviewers. In particular, we are indebted to one of them for two important technical remarks. The third author has been partially supported by MIUR under project PRIN No. 2010LYA9RH_006.

References

Marie-Catherine De Marneffe, Bill MacCartney, and Christopher D. Manning. 2006. Generating typed dependency parses from phrase structure parses. In *Proceedings of the 5th International Conference on Language Resources and Evaluation (LREC)*, volume 6, pages 449–454.

Yoav Goldberg and Joakim Nivre. 2012. A dynamic oracle for arc-eager dependency parsing. In *Proc. of the 24th COLING*, Mumbai, India.

Yoav Goldberg and Joakim Nivre. 2013. Training deterministic parsers with non-deterministic oracles. *Transactions of the association for Computational Linguistics*, 1.

John E. Hopcroft and Jeffrey D. Ullman. 1979. *Introduction to Automata Theory, Languages and Computation*. Addison-Wesley, Reading, MA.

Liang Huang and Kenji Sagae. 2010. Dynamic programming for linear-time incremental parsing. In *Proceedings of the 48th Annual Meeting of the Association for Computational Linguistics*, July.

Marco Kuhlmann, Carlos Gómez-Rodríguez, and Giorgio Satta. 2011. Dynamic programming algorithms for transition-based dependency parsers. In *Proceedings of the 49th Annual Meeting of the Association for Computational Linguistics: Human Language Technologies*, pages 673–682, Portland, Oregon, USA, June. Association for Computational Linguistics.

Mitchell P. Marcus, Beatrice Santorini, and Mary Ann Marcinkiewicz. 1993. Building a large annotated corpus of english: The penn treebank. *Computational Linguistics*, 19(2):313–330.

Joakim Nivre, Johan Hall, Sandra Kübler, Ryan McDonald, Jens Nilsson, Sebastian Riedel, and Deniz Yuret. 2007. The CoNLL 2007 shared task on dependency parsing. In *Proceedings of EMNLP-CoNLL*.

Joakim Nivre. 2003. An efficient algorithm for projective dependency parsing. In *Proceedings of the Eighth International Workshop on Parsing Technologies (IWPT)*, pages 149–160, Nancy, France.

Joakim Nivre. 2004. Incrementality in deterministic dependency parsing. In *Workshop on Incremental Parsing: Bringing Engineering and Cognition Together*, pages 50–57, Barcelona, Spain.

Joakim Nivre. 2008. Algorithms for deterministic incremental dependency parsing. *Computational Linguistics*, 34(4):513–553.

Francesco Sartorio, Giorgio Satta, and Joakim Nivre. 2013. A transition-based dependency parser using a dynamic parsing strategy. In *Proceedings of the 51st Annual Meeting of the Association for Computational Linguistics (Volume 1: Long Papers)*, pages 135–144, Sofia, Bulgaria, August. Association for Computational Linguistics.

Yue Zhang and Stephen Clark. 2008. A tale of two parsers: Investigating and combining graph-based and transition-based dependency parsing. In *Proceedings of EMNLP*.

Joint Incremental Disfluency Detection and Dependency Parsing

Matthew Honnibal
Department of Computing
Macquarie University
Sydney, Australia
matthew.honnibal@mq.edu.edu.au

Mark Johnson
Department of Computing
Macquarie University
Sydney, Australia
mark.johnson@mq.edu.edu.au

Abstract

We present an incremental dependency parsing model that jointly performs disfluency detection. The model handles speech repairs using a novel non-monotonic transition system, and includes several novel classes of features. For comparison, we evaluated two pipeline systems, using state-of-the-art disfluency detectors. The joint model performed better on both tasks, with a parse accuracy of 90.5% and 84.0% accuracy at disfluency detection. The model runs in expected linear time, and processes over 550 tokens a second.

1 Introduction

Most unscripted speech contains filled pauses (*ums* and *uhs*), and errors that are usually edited on-the-fly by the speaker. Disfluency detection is the task of detecting these infelicities in spoken language transcripts. The task has some immediate value, as disfluencies have been shown to make speech recognition output much more difficult to read (Jones et al., 2003), but has also been motivated as a module in a natural language understanding pipeline, because disfluencies have proven problematic for PCFG parsing models.

Instead of a pipeline approach, we build on recent work in transition-based dependency parsing, to perform the two tasks jointly. There have been two small studies of dependency parsing on unscripted speech, both using entirely greedy parsing strategies, without a direct comparison against a pipeline architecture (Jorgensen, 2007; Rasooli and Tetreault, 2013). We go substantially beyond these pilot studies, and present a system that compares favourably to a pipeline consisting of state-of-the-art components. Our parser largely follows the design of Zhang and Clark (2011). We use a structured averaged perceptron model with beam-search decoding (Collins, 2002). Our feature set is based on Zhang and Clark (2011), and our transition-system is based on the arc-eager system of Nivre (2003).

We extend the transition system with a novel non-monotonic transition, Edit. It allows sentences like '*Pass the pepper uh salt*' to be parsed incrementally, without the need to guess early that *pepper* is disfluent. This is achieved by reprocessing the leftward children of the word Edit marks as disfluent. For instance, if the parser attaches *the* to *pepper*, but subsequently marks *pepper* as disfluent, *the* will be returned to the stack. We also exploit the ease with which the model can incorporate arbitrary features, and design a set of features that capture the 'rough copy' structure of some speech repairs, which motivated the Johnson and Charniak (2004) noisy channel model.

Our main comparison is against two pipeline systems, which use the two current state-of-the-art disfluency detection systems as pre-processors to our parser, minus the custom disfluency features and transition. The joint model compared favourably to the pipeline parsers at both tasks, with an unlabelled attachment score of 90.5%, and 84.0% accuracy at detecting speech repairs. An efficient implementation is available under an open-source license.[1] The future prospects of the system are also quite promising. Because the parser is incremental, it should be well suited to unsegmented text such as the output of a speech-recognition system. We consider our main contributions to be:

- a novel non-monotonic transition system, for speech repairs and restarts,

[1] http://github.com/syllog1sm/redshift

Transactions of the Association for Computational Linguistics, 2 (2014) 131–142. Action Editor: Joakim Nivre.
Submitted 11/2013; Revised 2/2014; Published 4/2014.

$$\text{A flight to } \underbrace{\text{um}}_{\text{FP}} \underbrace{\text{Boston}}_{\text{RM}} \underbrace{\text{I mean}}_{\text{IM}} \underbrace{\text{Denver}}_{\text{RP}} \text{ Tuesday}$$

Figure 1: A sentence with disfluencies annotated in the style of Shriberg (1994) and the Switchboard corpus. FP=Filled Pause, RM=Reparandum, IM=Interregnum, RP=Repair. We follow previous work in evaluating the system on the accuracy with which it identifies speech-repairs, marked *reparandum* above.

- several novel feature classes,
- direct comparison against the two best disfluency pre-processors, and
- state-of-the-art accuracy for both speech parsing and disfluency detection.

2 Switchboard Disfluency Annotations

The Switchboard portion of the Penn Treebank (Marcus et al., 1993) consists of telephone conversations between strangers about an assigned topic. Two annotation layers are provided: one for syntactic bracketing (MRG files), and one for disfluencies (DPS files). The disfluency layer marks elements with little or no syntactic function, such as filled pauses and discourse markers, and annotates speech repairs using the Shriberg (1994) system of reparandum/interregnum/repair. An example is shown in Figure 1.

In the syntactic annotation, edited words are covered by a special node labelled EDITED. The idea is to mark text which, if excised, would result in a grammatical sentence. The MRG files do not mark other types of disfluencies. We follow the evaluation defined by Charniak and Johnson (2001), which evaluates the accuracy of identifying speech repairs and restarts. This definition of the task is the standard in recent work. The reason for this is that filled pauses can be detected using a simple rule-based approach, and parentheticals have less impact on readability and down-stream processing accuracy.

The MRG and DPS layers have high but imperfect agreement over what tokens they mark as speech repairs: of the text annotated with both layers, 33,720 tokens are marked as disfluent in at least one layer, 32,310 are only marked as disfluent by the DPS files, and 32,742 are only marked as disfluent by the MRG layer.

The Switchboard annotation project was not fully completed. Because disfluency annotation is cheaper to produce, many of the DPS training files do not have matching MRG files. Only 619,236 of the 1,482,845 tokens in the DPS disfluency-detection training data have gold-standard syntactic parses. Our system requires the more expensive syntactic annotation, but we find that it outperforms the previous state-of-the-art (Qian and Liu, 2013), despite training on less than half the data.

2.1 Dependency Conversion

As is standard in statistical dependency parsing of English, we acquire our gold-standard dependencies from phrase-structure trees. We used the 2013-04-05 version of the Stanford dependency converter (de Marneffe et al., 2006). As is standard for English dependency parsing, we use the Basic Dependencies scheme, which produces strictly projective representations.

At first we feared that the filled pauses, disfluencies and meta-data tokens in the Switchboard corpus might disrupt the conversion process, by making it more difficult for the converter to recognise the underlying production rules.

To test this, we performed a small experiment. We prepared two versions of the corpus: one where EDITED nodes, filled pauses and meta-data were removed before the trees were transformed by the Stanford converter, and one where the disfluency removal was performed after the dependency conversion. The resulting corpora were largely identical: 99.54% of unlabelled and 98.7% of labelled dependencies were the same. The fact that the Stanford converter is quite robust to disfluencies was useful for our baseline joint model, which is trained on dependency trees that also included governors for disfluent words.

We follow previous work on disfluency detection by lower-casing the text and removing punctuation and partial words (words tagged XX and words ending in '-'). We also remove one-token sentences, as their syntactic analyses are trivial. We found that two additional simple pre-processes improved our results: discarding all 'um' and 'uh' tokens; and merging 'you know' and 'i mean' into single tokens.

These pre-processes can be completed on the input string without losing information: none of the 'um' or 'uh' tokens are semantically significant, and the bigrams *you know* and *i mean* have a dependency between the two tokens over 99.9% of the times they occur in the treebank, with *you* and *I* never having any children. This makes it easy to unmerge the tokens deterministically after parsing: all incoming and outgoing arcs will point to *know* or *mean*. The same pre-processing was performed for all our parsing systems.

3 Transition-based Dependency Parsing

A transition-based parser predicts the syntactic structure of a sentence incrementally, by making a sequence of classification decisions. We follow the architecture of Zhang and Clark (2011), who use beam-search for decoding, and a structured averaged perceptron for training. Despite its simplicity, this type of parser has produced highly competitive results on the Wall Street Journal: with the extended feature set described by Zhang and Nivre (2011), it achieves 93.5% unlabelled accuracy on Stanford basic dependencies (de Marneffe et al., 2006). Converting the constituency trees produced by the Charniak and Johnson (2005) reranking parser results in similar accuracy.

Briefly, the transition-based parser consists of a configuration (or 'state') which is sequentially manipulated by a set of possible transitions. For us, a state is a 4-tuple $c = (\sigma, \beta, A, D)$, where σ and β are disjoint sets of word indices termed the *stack* and *buffer* respectively, A is the set of dependency arcs, and D is the set of word indices marked disfluent. There are no arcs to or from members of D, so the dependencies and disfluencies can be implemented as a single vector (in our parser, a token is marked as disfluent by setting it as its own head).

We use the arc-eager transition system (Nivre, 2003, 2008), which consists of four parsing actions: **S**hift, **L**eft-Arc, **R**ight-Arc and Re**d**uce. We denote the stack with its topmost element to the right, and the buffer with its first element to the left. A vertical bar is used to indicate concatenation to the stack or buffer, e.g. $\sigma|i$ indicates a stack with the topmost element i and remaining elements σ. A dependency from a governor i to a child j is denoted $i \rightarrow j$. The four arc-eager transitions are shown in Figure 2.

The Shift action moves the first item of the buffer onto the stack. The Right-Arc does the same, but also adds an arc, so that the top two items on the stack are connected. The Reduce move and the Left-Arc both pop the stack, but the Left-Arc first adds an arc from the first word of the buffer to the word on top of the stack. Constraints on the Reduce and Left-Arc moves ensure that every word is assigned exactly one head in the final configuration. We follow the suggestion

$(\sigma, i|\beta, A, D) \vdash (\sigma|i, \beta, A, D)$ S

$(\sigma|i, j|\beta, A, D) \vdash (\sigma, j|\beta, A \cup \{j \rightarrow i\}, D)$ L

Only if i does not have an incoming arc.

$(\sigma|i, j|\beta, A, D) \vdash (\sigma|i|j, \beta, A \cup \{i \rightarrow j\}, D)$ R

$(\sigma|i, \beta, A, D) \vdash (\sigma, \beta, A, D)$ D

Only if i has an incoming arc.

$(\sigma|i, j|\beta, A, D) \vdash (\sigma|[x_1, x_n], j|\beta, A', D')$ E

Where

$A' = A \setminus \{x \rightarrow y \text{ or } y \rightarrow x : \forall x \in [i, j), \forall y \in \mathbb{N}\}$

$D' = D \cup [i, j)$

$x_1 ... x_n$ are the former left children of i

Figure 2: Our parser's transition system. The first four transitions are the standard arc-eager system; the fifth is our novel Edit transition.

of Ballesteros and Nivre (2013) and add a dummy token that governs root dependencies to the end of the sentence. Parsing terminates when this token is at the start of the buffer, and the stack is empty. Disfluencies are added to D via the Edit transition, E, which we now define.

4 A Non-Monotonic Edit Transition

One of the reasons disfluent sentences are hard to parse is that there often appear to be syntactic relationships between words in the reparandum and the fluent sentence. When these relations are considered in addition to the dependencies between fluent words, the resulting structure is not necessarily a projective tree.

Figure 3 shows a simple example, where the repair *square* replaces the reparandum *rectangle*. An incremental parser could easily become 'garden-pathed' and attach the repair *square* to the preceding words, constructing the dependencies shown dotted in Figure 3. Rather than attempting to devise an incremental model that avoids constructing such dependencies, we allow the parser to construct these dependencies and later delete them if the governor or child are marked disfluent.

Psycholinguistic models of human sentence processing have long posited *repair* mechanisms (Frazier and Rayner, 1982). Recently, Honnibal et al. (2013) showed that a limited amount of 'non-monotonic' behaviour can improve an incremental parser's accuracy. We here introduce a non-monotonic transition, Edit, for speech repairs.

The Edit transition marks the word i on top of the stack $\sigma|i$ as disfluent, along with its rightward descendents — i.e., all words in the sequence $i...j-1$, where j is the word at the start of the buffer. It then restores the words both preceding and formerly governed by i to the stack.

In other words, the word on top of the stack and

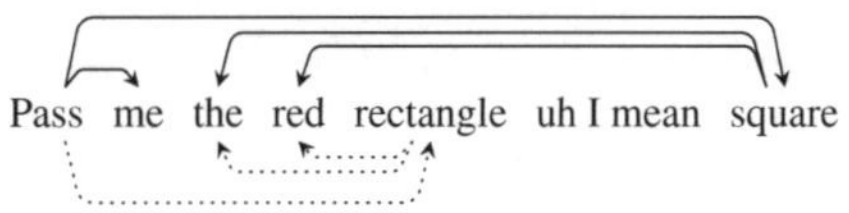

Figure 3: Example where apparent dependencies between the reparandum and the fluent sentence complicate parsing. The dotted edges are difficult for an incremental parser to avoid, but cannot be part of the final parse if it is to be a projective tree. Our solution is to make the transition system non-monotonic: the parser is able to delete edges.

its *rightward descendents* are all marked as disfluent, and the stack is popped. We then restore its leftward children to the stack, and all dependencies to and from words marked disfluent are deleted. The transition is *non-monotonic* in the sense that it can delete dependencies created by a previous transition, and replace tokens onto the stack that had been popped.

Why revisit the leftward children, but not the right? We are concerned about dependencies which might be mirrored between the reparandum and the repair. The rightward subtree of the disfluency might well be incorrect, but if it is, it would still be incorrect if the word on top of the stack were actually fluent. We therefore regard these as parsing errors that we will train our model to avoid. In contrast, avoiding the Left-Arc transitions would require the parser to predict that the head is disfluent when it has not necessarily seen any evidence indicating that.

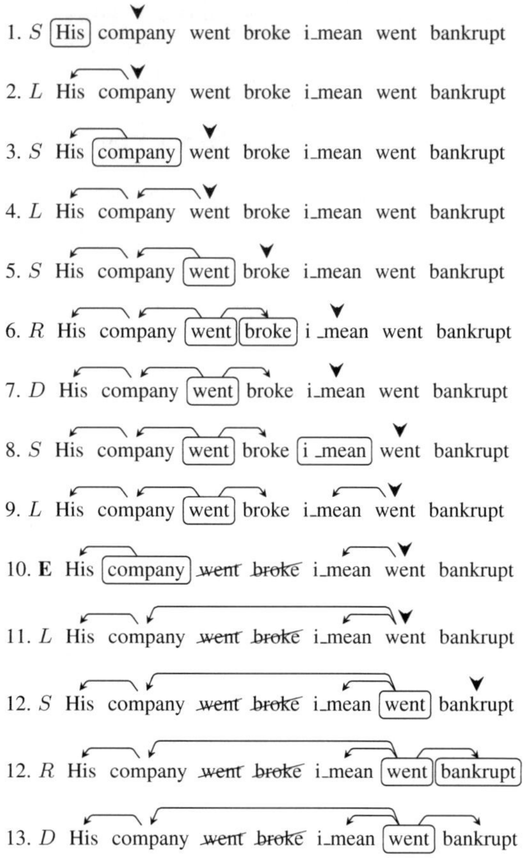

Figure 4: A gold-standard transition sequence using our EDIT transition. Each line specifies an action and shows the state resulting from it. Words on the stack are circled, and the arrow indicates the start of the buffer. Disfluent words are struck-through.

4.1 Worked Example

Figure 4 shows a gold-standard derivation for a disfluent sentence from the development data. Line 1 shows the state resulting from the initial Shift action. In the next three states, *His* is Left-Arced to *company*, which is then Shifted onto the stack, and Left-Arced to *went* in Line 4.

The dependency between *went* and *company* is not part of the gold-standard, because *went* is disfluent. The correct governor of *company* is the second *went* in the sentence. The Left-Arc move in Line 4 can still be considered correct, however, because the gold-standard analysis is still derivable from the resulting configuration, via the Edit transition. Another non-gold dependency is created in Line 6, between *broke* and *went*, before *broke* is Reduced from the stack in Line 7.

Lines 9 and 10 show the states before and after the Edit transition. The word on top of the stack in Line 9, *went*, has one leftward child, and one rightward child. After the Edit transition is applied, *went* and its rightward child *broke* are both marked disfluent, and *company* is returned to the stack. All of the previous dependencies to and from *went* and *broke* are deleted.

Parsing then proceeds as normal, with the correct governor of *company* being assigned by the Left-Arc in Line 11, and *bankrupt* being Right-Arced to *went* in Line 12. To conserve space, we have omitted the dummy ROOT token, which is placed at the end of the sentence, following the suggestion of Ballesteros and Nivre (2013). The final action will be a Left-Arc from the ROOT token to *went*.

4.2 Dynamic Oracle Training Algorithm

Our non-monotonic transition system introduces substantial *spurious ambiguity*: the gold-standard parse can be derived via many different transition sequences. Recent work has shown that this can be advantageous (Sartorio et al., 2013; Honnibal et al., 2013; Goldberg and Nivre, 2012), because difficult decisions can sometimes be delayed until more information is available.

Line 5 of Figure 4 shows a state that introduces spurious ambiguity. From this configuration, there are multiple actions that could be considered 'correct', in the sense that the gold-standard analysis can be derived from them. The Edit transition is correct because *went* is disfluent, but the Left-Arc and even the Right-Arc are also correct, in that there are continuations from them that lead to the gold-standard analysis.

We regard all transition sequences that can result in the correct analysis as equally valid, and want to avoid stipulating one of them during training. We achieve this by following Goldberg and Nivre (2012) in using a *dynamic oracle* to create partially labelled training data.[2] A dynamic oracle is a function that determines the cost of applying an action to a state, in terms of gold-standard arcs that are newly unreachable.

We follow Collins (2002) in training an averaged perceptron model to predict transition *sequences*, rather than individual transitions. This type of model is often referred to as a structured perceptron, or sometimes a global perceptron. During training, if the model does not predict the correct sequence, an update is performed, based on the gold-standard sequence and part of the sequence predicted by the current weights. Only part of the sequence is used to calculate the weight update, in order to account for search errors. We use the maximum violation strategy described by Huang et al. (2012) to select the subsequence to update from.

To train our model using the dynamic oracle, we use the latent-variable structured perceptron algorithm described by Sun et al. (2009). Beam-search is performed to find the highest-scoring gold-standard sequence, as well as the highest-scoring prediction. We use the same beam-width for both search procedures.

4.3 Path Length Normalisation

One problem introduced by the Edit transition is that the number of actions applied to a sentence is no longer constant — it is no longer guaranteed to be $2n - 1$, for a sentence of length n. When the Edit transition is applied to a word with leftward children, those children are returned to the stack, and processed again. This has little to no impact on the algorithm's empirical efficiency, although worst-case complexity is no longer linear, but it does pose a problem for decoding.

The perceptron model tends to assign large positive scores to its top prediction. We thus observed a problem when comparing paths of different lengths, at the end of the sentence. Paths that included Edit transitions were longer, so the sum of their scores tended to be higher.

The same problem has been observed during incremental PCFG parsing, by Zhu et al. (2013). They introduce an additional transition, IDLE, to ensure that paths are the same length. So long as one candidate in the beam is still being processed, all other candidates apply the IDLE transition.

We adopt a simpler solution. We normalise the figure-of-merit for a candidate state, which is used to rank it in the beam, by the length of its transition history. The new figure-of-merit is the arithmetic mean of the candidate's transition scores, where previously the figure-of-merit was the sum of the candidate's transition scores.

Interestingly, Zhu et al. (2013) report that they tried exactly this, and that it was less effective than their solution. We found that the features associated with the IDLE transition were uninformative (the state is at termination, so the stack and buffer are empty), and had nothing to do with how many edit transitions were earlier applied.

5 Features for the Joint Parser

Our baseline parser uses the feature set described by Zhang and Nivre (2011). The feature set contains 73 templates that mostly refer to the properties of 12 *context tokens*: the top of the stack (S0), its two leftmost and rightmost children ($S0_L$, $S0_{L2}$, $S0_R$, $S0_{R2}$), its parent and grand-parent ($S0_h$, $S0_{h2}$), the first word of the buffer and its two leftmost children (N0, $N0_L$, $N0_{LL}$), and the next two words of the buffer (N1, N2).

Atomic features consist of the word, part-of-speech tag, or dependency label for these tokens; and multiple feature atoms are often combined for feature templates. There are also features for the string-distance between S0 and N0, and the left and right valencies (total number of children) of

[2] The training data is partially labelled in the sense that instances can have multiple true labels. Equivalently, one might say that the transitions are latent variables, which generate the dependencies.

S0 and N0, as well as the set of their children's dependency labels. We restrict these to the first and last 2 children for implementation efficiency, as we found this had no effect on accuracy. Numeric features (for distance and valency) are binned with the function $\lambda x : \min(x, 5)$. There is only one bilexical feature template, which pairs the words of S0 and N0. There are also ten tri-tag templates.

Our feature set includes additional dependency label features not used by Zhang and Nivre (2011), as we found that disfluency detection errors often resulted in ungrammatical dependency label combinations. The additional templates combine the POS tag of S0 with two or three dependency labels from its left and right subtrees. Details can be found in the supplementary material.

5.1 Brown Cluster Features

The Brown clustering algorithm (Brown et al., 1992) is a well known source of semi-supervised features. The clustering algorithm is run over a large sample of unlabelled data, to generate a type-to-cluster map. This mapping is then used to generate features that sometimes generalise better than lexical features, and are helpful for out-of-vocabulary words (Turian et al., 2010).

Koo and Collins (2010) found that Brown cluster features greatly improved the performance of a graph-based dependency parser. On our transition-based parser, Brown cluster features bring a small but statistically significant improvement on the WSJ task (0.1-0.3% UAS). Other developers of transition-based parsers seem to have found similar results (personal communication). Since a Brown cluster mapping computed by Liang (2005) is easily available,[3] the features are simple to implement and cheap to compute.

Our templates follow Koo and Collins (2010) in including features that refer to cluster prefix strings, as well as the full clusters. We adapt their templates to transition-based parsing by replacing 'head' with 'item on top of the stack' and 'child' with 'first word of the buffer'. The exact templates can be found in the supplementary material.

The Brown cluster features are used in our 'baseline' parser, and in the parsers we use as part of our pipeline systems. They improved development set accuracy by 0.4%. We experimented with the other feature sets in these parsers, but found that they did not improve accuracy on fluent text.

[3] http://www.metaoptimize.com/projects/wordreps

5.2 Rough Copy Features

Johnson and Charniak (2004) point out that in speech repairs, the repair is often a 'rough copy' of the reparandum. The simplest case of this is where the repair is a single word repetition. It is common for the repair to differ from the reparandum by insertion, deletion or substitution of one or more words.

To capture this regularity, we first extend the feature-set with three new context tokens:[4]

1. $S0_{re}$: The rightmost edge of S0 descendants;
2. $S0_{le}$: The leftmost edge of S0 descendants;
3. $N0_{le}$: The leftmost edge of N0 descendants.

If a word has no leftward children, it will be its own left-edge, and similarly it will be its own rightward edge if it has no rightward children. Note that the token $S0_{re}$ is necessarily immediately before $N0_{le}$, unless some of the tokens between them are disfluent. We use the $S0_{le}$ and $N0_{le}$ to compute the following rough-copy features:

1. How long is the *prefix word match* between $S0_{le}$...S0 and $N0_{le}$...N0?

   If the parser were analysing *the red the blue square*, with *red* on the stack and *square* at N0, its value would be 1.
2. How long is the *prefix POS tag match* between $S0_{le}$...S0 and $N0_{le}$...N0?
3. Do the words in $S0_{le}$...S0 and $N0_{le}$...N0 match exactly?
4. Do the POS tags in $S0_{le}$...S0 and $N0_{le}$...N0 match exactly?

   If the parser were analysing *the red square the blue rectangle*, with *square* on the stack and *rectangle* at N0, its value would be *true*.

The prefix-length features are binned using the function $\lambda x : \min(x, 5)$.

5.3 Match Features

This class of features ask which pairs of the *context tokens* match, in word or POS tag. The context tokens in the Zhang and Nivre (2011) feature set are the top of the stack (S0), its head and

[4] As is common in this type of parser, our implementation has a number of vectors for properties that are defined before parsing, such as word forms, POS tags, Brown clusters, etc. A context token is an index into these vectors, allowing features considering these properties to be computed.

grandparent ($S0_h$, $S0_{h2}$), its two left- and rightmost children ($S0_L$, $S0_{L2}$, $S0_R$, $S0_{R2}$), the first three words of the buffer (N0, N1, N2), and the two leftmost children of N0 ($N0_L$, $N0_{LL}$). We extend this set with the $S0_{le}$, $S0_{re}$ and $N0_{le}$ tokens described above, and also the first left and right child of S0 and N0 ($S0_{L0}$, $S0_{R0}$, $N0_{L0}$).

All up, there are 18 context tokens, so $\binom{18}{2} = 153$ token pairs. For each pair of these tokens, we add two binary features, indicating whether the two tokens match in word form or POS tag. We also have two further classes of features: if the words do match, a feature is added indicating the word form; if the tags match, a feature is added indicating the tag. These finer grained versions help the model adjust for the fact that some words can be duplicated in grammatical sentences (e.g. 'that that'), while most rare words cannot.

5.4 Edited Neighbour Features

Disfluencies are usually string contiguous, even if they do not form a single constituent. In these situations, our model has to make multiple transitions to mark a single disfluency. For instance, if an utterance begins *and the and a*, the stack will contain two entries, for *and* and *the*, and two Edit transitions will be required.

To mitigate this disadvantage of our model, we add four binary features. Two fire when the word or pair of words immediately preceding N0 have been marked disfluent; the other two fire when the word or pair of words immediately following S0 have been marked disfluent. These features provide an additional string-based view that the parser would otherwise be missing. Speakers tend be disfluent in bursts: if the previous word is disfluent, the next word is more likely to be disfluent. These four features are therefore all associated with positive weights for the Edit transition. Without these features, we would miss an aspect of disfluency processing that sequence models naturally capture.

6 Part-of-Speech Tagging

We adopt the standard strategy of using a POS tagger as a pre-process before parsing. Most transition-based parsers use a structured averaged perceptron model with beam-search for tagging, as this model achieves competitive accuracy and matches the standard dependency parsing architecture. Our tagger also uses this architecture.

We performed some additional feature engineering for the tagger, in order to improve its accuracy given the lack of case distinctions and punctuation in the data. Our additional features use two sources of unsupervised information. First, we follow the suggestion of Manning (2011) by using Brown cluster features to improve the tagger's accuracy on unknown words. Second, we compensate for the lack of case distinctions by including features that ask what percentage of the time a word form was seen title-cased, upper-cased and lower-cased in the Google Web1T corpus.

Where most previous work uses cross-fold training for the tagger, to ensure that the parser is trained on tags that reflect run-time accuracies, we do online training of the tagger alongside the parser, using the current tagger model to produce tags during parser training. This had no impact on parse accuracy, and made it slightly easier to develop our tagger alongside the parser.

The tagger achieved 96.5% accuracy on the development data, but when we ran our final test experiments, we found its accuracy dropped to 96.0%, indicating some over-fitting during our feature engineering. On the development data, our parser accuracy improves by about 1% when gold-standard tags are used.

7 Experiments

We use the Switchboard portion of the Penn Treebank (Marcus et al., 1993), as described in Section 2, to train our joint models and evaluate them on dependency parsing and disfluency detection. The pre-processing and dependency conversion are described in Section 2.1. We use the standard train/dev/test split from Charniak and Johnson (2001): Sections 2 and 3 for training, and Section 4 divided into three held-out sections, the first of which is used for final evaluation.

Our parser evaluation uses the SPARSEVAL (Roark et al., 2006) metric. However, we wanted to use the Stanford dependency converter, for the reasons described in Section 2.1, so we used our own implementation. Because we do not need to deal with recognition errors, we do not need to report our parsing results using $P/R/F$-measures. Instead, we report an unlabelled accuracy score, which refers to the percentage of fluent words whose governors were assigned correctly. Note that words marked as disfluent cannot have any incoming or out-going dependencies, so if a word is incorrectly marked as disfluent, all of its dependencies will be incorrect.

We follow Johnson and Charniak (2004) and others in restricting our disfluency evaluation to speech repairs, which we identify as words that have a node labelled EDITED as an ancestor. Unlike most other disfluency detection research, we train only on the MRG files, giving us 619,236 words of training data instead of the 1,482,845 used by the pipeline systems. It may be possible to improve our system's disfluency detection by leveraging the additional data that does not have syntactic annotation in some way.

All parsing models were trained for 15 iterations. We found that optimising the number of iterations on a development set led to small improvements that did not transfer to a second development set (part of Section 4, which Charniak and Johnson (2001) reserved for 'future use').

We test for statistical significance in our results by training 20 models for each experimental configuration, using different random seeds. The random seeds control how the sentences are shuffled during training, which the perceptron model is quite sensitive to. We use the Wilcoxon rank-sums non-parametric test. The standard deviation in UAS for a sample was typically around 0.05%, and 0.5% for disfluency F-measure.

All of our models use beam-search decoding, with a beam width of 32. We found that a beam width of 64 brought a very small accuracy improvement (about 0.1%), at the cost of 50% slower run-time. Wider beams than this brought no accuracy improvement. Accuracy seems to plateau with slightly narrower beams than on newswire text. This is probably due to the shorter sentences in Switchboard.

The baseline and pipeline systems are configured in the same way, except that the baseline parser is modified slightly to allow it to predict disfluencies, using a special dependency label, ERASED. All descendants of a word attached to its head by this label are marked as disfluent. Both the baseline and pipeline/oracle parsers use the same feature set: the Zhang and Nivre (2011) features, plus our Brown cluster features.

The baseline system is a standard arc-eager transition-based parser with a structured averaged perceptron model and beam-search decoding. The model is trained in the standard way, with a 'static' oracle and maximum-violation update, following (Huang et al., 2012).

7.1 Comparison with Pipeline Approaches

The accuracy of incremental dependency parsers is well established on the Wall Street Journal, but there are no dependency parsing results in the literature that make it easy to put our joint model's parsing accuracy into context. We therefore compare our joint model to two pipeline systems, which consist of a disfluency detector, followed by our dependency parser. We also evaluate parse accuracies after oracle pre-processing, to gauge the net effect of disfluencies on our parser's accuracy.

The dependency parser for the pipeline systems was trained on text with all disfluencies removed, following Charniak and Johnson (2001). The two disfluency detection systems we used were the Qian and Liu (2013) sequence-tagging model, and a version of the Johnson and Charniak (2004) noisy channel model, using the Charniak (2001) syntactic language model and the reranking features of Zwarts and Johnson (2011). They are the two best published disfluency detection systems.

8 Results

Table 1 shows the development set accuracies for our joint parser. Both the disfluency features and the Edit transition make statistically significant improvements, in both disfluency F-measure, unlabelled attachment score (UAS), and labelled attachment score (LAS).

The **Oracle pipeline** system, which uses the gold-standard to clean disfluencies prior to parsing, shows the total impact of speech-errors on the parser. The baseline parser, which uses the Zhang and Nivre (2011) feature set plus the Brown cluster features, scores 1.8% UAS lower than the oracle.

When we add the features described in Sections 5.2, 5.3 and 5.4, the gap is reduced to 1.2% (**+Features**). Finally, the improved transition system reduces the gap further still, to 0.8% UAS (**+Edit transition**). We also tested these features in the Oracle parser, but found they were ineffective on fluent text.

The **w/s** column shows the tokens analysed per second for each system, including disfluencies, with a single thread on a 2.4GHz Intel Xeon. The additional features reduce efficiency, but the non-monotonic Edit transition does not. The system is easily efficient enough for real-time use.

	P	R	F	UAS	LAS	w/s
Baseline joint	79.4	70.1	74.5	89.9	86.9	711
+Features	86.0	77.2	81.3	90.5	87.5	539
+Edit transition	92.2	80.2	85.8	90.9	87.9	555
Oracle pipeline	100	100	100	91.7	88.6	782

Table 1: Development results for the joint models. For the baseline model, disfluencies reduce parse accuracy by 1.7% Unlabelled Attachment Score (UAS). Our features and Edit transition reduce the gap to 0.7%, and improve disfluency detection by 11.3% F-measure.

	Disfl. F	UAS
Johnson et al pipeline	82.1	90.3
Qian and Liu pipeline	83.9	90.1
Baseline joint parser	73.9	89.4
Final joint parser	84.1	**90.5**

Table 2: Test-set parse and disfluency accuracies. The joint parser is improved by the features and Edit transition, and is better than pre-processing the text with state-of-the-art disfluency detectors.

Table 2 shows the final evaluation. Our main comparison is with the two pipeline systems, described in Section 7.1. The Johnson and Charniak (2004) system was 1.8% less accurate at disfluency detection than the other disfluency detector we evaluated, the state-of-the-art Qian and Liu (2013) system. However, when we evaluated the two systems as pre-processors before our parser, we found that the **Johnson et al pipeline** achieved 0.2% better unlabelled attachment score than the **Qian and Liu pipeline**. We attribute this to the use of the Charniak and Johnson (2001) syntactic language model in the Johnson et al pipeline, which would help the system produce more syntactically consistent output.

Our joint model achieved an unlabelled attachment score of 90.5%, out-performing both pipeline systems. The **Baseline joint parser**, which did not include the Edit transition or disfluency features, scores 1.1% below the **Final joint parser**. All of the parse accuracy differences were found to be statistically significant ($p < 0.001$).

The Edit transition and disfluency features together brought a 10.1% improvement in disfluency F-measure, which was also found to be statistically significant. The final joint parser achieved 0.2% higher disfluency detection accuracy than the previous state-of-the-art, the Qian and Liu (2013) system,[5] despite having approximately half as much training data (we require syntactic annotation, for which there is less data).

Our significance testing regime involved using 20 different random seeds when training each of our models, which the perceptron algorithm is sensitive to. This could not be applied to the other two disfluency detectors, so we cannot test those differences for significance. However, we note that the 20 samples for our disfluency detector ranged in accuracy from 83.3-84.6, so we doubt that 0.2% mean improvement over the Qian and Liu (2013) result is meaningful.

Although we did not systematically optimise on the development set, our test scores are lower than our development accuracies. Much of the over-fitting seems to be in the POS tagger, which dropped in accuracy by 0.5%.

9 Analysis of Edit Behaviour

In order to understand how the parser applies the Edit transition, we collected some additional statistics over the development data. The parser predicted 2,558 Edit transitions, which together marked 2,706 words disfluent (2,495 correctly). The Edit transition can mark multiple words disfluent when S0 has one or more rightward descendants. It turns out this case is uncommon; the parser largely assigns disfluency labels word-by-word, only sometimes marking words with rightward descendents as disfluent.

Of the 2,558 Edit transitions, there were 682 cases were at least one leftward child was returned to the stack, and the total number of leftward children returned was 1,132. The most common type of construction that caused the parser to return words to the stack were disfluent predicates, which often have subjects and discourse conjunctions as leftward children. An example of a disfluent predicate with a fluent subject is shown in Figure 4.

There were only 48 cases of the same word being returned to the stack twice. The possibility of words being returned to the stack multiple times is what gives our system worse than linear worst-case complexity. In the worst case, the ith word of a sentence of length n could be returned to the stack $n - (i + 1)$ times. Empirically, the Edit transition made no difference to run-time.

Once a word has been returned to the stack by the Edit transition, how does the parser end up analysing it? If it turned out that almost all of the former leftward children of disfluent words are subsequently marked as disfluent, there would be

[5] Our scores refer to an updated version of the system that corrects minor pre-processing problems. We thank Qian Xian for making his code available.

little point in returning them to the stack — we could just mark them as disfluent in the original Edit transition. On the other hand, if they are almost all marked as fluent, perhaps they can just be attached as children to the first word of the buffer.

In fact the two cases are almost equally common. Of the 1,132 words returned to the stack, 547 were subsequently marked disfluent, and 584 were not. The parser was also quite accurate in its decisions over these tokens. Of the 547 tokens marked disfluent, 500 were correct — similar to the overall development set precision, 92.2%.

Accuracy over the words returned to the stack might be improved in future by features referring to their former heads. For instance, in *He went broke uh became bankrupt*, we do not currently have features that record the deleted dependency became *he* and *went*. We thank one of the anonymous reviewers for this suggestion.

10 Related Work

The most similar system to ours was published very recently. Rasooli and Tetreault (2013) describe a joint model of dependency parsing and disfluency detection. They introduce a second classification step, where they first decide whether to apply a disfluency transition, or a regular parsing move. Disfluency transitions operate either over a sequence of words before the start of the buffer, or a sequence of words from the start of the buffer forward. Instead of the dynamic oracle training method that we employ, they use a two-stage bootstrap-style process.

Direct comparison between our model and theirs is difficult, as they use the Penn2MALT scheme, and their parser uses greedy decoding, where we use beam search. They also use gold-standard part-of-speech tags, which would improve our scores by around 1%. The use of beam-search may explain much of our performance advantage: they report an unlabelled attachment score of 88.6, and a disfluency detection F-measure of 81.4%. Our training algorithm would be applicable to a beam-search version of their parser, as their transition-system also introduces substantial spurious ambiguity, and some non-monotonic behaviour.

A hybrid transition system would also be possible, as the two types of Edit transition seem to be complementary. The Rasooli and Tetreault system offers a token-based view of disfluencies, which is useful for examples such as, *and the and the*, which would require two applications of our transition. On the other hand, our Edit transition may have the advantage for more syntactically complicated examples, particularly for disfluent verbs.

The importance of syntactic features for disfluency detection was demonstrated by Johnson and Charniak (2004). Despite this, most subsequent work has used sequence models, rather than syntactic parsers. The other disfluency system that we compare our model to, developed by Qian and Liu (2013), uses a cascade of Maximum Margin Markov Models to perform disfluency detection with minimal syntactic information.

One motivation for sequential approaches is that most applications of these models will be over unsegmented text, as segmenting unpunctuated text is a difficult task that benefits from syntactic features (Zhang et al., 2013).

We consider the most promising aspect of our system to be that it is naturally incremental, so it should be straightforward to extend the system to operate on unsegmented text in subsequent work. Due to its use of syntactic features, from the joint model, the system is substantially more accurate than the previous state-of-the-art in incremental disfluency detection, 77% (Zwarts et al., 2010).

11 Conclusion

We have presented an efficient and accurate joint model of dependency parsing and disfluency detection. The model out-performs pipeline approaches using state-of-the-art disfluency detectors, and is highly efficient, processing over 550 tokens a second. Because the system is incremental, it should be straight-forward to apply it to unsegmented text. The success of an incremental, non-monotonic parser at disfluent speech parsing may also be of some psycholinguistic interest.

Acknowledgments

The authors would like to thank the anonymous reviewers for their valuable comments. This research was supported under the Australian Research Council's Discovery Projects funding scheme (project numbers DP110102506 and DP110102593).

References

Miguel Ballesteros and Joakim Nivre. 2013. Going to the roots of dependency parsing. *Computational Linguistics. 39:1.*

Peter F. Brown, Peter V. deSouza, Robert L. Mercer, Vincent J. Della Pietra, and Jenifer C. Lai. 1992. Class-based n-gram models of natural language. *Computational Linguistics*, 18:467–479.

Eugene Charniak. 2001. Immediate-head parsing for language models. In *Proceedings of 39th Annual Meeting of the Association for Computational Linguistics*, pages 124–131. Association for Computational Linguistics, Toulouse, France.

Eugene Charniak and Mark Johnson. 2001. Edit detection and parsing for transcribed speech. In *Proceedings of the 2nd Meeting of the North American Chapter of the Association for Computational Linguistics*, pages 118–126. The Association for Computational Linguistics.

Eugene Charniak and Mark Johnson. 2005. Coarse-to-fine n-best parsing and MaxEnt discriminative reranking. In *Proceedings of the 43rd Annual Meeting of the Association for Computational Linguistics*, pages 173–180. Association for Computational Linguistics, Ann Arbor, Michigan.

Michael Collins. 2002. Discriminative training methods for hidden Markov models: Theory and experiments with perceptron algorithms. In *Proceedings of the 2002 Conference on Empirical Methods in Natural Language Processing*, pages 1–8. Association for Computational Linguistics.

Marie-Catherine de Marneffe, Bill MacCartney, and Christopher D. Manning. 2006. Generating typed dependency parses from phrase structure parses. In *Proceedings of the 5th International Conference on Language Resources and Evaluation (LREC)*.

Lyn Frazier and Keith Rayner. 1982. Making and correcting errors during sentence comprehension: Eye movements in the analysis of structurally ambiguous sentences. *Cognitive Psychology*, 14(2):178–210.

Yoav Goldberg and Joakim Nivre. 2012. A dynamic oracle for arc-eager dependency parsing. In *Proceedings of the 24th International Conference on Computational Linguistics (Coling 2012)*. Association for Computational Linguistics, Mumbai, India.

Matthew Honnibal, Yoav Goldberg, and Mark Johnson. 2013. A non-monotonic arc-eager transition system for dependency parsing. In *Proceedings of the Seventeenth Conference on Computational Natural Language Learning*, pages 163–172. Association for Computational Linguistics, Sofia, Bulgaria.

Liang Huang, Suphan Fayong, and Yang Guo. 2012. Structured perceptron with inexact search. In *Proceedings of the 2012 Conference of the North American Chapter of the Association for Computational Linguistics: Human Language Technologies*, pages 142–151. Association for Computational Linguistics, Montréal, Canada.

Mark Johnson and Eugene Charniak. 2004. A TAG-based noisy channel model of speech repairs. In *Proceedings of the 42nd Annual Meeting of the Association for Computational Linguistics*, pages 33–39.

Douglas A. Jones, Florian Wolf, Edward Gibson, Elliott Williams, Evelina Fedorenko, Douglas A. Reynolds, and Marc A. Zissman. 2003. Measuring the readability of automatic speech-to-text transcripts. In *INTERSPEECH*. ISCA.

Fredrik Jorgensen. 2007. The effects of disfluency detection in parsing spoken language. In Joakim Nivre, Heiki-Jaan Kaalep, Kadri Muischnek, and Mare Koit, editors, *Proceedings of the 16th Nordic Conference of Computational Linguistics NODALIDA-2007*, pages 240–244.

Terry Koo and Michael Collins. 2010. Efficient third-order dependency parsers. In *Proceedings of the 48th Annual Meeting of the Association for Computational Linguistics (ACL)*, pages 1–11.

Percy Liang. 2005. *Semi-supervised learning for natural language*. Ph.D. thesis, MIT.

Christopher D. Manning. 2011. Part-of-speech tagging from 97linguistics? In *Proceedings of the 12th international conference on Computational linguistics and intelligent text processing - Volume Part I*, CICLing'11, pages 171–189. Springer-Verlag, Berlin, Heidelberg.

Michell P. Marcus, Beatrice Santorini, and Mary Ann Marcinkiewicz. 1993. Building a large annotated corpus of English: The Penn Treebank. *Computational Linguistics*, 19(2):313–330.

Joakim Nivre. 2003. An efficient algorithm for projective dependency parsing. In *Proceedings of the 8th International Workshop on Parsing Technologies (IWPT)*, pages 149–160.

Joakim Nivre. 2008. Algorithms for deterministic incremental dependency parsing. *Computational Linguistics*, 34:513–553.

Xian Qian and Yang Liu. 2013. Disfluency detection using multi-step stacked learning. In *Proceedings of the 2013 Conference of the North American Chapter of the Association for Computational Linguistics: Human Language Technologies*, pages 820–825. Association for Computational Linguistics, Atlanta, Georgia.

Mohammad Sadegh Rasooli and Joel Tetreault. 2013. Joint parsing and disfluency detection in linear time. In *Proceedings of the 2013 Conference on Empirical Methods in Natural Language Processing*, pages 124–129. Association for Computational Linguistics, Seattle, Washington, USA.

Brian Roark, Mary Harper, Eugene Charniak, Bonnie Dorr, Mark Johnson, Jeremy Kahn, Yang Liu, Mary Ostendorf, John Hale, Anna Krasnyanskaya, Matthew Lease, Izhak Shafran, Matthew Snover, Robin Stewart, and LisaYung. 2006. Sparseval: Evaluation metrics for parsing speech. In *Proceedings of Language Resource and Evaluation Conference*, pages 333–338. European Language Resources Association (ELRA), Genoa, Italy.

Francesco Sartorio, Giorgio Satta, and Joakim Nivre. 2013. A transition-based dependency parser using a dynamic parsing strategy. In *Proceedings of the 51st Annual Meeting of the Association for Computational Linguistics*, pages 135–144. Association for Computational Linguistics, Sofia, Bulgaria.

Elizabeth Shriberg. 1994. *Preliminaries to a Theory of Speech Disfluencies*. Ph.D. thesis, University of California, Berkeley.

Xu Sun, Takuya Matsuzaki, Daisuke Okanohara, and Jun'ichi Tsujii. 2009. Latent variable perceptron algorithm for structured classification. In *IJCAI*, pages 1236–1242.

Joseph Turian, Lev-Arie Ratinov, and Yoshua Bengio. 2010. Word representations: A simple and general method for semi-supervised learning. In *Proceedings of the 48th Annual Meeting of the Association for Computational Linguistics*, pages 384–394. Association for Computational Linguistics, Uppsala, Sweden.

Dongdong Zhang, Shuangzhi Wu, Nan Yang, and Mu Li. 2013. Punctuation prediction with transition-based parsing. In *Proceedings of the 51st Annual Meeting of the Association for Computational Linguistics*, pages 752–760. Association for Computational Linguistics, Sofia, Bulgaria.

Yue Zhang and Stephen Clark. 2011. Syntactic processing using the generalized perceptron and beam search. *Computational Linguistics*, 37(1):105–151.

Yue Zhang and Joakim Nivre. 2011. Transition-based dependency parsing with rich non-local features. In *Proceedings of the 49th Annual Meeting of the Association for Computational Linguistics: Human Language Technologies*, pages 188–193. Association for Computational Linguistics, Portland, USA.

Muhua Zhu, Yue Zhang, Wenliang Chen, Min Zhang, and Jingbo Zhu. 2013. Fast and accurate shift-reduce constituent parsing. In *Proceedings of the 51st Annual Meeting of the Association for Computational Linguistics*, pages 434–443. Association for Computational Linguistics, Sofia, Bulgaria.

Simon Zwarts and Mark Johnson. 2011. The impact of language models and loss functions on repair disfluency detection. In *Proceedings of the 49th Annual Meeting of the Association for Computational Linguistics: Human Language Technologies*, pages 703–711. Association for Computational Linguistics, Portland, USA.

Simon Zwarts, Mark Johnson, and Robert Dale. 2010. Detecting speech repairs incrementally using a noisy channel approach. In *Proceedings of the 23rd International Conference on Computational Linguistics (Coling 2010)*, pages 1371–1378. Coling 2010 Organizing Committee, Beijing, China.

Temporal Annotation in the Clinical Domain

William F. Styler IV[1], **Steven Bethard**[2], **Sean Finan**[3], **Martha Palmer**[1], **Sameer Pradhan**[3], **Piet C de Groen**[4], **Brad Erickson**[4], **Timothy Miller**[3], **Chen Lin**[3], **Guergana Savova**[3] and **James Pustejovsky**[5]
[1] Department of Linguistics, University of Colorado at Boulder
[2] Department of Computer and Information Sciences, University of Alabama at Birmingham
[3] Children's Hospital Boston Informatics Program and Harvard Medical School
[4] Mayo Clinic College of Medicine, Mayo Clinic, Rochester, MN
[5] Department of Computer Science, Brandeis University

Abstract

This article discusses the requirements of a formal specification for the annotation of temporal information in clinical narratives. We discuss the implementation and extension of ISO-TimeML for annotating a corpus of clinical notes, known as the THYME corpus. To reflect the information task and the heavily inference-based reasoning demands in the domain, a new annotation guideline has been developed, "the THYME Guidelines to ISO-TimeML (THYME-TimeML)". To clarify what relations merit annotation, we distinguish between linguistically-derived and inferentially-derived temporal orderings in the text. We also apply a top performing TempEval 2013 system against this new resource to measure the difficulty of adapting systems to the clinical domain. The corpus is available to the community and has been proposed for use in a SemEval 2015 task.

1 Introduction

There is a long-standing interest in temporal reasoning within the biomedical community (Savova et al., 2009; Hripcsak et al., 2009; Meystre et al., 2008; Bramsen et al., 2006; Combi et al., 1997; Keravnou, 1997; Dolin, 1995; Irvine et al., 2008; Sullivan et al., 2008). This interest extends to the automatic extraction and interpretation of temporal information from medical texts, such as electronic discharge summaries and patient case summaries. Making effective use of temporal information from such narratives is a crucial step in the intelligent analysis of informatics for medical researchers, while an awareness of temporal information (both implicit and explicit) in a text is also necessary for many data mining tasks.

It has also been demonstrated that the temporal information in clinical narratives can be usefully mined to provide information for some higher-level temporal reasoning (Zhao et al., 2005). Robust temporal understanding of such narratives, however, has been difficult to achieve, due to the complexity of determining temporal relations among events, the diversity of temporal expressions, and the interaction with broader computational linguistic issues.

Recent work on Electronic Health Records (EHRs) points to new ways to exploit and mine the information contained therein (Savova et al., 2009; Roberts et al., 2009; Zheng et al., 2011; Turchin et al., 2009). We target two main use cases for extracted data. First, we hope to enable interactive displays and summaries of the patient's records to the physician at the time of visit, making a comprehensive review of the patient's history both faster and less prone to oversights. Second, we hope to enable temporally-aware secondary research across large databases of medical records (e.g., "What percentage of patients who undergo procedure X develop side-effect Y within Z months?"). Both of these applications require the extraction of time and date associations for critical events and the relative ordering of events during the patient's period of care, all from the various records which make up a patient's EHR. Although we have these two specific applications in mind, the schema we have developed is generalizable and could potentially be embedded in a wide variety of biomedical use cases.

Narrative texts in EHRs are temporally rich documents that frequently contain assertions about the timing of medical events, such as visits, laboratory values, symptoms, signs, diagnoses, and procedures (Bramsen et al., 2006; Hripcsak et al., 2009; Zhou et al., 2008). Temporal representation and reasoning in the medical record are difficult due to: (1) the diversity of time expressions; (2) the complexity of determining temporal relations among events (which are often left to inference); (3) the difficulty of handling the temporal granularity of an event; and (4)

Transactions of the Association for Computational Linguistics, 2 (2014) 143–154. Action Editor: Ellen Riloff.
Submitted 9/2013; Revised 2/2014; Published 4/2014.

general issues in natural language processing (e.g., ambiguity, anaphora, ellipsis, conjunction). As a result, the signals used for reconstructing a timeline can be both domain-specific and complex, and are often left implicit, requiring significant domain knowledge to accurately detect and interpret.

In this paper, we discuss the demands on accurately annotating such temporal information in clinical notes. We describe an implementation and extension of ISO-TimeML (Pustejovsky et al., 2010), developed specifically for the clinical domain, which we refer to as the "THYME Guidelines to ISO-TimeML" ("THYME-TimeML"), where THYME stands for "Temporal Histories of Your Medical Events". A simplified version of these guidelines formed the basis for the 2012 i2b2 medical-domain temporal relation challenge (Sun et al., 2013a).

This is being developed in the context of the THYME project, whose goal is to both create robust gold standards for semantic information in clinical notes, as well as to develop state-of-the-art algorithms to train and test on this dataset.

Deriving timelines from news text requires the concrete realization of context-dependent assumptions about temporal intervals, orderings and organization, underlying the explicit signals marked in the text (Pustejovsky and Stubbs, 2011). Deriving patient history timelines from clinical notes also involves these types of assumptions, but there are special demands imposed by the characteristics of the clinical narrative. Due to both medical shorthand practices and general domain knowledge, many event-event relations are not signaled in the text at all, and rely on a shared understanding and common conceptual models of the progressions of medical procedures available only to readers familiar with language use in the medical community.

Identifying these implicit relations and temporal properties puts a heavy burden on the annotation process. As such, in the THYME-TimeML guideline, considerable effort has gone into both describing and proscribing the annotation of temporal orderings that are inferable only through domain-specific temporal knowledge.

Although the THYME guidelines describe a number of departures from the ISO-TimeML standard for expediency and ease of annotation, this paper will focus on those differences specifically motivated by the needs of the clinical domain, and on the consequences for systems built to extract temporal data in both the clinical and general domain.

2 The Nature of Clinical Documents

In the THYME corpus, we have been examining 1,254 de-identified[1] notes from a large healthcare practice (the Mayo Clinic), representing two distinct fields within oncology: brain cancer, and colon cancer. To date, we have principally examined two different general types of clinical narrative in our EHRs: clinical notes and pathology reports.

Clinical notes are records of physician interactions with a patient, and often include multiple, clearly delineated sections detailing different aspects of the patient's care and present illness. These notes are fairly generic across institutions and specialities, and although some terms and inferences may be specific to a particular type of practice (such as oncology), they share a uniform structure and pattern. The 'History of Present Illness', for example, summarizes the course of the patient's chief complaint, as well as the interventions and diagnostics which have been thus far attempted. In other sections, the doctor may outline her current plan for the patient's treatment, then later describe the patient's specific medical history, allergies, care directives, and so forth.

Most critically for temporal reasoning, each clinical note reflects a single time in the patient's treatment history at which all of the doctor's statements are accurate (the DOCTIME), and each section tends to describe events of a particular timeframe. For example, 'History of Present illness' predominantly describes events occuring before DOCTIME, whereas 'Medications' provides a snapshot at DOCTIME and 'Ongoing Care Orders' discusses events which have not yet occurred.[2]

Clinical notes contain rich temporal information and background, moving fluidly from prior treatments and symptoms to present conditions to future interventions. They are also often rich with hypothetical statements ("if the tumor recurs, we can..."), each of which can form its own separate timeline.

By constrast, pathology notes are quite different. Such notes are generated by a medical pathologist

[1]Although most patient information was removed, dates and temporal information were not modified according to this project's specific data use agreement.

[2]One complication is the propensity of doctors and automated systems to later update sections in a note without changing the timestamp or metadata. We have added a SECTIONTIME to keep these updated sections from affecting our overall timeline.

upon receipt and analysis of specimens (ranging from tissue samples from biopsy to excised portions of tumor or organs). Pathology notes provide crucial information to the patient's doctor confirming the malignancy (cancer) in samples, describing surgical margins (which indicate whether a tumor was completely excised), and classifying and 'staging' a tumor, describing the severity and spread of the cancer. Because the information in such notes pertains to samples taken at a single moment in time, they are temporally sparse, seldom referring to events before or after the examination of the specimen. However, they contain critical information about the state of the patient's illness and about the cancer itself, and must be interpreted to understand the history of the patient's illness.

Most importantly, in all EHRs, we must contend with the results of a fundamental tension in modern medical records: hyper-detailed records provide a crucial defense against malpractice litigation, but including such detail takes enormous time, which doctors seldom have. Given that these notes are written by and for medical professionals (who form a relatively insular speech community), a great many non-standard expressions, abbreviations, and assumptions of shared knowledge are used, which are simultaneously concise and detail-rich for others who have similar backgrounds.

These time-saving devices can range from temporally loaded acronyms (e.g., 'qid', Latin for *quater in die*, 'four times daily'), to assumed orderings (a diagnostic test for a disorder is assumed to come before the procedure which treats it), and even to completely implicit events and temporal details. For example, consider the sentence in (1).

(1) **Colonoscopy** 3/12/10, nodule **biopsies** negative

We must understand that during the colonoscopy, the doctor obtained biopsies of nodules, which were packaged and sent to a pathologist, who reviewed them and determined them to be 'negative' (non-cancerous).

In such documents, we must recover as much temporal detail as possible, even though it may be expressed in a way which is not easily understood outside of the medical community, let alone by linguists or automated systems. We must also be aware of the legal relevance of some events (e.g., "We **discussed** the possible side effects"), even when they may not seem relevant to the patient's actual care.

Finally, each specialty and note type has separate conventions. Within colon cancer notes, the American Joint Committee on Cancer (AJCC) Staging Codes (e.g., *T4N1*, indicating the nature of the tumor, lymph node and metastasis involvement) are meticulously recorded, but are largely absent in the brain cancer notes which make up the second corpus in our project. So, although clinical notes share many similarities, annotators without sufficient domain expertise may require additional training to adapt to the inferences and nuances of a new clinical subdomain.

3 Interpreting 'Event' and Temporal Expressions in the Clinical Domain

Much prior work has been done on standardizing the annotation of events and temporal expressions in text. The most widely used approach is the ISO-TimeML specification (Pustejovsky et al., 2010), an ISO standard that provides a common framework for annotating and analyzing time, events, and event relations. As defined by ISO-TimeML, an EVENT refers to anything that can be said "to obtain or hold true, to happen or to occur". This is a broad notion of event, consistent with Bach's use of the term "eventuality" (Bach, 1986) as well as the notion of fluents in AI (McCarthy, 2002).

Because the goals of the THYME project involve automatically identifying the clinical timeline for a patient from clincal records, the scope of what should be admitted into the domain of events is interpreted more broadly than in ISO-TimeML[3]. Within the THYME-TimeML guideline, an EVENT is *anything* relevant to the clinical timeline, i.e., anything that would show up on a detailed timeline of the patient's care or life. The best single-word syntactic head for the EVENT is then used as its span. For example, a *diagnosis* would certainly appear on such a timeline, as would a *tumor*, *illness*, or *procedure*. On the other hand, entities that persist throughout the relevant temporal period of the clinical timeline (*endurants* in ontological circles) would not be considered as event-like. This includes the patient, other humans mentioned (the patient's mother-in-law or the doctor), organizations (the emergency room), non-anatomical objects (the patient's car), or individual parts of the patient's anatomy (an arm is not an EVENT unless missing or otherwise notable).

To meet our explicit goals, the THYME-TimeML guideline introduces two additional levels of interpre-

[3]Our use of the term 'EVENT' corresponds with the less specific ISO-TimeML term 'Eventuality'

tation beyond that specified by ISO-TimeML: (i) a well-defined task; and (ii) a clearly identified domain. By focusing on the creation of a *clinical timeline* from *clinical narrative*, the guideline imposes constraints that cannot be assumed for a broadly defined and domain independent annotation schema.

Some EVENTs annotated under our guideline are considered meaningful and eventive mostly by virtue of a specific clinical or legal value. For example, AJCC Staging Codes (discussed in Section 2) are eventive only in the sense of the code being assigned to a tumor at a given moment in the patient's care. However, they are of such critical importance and informative value to doctors that we have chosen to annotate them *specifically so that they will show up on the patient's timeline in a clinical setting*.

Similarly, because of legal pressures to establish informed consent and patient knowledge of risk, entire paragraphs of clinical notes are dedicated to documenting the doctor's discussion of risks, plans, and alternative strategies. As such, we annotate verbs of discussion ("We **talked** about the risks of this drug"), consent ("She **agreed** with the current plan"), and comprehension ("Mrs. Larsen **repeated** the potential side effects back to me"), even though they are more relevant to legal defense than medical treatment.

It is also because of this grounding in clinical language that entities and other non-events are often interpreted in terms of their associated eventive properties. There are two major types for which this is a significant shift in semantic interpretation:

(2) a Medication as Event:
Orders: Lariam twice daily.
b Disorder as Event:
Tumor of the left lung.

In both these cases, entities which are not typically marked as events are identified as such, because they contribute significant information to the clinical timeline being constructed. In (2a), for example, the TIMEX3 "twice daily" is interpreted as scoping over the eventuality of the patient *taking* the medication, not the prescription event. In sentence (2b), the "tumor" is interpreted as a stative eventuality of the patient *having* a tumor located within an anatomical region, rather than an entity within an entity.

Within the medical domain, these eventive interpretations of medications, growths and status codes are unambiguous and consistent. Doctors in clinical notes (unlike in biomedical research texts) do not discuss medications without an associated (implicit) administering EVENT (though some mentions may be hypothetical, generic or negated). Similarly, mentions of symptoms or disorders reflect occurrences in a patient's life, rather than abstract entities. With these interpretations in mind, we can safely infer, for instance, that all UMLS (Unified Medical Language System, (Bodenreider, 2004)) entities of the types Disorder, Chemical/Drug, Procedure and Sign/Symptom will be EVENTs.

In general, in the medical domain, it is essential to read "between the lines" of the shorthand expressions used by the doctors, and recognize implicit events that are being referred to by specific anatomical sites or medications.

4 Modifications to ISO-TimeML for the Clinical Domain

Overall, we have found that the specification required for temporal annotation in the clinical domain does not require substantial modification from existing specifications for the general domain. The clinical domain includes no shortage of inferences, shorthands, and unusual use of language, but the structure of the underlying timeline is not unique.

As a result of this, we have been able to adopt most of the framework from ISO-TimeML, adapting the guidelines where needed, as well as reframing the focus of what gets annotated. This is reflected in a comprehensive guideline, incorporating the specific patterns and uses of events and temporal expressions as seen in clinical data. This approach allows the resulting annotations to be interoperable with existing solutions, while still accommodating the major differences in the nature of the texts. Our guidelines, as well as the annotated data, are available at `http://thyme.healthnlp.org`[4]

Our extensions of the ISO-TimeML specification to the clinical domain are intended to address specific constructions, meanings, and phenomena in medical texts. Our schema differs from ISO-TimeML in a few notable ways.

EVENT Properties We have both simplified the ISO-TimeML coding of EVENTs, and extended it to meet the needs of the clinical domain and the specific language goals of the clinical narrative.

[4]Access to the corpus will require a data use agreement. More information about this process is available from the corpus website.

Consider, for example, how modal subordination is handled in ISO-TimeML. This involves the semantic characterization of an event as "likely", "possible", or as presented by observation, evidence, or hearsay. All of these are accounted for compositionally in ISO-TimeML within the SLINK (Subordinating Link) relation (Pustejovsky et al., 2005). While accepting ISO-TimeML's definition of event modality, we have simplified the annotation task within the current guideline, so that EVENTs now carry attributes for "contextual modality", "contextual aspect" and "permanence".

Contextual modality allows the values ACTUAL, HYPOTHETICAL, HEDGED, and GENERIC. ACTUAL covers EVENTs which have actually happened, e.g., "We've noted a tumor". HYPOTHETICAL covers conditionals and possibilities, e.g., "If she develops a tumor". HEDGED is for situations where doctors proffer a diagnosis, but do so cautiously, to avoid legal liability for an incorrect diagnosis or for overlooking a correct one. For example:

(3) a. The signal in the MRI is not inconsistent with a **tumor** in the spleen.
b. The rash appears to be **measles**, awaiting antibody test to confirm.

These HEDGED EVENTs are more real than a hypothetical diagnosis, and likely merit inclusion on a timeline as part of the diagnostic history, but must not be conflated with confirmed fact. These (and other forms of uncertainty in the medical domain) are discussed extensively in (Vincze et al., 2008). In contrast, GENERIC EVENTs do not refer to the patient's illness or treatment, but instead discuss illness or treatment in general (often in the patient's specific demographic). For example:

(4) In other patients without significant **comorbidity** that can **tolerate** adjuvant **chemotherapy**, there is a **benefit** to systemic adjuvant **chemotherapy**.

These sections would be true if pasted into any patient's note, and are often identical chunks of text repeatedly used to justify a course of action or treatment as well as to defend against liability.

Contextual Aspect (to distinguish from grammatical aspect), allows the clinically-necessary category, INTERMITTENT. This serves to distinguish intermittent EVENTs (such as vomiting or seizures) from constant, more stative EVENTs (such as fever or soreness). For example, the bolded EVENT in (5a) would be marked as INTERMITTENT, while that in (5b) would not:

(5) a She has been **vomiting** since June.
b She has had **swelling** since June.

In the first case, we assume that her vomiting has been intermittent, i.e., there were several points since June in which she was not actively vomiting. In the second case, unless made otherwise explicit ("she has had occasional swelling"), we assume that swelling was a constant state. This property is also used when a particular instance of an EVENT is intermittent, even though it generally would not be:

(6) Since starting her new regime, she has had occasional bouts of **fever**, but is feeling much better.

The permanence attribute has two values, FINITE and PERMANENT. Permanence is a property of diseases themselves, roughly corresponding to the medical concept of "chronic" vs. "acute" disease, which marks whether a disease is persistent following diagnosis. For example, a (currently) uncurable disease like Multiple Sclerosis would be classed as PERMANENT, and thus, once mentioned in a patient's note, will be assumed to persist through the end of the patient's timeline. This is compared with FINITE disorders like "Influenza" or "fever", which, if not mentioned in subsequent notes, should be considered cured and no longer belongs on the patient's timeline. Because it requires domain-specific knowledge, although present in the specification, Permanence is not currently annotated. However, annotators are trained on the basic idea and told about subsequent axiomatic assignment. The addition of this property to our schema is designed to relieve annotators of any feeling of obligation to express this inferred information in some other way.

TIMEX3 Types Temporal expressions (TIMEX3s) in the clinical domain function the same as in the general linguistic community, with two notable exceptions. ISO-TimeML SETs (statements of frequency) occur quite frequently in the medical domain, particularly with regard to medications and treatments. Medication sections within notes often contain long lists of medications, each with a particular associated set ("Claritin 30mg *twice daily*"), and further temporal specification is not uncommon (e.g., "three times per day at meals", "once a week at bedtime").

The second major change for the medical domain is a new type of TIMEX3 which we call PREPOSTEXP. This covers temporally complex terms like "preoperative", "postoperative", and "intraoperative". These temporal expressions designate a span of time bordered, usually only on one side, by the incorporated event (an operation, in the previous EVENTs). In many cases, the referent is clear:

(7) She underwent **hemicolectomy** *last week*, and had some postoperative **bleeding**.

Here we understand that "postoperative" refers to "the period of time following the hemicolectomy". In these cases, the PREPOSTEXP makes explicit a temporal link between the bleeding and the hemicolectomy. In other cases, no clear referent is present:

(8) Patient shows some **post-procedure** scarring.

In these situations, where no procedure is mentioned (or the reference is never explicitly resolved), we treat the PREPOSTEXP as a narrative container (see Section 5), covering the span of time following the unnamed procedure.

Finally, it is worth noting that the process of normalizing those TIMEX3s is significantly more complex relative to the general domain, because many temporal expressions are anchored not to dates or times, but to other EVENTs (whose dates are often not mentioned or not known by the physician). As we move towards a complete system, we are working to expand the ISO-TimeML system for TIMEX3 normalization to allow some value to be assigned to a phrase like "in the months after her hemicolectomy" when no referent date is present. ISO-TimeML, in discussion with ISO TC 37SC 4, plans to reference to such TIMEX3s in a future release of the standard.

5 Temporal Ordering and Narrative Containers

The semantic content and informational impact of a timeline is encoded in the ordering relations that are identified between the temporal and event expressions present in clinical notes. ISO-TimeML specifies the standard thirteen "Allen relations" from the interval calculus (Allen, 1983), which it refers to as TLINK values. For unguided, general-purpose annotation, the number of relations that could be annotated grows quadratically with the number of events and times, and the task quickly becomes unmanageable. There are, however, strategies that we can adopt to make this labeling task more tractable. Temporal ordering relations in text are of three kinds:

1. Relations between two events
2. Relations between two times
3. Relations between a time and an event.

ISO-TimeML, as a formal specification of the temporal information conveyed in language, makes no distinction between these ordering types. Humans, however, do make distinctions, based on local temporal markers and the discourse relations established in a narrative (Miltsakaki et al., 2004; Poesio, 2004).

Because of the difficulty of humans capturing every relationship present in the note (and the disagreement which arises when annotators attempt to do so), it is vital that the annotation guidelines describe an approach that reduces the number of relations that must be considered, but still results in maximally informative temporal links. We have found that many of the weaknesses in prior annotation approaches stem from interaction between two competing goals:

- The guideline should specify certain types of annotations that *should* be performed;
- The guideline should not force annotations to be performed when they need not be.

Failing in the first goal will result in under-annotation and the neglect of relations which provide necessary information for inference and analysis. Failure in the second goal results in over-annotation, creating complex webs of temporal relations which yield mostly inferable information, but which complicate annotation and adjudication considerably.

Our method of addressing both goals in temporal relations annotation is that of the narrative container, discussed in Pustejovsky and Stubbs (2011). A narrative container can be thought of as a temporal bucket into which an EVENT or series of EVENTs may fall, or a natural cluster of EVENTs around a given time or situation. These narrative containers are often represented (or "anchored") by dates or other temporal expressions (within which a variety of different EVENTs occur), although they can also be anchored to more abstract concepts ("recovery" which might involve a variety of EVENTs) or even durative EVENTs (many other EVENTs can occur during a surgery). Rather than marking every possible TLINK between each EVENT, we instead try to link all EVENTs to their narrative containers, and then link those containers so that the contained EVENTs can be linked by inference.

First, annotators assign each event to one of four broad narrative containers: before the DOCTIME, before and overlapping the DOCTIME, just overlapping the DOCTIME or after the DOCTIME. This narrative container is identified by the EVENT attribute DocTimeRel. After the assignment of DocTimeRel, the remainder of the narrative container relations must be specified using temporal links (TLINKs). There are five different temporal relations used for such TLINKs: BEFORE, OVERLAP, BEGINS-ON, ENDS-ON and CONTAINS[5]. Due to our narrative container approach, CONTAINS is the most frequent relation by a large margin.

EVENTs serving as narrative container anchors are not tagged as containers per-se. Instead, annotators use the narrative container idea to help them visualize the temporal relations within a document, and then make a series of CONTAINS TLINK annotations which establish EVENTs and TIMEX3s as anchors, and specify their contents. If the annotators do their jobs correctly, properly implementing DocTimeRel and creating accurate TLINKs, a good understanding of the narrative containers present in a document will naturally emerge from the annotated text.

The major advantage introduced with narrative containers is this: a narrative event is placed *within* a bounding temporal interval which is explicitly mentioned in the text. This allows EVENTs within separate containers to be linked by post-hoc inference, temporal reasoning, and domain knowledge, rather than by explicit (and time-consuming) one-by-one temporal relations annotation.

A secondary advantage is that this approach works nicely with the general structure of story-telling in both the general and clinical domains, and provides a compelling and useful metaphor for interpreting timelines. Often, especially in clinical histories, doctors will cluster discussions of symptoms, interventions and diagnoses around a given date (e.g. a whole paragraph starting "June 2009:"), a specific hospitalization ("During her January stay at Mercy"), or a given illness or treatment ("While she underwent Chemo"). Even when specific EVENTs are not explicitly ordered within a cluster (often because the order can be easily inferred with domain knowledge), it is often quite easy to place the EVENTs into containers, and just a few TLINKs can order the containers relative to one another with enough detail to create a clinically useful understanding of the overall timeline.

Narrative containers also allow the inference of relations between sub-events within nested containers:

(9) December 19th: The patient underwent an **MRI** and **EKG** as well as emergency **surgery**. During the **surgery**, the patient experienced mild **tachycardia**, and she also **bled** significantly during the initial **incision**.

1. December 19th CONTAINS **MRI**
2. December 19th CONTAINS **EKG**
3. December 19th CONTAINS **surgery**

a. **surgery** CONTAINS **tachycardia**
b. **surgery** CONTAINS **incision**
c. **incision** CONTAINS **bled**

Through our container nesting, we can automatically infer that 'bled' occurred on December 19th (because '19th' CONTAINS 'surgery' which CONTAINS 'incision' which CONTAINS 'bled'). This also allows the capture of EVENT/sub-event relations, and the rapid expression of complex temporal interactions.

6 Explicit vs. Inferable Annotation

Given a specification language, there are essentially two ways of introducing the elements into the document (data source) being annotated:[6]

- Manual annotation: Elements are introduced into the document directly by the human annotator following the guideline.
- Automatic (inferred) annotation: Elements are created by applying an automated procedure that introduces new elements that are derivable from the human annotations.

As such, there is a complex interaction between specification and guideline, and we focus on how the clinical annotation task has helped shape and refine the annotation guidelines. It is important to note that an annotation guideline does not necessarily force the markup of certain elements in a text, even though the specification language (and the eventual goal of the project) might require those annotations to exist.

In some cases, these added annotations are derived logically from human annotations. Explicitly marked temporal relations can be used to infer others that are not marked but exist implicitly through closure. For instance, given EVENTs A, B and C and TLINKs 'A BEFORE B' and 'B BEFORE C', the TLINK 'A BEFORE C' can be automatically inferred. Repeatedly applying such inference rules allows all inferable

[5] This is a subset of the ISO-TimeML TLINK types, excluding those seldom occurring in medical records, like 'simultaneous' as well as inverse relations like 'during' or 'after'.

[6] We ignore the application of automatic techniques, such as classifiers trained on external datasets, as our focus here is on the preparation of the gold standard used for such classifiers.

TLINKs to be generated (Verhagen, 2005). We can use this idea of closure to show our annotators which annotations need not be marked explicitly, saving time and effort. We have also incorporated these closure rules into our inter-annotator agreement (IAA) calculation for temporal relations, described further in Section 7.2.

The automatic application of rules following the annotation of the text is not limited to the marking of logically inferable relations or EVENTs. In the clinical domain, the combination of within-group shared knowledge and pressure towards concise writing leads to a number of common, inferred relations. Take, for example, the sentence:

(10) Jan 2013: **Colonoscopy**, **biopsies**. **Pathology** showed **adenocarcinoma**, **resected** at Mercy. **Diagnosis T3N1 Adenocarcinoma**.

In this sentence, only the CONTAINS relations between "Jan 2013" and the EVENTs (in bold) are explicitly stated. However, based on the known progression-of-care for colon cancer, we can infer that the colonoscopy occurs first, biopsies occur during the colonoscopy, pathology happens afterwards, a diagnosis (here, adenocarcinoma) is returned after pathology, and resection of the tumor occurs after diagnosis. The presence of the AJCC staging information in the final sentence (along with the confirmation of the adenocarcinoma diagnosis) implies a post-surgical pathology exam of the resected specimen, as the AJCC staging information cannot be determined without this additional examination.

These inferences come naturally to domain experts but are largely inaccessible to people outside the medical community without considerable annotator training. Making explicit our understanding of these "understood orderings" is crucial; although they are not marked by human annotators in our schema, the annotators often found it initially frustrating to leave these (purely inferential) relations unstated. Although many of our (primarily linguistically trained) annotators learned to see these patterns, we chose to exclude them from the manual task since newer annotators with varying degrees of domain knowledge may struggle if asked to manually annotate them.

Similar unspoken-but-understood orderings are found throughout the clinical domain. As mentioned in Section 3, both Permanence and Contextual Aspect:Intermittent are properties of symptoms and diseases themselves, rather than of the patient's particular situation. As such, these properties could easily be identified and marked across a medical ontology, and then be automatically assigned to EVENTs recognized as specific medical named entities.

Annotation Type	Raw Count
EVENT	15,769
TIMEX3	1,426
LINK	7935
Total	25,130

Table 1: Raw Frequency of Annotation Types

TLINK Type	Raw Count	% of TLINKs
CONTAINS	5,112	64.42%
OVERLAP	1,205	15.19%
BEFORE	1,004	12.65%
BEGINS-ON	488	6.15%
ENDS-ON	126	1.59%
Total	7,935	100.00%

Table 2: Relative Frequency of TLINK types

Finally, due to the peculiarities of EHR systems, some annotations *must* be done programatically. Exact dates of patient visit (or of pathology/radiology consult) are often recorded as metadata on the EHR itself, rather than within the text, making the canonical DOCTIME (or time of automatic section modifications) difficult to access in de-identified plaintext data, but easy to find automatically.

7 Results

We report results on the annotations from the here-released subset of the THYME colon cancer corpus, which includes clinical notes and pathology reports for 35 patients diagnosed with colon cancer for a total of 107 documents. Each note was annotated by a pair of graduate or undergraduate students in Linguistics at the University of Colorado, then adjudicated by a domain expert. These clinical narratives were sampled from the EHRs of a major healthcare center (the Mayo Clinic). They were deidentified for all patient-sensitive information; however, original dates were retained.

7.1 Descriptive Statistics

Table 1 presents the raw counts for events, temporal expressions and links in the adjudicated gold annotations. Table 2 presents the number and percentage of TLINKs by type in the adjudicated relations gold annotations.

Annotation Type	F1-Score	Alpha
EVENT	0.8038	0.7899
TIMEX3	0.8047	0.6705
LINK: Participants only	0.5012	0.4999
LINK: Participants+type	0.4506	0.4503
LINK: CONTAINS	0.5630	0.5626

Table 3: IAA (F1-Score and Alpha) by annotation type

EVENT Property	F1-Score	Alpha
DocTimeRel	0.7189	0.6889
Cont.Aspect	0.9947	0.9930
Cont.Modality	0.9547	0.9420

Table 4: IAA (F1-Score and Alpha) for EVENT properties

7.2 Inter-annotator Agreement

We report inter-annotator agreement (IAA) results on the THYME corpus. Each note was annotated by two independent annotators. The final gold standard was produced after disagreement adjudication by a third annotator was performed.

We computed the IAA as F1-score and Krippendorff's Alpha (Krippendorff, 2012) by applying closure, using explicitly marked temporal relations to identify others that are not marked but exist implicitly. In the computation of the IAA, inferred-only TLINKs do not contribute to the score, matched or unmatched. For instance, if both annotators mark A BEFORE B and B BEFORE C, to prevent artificially inflating the agreement score, the inferred A BEFORE C is ignored. Likewise, if one annotator marked A BEFORE B and B BEFORE C and the other annotator did not, the inferred A BEFORE C is not counted. However, if one annotator did explicitly mark A BEFORE C, then an equivalent inferred TLINK would be used to match it. EVENT and TIMEX3 IAA was generated based on exact and overlapping spans, respectively. These results are reported in Table 3.

The THYME corpus also differs from ISO-TimeML in terms of EVENT properties, with the addition of DocTimeRel, ContextualModality and ContextualAspect. IAA for these properties is in Table 4.

7.3 Baseline Systems

To get an idea of how much work will be necessary to adapt existing temporal information extraction systems to the clinical domain, we took the freely available ClearTK-TimeML system (Bethard, 2013), which was among the top performing systems in TempEval 2013 (UzZaman et al., 2013), and evaluated its performance on the THYME corpus.

	TempEval 2013			THYME Corpus		
	P	R	F_1	P	R	F_1
TIMEX3	83.2	71.7	77.0	59.3	42.8	49.7
EVENT	81.4	76.4	78.8	78.9	23.9	36.6
DocTimeRel	-	-	-	47.4	47.4	47.4
LINK[7]	28.6	30.9	26.6	22.7	18.6	20.4
EVENT-TIMEX3	-	-	-	32.3	60.7	42.1
EVENT-EVENT	-	-	-	7.0	3.0	4.2

Table 5: Performance of ClearTK-TimeML models, as reported in the TempEval 2013 competition, and as applied to the THYME Corpus development set.

ClearTK-TimeML uses support vector machine classifiers trained on the TempEval 2013 training data, employing a small set of features including character patterns, tokens, stems, part-of-speech tags, nearby nodes in the constituency tree, and a small time word gazetteer. For EVENTs and TIMEX3s, the ClearTK-TimeML system could be applied directly to the THYME corpus. For DocTimeRels, the relation for an EVENT was taken from the TLINK between that EVENT and the document creation time, after mapping INCLUDES to OVERLAP. EVENTs with no such TLINK were assumed to have a DocTimeRel of OVERLAP. For other temporal relations, INCLUDES was mapped to CONTAINS.

Results of this system on TempEval 2013 and the THYME corpus are shown in Table 5. For time expressions, performance when moving to the clinical data degrades about 25%, from F_1 of 77.0 to 49.7. For events, the degradation is much larger, about 40%, from 78.8 to 36.6, most likely because of the large number of clinical symptoms, diseases, disorders, etc. which have never been observed by the system during training. Temporal relations are a bit more difficult to compare because TempEval lumped DocTimeRel and other temporal relations together and had several differences in their evaluation metric[7]. However, we at least can see that performance of the ClearTK-TimeML system on temporal relations is low on clinical text, achieving only F_1 of 20.4.

These results suggest that clinical narratives do

[7]The TempEval 2013 evaluation metric penalized systems for parts of the text that were not examined by annotators, and used different variants of closure-based precision and recall.

indeed present new challenges for temporal information extraction systems, and that having access to domain specific training data will be crucial for accurate extraction in the clinical domain. At the same time, it is encouraging that we were able to apply existing ISO-TimeML-based systems to our corpus, despite the several extensions to ISO-TimeML that were necessary for clinical narratives.

8 Discussion

CONTAINS plays a large role in the THYME corpus, representing 66% of TLINK annotations made, compared with only 14.6% for OVERLAP, the second most frequent type. We also see that BEFORE links are relatively less common than OVERLAP and CONTAINS, illustrating that much of the temporal ordering on the timeline is accomplished by using many vertical links (CONTAINS, OVERLAP) to build containers, and few horizontal links (BEFORE, BEGINS-ON, ENDS-ON) to order them.

IAA on EVENTs and Temporal Expressions is strong, although differentiating implicit EVENTs (which should not be marked) from explicit, markable EVENTs remains one of the biggest sources of disagreement. When compared to the data from the 2012 i2b2 challenge (Sun et al., 2013b), our IAA figures are quite similar. Even with our more complex schema, we achieved an F1-score of 0.8038 for EVENTs (compared to the i2b2 score of 0.87 for partial match). For TIMEX3s, our F1-score was 0.8047, compared to an F1-score of 0.89 for i2b2.

TLINKing medical EVENTs remains a very difficult task. By using our narrative container approach to constrain the number of necessary annotations and by eliminating often-confusing inverse relations (like 'after' and 'during') (neither of which were done for the i2b2 data), we were able to significantly improve on the i2b2 TLINK span agreement F1-score of 0.39, achieving an agreement score of 0.5012 for all LINKs across our corpus. The majority of remaining annotator disagreement comes from different opinions about whether any two EVENTs require an explicit TLINK between them or an inferred one, rather than what type of TLINK it would be (e.g. BEFORE vs. CONTAINS). Although our results are still significantly higher than the results reported for i2b2, and in line with previously reported general news figures, we are not satisfied. Improving IAA is an important goal for future work, and with further training, specification, experience, and standardization, we hope to clarify contexts for explicit TLINKS.

News-trained temporal information extraction systems see a significant drop in performance when applied to the clinical texts of the THYME corpus. But as the corpus is an extension of ISO-TimeML, future work will be able to train ISO-TimeML compliant systems on the annotations of the THYME corpus to reduce or eliminate this performance gap.

Some applications that our work may enable include (1) better understanding of event semantics, such as whether a disease is chronic or acute and its usual natural history, (2) typical event duration for these events, (3) the interaction of general and domain-specific events and their importance in the final timeline, and, more generally, (4) the importance of rough temporality and narrative containers as a step towards finer-grained timelines.

We have several avenues of ongoing and future work. First, we are working to demonstrate the utility of the THYME corpus for training machine learning models. We have designed support vector machine models with constituency tree kernels that were able to reach an F1-score of 0.737 on an EVENT-TIMEX3 narrative container identification task (Miller et al., 2013), and we are working on training models to identify events, times and the remaining types of temporal relations. Second, as per our motivating use cases, we are working to integrate this annotation data with timeline visualization tools and to use these annotations in quality-of-care research. For example, we are using temporal reasoning built on this work to investigate the liver toxicity of methotrexate across a large corpus of EHRs (Lin et al., under review)]. Finally, we plan to explore the application of our notion of an event (anything that should be visible on a domain-appropriate timeline) to other domains. It should transfer naturally to clinical notes about other (non-cancer) conditions, and even to other types of clinical notes, as certain basic events should always be included in a patient's timeline. Applying our notion of event to more distant domains, such as legal opinions, would require first identifying a consensus within the domain about which events must appear on a timeline.

9 Conclusion

Much of the information in clinical notes critical to the construction of a detailed timeline is left implicit by the concise shorthand used by doctors. Many events are referred to only by a term such as "tumor", while properties of the event itself, such as "intermittent", may not be specified. In addition, the ordering of events on a timeline is often left to the reader to infer, based on domain-specific knowledge. It is incumbent upon the annotation guideline to indicate that only informative event orderings should be annotated, while leaving domain-specific orderings to post-annotation inference. This document has detailed our approach to adapting the existing ISO-TimeML standard to this recovery of implicit information, and defining guidelines that support annotation within this complex domain. Our guidelines, as well as the annotated data, are available at `http://thyme.healthnlp.org`, and the full corpus has been proposed for use in a SemEval 2015 shared task.

Acknowledgments

The project described is supported by Grant Number R01LM010090 and U54LM008748 from the National Library Of Medicine. The content is solely the responsibility of the authors and does not necessarily represent the official views of the National Library Of Medicine or the National Institutes of Health.

We would also like to thank Dr. Piet C. de Groen and Dr. Brad Erickson at the Mayo Clinic, as well as Dr. William F. Styler III, for their contributions to the schema and to our understanding of the intricacies of clinical language.

References

James F Allen. 1983. Maintaining knowledge about temporal intervals. *Communications of the ACM*, 26(11):832–843.

Emmon Bach. 1986. The algebra of events. *Linguistics and philosophy*, 9(1):5–16.

Steven Bethard. 2013. Cleartk-timeml: A minimalist approach to tempeval 2013. In *Second Joint Conference on Lexical and Computational Semantics (*SEM), Volume 2: Proceedings of the Seventh International Workshop on Semantic Evaluation (SemEval 2013)*, pages 10–14, Atlanta, Georgia, USA, June. Association for Computational Linguistics.

Olivier Bodenreider. 2004. The Unified Medical Language System (UMLS): integrating biomedical terminology. *Nucleic acids research*, 32(Database issue):D267–D270, January.

Philip Bramsen, Pawan Deshpande, Yoong Keok Lee, and Regina Barzilay. 2006. Finding temporal order in discharge summaries. In *AMIA Annual Symposium Proceedings*, volume 2006, page 81. American Medical Informatics Association.

Carlo Combi, Yuval Shahar, et al. 1997. Temporal reasoning and temporal data maintenance in medicine: issues and challenges. *Computers in biology and medicine*, 27(5):353–368.

Robert H Dolin. 1995. Modeling the temporal complexities of symptoms. *Journal of the American Medical Informatics Association*, 2(5):323–331.

George Hripcsak, Nicholas D Soulakis, Li Li, Frances P Morrison, Albert M Lai, Carol Friedman, Neil S Calman, and Farzad Mostashari. 2009. Syndromic surveillance using ambulatory electronic health records. *Journal of the American Medical Informatics Association*, 16(3):354–361.

Ann K Irvine, Stephanie W Haas, and Tessa Sullivan. 2008. Tn-ties: A system for extracting temporal information from emergency department triage notes. In *AMIA Annual Symposium proceedings*, volume 2008, page 328. American Medical Informatics Association.

Elpida T Keravnou. 1997. Temporal abstraction of medical data: Deriving periodicity. In *Intelligent Data Analysis in Medicine and Pharmacology*, pages 61–79. Springer.

Klaus H. Krippendorff. 2012. *Content Analysis: An Introduction to Its Methodology*. SAGE Publications, Inc, third edition edition, April.

Chen Lin, Elizabeth Karlson, Dmitriy Dligach, Monica Ramirez, Timothy Miller, Huan Mo, Natalie Braggs, Andrew Cagan, Joshua Denny, and Guergana. Savova. under review. Automatic identification of methotrexade-induced liver toxicity in rheumatoid arthritis patients from the electronic medical records. *Journal of the Medical Informatics Association*.

John McCarthy. 2002. Actions and other events in situation calculus. In *Proceedings of the International conference on Principles of Knowledge Representation and Reasoning*, pages 615–628. Morgan Kaufmann Publishers; 1998.

Stéphane M Meystre, Guergana K Savova, Karin C Kipper-Schuler, John F Hurdle, et al. 2008. Extracting information from textual documents in the electronic health record: a review of recent research. *Yearb Med Inform*, 35:128–44.

Timothy Miller, Steven Bethard, Dmitriy Dligach, Sameer Pradhan, Chen Lin, and Guergana Savova. 2013. Discovering temporal narrative containers in clinical text. In *Proceedings of the 2013 Workshop on Biomedical Natural Langua ge Processing*, pages 18–26, Sofia, Bulgaria, August. Association for Computational Linguistics.

Eleni Miltsakaki, Rashmi Prasad, Aravind Joshi, and Bonnie Webber. 2004. The penn discourse treebank. In *In Proceedings of LREC 2004*.

Massimo Poesio. 2004. Discourse annotation and semantic annotation in the gnome corpus. In *In Proceedings of the ACL Workshop on Discourse Annotation*.

James Pustejovsky and Amber Stubbs. 2011. Increasing informativeness in temporal annotation. In *Proceedings of the 5th Linguistic Annotation Workshop*, pages 152–160. Association for Computational Linguistics.

James Pustejovsky, Robert Knippen, Jessica Littman, and Roser Sauri. 2005. Temporal and event information in natural language text. *Language Resources and Evaluation*, 39(2-3):123–164.

James Pustejovsky, Kiyong Lee, Harry Bunt, and Laurent Romary. 2010. Iso-timeml: An international standard for semantic annotation. In *Proceedings of the Seventh International Conference on Language Resources and Evaluation (LREC 2010)*, Valletta, Malta.

Angus Roberts, Robert Gaizauskas, Mark Hepple, George Demetriou, Yikun Guo, and Ian Roberts. 2009. Building a semantically annotated corpus of clinical texts. *Journal of biomedical informatics*, 42(5):950–966.

Guergana Savova, Steven Bethard, Will Styler, James Martin, Martha Palmer, James Masanz, and Wayne Ward. 2009. Towards temporal relation discovery from the clinical narrative. In *AMIA Annual Symposium Proceedings*, volume 2009, page 568. American Medical Informatics Association.

Tessa Sullivan, Ann Irvine, and Stephanie W Haas. 2008. It's all relative: usage of relative temporal expressions in triage notes. *Proceedings of the American Society for Information Science and Technology*, 45(1):1–8.

Weiyi Sun, Anna Rumshisky, and Ozlem Uzuner. 2013a. Evaluating temporal relations in clinical text: 2012 i2b2 challenge. *Journal of the American Medical Informatics Association*.

Weiyi Sun, Anna Rumshisky, and Ozlem Uzuner. 2013b. Evaluating temporal relations in clinical text: 2012 i2b2 challenge. *Journal of the American Medical Informatics Association*, 20(5):806–813.

Alexander Turchin, Maria Shubina, Eugene Breydo, Merri L Pendergrass, and Jonathan S Einbinder. 2009. Comparison of information content of structured and narrative text data sources on the example of medication intensification. *Journal of the American Medical Informatics Association*, 16(3):362–370.

Naushad UzZaman, Hector Llorens, Leon Derczynski, James Allen, Marc Verhagen, and James Pustejovsky. 2013. Semeval-2013 task 1: Tempeval-3: Evaluating time expressions, events, and temporal relations. In *Second Joint Conference on Lexical and Computational Semantics (*SEM), Volume 2: Proceedings of the Seventh International Workshop on Semantic Evaluation (SemEval 2013)*, pages 1–9, Atlanta, Georgia, USA, June. Association for Computational Linguistics.

Marc Verhagen. 2005. Temporal Closure in an Annotation Environment. *Language Resources and Evaluation*, 39(2):211–241.

Veronika Vincze, Gyrgy Szarvas, Richrd Farkas, Gyrgy Mra, and Jnos Csirik. 2008. The bioscope corpus: biomedical texts annotated for uncertainty, negation and their scopes. *BMC Bioinformatics*, 9(Suppl 11):1–9.

Ying Zhao, George Karypis, and Usama M. Fayyad. 2005. Hierarchical clustering algorithms for document datasets. *Data Mining and Knowledge Discovery*, 10:141–168.

Jiaping Zheng, Wendy W Chapman, Rebecca S Crowley, and Guergana K Savova. 2011. Coreference resolution: A review of general methodologies and applications in the clinical domain. *Journal of biomedical informatics*, 44(6):1113–1122.

Li Zhou, Simon Parsons, and George Hripcsak. 2008. The evaluation of a temporal reasoning system in processing clinical discharge summaries. *Journal of the American Medical Informatics Association*, 15(1):99–106.

Senti-LSSVM: Sentiment-Oriented Multi-Relation Extraction with Latent Structural SVM

Lizhen Qu
Max Planck Institute
for Informatics
lqu@mpi-inf.mpg.de

Yi Zhang
Nuance Communications
yi.zhang@nuance.com

Rui Wang
DFKI GmbH
mars198356@hotmail.com

Lili Jiang
Max Planck Institute
for Informatics
ljiang@mpi-inf.mpg.de

Rainer Gemulla
Max Planck Institute
for Informatics
rgemulla@mpi-inf.mpg.de

Gerhard Weikum
Max Planck Institute
for Informatics
weikum@mpi-inf.mpg.de

Abstract

Extracting instances of sentiment-oriented relations from user-generated web documents is important for online marketing analysis. Unlike previous work, we formulate this extraction task as a structured prediction problem and design the corresponding inference as an integer linear program. Our latent structural SVM based model can learn from training corpora that do not contain explicit annotations of sentiment-bearing expressions, and it can simultaneously recognize instances of both binary (polarity) and ternary (comparative) relations with regard to entity mentions of interest. The empirical evaluation shows that our approach significantly outperforms state-of-the-art systems across domains (cameras and movies) and across genres (reviews and forum posts). The gold standard corpus that we built will also be a valuable resource for the community.

1 Introduction

Sentiment-oriented relation extraction (Choi et al., 2006) is concerned with recognizing sentiment polarities and comparative relations between entities from natural language text. Identifying such relations often requires syntactic and semantic analysis at both sentence and phrase level. Most prior work on sentiment analysis consider either i) subjective sentence detection (Yu and Kübler, 2011), ii) polarity classification (Johansson and Moschitti, 2011; Wilson et al., 2005), or iii) comparative relation identification (Jindal and Liu, 2006; Ganapathibhotla and Liu, 2008). In practice, however, different types of sentiment-oriented relations frequently coexist in documents. In particular, we found that more than 38% of the sentences in our test corpus contain more than one type of relations. The isolated analysis approach is inappropriate because i) it sacrifices acuracy by ignoring the intricate interplay among different types of relations; ii) it could lead to conflicting predictions such as estimating a relation candidate as both negative and comparative. Therefore, in this paper, we identify instances of both sentiment polarities and comparative relations for entities of interest *simultaneously*. We assume that all the mentions of entities and attributes are given, and entities are disambiguated. It is a widely used assumption when evaluating a module in a pipeline system that the outputs of preceding modules are error-free.

To the best of our knowledge, the only existing system capable of extracting both comparisons and sentiment polarities is a rule-based system proposed by Ding et al. (2009). We argue that it is better to tackle the task by using a *unified model* with *structured outputs*. It allows us to consider a set of correlated relation instances *jointly* and characterize their interaction through a set of soft and hard constraints. For example, we can encode constraints to discourage an attribute to participate in a polarity relation and a comparative relation at the same time. As a result, the system extracts a set of correlated instances of sentiment-oriented relations from a given sentence. For example, with the sentence about the camera Canon 7D, *"The sensor is great, but the price is higher than Nikon D7000."* the expected output is *positive*(`Canon 7D`, *sensor*)

Transactions of the Association for Computational Linguistics, 2 (2014) 155–168. Action Editor: Janyce Wiebe.
Submitted 6/2013; Revised 11/2013; Published 4/2014.

and *preferred*(Nikon D7000, Canon 7D, textit-price).

However, constructing a fully annotated training corpus for this task is labor-intensive and requires strong linguistic background. We minimize this overhead by applying a simplified annotation scheme, in which annotators mark mentions of entities and attributes, disambiguate the entities, and label instances of relations for each sentence. Based on the new scheme, we have created a small Sentiment Relation Graph (SRG) corpus for the domains of cameras and movies, which significantly differs from the corpora used in prior work (Wei and Gulla, 2010; Kessler et al., 2010; Toprak et al., 2010; Wiebe et al., 2005; Hu and Liu, 2004) in the following ways: i) both sentiment polarities and comparative relations are annotated; ii) all mentioned entities are disambiguated; and iii) no subjective expressions are annotated, unless they are part of entity mentions.

The new annotation scheme raises a new challenge for learning algorithms in that they need to automatically find textual evidences for each annotated relation during training. For example, with the sentence *"I like the Rebel a little better, but that is another price jump"*, simply assigning a sentiment-bearing expression to the nearest relation candidate is insufficient, especially when the sentiment is not explicitly expressed.

In this paper, we propose SENTI-LSSVM, a latent structural SVM based model for sentiment-oriented relation extraction. SENTI-LSSVM is applied to find the most likely set of the relation instances expressed in a given sentence, where the latent variables are used to assign the most appropriate textual evidences to the respective instances.

In summary, the contributions of this paper are the following:

- We propose SENTI-LSSVM: the first unified statistical model with the capability of extracting instances of both binary and ternary sentiment-oriented relations.
- We design a task-specific integer linear programming (ILP) formulation for inference.
- We construct a new SRG corpus as a valuable asset for the evaluation of sentiment relation extraction.
- We conduct extensive experiments with online reviews and forum posts, showing that SENTI-LSSVM model can effectively learn from a training corpus without explicitly annotated subjective expressions and that its performance significantly outperforms state-of-the-art systems.

2 Related Work

There are ample works on analyzing sentiment polarities and entity comparisons, but the majority of them studied the two tasks in isolation.

Most prior approaches for fine-grained sentiment analysis focus on polarity classification. Supervised approaches on expression-level analysis require the annotation of sentiment-bearing expressions as training data (Jin et al., 2009; Choi and Cardie, 2010; Johansson and Moschitti, 2011; Yessenalina and Cardie, 2011; Wei and Gulla, 2010). However, the corresponding annotation process is time-consuming. Although sentence-level annotations are easier to obtain, the analysis at this level cannot cope with sentences conveying relations of multiple types (McDonald et al., 2007; Täckström and McDonald, 2011; Socher et al., 2012). Lexicon-based approaches require no training data (Ku et al., 2006; Kim and Hovy, 2006; Godbole et al., 2007; Ding et al., 2008; Popescu and Etzioni, 2005; Liu et al., 2005) but suffer from inferior performance (Wilson et al., 2005; Qu et al., 2012). In contrast, our method requires no annotation of sentiment-bearing expressions for training and can predict both sentiment polarities and comparative relations.

Sentiment-oriented comparative relations have been studied in the context of user-generated discourse (Jindal and Liu, 2006; Ganapathibhotla and Liu, 2008). Approaches rely on linguistically motivated rules and assume the existence of independent keywords in sentences which indicate comparative relations. Therefore, these methods fall short of extracting comparative relations based on domain dependent information.

Both Johansson and Moschitti (2011) and Wu et al. (2011) formulate fine-grained sentiment analysis as a learning problem with structured outputs. However, they focus only on polarity classification of expressions and require annotation of sentiment-bearing expressions for training as well.

While ILP has been previously applied for inference in sentiment analysis (Choi and Cardie, 2009; Somasundaran and Wiebe, 2009; Wu et al., 2011), our task requires a complete ILP reformulation due to 1) the absence of annotated sentiment expressions and 2) the constraints imposed by the joint extraction of both sentiment polarity and comparative relations.

3 System Overview

This section gives an overview of the whole system for extracting sentiment-oriented relation instances. Prior to presenting the system architecture, we introduce the essential concepts and the definitions of two kinds of directed hypergraphs as the representation of correlated relation instances extracted from sentences.

3.1 Concepts and Definitions

Entity. An *entity* is an abstract or concrete thing, which needs not be of material existence. An entity in this paper refers to either a product or a brand.

Attribute. An *attribute* is an object closely associated with or belonging to an entity, such as the lens of digital camera.

Sentiment-Oriented Relation. A *sentiment-oriented relation* is either a sentiment polarity or a comparative relation, defined on tuples of entities and attributes. A *sentiment polarity* relation conveys either a positive or a negative attitude towards entities or their attributes, whereas a *comparative relation* indicates the preference of one entity over the other entity w.r.t. an attribute.

Relation Instance. An instance of *sentiment polarity* takes the form *r*(entity, attribute) with *r* ∈ {*positive, negative*}, such as *positive*(`Canon 7D`, *sensor*). The polarity instances expressed in the form of unary relations, such as "Nikon D7000 is excellent.", are denoted as binary relations *r*(entity, *whole*), where the attribute *whole* indicates the entity as a whole. In contrast, an instance of *comparative relation* is in the form of *preferred*{entity, entity, attribute}, e.g. *preferred*(`Canon 7D`, `Nikon D7000`, *price*). For brevity, we refer to an instance set of sentiment-oriented relations extracted from a sentence as an **sSoR**. To represent the instances of the remaining relations, we represent them as *other*{entity, attribute}, such as textitpartOf{*wheel*, `car`}. These relations include objective relations and the subjective relations other than sentiment-oriented relations.

Mention-Based Relation Instances. A mention-based relation instance refers to a tuple of entity mentions with a certain relation. This concept is introduced as the representation of instances in a sentence by replacing entities with the corresponding entity mentions, such as *positive*("Canon SD880i", "wide angle view").

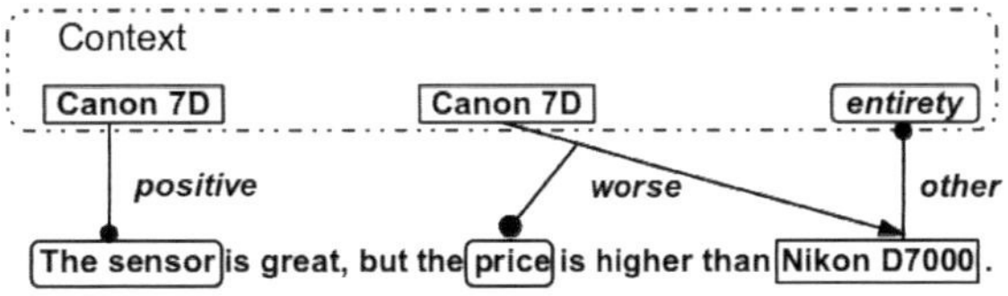

Figure 1: An example of MRG.

Mention-Based Relation Graph. A mention-based relation graph (or **MRG**) represents a collection of mention-based relation instances expressed in a sentence. As illustrated in Figure 1, an MRG is a directed hypergraph $G = \langle M, E \rangle$ with a vertex set M and an edge set E. A vertex $m_i \in M$ denotes a mention of an entity or an attribute occurring either within the sentence or in its context. We say that a mention is from the context if it is mentioned in the previous sentence or is an attribute implied in the current sentence. An instance of a binary relation in an MRG takes the form of a binary edge $e_l = (m_i, m_a)$, where m_i and m_a denote an entity mention and an attribute mention respectively, and the type $l \in$ {*positive, negative, other*}. A ternary edge e_l indicating comparative relation is represented as $e_l = (m_i, m_j, m_a)$, where two entity mentions m_i and m_j are compared with respect to the attribute mention m_a. We define the type $l \in$ {*better,worse*} to indicate two possible directions of the relation and assume m_i occurs before m_j. As a result, we have a set L of five *relation types*: *positive, negative, better, worse* or *other*. According to these definitions, the annotations in the SRG corpus are actually MRGs and disambiguated entities. If there are multiple mentions referring to the same entity, annotators are asked to choose the most obvious one because it saves annotation time and is less demanding for the entity recognition and diambiguation modules.

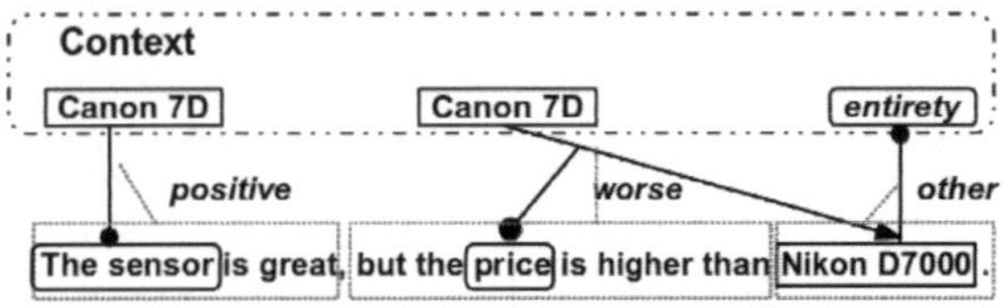

Figure 2: An example of eMRG. The textual evidences are wrapped by green dashed boxes.

Evidentiary Mention-Based Relation Graph. An *evidentiary* mention-based relation graph, coined **eMRG** , extends an MRG by associating each edge with a textual evidence to support the corresponding relation assertions (see Figure 2). Consequently, an edge in an eMRG is denoted by a pair (a, c), where a represents a mention-based relation instance and c is the associated textual evidence. It is also referred to as an *evidentiary* edge. represented as $e_l = (m_i, m_j, m_a)$, an MRG as an **evidentiary MRG (eMRG)** and the edges of eMRGs as **evidentiary** edges, as shown in Figure 2.

3.2 System Architecture

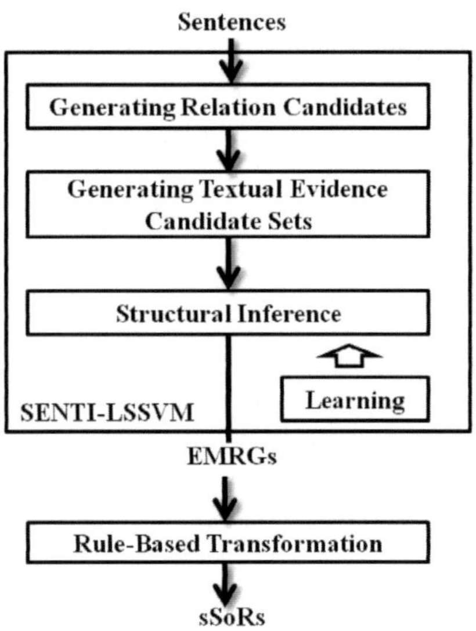

Figure 3: System architecture.

As illustrated by Figure 3, at the core of our system is the SENTI-LSSVM model, which extracts sets of mention-based relationships in the form of eMRGs from sentences. For a given sentence with known entity mentions, we select all possible mention sets as *relation candidates*, where each set includes at least one entity mention. Then we associate each relation candidate with a set of constituents or the whole sentence as the textual evidence candidates (cf. Section 6.1). Subsequently, the inference component aims to find the most likely eMRG from all possible combinations of mention-based relation instances and their textual evidences (cf. Section 6.2). The representation eMRG is chosen because it characterizes exactly the model outputs by letting each edge correspond to an instance of mention-based relation and the associated textual evidence. Finally, the model parameters of this model are learned by an online algorithm (cf. Section 7).

Since instance sets of sentiment-oriented relations (sSoRs) are the expected outputs, we can obtain sSoRs from MRGs by using a simple rule-based algorithm. The algorithm essentially maps the mentions from an MRG into entities and attributes in an sSoR and label the corresponding tuples with the relation types of the edges from an MRG. For instances of comparative relation, the label *better* or *worse* is mapped to the relation type *preferred.*

4 SENTI-LSSVM Model

The task of sentiment-oriented relation extraction is to determine the most likely sSoR in a sentence. Since sSoRs are derived from the corresponding MRGs as described in Section 3, the task is reduced to find the most likely MRG for each sentence. Since an MRG is created by assigning relation types to a subset of all *relation candidates*, which are possible tuples of mentions with unknown relation types, the number of MRGs can be extremely high.

To tackle the task, one solution is to employ an edge-factored linear model in the framework of structural SVM (Martins et al., 2009; Tsochantaridis et al., 2004). The model suggests that a bag of features should be specified for each relation candidate, and then the model predicts the most likely candidate sets along with their relation types to form the optimal MRGs. As we observed, for a relation candidate, the most informative features are the words near its entity mentions in the original text. However, if we represent a candidate by all these words, it is very likely that the instances of different relation types share overly similar features, because a mention is often involved in more than one relation candidate, as shown in Figure 2. As a consequence, the instances of different relations represented by overly similar features can easily confuse the learning algorithm. Thus, it is critical to select proper constituents or sentences as textual evidences for each relation candidate in both training and testing.

Consequently, we divide the task of sentiment-oriented relation extraction into two subtasks : i) identifying the most likely MRGs; ii) assigning proper textual evidences to each edge of MRGs to support their relation assertions. It is desirable to carry out the two subtasks *jointly* as these two subtasks could enhance each other. First, the identification of relation types requires proper textual evidences; second, the soft and hard constraints imposed by the correlated relation instances facilitate the recognition of the corresponding textual evidences. Since the eMRGs are created by attaching every MRG with a set of textual evidences, tackling the two subtasks simultaneously is equivalent to selecting the most likely eMRG from a set of eMRG candidates. It is challenging because our SRG corpus does not contain any annotation of textual evidences.

Formally, let $\mathcal{X}$ denote the set of all available sentences, and we define $y \in \mathcal{Y}(x)(x \in \mathcal{X})$ as the set of labeled edges of an MRG and $\mathcal{Y} = \cup_{x \in \mathcal{X}} \mathcal{Y}(x)$. Since the assignments of textual evidences are not observed, an assignment of evidences to y is denoted by a latent variable $h \in \mathcal{H}(x)$ and $\mathcal{H} = \cup_{x \in \mathcal{X}} \mathcal{H}(x)$. Then (y, h) corresponds to an eMRG, and $(a, c) \in (y, h)$ is a labeled edge a attached with a textual evidence c. Given a labeled dataset $D = \{(x_1, y_1), ..., (x_n, y_n)\} \in (\mathcal{X} \times \mathcal{Y})^n$, we aim to learn a discriminant function $f : \mathcal{X} \to \mathcal{Y} \times \mathcal{H}$ that outputs the optimal eMRG $(y, h) \in \mathcal{Y}(x) \times \mathcal{H}(x)$ for a given sentence x.

Due to the introduction of latent variables, we adopt the latent structural SVM (Yu and Joachims, 2009) for structural classification. Our discriminant function is defined as

$$f(x) = \text{argmax}_{(y,h) \in \mathcal{Y}(x) \times \mathcal{H}(x)} \boldsymbol{\beta}^\top \Phi(x, y, h) \quad (1)$$

where $\Phi(x, y, h)$ is the feature function of an eMRG (y, h) and $\boldsymbol{\beta}$ is the corresponding weight vector.

To ensure tractability, we also employ edge-based factorization for our model. Let M_p denote a set of entity mentions and $y_r(m_i)$ be a set of edges labeled with sentiment-oriented relations incident to m_i, the factorization of $\Phi(x, y, h)$ is given as

$$\begin{aligned}\Phi(x, y, h) \;=\; & \sum_{(a,c) \in (y,h)} \Phi_e(x, a, c) + \\ & \sum_{m_i \in M_p} \sum_{a, a' \in y_r(m_i), a \neq a'} \Phi_c(a, a')\end{aligned} \quad (2)$$

where $\Phi_e(x, a, c)$ is a local edge feature function for a labeled edge a attached with a textual evidence c and $\Phi_c(a, a')$ is a feature function capturing co-occurrence of two labeled edges a_{m_i} and a'_{m_i} incident to an entity mention m_i.

5 Feature Space

The following features are used in the feature functions (Equation 2):

Unigrams: As mentioned before, a textual evidence attached to an edge in MRG is either a word, phrase or sentence. We consider all lemmatized unigrams in the textual evidence as unigram features.

Context: Since web users usually express related sentiments about the same entity across sentence boundaries, we describe the sentiment flow using a set of contextual binary features. For example, if entity A is mentioned in both the previous sentence and the current sentence, a set of contextual binary features are used to indicate all possible combinations of the current and the previous mentioned sentiment-oriented relations regarding to entity A.

Co-occurrence: We have mentioned the co-occurrence feature in Equation 2, indicated by $\Phi_c(a, a')$. It captures the co-occurrence of two labeled edges incident to the same entity mention. Note that the co-occurrence feature function is considered only if there is a contrast conjunction such as *"but"* between the non-shared entity mentions incident to the two labeled edges.

Senti-predictors: Following the idea of (Qu et al., 2012), we encode the prediction results from the rule-based phrase-level multi-relation predictor (Ding et al., 2009) and from the bag-of-opinions predictor (Qu et al., 2010) as features based on the textual evidence. The output of the first predictor is an integer value, while the output of the second predictor is a sentiment relation, such as "positive", "negative", "better" or "worse". We map the relational outputs into integer values and then encode the outputs from both predictors as senti-predictor features.

Others: The commonly used part-of-speech tags are also included as features. Moreover, for an edge candidate, a set of binary features are used to denote the types of the edge and its entity mentions. For instance, a binary feature indicates whether an edge is a binary edge related to an entity mentioned in context. To characterize the syntactic dependencies between two adjacent entity mentions, we use the path in the dependency tree between the heads of the corresponding constituents, the number of words and other mentions in-between as features. Additionally, if the textual evidence is a constituent, its feature w.r.t. an edge is the dependency path to the closest mention of the edge that does not overlap with this constituent.

6 Structural Inference

In order to find the best eMRG for a given sentence with a well trained model, we need to determine the most likely relation type for each relation candidate and support the corresponding assertions with proper textual evidences. We formulate this task as an Integer Linear Programming (ILP). Instead of considering all constituents of a sentence, we empirically select a subset as textual evidences for each relation candidate.

6.1 Textual Evidence Candidates Selection

Textual evidences are selected based on the constituent trees of sentences parsed by the Stanford parser (Klein and Manning, 2003). For each mention in a sentence, we first locate a constituent in the tree with the maximal overlap by Jaccard similarity. Starting from this constituent, we consider two types of candidates: *type I* candidates are constituents at the highest level which contain neither any word of another mention nor any contrast conjunctions such as *"but"*; *type II* candidates are constituents at the highest level which cover exactly two mentions of an edge and do not overlap with any other mentions. For a binary edge connecting an entity mention and an attribute mention, we consider a *type I* candidate starting from the attribute mention. For a binary edge connecting two entity mentions, we consider *type I* candidates starting from both mentions. Moreover, for a comparative ternary edge, we consider both *type I* and *type II* candidates starting from the attribute mention. This strategy is based on our observation that these candidates often cover the most important information w.r.t. the covered entity mentions.

6.2 ILP Formulation

We formulate the inference problem of finding the best eMRG as an ILP problem due to its convenient integration of both soft and hard constraints.

Given the model parameters $\boldsymbol{\beta}$, we reformulate the score of an eMRG in the discriminant function (1) as follows,

$$\boldsymbol{\beta}^\top \Phi(x, y, h) = \sum_{(a,c)\in(y,h)} s_{ac} z_{ac} + \sum_{m_i \in M_p} \sum_{a,a' \in y_r(m_i), a \neq a'} s_{aa'} z_{aa'}$$

where $s_{ac} = \boldsymbol{\beta}^\top \Phi_e(x, a, c)$ denotes the score of a labeled edge a attached with a textual evidence c, $s_{aa'} = \boldsymbol{\beta}^\top \Phi_c(a, a')$ is the edge co-occurrence score, the binary variable z_{ac} indicates the presence or absence of the corresponding edge, and $z_{aa'}$ indicates if two edges co-occurr. As not every edge set can form an eMRG, we require that a valid eMRG should satisfy a set of linear constraints, which form our *constraint space*. Then function (1) is equivalent to

$$\begin{aligned} \max_{\mathbf{z}\in\mathbb{B}} \quad & \mathbf{s}^\top \mathbf{z} + \mu \mathbf{z}^d \\ \text{s.t.} \quad & \mathbf{A} \begin{bmatrix} \mathbf{z} \\ \boldsymbol{\eta} \\ \boldsymbol{\tau} \end{bmatrix} \leq \mathbf{d} \\ & \mathbf{z}, \boldsymbol{\eta}, \boldsymbol{\tau} \in \mathbb{B} \end{aligned}$$

where $\mathbb{B} = 2^S$ with $S = \{0, 1\}$, and $\boldsymbol{\eta}$ and $\boldsymbol{\tau}$ are auxiliary binary variables that help define the constraint space. The above optimization problem takes exactly the form of an ILP because both the constraints and the objective function are linear, and all variables take only integer values.

In the following, we consider two types of constraint space, 1) an eMRG with only binary edges and 2) an eMRG with both binary and ternary edges.

eMRG with only Binary Edges: An eMRG has only binary edges if a sentence contains no attribute mention or at most one entity mention. We expect that each edge has only one relation type and is supported by a single textual evidence. To facilitate the formulation of constraints, we introduce η_{e_l} to denote the presence or absence of a labeled edge e_l, and η_{ec} to indicate if a textual evidence c is assigned to an unlabeled edge e. Then the binary variable for the corresponding evidentiary edge $z_{e_l c} = \eta_{ec} \wedge \eta_{e_l}$, where the ILP formulation of conjunction can be found in (Martins et al., 2009).

Let C_e denote the set of textual evidence candidates of an unlabeled edge e. The constraint of *at most one textual evidence per edge* is formulated as:

$$\sum_{c \in C_e} \eta_{ec} \leq 1 \tag{3}$$

Once a textual evidence is assigned to an edge, their relation labels should match and the number of labeled edges must agree with the number of attached textual evidences. Further, we assume that a textual evidence c conveys at most one relation so that an evidence will not be assigned to the relations of different types, which is the main problem for the structural SVM based model. Let η_{cl} indicate that the textual evidence c is labeled by the relation type l. The corresponding constraints are expressed as,

$$\sum_{l \in L_e} \eta_{e_l} = \sum_{c \in C_e} \eta_{ec}; \quad z_{e_l c} \leq \eta_{cl}; \quad \sum_{l \in L} \eta_{cl} \leq 1$$

where L_e denotes the set of all possible labels for an unlabeled edge e, and L is the set of all relation types of MRGs (cf. Section 3).

In order to avoid a textual evidence being overly reused by multiple relation candidates, we first penalize the assignment of a textual evidence c to a labeled edge a by associating the corresponding z_{ac} with a fixed negative cost $-\mu$ in the objective function. Then the selection of one textual evidence per edge a is encouraged by associating μ to z_c^d in the objective function, where $z_c^d = \bigvee_{e \in S_c} \eta_{ec}$ and S_c is the set of edges that the textual evidence c serves as a candidate. The disjunction z_c^d is expressed as:

$$\begin{aligned} z_c^d &\geq \eta_e, e \in S_c \\ z_c^d &\leq \sum_{e \in S_c} \eta_e \end{aligned}$$

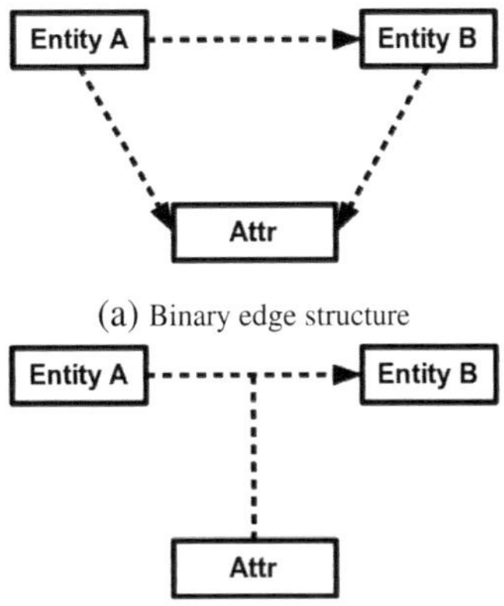

(a) Binary edge structure

(b) Ternary edge structure

Figure 4: Alternative structures associated with an attribute mention.

This soft constraint not only encourages one textual evidence per edge, but also keeps it eligible for multiple assignments.

For any two labeled edge a and a' incident to the same entity mention, the edge-to-edge co-occurrence is described by $z^c_{a,a'} = z_a \wedge z_{a'}$.

eMRG with both Binary and Ternary Edges: If there are more than one entity mentions and at least one attribute mention in a sentence, an eMRG can potentially have both binary and ternary edges. In this case, we assume that each mention of attributes can participate either in binary relations or in ternary relations. The assumption holds in more than 99.9% of the sentences in our SRG corpus, thus we describe it as a set of hard constraints. Geometrically, the assumption can be visualized as the selection between two alternative structures incident to the same attribute mention, as shown in Figure 4. Note that, in the binary edge structure, we include not only the edges incident to the attribute mention but also the edge between the two entity mentions.

Let $S^b_{m_i}$ be the set of all possible labeled edges in a binary edge structure of an attribute mention m_i. Variable $\tau^b_{m_i} = \bigvee_{e_l \in S^b_{m_i}} \eta_{e_l}$ indicates whether the attribute mention is associated with a binary edge structure or not. In the same manner, we use $\tau^t_{m_i} = \bigvee_{e_l \in S^t_{m_i}} \eta_{e_l}$ to indicate the association of the an attribute mention m_i with an ternary edge structure from the set of all incident ternary edges $S^t_{m_i}$. The selection between two alternative structures is formulated as $\tau^b_{m_i} + \tau^t_{m_i} = 1$. As this influences only the edges incident to an attribute mention, we keep all the constraints introduced in the previous section unchanged except for constraint (3), which is modified as

$$\sum_{c \in C_e} \eta_{ec} \leq \tau^b_{m_i}; \qquad \sum_{c \in C_e} \eta_{ec} \leq \tau^t_{m_i}$$

Therefore, we can have either binary edges or ternary edges for an attribute mention.

7 Learning Model Parameters

Given a set of training sentences $D = \{(x_1, y_1), \ldots, (x_n, y_n)\}$, the best weight vector $\boldsymbol{\beta}$ of the discriminant function (1) is found by solving the following optimization problem:

$$\min_{\boldsymbol{\beta}} \frac{1}{n} \sum_{i=1}^{n} [\max_{(\hat{y}, \hat{h}) \in \mathcal{Y}(x) \times \mathcal{H}(x)} (\boldsymbol{\beta}^\top \Phi(x, \hat{y}, \hat{h}) + \delta(\hat{h}, \hat{y}, y)) - \max_{\bar{h} \in \mathcal{H}(x)} \boldsymbol{\beta}^\top \Phi(x, y, \bar{h})] + \rho |\boldsymbol{\beta}|] \quad (4)$$

where $\delta(\hat{h}, \hat{y}, y)$ is a loss function measuring the discrepancies between an eMRG $(y, \bar{h})$ with gold standard edge labels y and an eMRG $(\hat{y}, \hat{h})$ with inferred labeled edges $\hat{y}$ and textual evidences $\hat{h}$. Due to the sparse nature of the lexical features, we apply L1 regularizer to the weight vector $\boldsymbol{\beta}$, and the degree of sparsity is controlled by the hyperparameter ρ.

Since the L1 norm in the above optimization problem is not differentiable at zero, we apply the online *forward-backward splitting* (FOBOS) algorithm (Duchi and Singer, 2009). It requires two steps for updating the weight vector $\boldsymbol{\beta}$ by using a single training sentence x on each iteration t.

$$\begin{aligned} \boldsymbol{\beta}_{t+\frac{1}{2}} &= \boldsymbol{\beta}_t - \varepsilon_t \Delta_t \\ \boldsymbol{\beta}_{t+1} &= \arg\min_{\boldsymbol{\beta}} \frac{1}{2} \|\boldsymbol{\beta} - \boldsymbol{\beta}_t\|^2 + \varepsilon_t \rho |\boldsymbol{\beta}| \end{aligned}$$

where Δ_t is the subgradient computed without considering the L1 norm and ε_t is the learning rate. For a labeled sentence x, $\Delta_t = \Phi(x, \hat{y}^*, \hat{h}^*) - \Phi(x, y, \bar{h}^*)$, where the feature functions of the corresponding eMRGs are inferred by solving $(\hat{y}^*, \hat{h}^*) = \arg\max_{(\hat{h}, \hat{y}) \in \mathcal{H}(x) \times \mathcal{Y}(x)} [\boldsymbol{\beta}^\top \Phi(x, \hat{y}, \hat{h}) + \delta(\hat{h}, \hat{y}, y)]$ and $(y, \bar{h}^*) = \arg\max_{\bar{h} \in \mathcal{H}(x)} \boldsymbol{\beta}^\top \Phi(x, y, \bar{h})$, as indicated in the optimization problem (4).

The former inference problem is similar to the one we considered in the previous section except the inclusion of the loss function. We incorporate the loss function into the ILP formulation by defining the loss between an MRG (y, h) and a gold standard MRG as the sum of per-edge costs. In our experiments, we consider a positive cost φ for each wrongly labeled edge a, so that if an edge a has a different label from the gold standard, we add φ to the coefficient s_{ac} of the corresponding variable z_{ac} in the objective function of the ILP formulation.

In addition, since the non-positive weights of edge labels in the initial learning phrase often lead to eMRGs with many unlabeled edges, which harms the learning performance, we fix it by adding a constraint for the minimal number of labeled edges in an eMRG,

$$\sum_{a \in A} \sum_{c \in C_a} \eta_{ac} \geq \zeta \quad (5)$$

where A is the set of all labeled edge candidates and ζ denotes the minimal number of labeled edges.

Empirically, the best way to determine ζ is to make it equal to the maximal number of labeled edges in an eMRG with the restriction that a textual evidence can be assigned to at most one edge. By considering all the edge candidates A and all the textual evidence candidates C as two vertex sets in a bipartite graph $\hat{G} = \langle V = (A, C), E \rangle$ (with edges in E indicating which textual evidence can be assigned to which edge), ζ corresponds to exactly the size of a maximum matching of the bipartite graph[1].

To find the optimal eMRG $(y, \bar{h}^*)$, for the gold label k of each edge, we consider the following set of constraints for inference since the labels of the edges are known for the training data,

$$\sum_{c \in C_e} \eta_{ec} \leq 1; \qquad \eta_{ec} \leq l_{ck}$$

$$\sum_{k' \in L} l_{ck'} \leq 1; \qquad \sum_{e \in S_c} \eta_{ec} \leq 1$$

We include also the soft constraints, which avoid a textual evidence being overly reused by multiple relations, and the constraints similar to (5) to ensure a minimal number of labeled edges and a minimal number of sentiment-oriented relations.

[1]It is computed by the Hopcroft-Karp algorithm (Hopcroft and Karp, 1973) in our implementation.

8 SRG Corpus

For evaluation we constructed the SRG corpus, which in total consists of 1686 manually annotated online reviews and forum posts in the digital camera and movie domains[2]. For each domain, we maintain a set of attributes and a list of entity names.

The annotation scheme for the sentiment representation asserts minimal linguistic knowledge from our annotators. By focusing on the meanings of the sentences, the annotators make decisions based on their language intuition, not restricted by specific syntactic structures. Taking the example in Figure 2, the annotators only need to mark the mentions of entities and attributes from both the sentences and the context, disambiguate them, and label ("Canon 7D", "Nikon D7000", *price*) as *worse* and ("Canon 7D", "sensor") as *positive*, whereas in prior work, people have annotated the sentiment-bearing expressions such as "great" and link them to the respective relation instances as well. This also enables them to annotate instances of both sentiment polarity and comparative relaton, which are conveyed by not only explicit sentiment-bearing expressions like *"excellent performance"*, but also factual expressions implying evaluations such as *"The 7V has 10x optical zoom and the 9V has 16x."*.

	Camera		Movie	
	Reviews	Forums	Reviews	Forums
positive	386	1539	879	905
negative	165	363	529	331
comparison	30	480	39	35

Table 1: Distribution of relation instances in SRG corpus.

14 annotators participated in the annotation project. After a short training period, annotators worked on randomly assigned documents one at a time. For product reviews, the system lists all relevant information about the entity and the predefined attributes. For forum posts, the system shows only the attribute list. For each sentence in a document, the annotator first determines if it refers to an entity of interest. If not, the sentence is marked as *off-topic*. Otherwise, the annotator will identify the most obvious mentions, disambiguate them, and mark the MRGs. We evaluate the inter-annotator agreement on sSoRs in terms of Cohen's Kappa (κ) (Cohen, 1968). An average Kappa value of 0.698 was achieved on a randomly selected set consisting of 412 sentences.

Table 1 shows the corpus distribution after normalizing them into sSoRs. Camera forum posts contain the largest proportion of comparisons because they are mainly about the recommendation of digital cameras. In contrast, web users are much less interested in comparing movies, in both reviews and forums. In all subsets, positive relations play a dominant role since web users intend to express more positive attitudes online than negative ones (Pang and Lee, 2007).

9 Experiments

This section describes the empirical evaluation of SENTI-LSSVM together with two competitive baselines on the SRG corpus.

9.1 Experimental Setup

We implemented a rule-based baseline (DING-RULE) and a structural SVM (Tsochantaridis et al., 2004) baseline (SENTI-SSVM) for comparison. The former system extends the work of Ding et al. (2009), which designed several linguistically-motivated rules based on a sentiment polarity lexicon for relation identification and assumes there is only one type of sentiment relation in a sentence. In our implementation, we keep all the rules of (Ding et al., 2009) and add one phrase-level rule when there are more than one mention in a sentence. The additional rule assigns sentiment-bearing words and negators to its nearest relation candidates based on the absolute surface distance between the words and the corresponding mentions. In this case, the phrase-level sentiment-oriented relations depend only on the assigned sentiment words and negators. The latter system is based on a structural SVM and does not consider the assignment of textual evidences to relation instances during inference. The textual features of a relation candidate are all lexical and sentiment predictor features within a surface distance of four words from the mentions of the candidate.

[2]The 107 camera reviews are from *bestbuy.com* and *Amazon.com*; the 667 camera forum posts are downloaded from *forum.digitalcamerareview.com*; the 138 movie reviews and 774 forum posts are from *imdb.com* and *boards.ie* respectively

Thus, this baseline does not need the inference constraints of SENTI-LSSVM for the selection of textual evidences. To gain more insights into the model, we also evaluate the contribution of individual features of SENTI-LSSVM. In addition, to show if identifying sentiment polarities and comparative relations *jointly* works better than tackling each task on its own, we train SENTI-LSSVM for each task separately and combine their predictions according to compatibility rules and the corresponding graph scores.

For each domain and text genre, we withheld 15% documents for development and use the remaining for cross validation. The hyperparameters of all systems are tuned on the development datasets. For all experiments of SENTI-LSSVM, we use $\rho = 0.0001$ for the L1 regularizer in Eq.(4) and $\varphi = 0.05$ for the loss function; and for SENTI-SSVM, $\rho = 0.0001$ and $\varphi = 0.01$. Since the relation type of *off-topic* sentences is certainly *other*, we evaluate all systems with 5-fold cross-validation only on the *on-topic* sentences in the evaluation dataset. Since the same SSOR can have several equivalent MRGs and the relation type *other* is not of our interest, we evaluate the SSORs in terms of precision, recall and F-measure. All reported numbers are averages over the 5 folds.

9.2 Results

Table 2 shows the complete results of all systems. Here our model SENTI-LSSVM outperformed all baselines in terms of the average F-measure scores and recalls by a large margin. The F-measure on movie reviews is about 14% over the best baseline. The rule-based system has higher precision than recall in most cases. However, simply increasing the coverage of the domain independent sentiment polarity lexicon might lead to worse performance (Taboada et al., 2011) because many sentiment oriented relations are conveyed by domain dependent expressions and factual expressions implying evaluations, such as *"This camera does not have manual control."* Compared to DING-RULE, SENTI-SSVM performs better in the camera domain but worse for the movies due to many misclassification of *negative* relation instances as *other*. It also wrongly predicted more *positive* instances as *other* than SENTI-LSSVM. We found that the recalls of these instances are low because they often have overly similar features with the instances of the type *other* linking to the same mentions. The problem gets worse in the movie domain since i) many sentences contain no explicit sentiment-bearing words; ii) the prior polarity of the sentiment-bearing words do not agree with their contextual polarity in the sentences. Consider the following example from a forum post about the movie *"Superman Returns"*: *"Have a look at Superman: the Animated Series or Justice League Unlimited ... that is how the characters of Superman and Lex Luthor should be."*. In contrast, our model minimizes the overlapping features by assigning them to the most likely relation candidates. This leads to significantly better performance. Although SENTI-SSVM has low recall for both *positive* and *negative* relations, it achieves the highest recall for the comparative relation among all systems in the movie domain and camera reviews. Since less than 1% of all instances are for comparative relations in these document sets and all models are trained to optimize the overall accuracy, SENTI-LSSVM intends to trade off the minority class for the overall better performance. This advantage disappears on the camera forum posts, where the number of instances of comparative relation is 12 times more than that in the other data sets.

All systems perform better in predicting positive relations than the negative ones. This corresponds well to the empirical findings in (Wilson, 2008) that people intend to use more complex expressions for negative sentiments than their affirmative counterparts. It is also in accordance with the distribution of these relations in our SRG corpus which is randomly sampled from the online documents. For learning systems, it can also be explained by the fact that the training data for positive relations are considerably more than those for negative ones. The comparative relation is the hardest one to process since we found that many corresponding expressions do not contain explicit keywords for comparison.

To understand the performance of the key feature groups in our model better, we remove each group from the full SENTI-LSSVM system and evaluate the variations with movie reviews and camera forum posts, which have relatively balanced distribution of relation types. As shown in Table 3, the features from the sentiment predictors make significant contributions for both datasets. The different drops of the performance indicate that the po-

		Positive			Negative			Comparison			Micro-average		
		P	R	F	P	R	F	P	R	F	P	R	F
Camera Forum	DING-RULE	56.4	39.0	46.1	46.2	24.0	31.6	42.6	14.0	21.0	53.4	30.8	39.0
	SENTI-SSVM	60.2	35.6	44.8	44.2	38.5	41.2	28.0	**40.1**	32.9	43.7	36.7	39.9
	SENTI-LSSVM	**69.2**	38.9	**49.8**	**50.8**	**39.3**	**44.3**	42.6	35.1	**38.5**	**56.5**	**38.0**	**45.4**
Camera Re-view	DING-RULE	**83.6**	69.0	75.6	68.6	38.8	49.6	**30.0**	16.9	21.6	**81.1**	58.6	68.1
	SENTI-SSVM	72.6	75.4	74.0	63.9	**62.5**	63.2	28.0	**38.9**	**32.5**	68.1	70.4	69.3
	SENTI-LSSVM	77.3	**85.4**	**81.2**	68.9	61.3	**64.9**	22.3	20.7	21.6	73.1	**73.4**	**73.7**
Movie Forum	DING-RULE	63.7	37.4	47.1	27.6	34.3	30.6	8.9	5.6	6.8	48.2	35.9	41.2
	SENTI-SSVM	**66.2**	30.1	41.3	25.6	17.3	20.7	**44.2**	**56.7**	**49.7**	**53.3**	27.9	36.6
	SENTI-LSSVM	63.3	**44.2**	**52.1**	**29.7**	**45.6**	**36.0**	40.1	45.0	42.4	49.7	**44.6**	**47.0**
Movie Re-view	DING-RULE	**66.5**	47.2	55.2	42.0	39.1	40.5	**31.4**	12.0	17.4	56.2	44.0	49.4
	SENTI-SSVM	61.3	54.0	57.4	45.2	13.7	21.1	24.5	**63.3**	**35.3**	54.6	39.2	45.7
	SENTI-LSSVM	59.0	**79.1**	**67.6**	**53.3**	**51.4**	**52.3**	28.3	34.0	30.9	**57.9**	**68.8**	**62.9**

Table 2: Evaluation results for DING-RULE, SENTI-SSVM and SENTI-LSSVM. Boldface figures are statistically significantly better than all others in the same comparison group under t-test with $p = 0.05$.

Feature Models	Movie Reviews	Camera Forums
full system	62.9	45.4
¬unigram	63.2 (+0.3)	41.2 (-4.2)
¬context	54.5 (-8.4)	46.0 (+0.6)
¬co-occurrence	62.6 (-0.3)	44.9 (-0.5)
¬senti-predictors	61.3 (-1.6)	34.3 (-11.1)

Table 3: Micro-average F-measure of SENTI-LSSVM with different feature models

larities predicted by rules are more consistent in camera forum posts than in movie reviews. Due to the complexity of expressions in the movie reviews our model cannot benefit from the unigram features but these features are a good compensation for the sentiment predictor features in camera forum posts. The sharp drop by removing the context features from our model on movie reviews indicates that the sentiments in movie reviews depend highly on the relations of the previous sentences. In contrast, the sentiment-oriented relations of the previous sentences could be a reason of overfitting for camera forum data. The edge co-occurrence features do not play an important role in our model since the number of co-occurred sentiment-oriented relations in the sentences with contrast conjunctions like *"but"* is small. However, we found that allowing the co-occurrence of any sentiment-oriented relations would harm the performance of the model.

In addition, our experiments showed that the separated approach, which trains a model for sentiment polarities and comparative relations respectively, leads to a decrease by almost 1% in terms of the F-measure averaged over all four datasets. The largest drop of F-measure is 3% on camera forum posts, since this dataset contains the largest proportion of comparative relations. We found that the errors are increased when the trained models make conflicting predictions. In this case, the joint approach can take all factors into account and make more consistent decisions than the separated approaches.

10 Conclusion

We proposed SENTI-LSSVM model for extracting instances of both sentiment polarities and comparative relations. For evaluating and training the model, we created an SRG corpus by using a lightweight annotation scheme. We showed that our model can automatically find textual evidences to support its relation predictions and achieves significantly better F-measure scores than alternative state-of-the-art methods.

References

Yejin Choi and Claire Cardie. 2009. Adapting a polarity lexicon using integer linear programming for domain-specific sentiment classification. In *Proceedings of the 2009 Conference on Empirical Methods in Natural*

Language Processing: Volume 2 - Volume 2, EMNLP '09, pages 590–598, Stroudsburg, PA, USA. Association for Computational Linguistics.

Yejin Choi and Claire Cardie. 2010. Hierarchical sequential learning for extracting opinions and their attributes. In *Proceedings of the Annual meeting of the Association for Computational Linguistics*, pages 269–274. Association for Computational Linguistics.

Yejin Choi, Eric Breck, and Claire Cardie. 2006. Joint extraction of entities and relations for opinion recognition. In *Proceedings of the Conference on Empirical Methods in Natural Language Processing*, pages 431–439, Stroudsburg, PA, USA. Association for Computational Linguistics.

Jacob Cohen. 1968. Weighted Kappa: Nominal Scale Agreement Provision for Scaled Disagreement or Partial Credit. *Psychological bulletin*, 70(4):213.

Xiaowen Ding, Bing Liu, and Philip S. Yu. 2008. A holistic lexicon-based approach to opinion mining. In *Proceedings of the 2008 International Conference on Web Search and Data Mining*, pages 231–240, New York, NY, USA. ACM.

Xiaowen Ding, Bing Liu, and Lei Zhang. 2009. Entity discovery and assignment for opinion mining applications. In *Proceedings of the ACM SIGKDD Conference on Knowledge Discovery and Data Mining*, pages 1125–1134.

John Duchi and Yoram Singer. 2009. Efficient online and batch learning using forward backward splitting. *The Journal of Machine Learning Research*, 10:2899–2934.

Murthy Ganapathibhotla and Bing Liu. 2008. Mining opinions in comparative sentences. In *Proceedings of the 22nd International Conference on Computational Linguistics - Volume 1*, pages 241–248, Stroudsburg, PA, USA. Association for Computational Linguistics.

Namrata Godbole, Manjunath Srinivasaiah, and Steven Skiena. 2007. Large-scale sentiment analysis for news and blogs (system demonstration). In *Proceedings of the International AAAI Conference on Weblogs and Social Media*.

John E Hopcroft and Richard M Karp. 1973. An n^5/2 algorithm for maximum matchings in bipartite graphs. *SIAM Journal on computing*, 2(4):225–231.

Minqing Hu and Bing Liu. 2004. Mining and summarizing customer reviews. In *Proceedings of the tenth ACM SIGKDD international conference on Knowledge discovery and data mining*, Proceedings of the ACM SIGKDD Conference on Knowledge Discovery and Data Mining, pages 168–177, New York, NY, USA. ACM.

Wei Jin, Hung Hay Ho, and Rohini K. Srihari. 2009. Opinionminer: a novel machine learning system for web opinion mining and extraction. In *Proceedings of the 15th ACM SIGKDD international conference on Knowledge discovery and data mining*, pages 1195–1204, New York, NY, USA. ACM.

Nitin Jindal and Bing Liu. 2006. Mining comparative sentences and relations. In *Proceedings of the 21st International Conference on Artificial Intelligence - Volume 2*, AAAI'06, pages 1331–1336. AAAI Press.

Richard Johansson and Alessandro Moschitti. 2011. Extracting opinion expressions and their polarities–exploration of pipelines and joint models. In *Proceedings of the Annual meeting of the Association for Computational Linguistics*, volume 11, pages 101–106.

Jason S. Kessler, Miriam Eckert, Lyndsie Clark, and Nicolas Nicolov. 2010. The 2010 icwsm jdpa sentment corpus for the automotive domain. In *4th International AAAI Conference on Weblogs and Social Media Data Workshop Challenge (ICWSM-DWC 2010)*.

Soo-Min Kim and Eduard Hovy. 2006. Extracting opinions, opinion holders, and topics expressed in online news media text. In *Proceedings of the Workshop on Sentiment and Subjectivity in Text*, SST '06, pages 1–8, Stroudsburg, PA, USA. Association for Computational Linguistics.

Dan Klein and Christopher D. Manning. 2003. Accurate unlexicalized parsing. In *Proceedings of the 41st Annual Meeting on Association for Computational Linguistics - Volume 1*, ACL '03, pages 423–430, Stroudsburg, PA, USA. Association for Computational Linguistics.

Lun-Wei Ku, Yu-Ting Liang, and Hsin-Hsi Chen. 2006. Opinion extraction, summarization and tracking in news and blog corpora. In *AAAI Spring Symposium: Computational Approaches to Analyzing Weblogs*, pages 100–107.

Bing Liu, Minqing Hu, and Junsheng Cheng. 2005. Opinion observer: analyzing and comparing opinions on the web. In *Proceedings of the 14th international conference on World Wide Web*, pages 342–351, New York, NY, USA. ACM.

André L. Martins, Noah A. Smith, and Eric P. Xing. 2009. Concise integer linear programming formulations for dependency parsing. In *Proceedings of the Annual meeting of the Association for Computational Linguistics*, pages 342–350.

Ryan T. McDonald, Kerry Hannan, Tyler Neylon, Mike Wells, and Jeffrey C. Reynar. 2007. Structured models for fine-to-coarse sentiment analysis. In *Proceedings of the Annual meeting of the Association for Computational Linguistics*.

Bo Pang and Lillian Lee. 2007. Opinion mining and sentiment analysis. *Foundations and Trends in Information Retrieval*, 2(1-2):1–135.

Ana-Maria Popescu and Oren Etzioni. 2005. Extracting product features and opinions from reviews. In *Proceedings of the conference on Human Language Technology and Empirical Methods in Natural Language Processing*, HLT '05, pages 339–346, Stroudsburg, PA, USA. Association for Computational Linguistics.

Lizhen Qu, Georgiana Ifrim, and Gerhard Weikum. 2010. The bag-of-opinions method for review rating prediction from sparse text patterns. In Chu-Ren Huang and Dan Jurafsky, editors, *Proceedings of the 23rd International Conference on Computational Linguistics (Coling 2010)*, ACL Anthology, pages 913–921, Beijing, China. Tsinghua University Press.

Lizhen Qu, Rainer Gemulla, and Gerhard Weikum. 2012. A weakly supervised model for sentence-level semantic orientation analysis with multiple experts. In *Joint Conference on Empirical Methods in Natural Language Processing and Computational Natural Language Learning (EMNLP-CoNLL)*, pages 149–159, Jeju Island, Korea, July. Proceedings of the Annual meeting of the Association for Computational Linguistics.

Richard Socher, Brody Huval, Christopher D. Manning, and Andrew Y. Ng. 2012. Semantic compositionality through recursive matrix-vector spaces. In *Proceedings of the Conference on Empirical Methods in Natural Language Processing*, pages 1201–1211.

Swapna Somasundaran and Janyce Wiebe. 2009. Recognizing stances in online debates. In *Proceedings of the Joint conference of the 47th Annual Meeting of the Association for Computational Linguistics and the 4th International Joint Conference on Natural Language Processing of the Asian Federation of Natural Language Processing*, pages 226–234.

Maite Taboada, Julian Brooke, Milan Tofiloski, Kimberly D. Voll, and Manfred Stede. 2011. Lexicon-based methods for sentiment analysis. *Computational Linguistics*, 37(2):267–307.

Oscar Täckström and Ryan McDonald. 2011. Discovering fine-grained sentiment with latent variable structured prediction models. In *Proceedings of the 33rd European conference on Advances in information retrieval*, ECIR'11, pages 368–374, Berlin, Heidelberg. Springer-Verlag.

Cigdem Toprak, Niklas Jakob, and Iryna Gurevych. 2010. Sentence and expression level annotation of opinions in user-generated discourse. In *Proceedings of the 48th Annual Meeting of the Association for Computational Linguistics*, ACL '10, pages 575–584, Stroudsburg, PA, USA. Association for Computational Linguistics.

Ioannis Tsochantaridis, Thomas Hofmann, Thorsten Joachims, and Yasemin Altun. 2004. Support vector machine learning for interdependent and structured output spaces. In *Proceedings of the International Conference on Machine Learning*, pages 104–112.

Wei Wei and Jon Atle Gulla. 2010. Sentiment learning on product reviews via sentiment ontology tree. In *Proceedings of the Annual meeting of the Association for Computational Linguistics*, pages 404–413.

Janyce Wiebe, Theresa Wilson, and Claire Cardie. 2005. Annotating expressions of opinions and emotions in language. *Language Resources and Evaluation*, 39(2-3):165–210.

Theresa Wilson, Janyce Wiebe, and Paul Hoffmann. 2005. Recognizing contextual polarity in phrase-level sentiment analysis. In *Proceedings of the conference on Human Language Technology and Empirical Methods in Natural Language Processing*, HLT '05, pages 347–354, Stroudsburg, PA, USA. Association for Computational Linguistics.

Theresa Ann Wilson. 2008. *Fine-grained subjectivity and sentiment analysis: recognizing the intensity, polarity, and attitudes of private states*. Ph.D. thesis, UNIVERSITY OF PITTSBURGH.

Yuanbin Wu, Qi Zhang, Xuanjing Huang, and Lide Wu. 2011. Structural opinion mining for graph-based sentiment representation. In *Proceedings of the Conference on Empirical Methods in Natural Language Processing*, pages 1332–1341.

Ainur Yessenalina and Claire Cardie. 2011. Compositional matrix-space models for sentiment analysis. In *Proceedings of the Conference on Empirical Methods in Natural Language Processing*, pages 172–182.

Chun-Nam John Yu and Thorsten Joachims. 2009. Learning structural svms with latent variables. In *Proceedings of the International Conference on Machine Learning*, page 147.

Ning Yu and Sandra Kübler. 2011. Filling the gap: Semi-supervised learning for opinion detection across domains. In *Proceedings of the Fifteenth Conference on Computational Natural Language Learning*, pages 200–209. Association for Computational Linguistics.

Segmentation for Efficient Supervised Language Annotation with an Explicit Cost-Utility Tradeoff

Matthias Sperber[1], **Mirjam Simantzik**[2], **Graham Neubig**[3], **Satoshi Nakamura**[3], **Alex Waibel**[1]
[1]Karlsruhe Institute of Technology, Institute for Anthropomatics, Germany
[2]Mobile Technologies GmbH, Germany
[3]Nara Institute of Science and Technology, AHC Laboratory, Japan
matthias.sperber@kit.edu, mirjam.simantzik@jibbigo.com, neubig@is.naist.jp
s-nakamura@is.naist.jp, waibel@kit.edu

Abstract

In this paper, we study the problem of manually correcting automatic annotations of natural language in as efficient a manner as possible. We introduce a method for automatically segmenting a corpus into chunks such that many uncertain labels are grouped into the same chunk, while human supervision can be omitted altogether for other segments. A tradeoff must be found for segment sizes. Choosing short segments allows us to reduce the number of highly confident labels that are supervised by the annotator, which is useful because these labels are often already correct and supervising correct labels is a waste of effort. In contrast, long segments reduce the cognitive effort due to context switches. Our method helps find the segmentation that optimizes supervision efficiency by defining user models to predict the cost and utility of supervising each segment and solving a constrained optimization problem balancing these contradictory objectives. A user study demonstrates noticeable gains over pre-segmented, confidence-ordered baselines on two natural language processing tasks: speech transcription and word segmentation.

1 Introduction

Many natural language processing (NLP) tasks require human supervision to be useful in practice, be it to collect suitable training material or to meet some desired output quality. Given the high cost of human intervention, how to minimize the supervision effort is an important research problem. Previous works in areas such as active learning, post editing, and interactive pattern recognition have investigated this question with notable success (Settles, 2008; Specia, 2011; González-Rubio et al., 2010).

(a) It was a bright cold **(they)** in **(apron)**, and **(a)** clocks were striking thirteen.

(b) It was a bright cold **(they)** in **(apron)**, and **(a)** clocks were striking thirteen.

(c) It was a bright cold **(they)** in **(apron)**, and **(a)** clocks were striking thirteen.

Figure 1: Three automatic transcripts of the sentence "It was a bright cold day in April, and the clocks were striking thirteen", with recognition errors in parentheses. The underlined parts are to be corrected by a human for (a) sentences, (b) words, or (c) the proposed segmentation.

The most common framework for efficient annotation in the NLP context consists of training an NLP system on a small amount of baseline data, and then running the system on unannotated data to estimate confidence scores of the system's predictions (Settles, 2008). Sentences with the lowest confidence are then used as the data to be annotated (Figure 1 (a)). However, it has been noted that when the NLP system in question already has relatively high accuracy, annotating entire sentences can be wasteful, as most words will already be correct (Tomanek and Hahn, 2009; Neubig et al., 2011). In these cases, it is possible to achieve much higher benefit per annotated word by annotating sub-sentential units (Figure 1 (b)).

However, as Settles et al. (2008) point out, simply maximizing the benefit per annotated instance is not enough, as the real supervision effort varies

Transactions of the Association for Computational Linguistics, 2 (2014) 169–180. Action Editor: Eric Fosler-Lussier.
Submitted 11/2013; Revised 2/2014; Published 4/2014. ©2014 Association for Computational Linguistics.

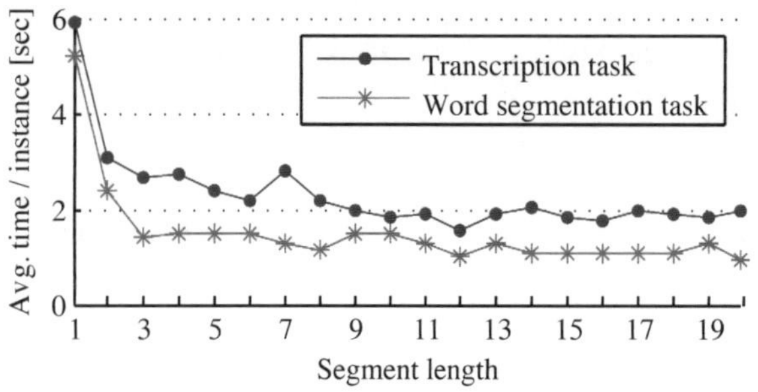

Figure 2: Average annotation time per instance, plotted over different segment lengths. For both tasks, the effort clearly increases for short segments.

greatly across instances. This is particularly important in the context of choosing segments to annotate, as human annotators heavily rely on semantics and context information to process language, and intuitively, a consecutive sequence of words can be supervised faster and more accurately than the same number of words spread out over several locations in a text. This intuition can also be seen in our empirical data in Figure 2, which shows that for the speech transcription and word segmentation tasks described later in Section 5, short segments had a longer annotation time per word. Based on this fact, we argue it would be desirable to present the annotator with a segmentation of the data into easily supervisable chunks that are both large enough to reduce the number of context switches, and small enough to prevent unnecessary annotation (Figure 1 (c)).

In this paper, we introduce a new strategy for natural language supervision tasks that attempts to optimize supervision efficiency by choosing an appropriate segmentation. It relies on a user model that, given a specific segment, predicts the cost and the utility of supervising that segment. Given this user model, the goal is to find a segmentation that minimizes the total predicted cost while maximizing the utility. We balance these two criteria by defining a constrained optimization problem in which one criterion is the optimization objective, while the other criterion is used as a constraint. Doing so allows specifying practical optimization goals such as "remove as many errors as possible given a limited time budget," or "annotate data to obtain some required classifier accuracy in as little time as possible."

Solving this optimization task is computationally difficult, an NP-hard problem. Nevertheless, we demonstrate that by making realistic assumptions about the segment length, an optimal solution can be found using an integer linear programming formulation for mid-sized corpora, as are common for supervised annotation tasks. For larger corpora, we provide simple heuristics to obtain an approximate solution in a reasonable amount of time.

Experiments over two example scenarios demonstrate the usefulness of our method: Post editing for speech transcription, and active learning for Japanese word segmentation. Our model predicts noticeable efficiency gains, which are confirmed in experiments with human annotators.

2 Problem Definition

The goal of our method is to find a segmentation over a corpus of word tokens w_1^N that optimizes supervision efficiency according to some predictive user model. The user model is denoted as a set of functions $u_{l,k}(w_a^b)$ that evaluate any possible subsequence w_a^b of tokens in the corpus according to criteria $l \in L$, and supervision modes $k \in K$.

Let us illustrate this with an example. Sperber et al. (2013) defined a framework for speech transcription in which an initial, erroneous transcript is created using automatic speech recognition (ASR), and an annotator corrects the transcript either by correcting the words by keyboard, by respeaking the content, or by leaving the words as is. In this case, we could define $K = \{\text{TYPE}, \text{RESPEAK}, \text{SKIP}\}$, each constant representing one of these three supervision modes. Our method will automatically determine the appropriate supervision mode for each segment.

The user model in this example might evaluate every segment according to two criteria L, a cost criterion (in terms of supervision time) and a utility criterion (in terms of number of removed errors), when using each mode. Intuitively, respeaking should be assigned both lower cost (because speaking is faster than typing), but also lower utility than typing on a keyboard (because respeaking recognition errors can occur). The SKIP mode denotes the special, unsupervised mode that always returns 0 cost and 0 utility.

Other possible supervision modes include multiple input modalities (Suhm et al., 2001), several human annotators with different expertise and cost

(Donmez and Carbonell, 2008), and correction vs. translation from scratch in machine translation (Specia, 2011). Similarly, cost could instead be expressed in monetary terms, or the utility function could predict the improvement of a classifier when the resulting annotation is not intended for direct human consumption, but as training data for a classifier in an active learning framework.

3 Optimization Framework

Given this setting, we are interested in simultaneously finding optimal locations and supervision modes for all segments, according to the given criteria. Each resulting segment will be assigned exactly one of these supervision modes. We denote a segmentation of the N tokens of corpus w_1^N into $M \leq N$ segments by specifying segment boundary markers $s_1^{M+1} = (s_1 = 1, s_2, \ldots, s_{M+1} = N+1)$. Setting a boundary marker $s_i = a$ means that we put a segment boundary before the a-th word token (or the end-of-corpus marker for $a = N+1$). Thus our corpus is segmented into token sequences $[(w_{s_j}, \ldots, w_{s_{j+1}-1})]_{j=1}^{M}$. The supervision modes assigned to each segment are denoted by m_j. We favor those segmentations that minimize the cumulative value $\sum_{j=1}^{M} [u_{l,m_j}(w_{s_j}^{s_{j+1}})]$ for each criterion l. For any criterion where larger values are intuitively better, we flip the sign before defining $u_{l,m_j}(w_{s_j}^{s_{j+1}})$ to maintain consistency (e.g. negative number of errors removed).

3.1 Multiple Criteria Optimization

In the case of a single criterion ($|L| = 1$), we obtain a simple, single-objective unconstrained linear optimization problem, efficiently solvable via dynamic programming (Terzi and Tsaparas, 2006). However, in practice one usually encounters several competing criteria, such as cost and utility, and here we will focus on this more realistic setting. We balance competing criteria by using one as an optimization objective, and the others as constraints.[1] Let crite-

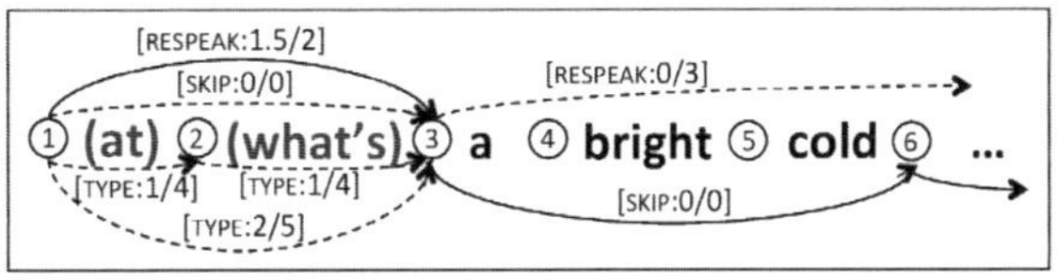

Figure 3: Excerpt of a segmentation graph for an example transcription task similar to Figure 1 (some edges are omitted for readability). Edges are labeled with their mode, predicted number of errors that can be removed, and necessary supervision time. A segmentation scheme might prefer solid edges over dashed ones in this example.

rion l' be the optimization objective criterion, and let C_l denote the constraining constants for the criteria $l \in L_{-l'} = L \setminus \{l'\}$. We state the optimization problem:

$$\min_{M; s_1^{M+1}; m_1^M} \sum_{j=1}^{M} \left[u_{l',m_j} \left(w_{s_j}^{s_{j+1}} \right) \right]$$

$$\text{s.t.} \sum_{j=1}^{M} \left[u_{l,m_j} \left(w_{s_j}^{s_{j+1}} \right) \right] \leq C_l \qquad (\forall l \in L_{-l'})$$

This constrained optimization problem is difficult to solve. In fact, the NP-hard multiple-choice knapsack problem (Pisinger, 1994) corresponds to a special case of our problem in which the number of segments is equal to the number of tokens, implying that our more general problem is NP-hard as well.

In order to overcome this problem, we reformulate search for the optimal segmentation as a resource-constrained shortest path problem in a directed, acyclic multigraph. While still not efficiently solvable in theory, this problem is well studied in domains such as vehicle routing and crew scheduling (Irnich and Desaulniers, 2005), and it is known that in many practical situations the problem can be solved reasonably efficiently using integer linear programming relaxations (Toth and Vigo, 2001).

In our formalism, the set of nodes V represents the spaces between neighboring tokens, at which the algorithm may insert segment boundaries. A node with index i represents a segment break before the i-th token, and thus the sequence of the indices in a path directly corresponds to s_1^{M+1}. Edges E denote the grouping of tokens between the respective

[1] This approach is known as the *bounded objective function method* in multi-objective optimization literature (Marler and Arora, 2004). The very popular *weighted sum method* merges criteria into a single efficiency measure, but is problematic in our case because the number of supervised tokens is unspecified. Unless the weights are carefully chosen, the algorithm might find, e.g., the completely unsupervised or completely supervised segmentation to be most "efficient."

nodes into one segment. Edges are always directed from left to right, and labeled with a supervision mode. In addition, each edge between nodes i and j is assigned $u_{l,k}(w_i^{j-1})$, the corresponding predicted value for each criterion $l \in L$ and supervision mode $k \in K$, indicating that the supervision mode of the j-th segment in a path directly corresponds to m_j.

Figure 3 shows an example of what the resulting graph may look like. Our original optimization problem is now equivalent to finding the shortest path between the first and last nodes according to criterion l', while obeying the given resource constraints. According to a widely used formulation for the resource constrained shortest path problem, we can define E_{ij} as the set of competing edges between i and j, and express this optimization problem with the following integer linear program (ILP):

$$\min_{\mathbf{x}} \sum_{i,j \in V} \sum_{k \in E_{ij}} x_{ijk} u_{l',k}(s_i^{j-1}) \tag{1}$$

$$\text{s.t.} \sum_{i,j \in V} \sum_{k \in E_{ij}} x_{ijk} u_{l,k}(s_i^{j-1}) \leq C_l \qquad (\forall l \in L_{-l'}) \tag{2}$$

$$\sum_{\substack{i \in V \\ k \in E_{ij}}} x_{ijk} = \sum_{\substack{i \in V \\ k \in E_{ij}}} x_{jik} \qquad (\forall j \in V \backslash \{1, n\}) \tag{3}$$

$$\sum_{\substack{j \in V \\ k \in E_{1j}}} x_{1jk} = 1 \tag{4}$$

$$\sum_{\substack{i \in V \\ k \in E_{in}}} x_{ink} = 1 \tag{5}$$

$$x_{ijk} \in \{0, 1\} \qquad (\forall x_{ijk} \in \mathbf{x}) \tag{6}$$

The variables $\mathbf{x}=\{x_{ijk} | i, j \in V, k \in E_{ij}\}$ denote the activation of the k'th edge between nodes i and j. The shortest path according to the minimization objective (1), that still meets the resource constraints for the specified criteria (2), is to be computed. The degree constraints (3,4,5) specify that all but the first and last nodes must have as many incoming as outgoing edges, while the first node must have exactly one outgoing, and the last node exactly one incoming edge. Finally, the integrality condition (6) forces all edges to be either fully activated or fully deactivated. The outlined problem formulation can solved directly by using off-the-shelf ILP solvers, here we employ GUROBI (Gurobi Optimization, 2012).

3.2 Heuristics for Approximation

In general, edges are inserted for every supervision mode between every combination of two nodes. The search space can be constrained by removing some of these edges to increase efficiency. In this study, we only consider edges spanning at most 20 tokens.

For cases in which larger corpora are to be annotated, or when the acceptable delay for delivering results is small, a suitable segmentation can be found approximately. The easiest way would be to partition the corpus, e.g. according to its individual documents, divide the budget constraints evenly across all partitions, and then segment each partition independently. More sophisticated methods might approximate the Pareto front for each partition, and distribute the budgets in an intelligent way.

4 User Modeling

While the proposed framework is able to optimize the segmentation with respect to each criterion, it also rests upon the assumption that we can provide user models $u_{l,k}(w_i^{j-1})$ that accurately evaluate every segment according to the specified criteria and supervision modes. In this section, we discuss our strategies for estimating three conceivable criteria: annotation cost, correction of errors, and improvement of a classifier.

4.1 Annotation Cost Modeling

Modeling cost requires solving a regression problem from features of a candidate segment to annotation cost, for example in terms of supervision time. Appropriate input features depend on the task, but should include notions of complexity (e.g. a confidence measure) and length of the segment, as both are expected to strongly influence supervision time.

We propose using Gaussian process (GP) regression for cost prediction, a start-of-the-art nonparametric Bayesian regression technique (Rasmussen and Williams, 2006)[2]. As reported on a similar task by Cohn and Specia (2013), and confirmed by our preliminary experiments, GP regression significantly outperforms popular techniques such as sup-

[2]Code available at http://www.gaussianprocess.org/gpml/

port vector regression and least-squares linear regression. We also follow their settings for GP, employing GP regression with a squared exponential kernel with automatic relevance determination. Depending on the number of users and amount of training data available for each user, models may be trained separately for each user (as we do here), or in a combined fashion via multi-task learning as proposed by Cohn and Specia (2013).

It is also crucial for the predictions to be reliable throughout the whole relevant space of segments. If the cost of certain types of segments is systematically underpredicted, the segmentation algorithm might be misled to prefer these, possibly a large number of times.[3] An effective trick to prevent such underpredictions is to predict the log time instead of the actual time. In this way, errors in the critical low end are penalized more strongly, and the time can never become negative.

4.2 Error Correction Modeling

As one utility measure, we can use the number of errors corrected, a useful measure for post editing tasks over automatically produced annotations. In order to measure how many errors can be removed by supervising a particular segment, we must estimate both how many errors are in the automatic annotation, and how reliably a human can remove these for a given supervision mode.

Most machine learning techniques can estimate confidence scores in the form of posterior probabilities. To estimate the number of errors, we can sum over one minus the posterior for all tokens, which estimates the Hamming distance from the reference annotation. This measure is appropriate for tasks in which the number of tokens is fixed in advance (e.g. a part-of-speech estimation task), and a reasonable approximation for tasks in which the number of tokens is not known in advance (e.g. speech transcription, cf. Section 5.1.1).

Predicting the particular tokens at which a human will make a mistake is known to be a difficult task (Olson and Olson, 1990), but a simplifying constant human error rate can still be useful. For example, in the task from Section 2, we may suspect a certain number of errors in a transcript segment, and predict, say, 95% of those errors to be removed via typing, but only 85% via respeaking.

4.3 Classifier Improvement Modeling

Another reasonable utility measure is accuracy of a classifier trained on the data we choose to annotate in an active learning framework. Confidence scores have been found useful for ranking particular tokens with regards to how much they will improve a classifier (Settles, 2008). Here, we may similarly score segment utility as the sum of its token confidences, although care must be taken to normalize and calibrate the token confidences to be linearly comparable before doing so. While the resulting utility score has no interpretation in absolute terms, it can still be used as an optimization objective (cf. Section 5.2.1).

5 Experiments

In this section, we present experimental results examining the effectiveness of the proposed method over two tasks: speech transcription and Japanese word segmentation.[4]

5.1 Speech Transcription Experiments

Accurate speech transcripts are a much-demanded NLP product, useful by themselves, as training material for ASR, or as input for follow-up tasks like speech translation. With recognition accuracies plateauing, manually correcting (post editing) automatic speech transcripts has become popular. Common approaches are to identify words (Sanchez-Cortina et al., 2012) or (sub-)sentences (Sperber et al., 2013) of low confidence, and have a human editor correct these.

5.1.1 Experimental Setup

We conduct a user study in which participants post-edited speech transcripts, given a fixed goal word error rate. The transcription setup was such that the transcriber could see the ASR transcript of parts before and after the segment that he was editing, providing context if needed. When imprecise time alignment resulted in segment breaks that were

[3]For instance, consider a model that predicts well for segments of medium size or longer, but underpredicts the supervision time of single-token segments. This may lead the segmentation algorithm to put every token into its own segment, which is clearly undesirable.

[4]Software and experimental data can be downloaded from http://www.msperber.com/research/tacl-segmentation/

slightly "off," as happened occasionally, that context helped guess what was said. The segment itself was transcribed from scratch, as opposed to editing the ASR transcript; besides being arguably more efficient when the ASR transcript contains many mistakes (Nanjo et al., 2006; Akita et al., 2009), preliminary experiments also showed that supervision time is far easier to predict this way. Figure 4 illustrates what the setup looked like.

We used a self-developed transcription tool to conduct experiments. It presents our computed segments one by one, allows convenient input and playback via keyboard shortcuts, and logs user interactions with their time stamps. A selection of TED talks[5] (English talks on technology, entertainment, and design) served as experimental data. While some of these talks contain jargon such as medical terms, they are presented by skilled speakers, making them comparably easy to understand. Initial transcripts were created using the Janus recognition toolkit (Soltau et al., 2001) with a standard, TED-optimized setup. We used confusion networks for decoding and obtaining confidence scores.

For reasons of simplicity, and better comparability to our baseline, we restricted our experiment to two supervision modes: TYPE and SKIP. We conducted experiments with 3 participants, 1 with several years of experience in transcription, 2 with none. Each participant received an explanation on the transcription guidelines, and a short hands-on training to learn to use our tool. Next, they transcribed a balanced selection of 200 segments of varying length and quality in random order. This data was used to train the user models.

Finally, each participant transcribed another 2 TED talks, with word error rate (WER) 19.96% (predicted: 22.33%). We set a target (predicted) WER of 15% as our optimization constraint,[6] and minimize the predicted supervision time as our objective function. Both TED talks were transcribed once using the baseline strategy, and once using the proposed strategy. The order of both strategies was reversed between talks, to minimize learning bias due to transcribing each talk twice.

The baseline strategy was adopted according to Sperber et al. (2013): We segmented the talk into natural, subsentential units, using Matusov et al. (2006)'s segmenter, which we tuned to reproduce the TED subtitle segmentation, producing a mean segment length of 8.6 words. Segments were added in order of increasing average word confidence, until the user model predicted a WER$<15\%$. The second segmentation strategy was the proposed method, similarly with a resource constraint of WER$<15\%$.

Supervision time was predicted via GP regression (cf. Section 4.1), using segment length, audio duration, and mean confidence as input features. The output variable was assumed subject to additive Gaussian noise with zero mean, a variance of 5 seconds was chosen empirically to minimize the mean squared error. Utility prediction (cf. Section 4.2) was based on posterior scores obtained from the confusion networks. We found it important to calibrate them, as the posteriors were overconfident especially in the upper range. To do so, we automatically transcribed a development set of TED data, grouped the recognized words into buckets according to their posteriors, and determined the average number of errors per word in each bucket from an alignment with the reference transcript. The mapping from average posterior to average number of errors was estimated via GP regression. The result was summed over all tokens, and multiplied by a constant human confidence, separately determined for each participant.[7]

5.1.2 Simulation Results

To convey a better understanding of the potential gains afforded by our method, we first present a simulated experiment. We assume a transcriber who makes no mistakes, and needs exactly the amount of time predicted by a user model trained on the data of a randomly selected participant. We compare three scenarios: A baseline simulation, in which the baseline segments are transcribed in ascending order of confidence; a simulation using the proposed method, in which we change the WER constraint in small increments; finally, an oracle simulation, which uses

[5] www.ted.com

[6] Depending on the level of accuracy required by our final application, this target may be set lower or higher.

[7] More elaborate methods for WER estimation exist, such as by Ogawa et al. (2013), but if our method achieves improvements using simple Hamming distance, incorporating more sophisticated measures will likely achieve similar, or even better accuracy.

(3) SKIP: "nineteen forty six until today you see the green"

(4) TYPE: <annotator types: "is the traditional">

(5) SKIP: "Interstate conflict"

(6) TYPE: <annotator types: "the ones we used to">

(7) SKIP: ...

Figure 4: Result of our segmentation method (excerpt). TYPE segments are displayed empty and should be transcribed from scratch. For SKIP segments, the ASR transcript is displayed to provide context. When annotating a segment, the corresponding audio is played back.

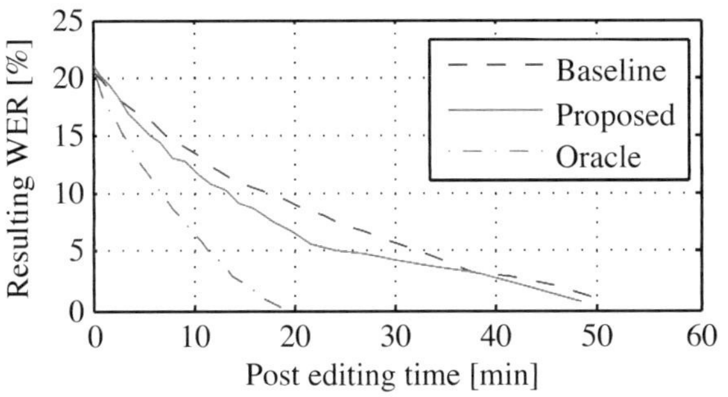

Figure 5: Simulation of post editing on example TED talk. The proposed method reduces the WER considerably faster than the baseline at first, later both converge. The much superior oracle simulation indicates room for further improvement.

the proposed method, but uses a utility model that knows the actual number of errors in each segment. For each supervised segment, we simply replace the ASR output with the reference, and measure the resulting WER.

Figure 5 shows the simulation on an example TED talk, based on an initial transcript with 21.9% WER. The proposed method is able to reduce the WER faster than the baseline, up to a certain point where they converge. The oracle simulation is even faster, indicating room for improvement through better confidence scores.

5.1.3 User Study Results

Table 1 shows the results of the user study. First, we note that the WER estimation by our utility model was off by about 2.5%: While the predicted improvement in WER was from 22.33% to 15.0%, the actual improvement was from 19.96% to about 12.5%. The actual resulting WER was consistent across all users, and we observe strong, consistent reductions in supervision time for all participants. Prediction of the necessary supervision time was accurate: Averaged over participants, 45:41 minutes were predicted for the baseline, 44:22 minutes measured. For the proposed method, 32:11 minutes were predicted, 33:37 minutes measured. On average, participants removed 6.68 errors per minute using the baseline, and 8.93 errors per minute using the proposed method, a speed-up of 25.2%.

Participant	**Baseline**		**Proposed**	
	WER	Time	WER	Time
P_1	12.26	44:05	12.18	33:01
P_2	12.75	36:19	12.77	29:54
P_3	12.70	52:42	12.50	37:57
AVG	12.57	44:22	12.48	33:37

Table 1: Transcription task results. For each user, the resulting WER [%] after supervision is shown, along with the time [min] they needed. The unsupervised WER was 19.96%.

Note that predicted and measured values are not strictly comparable: In the experiments, to provide a fair comparison participants transcribed the same talks twice (once using baseline, once the proposed method, in alternating order), resulting in a noticeable learning effect. The user model, on the other hand, is trained to predict the case in which a transcriber conducts only one transcription pass.

As an interesting finding, without being informed about the order of baseline and proposed method, participants reported that transcribing according to the proposed segmentation seemed harder, as they found the baseline segmentation more linguistically reasonable. However, this perceived increase in difficulty did not show in efficiency numbers.

5.2 Japanese Word Segmentation Experiments

Word segmentation is the first step in NLP for languages that are commonly written without word boundaries, such as Japanese and Chinese. We apply our method to a task in which we domain-adapt a word segmentation classifier via active learning. In this experiment, participants annotated whether or not a word boundary occurred at certain positions in a Japanese sentence. The tokens to be grouped into segments are positions between adjacent characters.

5.2.1 Experimental Setup

Neubig et al. (2011) have proposed a pointwise method for Japanese word segmentation that can be trained using partially annotated sentences, which makes it attractive in combination with active learning, as well as our segmentation method. The authors released their method as a software package "KyTea" that we employed in this user study. We used KyTea's active learning domain adaptation toolkit[8] as a baseline.

For data, we used the Balanced Corpus of Contemporary Written Japanese (BCCWJ), created by Maekawa (2008), with the *internet Q&A subcorpus* as in-domain data, and the *whitepaper* subcorpus as background data, a domain adaptation scenario. Sentences were drawn from the in-domain corpus, and the manually annotated data was then used to train KyTea, along with the pre-annotated background data. The goal (objective function) was to improve KyTea's classification accuracy on an in-domain test set, given a constrained time budget of 30 minutes. There were again 2 supervision modes: ANNOTATE and SKIP. Note that this is essentially a batch active learning setup with only one iteration.

We conducted experiments with one expert with several years of experience with Japanese word segmentation annotation, and three non-expert native speakers with no prior experience. Japanese word segmentation is not a trivial task, so we provided non-experts with training, including explanation of the segmentation standard, a supervised test with immediate feedback and explanations, and hands-on training to get used to the annotation software.

Supervision time was predicted via GP regression (cf. Section 4.1), using the segment length and mean confidence as input features. As before, the output variable was assumed subject to additive Gaussian noise with zero mean and 5 seconds variance. To obtain training data for these models, each participant annotated about 500 example instances, drawn from the adaptation corpus, grouped into segments and balanced regarding segment length and difficulty.

For utility modeling (cf. Section 4.3), we first normalized KyTea's confidence scores, which are given in terms of SVM margin, using a sigmoid function (Platt, 1999). The normalization parameter was selected so that the mean confidence on a development set corresponded to the actual classifier accuracy. We derive our measure of classifier improvement for correcting a segment by summing over one minus the calibrated confidence for each of its tokens. To analyze how well this measure describes the actual training utility, we trained KyTea using the background data plus disjoint groups of 100 in-domain instances with similar probabilities and measured the achieved reduction of prediction errors. The correlation between each group's mean utility and the achieved error reduction was 0.87. Note that we ignore the decaying returns usually observed as more data is added to the training set. Also, we did not attempt to model user errors. Employing a constant base error rate, as in the transcription scenario, would change segment utilities only by a constant factor, without changing the resulting segmentation.

After creating the user models, we conducted the main experiment, in which each participant annotated data that was selected from a pool of 1000 in-domain sentences using two strategies. The first, baseline strategy was as proposed by Neubig et al. (2011). Queries are those instances with the lowest confidence scores. Each query is then extended to the left and right, until a word boundary is predicted. This strategy follows similar reasoning as was the premise to this paper: To decide whether or not a position in a text corresponds to a word boundary, the annotator has to acquire surrounding context information. This context acquisition is relatively time consuming, so he might as well label the surrounding instances with little additional effort. The second strategy was our proposed, more principled approach. Queries of both methods were shuffled to minimize bias due to learning effects. Finally, we trained KyTea using the results of both methods, and compared the achieved classifier improvement and supervision times.

5.2.2 User Study Results

Table 2 summarizes the results of our experiment. It shows that the annotations by each participant resulted in a better classifier for the proposed method than the baseline, but also took up considerably more time, a less clear improvement than for the transcription task. In fact, the total error for time predictions was as high as 12.5% on average,

[8] http://www.phontron.com/kytea/active.html

Participant	Baseline		Proposed	
	Time	Acc.	Time	Acc.
Expert	25:50	96.17	32:45	96.55
$NonExp_1$	22:05	95.79	26:44	95.98
$NonExp_2$	23:37	96.15	31:28	96.21
$NonExp_3$	25:23	96.38	33:36	96.45

Table 2: Word segmentation task results, for our expert and 3 non-expert participants. For each participant, the resulting classifier accuracy [%] after supervision is shown, along with the time [min] they needed. The unsupervised accuracy was 95.14%.

where the baseline method tended take less time than predicted, the proposed method more time. This is in contrast to a much lower total error (within 1%) when cross-validating our user model training data. This is likely due to the fact that the data for training the user model was selected in a balanced manner, as opposed to selecting difficult examples, as our method is prone to do. Thus, we may expect much better predictions when selecting user model training data that is more similar to the test case.

Plotting classifier accuracy over annotation time draws a clearer picture. Let us first analyze the results for the expert annotator. Figure 6 (E.1) shows that the proposed method resulted in consistently better results, indicating that time predictions were still effective. Note that this comparison may put the proposed method at a slight disadvantage by comparing intermediate results despite optimizing globally.

For the non-experts, the improvement over the baseline is less consistent, as can be seen in Figure 6 (N.1) for one representative. According to our analysis, this can be explained by two factors: (1) The non-experts' annotation error (6.5% on average) was much higher than the expert's (2.7%), resulting in a somewhat irregular classifier learning curve. (2) The variance in annotation time per segment was consistently higher for the non-experts than the expert, indicated by an average per-segment prediction error of 71% vs. 58% relative to the mean actual value, respectively. Informally speaking, non-experts made more mistakes, and were more strongly influenced by the difficulty of a particular segment (which was higher on average with the proposed method, as indicated by a

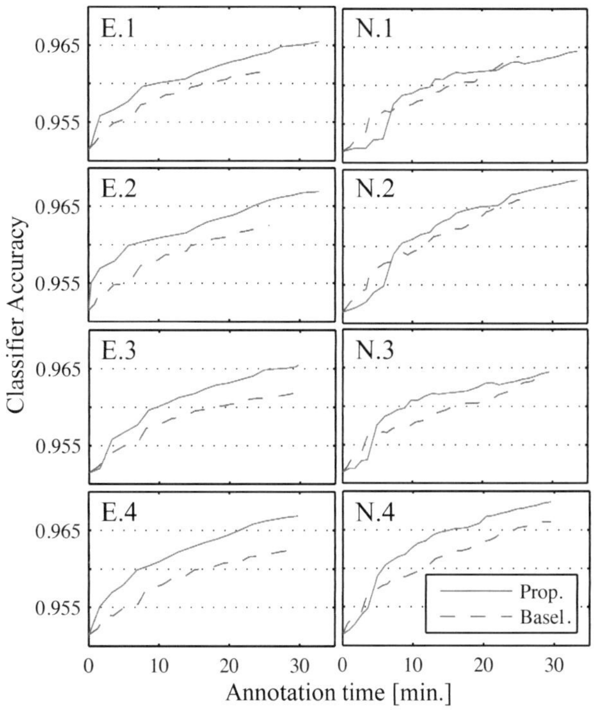

Figure 6: Classifier improvement over time, depicted for the expert (E) and a non-expert (N). The graphs show numbers based on (1) actual annotations and user models as in Sections 4.1 and 4.3, (2) error-free annotations, (3) measured times replaced by predicted times, and (4) both reference annotations and replaced time predictions.

lower average confidence).[9]

In Figures 6 (2-4) we present a simulation experiment in which we first pretend as if annotators made no mistakes, then as if they needed exactly as much time as predicted for each segment, and then both. This cheating experiment works in favor of the proposed method, especially for the non-expert. We may conclude that our segmentation approach is effective for the word segmentation task, but requires more accurate time predictions. Better user models will certainly help, although for the presented scenario our method may be most useful for an expert annotator.

[9]Note that the non-expert in the figure annotated much faster than the expert, which explains the comparable classification result despite making more annotation errors. This is in contrast to the other non-experts, who were slower.

5.3 Computational Efficiency

Since our segmentation algorithm does not guarantee polynomial runtime, computational efficiency was a concern, but did not turn out problematic. On a consumer laptop, the solver produced segmentations within a few seconds for a single document containing several thousand tokens, and within hours for corpora consisting of several dozen documents. Runtime increased roughly quadratically with respect to the number of segmented tokens. We feel that this is acceptable, considering that the time needed for human supervision will likely dominate the computation time, and reasonable approximations can be made as noted in Section 3.2.

6 Relation to Prior Work

Efficient supervision strategies have been studied across a variety of NLP-related research areas, and received increasing attention in recent years. Examples include post editing for speech recognition (Sanchez-Cortina et al., 2012), interactive machine translation (González-Rubio et al., 2010), active learning for machine translation (Haffari et al., 2009; González-Rubio et al., 2011) and many other NLP tasks (Olsson, 2009), to name but a few studies.

It has also been recognized by the active learning community that correcting the most useful parts first is often not optimal in terms of efficiency, since these parts tend to be the most difficult to manually annotate (Settles et al., 2008). The authors advocate the use of a user model to predict the supervision effort, and select the instances with best "bang-for-the-buck." This prediction of supervision effort was successful, and was further refined in other NLP-related studies (Tomanek et al., 2010; Specia, 2011; Cohn and Specia, 2013). Our approach to user modeling using GP regression is inspired by the latter.

Most studies on user models consider only supervision effort, while neglecting the accuracy of human annotations. The view on humans as a perfect oracle has been criticized (Donmez and Carbonell, 2008), since human errors are common and can negatively affect supervision utility. Research on human-computer-interaction has identified the modeling of human errors as very difficult (Olson and Olson, 1990), depending on factors such as user experience, cognitive load, user interface design, and fatigue. Nevertheless, even the simple error model used in our post editing task was effective.

The active learning community has addressed the problem of balancing utility and cost in some more detail. The previously reported "bang-for-the-buck" approach is a very simple, greedy approach to combine both into one measure. A more theoretically founded scalar optimization objective is the net benefit (utility minus costs) as proposed by Vijayanarasimhan and Grauman (2009), but unfortunately is restricted to applications where both can be expressed in terms of the same monetary unit. Vijayanarasimhan et al. (2010) and Donmez and Carbonell (2008) use a more practical approach that specifies a constrained optimization problem by allowing only a limited time budget for supervision. Our approach is a generalization thereof and allows either specifying an upper bound on the predicted cost, or a lower bound on the predicted utility.

The main novelty of our presented approach is the explicit modeling and selection of segments of various sizes, such that annotation efficiency is optimized according to the specified constraints. While some works (Sassano and Kurohashi, 2010; Neubig et al., 2011) have proposed using subsentential segments, we are not aware of any previous work that explicitly optimizes that segmentation.

7 Conclusion

We presented a method that can effectively choose a segmentation of a language corpus that optimizes supervision efficiency, considering not only the actual usefulness of each segment, but also the annotation cost. We reported noticeable improvements over strong baselines in two user studies. Future user experiments with more participants would be desirable to verify our observations, and allow further analysis of different factors such as annotator expertise. Also, future research may improve the user modeling, which will be beneficial for our method.

Acknowledgments

The research leading to these results has received funding from the European Union Seventh Framework Programme (FP7/2007-2013) under grant agreement n 287658 Bridges Across the Language Divide (EU-BRIDGE).

References

Yuya Akita, Masato Mimura, and Tatsuya Kawahara. 2009. Automatic Transcription System for Meetings of the Japanese National Congress. In *Interspeech*, pages 84–87, Brighton, UK.

Trevor Cohn and Lucia Specia. 2013. Modelling Annotator Bias with Multi-task Gaussian Processes: An Application to Machine Translation Quality Estimation. In *Association for Computational Linguistics Conference (ACL)*, Sofia, Bulgaria.

Pinar Donmez and Jaime Carbonell. 2008. Proactive Learning : Cost-Sensitive Active Learning with Multiple Imperfect Oracles. In *Conference on Information and Knowledge Management (CIKM)*, pages 619–628, Napa Valley, CA, USA.

Jesús González-Rubio, Daniel Ortiz-Martínez, and Francisco Casacuberta. 2010. Balancing User Effort and Translation Error in Interactive Machine Translation Via Confidence Measures. In *Association for Computational Linguistics Conference (ACL), Short Papers Track*, pages 173–177, Uppsala, Sweden.

Jesús González-Rubio, Daniel Ortiz-Martínez, and Francisco Casacuberta. 2011. An active learning scenario for interactive machine translation. In *International Conference on Multimodal Interfaces (ICMI)*, pages 197–200, Alicante, Spain.

Gurobi Optimization. 2012. Gurobi Optimizer Reference Manual.

Gholamreza Haffari, Maxim Roy, and Anoop Sarkar. 2009. Active Learning for Statistical Phrase-based Machine Translation. In *North American Chapter of the Association for Computational Linguistics - Human Language Technologies Conference (NAACL-HLT)*, pages 415–423, Boulder, CO, USA.

Stefan Irnich and Guy Desaulniers. 2005. Shortest Path Problems with Resource Constraints. In *Column Generation*, pages 33–65. Springer US.

Kikuo Maekawa. 2008. Balanced Corpus of Contemporary Written Japanese. In *International Joint Conference on Natural Language Processing (IJCNLP)*, pages 101–102, Hyderabad, India.

R. Timothy Marler and Jasbir S. Arora. 2004. Survey of multi-objective optimization methods for engineering. *Structural and Multidisciplinary Optimization*, 26(6):369–395, April.

Evgeny Matusov, Arne Mauser, and Hermann Ney. 2006. Automatic Sentence Segmentation and Punctuation Prediction for Spoken Language Translation. In *International Workshop on Spoken Language Translation (IWSLT)*, pages 158–165, Kyoto, Japan.

Hiroaki Nanjo, Yuya Akita, and Tatsuya Kawahara. 2006. Computer Assisted Speech Transcription System for Efficient Speech Archive. In *Western Pacific Acoustics Conference (WESPAC)*, Seoul, Korea.

Graham Neubig, Yosuke Nakata, and Shinsuke Mori. 2011. Pointwise Prediction for Robust , Adaptable Japanese Morphological Analysis. In *Association for Computational Linguistics: Human Language Technologies Conference (ACL-HLT)*, pages 529–533, Portland, OR, USA.

Atsunori Ogawa, Takaaki Hori, and Atsushi Nakamura. 2013. Discriminative Recognition Rate Estimation For N-Best List and Its Application To N-Best Rescoring. In *International Conference on Acoustics, Speech, and Signal Processing (ICASSP)*, pages 6832–6836, Vancouver, Canada.

Judith Reitman Olson and Gary Olson. 1990. The Growth of Cognitive Modeling in Human-Computer Interaction Since GOMS. *Human-Computer Interaction*, 5(2):221–265, June.

Fredrik Olsson. 2009. A literature survey of active machine learning in the context of natural language processing. Technical report, SICS Sweden.

David Pisinger. 1994. A Minimal Algorithm for the Multiple-Choice Knapsack Problem. *European Journal of Operational Research*, 83(2):394–410.

John C. Platt. 1999. Probabilistic Outputs for Support Vector Machines and Comparisons to Regularized Likelihood Methods. In *Advances in Large Margin Classifiers*, pages 61–74. MIT Press.

Carl E. Rasmussen and Christopher K.I. Williams. 2006. *Gaussian Processes for Machine Learning*. MIT Press, Cambridge, MA, USA.

Isaias Sanchez-Cortina, Nicolas Serrano, Alberto Sanchis, and Alfons Juan. 2012. A prototype for Interactive Speech Transcription Balancing Error and Supervision Effort. In *International Conference on Intelligent User Interfaces (IUI)*, pages 325–326, Lisbon, Portugal.

Manabu Sassano and Sadao Kurohashi. 2010. Using Smaller Constituents Rather Than Sentences in Active Learning for Japanese Dependency Parsing. In *Association for Computational Linguistics Conference (ACL)*, pages 356–365, Uppsala, Sweden.

Burr Settles, Mark Craven, and Lewis Friedland. 2008. Active Learning with Real Annotation Costs. In *Neural Information Processing Systems Conference (NIPS) - Workshop on Cost-Sensitive Learning*, Lake Tahoe, NV, United States.

Burr Settles. 2008. An Analysis of Active Learning Strategies for Sequence Labeling Tasks. In *Conference on Empirical Methods in Natural Language Processing (EMNLP)*, pages 1070–1079, Honolulu, USA.

Hagen Soltau, Florian Metze, Christian Fügen, and Alex Waibel. 2001. A One-Pass Decoder Based on Polymorphic Linguistic Context Assignment. In *Automatic Speech Recognition and Understanding Work-*

shop (ASRU), pages 214–217, Madonna di Campiglio, Italy.

Lucia Specia. 2011. Exploiting Objective Annotations for Measuring Translation Post-editing Effort. In *Conference of the European Association for Machine Translation (EAMT)*, pages 73–80, Nice, France.

Matthias Sperber, Graham Neubig, Christian Fügen, Satoshi Nakamura, and Alex Waibel. 2013. Efficient Speech Transcription Through Respeaking. In *Interspeech*, pages 1087–1091, Lyon, France.

Bernhard Suhm, Brad Myers, and Alex Waibel. 2001. Multimodal error correction for speech user interfaces. *Transactions on Computer-Human Interaction*, 8(1):60–98.

Evimaria Terzi and Panayiotis Tsaparas. 2006. Efficient algorithms for sequence segmentation. In *SIAM Conference on Data Mining (SDM)*, Bethesda, MD, USA.

Katrin Tomanek and Udo Hahn. 2009. Semi-Supervised Active Learning for Sequence Labeling. In *International Joint Conference on Natural Language Processing (IJCNLP)*, pages 1039–1047, Singapore.

Katrin Tomanek, Udo Hahn, and Steffen Lohmann. 2010. A Cognitive Cost Model of Annotations Based on Eye-Tracking Data. In *Association for Computational Linguistics Conference (ACL)*, pages 1158–1167, Uppsala, Sweden.

Paolo Toth and Daniele Vigo. 2001. *The Vehicle Routing Problem*. Society for Industrial & Applied Mathematics (SIAM), Philadelphia.

Sudheendra Vijayanarasimhan and Kristen Grauman. 2009. Whats It Going to Cost You?: Predicting Effort vs. Informativeness for Multi-Label Image Annotations. In *Conference on Computer Vision and Pattern Recognition (CVPR)*, pages 2262–2269, Miami Beach, FL, USA.

Sudheendra Vijayanarasimhan, Prateek Jain, and Kristen Grauman. 2010. Far-sighted active learning on a budget for image and video recognition. In *Conference on Computer Vision and Pattern Recognition (CVPR)*, pages 3035–3042, San Francisco, CA, USA, June.

Dynamic Language Models for Streaming Text

Dani Yogatama* **Chong Wang*** **Bryan R. Routledge†** **Noah A. Smith*** **Eric P. Xing***
*School of Computer Science
†Tepper School of Business
Carnegie Mellon University
Pittsburgh, PA 15213, USA
*{dyogatama,chongw,nasmith,epxing}@cs.cmu.edu, †routledge@cmu.edu

Abstract

We present a probabilistic language model that captures temporal dynamics and conditions on arbitrary *non-linguistic* context features. These context features serve as important indicators of language changes that are otherwise difficult to capture using text data by itself. We learn our model in an efficient online fashion that is scalable for large, streaming data. With five streaming datasets from two different genres—economics news articles and social media—we evaluate our model on the task of sequential language modeling. Our model consistently outperforms competing models.

1 Introduction

Language models are a key component in many NLP applications, such as machine translation and exploratory corpus analysis. Language models are typically assumed to be static—the word-given-context distributions do not change over time. Examples include n-gram models (Jelinek, 1997) and probabilistic topic models like latent Dirichlet allocation (Blei et al., 2003); we use the term "language model" to refer broadly to probabilistic models of text.

Recently, streaming datasets (e.g., social media) have attracted much interest in NLP. Since such data evolve rapidly based on events in the real world, assuming a static language model becomes unrealistic. In general, more data is seen as better, but treating all past data equally runs the risk of distracting a model with irrelevant evidence. On the other hand, cautiously using only the most recent data risks overfitting to short-term trends and missing important time-insensitive effects (Blei and Lafferty, 2006; Wang et al., 2008). Therefore, in this paper, we take steps toward methods for capturing long-range temporal dynamics in language use.

Our model also exploits observable context variables to capture temporal variation that is otherwise difficult to capture using only text. Specifically for the applications we consider, we use stock market data as exogenous evidence on which the language model depends. For example, when an important company's price moves suddenly, the language model should be based not on the very recent history, but should be similar to the language model for a day when a similar change happened, since people are likely to say similar things (either about that company, or about conditions relevant to the change). Non-linguistic contexts such as stock price changes provide useful auxiliary information that might indicate the similarity of language models across different timesteps.

We also turn to a fully online learning framework (Cesa-Bianchi and Lugosi, 2006) to deal with nonstationarity and dynamics in the data that necessitate adaptation of the model to data in real time. In online learning, streaming examples are processed only when they arrive. Online learning also eliminates the need to store large amounts of data in memory. Strictly speaking, online learning is distinct from *stochastic* learning, which for language models built on massive datasets has been explored by Hoffman et al. (2013) and Wang et al. (2011). Those techniques are still for static modeling. Language modeling for streaming datasets in the context of machine translation was considered by Levenberg and Osborne (2009) and Levenberg et al. (2010). Goyal et al. (2009) introduced a streaming algorithm for large scale language modeling by approximating n-gram frequency counts. We propose a general online learning algorithm for language modeling that draws inspiration from regret minimization in sequential predictions (Cesa-Bianchi and Lugosi, 2006) and on-

Transactions of the Association for Computational Linguistics, 2 (2014) 181–192. Action Editor: Eric Fosler-Lussier.
Submitted 10/2013; Revised 2/2014; Published 4/2014.

line variational algorithms (Sato, 2001; Honkela and Valpola, 2003).

To our knowledge, our model is the first to bring together temporal dynamics, conditioning on non-linguistic context, and scalable online learning suitable for streaming data and extensible to include topics and n-gram histories. The main idea of our model is independent of the choice of the base language model (e.g., unigrams, bigrams, topic models, etc.). In this paper, we focus on unigram and bigram language models in order to evaluate the basic idea on well understood models, and to show how it can be extended to higher-order n-grams. We leave extensions to topic models for future work.

We propose a novel task to evaluate our proposed language model. The task is to predict economics-related text at a given time, taking into account the changes in stock prices up to the corresponding day. This can be seen an inverse of the setup considered by Lavrenko et al. (2000), where news is assumed to influence stock prices. We evaluate our model on economics news in various languages (English, German, and French), as well as Twitter data.

2 Background

In this section, we first discuss the background for sequential predictions then describe how to formulate online language modeling as sequential predictions.

2.1 Sequential Predictions

Let $w_1, w_2, \ldots, w_T$ be a sequence of response variables, revealed one at a time. The goal is to design a good learner to predict the next response, given previous responses and additional evidence which we denote by $\boldsymbol{x}_t \in \mathbb{R}^M$ (at time t). Throughout this paper, we use the term *features* for $\boldsymbol{x}$. Specifically, at each round t, the learner receives $\boldsymbol{x}_t$ and makes a prediction $\hat{w}_t$, by choosing a parameter vector $\boldsymbol{\alpha}_t \in \mathbb{R}^M$. In this paper, we refer to $\boldsymbol{\alpha}$ as *feature coefficients*.

There has been an enormous amount of work on online learning for sequential predictions, much of it building on convex optimization. For a sequence of loss functions $\ell_1, \ell_2, \ldots, \ell_T$ (parameterized by $\boldsymbol{\alpha}$), an online learning algorithm is a strategy to minimize the regret, with respect to the best fixed $\boldsymbol{\alpha}^*$ in hindsight.[1] Regret guarantees assume a Lipschitz condition on the loss function ℓ that can be prohibitive for complex models. See Cesa-Bianchi and Lugosi (2006), Rakhlin (2009), Bubeck (2011), and Shalev-Shwartz (2012) for in-depth discussion and review.

There has also been work on online and stochastic learning for Bayesian models (Sato, 2001; Honkela and Valpola, 2003; Hoffman et al., 2013), based on variational inference. The goal is to approximate posterior distributions of latent variables when examples arrive one at a time.

In this paper, we will use both kinds of techniques to learn language models for streaming datasets.

2.2 Problem Formulation

Consider an online language modeling problem, in the spirit of sequential predictions. The task is to build a language model that accurately predicts the texts generated on day t, conditioned on observable features up to day t, $\boldsymbol{x}_{1:t}$. Every day, after the model makes a prediction, the actual texts $\boldsymbol{w}_t$ are revealed and we suffer a loss. The loss is defined as the negative log likelihood of the model $\ell_t = -\log p(\boldsymbol{w}_t \mid \boldsymbol{\alpha}, \boldsymbol{\beta}_{1:t-1}, \boldsymbol{x}_{1:t-1}, \boldsymbol{n}_{1:t-1})$, where $\boldsymbol{\alpha}$ and $\boldsymbol{\beta}_{1:T}$ are the model parameters and $\boldsymbol{n}$ is a background distribution (details are given in §3.2). We can then update the model and proceed to day $t+1$. Notice the similarity to the sequential prediction described above. Importantly, this is a realistic setup for building evolving language models from large-scale streaming datasets.

3 Model

3.1 Notation

We index timesteps by $t \in \{1, \ldots, T\}$ and word types by $v \in \{1, \ldots, V\}$, both are always given as subscripts. We denote vectors in boldface and use $1:T$ as a shorthand for $\{1, 2, \ldots, T\}$. We assume words of the form $\{\boldsymbol{w}_t\}_{t=1}^T$ for $\boldsymbol{w}_t \in \mathbb{R}^V$, which is the vector of word frequences at timetstep t. Non-linguistic context features are $\{\boldsymbol{x}_t\}_{t=1}^T$ for $\boldsymbol{x}_t \in \mathbb{R}^M$. The goal is to learn parameters $\boldsymbol{\alpha}$ and $\boldsymbol{\beta}_{1:T}$, which will be described in detail next.

3.2 Generative Story

The main idea of our model is illustrated by the following generative story for the unigram language

[1]Formally, the regret is defined as $\text{Regret}_T(\boldsymbol{\alpha}^*) = \sum_{t=1}^T \ell_t(\boldsymbol{x}_t, \boldsymbol{\alpha}_t, w_t) - \inf_{\boldsymbol{\alpha}^*} \sum_{t=1}^T \ell_t(\boldsymbol{x}_t, \boldsymbol{\alpha}^*, w_t)$.

model. (We will discuss the extension to higher-order language models later.) A graphical representation of our proposed model is given in Figure 1.

1. Draw feature coefficients $\boldsymbol{\alpha} \sim \mathcal{N}(0, \lambda \mathbf{I})$.[2] Here $\boldsymbol{\alpha}$ is a vector in $\mathbb{R}^M$, where M is the dimensionality of the feature vector.
2. For each timestep t:
   (a) Observe non-linguistic context features $\boldsymbol{x}_t$.
   (b) Draw $\boldsymbol{\beta}_t \sim$ $\mathcal{N}\left(\sum_{k=1}^{t-1} \delta_k \frac{\exp(\boldsymbol{\alpha}^\top \boldsymbol{f}(\boldsymbol{x}_t, \boldsymbol{x}_k))}{\sum_{j=1}^{t-1} \delta_j \exp(\boldsymbol{\alpha}^\top \boldsymbol{f}(\boldsymbol{x}_t, \boldsymbol{x}_j))} \boldsymbol{\beta}_k, \varphi \mathbf{I}\right)$. Here, $\boldsymbol{\beta}_t$ is a vector in $\mathbb{R}^V$, where V is the size of the word vocabulary, φ is the variance parameter and δ_k is a fixed hyperparameter; we discuss them below.
   (c) For each word $w_{t,v}$, draw $w_{t,v} \sim$ Categorical $\left(\frac{\exp(n_{1:t-1,v} + \beta_{t,v})}{\sum_{j \in V} \exp(n_{1:t-1,j} + \beta_{t,j})}\right)$.

In the last step, $\boldsymbol{\beta}_t$ and $\boldsymbol{n}$ are mapped to the V-dimensional simplex, forming a distribution over words. $\boldsymbol{n}_{1:t-1} \in \mathbb{R}^V$ is a background (log) distribution, inspired by a similar idea in Eisenstein et al. (2011). In this paper, we set $n_{1:t-1,v}$ to be the log-frequency of v up to time $t-1$. We can interpret $\boldsymbol{\beta}$ as a time-dependent deviation from the background log-frequencies that incorporates world-context. This deviation comes in the form of a weighted average of earlier deviation vectors.

The intuition behind the model is that the probability of a word appearing at day t depends on the background log-frequencies, the deviation coefficients of the word at previous timesteps $\boldsymbol{\beta}_{1:t-1}$, and the similarity of current conditions of the world (based on observable features $\boldsymbol{x}$) to previous timesteps through $\boldsymbol{f}(\boldsymbol{x}_t, \boldsymbol{x}_k)$. That is, $\boldsymbol{f}$ is a function that takes d-dimensional feature vectors at two timesteps $\boldsymbol{x}_t$ and $\boldsymbol{x}_k$ and returns a similarity vector $\boldsymbol{f}(\boldsymbol{x}_t, \boldsymbol{x}_k) \in \mathbb{R}^M$ (see §6.1.1 for an example of $\boldsymbol{f}$ that we use in our experiments). The similarity is parameterized by $\boldsymbol{\alpha}$, and decays over time with rate δ_k. In this work, we assume a fixed window size c (i.e., we consider c most recent timesteps), so that $\delta_{1:t-c-1} = 0$ and $\delta_{t-c:t-1} = 1$. This allows up to cth order dependencies.[3] Setting δ this way allows us to bound the number of past vectors $\boldsymbol{\beta}$ that need to be kept in memory. We set $\boldsymbol{\beta}_0$ to $\mathbf{0}$.

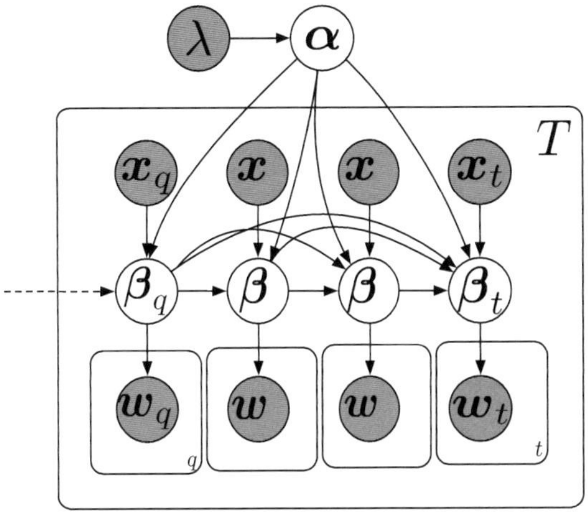

Figure 1: Graphical representation of the model. The subscript indices q, r, s are shorthands for the previous timesteps $t-3, t-2, t-1$. Only four timesteps are shown here. There are arrows from previous $\boldsymbol{\beta}_{t-4}, \boldsymbol{\beta}_{t-5}, \ldots, \boldsymbol{\beta}_{t-c}$ to $\boldsymbol{\beta}_t$, where c is the window size as described in §3.2. They are not shown here, for readability.

Although the generative story described above is for unigram language models, extensions can be made to more complex models (e.g., mixture of unigrams, topic models, etc.) and to longer n-gram contexts. In the case of topic models, the model will be related to dynamic topic models (Blei and Lafferty, 2006) augmented by context features, and the learning procedure in §4 can be used to perform online learning of dynamic topic models. However, our model captures longer-range dependencies than dynamic topic models, and can condition on non-linguistic features or metadata. In the case of higher-order n-grams, one simple way is to draw more $\boldsymbol{\beta}$, one for each history. For example, for a bigram model, $\boldsymbol{\beta}$ is in $\mathbb{R}^{V^2}$, rather than $\mathbb{R}^V$ in the unigram model. We consider both unigram and bigram language models in our experiments in §6. However, the main idea presented in this paper is largely independent of the base model.

Related work. Mimno and McCallum (2008) and Eisenstein et al. (2010) similarly conditioned text on

[2]Feature coefficients $\boldsymbol{\alpha}$ can be also drawn from other distributions such as $\boldsymbol{\alpha} \sim \text{Laplace}(0, \lambda)$.

[3]In online Bayesian learning, it is known that forgetting inaccurate estimates from earlier timesteps is important (Sato, 2001; Honkela and Valpola, 2003). Since we set $\delta_{1:t-c-1} = 0$, at every timestep t, δ_k leads to forgetting older examples.

observable features (e.g., author, publication venue, geography, and other document-level metadata), but conducted inference in a batch setting, thus their approaches are not suitable for streaming data. It is not immediately clear how to generalize their approach to dynamic settings. Algorithmically, our work comes closest to the online dynamic topic model of Iwata et al. (2010), except that we also incorporate context features.

4 Learning and Inference

The goal of the learning procedure is to minimize the overall negative log likelihood,

$$-\log \mathcal{L}(\mathcal{D}) = \\ -\log \int d\boldsymbol{\beta}_{1:T} p(\boldsymbol{\beta}_{1:T} \mid \boldsymbol{\alpha}, \boldsymbol{x}_{1:T}) p(\boldsymbol{w}_{1:T} \mid \boldsymbol{\beta}_{1:T}, \boldsymbol{n}).$$

However, this quantity is intractable. Instead, we derive an upper bound for this quantity and minimize that upper bound. Using Jensen's inequality, the variational upper bound on the negative log likelihood is:

$$-\log \mathcal{L}(\mathcal{D}) \leq -\int d\boldsymbol{\beta}_{1:T} q(\boldsymbol{\beta}_{1:T} \mid \gamma_{1:T}) \quad (4) \\ \log \frac{p(\boldsymbol{\beta}_{1:T} \mid \boldsymbol{\alpha}, \boldsymbol{x}_{1:T}) p(\boldsymbol{w}_{1:T} \mid \boldsymbol{\beta}_{1:T}, \boldsymbol{n})}{q(\boldsymbol{\beta}_{1:T} \mid \gamma_{1:T})}.$$

Specifically, we use mean-field variational inference where the variables in the variational distribution q are completely independent. We use Gaussian distributions as our variational distributions for $\boldsymbol{\beta}$, denoted by $\boldsymbol{\gamma}$ in the bound in Eq. 4. We denote the parameters of the Gaussian variational distribution for $\beta_{t,v}$ (word v at timestep t) by $\mu_{t,v}$ (mean) and $\sigma_{t,v}$ (variance).

Figure 2 shows the functional form of the variational bound that we seek to minimize, denoted by $\hat{\mathcal{B}}$. The two main steps in the optimization of the bound are inferring $\boldsymbol{\beta}_t$ and updating feature coefficients $\boldsymbol{\alpha}$. We next describe each step in detail.

4.1 Learning

The goal of the learning procedure is to minimize the upper bound in Figure 2 with respect to $\boldsymbol{\alpha}$. However, since the data arrives in an online fashion, and speed is very important for processing streaming datasets, the model needs to be updated at every timestep t (in our experiments, daily).

Notice that at timestep t, we only have access to $\boldsymbol{x}_{1:t}$ and $\boldsymbol{w}_{1:t}$, and we perform learning at *every* timestep *after* the text for the current timestep $\boldsymbol{w}_t$ is revealed. We do not know $\boldsymbol{x}_{t+1:T}$ and $\boldsymbol{w}_{t+1:T}$. Nonetheless, we want to update our model so that it can make a better prediction at $t+1$. Therefore, we can only minimize the bound until timestep t. Let $C_k \triangleq \frac{\exp(\boldsymbol{\alpha}^\top \boldsymbol{f}(\boldsymbol{x}_t, \boldsymbol{x}_k))}{\sum_{j=t-c}^{t-1} \exp(\boldsymbol{\alpha}^\top \boldsymbol{f}(\boldsymbol{x}_t, \boldsymbol{x}_j))}$. Our learning algorithm is a variational Expectation-Maximization algorithm (Wainwright and Jordan, 2008).

E-step Recall that we use variational inference and the variational parameters for $\boldsymbol{\beta}$ are $\boldsymbol{\mu}$ and $\boldsymbol{\sigma}$. As shown in Figure 2, since the log-sum-exp in the last term of $\mathcal{B}$ is problematic, we introduce additional variational parameters $\boldsymbol{\zeta}$ to simplify $\mathcal{B}$ and obtain $\hat{\mathcal{B}}$ (Eqs. 2–3). The E-step deals with all the local variables $\boldsymbol{\mu}$, $\boldsymbol{\sigma}$, and $\boldsymbol{\zeta}$.

Fixing other variables and taking the derivative of the bound $\hat{\mathcal{B}}$ w.r.t. ζ_t and setting it to zero, we obtain the closed-form update for ζ_t: $\zeta_t = \sum_{v \in V} \exp(n_{1:t-1,v}) \exp\left(\mu_{t,v} + \frac{\sigma_{t,v}}{2}\right)$.

To minimize with respect to $\boldsymbol{\mu}_t$ and $\boldsymbol{\sigma}_t$, we apply gradient-based methods since there are no closed-form solutions. The derivative w.r.t. $\mu_{t,v}$ is:

$$\frac{\partial \hat{\mathcal{B}}}{\partial \mu_{t,v}} = \frac{\mu_{t,v} - C_k \mu_{k,v}}{\varphi} \\ - n_{t,v} + \frac{n_t}{\zeta_t} \exp(n_{1:t-1,v}) \exp\left(\mu_{t,v} + \frac{\sigma_{t,v}}{2}\right),$$

where $n_t = \sum_{v \in V} n_{t,v}$.

The derivative w.r.t. $\sigma_{t,v}$ is:

$$\frac{\partial \hat{\mathcal{B}}}{\partial \sigma_{t,v}} = \frac{1}{2\sigma_{t,v}} + \frac{1}{2\varphi} + \frac{n_t}{2\zeta_t} \exp(n_{1:t-1,v}) \exp\left(\mu_{t,v} + \frac{\sigma_{t,v}}{2}\right).$$

Although we require iterative methods in the E-step, we find it to be reasonably fast in practice.[4] Specifically, we use the L-BFGS quasi-Newton algorithm (Liu and Nocedal, 1989).

We can further improve the bound by updating the variational parameters for timestep $1:t-1$, i.e., $\boldsymbol{\mu}_{1:t-1}$ and $\boldsymbol{\sigma}_{1:t-1}$, as well. However, this will require storing the texts from previous timesteps. Additionally, this will complicate the M-step update described

[4] Approximately 16.5 seconds/day (walltime) to learn the model on the EN:NA dataset on a 2.40GHz CPU with 24GB memory.

$$\mathcal{B} = -\sum_{t=1}^{T}\mathbb{E}_q[\log p(\boldsymbol{\beta}_t \mid \boldsymbol{\beta}_k, \boldsymbol{\alpha}, \boldsymbol{x}_t)] - \sum_{t=1}^{T}\mathbb{E}_q[\log p(\boldsymbol{w}_t \mid \boldsymbol{\beta}_t, \boldsymbol{n}_t)] - \mathbb{H}(q) \tag{1}$$

$$= \sum_{t=1}^{T}\left\{\frac{1}{2}\sum_{j\in V}\log\frac{\sigma_{t,j}}{\varphi} - \mathbb{E}_q\left[-\frac{\left(\boldsymbol{\beta}_t - \sum_{k=t-c}^{t-1} C_k\boldsymbol{\beta}_k\right)^2}{2\varphi}\right] - \mathbb{E}_q\left[\sum_{v\in\boldsymbol{w}_t} n_{1:t-1,v} + \beta_{t,v} - \log\sum_{j\in V}\exp(n_{1:t-1,j} + \beta_{t,j})\right]\right\} \tag{2}$$

$$\leq \sum_{t=1}^{T}\left\{\frac{1}{2}\sum_{j\in V}\log\frac{\sigma_{t,v}}{\varphi} + \frac{\left(\boldsymbol{\mu}_t - \sum_{k=t-c}^{t-1} C_k\boldsymbol{\mu}_k\right)^2}{2\varphi} + \frac{\boldsymbol{\sigma}_t + \sum_{k=t-c}^{t-1} C_k^2\boldsymbol{\sigma}_k}{2\varphi}\right.$$

$$\left. - \sum_{v\in\boldsymbol{w}_t}\left(\mu_{t,v} - \log\zeta_t - \frac{1}{\zeta_t}\sum_{j\in V}\exp\left(n_{1:t-1,j}\right)\exp\left(\mu_{t,j} + \frac{\sigma_{t,j}}{2}\right)\right)\right\} + \text{const} \tag{3}$$

Figure 2: The variational bound that we seek to minimize, $\mathcal{B}$. $\mathbb{H}(q)$ is the entropy of the variational distribution q. The derivation from line 1 to line 2 is done by replacing the probability distributions $p(\boldsymbol{\beta}_t \mid \boldsymbol{\beta}_k, \boldsymbol{\alpha}, \boldsymbol{x}_t)$ and $p(\boldsymbol{w}_t \mid \boldsymbol{\beta}_t, \boldsymbol{n}_t)$ by their respective functional forms. Notice that in line 3 we compute the expectations under the variational distributions and further bound $\mathcal{B}$ by introducing additional variational parameters $\boldsymbol{\zeta}$ using Jensen's inequality on the log-sum-exp in the last term. We denote the new bound $\hat{\mathcal{B}}$.

below. Therefore, for each $s < t$, we choose to fix $\boldsymbol{\mu}_s$ and $\boldsymbol{\sigma}_s$ once they are learned at timestep s.

M-step In the M-step, we update the global parameter $\boldsymbol{\alpha}$, fixing $\boldsymbol{\mu}_{1:t}$. Fixing other parameters and taking the derivative of $\hat{\mathcal{B}}$ w.r.t. $\boldsymbol{\alpha}$, we obtain:[5]

$$\frac{\partial\hat{\mathcal{B}}}{\partial\alpha} = \frac{(\boldsymbol{\mu}_t - \sum_{k=t-c}^{t-1} C_k\boldsymbol{\mu}_k)(-\sum_{k=t-c}^{t-1}\frac{\partial C_k}{\partial\boldsymbol{\alpha}})}{\varphi} + \frac{\sum_{k=t-c}^{t-1} C_k\boldsymbol{\sigma}_k\frac{\partial C_k}{\partial\boldsymbol{\alpha}}}{\varphi},$$

where:

$$\frac{\partial C_k}{\partial\boldsymbol{\alpha}} = C_k\boldsymbol{f}(\boldsymbol{x}_t, \boldsymbol{x}_k) - C_k\frac{\sum_{s=t-c}^{t-1}\boldsymbol{f}(\boldsymbol{x}_t, \boldsymbol{x}_s)\exp(\boldsymbol{\alpha}^\top\boldsymbol{f}(\boldsymbol{x}_t, \boldsymbol{x}_s))}{\sum_{s=t-c}^{t-1}\exp(\boldsymbol{\alpha}^\top\boldsymbol{f}(\boldsymbol{x}_t, \boldsymbol{x}_s))}.$$

We follow the convex optimization strategy and simply perform a stochastic gradient update: $\boldsymbol{\alpha}_{t+1} = \boldsymbol{\alpha}_t + \eta_t\frac{\partial\hat{\mathcal{B}}}{\partial\boldsymbol{\alpha}_t}$ (Zinkevich, 2003). While the variational bound $\hat{\mathcal{B}}$ is not convex, given the local variables $\boldsymbol{\mu}_{1:t}$ and $\boldsymbol{\sigma}_{1:t}$, optimizing $\boldsymbol{\alpha}$ at timestep t without knowing the future becomes a convex problem.[6] Since we do not reestimate $\boldsymbol{\mu}_{1:t-1}$ and $\boldsymbol{\sigma}_{1:t-1}$ in the E-step, the choice to perform online gradient descent instead of iteratively performing batch optimization at every timestep is theoretically justified.

Notice that our overall learning procedure is still to minimize the variational upper bound $\hat{\mathcal{B}}$. All these choices are made to make the model suitable for learning in real time from large streaming datasets. Preliminary experiments showed that performing more than one EM iteration per day does not considerably improve performance, so in our experiments we perform one EM iteration per day.

To learn the parameters of the model, we rely on approximations and optimize an upper bound $\hat{\mathcal{B}}$. We have opted for this approach over alternatives (such as MCMC methods) because of our interest in the online, large-data setting. Our experiments show that we are still able to learn reasonable parameter estimates by optimizing $\hat{\mathcal{B}}$. Like online variational methods for other latent-variable models such as LDA (Sato, 2001; Hoffman et al., 2013), open questions remain about the tightness of such approximations and the identifiability of model parameters. We note, how-

[5]In our implementation, we augment $\boldsymbol{\alpha}$ with a squared L_2 regularization term (i.e., we assume that $\boldsymbol{\alpha}$ is drawn from a normal distribution with mean zero and variance λ) and use the FOBOS algorithm (Duchi and Singer, 2009). The derivative of the regularization term is simple and is not shown here. Of course, other regularizers (e.g., the L_1-norm, which we use for other parameters, or the $L_{1/\infty}$-norm) can also be explored.

[6]As a result, our algorithm is Hannan consistent w.r.t. the best fixed $\boldsymbol{\alpha}$ (for $\hat{\mathcal{B}}$) in hindsight; i.e., the average regret goes to zero as T goes to ∞.

ever, that our model does not include latent mixtures of topics and may be generally easier to estimate.

5 Prediction

As described in §2.2, our model is evaluated by the loss suffered at every timestep, where the loss is defined as the negative log likelihood of the model on text at timestep $\boldsymbol{w}_t$. Therefore, at each timestep t, we need to *predict* (the distribution of) $\boldsymbol{w}_t$. In order to do this, for each word $v \in V$, we simply compute the deviation means $\boldsymbol{\beta}_{t,v}$ as weighted combinations of previous means, where the weights are determined by the world-context similarity encoded in $\boldsymbol{x}$:

$$\mathbb{E}_q[\beta_{t,v} \mid \mu_{t,v}] = \sum_{k=t-c}^{t-1} \frac{\exp(\boldsymbol{\alpha}^\top \boldsymbol{f}(\boldsymbol{x}_t, \boldsymbol{x}_k))}{\sum_{j=t-c}^{t-1} \exp(\boldsymbol{\alpha}^\top \boldsymbol{f}(\boldsymbol{x}_t, \boldsymbol{x}_j))} \mu_{k,v}.$$

Recall that the word distribution that we use for prediction is obtained by applying the operator π that maps $\boldsymbol{\beta}_t$ and $\boldsymbol{n}$ to the V-dimensional simplex, forming a distribution over words: $\pi(\boldsymbol{\beta}_t, \boldsymbol{n}_{1:t-1})_v = \frac{\exp(n_{1:t-1,v} + \beta_{t,v})}{\sum_{j \in V} \exp(n_{1:t-1,j} + \beta_{t,j})}$, where $n_{1:t-1,v} \in \mathbb{R}^V$ is a background distribution (the log-frequency of word v observed up to time $t-1$).

6 Experiments

In our experiments, we consider the problem of predicting economy-related text appearing in news and microblogs, based on observable features that reflect current economic conditions in the world at a given time. In the following, we describe our dataset in detail, then show experimental results on text prediction. In all experiments, we set the window size $c = 7$ (one week) or $c = 14$ (two weeks), $\lambda = \frac{1}{2|V|}$ (V is the size of vocabulary of the dataset under consideration), and $\varphi = 1$.

6.1 Dataset

Our data contains metadata and text corpora. The metadata is used as our features, whereas the text corpora are used for learning language models and predictions. The dataset (excluding Twitter) can be downloaded at `http://www.ark.cs.cmu.edu/DynamicLM`.

6.1.1 Metadata

We use end-of-day stock prices gathered from `finance.yahoo.com` for each stock included in the Standard & Poor's 500 index (S&P 500). The index includes large (by market value) companies listed on US stock exchanges.[7] We calculate daily (continuously compounded) returns for each stock, o: $r_{o,t} = \log P_{o,t} - \log P_{o,t-1}$, where $P_{o,t}$ is the closing stock price.[8] We make a simplifying assumption that text for day t is generated after $P_{o,t}$ is observed.[9] In general, stocks trade Monday to Friday (except for federal holidays and natural disasters). For days when stocks do not trade, we set $r_{o,t} = 0$ for all stocks since any price change is not observed.

We transform returns into similarity values as follows: $f(x_{o,t}, x_{o,k}) = 1$ iff $\text{sign}(r_{o,t}) = \text{sign}(r_{o,k})$ and 0 otherwise. While this limits the model by ignoring the magnitude of price changes, it is still reasonable to capture the similarity between two days.[10] There are 500 stocks in the S&P 500, so $\boldsymbol{x}_t \in \mathbb{R}^{500}$ and $\boldsymbol{f}(\boldsymbol{x}_t, \boldsymbol{x}_k) \in \mathbb{R}^{500}$.

6.1.2 Text data

We have five streams of text data. The first four corpora are news streams tracked through Reuters.[11] Two of them are written in English, North American Business Report (EN:NA) and Japanese Investment News (EN:JP). The remaining two are German Economic News Service (DE, in German) and French Economic News Service (FR, in French). For all four of the Reuters streams, we collected news data over a period of thirteen months (392 days), 2012-05-26 to 2013-06-21. See Table 1 for descriptive statistics of these datasets. Numerical terms are mapped to a single word, and all letters are downcased.

The last text stream comes from the Decahose/Gardenhose stream from Twitter. We collected public tweets that contain ticker symbols (i.e., symbols that are used to denote stocks of a particular company in a stock market), preceded by the dollar

[7] For a list of companies listed in the S&P 500 as of 2012, see `http://en.wikipedia.org/wiki/List_of_S\%26P_500_companies`. This set was fixed during the time periods of all our experiments.

[8] We use the "adjusted close" on Yahoo that includes interim dividend cash flows and also adjusts for "splits" (changes in the number of outstanding shares).

[9] This is done in order to avoid having to deal with hourly timesteps. In addition, intraday price data is only available through commercial data provided.

[10] Note that daily stock returns are equally likely to be positive or negative and display little serial correlation.

[11] `http://www.reuters.com`

Dataset	Total # Doc.	Avg. # Doc.	#Days	Unigrams		Bigrams	
				Total # Tokens	Size Vocab.	Total # Tokens	Size Vocab.
EN:NA	86,683	223	392	28,265,550	10,000	11,804,201	5,000
EN:JP	70.807	182	392	16,026,380	10,000	7,047,095	5,000
FR	62,355	160	392	11,942,271	10,000	3,773,517	5,000
DE	51,515	132	392	9,027,823	10,000	3,499,965	5,000
Twitter	214,794	336	639	1,660,874	10,000	551,768	5,000

Table 1: Statistics about the datasets. Average number of documents (third column) is per day.

sign $ (e.g., $GOOG, $MSFT, $AAPL, etc.). These tags are generally used to indicate tweets about the stock market. We look at tweets from the period 2011-01-01 to 2012-09-30 (639 days). As a result, we have approximately 100–800 tweets per day. We tokenized the tweets using the CMU ARK TweetNLP tools,[12] numerical terms are mapped to a single word, and all letters are downcased.

We perform two experiments using unigram and bigram language models as the base models. For each dataset, we consider the top 10,000 unigrams after removing corpus-specific stopwords (the top 100 words with highest frequencies). For the bigram experiments, we only use 5,000 words to limit the number of unique bigrams so that we can simulate experiments for the entire time horizon in a reasonable amount of time. In standard open-vocabulary language modeling experiments, the treatment of unknown words deserves care. We have opted for a controlled, closed-vocabulary experiment, since standard smoothing techniques will almost surely interact with temporal dynamics and context in interesting ways that are out of scope in the present work.

6.2 Baselines

Since this is a forecasting task, at each timestep, we only have access to data from previous timesteps. Our model assumes that all words in all documents in a corpus come from a single multinomial distribution. Therefore, we compare our approach to the corresponding base models (standard unigram and bigram language models) over the same vocabulary (for each stream). The first one maintains counts of every word and updates the counts at each timestep. This corresponds to a base model that uses all of the available data up to the current timestep ("base all"). The second one *replaces* counts of every word with the counts from the previous timestep ("base one"). Additionally, we also compare with a base model whose counts decay exponentially ("base exp"). That is, the counts from previous timesteps decay by $\exp(-\gamma s)$, where s is the distance between previous timesteps and the current timestep and γ is the decay constant. We set the decay constant $\gamma = 1$. We put a symmetric Dirichlet prior on the counts ("add-one" smoothing); this is analogous to our treatment of the background frequencies $\boldsymbol{n}$ in our model. Note that our model, similar to "base all," uses *all* available data up to timestep $t-1$ when making predictions for timestep t. The window size c only determines which previous timesteps' models can be chosen for making a prediction today. The past models themselves are estimated from all available data up to their respective timesteps.

We also compare with two strong baselines: a linear interpolation of "base one" models for the past week ("int. week") and a linear interpolation of "base all" and "base one" ("int one all"). The interpolation weights are learned online using the normalized exponentiated gradient algorithm (Kivinen and Warmuth, 1997), which has been shown to enjoy a stronger regret guarantee compared to standard online gradient descent for learning a convex combination of weights.

6.3 Results

We evaluate the perplexity on unseen dataset to evaluate the performance of our model. Specifically, we use per-word predictive perplexity:

$$\text{perplexity} = \exp\left(-\frac{\sum_{t=1}^{T} \log p(\boldsymbol{w}_t \mid \boldsymbol{\alpha}, \boldsymbol{x}_{1:t}, \boldsymbol{n}_{1:t-1})}{\sum_{t=1}^{T} \sum_{j \in V} w_{t,j}}\right).$$

Note that the denominator is the number of tokens up to timestep T. Lower perplexity is better.

Table 2 and Table 3 show the perplexity results for

[12]https://www.ark.cs.cmu.edu/TweetNLP

Dataset	base all	base one	base exp	int. week	int. one all	$c = 7$	$c = 14$
EN:NA	3,341	3,677	3,486	3,403	3,271	**3,262**	3,285
EN:JP	2,802	3,212	2,750	2,949	2,708	**2,656**	2,689
FR	3,603	3,910	3,678	3,625	3,416	**3,404**	3,438
DE	3,789	4,199	3,979	3,926	**3,634**	3,649	3,687
Twitter	3,880	6,168	5,133	5,859	4,047	**3,801**	3,819

Table 2: Perplexity results for our five data streams in the unigram experiments. The base models in "base all," "base one," and "base exp" are unigram language models. "int. week" is a linear interpolation of "base one" from the past week. "int. one all" is a linear interpolation of "base one" and "base all". The rightmost two columns are versions of our model. Best results are highlighted in bold.

Dataset	base all	base one	base exp	int. week	int. one all	$c = 7$
EN:NA	242	2,229	1,880	2,200	244	**223**
EN:JP	185	2,101	1,726	2,050	189	**167**
FR	159	2,084	1,707	2,068	166	**139**
DE	268	2,634	2,267	2,644	282	**243**
Twitter	756	4,245	4,253	5,859	4,046	**739**

Table 3: Perplexity results for our five data streams in the bigram experiments. The base models in "base all," "base one," and "base exp" are bigram language models. "int. week" is a linear interpolation of "base one" from the past week. "int. one all" is a linear interpolation of "base one" and "base all". The rightmost column is a version of our model with $c = 7$. Best results are highlighted in bold.

each of the datasets for unigram and bigram experiments respectively. Our model outperformed other competing models in all cases but one. Recall that we only define the similarity function of world context as: $f(x_{o,t}, x_{o,k}) = 1$ iff $\text{sign}(r_{o,t}) = \text{sign}(r_{o,k})$ and 0 otherwise. A better similarity function (e.g., one that takes into account market size of the company and the magnitude of increase or decrease in the stock price) might be able to improve the performance further. We leave this for future work. Furthermore, the variations can be captured using models from the past week. We discuss why increasing c from 7 to 14 did not improve performance of the model in more detail in §6.4.

We can also see how the models performed over time. Figure 4 traces perplexity for four Reuters news stream datasets.[13] We can see that in some cases the performance of the "base all" model degraded over time, whereas our model is more robust to temporal shifts.

In the bigram experiments, we only ran our model with $c = 7$, since we need to maintain $\boldsymbol{\beta}$ in $\mathbb{R}^{V^2}$, instead of $\mathbb{R}^V$ in the unigram model. The goal of this experiment is to determine whether our method still adds benefit to more expressive language models. Note that the weights of the linear interpolation models are also learned in an online fashion since there are no classical training, development, and test sets in our setting. Since the "base one" model performed poorly in this experiment, the performance of the interpolated models also suffered. For example, the "int. one all" model needed time to learn that the "base one" model has to be downweighted (we started with all interpolated models having uniform weights), so it was not able to outperform even the "base all" model.

6.4 Analysis and Discussion

It should not be surprising that conditioning on world-context reduces perplexity (Cover and Thomas, 1991). A key attraction of our model, we believe, lies in the ability to inspect its parameters.

Deviation coefficients. Inspecting the model allows us to gain insight into temporal trends. We

[13] In both experiments, in order to manage the time and space complexities of updating $\boldsymbol{\beta}$, we apply a sparsity shrinkage technique by using OWL-QN (Andrew and Gao, 2007) when maximizing it, with regularization constant set to 1. Intuitively, this is equivalent to encouraging the deviation vector to be sparse (Eisenstein et al., 2011).

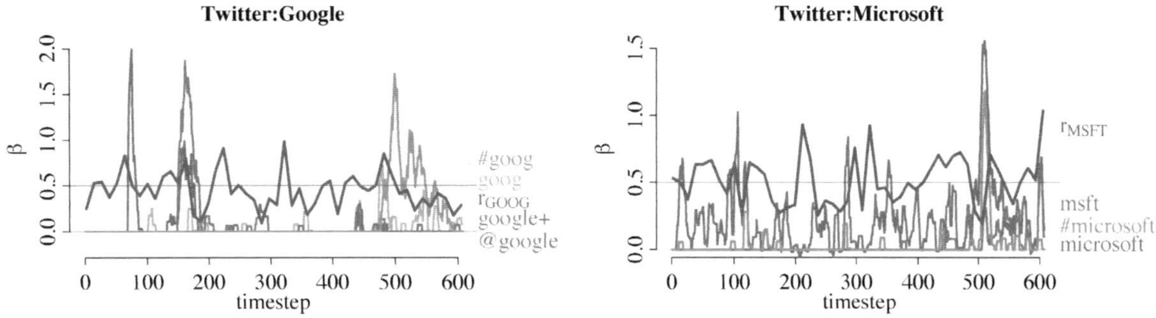

Figure 3: Deviation coefficients $\boldsymbol{\beta}$ over time for Google- and Microsoft-related words on Twitter with unigram base model ($c = 7$). Significant changes (increases or decreases) in the returns of Google and Microsoft stocks are usually followed by increases in β of related words.

investigate the deviations learned by our model on the Twitter dataset. Examples are shown in Figure 3. The left plot shows β for four words related to Google: `goog`, `#goog`, `@google`, `google+`. For comparison, we also show the return of Google stock for the corresponding timestep (scaled by 50 and centered at 0.5 for readability, smoothed using loess (Cleveland, 1979), denoted by r_{GOOG} in the plot). We can see that significant changes of return of Google stocks (e.g., the r_{GOOG} spikes between timesteps 50–100, 150–200, 490–550 in the plot) occurred alongside an increase in β of Google-related words. Similar trends can also be observed for Microsoft-related words in the right plot. The most significant loss of return of Microsoft stocks (the downward spike near timestep 500 in the plot) is followed by a sudden sharp increase in β of the words `#microsoft` and `microsoft`.

Feature coefficients. We can also inspect the learned feature coefficients $\boldsymbol{\alpha}$ to investigate which stocks have higher associations with the text that is generated. Our feature coefficients are designed to reflect which changes (or lack of changes) in stock prices influence the word distribution more, not which stocks are talked about more often. We find that the feature coefficients do not correlate with obvious company characteristics like market capitalization (firm size). For example, on the Twitter dataset with bigram base models, the five stocks with the highest weights are: ConAgra Foods Inc., Intel Corp., Bristol-Myers Squibb, Frontier Communications Corp., and Amazon.com Inc. Strongly negative weights tended to align with streams with less activity, suggesting that these were being used to smooth across all c days of history. A higher weight for stock o implies an increase in probability of choosing models from previous timesteps s, when the state of the world for the current timestep t and timestep s is the same (as represented by our similarity function) with respect to stock o (all other things being equal), and a decrease in probability for a lower weight.

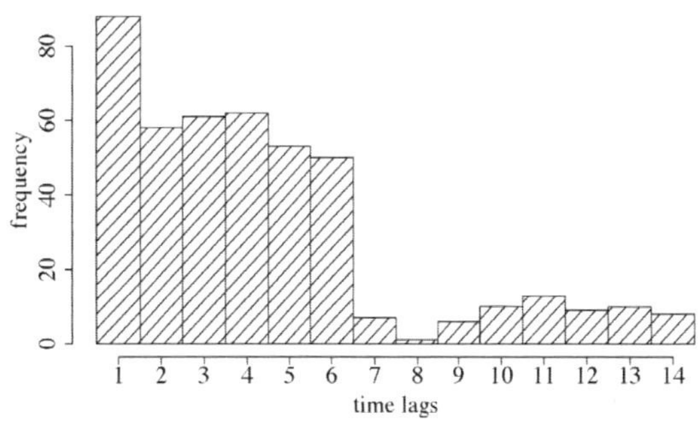

Figure 5: Distributions of the selection probabilities of models from the previous $c = 14$ timesteps, on the EN:NA dataset with unigram base model. For simplicity, we show E-step modes. The histogram shows that the model tends to favor models from days closer to the current date.

Selected models. Besides feature coefficients, our model captures temporal shift by modeling similarity across the most recent c days. During inference, our model weights different word distributions from the past. The similarity is encoded in the pairwise features $\boldsymbol{f}(\boldsymbol{x}_t, \boldsymbol{x}_k)$ and the parameters $\boldsymbol{\alpha}$. Figure 5 shows the distributions of the strongest-posterior models from previous timesteps, based on how far

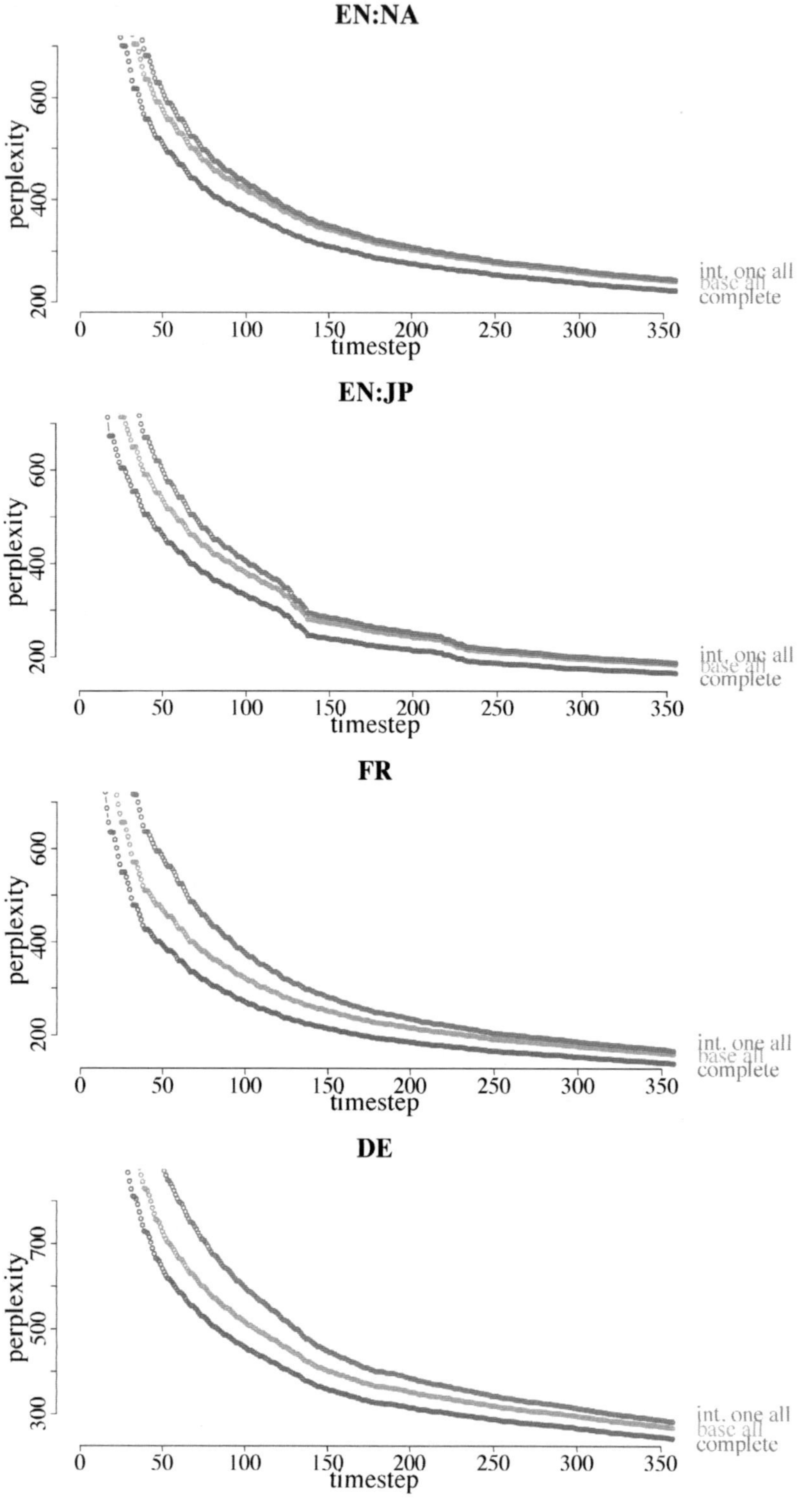

Figure 4: Perplexity over time for four Reuters news streams ($c = 7$) with bigram base models.

in the past they are at the time of use, aggregated across rounds on the EN:NA dataset, for window size $c = 14$. It shows that the model tends to favor models from days closer to the current date, with the $t - 1$ models selected the most, perhaps because the state of the world today is more similar to dates closer to today compare to more distant dates. The plot also explains why increasing c from 7 to 14 did not improve performance of the model, since most of the variation in our datasets can be captured with models from the past week.

Topics. Latent topic variables have often figured heavily in approaches to dynamic language modeling. In preliminary experiments incorporating single-membership topic variables (i.e., each document belongs to a single topic, as in a mixture of unigrams), we saw no benefit to perplexity. Incorporating topics also increases computational cost, since we must maintain and estimate one language model per topic, per timestep. It is straightforward to design models that incorporate topics with single- or mixed-membership as in LDA (Blei et al., 2003), an interesting future direction.

Potential applications. Dynamic language models like ours can be potentially useful in many applications, either as a standalone language model, e.g., predictive text input, whose performance may depend on the temporal dimension; or as a component in applications like machine translation or speech recognition. Additionally, the model can be seen as a step towards enhancing text understanding with numerical, contextual data.

7 Conclusion

We presented a dynamic language model for streaming datasets that allows conditioning on observable real-world context variables, exemplified in our experiments by stock market data. We showed how to perform learning and inference in an online fashion for this model. Our experiments showed the predictive benefit of such conditioning and online learning by comparing to similar models that ignore temporal dimensions and observable variables that influence the text.

Acknowledgements

The authors thank several anonymous reviewers for helpful feedback on earlier drafts of this paper and Brendan O'Connor for help with collecting Twitter data. This research was supported in part by Google, by computing resources at the Pittsburgh Supercomputing Center, by National Science Foundation grant IIS-1111142, AFOSR grant FA95501010247, ONR grant N000140910758, and by the Intelligence Advanced Research Projects Activity via Department of Interior National Business Center contract number D12PC00347. The U.S. Government is authorized to reproduce and distribute reprints for Governmental purposes notwithstanding any copyright annotation thereon. The views and conclusions contained herein are those of the authors and should not be interpreted as necessarily representing the official policies or endorsements, either expressed or implied, of IARPA, DoI/NBC, or the U.S. Government.

References

Galen Andrew and Jianfeng Gao. 2007. Scalable training of l_1-regularized log-linear models. In *Proc. of ICML*.

David M. Blei and John D. Lafferty. 2006. Dynamic topic models. In *Proc. of ICML*.

David M. Blei, Andrew Y. Ng, and Michael I. Jordan. 2003. Latent Dirichlet allocation. *Journal of Machine Learning Research*, 3:993–1022.

Sébastien Bubeck. 2011. Introduction to online optimization. Technical report, Department of Operations Research and Financial Engineering, Princeton University.

Nicolò Cesa-Bianchi and Gábor Lugosi. 2006. *Prediction, Learning, and Games*. Cambridge University Press.

William S. Cleveland. 1979. Robust locally weighted regression and smoothing scatterplots. *Journal of the American Statistical Association*, 74(368):829–836.

Thomas M. Cover and Joy A. Thomas. 1991. *Elements of Information Theory*. John Wiley & Sons.

John Duchi and Yoram Singer. 2009. Efficient online and batch learning using forward backward splitting. *Journal of Machine Learning Research*, 10(7):2899–2934.

Jacob Eisenstein, Brendan O'Connor, Noah A. Smith, and Eric P. Xing. 2010. A latent variable model for geographic lexical variation. In *Proc. of EMNLP*.

Jacob Eisenstein, Amr Ahmed, and Eric P. Xing. 2011. Sparse additive generative models of text. In *Proc. of ICML*.

Amit Goyal, Hal Daume III, and Suresh Venkatasubramanian. 2009. Streaming for large scale NLP: Language modeling. In *Proc. of HLT-NAACL*.

Matt Hoffman, David M. Blei, Chong Wang, and John Paisley. 2013. Stochastic variational inference. *Journal of Machine Learning Research*, 14:1303–1347.

Antti Honkela and Harri Valpola. 2003. On-line variational Bayesian learning. In *Proc. of ICA*.

Tomoharu Iwata, Takeshi Yamada, Yasushi Sakurai, and Naonori Ueda. 2010. Online multiscale dynamic topic models. In *Proc. of KDD*.

Frederick Jelinek. 1997. *Statistical Methods for Speech Recognition*. MIT Press.

Jyrki Kivinen and Manfred K. Warmuth. 1997. Exponentiated gradient versus gradient descent for linear predictors. *Information and Computation*, 132:1–63.

Victor Lavrenko, Matt Schmill, Dawn Lawrie, Paul Ogilvie, David Jensen, and James Allan. 2000. Mining of concurrent text and time series. In *Proc. of KDD Workshop on Text Mining*.

Abby Levenberg and Miles Osborne. 2009. Stream-based randomised language models for SMT. In *Proc. of EMNLP*.

Abby Levenberg, Chris Callison-Burch, and Miles Osborne. 2010. Stream-based translation models for statistical machine translation. In *Proc. of HLT-NAACL*.

Dong C. Liu and Jorge Nocedal. 1989. On the limited memory BFGS method for large scale optimization. *Mathematical Programming B*, 45(3):503–528.

David Mimno and Andrew McCallum. 2008. Topic models conditioned on arbitrary features with Dirichlet-multinomial regression. In *Proc. of UAI*.

Alexander Rakhlin. 2009. Lecture notes on online learning. Technical report, Department of Statistics, The Wharton School, University of Pennsylvania.

Masaaki Sato. 2001. Online model selection based on the variational bayes. *Neural Computation*, 13(7):1649–1681.

Shai Shalev-Shwartz. 2012. Online learning and online convex optimization. *Foundations and Trends in Machine Learning*, 4(2):107–194.

Martin J. Wainwright and Michael I. Jordan. 2008. Graphical models, exponential families, and variational inference. *Foundations and Trends in Machine Learning*, 1(1–2):1–305.

Chong Wang, David M. Blei, and David Heckerman. 2008. Continuous time dynamic topic models. In *Proc. of UAI*.

Chong Wang, John Paisley, and David M. Blei. 2011. Online variational inference for the hierarchical Dirichlet process. In *Proc. of AISTATS*.

Martin Zinkevich. 2003. Online convex programming and generalized infinitesimal gradient ascent. In *Proc. of ICML*.

Discriminative Lexical Semantic Segmentation with Gaps: Running the MWE Gamut

Nathan Schneider **Emily Danchik** **Chris Dyer** **Noah A. Smith**
School of Computer Science
Carnegie Mellon University
Pittsburgh, PA 15213, USA
{nschneid,emilydan,cdyer,nasmith}@cs.cmu.edu

Abstract

We present a novel representation, evaluation measure, and supervised models for the task of identifying the multiword expressions (MWEs) in a sentence, resulting in a *lexical semantic segmentation*. Our approach generalizes a standard chunking representation to encode MWEs containing gaps, thereby enabling efficient sequence tagging algorithms for feature-rich discriminative models. Experiments on a new dataset of English web text offer the first linguistically-driven evaluation of MWE identification with truly heterogeneous expression types. Our statistical sequence model greatly outperforms a lookup-based segmentation procedure, achieving nearly 60% F_1 for MWE identification.

1. **MW named entities:** *Prime Minister Tony Blair*
2. **MW compounds:** *hot air balloon, skinny dip*
3. **conventionally SW compounds:** *somewhere*
4. **verb-particle:** *pick up, dry out, take over, cut short*
5. **verb-preposition:** *refer to, depend on, look for*
6. **verb-noun(-preposition):** *pay attention (to)*
7. **support verb:** *make decisions, take pictures*
8. **other phrasal verb:** *put up with, get rid of*
9. **PP modifier:** *above board, at all, from time to time*
10. **coordinated phrase:** *cut and dry, more or less*
11. **connective:** *as well as, let alone, in spite of*
12. **semi-fixed VP:** *pick up where* <one> *left off*
13. **fixed phrase:** *scared to death, leave of absence*
14. **phatic:** *You're welcome. Me neither!*
15. **proverb:** *Beggars can't be choosers.*

Figure 1: Some of the classes of idioms in English. The examples included here contain multiple lexicalized words—with the exception of those in (3), if the conventional single-word (SW) spelling is used.

1 Introduction

Language has a knack for defying expectations when put under the microscope. For example, there is the notion—sometimes referred to as *compositionality*—that words will behave in predictable ways, with individual meanings that combine to form complex meanings according to general grammatical principles. Yet language is awash with examples to the contrary: in particular, idiomatic expressions such as *awash with* NP, *have a knack for* $\text{VP}_{\text{-}ing}$, *to the contrary*, and *defy expectations*. Thanks to processes like metaphor and grammaticalization, these are (to various degrees) semantically opaque, structurally fossilized, and/or statistically idiosyncratic. In other words, idiomatic expressions may be exceptional in form, function, or distribution. They are so diverse, so unruly, so difficult to circumscribe, that entire theories of syntax are predicated on the notion that constructions with idiosyncratic form-meaning mappings (Fillmore et al., 1988; Goldberg, 1995) or statistical properties (Goldberg, 2006) offer crucial evidence about the grammatical organization of language.

Here we focus on **multiword expressions** (MWEs): *lexicalized* combinations of two or more words that are exceptional enough to be considered as single units in the lexicon. As figure 1 illustrates, MWEs occupy diverse syntactic and semantic functions. Within MWEs, we distinguish (a) proper names and (b) lexical idioms. The latter have proved themselves a "pain in the neck for NLP" (Sag et al., 2002). Automatic and efficient detection of MWEs, though far from solved, would have diverse appli-

Transactions of the Association for Computational Linguistics, 2 (2014) 193–206. Action Editor: Joakim Nivre.
Submitted 12/2013; Revised 1/2014; Published 4/2014.

cations including machine translation (Carpuat and Diab, 2010), information retrieval (Newman et al., 2012), opinion mining (Berend, 2011), and second language learning (Ellis et al., 2008).

It is difficult to establish any comprehensive taxonomy of multiword idioms, let alone develop linguistic criteria and corpus resources that cut across these types. Consequently, the voluminous literature on MWEs in computational linguistics—see §7, Baldwin and Kim (2010), and Ramisch (2012) for surveys—has been fragmented, looking (for example) at subclasses of phrasal verbs or nominal compounds in isolation. To the extent that MWEs have been annotated in existing corpora, it has usually been as a secondary aspect of some other scheme. Traditionally, such resources have prioritized certain kinds of MWEs to the exclusion of others, so they are not appropriate for evaluating general-purpose identification systems.

In this article, we briefly review a shallow form of analysis for MWEs that is neutral to expression type, and that facilitates free text annotation without requiring a prespecified MWE lexicon (§2). The scheme applies to gappy (discontinuous) as well as contiguous expressions, and allows for a qualitative distinction of association strengths. In Schneider et al. (2014) we have applied this scheme to fully annotate a 55,000-word corpus of English web reviews (Bies et al., 2012a), a conversational genre in which colloquial idioms are highly salient. This article's main contribution is to show that the representation—constrained according to linguistically motivated assumptions (§3)—can be transformed into a sequence tagging scheme that resembles standard approaches in named entity recognition and other text chunking tasks (§4). Along these lines, we develop a discriminative, structured model of MWEs in context (§5) and train, evaluate, and examine it on the annotated corpus (§6). Finally, in §7 and §8 we comment on related work and future directions.

2 Annotated Corpus

To build and evaluate a multiword expression analyzer, we use the MWE-annotated corpus of Schneider et al. (2014). It consists of informal English web text that has been specifically and completely annotated for MWEs, without reference to any particular lexicon. To the best of our knowledge, this corpus is the first to be freely annotated for many kinds of MWEs (without reference to a lexicon), and is also the first dataset of social media text with MWE annotations beyond named entities. This section gives a synopsis of the annotation conventions used to develop that resource, as they are important to understanding our models and evaluation.

Rationale. The multiword expressions community has lacked a canonical corpus resource comparable to benchmark datasets used for problems such as NER and parsing. Consequently, the MWE literature has been driven by lexicography: typically, the goal is to acquire an MWE lexicon with little or no supervision, or to apply such a lexicon to corpus data. Studies of MWEs in context have focused on various subclasses of constructions in isolation, necessitating special-purpose datasets and evaluation schemes. By contrast, Schneider et al.'s (2014) corpus creates an opportunity to tackle *general-purpose* MWE identification, such as would be desirable for use by high-coverage downstream NLP systems. It is used to train and evaluate our models below. The corpus is publicly available as a benchmark for further research.[1]

Data. The documents in the corpus are online user reviews of restaurants, medical providers, retailers, automotive services, pet care services, etc. Marked by conversational and opinionated language, this genre is fertile ground for colloquial idioms (Nunberg et al., 1994; Moon, 1998). The 723 reviews (55,000 words, 3,800 sentences) in the English Web Treebank (WTB; Bies et al., 2012b) were collected by Google, tokenized, and annotated with phrase structure trees in the style of the Penn Treebank (Marcus et al., 1993). MWE annotators used the sentence and word tokenizations supplied by the treebank.[2]

Annotation scheme. The annotation scheme itself was designed to be as simple as possible. It consists of grouping together the tokens in each sentence that belong to the same MWE instance. While annotation guidelines provide examples of MWE groupings in a wide range of constructions, the annotator is not

[1] `http://www.ark.cs.cmu.edu/LexSem/`

[2] Because we use treebank data, syntactic parses are available to assist in post hoc analysis. Syntactic information was not shown to annotators.

	# of constituent tokens				*# of gaps*		
	2	**3**	**≥4**	**total**	**0**	**1**	**2**
strong	2257	595	172	3024	2626	394	4
weak	269	121	69	459	322	135	2
	2526	716	241	3483	2948	529	6

Table 1: Counts in the MWE corpus.

tied to any particular taxonomy or syntactic structure. This simplifies the number of decisions that have to be made for each sentence, even if some are difficult.

Further instructions to annotators included:

- Groups should include only the lexically fixed parts of an expression (modulo inflectional morphology); this generally excludes determiners and pronouns: ***made*** *the* ***mistake***, ***pride*** *themselves* ***on***.
- Multiword proper names count as MWEs.
- Misspelled or unconventionally spelled tokens are interpreted according to the intended word if clear.
- Overtokenized words (spelled as two tokens, but conventionally one word) are joined as multiwords. Clitics separated by the tokenization in the corpus—negative *n't*, possessive *'s*, etc.—are joined if functioning as a fixed part of a multiword (e.g., ***T 's Cafe***), but not if used productively.

Gaps. There are, broadly speaking, three reasons to group together tokens that are not fully contiguous. Most commonly, gaps contain internal modifiers, such as *good* in ***make*** *good* ***decisions***. Syntactic constructions such as the passive can result in gaps that might not otherwise be present: in *good* ***decisions*** *were* ***made***, there is instead a gap filled by the passive auxiliary. Finally, some MWEs may take internal arguments: *they* ***gave*** *me* ***a break***. Figure 1 has additional examples. Multiple gaps can occur even within the same expression, though it is rare: *they agreed to* ***give*** *Bob* ***a*** *well-deserved* ***break***.

Strength. The annotation scheme has two "strength" levels for MWEs. Clearly idiomatic expressions are marked as strong MWEs, while mostly compositional but especially frequent collocations/ phrases (e.g., *abundantly clear* and *patently obvious*) are marked as weak MWEs. Weak multiword groups are allowed to include strong MWEs as constituents (but not vice versa). Strong groups are required to cohere when used inside weak groups: that is, a weak group cannot include only part of a strong group. For purposes of annotation, there were no constraints hinging on the ordering of tokens in the sentence.

Process. MWE annotation proceeded one sentence at a time. The 6 annotators referred to and improved the guidelines document on an ongoing basis. Every sentence was seen independently by at least 2 annotators, and differences of opinion were discussed and resolved (often by marking a weak MWE as a compromise). See Schneider et al. (2014) for details.

Statistics. The annotated corpus consists of 723 documents (3,812 sentences). MWEs are frequent in this domain: 57% of sentences (72% of sentences over 10 words long) and 88% of documents contain at least one MWE. 8,060/55,579=15% of tokens belong to an MWE; in total, there are 3,483 MWE instances. 544 (16%) are strong MWEs containing a gold-tagged proper noun—most are proper names. A breakdown appears in table 1.

3 Representation and Task Definition

We define a **lexical segmentation** of a sentence as a partitioning of its tokens into segments such that each segment represents a single unit of lexical meaning. A *multiword* lexical expression may contain **gaps**, i.e. interruptions by other segments. We impose two restrictions on gaps that appear to be well-motivated linguistically:

- **Projectivity:** Every expression filling a gap must be completely contained within that gap; gappy expressions may not interleave.
- **No nested gaps:** A gap in an expression may be filled by other single- or multiword expressions, so long as those do not themselves contain gaps.

Formal grammar. Our scheme corresponds to the following extended CFG (Thatcher, 1967), where S is the full sentence and terminals w are word tokens:

$$\begin{aligned} S &\rightarrow X^+ \\ X &\rightarrow \underline{w^+}\ (Y^+\ \underline{w^+})^* \\ Y &\rightarrow \underline{w^+} \end{aligned}$$

Each expression X or Y is lexicalized by the words in one or more underlined variables on the right-hand side. An X constituent may optionally contain one or more gaps filled by Y constituents, which must not contain gaps themselves.[3]

[3]MWEs with multiple gaps are rare but attested in data: e.g., ***putting*** *me* ***at*** *my* ***ease***. We encountered one violation of the gap nesting constraint in the reviews data: *I* $have_1^2$ $nothing_1^2$ but_1^2 *fantastic* $things^2$ to_1^2 say_1^2 . Additionally, the interrupted phrase

Denoting multiword groupings with subscripts, *My wife had* *taken*$_1$ | *her '07*$_2$ *Ford*$_2$ *Fusion*$_2$ | *in*$_1$ *for a routine* *oil*$_3$ *change*$_3$ contains 3 multiword groups—{*taken, in*}, {*'07, Ford, Fusion*}, {*oil, change*}—and 7 single-word groups. The first MWE is gappy (accentuated by the box); a single word and a contiguous multiword group fall within the gap. The projectivity constraint forbids an analysis like *taken*$_1$ *her '07*$_2$ *Ford*$_1$ *Fusion*$_2$, while the gap nesting constraint forbids *taken*$_1$ | *her*$_2$ | *'07* | *Ford*$_2$ *Fusion*$_2$ | *in*$_1$.

3.1 Two-level Scheme: Strong vs. Weak MWEs

Our annotated data distinguish two strengths of MWEs as discussed in §2. Augmenting the grammar of the previous section, we therefore designate nonterminals as strong ($\bar{X}, \bar{Y}$) or weak ($\tilde{X}, \tilde{Y}$):

$$\begin{array}{lcl} S & \rightarrow & \tilde{X}^{+} \\ \tilde{X} & \rightarrow & \underline{\bar{X}}^{+} \ (\tilde{Y}^{+} \ \underline{\bar{X}}^{+})^{*} \\ \bar{X} & \rightarrow & \underline{w}^{+} \ (\tilde{Y}^{+} \ \underline{w}^{+})^{*} \\ \tilde{Y} & \rightarrow & \underline{\bar{Y}}^{+} \\ \bar{Y} & \rightarrow & \underline{w}^{+} \end{array}$$

A weak MWE may be lexicalized by single words and/or strong multiwords. Strong multiwords cannot contain weak multiwords except in gaps. Further, the contents of a gap cannot be part of any multiword that extends outside the gap.[4]

For example, consider the segmentation: *he was willing to budge*$_1$ *a*$_2$ *little*$_2$ *on*$_1$ *the price which means*^{4} *a*$_3^4$ *lot*$_3^4$ *to*^{4} *me*^{4}. Subscripts denote strong MW groups and superscripts weak MW groups; unmarked tokens serve as single-word expressions. The MW groups are thus {*budge, on*}, {*a, little*}, {*a, lot*}, and {*means*, {*a, lot*}, *to, me*}. As should be evident from the grammar, the projectivity and gap-nesting constraints apply here just as in the 1-level scheme.

3.2 Evaluation

Matching criteria. Given that most tokens do not belong to an MWE, to evaluate MWE identification we adopt a precision/recall-based measure from the coreference resolution literature. The MUC criterion (Vilain et al., 1995) measures precision and recall of links in terms of groups (units) implied by the transitive closure over those links.[5] It can be defined as follows:

Let $a - b$ denote a link between two elements in the gold standard, and $a \hat{-} b$ denote a link in the system prediction. Let the $*$ operator denote the transitive closure over all links, such that $[\![a -^{*} b]\!]$ is 1 if a and b belong to the same (gold) set, and 0 otherwise. Assuming there are no redundant[6] links within any annotation (which in our case is guaranteed by linking consecutive words in each MWE), we can write the MUC precision and recall measures as:

$$P = \frac{\sum_{a,b:a \hat{-} b} [\![a -^{*} b]\!]}{\sum_{a,b:a \hat{-} b} 1} \qquad R = \frac{\sum_{a,b:a - b} [\![a \hat{-}^{*} b]\!]}{\sum_{a,b:a - b} 1}$$

This awards partial credit when predicted and gold expressions overlap in part. Requiring full MWEs to match exactly would arguably be too stringent, overpenalizing larger MWEs for minor disagreements. We combine precision and recall using the standard F_1 measure of their harmonic mean. This is the **link-based** evaluation used for most of our experiments. For comparison, we also report some results with a more stringent **exact match** evaluation where the span of the predicted MWE must be identical to the span of the gold MWE for it to count as correct.

Strength averaging. Recall that the 2-level scheme (§3.1) distinguishes *strong* vs. *weak* links/groups, where the latter category applies to reasonably compositional collocations as well as ambiguous or difficult cases. If where one annotation uses a weak link the other has a strong link or no link at all, we want to penalize the disagreement less than if one had a strong link and the other had no link. To accommodate the 2-level scheme, we therefore average $F_1^{\uparrow}$, in which all weak links have been converted to strong links, and $F_1^{\downarrow}$, in which they have been removed: $F_1 = \frac{1}{2}(F_1^{\uparrow} + F_1^{\downarrow})$.[7] If neither annotation contains any weak links, this equals the MUC

great gateways never^1 *before*^{1} , *so*$_3^2$ *far*$_3^2$ *as*$_3^2$ *Hudson knew*^{2} , *seen*^{1} *by Europeans* was annotated in another corpus.

[4]This was violated 6 times in our annotated data: modifiers within gaps are sometimes collocated with the gappy expression, as in *on*$_2^1$ *a*$_2^1$ *tight*^{1} *budget*$_2^1$ and *have*$_2^1$ *little*^{1} *doubt*$_2^1$.

[5]As a criterion for coreference resolution, the MUC measure has perceived shortcomings which have prompted several other measures (see Recasens and Hovy, 2011 for a review). It is not clear, however, whether any of these criticisms are relevant to MWE identification.

[6]A link between a and b is redundant if the other links already imply that a and b belong to the same set. A set of N elements is expressed non-redundantly with exactly $N-1$ links.

[7]Overall precision and recall are likewise computed by averaging "strengthened" and "weakened" measurements.

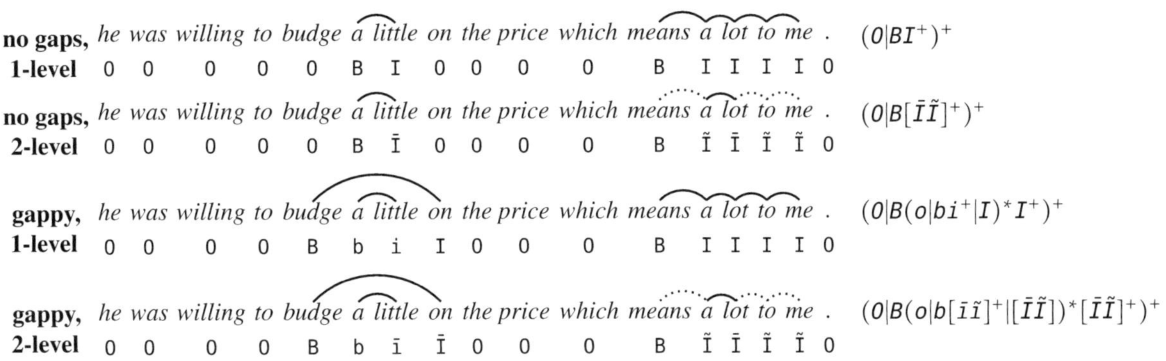

Figure 2: Examples and regular expressions for the 4 tagging schemes. Strong links are depicted with solid arcs, and weak links with dotted arcs. The bottom analysis was provided by an annotator; the ones above are simplifications.

score because $F_1 = F_1^{\uparrow} = F_1^{\downarrow}$. This method applies to both the link-based and exact match evaluation criteria.

4 Tagging Schemes

Following (Ramshaw and Marcus, 1995), shallow analysis is often modeled as a sequence-chunking task, with tags containing chunk-positional information. The BIO scheme and variants (e.g., BILOU; Ratinov and Roth, 2009) are standard for tasks like named entity recognition, supersense tagging, and shallow parsing.

The language of derivations licensed by the grammars in §3 allows for a tag-based encoding of MWE analyses with only bigram constraints. We describe 4 tagging schemes for MWE identification, starting with BIO and working up to more expressive variants. They are depicted in figure 2.

No gaps, 1-level (3 tags). This is the standard contiguous chunking representation from Ramshaw and Marcus (1995) using the tags {O B I}. O is for tokens **o**utside any chunk; B marks tokens **b**eginning a chunk; and I marks other tokens **i**nside a chunk. Multiword chunks will thus start with B and then I. B must always be followed by I; I is not allowed at the beginning of the sentence or following O.

No gaps, 2-level (4 tags). We can distinguish strength levels by splitting I into two tags: Ī for strong expressions and Ĩ for weak expressions. To express strong and weak contiguous chunks requires 4 tags: {O B Ī Ĩ}. (Marking B with a strength as well would be redundant because MWEs are never length-one chunks.) The constraints on Ī and Ĩ are the same as the constraints on I in previous schemes. If Ī and Ĩ occur next to each other, the strong attachment will receive higher precedence, resulting in analysis of strong MWEs as nested within weak MWEs.

Gappy, 1-level (6 tags). Because gaps cannot themselves contain gappy expressions (we do not support full recursivity), a finite number of additional tags are sufficient to encode gappy chunks. We therefore add lowercase tag variants representing tokens *within a gap*: {O o B b I i}. In addition to the constraints stated above, no within-gap tag may occur at the beginning or end of the sentence or immediately following or preceding O. Within a gap, b, i, and o behave like their out-of-gap counterparts.

Gappy, 2-level (8 tags). 8 tags are required to encode the 2-level scheme with gaps: {O o B b Ī ī Ĩ ĩ}. Variants of the inside tag are marked for strength of the incoming link—this applies gap-externally (capitalized tags) and gap-internally (lowercase tags). If Ī or Ĩ immediately follows a gap, its diacritic reflects the strength of the gappy expression, not the gap's contents.

5 Model

With the above representations we model MWE identification as sequence tagging, one of the paradigms that has been used previously for identifying *contiguous* MWEs (Constant and Sigogne, 2011, see §7).[8] Constraints on legal tag bigrams are sufficient to ensure the full tagging is well-formed subject to the regular expressions in figure 2; we enforce these

[8] Hierarchical modeling based on our representations is left to future work.

constraints in our experiments.[9]

In NLP, conditional random fields (Lafferty et al., 2001) and the structured perceptron (Collins, 2002) are popular techniques for discriminative sequence modeling with a convex loss function. We choose the second approach for its speed: learning and inference depend mainly on the runtime of the Viterbi algorithm, whose asymptotic complexity is linear in the length of the input and (with a first-order Markov assumption) quadratic in the number of tags. Below, we review the structured perceptron and discuss our cost function, features, and experimental setup.

5.1 Cost-Augmented Structured Perceptron

The structured perceptron's (Collins, 2002) learning procedure, algorithm 1, generalizes the classic perceptron algorithm (Freund and Schapire, 1999) to incorporate a structured decoding step (for sequences, the Viterbi algorithm) in the inner loop. Thus, training requires only max inference, which is fast with a first-order Markov assumption. In training, features are adjusted where a tagging error is made; the procedure can be viewed as optimizing the structured hinge loss. The output of learning is a weight vector that parametrizes a feature-rich scoring function over candidate labelings of a sequence.

To better align the learning algorithm with our F-score–based MWE evaluation (§3.2), we use a cost-augmented version of the structured perceptron that is sensitive to different kinds of errors during training. When recall is the bigger obstacle, we can adopt the following cost function: given a sentence $\mathbf{x}$, its gold labeling $\mathbf{y}^*$, and a candidate labeling $\mathbf{y}'$,

$$cost(\mathbf{y}^*, \mathbf{y}', \mathbf{x}) = \sum_{j=1}^{|\mathbf{y}^*|} c(y_j^*, y_j') \quad \text{where}$$

$$c(y^*, y') = [\![y^* \neq y']\!] + \rho[\![y^* \in \{\mathsf{B}, \mathsf{b}\} \wedge y' \in \{\mathsf{O}, \mathsf{o}\}]\!]$$

A single nonnegative hyperparameter, ρ, controls the tradeoff between recall and accuracy; higher ρ biases the model in favor of recall (possibly hurting accuracy and precision). This is a slight variant of the recall-oriented cost function of Mohit et al. (2012). The difference is that we only penalize *beginning-of-expression* recall errors. Preliminary experiments showed that a cost function penalizing all recall errors—i.e., with $\rho[\![y^* \neq \mathsf{O} \wedge y' = \mathsf{O}]\!]$ as the second term, as in Mohit et al.—tended to append additional tokens to high-confidence MWEs (such as proper names) rather than encourage new MWEs, which would require positing at least two new non-outside tags.

[9]The 8-tag scheme licenses 42 tag bigrams: sequences such as B O and o ī are prohibited. There are also constraints on the allowed tags at the beginning and end of the sequence.

```
Input: data ⟨⟨x^(n), y^(n)⟩⟩_{n=1}^N; number of iterations M
w ← 0
w̄ ← 0
t ← 1
for m = 1 to M do
    for n = 1 to N do
        ⟨x, y⟩ ← ⟨x^(n), y^(n)⟩
        ŷ ← argmax_y' (w^T g(x, y') + cost(y, y', x))
        if ŷ ≠ y then
            w ← w + g(x, y) − g(x, ŷ)
            w̄ ← w̄ + t g(x, y) − t g(x, ŷ)
        end
        t ← t + 1
    end
end
Output: w − (w̄/t)
```

Algorithm 1: Training with the averaged perceptron. (Adapted from Daumé, 2006, p. 19.)

5.2 Features

Basic features. These are largely based on those of Constant et al. (2012): they look at word unigrams and bigrams, character prefixes and suffixes, and POS tags, as well as lexicon entries that match lemmas[10] of multiple words in the sentence. Appendix A lists the basic features in detail.

Some of the basic features make use of *lexicons*. We use or construct 10 lists of English MWEs: all multiword entries in **WordNet** (Fellbaum, 1998); all multiword chunks in **SemCor** (Miller et al., 1993); all multiword entries in English **Wiktionary**;[11] the **WikiMwe** dataset mined from English Wikipedia (Hartmann et al., 2012); the **SAID** database of phrasal lexical idioms (Kuiper et al., 2003); the named entities and other MWEs in the WSJ corpus on the English side of the **CEDT** (Hajič et al., 2012);

[10]The WordNet API in NLTK (Bird et al., 2009) was used for lemmatization.

[11]`http://en.wiktionary.org`; data obtained from `https://toolserver.org/~enwikt/definitions/enwikt-defs-20130814-en.tsv.gz`

preexisting lexicons	entries	max gap length	LOOKUP $\bar{P}$	$\bar{R}$	$\bar{F_1}$	σ	SUPERVISED MODEL $\bar{P}$	$\bar{R}$	$\bar{F_1}$	σ
none	0						74.39	44.43	55.57	2.19
WordNet + SemCor	71k	0	46.15	28.41	35.10	2.44	74.51	45.79	56.64	1.90
6 lexicons	420k	0	35.05	46.76	40.00	2.88	76.08	**52.39**	**61.95**	1.67
10 lexicons	437k	0	33.98	47.29	39.48	2.88	75.95	51.39	61.17	2.30
best configuration with in-domain lexicon		1	**46.66**	**47.90**	**47.18**	2.31	**76.64**	51.91	61.84	1.65
			2 lexicons + *MWtypes*(train)$_{\geq 1}$				6 lexicons + *MWtypes*(train)$_{\geq 2}$			

Table 2: Use of lexicons for lookup-based vs. statistical segmentation. Supervised learning used only basic features and the structured perceptron, with the 8-tag scheme. Results are with the link-based matching criterion for evaluation.

Top: Comparison of preexisting lexicons. "6 lexicons" refers to WordNet and SemCor plus SAID, WikiMwe, Phrases.net, and English Wiktionary; "10 lexicons" adds MWEs from CEDT, VNC, LVC, and Oyz. (In these lookup-based configurations, allowing gappy MWEs never helps performance.)

Bottom: Combining preexisting lexicons with a lexicon derived from MWEs annotated in the training portion of each cross-validation fold at least once (lookup) or twice (model).

All precision, recall, and F_1 percentages are averaged across 8 folds of cross-validation on **train**; standard deviations are shown for the F_1 score. In each column, the highest value using only preexisting lexicons is underlined, and the highest overall value is bolded. The boxed row indicates the configuration used as the basis for subsequent experiments.

the **verb-particle constructions** (VPCs) dataset of (Baldwin, 2008); a list of **light verb constructions** (LVCs) provided by Claire Bonial; and two idioms websites.[12] After preprocessing, each lexical entry consists of an ordered sequence of word lemmas, some of which may be variables like <*something*>.

Given a sentence and one or more of the lexicons, lookup proceeds as follows: we enumerate entries whose lemma sequences match a sequence of lemmatized tokens, and build a lattice of possible analyses over the sentence. We find the shortest path (i.e., using as few expressions as possible) with dynamic programming, allowing gaps of up to length 2.[13]

Unsupervised word clusters. Distributional clustering on large (unlabeled) corpora can produce lexical generalizations that are useful for syntactic and semantic analysis tasks (e.g.: Miller et al., 2004; Koo et al., 2008; Turian et al., 2010; Owoputi et al., 2013; Grave et al., 2013). We were interested to see whether a similar pattern would hold for MWE identification, given that MWEs are concerned with what is lexically *idiosyncratic*—i.e., backing off from specific lexemes to word classes may lose the MWE-relevant information. Brown clustering[14] (Brown et al., 1992) on the 21-million-word Yelp Academic Dataset[15] (which is similar in genre to the annotated web reviews data) gives us a hard clustering of word types. To our tagger, we add features mapping the previous, current, and next token to Brown cluster IDs. The feature for the current token conjoins the word lemma with the cluster ID.

Part-of-speech tags. We compared three PTB-style POS taggers on the full REVIEWS subcorpus (**train+test**). The Stanford CoreNLP tagger[16] (Toutanova et al., 2003) yields an accuracy of 90.4%. The ARK TweetNLP tagger v. 0.3.2 (Owoputi et al., 2013) achieves 90.1% with the model[17] trained on the Twitter corpus of Ritter et al. (2011), and 94.9% when trained on the ANSWERS, EMAIL, NEWSGROUP, and WEBLOG subcorpora of WTB. We use this third configuration to produce automatic POS tags for training and testing our MWE tagger. (A comparison condition in §6.3 uses oracle POS tags.)

5.3 Experimental Setup

The corpus of web reviews described in §2 is used for training and evaluation. 101 arbitrarily chosen documents (500 sentences, 7,171 words) were held

[12] `http://www.phrases.net/` and `http://home.postech.ac.kr/~oyz/doc/idiom.html`

[13] Each top-level lexical expression (single- or multiword) incurs a cost of 1; each expression within a gap has cost 1.25.

[14] With Liang's (2005) implementation: `https://github.com/percyliang/brown-cluster`. We obtain 1,000 clusters from words appearing at least 25 times.

[15] `https://www.yelp.com/academic_dataset`

[16] v. 3.2.0, with `english-bidirectional-distsim`

[17] `http://www.ark.cs.cmu.edu/TweetNLP/model.ritter_ptb_alldata_fixed.20130723`

configuration	M	ρ	$\|\mathbf{w}\|$	LINK-BASED P	R	F_1	EXACT MATCH P	R	F_1
base model	5	—	1,765k	69.27	50.49	58.35	60.99	48.27	53.85
+ recall cost	4	150	1,765k	61.09	57.94	59.41	53.09	55.38	54.17
+ clusters	3	100	2,146k	63.98	55.51	59.39	56.34	53.24	54.70
+ oracle POS	4	100	2,145k	66.19	59.35	62.53	58.51	57.00	57.71

Table 3: Comparison of supervised models on **test** (using the 8-tag scheme). The base model corresponds to the boxed result in table table 2, but here evaluated on **test**. For each configuration, the number of training iterations M and (except for the base model) the recall-oriented hyperparameter ρ were tuned by cross-validation on **train**.

out as a final **test** set. This left 3,312 sentences/ 48,408 words for training/development (**train**). Feature engineering and hyperparameter tuning were conducted with 8-fold cross-validation on **train**. The 8-tag scheme is used except where otherwise noted.

In learning with the structured perceptron (algorithm 1), we employ two well-known techniques that can both be viewed as regularization. First, we use the average of parameters over all timesteps of learning. Second, within each cross-validation fold, we determine the number of training iterations (epochs) M by early stopping—that is, after each iteration, we use the model to decode the held-out data, and when that accuracy ceases to improve, use the previous model. The two hyperparameters are the number of iterations and the value of the recall cost hyperparameter (ρ). Both are tuned via cross-validation on **train**; we use the multiple of 50 that maximizes average link-based F_1. The chosen values are shown in table 3. Experiments were managed with the `ducttape` tool.[18]

6 Results

We experimentally address the following questions to probe and justify our modeling approach.

6.1 Is supervised learning necessary?

Previous MWE identification studies have found benefit to statistical learning over heuristic lexicon lookup (Constant and Sigogne, 2011; Green et al., 2012). Our first experiment tests whether this holds for comprehensive MWE identification: it compares our supervised tagging approach with baselines of heuristic lookup on preexisting lexicons. The baselines construct a lattice for each sentence using the same method as lexicon-based model features (§5.2). If multiple lexicons are used, the union of their entries is used to construct the lattice. The resulting segmentation—which does not encode a strength distinction—is evaluated against the gold standard.

Table 2 shows the results. Even with just the labeled training set as input, the supervised approach beats the strongest heuristic baseline (that incorporates in-domain lexicon entries extracted from the training data) by 30 precision points, while achieving comparable recall. For example, the baseline (but not the statistical model) incorrectly predicts an MWE in *places to **eat in** Baltimore* (because *eat in*, meaning 'eat at home,' is listed in WordNet). The supervised approach has learned not to trust WordNet too much due to this sort of ambiguity. Downstream applications that currently use lexicon matching for MWE identification (e.g., Ghoneim and Diab, 2013) likely stand to benefit from our statistical approach.

6.2 How best to exploit MWE lexicons (type-level information)?

For statistical tagging (right portion of table 2), using more *preexisting* (out-of-domain) lexicons generally improves recall; precision also improves a bit.

A lexicon of MWEs occurring in the non-held-out training data *at least twice*[19] (table 2, bottom right) is marginally worse (better precision/worse recall) than the best result using only preexisting lexicons.

6.3 Variations on the base model

We experiment with some of the modeling alternatives discussed in §5. Results appear in table 3 under both the link-based and exact match evaluation criteria. We note that the exact match scores are (as expected) several points lower.

[18] `https://github.com/jhclark/ducttape/`

[19] If we train with access to the full lexicon of *training set* MWEs, the learner credulously overfits to relying on that lexicon—after all, it has perfect coverage of the training data!—which proves fatal for the model at test time.

Recall-oriented cost. The recall-oriented cost adds about 1 link-based F_1 point, sacrificing precision in favor of recall.

Unsupervised word clusters. When combined with the recall-oriented cost, these produce a slight improvement to precision/degradation to recall, improving exact match F_1 but not affecting link-based F_1. Only a few clusters receive high positive weight; one of these consists of *matter*, *joke*, *biggie*, *pun*, *avail*, *clue*, *corkage*, *frills*, *worries*, etc. These words are diverse semantically, but all occur in collocations with *no*, which is what makes the cluster coherent and useful to the MWE model.

Oracle part-of-speech tags. Using human-annotated rather than automatic POS tags improves MWE identification by about 3 F_1 points on **test** (similar differences were observed in development).

6.4 What are the highest-weighted features?

An advantage of the linear modeling framework is that we can examine learned feature weights to gain some insight into the model's behavior.

In general, the highest-weighted features are the lexicon matching features and features indicative of proper names (POS tag of proper noun, capitalized word not at the beginning of the sentence, etc.).

Despite the occasional cluster capturing collocational or idiomatic groupings, as described in the previous section, the clusters appear to be mostly useful for identifying words that tend to belong (or not) to proper names. For example, the cluster with *street*, *road*, *freeway*, *highway*, *airport*, etc., as well as words outside of the cluster vocabulary, weigh in favor of an MWE. A cluster with everyday destinations (*neighborhood*, *doctor*, *hotel*, *bank*, *dentist*) prefers non-MWEs, presumably because these words are not typically part of proper names in this corpus. This was from the best model using non-oracle POS tags, so the clusters are perhaps useful in correcting for proper nouns that were mistakenly tagged as common nouns. One caveat, though, is that it is hard to discern the impact of these specific features where others may be capturing essentially the same information.

6.5 How heterogeneous are learned MWEs?

On **test**, the final model (with automatic POS tags) predicts 365 MWE instances (31 are gappy; 23 are weak). There are 298 unique MWE types.

POS pattern	#	examples (lowercased lemmas)
NOUN NOUN	53	*customer service, oil change*
VERB PREP	36	*work with, deal with, yell at*
PROPN PROPN	29	*eagle transmission, comfort zone*
ADJ NOUN	21	*major award, top notch, mental health*
VERB PART	20	*move out, end up, pick up, pass up*
VERB ADV	17	*come back, come in, come by, stay away*
PREP NOUN	12	*on time, in fact, in cash, for instance*
VERB NOUN	10	*take care, make money, give crap*
VERB PRON	10	*thank you, get it*
PREP PREP	8	*out of, due to, out ta, in between*
ADV ADV	6	*no matter, up front, at all, early on*
DET NOUN	6	*a lot, a little, a bit, a deal*
VERB DET NOUN	6	*answer the phone, take a chance*
NOUN PREP	5	*kind of, care for, tip on, answer to*

Table 4: Top predicted POS patterns and frequencies.

Organizing the predicted MWEs by their coarse POS sequence reveals that the model is not too prejudiced in the kinds of expressions it recognizes: the 298 types fall under 89 unique POS+strength patterns. Table 4 shows the 14 POS sequences predicted 5 or more times as strong MWEs. Some of the examples (*major award*, *a deal*, *tip on*) are false positives, but most are correct. Singleton patterns include PROPN VERB (*god forbid*), PREP DET (*at that*), ADJ PRON (*worth it*), and PREP VERB PREP (*to die for*).

True positive MWEs mostly consist of (a) named entities, and (b) lexical idioms seen in training and/or listed in one of the lexicons. Occasionally the system correctly guesses an unseen and OOV idiom based on features such as hyphenation (*walk - in*) and capitalization/OOV words (*Chili Relleno*, *BIG MISTAKE*). On **test**, 244 gold MWE types were unseen in training; the system found 93 true positives (where the type was predicted at least once), 109 false positives, and 151 false negatives—an unseen type recall rate of 38%. Removing types that occurred in lexicons leaves 35 true positives, 61 false positives, and 111 false negatives—a unseen and OOV type recall rate of 24%.

6.6 What kinds of mismatches occur?

Inspection of the output turns up false positives due to ambiguity (e.g., *Spongy and* ***sweet bread***); false negatives (*top to bottom*); and overlap (***get high*** *quality service*, gold *get* ***high quality*** *service*; ***live up*** *to*, gold ***live up to***). A number of the mismatches turn

scheme	$\lvert\mathcal{Y}\rvert$	ρ	$\overline{M}$	$\overline{\lvert\mathbf{w}\rvert}$	$\overline{\mathrm{P}}$	$\overline{\mathrm{R}}$	$\overline{F_1}$
no gaps, 1-level	3	100	2.1	733k	73.33	55.72	63.20
no gaps, 2-level	4	150	3.3	977k	72.60	59.11	65.09
gappy, 1-level	6	200	1.6	1,466k	66.48	61.26	63.65
gappy, 2-level	8	100	3.5	1,954k	73.27	60.44	66.15

Table 5: Training with different tagging schemes. Results are cross-validation averages on **train**. All schemes are evaluated against the full gold standard (8 tags).

out to be problems with the gold standard, like *having our water **shut off*** (gold *having our **water shut off***). This suggests that even noisy automatic taggers might help identify annotation inconsistencies and errors for manual correction.

6.7 Are gappiness and the strength distinction learned in practice?

Three quarters of MWEs are strong and contain no gaps. To see whether our model is actually sensitive to the phenomena of gappiness and strength, we train on data simplified to remove one or both distinctions—as in the first 3 labelings in figure 2—and evaluate against the full 8-tag scheme. For the model with the recall cost, clusters, and oracle POS tags, we evaluate each of these simplifications of the training data in table 5. The gold standard for evaluation remains the same across all conditions.

If the model was unable to recover gappy expressions or the strong/weak distinction, we would expect it to do no better when trained with the full tagset than with the simplified tagset. However, there is some loss in performance as the tagset for learning is simplified, which suggests that gappiness and strength are being learned to an extent.

7 Related Work

Our annotated corpus (Schneider et al., 2014) joins several resources that indicate certain varieties of MWEs: lexicons such as WordNet (Fellbaum, 1998), SAID (Kuiper et al., 2003), and WikiMwe (Hartmann et al., 2012); targeted lists (Baldwin, 2005, 2008; Cook et al., 2008; Tu and Roth, 2011, 2012); websites like Wiktionary and Phrases.net; and large-scale corpora such as SemCor (Miller et al., 1993), the French Treebank (Abeillé et al., 2003), the Szeged-ParalellFX corpus (Vincze, 2012), and the Prague Czech-English Dependency Treebank (Čmejrek et al., 2005). The difference is that Schneider et al. (2014) pursued *a comprehensive annotation approach* rather than targeting specific varieties of MWEs or relying on a preexisting lexical resource. The annotations are *shallow*, not relying explicitly on syntax (though in principle they could be mapped onto the parses in the Web Treebank).

In terms of modeling, the use of machine learning classification (Hashimoto and Kawahara, 2008; Shigeto et al., 2013) and specifically BIO sequence tagging (Diab and Bhutada, 2009; Constant and Sigogne, 2011; Constant et al., 2012; Vincze et al., 2013) for contextual recognition of MWEs is not new. Lexical semantic classification tasks like named entity recognition (e.g., Ratinov and Roth, 2009), supersense tagging (Ciaramita and Altun, 2006; Paaß and Reichartz, 2009), and index term identification (Newman et al., 2012) also involve chunking of certain MWEs. But our discriminative models, facilitated by the new corpus, *broaden the scope of the MWE identification task* to include many varieties of MWEs at once, including explicit marking of gaps and a strength distinction. By contrast, the aforementioned identification systems, as well as some MWE-enhanced syntactic parsers (e.g., Green et al., 2012), have been restricted to contiguous MWEs. However, Green et al. (2011) allow gaps to be described as constituents in a syntax tree. Gimpel and Smith's (2011) shallow, gappy language model allows arbitrary token groupings within a sentence, whereas our model imposes projectivity and nesting constraints (§3). Blunsom and Baldwin (2006) present a sequence model for HPSG supertagging, and evaluate performance on discontinuous MWEs, though the sequence model treats the non-adjacent component supertags like other labels—it cannot enforce that they mutually require one another, as we do via the gappy tagging scheme (§3.1). The lexicon lookup procedures of Bejček et al. (2013) can match gappy MWEs, but are nonstatistical and extremely error-prone when tuned for high oracle recall.

Another major thread of research has pursued *unsupervised* discovery of multiword types from raw corpora, such as with statistical association measures (Church et al., 1991; Pecina, 2010; Ramisch et al., 2012, *inter alia*), parallel corpora (Melamed, 1997; Moirón and Tiedemann, 2006; Tsvetkov and Wintner, 2010), or a combination thereof (Tsvetkov and

Wintner, 2011); this may be followed by a lookup-and-classify approach to contextual identification (Ramisch et al., 2010). Though preliminary experiments with our models did not show benefit to incorporating such automatically constructed lexicons, we hope these two perspectives can be brought together in future work.

8 Conclusion

This article has presented the first supervised model for identifying heterogeneous multiword expressions in English text. Our feature-rich discriminative sequence tagger performs shallow chunking with a novel scheme that allows for MWEs containing gaps, and includes a strength distinction to separate highly idiomatic expressions from collocations. It is trained and evaluated on a corpus of English web reviews that are comprehensively annotated for multiword expressions. Beyond the training data, its features incorporate evidence from external resources—several lexicons as well as unsupervised word clusters; we show experimentally that this statistical approach is far superior to identifying MWEs by heuristic lexicon lookup alone. Future extensions might integrate additional features (e.g., exploiting statistical association measures computed over large corpora), enhance the lexical representation (e.g., by adding semantic tags), improve the expressiveness of the model (e.g., with higher-order features and inference), or integrate the model with other tasks (such as parsing and translation).

Our data and open source software are released at `http://www.ark.cs.cmu.edu/LexSem/`.

Acknowledgments

This research was supported in part by NSF CAREER grant IIS-1054319, Google through the Reading is Believing project at CMU, and DARPA grant FA8750-12-2-0342 funded under the DEFT program. We are grateful to Kevin Knight, Martha Palmer, Claire Bonial, Lori Levin, Ed Hovy, Tim Baldwin, Omri Abend, members of JHU CLSP, the NLP group at Berkeley, and the Noah's ARK group at CMU, and anonymous reviewers for valuable feedback.

A Basic Features

All are conjoined with the current label, y_i.

Label Features

1. previous label (the only first-order feature)

Token Features

Original token

2. $i = \{1, 2\}$
3. $i = |\mathbf{w}| - \{0, 1\}$
4. capitalized $\wedge$ $[\![i = 0]\!]$
5. word shape

Lowercased token

6. prefix: $[w_i]_1^k |_{k=1}^4$
7. suffix: $[w_i]_j^{|w|} |_{j=|w|-3}^{|w|}$
8. has digit
9. has non-alphanumeric c
10. context word: $w_j |_{j=i-2}^{i+2}$
11. context word bigram: $\mathbf{w}_j^{j+1} |_{j=i-2}^{i+1}$

Lemma Features

12. lemma + context lemma if one of them is a verb and the other is a noun, verb, adjective, adverb, preposition, or particle: $\lambda_i \wedge \lambda_j |_{j=i-2}^{i+2}$

Part-of-speech Features

13. context POS: $pos_j |_{j=i-2}^{i+2}$
14. context POS bigram: $\mathbf{pos}_j^{j+1} |_{j=i-2}^{i+1}$
15. word + context POS: $w_i \wedge pos_{i\pm1}$
16. context word + POS: $w_{i\pm1} \wedge pos_i$

Lexicon Features (unlexicalized)

WordNet only

17. OOV: λ_i is not in WordNet as a unigram lemma $\wedge$ pos_i
18. compound: non-punctuation lemma λ_i and the {previous, next} lemma in the sentence (if it is non-punctuation; an intervening hyphen is allowed) form an entry in WordNet, possibly separated by a hyphen or space
19. compound-hyphen: pos_i = HYPH $\wedge$ previous and next tokens form an entry in WordNet, possibly separated by a hyphen or space
20. ambiguity class: if content word unigram λ_i is in WordNet, the set of POS categories it can belong to; else pos_i if not a content POS $\wedge$ the POS of the longest MW match to which λ_i belongs (if any) $\wedge$ the position in that match (B or I)

For each multiword lexicon

21. lexicon name $\wedge$ status of token i in the shortest path segmentation (O, B, or I) $\wedge$ subcategory of lexical entry whose match includes token i, if matched $\wedge$ whether the match is gappy
22. the above $\wedge$ POS tags of the first and last matched tokens in the expression

Over all multiword lexicons

23. at least k lexicons contain a match that includes this token (if $n \geq 1$ matches, n active features)
24. at least k lexicons contain a match that includes this token, starts with a given POS, and ends with a given POS

References

Anne Abeillé, Lionel Clément, and François Toussenel. 2003. Building a treebank for French. In Anne Abeillé and Nancy Ide, editors, *Treebanks*, volume 20 of *Text, Speech and Language Technology*, pages 165–187. Kluwer Academic Publishers, Dordrecht, The Netherlands.

Timothy Baldwin. 2005. Looking for prepositional verbs in corpus data. In *Proc. of the Second ACL-SIGSEM Workshop on the Linguistic Dimensions of Prepositions and their Use in Computational Linguistics Formalisms and Applications*, pages 115–126. Colchester, UK.

Timothy Baldwin. 2008. A resource for evaluating the deep lexical acquisition of English verb-particle constructions. In *Proc. of MWE*, pages 1–2. Marrakech, Morocco.

Timothy Baldwin and Su Nam Kim. 2010. Multiword expressions. In Nitin Indurkhya and Fred J. Damerau, editors, *Handbook of Natural Language Processing, Second Edition*. CRC Press, Taylor and Francis Group, Boca Raton, Florida, USA.

Eduard Bejček, Pavel Straňák, and Pavel Pecina. 2013. Syntactic identification of occurrences of multiword expressions in text using a lexicon with dependency structures. In *Proc. of the 9th Workshop on Multiword Expressions*, pages 106–115. Atlanta, Georgia, USA.

Gábor Berend. 2011. Opinion expression mining by exploiting keyphrase extraction. In *Proc. of 5th International Joint Conference on Natural Language Processing*, pages 1162–1170. Chiang Mai, Thailand.

Ann Bies, Justin Mott, Colin Warner, and Seth Kulick. 2012a. English Web Treebank. Technical Report LDC2012T13, Linguistic Data Consortium, Philadelphia, Pennsylvania, USA.

Ann Bies, Justin Mott, Colin Warner, and Seth Kulick. 2012b. English Web Treebank. Technical Report LDC2012T13, Linguistic Data Consortium, Philadelphia, Pennsylvania, USA.

Steven Bird, Ewan Klein, and Edward Loper. 2009. *Natural Language Processing with Python: Analyzing Text with the Natural Language Toolkit*. O'Reilly Media, Inc., Sebastopol, California, USA.

Phil Blunsom and Timothy Baldwin. 2006. Multilingual deep lexical acquisition for HPSGs via supertagging. In *Proc. of EMNLP*, pages 164–171. Sydney, Australia.

Peter F. Brown, Peter V. deSouza, Robert L. Mercer, Vincent J. Della Pietra, and Jenifer C. Lai. 1992. Class-based n-gram models of natural language. *Computational Linguistics*, 18(4):467–479.

Marine Carpuat and Mona Diab. 2010. Task-based evaluation of multiword expressions: a pilot study in statistical machine translation. In *Proc. of NAACL-HLT*, pages 242–245. Los Angeles, California, USA.

Kenneth Church, William Gale, Patrick Hanks, and Donald Hindle. 1991. Using statistics in lexical analysis. In Uri Zernik, editor, *Lexical acquisition: exploiting on-line resources to build a lexicon*, pages 115–164. Lawrence Erlbaum Associates, Hillsdale, New Jersey, USA.

Massimiliano Ciaramita and Yasemin Altun. 2006. Broad-coverage sense disambiguation and information extraction with a supersense sequence tagger. In *Proc. of EMNLP*, pages 594–602. Sydney, Australia.

Michael Collins. 2002. Discriminative training methods for Hidden Markov Models: theory and experiments with perceptron algorithms. In *Proc. of EMNLP*, pages 1–8. Philadelphia, Pennsylvania, USA.

Matthieu Constant and Anthony Sigogne. 2011. MWU-aware part-of-speech tagging with a CRF model and lexical resources. In *Proc. of the Workshop on Multiword Expressions: from Parsing and Generation to the Real World*, pages 49–56. Portland, Oregon, USA.

Matthieu Constant, Anthony Sigogne, and Patrick Watrin. 2012. Discriminative strategies to integrate multiword expression recognition and parsing. In *Proc. of ACL*, pages 204–212. Jeju Island, Korea.

Paul Cook, Afsaneh Fazly, and Suzanne Stevenson. 2008. The VNC-Tokens dataset. In *Proc. of MWE*, pages 19–22. Marrakech, Morocco.

Hal Daumé, III. 2006. *Practical structured learning techniques for natural language processing*. Ph.D. dissertation, University of Southern California, Los Angeles, California, USA. URL `http://hal3.name/docs/daume06thesis.pdf`.

Mona Diab and Pravin Bhutada. 2009. Verb noun construction MWE token classification. In *Proc. of MWE*, pages 17–22. Suntec, Singapore.

Nick C. Ellis, Rita Simpson-Vlach, and Carson Maynard. 2008. Formulaic language in native and second language speakers: psycholinguistics, corpus linguistics, and TESOL. *TESOL Quarterly*, 42(3):375–396.

Christiane Fellbaum, editor. 1998. *WordNet: an electronic lexical database*. MIT Press, Cambridge, Massachusetts, USA.

Charles J. Fillmore, Paul Kay, and Mary Catherine O'Connor. 1988. Regularity and idiomaticity in grammatical constructions: the case of 'let alone'. *Language*, 64(3):501–538.

Yoav Freund and Robert E. Schapire. 1999. Large margin classification using the perceptron algorithm. *Machine Learning*, 37(3):277–296.

Mahmoud Ghoneim and Mona Diab. 2013. Multiword expressions in the context of statistical machine translation. In *Proc. of IJCNLP*, pages 1181–1187. Nagoya, Japan.

Kevin Gimpel and Noah A. Smith. 2011. Generative models of monolingual and bilingual gappy patterns. In *Proc. of WMT*, pages 512–522. Edinburgh, Scotland, UK.

Adele E. Goldberg. 1995. *Constructions: a construction grammar approach to argument structure*. University of Chicago Press, Chicago, Illinois, USA.

Adele E. Goldberg. 2006. *Constructions at work: the nature of generalization in language*. Oxford University Press, Oxford, UK.

Edouard Grave, Guillaume Obozinski, and Francis Bach. 2013. Hidden Markov tree models for semantic class induction. In *Proc. of CoNLL*, pages 94–103. Sofia, Bulgaria.

Spence Green, Marie-Catherine de Marneffe, John Bauer, and Christopher D. Manning. 2011. Multiword expression identification with tree substitution grammars: a parsing tour de force with French. In *Proc. of EMNLP*, pages 725–735. Edinburgh, Scotland, UK.

Spence Green, Marie-Catherine de Marneffe, and Christopher D. Manning. 2012. Parsing models for identifying multiword expressions. *Computational Linguistics*, 39(1):195–227.

Jan Hajič, Eva Hajičová, Jarmila Panevová, Petr Sgall, Silvie Cinková, Eva Fučíková, Marie Mikulová, Petr Pajas, Jan Popelka, Jiří Semecký, Jana Šindlerová, Jan Štěpánek, Josef Toman, Zdeňka Urešová, and Zdeněk Žabokrtský. 2012. Prague Czech-English Dependency Treebank 2.0. Technical Report LDC2012T08, Linguistic Data Consortium, Philadelphia, Pennsylvania, USA. URL `http://www.ldc.upenn.edu/Catalog/catalogEntry.jsp?catalogId=LDC2003T10`.

Silvana Hartmann, György Szarvas, and Iryna Gurevych. 2012. Mining multiword terms from Wikipedia. In Maria Teresa Pazienza and Armando Stellato, editors, *Semi-Automatic Ontology Development*. IGI Global, Hershey, Pennsylvania, USA.

Chikara Hashimoto and Daisuke Kawahara. 2008. Construction of an idiom corpus and its application to idiom identification based on WSD incorporating idiom-specific features. In *Proc. of EMNLP*, pages 992–1001. Honolulu, Hawaii, USA.

Terry Koo, Xavier Carreras, and Michael Collins. 2008. Simple semi-supervised dependency parsing. In *Proc. of ACL-08: HLT*, pages 595–603. Columbus, Ohio.

Koenraad Kuiper, Heather McCann, Heidi Quinn, Therese Aitchison, and Kees van der Veer. 2003. SAID. Technical Report LDC2003T10, Linguistic Data Consortium, Philadelphia, Pennsylvania, USA. URL `http://www.ldc.upenn.edu/Catalog/catalogEntry.jsp?catalogId=LDC2003T10`.

John D. Lafferty, Andrew McCallum, and Fernando C. N. Pereira. 2001. Conditional random fields: probabilistic models for segmenting and labeling sequence data. In *Proc. of ICML*, pages 282–289.

Percy Liang. 2005. *Semi-supervised learning for natural language*. Master's thesis, Massachusetts Institute of Technology, Cambridge, Massachusetts, USA. URL `http://people.csail.mit.edu/pliang/papers/meng-thesis.pdf`.

Mitchell P. Marcus, Beatrice Santorini, and Mary Ann Marcinkiewicz. 1993. Building a large annotated corpus of English: the Penn Treebank. *Computational Linguistics*, 19(2):313–330.

I. Dan Melamed. 1997. Automatic discovery of non-compositional compounds in parallel data. In *Proc. of EMNLP*, pages 97–108. Providence, Rhode Island, USA.

George A. Miller, Claudia Leacock, Randee Tengi, and Ross T. Bunker. 1993. A semantic concordance. In *Proc. of HLT*, pages 303–308. Plainsboro, New Jersey, USA.

Scott Miller, Jethran Guinness, and Alex Zamanian. 2004. Name tagging with word clusters and discriminative training. In *Proc. of HLT-NAACL*, pages 337–342. Boston, Massachusetts, USA.

Behrang Mohit, Nathan Schneider, Rishav Bhowmick, Kemal Oflazer, and Noah A. Smith. 2012. Recall-oriented learning of named entities in Arabic Wikipedia. In *Proc. of EACL*, pages 162–173. Avignon, France.

Begona Villada Moirón and Jörg Tiedemann. 2006. Identifying idiomatic expressions using automatic word-alignment. In *Proc. of the EACL 2006 Workshop on Multi-word Expressions in a Multilingual Context*, pages 33–40. Trento, Italy.

Rosamund Moon. 1998. *Fixed expressions and idioms in English: a corpus-based approach*. Oxford Studies in Lexicography and Lexicology. Clarendon Press, Oxford, UK.

David Newman, Nagendra Koilada, Jey Han Lau, and Timothy Baldwin. 2012. Bayesian text segmentation for index term identification and keyphrase extraction. In *Proc. of COLING 2012*, pages 2077–2092. Mumbai, India.

Geoffrey Nunberg, Ivan A. Sag, and Thomas Wasow. 1994. Idioms. *Language*, 70(3):491–538.

Olutobi Owoputi, Brendan O'Connor, Chris Dyer, Kevin Gimpel, Nathan Schneider, and Noah A. Smith. 2013. Improved part-of-speech tagging for online conversational text with word clusters. In *Proc. of NAACL-HLT*, pages 380–390. Atlanta, Georgia, USA.

Gerhard Paaß and Frank Reichartz. 2009. Exploiting

semantic constraints for estimating supersenses with CRFs. In *Proc. of the Ninth SIAM International Conference on Data Mining*, pages 485–496. Sparks, Nevada, USA.

Pavel Pecina. 2010. Lexical association measures and collocation extraction. *Language Resources and Evaluation*, 44(1):137–158.

Carlos Ramisch. 2012. *A generic and open framework for multiword expressions treatment: from acquisition to applications*. Ph.D. dissertation, University of Grenoble and Federal University of Rio Grande do Sul, Grenoble, France. URL http://www.inf.ufrgs.br/~ceramisch/download_files/thesis-getalp.pdf.

Carlos Ramisch, Vitor De Araujo, and Aline Villavicencio. 2012. A broad evaluation of techniques for automatic acquisition of multiword expressions. In *Proc. of ACL 2012 Student Research Workshop*, pages 1–6. Jeju Island, Korea.

Carlos Ramisch, Aline Villavicencio, and Christian Boitet. 2010. mwetoolkit: a framework for multiword expression identification. In *Proc. of LREC*, pages 662–669. Valletta, Malta.

Lance A. Ramshaw and Mitchell P. Marcus. 1995. Text chunking using transformation-based learning. In *Proc. of the Third ACL Workshop on Very Large Corpora*, pages 82–94. Cambridge, Massachusetts, USA.

Lev Ratinov and Dan Roth. 2009. Design challenges and misconceptions in named entity recognition. In *Proc. of CoNLL*, pages 147–155. Boulder, Colorado, USA.

Marta Recasens and Eduard Hovy. 2011. BLANC: Implementing the Rand index for coreference evaluation. *Natural Language Engineering*, 17(04):485–510.

Alan Ritter, Sam Clark, Mausam, and Oren Etzioni. 2011. Named entity recognition in tweets: an experimental study. In *Proc. of EMNLP*, pages 1524–1534. Edinburgh, Scotland, UK.

Ivan Sag, Timothy Baldwin, Francis Bond, Ann Copestake, and Dan Flickinger. 2002. Multiword expressions: a pain in the neck for NLP. In Alexander Gelbukh, editor, *Computational Linguistics and Intelligent Text Processing*, volume 2276 of *Lecture Notes in Computer Science*, pages 189–206. Springer, Berlin, Germany.

Nathan Schneider, Spencer Onuffer, Nora Kazour, Emily Danchik, Michael T. Mordowanec, Henrietta Conrad, and Noah A. Smith. 2014. Comprehensive annotation of multiword expressions in a social web corpus. In *Proc. of LREC*. Reykjavík, Iceland.

Yutaro Shigeto, Ai Azuma, Sorami Hisamoto, Shuhei Kondo, Tomoya Kouse, Keisuke Sakaguchi, Akifumi Yoshimoto, Frances Yung, and Yuji Matsumoto. 2013. Construction of English MWE dictionary and its application to POS tagging. In *Proc. of the 9th Workshop on Multiword Expressions*, pages 139–144. Atlanta, Georgia, USA.

James W. Thatcher. 1967. Characterizing derivation trees of context-free grammars through a generalization of finite automata theory. *Journal of Computer and System Sciences*, 1(4):317–322.

Kristina Toutanova, Dan Klein, Christopher D. Manning, and Yoram Singer. 2003. Feature-rich part-of-speech tagging with a cyclic dependency network. In *Proc. of HLT-NAACL*, pages 173–180. Edmonton, Alberta, Canada.

Yulia Tsvetkov and Shuly Wintner. 2010. Extraction of multi-word expressions from small parallel corpora. In *Coling 2010: Posters*, pages 1256–1264. Beijing, China.

Yulia Tsvetkov and Shuly Wintner. 2011. Identification of multi-word expressions by combining multiple linguistic information sources. In *Proc. of EMNLP*, pages 836–845. Edinburgh, Scotland, UK.

Yuancheng Tu and Dan Roth. 2011. Learning English light verb constructions: contextual or statistical. In *Proc. of the Workshop on Multiword Expressions: from Parsing and Generation to the Real World*, pages 31–39. Portland, Oregon, USA.

Yuancheng Tu and Dan Roth. 2012. Sorting out the most confusing English phrasal verbs. In *Proc. of *SEM*, pages 65–69. Montréal, Quebec, Canada.

Joseph Turian, Lev-Arie Ratinov, and Yoshua Bengio. 2010. Word representations: a simple and general method for semi-supervised learning. In *Proc. of ACL*, pages 384–394. Uppsala, Sweden.

Martin Čmejrek, Jan Cuřín, Jan Hajič, and Jiří Havelka. 2005. Prague Czech-English Dependency Treebank: resource for structure-based MT. In *Proc. of EAMT*, pages 73–78. Budapest, Hungary.

Marc Vilain, John Burger, John Aberdeen, Dennis Connolly, and Lynette Hirschman. 1995. A model-theoretic coreference scoring scheme. In *Proc. of MUC-6*, pages 45–52. Columbia, Maryland, USA.

Veronika Vincze. 2012. Light verb constructions in the SzegedParalellFX English-Hungarian parallel corpus. In *Proc. of LREC*. Istanbul, Turkey.

Veronika Vincze, István Nagy T., and János Zsibrita. 2013. Learning to detect English and Hungarian light verb constructions. *ACM Transactions on Speech and Language Processing*, 10(2):6:1–6:25.

Grounded Compositional Semantics for Finding and Describing Images with Sentences

Richard Socher, Andrej Karpathy, Quoc V. Le*, Christopher D. Manning, Andrew Y. Ng
Stanford University, Computer Science Department, *Google Inc.
richard@socher.org, karpathy@cs.stanford.edu,
qvl@google.com, manning@stanford.edu, ang@cs.stanford.edu

Abstract

Previous work on Recursive Neural Networks (RNNs) shows that these models can produce compositional feature vectors for accurately representing and classifying sentences or images. However, the sentence vectors of previous models cannot accurately represent visually grounded meaning. We introduce the DT-RNN model which uses dependency trees to embed sentences into a vector space in order to retrieve images that are described by those sentences. Unlike previous RNN-based models which use constituency trees, DT-RNNs naturally focus on the action and agents in a sentence. They are better able to abstract from the details of word order and syntactic expression. DT-RNNs outperform other recursive and recurrent neural networks, kernelized CCA and a bag-of-words baseline on the tasks of finding an image that fits a sentence description and vice versa. They also give more similar representations to sentences that describe the same image.

1 Introduction

Single word vector spaces are widely used (Turney and Pantel, 2010) and successful at classifying single words and capturing their meaning (Collobert and Weston, 2008; Huang et al., 2012; Mikolov et al., 2013). Since words rarely appear in isolation, the task of learning compositional meaning representations for longer phrases has recently received a lot of attention (Mitchell and Lapata, 2010; Socher et al., 2010; Socher et al., 2012; Grefenstette et al., 2013). Similarly, classifying whole images into a fixed set of classes also achieves very high performance (Le et al., 2012; Krizhevsky et al., 2012). However, similar to words, objects in images are often seen in relationships with other objects which are not adequately described by a single label.

In this work, we introduce a model, illustrated in Fig. 1, which learns to map sentences and images into a common embedding space in order to be able to retrieve one from the other. We assume word and image representations are first learned in their respective single modalities but finally mapped into a jointly learned multimodal embedding space.

Our model for mapping sentences into this space is based on ideas from Recursive Neural Networks (RNNs) (Pollack, 1990; Costa et al., 2003; Socher et al., 2011b). However, unlike all previous RNN models which are based on constituency trees (CT-RNNs), our model computes compositional vector representations inside dependency trees. The compositional vectors computed by this new dependency tree RNN (DT-RNN) capture more of the meaning of sentences, where we define meaning in terms of similarity to a "visual representation" of the textual description. DT-RNN induced vector representations of sentences are more robust to changes in the syntactic structure or word order than related models such as CT-RNNs or Recurrent Neural Networks since they naturally focus on a sentence's action and its agents.

We evaluate and compare DT-RNN induced representations on their ability to use a sentence such as *"A man wearing a helmet jumps on his bike near a beach."* to find images that show such a scene. The goal is to learn sentence representations that capture

Transactions of the Association for Computational Linguistics, 2 (2014) 207–218. Action Editor: Alexander Clark.
Submitted 10/2013; Revised 3/2014; Published 4/2014.

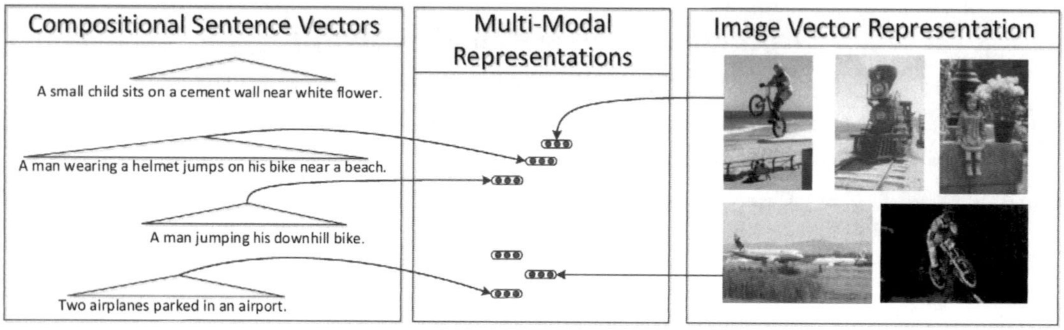

Figure 1: The DT-RNN learns vector representations for sentences based on their dependency trees. We learn to map the outputs of convolutional neural networks applied to images into the same space and can then compare both sentences and images. This allows us to query images with a sentence and give sentence descriptions to images.

the visual scene described and to find appropriate images in the learned, multi-modal sentence-image space. Conversely, when given a query image, we would like to find a description that goes beyond a single label by providing a correct sentence describing it, a task that has recently garnered a lot of attention (Farhadi et al., 2010; Ordonez et al., 2011; Kuznetsova et al., 2012). We use the dataset introduced by (Rashtchian et al., 2010) which consists of 1000 images, each with 5 descriptions. On all tasks, our model outperforms baselines and related models.

2 Related Work

The presented model is connected to several areas of NLP and vision research, each with a large amount of related work to which we can only do some justice given space constraints.

Semantic Vector Spaces and Their Compositionality. The dominant approach in semantic vector spaces uses distributional similarities of single words. Often, co-occurrence statistics of a word and its context are used to describe each word (Turney and Pantel, 2010; Baroni and Lenci, 2010), such as tf-idf. Most of the compositionality algorithms and related datasets capture two-word compositions. For instance, (Mitchell and Lapata, 2010) use two-word phrases and analyze similarities computed by vector addition, multiplication and others. Compositionality is an active field of research with many different models and representations being explored (Grefenstette et al., 2013), among many others. We compare to supervised compositional models that can learn task-specific vector representations such as constituency tree recursive neural networks (Socher et al., 2011b; Socher et al., 2011a), chain structured recurrent neural networks and other baselines. Another alternative would be to use CCG trees as a backbone for vector composition (K.M. Hermann, 2013).

Multimodal Embeddings. Multimodal embedding methods project data from multiple sources such as sound and video (Ngiam et al., 2011) or images and text. Socher et al. (Socher and Fei-Fei, 2010) project words and image regions into a common space using kernelized canonical correlation analysis to obtain state of the art performance in annotation and segmentation. Similar to our work, they use unsupervised large text corpora to learn semantic word representations. Among other recent work is that by Srivastava and Salakhutdinov (2012) who developed multimodal Deep Boltzmann Machines. Similar to their work, we use techniques from the broad field of deep learning to represent images and words.

Recently, single word vector embeddings have been used for zero shot learning (Socher et al., 2013c). Mapping images to word vectors enabled their system to classify images as depicting objects such as "cat" without seeing any examples of this class. Related work has also been presented at NIPS (Socher et al., 2013b; Frome et al., 2013). This work moves zero-shot learning beyond single categories per image and extends it to unseen phrases and full length sentences, making use of similar ideas of semantic spaces grounded in visual knowledge.

Detailed Image Annotation. Interactions between images and texts is a growing research field. Early work in this area includes generating single words or fixed phrases from images (Duygulu et al., 2002; Barnard et al., 2003) or using contextual information to improve recognition (Gupta and Davis, 2008; Torralba et al., 2010).

Apart from a large body of work on single object image classification (Le et al., 2012), there is also work on attribute classification and other mid-level elements (Kumar et al., 2009), some of which we hope to capture with our approach as well.

Our work is close in spirit with recent work in describing images with more detailed, longer textual descriptions. In particular, Yao et al. (2010) describe images using hierarchical knowledge and humans in the loop. In contrast, our work does not require human interactions. Farhadi et al. (2010) and Kulkarni et al. (2011), on the other hand, use a more automatic method to parse images. For instance, the former approach uses a single triple of objects estimated for an image to retrieve sentences from a collection written to describe similar images. It forms representations to describe 1 object, 1 action, and 1 scene. Kulkarni et al. (2011) extends their method to describe an image with multiple objects. None of these approaches have used a compositional sentence vector representation and they require specific language generation techniques and sophisticated inference methods. Since our model is based on neural networks inference is fast and simple. Kuznetsova et al. (2012) use a very large parallel corpus to connect images and sentences. Feng and Lapata (2013) use a large dataset of captioned images and experiments with both extractive (search) and abstractive (generation) models.

Most related is the very recent work of Hodosh et al. (2013). They too evaluate using a ranking measure. In our experiments, we compare to kernelized Canonical Correlation Analysis which is the main technique in their experiments.

3 Dependency-Tree Recursive Neural Networks

In this section we first focus on the DT-RNN model that computes compositional vector representations for phrases and sentences of variable length and syntactic type. In section 5 the resulting vectors will then become multimodal features by mapping images that show what the sentence describes to the same space and learning both the image and sentence mapping jointly.

The most common way of building representations for longer phrases from single word vectors is to simply linearly average the word vectors. While this bag-of-words approach can yield reasonable performance in some tasks, it gives all the words the same weight and cannot distinguish important differences in simple visual descriptions such as *The bike crashed into the standing car.* vs. *The car crashed into the standing bike.*.

RNN models (Pollack, 1990; Goller and Küchler, 1996; Socher et al., 2011b; Socher et al., 2011a) provided a novel way of combining word vectors for longer phrases that moved beyond simple averaging. They combine vectors with an RNN in binary constituency trees which have potentially many hidden layers. While the induced vector representations work very well on many tasks, they also inevitably capture a lot of syntactic structure of the sentence. However, the task of finding images from sentence descriptions requires us to be more invariant to syntactic differences. One such example are active-passive constructions which can collapse words such as "by" in some formalisms (de Marneffe et al., 2006), relying instead on the semantic relationship of "agent". For instance, *The mother hugged her child.* and *The child was hugged by its mother.* should map to roughly the same visual space. Current Recursive and Recurrent Neural Networks do not exhibit this behavior and even bag of words representations would be influenced by the words *was* and *by*. The model we describe below focuses more on recognizing actions and agents and has the potential to learn representations that are invariant to active-passive differences.

3.1 DT-RNN Inputs: Word Vectors and Dependency Trees

In order for the DT-RNN to compute a vector representation for an ordered list of m words (a phrase or sentence), we map the single words to a vector space and then parse the sentence.

First, we map each word to a d-dimensional vector. We initialize these word vectors with the un-

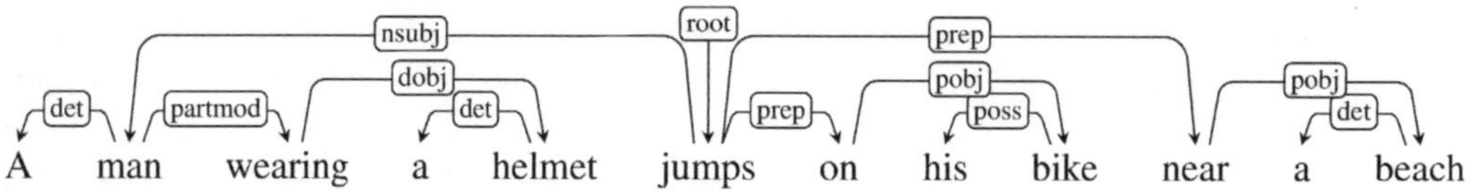

Figure 2: Example of a full dependency tree for a longer sentence. The DT-RNN will compute vector representations at every word that represents that word and an arbitrary number of child nodes. The final representation is computed at the *root* node, here at the verb *jumps*. Note that more important activity and object words are higher up in this tree structure.

supervised model of Huang et al. (2012) which can learn single word vector representations from both local and global contexts. The idea is to construct a neural network that outputs high scores for windows and documents that occur in a large unlabeled corpus and low scores for window-document pairs where one word is replaced by a random word. When such a network is optimized via gradient descent the derivatives backpropagate into a word embedding matrix A which stores word vectors as columns. In order to predict correct scores the vectors in the matrix capture co-occurrence statistics. We use $d = 50$ in all our experiments. The embedding matrix X is then used by finding the column index i of each word: $[w] = i$ and retrieving the corresponding column x_w from X. Henceforth, we represent an input sentence s as an ordered list of (word,vector) pairs: $s = ((w_1, x_{w_1}), \ldots, (w_m, x_{w_m}))$.

Next, the sequence of words $(w_1, \ldots, w_m)$ is parsed by the dependency parser of de Marneffe et al. (2006). Fig. 2 shows an example. We can represent a dependency tree d of a sentence s as an ordered list of (child,parent) indices: $d(s) = \{(i, j)\}$, where every child word in the sequence $i = 1, \ldots, m$ is present and has any word $j \in \{1, \ldots, m\} \cup \{0\}$ as its parent. The root word has as its parent 0 and we notice that the same word can be a parent between zero and m number of times. Without loss of generality, we assume that these indices form a tree structure. To summarize, the input to the DT-RNN for each sentence is the pair (s, d): the words and their vectors and the dependency tree.

3.2 Forward Propagation in DT-RNNs

Given these two inputs, we now illustrate how the DT-RNN computes parent vectors. We will use the following sentence as a running example: *Students*$_1$ *ride*$_2$ *bikes*$_3$ *at*$_4$ *night*$_5$. Fig. 3 shows its tree and computed vector representations. The dependency tree for this sentence can be summarized by the following set of (child, parent) edges: $d = \{(1, 2), (2, 0), (3, 2), (4, 2), (5, 4)\}$.

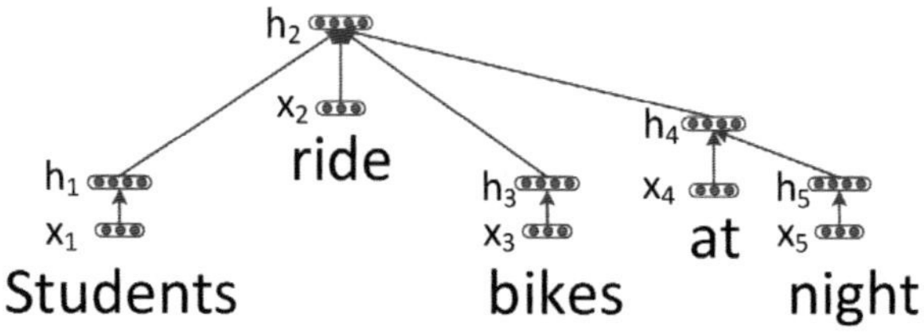

Figure 3: Example of a DT-RNN tree structure for computing a sentence representation in a bottom up fashion.

The DT-RNN model will compute parent vectors at each word that include all the dependent (children) nodes in a bottom up fashion using a compositionality function g_θ which is parameterized by all the model parameters θ. To this end, the algorithm searches for nodes in a tree that have either (i) no children or (ii) whose children have already been computed and then computes the corresponding vector.

In our example, the words x_1, x_3, x_5 are leaf nodes and hence, we can compute their corresponding hidden nodes via:

$$h_c = g_\theta(x_c) = f(W_v x_c) \quad \text{for } c = 1, 3, 5, \quad (1)$$

where we compute the hidden vector at position c via our general composition function g_θ. In the case of leaf nodes, this composition function becomes simply a linear layer, parameterized by $W_v \in \mathbb{R}^{n \times d}$, followed by a nonlinearity. We cross-validate over using no nonlinearity ($f = \text{id}$), $\tanh$, sigmoid or rectified linear units ($f = \max(0, x)$, but generally find $\tanh$ to perform best.

The final sentence representation we want to compute is at h_2, however, since we still do not have h_4, we compute that one next:

$$h_4 = g_\theta(x_4, h_5) = f(W_v x_4 + W_{r1} h_5), \quad (2)$$

where we use the same W_v as before to map the word vector into hidden space but we now also have a linear layer that takes as input h_5, the only child of the fourth node. The matrix $W_{r1} \in \mathbb{R}^{n \times n}$ is used because node 5 is the first child node on the right side of node 4. Generally, we have multiple matrices for composing with hidden child vectors from the right and left sides: $W_{r\cdot} = (W_{r1}, \ldots, W_{rk_r})$ and $W_{l\cdot} = (W_{l1}, \ldots, W_{lk_l})$. The number of needed matrices is determined by the data by simply finding the maximum numbers of left k_l and right k_r children any node has. If at test time a child appeared at an even large distance (this does not happen in our test set), the corresponding matrix would be the identity matrix.

Now that all children of h_2 have their hidden vectors, we can compute the final sentence representation via:

$$h_2 = g_\theta(x_2, h_1, h_3, h_4) = \quad (3)$$
$$f(W_v x_2 + W_{l1} h_1 + W_{r1} h_3 + W_{r2} h_4).$$

Notice that the children are multiplied by matrices that depend on their location relative to the current node.

Another modification that improves the mean rank by approximately 6 in image search on the dev set is to weight nodes by the number of words underneath them and normalize by the sum of words under all children. This encourages the intuitive desideratum that nodes describing longer phrases are more important. Let $\ell(i)$ be the number of leaf nodes (words) under node i and $C(i, y)$ be the set of child nodes of node i in dependency tree y. The final composition function for a node vector h_i becomes:

$$h_i = f\left(\frac{1}{\ell(i)}\left(W_v x_i + \sum_{j \in C(i)} \ell(j) W_{\text{pos}(i,j)} h_j\right)\right), \quad (4)$$

where by definition $\ell(i) = 1 + \sum_{j \in C(i)} \ell(j)$ and $\text{pos}(i, j)$ is the relative position of child j with respect to node i, e.g. $l1$ or $r2$ in Eq. 3.

3.3 Semantic Dependency Tree RNNs

An alternative is to condition the weight matrices on the semantic relations given by the dependency parser. We use the collapsed tree formalism of the Stanford dependency parser (de Marneffe et al., 2006). With such a semantic untying of the weights, the DT-RNN makes better use of the dependency formalism and could give active-passive reversals similar semantic vector representation. The equation for this semantic DT-RNN (**SDT-RNN**) is the same as the one above except that the matrices $W_{\text{pos}(i,j)}$ are replaced with matrices based on the dependency relationship. There are a total of 141 unique such relationships in the dataset. However, most are very rare. For examples of semantic relationships, see Fig. 2 and the model analysis section 6.7.

This forward propagation can be used for computing compositional vectors and in Sec. 5 we will explain the objective function in which these are trained.

3.4 Comparison to Previous RNN Models

The DT-RNN has several important differences to previous RNN models of Socher et al. (2011a) and (Socher et al., 2011b; Socher et al., 2011c). These constituency tree RNNs (CT-RNNs) use the following composition function to compute a hidden parent vector h from exactly two child vectors (c_1, c_2) in a binary tree: $h = f\left(W \begin{bmatrix} c_1 \\ c_2 \end{bmatrix}\right)$, where $W \in \mathbb{R}^{d \times 2d}$ is the main parameter to learn. This can be rewritten to show the similarity to the DT-RNN as $h = f(W_{l1} c_1 + W_{r1} c_2)$. However, there are several important differences.

Note first that in previous RNN models the parent vectors were of the same dimensionality to be recursively compatible and be used as input to the next composition. In contrast, our new model first maps single words into a hidden space and then parent nodes are composed from these hidden vectors. This allows a higher capacity representation which is especially helpful for nodes that have many children.

Secondly, the DT-RNN allows for n-ary nodes in the tree. This is an improvement that is possible even for constituency tree CT-RNNs but it has not been explored in previous models.

Third, due to computing parent nodes in constituency trees, previous models had the problem that words that are merged last in the tree have a larger weight or importance in the final sentence rep-

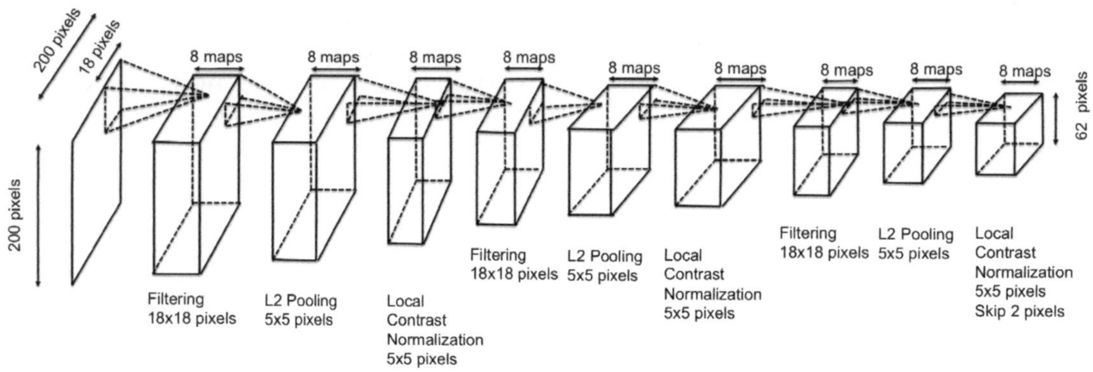

Figure 4: The architecture of the visual model. This model has 3 sequences of filtering, pooling and local contrast normalization layers. The learnable parameters are the filtering layer. The filters are not shared, i.e., the network is nonconvolutional.

resentation. This can be problematic since these are often simple non-content words, such as a leading 'But,'. While such single words can be important for tasks such as sentiment analysis, we argue that for describing visual scenes the DT-RNN captures the more important effects: The dependency tree structures push the central content words such as the main action or verb and its subject and object to be merged last and hence, by construction, the final sentence representation is more robust to less important adjectival modifiers, word order changes, etc.

Fourth, we allow some untying of weights depending on either how far away a constituent is from the current word or what its semantic relationship is.

Now that we can compute compositional vector representations for sentences, the next section describes how we represent images.

4 Learning Image Representations with Neural Networks

The image features that we use in our experiments are extracted from a deep neural network, replicated from the one described in (Le et al., 2012). The network was trained using both unlabeled data (random web images) and labeled data to classify 22,000 categories in ImageNet (Deng et al., 2009). We then used the features at the last layer, before the classifier, as the feature representation in our experiments. The dimension of the feature vector of the last layer is 4,096. The details of the model and its training procedures are as follows.

The architecture of the network can be seen in Figure 4. The network takes 200x200 pixel images as inputs and has 9 layers. The layers consist of three sequences of filtering, pooling and local contrast normalization (Jarrett et al., 2009). The pooling function is L2 pooling of the previous layer (taking the square of the filtering units, summing them up in a small area in the image, and taking the square-root). The local contrast normalization takes inputs in a small area of the lower layer, subtracts the mean and divides by the standard deviation.

The network was first trained using an unsupervised objective: trying to reconstruct the input while keeping the neurons sparse. In this phase, the network was trained on 20 million images randomly sampled from the web. We resized a given image so that its short dimension has 200 pixels. We then cropped a fixed size 200x200 pixel image right at the center of the resized image. This means we may discard a fraction of the long dimension of the image.

After unsupervised training, we used ImageNet (Deng et al., 2009) to adjust the features in the entire network. The ImageNet dataset has 22,000 categories and 14 million images. The number of images in each category is equal across categories. The 22,000 categories are extracted from WordNet.

To speed up the supervised training of this network, we made a simple modification to the algorithm described in Le et al. (2012): adding a "bottleneck" layer in between the last layer and the classifier. to reduce the number of connections. We added one "bottleneck" layer which has 4,096 units in between the last layer of the network and the softmax layer. This newly-added layer is fully connected to the previous layer and has a linear activation function. The total number of connections of this network is approximately 1.36 billion.

The network was trained again using the supervised objective of classifying the 22,000 classes in ImageNet. Most features in the networks are local, which allows model parallelism. Data parallelism by asynchronous SGD was also employed as in Le et al. (2012). The entire training, both unsupervised and supervised, took 8 days on a large cluster of machines. This network achieves 18.3% precision@1 on the full ImageNet dataset (Release Fall 2011).

We will use the features at the bottleneck layer as the feature vector z of an image. Each scaled and cropped image is presented to our network. The network then performs a feedforward computation to compute the values of the bottleneck layer. This means that every image is represented by a fixed length vector of 4,096 dimensions. Note that during training, no aligned sentence-image data was used and the ImageNet classes do not fully intersect with the words used in our dataset.

5 Multimodal Mappings

The previous two sections described how we can map sentences into a $d = 50$-dimensional space and how to extract high quality image feature vectors of 4096 dimensions. We now define our final multimodal objective function for learning joint image-sentence representations with these models. Our training set consists of N images and their feature vectors z_i and each image has 5 sentence descriptions $s_{i1}, \ldots, s_{i5}$ for which we use the DT-RNN to compute vector representations. See Fig. 5 for examples from the dataset. For training, we use a max-margin objective function which intuitively trains pairs of correct image and sentence vectors to have high inner products and incorrect pairs to have low inner products. Let $v_i = W_I z_i$ be the mapped image vector and $y_{ij} = DTRNN_\theta(s_{ij})$ the composed sentence vector. We define $\mathcal{S}$ to be the set of all sentence indices and $\mathcal{S}(i)$ the set of sentence indices corresponding to image i. Similarly, $\mathcal{I}$ is the set of all image indices and $\mathcal{I}(j)$ is the image index of sentence j. The set $\mathcal{P}$ is the set of all correct image-sentence training pairs (i, j). The ranking cost function to minimize is then: $J(W_I, \theta) =$

$$\sum_{(i,j)\in\mathcal{P}} \sum_{c\in\mathcal{S}\setminus\mathcal{S}(i)} \max(0, \Delta - v_i^T y_j + v_i^T y_c)$$

$$+ \sum_{(i,j)\in\mathcal{P}} \sum_{c\in\mathcal{I}\setminus\mathcal{I}(j)} \max(0, \Delta - v_i^T y_j + v_c^T y_j), \quad (5)$$

where θ are the language composition matrices, and both second sums are over other sentences coming from different images and vice versa. The hyperparameter Δ is the margin. The margin is found via cross validation on the dev set and usually around 1.

The final objective also includes the regularization term $\lambda/left(\|\theta\|_2^2 + \|W_I\|_F)$. Both the visual model and the word vector learning require a very large amount of training data and both have a huge number of parameters. Hence, to prevent overfitting, we assume their weights are fixed and only train the DT-RNN parameters W_I. If larger training corpora become available in the future, training both jointly becomes feasible and would present a very promising direction. We use a modified version of AdaGrad (Duchi et al., 2011) for optimization of both W_I and the DT-RNN as well as the other baselines (except kCCA). Adagrad has achieved good performance previously in neural networks models (Dean et al., 2012; Socher et al., 2013a). We modify it by resetting all squared gradient sums to 1 every 5 epochs. With both images and sentences in the same multimodal space, we can easily query the model for similar images or sentences by finding the nearest neighbors in terms of negative inner products.

An alternative objective function is based on the squared loss $J(W_I, \theta) = \sum_{(i,j)\in\mathcal{P}} \|v_i - y_j\|_2^2$. This requires an alternating minimization scheme that first trains only W_I, then fixes W_I and trains the DT-RNN weights θ and then repeats this several times. We find that the performance with this objective function (paired with finding similar images using Euclidean distances) is worse for all models than the margin loss of Eq. 5. In addition kCCA also performs much better using inner products in the multimodal space.

6 Experiments

We use the dataset of Rashtchian et al. (2010) which consists of 1000 images, each with 5 sentences. See Fig. 5 for examples.

We evaluate and compare the DT-RNN in three different experiments. First, we analyze how well the sentence vectors capture similarity in visual meaning. Then we analyze *Image Search with Query Sentences*: to query each model with a sentence in order to find an image showing that sen-

1. A woman and her dog watch the cameraman in their living with wooden floors.
2. A woman sitting on the couch while a black faced dog runs across the floor.
3. A woman wearing a backpack sits on a couch while a small dog runs on the hardwood floor next to her.
4. A women sitting on a sofa while a small Jack Russell walks towards the camera.
5. White and black small dog walks toward the camera while woman sits on couch, desk and computer seen in the background as well as a pillow, teddy bear and moggie toy on the wood floor.

1. A man in a cowboy hat check approaches a small red sports car.
2. The back and left side of a red Ferrari and two men admiring it.
3. The sporty car is admired by passer by.
4. Two men next to a red sports car in a parking lot.
5. Two men stand beside a red sports car.

Figure 5: Examples from the dataset of images and their sentence descriptions (Rashtchian et al., 2010). Sentence length varies greatly and different objects can be mentioned first. Hence, models have to be invariant to word ordering.

tence's visual 'meaning.' The last experiment *Describing Images by Finding Suitable Sentences* does the reverse search where we query the model with an image and try to find the closest textual description in the embedding space.

In our comparison to other methods we focus on those models that can also compute fixed, continuous vectors for sentences. In particular, we compare to the RNN model on constituency trees of Socher et al. (2011a), a standard recurrent neural network; a simple bag-of-words baseline which averages the words. All models use the word vectors provided by Huang et al. (2012) and do not update them as discussed above. Models are trained with their corresponding gradients and backpropagation techniques. A standard recurrent model is used where the hidden vector at word index t is computed from the hidden vector at the previous time step and the current word vector: $h_t = f(W_h h_{t-1} + W_x x_t)$. During training, we take the last hidden vector of the sentence chain and propagate the error into that. It is also this vector that is used to represent the sentence.

Other possible comparisons are to the very different models mentioned in the related work section. These models use a lot more task-specific engineering, such as running object detectors with bounding boxes, attribute classifiers, scene classifiers, CRFs for composing the sentences, etc. Another line of work uses large sentence-image aligned resources (Kuznetsova et al., 2012), whereas we focus on easily obtainable training data of each modality separately and a rather small multimodal corpus.

In our experiments we split the data into 800 training, 100 development and 100 test images. Since there are 5 sentences describing each image, we have 4000 training sentences and 500 testing sentences. The dataset has 3020 unique words, half of which only appear once. Hence, the unsupervised, pre-trained semantic word vector representations are crucial. Word vectors are not fine tuned during training. Hence, the main parameters are the DT-RNN's $W_{l\cdot}, W_{r\cdot}$ or the semantic matrices of which there are 141 and the image mapping W_I. For both DT-RNNs the weight matrices are initialized to block identity matrices plus Gaussian noise. Word vectors and hidden vectors are set o length 50. Using the development split, we found $\lambda = 0.08$ and the learning rate of AdaGrad to 0.0001. The best model uses a margin of $\Delta = 3$.

Inspired by Socher and Fei-Fei (2010) and Hodosh et al. (2013) we also compare to kernelized Canonical Correlation Analysis (kCCA). We use the average of word vectors for describing sentences and the same powerful image vectors as before. We use the code of Socher and Fei-Fei (2010). Technically, one could combine the recently introduced deep CCA Andrew et al. (2013) and train the recursive neural network architectures with the CCA objective. We leave this to future work. With linear kernels, kCCA does well for image search but is worse for sentence self similarity and describing images with sentences close-by in embedding space. All other models are trained by replacing the DT-RNN function in Eq. 5.

6.1 Similarity of Sentences Describing the Same Image

In this experiment, we first map all 500 sentences from the test set into the multi-modal space. Then for each sentence, we find the nearest neighbor sen-

Sentences Similarity for Image		*Image Search*		*Describing Images*	
Model	Mean Rank	Model	Mean Rank	Model	Mean Rank
Random	101.1	Random	52.1	Random	92.1
BoW	11.8	BoW	14.6	BoW	21.1
CT-RNN	15.8	CT-RNN	16.1	CT-RNN	23.9
Recurrent NN	18.5	Recurrent NN	19.2	Recurrent NN	27.1
kCCA	10.7	kCCA	15.9	kCCA	18.0
DT-RNN	11.1	DT-RNN	13.6	DT-RNN	19.2
SDT-RNN	**10.5**	SDT-RNN	**12.5**	SDT-RNN	**16.9**

Table 1: **Left:** Comparison of methods for sentence similarity judgments. Lower numbers are better since they indicate that sentences describing the same image rank more highly (are closer). The ranks are out of the 500 sentences in the test set. **Center:** Comparison of methods for image search with query sentences. Shown is the average rank of the single correct image that is being described. **Right:** Average rank of a correct sentence description for a query image.

tences in terms of inner products. We then sort these neighbors and record the rank or position of the nearest sentence *that describes the same image*. If all the images were very unique and the visual descriptions close-paraphrases and consistent, we would expect a very low rank. However, usually a handful of images are quite similar (for instance, there are various images of airplanes flying, parking, taxiing or waiting on the runway) and sentence descriptions can vary greatly in detail and specificity for the same image.

Table 1 (left) shows the results. We can see that averaging the high quality word vectors already captures a lot of similarity. The chain structure of a standard recurrent neural net performs worst since its representation is dominated by the last words in the sequence which may not be as important as earlier words.

6.2 Image Search with Query Sentences

This experiment evaluates how well we can find images that display the visual meaning of a given sentence. We first map a query sentence into the vector space and then find images in the same space using simple inner products. As shown in Table 1 (center), the new DT-RNN outperforms all other models.

6.3 Describing Images by Finding Suitable Sentences

Lastly, we repeat the above experiments but with roles reversed. For an image, we search for suitable textual descriptions again simply by finding close-by sentence vectors in the multi-modal embedding space. Table 1 (right) shows that the DT-RNN again outperforms related models. Fig. 2assigned to images. The average ranking of 25.3 for a correct sentence description is out of 500 possible sentences. A random assignment would give an average ranking of 100.

Image Search		*Describing Images*	
Model	mRank	Model	mRank
BoW	24.7	BoW	30.7
CT-RNN	22.2	CT-RNN	29.4
Recurrent NN	28.4	Recurrent NN	31.4
kCCA	13.7	kCCA	38.0
DT-RNN	13.3	DT-RNN	26.8
SDT-RNN	15.8	SDT-RNN	37.5

Table 2: Results of multimodal ranking when models are trained with a squared error loss and using Euclidean distance in the multimodal space. Better performance is reached for all models when trained in a max-margin loss and using inner products as in the previous table.

6.4 Analysis: Squared Error Loss vs. Margin Loss

We analyze the influence of the multimodal loss function on the performance. In addition, we compare using Euclidean distances instead of inner products. Table 2 shows that performance is worse for all models in this setting.

6.5 Analysis: Recall at n vs Mean Rank

Hodosh et al. (2013) and other related work use recall at n as an evaluation measure. Recall at n captures how often one of the top n closest vectors were a correct image or sentence and gives a good intuition of how a model would perform in a ranking task that presents n such results to a user. Below, we compare three commonly used and high performing models: bag of words, kCCA and our SDT-RNN on

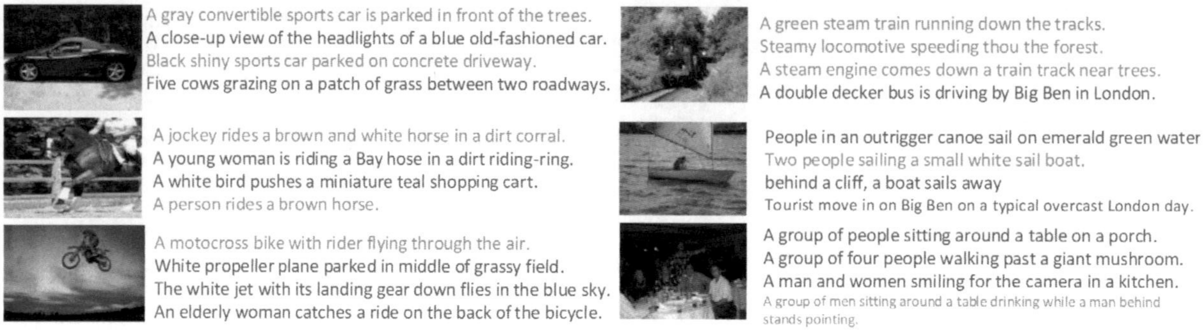

Figure 6: Images and their sentence descriptions assigned by the DT-RNN.

	Image Search			
Model	mRank △	R@1 ▽	R@5 ▽	R@10 ▽
BoW	14.6	15.8	42.2	60.0
kCCA	15.9	**16.4**	41.4	58.0
SDT-RNN	**12.5**	**16.4**	**46.6**	**65.6**
	Describing Images			
BoW	21.1	19.0	38.0	57.0
kCCA	18.0	21.0	**47.0**	61.0
SDT-RNN	**16.9**	**23.0**	45.0	**63.0**

Table 3: Evaluation comparison between mean rank of the closest correct image or sentence (lower is better △) with recall at different thresholds (higher is better, ▽). With one exception (R@5, bottom table), the SDT-RNN outperforms the other two models and all other models we did not include here.

this different metric. Table 3 shows that the measures do correlate well and the SDT-RNN also performs best on the multimodal ranking tasks when evaluated with this measure.

6.6 Error Analysis

In order to understand the main problems with the composed sentence vectors, we analyze the sentences that have the worst nearest neighbor rank between each other. We find that the main failure mode of the SDT-RNN occurs when a sentence that should describe the same image does not use a verb but the other sentences of that image do include a verb. For example, the following sentence pair has vectors that are very far apart from each other even though they are supposed to describe the same image:

1. A blue and yellow airplane flying straight down while emitting white smoke

2. Airplane in dive position

Generally, as long as both sentences either have a verb or do not, the SDT-RNN is more robust to different sentence lengths than bag of words representations.

6.7 Model Analysis: Semantic Composition Matrices

The best model uses composition matrices based on semantic relationships from the dependency parser. We give some insights into what the model learns by listing the composition matrices with the largest Frobenius norms. Intuitively, these matrices have learned larger weights that are being multiplied with the child vector in the tree and hence that child will have more weight in the final composed parent vector. In decreasing order of Frobenius norm, the relationship matrices are: nominal subject, possession modifier (e.g. their), passive auxiliary, preposition at, preposition in front of, passive auxiliary, passive nominal subject, object of preposition, preposition in and preposition on.

The model learns that nouns are very important as well as their spatial prepositions and adjectives.

7 Conclusion

We introduced a new recursive neural network model that is based on dependency trees. For evaluation, we use the challenging task of mapping sentences and images into a common space for finding one from the other. Our new model outperforms baselines and other commonly used models that can compute continuous vector representations for sentences. In comparison to related models, the DT-RNN is more invariant and robust to surface changes such as word order.

References

G. Andrew, R. Arora, K. Livescu, and J. Bilmes. 2013. Deep canonical correlation analysis. In *ICML*, Atlanta, Georgia.

K. Barnard, P. Duygulu, N. de Freitas, D. Forsyth, D. Blei, and M. Jordan. 2003. Matching words and pictures. *JMLR*.

M. Baroni and A. Lenci. 2010. Distributional memory: A general framework for corpus-based semantics. *Computational Linguistics*, 36(4):673–721.

R. Collobert and J. Weston. 2008. A unified architecture for natural language processing: deep neural networks with multitask learning. In *Proceedings of ICML*, pages 160–167.

F. Costa, P. Frasconi, V. Lombardo, and G. Soda. 2003. Towards incremental parsing of natural language using recursive neural networks. *Applied Intelligence*.

M. de Marneffe, B. MacCartney, and C. D. Manning. 2006. Generating typed dependency parses from phrase structure parses. In *LREC*.

J. Dean, G. S. Corrado, R. Monga, K. Chen, M. Devin, Q. V. Le, M. Z. Mao, M. Ranzato, A. Senior, P. Tucker, K. Yang, and A.Y. Ng. 2012. Large scale distributed deep networks. In *NIPS*.

J. Deng, W. Dong, R. Socher, L.-J. Li, K. Li, and L. Fei-Fei. 2009. ImageNet: A Large-Scale Hierarchical Image Database. In *CVPR*.

J. Duchi, E. Hazan, and Y. Singer. 2011. Adaptive subgradient methods for online learning and stochastic optimization. *JMLR*, 12, July.

P. Duygulu, K. Barnard, N. de Freitas, and D. Forsyth. 2002. Object recognition as machine translation. In *ECCV*.

A. Farhadi, M. Hejrati, M. A. Sadeghi, P. Young, C. Rashtchian, J. Hockenmaier, and D. Forsyth. 2010. Every picture tells a story: Generating sentences from images. In *ECCV*.

Y. Feng and M. Lapata. 2013. Automatic caption generation for news images. *IEEE Trans. Pattern Anal. Mach. Intell.*, 35.

A. Frome, G. Corrado, J. Shlens, S. Bengio, J. Dean, M. Ranzato, and T. Mikolov. 2013. Devise: A deep visual-semantic embedding model. In *NIPS*.

C. Goller and A. Küchler. 1996. Learning task-dependent distributed representations by backpropagation through structure. In *Proceedings of the International Conference on Neural Networks*.

E. Grefenstette, G. Dinu, Y.-Z. Zhang, M. Sadrzadeh, and M. Baroni. 2013. Multi-step regression learning for compositional distributional semantics. In *IWCS*.

A. Gupta and L. S. Davis. 2008. Beyond nouns: Exploiting prepositions and comparative adjectives for learning visual classifiers. In *ECCV*.

M. Hodosh, P. Young, and J. Hockenmaier. 2013. Framing image description as a ranking task: Data, models and evaluation metrics. *J. Artif. Intell. Res. (JAIR)*, 47:853–899.

E. H. Huang, R. Socher, C. D. Manning, and A. Y. Ng. 2012. Improving Word Representations via Global Context and Multiple Word Prototypes. In *ACL*.

K. Jarrett, K. Kavukcuoglu, M.A. Ranzato, and Y. LeCun. 2009. What is the best multi-stage architecture for object recognition? In *ICCV*.

P. Blunsom. K.M. Hermann. 2013. The role of syntax in vector space models of compositional semantics. In *ACL*.

A. Krizhevsky, I. Sutskever, and G. E. Hinton. 2012. Imagenet classification with deep convolutional neural networks. In *NIPS*.

G. Kulkarni, V. Premraj, S. Dhar, S. Li, Y. Choi, A. C. Berg, and T. L. Berg. 2011. Baby talk: Understanding and generating image descriptions. In *CVPR*.

N. Kumar, A. C. Berg, P. N. Belhumeur, , and S. K. Nayar. 2009. Attribute and simile classifiers for face verification. In *ICCV*.

P. Kuznetsova, V. Ordonez, A. C. Berg, T. L. Berg, and Yejin Choi. 2012. Collective generation of natural image descriptions. In *ACL*.

Q. V. Le, M.A. Ranzato, R. Monga, M. Devin, K. Chen, G.S. Corrado, J. Dean, and A. Y. Ng. 2012. Building high-level features using large scale unsupervised learning. In *ICML*.

T. Mikolov, W. Yih, and G. Zweig. 2013. Linguistic regularities in continuous spaceword representations. In *HLT-NAACL*.

J. Mitchell and M. Lapata. 2010. Composition in distributional models of semantics. *Cognitive Science*, 34(8):1388–1429.

J. Ngiam, A. Khosla, M. Kim, J. Nam, H. Lee, and A.Y. Ng. 2011. Multimodal deep learning. In *ICML*.

V. Ordonez, G. Kulkarni, and T. L. Berg. 2011. Im2text: Describing images using 1 million captioned photographs. In *NIPS*.

J. B. Pollack. 1990. Recursive distributed representations. *Artificial Intelligence*, 46, November.

C. Rashtchian, P. Young, M. Hodosh, and J. Hockenmaier. 2010. Collecting image annotations using Amazon's Mechanical Turk. In *Workshop on Creating Speech and Language Data with Amazon's MTurk*.

R. Socher and L. Fei-Fei. 2010. Connecting modalities: Semi-supervised segmentation and annotation of images using unaligned text corpora. In *CVPR*.

R. Socher, C. D. Manning, and A. Y. Ng. 2010. Learning continuous phrase representations and syntactic parsing with recursive neural networks. In *Proceedings of the NIPS-2010 Deep Learning and Unsupervised Feature Learning Workshop*.

R. Socher, E. H. Huang, J. Pennington, A. Y. Ng, and C. D. Manning. 2011a. Dynamic Pooling and Unfolding Recursive Autoencoders for Paraphrase Detection. In *NIPS*.

R. Socher, C. Lin, A. Y. Ng, and C.D. Manning. 2011b. Parsing Natural Scenes and Natural Language with Recursive Neural Networks. In *ICML*.

R. Socher, J. Pennington, E. H. Huang, A. Y. Ng, and C. D. Manning. 2011c. Semi-Supervised Recursive Autoencoders for Predicting Sentiment Distributions. In *EMNLP*.

R. Socher, B. Huval, C. D. Manning, and A. Y. Ng. 2012. Semantic Compositionality Through Recursive Matrix-Vector Spaces. In *EMNLP*.

R. Socher, J. Bauer, C. D. Manning, and A. Y. Ng. 2013a. Parsing With Compositional Vector Grammars. In *ACL*.

R. Socher, M. Ganjoo, C. D. Manning, and A. Y. Ng. 2013b. Zero-Shot Learning Through Cross-Modal Transfer. In *NIPS*.

R. Socher, M. Ganjoo, H. Sridhar, O. Bastani, and A. Y. Ng. C. D. Manning and. 2013c. Zero-shot learning through cross-modal transfer. In *Proceedings of the International Conference on Learning Representations (ICLR, Workshop Track)*.

N. Srivastava and R. Salakhutdinov. 2012. Multimodal learning with deep boltzmann machines. In *NIPS*.

A. Torralba, K. P. Murphy, and W. T. Freeman. 2010. Using the forest to see the trees: exploiting context for visual object detection and localization. *Communications of the ACM*.

P. D. Turney and P. Pantel. 2010. From frequency to meaning: Vector space models of semantics. *Journal of Artificial Intelligence Research*, 37:141–188.

B. Yao, X. Yang, L. Lin, M. W. Lee, and S.-C. Zhu. 2010. I2t:image parsing to text description. *IEEE Xplore*.

Back to Basics for Monolingual Alignment: Exploiting Word Similarity and Contextual Evidence

Md Arafat Sultan[†], **Steven Bethard**[‡] **and Tamara Sumner**[†]
[†]Institute of Cognitive Science and Department of Computer Science
University of Colorado Boulder
[‡]Department of Computer and Information Sciences
University of Alabama at Birmingham
arafat.sultan@colorado.edu, bethard@cis.uab.edu, sumner@colorado.edu

Abstract

We present a simple, easy-to-replicate monolingual aligner that demonstrates state-of-the-art performance while relying on almost no supervision and a very small number of external resources. Based on the hypothesis that words with similar meanings represent potential pairs for alignment if located in similar contexts, we propose a system that operates by finding such pairs. In two intrinsic evaluations on alignment test data, our system achieves F_1 scores of 88–92%, demonstrating 1–3% absolute improvement over the previous best system. Moreover, in two extrinsic evaluations our aligner outperforms existing aligners, and even a naive application of the aligner approaches state-of-the-art performance in each extrinsic task.

1 Introduction

Monolingual alignment is the task of discovering and aligning similar semantic units in a pair of sentences expressed in a natural language. Such alignments provide valuable information regarding how and to what extent the two sentences are related. Consequently, alignment is a central component of a number of important tasks involving text comparison: textual entailment recognition, textual similarity identification, paraphrase detection, question answering and text summarization, to name a few.

The high utility of monolingual alignment has spawned significant research on the topic in the recent past. Major efforts that have treated alignment as a standalone problem (MacCartney et al., 2008; Thadani and McKeown, 2011; Yao et al., 2013a) are primarily supervised, thanks to the manually aligned corpus with training and test sets from Microsoft Research (Brockett, 2007). Primary concerns of such work include both quality and speed, due to the fact that alignment is frequently a component of larger NLP tasks.

Driven by similar motivations, we seek to devise a lightweight, easy-to-construct aligner that produces high-quality output and is applicable to various end tasks. Amid a variety of problem formulations and ingenious approaches to alignment, we take a step back and examine closely the effectiveness of two frequently made assumptions: 1) Related semantic units in two sentences must be similar or related in their meaning, and 2) Commonalities in their semantic contexts in the respective sentences provide additional evidence of their relatedness (MacCartney et al., 2008; Thadani and McKeown, 2011; Yao et al., 2013a; Yao et al., 2013b). Alignment, based solely on these two assumptions, reduces to finding the best combination of pairs of similar semantic units in similar contexts.

Exploiting existing resources to identify similarity of semantic units, we search for robust techniques to identify contextual commonalities. Dependency trees are a commonly used structure for this purpose. While they remain a central part of our aligner, we expand the horizons of dependency-based alignment beyond exact matching by systematically exploiting the notion of "type equivalence" with a small hand-crafted set of equivalent dependency types. In addition, we augment dependency-based alignment with surface-level text analysis.

While phrasal alignments are important and have

Transactions of the Association for Computational Linguistics, 2 (2014) 219–230. Action Editor: Alexander Koller.
Submitted 11/2013; Revised 1/2014; Published 5/2014.

been investigated in multiple studies, we focus primarily on word alignments (which have been shown to form the vast majority of alignments ($\geq 95\%$) in multiple human-annotated corpora (Yao et al., 2013b)), keeping the framework flexible enough to allow incorporation of phrasal alignments in future.

Evaluation of our aligner on the benchmark dataset reported in (Brockett, 2007) shows an F_1 score of 91.7%: a 3.1% absolute improvement over the previous best system (Yao et al., 2013a), corresponding to a 27.2% error reduction. It shows superior performance also on the dataset reported in (Thadani et al., 2012). Additionally, we present results of two extrinsic evaluations, namely textual similarity identification and paraphrase detection. Our aligner not only outperforms existing aligners in each task, but also approaches top systems for the extrinsic tasks.

2 Background

Monolingual alignment has been applied to various NLP tasks including textual entailment recognition (Hickl et al., 2006; Hickl and Bensley, 2007), paraphrase identification (Das and Smith, 2009; Madnani et al., 2012), and textual similarity assessment (Bär et al., 2012; Han et al., 2013) – in some cases explicitly, i.e., as a separate module. But many such systems resort to simplistic and/or ad-hoc strategies for alignment and in most such work, the alignment modules were not separately evaluated on alignment benchmarks, making their direct assessment difficult.

With the introduction of the MSR alignment corpus (Brockett, 2007) developed from the second Recognizing Textual Entailment challenge data (Bar-Haim et al., 2006), direct evaluation and comparison of aligners became possible. The first aligner trained and evaluated on the corpus was a phrasal aligner called MANLI (MacCartney et al., 2008). It represents alignments as sets of different *edit* operations (where a sequence of edits turns one input sentence into the other) and finds an optimal set of edits via a simulated annealing search. Weights of different edit features are learned from the training set of the MSR alignment corpus using a perceptron learning algorithm. MANLI incorporates only shallow features characterizing contextual similarity: relative positions of the two phrases being aligned (or not) in the two sentences and boolean features representing whether or not the preceding and following tokens of the two phrases are similar.

Thadani and McKeown (2011) substituted MANLI's simulated annealing-based decoding with integer linear programming, and achieved a considerable speed-up. More importantly for our discussion, they found contextual evidence in the form of syntactic constraints useful in better aligning stop words. Thadani et al. (2012) further extended the model by adding features characterizing dependency *arc edits*, effectively bringing stronger influence of contextual similarity into alignment decisions. Again the performance improved consequently.

The most successful aligner to date both in terms of accuracy and speed, called JacanaAlign, was developed by Yao et al. (2013a). In contrast to the earlier systems, JacanaAlign is a word aligner that formulates alignment as a sequence labeling problem. Each word in the source sentence is labeled with the corresponding target word index if an alignment is found. It employs a conditional random field to assign the labels and uses a feature set similar to MANLI's in terms of the information they encode (with some extensions). Contextual features include only semantic match of the left and the right neighbors of the two words and their POS tags. Even though JacanaAlign outperformed the MANLI enhancements despite having less contextual features, it is difficult to compare the role of context in the two models because of the large paradigmatic disparity. An extension of JacanaAlign was proposed for phrasal alignments in (Yao et al., 2013b), but the contextual features remained largely unchanged.

Noticeable in all the above systems is the use of contextual evidence as a feature for alignment, but in our opinion, not to an extent sufficient to harness its full potential. Even though deeper dependency-based modeling of contextual commonalities can be found in some other studies (Kouylekov and Magnini, 2005; Chambers et al., 2007; Chang et al., 2010; Yao et al., 2013c), we believe there is further scope for systematic exploitation of contextual evidence for alignment, which we aim to do in this work.

On the contrary, word semantic similarity has been a central component of most aligners; various measures of word similarity have been utilized, including string similarity, resource-based similarity (derived from one or more lexical resources like WordNet)

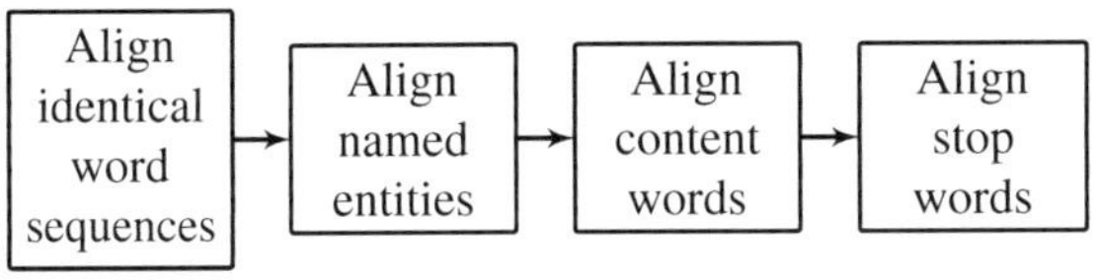

Figure 1: System overview

and distributional similarity (computed from word co-occurrence statistics in large corpora). An important trade-off between precision, coverage and speed exists here and aligners commonly rely on only a subset of these measures (Thadani and McKeown, 2011; Yao et al., 2013a). We use the Paraphrase Database (PPDB) (Ganitkevitch et al., 2013), which is a large resource of lexical and phrasal paraphrases constructed using bilingual pivoting (Bannard and Callison-Burch, 2005) over large parallel corpora.

3 System

Our system operates as a pipeline of alignment modules that differ in the types of word pairs they align. Figure 1 is a simplistic representation of the pipeline. Each module makes use of contextual evidence to make alignment decisions. In addition, the last two modules are informed by a word semantic similarity algorithm. Because of their phrasal nature, we treat named entities separately from other content words. The rationale behind the order in which the modules are arranged is discussed later in this section (3.3.5).

Before discussing each alignment module in detail, we describe the system components that identify word and contextual similarity.

3.1 Word Similarity

The ability to correctly identify semantic similarity between words is crucial to our aligner, since contextual evidence is important only for similar words. Instead of treating word similarity as a continuous variable, we define three levels of similarity.

The first level is an exact word or lemma match which is represented by a similarity score of 1. The second level represents semantic similarity between two terms which are not identical. To identify such word pairs, we employ the Paraphrase Database (PPDB)[1]. We use the largest (XXXL) of the PPDB's lexical paraphrase packages and treat all pairs identically by ignoring the accompanying statistics. We customize the resource by removing pairs of identical words or lemmas and adding lemmatized forms of the remaining pairs. For now, we use the term *ppdbSim* to refer to the similarity of each word pair in this modified version of PPDB (which is a value in (0, 1)) and later explain how we determine it (Section 3.3.5). Finally, any pair of different words which is absent in PPDB is assigned a zero similarity score.

3.2 Extracting Contextual Evidence

Our alignment modules collect contextual evidence from two complementary sources: syntactic dependencies and words occurring within a small textual vicinity of the two words to be aligned. The application of each kind assumes a common principle of *minimal* evidence. Formally, given two input sentences S and T, we consider two words $s \in S$ and $t \in T$ to form a candidate pair for alignment if $\exists r_s \in S$ and $\exists r_t \in T$ such that:

1. $(s, t) \in \Re_{Sim}$ and $(r_s, r_t) \in \Re_{Sim}$, where $\Re_{Sim}$ is a binary relation indicating *sufficient* semantic relatedness between the members of each pair ($\geq ppdbSim$ in our case).
2. $(s, r_s) \in \Re_{C_1}$ and $(t, r_t) \in \Re_{C_2}$, such that $\Re_{C_1} \approx \Re_{C_2}$; where $\Re_{C_1}$ and $\Re_{C_2}$ are binary relations representing specific types of contextual relationships between two words in a sentence (e.g., an *nsubj* dependency between a verb and a noun). The symbol $\approx$ represents equivalence between two relationships, including identicality.

Note that the minimal-evidence assumption holds a single piece of contextual evidence as sufficient support for a potential alignment; but as we discuss later in this section, an evidence for word pair (s, t) (where $s \in S$ and $t \in S$) may not lead to an alignment if there exists a competing pair (s', t) or (s, t') with more evidence (where $s' \in S$ and $t' \in T$).

In the rest of this section, we elaborate the different forms of contextual relationships we exploit along with the notion of equivalence between relationships.

3.2.1 Syntactic Dependencies

Dependencies can be important sources of contextual evidence. Two *nsubj* children r_s and r_t of two verbs $s \in S$ and $t \in T$, for example, provide evidence for not only an (s, t) alignment, but

[1]http://paraphrase.org

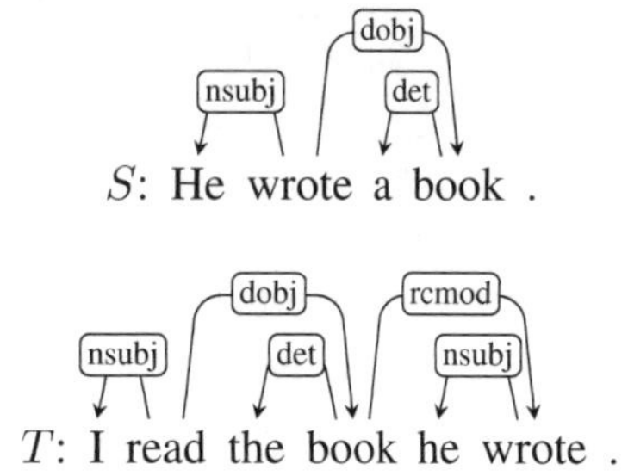

Figure 2: Equivalent dependency types: *dobj* and *rcmod*

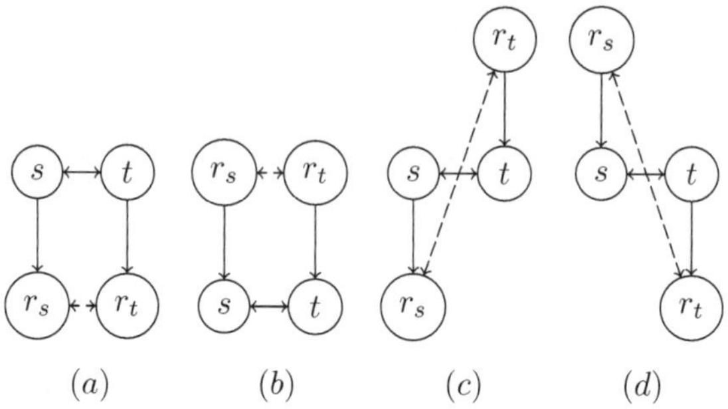

Figure 3: Parent-child orientations in dependencies

also an (r_s, r_t) alignment if $(s,t) \in \Re_{Sim}$ and $(r_s, r_t) \in \Re_{Sim}$. (We adopt the Stanford typed dependencies (de Marneffe and Manning, 2008).)

Moreover, dependency types can exhibit equivalence; consider the two sentences in Figure 2. The *dobj* dependency in S is equivalent to the *rcmod* dependency in T (*dobj* $\approx$ *rcmod*, following our earlier notation) since they represent the same semantic relation between identical word pairs in the two sentences. To be able to use such evidence for alignment, we need to go beyond exact matching of dependencies and develop a mapping among dependency types that encodes such equivalence. Note also that the parent-child roles are opposite for the two dependency types in the above example, a scenario that such a mapping must accommodate.

The four possible such scenarios regarding parent-child orientations are shown in Figure 3. If $(s,t) \in \Re_{Sim}$ and $(r_s, r_t) \in \Re_{Sim}$ (represented by bidirectional arrows), then each orientation represents a set of possible ways in which the S and T dependencies (unidirectional arrows) can provide evidence of similarity between the contexts of s in S and t in T. Each such set comprises equivalent dependency type pairs for that orientation. In the example of Figure 2, *(dobj, rcmod)* is such a pair for orientation (c), given $s = t =$ "*wrote*" and $r_s = r_t =$ "*book*".

We apply the notion of dependency type equivalence to intra-category alignment of content words in four major lexical categories: *verbs*, *nouns*, *adjectives* and *adverbs* (the Stanford POS tagger (Toutanova et al., 2003) is used to identify the categories). Table 1 shows dependency type equivalences for each lexical category of s and t.

The '$\leftarrow$' sign on column 5 of some rows represents a duplication of the column 4 content of the same row. For each row, columns 4 and 5 show two sets of dependency types; each member of the first is equivalent to each member of the second for the current orientation (column 1) and lexical categories of the associated words (columns 2 and 3). For example, row 2 represents the fact that an *agent* relation (between s and r_s; s is the parent) is equivalent to an *nsubj* relation (between t and r_t; t is the parent).

Note that the equivalences are fundamentally redundant across different orientations. For example, row 2 (which is presented as an instance of orientation *(a)*) can also be presented as an instance of orientation *(b)* with *POS*(s)=*POS*(t)=*noun* and *POS*(r_s)=*POS*(r_t)=*verb*. We avoid such redundancy for compactness. For the same reason, the equivalence of *dobj* and *rcmod* in Figure 2 is shown in the table only as an instance of orientation *(c)* and not as an instance of orientation *(d)* (in general, this is why orientations *(b)* and *(d)* are absent in the table).

We present dependency-based contextual evidence extraction in Algorithm 1. (The Stanford dependency parser (de Marneffe et al., 2006) is used to extract the dependencies.) Given a word pair (s_i, t_j) from the input sentences S and T, it collects contextual evidence (as indexes of r_{s_i} and r_{t_j} with a positive similarity) for each matching row in Table 1. An exact match of the two dependencies is also considered a piece of evidence. Note that Table 1 only considers content word pairs (s_i, t_j) such that *POS*(s_i)=*POS*(t_j), but as 90% of all content word alignments in the MSR alignment *dev* set are within the same lexical category, this is a reasonable set to start with.

3.2.2 Textual Neighborhood

While equivalent dependencies can provide strong contextual evidence, they can not ensure high recall because, a) the ability to accurately extract depen-

Orientation	POS(s,t)	POS(r_s,r_t)	S Dependency Types	T Dependency Types
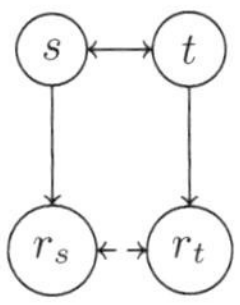 (a)	verb	verb	{purpcl, xcomp}	⟵
		noun	{agent, nsubj, xsubj}	⟵
			{dobj, nsubjpass, rel}	⟵
			{tmod, prep_in, prep_at, prep_on}	⟵
			{iobj, prep_to}	⟵
	noun	verb	{infmod, partmod, rcmod}	⟵
		noun	{pos, nn, prep_of, prep_in, prep_at, prep_for}	⟵
		adjective	{amod, rcmod}	⟵
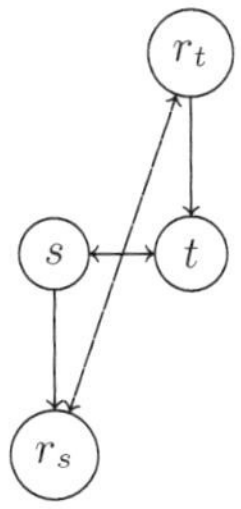 (c)	verb	verb	{conj_and}	⟵
			{conj_or}	⟵
			{conj_nor}	⟵
		noun	{dobj, nsubjpass, rel}	{infmod, partmod, rcmod}
		adjective	{acomp}	{cop, csubj}
	noun	noun	{conj_and}	⟵
			{conj_or}	⟵
			{conj_nor}	⟵
		adjective	{amod, rcmod}	{nsubj}
	adjective	adjective	{conj_and}	⟵
			{conj_or}	⟵
			{conj_nor}	⟵
	adverb	adverb	{conj_and}	⟵
			{conj_or}	⟵
			{conj_nor}	⟵

Table 1: Equivalent dependency structures

Algorithm 1: $depContext(S, T, i, j, EQ)$

Input:

1. S, T: Sentences to be aligned
2. i: Index of a word in S
3. j: Index of a word in T
4. EQ: Dependency type equivalences (Table 1)

Output: $context = \{(k, l)\}$: pairs of word indexes

$context \leftarrow \{(k, l) : wordSim(s_k, t_l) > 0$
$\quad \wedge\, (i, k, \tau_s) \in dependencies(S)$
$\quad \wedge\, (j, l, \tau_t) \in dependencies(T)$
$\quad \wedge\, POS(s_i) = POS(t_j) \wedge POS(s_k) = POS(t_l)$
$\quad \wedge\, (\tau_s = \tau_t$
$\qquad \vee\, (POS(s_i), POS(s_k), \tau_s, \tau_t) \in EQ))\}$

Algorithm 2: $textContext(S, T, i, j, \textsc{Stop})$

Input:

1. S, T: Sentences to be aligned
2. i: Index of a word in S
3. j: Index of a word in T
4. STOP: A set of stop words

Output: $context = \{(k, l)\}$: pairs of word indexes

$C_i \leftarrow \{k : k \in [i-3, i+3] \wedge k \neq i \wedge s_k \notin \textsc{Stop}\}$
$C_j \leftarrow \{l : l \in [j-3, j+3] \wedge l \neq j \wedge t_l \notin \textsc{Stop}\}$
$context \leftarrow C_i \times C_j$

dencies is limited by the accuracy of the parser, and b) we investigate equivalence types for only inter-lexical-category alignment in this study. Therefore we apply an additional model of word context: the textual neighborhood of s in S and t in T.

Extraction of contextual evidence for content words from textual neighborhood is described in Algorithm 2. Like the dependency-based module, it accumulates evidence for each (s_i, t_j) pair by inspecting multiple pairs of neighboring words. But instead of aligning only words within a lexical category, this module also performs inter-category alignment, considering content words within a $(3, 3)$ window of s_i and t_j as neighbors. We implement relational equivalence ($\approx$) here by holding any two positions within the window equally contributive and mutually comparable as sources of contextual evidence.

3.3 The Alignment Algorithm

We now describe each alignment module in the pipeline and their sequence of operation.

3.3.1 Identical Word Sequences

The presence of a common word sequence in S and T is indicative of an (a) identical, and (b) contextually similar word in the other sentence for each word in the sequence. We observe the results of aligning identical words in such sequences of length n containing at least one content word. This simple heuristic demonstrates a high precision ($\approx 97\%$) on the MSR alignment *dev* set for $n \geq 2$, and therefore we consider membership in such sequences as the simplest form of contextual evidence in our system and align all identical word sequence pairs in S and T containing at least one content word. From this point on, we will refer to this module as *wsAlign*.

3.3.2 Named Entities

We align named entities separately to enable the alignment of full and partial mentions (and acronyms) of the same entity. We use the Stanford Named Entity Recognizer (Finkel et al., 2005) to identify named entities in S and T. After aligning the exact term matches, any unmatched term of a partial mention is aligned to all terms in the full mention. The module recognizes only first-letter acronyms and aligns an acronym to all terms in the full mention of the corresponding name.

Since named entities are instances of nouns, named entity alignment is also informed by contextual evidence (which we discuss in the next section), but happens before alignment of other generic content words. Parents (or children) of a named entity are simply the parents (or children) of its head word. We will refer to this module as a method named *neAlign* from this point on.

3.3.3 Content Words

Extraction of contextual evidence for promising content word pairs has already been discussed in Section 3.2, covering both dependency-based context and textual context.

Algorithm 3: $cwDepAlign(S, T, EQ, A_E, w, \text{STOP})$

Input:

1. S, T: Sentences to be aligned
2. EQ: Dependency type equivalences (Table 1)
3. A_E: Already aligned word pair indexes
4. w: Weight of word similarity relative to contextual similarity
5. STOP: A set of stop words

Output: $A = \{(i, j)\}$: word index pairs of aligned words $\{(s_i, t_j)\}$ where $s_i \in S$ and $t_j \in T$

1 $\Psi \leftarrow \varnothing$; $\Lambda_\Psi \leftarrow \varnothing$; $\Phi \leftarrow \varnothing$
2 **for** $s_i \in S, t_j \in T$ **do**
3   **if** $s_i \notin \text{STOP} \wedge \neg\exists t_l : (i, l) \in A_E$
4     $\wedge\, t_j \notin \text{STOP} \wedge \neg\exists s_k : (k, j) \in A_E$
5     $\wedge\, wordSim(s_i, t_j) > 0$ **then**
6         $context \leftarrow depContext(S, T, i, j, EQ)$
7         $contextSim \leftarrow \sum_{(k,l) \in context} wordSim(s_k, t_l)$
8   **if** $contextSim > 0$ **then**
9             $\Psi \leftarrow \Psi \cup \{(i, j)\}$
10             $\Lambda_\Psi(i, j) \leftarrow context$
11             $\Phi(i, j) \leftarrow w * wordSim(s_i, t_j)$
12                 $+ (1 - w) * contextSim$
13 Linearize and sort Ψ in decreasing order of $\Phi(i, j)$
14 $A \leftarrow \varnothing$
15 **for** $(i, j) \in \Psi$ **do**
16   **if** $\neg\exists l : (i, l) \in A$
17     $\wedge \neg\exists k : (k, j) \in A$ **then**
18         $A \leftarrow A \cup \{(i, j)\}$
19   **for** $(k, l) \in \Lambda_\Psi(i, j)$ **do**
20   **if** $\neg\exists q : (k, q) \in A \cup A_E$
21         $\wedge \neg\exists p : (p, l) \in A \cup A_E$ **then**
22             $A \leftarrow A \cup \{(k, l)\}$

Algorithm 3 (*cwDepAlign*) describes the dependency-based alignment process. For each potentially alignable pair (s_i, t_j), the dependency-based context is extracted as described in Algorithm 1, and context similarity is calculated as the sum of the word similarities of the (s_k, t_l) context word pairs (lines 2-7). (The *wordSim* method returns a similarity score in $\{0, ppdbSim, 1\}$.) The alignment score of the (s_i, t_j) pair is then a weighted sum of word and contextual similarity (lines 8-12). (We discuss how the weights are set in Section 3.3.5.) The module then aligns (s_i, t_j) pairs with non-zero evidence in decreasing order of this score (lines 13-18). In addition, it aligns all the pairs that contributed contextual evidence for the (s_i, t_j) alignment (lines 19-22). Note that we implement a one-to-one alignment whereby a word gets aligned at most once within the module.

Algorithm 4 (*cwTextAlign*) presents alignment based on similarities in the textual neighborhood. For each potentially alignable pair (s_i, t_j), Algorithm 2 is used to extract the context, which is a set of neighboring content word pairs (lines 2-7). The contextual similarity is the sum of the similarities of these pairs

Algorithm 4: $cwTextAlign(S, T, A_E, w, \text{STOP})$

Input:

1. S, T: Sentences to be aligned
2. A_E: Existing alignments by word indexes
3. w: Weight of word similarity relative to contextual similarity
4. STOP: A set of stop words

Output: $A = \{(i, j)\}$: word index pairs of aligned words $\{(s_i, t_j)\}$ where $s_i \in S$ and $t_j \in T$

1 $\Psi \leftarrow \varnothing; \Phi \leftarrow \varnothing$
2 **for** $s_i \in S, t_j \in T$ **do**
3   **if** $s_i \notin \text{STOP} \land \neg\exists t_l : (i, l) \in A_E$
4     $\land\, t_j \notin \text{STOP} \land \neg\exists s_k : (k, j) \in A_E$
5     $\land\, wordSim(s_i, t_j) > 0$ **then**
6         $\Psi \leftarrow \Psi \cup \{(i, j)\}$
7         $context \leftarrow textContext(S, T, i, j, \text{STOP})$
8         $contextSim \leftarrow \sum_{(k,l) \in context} wordSim(s_k, t_l)$
9         $\Phi(i, j) \leftarrow w * wordSim(s_i, t_j)$
10             $+ (1 - w) * contextSim$
11 Linearize and sort Ψ in decreasing order of $\Phi(i, j)$
12 $A \leftarrow \varnothing$
13 **for** $(i, j) \in \Psi$ **do**
14   **if** $\neg\exists l : (i, l) \in A$
15     $\land \neg\exists k : (k, j) \in A$ **then**
16         $A \leftarrow A \cup \{(i, j)\}$

(line 8), and the alignment score is a weighted sum of word similarity and contextual similarity (lines 9, 10). The alignment score is then used to make one-to-one word alignment decisions (lines 11-16). Considering textual neighbors as weaker sources of evidence, we do not align the neighbors.

Note that in *cwTextAlign* we also align semantically similar content word pairs (s_i, t_j) with no contextual similarities if no pairs (s_k, t_j) or (s_i, t_l) exist with a higher alignment score. This is a consequence of our observation of the MSR alignment *dev* data, where we find that more often than not content words are inherently sufficiently meaningful to be aligned even in the absence of contextual evidence when there are no competing pairs.

The content word alignment module is thus itself a pipeline of *cwDepAlign* and *cwTextAlign*.

3.3.4 Stop Words

We follow the contextual evidence-based approach to align stop words as well, some of which get aligned as part of word sequence alignment as discussed in Section 3.3.1, and neighbor alignment as discussed in Section 3.3.3. For the rest we utilize dependencies and textual neighborhoods as before, with three adjustments.

Firstly, since stop word alignment is the last module in our pipeline, rather than considering all semantically similar word pairs for contextual similarity, we consider only aligned pairs. Secondly, since many stop words (e.g. determiners, modals) typically demonstrate little variation in the dependencies they engage in, we ignore type equivalences for stop words and implement only exact matching of dependencies. (Stop words in general can participate in equivalent dependencies, but we leave constructing a corresponding mapping for future work.) Finally, for textual neighborhood, we separately check alignments of the left and the right neighbors and aggregate the evidences to determine alignment – again due to the primarily syntactic nature of interaction of stop words with their neighbors.

Thus stop words are also aligned in a sequence of dependency and textual neighborhood-based alignments. We assume two corresponding modules named *swDepAlign* and *swTextAlign*, respectively.

Algorithm 5: $align(S, T, EQ, w, \text{STOP})$

Input:

1. S, T: Sentences to be aligned
2. EQ: Dependency type equivalences (Table 1)
3. w: Weight of word similarity relative to contextual similarity
4. STOP: A set of stop words

Output: $A = \{(i, j)\}$: word index pairs of aligned words $\{(s_i, t_j)\}$ where $s_i \in S$ and $t_j \in T$

$A \leftarrow wsAlign(S, T)$
$A \leftarrow A \cup neAlign(S, T, EQ, A, w)$
$A \leftarrow A \cup cwDepAlign(S, T, EQ, A, w, \text{STOP})$
$A \leftarrow A \cup cwTextAlign(S, T, A, w, \text{STOP})$
$A \leftarrow A \cup swDepAlign(S, T, A, w, \text{STOP})$
$A \leftarrow A \cup swTextAlign(S, T, A, w, \text{STOP})$

3.3.5 The Algorithm

Our full alignment pipeline is shown as the method $align$ in Algorithm 5. Note that the strict order of the alignment modules limits the scope of downstream modules since each such module discards any word that has already been aligned by an earlier module (this is accomplished via the variable A; the corresponding parameter in Algorithms 3 and 4 is A_E).

The rationales behind the specific order of the modules can now be explained: (1) *wsAlign* is a module with relatively higher precision, (2) it is convenient to align named entities before other content words to enable alignment of entity mentions of different lengths, (3) dependency-based evidence was observed to be more reliable (i.e. of higher precision) than textual evidence in the MSR alignment *dev* set, and (4) stop word alignments are dependent on existing content word alignments.

The aligner assumes two free parameters: $ppdbSim$ and w (in Algorithms 3 and 4). To determine their values, we exhaustively search through the two-dimensional space $(ppdbSim, w)$ for $ppdbSim, w \in \{0.1, ..., 0.9, 1\}$ and the combination $(0.9, 0.9)$ yields the best F_1 score for the MSR alignment *dev* set. We use these values for the aligner in all of its subsequent applications.

4 Evaluation

We evaluate the performance of our aligner both intrinsically and extrinsically on multiple corpora.

4.1 Intrinsic Evaluation

The MSR alignment dataset[2] (Brockett, 2007) was designed to train and directly evaluate automated aligners. Three annotators individually aligned words and phrases in 1600 pairs of *premise* and *hypothesis* sentences from the RTE2 challenge data (divided into *dev* and *test* sets, each consisting of 800 sentences). The dataset has subsequently been used to assess several top performing aligners (MacCartney et al., 2008; Thadani and McKeown, 2011; Yao et al., 2013a; Yao et al., 2013b). We use the *test* set for evaluation in the same manner as these studies: (a) we apply majority rule to select from the three sets of annotations for each sentence and discard three-way disagreements, (b) we evaluate only on the *sure* links (word pairs that annotators mentioned should certainly be aligned, as opposed to *possible* links).

We test the generalizability of the aligner by evaluating it, unchanged (i.e. with identical parameter values), on a second alignment corpus: the Edinburgh++[3] (Thadani et al., 2012) corpus. The *test* set consists of 306 pairs; each pair is aligned by at most two annotators and we adopt the random selection policy described in (Thadani et al., 2012) to resolve disagreements.

	System	**P%**	**R%**	**F_1%**	**E%**
MSR	MacCartney et al. (2008)	85.4	85.3	85.3	21.3
	Thadani & McKeown (2011)	89.5	86.2	87.8	33.0
	Yao et al. (2013a)	**93.7**	84.0	88.6	35.3
	Yao et al. (2013b)	92.1	82.8	86.8	29.1
	This Work	**93.7**	**89.8**	**91.7**	**43.8**
EDB++	Yao et al. (2013a)	91.3	82.0	86.4	15.0
	Yao et al. (2013b)	90.4	81.9	85.9	13.7
	This Work	**93.5**	**82.5**	**87.6**	**18.3**

Table 2: Results of intrinsic evaluation on two datasets

Table 2 shows the results. For each corpus, it shows *precision* (% alignments that matched with gold annotations), *recall* (% gold alignments discovered by the aligner), F_1 score and the percentage of sentences that received the exact gold alignments (denoted by E) from the aligner.

On the MSR test set, our aligner shows a 3.1% improvement in F_1 score over the previous best system (Yao et al., 2013a) with a 27.2% error reduction. Importantly, it demonstrates a considerable increase in recall without a loss of precision. The E score also increases as a consequence.

On the Edinburgh++ test set, our system achieves a 1.2% increase in F_1 score (an error reduction of 8.8%) over the previous best system (Yao et al., 2013a), with improvements in both precision and recall. This is a remarkable result that demonstrates the general applicability of the aligner, as no parameter tuning took place.

4.1.1 Ablation Test

We perform a set of ablation tests to assess the importance of the aligner's individual components. Each row of Table 3 beginning with (-) shows a feature excluded from the aligner and two associated sets of metrics, showing the performance of the resulting algorithm on the two alignment corpora.

Without a word similarity module, recall drops as would be expected. Without contextual evidence (word sequences, dependencies and textual neighbors) precision drops considerably and recall also falls. Without dependencies, the aligner still gives

[2]http://www.cs.biu.ac.il/ nlp/files/RTE_2006_Aligned.zip

[3]http://www.ling.ohio-state.edu/~scott/#edinburgh-plusplus

	MSR			EDB++		
Feature	**P%**	**R%**	**F_1%**	**P%**	**R%**	**F_1%**
Original	93.7	89.8	91.7	93.5	82.5	87.6
(-) Word Similarity	95.2	86.3	90.5	95.1	77.3	85.3
(-) Contextual Evidence	81.3	86.0	83.6	86.4	80.6	83.4
(-) Dependencies	94.2	88.8	91.4	93.8	81.3	87.1
(-) Text Neighborhood	85.5	90.4	87.9	90.4	84.3	87.2
(-) Stop Words	94.2	88.3	91.2	92.2	80.0	85.7

Table 3: Ablation test results

state-of-the-art results, which points to the possibility of a very fast yet high-performance aligner. Without evidence from textual neighbors, however, the precision of the aligner suffers badly. Textual neighbors find alignments across different lexical categories, a type of alignment that is currently not supported by our dependency equivalences. Extending the set of dependency equivalences might alleviate this issue. Finally, without stop words (i.e. while aligning content words only) recall drops just a little for each corpus, which is expected as content words form the vast majority of non-identical word alignments.

4.2 Extrinsic Evaluation

We extrinsically evaluate our system on textual similarity identification and paraphrase detection. Here we discuss each task and the results of evaluation.

4.2.1 Semantic Textual Similarity

Given two short input text fragments (commonly sentences), the goal of this task is to identify the degree to which the two fragments are semantically similar. The *SEM 2013 STS task (Agirre et al., 2013) assessed a number of STS systems on four test datasets by comparing their output scores to human annotations. Pearson correlation coefficient with human annotations was computed individually for each test set and a weighted sum of the correlations was used as the final evaluation metric (the weight for each dataset was proportional to its size).

We apply our aligner to the task by aligning each sentence pair and taking the proportion of content words aligned in the two sentences (by normalizing with the harmonic mean of their number of content words) as a proxy of their semantic similarity. Only three of the four STS 2013 datasets are freely available[4] (*headlines*, *OnWN*, and *FNWN*), which we use for our experiments (leaving out the *SMT* dataset).

[4]http://ixa2.si.ehu.es/sts/

System	Correl.%	Rank
Han et al. (2013)	**73.7**	1 (original)
JacanaAlign	46.2	66
This Work	67.2	7

Table 4: Extrinsic evaluation on STS 2013 data

These three sets contain 1500 annotated sentence pairs in total.

Table 4 shows the results. The first row shows the performance of the top system in the task. With a direct application of our aligner (no parameter tuning), our STS algorithm acheives a 67.15% weighted correlation, which would earn it the 7th rank among 90 participating systems. Considering the fact that alignment is one of many components of STS, this result is truly promising.

For comparison, we also evaluate the previous best aligner named JacanaAlign (Yao et al., 2013a) on STS 2013 data (the JacanaAlign public release[5] is used, which is a version of the original aligner with extra lexical resources). We apply three different values derived from its output as proxies of semantic similarity: a) aligned content word proportion, b) the Viterbi decoding score, and c) the normalized decoding score. Of the three, (b) gives the best results, which we show in row 2 of Table 4. Our aligner outperforms JacanaAlign by a large margin.

4.2.2 Paraphrase Identification

The goal of paraphrase identification is to decide if two sentences have the same meaning. The output is a yes/no decision instead of a real-valued similarity score as in STS. We use the MSR paraphrase corpus[6] (4076 *dev* pairs, 1725 *test* pairs) (Dolan et al., 2004) to evaluate our aligner and compare with other aligners. Following earlier work (MacCartney et al., 2008; Yao et al., 2013b), we use a normalized alignment score of the two sentences to make a decision based on a threshold which we set using the *dev* set. Alignments with a higher-than-threshold score are taken to be paraphrases and the rest non-paraphrases.

Again, this is an oversimplified application of the aligner, even more so than in STS, since a small change in linguistic properties of two sentences (e.g. polarity or modality) can turn them into non-

[5]https://code.google.com/p/jacana/

[6]http://research.microsoft.com/en-us/downloads/607d14d9-20cd-47e3-85bc-a2f65cd28042/

System	Acc.%	P%	R%	F_1%
Madnani et al. (2012)	**77.4**	***79.0***	*89.9*	**84.1**
Yao et al. (2013a)	70.0	72.6	88.1	*79.6*
Yao et al. (2013b)	68.1	68.6	**95.8**	*79.9*
This Work	73.4	76.6	86.4	81.2

Table 5: Extrinsic evaluation on MSR paraphrase data

paraphrases despite having a high degree of alignment. So the aligner was not expected to demonstrate state-of-the-art performance, but still it gets close as shown in Table 5. The first column shows the accuracy of each system in classifying the input sentences into one of two classes: *true* (paraphrases) and *false* (non-paraphrases). The rest of the columns show the performance of the system for the true class in terms of precision, recall, and F_1 score. *Italicized* numbers represent scores that were not reported by the authors of the corresponding papers, but have been reconstructed from the reported data (and hence are likely to have small precision errors).

The first row shows the best performance by any system on the test set to the best of our knowledge. The next two rows show the performances of two state-of-the-art aligners (performances of both systems were reported in (Yao et al., 2013b)). The last row shows the performance of our aligner. Although it does worse than the best paraphrase system, it outperforms the other aligners.

5 Discussion

Our experiments reveal that a word aligner based on simple measures of lexical and contextual similarity can demonstrate state-of-the-art accuracy. However, as alignment is frequently a component of larger tasks, high accuracy alone is not always sufficient. Other dimensions of an aligner's usability include speed, consumption of computing resources, replicability, and generalizability to different applications. Our design goals include achieving a balance among such multifarious and conflicting goals.

A speed advantage of our aligner stems from formulating the problem as one-to-one word alignment and thus avoiding an expensive decoding phase. The presence of multiple phases is offset by discarding already aligned words in subsequent phases. The use of PPDB as the only (hashable) word similarity resource helps in reducing latency as well as space requirements. As shown in Section 4.1.1, further speedup could be achieved with only a small performance degradation by considering only the textual neighborhood as source of contextual evidence.

However, the two major goals that we believe the aligner achieves to the greatest extent are replicability and generalizability. The easy replicability of the aligner stems from its use of only basic and frequently used NLP modules (a lemmatizer, a POS tagger, an NER module, and a dependency parser: all available as part of the Stanford CoreNLP suite[7]; we use a Python wrapper[8]) and a single word similarity resource (PPDB).

We experimentally show that the aligner can be successfully applied to different alignment datasets as well as multiple end tasks. We believe a design characteristic that enhances the generalizability of the aligner is its minimal dependence on the MSR alignment training data, which originates from a textual entailment corpus having unique properties such as disparities in the lengths of the input sentences and a directional nature of their relationship (i.e., the premise implying the hypothesis, but not vice versa). A related potential reason is the symmetry of the aligner's output (caused by its assumption of no directionality) – the fact that it outputs the same set of alignments regardless of the order of the input sentences, in contrast to most existing aligners.

Major limitations of the aligner include the inability to align phrases, including multiword expressions. It is incapable of capturing and exploiting long distance dependencies among words (e.g. coreferences). No word similarity resource is perfect and PPDB is no exception, therefore certain word alignments also remain undetected.

6 Conclusions

We show how contextual evidence can be used to construct a monolingual word aligner with certain desired properties, including state-of-the-art accuracy, easy replicability, and high generalizability. Some potential avenues for future work include: allowing phrase-level alignment via phrasal similarity resources (e.g. the phrasal paraphrases of PPDB), including other sources of similarity such as vector space models or WordNet relations, expanding the set

[7]http://nlp.stanford.edu/downloads/corenlp.shtml

[8]https://github.com/dasmith/stanford-corenlp-python

of dependency equivalences and/or using semantic role equivalences, and formulating our alignment algorithm as objective optimization rather than greedy search.

The aligner is available for download at `https://github.com/ma-sultan/monolingual-word-aligner`.

Acknowledgments

This material is based in part upon work supported by the National Science Foundation under Grant Numbers EHR/0835393 and EHR/0835381. Any opinions, findings, and conclusions or recommendations expressed in this material are those of the author(s) and do not necessarily reflect the views of the National Science Foundation.

References

Eneko Agirre, Daniel Cer, Mona Diab, Aitor Gonzalez-Agirre, and Weiwei Guo. 2013. *SEM 2013 shared task: Semantic Textual Similarity. In *Proceedings of the Second Joint Conference on Lexical and Computational Semantics.* Association for Computational Linguistics, 32-43.

Colin Bannard and Chris Callison-Burch. 2005. Paraphrasing with Bilingual Parallel Corpora. In *Proceedings of the 43rd Annual Meeting on Association for Computational Linguistics.* Association for Computational Linguistics, 597-604.

Daniel Bär, Chris Biemann, Iryna Gurevych, and Torsten Zesch. 2012. UKP: computing semantic textual similarity by combining multiple content similarity measures. In *Proceedings of the First Joint Conference on Lexical and Computational Semantics.* Association for Computational Linguistics, 435-440.

Roy Bar-Haim, Ido Dagan, Bill Dolan, Lisa Ferro, Danilo Giampiccolo, Bernardo Magnini, and Idan Szpektor. 2006. The Second PASCAL Recognising Textual Entailment Challenge. In *Proceedings of The Second PASCAL Recognising Textual Entailment Challenge.*

Chris Brockett. 2007. Aligning the RTE 2006 Corpus. Technical Report MSR-TR-2007-77, Microsoft Research.

Nathanael Chambers, Daniel Cer, Trond Grenager, David Hall, Chloe Kiddon, Bill MacCartney, Marie-Catherine de Marneffe, Daniel Ramage, Eric Yeh, and Christopher D Manning. 2007. Learning alignments and leveraging natural logic. In *Proceedings of the ACL-PASCAL Workshop on Textual Entailment and Paraphrasing* Association for Computational Linguistics, 165-170.

Ming-Wei Chang, Dan Goldwasser, Dan Roth, and Vivek Srikumar. 2010. Discriminative Learning over Constrained Latent Representations. In *Proceedings of the 2010 Annual Conference of the North American Chapter of the Association for Computational Linguistics* Association for Computational Linguistics, 429-437.

Dipanjan Das and Noah A. Smith. 2009. Paraphrase Identication as Probabilistic Quasi-Synchronous Recognition. In *Proceedings of the Joint Conference of the 47th Annual Meeting of the ACL and the 4th International Joint Conference on Natural Language Processing of the AFNLP.* Association for Computational Linguistics, 468-476.

Marie-Catherine de Marneffe, Bill MacCartney, and Christopher D. Manning. 2006. Generating Typed Dependency Parses from Phrase Structure Parses. In *Proceedings of the International Conference on Language Resources and Evaluation.* 449-454.

Marie-Catherine de Marneffe and Christopher D. Manning. 2008. Stanford typed dependencies manual. Technical Report, Stanford University.

Bill Dolan, Chris Quirk, and Chris Brockett. 2004. Unsupervised Construction of Large Paraphrase Corpora: Exploiting Massively Parallel News Sources. In *Proceedings of the International Conference on Computational Linguistics.* Association for Computational Linguistics, 350-356.

Jenny Rose Finkel, Trond Grenager, and Christopher Manning. 2005. Incorporating Non-local Information into Information Extraction Systems by Gibbs Sampling. In *Proceedings of the 43rd Annual Meeting of the Association for Computational Linguistics.* Association for Computational Linguistics, 363-370.

Juri Ganitkevitch, Benjamin Van Durme, and Chris Callison-Burch. 2013. PPDB: The Paraphrase Database. In *Proceedings of the 2013 Conference of the North American Chapter of the Association for Computational Linguistics.* Association for Computational Linguistics, 758-764.

Lushan Han, Abhay Kashyap, Tim Finin, James Mayeld, and Jonathan Weese. 2013. UMBC EBIQUITY-CORE: Semantic Textual Similarity Systems. In *Proceedings of the Second Joint Conference on Lexical and Computational Semantics, Volume 1.* Association for Computational Linguistics, 44-52.

Andrew Hickl and Jeremy Bensley. 2007. A Discourse Commitment-Based Framework for Recognizing Textual Entailment. In *Proceedings of the ACL-PASCAL Workshop on Textual Entailment and Paraphrasing.* Association for Computational Linguistics, 171-176.

Andrew Hickl, Jeremy Bensley, John Williams, Kirk Roberts, Bryan Rink, and Ying Shi. 2006. Recognizing Textual Entailment with LCCs GROUNDHOG

System. In *Proceedings of the Second PASCAL Challenges Workshop on Recognizing Textual Entailment.*

Milen Kouylekov and Bernardo Magnini. 2005. Recognizing textual entailment with tree edit distance algorithms. In *Proceedings of the PASCAL Challenges Workshop: Recognising Textual Entailment Challenge* 17-20.

Bill MacCartney, Michel Galley, and Christopher D. Manning. 2008. A Phrase-Based Alignment Model for Natural Language Inference. In *Proceedings of the 2008 Conference on Empirical Methods in Natural Language Processing.* Association for Computational Linguistics, 802-811.

Nitin Madnani, Joel Tetreault, and Martin Chodorow. 2012. Re-examining Machine Translation Metrics for Paraphrase Identification. In *Proceedings of 2012 Conference of the North American Chapter of the Association for Computational Linguistics.* Association for Computational Linguistics, 182-190.

Kapil Thadani and Kathleen McKeown. 2011. Optimal and Syntactically-Informed Decoding for Monolingual Phrase-Based Alignment. In *Proceedings of the 49th Annual Meeting of the Association for Computational Linguistics: Human Language Technologies.* Association for Computational Linguistics, 254-259.

Kapil Thadani, Scott Martin, and Michael White. 2012. A Joint Phrasal and Dependency Model for Paraphrase Alignment. In *Proceedings of COLING 2012: Posters.* 1229-1238.

Kristina Toutanova, Dan Klein, Christopher D. Manning, and Yoram Singer. 2003 Feature-rich Part-of-speech Tagging with a Cyclic Dependency Network In *Proceedings of the 2003 Human Language Technology Conference of the North American Chapter of the Association for Computational Linguistics.* Association for Computational Linguistics, 173-180.

Xuchen Yao, Benjamin Van Durme, Chris Callison-Burch, and Peter Clark. 2013a. A Lightweight and High Performance Monolingual Word Aligner. In *Proceedings of the 51st Annual Meeting of the Association for Computational Linguistics.* Association for Computational Linguistics, 702-707.

Xuchen Yao, Benjamin Van Durme, Chris Callison-Burch, and Peter Clark. 2013b. Semi-Markov Phrase-based Monolingual Alignment. In *Proceedings of the 2013 Conference on Empirical Methods in Natural Language Processing.* Association for Computational Linguistics, 590-600.

Xuchen Yao, Benjamin Van Durme, Chris Callison-Burch, and Peter Clark. 2013c. Answer Extraction as Sequence Tagging with Tree Edit Distance. In *Proceedings of the 2013 Conference of the North American Chapter of the Association for Computational Linguistics.* Association for Computational Linguistics, 858-867.

Entity Linking meets Word Sense Disambiguation: a Unified Approach

Andrea Moro, Alessandro Raganato, Roberto Navigli
Dipartimento di Informatica,
Sapienza Università di Roma,
Viale Regina Elena 295, 00161 Roma, Italy
{moro,navigli}@di.uniroma1.it
ale.raganato@gmail.com

Abstract

Entity Linking (EL) and Word Sense Disambiguation (WSD) both address the lexical ambiguity of language. But while the two tasks are pretty similar, they differ in a fundamental respect: in EL the textual mention can be linked to a named entity which may or may not contain the exact mention, while in WSD there is a perfect match between the word form (better, its lemma) and a suitable word sense.

In this paper we present Babelfy, a unified graph-based approach to EL and WSD based on a loose identification of candidate meanings coupled with a densest subgraph heuristic which selects high-coherence semantic interpretations. Our experiments show state-of-the-art performances on both tasks on 6 different datasets, including a multilingual setting. Babelfy is online at `http://babelfy.org`

1 Introduction

The automatic understanding of the meaning of text has been a major goal of research in computational linguistics and related areas for several decades, with ambitious challenges, such as Machine Reading (Etzioni et al., 2006) and the quest for knowledge (Schubert, 2006). Word Sense Disambiguation (WSD) (Navigli, 2009; Navigli, 2012) is a historical task aimed at assigning meanings to single-word and multi-word occurrences within text, a task which is more alive than ever in the research community.

Recently, the collaborative creation of large semi-structured resources, such as Wikipedia, and knowledge resources built from them (Hovy et al., 2013), such as BabelNet (Navigli and Ponzetto, 2012a), DBpedia (Auer et al., 2007) and YAGO2 (Hoffart et al., 2013), has favoured the emergence of new tasks, such as Entity Linking (EL) (Rao et al., 2013), and opened up new possibilities for tasks such as Named Entity Disambiguation (NED) and Wikification. The aim of EL is to discover mentions of entities within a text and to link them to the most suitable entry in a reference knowledge base. However, in contrast to WSD, a mention may be partial while still being unambiguous thanks to the context. For instance, consider the following sentence:

(1) Thomas and Mario are strikers playing in Munich.

This example makes it clear how intertwined the two tasks of WSD and EL are. In fact, on the one hand, *striker* and *play* are polysemous words which can be disambiguated by selecting the game/soccer playing senses of the two words in a dictionary; on the other hand, *Thomas* and *Mario* are partial mentions which have to be linked to the appropriate entries of a knowledge base, that is, *Thomas Müller* and *Mario Gomez*, two well-known soccer players.

The two main differences between WSD and EL lie, on the one hand, in the kind of inventory used, i.e., dictionary vs. encyclopedia, and, on the other hand, in the assumption that the mention is complete or potentially partial. Notwithstanding these differences, the tasks are similar in nature, in that they both involve the disambiguation of textual fragments according to a reference inventory. However, the research community has so far tackled the two tasks separately, often duplicating efforts and solutions.

In contrast to this trend, research in knowledge acquisition is now heading towards the seamless in-

Transactions of the Association for Computational Linguistics, 2 (2014) 231–244. Action Editor: Noah Smith.
Submitted 9/2013; Revised 1/2014; Published 5/2014.

tegration of encyclopedic and lexicographic knowledge into structured language resources (Hovy et al., 2013), and the main representative of this new direction is undoubtedly BabelNet (Navigli and Ponzetto, 2012a). Given such structured language resources it seems natural to suppose that they might provide a common ground for the two tasks of WSD and EL.

More precisely, in this paper we explore the hypothesis that the lexicographic knowledge used in WSD is also useful for tackling the EL task, and, vice versa, that the encyclopedic information utilized in EL helps disambiguate nominal mentions in a WSD setting. We propose Babelfy, a novel, unified graph-based approach to WSD and EL, which performs two main steps: i) it exploits random walks with restart, and triangles as a support for reweighting the edges of a large semantic network; ii) it uses a densest subgraph heuristic on the available semantic interpretations of the input text to perform a joint disambiguation with both concepts and named entities. Our experiments show the benefits of our synergistic approach on six gold-standard datasets.

2 Related Work

2.1 Word Sense Disambiguation

Word Sense Disambiguation (WSD) is the task of choosing the right sense for a word within a given context. Typical approaches for this task can be classified as i) supervised, ii) knowledge-based, and iii) unsupervised. However, supervised approaches require huge amounts of annotated data (Zhong and Ng, 2010; Shen et al., 2013; Pilehvar and Navigli, 2014), an effort which cannot easily be repeated for new domains and languages, while unsupervised ones suffer from data sparsity and an intrinsic difficulty in their evaluation (Agirre et al., 2006; Brody and Lapata, 2009; Manandhar et al., 2010; Van de Cruys and Apidianaki, 2011; Di Marco and Navigli, 2013). On the other hand, knowledge-based approaches are able to obtain good performance using readily-available structured knowledge (Agirre et al., 2010; Guo and Diab, 2010; Ponzetto and Navigli, 2010; Miller et al., 2012; Agirre et al., 2014). Some of these approaches marginally take into account the structural properties of the knowledge base (Mihalcea, 2005). Other approaches, instead, leverage the structural properties of the knowledge base by exploiting centrality and connectivity measures (Sinha and Mihalcea, 2007; Tsatsaronis et al., 2007; Agirre and Soroa, 2009; Navigli and Lapata, 2010).

One of the key steps of many knowledge-based WSD algorithms is the creation of a graph representing the semantic interpretations of the input text. Two main strategies to build this graph have been proposed: i) exploiting the direct connections, i.e., edges, between the considered sense candidates; ii) populating the graph according to (shortest) paths between them. In our approach we manage to unify these two strategies by automatically creating edges between sense candidates performing Random Walk with Restart (Tong et al., 2006).

The recent upsurge of interest in multilinguality has led to the development of cross-lingual and multilingual approaches to WSD (Lefever and Hoste, 2010; Lefever and Hoste, 2013; Navigli et al., 2013). Multilinguality has been exploited in different ways, e.g., by using parallel corpora to build multilingual contexts (Guo and Diab, 2010; Banea and Mihalcea, 2011; Lefever et al., 2011) or by means of ensemble methods which exploit complementary sense evidence from translations in different languages (Navigli and Ponzetto, 2012b). In this work, we present a novel exploitation of the structural properties of a multilingual semantic network.

2.2 Entity Linking

Entity Linking (Erbs et al., 2011; Rao et al., 2013; Cornolti et al., 2013) encompasses a set of similar tasks, which include Named Entity Disambiguation (NED), that is the task of linking entity mentions in a text to a knowledge base (Bunescu and Pasca, 2006; Cucerzan, 2007), and Wikification, i.e., the automatic annotation of text by linking its relevant fragments of text to the appropriate Wikipedia articles. Mihalcea and Csomai (2007) were the first to tackle the Wikification task. In their approach they disambiguate each word in a sentence independently by exploiting the context in which it occurs. However, this approach is local in that it lacks a collective notion of coherence between the selected Wikipedia pages. To overcome this problem, Cucerzan (2007) introduced a global approach based on the simultaneous disambiguation of all the terms in a text and the use of lexical context to disambiguate the mentions. To maximize the semantic agreement Milne and Witten (2008) introduced the analysis of the semantic relations between the candidate senses and the unambiguous context, i.e., words with a single sense candidate. However, the performance of this algorithm depends heavily on the number of links incident to the target senses and on the availability of unambiguous words within the input text. To overcome this issue a novel class of approaches have been proposed (Kulkarni et al., 2009; Ratinov et al., 2011; Hoffart et al., 2011) that exploit global and local features. However, these systems either rely on a difficult NP-hard formalization of the problem which is infeasible for long text, or exploit popularity measures which are domain-dependent. In contrast, we show that the semantic network structure can be leveraged to obtain state-of-the-art performance by synergistically disambiguating both word senses and named entities at the same time.

Recently, the explosion of on-line social networking services, such as Twitter and Facebook, have contributed to the development of new methods for the efficient disambiguation of short texts (Ferragina and Scaiella, 2010; Hoffart et al., 2012; Böhm et al., 2012). Thanks to a loose candidate identification technique coupled with a densest subgraph heuristic, we show that our approach is particularly suited for short and highly ambiguous text disambiguation.

2.3 The Best of Two Worlds

Our main goal is to bring together the two worlds of WSD and EL. On the one hand, this implies relaxing the constraint of a perfect association between mentions and meanings, which is, instead, assumed in WSD. On the other hand, this relaxation leads to the inherent difficulty of encoding a full-fledged sense inventory for EL. Our solution to this problem is to keep the set of candidate meanings for a given mention as open as possible (see Section 6), so as to enable high recall in linking partial mentions, while providing an effective method for handling this high ambiguity (see Section 7).

A key assumption of our work is that the lexicographic knowledge used in WSD is also useful for tackling the EL task, and vice versa the encyclopedic information utilized in EL helps disambiguate nominal mentions in a WSD setting. We enable the joint treatment of concepts and named entities by enforcing high coherence in our semantic interpretations.

3 WSD and Entity Linking Together

Task. Our task is to disambiguate and link all nominal and named entity mentions occurring within a text. The linking task is performed by associating each mention with the most suitable entry of a given knowledge base.[1]

We point out that our definition is unconstrained in terms of what to link, i.e., unlike Wikification and WSD, we can link overlapping fragments of text. For instance, given the text fragment *Major League Soccer*, we identify and disambiguate several different nominal and entity mentions: *Major League Soccer*, *major league*, *league* and *soccer*. In contrast to EL, we link not only named entity mentions, such as *Major League Soccer*, but also nominal mentions, e.g., *major league*, to their corresponding meanings in the knowledge base.

Babelfy. We provide a unified approach to WSD and entity linking in three steps:

1. Given a lexicalized semantic network, we associate with each vertex, i.e., either concept or named entity, a semantic signature, that is, a set of related vertices (Section 5). This is a preliminary step which needs to be performed only once, independently of the input text.

2. Given a text, we extract all the linkable fragments from this text and, for each of them, list the possible meanings according to the semantic network (Section 6).

3. We create a graph-based semantic interpretation of the whole text by linking the candidate meanings of the extracted fragments using the previously-computed semantic signatures. We then extract a dense subgraph of this representation and select the best candidate meaning for each fragment (Section 7).

4 Semantic Network

Our approach requires the availability of a wide-coverage semantic network which encodes structural and lexical information both of an encyclopedic and of a lexicographic kind. Although in principle any semantic network with these properties

[1]Mentions which are not contained in the reference knowledge base are not taken into account.

could be utilized, in our work we used the BabelNet[2] 1.1.1 semantic network (Navigli and Ponzetto, 2012a) since it is the largest multilingual knowledge base, obtained from the automatic seamless integration of Wikipedia[3] and WordNet (Fellbaum, 1998). We consider BabelNet as a directed multigraph which contains both concepts and named entities as its vertices and a multiset of semantic relations as its edges. We leverage the multilingual lexicalizations of the vertices of BabelNet to identify mentions in the input text. For example, the entity *FC Bayern Munich* can be lexicalized in different languages, e.g., *F.C. Bayern de Múnich* in Spanish, *Die Roten* in English and *Bayern München* in German, among others. As regards semantic relations, the only information we use is that of the end points, i.e., vertices, that these relations connect, while neglecting the relation type.

5 Building Semantic Signatures

One of the major issues affecting both manually-curated and automatically constructed semantic networks is data sparsity. For instance, we calculated that the average number of incident edges is roughly 10 in WordNet, 50 in BabelNet and 80 in YAGO2, to mention a few. Although automatically-built resources typically provide larger amounts of edges, two issues have to be taken into account: concepts which should be related might not be directly connected despite being structurally close within the network, and, vice versa, weakly-related or even unrelated concepts can be erroneously connected by an edge. For instance, in BabelNet we do not have an edge between *playmaker* and *Thomas Müller*, while we have an incorrect edge connecting *FC Bayern Munich* and *Yellow Submarine (song)*. However, this crisp notion of relatedness can be overcome by exploiting the global structure of the semantic network, thereby obtaining a more precise and higher-coverage measure of relatedness. We address this issue in two steps: first, we provide a structural weighting of the network's edges; second, for each vertex we create a set of related vertices using random walks with restart.

[2]http://babelnet.org

[3]http://www.wikipedia.org

Structural weighting. Our first objective is to assign higher weights to edges which are involved in more densely connected areas of the directed network. To this end, inspired by the local clustering coefficient measure (Watts and Strogatz, 1998) and its recent success in Word Sense Induction (Di Marco and Navigli, 2013), we use directed triangles, i.e., directed cycles of length 3, and weight each edge (v, v') by the number of directed triangles it occurs in:

$$weight(v, v') := |\{(v, v', v'') : (v, v'), (v', v''), (v'', v) \in E\}| + 1 \quad (1)$$

We add one to each weight to ensure the highest degree of reachability in the network.

Random Walk with Restart. Our goal is to create a *semantic signature* (i.e., a set of highly related vertices) for each concept and named entity of the semantic network. To do this, we perform a Random Walk with Restart (RWR) (Tong et al., 2006), that is, a stochastic process that starts from an initial vertex of the graph[4] and then, for a fixed number n of steps or until convergence, explores the graph by choosing the next vertex within the current neighborhood or by restarting from the initial vertex with a given, fixed *restart probability* α. For each edge (v, v') in the network, we model the conditional probability $P(v'|v)$ as the normalized weight of the edge:

$$P(v'|v) = \frac{weight(v, v')}{\sum_{v'' \in V} weight(v, v'')}$$

where V is the set of vertices of the semantic network and $weight(v, v')$ is the function defined in Equation 1. We then run the RWR from each vertex v of the semantic network for a fixed number n of steps (we show in Algorithm 1 our RWR pseudocode). We keep track of the encountered vertices using the map $counts$, i.e., we increase the counter associated with vertex v' in $counts$ every time we hit v' during a RWR started from v (see line 11). As a result, we obtain a frequency distribution over the whole set of concepts and entities. To eliminate weakly-related vertices we keep only those items that were hit at least η times (see lines 16–18). Finally, we save the remaining vertices in the set $semSign_v$ which is the semantic signature of v (see line 19).

[4]RWR can be used with an initial set of vertices, however in this paper we use a single initial vertex.

Algorithm 1 Random walk with restart.

```
input: v, the starting vertex;
       α, the restart probability;
       n, the number of steps to be executed;
       P, the transition probabilities;
       η, the frequency threshold.
output: semSign_v, set of related vertices for v.
function RWR(v, α, n, P, η)
    v' := v
    counts := new Map < Synset, Integer >
    while n > 0 do
        if random() > α then
            given the transition probabilities P(·|v')
            of v', choose a random neighbor v''
            v' := v''
            counts[v'] ++
        else
            restart the walk
            v' := v
        n := n − 1
    for each v' in counts.keys() do
        if counts[v'] < η then
            remove v' from counts.keys()
    return semSign_v = counts.keys()
```

The creation of our set of semantic signatures, one for each vertex in the semantic network, is a preliminary step carried out once only before starting processing any input text. We now turn to the candidate identification and disambiguation steps.

6 Candidate Identification

Given a text as input, we apply part-of-speech tagging and identify the set F of all the textual fragments, i.e., all the sequences of words of maximum length five, which contain at least one noun and that are substrings of lexicalizations in BabelNet, i.e., those fragments that can potentially be linked to an entry in BabelNet. For each textual fragment $f \in F$, i.e., a single- or multi-word expression of the input text, we look up the semantic network for candidate meanings, i.e., vertices that contain f or, only for named entities, a superstring of f as their lexicalization. For instance, for sentence (1) in the introduction, we identify the following textual fragments: *Thomas*, *Mario*, *strikers*, *Munich*. This output is obtained thanks to our loose candidate identification routine, i.e., based on superstring matching instead of exact matching, which, for instance, enables us to recognize the right candidate *Mario Gomez* for the mention *Mario* even if this named entity does not have *Mario* as one of its lexicalizations (for an analysis of the impact of this routine against the exact matching approach see the discussion in Section 9).

Moreover, as we stated in Section 3, we allow overlapping fragments, e.g., for *major league* we recognize *league* and *major league*. We denote with $cand(f)$ the set of all the candidate meanings of fragment f. For instance, for the noun *league* we have that $cand(league)$ contains among others the *sport* word sense and the *TV series* named entity.

7 Candidate Disambiguation

Semantic interpretation graph. After the identification of fragments (F) and their candidate meanings ($cand(\cdot)$), we create a directed graph $G_I = (V_I, E_I)$ of the semantic interpretations of the input text. We show the pseudocode in Algorithm 2. V_I contains all the candidate meanings of all fragments, that is, $V_I := \{(v, f) : v \in cand(f), f \in F\}$, where f is a fragment of the input text and v is a candidate Babel synset that has a lexicalization which is equal to or is a superstring of f (see lines 4–8). The set of edges E_I connects related meanings and is populated as follows: we add an edge from (v, f) to (v', f') if and only if $f \neq f'$ and $v' \in semSign_v$ (see lines 9–11). In other words, we connect two candidate meanings of different fragments if one is in the semantic signature of the other. For instance, we add an edge between (*Mario Gomez, Mario*) and (*Thomas Müller, Thomas*), while we do not add one between (*Mario Gomez, Mario*) and (*Mario Basler, Mario*) since these are two candidate meanings of the same fragment, i.e., *Mario*. In Figure 1, we show an excerpt of our graph for sentence (1).

At this point we have a graph-based representation of all the possible interpretations of the input text. In order to drastically reduce the degree of ambiguity while keeping the interpretation coherence as high as possible, we apply a novel densest subgraph heuristic (see line 12), whose description we defer to the next paragraph. The result is a subgraph which contains those semantic interpretations that are most coherent to each other. However, this subgraph might still contain multiple interpretations for the same fragment, and even unambiguous fragments which are not correct. Therefore, the final

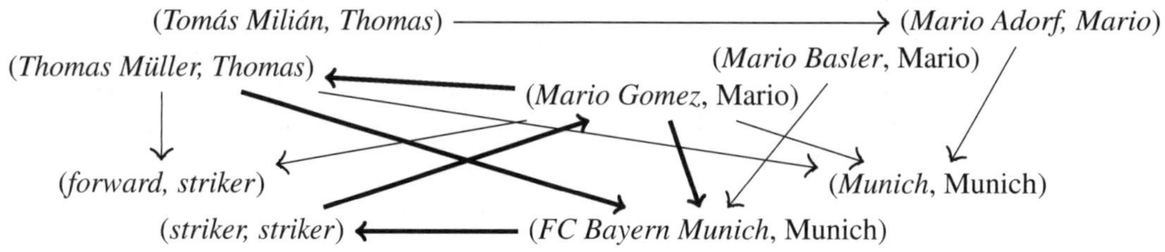

Figure 1: An excerpt of the semantic interpretation graph automatically built for the sentence *Thomas and Mario are strikers playing in Munich* (the edges connecting the correct meanings are in bold).

step is the selection of the most suitable candidate meaning for each fragment f given a threshold θ to discard semantically unrelated candidate meanings. We score each meaning $v \in cand(f)$ with its normalized weighted degree[5] in the densest subgraph:

$$score((v,f)) = \frac{w_{(v,f)} \cdot deg((v,f))}{\sum\limits_{v' \in cand(f)} w_{(v',f)} \cdot deg((v',f))} \quad (2)$$

where $w_{(v,f)}$ is the fraction of fragments the candidate meaning v connects to:

$$w_{(v,f)} := \frac{\begin{array}{r} |\{f' \in F : \exists v' \; s.t. \; ((v,f),(v',f')) \\ \text{or } ((v',f'),(v,f)) \in E_I\}| \end{array}}{|F| - 1}$$

The rationale behind this scoring function is to take into account both the semantic coherence, using a graph centrality measure among the candidate meanings, and the lexical coherence, in terms of the number of fragments a candidate relates to.

Finally, we link each f to the highest ranking candidate meaning $v^\star$ if $score((v^\star, f)) \geq \theta$, where θ is a fixed threshold (see lines 14–18 of Algorithm 2). For instance, in sentence (1) and for the fragment *Mario* we select *Mario Gomez* as our final candidate meaning and link it to the fragment.

Linking by densest subgraph. We now illustrate our novel densest subgraph heuristic, used in line 12 of Algorithm 2, for reducing the level of ambiguity of the initial semantic interpretation graph G_I. The main idea here is that the most suitable meanings of each text fragment will belong to the densest area of the graph. For instance, in Figure 1 the (candidate, fragment) pairs *(Thomas Müller, Thomas), (Mario Gomez, Mario), (striker, striker)* and *(FC Bayern Munich, Munich)* form a dense subgraph supporting their relevance for sentence (1).

Algorithm 2 Candidate Disambiguation.

1: **input:** F, the fragments in the input text;
  $semSign$, the semantic signatures;
  μ, ambiguity level to be reached;
  $cand$, fragments to candidate meanings.
2: **output:** $selected$, disambiguated fragments.
3: **function** DISAMB($F, semSign, \mu, cand$)
4:   $V_I := \emptyset; E_I := \emptyset$
5:   $G_I := (V_I, E_I)$
6:   **for each** fragment $f \in F$ **do**
7:     **for each** candidate $v \in cand(f)$ **do**
8:       $V_I := V_I \cup \{(v, f)\}$
9:   **for each** $((v,f),(v',f')) \in V_I \times V_I$ **do**
10:     **if** $f \neq f'$ **and** $v' \in semSign_v$ **then**
11:       $E_I := E_I \cup \{((v,f),(v',f'))\}$
12:   $G_I^\star :=$ DENSSUB($F, cand, G_I, \mu$)
13:   $selected :=$ **new** $Map < String, Synset >$
14:   **for each** $f \in F \; s.t. \; \exists (v,f) \in V_I^\star$ **do**
15:     $cand^\star(f) := \{v : (v,f) \in V_I^\star\}$
16:     $v^\star := \arg\max_{v \in cand^\star(f)} score((v,f))$
17:     **if** $score((v^\star, f)) \geq \theta$ **then**
18:       $selected(f) := v^\star$
19:   **return** $selected$

The problem of identifying the densest subgraph of size at least k is NP-hard (Feige et al., 1999). Therefore, we define a heuristic for k-partite graphs inspired by a 2-approximation greedy algorithm for arbitrary graphs (Charikar, 2000; Khuller and Saha, 2009). Our adapted strategy for selecting a dense subgraph of G_I is based on the iterative removal of low-coherence vertices, i.e., fragment interpretations. We show the pseudocode in Algorithm 3.

We start with the initial graph $G_I^{(0)}$ at step $t = 0$ (see line 5). For each step t (lines 7–16), first, we identify the most ambiguous fragment f_{max}, i.e., the one with the maximum number of candidate mean-

[5] We denote with $deg(v)$ the overall number of incoming and outgoing edges, i.e., $deg(v) := deg^+(v) + deg^-(v)$.

Algorithm 3 Densest Subgraph.

1: **input:** F, the set of all fragments in the input text;
 $cand$, from fragments to candidate meanings;
 $G_I^{(0)}$, the full semantic interpretation graph;
 μ, ambiguity level to be reached.
2: **output:** $G_I^\star$, a dense subgraph.
3: **function** DENSSUB($F, cand, G_I^{(0)}, \mu$)
4: $t := 0$
5: $G_I^\star := G_I^{(0)}$
6: **while** true **do**
7: $f_{max} := \arg\max_{f \in F} |\{v : \exists(v, f) \in V_I^{(t)}\}|$
8: **if** $|\{v : \exists(v, f_{max}) \in V_I^{(t)}\}| \leq \mu$ **then**
9: **break**;
10: $v_{min} := \underset{v \in cand(f_{max})}{\text{argmin}} \; score((v, f_{max}))$
11: $V_I^{(t+1)} := V_I^{(t)} \setminus \{(v_{min}, f_{max})\}$
12: $E_I^{(t+1)} := E_I^{(t)} \cap V_I^{(t+1)} \times V_I^{(t+1)}$
13: $G_I^{(t+1)} := (V_I^{(t+1)}, E_I^{(t+1)})$
14: **if** $avgdeg(G_I^{(t+1)}) > avgdeg(G_I^\star)$ **then**
15: $G_I^\star := G_I^{(t+1)}$
16: $t := t + 1$
17: **return** $G_I^\star$

ings in the graph (see line 7). Next, we discard the weakest interpretation of the current fragment f_{max}. To do so, we determine the lexical and semantic coherence of each candidate meaning (v, f_{max}) using Formula 2 (see line 10). We then remove from our graph $G_I^{(t)}$ the lowest-coherence vertex (v_{min}, f_{max}), i.e., the one whose score is minimum (see lines 11–13). For instance, in Figure 1, f_{max} is the fragment *Mario* and we have: $score$((*Mario Gomez, Mario*)) $\propto \frac{3}{3} \cdot 5 = 5$, $score$((*Mario Basler, Mario*)) $\propto \frac{1}{3} \cdot 1 = 0.\overline{3}$ and $score$((*Mario Adorf, Mario*)) $\propto \frac{2}{3} \cdot 2 = 1.\overline{3}$, so we remove (*Mario Basler, Mario*) from the graph since its score is minimum.

We then move to the next step, i.e., we set $t := t + 1$ (see line 16) and repeat the low-coherence removal step. We stop when the number of remaining candidates for each fragment is below a threshold μ, i.e., $|\{v : \exists(v, f) \in V_I^{(t)}\}| \leq \mu \; \forall f \in F$ (see lines 8–9). During each iteration step t we compute the average degree of the current graph $G_I^{(t)}$, i.e., $avgdeg(G_I^{(t)}) = \frac{2|E_I^{(t)}|}{|V_I^{(t)}|}$. Finally, we select as the densest subgraph of the initial semantic interpretation graph G_I the graph $G_I^\star$ that maximizes the average degree (see lines 14–15).

8 Experimental Setup

Datasets. We carried out our experiments on six datasets, four for WSD and two for EL:

- The SemEval-2013 task 12 dataset for multilingual WSD (Navigli et al., 2013), which consists of 13 documents in different domains, available in 5 languages. For each language, all noun occurrences were annotated using BabelNet, thereby providing Wikipedia and WordNet annotations wherever applicable. The number of mentions to be disambiguated roughly ranges from 1K to 2K per language in the different setups.
- The SemEval-2007 task 7 dataset for coarse-grained English all-words WSD (Navigli et al., 2007). We take into account only nominal mentions obtaining a dataset containing 1107 nouns to be disambiguated using WordNet.
- The SemEval-2007 task 17 dataset for fine-grained English all-words WSD (Pradhan et al., 2007). We considered only nominal mentions resulting in 158 nouns annotated with WordNet synsets.
- The Senseval-3 dataset for English all-words WSD (Snyder and Palmer, 2004), which contains 899 nouns to be disambiguated using WordNet.
- KORE50 (Hoffart et al., 2012), which consists of 50 short English sentences (mean length of 14 words) with a total number of 144 mentions manually annotated using YAGO2, for which a Wikipedia mapping is available. This dataset was built with the idea of testing against a high level of ambiguity for the EL task.
- AIDA-CoNLL[6] (Hoffart et al., 2011), which consists of 1392 English articles, for a total of roughly 35K named entity mentions annotated with YAGO concepts separated in development, training and test sets.

We exploited the POS tags already available in the SemEval and Senseval datasets, while we used the Stanford POS tagger (Toutanova et al., 2003) for the English sentences in the last two datasets.

[6] We used AIDA-CoNLL as it is the most recent and largest available dataset for EL (Hachey et al., 2013). The TAC KBP datasets are available only to participants.

Parameters. We fixed the parameters of RWR (Section 5) to the values $\alpha = .85$, $\eta = 100$ and $n = 1M$ which maximize F1 on a manually created tuning set made up of 10 gold-standard semantic signatures. We tuned our two disambiguation parameters $\mu = 10$ and $\theta = 0.8$ by optimizing $F1$ on the trial dataset of the SemEval-2013 task on multilingual WSD (Navigli et al., 2013). We used the same parameters on all the other WSD datasets. As for EL, we used the training part of AIDA-CoNLL (Hoffart et al., 2011) to set $\mu = 5$ and $\theta = 0.0$.

8.1 Systems

Multilingual WSD. We evaluated our system on the SemEval-2013 task 12 by comparing it with the participating systems:

- UMCC-DLSI (Gutiérrez et al., 2013) a state-of-the-art Personalized PageRank-based approach that exploits the integration of different sources of knowledge, such as WordNet Domains/Affect (Strapparava and Valitutti, 2004), SUMO (Zouaq et al., 2009) and the eXtended WordNet (Mihalcea and Moldovan, 2001);
- DAEBAK! (Manion and Sainudiin, 2013) which performs WSD on the basis of peripheral diversity within subgraphs of BabelNet;
- GETALP (Schwab et al., 2013) which uses an Ant Colony Optimization technique together with the classical measure of Lesk (1986).

We also compared with UKB w2w (Agirre and Soroa, 2009), a state-of-the-art approach for knowledge-based WSD, based on Personalized PageRank (Haveliwala, 2002). We used the same mapping from words to senses that we used in our approach, default parameters[7] and BabelNet as the input graph. Moreover, we compared our system with IMS (Zhong and Ng, 2010), a state-of-the-art supervised English WSD system which uses an SVM trained on sense-annotated corpora, such as SemCor (Miller et al., 1993) and DSO (Ng and Lee, 1996), among others. We used the IMS model out-of-the-box with Most Frequent Sense (MFS) as backoff routine since the model obtained using the task trial data performed worse.

We followed the original task formulation and evaluated the synsets in three different settings, i.e., when using BabelNet senses, Wikipedia senses and WordNet senses, thanks to BabelNet being a superset of the other two inventories. We ran our system on a document-by-document basis, i.e., disambiguating each document at once, so as to test its effectiveness on long coherent texts. Performance was calculated in terms of F1 score. We also compared the systems with the MFS baseline computed for the three inventories (Navigli et al., 2013).

Coarse-grained WSD. For the SemEval-2007 task 7 we compared our system with the two top-ranked approaches, i.e., NUS-PT (Chan et al., 2007) and UoR-SSI (Navigli, 2008), which respectively exploited parallel texts and enriched semantic paths in a semantic network, the previously described UKB w2w system,[8] a knowledge-based WSD approach (Ponzetto and Navigli, 2010) which exploits an automatic extension of WordNet, and, as baseline, the MFS.

Fine-grained WSD. For the remaining fine-grained WSD datasets, i.e., Senseval-3 and SemEval-2007 task 17, we compared our approach with the previously described state-of-the-art systems UKB and IMS, and, as baseline, the MFS.

KORE50 and AIDA-CoNLL. For the KORE50 and AIDA-CoNLL datasets we compared our system with six approaches, including state-of-the-art ones (Hoffart et al., 2012; Cornolti et al., 2013):

- MW, i.e., the Normalized Google Distance as defined by Milne and Witten (2008);
- KPCS (Hoffart et al., 2012), which calculates a Mutual Information weighted vector of keyphrases for each candidate and then uses the cosine similarity to obtain candidates' scores;
- KORE and its variants KORE_{LSH-G} and KORE_{LSH-F} (Hoffart et al., 2012), based on similarity measures that exploit the overlap between phrases associated with the considered entities (KORE) and a hashing technique to reduce the space needed by the keyphrases associated with the entities (LSH-G, LSH-F);
- Tagme 2.0[9] (Ferragina and Scaiella, 2012) which uses the relatedness measure defined

[7] ./ukb_wsd -D dict.txt -K kb.bin --ppr_w2w ctx.txt

[8] We report the results as given by Agirre et al. (2014).

[9] We used the out-of-the-box RESTful API available at http://tagme.di.unipi.it

	Sens3	Sem07	SemEval-2013 English			French		German		Italian		Spanish	
System	WN	WN	WN	Wiki	BN	Wiki	BN	Wiki	BN	Wiki	BN	Wiki	BN
Babelfy	68.3	62.7	**65.9**	**87.4**	**69.2**	**71.6**	$\star$56.9	81.6	**69.4**	**84.3**	66.6	**83.8**	69.5
IMS	**71.2**	63.3	65.7	–	–	–	–	–	–	–	–	–	–
UKB w2w	$\star$65.3	$\star$56.0	61.3	–	60.8	–	**60.8**	–	66.2	–	**67.3**	–	70.0
UMCC-DLSI	–	–	64.7	54.8	68.5	$\star$60.5	60.5	$\star$58.1	62.8	$\star$58.3	65.8	$\star$61.0	**71.0**
DAEBAK!	–	–	–	–	60.4	–	53.8	–	59.1	–	$\star$61.3	–	60.0
GETALP-BN	–	–	51.4	–	58.3	–	48.3	–	52.3	–	52.8	–	57.8
MFS	70.3	**65.8**	$\star$63.0	$\star$80.3	$\star$66.5	69.4	45.3	**83.1**	$\star$67.4	82.3	57.5	82.4	$\star$64.4
Babelfy unif. weights	67.0	65.2	65.0	87.0	68.5	71.9	57.2	81.2	69.8	83.7	66.8	83.8	70.8
Babelfy w/o dens. sub.	68.3	63.3	65.4	87.3	68.7	71.6	57.0	81.7	69.1	84.4	66.5	83.9	69.5
Babelfy only concepts	68.2	62.7	65.5	83.0	68.7	70.2	56.6	79.3	69.3	83.0	66.3	84.0	69.7
Babelfy on sentences	66.0	65.2	63.5	84.0	67.1	70.7	53.6	82.3	68.1	83.8	64.2	83.5	68.7

Table 1: F1 scores (percentages) of the participating systems of SemEval-2013 task 12 together with MFS, UKB w2w, IMS, our system and its ablated versions on the Senseval-3, SemEval-2007 task 17 and SemEval-2013 datasets. The first system which has a statistically significant difference from the top system is marked with $\star$ (χ^2, $p < 0.05$).

by Milne and Witten (2008) weighted with the commonness of a sense together with the keyphraseness measure defined by Mihalcea and Csomai (2007) to exploit the context around the target word;

- Illinois Wikifier[10] (Cheng and Roth, 2013) which combines local features, such as commonness and TF-IDF between mentions and Wikipedia pages, with global coherence features based on Wikipedia links and relational inference;
- DBpedia Spotlight[11] (Mendes et al., 2011) which uses LingPipe's string matching algorithm implementation together with a weighted cosine similarity measure to recognize and disambiguate mentions.

We also compared with UKB w2w, introduced above. Note that we could not use supervised systems, as the training data of AIDA-CoNLL covers less than half of the mentions used in the testing part and less than 10% of the entities considered in KORE50. To enable a fair comparison, we ran our system by restricting the BabelNet sense inventory of the target mentions to the English Wikipedia. As is customary in the literature, we calculated the systems' accuracy for both Entity Linking datasets.

[10]We used the out-of-the-box Java API available from http://cogcomp.cs.illinois.edu/page/download_view/Wikifier

[11]We used the 2011 version of DBpedia Spotlight as it obtains better scores on the considered datasets in comparison to the new version (Daiber et al., 2013). We used the out-of-the-box RESTful API available at http://spotlight.dbpedia.org

9 Results

Multilingual WSD. In Table 1 we show the F1 performance on the SemEval-2013 task 12 for the three setups: WordNet, Wikipedia and BabelNet. Using BabelNet we surpass all systems on English and German and obtain performance comparable with the best systems on two other languages (UKB on Italian and UMCC-DLSI on Spanish). Using the WordNet sense inventory, our results are on a par with the best system, i.e., IMS. On Wikipedia our results range between 71.6% (French) and 87.4% F1 (English), i.e., more than 10 points higher than the current state of the art (UMCC-DLSI) in all 5 languages. As for the MFS baseline, which is known to be very competitive in WSD (Navigli, 2009), we beat it in all setups except for German on Wikipedia. Interestingly, we surpass the WordNet MFS by 2.9 points, a significant result for a knowledge-based system (see also (Pilehvar and Navigli, 2014)).

Coarse- and fine-grained WSD. In Table 2, we show the results of the systems on the SemEval-2007 coarse-grained WSD dataset. As can be seen, we obtain the second best result after Ponzetto and Navigli (2010). In Table 1 (first two columns), we show the results of IMS and UKB on the Senseval-3 and SemEval-2007 task 17 datasets. We rank second on both datasets after IMS. However, the differences are not statistically significant. Moreover, Agirre et al. (2014, Table 5) note that using WordNet 3.0, instead of 1.7 or 2.1, to annotate these datasets can cause a more than one percent drop in performance.

System	F1
(Ponzetto and Navigli, 2010)	**85.5**
Babelfy	84.6
UoR-SSI	84.1
UKB w2w	83.6
NUS-PT	⋆82.3
MFS	77.4
Babelfy unif. weights	85.7
Babelfy w/o dens. sub.	84.9
Babelfy only concepts	85.3
Babelfy on sentences	82.3

Table 2: F1 score (percentages) on the SemEval-2007 task 7. The first system which has a statistically significant difference from the top system is marked with ⋆ (χ^2, $p < 0.05$).

System	KORE50	CoNLL
Babelfy	**71.5**	82.1
KORE-LSH-G	64.6	81.8
KORE	63.9	⋆80.7
MW	⋆57.6	**82.3**
Tagme	56.3	70.1
KPCS	55.6	82.2
KORE-LSH-F	53.2	81.2
UKB w2w (on BabelNet)	52.1	71.8
Illinois Wikifier	41.7	72.4
DBpedia Spotlight	35.4	34.0
Babelfy unif. weights	69.4	81.7
Babelfy w/o dens. sub.	62.5	78.1
Babelfy only NE	68.1	78.8

Table 3: Accuracy (percentages) of state-of-the-art EL systems and our system on KORE50 and AIDA-CoNLL. The first system with a statistically significant difference from the top system is marked with ⋆ (χ^2, $p < 0.05$).

Entity Linking. In Table 3 we show the results on the two Entity Linking datasets, i.e., KORE50 and AIDA-CoNLL. Our system outperforms all other approaches, with KORE-LSH-G getting closest, and Tagme and Wikifier lagging behind on the KORE50 dataset. For the AIDA-CoNLL dataset we obtain the third best performance after MW and KPCS, however the difference is not statistically significant.

We note the low performance of DBpedia Spotlight which, even if it achieves almost 100% precision on the identified mentions on both datasets, suffers from low recall due to its candidate identification step, confirming previous evaluations (Derczynski et al., 2013; Hakimov et al., 2012; Ludwig and Sack, 2011). This problem becomes even more accentuated in the latest version of this system (Daiber et al., 2013). Finally, UKB using BabelNet obtains low performance on EL, i.e., 19.4-10.5 points below the state of the art. This result is discussed below.

Discussion. The results obtained by UKB show that the high performance of our unified approach to EL and WSD is not just a mere artifact of the use of a rich multilingual semantic network, that is, BabelNet. In other words, it is not true that any graph-based algorithm could be applied to perform both EL and WSD at the same time equally well. This also shows that BabelNet by itself is not sufficient for achieving high performances for both tasks and that, instead, an appropriate processing of the structural and lexical information of the semantic network is needed. A manual analysis revealed that the main cause of error for UKB in the EL setup stems from its inability to enforce high coherence, e.g., by jointly disambiguating all the words, which is instead needed when considering the high level of ambiguity that we have in our semantic interpretation graph (Cucerzan, 2007). For instance, for sentence (1) in the introduction, UKB disambiguates *Thomas* as a cricket player and *Mario* as the popular video game rather than the two well-known soccer players, and *Munich* as the German city, rather than the soccer team in which they play. Our approach, instead, by enforcing highly coherent semantic interpretations, correctly identifies all the soccer-related entities.

In order to determine the need of our loose candidate identification heuristic (see Section 6), we compared the percentage of times a candidate set contains the correct entity against that obtained by an exact string matching between the mention and the sense inventory. On KORE50, our heuristic retrieves the correct entity 98.6% of the time vs. 42.4% when exact matching is used. This demonstrates the inadequacy of exact matching for EL, and the need for a comprehensive sense inventory, as is done in our approach.

We also performed different ablation tests by experimenting with the following variants of our system (reported at the bottom of Tables 1, 2 and 3):

- Babelfy using uniform distribution during the RWR to obtain the concepts' semantic signatures; this test assesses the impact of our weighting and edge creation strategy.

- Babelfy without performing the densest subgraph heuristic, i.e., when line 12 in Algorithm 2 is $G_I^\star = G_I$, so as to verify the impact of identifying the most coherent interpretations.
- Babelfy applied to the BabelNet subgraph induced by the entire set of named entity vertices, for the EL task, and that induced by word senses only, for the WSD task; this test aims to stress the impact of our unified approach.
- Babelfy applied on sentences instead of on whole documents.

The component which has a smaller impact on the performance is our triangle-based weighting scheme. The main exception is on the smallest dataset, i.e., SemEval-2007 task 17, for which this version attains an improvement of 2.5 percentage points.

Babelfy without the densest subgraph algorithm is the version which attains the lowest performances on the EL task, with a 9% performance drop on the KORE50 dataset, showing the need for a specially designed approach to cope with the high level of ambiguity that is encountered on this task. On the other hand, in the WSD datasets this version attains almost the same results as the full version, due to the lower number of candidate word senses.

Babelfy applied on sentences instead of on whole documents shows a lower performance, confirming the significance of higher semantic coherence on whole documents (notwithstanding the two exceptions on the SemEval-2007 task 17 and on the SemEval-2013 German Wikipedia datasets).

Finally, the version in which we restrict our system to named entities only (for EL) and concepts only (for WSD) consistently obtains lower results (notwithstanding the three exceptions on the Spanish SemEval-2013 task 12 using BabelNet and Wikipedia, and on the SemEval 2007 coarse-grained task). This highlights the benefit of our joint use of lexicographic and encyclopedic structured knowledge, on each of the two tasks. The 3.4% performance drop attained on KORE50 is of particular interest, since this dataset aims at testing performance on highly ambiguous mentions within short sentences. This indicates that the semantic analysis of small contexts can be improved by leveraging the coherence between concepts and named entities.

10 Conclusion

In this paper we presented Babelfy, a novel, integrated approach to Entity Linking and Word Sense Disambiguation, available at `http://babelfy.org`. Our joint solution is based on three key steps: i) the automatic creation of semantic signatures, i.e., related concepts and named entities, for each node in the reference semantic network; ii) the unconstrained identification of candidate meanings for all possible textual fragments; iii) linking based on a high-coherence densest subgraph algorithm. We used BabelNet 1.1.1 as our multilingual semantic network.

Our graph-based approach exploits the semantic network structure to its advantage: two key features of BabelNet, that is, its multilinguality and its integration of lexicographic and encyclopedic knowledge, make it possible to run our general, unified approach on the two tasks of Entity Linking and WSD in any of the languages covered by the semantic network. However, we also demonstrated that BabelNet in itself does not lead to state-of-the-art accuracy on both tasks, even when used in conjunction with a high-performance graph-based algorithm like Personalized PageRank. This shows the need for our novel unified approach to EL and WSD.

At the core of our approach lies the effective treatment of the high degree of ambiguity of partial textual mentions by means of a 2-approximation algorithm for the densest subgraph problem, which enables us to output a semantic interpretation of the input text with drastically reduced ambiguity, as was previously done with SSI (Navigli, 2008).

Our experiments on six gold-standard datasets show the state-of-the-art performance of our approach, as well as its robustness across languages. Our evaluation also demonstrates that our approach fares well both on long texts, such as those of the WSD tasks, and short and highly-ambiguous sentences, such as the ones in KORE50. Finally, ablation tests and further analysis demonstrate that each component of our system is needed to contribute state-of-the-art performances on both EL and WSD.

As future work, we plan to use Babelfy for information extraction, where semantics is taking the lead (Moro and Navigli, 2013), and for the validation of semantic annotations (Vannella et al., 2014).

Acknowledgments

The authors gratefully acknowledge the support of the ERC Starting Grant MultiJEDI No. 259234.

References

Eneko Agirre and Aitor Soroa. 2009. Personalizing PageRank for Word Sense Disambiguation. In *Proc. of EACL*, pages 33–41.

Eneko Agirre, David Martínez, Oier López de Lacalle, and Aitor Soroa. 2006. Two graph-based algorithms for state-of-the-art WSD. In *Proc. of EMNLP*, pages 585–593.

Eneko Agirre, Aitor Soroa, and Mark Stevenson. 2010. Graph-based Word Sense Disambiguation of biomedical documents. *Bioinformatics*, 26(22):2889–2896.

Eneko Agirre, Oier Lopez de Lacalle, and Aitor Soroa. 2014. Random Walks for Knowledge-Based Word Sense Disambiguation. *Computational Linguistics*, 40(1):57–84.

Sören Auer, Christian Bizer, Georgi Kobilarov, Jens Lehmann, Richard Cyganiak, and Zachary Ives. 2007. DBpedia: A Nucleus for a Web of Open Data. In *Proc. of ISWC/ASWC*, pages 722–735.

Carmen Banea and Rada Mihalcea. 2011. Word Sense Disambiguation with multilingual features. In *Proc. of IWCS*, pages 25–34.

Christoph Böhm, Gerard de Melo, Felix Naumann, and Gerhard Weikum. 2012. LINDA: distributed web-of-data-scale entity matching. In *Proc. of CIKM*, pages 2104–2108.

Samuel Brody and Mirella Lapata. 2009. Bayesian Word Sense Induction. In *Proc. of EACL*, pages 103–111.

Razvan C. Bunescu and Marius Pasca. 2006. Using encyclopedic knowledge for named entity disambiguation. In *Proc. of EACL*, pages 9–16.

Yee Seng Chan, Hwee Tou Ng, and Zhi Zhong. 2007. NUS-PT: Exploiting Parallel Texts for Word Sense Disambiguation in the English All-Words Tasks. In *Proc. of SemEval-2007*, pages 253–256.

Moses Charikar. 2000. Greedy approximation algorithms for finding dense components in a graph. In *Proc. of APPROX*, pages 84–95.

Xiao Cheng and Dan Roth. 2013. Relational Inference for Wikification. In *Proc. of EMNLP*, pages 1787–1796.

Marco Cornolti, Paolo Ferragina, and Massimiliano Ciaramita. 2013. A framework for benchmarking entity-annotation systems. In *Proc. of WWW*, pages 249–260.

Silviu Cucerzan. 2007. Large-Scale Named Entity Disambiguation Based on Wikipedia Data. In *Proc. of EMNLP-CoNLL*, pages 708–716.

Joachim Daiber, Max Jakob, Chris Hokamp, and Pablo N. Mendes. 2013. Improving efficiency and accuracy in multilingual entity extraction. In *Proc. of I-Semantics*, pages 121–124.

Leon Derczynski, Diana Maynard, Niraj Aswani, and Kalina Bontcheva. 2013. Microblog-genre noise and impact on semantic annotation accuracy. In *Proc. of Hypertext*, pages 21–30.

Antonio Di Marco and Roberto Navigli. 2013. Clustering and Diversifying Web Search Results with Graph-Based Word Sense Induction. *Computational Linguistics*, 39(3):709–754.

Nicolai Erbs, Torsten Zesch, and Iryna Gurevych. 2011. Link discovery: A comprehensive analysis. In *Proc. of ICSC*, pages 83–86.

Oren Etzioni, Michele Banko, and Michael J Cafarella. 2006. Machine Reading. In *Proc. of AAAI*, pages 1517–1519.

Uriel Feige, Guy Kortsarz, and David Peleg. 1999. The dense k-subgraph problem. *Algorithmica*, 29:2001.

Christiane Fellbaum. 1998. *WordNet: An Electronic Lexical Database*. MIT Press.

Paolo Ferragina and Ugo Scaiella. 2010. TAGME: On-the-fly Annotation of Short Text Fragments (by Wikipedia Entities). In *Proc. of CIKM*, pages 1625–1628.

Paolo Ferragina and Ugo Scaiella. 2012. Fast and Accurate Annotation of Short Texts with Wikipedia Pages. *IEEE Software*, 29(1):70–75.

Weiwei Guo and Mona T. Diab. 2010. Combining Orthogonal Monolingual and Multilingual Sources of Evidence for All Words WSD. In *Proc. of ACL*, pages 1542–1551.

Yoan Gutiérrez, Yenier Castañeda, Andy González, Rainel Estrada, Dennys D. Piug, Jose I. Abreu, Roger Pérez, Antonio Fernández Orquín, Andrés Montoyo, Rafael Muñoz, and Franc Camara. 2013. UMCC_DLSI: Reinforcing a Ranking Algorithm with Sense Frequencies and Multidimensional Semantic Resources to solve Multilingual Word Sense Disambiguation. In *Proc. of SemEval-2013*, pages 241–249.

Ben Hachey, Will Radford, Joel Nothman, Matthew Honnibal, and James R. Curran. 2013. Evaluating Entity Linking with Wikipedia. *Artificial Intelligence*, 194:130–150.

Sherzod Hakimov, Salih Atilay Oto, and Erdogan Dogdu. 2012. Named entity recognition and disambiguation using linked data and graph-based centrality scoring. In *Proc. of SWIM*, pages 4:1–4:7.

Taher H. Haveliwala. 2002. Topic-sensitive PageRank. In *Proc. of WWW*, pages 517–526.

Johannes Hoffart, Mohamed Amir Yosef, Ilaria Bordino, Hagen Fürstenau, Manfred Pinkal, Marc Spaniol, Bilyana Taneva, Stefan Thater, and Gerhard Weikum. 2011. Robust disambiguation of named entities in text. In *Proc. of EMNLP*, pages 782–792.

Johannes Hoffart, Stephan Seufert, Dat Ba Nguyen, Martin Theobald, and Gerhard Weikum. 2012. KORE: keyphrase overlap relatedness for entity disambiguation. In *Proc. of CIKM*, pages 545–554.

Johannes Hoffart, Fabian M Suchanek, Klaus Berberich, and Gerhard Weikum. 2013. YAGO2: A spatially and temporally enhanced knowledge base from Wikipedia. *Artificial Intelligence*, 194:28–61.

Eduard H. Hovy, Roberto Navigli, and Simone P. Ponzetto. 2013. Collaboratively built semi-structured content and Artificial Intelligence: The story so far. *Artificial Intelligence*, 194:2–27.

Samir Khuller and Barna Saha. 2009. On finding dense subgraphs. In *Proc. of ICALP*, pages 597–608.

Sayali Kulkarni, Amit Singh, Ganesh Ramakrishnan, and Soumen Chakrabarti. 2009. Collective Annotation of Wikipedia Entities in Web Text. In *Proc. of KDD*, pages 457–466.

Els Lefever and Véronique Hoste. 2010. Semeval-2010 task 3: Cross-lingual Word Sense Disambiguation. In *Proc. of SemEval-2010*, pages 15–20.

Els Lefever and Véronique Hoste. 2013. SemEval-2013 Task 10: Cross-lingual Word Sense Disambiguation. In *Proc. of SemEval-2013*, pages 158–166.

Els Lefever, Véronique Hoste, and Martine De Cock. 2011. Parasense or how to use parallel corpora for Word Sense Disambiguation. In *Proc. of ACL-HLT*, pages 317–322.

Michael E. Lesk. 1986. Automatic Sense Disambiguation Using Machine Readable Dictionaries: How to Tell a Pine Cone from an Ice Cream Cone. In *Proc. of the International Conference on Systems Documentation*, pages 24–26.

Nadine Ludwig and Harald Sack. 2011. Named entity recognition for user-generated tags. In *Proc. of DEXA*, pages 177–181.

Suresh Manandhar, Ioannis P. Klapaftis, Dmitriy Dligach, and Sameer S. Pradhan. 2010. SemEval-2010 task 14: Word sense induction & disambiguation. In *Proc. of SemEval-2010*, pages 63–68.

Steve L. Manion and Raazesh Sainudiin. 2013. DAEBAK!: Peripheral Diversity for Multilingual Word Sense Disambiguation. In *Proc. of SemEval-2013*, pages 250–254.

Pablo N. Mendes, Max Jakob, Andrés García-Silva, and Christian Bizer. 2011. DBpedia spotlight: shedding light on the web of documents. In *Proc. of I-Semantics*, pages 1–8.

Rada Mihalcea and Andras Csomai. 2007. Wikify!: linking documents to encyclopedic knowledge. In *Proc. of CIKM*, pages 233–242.

Rada Mihalcea and Dan I Moldovan. 2001. Extended WordNet: Progress report. In *Proc. of NAACL Workshop on WordNet and Other Lexical Resources*, pages 95–100.

Rada Mihalcea. 2005. Unsupervised large-vocabulary word sense disambiguation with graph-based algorithms for sequence data labeling. In *Proc. of HLT/EMNLP*, pages 411–418.

George A. Miller, Claudia Leacock, Randee Tengi, and Ross T. Bunker. 1993. A semantic concordance. In *Proc. of HLT*, pages 303–308.

Tristan Miller, Chris Biemann, Torsten Zesch, and Iryna Gurevych. 2012. Using Distributional Similarity for Lexical Expansion in Knowledge-based Word Sense Disambiguation. In *Proc. of COLING*, pages 1781–1796.

David Milne and Ian H. Witten. 2008. Learning to link with Wikipedia. In *Proc. of CIKM*, pages 509–518.

Andrea Moro and Roberto Navigli. 2013. Integrating Syntactic and Semantic Analysis into the Open Information Extraction Paradigm. In *Proc. of IJCAI*, pages 2148–2154.

Roberto Navigli and Mirella Lapata. 2010. An Experimental Study of Graph Connectivity for Unsupervised Word Sense Disambiguation. *TPAMI*, 32(4):678–692.

Roberto Navigli and Simone Paolo Ponzetto. 2012a. BabelNet: The automatic construction, evaluation and application of a wide-coverage multilingual semantic network. *Artificial Intelligence*, 193:217–250.

Roberto Navigli and Simone Paolo Ponzetto. 2012b. Joining forces pays off: Multilingual Joint Word Sense Disambiguation. In *Proc. of EMNLP*, pages 1399–1410.

Roberto Navigli, Kenneth C. Litkowski, and Orin Hargraves. 2007. SemEval-2007 Task 07: Coarse-Grained English All-Words Task. In *Proc. of SemEval-2007*, pages 30–35.

Roberto Navigli, David Jurgens, and Daniele Vannella. 2013. SemEval-2013 Task 12: Multilingual Word Sense Disambiguation. In *Proc. of SemEval-2013*, pages 222–231.

Roberto Navigli. 2008. A structural approach to the automatic adjudication of word sense disagreements. *Natural Language Engineering*, 14(4):293–310.

Roberto Navigli. 2009. Word Sense Disambiguation: A survey. *ACM Computing Surveys*, 41(2):1–69.

Roberto Navigli. 2012. A Quick Tour of Word Sense Disambiguation, Induction and Related Approaches. In *Proc. of SOFSEM*, pages 115–129.

Hwee Tou Ng and Hian Beng Lee. 1996. Integrating multiple knowledge sources to disambiguate word sense: An exemplar-based approach. In *Proc. of ACL*, pages 40–47.

Mohammad Taher Pilehvar and Roberto Navigli. 2014. A Large-scale Pseudoword-based Evaluation Framework for State-of-the-Art Word Sense Disambiguation. *Computational Linguistics*.

Simone P. Ponzetto and Roberto Navigli. 2010. Knowledge-rich Word Sense Disambiguation rivaling supervised system. In *Proc. of ACL*, pages 1522–1531.

Sameer S. Pradhan, Edward Loper, Dmitriy Dligach, and Martha Palmer. 2007. SemEval-2007 task 17: English lexical sample, SRL and all words. In *Proc. of SemEval-2007*, pages 87–92. Association for Computational Linguistics.

Delip Rao, Paul McNamee, and Mark Dredze. 2013. Entity Linking: Finding Extracted Entities in a Knowledge Base. In *Multi-source, Multilingual Information Extraction and Summarization*, Theory and Applications of Natural Language Processing, pages 93–115. Springer Berlin Heidelberg.

Lev-Arie Ratinov, Dan Roth, Doug Downey, and Mike Anderson. 2011. Local and Global Algorithms for Disambiguation to Wikipedia. In *Proc. of ACL*, pages 1375–1384.

Lenhart K. Schubert. 2006. Turing's dream and the knowledge challenge. In *Proc. of NCAI*, pages 1534–1538.

Didier Schwab, Andon Tchechmedjiev, Jérôme Goulian, Mohammad Nasiruddin, Gilles Sérasset, and Hervé Blanchon. 2013. GETALP System: Propagation of a Lesk Measure through an Ant Colony Algorithm. In *Proc. of SemEval-2013*, pages 232–240.

Hui Shen, Razvan Bunescu, and Rada Mihalcea. 2013. Coarse to Fine Grained Sense Disambiguation in Wikipedia. In *Proc. of *SEM*, pages 22–31.

Ravi Sinha and Rada Mihalcea. 2007. Unsupervised Graph-based Word Sense Disambiguation Using Measures of Word Semantic Similarity. In *Proc. of ICSC*, pages 363–369.

Benjamin Snyder and Martha Palmer. 2004. The English all-words task. In *Proc. of Senseval-3*, pages 41–43.

Carlo Strapparava and Alessandro Valitutti. 2004. WordNet Affect: an Affective Extension of WordNet. In *Proc. of LREC*, pages 1083–1086.

Hanghang Tong, Christos Faloutsos, and Jia-Yu Pan. 2006. Fast Random Walk with Restart and Its Applications. In *Proc. of ICDM*, pages 613–622.

Kristina Toutanova, Dan Klein, Christopher D. Manning, and Yoram Singer. 2003. Feature-rich part-of-speech tagging with a cyclic dependency network. In *Proc. of NAACL-HLT*, pages 173–180.

George Tsatsaronis, Michalis Vazirgiannis, and Ion Androutsopoulos. 2007. Word Sense Disambiguation with Spreading Activation Networks Generated from Thesauri. In *Proc. of IJCAI*, pages 1725–1730.

Tim Van de Cruys and Marianna Apidianaki. 2011. Latent Semantic Word Sense Induction and Disambiguation. In *Proc. of ACL*, pages 1476–1485.

Daniele Vannella, David Jurgens, Daniele Scarfini, Domenico Toscani, and Roberto Navigli. 2014. Validating and Extending Semantic Knowledge Bases using Video Games with a Purpose. In *Proc. of ACL*.

Duncan J. Watts and Steven H. Strogatz. 1998. Collective dynamics of 'small-world' networks. *Nature*, 393(6684):409–10.

Zhi Zhong and Hwee Tou Ng. 2010. It Makes Sense: A Wide-Coverage Word Sense Disambiguation System for Free Text. In *Proc. of ACL (Demo)*, pages 78–83.

Amal Zouaq, Michel Gagnon, and Benoit Ozell. 2009. A SUMO-based Semantic Analysis for Knowledge Extraction. In *Proc of LTC*.

Crosslingual and Multilingual Construction of Syntax-Based Vector Space Models

Jason Utt and **Sebastian Padó**
Institut für Maschinelle Sprachverarbeitung
Universität Stuttgart
[uttjn|pado]@ims.uni-stuttgart.de

Abstract

Syntax-based distributional models of lexical semantics provide a flexible and linguistically adequate representation of co-occurrence information. However, their construction requires large, accurately parsed corpora, which are unavailable for most languages.

In this paper, we develop a number of methods to overcome this obstacle. We describe (a) a *crosslingual* approach that constructs a syntax-based model for a new language requiring only an English resource and a translation lexicon; and (b) *multilingual* approaches that combine crosslingual with monolingual information, subject to availability. We evaluate on two lexical semantic benchmarks in German and Croatian. We find that the models exhibit complementary profiles: crosslingual models yield higher accuracies while monolingual models provide better coverage. In addition, we show that simple multilingual models can successfully combine their strengths.

1 Introduction

Building on the Distributional Hypothesis (Harris, 1954; Miller and Charles, 1991), which states that words occurring in similar contexts are similar in meaning, distributional semantic models (DSMs) represent a word's meaning via its occurrence in context in large corpora. Vector spaces, the most widely used type of DSMs, represent words as vectors in a high-dimensional space whose dimensions correspond to features of the words' contexts. *Word spaces* represent the simplest case of DSMs in which the dimensions are simply the context words (Schütze, 1992). A notable subclass of DSMs are *syntax-based models* (Lin, 1998; Baroni and Lenci, 2010) which use (lexicalized) syntactic relations as dimensions. They are able to model more fine-grained distinctions than word spaces and have been found to be useful for tasks such as selectional preference learning (Erk et al., 2010), verb class induction (Schulte im Walde, 2006), analogical reasoning (Turney, 2006), and alternation discovery (Joanis et al., 2006). Despite their flexibility and usefulness, syntax-based DSMs are used less often than word-based spaces. An important reason is that their construction requires accurate parsers, which are unavailable for many languages. In addition, syntax-based DSMs are inherently more sparse than word spaces, which calls for a large corpus of well parsable data. It is thus not surprising that besides English (Baroni and Lenci, 2010), only few other languages possess large-scale syntax-based DSMs (Padó and Utt, 2012; Šnajder et al., 2013).

This paper develops methods that take advantage of the *resource gradient* between English and other languages, exploiting the higher-quality resources of the former to induce resources for target languages among the latter, by *translating* the *word-link-word* co-occurrences that underlie syntax-based DSMs. This directly provides a *crosslingual method* to construct syntax-based DSMs for target languages without any target language data, requiring only an English syntax-based DSM and a translation lexicon. Such lexicons are available for many language pairs, and we outline a method to reduce ambiguity inherent in such dictionaries. We describe a set of *multilingual methods* that can combine corpus evidence from English and the target language to further improve the performance of the obtained DSM.

We consider two target languages, German and Croatian, as examples of one close and one more remote target language. For evaluation, we use two

Transactions of the Association for Computational Linguistics, 2 (2014) 245–258. Action Editor: Patrick Pantel.
Submitted 11/2013; Revised 3/2014; Published 10/2014.

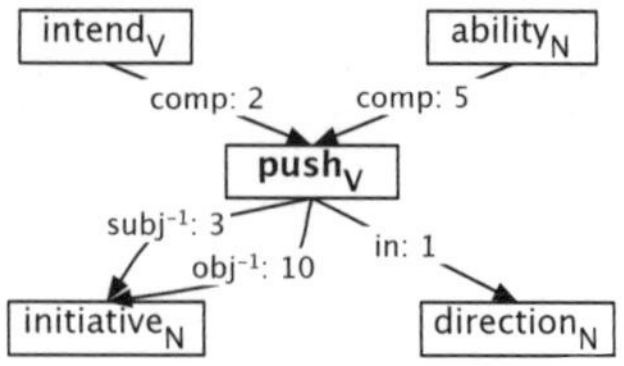

(a) DM as graph

$W \times LW$	push
$\langle$comp^{-1}, intend$\rangle$	2
$\langle$comp^{-1}, ability$\rangle$	5
$\langle$subj^{-1}, initiative$\rangle$	3
$\langle$obj^{-1}, initiative$\rangle$	10
$\langle$in, direction$\rangle$	1

(b) DM as $W \times LW$ matrix

$WL \times W$	$\langle$push, comp$^{-1}\rangle$	$\langle$push, in$\rangle$	$\langle$push, obj$^{-1}\rangle$	$\langle$push, subj$^{-1}\rangle$
ability	5	0	0	0
direction	0	1	0	0
initiative	0	0	10	3
intend	2	0	0	0

(c) DM as $WL \times W$ matrix

Figure 1: Distributional Memory sample around *to push* represented as a graph (a) and two matrices (b, c)

tasks, namely synonym choice and semantic similarity prediction. For both languages and tasks, monolingually constructed DSMs can provide strong baselines. We find similar patterns across tasks and target languages: the crosslingually constructed DSM can be parametrized so that it becomes superior to an existing monolingual DSM in quality, even if inferior in coverage. A simple multilingual backoff can combine the crosslingual model's high quality with the monolingual model's high coverage.

Structure of the paper. We begin by sketching the structure of Distributional Memory, a general framework for syntax-based semantic spaces, in Section 2. Our main contributions follow in Sections 3 and 4, namely, a family of models for the crosslingual and multilingual construction of DSMs. The second part of the paper is concerned with evaluation. Section 5 describes our experimental setup after which we discuss our results for German (Section 6) and Croatian (Section 7). The paper concludes with related work (Section 8) and a general discussion (Section 9).

2 Distributional Memory: A General Model of Syntax-based Vector Spaces

2.1 Motivation and Definition

Simple syntax-based DSMs represent target words in terms of dimensions labeled with word-relation pairs (Lin, 1998; Grefenstette, 1994). Unfortunately, this representation only supports tasks that compare pairs of words with regard to their meaning (e.g., in synonymy detection or selectional preferences), but not for tasks such as analogical reasoning, where sets of word pairs are compared (Turney, 2006).

To unify syntax-based DSMs, Baroni and Lenci (2010) proposed the *Distributional Memory* (DM) model which captures distributional information at the more general level of word-link-word triples, stored as a third order co-occurrence tensor. The DM tensor can be seen as a set of ordered *word-link-word* tuples such as $\langle$*pencil obj use*$\rangle$ associated with a scoring function $\sigma\colon W \times L \times W \rightarrow \mathbb{R}^+$ that scores, for example, $\langle$*pencil obj use*$\rangle$ more highly than $\langle$*elephant obj use*$\rangle$.

The DM tensor can be visualized as a directed graph whose nodes are labeled with lemmas and whose edges are labeled with links and scores. As an example, Figure (1a) shows five links for the verb *push* in the English DM, including subject, object, prepositional adjunct, and governing verbs.

DSMs for individual tasks can be obtained by "matricizing" the tensor into two-dimensional matrices corresponding to standard vector spaces. The matrix in Figure (1b) shows the *word by link-word* space ($W \times LW$). It represents words w in terms of pairs $\langle l, w\rangle$ of a link and a context word. This space models similarity among words, e.g. for thesaurus construction (Lin, 1998). The example matrix in Figure (1c) represents a *word-link by word* space ($WL \times W$). It characterizes pairs $\langle w, l\rangle$ through context words w, which can be understood as selectional preferences.

DM does not assume a specific source for building the graph. However, all existing DM resources were extracted from large dependency-parsed corpora such as UKWAC (Baroni et al., 2008). In the simplest case, the set of labels L is (a subset of) the dependency relations in the corpus, and the scoring function σ is a measure of association between the governor and the dependent (see Baroni and Lenci (2010) for details). However, the most robust DMs (including Baroni and Lenci's LexDM and TypeDM) use both syntactic and lexicalized links, i.e. links which contain words themselves, as well as *surface form-based* links, e.g., observed *subject-verb-object* triples in the corpus lead to a $\langle$*subject verb object*$\rangle$ edge in the DM graph.

2.2 DMs for Other Languages

Given the appealing properties of Distributional Memory, it may be surprising that not many comparable resources exist for other languages. To our knowledge, comparable resources exist only for German (Padó and Utt, 2012) and Croatian (Šnajder et al., 2013). Both studies replicate the monolingual DM construction process outlined by Baroni and Lenci for the respective languages. For German, the process is relatively unproblematic, since German is relatively well-equipped in terms of corpora and parsers. In contrast, Šnajder et al. (2013) faced serious resource scarcity while building a Croatian DM and had to go to considerable lengths to clean a large web corpus and to optimize the linguistic processing tools. The resulting DM outperforms a monolingual context word model for nouns and verbs, but performs worse than the word-based model for (generally rarer) adjectives. As a direct consequence, high-quality syntax-based DSMs can only be constructed for a limited set of languages.

3 Crosslingual Construction of DMs

3.1 Motivation

As outlined in the previous section, there is a bottleneck in many languages regarding both large, clean corpora as well as processing pipelines that result in high-accuracy dependency parses. To address this problem, we propose to induce Distributional Memories for such languages crosslingually by *translating* a source language DM into the target language.

By adopting English as the source language we can take advantage of the *resource gradient*, that is, the higher maturity of English NLP techniques, such as parsers, compared to most other languages. For many languages, treebanks have become available only within the last ten years (Buchholz and Marsi, 2006), if at all, while English has been at the forefront of NLP development for several decades, and a number of highly accurate dependency parsers exist (McDonald et al., 2005; Nivre, 2006). At the same time, English arguably possesses the widest range of large and well-cleaned corpora of any language.

To make our approaches applicable to as many target languages as possible, we assume in this section that very few resources for the target language are available. The crosslingual methods we develop

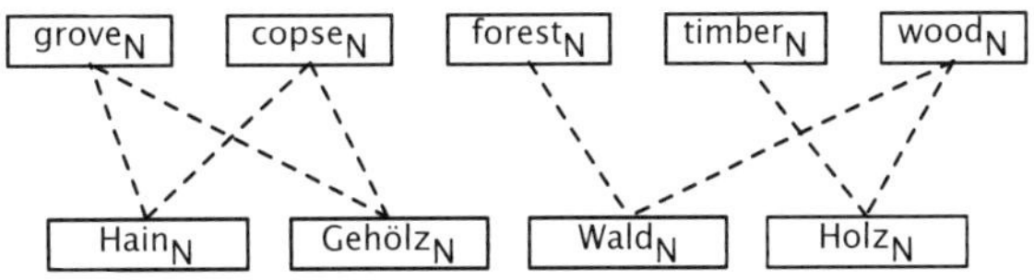

Figure 2: Sample of the English-German `dict.cc` dictionary; translations shown as dashed lines.

here work without any target language corpora, either monolingual or bilingual. The only knowledge we use is a simple *translation lexicon*, that is, a list of translation pairs without translation probabilities, as shown in Figure 2. Translation lexicons of this type are arguably the most common bilingual resource and accurate ones exist for virtually any language pair (Soderland et al., 2009), even for languages with few available corpora. Furthermore, such translation lexicons are often crowdsourced and are available for download. For example, the website `dict.cc` provides numerous such lexicons for German and English.

This approach promises in particular to yield models with a quality-coverage profile complementary to that of monolingual models (Mohammad et al., 2007; Peirsman and Padó, 2011): Crosslingual DMs are extracted from source language corpora which we assume to be parsed more accurately than target language corpora. In addition, the translation process can be designed to act as a further filtering step (cf. Section 3.4 below), thus optimizing crosslingual models for higher quality at the expense of coverage. In contrast, monolingual models – in particular for under-resourced languages – often hit a quality ceiling, but can generally guarantee high coverage.

3.2 Translating DMs with Translation Lexicons

We conceptualize DM as a directed graph (see Figure 1), which allows us to phrase translation in graph terms (Mihalcea and Radev, 2011). A DM is a triple (V, E, σ) where V is a set of vertices (i.e., the vocabulary), E a set of typed edges between words, represented as word-link-word triples (cf. Section 2), and σ, an edge-weighting function. We will use S and T to refer to the source and target language vocabularies, respectively, and (V_S, E_S, σ_S) and (V_T, E_T, σ_T) to denote source and target language DMs.

We can now ask how the shape of the graph

changes under translation. In an ideal world, a translation lexicon would be a bijective function between the source and target language vocabularies: $\text{Tr} : S \rightarrow T$. Then, the transformation would merely constitute a relabeling. We would then construct the German DM graph by exchanging all English node labels with German node labels, i.e., $V_T = T$, and creating a German edge for each English edge.[1]

3.3 Ambiguity in Unfiltered Translation

The dictionary fragment in Figure 2 shows that translation is not bijective but a many-to-many relation. In fact, taking the English–German `dict.cc` lexicon as an example, there is an average of 2.3 German translations for each English lemma, and an average of 1.9 English translations for each German lemma. We model this situation using two functions: $\text{Tr} : S \rightarrow 2^T$ translates source words into sets of target words, and $\text{Tr}^{-1} : T \rightarrow 2^S$ translates target words back into the source language.

The naive way to translate nodes using Tr is to use *all* translations for a given word. Thus, for each edge in the source DM between lemmas s_1 and s_2, we obtain $|\,\text{Tr}(s_1)| \cdot |\,\text{Tr}(s_2)|$ edges in the target language:

$$E_T = \{(t_1, l, t_2) \,|\, \exists(s_1, l, s_2) \in E_S : t_1 \in \text{Tr}(s_1) \wedge t_2 \in \text{Tr}(s_2)\} \quad (1)$$

The score σ_T of a target edge is defined as the mean of the scores of all source edges that map to it.

$$\sigma_T(t_1, l, t_2) = \sum_{\substack{s_1 \in \text{Tr}^{-1}(t_1) \\ s_2 \in \text{Tr}^{-1}(t_2)}} \frac{\sigma_S(s_1, l, s_2)}{|\,\text{Tr}^{-1}(t_1)| \cdot |\,\text{Tr}^{-1}(t_2)|} \quad (2)$$

We take the mean as it is less sensitive to outliers than maximum or minimum. In addition, unlike taking the sum, it is also automatically normalized regarding the number of translations, thus penalizing words with many unrelated senses.

A look at Figures 1 and 3, however, indicates that this procedure overgenerates. This is problematic on two levels. First, the target language graph will contain a very large number of edges (e.g., using `dict.cc`, the edge ⟨*text sbj_tr use*⟩ has 42 German

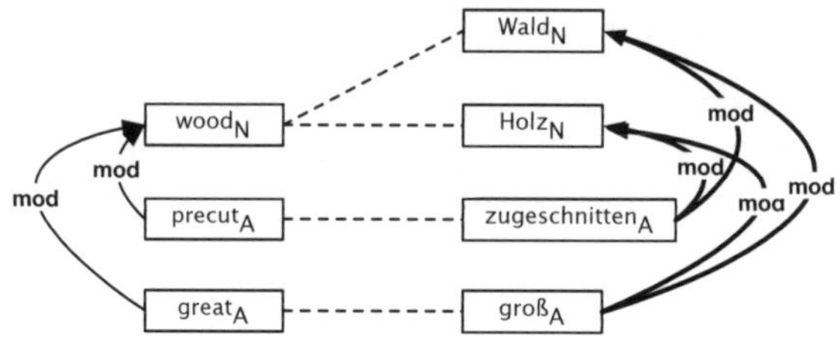

Figure 3: Unfiltered edge translation (EN–DE)

translations). Second, the correctness of the target DM suffers. For some cases, such as *copse – Gehölz, Hain*, the various translations are synonymous, and Eq. (1) is appropriate. In other cases, multiple translations indicate *lexical ambiguity* of the source term. For example, the two translations of *wood* correspond to its senses as *forest (Wald)* and *timber (Holz)*, respectively. In such cases, Eq. (1) confuses the senses, as the example in Figure 3 illustrates. The left-hand side shows DM edges between *wood* and two adjectival modifiers, namely *precut* (which is more plausible for the *timber* sense) and *great* (which is more plausible for the *forest* sense). The right-hand side shows (part of) the German translations according to Eq. (1): both *Holz (timber)* and *Wald (forest)* are linked to both adjectives, leading to spurious edges in the German DM.

3.4 Filtering by Backtranslation

Since the nature of the translation is not indicated in the translation lexicon, we exploit typical redundancies in the source DM, which often contains "quasi-synonymous" edges that express the same relation with different words, e.g., ⟨*book obj read*⟩ and ⟨*novel obj read*⟩. This allows us to score target edge candidates by how well we can "backtranslate" (Somers, 2005) them into the source language.

This idea is illustrated in Figure 4. We still assume, as above, that *wood* has two translations, but that *precut* has only one. For the English edge ⟨*precut mod wood*⟩, we obtain two German candidate edges, namely ⟨*zugeschnitten mod Holz*⟩ and ⟨*zugeschnitten mod Wald*⟩. When backtranslating these candidates, the first one, ⟨*zugeschnitten mod Wald*⟩, maps only onto the original edge. The second one, ⟨*zugeschnitten mod Holz*⟩, is backtranslated into a different source edge, ⟨*precut mod timber*⟩, which makes it more probable.

[1]We build on the assumption that dependency relations are language-independent which, while incorrect, represents a reasonable simplification (McDonald et al., 2013).

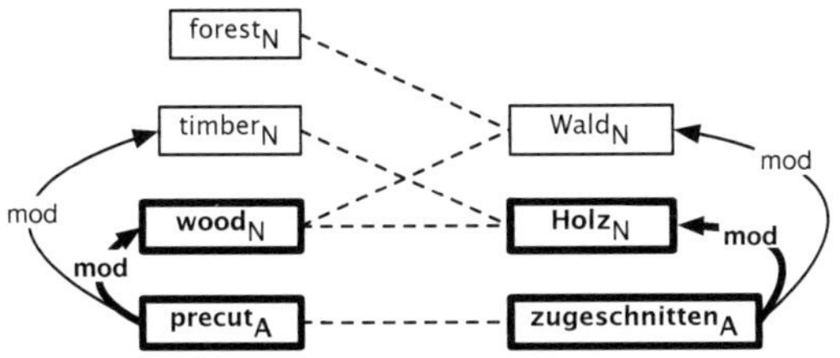

Figure 4: Backtranslation filtering. Original and winning edges shown in boldface.

Model	Covered items Corr.	Cov.
DM.DE (AllL)	.43	.60
DM.DE (SPrfL)	.43	.60
DM.XL EN→DE filter (AllL)	.42	**.61**
DM.XL EN→DE filter (SPrfL)	**.49**	.49

Table 1: Coverage and Correlation (Pearson's r) for predicting word similarity, contrasting link types (all links vs. selectional preference links)

We operationalize this by adding another condition to Eq. (1), namely that target edges must be among the highest-scoring edges for some source edge. Recall that our target scores σ_T are already defined in terms of source edge scores, so no redefinition of the scoring function is necessary.

$$E_T = \{(t_1, l, t_2) \mid \exists (s_1, l, s_2) \in E_S : t_1 \in \mathrm{Tr}(s_1) \wedge t_2 \in \mathrm{Tr}(s_2) \wedge \sigma_T(t_1, l, t_2) = \max_{\substack{t \in \mathrm{Tr}(s_1) \\ t' \in \mathrm{Tr}(s_2)}} \sigma_T(t, l, t'), \} \quad (3)$$

where $\sigma_T(t, l, t')$ is the score as defined in Eq. 2. This filtering scheme is fairly liberal: we do not limit the number of target edges that a source edge can translate to. A stricter variant could, e.g., abstain from translating a source edge if no unique best edge exists. We leave such variants to future work.

3.5 Defining Similarity

Recall from Figure 1 that DM contains information about both "incoming" as well as "outgoing" links. Monolingually constructed DMs by default use all of these relations since the information is reliable. The situation is not as clear in a crosslingual setting. Our intuition is that *selectional preferences* are most informative and most likely to survive translation. For example, for verbs we expect knowledge about their arguments to be more informative than about their governors. Conversely, for nouns we want to use knowledge about the verbs that they occur with rather than their arguments or modifiers.

We implement this idea by computing semantic similarity between word vectors either on complete vectors (condition "AllL") or on a filtered version that uses only inverse links for verbs and only regular links for nouns and adjectives (condition "SPrfL"). Table 1 shows the results of preliminary experiments on a semantic similarity dataset (details in Section 5). They bear out our hypothesis: in the monolingual setting, there is almost no difference. Thus, in line with previous work, we adopt (AllL) for DM.DE. In contrast, we see a clear quality-coverage trade-off in the crosslingual scenario, with a higher quality for (SPrfL). Since this corresponds to our focus on higher precision for crosslingual models, we will adopt (SPrfL) for all crosslingual DMs.

4 Multilingual Construction of DMs

The crosslingual models described in the previous section do not use any corpus information from the target language: As previously discussed, our rationale is to make the methods as widely applicable as possible. However, this assumption may be too cautious as more corpora and parsers continually become available. In order to take advantage of such developments, this section discusses two simple methods for combining monolingually and crosslingually constructed DMs, thereby combining corpus evidence from both the source and the target language.

We concentrate on methods that can be applied to DMs directly, e.g. by researchers who do not have access to the source corpora. Moreover, we combine not the graphs, but the resulting semantic similarities.[2] We take our inspiration from work on combining and smoothing n-gram language models, where the usual operations are interpolation and back-off (Chen and Goodman, 1998). Note that in our case, the two models to be combined are assumed to have complementary properties, with the monolin-

[2]We conducted experiments with graph merging but found that the different topologies of the monolingual and crosslingual DMs make it difficult to merge the graphs in a manner that combines the information from both graphs.

gual model having higher coverage and the crosslingual model higher quality (cf. Section 3.1). For this reason, we assume that a linear interpolation of the models' similarities for each word pair will not perform well. Our first strategy is a simple backoff combination (DM.MULTI Backoff) that starts with the crosslingual model and falls back to the monolingual model in the case of zero-similarities. Our second strategy follows the intuition that both noise and sparse data tend to result in underestimated similarities. This leads us to the DM.MULTI MaxSim model: It takes the predictions from the monolingual and crosslingual model and takes the higher one.

Both DM.MULTI variants combine predictions from two models and implicitly assume that the predictions are drawn from the same score distribution. Since this is not guaranteed, we standardize all scores before combination, that is, we linearly transform the values so that the resulting distribution has a mean of 0 and a standard deviation of 1.

	Demagoge		**demagogue**
1	*Miesmacher*	×	*grinch*
2	*guter Redner*	×	*able speaker*
3	*skrupelloser Hetzer*	✓	*unscrupulous agitator*
4	*Meinungsforscher*	×	*pollster*

(a) Task 1: synonym target with four candidates

Word Pair	Similarity
Absage - ablehnen *(rejection - refuse)*	3.5
Absage - Stellenanzeige *(rejection - job advertisement)*	1.875
Affe - Gepäckkontrolle *(monkey - luggage inspection)*	0.125

(b) Task 2: semantic similarity (range: 0–4)

Table 2: Example items from evaluation tasks

5 Experimental Setup

To show the benefits of our crosslingual methods, we perform experiments for the language pairs English–German and English–Croatian. These languages exemplify variability on the resource gradient: The resource situation is best for English, still relatively good for German, and most difficult for Croatian.

This section outlines the experiments for German; Section 7 focuses on Croatian. We evaluate our models on two standard tasks from lexical semantics: synonym choice and the prediction of human relatedness judgments. Even though these two tasks are *in-vitro*, they are widely used for model selection in distributional space models and we can compare the results of our models against previous work. The two tasks test how well the models can account for two different aspects of lexical semantics, namely a specific lexical relation (synonymy) and general semantic relatedness.

5.1 Tasks and Datasets

Our first task is synonym detection, where models have to identify the true synonym for a target word from four candidates. We use the German Reader's Digest Word Power (RDWP) dataset (Wallace and Wallace, 2005) which contains 984 items.[3] RDWP is similar to the English TOEFL data (Landauer and Dumais, 1997), but can contain short phrases among the candidates (cf. example in Table 2a).

Our second evaluation tests how well the models predict similarities for German word pairs including closely related, somewhat related, and unrelated word pairs (cf. Table 2b). We use the Gur350 dataset[4] which contains 350 word pairs scored for relatedness by native German taggers on a five-point Likert scale between 0 (unrelated) and 4 (synonymous). Both datasets contain nouns, verbs and adjectives.

5.2 Procedure

Starting from a DM model, we matricize it into a word by link-word space ($W \times LW$) and compute similarities between words with Cosine similarity. In Exp. 1, we compute the semantic similarities of the target with each candidate and predict the candidate with the highest similarity to the target. For phrasal candidates, we compute the similarity between the target and all constituent words and take the maximum. We follow Mohammad et al. (2007) in assigning partial credit to a model when the candidates of a target are tied for maximal similarity. We evaluate the models on Exp. 2 by calculating the strength of the correlation between the model predictions and the

[3]Available from: `http://goo.gl/PN42E`
[4]Available from: `http://goo.gl/3Dflf1`

human relatedness judgments. We use Pearson's correlation coefficient since it is the de facto evaluation measure in relevant earlier work.[5]

On both tasks, we compare the models in two conditions. In the first condition ("All"), models are forced to make predictions for all items in the dataset even if they have no information about the item. In the second condition ("Covered"), models are allowed to abstain in the case of zero similarities. For Exp. 1, we report the accuracy (the number of correctly recognized synonyms divided by the number of attempted problems) and coverage (the ratio of items attempted; always 1 for the "All" condition). Items are considered covered if at least one candidate has a non-zero similarity to the target. In Exp. 2, we measure the correlation between the semantic similarities and human judgments for word pairs. Coverage is calculated as the percentage of items with similarity greater 0.

Differences between models are tested for significance using bootstrap resampling (Efron and Tibshirani, 1993), always in the "All" condition.

5.3 Models

We consider three types of DM models (monolingual, crosslingual and multilingual), bag-of-words models and a set of models proposed in the literature.

Monolingual model. We use DM.DE (Padó and Utt, 2012), constructed from a 900M-token web corpus, SDEWAC, parsed with MATE (Bohnet, 2010).[6] As discussed in Section 3.5, we consider all links (AllL) for the monolingual model.

Crosslingual models. The starting point for the crosslingual models is Baroni and Lenci (2010)'s English TypeDM model extracted from approximately 3B tokens of Wikipedia and web corpus text parsed with MaltParser (Nivre, 2006).[7] DM.XL *naive* implements Eq. (1), and DM.XL *filter* implements Eq. (3). As our translation lexicon, we use the community-built English–German `dict.cc` online dictionary.[8]

	Adj	Noun	Verbs	Total
English	37K	78K	8K	123K
German	35L	99K	9K	143K
Translation pairs	77K	172K	28K	277K

Table 3: Size of the `dict.cc` dictionary

Class	Model	Nodes	Edges
monolingual	DM.DE (DE)	3.5M	78M
	TYPEDM (EN)	31K	131M
crosslingual & multilingual (DE)	DM.XL naive	63K	5B
	DM.XL filter	63K	1.7B

Table 4: Sizes of various DM resources

The statistics of the dictionary in Table 3 show that it is quite large and covers many adjectives and nouns, but relatively few verbs. We had to exclude much verbal data due to ill-structured entries or phrasal entries. Following Section 3.5, we only consider selectional preference links (SPrfL) for the crosslingual model.

Multilingual models. We consider the two models described in Section 4, namely DM.MULTI Backoff and DM.MULTI MaxSim, each combining DM.DE (AllL) with DM.XL *filter* (SPrfL).

Bag-of-words models. We build a standard BOW model from the same German corpus SDEWAC used for DM.DE. We assume a window of 10 context words to the left and right. We use the top 10K most frequent content words (nouns, adjectives, verbs and adverbs) as dimensions. Our second BOW model (BOW PCA_{500}) was reduced to 500 dimensions by applying principle component analysis, a technique generally used to increase robustness to parameter choice and to combat sparsity.[9]

Models from the literature. We compare our models against the state of the art, represented by the respective best models from two previous studies (Zesch et al., 2007; Mohammad et al., 2007). They comprise monolingual ontology-based models that use GermaNet, (German) Wikipedia, or both (Lin_{GN},

[5]We note that since the data are not normally distributed, a non-parametric correlation coefficient would be more appropriate. While we omitted them due to space limitations in this paper, we will provide Spearman ρ results for all models online at `http://goo.gl/uxuffp`.

[6]Available from `http://goo.gl/H6gViT`.

[7]Available from `http://goo.gl/63ajCI`.

[8]Available from `http://goo.gl/re44Hg`.

[9]We also built models using smaller context windows and Latent Semantic Analysis (LSA, Landauer, 1997), both with 500 dimensions and with an automatically optimized number of dimensions (Wild et al., 2008). Since these spaces did not consistently yield better results than the reported models using PCA, we do not report the results in detail.

Model	All Acc	Covered Acc	Cov
Baselines and word-based DSMs			
1 Random	.25	.25	**1**
2 Frequency	.31	.31	**1**
3 BOW	.46	.46	.98
4 BOW PCA_{500}	**.55**	**.55**	.98
Syntax-based DSMs			
5 DM.DE (AllL)	.48	.53	.84
6 DM.XL EN→DE naive (SPrfL)	.47	**.63**	.58
7 DM.XL EN→DE filter (SPrfL)	.46	.61	.58
8 DM.MULTI Backoff(7,5)	.54	.58	**.89**
9 DM.MULTI MaxSim(7,5)	**.55**	.59	**.89**
Models from the literature			
10 Lin_{dist} [MGHZ07]	NA	.52	**.45**
11 HPG [MGHZ07]	NA	**.77**	.22
12 JC [MGHZ07]	NA	.44	.36

Table 5: Exp. 1: Accuracy and Coverage for synonym choice on the Reader's Digest Word Choice dataset. MGHZ07: Mohammad et al. (2007). Best results for each model class in bold.

Model	All Corr	Covered Corr	Cov
Baselines and word-based DSMs			
1 Frequency	.13	.13	**1**
2 BOW	.20	.21	.97
3 BOW PCA_{500}	**.34**	**.37**	.97
Syntax-based DSMs			
4 DM.DE (AllL) [PU12]	.38	.43	.60
5 DM.XL EN→DE naive (SPrfL)	.28	.45	.49
6 DM.XL EN→DE filter (SPrfL)	.33	**.49**	.49
7 DM.MULTI Backoff(6,4)	.40	.45	**.69**
8 DM.MULTI MaxSim(6,4)	**.42**	.47	**.69**
Models from the literature			
9 Lin_{GN} [MGHZ07]	NA	.50	.26
10 Lin_{dist} [MGHZ07]	NA	**.51**	.26
11 JC_{GN}+PL_{WP} [ZGM07]	NA	**.59**	**.33**

Table 6: Exp. 2: Coverage and correlation (Pearson's r) for predicting word similarity on the Gur350 dataset. MGHZ07: Mohammad et al. (2007)[8], ZGM07: Zesch et al. (2007)[9], PU12: Padó and Utt (2012). Best results for each model class in bold.

HPG, JC, PL); and crosslingual distributional models that represent the meaning of German lemmas in terms English thesaurus categories (Lin_{dist}).

DM model statistics. Table 4 shows the sizes of the various DMs. The German and English monolingual DMs are markedly different: the English DM is much more compact, covering only 30K lemmas while the German DM covers 3.5M lemmas, and at the same time much denser. This discrepancy is due to the larger English corpus and the inclusion of very low-frequency items in DM.DE. The crosslingual models created from TYPEDM cover 63K lemmas in German, about twice the English coverage but still almost two orders of magnitude below the monolingual DM.DE. They become very large: naive translation increases the number of edges by a factor of 30, and filtered translation still by a factor of 13. This means filtering does reduce the size of the resulting DM, but there is still considerable overgeneration.

6 Experimental Evaluation on German

The experimental results for the two experiments are shown in Tables 5 and 6, structured by model type. We observe similar patterns for the two experiments.

Baselines and word-based DSMs. In both cases, uninformed baselines (random and frequency) perform badly. (In Exp. 1, the frequency baseline predicts the most frequent item as synonym; in Exp. 2, it predicts $min(f(w_1), f(w_2))$.) In contrast, word-based DSMs perform quite well, particularly the dimensionality-reduced model (BOW PCA).

Syntax-based DSM. We see a consistent quality versus coverage tradeoff among the different classes of syntax-based DSMs. The monolingual DM.DE model is significantly outperformed by the BOW model on Exp. 1 ($p<0.01$), but numerically outperforms it on Exp. 2 (difference not significant).

In both tasks, the crosslingual DM.XL models outperform both DM.DE and BOW PCA in terms of quality: They achieve the numerically highest accuracy (and correlation, respectively) among all syntax-based models. This high quality comes at a low coverage, matching our intuitions about the profile of the

[8] Mohammad et al. (2007) do not provide coverage numbers in their paper. We appreciate the support of Torsten Zesch and Saif Mohammad in recovering the necessary information.

[9] Zesch et al. (2007) report results for the subset of Gur350 in the intersection of GermaNet and Wikipedia. Thus, their models may have higher coverage on the complete Gur350, but to our knowledge these numbers have not been published.

crosslingual model. Filtering leads to a significant improvement in Exp. 2 ($p<0.05$) but not in Exp. 1.

The multilingual models (DM.MULTI) perform even better. They nearly retain the quality of the crosslingual models (accuracy of .59 vs. .63 for Exp. 1, correlation of .47 vs. .49 for Exp. 2) but attain higher coverage (89% in Exp. 1 and 69% in Exp. 2) Notably, the coverage is even higher than that of the DM.DE models, attesting to the complementarity of mono- and crosslingual information.

The differences among the DM.MULTI models are small, but MaxSim does a little better and performs best overall. In Exp. 1, it does significantly better in the all-items evaluation than all other syntax-based models ($p<0.01$). The differences in Exp. 2 are only significant at $p<0.05$ for the model pair 6–8; we attribute this to the smaller size of the dataset.

In sum, we can construct crosslingual DMs without any use of target language corpora that mirror or even exceed the performance of monolingual DMs. If monolingual data is available, the combination of corpus evidence provides a substantial advantage over both monolingual and crosslingual models, even for German, a language with large, relatively reliably parsed corpora. Users can choose among different models with different coverage/quality tradeoffs.

Comparison to models from the literature. Models from the literature are shown at the bottom of the two tables. They generally obtain the highest accuracy (or correlation, respectively), but only cover a relatively small part of the datasets. In particular, the models with a quality higher than the DM variants (11 in Exp. 1 and 10 and 11 in Exp. 2) exhibit a coverage of less than half than that of the DM.MULTI models. This appears to show the usual trade-off between hand-constructed knowledge and automatically acquired knowledge (Gildea and Jurafsky, 2002). However, we can similarly bias our DMs towards accuracy with the aid of a simple frequency filter that only permits predictions for items where all involved lemmas occur more frequently in the German corpus than some threshold. Setting these thresholds to match the coverage figures of the best ontology-based models, DM.MULTI MaxSim almost reaches the ontology-based results: On Exp. 1, for a coverage of .22 we obtain an accuracy of .68 (ontology-based model: .77), and on Exp. 2, we obtain a correlation of .60 (ontology-based model: .59) at a coverage of .33.[10] Thus, our DM models approximate the quality of ontology-based models without using any handcrafted resources.

Nouns	*Couscous (couscous), Albino (albino)*
Adjectives	*kursorisch (cursory), süffisant (smug)*
Verbs	*erodieren (to erode), moussieren (to fizz)*

Table 7: Words of foreign origin better represented by the multilingual model

Differences between Exp. 1 and 2. The two main differences between the experiments are (a) the performance of DM relative to the BOW baseline, and (b) the impact of backtranslation filtering. In Exp. 1, the BOW performs as well as DM.MULTI, and the unfiltered DM.XL has a slight edge (2% accuracy) over the filtered one. In contrast, in Exp. 2 filtering leads to a major improvement and DM.MULTI does substantially better than BOW PCA. Our analyses attribute this difference to the nature of the two tasks (cf. Section 5). Exp. 1 requires the recognition of synonyms. Here, the main determinant of success is whether the actual synonym receives the highest similarity or not, irrespective of the margin to the competing candidates. This margin does increase from 0.09 in the naive to 0.11 in the filtered DM.XL, but the overall number of correct predictions remains almost unchanged. In contrast, Exp. 2 covers the whole range from highly similar to unrelated word pairs, and the correlation evaluation is sensitive to the relative size of similarities produced by the DM across many word pairs. The improvement we see indicates that filtering improves the overall scaling of the similarities, but this effect is masked by the decision criterion in Exp. 1.

Qualitative analysis. Comparing DM.DE with DM.MULTI, the question arises: can we further characterize the benefits that the inclusion of crosslingual corpus evidence confers to monolingual models? We first inspected Exp. 1 for synonyms that were correctly recognized by DM.MULTI MaxSim but not DM.DE, and found a large number of words of foreign origin (see Table 7). These words tend to be rare in the German corpus in the form of technical, slang,

[10]We cannot provide significance tests since we do not have item-wise predictions for the models from the literature.

or elevated register terms. Due to their low level of ambiguity as well as the fact that their English translations are often more frequent, the crosslingual model represents them more sensibly.

We then inspected Exp. 2 in a similar way but found it more difficult to identify salient improved classes since the improvement is mostly in terms of coverage. The data set for Exp. 2 includes proper nouns, such as *Berlin/Berlin-Kreuzberg, Benedetto/Benedikt*, which are unlikely to be covered by a translation lexicon. It also contains items that encode world knowledge such as *Ratzinger/Papst (pope)* which has a better chance of being covered by target language corpora. This pair is not covered by the DM.XL models, but the monolingual models (DM.DE, BOW, and BOW PCA) assign it the similarities .23, .66, and .89, respectively.

7 Experimental Evaluation on Croatian

Our third experiment considers a language that is more different from English than German, namely Croatian, a Slavic language. Available resources for Croatian are more limited than for English or German. Since syntactic analysis used to be a bottleneck, the first syntax-based DSM for Croatian, DM.HR, became available only last year (Šnajder et al., 2013). As for evaluation datasets, there are no human similarity judgments, but there is a synonym choice dataset (CroSyn – see Karan et al. (2012) for details).

Thus, our Croatian evaluation is a synonym choice task parallel to Exp. 1 for German. We take DM.HR as the monolingual model which was built from a dependency-parsed Croatian web corpus of 1.2B tokens. We construct a crosslingual model by starting from Baroni and Lenci's English TypeDM and using Taktika Nova's freely available English–Croatian dictionary[11] with 105K translation pairs. After removing entries with more than one word per language, we were left with 95K pairs, considerably fewer than for English–German. We apply the methods from Section 3 for edge translation and filtering. The resulting filtered Croatian DM.XL has 47K nodes and 315M edges, about one order of magnitude smaller than the German crosslingual resource. Finally, we combined DM.HR with the crosslingual DM (as in Section 4) to obtain multilingual Croatian DMs.

[11]Available from `http://goo.gl/xHUjJH`

Model	All Acc	Covered Acc	Covered Cov
Word-based DSMs			
1 BOW-LSA [SPA13]	.66	.66	**1**
Syntax-based DSMs			
2 DM.HR (AllL)	.65	.65	**.99**
3 DM.XL EN→HR naive (SPrfL)	.43	.50	.71
4 DM.XL EN→HR filter (SPrfL)	.58	**.71**	.71
5 DM.MULTI Backoff(4,2)	.69	.69	**.99**
6 DM.MULTI MaxSim(4,2)	**.70**	.70	**.99**

Table 8: Experiment 3: Accuracy and Coverage for synonym choice on the CroSyn dataset. SPA13: Šnajder et al. (2013). In boldface: best results.

Table 8 shows the results which correspond closely to those for Exp. 1. A dimensionality-reduced BOW space performs competitively with the monolingual DM.HR (Šnajder et al., 2013). The crosslingual DM is again able to improve accuracy over DM.HR (by 6%) but drops in coverage. Again, the multilingual models perform best: DM.MULTI MaxSim loses only 1% accuracy compared to the crosslingual model but achieves almost perfect coverage. The differences to DM.HR and DM.XL are both significant ($p<0.01$).[12]

The two major differences to the German synonym choice task (Exp. 1) are that (a) filtering plays an essential role for Croatian (increase in accuracy by 15%) and (b) DM.MULTI clearly outperforms the BOW model. We attribute the difference to the semi-automatic construction of the Croatian dataset from machine-readable dictionaries. Overall, the results for Croatian are encouraging. They demonstrate that languages where parsing technology is still developing can in particular profit from cross- and multilingual methods. This is true even for relatively small translation dictionaries, matching previous results from the literature (Peirsman and Padó, 2011).

8 Related Work

Given the resource gradient between English and other languages, the crosslingual induction of linguistic information has been an active topic of research.

Many studies use parallel corpora. Annotation projection (Yarowsky and Ngai, 2001) transfers source language annotation directly onto target language

[12]We cannot provide significances for the BOW results because we again do not have per-item predictions.

sentence. It has been applied to various linguistic levels such as POS tagging and syntax (Hi and Hwa, 2005; Hwa et al., 2005, among others). Other studies use parallel data as indirect supervision for monolingual tasks. Diab and Resnik (2002) use translations as word sense labels; van der Plas and Tiedemann (2006) exploit multilingual distributional semantics for robust synonymy extraction. Naseem et al. (2009) learn unsupervised POS taggers on multilingual parallel data, exploiting the differences between languages as soft constraints. Titov and Klementiev (2012) and Kozhevnikov and Titov (2013) induce shallow semantic parsers from parallel data. Klementiev et al. (2012) approach document classification with multitask learning, inducing a multilingual DSM.

Since parallel corpora are not available in large quantities, other studies use *comparable corpora* which can provide additional features from the other language. For example, Merlo et al. (2002) improve English verb classification with new features derived from Chinese translations. De Smet and Moens (2009) learn multilingual topic models for news aggregation. Peirsman and Padó (2011) use comparable corpora to transfer selectional preferences and sentiment labels. Wikipedia can be seen as a particularly rich type of comparable corpus with additional link structure. It has been used to compute semantic relatedness (Navigli and Ponzetto, 2012; Navigli and Ponzetto, 2010) and to compute conceptual document representations for crosslingual information retrieval (Potthast et al., 2008; Cimiano et al., 2009).

Our work, does not require parallel or comparable corpora. We note, however, that translation lexicons such as the ones we use can be extracted from comparable corpora (Rapp, 1999; Vulić and Moens, 2012, and many others), though few papers are concerned with the translation at the level of semantic relations, as we are. Similar in this respect is Fung and Chen (2004), who translate FrameNet (Baker et al., 1998) into Chinese with a bilingual ontology. They use a relation-based pruning scheme that is somewhat comparable to our backtranslation filtering.

To our knowledge, the most similar work to ours is (Mohammad et al., 2007), which also considers DSMs, albeit a different variety, namely *concept-based* DSMs where targets are characterized in terms of their distribution over categories of Roget's thesaurus. Like our work, their study creates crosslingual DSMs for German using a translation lexicon. It follows a different strategy, however: it collects co-occurrence counts from a German corpus and translates the context dimensions into the English Roget categories. Therefore, it crucially requires a large target language corpus, which our crosslingual methods (Section 3) avoid. Its use of a target language corpus resembles our multilingual methods (Section 4), but unlike them, does not combine corpus evidence from both languages. In sum, we believe that our methods are more adaptable to different scenarios, being able to use whatever data is available in either language.

9 Conclusion

The appeal of syntax-based distributional spaces lies in their promise of flexible and linguistically more appropriate models for many phenomena in lexical semantics. A major obstacle to their adoption for novel languages has been the significantly higher requirements on resources compared to word spaces.

In this paper, we have demonstrated that this obstacle can be overcome by transferring English distributional information along the resource gradient into target languages such as German and Croatian. The simplest models, which are based solely on the English Distributional Memory (DM) resource and a translation lexicon, already beat monolingual DMs in quality. These crosslingual models suffer from lower coverage but can be combined with the monolingual DM yielding a multilingual DM that maintains competitive accuracy while achieving significantly higher coverage than either individual model. The outcomes of our experiments are mostly stable across the languages and tasks presented, which leads us to assume the methodology successfully generalizes.[13]

Directions for future research include (a), more stringent filtering of spurious edges in DM.XL models to make the graph topology more similar to monolingual models and enable graph merging to obtain unified multilingual models; (b), the extension of our approach to more than two languages; (c), dimensionality reduction for tensor-based DSMs both for efficiency reasons and to improve performance.

[13]The German DMs are publicly available from `http://goo.gl/uxuffp`.

Acknowledgments

We gratefully acknowledge partial funding of our research by the DFG (SFB 732, Project D6) and the EC (Project EXCITEMENT, FP7 ICT-287923).

References

Collin F. Baker, Charles J. Fillmore, and John B. Lowe. 1998. The Berkeley FrameNet Project. In *Proceedings of the joint Annual Meeting of the Association for Computational Linguistics and International Conference on Computational Linguistics*, pages 86–90, Montréal, QC.

Marco Baroni and Alessandro Lenci. 2010. Distributional memory: A general framework for corpus-based semantics. *Computational Linguistics*, 36(4):1–49.

Marco Baroni, Silvia Bernardini, Adriano Ferraresi, and Eros Zanchetta. 2008. The WaCky Wide Web: A Collection of Very Large Linguistically Processed Web-Crawled Corpora. *Language Resources and Evaluation*, 43(3):209–226.

Bernd Bohnet. 2010. Top accuracy and fast dependency parsing is not a contradiction. In *Proceedings of the 23rd International Conference on Computational Linguistics*, pages 89–97, Beijing, China.

Sabine Buchholz and Erwin Marsi. 2006. CoNLL-X shared task on multilingual dependency parsing. In *Proceedings of the Tenth Conference on Computational Natural Language Learning*, pages 149–164, New York, NY.

Stanley F. Chen and Joshua Goodman. 1998. An empirical study of smoothing techniques for language modeling. Technical Report TR-10-98, Center for Research in Computing Technology, Harvard University.

Philipp Cimiano, Antje Schultz, Sergej Sizov, Philipp Sorg, and Steffen Staab. 2009. Explicit vs. latent concept models for cross-language information retrieval. In *Proceedings of the International Joint Conference on Artificial Intelligence*, pages 1513–1518, Pasadena, CA.

Wim De Smet and Marie-Francine Moens. 2009. Cross-language linking of news stories on the web using interlingual topic modelling. In *Proceedings of the CIKM Workshop on Social Web Search and Mining*, pages 57–64, Hong Kong.

Mona Diab and Philip Resnik. 2002. An unsupervised method for word sense tagging using parallel corpora. In *Proceedings of the 40th Annual Meeting of the Association for Computational Linguistics*, pages 255–262, Philadelphia, PA.

Bradley Efron and Robert J. Tibshirani. 1993. *An Introduction to the Bootstrap*. Chapman and Hall, New York, NY.

Katrin Erk, Sebastian Padó, and Ulrike Padó. 2010. A Flexible, Corpus-Driven Model of Regular and Inverse Selectional Preferences. *Computational Linguistics*, 36(4):723–763.

Pascale Fung and Benfeng Chen. 2004. BiFrameNet: Bilingual Frame Semantics Resources Construction by crosslingual Induction. In *Proceedings of the 20th International Conference on Computational Linguistics*, pages 931–935, Geneva, Switzerland.

Daniel Gildea and Daniel Jurafsky. 2002. Automatic labeling of semantic roles. *Computational Linguistics*, 28(3):245–288.

Gregory Grefenstette. 1994. *Explorations in Automatic Thesaurus Discovery*. Kluwer Academic Publishers, Boston/Norwell, MA.

Zelig S. Harris. 1954. Distributional structure. *Word*, 10(23):146–162.

Chenhai Hi and Rebecca Hwa. 2005. A Backoff Model for Bootstrapping Resources for Non-English Languages. In *Proceedings of the joint Human Language Technology Conference and Conference on Empirical Methods in Natural Language Processing*, pages 851–858, Vancouver, BC.

Rebecca Hwa, Philipp Resnik, Amy Weinberg, Clara Cabezas, and Okan Kolak. 2005. Bootstrapping Parsers via Syntactic Projection across Parallel Texts. *Journal of Natural Language Engineering*, 11(3):311–325.

Eric Joanis, Suzanne Stevenson, and David James. 2006. A general feature space for automatic verb classification. *Natural Language Engineering*, 14(03):337–367.

Mladen Karan, Jan Šnajder, and Bojana Dalbelo Bašić. 2012. Distributional semantics approach to detecting synonyms in Croatian language. In *Proceedings of the Eighth Language Technologies Conference*, Ljubljana, Slovenia.

Alexandre Klementiev, Ivan Titov, and Binod Bhattarai. 2012. Inducing crosslingual distributed representations of words. In *Proceedings of the International Conference on Computational Linguistics*, pages 1459–1474, Mumbai, India.

Mikhail Kozhevnikov and Ivan Titov. 2013. Crosslingual transfer of semantic role models. In *Proceedings of the 51th Annual Meeting of the Association for Computational Linguistics*, pages 1190–1200, Sofia, Bulgaria.

Thomas K Landauer and Susan T Dumais. 1997. A solution to Plato's problem: The latent semantic analysis theory of acquisition, induction, and representation of knowledge. *Psychological Review*, 104(2):211–240.

Dekang Lin. 1998. Automatic retrieval and clustering of similar words. In *Proceedings of the joint Annual Meeting of the Association for Computational Linguistics and International Conference on Computational Linguistics*, pages 768–774, Montreal, QC.

Ryan McDonald, Fernando Pereira, Kiril Ribarov, and Jan Hajič. 2005. Non-projective dependency parsing using spanning tree algorithms. In *Proceedings of the Conference on Human Language Technology and Empirical Methods in Natural Language Processing*, pages 523–530, Vancouver, BC.

Ryan McDonald, Joakim Nivre, Yvonne Quirmbach-Brundage, Yoav Goldberg, Dipanjan Das, Kuzman Ganchev, Keith Hall, Slav Petrov, Hao Zhang, Oscar Täckström, Claudia Bedini, Núria Bertomeu Castelló, and Jungmee Lee. 2013. Universal dependency annotation for multilingual parsing. In *Proceedings of the 51st Annual Meeting of the Association for Computational Linguistics*, pages 92–97, Sofia, Bulgaria.

Paola Merlo, Suzanne Stevenson, Vivian Tsang, and Gianluca Allaria. 2002. A multilingual paradigm for automatic verb classification. In *Proceedings of the 40th Annual Meeting on Association for Computational Linguistics*, pages 207–214, Philadelphia, PA.

Rada Mihalcea and Dragomir Radev. 2011. *Graph-based Natural Language Processing and Information Retrieval*. Cambridge University Press, Cambridge, UK.

George A. Miller and Walter G. Charles. 1991. Contextual correlates of semantic similarity. *Language and Cognitive Processes*, 6(1):1–28.

Saif Mohammad, Iryna Gurevych, Graeme Hirst, and Torsten Zesch. 2007. Crosslingual distributional profiles of concepts for measuring semantic distance. In *Proceedings of the Joint Conference on Empirical Methods in Natural Language Processing and Computational Natural Language Learning*, pages 571–580, Prague, Czech Republic.

Tahira Naseem, Benjamin Snyder, Jacob Eisenstein, and Regina Barzilay. 2009. Multilingual Part-of-Speech Tagging : Two Unsupervised Approaches. *Journal of Artificial Intelligence Research*, 36:1–45.

Roberto Navigli and Simone Paolo Ponzetto. 2010. BabelNet: Building a very large multilingual semantic network. In *Proceedings of the 48th Annual Meeting of the Association for Computational Linguistics*, pages 216–225, Uppsala, Sweden.

Roberto Navigli and Simone Paolo Ponzetto. 2012. Babelrelate! a joint multilingual approach to computing semantic relatedness. In *Proceedings of the 26th Conference on Artificial Intelligence*, pages 108–114, Toronto, ON.

Joakim Nivre. 2006. *Inductive Dependency Parsing*. Springer, Dordrecht, Netherlands.

Sebastian Padó and Jason Utt. 2012. A distributional memory for German. In *Proceedings of the KONVENS 2012 workshop on recent developments and applications of lexical-semantic resources*, pages 462–470, Vienna, Austria.

Yves Peirsman and Sebastian Padó. 2011. Semantic relations in bilingual lexicons. *ACM Transactions in Speech and Language Processing*, 8(2):3:1–3:21.

Lonneke van der Plas and Jörg Tiedemann. 2006. Finding synonyms using automatic word alignment and measures of distributional similarity. In *Proceedings of joint Annual Meeting of the Association for Computational Linguistics and International Conference on Computational Linguistics*, pages 866–873, Sydney, Australia.

Martin Potthast, Benno Stein, and Maik Anderka. 2008. A wikipedia-based multilingual retrieval model. In *Proceedings of the European Conference on Information Retrieval*, pages 522–530, Glasgow, Scotland.

Reinhard Rapp. 1999. Automatic identification of word translations from unrelated English and German corpora. In *Proceedings of the 37th Annual Meeting of the Association for Computational Linguistics on Computational Linguistics*, pages 519–526, College Park, MD.

Sabine Schulte im Walde. 2006. Experiments on the Automatic Induction of German Semantic Verb Classes. *Computational Linguistics*, 32(2):159–194.

Hinrich Schütze. 1992. Dimensions of meaning. In *Proceedings of Supercomputing '92*, pages 787–796, Minneapolis, MN.

Stephen Soderland, Oren Etzioni, Daniel S Weld, Michael Skinner, Jeff Bilmes, et al. 2009. Compiling a Massive, Multilingual Dictionary via Probabilistic Inference. In *Proceedings of the Joint Conference of the 47th Annual Meeting of the ACL and the 4th International Joint Conference on Natural Language Processing*, pages 262–270, Suntec, Singapore.

Harold Somers. 2005. Round-trip translation: What is it good for? In *Proceedings of the Australasian Language Technology Workshop*, pages 127–133, Sydney, Australia.

Jan Šnajder, Sebastian Padó, and Željko Agić. 2013. Building and evaluating a distributional memory for Croatian. In *Proceedings of the 51st Annual Meeting of the Association for Computational Linguistics*, pages 784–789, Sofia, Bulgaria.

Ivan Titov and Alexandre Klementiev. 2012. Crosslingual induction of semantic roles. In *Proceedings of the 50th Annual Meeting of the Association for Computational Linguistics*, pages 647–656, Jeju Island, South Korea.

Peter Turney. 2006. Similarity of semantic relations. *Computational Linguistics*, 32(3):379–416.

Ivan Vulić and Marie-Francine Moens. 2012. Detecting highly confident word translations from comparable corpora without any prior knowledge. In *Proceedings of the 13th Conference of the European Chapter of the Association for Computational Linguistics*, pages 449–459, Avignon, France.

DeWitt Wallace and Lila Acheson Wallace. 2005. *Reader's Digest, das Beste für Deutschland.* Verlag Das Beste, Stuttgart, Germany.

Fridolin Wild, Christina Stahl, Gerald Stermsek, and Gustaf Neumann. 2008. Parameters driving effectiveness of automated essay scoring with LSA. In *Proceedings of the 9th Computer-Aided Assessment Conference*, pages 485–494, Loughborough, UK.

David Yarowsky and Grace Ngai. 2001. Inducing Multilingual POS Taggers and NP Bracketers via Robust Projection across Aligned Corpora. In *Proceedings of the 2nd Annual Meeting of the North American Chapter of the Association for Computational Linguistics*, pages 200–207, Pittsburgh, PA.

Torsten Zesch, Iryna Gurevych, and Max Mühlhäuser. 2007. Comparing Wikipedia and German Wordnet by evaluating semantic relatedness on multiple datasets. In *Human Language Technologies 2007: The Conference of the North American Chapter of the Association for Computational Linguistics*, pages 205–208, Rochester, NY.

Entity Linking on Microblogs with Spatial and Temporal Signals

Yuan Fang *†
University of Illinois at Urbana-Champaign
201 N. Goodwin Avenue
Urbana, IL 61801, USA
fang2@illinois.edu

Ming-Wei Chang
Microsoft Research
1 Microsoft Way
Redmond, WA 98052, USA
minchang@microsoft.com

Abstract

Microblogs present an excellent opportunity for monitoring and analyzing world happenings. Given that words are often ambiguous, entity linking becomes a crucial step towards understanding microblogs. In this paper, we re-examine the problem of entity linking on microblogs. We first observe that spatiotemporal (*i.e.*, spatial and temporal) signals play a key role, but they are not utilized in existing approaches. Thus, we propose a novel entity linking framework that incorporates spatiotemporal signals through a weakly supervised process. Using entity annotations[1] on real-world data, our experiments show that the spatiotemporal model improves F1 by more than 10 points over existing systems. Finally, we present a qualitative study to visualize the effectiveness of our approach.

1 Introduction

Microblogging services provide an immense platform for intelligence gathering, such as market research (Asur and Huberman, 2010), disaster monitoring (Sadilek et al., 2012) and political analysis (Tumasjan et al., 2010). Extracting entities from microblogs is an essential step for many such applications. Suppose that a marketing firm is interested in the sentiment about some product on Twitter. However, any sentiment analysis is potentially misleading if we cannot correctly retrieve the tweets mentioning the target product.

To retrieve tweets for a given entity (*e.g.*, a product or an organization), a straightforward approach is to formulate a keyword query. However, simple keyword matching is largely ineffective, since keywords are often ambiguous. For instance, "spurs" can refer to two distinct sports teams (San Antonio Spurs, which is a basketball team in the US, and Tottenham Hotspur F.C., which is a soccer team in the UK), besides being a non-entity verb or noun. Thus, retrieving tweets via keyword queries inevitably mixes different entities.

Given the ambiguity of keywords, in this paper, we study the task of entity linking (Bunescu and Pasca, 2006) on microblogs. As *input*, we are given a short message (*e.g.*, a tweet) and an entity database (*e.g.*, Wikipedia where each article is an entity). As *output*, we map every surface form (*e.g.*, "spurs") in the message to an entity (*e.g.*, San Antonio Spurs) or to $\emptyset$ (*i.e.*, a non-entity). This task is particularly challenging for microblogs due to their short, noisy and colloquial nature. Fortunately, we also observe two new opportunities, which are often missing in traditional data.

First, microblogs usually embed rich meta-data, most notably *spatiotemporal* (*i.e.*, spatial and temporal) signals. Specifically, all tweets are associated with a timestamp, and many can be mapped to a location. We observe that entity priors often change across time and location. Consider the example tweets in Fig. 1. To understand the meaning of the word "spurs," it is challenging to only rely on the textual features. However, with the help of lo-

*Work done during an internship at Microsoft Research.
†Also affiliated with Agency for Science, Technology and Research, 1 Fusionopolis Way, Singapore 138632.
[1]Can be downloaded at http://research.microsoft.com/en-us/downloads/84ac9d88-c353-4059-97a4-87d129db0464/.

Transactions of the Association for Computational Linguistics, 2 (2014) 259–272. Action Editor: Noah Smith.
Submitted 11/2013; Revised 3/2014; Published 10/2014.

	Tweets mentioning Tottenham Hotspur F.C., a soccer team in the UK
UK:	Who scored the 2 goals for **spurs** I had to go out or 5 mins and missed it all
UK:	Defoe again 3 nil to **spurs** how you doing @USER at Arsenal
	Tweets mentioning San Antonio Spurs, a basketball team in the US
US:	@USER who cares, nobody wanna see the **spurs** play. Remember they're boring. He's a great coach ...
US:	The fine on the **spurs** for 250k is ridiculous! I'm a laker fan; still think this is too much

Figure 1: **Examples illustrating the importance of spatiotemporal signals to entity linking.** The "UK" or "US" tag indicates the location of the posting user. Based on deep semantic understanding of lexical items and additional resources (such as the entire conversation and attached URL), the annotators can label "spurs" in the first two tweets as the soccer team, and in the other two as the basketball team. While most entity linking systems handle merely textual features, the task obviously becomes easier with location information.

cation information, the two teams can be easily distinguished. In particular, based on our labeled data, San Antonio Spurs accounts for 91% of the "spurs" tweets in the US, whereas it only accounts for 8% in the UK. Similar trends also exist across different time periods. Therefore, exploiting spatiotemporal signals is crucial to entity linking.

Second, we can leverage the predictions from the tweets carrying an easier surface form to help link the tweets carrying an ambiguous surface form at a similar time or location. The intuition is that certain surface forms are easier to disambiguate than others. For instance, while only saying "spurs" in a tweet can be quite ambiguous, many other tweets around the same time or location might carry an easier surface form, such as "SA spurs" or "san antonio spurs," which are not ambiguous.

In this work, we focus on the *offline* mining setting, where a corpus has been collected for analysis offline. Developing algorithms for the streaming setting is an important direction of future work. Our contributions are summarized as follows:

- We propose a spatiotemporal framework for entity linking on microblogs. To our best knowledge, this is the first work to model spatiotemporal signals for entity linking.
- We demonstrate the effectiveness of our framework through extensive quantitative experiments. In particular, we improve F1 by more than 10 points over the existing state of the art.
- We point out that entity linking should be evaluated for both information extraction and retrieval needs. In the former, we evaluate the extraction of entities from tweets, while in the latter we evaluate the retrieval of tweets for a query entity. A qualitative study is also presented for the latter.

2 Related Work

Earlier research on entity linking (Bunescu and Pasca, 2006; Cucerzan, 2007; Milne and Witten, 2008) has been focused on well-written documents such as news and encyclopedia articles. The TAC KBP track (Ji et al., 2010; Ji and Grishman, 2011) also includes an entity linking task with a slightly different setting—to link a given mention based on a background document. These efforts exploit the statistical power aggregated by a semantic knowledge bases, most notably Wikipedia. Various features in the target document are also leveraged (Han et al., 2011; Kulkarni et al., 2009; Hoffart et al., 2011; Shen et al., 2012) to assess both local compatibility and global coherence.

These techniques have also been adapted and tailored to short texts including tweets, for the problem of entity linking (Ferragina and Scaiella, 2010; Meij et al., 2012; Guo et al., 2013) as well as the related problem of named entity recognition (NER) (Ritter et al., 2011; Li et al., 2012a). However, given the short and noisy nature of microblogs, these approaches, which largely depend on textual features, often result in unsatisfactory performance. Fortunately, additional non-textual meta-data in microblogs can often help. A recent study (Shen et al., 2013) improves entity linking by utilizing user account information, based on the intuition that all tweets posted by the same user share an underlying topic distribution.

Inspired by the use of non-textual features, we explore the spatiotemporal signals associated with tweets. Although the spatiotemporal aspect of social media has been studied in many papers, including temporal cycle tracking (Leskovec et al., 2009), spatial object matching (Dalvi et al., 2012), mining emerging topics (Mei et al., 2006; Cataldi et al., 2010; Yin et al., 2011), event monitoring (Sakaki et al., 2010; Xu et al., 2012), and identifying geographical linguistic variations (Eisenstein et al., 2010; Wing and Baldridge, 2011), none of them addresses the problem of entity linking. In this paper, we propose a novel spatiotemporal framework for entity linking, building upon some of the previously observed patterns in social media.

While we believe that entity linking is the first step towards intelligence gathering, many existing studies filter or cluster tweets based on merely keywords. On the one hand, manual selection of keywords (Sakaki et al., 2010; Tumasjan et al., 2010) requires significant labor, and thus is not scalable to the vast number of entities. On the other hand, automatic approaches (Li et al., 2013) only identify coarse-grained topics (*e.g.*, crime or sports), falling short of recognizing specific entities.

Lastly, there is a line of research on record extraction from social media (Benson et al., 2011; Ritter et al., 2012). Although the problem is different from entity linking, they present an interesting insight into social media. They observe that the same record is often referenced by multiple messages, and exploit this redundancy to help with extraction. The redundant nature of social media can be potentially leveraged to improve entity linking as well.

3 Spatiotemporal Entity Linking

Our spatiotemporal framework for entity linking requires an input tweet m, as well as its associated timestamp t and location l. For each tweet m, the goal is to predict an output set $\{e_1, e_2, \dots\}$ of entities that are mentioned in m.

3.1 Background

To build an entity linking system, we need both a *database* and a *lexicon*.

A database is a set of entities that a tweet can link to. Following earlier work (Sil and Yates, 2013), our database consists of the intersection of Freebase and Wikipedia. We then select the entities belonging to the *core* types (Guo et al., 2013)[2] based on the Freebase type information. In total, there are 2.7 million entities in our database.

A lexicon is a dictionary that maps a candidate anchor a (*i.e.*, a surface form) to its possible entity set $\mathcal{E}(a)$. Similar to existing studies (Cucerzan, 2007; Guo et al., 2013), our lexicon comprises information from disambiguation pages, redirect pages and anchor texts in Wikipedia[3]. To handle the case where a is not an entity, we add a special symbol $\emptyset$ to every $\mathcal{E}(a)$. We have 6 million anchors in total.

Given a tweet, the system generates a set of candidate anchors based on the lexicon. Specifically, each tweet is tokenized into individual words, keeping each punctuation as a separate token. To identify if any sequence of tokens matches an anchor in the lexicon, we use exact matching, but allow for case-insensitivity. Furthermore, we employ an NER system trained using structural perceptron (Collins, 2002) to filter the anchors of type *person*, *loc* or *org*, such that only the anchors recognized by the NER are retained.

3.2 Incorporating Spatiotemporal Signals

Consider a tweet m with timestamp t and location l. Given anchor a in tweet m, our system links a to the candidate entity e^* as follows:

$$\begin{aligned} e^* &= \arg\max_{e \in \mathcal{E}(a)} P(e|m, a, t, l) \\ &= \arg\max_{e \in \mathcal{E}(a)} P(e, m, a, t, l) \end{aligned} \quad (1)$$

We further adopt the following conditional independence assumption in our model.

ASSUMPTION: Given an entity e, *how* e is expressed (m, a), and *when* or *where* e is published (t, l), are conditionally independent. In other words, we have $P(m, a|t, l, e) = P(m, a|e)$. ■

Intuitively, the expression (m, a) of a given entity e is stable across most times and locations (t, l), which could be attributed to the imitation nature (Leskovec et al., 2009) of social media. That is, as stories of e propagate on the social media, users over different t and l often imitate each other (disregarding cross-lingual scenarios). While there could be a "burn-in" period for recent events of e, the distribution of m and a would eventually "stabilize" over most t and l.

[2]Their core types include *person*, *organization* (*org*), *location* (*loc*), *book*, *tvshow* and *movie*. We deal with two additional types, namely, *event* and *product*.

[3]We use a snapshot of Wikipedia taken on 04/03/2013.

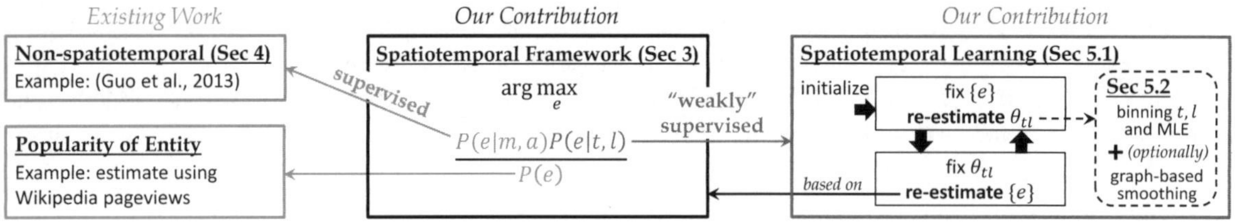

Figure 2: Overall framework of spatiotemporal entity linking.

Subsequently, we decompose the model below, to enable the reuse of existing non-spatiotemporal models for $P(e|m, a)$, as we shall see later.

$$\begin{aligned} & P(e, m, a, t, l) \\ &= P(m, a|t, l, e)P(t, l, e) \\ &= P(m, a|e)P(t, l, e) \\ &= P(e|m, a)P(m, a)P(e|t, l)P(t, l)/P(e) \end{aligned} \quad (2)$$

Note that in (2), we choose to rewrite $P(t, l, e)$ as $P(e|t, l)P(t, l)$ instead of $P(t, l|e)P(e)$. The choice is due to computational issues. In the latter, we need to estimate one distribution for every e; in the former, we need to estimate one distribution for every t, l. There are 2.7 million entities in our database, but with appropriate quantization the number of t, l "bins" are only on the order of thousands.

Thus, the prediction model (1) is equivalent to

$$e^* = \arg\max_{e \in \mathcal{E}(a)} P(e|m, a)P(e|t, l)/P(e). \quad (3)$$

Intuitively, if e at some t, l is more popular than usual, *i.e.*, $P(e|t, l) > P(e)$, we should promote e for a tweet at t, l; otherwise we should demote e.

The overall framework is summarized in Fig. 2, which boils down to the three factors in (3), namely, $P(e|m, a)$, $P(e|t, l)$ and $P(e)$. In Sect. 4, we will discuss briefly how $P(e|m, a)$ is modeled based on previous work. In Sect. 5, we will estimate spatiotemporal signals in the form of $P(e|t, l)$, which is jointly optimized with entity assignments. Lastly, we discuss $P(e)$ here.

$P(e)$ measures the popularity of e, and is estimated by making it proportional to the Wikipedia pageviews of e. While this is a fair proxy for a general social media corpus, we acknowledge that more advanced method is required for a specialized corpus (*e.g.*, for users of a sub-community). Note that $P(e)$ is not estimated based on the joint optimization technique for $P(e|t, l)$ in Sect. 5. The reason is that our tweets used in the experiments only cover a one-month period, which does not necessarily reflect the general popularity of the entities.

4 End-to-End Entity Linking

The goal of this section is to describe our base system that does not consider spatiotemporal signals, *i.e.*, to model $P(e|m, a)$. Specifically, we adopt an end-to-end entity linking system (E2E), which is designed to jointly detect mentions and disambiguate entities. E2E is a supervised method largely based on a previous study (Guo et al., 2013).

For efficiency, we only adopt the first order model. Therefore, the prediction function can be decomposed for each anchor a independently,

$$e^* = \arg\max_{e \in \mathcal{E}(a)} \mathbf{w}^T \Phi(m, a, e). \quad (4)$$

where $\mathbf{w}$ is a linear model trained using structural SVM, and Φ is a feature function over message m, anchor a, and candidate output e.

We use all the basic features and the cohesiveness score feature (Guo et al., 2013)[4]. Additional features are also included. First, for each mention and candidate entity pair, we add a feature to capture the number of highly correlated candidates carried by other mentions in the same tweet with respect to the current candidate. Second, we include a binary feature that will be active if the type of the mention (when recognized by our NER system) and the type of the candidate entity (according to the Freebase type information) agree with each other.

Probability conversion. It is crucial to have a well calibrated probability distribution for the predictions. In order to convert the output of the structural SVM model, we adapt an existing approach

[4]Described in Table 4 and Sect. 4.3 of the reference.

(Platt, 2000) to our case. We define

$$P(e|m,a)=\frac{\exp(b_1+b_2\mathbf{w}^T\Phi(m,a,e))}{\sum_{e'\in\mathcal{E}(a)}\exp(b_1+b_2\mathbf{w}^T\Phi(m,a,e'))},$$

where b_1 and b_2 are the calibration parameters that will be tuned using labeled data.

Given a labeled development set, let $G(e|m,a)=1$ if and only if anchor a in tweet m is labeled to link to entity e, and let $G(\emptyset|m,a)=1$ if and only if a in m is not labeled to link to any entity. Note that $\sum_{e\in\mathcal{E}(a)}G(e|m,a)=1$. Thus, G represents the ground-truth distribution, and we want $P(e|m,a)$ to be as close to $G(e|m,a)$ as possible. To this end, we optimize b_1 and b_2 by minimizing the cross entropy between G and P:

$$\min_{b_1,b_2}\ -\sum_{m,a}G(e|m,a)\log P(e|m,a).$$

Alternative base system. We also consider *Link-Probability* (LP) as an additional base system. As pointed out earlier (Guo et al., 2013), mention detection is an important step for end-to-end entity linking, and its design is crucial to the ultimate performance. Hence, to detect candidate anchors, LP uses the same design of database and lexicon discussed in this paper and elsewhere (Cucerzan, 2007; Guo et al., 2013), which is believed to be effective. Given a potential anchor a in message m, $P(e|m,a)$ is simply modeled as $P(e|a)$, which can be estimated from Wikipedia anchor statistics. In fact, anchor statistics constitute one of the most useful features in more sophisticated systems (Shen et al., 2012; Guo et al., 2013). Given its robust mention detection mechanism and the utility of anchor statistics, the simple LP turns out surprisingly well.

5 Estimating Spatiotemporal Signals

There are two critical challenges for successfully estimating the spatiotemporal signals in the form of $P(e|t,l)$. First, it is impractical to collect sufficient labeled data to directly estimate it. Second, we need to properly handle the continuous space of the spatiotemporal signals.

In the following, we detail the overall model for learning spatiotemporal signals in a weakly supervised fashion (Sect. 5.1), and then discuss two ways of handling continuous signals (Sect. 5.2).

5.1 Spatiotemporal Learning Model

We model the spatiotemporal signals by a generative model $P(e|t,l)\sim \text{Multi}(\theta_{tl})$, where θ_{tl} is the parameter for the multinomial distribution over all entities at t,l. Since there is no ground truth of the entity assignment, our model will jointly optimize the entity assignment and θ_{tl}. Based on (3), we use the following objective function $\Omega(\{e\},\theta_{tl})$:

$$\sum_{m,a}(\log P(e|m,a)+\log P(e|\theta_{tl})-\log P(e)),$$

where m is an unlabeled message at time t and location l, a is an anchor in m, and $\{e\}$ is a set of entity assignments for the set of m.

We use a block-coordinate ascent method to find the best θ_{tl} and $\{e\}$ iteratively. For each iteration, the following two steps will be executed.

- Fix θ_{tl}. Find the entity assignments $\{e\}$ that maximizes Ω. Note that if θ_{tl} is fixed, the most likely assignment can be found using

  $$\arg\max_e(\log P(e|m,a)+\log P(e|\theta_{tl})-\log P(e)).$$

  In fact, this equation is the same as (3), where $P(e|m,a)$ can be estimated by a supervised base system (*e.g.*, E2E or LP, see Sect. 4).

- Fix $\{e\}$. Re-estimate θ_{tl} by maximizing Ω. Once the assignment of entities has been generated by the previous step, we can re-estimate it by maximizing the objective function with

  $$\arg\max_{\theta_{tl}}\sum_{m,a}\log P(e|\theta_{tl}).$$

  In other words, we are looking for the maximum likelihood estimate (MLE) of θ_{tl}, given the (previously inferred) entity assignments $\{e\}$. Since θ_{tl} is multinomial, its MLE can be computed as the relative frequency of each e, that is,

  $$\theta_{tl}(e)=\frac{\text{\# tweets containing } e \text{ at } t,l}{\sum_{e'}\text{\# tweets containing } e' \text{ at } t,l}.$$

  Of course, t,l are continuous, so direct counting is infeasible. Instead, we resort to discrete bins, which will be treated in Sect. 5.2.

This process will be executed repeatedly, and can be considered as a variant of the Hard EM algorithm. In practice, we run it for up to five iterations, as Hard EM often converges fast.

We call this learning process a "weakly supervised" model. For some time t and location l, the objective function $\Omega(\{e\}, \theta_{tl})$ sums over all messages at t, l. These messages themselves are unlabeled, but some supervision is provided by the base system indirectly. In other words, even though we do not know the ground truth entity assignments in the messages, we can leverage the predictions from the base system to update the entity assignments.

5.2 Handling Continuous Time and Location

Given the continuous space of time t and location l, we propose two methods to estimate θ_{tl}. While it could be cast as an instance of the well-studied density estimation problem (Vapnik and Mukherjee, 1999; Scott, 2009), we resort to a simple binning method, which has also been applied to other spatiotemporal contexts (Wing and Baldridge, 2011; Xu et al., 2012). The binning approach can already demonstrate the significance of spatiotemporal signals in entity linking.

Binning. Our first approach segments the continuous space into discrete bins. Time is divided into a set of equal intervals Δ_{T} (*e.g.*, every one hour), and location is divided into a set of equal squares Δ_{L} (*e.g.*, each 100×100 sqkm area[5]). Let $\Delta = \Delta_{\mathrm{T}} \times \Delta_{\mathrm{L}}$ denote the set of bins over time and location. We further index the bins by $\mathcal{I} = \{1, \ldots, n\}$ where $n = |\Delta|$, and refer to each bin δ_i through its index $i \in \mathcal{I}$. Correspondingly, we denote the multinomial parameter at bin δ_i by θ_i, which can be estimated using maximum likelihood (*i.e.*, relative frequency of entities in δ_i).

It can be shown that with sufficiently small bins, θ_{tl} can be approximated accurately by θ_i when $t, l \in \delta_i$. In practice, if the bins are too small, there are often inadequate tweets in a bin, and thus θ_i cannot be well estimated. On the contrary, if the bins are too large, θ_i cannot reliably model θ_{tl}. In this paper, we tune the bin size using development data.

Graph-based smoothing. Our algorithm contains two steps: first, we estimate $\hat{\theta}_i$ for each bin δ_i as in the above binning approach; next, we smooth the initial estimate to obtain the final estimate θ_i using graph-based regularization.

[5]The location grid is actually defined in longitude and latitude. Here we show the equivalent distance on Earth's surface.

As a common insight in graph-based learning (Zhu et al., 2003; Fang et al., 2012; Fang et al., 2014), if δ_i and δ_j are close to each other, θ_i and θ_j should be similar. Moreover, θ_i should not deviate too much from the initial estimate $\hat{\theta}_i$. The intuition can be captured by the following optimization:

$$\min_{(\theta_1,\ldots,\theta_n)} \tfrac{1}{2}(1-\epsilon)\textstyle\sum_{i,j\in\mathcal{I}} W_{ij}\|\theta_i - \theta_j\|^2 + \epsilon \textstyle\sum_{i\in\mathcal{I}} D_{ii}\|\theta_i - \hat{\theta}_i\|^2, \quad (5)$$

where $\epsilon \in (0, 1)$ is a regularization parameter, W is an affinity matrix such that W_{ij} measures the "closeness" of δ_i and δ_j, and D is a diagonal matrix such that $D_{ii} = \sum_{j\in\mathcal{I}} W_{ij}$. In particular, we design the affinity matrix as follows:

$$W_{ij} = \begin{cases} (d_0 + d(\delta_i, \delta_j))^\gamma & i \neq j \\ 0 & i = j, \end{cases} \quad (6)$$

where $d_0 > 0$ and $\gamma < 0$ are parameters, and $d(\cdot)$ is a symmetric distance function for bins. Given that $\gamma < 0$, W_{ij} follows a polynomial decay when δ_i and δ_j become farther apart, as previously suggested (Dalvi et al., 2012).

It can be shown that the optimization problem (5) is equivalent to finding θ_i such that $\forall i \in \mathcal{I}$,

$$\theta_i = (1-\epsilon)\textstyle\sum_{j\in\mathcal{I}} \frac{W_{ij}}{D_{ii}}\theta_j + \epsilon\hat{\theta}_i. \quad (7)$$

Interestingly, we can consider (7) as a generalization of previous observations on social media. It is proposed that the temporal model on social media needs to account for two factors: *imitation* and *recency* (Leskovec et al., 2009). For imitation, users often imitate one another, so that a past story can be picked up and propagated by other users by writing new articles about the same story. For *recency*, more recent stories are more likely to be imitated. We generalize their idea to both temporal and spatial signals, and extend it to entity linking. Specifically, (7) can be interpreted as a result of imitation: tweets mentioning entity e in δ_i are imitated from those in δ_j. In addition, a closer δ_j has a higher chance to be imitated, which captures recency.

To solve (7), let $Q = [\theta_1, \ldots, \theta_n]^T$ and $\hat{Q} = [\hat{\theta}_1, \ldots, \hat{\theta}_n]^T$, treating θ_i and $\hat{\theta}_i$ as column vectors. Through the following iterative updates (Fang et al., 2013), $Q^{(t)}$ converges to Q as $t \to \infty$, starting from an arbitrary $Q^{(0)}$:

$$Q^{(t+1)} = (1-\epsilon)(D^{-1}W)Q^{(t)} + \epsilon\hat{Q}. \quad (8)$$

The time complexity is $O(tnk)$, where k is the number of neighboring bins on the graph. Such cost is reasonable, given that the update generally converges for $t < 50$, and k is a constant if we only consider k nearest neighbors on the graph.

Joint vs. separate modeling. Finally, while modeling time and location *jointly* is more expressive than modeling each signal separately, the joint approach also creates much more bins (and hence more multinomial parameters), making data scarcity a severe issue. In particular, jointly we have $|\Delta_T| \times |\Delta_L|$ bins, but separately we only have $|\Delta_T| + |\Delta_L|$ bins. By assuming the conditional independence of t and l given e, we can rewrite (3) to model time and location separately:

$$e^* = \arg\max_{e \in \mathcal{E}(a)} P(e|m,a)P(e|t)P(e|l)/P(e)^2 \quad (9)$$

We refer to the joint model (3) as "T×L", and the separate model as "T+L" (9). For "T+L", graph-based smoothing can be carried out separately for the time bins and the location bins. The two models will be compared in our experiments.

6 Experiments

In this section, we assess the effectiveness of our approach through quantitative experiments.

6.1 Settings

Dataset. Our experiments are conducted on Twitter data. We collect all English tweets from verified accounts in December 2012, excluding retweets.[6] These tweets amount to 7 million. As we assume an offline analysis scenario instead of an online streaming scenario, these tweets are fetched and stored locally in advance.

We further select tweets with both spatial and temporal information. For time, we take the posting time of each tweet. Locations are harder to obtain, given that fewer than 5% of our tweets are geotagged. For tweets without geo-coordinates, we use the location in the user profile and map it to coordinates based on a lookup table containing major cities in the US[7]. Such mapping exists for about 25% of the tweets. For the remaining tweets, their user profiles are either uninformative (*e.g.*, "home") or report a non-US location. In the end, 1.8 million tweets remain in our dataset. Note that some studies (Dalvi et al., 2012; Li et al., 2012b) enable the inference of missing locations based on user generated content or user network. We do not apply these methods, which are beyond our focus.

Lastly, we collect the Wikipedia pageviews in the year 2012 in order to estimate $P(e)$ in (3).

Development set. We randomly sample 250 tweets as the development set and label their *core* entities (see Sect. 3.1). There are two human annotators. Each annotator labels half of the tweets, which are then counter-checked by the other to reach an agreement. To label a tweet, the annotators are given all available information to understand its content, *e.g.*, the attached URL and the conversation.

On the other hand, the base system E2E is trained on an independent set of 1000 tweets randomly sampled from the year 2010.

Algorithms. For the binning approach, we tune the bin size on the development set, ranging from 10 minutes to 1 day for time, and from 10×10 sqkm to 1500×1500 sqkm for location. Although the optimal bin size may be entity specific, we use the same size optimized over all entities for scalability considerations. That said, if we are only interested in a small set of target entities, it is possible to optimize the bin size for each entity, in order to attain better performance. Unless otherwise stated, in the rest of the paper, binning is the default method to estimate spatiotemporal signals.

For graph-based smoothing, we use the finest bin for both time and location, and tune its parameters $\epsilon \in \{.01, .05, .1, .5\}$, $d_0 = \{1, 10\}$ and $\gamma \in \{\text{-}.5, \text{-}1, \text{-}2, \text{-}4, \text{-}8\}$ on the development set. To construct the graph, we also need to define the distance function $d(\cdot)$ in (6). For time bins, we use the

[6]The identities of *verified accounts* are validated by Twitter, and thus their tweets contain little spam. Moreover, we ignore retweets here as their spatiotemporal behavior might significantly differ from that of the original tweets.

[7]The lookup table is compiled from geonames.org. We only consider city and state names in the US, discarding all others. As city names may be ambiguous, we apply conservative matching using city-state pair. We also account for popular abbreviations (*e.g.*, IL for Illinois and NYC for New York City).

elapsed time between the middle timestamps of two bins. For location bins, we use the distance between the geographical centers of two bins on Earth's surface. For joint time-location bins, we take the average of time (min) and location (km) distances.

Finally, in both of the above, we use the inferred entity assignments $\{e\}$ to estimate θ_{tl} (see Sect 5.1). Since the inferred assignments can be quite noisy, we only count confident ones such that their inferred probability is at least 0.5.

6.2 Evaluation Methodology

We adopt two different evaluation policies, which are driven by information *extraction* (IE) and *retrieval* (IR) needs, respectively.

IE-driven evaluation. The IE-driven evaluation is similar to the standard evaluation for an end-to-end entity linking system, which evaluates the entities "extracted" by linking. We randomly sample 250 tweets as the test set, which are labeled in the same manner as the development set. For evaluation, we compute the F1 score over the test set, as defined earlier (Guo et al., 2013).

According to the labels, 40% of the tweets in the test set contain at least one entity. A total of 179 entity instances are identified, or an average of 0.72 per tweet. These entities belong to different types, including *person* (24%), *org* (36%), *loc* (16%), *event* (9%), and others (15%).

IR-driven evaluation. One key application of entity linking is to enable intelligence gathering for a *query entity*, where the first step is to "retrieve" the tweets mentioning the query entity. As listed in Table 1, we sample ten query entities of different types, where each entity is known to be influenced by spatiotemporal signals, and has one or more ambiguous anchors. For instance, Hillary Rodham Clinton may be mentioned by "clinton" only, which could be mistakenly linked to Bill Clinton.

Type	Query entity	
person	Hillary Rodham Clinton*	Catherine, Duchess of Cambridge*
org	San Antonia Spurs*	Big Bang (South Korean band)*
loc	Washington (state)*	Newtown, Connecticut
event	Hanukkah*	Winter solstice
movie	Les Misérables (2012 film)	Django unchained (2012 film)

Table 1: Query entities for IR-driven evaluation.

For each query entity, we randomly sample 100 tweets as the test set (totaling 1000 tweets), such that each tweet contains an ambiguous anchor of the entity (through a lookup from our lexicon). Each tweet is labeled to indicate whether it mentions the query entity or not. About 37% of the sampled tweets did not actually mention the query entity since the anchors are ambiguous. For evaluation, we test if the system can correctly identify the presence or absence of the query entity in every tweet. In particular, we compute the F1 score over the test set.

Note that this task is harder than it seems. Besides ambiguous anchors, many entities are not dominant for their anchor. For instance, for the anchor "big bang", Big Bang (South Korean band) is less popular than The Big Bang Theory (a TV show). In fact, six of the entities are not dominant, marked by $\star$ in Table 1. Thus, merely linking to the most popular one (*i.e.*, the base system LP) is not a good strategy.

Significance test. To establish the statistical significance of our results, we randomly divide the test set into 10 splits of equal number of tweets, and compute the F1 score on each split for each algorithm. Two-tail paired t-test is then applied to determine if the F1 scores of two algorithms over the 10 splits are significantly different.

6.3 Results and Discussion

We present the empirical findings for the following research questions.

Q1: How do our base systems perform?
Q2: Are spatiotemporal signals indeed useful?
Q3: Does the graph-based smoothing help?
Q4: What causes the errors? How to recover them?

Base system comparison (Q1). To show that our base systems, in particular E2E, already outperform other systems, we compare with Wikiminer (Milne and Witten, 2008) and Illinois (Ratinov et al., 2011) systems.[8] As existing systems are more geared for the IE scenario, we report in Table 2 the IE-drive F1 on the test set.

[8]We use the authors' implementations. AIDA (Hoffart et al., 2011) is not compared, as it mostly links to *person*, *org* and *loc* only. TAGME (Ferragina and Scaiella, 2010) and Cucerzan (Cucerzan, 2007) were already compared in an earlier paper (Guo et al., 2013) which E2E is largely based on. To be fair, we discard non-core entities linked by Wikiminer or Illinois.

	E2E				LP			
	IE		IR		IE		IR	
base	57.0	–	58.4	–	48.3	–	48.5	–
+T	64.9	***	71.4	***	**52.4**	*	59.7	***
+L	65.0	**	76.1	***	50.3	*	**61.8**	***
+T+L	**68.6**	***	**79.0**	***	49.0		53.3	***
+T×L	66.2	***	74.1	***	50.6		61.2	***

(a) F1 scores

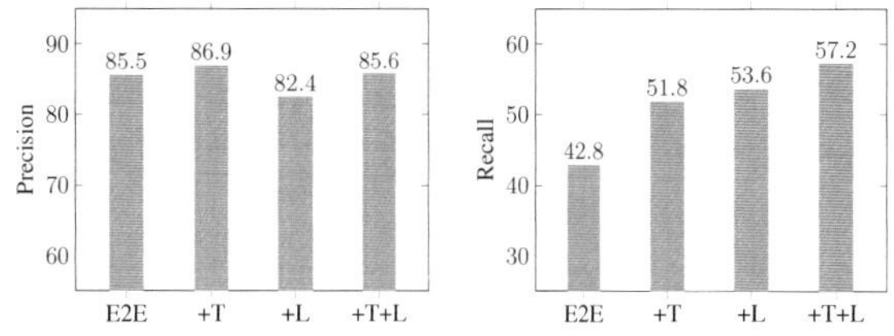

(b) Precision (c) Recall

Figure 3: **Effect of using spatiotemporal signals.** (a) F1 scores. ***, **, *: Significantly different from the base system at .01, .05, .1 levels. (b, c) IE-driven evaluation of precision and recall, using E2E as the base system.

The results clearly show that E2E performs better than other base systems. Also note that LP obtains similar or better F1 than Illinois or Wikiminer, although its precision is lower.

	Precision	Recall	F1	Significance
Wikiminer	78.9	24.7	37.6	***
Illinois	77.3	34.9	48.1	**
LP	49.7	**47.0**	48.3	**
E2E	**85.5**	42.8	**57.0**	–

Table 2: IE-driven comparison of base systems. ***, **, *: Significantly different from E2E at .01, .05, .1 levels.

Spatiotemporal signals (Q2). To showcase our key insight that spatiotemporal signals are crucial for entity linking, we compare the base systems with their time or location-aware counterparts.

As reported in Fig. 3a, using either temporal (+T) or spatial (+L) signal can indeed improve entity linking over the base systems. In particular, the improvements in IR-driven evaluation are more significant since the chosen entities are known to be influenced by time or location.

Next, we combine both temporal and spatial signals. As Sect. 5 discussed, while the joint model (+T×L) is ideal in theory, it is not necessarily better than the separate model (+T+L) due to data scarcity, as shown in the last two rows of Fig. 3a. In the following, we will use "+T+L" as the default setting. Also note that using both time and location on LP may be worse than using either alone, given that LP has low precision and thus employing both signals may aggregate more errors.

Let us also examine the precision and recall in Fig. 3b and 3c. Interestingly, while precision is not compromised, recall is greatly increased with spatiotemporal signals. The reason is that E2E has high precision, but misses a lot of mentions (*i.e.*, linking them to $\emptyset$). However, if an entity e is "trending" at some time t or location l, that is, e is mentioned by more tweets than usual at t or l, we shall expect $P(e|t,l) > P(e)$. Thus, the system is more likely to link to e instead of $\emptyset$ based on our spatiotemporal model (3), resulting in higher recall. A more in-depth error analysis will be presented in Q4.

Graph-based smoothing (Q3). Next, we evaluate the utility of smoothing in Fig. 4. The model called "Fine" discretizes time and location using the finest bins. The one called "Fine+Smoothing" is our graph-based smoothing algorithm applied to the "Fine" model. We also compare with "Optimal", which discretizes time and location using the optimal bins tuned on the development set.

As we can see, smoothing is crucial when a small bin size is used. Compared to "Optimal", our smoothing is better on LP but not on E2E. However, smoothing is still useful, as "Optimal" depends a lot on choosing the right bin size, while smoothing is less sensitive to its parameters.

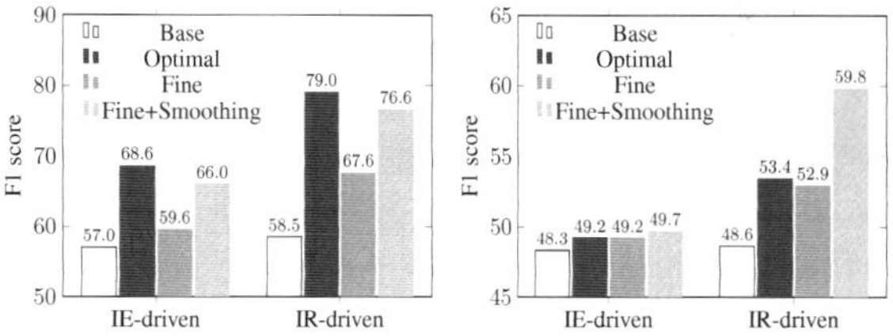

(a) Base system: E2E (b) Base system: LP

Figure 4: F1 scores by different ways of estimating spatiotemporal signals in the +T+L setting.

Error analysis (Q4). Let us investigate what causes the errors. In Table 3, we first break down the errors into false positives and false negatives. Each type is further categorized as "mention" (the mention itself is wrong) or "linking" (the mention is correct but linking is wrong). Note that if the mention is wrong, the linking would also be wrong.

	False Positives			False Negatives		
	mention	linking	total	mention	linking	total
E2E	7	5	12	90	5	95
+T+L	9	7	16	64	7	71

Table 3: Sources of error in IE-driven evaluation.

On the one hand, both systems make few false positives, suggesting high precision (see Fig. 3b). On the other hand, while the base system (E2E) makes many false negatives, the spatiotemporal model (+T+L) substantially reduces these errors, resulting in a significant increase in recall (see Fig. 3c). +T+L is particularly effective in recovering false negatives due to incorrect mention, *i.e.*, linking to $\emptyset$ when it should not, which account for the vast majority (84%) of all the errors in E2E.

Next, we examine how these errors can be recovered in +T+L. We zoom into entity types of *person*, *org*, *loc* and *event*, which collectively cover 85% of the entities in the test set. Fig. 5a reveals that +T+L is consistently helpful to different types of entities. In particular, +T+L improves the *event* entities the most, since events are generally more correlated to time and location, which are useful signals for recovering the errors.

We illustrate in Fig. 5b some entities that are missed by E2E, but recovered by useful spatial or temporal signals. Taking tweet #2 for illustration, E2E is not confident linking to the entity California State University, Fullerton based on textual content alone, and thus incorrectly links to $\emptyset$. This is a false negative due to incorrect mention, the most frequent kind in E2E (see Table 3). Fortunately, +T+L is confident linking to the entity correctly, given that 1) the tweet was posted during a campus emergency, *when* many other tweets were also discussing this entity; and 2) the posting user was in California, *where* the users of many other tweets discussing this entity were also located.

7 Qualitative Study: Entity vs. Keyword

The goal of this section is twofold. First, we provide a qualitative analysis to visualize the performance of our entity linking system. The results show that our system can consistently recover the real-world happenings or physical locations of the query entities. Second, we show that entity linking is more effective than keyword matching in the retrieving scenario (see Sect. 6.2).

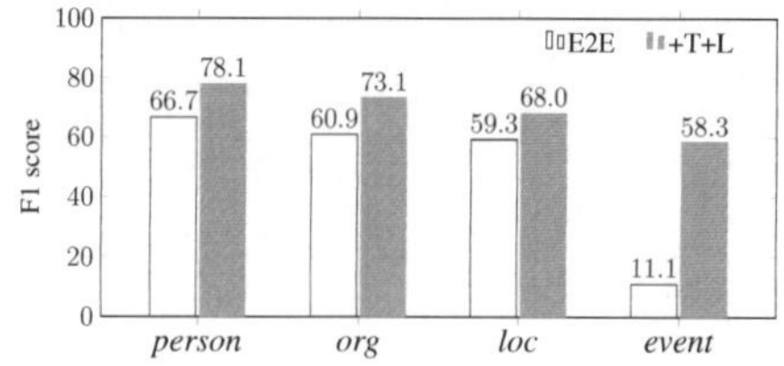

(a) F1 scores

Tweet	Example entity	Posting time	User location
#1	*person*: Colin Kaepernick	during his game	*(not useful)*
#2	*org*: Cali. State U. Fullerton	in campus emergency	California
#3	*loc*: Los Angeles	*(not useful)*	California
#4	*event*: New Year's Eve	on 31 December	*(not useful)*

(b) Example entities recovered by spatiotemporal signals

Figure 5: IE-driven evaluation by entity type.

Approach. We can retrieve a tweet by entity linking or keywords. For entity linking, we classify all the tweets using E2E+T+L, and a tweet is positive (*i.e.*, it will be retrieved) if its predictions contain the query entity. For keyword matching, a tweet is positive if it contains the given keywords which describe the query entity.

To visualize the retrieved tweets, we discretize time into 24-hour bins, and location into 100×100 sqkm bins. In a bin δ_i, define the *intensity* of an entity e as $\#(e, \delta_i)/\#(\delta_i)$, where $\#(e, \delta_i)$ is the number of positive tweets for e in δ_i, and $\#(\delta_i)$ is the total number of tweets in δ_i. To visualize the intensity of multiple entities simultaneously, we further compute the *normalized intensity* of e, which normalizes e's intensity by its maximum over all the bins.

Case study 1: "washington." We retrieve tweets with keyword "washington", a common anchor for three entities: Washington (state), Wasghinton D.C. and Washington Redskins. We also retrieve tweets for each of them with entity linking.

We first examine the intensity of the entities over December 2012. In Fig. 6a, the intensity based on keyword "washington" inevitably represents a mixture of different entities—it is unclear which "washington" entity corresponds to each intensity peak. Fortunately, entity linking separates the three enti-

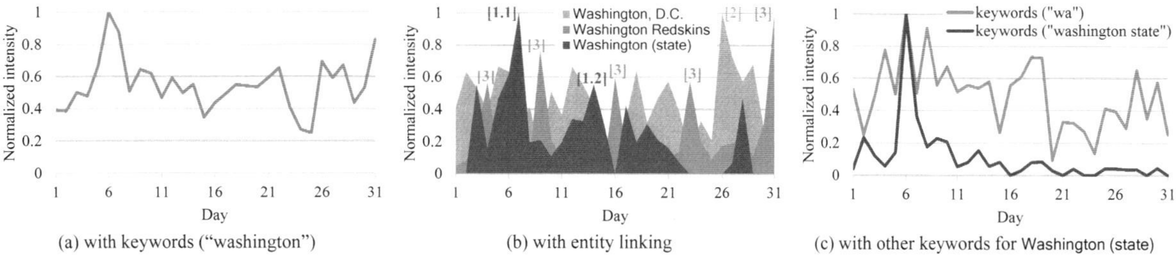

Figure 6: **Intensity of "washington" over December 2012.** In particular, entity linking (b) reveals the correspondence to several real-world happenings: *legalization of marijuana* in Washington (state) [1.1] and *Obama's response* [1.2], *fiscal cliff and weather alert* in Washington D.C. [2], *games* of Washington Redskins [3].

ties in Fig. 6b, where major intensity peaks correspond to real-world happenings for each entity. We also use alternative keywords specifically targeted for Washington (state), namely, "washington state" and "wa". While they are more precise than "washington" for the given entity, they have lower recall, resulting in different intensity profiles in Fig. 6c.

Lastly, we examine their intensity over the US. Using keywords, Fig. 6a does not isolate different entities. In contrast, using entity linking, Fig. 6b reveals more information about the three entities. For instance, tweets for Washington (state) are mostly concentrated in that state, and those for Washington Redskins are mostly in their home location but also have occurrences all over the US.

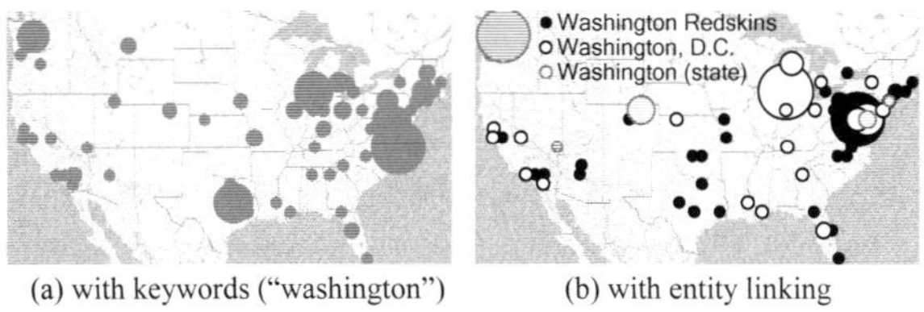

Figure 7: Intensity of "washington" over the US. The size of dots indicates the normalized intensity.

Case study 2: "spurs." We retrieve tweets with keyword "spurs", a popular anchor for both San Antonio Spurs and Tottenham Hotspur F.C. We also retrieve tweets for each of them with entity linking.

As illustrated in Fig. 8, the intensity based on keyword "spurs" roughly matches that of San Antonio Spurs based on entity linking, but significantly differs from Tottenham Hotspur F.C. In other words, "spurs" only accounts for the former entity, even though it is also a standard anchor for the latter. The reason is that an overwhelming majority of the mentions of "spurs" in the US refer to San Antonio Spurs. That means, while keywords may work for the dominating entity, they are particularly weak for the other entity. In contrast, with entity linking, both entities can be identified, where the major peaks correspond to the game days of each team.

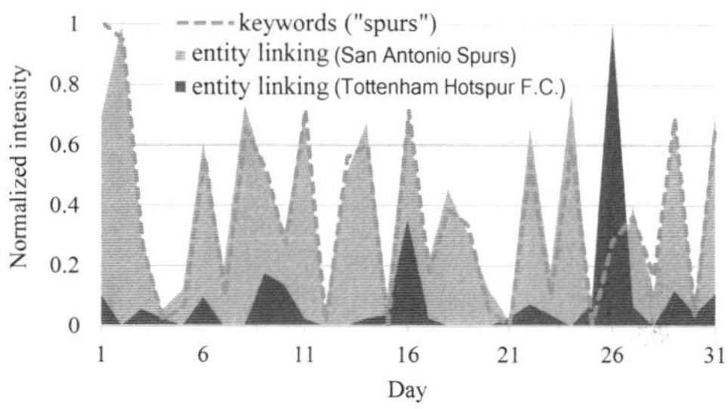

Figure 8: Intensity of "spurs" over December 2012.

8 Conclusion

As microblogging and other social media services become increasingly popular, the number of short and noisy messages are growing at an unprecedented rate. We demonstrate, for the first time, that spatiotemporal signals are critical in advancing entity linking. After all, it might not be a mere text-based language processing problem.

There are some important future directions for this work. First, updating the spatiotemporal model on the fly is a useful extension to cater to the online streaming setting. Second, we foresee a more general framework to integrate various meta-data such as authorship, surrounding conversation, attached URL and hashtags, in addition to the spatiotemporal signals. Finally, it would also pay off to analyze the interactions between the meta-data and the use of language. We believe that exploring the meta-data for entity linking on microblogs will be an interesting and active line of research.

References

S. Asur and B.A. Huberman. 2010. Predicting the future with social media. In *Web Intelligence*, pages 492–499.

E. Benson, A. Haghighi, and R. Barzilay. 2011. Event discovery in social media feeds. In *Proceedings of the Annual Meeting of the Association for Computational Linguistics (ACL)*, pages 389–398.

R. C Bunescu and M. Pasca. 2006. Using encyclopedic knowledge for named entity disambiguation. In *Proceedings of the European Chapter of the ACL (EACL)*, pages 9–16.

M. Cataldi, L. Di Caro, and C. Schifanella. 2010. Emerging topic detection on twitter based on temporal and social terms evaluation. In *Proceedings of the International Workshop on Multimedia Data Mining (MDMKDD)*, pages 4:1–10.

M. Collins. 2002. Discriminative training methods for hidden Markov models: Theory and experiments with perceptron algorithms. In *Proceedings of the Conference on Empirical Methods for Natural Language Processing (EMNLP)*.

S. Cucerzan. 2007. Large-scale named entity disambiguation based on Wikipedia data. In *Proceedings of the Joint Conference on Empirical Methods in Natural Language Processing and Computational Natural Language Learning (EMNLP-CoNLL)*, pages 708–716.

N. Dalvi, R. Kumar, and B. Pang. 2012. Object matching in tweets with spatial models. In *Proceedings of International Conference on Web Search and Web Data Mining (WSDM)*, pages 43–52.

J. Eisenstein, B. O'Connor, N.A. Smith, and E.P. Xing. 2010. A latent variable model for geographic lexical variation. In *Proceedings of the Conference on Empirical Methods for Natural Language Processing (EMNLP)*, pages 1277–1287.

Y. Fang, B.-J. Hsu, and K. C.-C. Chang. 2012. Confidence-aware graph regularization with heterogeneous pairwise features. In *Proceedings of International Conference on Research and Development in Information Retrieval (SIGIR)*, pages 951–960.

Y. Fang, K. C.-C. Chang, and H.W. Lauw. 2013. Roundtriprank: Graph-based proximity with importance and specificity. In *Proceedings of International Conference on Data Engineering (ICDE)*, pages 613–624.

Y. Fang, K. C.-C. Chang, and H.W. Lauw. 2014. Graph-based semi-supervised learning: Realizing pointwise smoothness probabilistically. In *Proceedings of the International Conference on Machine Learning (ICML)*.

P. Ferragina and U. Scaiella. 2010. TAGME: on-the-fly annotation of short text fragments (by Wikipedia entities). In *Proceedings of ACM Conference on Information and Knowledge Management (CIKM)*, pages 1625–1628.

S. Guo, M.-W. Chang, and E. Kıcıman. 2013. To link or not to link? A study on end-to-end tweet entity linking. In *Proceedings of the Annual Meeting of the North American Association of Computational Linguistics (NAACL)*, pages 1020–1030.

X. Han, L. Sun, and J. Zhao. 2011. Collective entity linking in web text: a graph-based method. In *Proceedings of International Conference on Research and Development in Information Retrieval (SIGIR)*, pages 765–774.

J. Hoffart, M. Amir Yosef, I. Bordino, H. Fürstenau, M. Pinkal, M. Spaniol, B. Taneva, S. Thater, and G. Weikum. 2011. Robust disambiguation of named entities in text. In *Proceedings of the Conference on Empirical Methods for Natural Language Processing (EMNLP)*, pages 782–792.

H. Ji and R. Grishman. 2011. Knowledge base population: Successful approaches and challenges. In *Proceedings of the Annual Meeting of the Association for Computational Linguistics (ACL)*, pages 1148–1158.

H. Ji, R. Grishman, H.T. Dang, K. Griffitt, and J. Ellis. 2010. Overview of the TAC 2010 knowledge base population track. In *Text Analysis Conference (TAC)*.

S. Kulkarni, A. Singh, G. Ramakrishnan, and S. Chakrabarti. 2009. Collective annotation of Wikipedia entities in web text. In *Proceedings of International Conference on Knowledge Discovery and Data Mining (KDD)*, pages 457–466.

J. Leskovec, L. Backstrom, and J. Kleinberg. 2009. Meme-tracking and the dynamics of the news cycle. In *Proceedings of International Conference on Knowledge Discovery and Data Mining (KDD)*, pages 497–506.

C. Li, J. Weng, Q. He, Y Yao, A. Datta, A. Sun, and B.-S. Lee. 2012a. TwiNER: named entity recognition in targeted twitter stream. In *Proceedings of International Conference on Research and Development in Information Retrieval (SIGIR)*, pages 721–730.

R. Li, S. Wang, H. Deng, R. Wang, and K. Chen-Chuan Chang. 2012b. Towards social user profiling: unified and discriminative influence model for inferring home locations. In *Proceedings of International Conference on Knowledge Discovery and Data Mining (KDD)*, pages 1023–1031.

R. Li, S. Wang, and K. Chen-Chuan Chang. 2013. Towards social data platform: Automatic topic-focused monitor for twitter stream. *Proceedings of the VLDB Endowment (PVLDB)*, 6(14).

Q. Mei, C. Liu, H. Su, and C.-X. Zhai. 2006. A probabilistic approach to spatiotemporal theme pattern mining on weblogs. In *Proceedings of the International World Wide Web Conference (WWW)*, pages 533–542.

E. Meij, W. Weerkamp, and M. de Rijke. 2012. Adding semantics to microblog posts. In *Proceedings of International Conference on Web Search and Web Data Mining (WSDM)*, pages 563–572.

D. Milne and I. H. Witten. 2008. Learning to link with Wikipedia. In *Proceedings of ACM Conference on Information and Knowledge Management (CIKM)*, pages 509–518.

J. Platt. 2000. Probabilistic outputs for support vector machines and comparison to regularize likelihood methods. In *Advances in Large Margin Classifiers*, pages 61–74.

L. Ratinov, D. Roth, D. Downey, and M. Anderson. 2011. Local and global algorithms for disambiguation to Wikipedia. In *Proceedings of the Annual Meeting of the Association for Computational Linguistics (ACL)*, pages 1375–1384.

A. Ritter, S. Clark, Mausam, and O. Etzioni. 2011. Named entity recognition in tweets: an experimental study. In *Proceedings of the Conference on Empirical Methods for Natural Language Processing (EMNLP)*, pages 1524–1534.

A. Ritter, Mausam, O. Etzioni, and S. Clark. 2012. Open domain event extraction from Twitter. In *Proceedings of International Conference on Knowledge Discovery and Data Mining (KDD)*, pages 1104–1112.

A. Sadilek, H. Kautz, and V. Silenzio. 2012. Modeling spread of disease from social interactions. In *Proceedings of the International Conference on Weblogs and Social Media (ICWSM)*.

T. Sakaki, M. Okazaki, and Y. Matsuo. 2010. Earthquake shakes Twitter users: real-time event detection by social sensors. In *Proceedings of the International World Wide Web Conference (WWW)*, pages 851–860.

D.W. Scott. 2009. *Multivariate density estimation: theory, practice, and visualization*. John Wiley & Sons.

W. Shen, J. Wang, P. Luo, and M. Wang. 2012. LINDEN: linking named entities with knowledge base via semantic knowledge. In *Proceedings of the International World Wide Web Conference (WWW)*, pages 449–458.

W. Shen, J. Wang, P. Luo, and M. Wang. 2013. Linking named entities in tweets with knowledge base via user interest modeling. In *Proceedings of International Conference on Knowledge Discovery and Data Mining (KDD)*, pages 68–76.

A. Sil and A. Yates. 2013. Re-ranking for joint named-entity recognition and linking. In *Proceedings of ACM Conference on Information and Knowledge Management (CIKM)*.

A. Tumasjan, T. O. Sprenger, P. G Sandner, and I. M Welpe. 2010. Predicting elections with Twitter: What 140 characters reveal about political sentiment. In *Proceedings of the International Conference on Weblogs and Social Media (ICWSM)*, pages 178–185.

V. Vapnik and S. Mukherjee. 1999. Support vector method for multivariate density estimation. In *Proceedings of the Conference on Advances in Neural Information Processing Systems (NIPS)*, pages 659–665.

B.P. Wing and J. Baldridge. 2011. Simple supervised document geolocation with geodesic grids. In *Proceedings of the Annual Meeting of the Association for Computational Linguistics (ACL)*, pages 955–964.

J.-M. Xu, A. Bhargava, R. Nowak, and X. Zhu. 2012. Socioscope: Spatio-temporal signal recovery from social media. In *Proceedings of the European Conference on Machine Learning (ECML)*, pages 644–659.

Z. Yin, L. Cao, J. Han, C. Zhai, and T. Huang. 2011. Geographical topic discovery and comparison. In *Proceedings of the International World Wide Web Conference (WWW)*, pages 247–256.

X. Zhu, Z. Ghahramani, J. Lafferty, et al. 2003. Semi-supervised learning using Gaussian fields and harmonic functions. In *Proceedings of the International Conference on Machine Learning (ICML)*, pages 912–919.

Dense Event Ordering with a Multi-Pass Architecture

Nathanael Chambers
United States Naval Academy
nchamber@usna.edu

Taylor Cassidy
Army Research Lab
IBM Research
taylorcassidy64@gmail.com

Bill McDowell
Carnegie Mellon University
forkunited@gmail.com

Steven Bethard
University of Alabama at Birmingham
bethard@cis.uab.edu

Abstract

The past 10 years of event ordering research has focused on learning partial orderings over document events and time expressions. The most popular corpus, the TimeBank, contains a small subset of the possible ordering graph. Many evaluations follow suit by only testing certain pairs of events (e.g., only main verbs of neighboring sentences). This has led most research to focus on specific learners for partial labelings. This paper attempts to nudge the discussion from identifying *some* relations to *all* relations. We present new experiments on strongly connected event graphs that contain ~10 times more relations per document than the TimeBank. We also describe a shift away from the single learner to a sieve-based architecture that naturally blends multiple learners into a precision-ranked cascade of sieves. Each sieve adds labels to the event graph one at a time, and earlier sieves inform later ones through transitive closure. This paper thus describes innovations in both approach and task. We experiment on the densest event graphs to date and show a 14% gain over state-of-the-art.

1 Introduction

Event ordering in the NLP community usually refers to a specific labeling task: given pairs of events and time expressions, choose ordering relations for them. The TimeBank corpus (Pustejovsky et al., 2003) provided a corpus of labeled pairs that motivated machine learning approaches to this task. However, only a small subset of possible pairs are labeled. The annotators identified the most central and obvious relations, and left the rest unlabeled. Partly because of this, there has been little research into complete event graphs. This paper describes our recent exploration into the dramatic changes required of both learning algorithms and experimental setup when faced with the task of a more complete graph labeling.

The most obvious shift required of a complete graph labeling algorithm is that of *relation identification*. Research on the TimeBank and in the TempEval contests has largely focused on *relation classification*. The event pairs are given, and the task is to classify them. We are now forced to first determine which events should be paired up before classification. Our experiments here fully integrate and evaluate both identification and classification.

We are not the first to approach relation identification with classification, but this paper is the first to directly and comprehensively address it. Most recently, TempEval 3 (UzZaman et al., 2013a) proposed a labeling of raw text without prior relation identification, but the challenge ultimately relied on the TimeBank. Systems were only evaluated on its subset of labeled event pairs. This meant that relation identification was largely ignored. The top system optimized only relation classification and intentionally left many pairs unlabeled (Bethard, 2013).

This paper presents CAEVO, a CAscading EVent Ordering architecture. It is a novel sieve-based architecture for temporal event ordering that directly addresses the interplay between identification and classification. We shift away from the idea of monolithic learners, and propose smaller specialized classifiers. Inspiration comes from the recent success in named entity coreference with sieve-based learning (Lee et al., 2013). CAEVO contains a host of classi-

Transactions of the Association for Computational Linguistics, 2 (2014) 273–284. Action Editor: Ellen Riloff.
Submitted 11/2013; Revised 5/2014; Published 10/2014.

fiers that each specialize on different types of edges. The classifiers are ordered by their individual precision, and run in order starting with the most precise. Each sieve informs those below it by passing on its decisions as graph constraints. These more precise constraints are then used by later sieves to assist their less precise decisions.

One of the main advantages of this CAEVO architecture is the natural inclusion of transitive reasoning. After each sieve proposes its labels, the architecture infers transitive links from the new labels and adds them to the graph. This type of expansion has not been adequately evaluated due to our community's sparsely labeled corpora. We are the first to report the surprising result that edges from transitive closure are more precise than the original sieve-provided labels.

Finally, CAEVO enables quick experimentation. Classifiers are pulled in and out with ease, quickly testing new theories. As in D'Souza and Ng (2013), we created rule-based classifiers based on linguistic theory. We naturally integrate these with machine learned classifiers using the sieve architecture. Each classifier focuses on its independent decisions, and the architecture then imposes transitivity constraints. CAEVO contains 12 sieves ordered by precision, and it outperforms the top systems in event ordering.

2 Previous Work

Two lines of research are particularly relevant to our work: research on event ordering annotation, and research on event ordering models. We briefly review both here.

2.1 Event Ordering Annotation

Most prior annotation efforts constructed corpora with only a small subset of temporal relations annotated. In the TimeBank (Pustejovsky et al., 2003), temporal relations were only annotated when the relation was judged to be salient by the annotator. The TempEval competitions (Verhagen et al., 2007; Verhagen et al., 2010; UzZaman et al., 2013b) aimed to improve coverage by annotating relations between all events and times in the same sentence. However, event tokens that were mentioned fewer than 20 times were excluded and only one TempEval task considered relations between events in different sentences.

	Events	Times	Relations	R
TimeBank	7935	1414	6418	0.7
Bramsen 2006	627	–	615	1.0
TempEval 2007	6832	1249	5790	0.7
TempEval 2010	5688	2117	4907	0.6
TempEval 2013	11145	2078	11098	0.8
Kolomiyets 2012	1233	–	1139	0.9
Do 2012[1]	324	232	3132	5.6
This work	1729	289	**12715**	**6.3**

Table 1: Events, times, temporal relations and the ratio of relations to events + times (R) in various corpora.

To avoid such sparse annotations, researchers have explored schemes that encourage annotators to connect all events. Bramsen et al. (2006) annotated timelines as directed acyclic graphs, though they annotated multi-sentence segments of text rather than individual events. Kolomiyets et al. (2012) annotated "temporal dependency structures" (i.e. dependency trees of temporal relations), though they only focused on pairs of events. In Do et al. (2012), "the annotator was not required to annotate all pairs of event mentions, but as many as possible", and then more relations were automatically inferred after the annotation was complete. In contrast, in our work we *required* annotators to label every possible pair of events/times in a given window, and our event graphs are guaranteed to be strongly connected, with every edge verified by the annotators. Table 1 compares the density of relation annotation across various corpora.

A major dilemma from this prior work is that unlabeled event/time pairs are inherently ambiguous. The unlabeled pair holds 3 possibilities:

1. The annotator looked at the pair of events and decided that multiple valid relations could apply.
2. The annotator looked at the pair of events and decided that no temporal relation exists
3. The annotator failed to look at the pair of events, so a single relation may exist.

This ambiguity makes accurate training and evaluation difficult. In the current work, we adopt the VAGUE relation, introduced by TempEval 2007, and force our annotators to indicate pairs for which no clear temporal relation exists. We are thus the first to eliminate the 3rd possibility from our corpus.

[1]Do 2012 reports 6264 relations, but we list half of this because they include relations and their inverses in the count.

2.2 Event Ordering Models

In part because of the sparsity of temporal relations in the available training corpora, most existing models formulate temporal ordering as a pair-wise *classification* task, where each pair of events and/or times is examined and classified as having a temporal relation or not. Early work on the TimeBank took this approach (Boguraev and Ando, 2005), classifying relations between all events and times within 64 tokens of each other. Most of the top-performing systems in the TempEval competitions also took this pair-wise classification approach for both event-time and event-event temporal relations (Bethard and Martin, 2007; Cheng et al., 2007; UzZaman and Allen, 2010; Llorens et al., 2010; Bethard, 2013). These systems have sometimes even explicitly focused on a small subset of temporal relations; for example, the top-ranked ordering system in TempEval 2013 (Bethard, 2013) only classified relations in certain syntactic constructions and with certain relation types.

Systems have tried to take advantage of global information to ensure that the pair-wise classifications satisfy temporal logic transitivity constraints, using frameworks like integer linear programming and Markov logic networks (Bramsen et al., 2006; Chambers and Jurafsky, 2008; Tatu and Srikanth, 2008; Yoshikawa et al., 2009; UzZaman and Allen, 2010). The gains have been small, likely because of the disconnectedness that is common in sparsely annotated corpora (Chambers and Jurafsky, 2008).

An approach that has not been leveraged for event ordering, but that has been successful in the coreference community is the sieve-based architecture. The top performer in CoNLL-2011 shared task was one such system (Lee et al., 2013). The core idea is to begin with the most reliable classifier first, and inform those below it. This idea also appeared in the early IBM MT models (Brown et al., 1993) and in the "islands of reliability" approaches to parsing and speech (Borghesi and Favareto, 1982; Corazza et al., 1991). D'Souza and Ng (2013) recently combined a rule-based model with a machine learned model, but lacked the fine-grained formality of a cascade of sieves. This paper is inspired by the above and is the first to apply it to temporal ordering as an extensible, formal architecture.

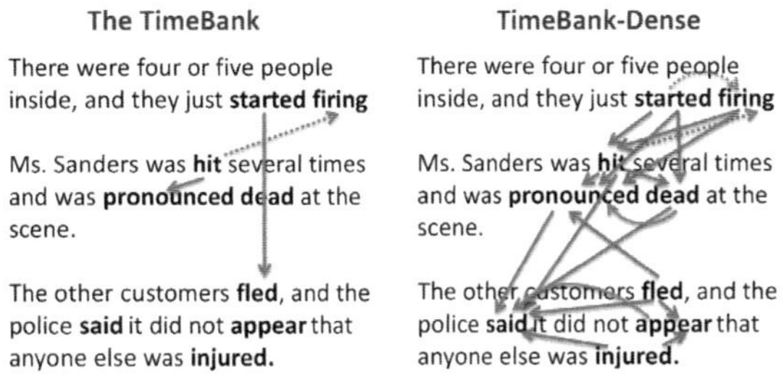

Figure 1: TimeBank document on the left with TimeBank-Dense on the right. Solid arrows indicate BEFORE and dotted INCLUDED IN. Relations with the DCT not shown.

3 TimeBank-Dense: A Dense Ordering

We use a new corpus, called TimeBank-Dense (Cassidy et al., 2014), to motivate and evaluate our architecture. This section highlights its main features.

The TimeBank-Dense corpus was created to address the sparsity in current corpora. It is unique in that the annotators were forced to label all local edges, even in ambiguous cases. The corpus is not a complete graph over events and time expressions, but it approximates completeness by labeling locally complete graphs over neighboring sentences. All pairs of events and time expressions in the same sentence and all pairs of events and time expressions in the immediately following sentence were labeled. It also includes edges between every event and the document creation time (DCT). The document event graphs in TimeBank-Dense are thus strongly connected[2], but they are not complete graphs because edges that cross 2 or more sentences are not explicitly included[3]. See Figure 1 for an illustration of the significant difference between a TimeBank document and a TimeBank-Dense document. The specific edges that were labeled are as follows:

1. Event-Event, Event-Time, and Time-Time pairs in the same sentence
2. Event-Event, Event-Time, and Time-Time pairs between the current and next sentence
3. Event-DCT pairs for every event in the document (DCT is the document creation time)
4. Time-DCT pairs for every time expression in the document

[2]Viewed as an undirected graph: since all events connect the DCT, there exists a path from every event to every other event.

[3]Though many are inferred through transitive closure.

TimeBank-Dense contains 12,715 labeled relations over 36 TimeBank newspaper articles. It uses TimeBank annotated events and time expressions, and then annotates the edges between them. The set of temporal relations are a subset of the 13 original Allen relations (Allen, 1983). The TempEval contests have used both a smaller set of relations (TempEval 1) and all 13 relations (TempEval 3). Published work mirrors this trend, and different groups focus on different aspects of the semantics. The TimeBank-Dense set is a middle ground between coarse and fine-grained distinctions: BEFORE, AFTER, INCLUDES, IS INCLUDED, SIMULTANEOUS, and VAGUE.

The main reason for not using a more fine-grained set is because we annotate pairs that are more ambiguous than those considered in previous efforts. Decisions between relations like BEFORE and IMMEDIATELY BEFORE complicate an already difficult task. The added benefit of a system that makes fine-grained distinctions is also not clear. We lean toward higher annotator agreement by using relations that have a greater separation between their semantics.[4]

Annotators of TimeBank-Dense also had to mutually agree on each labeled edge, otherwise it was labeled VAGUE. Precision between annotators averaged 65.1%, and the kappa ranged from .56 to .64. For comparison, TimeBank annotators averaged 77% precision with a .71 kappa. The breakdown of relation counts is shown in Table 2. **T3** refers to TempEval-3. TempEval-3 used TimeBank documents, but removed a small portion of its events. This paper evaluates on T3 data to maintain a connection to the recent competition, but this resulted in the removal of a portion of the densely annotated edges.

The most significant change in this new corpus is the inclusion of the VAGUE relation. This allows a system to separate relation identification from classification, if desired. The VAGUE relation makes up 46% of the annotated graph. This is the first empirical measurement of how many edges do not carry a clear semantics. This annotation eliminates 1 of the 3 ambiguities (discussed in Section 2) that has plagued ordering research: *the annotator failed to look at the pair of events, so a single relation may exist.*

[4]For instance, a relation like STARTS is a special case of INCLUDES if events are viewed as open intervals, and IMMEDIATELY BEFORE is a special case of BEFORE. We avoid this overlap and only use INCLUDES and BEFORE.

TimeBank-Dense Relation Count

	b	a	i	ii	s	v	Total
All	2590	2104	836	1060	215	5910	12715
T3 train	1444	1148	473	629	120	3013	6827
T3 dev	242	218	37	73	20	359	949
T3 test	589	428	116	159	39	900	2231

Table 2: The number of each relation type in the TimeBank-Dense corpus. T3 is the TempEval3 version used in this paper's experiments.

# of Mutual Vague	Partial Vague	No Vague
1657 (28%)	3234 (55%)	1019 (17%)

Table 3: VAGUE relation origins. Partial vague: one annotator does not choose vague. No vague: neither annotator chooses vague, but they disagree on the specific relation.

This is a significant improvement over previous ordering annotations. Several questions can now be answered to benefit learning algorithms. Which set of edges in the graph are unambiguous? Can I know for certain that I have all BEFORE relations in this document? These questions are critical to supervised learning, and we see the removal of this ambiguity as an important step toward better classification.

Of course, an ambiguity still remains: does VAGUE mean that no relation exists, or that multiple relations are possible? This is not unique to our corpus, but is present in all current ordering corpora. We erred on the side of caution because it is not clear how this can be resolved. Though we don't solve this problem here, we can more deeply analyze how VAGUE relations come about during annotation. Table 3 shows the 3 annotation scenarios that result in a VAGUE relation, and how often each occurred: (1) mutual vague: annotators agreed on VAGUE, (2) partial vague: one annotator chose VAGUE but the other chose a non-vague relation, and (3) no vague: annotators chose different non-vague relations. These disagreements will be released with the corpus, enabling future research into distinguishing these fine-grained semantics.

TimeBank-Dense is split into a 22 document training set, 5 document dev set, and a 9 document test set [5]. We follow this split in all experiments.

[5]Available at http://www.usna.edu/Users/cs/nchamber/caevo/

4 Sieve-Based Temporal Ordering

The sieve architecture applies a sequence of temporal relation classifiers, one at a time, to label the edges of a graph of events and time expressions. The individual classifiers are called sieves, and each sieve passes its temporal relation decisions onto the next sieve. The input to each sieve is the partially labeled graph from previous sieves. These previous decisions can help inform a sieve's own decisions. The sieves are ordered by precision, running the most precise models first. Events and time expressions are assumed to be annotated with their standard attributes (such as verb tense). This work uses gold event attributes for consistent analysis of ordering decisions.

One of the benefits of this architecture is the seamless enforcement of transitivity constraints. Independent pairwise classifiers often produce inconsistent labelings. The architecture avoids inconsistent graphs by inferring all transitive relations from each sieve's output before the graph is passed on to the next one. Specifically, the nth sieve cannot add an inconsistent edge that is inferrable from the previous $n-1$ sieves. Transitive inference is run after each stage, so it is not possible to relabel an already inferred edge. In a similar fashion, the architecture enforces the *precision preference rule*: the nth sieve may not label edge e if one of the previous $n-1$ sieves has already labeled it. Transitive inferences are made with all possible relations (e.g., A before B and B includes C infers A before C). The only relation that does not infer new edges is VAGUE.

This architecture facilitates a seamless integration of a wide variety of classifiers. We experimented with both rule-based and machine learned classifiers. The following subsections describe the final set of 12 temporal classifiers in CAEVO. We begin with the deterministic rule-based sieves.

4.1 Deterministic Sieves

The most precise sieves come from linguistic insight into syntactic and semantic patterns. Many pairs of events share common syntactic attributes that clearly indicate a temporal relation. Machine learning is not needed for these known linguistic phenomena, and a trained classifier can incorrectly label these obvious pairs if other features incorrectly override the decision. We therefore rely on deterministic rule-based approaches to capture these phenomena.

4.1.1 Verb/Timex Adjacency

Many prepositions in English carry either explicit (e.g., before, during) or implicit temporal semantics (e.g., in, over). Several are so reliable that a simple series of rules can label event-timex edges with very high precision. This Verb/Timex Adjacency sieve thus applies to event words and time expressions that are connected by a direct path in the syntactic parse tree, as well as all event/time pairs such that the event is at most 2 tokens before the time expression.

Time expressions under a preposition are handled with specific rules. For instance, *in, on, over, during*, and *within* all resolve to IS INCLUDED. The prepositions *for, at*, and *throughout* resolve to SIMULTANEOUS. In the absence of a preposition, a timex might simply be a modifier of the verb. The following is one such example.

> Police confirmed Friday that the body found along a highway...

The *confirmed* event IS INCLUDED in *Friday*. The edge between an event and a direct time modifier all default to IS INCLUDED. The precision of this sieve on the development set is 92%, the top performer.

4.1.2 Timex-Timex Relations

One of the most precise sieves is a small set of deterministic rules that address relations between time expressions (including the DCT). This sieve uses the normalized time values for time expressions to compare their start/end times. Given two time spans with defined starting and ending time points, the temporal relation is unambiguous.

The more difficult cases involve time expressions without stated start/end points. Examples of these include references to the abstract future or past, such as in phrases like 'last year' and 'next quarter'. This sieve chooses BEFORE if the abstract references are not the same, but in clear opposition to each other. For instance, a past reference and a future reference are labeled BEFORE. If the abstract references are the same, then VAGUE is typically applied. We defer to the publicly released code for further details.

4.1.3 Reporting Event with DCT

Newspaper articles contain an abundance of reporting events (e.g., said, reply, tell). We crafted a targeted sieve to handle this genre-specific phenomena. Since the document creation time is often the day of the reporting events, edges between reporting events and the DCT are labeled as IS INCLUDED. This is essentially a high baseline for event-DCT edges. One of the advantages of the sieve-based architecture is that this sieve can be placed later in the cascade of sieves. More sophisticated reasoners run before this one, making more informed decisions when appropriate, and this sieve cleans up the remaining reporting-DCT edges that are still unlabeled.

4.1.4 Reporting Event with Dominated Event

We also created rules for edges between a reporting event and another event that is syntactically dominated by the reporting event. Statistical classifiers can pick up patterns for reporting verbs, but the labels are consistent enough that a few deterministic rules can handle many of the cases. The following rules are solely based on the tense and grammatical aspect of each event.

The following is a sampling of these rules, where *gov* is the governing event and *dep* the dependent.

1. If gov is present, and dep is past
   then (gov AFTER dep)
2. If gov is present, and dep is present perfect
   then (gov AFTER dep)
3. If gov is present, and dep is future
   then (gov BEFORE dep)
4. If gov is past, and dep is past perfective
   then (gov AFTER dep)
5. If gov is past, and dep is past progressive
   then (gov IS INCLUDED dep)

4.1.5 General Event with Dominated Event

We generalized the above reporting-event sieve to apply to all types of events. This 'backoff' sieve handles the non-reporting event pairs where one event immediately dominates another. It operates similar to the preceding sieve and uses event features like tense and aspect to make its decisions. However, unlike the preceding, the decisions are split into different rule sets based on the specific typed dependency relation that connects the two events. We have separate rules nsubj, dobj, xcomp, ccomp, advcl, and conj.

4.1.6 Reichenbach Rules

Reichenbach (1947) defined the role played by the various tenses of English verbs in conveying temporal information in a discourse. Each tense is distinguished in terms of the relative ordering of the following time points:

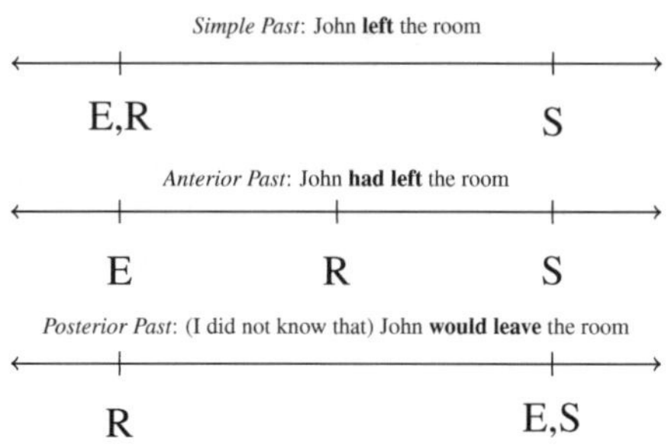

Figure 2: Timelines in which the ordering $S < R$ is fixed because the verb *to leave* is in the past tense.

- ***Point of speech*** (S) The time at which an act of speech is performed.
- ***Point of event*** (E) The time at which the the event referred to by the verb occurs.
- ***Point of reference*** (R) A single time with respect to which S is ordered by one dimension of tense, and to which E is ordered by another.

Reichenbach's account maps the set of possible orderings of S, E, and R, where each pair of elements can be ordered with $<$ (before), $=$ (simultaneous), or $>$ (after), onto a set of tense names given by: $\{anterior, simple, posterior\} \times \{past, present, future\}$. The relative ordering of E and R is indicated by the first dimension, while that of S and R is given by the second. Figure 2 depicts examples of the ordering $R < S$.

Similar to Derczynski and Gaizauskas (2013) we map a subset of Reichenbach's tenses onto pairs of TimeML tense and aspect attribute values, which are given by $\{simple, perfect, progressive\} \times \{past, present, future\}$, where the first dimension is *grammatical aspect* and the second is *tense*. We refer to an event's tense/aspect combination as its *tense-aspect profile*. Consider two events e_1 and e_2 associated with $S_1/E_1/R_1$ and $S_2/E_2/R_2$. Intuitively, given $R_1 = R_2$ and the time point orderings for each event (derived from its tense-aspect profile) we can enumerate the possible interval relations that might hold between E_1 and E_2, which we can interpret as a disjunction of the possible orderings of e_1 and e_2 (Derczynski and Gaizauskas, 2013). We identify a subset of tense/aspect profile pairs that unambiguously yield an interval relation from our 6 relations, and implement them as rules in the *Reichenbach Sieve*. Three such rules are given here:

1. If $e1$ is *past/simple* and $e2$ is *past/perfect* then ($e1$ AFTER $e2$)
2. If $e1$ is *future/simple* and $e2$ is *present/perfect* then ($e1$ AFTER $e2$)
3. If $e1$ is *past/simple* and $e2$ is *future/simple* then ($e1$ BEFORE $e2$)

The Reichenbach sieve achieved a precision of 61% on the entire dataset, and 91% when links labeled VAGUE were excluded, a notably larger increase over other sieves. The lower 61% is primarily due to the abundance of non-canonical usages of various tense/aspect profiles. For example, the present tense may convey habitual action, an event conveyed with the future tense in a quotation may have already occurred, the present perfect may be used to indicate that an event occurred at least once in the past, etc.

4.1.7 WordNet Rules

Determining whether two words are precisely co-referent is notoriously difficult (Hovy et al., 2013). Synonymous words, or even those sharing the same surface form may be only partially co-referent and thus likely labeled VAGUE by annotators. For example, news articles state what someone *said* multiple times without revealing temporal ordering between the events. Event-event edges whose events share the same lemma, or are each a member of the same synset are thus labeled VAGUE. Time-time edges with the same lemma/synset are labeled SIMULTANEOUS.

4.1.8 All Vague

The majority class baseline for this task is to label all edges as VAGUE. This sieve is added to the end of the gauntlet, labeling any remaining unlabeled edges.

4.2 Machine Learned Sieves

Current state-of-the-art models for temporal ordering are machine learned classifiers. The top systems in the latest TempEval-3 contest used supervised classifiers for the different types of edges in the event graph (Bethard, 2013; Chambers, 2013). In the spirit of the sieve architecture, rather than training one large classifier for all types of edges, we create targeted classifiers for each type of edge. The resulting models are again ranked by precision and mutually inform each other through the architecture's transitive constraints. All models use the MaxEnt classifier from the Stanford CoreNLP with its default settings. Below we describe the features for each sieve.

Event-Time Features
Token, lemma, POS tag of event
Tense, aspect, class of event
Bigram of event and time expression words
Token path from event to time
Syntactic parse tree path between the event and time
Typed dependency edge path between the events
Boolean: syntactically dominates or is-dominated
Boolean: time expression concludes sentence?
Boolean: time expression day of week?
Full time expression phrase

Figure 3: Features for event-time edges.

4.2.1 Event-Time Edges

We created two different sieves for labeling edges between an event and a time expression. Similar to the event-event distinction, one classifier applies to intra-sentence edges and the other to inter-sentence. The features for these classifiers are shown in Figure 3. The same features from the above event-event classifier are used where applicable. These include the parse paths, syntactic dominance, and event features with POS tags and token context. Features specific to event-time edges include the event word's tense, aspect, and class (included independently from the time expression). Time features included a boolean feature if it was a day of the week, the head word of the expression, and the entire expression if it is more than one word. A boolean feature indicating if the time expression ended the sentence is also included.

4.2.2 Event-Event Edges

We created three different sieves for event-event edges. They use the same features, but are trained and applied to different subsets of the graph edges.

1. intra-sentence: Label edges between all event pairs that occur in the same sentence.
2. intra-sentence dominance: Label edges between all event pairs that occur in the same sentence *and* one event dominates the other in the syntactic parse tree.
3. inter-sentence: Label edges between all event pairs that occur in neighboring sentences.

Event-Event Features

Text order normalized (put the first event first)
Boolean: syntactically dominates or is-dominated
Boolean: is there an event in between these two?
Syntactic parse tree path between the events
Typed dependency edge path between the events
Token n-grams, POS tag n-grams
Pairs of tense, aspect, event class
Prepositions attached to each event, if any

Figure 4: Features for intra-sentence event-event edges.

The features for these classifiers are summarized in Figure 4. The POS tag features for each event include its previous two tags, the event word's tag, and the POS bigram ending on the event word. A POS bigram is also created from the POS tag of each event. The token word, its lemma, its WordNet synset, and the token bigram from each event word are also used. Various syntactic features are used, including preposition words that dominate either event, boolean dominance features if one event is above the other in the parse tree, the parse path between the two events (append the non-terminals together), and the typed dependency path between the two. Finally, we use event attributes of tense, aspect, and class to create event pairs of their values (e.g., if both events are past tense, then the feature's value is 'past past').

The final CAEVO architecture includes both intra-sentence learners, but not inter-sentence. The latter's precision was not high enough to warrant its inclusion. As mirrored in recent TempEval competition results, inter-sentence event relations continue to be an area of future research.

4.2.3 Event-DCT Edges

Temporal relations between events and the document creation time (DCT) are also separately classified. The features for this machine-learned sieve focus solely on the event word, including its POS tag, the two previous POS tags, event lemma, WordNet synset, token unigrams from a window of size 2, and event attributes: tense, aspect, and class. Since this sieve relies entirely on the event's features with no DCT specific features, it can be viewed as a single-event classifier. We also experimented with a number of rule-based sieves for Event-DCT classification, but they were all outperformed by the machine-learning sieve on the training and development sets.

4.3 The Complete Sieve Gauntlet

We now present the sieves used by CAEVO. Although the final system contains 12 sieves, we experimented with over 25 different classifiers. The final set of 12 are sorted by precision:

$$precision(sieve) = \frac{\#\text{correct}}{\#\text{proposed by } sieve} \quad (1)$$

Transitive closure is not included when calculating precision. Sieves are ranked according to precision, placed in order from highest to lowest. Sieves with a precision lower than the All Vague baseline were removed. Table 4 shows the final sieve order.

5 Experiments and Results

We now present the first experiments on the TimeBank-Dense corpus, using the set of events used for TempEval-3. These experiments highlight two separate contributions. The first is a new approach to temporal ordering, the CAEVO architecture with a cascade of classifiers. The second is an evaluation of an ordering system on the densest event graphs to date. We provide per-sieve results and compare against two state-of-the-art systems.

All sieves were developed on and motivated by the TimeBank-Dense training data. Precision was initially computed on the development set, and final sieve ordering is based on individual performance. Final performance is reported on the test set.

We compare against the *All Vague* baseline that labels all edges as VAGUE. We also compare against the winner of TempEval-3, ClearTK (Bethard, 2013). We include ClearTK in four configurations: (1) the base TempEval-3 system, (2) with CAEVO transitivity, (3) with transitivity and altered to output a VAGUE relation where it normally would have skipped the decision, and (4) retrained models on TimeBank-Dense with transitivity and all VAGUE. We also include the second place TempEval-3 system, NavyTime (Chambers, 2013), retrained and run as (3) and (4). Results are shown in Table 5. The optimized TempEval-3 systems ultimately achieve ~44 F1. The transitivity architecture automatically boosted ClearTK from .147 to .264 with no additional changes. CAEVO outperforms at 50.7 F1, improving over the retrained TempEval-3 systems by 14% relative F1.

Ordered Sieves

		Dev		Test	
Sieve	**Brief Description**	**P**	**R**	**P**	**R**
Verb/Time Adjacent	Rules for edges between one verbal event and one Timex	.92	.01	.74	.01
TimeTime	Rules for edges between two Timex	.88	.02	.90	.02
Reporting Governor	Rules for when a reporting event dominates an event	.69	.01	.91	.01
Reichenbach	Rules following Reichenbach theory for edges between two events	.63	.02	.67	.03
General Governor	Rules for edges where one event dominates another via typed dependencies	.63	.04	.51	.02
WordNet	Rules for edges between two events/times based on WordNet synonym lookup	.52	.02	.57	.01
Reporting DCT	Rules for reporting events and the DCT	1.0	.00	1.0	.00
ML-E-T SameSent	Trained classifier for event-time edges	.50	.03	.42	.03
ML-E-E SameSent	Trained classifier for all intra-sentence event-event edges	.45	.11	.44	.10
ML-E-E Dominate	Trained classifier for edges where one event syntactically dominates another	.41	.05	.44	.05
ML-E-DCT	Trained classifier for all event-DCT edges	.40	.06	.53	.07
AllVague	Labels all edges as VAGUE	.38	.38	.40	.40

Table 4: The final order of sieves in CAEVO. Precision was computed on the development set. ReportingDCT only matched one pair in the dev set, so we moved it below the other more common rule-based sieves.

System Comparison

System	P	R	F1
ClearTK	.397	.091	.147
ClearTK + trans	.390	.199	.264
ClearTK VAGUE + trans	.431	.431	.431
ClearTK Dense VAGUE + trans	.460	.426	.442
NavyT Dense VAGUE	.485	.415	.447
NavyT Dense VAGUE + trans	.483	.427	.453
Baseline: All Vague	.405	.405	.405
CAEVO	**.508**	**.506**	**.507**

Table 5: Comparison with top systems. The "Dense" systems were retrained on TimeBank-Dense. The "Opt" systems were optimized to label unknown edges as *VAGUE*.

CAEVO Component Ablation

	P	R	F1
CAEVO with only ML Sieves	.458	.202	.280
+ Rule-Based Sieves	.486	.240	.321
+ Transitivity	.505	.328	.398
+ All Vague Sieve	.507	.507	.507
Direct Sieve Predictions	.498	.398	.442
Predictions from Transitivity	.544	.109	.182

Table 6: System precision on the test set with and without transitivity, and precision of transitive labels.

The bottom of Table 6 illustrates the contribution of transitive closure in the labeling decisions. Prior research has hypothesized that transitive closure should help individual decisions (Chambers and Jurafsky, 2008; Yoshikawa et al., 2009), but this has not been adequately tested due to the sparsely labeled graphs available to the community. We computed the precision of edges directly labeled by sieves, and the precision of edges inferred from transitive closure. Transitive inferences achieve *better* performance than directly classified edges (54.5% to 49.8% precision).

Table 7 breaks apart precision by edge type. Since CAEVO labels all edges, precision and recall are the same. Edges between an event and the DCT show 55% precision, while event-event and event-time edges achieve the lowest performance at 49%. Linking time expressions to each other is helpful. While far less numerous, time-time edges are the easiest to classify (71% precision). Upon removing the Time-Time sieve, overall results drop almost 5%, despite the time-time edges only making up a smaller 2.6% of the data. Combined with transitive closure, they positively influence the other event decisions.

Finally, Table 8 shows CAEVO's per-relation results. We also reversed the order of sieves (but with all vague still last) to see what effect it has. Performance on the dev set dropped from .48 F1 to .46.

6 Discussion

These are the first experiments on event ordering where the document event graphs were annotated so as to guarantee high density of relations and strong

Edge Type Performance

Edge Type	Total	P/R/F1
Event-Event Edges	1427	.494
Event-Time Edges	423	.494
Event-DCT	311	.553
Time-Time Edges	59	.712

Table 7: The number of edges for each edge type, and the system's overall precision on each. Since CAEVO labels all possible edges, precision and recall are the same.

Per-Relation Performance

Relation	P	R	F1
BEFORE	.52	.45	.49
AFTER	.55	.38	.45
INCLUDES	.44	.21	.28
IS INCLUDED	.57	.43	.49
SIMULTANEOUS	.71	.31	.43
VAGUE	.48	.66	.56

Table 8: Performance on individual relation types.

connectivity. Most related to our experiments is the dense annotation work of Do et al. (2012), but as they did not force annotators to label every pair, unannotated pairs in their corpus are ambiguous between a VAGUE relation and a relation that was simply missed by the annotators. This ambiguity causes problems for evaluation that are not present in a corpus where annotators were required to annotate all pairs.

Constructing event ordering systems that will be evaluated on dense, strongly connected document event graphs is fundamentally different than optimizing a system to label a subset of edges. This can be seen in the performance of the ClearTK-TimeML system, which achieved the top performance (36.26) on the sparse relation task of TempEval 2013, but performed dramatically worse (15.8) on our dense relation task. This is not to fault ClearTK, but to illustrate the difference of evaluating only a subset of an event graph's edges rather than the entire graph.

We also presented the first sieve-based architecture for event/time ordering. The CAEVO architecture allowed us to focus on specific classifiers for local decisions, and leave constraint enforcement to the architecture itself. There are several intangible benefits to this setup that don't appear in the results: (1) seamless integration of new/existing classifiers, (2) extremely quick ablation experiments by adding/removing sieves, and (3) facilitation of the development of specific classifiers that are agnostic to global constraints.

The final results are encouraging. Our multi-pass system achieved an F1 of 50.7, a full 10 F1 points over the All-Vague baseline, and a 14% relative increase over the top two systems in TempEval 3. This increase is based not just on the top systems out of the box, but after retraining them with TimeBank-Dense. The largest factor contributing to this gain is the enforcement of global constraints. Transitive inference alone boosted performance by about 10%.

Finally, we note that a lot of effort was put into linguistically motivated rule-based classifiers. The overall gain from these high precision sieves was 2 F1 points. The Reichenbach sieve's application of a more traditional linguistic theory of time helped increase performance. Error analysis reveals there are inherent difficulties in relying solely on tense and aspect for ordering decisions, but we hope to continue experiments into this and other theories.

CAEVO and its code is now publicly available[6]. In addition to temporal classification (the focus of this paper), it also automatically extracts events and time expressions. CAEVO is a complete system that produces dense event/time graphs from raw text. We hope it provides a new platform for quick experimentation and development. The TimeBank-Dense corpus is also publicly available, as well as the new annotation tool that forces annotators to label all edges. It is a unique tool that helps with transitive inference as annotators work. We hope it encourages further dense data creation for temporal research.

Acknowledgments

This work was supported, in part, by the Johns Hopkins Human Language Technology Center of Excellence. Any opinions, findings, and conclusions or recommendations expressed in this material are those of the authors. It was also supported by Grant Number R01LM010090 from the National Library Of Medicine. Finally, thanks to Benjamin Van Durme for assistance and insight.

[6]http://www.usna.edu/Users/cs/nchamber/caevo

References

James F Allen. 1983. Maintaining knowledge about temporal intervals. *Communications of the ACM*, 26(11):832–843.

Steven Bethard and James H. Martin. 2007. CU-TMP: Temporal relation classification using syntactic and semantic features. In *Proceedings of the Fourth International Workshop on Semantic Evaluations (SemEval-2007)*, pages 129–132, Prague, Czech Republic, June. Association for Computational Linguistics.

Steven Bethard. 2013. ClearTK-TimeML: A minimalist approach to tempeval 2013. In *Second Joint Conference on Lexical and Computational Semantics (*SEM), Volume 2: Proceedings of the Seventh International Workshop on Semantic Evaluation (SemEval 2013)*, pages 10–14, Atlanta, Georgia, USA, June. Association for Computational Linguistics.

Branimir Boguraev and Rie Kubota Ando. 2005. TimeBank-driven TimeML analysis. In *Annotating, Extracting and Reasoning about Time and Events*. Springer.

Luigi Borghesi and Chiara Favareto. 1982. Flexible parsing of discretely uttered sentences. In *Proceedings of the 9th conference on Computational linguistics-Volume 1*, pages 37–42. Academia Praha.

Philip Bramsen, Pawan Deshpande, Yoong Keok Lee, and Regina Barzilay. 2006. Inducing temporal graphs. In *Proceedings of the 2006 Conference on Empirical Methods in Natural Language Processing*, pages 189–198. Association for Computational Linguistics.

Peter F Brown, Vincent J Della Pietra, Stephen A Della Pietra, and Robert L Mercer. 1993. The mathematics of statistical machine translation: Parameter estimation. *Computational linguistics*, 19(2):263–311.

Taylor Cassidy, Bill McDowell, Nathanael Chambers, and Steven Bethard. 2014. An annotation framework for dense event ordering. In *The 52nd Annual Meeting of the Association for Computational Linguistics*, Baltimore, MD, USA, June. Association for Computational Linguistics.

Nathanael Chambers and Dan Jurafsky. 2008. Jointly combining implicit constraints improves temporal ordering. In *Proceedings of the Conference on Empirical Methods in Natural Language Processing*, pages 698–706. Association for Computational Linguistics.

Nathanael Chambers. 2013. Navytime: Event and time ordering from raw text. In *Second Joint Conference on Lexical and Computational Semantics (*SEM), Volume 2: Proceedings of the Seventh International Workshop on Semantic Evaluation (SemEval 2013)*, Atlanta, Georgia, USA, June. Association for Computational Linguistics.

Yuchang Cheng, Masayuki Asahara, and Yuji Matsumoto. 2007. NAIST.Japan: Temporal relation identification using dependency parsed tree. In *Proceedings of the Fourth International Workshop on Semantic Evaluations (SemEval-2007)*, pages 245–248, Prague, Czech Republic, June. Association for Computational Linguistics.

A Corazza, R De Mori, R Gretter, and G Satta. 1991. Stochastic context-free grammars for island-driven probabilistic parsing. In *Proceedings of Second International Workshop on Parsing Technologies (IWPT91)*, pages 210–217.

Leon Derczynski and Robert Gaizauskas. 2013. Empirical validation of reichenbach's tense framework. In *Proceedings of the 10th International Conference on Computational Semantics (IWCS 2013)*, pages 71–82.

Quang Do, Wei Lu, and Dan Roth. 2012. Joint inference for event timeline construction. In *Proceedings of the 2012 Joint Conference on Empirical Methods in Natural Language Processing and Computational Natural Language Learning*, pages 677–687, Jeju Island, Korea, July. Association for Computational Linguistics.

Jennifer DSouza and Vincent Ng. 2013. Classifying temporal relations with rich linguistic knowledge. In *Proceedings of NAACL-HLT*, pages 918–927.

Eduard Hovy, Teruko Mitamura, Felisa Verdejo, Jun Araki, and Andrew Philpot. 2013. Events are not simple: Identity, non-identity, and quasi-identity. *NAACL HLT 2013*.

Oleksandr Kolomiyets, Steven Bethard, and Marie-Francine Moens. 2012. Extracting narrative timelines as temporal dependency structures. In *Proceedings of the 50th Annual Meeting of the Association for Computational Linguistics (Volume 1: Long Papers)*, pages 88–97, Jeju Island, Korea, July. Association for Computational Linguistics.

Heeyoung Lee, Angel Chang, Yves Peirsman, Nathanael Chambers, Mihai Surdeanu, and Dan Jurafsky. 2013. Deterministic coreference resolution based on entity-centric, precision-ranked rules. *Computational Linguistics*.

Hector Llorens, Estela Saquete, and Borja Navarro. 2010. TIPSem (English and Spanish): Evaluating CRFs and semantic roles in TempEval-2. In *Proceedings of the 5th International Workshop on Semantic Evaluation*, pages 284–291, Uppsala, Sweden, July. Association for Computational Linguistics.

James Pustejovsky, Patrick Hanks, Roser Sauri, Andrew See, Robert Gaizauskas, Andrea Setzer, Dragomir Radev, Beth Sundheim, David Day, Lisa Ferro, et al. 2003. The timebank corpus. In *Corpus linguistics*, volume 2003, page 40.

Hans Reichenbach. 1947. *Elements of Symbolic Logic*. Macmillan.

Marta Tatu and Munirathnam Srikanth. 2008. Experiments with reasoning for temporal relations between events. In *Proceedings of the 22nd International Conference on Computational Linguistics-Volume 1*, pages 857–864. Association for Computational Linguistics.

Naushad UzZaman and James Allen. 2010. TRIPS and TRIOS system for TempEval-2: Extracting temporal information from text. In *Proceedings of the 5th International Workshop on Semantic Evaluation*, pages 276–283, Uppsala, Sweden, July. Association for Computational Linguistics.

Naushad UzZaman, Hector Llorens, Leon Derczynski, James Allen, Marc Verhagen, and James Pustejovsky. 2013a. Semeval-2013 task 1: Tempeval-3: Evaluating time expressions, events, and temporal relations. In *Second Joint Conference on Lexical and Computational Semantics (*SEM), Volume 2: Proceedings of the Seventh International Workshop on Semantic Evaluation (SemEval 2013)*, pages 1–9, Atlanta, Georgia, USA, June. Association for Computational Linguistics.

Naushad UzZaman, Hector Llorens, Leon Derczynski, Marc Verhagen, James Allen, and James Pustejovsky. 2013b. Semeval-2013 task 1: Tempeval-3: Evaluating time expressions, events, and temporal relations. In *Proceedings of the 7th International Workshop on Semantic Evaluation*. Association for Computational Linguistics.

Marc Verhagen, Robert Gaizauskas, Frank Schilder, Mark Hepple, Graham Katz, and James Pustejovsky. 2007. Semeval-2007 task 15: Tempeval temporal relation identification. In *Proceedings of the 4th International Workshop on Semantic Evaluations*, pages 75–80. Association for Computational Linguistics.

Marc Verhagen, Roser Sauri, Tommaso Caselli, and James Pustejovsky. 2010. Semeval-2010 task 13: Tempeval-2. In *Proceedings of the 5th International Workshop on Semantic Evaluation*, pages 57–62. Association for Computational Linguistics.

Katsumasa Yoshikawa, Sebastian Riedel, Masayuki Asahara, and Yuji Matsumoto. 2009. Jointly identifying temporal relations with Markov Logic. In *Proceedings of the Joint Conference of the 47th Annual Meeting of the ACL and the 4th International Joint Conference on Natural Language Processing of the AFNLP*, pages 405–413. Association for Computational Linguistics.

Multi-Modal Models for Concrete and Abstract Concept Meaning

Felix Hill
Computer Laboratory
University of Cambridge
fh295@cam.ac.uk

Roi Reichart
Technion - IIT
Haifa, Israel
roiri@ie.technion.ac.il

Anna Korhonen
Computer Laboratory
University of Cambridge
alk23@cam.ac.uk

Abstract

Multi-modal models that learn semantic representations from both linguistic and perceptual input outperform language-only models on a range of evaluations, and better reflect human concept acquisition. Most perceptual input to such models corresponds to concrete noun concepts and the superiority of the multi-modal approach has only been established when evaluating on such concepts. We therefore investigate which concepts can be effectively learned by multi-modal models. We show that concreteness determines both which linguistic features are most informative and the impact of perceptual input in such models. We then introduce *ridge regression* as a means of propagating perceptual information from concrete nouns to more abstract concepts that is more robust than previous approaches. Finally, we present *weighted gram matrix combination*, a means of combining representations from distinct modalities that outperforms alternatives when both modalities are sufficiently rich.

1 Introduction

What information is needed to learn the meaning of a word? Children learning words are exposed to a diverse mix of information sources. These include clues in the language itself, such as nearby words or speaker intention, but also what the child perceives about the world around it when the word is heard. Learning the meaning of words requires not only a sensitivity to both linguistic and perceptual input, but also the ability to process and combine information from these modalities in a productive way.

Many computational semantic models represent words as real-valued vectors, encoding their relative frequency of occurrence in particular forms and contexts in linguistic corpora (Sahlgren, 2006; Turney et al., 2010). Motivated both by parallels with human language acquisition and by evidence that many word meanings are *grounded* in the perceptual system (Barsalou et al., 2003), recent research has explored the integration into text-based models of input that approximates the visual or other sensory modalities (Silberer and Lapata, 2012; Bruni et al., 2014). Such models can learn higher-quality semantic representations than conventional corpus-only models, as evidenced by a range of evaluations.

However, the majority of perceptual input for the models in these studies corresponds directly to concrete noun concepts, such as *chocolate* or *cheeseburger*, and the superiority of the multi-modal over the corpus-only approach has only been established when evaluations include such concepts (Leong and Mihalcea, 2011; Bruni et al., 2012; Roller and Schulte im Walde, 2013; Silberer and Lapata, 2012). It is thus unclear if the multi-modal approach is effective for more abstract words, such as *guilt* or *obesity*. Indeed, since empirical evidence indicates differences in the representational frameworks of both concrete and abstract concepts (Paivio, 1991; Hill et al., 2013), and verb and noun concepts (Markman and Wisniewski, 1997), perceptual information may not fulfill the same role in the representation of the various concept types. This potential challenge to the multi-modal approach is of particular practical importance since concrete nouns constitute only a small proportion of the open-class, meaning-bearing

Transactions of the Association for Computational Linguistics, 2 (2014) 285–296. Action Editor: Rada Mihalcea.
Submitted 12/2013; Revised 6/2014; Published 10/2014.

words in everyday language (Section 2).

In light of these considerations, this paper addresses three questions: (1) Which information sources (modalities) are important for acquiring concepts of different types? (2) Can perceptual input be propagated effectively from concrete to more abstract words? (3) What is the best way to combine information from the different sources?

We construct models that acquire semantic representations for four sets of concepts: concrete nouns, abstract nouns, concrete verbs and abstract verbs. The linguistic input to the models comes from the recently released Google Syntactic N-Grams Corpus (Goldberg and Orwant, 2013), from which a selection of linguistic features are extracted. Perceptual input is approximated by data from the McRae et al. (2005) norms, which encode perceptual properties of concrete nouns, and the ESPGame dataset (Von Ahn and Dabbish, 2004), which contains manually generated descriptions of 100,000 images.

To address (1) we extract representations for each concept type from combinations of information sources. We first focus on different classes of linguistic features, before extending our models to the multi-modal context. While linguistic information overall effectively reflects the meaning of all concept types, we show that features encoding syntactic patterns are only valuable for the acquisition of abstract concepts. On the other hand, perceptual information, whether directly encoded or propagated through the model, plays a more important role in the representation of concrete concepts.

In addressing (2), we propose *ridge regression* (Myers, 1990) as a means of propagating features from concrete nouns to more abstract concepts. The regularization term in ridge regression encourages solutions that generalize well across concept types. We show that ridge regression effectively propagates perceptual information to abstract nouns and concrete verbs, and is overall preferable to both linear regression and the method of Johns and Jones (2012) applied to a similar task by Silberer and Lapata (2012). However, for all propagation methods, the impact of integrating perceptual information depends on the concreteness of the target concepts. Indeed, for abstract verbs, the most abstract concept type in our evaluations, perceptual input actually degrades representation quality. This highlights the need to consider the concreteness of the target domain when constructing multi-modal models.

To address (3), we present various means of combining information from different modalities. We propose *weighted gram matrix combination*, a technique in which representations of distinct modalities are mapped to a space of common dimension where coordinates reflect proximity to other concepts. This transformation, which has been shown to enhance semantic representations in the context of verb-clustering (Reichart and Korhonen, 2013), reduces representation sparsity and facilitates a product-based combination that results in greater inter-modal dependency. Weighted gram matrix combination outperforms alternatives such as concatenation and Canonical Correlation Analysis (CCA) (Hardoon et al., 2004) when combining representations from two similarly rich information sources.

In Section 3, we present experiments with linguistic features designed to address question (1). These analyses are extended to multi-modal models in Section 4, where we also address (2) and (3). We first discuss the relevance of concreteness and part-of-speech (lexical function) to concept representation.

2 Concreteness and Word Meaning

A large and growing body of psychological evidence indicates differences between abstract and concrete concepts.[1] It has been shown that concrete words are more easily learned, remembered and processed than abstract words (Paivio, 1991; Schwanenflugel and Shoben, 1983), while neuroimaging studies demonstrate differences in brain activity when subjects are presented with stimuli corresponding to the two concept types (Binder et al., 2005).

The abstract/concrete distinction is important to computational semantics for various reasons. While many models construct representations of concrete words (Andrews et al., 2009; Landauer and Dumais, 1997), abstract words are in fact far more common in everyday language. For instance, based on an analysis of those noun concepts in the University of South Florida dataset (USF) and their occurrence in the British National Corpus (BNC) (Leech et al., 1994), 72% of noun tokens in corpora are rated by human

[1] Here *concreteness* is understood intuitively, as per the psychological literature (Rosen, 2001; Gallese and Lakoff, 2005).

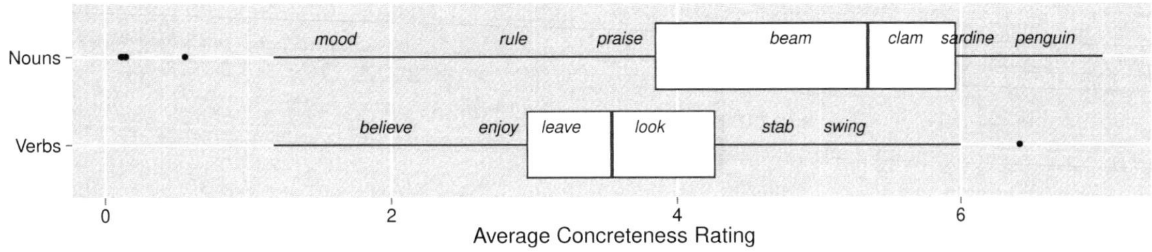

Figure 1: Boxplot of concreteness distributions for noun and verb concepts in the USF data, with selected example concepts. The bold vertical line is the mean, boxes extend from the first to the third quartile, and dots represent outliers.

judges as more abstract than the noun *war*, a concept that many would already consider quite abstract.[2]

The recent interest in multi-modal semantics further motivates a principled modelling approach to lexical concreteness. Many multi-modal models implicitly distinguish concrete and abstract concepts since their perceptual input corresponds only to concrete words (Bruni et al., 2012; Silberer and Lapata, 2012; Roller and Schulte im Walde, 2013). However, given that many abstract concepts express relations or modifications of concrete concepts (Gentner and Markman, 1997), it is reasonable to expect that perceptual information about concrete concepts could also enhance the quality of more abstract representations in an appropriately constructed model.

Moreover, concreteness is closely related to more functional lexical distinctions, such as those between adjectives, nouns and verbs. An analysis of the USF dataset, which includes concreteness ratings for over 4,000 words collected from thousands of participants, indicates that on average verbs (mean concreteness, 3.64) are considered more abstract than nouns (mean concreteness, 4.91), an effect illustrated in Figure 1. This connection between lexical function and concreteness suggests that a sensitivity to concreteness could improve models that already make principled distinctions between words based on their part-of-speech (POS) (Im Walde, 2006; Baroni and Zamparelli, 2010).

Although the focus of this paper is on multi-modal models, few conventional semantic models make principled distinctions between concepts based on function or concreteness. Before turning to the multi-modal case, we thus investigate whether these distinctions are pertinent to text-only models.

[2]This sample covers 15.2% of all noun tokens in the BNC.

3 Concreteness and Linguistic Features

It has long been known that aspects of word meaning can be inferred from nearby words in corpora. Approaches that exploit this fact are often called *distributional models* (Sahlgren, 2006; Turney et al., 2010). We take a distributional approach to learning linguistic representations. The advantage of using distributional methods to learn representations from corpora versus approaches that rely on knowledge bases (Pedersen et al., 2004; Leong and Mihalcea, 2011) is that they are more scalable, easily applicable across languages and plausibly reflect the process of human word learning (Landauer and Dumais, 1997; Griffiths et al., 2007). We group distributional features into three classes to test which forms of linguistic information are most pertinent to the abstract/concrete and verb/noun distinctions.

All features are extracted from The Google Syntactic N-grams Corpus. The dataset contains counted dependency-tree fragments for over 10bn words of the English Google Books Corpus.

3.1 Feature Classes

Lexical Features Our lexical features are the co-occurrence counts of a concept word with each of the other 2,529 concepts in the USF data. Co-occurrences are counted in a 5-word window, and, as elsewhere (Erk and Padó, 2008), weighted by point-wise mutual information (PMI) to control for the underlying frequency of both concept and word.

POS-tag Features Many words function as more than one POS, and this variation can be indicative of meaning (Manning, 2011). For example, deverbal

	Context	Example
Noun Concepts	indirect object	*gave it to the* ***man***
	direct object	*gave the* ***pie*** *to him*
	subject	*the* ***man*** *grinned*
	in PP	*was in his* ***mouth***
	adject. modifier	*the portly* ***man***
Verb Concepts	infinitive clause	*to* ***eat*** *is human*
	transitive	*he* ***bit*** *the steak*
	intransitive	*he* ***salivated***
	distransitive	***put*** *jam on the toast*
	phrasal verb	*he* ***gobbled*** *it up*
	infinitival comp.	*he* ***wants*** *to snooze*
	clausal comp.	*I* ***bet*** *he won't diet*

Table 1: Grammatical features for noun/verb concepts

nouns, such as *shiver* or *walk*, often refer to processes rather than entities. To capture such effects, we count the frequency of occurrence with the POS categories *ajdective, adverb, noun* and *verb*.

Grammatical Features Grammatical role is a strong predictor of semantics (Gildea and Jurafsky, 2002). For instance, the subject of transitive verbs is more likely to refer to an animate entity than a noun chosen at random. Syntactic context also predicts verb semantics (Kipper et al., 2008). We thus count the frequency of nouns in a range of (non-lexicalized) syntactic contexts, and of verbs in one of the six most common *subcategorization-frame* classes as defined in Van de Cruys et al. (2012). These contexts are detailed in Table 1.

3.2 Evaluation Sets

We create evaluation sets of abstract and concrete concepts, and introduce a complementary dichotomy between nouns and verbs, the two POS categories most fundamental to propositional meaning. To construct these sets, we extract nouns and verbs from word pairs in the USF data based on their majority POS-tag in the lemmatized BNC (Leech et al., 1994), excluding any word not assigned to either of the POS categories in more than 70% of instances. From the resulting 2175 nouns and 354 verbs, the abstract-concrete distinction is drawn by ordering words according to concreteness and sampling at random from the first and fourth quartiles. Any concrete nouns not occurring in the McRae et al. (2005) Property Norm dataset were also excluded.

Concept Type	Words	Pairs	Examples
concrete nouns	303	1280	*yacht, cup*
abstract nouns	100	295	*fear, respect*
all nouns	403	1716	*cup, respect*
concrete verbs	50	66	*kiss, launch*
abstract verbs	50	127	*differ, obey*
all verbs	100	221	*kiss, differ*

Table 2: Evaluation sets used throughout. *All nouns* and *all verbs* are the union of abstract and concrete subsets and mixed *abstract-concrete* or *concrete-abstract* pairs.

For each list of concepts L = *concrete nouns, concrete verbs, abstract nouns, abstract verbs*, together with lists *all nouns* and *all verbs*, a corresponding set of pairs $\{(w_1, w_2) \in USF : w_1, w_2 \in L\}$ is defined for evaluation. These details are summarized in Table 2. Evaluation lists, sets of pairs and USF scores are downloadable from our website.

3.3 Evaluation Methodology

All models are evaluated by measuring correlations with the *free-association* scores in the USF dataset (Nelson et al., 2004). This dataset contains the free-association strength of over 150,000 word pairs.[3] These data reflect the cognitive proximity of concepts and have been widely used in NLP as a gold-standard for computational models (Andrews et al., 2009; Feng and Lapata, 2010; Silberer and Lapata, 2012; Roller and Schulte im Walde, 2013).

For evaluation pairs (c_1, c_2) we calculate the cosine similarity between our learned feature representations for c_1 and c_2, a standard measure of the proximity of two vectors (Turney et al., 2010), and follow previous studies (Leong and Mihalcea, 2011; Huang et al., 2012) in using Spearman's ρ as a measure of correlation between these values and our gold-standard.[4] All representations in this section are combined by concatenation, since the present focus is not on combination methods.[5]

[3] Free-association strength is measured by presenting subjects with a cue word and asking them to produce the *first word they can think of that is associated with that cue word.*

[4] We consider Spearman's ρ, a non-parametric ranking correlation, to be more appropriate than Pearson's r for free association data, which is naturally skewed and non-continuous.

[5] When combining multiple representations we normalize

Feature Type	All Nouns	Conc. Nouns	Abs. Nouns	All Verbs	Conc. Verbs	Abs. Verbs
(1) Lexical	0.168*	**0.199***	**0.248***	**0.173***	**0.268***	0.109
(2) POS-tag	0.059*	0.012	0.119*	0.052	-0.074	**0.123**
(3) Grammatical	0.078*	0.027	0.121*	0.009	-0.017	0.114
(1)+(2)+(3)	**0.182** *	0.181*	0.247*	0.172*	0.267*	0.108

Table 3: Spearman correlation ρ of cosine similarity between vector representations derived from three feature classes with USF scores. * indicates statistically significant correlations ($p < 0.05$).

3.4 Results

The performance of each feature class on the evaluation sets is detailed in Table 3. When all linguistic features are included, performance is somewhat better on noun concepts ($\rho = 0.182$) than verbs ($\rho = 0.172$). However, while correlations are significant on concrete ($\rho = 0.181$) and abstract nouns ($\rho = 0.247$) and concrete verbs, the effect is not significant on abstract verbs (although it is on verbs overall). The highest correlations for the linguistic features together are on abstract nouns ($\rho = 0.247$) and concrete verbs ($\rho = 0.267$). Referring back to the continuum in Figure 1, it is possible that there is an optimum concreteness level, exhibited by abstract nouns and concrete verbs, at which conceptual meaning is best captured by linguistic models.

The results indicate that the three feature classes convey distinct information. It is perhaps unsurprising that lexical features produce the best performance in the majority of cases; the value of lexical co-occurrence statistics in conveying word meaning is expressed in the well known *distributional hypothesis* (Harris, 1954). More interestingly, on abstract concepts the contribution of POS-tag (nouns, $\rho = 0.119$; verbs, $\rho = 0.123$) and grammatical features (nouns, $\rho = 0.121$; verbs, $\rho = 0.114$) is notably higher than on the corresponding concrete concepts. The importance of such features to modelling free-association between abstract concepts suggests that they may convey information about how concepts are (subjectively) organized and interrelated in the minds of language users, independent of their realisation in the physical world. Indeed, since abstract representations rely to a lesser extent than concrete representations on perceptual input (Section 4), it is perhaps unsurprising that more of their meaning is reflected in subtle linguistic patterns.

The results in this section demonstrate that different information is required to learn representations for abstract and concrete concepts and for noun and verb concepts. In the next section, we investigate how perceptual information fits into this equation.

4 Acquiring Multi-Modal Representations

As noted in Section 2, there is experimental evidence that perceptual information plays a distinct role in the representation of different concept types. We explore whether this finding extends to computational models by integrating such information into our corpus-based approaches. We focus on two aspects of the integration process. *Propagation*: Can models infer useful information about abstract nouns and verbs from perceptual information corresponding to concrete nouns? And *combination*: How can linguistic and (propagated or actual) perceptual information be integrated into a single, multi-modal representation? We begin by introducing the two sources of perceptual information.

4.1 Perceptual Information Sources

The McRae Dataset The McRae et al. (2005) Property Norms dataset is commonly used as a perceptual information source in cognitively-motivated semantic models (Kelly et al., 2010; Roller and Schulte im Walde, 2013). The dataset contains properties of over 500 concrete noun concepts produced by 30 human annotators. The proportion of subjects producing each property gives a measure of the strength of that property for a given concept. We encode this data in vectors with coordinates for each of the 2,526 properties in the dataset. A concept representation contains (real-valued) feature strengths in places corresponding to the features of that concept and zeros elsewhere. Having defined the concrete noun evaluation set as the 303 concepts found in both the USF and McRae datasets, this information is available for all concrete nouns.

each representation, then concatenate and then renormalize.

The ESP-Game Dataset To complement the cognitively-driven McRae data with a more explicitly visual information source, we also extract information from the ESP-Game dataset (Von Ahn and Dabbish, 2004) of 100,000 photographs, each annotated with a list of entities depicted in that image. This input enables connections to be made between concepts that co-occur in scenes, and thus might be experienced together by language learners at a given time. Because we want our models to reflect human concept learning in inferring conceptual knowledge from comparatively unstructured data, we use the ESP-Game dataset in preference to resources such as ImageNet (Deng et al., 2009), in which the conceptual hierarchy is directly encoded by expert annotators. An additional motivation is that ESP-Game was produced by crowdsourcing a simple task with untrained annotators, and thus represents a more scalable class of data source.

We represent the ESP-Game data in 100,000 dimensional vectors, with co-ordinates corresponding to each image in the dataset. A concept representation contains a 1 in any place that corresponds to an image in which the concept appears, and a 0 otherwise. Although it is possible to portray actions and processes in static images, and several of the ESP-Game images are annotated with verb concepts, for a cleaner analysis of the information propagation process we only include ESP input in our models for the concrete nouns in the evaluation set.

The data encoding outlined above results in perceptual representations of dimension $\approx 100,000$, for which, on average, fewer than 0.5% of entries are non-zero [6]. In contrast, in our full linguistic representations of nouns (dimension $\approx 4,000$) and verbs (dimension $\approx 8,000$) (Section 3), an average of 24% of entries are non-zero. One of the challenges for the propagation and combination methods described in the following subsections is therefore to manage the differences in dimension and sparsity between linguistic and perceptual representations.

4.2 Information Propagation

Johns and Jones Silberer and Lapata (2012) apply a method designed by Johns and Jones (2012) to infer quasi-perceptual representations for a concept in the case that actual perceptual information is not available. Translating their approach to the present context, for verbs and abstract nouns we infer quasi-perceptual representations based on the perceptual features of concrete nouns that are nearby in the semantic space defined by the linguistic features.

In the first step of their two-step method, for each abstract noun or verb $\mathbf{k}$, a quasi-perceptual representation is computed as an average of the perceptual representations of the concrete nouns, weighted by the proximity between these nouns and $\mathbf{k}$

$$\mathbf{k}^p = \sum_{\mathbf{c} \in \bar{C}} S(\mathbf{k}^l, \mathbf{c}^l)^\lambda \cdot \mathbf{c}^p$$

where $\bar{C}$ is the set of concrete nouns, $\mathbf{c}^p$ and $\mathbf{k}^p$ are the perceptual representations for $\mathbf{c}$ and $\mathbf{k}$ respectively, and $\mathbf{c}^l$ and $\mathbf{k}^l$ the linguistic representations. The exponent parameter λ reflects the learning rate.

Following Johns and Jones (2012), we define the proximity function S between noun concepts to be cosine similarity. However, because our verb and noun representations are of different dimension, we take verb-noun proximity to be the PMI between the two words in the corpus, with co-occurrences counted within a 5-word window.

In step two, the initial quasi-perceptual representations are inferred for a second time, but with the weighted average calculated over the perceptual or initial quasi-perceptual representations of all other words, not just concrete nouns. As with Johns and Jones (2012), we set the learning rate parameter λ to be 3 in the first step and 13 in the second.

Ridge Regression As an alternative propagation method we propose ridge regression (Myers, 1990). Ridge regression is a variant of least squares regression in which a regularization term is added to the training objective to favor solutions with certain properties. Here we apply it to learn parameters for linear maps from linguistic representations of concrete nouns to features in their perceptual representations. For concepts with perceptual representations of dimension n_p, we learn n_p linear functions $f_i : \mathbb{R}^{n_l} \rightarrow \mathbb{R}$ that map the linguistic representations (of dimension n_l) to a particular perceptual feature i. These functions are then applied together to map

[6] The ESP-Game and McRae representations are of approximately equal sparsity.

the linguistic representations of abstract nouns and verbs to full quasi-perceptual representations.[7]

As our model is trained on concrete nouns but applied to other concept types, we do not wish the mapping to reflect the training data too faithfully. To mitigate against this we define our regularization term as the Euclidian l_2 norm of the inferred parameter vector. This term ensures that the regression favors lower coefficients and a smoother solution function, which should provide better generalization performance than simple linear regression. The objective for learning the f_i is then to minimize

$$\|\mathbf{a}X - Y_i\|_2^2 + \|\mathbf{a}\|_2^2$$

where $\mathbf{a}$ is the vector of regression coefficients, X is a matrix of linguistic representations and Y_i a vector of perceptual feature i for the set of concrete nouns.

We now investigate ways in which the (quasi-) perceptual representations acquired via these methods can be combined with linguistic representations.

4.3 Information Combination

Canonical Correlation Analysis Canonical correlation analysis (CCA) (Hardoon et al., 2004) is an established statistical method for exploring relationships between two sets of random variables. The method determines a linear transformation of the space spanned by each of the sets of variables, such that the correlations between the sets of transformed variables is maximized.

Silberer and Lapata (2012) apply CCA in the present context of information fusion, with one set of random variables corresponding to perceptual features and another corresponding to linguistic features. Applied in this way, CCA provides a mechanism for reducing the dimensionality of the linguistic and perceptual representations such that the important interactions between them are preserved.[8] The transformed linguistic and perceptual vectors are then concatenated. We follow Silberer and Lapata by applying a kernalized variant of CCA.[9]

[7]Because the POS-tag and grammatical features are different for nouns and for verbs, we exclude them from our linguistic representations when implementing ridge regression.

[8]Dimensionality reduction is desirable in the present context because of the sparsity of our perceptual representations.

[9]The KernelCCA package in Python: http://pythonhosted.org/apgl/KernelCCA.html

Weighted Gram Matrix Combination The method we propose as an alternative means of fusing linguistic and extra-linguistic information is *weighted gram matrix combination*, which derives from an information combination technique applied to verb clustering by Reichart and Korhonen (2013). For a set of concepts $C = \{c_1, \ldots, c_n\}$ with representations $\{r_1, \ldots, r_n\}$, the method involves creating an $n \times n$ *weighted gram matrix* L in which

$$L_{ij} = S(r_i, r_j) \cdot \phi(r_i) \cdot \phi(r_j).$$

Here, S is again a similarity function (we use cosine similarity), and $\phi(r)$ is the *quality score* of r.

The quality scoring function ϕ can be any mapping $\mathbb{R}^n \to \mathbb{R}$ that reflects the importance of a concept relative to other concepts in C. In the present context, we follow Reichart and Korhonen (2013) in defining a quality score ϕ as the average cosine similarity of a concept with all other concepts in C

$$\phi(r_j) = \frac{1}{n} \sum_{i=1}^{n} S(r_i, r_j).$$

For $c_j \in C$, the matrix L then encodes a scalar projection of r_j onto the other members $r_{i \leq n}$, weighted by their quality. Each word representation in the set is thus mapped into a new space of dimension n determined by the concepts in C.

Converting concept representations to weighted gram matrix form has several advantages in the present context. First, both when evaluating and applying semantic representations, we generally require models to determine relations between concepts relative to others. We might, for instance, require close associates of a given word, a selection of potential synonyms, or the two most similar search queries in a given set. This relative nature of semantics is reflected by projecting representations into a space defined by the set of concepts themselves, rather than low-level features. It is also captured by the quality weighting, which lends primacy to concept dimensions that are central to the space.

Second, mapping representations of different dimension into vector spaces of equal dimension results in dense representations of equal dimension for each modality. This naturally lends equal weighting or status to each modality and resolves any issues

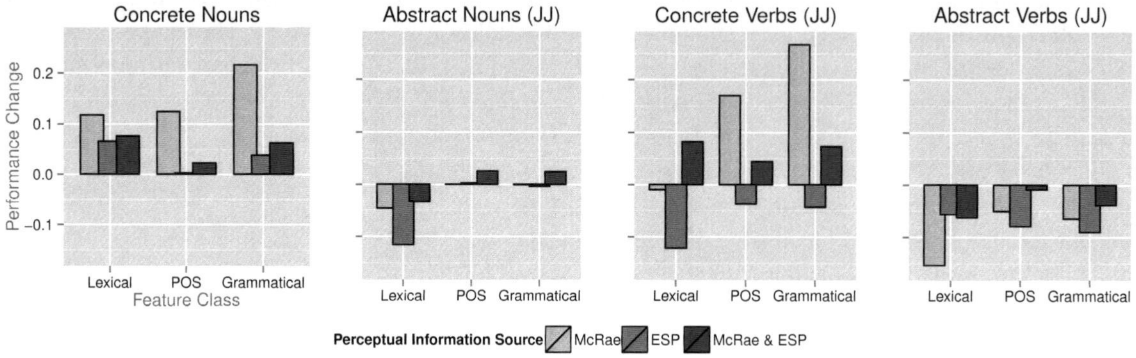

Figure 2: Additive change in Spearman's ρ when representations acquired from particular classes of linguistic features are combined with (actual or inferred) perceptual representations. Perceptual representations are derived from either the McRae Dataset, the ESP-Game Dataset or both (concatenated). For concepts other than concrete nouns, perceptual information is propagated using the Johns and Jones (JJ) method, and combined with simple concatenation.

of representations sparsity. In addition, the dimension equality in particular enables a wider range of mathematical operations for combining information sources. Here, we follow Reichart and Korhonen (2013) in taking the product of the linguistic and perceptual weighted gram matrices L and P, producing a new matrix containing fused representations for each concept

$$M = LPPL.$$

By taking the composite product $LPPL$ rather than LP or PL, M is symmetric and no ad hoc status is conferred to one modality over the other.

4.4 Results

The experiments in this section were designed to address the three questions specified in Section 1: (1) Which information sources are important for acquiring word concepts of different types? (2) Can perceptual information be propagated from concrete to abstract concepts? (3) What is the best way to combine the information from the different sources?

Question (1) To build on insights from Section 3, we first examined how perceptual input interacts with the three classes of linguistic features defined there. Figure 2 shows the additive difference in correlation between (i) models in which perceptual and particular linguistic features are concatenated and (ii) models based on just the linguistic features.

For concrete nouns and concrete verbs, (actual or inferred) perceptual information was beneficial in almost all cases. The largest improvement for both concept types was over grammatical features, achieved by including only the McRae data. This signals from this perceptual input and the grammatical features clearly reflect complementary aspects of the meaning of these concepts. We hypothesize that grammatical features (and POS features, which also perform strongly in this combination) confer information to concrete representations about the function and mutual interaction of concepts (the most 'relational' aspects of their meaning (Gentner, 1978)) which complements the more intrinsic properties conferred by perceptual features.

For abstract concepts, it is perhaps unsurprising that the overall contribution of perceptual information was smaller. Indeed, combining linguistic and perceptual information actually harmed performance on abstract verbs in all cases. For these concepts, the inferred perceptual features seem to obscure or contradict some of the information conveyed in the linguistic representations.

While the McRae data was clearly the most valuable source of perceptual input for concrete nouns and concrete verbs, for abstract nouns the combination of ESP-Game and McRae data was most informative. Both inspection of the data and cognitive theories (Rosch et al., 1976) suggest that entities identified in scenes, as in the ESP-Game dataset, generally correspond to a particular (basic) level of

Model	All Nouns	Conc. Nouns†	Abs. Nouns	All Verbs	Conc. Verbs	Abs. Verbs
Linguistic	0.175 — 0.335	0.169 — 0.317	0.233 — **0.344**	0.148 — 0.178	0.204 — 0.191	0.094 — **0.330**
(JJ)+Concat	0.116 — 0.375	0.258 — 0.442	0.190 — 0.267	0.129 — 0.162	**0.301** — 0.062	0.019 — 0.280
(JJ)+CCA	0.082 — 0.021	0.001 — 0.067	0.085 — -0.018	0.027— 0.213	0.079 — 0.276	**0.095** — 0.200
(JJ)+WGM	0.098 — 0.213	**0.397** — **0.523**	0.238 — 0.329	0.059 — 0.169	0.253 — 0.064	-0.080 — 0.254
RR+Concat	**0.232** — **0.432**		**0.248** — 0.343	0.013 — **0.212**	0.046 — **0.484**	0.023 — 0.133
RR+CCA	0.033 — -0.045		0.044 — -0.023	0.001 — -0.006	0.018 — 0.344	0.018 — 0.085
RR+WGM	0.094 — 0.069		0.232 — 0.327	**0.159** — 0.131	0.244 — 0.194	0.075 — 0.283
LR+	0.216 — 0.402		0.216 — 0.282	0.004 — 0.051	-0.051 — 0.139	-0.008 — 0.197

Table 4: Performance of different methods of information propagation (JJ = Johns and Jones, RR = ridge regression, LR = linear regression) and combination (Concat = concatenation, CCA = canonical correlation analysis, WGM = weighted gram matrix multiplication) across evaluation sets. Values are Spearman's ρ correlation with USF scores (left hand side of columns) and WordNet path similarity (right hand side). For the LR baseline we only report the highest score across the three combination types. †No propagation takes place for concrete nouns; this column reflects the performance of combination methods only.

the conceptual hierarchy. The ESP-Game data reflects relations between these basic-level concepts in the world, whereas the McRae data typically describes their (intrinsic) properties. Together, these sources seem to combine information on the properties of, and relations between, concepts in a way that particularly facilitates the learning of abstract nouns.

Question (2) The performance of different methods of information propagation and combination is presented in Table 4. The underlying linguistic representations in this case contained all three distributional feature classes. For more robust conclusions, in addition to the USF gold-standard we also measured the correlation between model output and the WordNet *path similarity* of words in our evaluation pairs. The path similarity between words w_1 and w_2 is the shortest distance between synsets of w_1 and w_2 in the WordNet taxonomy (Fellbaum, 1999), which correlates significantly with human judgements of concept similarity (Pedersen et al., 2004).[10]

The correlations with the USF data (left hand column, Table 4) of our linguistic-only models ($\rho = 0.094 - 0.233$) and best performing multi-modal models (on both concrete nouns, $\rho = 0.397$, and more abstract concepts, $\rho = 0.095 - 0.301$) were higher than the best comparable models described elsewhere (Feng and Lapata, 2010; Silberer and Lapata, 2012; Silberer et al., 2013).[11] This confirms both that the underlying linguistic space is of high quality and that the ESP and McRae perceptual input is similarly or more informative than the input applied in previous work.

Consistent with previous studies, adding perceptual input improved the quality of concrete noun representations as measured against both USF and path similarity gold-standards. Further, effective information propagation was indeed possible for both abstract nouns (USF evaluation) and concrete verbs (both evaluations). Interestingly, however, this was not the case for abstract verbs, for which no mix of propagation and combination methods produced an improvement on the linguistic-only model on either evaluation set. Indeed, as shown in Figure 2, no type of perceptual input generated an improvement in abstract verb representations, regardless of the underlying class of linguistic features.

This result underlines the link between concreteness, cognition and perception proposed in the psychological literature. More practically, it shows that concreteness can determine if propagation of perceptual input will be effective and, if so, the potential degree of improvement over text-only models.

Turning to means of propagation, both the Johns and Jones method and ridge regression outperformed the linear regression baseline on the majority of concept types in our evaluation. Across the five sets and ten evaluations on which propagation

[10]Other widely-used evaluation gold-standards, such as *WordSim 353* and the *MEN* dataset, do not contain a sufficient number of abstract concepts for the current purpose.

[11]Feng and Lapata (2010) report $\rho = .08$ for language-only and .12 for multi-modal models evaluated on USF over concrete and abstract concepts. Silberer and Lapata (2012) report $\rho = .14$ (language-only) and .35 (multi-modal) over concrete nouns.

takes place (*All Nouns, Abstract Nouns, All Verbs, Abstract Verbs* and *Concrete Verbs*), ridge regression performed more robustly, achieving the best performance on six evaluation sets compared to two for the Johns and Jones method.[12]

Question (3) Weighted gram matrix multiplication ($\rho = 0.397$ on USF and $\rho = 0.523$ on path similarity) outperformed both simple vector concatenation ($\rho = 0.258$ and $\rho = 0.442$) and CCA ($\rho = 0.001$ and $\rho = 0.067$) on concrete nouns. In the case of both abstract nouns and concrete verbs, however, the most effective means of combining quasi-perceptual information with linguistic representations was concatenation (abstract nouns, $\rho = 0.248$ and $\rho = 0.343$, concrete verbs, $\rho = 0.301$ and $\rho = 0.484$). One evident drawback of multiplicative methods such as weighted gram matrix combination is the greater inter-dependence of the information sources; a weak signal from one modality can undermine the contribution of the other modality. We hypothesize that this underlines the comparatively poor performance of the method on verbs and abstract nouns, as the perceptual input for concrete nouns is clearly a richer information source than the propagated features of more abstract concepts.

5 Conclusion

Motivated by the inherent difference between abstract and concrete concepts and the observation that abstract words occur more frequently in language, in this paper we have addressed the question of whether multi-modal models can enhance semantic representations of both concept types.

In Section 3, we demonstrated that different information sources are important for acquiring concrete and abstract noun and verb concepts. Within the linguistic modality, while lexical features are informative for all concept types, syntactic features are only significantly informative for abstract concepts.

In contrast, in Section 4 we observed that perceptual input is a more valuable information source for concrete concepts than abstract concepts. Nevertheless, perceptual input can be effectively propagated from concrete nouns to enhance representations of both abstract nouns and concrete verbs. Indeed, conceptual concreteness appears to determine the degree to which perceptual input is beneficial, since representations of abstract verbs, the most abstract concepts in our experiments, were actually degraded by this additional information. One important contribution of this work is therefore an insight into when multi-modal models should or should not aim to combine and/or propagate perceptual input to ensure that optimal representations are learned. In this respect, our conclusions align with the findings of Kiela and Hill (2014), who take an explicitly visual approach to resolving the same question.

Various methods for propagating and combining perceptual information with linguistic input were presented. We proposed ridge regression for inferring perceptual representations for abstract concepts, which proved more robust than alternatives across the range of concept types. This approach is particularly simple to implement, since it is based on an established statistical prodedure. In addition, we introduced weighted gram matrix combination for combining representations from distinct modalities of differing sparsity and dimension. This method produces the highest quality composite representations for concrete nouns, where both modalities represent high quality information sources.

Overall, our results demonstrate that the potential practical benefits of multi-modal models extend beyond concrete domains into a significant proportion of the lexical concepts found in language. In future work we aim to extend our experiments to concept types such as adjectives and adverbs, and to develop models that further improve the propagation and combination of extra-linguistic input.

Moreover, while we cannot draw definitive conclusions about human language processing, the effectiveness of the methods presented in this paper offer tentative support for the idea that even abstract concepts are *grounded* in the perceptual system (Barsalou et al., 2003). As such, it may be that, even in the more abstract cases of human communication, we find ways to see what people mean precisely by finding ways to see what they mean.

Acknowledgements

We thank The Royal Society and St John's College for their support.

[12]For these comparisons, the optimal combination method is selected in each case.

References

Mark Andrews, Gabriella Vigliocco, and David Vinson. 2009. Integrating experiential and distributional data to learn semantic representations. *Psychological Review*, 116(3):463.

Marco Baroni and Roberto Zamparelli. 2010. Nouns are vectors, adjectives are matrices: Representing adjective-noun constructions in semantic space. In *Proceedings of the 2010 Conference on Empirical Methods in Natural Language Processing*, pages 1183–1193. Association for Computational Linguistics.

Lawrence W Barsalou, W Kyle Simmons, Aron K Barbey, and Christine D Wilson. 2003. Grounding conceptual knowledge in modality-specific systems. *Trends in cognitive sciences*, 7(2):84–91.

Jeffrey R Binder, Chris F Westbury, Kristen A McKiernan, Edward T Possing, and David A Medler. 2005. Distinct brain systems for processing concrete and abstract concepts. *Journal of Cognitive Neuroscience*, 17(6):905–917.

Elia Bruni, Gemma Boleda, Marco Baroni, and Nam-Khanh Tran. 2012. Distributional semantics in technicolor. In *Proceedings of the 50th Annual Meeting of the Association for Computational Linguistics: Long Papers-Volume 1*, pages 136–145. Association for Computational Linguistics.

Elia Bruni, Nam Khanh Tran, and Marco Baroni. 2014. Multimodal distributional semantics. *Journal of Artificial Intelligence Research*, 49:1–47.

Jia Deng, Wei Dong, Richard Socher, Li-Jia Li, Kai Li, and Li Fei-Fei. 2009. Imagenet: A large-scale hierarchical image database. In *Computer Vision and Pattern Recognition, 2009. CVPR 2009*, pages 248–255. IEEE.

Katrin Erk and Sebastian Padó. 2008. A structured vector space model for word meaning in context. In *Proceedings of the Conference on Empirical Methods in Natural Language Processing*, pages 897–906. Association for Computational Linguistics.

Christiane Fellbaum. 1999. *WordNet*. Wiley Online Library.

Yansong Feng and Mirella Lapata. 2010. Visual information in semantic representation. In *Human Language Technologies: The 2010 Annual Conference of the North American Chapter of the Association for Computational Linguistics*, pages 91–99. Association for Computational Linguistics.

Vittorio Gallese and George Lakoff. 2005. The brain's concepts: The role of the sensory-motor system in conceptual knowledge. *Cognitive neuropsychology*, 22(3-4):455–479.

Dedre Gentner and Arthur B Markman. 1997. Structure mapping in analogy and similarity. *American psychologist*, 52(1):45.

Dedre Gentner. 1978. On relational meaning: The acquisition of verb meaning. *Child development*, pages 988–998.

Daniel Gildea and Daniel Jurafsky. 2002. Automatic labeling of semantic roles. *Computational linguistics*, 28(3):245–288.

Yoav Goldberg and Jon Orwant. 2013. A dataset of syntactic-ngrams over time from a very large corpus of english books. In *Second Joint Conference on Lexical and Computational Semantics, Association for Computational Linguistics*, pages 241–247. Association for Computational Linguistics.

Thomas L Griffiths, Mark Steyvers, and Joshua B Tenenbaum. 2007. Topics in semantic representation. *Psychological review*, 114(2):211.

David R Hardoon, Sandor Szedmak, and John Shawe-Taylor. 2004. Canonical correlation analysis: An overview with application to learning methods. *Neural Computation*, 16(12):2639–2664.

Zellig Harris. 1954. Distributional structure. *Word*, 10(23):146–162.

Felix Hill, Anna Korhonen, and Christian Bentz. 2013. A quantitative empirical analysis of the abstract/concrete distinction. *Cognitive Science*.

Eric H Huang, Richard Socher, Christopher D Manning, and Andrew Y Ng. 2012. Improving word representations via global context and multiple word prototypes. In *Proceedings of the 50th Annual Meeting of the Association for Computational Linguistics: Long Papers-Volume 1*, pages 873–882. Association for Computational Linguistics.

Sabine Schulte Im Walde. 2006. Experiments on the automatic induction of german semantic verb classes. *Computational Linguistics*, 32(2):159–194.

Brendan T Johns and Michael N Jones. 2012. Perceptual inference through global lexical similarity. *Topics in Cognitive Science*, 4(1):103–120.

Colin Kelly, Barry Devereux, and Anna Korhonen. 2010. Acquiring human-like feature-based conceptual representations from corpora. In *Proceedings of the NAACL HLT 2010 First Workshop on Computational Neurolinguistics*, pages 61–69. Association for Computational Linguistics.

Douwe Kiela and Felix Hill. 2014. Improving multimodal representations using image dispersion: Why less is sometimes more. In *Proceedings of ACL 2014, Baltimore*. Association for Computational Linguistics.

Karin Kipper, Anna Korhonen, Neville Ryant, and Martha Palmer. 2008. A large-scale classification of english verbs. *Language Resources and Evaluation*, 42(1):21–40.

Thomas K Landauer and Susan T Dumais. 1997. A solution to plato's problem: The latent semantic analysis theory of acquisition, induction, and representation of knowledge. *Psychological review*, 104(2):211.

Geoffrey Leech, Roger Garside, and Michael Bryant. 1994. Claws4: the tagging of the British National Corpus. In *Proceedings of the 15th conference on Computational linguistics-Volume 1*, pages 622–628. Association for Computational Linguistics.

Chee Wee Leong and Rada Mihalcea. 2011. Going beyond text: A hybrid image-text approach for measuring word relatedness. In *IJCNLP*, pages 1403–1407.

Christopher D Manning. 2011. Part-of-speech tagging from 97% to 100%: is it time for some linguistics? In *Computational Linguistics and Intelligent Text Processing*, pages 171–189. Springer.

Arthur B Markman and Edward J Wisniewski. 1997. Similar and different: The differentiation of basic-level categories. *Journal of Experimental Psychology: Learning, Memory, and Cognition*, 23(1).

Ken McRae, George S Cree, Mark S Seidenberg, and Chris McNorgan. 2005. Semantic feature production norms for a large set of living and non-living things. *Behavior Research Methods*, 37(4):547–559.

Raymond H Myers. 1990. *Classical and modern regression with applications*, volume 2. Duxbury Press Belmont, CA.

Douglas L Nelson, Cathy L McEvoy, and Thomas A Schreiber. 2004. The University of South Florida free association, rhyme, and word fragment norms. *Behavior Research Methods, Instruments, & Computers*, 36(3):402–407.

Allan Paivio. 1991. Dual coding theory: Retrospect and current status. *Canadian Journal of Psychology/Revue Canadienne de Psychologie*, 45(3):255.

Ted Pedersen, Siddharth Patwardhan, and Jason Michelizzi. 2004. Wordnet:: Similarity: measuring the relatedness of concepts. In *Demonstration Papers at HLT-NAACL 2004*, pages 38–41. Association for Computational Linguistics.

Roi Reichart and Anna Korhonen. 2013. Improved lexical acquisition through dpp-based verb clustering. In *Proceedings of the Conference of the Association for Computational Linguistics (ACL)*. Association for Computational Linguistics.

Stephen Roller and Sabine Schulte im Walde. 2013. A multimodal LDA model integrating textual, cognitive and visual modalities. In *Proceedings of the 2013 Conference on Empirical Methods in Natural Language Processing*, pages 1146–1157, Seattle, Washington, USA, October. Association for Computational Linguistics.

Eleanor Rosch, Carolyn B Mervis, Wayne D Gray, David M Johnson, and Penny Boyes-Braem. 1976. Basic objects in natural categories. *Cognitive Psychology*, 8(3):382–439.

Gideon Rosen. 2001. Nominalism, naturalism, epistemic relativism. *Noûs*, 35(s15):69–91.

Magnus Sahlgren. 2006. *The Word-Space Model: Using distributional analysis to represent syntagmatic and paradigmatic relations between words in high-dimensional vector spaces*. Ph.D. thesis, Stockholm.

Paula J Schwanenflugel and Edward J Shoben. 1983. Differential context effects in the comprehension of abstract and concrete verbal materials. *Journal of Experimental Psychology: Learning, Memory, and Cognition*, 9(1):82.

Carina Silberer and Mirella Lapata. 2012. Grounded models of semantic representation. In *Proceedings of the 2012 Joint Conference on Empirical Methods in Natural Language Processing and Computational Natural Language Learning*, pages 1423–1433. Association for Computational Linguistics.

Carina Silberer, Vittorio Ferrari, and Mirella Lapata. 2013. Models of semantic representation with visual attributes. In *Proceedings of the 51th Annual Meeting of the Association for Computational Linguistics, Sofia, Bulgaria*.

Peter D Turney, Patrick Pantel, et al. 2010. From frequency to meaning: Vector space models of semantics. *Journal of artificial intelligence research*, 37(1):141–188.

Tim Van de Cruys, Laura Rimell, Thierry Poibeau, Anna Korhonen, et al. 2012. Multiway tensor factorization for unsupervised lexical acquisition. *COLING 2012: Technical Papers*, pages 2703–2720.

Luis Von Ahn and Laura Dabbish. 2004. Labeling images with a computer game. In *Proceedings of the SIGCHI conference on Human Factors in Computing Systems*, pages 319–326. ACM.

Exploiting Social Network Structure for Person-to-Person Sentiment Analysis

Robert West
Stanford University
west@cs.stanford.edu

Hristo S. Paskov
Stanford University
hpaskov@stanford.edu

Jure Leskovec
Stanford University
jure@cs.stanford.edu

Christopher Potts
Stanford University
cgpotts@stanford.edu

Abstract

Person-to-person evaluations are prevalent in all kinds of discourse and important for establishing reputations, building social bonds, and shaping public opinion. Such evaluations can be analyzed separately using signed social networks and textual sentiment analysis, but this misses the rich interactions between language and social context. To capture such interactions, we develop a model that predicts individual *A*'s opinion of individual *B* by synthesizing information from the signed social network in which *A* and *B* are embedded with sentiment analysis of the evaluative texts relating *A* to *B*. We prove that this problem is NP-hard but can be relaxed to an efficiently solvable hinge-loss Markov random field, and we show that this implementation outperforms text-only and network-only versions in two very different datasets involving community-level decision-making: the Wikipedia Requests for Adminship corpus and the Convote U.S. Congressional speech corpus.

1 Introduction

People's evaluations of one another are prevalent in all kinds of discourse, public and private, across ages, genders, cultures, and social classes (Dunbar, 2004). Such opinions matter for establishing reputations and reinforcing social bonds, and they are especially consequential in political contexts, where they take the form of endorsements, accusations, and assessments intended to sway public opinion.

The significance of such *person-to-person* evaluations means that there is a pressing need for computational models and technologies that can analyze them. Research on *signed social networks* suggests one path forward: how one person will evaluate another can often be predicted from the network they are embedded in. Linguistic sentiment analysis suggests another path forward: one could leverage textual features to predict the valence of evaluative texts describing people. Such independent efforts have been successful, but they generally neglect the ways in which social and linguistic features complement each other. In some settings, textual data is sparse but the network structure is largely observed; in others, text is abundant but the network is partly or unreliably recorded. In addition, we often see rich interactions between the two kinds of information—political allies might tease each other with negative language to enhance social bonds, and opponents often use sarcastically positive language in their criticisms. Separate sentiment or signed-network models will miss or misread these signals.

We develop (Sec. 3) a graphical model that synthesizes network and linguistic information to make more and better predictions about both. The objective of the model is to predict *A*'s opinion of *B* using a synthesis of the structural context around *A* and *B* inside the social network and sentiment analysis of the evaluative texts relating *A* to *B*. We prove that the problem is NP-hard but that it can be relaxed to an efficiently solvable hinge-loss Markov random field (Broecheler et al., 2010), and we show that this implementation outperforms text-only and network-only versions in two very different datasets involving community-level decision-making: the Wikipedia Requests for Adminship corpus, in which Wikipedia editors discuss and vote on who should be

Transactions of the Association for Computational Linguistics, 2 (2014) 297–310. Action Editor: Hal Daume III.
Submitted 5/2014; Revised 6/2014; Published 10/2014.

promoted within the Wikipedia hierarchy (Sec. 4), and the Convote U.S. Congressional speech corpus (Thomas et al., 2006), in which elected officials discuss political topics (Sec. 5). These corpora differ dramatically in size, in the style and quality of their textual data, and in the structure and observability of their networks. Together, they provide a clear picture of how joint models of text and network structure can excel where their component parts cannot.

2 Background and related work

2.1 Sentiment analysis

In NLP, the label *sentiment analysis* covers diverse phenomena concerning how information about emotions, attitudes, perspectives, and social identities is conveyed in language (Pang and Lee, 2008). Most work assumes a *dimensional model* in which emotions are defined primarily by valence/polarity and arousal/intensity (Russell, 1980; Feldman Barrett and Russell, 1998; Rubin and Talerico, 2009), and the dominant application is predicting the valence of product, company, and service reviews.

We adopt the conceptual assumptions of this work for our basic sentiment model, but our focus is on person-to-person evaluations and their social consequences. This involves elements of work on modeling political affiliation (Agrawal et al., 2003; Malouf and Mullen, 2008; Yu et al., 2008), bias (Yano et al., 2010; Recasens et al., 2013), and stance on debate topics (Thomas et al., 2006; Somasundaran and Wiebe, 2010; Lin et al., 2006; Anand et al., 2011), but these aspects of belief and social identity are not our primary concern. Rather, we expect them to be *predictive* of the sentiment classifications we aim to make—e.g., if two people share political views, they will tend to evaluate each other positively.

Recent work in sentiment analysis has brought in topical, contextual, and social information to make more nuanced predictions about language (Jurafsky et al., 2014; Wilson et al., 2005; Blitzer et al., 2007). We build on these insights with our model, which seeks to modulate sentiment predictions based on network information (and *vice versa*).

2.2 Signed-network analysis

Many social networks encode person-to-person sentiment information via *signed* edges between users summarizing their opinions of each other. In this setting, one can leverage sociological theories of pairwise relationships and group-level organization to identify and understand patterns in these relationships (Heider, 1946; Cartwright and Harary, 1956).

Balance theory is based on simple intuitions like 'a friend of my friend is my friend', 'an enemy of my enemy is my friend', and 'an enemy of my friend is my enemy'. In graph theory, these are statements about the edge signs of triangles of connected nodes: given the signs of two edges, balance theory predicts the third, as summarized in Fig. 1(a), where the two given edges (gray) determine the third (black).

For directed relationships, Leskovec et al. (2010b) formulate an alternative called *status theory,* which posits that networks organize according to social status: a node has positive edges to others with higher status and negative edges to those with lower status. Fig. 1(a) illustrates the structure of various directed signed triangles, where the sign of the third edge (black) can be inferred based on the signs and directions of the other two (gray).

Leskovec et al. (2010b) show that signed edges in networks emerge in a manner that is broadly consistent with both of these theories and that social-network structure alone can support accurate edge-sign predictions (Leskovec et al., 2010a). Kunegis et al. (2013) predict hidden positive and negative edges in a scenario where all observed edges are positive. Bach et al. (2013) and Huang et al. (2013) frame sign prediction as a hinge-loss Markov random field, a type of probabilistic graphical model introduced by Broecheler et al. (2010). Our model combines these ideas with a sentiment model to achieve even more robust predictions.

2.3 Synthesis of sentiment & network analysis

Models of sentiment and signed networks have been successful at a variety of tasks. However, missing from the current scientific picture is a deep understanding of the ways in which sentiment expression and social networks interact. To some extent, these interactions are captured by adding contextual and demographic features to a text-based sentiment model, but those features only approximate the rich relational structure encoded in a signed network.

Thomas et al. (2006) and Tan et al. (2011) capitalize on this insight using an elaboration of the

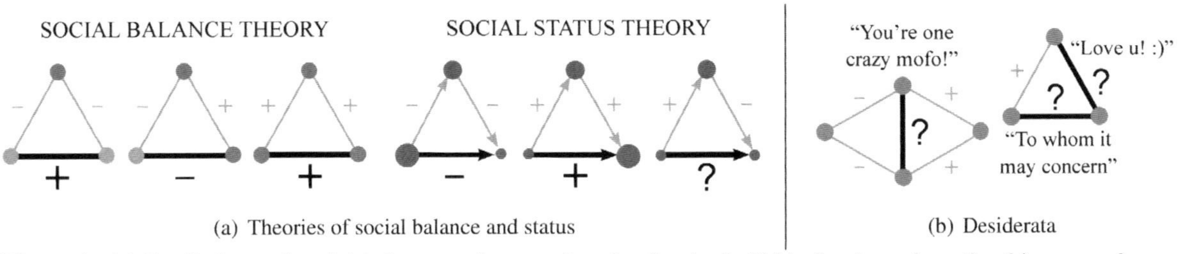

Figure 1: **(a)** Predictions of social balance and status theories for the bold black edge, given the thin gray edges. Balance theory reasons about undirected, status theory about directed, triangles. In the status diagrams, node size signifies social status. A positive edge may be replaced by a negative edge in the opposite direction, and *vice versa*, without changing the prediction. Status theory makes no prediction in the rightmost case. **(b)** Situations of the sort we aim to capture. At left, the network resolves textual ambiguity. At right, the text compensates for edge-label sparsity.

graph-cuts approach of Pang and Lee (2004). They are guided by an assumption of *homophily*, i.e., that certain social relationships correlate with agreement on certain topics: Thomas et al. (2006) use party affiliation and mentions in speeches to predict voting patterns, and Tan et al. (2011) use Twitter follows and mentions to predict attitudes about political and social events. Related ideas are pursued by Ma et al. (2011) and Hu et al. (2013), who add terms to their models enforcing homophily between friends with regard to their preferences.

We adopt some of the assumptions of the above authors, but our task is fundamentally different in two respects. First, whereas they model person-to-item evaluations, we model person-to-person evaluations; these are also the focus of Tang et al. (2013), who, though, use an unsigned network, whereas our work is geared toward distinguishing positive and negative edge labels. Second, the above models make overarching homophily assumptions, whereas we allow our model to explore the full set of triangle configurations suggested by Fig. 1(a).

3 Model

Here, we argue that combining textual and structural features can help predict edge signs. We formulate a model, show that it is computationally hard, and provide a relaxed version that is computationally tractable, building on work by Bach et al. (2013).

3.1 Desiderata

In many real-world scenarios, rich features are associated with edges between two people, such as comments they made about each other, messages they exchanged, or other behavioral features. Such features may contain a strong sentiment signal useful for predicting edge signs and may be used to fit a conventional sentiment model (Sec. 2.1).

However, the sign of an edge also depends on the signs of surrounding edges in the network (Sec. 2.2). A purely edge-feature–based sentiment model cannot account for the network structure, since it reasons about edges as independent of each other.

We argue that considering sentiment and network structure jointly can result in better predictions than either one on its own. Fig. 1(b) provides two illustrative examples. Here, the gray edge signs are observed, while the polarities of the black edges are to be predicted. In the left network, the text of the black edge (*'You're one crazy mofo!'*) might suggest a negative polarity. However, a negative black edge would make both triangles inconsistent with balance theory (Fig. 1(a)), whereas a positive black edge makes them consistent with the theory. So, in this case, the network context effectively helps detect the teasing, non-literal tone of the statement.

In the right network of Fig. 1(b), only one of three edge signs is observed. Predicting two positive edges would be consistent with balance theory, but the same would be true for predicting two negative edges. The text on the lower black edge (*'To whom it may concern'*) does not carry any clear sentiment signal, but the *'Love u! :)'* on the other edge strongly suggests a positive polarity. This lets us conclude that the bottom edge should probably be positive, too, since otherwise the triangle would contradict balance theory. This shows that combining sentiment and network features can help when jointly reasoning about several unknown edge signs.

3.2 Problem formulation

We now formulate a model capable of synthesizing textual and network features.

Notation. We represent the given social network as a signed graph $G = (V, E, x)$, where the vertices V represent people; the edges E, relationships between people in V; and the sign vector $x \in \{0,1\}^{|E|}$ represents edge polarities, i.e., $x_e = 1$ ($x_e = 0$) indicates a positive (negative) polarity for edge $e \in E$.

Some types of relationships imply directed edges (e.g., following a user on Twitter, or voting on a candidate in an election), whereas others imply undirected edges (e.g., friendship on Facebook, or agreement in a network of politicians). We formulate our problem for undirected graphs here, but the extension to directed graphs is straightforward. We define a *triangle* $t = \{e_1, e_2, e_3\} \subseteq E$ to be a set of three edges that form a cycle, and use T to indicate the set of all triangles in G. Finally, we use $x_t = (x_{e_1}, x_{e_2}, x_{e_3}) \in \{0,1\}^3$ to refer to t's edge signs.

Optimization problem. We assume that the structure of the network (i.e., V and E) is fully observed, whereas the edge signs x are only partially observed. Further, we assume that we have a sentiment model that outputs, for each edge e independently, an estimate p_e of the probability that e is of positive polarity, based on textual features associated with e. The task, then, is to *infer the unobserved edge signs* based on the observed information.

The high-level idea is that we want to infer edge signs that (1) agree with the predictions of the sentiment model, and (2) form triangles that agree with social theories of balance and status. It is not always possible to meet both objectives simultaneously for all edges and triangles, so we need to find a trade-off. This gives rise to a combinatorial optimization problem, which we term TRIANGLE BALANCE, that seeks to find edge signs x^* that minimize an objective consisting of both edge and triangle costs:[1]

$$x^* = \operatorname*{arg\,min}_{x \in \{0,1\}^{|E|}} \sum_{e \in E} c(x_e, p_e) + \sum_{t \in T} d(x_t). \quad (1)$$

The first term is the *total edge cost,* in which each edge e contributes a cost capturing how much its inferred sign x_e deviates from the prediction p_e of the sentiment model. The second term, the *total triangle cost,* penalizes each triangle t according to how undesirable its configuration is under its inferred signs x_t (e.g., if it contradicts status or balance theory).

We use the following edge cost function:

$$c(x_e, p_e) = \lambda_1 (1 - p_e) x_e + \lambda_0 p_e (1 - x_e). \quad (2)$$

Here, $\lambda_1, \lambda_0 \in \mathbb{R}_+$ are tunable parameters that allow for asymmetric costs for positive and negative edges, respectively, and p_e is the probability of edge e being positive according to the sentiment model alone. Intuitively, the more the inferred edge sign x_e deviates from the prediction p_e of the sentiment model, the higher the edge cost. (Note that at most one of the two sum factors of Eq. 2 is non-zero.)

The triangle cost for triangle t is signified by $d(x_t)$, which can only take on 8 distinct values because $x_t \in \{0,1\}^3$ (in practice, there are symmetries that decrease this number to 4). The parameters $d(x_t)$ may be tuned so that triangle configurations that agree with social theory have low costs, while those that disagree with it (e.g., 'the enemy of my friend is my friend') have high costs.

3.3 Computational complexity

The problem defined in Eq. 1 is intuitive, but, as with many combinatorial optimization problems, it is hard to find a good solution. In particular, we sketch a proof of this theorem in Appendix A:

Theorem 1. TRIANGLE BALANCE *is NP-hard.*

3.4 Relaxation as a Markov random field

The objective function of Eq. 1 may be seen as defining a Markov random field (MRF) over the underlying social network G, with edge potentials (defined by c) and triangle potentials (defined by d). Inference in MRFs (i.e., computing x^*) is a well-studied task for which a variety of methods have been proposed (Koller and Friedman, 2009). However, since our problem is NP-hard, no method can be expected to find x^* efficiently. One way of dealing with the computational hardness would be to find an *approximate binary* solution, using techniques such as Gibbs sampling or belief propagation. Another option is to consider a continuous relaxation of the binary problem and find an *exact non-binary* solution whose edge signs are continuous, i.e., $x_e \in [0,1]$.

[1]Of course, the entries of x^* corresponding to observed edges are not variable but fixed to their observed values in Eq. 1.

We take this latter approach and cast our problem as a *hinge-loss Markov random field* (HL-MRF). This is inspired by Bach et al. (2013), who also use an HL-MRF to predict edge signs based on triangle structure, but do not use any edge features. An HL-MRF is an MRF with continuous variables and with potentials that can be expressed as sums of hinge-loss terms of linear functions of the variables (cf. Broecheler et al. (2010) for details). HL-MRFs have the advantage that their objective function is convex so that, unlike binary MRFs (as defined by Eq. 1), exact inference is efficient (Bach et al., 2013).

We achieve a relaxation by using sums of hinge-loss terms to interpolate c over the continuous domain $[0,1]$ and d, over $[0,1]^3$ (even though they are defined only for binary domains). As a result, the HL-MRF formulation is equivalent to Eq. 1 when all x_e are binary, but it also handles continuous values gracefully. We now interpret a real-valued 'sign' $x_e \in [0,1]$ as the degree to which e is positive.

We start by showing how to transform c: even though it could be used in its current form (Eq. 2), we create a tighter relaxation by using

$$\tilde{c}(x_e, p_e) = \lambda_1 \|x_e - p_e\|_+ + \lambda_0 \|p_e - x_e\|_+, \quad (3)$$

where $\|y\|_+ = \max\{0, y\}$ is the hinge loss. At most one term can be active for any $x_e \in [0,1]$ due to the hinge loss, and $c(x_e, p_e) = \tilde{c}(x_e, p_e)$ for binary x_e.

To rewrite d, notice that, for any $x_t \in \{0,1\}^3$, we can write d as

$$d(x_t) = \sum_{z \in \{0,1\}^3} d(z)\, \delta(x_t, z), \quad (4)$$

where $\delta(x_t, z) = 1$ if $x_t = z$ and 0 otherwise. While δ is not convex, we can use

$$f(x_t, z) = \|1 - \|x_t - z\|_1\|_+ \quad (5)$$

as a convex surrogate. When x_t is binary, either $x_t = z$ so $\|x_t - z\|_1 = 0$ or $x_t \neq z$ so $\|x_t - z\|_1 \geq 1$, and hence $f(x_t, z) = \delta(x_t, z)$. To prove convexity, note that, for any fixed binary $z \in \{0,1\}^3$, $\|x - z\|_1 = \sum_{i=1}^{3} |x_i - z_i|$ is linear in $x \in [0,1]^3$, since $|x_i - z_i|$ equals either x_i (if $z_i = 0$) or $1 - x_i$ (if $z_i = 1$). It follows that f is a hinge-loss function of a linear transformation of x_t and therefore convex in x_t.

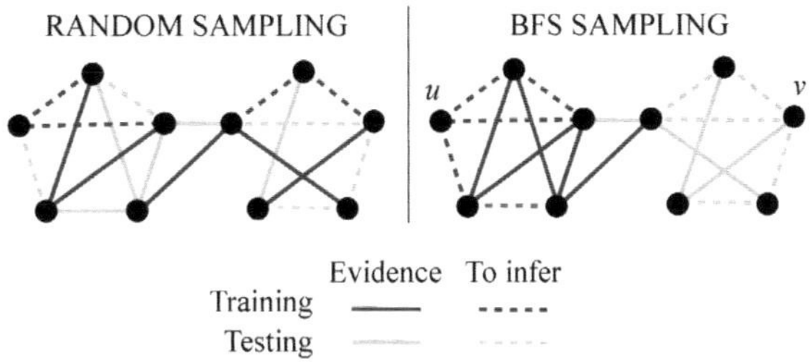

Figure 2: Options for training and testing our model.

Requiring the triangle cost $d(z)$ to be nonnegative for all triangle types $z \in \{0,1\}^3$, we can use

$$\tilde{d}(x_t) = \sum_{z \in \{0,1\}^3} d(z)\, f(x_t, z) \quad (6)$$

as a convex surrogate for d. Our overall optimization problem is then the following relaxation of Eq. 1:

$$x^* = \underset{x \in [0,1]^{|E|}}{\arg\min} \sum_{e \in E} \tilde{c}(x_e, p_e) + \sum_{t \in T} \tilde{d}(x_t). \quad (7)$$

This objective has the exact form of an HL-MRF, since it is a weighted sum of hinge losses of linear functions of x. We use the *Probabilistic Soft Logic* package[2] to perform the optimization, which is in turn based on the alternating-direction method of multipliers (ADMM) (Boyd et al., 2011).

Learning. Clearly, a solution is only useful if the cost parameters (λ_1, λ_0, and $d(z)$ for all $z \in \{0,1\}^3$) are set appropriately. One option would be to set the values heuristically, based on the predictions made by the social balance and status theories (Sec. 2.2). However, it is more principled to learn these parameters from data. For this purpose, we leverage the learning procedures included in the HL-MRF implementation we employ, which uses the voted-perceptron algorithm to perform maximum-likelihood estimation (Bach et al., 2013).

Since our data points (edges) interact with each other via the network, some words on how we perform training and testing are in order. Fig. 2 shows two options for obtaining training and testing sets (we use both options in our experiments). In the 'random sampling' paradigm, we randomly choose a set of edges for training (blue), and a disjoint set of edges for testing (yellow). In 'BFS sampling', we

[2]http://psl.umiacs.umd.edu

run a breadth-first search from seed node u to obtain a coherent training set (blue), and likewise from a seed node v to obtain a coherent testing set (yellow), taking care that no edges from the training set are also included in the testing set.

During both training and testing, an arbitrary portion of the edge signs may be fixed to observed values and need not be inferred. These are the solid edges in Fig. 2; we refer to them as *evidence*. Further, we define the *evidence ratio* as the number of evidence edges, divided by the number of all edges considered (solid and dashed).

The learning algorithm may use the structure (V and E) of the training graph induced by all blue edges (solid and dashed), the predictions p_e of the sentiment model for all blue edges, and the signs of the solid blue edges to predict the dashed blue edges.

During testing, the network structure of all yellow edges, the sentiment predictions for all yellow edges, and the signs of the solid yellow edges may be used to predict the dashed yellow edge signs. In principle, all training edges could be used as extra evidence for testing (i.e., all blue edges may be made solid yellow). However, in our experiments, we keep the training and testing sets fully disjoint.

Technical details. For clarity, we give further details. First, the distribution of positive and negative signs may be skewed; e.g., we observe a prior probability of 76% positive signs in our Wikipedia corpus (Sec. 4). Therefore, as also done by Bach et al. (2013), we add a cost term to our objective (Eq. 7) that penalizes deviations from this prior probability (as estimated on the training set). This ensures that the model can default to a reasonable prediction for edges that are not embedded in any triangles and about which the sentiment model is uncertain.

Second, intuitively, we should not penalize deviating from the sentiment model when it is itself uncertain about its prediction (i.e., when p_e is far from both 0 and 1). Rather, we want to rely more heavily on signals from the network structure in such cases. To achieve this, we introduce 10 pairs of cost parameters $(\lambda_1^{(1)}, \lambda_0^{(1)}), \ldots, (\lambda_1^{(10)}, \lambda_0^{(10)})$. Then, we divide the interval $[0,1]$ into 10 bins, and when p_e falls into the i-th bin, we use $\lambda_1^{(i)}$ and $\lambda_0^{(i)}$ in Eq. 3. This way, larger costs can be learned for the extreme bins close to 0 and 1 than for the intermediate bins around 0.5.

Finally, hinge-loss terms may optionally be squared in HL-MRFs. We use the squared hinge loss in Eq. 5, since initial experimentation showed this to perform slightly better than the linear hinge loss.

4 Wikipedia experiments

Our first set of experiments is conducted on the Wikipedia Requests for Adminship corpus, which allows us to evaluate our model's ability to predict person-to-person evaluations in Web texts that are informal but pertain to important social outcomes.

4.1 Dataset description

For a Wikipedia editor to become an administrator, a *request for adminship* (RfA)[3] must be submitted, either by the candidate or by another community member. Subsequently, any Wikipedia member may cast a supporting, neutral, or opposing vote. This induces a directed, signed network in which nodes represent Wikipedia members and edges represent votes (we discard neutral votes).

We crawled and parsed all votes since the adoption of the RfA process in 2003 through May 2013.[4] This signed network was previously analyzed by Leskovec et al. (2010b; 2010a). However, there is also a rich textual component that has so far remained untapped for edge-sign prediction: each vote is typically accompanied by a short comment (median/mean: 19/34 tokens). A typical positive comment reads, *'I've no concerns, will make an excellent addition to the admin corps'*, while an example of a negative comment is, *'Little evidence of collaboration with other editors and limited content creation.'* The presence of a voting network alongside textual edge features makes our method of Sec. 3 well-suited for this dataset.

The RfA network contains 11K nodes, 160K edges (76% positive), and close to 1M triangles.

4.2 Experimental setup

Train/test sets. We follow the train–test paradigm termed 'BFS sampling' in Sec. 3.4 and Fig. 2, choosing 10 random seed nodes, from each of which we perform a breadth-first search (following both in- and out-links) until we have visited 350 nodes. We

[3] http://en.wikipedia.org/wiki/Wikipedia:RfA

[4] Data available online (West, 2014).

thus obtain 10 subgraphs with 350 nodes each. We train a model for each subgraph i and test it on subgraph $i+1$ (mod 10), ensuring that edges from the training graph are removed from the testing graph.

The BFS sampling paradigm was used because the alternative ('random sampling' in Fig. 2) produces subgraphs with mostly isolated edges and only a few triangles—an unrealistic scenario.

Evaluated models. We evaluate three models:

1. A standard, text-based sentiment model that treats edges as independent data points;
2. our full model as specified in Sec. 3.4, which combines edge costs based on the predictions of the text-based sentiment model with triangle costs capturing network context;
3. a version of our model that considers only triangle costs, while ignoring the predictions of the text-based sentiment model (akin to the model proposed by Bach et al. (2013)).

We refer to these models as *'sentiment', 'combined',* and *'network',* respectively.

Sentiment model. Our text-based sentiment model is an L_2-regularized logistic-regression classifier whose features are term frequencies of the 10,000 overall most frequent words. The L_2-penalty is chosen via cross-validation on the training set. Since comments often explicitly contain the label (*'support'* or *'oppose'*), we remove all words with prefixes *'support'* or *'oppos'*. We train the model only once, on a random sample of 1,000 comments drawn from the set of all 160K comments (the vast majority of which will not appear in our 10 subgraphs).

Evidence ratio. Regarding the other two models, recall from Sec. 3.4 our definition of the *evidence ratio,* the fraction of edge signs that are fixed as evidence and need not be inferred. In our experiments, we explore the impact of the evidence ratio during training and testing, since we expect performance to increase as more evidence is available. (We use the same evidence ratio for training and testing, but this need not necessarily be so.)

Metrics. As our principal evaluation metrics, we use the areas under the curve (AUC) of the receiver operating characteristic (ROC) curve as well as the precision–recall (PR) curves. There are two PR curves, one for the positive class, the other for the negative one. Of these two, the positive class is less interesting: due to the class imbalance of 76% positive edges, even a random guesser would achieve an AUC of 0.76. The PR curve of the negative class is more informative: here, it is much harder to achieve high AUC, since random guessing yields only 0.24. Moreover, the negative edges are arguably more important, not only because they are rarer, but also because they indicate tensions in the network, which we might be interested in detecting and resolving. For these reasons, we report only the AUC under the negative PR curve (AUC/negPR) here.

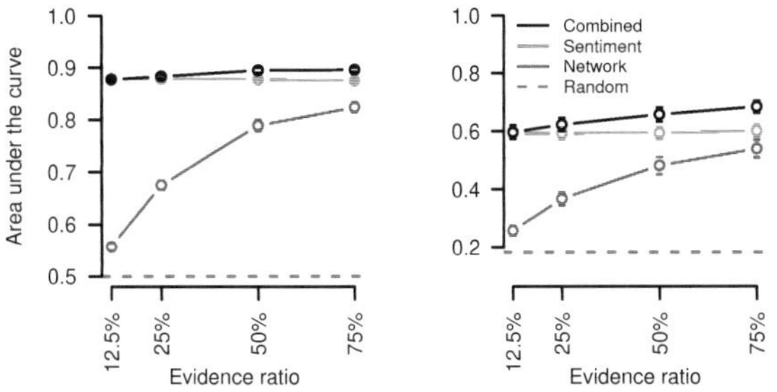

(a) AUC/ROC (b) AUC/negPR

Figure 3: AUC as function of evidence ratio (Wikipedia), with standard errors.

Additionally, we report the area under the ROC curve (AUC/ROC), a standard metric for quantifying classification performance on unbalanced data. It captures the probability of a random positive test example receiving a higher score than a random negative one (so guessing gives an AUC/ROC of 0.5).

4.3 Results

Performance as a function of evidence ratio. The AUCs as functions of the evidence ratio are shown in Fig. 3(a). (We emphasize that these plots are not themselves ROC and PR curves; rather, they are derived from those curves by measuring AUC for a range of models, parametrized by evidence ratio.)

Since we use the same sentiment model in all cases (Sec. 4.2), its performance (yellow) does not depend on the evidence ratio. It is remarkably high, at an AUC/ROC of 0.88, as a consequence of the highly indicative, sometimes even formulaic, language used in the comments (examples in Sec. 4.2).

The network-only model (blue) works poorly on very little evidence (AUC/ROC 0.56 for 12.5% ev-

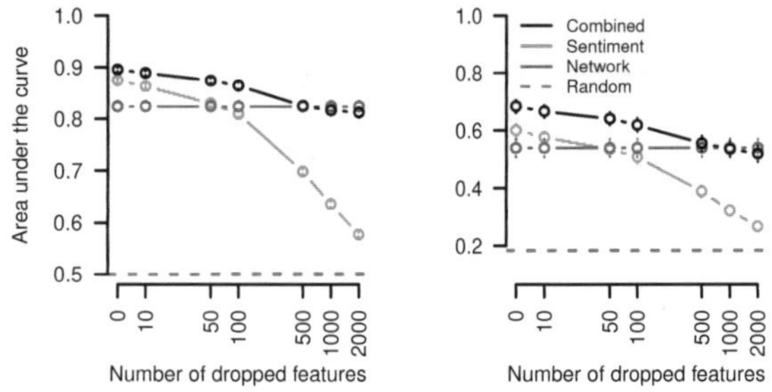

(a) AUC/ROC (b) AUC/negPR

Figure 4: AUC as function of number of dropped features (Wikipedia), with standard errors. Evidence ratio 75%.

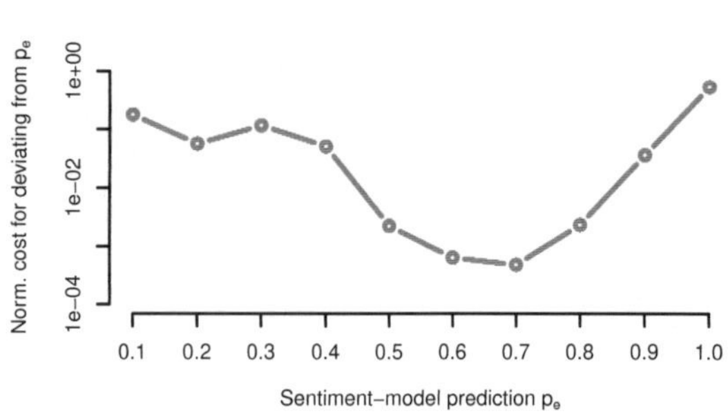

Figure 5: Normalized cost $\lambda^{(i)}$ (defined in Sec. 4.3; logarithmic scale) for deviating from sentiment-model predictions p_e, for bins $i = 1, \ldots, 10$ (Wikipedia). Upper bin boundaries on the x-axis. Values shown are averages over 10 folds. Evidence ratio 75%.

idence) but improves steadily as more evidence is used (AUC/ROC 0.82 for 75% evidence): this is intuitive, since more evidence means stronger context for each edge sign to be predicted.

Although the network-only model works poorly on little evidence, our full model (black), which synthesizes the sentiment and network models, is not affected by this and effectively defaults to the behavior of the sentiment-only model. Furthermore, although the network-only model never attains the performance of the sentiment-only model, combining the two in our full model (black) nonetheless yields a small performance boost in terms of AUC/ROC to 0.89 for 75% evidence. The gains are significantly larger when we consider AUC/negPR instead of AUC/ROC: while the sentiment model achieves 0.60, the combined model improves on this by 13%, to 0.68, at 75% evidence ratio.

Performance as a function of sentiment-model quality. It seems hard to improve by much on a sentiment model that achieves an AUC/ROC of 0.88 on its own; the Wikipedia corpus offers an exceptionally explicit linguistic signal. Hence, in our next experiment, we explore systematically how our model behaves under a less powerful sentiment model.

First, we measure, for each feature (i.e., word), how informative it is on its own for predicting the signs of edges (quantified by its mutual information with the edge sign), which induces a ranking of features in terms of informativeness. Now, to make the sentiment model less powerful in a controlled way, we drop the top m features and repeat the experiment described above for a range of m values (where we keep the evidence ratio fixed at 75%).

Fig. 4 shows that the performance of the sentiment model (yellow) declines drastically as more features are removed. The combined model (black), on the contrary, is much less affected: when the performance of the sentiment model drops to that of the network-only (blue; ROC/AUC 0.81), the combined model is still stronger than both (0.86). Even as the sentiment model approaches random performance, the combined model still never drops below the network-only model—it simply learns to disregard the predictions of the sentiment model altogether.

Learned edge costs. Recall from the final part of Sec. 3.4 that each output p_e of the sentiment model falls into one of 10 bins $[0, 0.1], \ldots, [0.9, 1]$, with separate edge-cost parameters $\lambda_1^{(i)}$ and $\lambda_0^{(i)}$ learned for each bucket i. The rationale was to give the model the freedom to trade off edge and triangle costs differently for each edge e, depending on how informative the sentiment model's prediction p_e is.

The goal of this section is to understand whether our model indeed exposes such behavior. Recall from Eq. 3 that λ_1 is the constant with which the absolute difference between p_e and the inferred edge sign x_e is multiplied when $x_e > p_e$, while λ_0 is the constant when $x_e < p_e$. If p_e falls into bin i, the sum $\lambda_1^{(i)} + \lambda_0^{(i)}$ expresses the cost of deviating from p_e in a single number; further, dividing this sum by the sum of all costs (i.e., $\lambda_1^{(i)}$ and $\lambda_0^{(i)}$ for all bins i, plus the costs $d(z)$ of all triangle types z) yields a normalized edge cost for each bin i, which we call $\lambda^{(i)}$.

Fig. 5 plots $\lambda^{(i)}$ for all bins $i = 1, \ldots, 10$. We observe that deviating from the sentiment model costs more when it makes a strong prediction (i.e., p_e

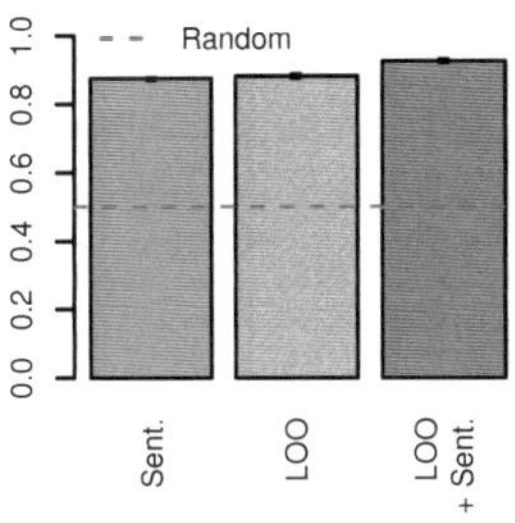

(a) AUC/ROC

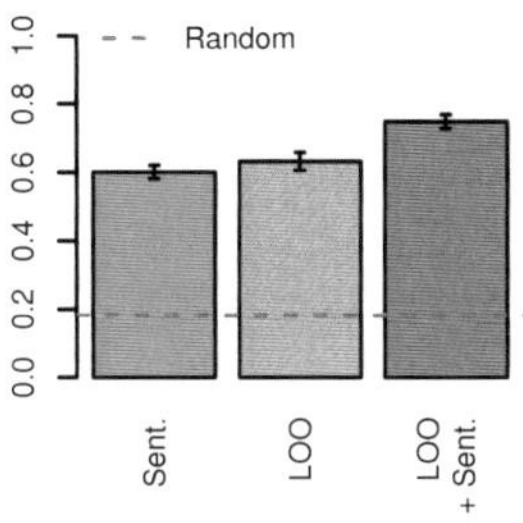

(b) AUC/negPR

Figure 6: Performance in a leave-one-out (LOO) scenario (Wikipedia), with standard errors. For comparison: performance of the sentiment model alone.

close to 0 or 1) than when it makes a non-informative one (e.g., $p_e \approx 0.5$). When $p_e \approx 1$, nearly 100% of the total cost is spent to ensure $x_e \approx p_e$, whereas that fraction is only around 0.1% when $p_e \approx 0.6$.

Leave-one-out setting. Our model predicts many missing edge signs simultaneously, using joint inference. Another scenario was proposed by Leskovec et al. (2010a), who predict signs one at a time, assuming all other edge signs are known. We call this a *leave-one-out* ('LOO' for short) setting. Assume we want to predict the sign of the edge (u, v) in the LOO setting, and that u, v, and w form a triangle. The type of this triangle can be described by the directions and known polarities of the two edges linking u to w, and v to w, respectively. The edge (u, v) may be embedded in several triangles, and the histogram over their types then serves as the feature vector of (u, v) in a logistic regression; as additional features, counts of u's positive/negative out-links and v's positive/negative in-links are used.

Since predictions in the LOO setup can draw on the full triangle neighborhood of the edge in question, we expect it to perform better than the network-only model in which edge signs in the triangle neighborhood are often missing. This expectation is confirmed by Fig. 6, which shows that the LOO model (gray) achieves an AUC/ROC (AUC/negPR) of 0.88 (0.63), with the network-only model (Fig. 3) at just 0.82 (0.54) at 75% evidence ratio.

However, LOO is outperformed by our combined model incorporating sentiment information (Fig. 3), which attains an AUC/ROC (AUC/negPR) of 0.89 (0.68). Finally, when we add the sentiment prediction as another feature to the LOO model ('LOO + Sent.' in Fig. 6), we do best, at 0.93 (0.75).

To summarize, we make two points: (1) By combining sentiment and network features, our model achieves better performance than a network-only model (LOO) that has access to significantly more network information. (2) Incorporating sentiment information helps not only in our setup as described in Sec. 4.2, but also in the previously proposed leave-one-out setup (Leskovec et al., 2010a).

5 U.S. Congress experiments

We now evaluate our model in a setting in which the linguistic person-to-person evaluations are less direct and reliable than in the RfA corpus but the signed network is considerably denser.

5.1 Dataset description

The 'Convote' corpus of Congressional speeches (Thomas et al., 2006) consists of 3,857 speech segments drawn from 53 debates from the U.S. House of Representatives in 2005. There is a mean of 72.8 speech segments per debate and 32.1 speakers per debate. Segments are annotated with the speaker, their party affiliation, the bill discussed, and how the speaker voted on that bill (positive or negative).

Thomas et al. (2006) and others represent this corpus as a bipartite person–item graph with signed edges from Congresspeople to the bills (items) they spoke about, and they add additional person–person edges encoding who mentioned whom in the speech segments. We take a different perspective, extracting from it a dense, undirected person–person graph by linking two Congresspeople if they ever voted on the same bill, labeling the edge as positive if they cast the same vote at least half of the time. We directly use the sentiment model trained by Thomas et al. The resulting graph has 276 nodes, 14,690 edges (54% positive), and 506,327 triangles.

5.2 Experimental setup

We split the network $G = (V, E)$ into 5 folds using the 'random sampling' technique described in Sec. 3.4 and Fig. 2: the set of nodes V is fixed across all folds, and the set of edges E is partitioned randomly so that each fold has 20% of all edges. In the full graph, there is one clique per debate, so each fold contains the overlay of several subgraphs, one per debate and each 20% complete on average.

Here, random sampling was used because the alternative ('BFS sampling' in Fig. 2) would produce nearly complete subgraphs, on which we found the prediction task to be overly easy (since the problem becomes more constrained; Sec. 5.3).

We compare the three models also used on the Wikipedia dataset (Sec. 4.2). Our sentiment model comes right out of the box with the Convote corpus: Thomas et al. (2006) distribute the text-level scores from their SVM classifier with the corpus, so we simply work with those, after transforming them into probabilities via logistic regression (a standard technique called Platt scaling (Platt, 1999)). Thus, let q_u and q_v be the probabilistic sentiment predictions for u and v on a given bill. The probability that u and v agree on the bill is $q_u q_v + (1 - q_u)(1 - q_v)$, and we define the probability p_e of a positive sign on the edge $e = \{u, v\}$ as the average agreement probability over all bills that u and v co-voted on.

For instance, the speech containing the sentence, *'Mr. Speaker, I do rise today in strong support of H.R. 810,'* receives a probability of 98% of expressing a positive opinion on H.R. (i.e., House of Representatives) bill 810, whereas the prediction for the speech containing the words, *'Therefore, I urge my colleagues to vote against both H.R. 810 and H.R. 2520,'* is only 1%. Hence, the edge between the two respective speakers has a probability of $98\% \times 1\% + 2\% \times 99\% = 3\%$ of being positive.

5.3 Results

Fig. 7 summarizes our results. As in the Wikipedia experiments, we report AUCs as a function of the evidence ratio. The sentiment model alone (yellow) achieves an AUC/ROC (AUC/negPR) of 0.65 (0.62), well above the random baselines at 0.5 (0.46). The network-only model (blue) performs much worse at the start, but it surpasses the sentiment model even with just 12.5% of the edges as evidence, a reflection of the dense, high-quality network structure with many triangles. When we combine the sentiment and network models (black), we consistently see the best results, with the largest gains in the realistic scenario where there is little evidence.

Eventually, the network-only model catches up to the combined model, simply because it reaches an upper bound on performance given available evidence. This owes mainly to the fact that, because we derived the person–person signs from person–item signs, only triangles with an even number of negative edges arise with noticeable frequency. To see why, suppose the corpus contained speeches about just one bill. In a triangle consisting of nodes u, v, and w, if u agreed with v and with w, then v and w must agree as well. (The fact that we have multiple bills in the corpus opens up the possibility for additional triangle types, but they rarely arise in the data.) This constrains the solution space and makes the problem easier than in the case of Wikipedia, where all triangle types are possible.

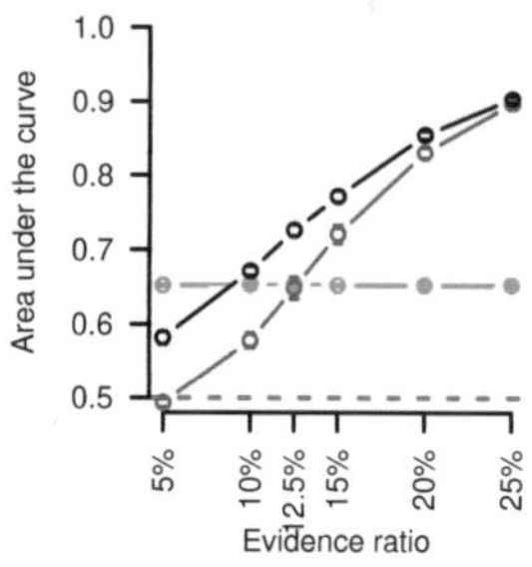

(a) AUC/ROC

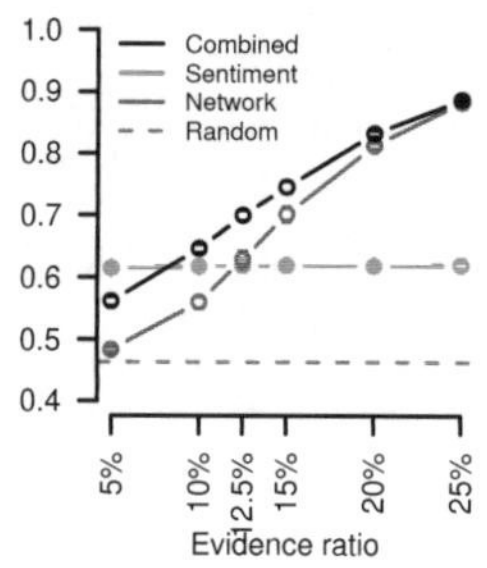

(b) AUC/negPR

Figure 7: AUC as function of evidence ratio (Convote), with standard errors.

Our plots so far have summarized precision–recall curves by measuring AUC. Here, it is also informative to inspect a concrete PR curve, as in Fig. 8, which shows all the values at 15% evidence ratio. The network-only model (blue) achieves very high precision up to a recall of about 0.20, where there is a sudden drop. The reason is that, according to the above argument about possible triangle types, the model can be very certain about some edges (e.g., because it is the only non-evidence edge in a triangle, making only a single triangle type possible), which causes the plateau for low recall. The combined model matches the precision on the plateau, but also maintains significantly higher precision as the network-only model starts to do more poorly: even if an edge e is not fully determined by surrounding evidence, the sentiment model might still give strong signals for e itself and its neighbors, such that the above reasoning effectively still applies.

6 Discussion

We developed a model that synthesizes textual and social-network information to jointly predict the po-

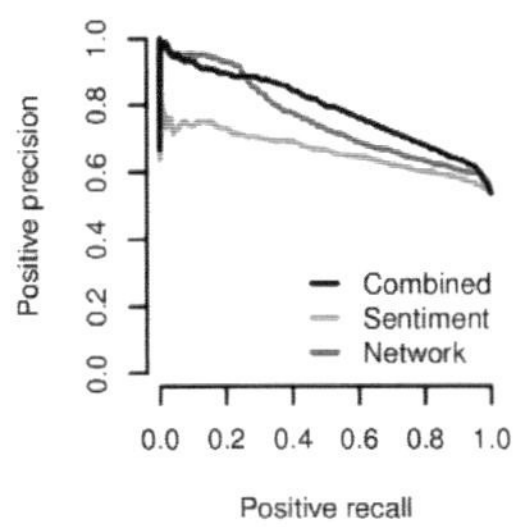

(a) Positive signs

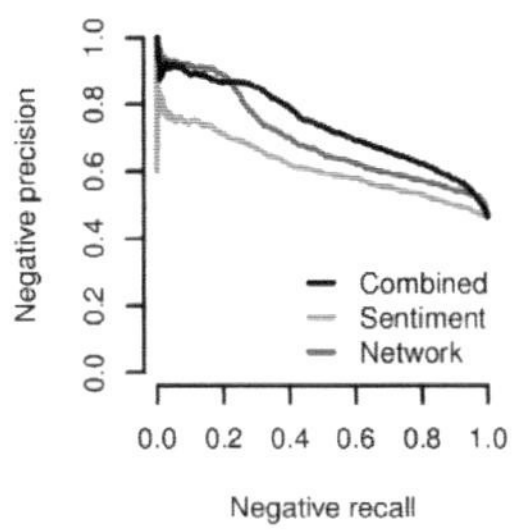

(b) Negative signs

Figure 8: Precision/recall (Convote, evidence ratio 15%).

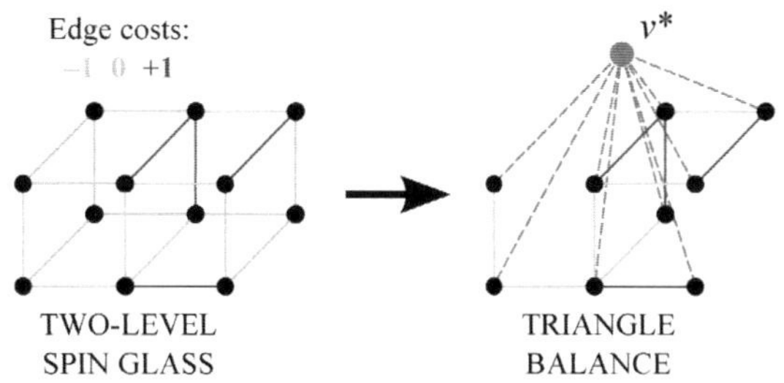

Figure 9: Reduction from TWO-LEVEL SPIN GLASS to TRIANGLE BALANCE.

larity of person-to-person evaluations, and we assessed this model in two datasets. Both involve communal decision making, where people's attitudes and opinions of each other have profound social consequences, but they are very different. In the Wikipedia corpus, the sentiment signal is strong because of established community norms for how to convey one's opinions, but the network is sparse. In the Convote corpus, the network is determined by fully observed voting patterns, making it strong, but the speech texts themselves only indirectly and noisily convey person-to-person opinions. In both cases, our method excels because it is adaptive: it learns from the data how best to combine the two signals.

Our model's adaptivity is important for real-world applications, where one is unlikely to know ahead of time which signals are most trustworthy. We envision the following use-case. One extracts a coherent subgraph of the network of interest, perhaps using one of our sampling methods (Fig. 2) and annotates its edges for their evaluativity. Then, in conjunction with a sentiment model (out-of-the-box or specially trained), one trains our combined model and uses it to predict new edge labels in the network. In this setting, the sentiment model might be unreliable, and one might have the time and resources to label only a small fraction of the edges. Individually, the network and sentiment models would likely perform poorly; in bringing the two together, our single model of joint inference could still excel.

Acknowledgements. This research has been supported in part by NSF IIS-1016909, CNS-1010921, IIS-1149837, IIS-1159679; ARO MURI; DARPA SMISC, GRAPHS; ONR N00014-13-1-0287; PayPal; Docomo; and Volkswagen. Robert West has been supported by a Facebook and a Stanford Graduate Fellowship.

A Proof sketch of Theorem 1

Due to space constraints, we only give a proof sketch here; the full proof is available online (West, 2014).

Proof sketch. By reduction from TWO-LEVEL SPIN GLASS (TLSG), a problem known to be NP-hard (Barahona, 1982). An instance of TLSG consists of vertices V arranged in two 2D grids, one stacked above the other, with edges E between nearest neighbors, and with an edge cost $c_{uv} \in \{-1, 0, +1\}$ associated with each edge $\{u, v\}$ (see Fig. 9 for a small instance). Given such an instance, TLSG asks for vertex signs $x \in \{-1, +1\}^{|V|}$ that minimize the total energy $H(x) = -\sum_{\{u,v\}\in E} c_{uv} x_u x_v$. The crucial observation is that TLSG defines vertex costs (implicitly all-zero) and edge costs, and asks for vertex signs, whereas TRIANGLE BALANCE defines edge costs and triangle costs, and asks for edge signs. That is, vertices (edges) in TLSG correspond to edges (triangles) in TRIANGLE BALANCE, and our proposed reduction transforms an original TLSG instance into a TRIANGLE BALANCE instance in which each edge corresponds to exactly one original vertex, and each triangle to exactly one original edge. As shown in Fig. 9, which depicts the reduction schematically, this is achieved by introducing a new vertex v^* that is connected to each original vertex and thus creates a triangle for each original edge. The full proof (West, 2014) shows how the edge and triangle costs can be constructed such that each optimal solution to the TLSG instance corresponds to an optimal solution to the TRIANGLE BALANCE instance, and *vice versa*. □

References

Rakesh Agrawal, Sridhar Rajagopalan, Ramakrishnan Srikant, and Yirong Xu. 2003. Mining newsgroups using networks arising from social behavior. In *Proceedings of the 12th International Conference on World Wide Web*.

Pranav Anand, Marilyn Walker, Rob Abbott, Jean E. Fox Tree, Robeson Bowmani, and Michael Minor. 2011. Cats rule and dogs drool! Classifying stance in online debate. In *Proceedings of the 2nd Workshop on Computational Approaches to Subjectivity and Sentiment Analysis*.

Stephen Bach, Bert Huang, Ben London, and Lise Getoor. 2013. Hinge-loss Markov random fields: Convex inference for structured prediction. In *Proceedings of the 29th Conference on Uncertainty in Artificial Intelligence*.

Francisco Barahona. 1982. On the computational complexity of Ising spin glass models. *Journal of Physics A: Mathematical and General*, 15(10):3241–3253.

John Blitzer, Mark Dredze, and Fernando Pereira. 2007. Biographies, bollywood, boom-boxes and blenders: Domain adaptation for sentiment classification. In *Proceedings of the 45th Annual Meeting of the Association of Computational Linguistics*.

Stephen Boyd, Neal Parikh, Eric Chu, Borja Peleato, and Jonathan Eckstein. 2011. Distributed optimization and statistical learning via the alternating direction method of multipliers. *Foundations and Trends in Machine Learning*, 3(1):1–122.

Matthias Broecheler, Lilyana Mihalkova, and Lise Getoor. 2010. Probabilistic similarity logic. In *Proceedings of the 26th Conference on Uncertainty in Artificial Intelligence*.

Dorwin Cartwright and Frank Harary. 1956. Structure balance: A generalization of Heider's theory. *Psychological Review*, 63(5):277–293.

Robin I. Dunbar. 2004. Gossip in evolutionary perspective. *Review of General Psychology*, 8(2):100–110.

Lisa Feldman Barrett and James A. Russell. 1998. Independence and bipolarity in the structure of affect. *Journal of Personality and Social Psychology*, 74(4):967–984.

Fritz Heider. 1946. Attitudes and cognitive organization. *The Journal of Psychology*, 21(1):107–112.

Xia Hu, Lei Tang, Jiliang Tang, and Huan Liu. 2013. Exploiting social relations for sentiment analysis in microblogging. In *Proceedings of the 6th ACM International Conference on Web Search and Data Mining*.

Bert Huang, Angelika Kimmig, Lise Getoor, and Jennifer Golbeck. 2013. A flexible framework for probabilistic models of social trust. In *Proceedings of the 2013 International Social Computing, Behavioral-Cultural Modeling and Prediction Conference*.

Dan Jurafsky, Victor Chahuneau, Bryan R. Routledge, and Noah A. Smith. 2014. Narrative framing of consumer sentiment in online restaurant reviews. *First Monday*, 19(4–7).

Daphne Koller and Nir Friedman. 2009. *Probabilistic Graphical Models: Principles and Techniques*. MIT Press.

Jérôme Kunegis, Julia Preusse, and Felix Schwagereit. 2013. What is the added value of negative links in online social networks? In *Proceedings of the 22nd International Conference on World Wide Web*.

Jure Leskovec, Daniel Huttenlocher, and Jon Kleinberg. 2010a. Predicting positive and negative links in online social networks. In *Proceedings of the 19th International Conference on World Wide Web*.

Jure Leskovec, Daniel Huttenlocher, and Jon Kleinberg. 2010b. Signed networks in social media. In *Proceedings of the SIGCHI Conference on Human Factors in Computing Systems*.

Wei-Hao Lin, Theresa Wilson, Janyce Wiebe, and Alexander Hauptmann. 2006. Which side are you on? Identifying perspectives at the document and sentence levels. In *Proceedings of the 10th Conference on Computational Natural Language Learning*.

Hao Ma, Dengyong Zhou, Chao Liu, Michael R Lyu, and Irwin King. 2011. Recommender systems with social regularization. In *Proceedings of the 4th ACM International Conference on Web Search and Data Mining*.

Robert Malouf and Tony Mullen. 2008. Taking sides: User classification for informal online political discourse. *Internet Research*, 18(2):177–190.

Bo Pang and Lillian Lee. 2004. A sentimental education: Sentiment analysis using subjectivity summarization based on minimum cuts. In *Proceedings of the 42nd Annual Meeting of the Association for Computational Linguistics*.

Bo Pang and Lillian Lee. 2008. Opinion mining and sentiment analysis. *Foundations and Trends in Information Retrieval*, 2(1):1–135.

John Platt. 1999. Probabilistic outputs for support vector machines and comparisons to regularized likelihood methods. *Advances in Large Margin Classifiers*, 10(3):61–74.

Marta Recasens, Cristian Danescu-Niculescu-Mizil, and Dan Jurafsky. 2013. Linguistic models for analyzing and detecting biased language. In *Proceedings of the 51st Annual Meeting of the Association for Computational Linguistics*.

David C. Rubin and Jennifer M. Talerico. 2009. A comparison of dimensional models of emotion. *Memory*, 17(8):802–808.

James A. Russell. 1980. A circumplex model of affect. *Journal of Personality and Social Psychology*, 39(6):1161–1178.

Swapna Somasundaran and Janyce Wiebe. 2010. Recognizing stances in ideological on-line debates. In *Proceedings of the NAACL HLT 2010 Workshop on Computational Approaches to Analysis and Generation of Emotion in Text*.

Chenhao Tan, Lillian Lee, Jie Tang, Long Jiang, Ming Zhou, and Ping Li. 2011. User-level sentiment analysis incorporating social networks. In *Proceedings of the 17th ACM SIGKDD International Conference on Knowledge Discovery and Data Mining*.

Jiliang Tang, Huiji Gao, Xia Hu, and Huan Liu. 2013. Exploiting homophily effect for trust prediction. In *Proceedings of the 6th ACM International Conference on Web Search and Data Mining*.

Matt Thomas, Bo Pang, and Lillian Lee. 2006. Get out the vote: Determining support or opposition from Congressional floor-debate transcripts. In *Proceedings of the 2006 Conference on Empirical Methods in Natural Language Processing*.

Robert West. 2014. Supplementary material. Online. http://infolab.stanford.edu/~west1/TACL2014/.

Theresa Wilson, Janyce Wiebe, and Paul Hoffmann. 2005. Recognizing contextual polarity in phrase-level sentiment analysis. In *Proceedings of Human Language Technology Conference and Conference on Empirical Methods in Natural Language Processing*.

Tae Yano, Philip Resnik, and Noah A. Smith. 2010. Shedding (a thousand points of) light on biased language. In *Proceedings of the NAACL-HLT Workshop on Creating Speech and Language Data With Amazon's Mechanical Turk*.

Bei Yu, Stefan Kaufmann, and Daniel Diermeier. 2008. Classifying party affiliation from political speech. *Journal of Information Technology and Politics*, 5(1):33–48.

The Benefits of a Model of Annotation

Rebecca J. Passonneau
Center for Computational Learning Systems
Columbia University
New York, NY USA
becky@ccls.columbia.edu

Bob Carpenter
Department of Statistics
Columbia University
New York, NY USA
carp@alias-i.com

Abstract

Standard agreement measures for interannotator reliability are neither necessary nor sufficient to ensure a high quality corpus. In a case study of word sense annotation, conventional methods for evaluating labels from trained annotators are contrasted with a probabilistic annotation model applied to crowdsourced data. The annotation model provides far more information, including a certainty measure for each gold standard label; the crowdsourced data was collected at less than half the cost of the conventional approach.

1 Introduction

The quality of annotated data for computational linguistics is generally assumed to be good enough if a few annotators can be shown to be consistent with one another. Standard practice relies on metrics that measure consistency, either in an absolute way, or in a chance-adjusted fashion. Such measures, however, merely report how often annotators agree, with no direct measure of corpus quality, nor of the quality of individual items. We argue that high chance-adjusted interannotator agreement is neither necessary nor sufficient to ensure high quality gold-standard labels. We contrast the use of agreement metrics with the use of probabilistic models to draw inferences about annotated data where the items have been labeled by many annotators. A probabilistic model to fit many annotators' observed labels produces much more information about the annotated corpus. In particular, there will be a confidence estimate for each ground truth label.

Probabilistic models of agreement and gold-standard inference have been used in psychometrics and marketing since the 1950s (e.g., IRT models or Bradley-Terry models) and in epidemiology since the 1970s (e.g., diagnostic disease prevalence models). More recently, crowdsourcing has motivated their application to data annotation for machine learning. The model we apply here (Dawid and Skene, 1979) assumes that annotators differ from one another in their accuracy at identifying the true label values, and that these true values occur at certain rates (their *prevalence*).

To contrast the two approaches to creation of an annotated corpus, we present a case study of word sense annotation. The items that were annotated are occurrences of words in their sentence contexts, and each label is a WordNet sense (Miller, 1995). Each item has sense labels from up to twenty-five different annotators, collected through crowdsourcing. Application of an annotation model does not require this many labels per item, and crowdsourced annotation data does not require a probabilistic model. The case study, however, shows how the two benefit each other.

MASC (Manually Annotated Sub-Corpus of the Open American National Corpus) contains a subsidiary word sense sentence corpus that consists of approximately one thousand sentences per word for 116 words. Word senses were annotated in their sentence contexts using WordNet sense labels. Chance-adjusted agreement levels ranged from very high to chance levels, with similar variation for pairwise agreement (Passonneau et al., 2012a). As a result, the annotations for certain words appear to be low

Transactions of the Association for Computational Linguistics, 2 (2014) 311–326. Action Editor: Chris Callison-Burch.
Submitted 2/2014; Revised 6/2014; Published 10/2014.

quality.[1] Our case study shows how we created a more reliable word sense corpus for a randomly selected subset of 45 of the same words, through crowdsourcing and application of the Dawid and Skene model. The model yields a certainty measure for each labeled instance. For most instances, the certainty of the estimated true labels is high, even on words where pairwise and chance-adjusted agreement of trained annotators were both low.

The paper first summarizes the limitations of agreement metrics, then presents the Dawid and Skene model. The next two sections present a case study of the crowdsourced data, and the annotation results. While many of the MASC words had low agreement from trained annotators on the small proportion of the data where agreement was assessed, the same words have many instances with highly confident labels estimated from the crowdsourced annotations. In the discussion section, we compare the model-based labels to the labels from the trained annotators. The final sections present related work and our conclusions.

2 Agreement Metrics versus a Model

A high-confidence ground truth label for each annotated instance is the ultimate goal of annotation, but can often be impractical or infeasible to achieve. On the grounds that more knowledge is always better, we argue that it is desirable to provide a confidence measure for each estimated label. This section first presents the case that the conventional steps to compute agreement provide at best an indirect measure of confidence on labels. We then present the Dawid and Skene model (1979), which estimates a probability of each label value on every instance. To motivate its application to the crowdsourced sense labels, we work through an example to show how true labels are inferred, and to illustrate that information about the true label is derived from both accurate and inaccurate annotators. With many annotators to compare, the value of gathering a label can be quantified using information gain and mutual information, as illustrated in Section 2.2.2.

[1]One potential use for the words with low agreement is to investigate whether features of the WordNet definitions, or sentence contexts, or both, correlate with low agreement.

2.1 Pairwise and Chance-Adjusted Agreement Measures

Current best practice for creating annotation standards involves iteration over four steps: 1) design or redesign the annotation task, 2) write or revise guidelines to instruct annotators how to carry out the task, possibly with some training, 3) have two or more annotators work independently to annotate a sample of data, 4) measure the interannotator agreement on the data sample. Once the desired agreement has been obtained, the final step is to create a gold standard dataset where each item is annotated by a single annotator. How much chance-adjusted agreement is sufficient has been much debated (Artstein and Poesio, 2008; di Eugenio and Glass, 2004; di Eugenio, 2000; Bruce and Wiebe, 1998). Surprisingly, little attention has been devoted to the question of whether the agreement subset is a representative sample of the corpus. Without such an assurance, there is little justification to take interannotator agreement as a quality measure of the corpus as a whole. Given the influence that a gold standard corpus can have on progress in our field, it is not clear that agreement measures on a corpus subset provide a sufficient guarantee of corpus quality.

While it is taken for granted that some annotators perform better than others,[2] agreement metrics do not differentiate annotators. Since there are many ways to be inaccurate, and only one way to be accurate, it is assumed that if annotators have high pairwise or chance-adjusted agreement, then the annotation must be accurate. This is not necessarily a correct inference, as we show below. If two annotators do not agree well, this method does not identify whether one annotator is more accurate. More importantly, no information is gained about the quality of the ground truth labels.

To assess the limitations of agreement metrics, consider how they are computed and what they measure. Let $i \in 1{:}I$ represent the items, $j \in 1{:}J$ the annotators, $k \in 1{:}K$ the label classes in a categorical labeling scheme (e.g., word senses), and $y_{i,j} \in 1{:}K$ the observed labels from annotator j for item i. Assume every annotator labels every item exactly once

[2]Some researchers believe that all that is needed is one trustworthy annotator, which begs the question of how trust is assessed.

(we later relax this constraint).

Agreement: Pairwise agreement $A_{m,n}$ between two annotators $m, n \in 1{:}J$ is defined as the proportion of items $i \in 1{:}I$ for which the annotators supplied the same label,

$$A_{m,n} = \frac{1}{I}\sum_{i=1}^{I} \mathbb{I}(y_{i,m} = y_{i,n}),$$

where $\mathbb{I}(s) = 1$ if s is true and 0 otherwise. In other words, $A_{m,n}$ is the maximum likelihood estimate of chance of agreement in a binomial model.

Pairwise agreement can be extended to the full set of annotators by averaging over all $\binom{J}{2}$ pairs:

$$A = \frac{1}{\binom{J}{2}} \sum_{m=1}^{J-1} \sum_{n=m+1}^{J} A_{m,n}.$$

In sum, A is the proportion of all pairs of items that annotators agreed on. It does not take into account the proportion of each label from $1{:}K$ in the data.

Chance-Adjusted Agreement: Agreement coefficients measure the proportion of observed agreements that are above the proportion expected by chance. Given an estimate $A_{m,n}$ of the probability that two annotators $m, n \in 1{:}J$ will agree on a label and an estimate of the probability $C_{m,n}$ that they will agree by chance, chance-adjusted agreement $\mathcal{IA}_{m,n} \in [-1, 1]$ is defined by

$$\mathcal{IA}_{m,n} = \frac{A_{m,n} - C_{m,n}}{1 - C_{m,n}}.$$

Chance agreement takes into account the prevalence of the individual labels in $1{:}K$. Specifically, it is defined to be the probability that a pair of labels drawn at random for two annotators will agree. There are two common ways to define this draw. Cohen's κ statistic (Cohen, 1960) assumes each annotator draws uniformly at random from her set of labels. Letting $\psi_{j,k} = \frac{1}{I}\sum_{i=1}^{I} \mathbb{I}(y_{i,j} = k)$ be the proportion of the label k in annotator j's labels, this notion of chance agreement for a pair of annotators m, n is estimated as the product of their proportions ψ:

$$C_{m,n} = \sum_{k=1}^{K} \psi_{m,k} \times \psi_{n,k}.$$

Krippendorff's α, another chance-adjusted metric in wide use, assumes each annotator draws uniformly at random from the pooled set of labels from all annotators (Krippendorff, 1980). Letting ϕ_k be the proportion of label k in the entire set of labels, this alternative estimate, $C'_{m,n} = \sum_{k=1}^{K} \phi_k^2$, does not depend on the identity of the annotators m and n.

Agreement coefficients suffer from multiple shortcomings. (1) They are intrinsically pairwise, although one can compare to a voted consensus or average over multiple pairwise agreements. (2) In agreement-based analyses, two wrongs make a right in the sense that if two annotators both make the same mistake, they agree. If annotators are 80% accurate on a binary task, then chance agreement on the wrong category occurs at a 4% rate. (3) Chance-adjusted agreement reduces to simple agreement as chance agreement approaches zero. When chance agreement is high, even high-accuracy annotators can have low chance-adjusted agreement, as when the data is skewed towards a few values, a typical case for NLP tasks. Feinstein and Cicchetti (1990) referred to this as the paradox of κ (see section 6). For example, in a binary task with 95% prevalence of one category, two 90% accurate annotators would have negative chance-adjusted agreements of $\frac{0.9-(.95^2+.05^2)}{1-(.95^2+.05^2)} = -.053$. Thus high chance-adjusted interannotator agreement is not a necessary condition for a high-quality corpus. An alternative metric discussed in Section 6 addresses skewed prevalence of label values, but has not been adopted in the NLP community (Gwet, 2008). (4) Interannotator agreement statistics implicitly assume annotators are unbiased; if they are biased in the same direction, e.g., the most prevalent category, then agreement is an overestimate of their accuracy. In the extreme case, in a binary labeling task, two adversarial annotators who always provide the wrong answer have a chance-adjusted agreement of 100%. (5) Item-level effects such as difficulty can inflate levels of agreement-in-error. For example, in a named-entity corpus one of the co-authors helped collect for MUC, hard-to-identify names have correlated false negatives among annotators, leading to higher agreement-in-error than would otherwise be expected. (6) Interannotator agreement statistics are rarely computed with confidence intervals, which can be quite wide even under optimistic assumptions of no annotator bias or item-level effects. Given a sample of 100 annotations, if the true gold standard categories were known (as opposed to being themselves estimated as in our setup here), an annotator getting 80 out of 100 items correct would produce a 95% interval for accuracy of roughly $(74\%, 86\%)$.[3] Agreement statistics have even wider error bounds. This introduces enough uncertainty to span the rather arbitrary decision boundaries for acceptability employed for inter-annotator agreement statistics. Note that bootstrapping is a reliable method to compute confidence intervals (Efron and Tibshirani, 1986). Briefly, given a sample of size N, a large number of samples of size N are drawn randomly with replacement from the original sample, the statistic of interest is computed for each random draw, and the mean $\pm$ 1.96 standard deviations gives the estimated value and its approximate 95% confidence interval.

2.2 A Probabilistic Annotation Model

A probabilistic model provides a recipe to randomly "generate" a dataset from a set of model parameters and constants.[4,5] The utility of such a model lies in its ability to support meaningful inferences from data, such as an estimate of the true prevalence of each category. Dawid and Skene (1979) proposed a model to determine a consensus among patient histories taken by multiple doctors. Inference is driven by accuracies and biases estimated for each annotator on a per-category basis. A graphical sketch of the model is shown in Figure 1.

Let K be the number of possible labels or categories for an item, I the number of items to annotate, J the number of annotators, and N the total number of labels provided by annotators, where each annotator may label each instance zero or more times. Because the data is not a simple $I \times J$ data matrix where every annotator labels every item exactly once, a database-like indexing scheme is used in which each annotation n is represented as a tuple of an item $ii[n] \in 1{:}I$, an annotator $jj[n] \in 1{:}J$, and a label $y[n] \in 1{:}K$.[6] Figure 2 illustrates how the annotations can be assembled in a table where each row is an annotation, and the column values are indices over items, annotators, and labels. The first two rows show that on item 1, annotators 1 and 3 assigned labels 4 and 1, respectively. The third row says that for item 192 annotator 17 provided label 5.

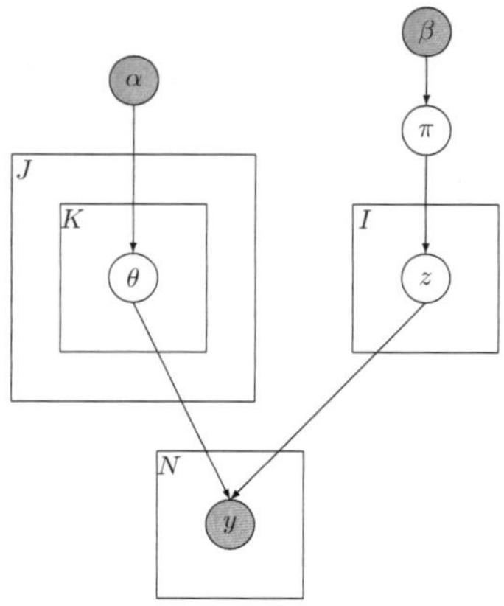

Figure 1: Graphical model sketch of the Dawid and Skene model enhanced with Dirichlet priors. *Sizes:* J number of annotators, K number of categories, I number of items, N number of labels collected. *Estimated parameters:* θ annotator accuracies/biases, π category prevalence, z true category. *Observed data:* y labels. *Hyperpriors:* α accuracies/biases, β prevalence.

n	ii_n	jj_n	y_n
1	1	1	4
2	1	3	1
3	192	17	5
⋮	⋮	⋮	⋮

Figure 2: Table of annotations y indexed by word instance ii and annotator jj.

Dawid and Skene's model includes parameters

- $z_i \in 1{:}K$ for the true category of item i,
- $\pi_k \in [0, 1]$ for the probability that an item is of category k, subject to $\sum_{k=1}^{K} \pi_k = 1$, and
- $\theta_{j,k,k'} \in [0, 1]$ for the probabilty that annotator j assigns the label k' to an item whose true category is k, subject to $\sum_{k'=1}^{K} \theta_{j,k,k'} = 1$.

The generative model first selects the true category for item i according to the prevalence of categories,

$$z_i \sim \mathsf{Categorical}(\pi).$$

[3] If items are not independent, as assumed here, the interval becomes wider.

[4] In a Bayesian setting, model parameters are also modeled as randomly generated from a prior distribution.

[5] The size constants defining the data collection are not generated as part of the model. In a "discriminative" model, only the outcomes and parameters are generated in this sense, not the predictors (i.e., features).

[6] For the data indexing, we use jj and ii to avoid confusion with the I items and J annotators of the model.

The observed labels y_n are generated based on annotator $jj[n]$'s responses $\theta_{jj[n],\, z[ii[n]]}$ to items $ii[n]$ whose true category is $z[ii[n]]$,

$$y_n \sim \mathsf{Categorical}(\theta_{jj[n],\, z[ii[n]]}).$$

We use additively smoothed maximum likelihood estimation (MLE) to stabilize inference.

$$\begin{aligned} \theta_{j,k} &\sim \mathsf{Dirichlet}(\alpha_k) \\ \pi &\sim \mathsf{Dirichlet}(\beta). \end{aligned}$$

The unsmoothed MLE is equivalent to the MAP estimate when α_k and β are unit vectors.

2.2.1 Estimated Senses

Given a set of annotators' labels for a word instance, the prevalence of senses, and the annotators' accuracies and biases, Bayes's rule can be used to estimate the true sense of each instance.

$$\begin{aligned} p(z_i|y,\theta,\pi) &\propto p(z_i|\pi)\, p(y|z_i,\theta) \\ &= \pi_{z[i]} \prod_{ii[n]=i} \theta_{jj[n],z[i],y[n]}. \end{aligned}$$

As a simple example, consider $K = 2$ outcomes with prevalences $\pi_1 = 0.2$, and $\pi_2 = 0.8$. Suppose three annotators with response matrices

$$\theta_1 = \begin{bmatrix} .75 & .25 \\ .40 & .60 \end{bmatrix} \theta_2 = \begin{bmatrix} .65 & .35 \\ .30 & .70 \end{bmatrix} \theta_3 = \begin{bmatrix} .9 & .1 \\ .2 & .8 \end{bmatrix}$$

supplied labels $y_1 = 1$, $y_2 = 1$, and $y_3 = 2$ for word instance i, respectively. Then

$$\Pr[z_i = 1|y,\theta,\pi] \propto \pi_1\, \theta_{1,1,1}\, \theta_{2,1,1}\, \theta_{3,1,2} = .00975$$

$$\Pr[z_i = 2|y,\theta,\pi] \propto \pi_2\, \theta_{1,2,1}\, \theta_{2,2,1}\, \theta_{3,2,2} = .0768.$$

By normalizing (and rounding),

$$\Pr[z_i = 1|y,\theta,\pi] = \frac{.00975}{.00975 + .0768} = .11$$

$$\Pr[z_i = 2|y,\theta,\pi] = \frac{.0768}{.00975 + .0768} = .89$$

Although the majority vote on i is for category 1, the estimated probability that the category is 1 is only 0.11, given the adjustments for annotators' accuracies and biases.

Comparison to voting. On the log scale, the annotation model is similar to a weighted additive voting scheme with maximum weight zero and no minimum weight; if $u \in (0, 1]$, then $\log u \in (-\infty, 0]$. As we discuss in the next section, the important difference is that the weighting is based on the true category, allowing the model to adjust for annotator bias.

Spam annotators. The Dawid and Skene model adjusts for annotations from noisy annotators. In the limit, a label for a word instance from an annotator whose response is independent of the true category provides no information about the true sense of that instance, and such a label provides no impact on the resulting category estimate. For example, in a binary task, a label from an annotator with response matrix

$$\theta_j = \begin{bmatrix} 0.9 & 0.1 \\ 0.9 & 0.1 \end{bmatrix}$$

provides no information on the true category. The model cancels the effect of such an annotator's label because $\Pr[z_i = 1|y', \theta_j, \pi] = \Pr[z_i = 1|\pi]$, which follows from the fact that

$$\frac{\pi_1 \times \theta_{j,1,1}}{\pi_2 \times \theta_{j,2,1}} = \frac{\pi_1}{\pi_2}.$$

Biased Annotators. Biased annotators can have low accuracy and low agreement with other annotators, yet still provide a great deal of information about the true label. For example, in a binary task, a positively biased annotator will return relatively more false positives and relatively fewer false negatives compared to an unbiased one. As shown in Section 4.2, our word sense task had fairly small estimated biases toward the high-frequency senses in most cases. Other tasks, such as ordinal ranking of author certainty for assertions, show systematically biased annotators. Annotators may be biased toward one end of an ordinal scale, or toward the center. These kinds of biases are apparent in the annotators in the annotation task described in (Rzhetsky et al., 2009), where biologists labeled sentences in biomedical research articles on a 1 to 7 scale of polarity and certainty.

Adversarial Annotators. An adversarial annotator who always returns the wrong answer exhibits an extreme bias. In a binary annotation case, it is clear how perfectly adversarial answers provide the same information as perfectly cooperative answers. Although it is possible to estimate the response matrix of an adversarial annotator, if too many of the annotators are adversarial, the Dawid and Skene model cannot separate the truth from the lies. None of the data sets we have collected showed any evidence of adversarial labeling.

2.2.2 How Much Information is in a Label?

By comparing the uncertainty before and after including a new label from an annotator, we can measure the reduction in uncertainty provided by the annotator's label. By considering the expected reduction in uncertainty due to observing a label from an annotator, we can quantify how much information the label is expected to provide.

Entropy. The information-theoretic notion of entropy makes the notion of uncertainty precise (Cover and Thomas, 1991). If Z_i is the random variable corresponding to the true label of word instance i with K possible labels and probability mass function p_{Z_i}, its entropy is

$$\mathrm{H}[Z_i] = -\sum_{k=1}^{K} p_{Z_i}(k)\ \log p_{Z_i}(k).$$

Conditional Entropy. Consider a label $Y_n = k'$ from annotator $j = jj_n$ for item $i = ii_n$. The entropy of Z_i conditioned on the observed label is

$$\mathrm{H}[Z_i|Y_n = k'] \\ = -\sum_{k=1}^{K} p_{Z_i|Y_n}(k|k') \log p_{Z_i|Y_n}(k|k').$$

Conditional entropy is defined by the expected entropy of Z_i after observing Y_n,

$$\mathrm{H}[Z_i|Y_n] = \sum_{k'=1}^{K} p_{Y_n}(k')\ \mathrm{H}[Z_i|Y_n = k'].$$

Conditional entropy can be generalized in the obvious way to condition on more than one observed label, for instance to compute the expected entropy of Z_i after observing two labels, Y_n and $Y_{n'}$.

Mutual Information. Mutual information is the expected reduction in entropy in the state of Z_i after observing one or more labels,

$$\mathrm{I}[Z_i;\ Y_n] = \mathrm{H}[Z_i] - \mathrm{H}[Z_i|Y_n].$$

Gibbs' inequality ensures that mutual information is positive. In theory at least, it never hurts to observe a label (in expectation), no matter how bad the annotator is. In practice, we may not have an accurate estimate of an annotator's response probabilities $p_{Y_n|Z_i}$. Using log base 2, which measures information in bits, consider the three hypothetical annotators illustrated above. Clearly the most accurate confusion matrix is θ_3. The conditional entropies of a new label for the three cases are, respectively, 0.71, 0.60 and 0.47 and the mutual information values are 0.01, 0.13 and 0.25.

Kinds of Annotators. A spam annotator provides zero information about a category, because $\mathrm{H}[Z_i|Y_n] = \mathrm{H}[Z_i]$. Spam annotators provide the minimum possible mutual information, i.e., $\mathrm{I}[Z_i; Y_n] = 0$.

A perfectly accurate annotator is one for whom $\Pr[Y_i = k|Z_i]$ is 1 if $k = Z_i$ and 0 otherwise. For such annotators, observing their label removes all uncertainty, so that $\mathrm{H}[Z_i|Y_n] = 0$. A perfect annotator provides maximum mutual information, i.e., $\mathrm{I}[Z_i;\ Y_n] = \mathrm{H}[Z_i]$.

A highly biased and hence inaccurate annotator can provide as much information as a more accurate annotator. This demonstrates that weighted voting schemes are not the correct approach to inference for true category labels.

2.2.3 Implementation and Priors

The results in this paper were derived by expectation maximization using software written in R. The code is distributed with the data under an open-source license.[7] Other implementations of the Dawid and Skene model should produce the same penalized maximum likelihood (equivalently maximum a posteriori) estimates.

The very weak Dirichlet priors added only arithmetic stabilization to the inferences, allowing an identified penalized maximum likelihood estimate in cases where an annotator did not label any instances of some sense for a word.

Bayesian posterior means provide similar results for this model; full Bayes would also quantify estimation uncertainty, which as noted above, is substantial for the data sizes discussed here. Carpenter (2008) discusses a more general approach based on a hierarchical model for the accuracy/bias parameters θ.

Modeling a random effect per item, such as item difficulty, widens confidence intervals on accuracies/biases, because observed labels may be the result of item ease/difficulty or annotator accuracy/bias. This would have been more realistic, and would have provided additional information,

[7] URL not given yet to preserve anonymity.

Word	*Pos*	Senses *All*	*Used*	α	*Agr.*
late	adj	9	7	0.85	0.90
high	adj	7	5	0.84	0.91
long	adj	8	7	0.67	0.81
full	adj	9	8	0.57	0.69
poor	adj	11	9	0.57	0.66
fair	adj	10	8	0.54	0.70
common	adj	12	6	0.40	0.53
particular	adj	7	5	0.20	0.48
normal	adj	4	4	0.02	0.38
work	noun	8	7	0.70	0.80
number	noun	7	7	0.62	0.95
book	noun	12	9	0.60	0.84
image	noun	17	9	0.57	0.71
paper	noun	10	7	0.57	0.66
board	noun	9	8	0.56	0.80
time	noun	12	8	0.56	0.63
sense	noun	8	5	0.54	0.65
way	noun	19	12	0.49	0.62
window	noun	10	8	0.48	0.62
date	noun	11	7	0.47	0.57
land	noun	14	10	0.47	0.55
life	noun	26	14	0.43	0.52
control	noun	13	9	0.34	0.47
level	noun	10	7	0.21	0.44
color	noun	12	7	0.15	0.66
family	noun	14	8	0.14	0.32
live	verb	14	7	0.69	0.78
read	verb	13	9	0.64	0.89
appear	verb	7	7	0.63	0.73
meet	verb	19	11	0.58	0.66
serve	verb	19	14	0.57	0.67
suggest	verb	5	4	0.56	0.78
add	verb	10	6	0.55	0.72
fold	verb	8	5	0.52	0.72
wait	verb	7	4	0.49	0.65
show	verb	13	11	0.46	0.53
tell	verb	10	8	0.44	0.59
lose	verb	16	10	0.43	0.59
know	verb	13	10	0.38	0.52
say	verb	14	11	0.37	0.56
find	verb	19	14	0.28	0.38
help	verb	9	6	0.26	0.58
kill	verb	14	12	0.26	0.76
win	verb	11	5	0.25	0.72
ask	verb	6	6	0.20	0.45

Figure 3: Krippendorff's α and pairwise agreement for the 45 MASC words in the crowdsourcing study, with number of WordNet senses available and used. Pairwise agreement was computed according to the formula in Section 2.

but we felt the increased model complexity, especially with multivariate outputs, would distract from our main point in contrasting model-based inference with agreement statistics.

3 Two Data Collections

3.1 MASC Word Sense Sentence Corpus

To motivate our case study, we briefly discuss some of the limitations of the MASC word sense sentence corpus, which is an addendum to the MASC corpus.[8] For convenience, we refer here to the word sense sentence corpus as the MASC corpus. This is a 1.3 million word corpus with approximately one thousand sentences per word, for 116 words nearly evenly balanced among nouns, adjectives and verbs (Passonneau et al., 2012a). Each sentence is drawn from the MASC corpus or the Open American National Corpus, exemplifies at least one of the 116 MASC words, and has been annotated by trained annotators who used WordNet senses as annotation labels. The annotation process is described in detail in (Passonneau et al., 2012a; Passonneau et al., 2012b).

The annotators were college students from Vassar, Barnard, and Columbia who were given general training in the annotation process, then were trained together on each word with a sample of fifty sentences, which included discussion with Christiane Fellbaum, one of the designers of WordNet. After the pre-annotation sample, annotators worked independently to label 1,000 sentences for each word using an annotation tool that presented the WordNet senses and example usages, plus four variants of *none of the above*. For each word, 100 of the 1,000 sentences were annotated by two to four annotators to assess inter-annotator reliability.

Figure 3 shows 45 randomly selected MASC words that were re-annotated using crowdsourcing. Shown are the part of speech, the number of WordNet senses, the number of senses used by annotators, the α value, and pairwise agreement. While the MASC word sense data demonstrates that annotators can agree on words with many senses, there are many words with low agreement, and correspondingly questionable ground truth labels. There is no correlation between the agreement and number of

[8] http://www.anc.org/data/masc/

available senses, or senses used by annotators (Passonneau et al., 2012a).

Due to limited resources, the project deviated from best practice in having only a single round of annotation per word, and no iteration to achieve an agreement threshold. All annotators, however, had at least two phases of training, and most annotated several rounds. Below we use mutual information to show that the quality of the crowdsourced labels is equivalent to or superior than labels from the trained MASC annotators.

3.2 Crowdsourced Word Sense Annotation

To collect the data, we relied on Amazon Mechanical Turk, a crowdsourcing marketplace that is used extensively in the NLP community (Callison-Burch and Dredze, 2010). Human Intelligence Tasks (HITs) are presented to Turkers by requesters. Certain aspects of the task were the same as for the MASC data: 45 randomly selected MASC words were used, sentences were drawn from the same pool, and the annotation labels were the same WordNet 3.0 senses. Instead of collecting a single label for most instances, however, we collected up to twenty-five. Other differences from the MASC data collection were: the annotators were not trained; the annotation interface differed, though it presented the same information; the sets of sentences were not identical; annotators labeled any number of instances for a word up to the limit of 25 labels per word; finally, the Turkers were not instructed to become familiar with WordNet.

In each HIT, Turkers were presented with ten sample sentences for each word, with the word's senses listed below each sentence. A short paragraph of instructions indicated there would be up to 100 HITs for each word. To encourage Turkers to do multiple HITs per word, so we could estimate annotator accuracies more tightly, the instructions indicated that Turkers could expect their time per HIT to decrease with increasing familiarity with the word's senses.

Most but not all crowdsourced instances had also been annotated by the trained annotators. Figures 7a-7b in Section 5, which compares the ground truth labels from the trained annotators with the crowdsourced labels, indicates for each word how many instances were annotated in common (e.g., 960 for *board (verb)*). Sentences were drawn from

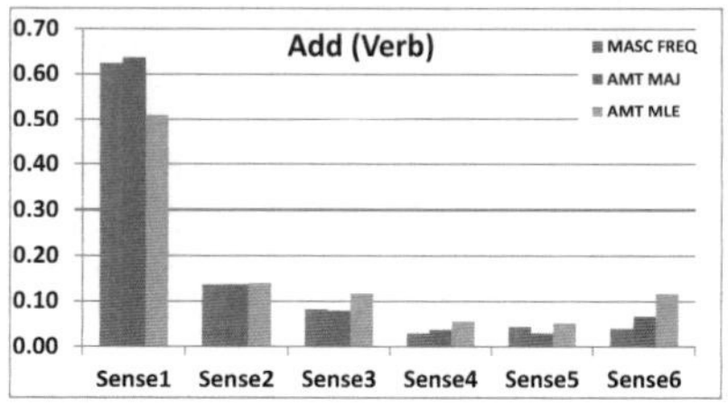

(a) *add (verb)* ($\alpha = 0.55$, agreement=0.72)

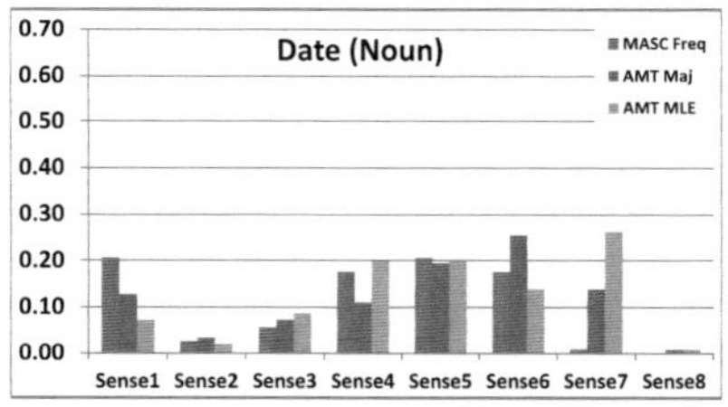

(b) *date (noun)* ($\alpha = 0.47$, agreement=0.57)

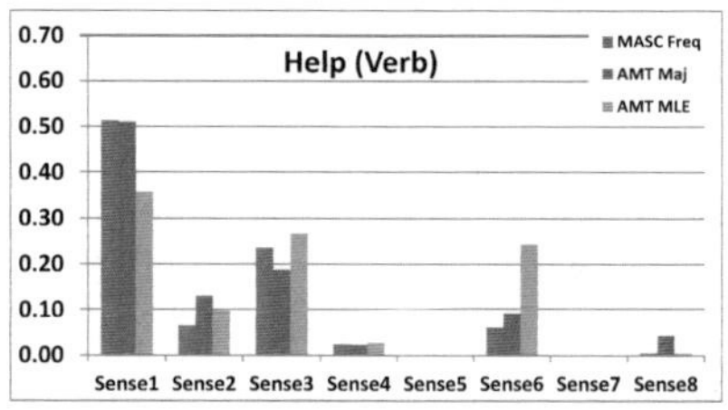

(c) *help (verb)* ($\alpha = 0.26$, agreement=0.58)

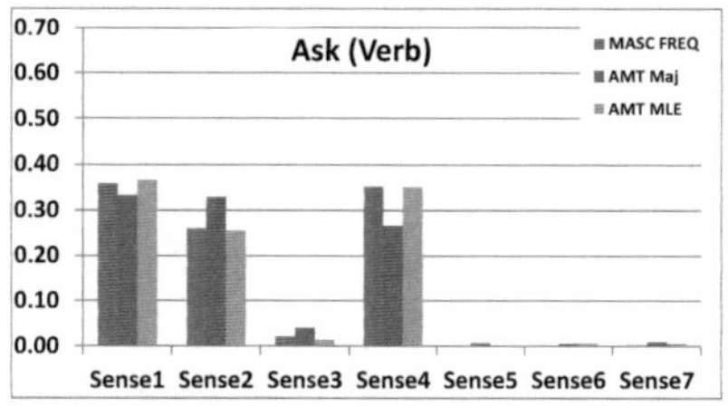

(d) *ask (verb)* ($\alpha = 0.20$, agreement=0.45)

Figure 4: Prevalence estimates for 4 words: the x-axis is the sense number, and the y-axis the proportion of instances assigned that sense. MASC FREQ: frequency of each sense in the singly-annotated instances from the trained MASC annotators; AMT MAJ: frequency of each majority vote sense for instances annotated by $\approx$25 Turkers; AMT MLE: estimated probability of each sense for instances annotated by $\approx$25 Turkers, using MLE.

Sense	≥ 0.99	Prop.
0	9	0.01
1	461	0.48
2	135	0.14
3	107	0.11
4	50	0.05
5	50	0.05
6	93	0.10
SubTot.	905	**0.94**
(Rest	62	0.06)
Total	962	1.00

(a) *add (verb)*: **94%**

Sense	≥ 0.99	Prop.
0	19	0.02
1	68	0.07
2	19	0.02
3	83	0.09
4	173	0.18
5	190	0.20
6	133	0.14
7	236	0.25
8	5	0.01
SubTot.	926	**0.97**
(Rest	33	0.03)
Total	959	1.00

(b) *date (noun)*: **97%**

Sense	≥ 0.99	Prop.
0	0	0.00
1	279	0.30
2	82	0.09
3	201	0.21
4	24	0.03
5	0	0.00
6	169	0.18
7	0	0.00
8	5	0.01
SubTot.	760	**0.81**
(Rest	180	0.19)
Total	940	1.00

(c) *help (verb)*: **81%**

Sense	≥ 0.99	Prop.
0	6	0.01
1	348	0.36
2	177	0.18
3	9	0.01
4	251	0.26
5	0	0
6	0	0
7	6	0.01
8	6	0.01
SubTot.	803	**0.83**
(Rest	163	0.17)
Total	966	1.00

(d) *ask (verb)*: **83%**

Figure 5: Proportion of instances where posterior probabilities ≥ 0.99

the same pool but in a few cases, the overlap is significantly less than the full 900-1,000 instances (e.g., *work (noun)* with 380).

Given 1,000 instances per word for a category whose prevalence is as low as 0.10 (100 examples expected), the 95% interval for sample prevalence, assuming examples are independent, will be 0.10 ± 0.06. We collected between 20 and 25 labels per item to get reasonable confidence intervals for the true label, and so that future models could incorporate item difficulty. The large number of labels sharpens our estimates of the true category significantly, as estimated error goes down as $\mathcal{O}(1/\sqrt{n})$ with n independent annotations. Confidence intervals must be expanded as correlation among annotator responses increases due to item-level effects such as difficulty or subject matter.

Requesters can control many aspects of HITs. To ensure a high proportion of instances with high quality inferred labels, we piloted the HIT design with two trials of two and three words each, and discussed both with Turkers on the Turker Nation message board. The HIT title we chose–*For American English Word Mavens*–targeted Turkers with an inherent interest in words and meanings, and we recruited Turkers with high performance ratings and a long history of good work. The final procedure and payment were as follows. To avoid spam workers, we required Turkers to have a 98% lifetime approval rating and to have successfully completed 20,000 HITs. HITs were automatically approved after fifteen minutes. We monitored performance of Turkers across HITs by comparing individual Turker's labels to the current majority labels. Turkers with very poor performance were warned to take more care, or be blocked from doing further HITs. Of 228 Turkers, five were blocked, with one subsequently unblocked. The blocked Turker data is included with the other Turker data in our analyses and in the full data release. As noted above, the model-based approach to annotation is effective at adjusting for inaccurate annotators.

4 Results

4.1 Estimates for Prevalence and Labels

Modeling annotators as having distinct biases and accuracies should match the intuitions of anyone who has compared the results of more than one annotator on a task. The power of the Dawid and Skene model, however, shows up in the estimates it yields for category prevalence and for the true labels on each instance. Figure 4 contrasts three ways to estimate sense prevalence, illustrated with four of the crowdsourced words. AMT MLE is the model estimate from Turkers' labels. MASC FREQ is a naive rate from the trained annotators' label distributions, rather than a true estimate. Majority voted labels for Turkers (AMT MAJ) are closer to the model estimates than MASC FREQ, but do not take annotators' biases into account.

The plots for the four words in Figure 4 are ordered by their α scores for the 100 instances that were annotated in common by four trained annotators: *add (0.55)* $>$ *date (0.47)* $>$ *help (0.26)* $>$

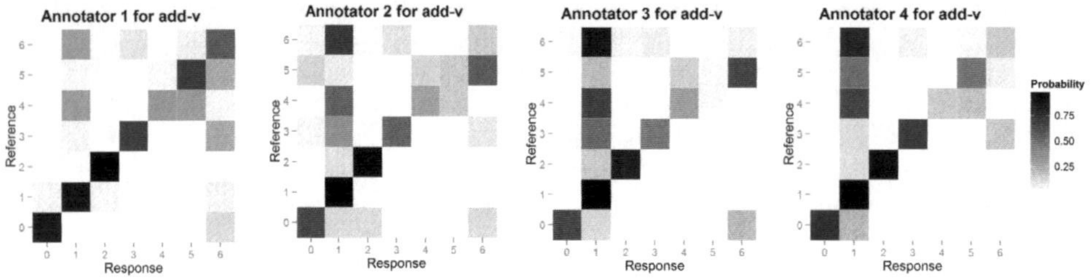

(a) Four of 57 annotators for *add (verb)*

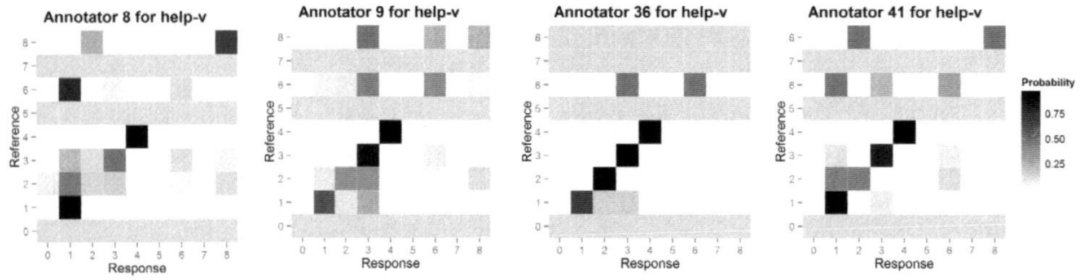

(b) Four of 49 annotators for *help (verb)*

Figure 6: Example confusion matrices of estimated annotator accuracies and biases

ask (0.20). The prevalence estimates diverge less on words where the agreement is higher. Notably, the plots for the first three words demonstrate one or more senses where the AMT MLE estimate differs markedly from all other estimates. In Figure 4a, the AMT MLE estimate for sense 1 is much lower (0.51) than the other two measures. In Figure 4b, the AMT MLE estimate for sense 4 is much closer to MASC FREQ than AMT MAJ, which sugggests that some Turkers are biased against sense 4. The AMT MLE estimates for senses 1, 6 and 7 are distinctive. For *help*, the AMT MLE estimates for senses 1 and 6 are particularly distinctive. For *ask* senses 2 and 4, the divergence of the AMT MAJ estimates is again evidence of bias in some Turkers.

The estimates of label quality on each item are perhaps the strongest reason for turning to model-based approaches to assess annotated data. For the same four words, Figure 5 shows the proportion of all instances that had an estimated true label where the label probability was greater than or equal to 0.99. This proportion ranges from 97% for *date* to 81% for *help*. Even for *help*, of the remaining 19% of instances of less confident estimated labels, 13% have posterior probabilities greater than 0.75. Figure 5 also shows that the high quality labels for each word are distributed across many of the senses. Of the 45 words studied here, 20 had α scores less than 0.50 from the trained annotators. For 42 of the same 45 words, 80% of the inferred true labels have a probability higher than 0.99.

4.2 Annotator Accuracy and Bias

Figure 6 shows confusion matrices in the form of heatmaps that plot annotator responses by the estimated true labels. Darker cells have higher probabilities. Perfect response accuracy (agreement with the inferred true label) would yield black squares on the diagonal and white on the off-diagonal. Figure 6a and Figure 6b show heatmaps for four annotators for the two words of the four that had the highest and third highest α values.

The two figures show that the Turkers were generally more accurate on *add (verb)* than on *help (verb)*, which is consistent with the differences in the inter-annotator agreement of trained annotators on these two words. In contrast to what can be learned from agreement metrics, inference based on the annotation model provides estimates of bias towards specific values. Figure 6a shows the bias of these annotators to overuse WordNet sense 1 for *help*. Further, there were no assignments of senses 6 or 8 for this word. The figures provide a succinct visual summary that there were more differences across the four annotators for *help* than for *add*, with more bias towards overuse of not only sense 1, but also senses 2 (annotators 8 and 41) and 3 (annotator 9). When annotator 8 uses sense 1, the true label is often sense 6, thus illustrating how annotators provide information about the true label even from inaccurate responses.

Mean accuracies per word ranged from 0.86 to 0.05, with most words showing a large spread across senses, and higher mean accuracy for the more frequent senses. Mean accuracy for *add* was 0.90 for sense 1, 0.79 for sense 2, and much lower for senses 6 (0.29) and 7 (0.19). For *help*, mean accuracy was best on sense 1 (0.73), which was also the most frequent, but it was also quite good on sense 4 (0.64), which was much less frequent. Mean accuracies on senses of *help* ranged from 0.11 (senses 5, 7, and other) to 0.73 (sense 1).

5 Discussion

For many of the words, the model yields the same label values as the trained annotator on a large majority of instances, yet for nearly as many words there is more disparity. After we discuss how the model-based and trained annotators labels line up with each other, we argue that the model estimates are better. The two sets of labels cannot be differentiated from one another by mutual information. In contrast to the model estimates, the trained annotator labels have no confidence value, and no estimate for the trained annotator's accuracy. We conclude the section with a cost comparison.

Figure 7 compares how many instances have the same labels from the trained annotators and of Turkers (blue); from the trained annotators and the model (red), and from the Turker Plurality and the model (green). Recall that about ninety percent of the instances labled by trained annotators have a single label; for the ten percent with two to four annotators, we used the majority label if there was one, else gave each tied sense a proportional amount of the vote. Figure 7a shows 22 words where all three comparisons have about the same relative proportion in common (70%-98% on average). Here sets with the least overlap are the trained annotators compared with the model, with the exception of *window (noun)*. The bottom figure shows the 23 words where the proportion in common is relatively lower (35%-75% on average), mostly due to the two comparisons for the trained annotators. Across the 45 words, the proportion of instances that had the same labels assigned by the trained annotators and the model does not correlate with the α scores for the words, or with pairwise agreement

Previous work has shown that model-based estimates are superior to majority-voting (Snow et al., 2008). Figure 7 shows that the trained annotators' labels match the model (red bars) consistently less often than they match the Turker plurality, which is often a majority (blue bars). There are a fair number of cases, however, with a large disparity between the trained annotators and Turkers. This is most apparent when the green bar is much higher than the red or blue bars. For the word *meet (verb)*, for example, in 19% of cases the trained annotator used sense 4 of WordNet 3.0 (glossed as "fill or meet a want or need") where the the plurality of Turkers selected sense 5 (glossed as "satisfy a condition or restriction"). Notably, in WordNet 3.1, two of the WordNet 3.0 senses for *meet (verb)* have been removed, including the sense 5 that the Turkers favored in our data. A similar situation occurs with *date (noun)*: 17% of cases where the trained annotator used sense 4, the plurality of Turkers used sense 5; the former sense 4 is no longer in WordNet 3.0.

For the trained annotators, interannotator agreement and pairwise agreement varied widely, as shown in Figure 3. Measures of the information provided by labels from Turkers and trained annotators give a similarly wide range across both groups. Figure 8 shows a histogram of estimated mutual information for Turkers and MASC annotators across the four words. The most striking feature of these plots is the large variation in mutual information scores within both groups of annotators for each word (note that *date* and *help* had many more trained annotators than *add* or *ask*). There is no evidence that a label from a trained annotator provides more information than a Turker's. Thus we conclude that a model-based label derived from many Turkers is preferable to a label from a single trained annotator.

In contrast to current best practice, an annotation model yields far more information about the most essential aspect of annotation efforts, namely how

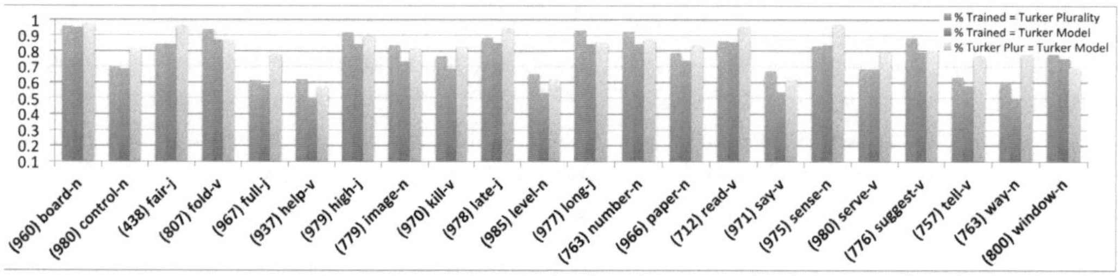

(a) For these 22 words, the three sets of labels (trained annotators, Turker plurality, Turker model) have a high proportion in common and lower variance.

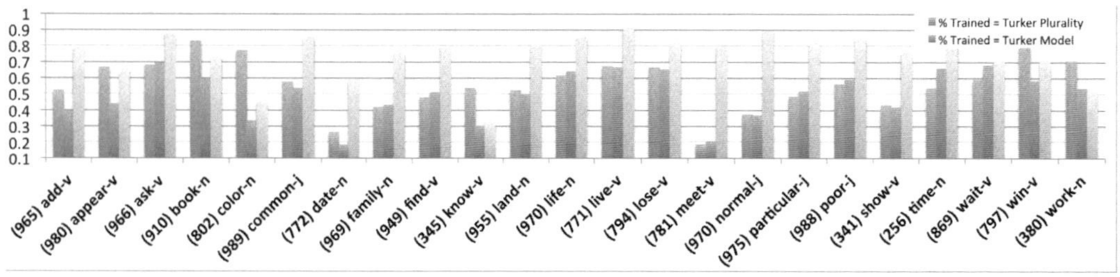

(b) For these 23 the words, the three sets of labels (trained annotators, Turker plurality, Turker model) have a lower proportion in common and higher variance.

Figure 7: Proportion of instances labeled by both trained annotators and Turkers (total instances in parentheses) where the trained annotator label matches the Turker plurality (blue), where the trained annotator label matches the model (red), and where the Turker plurality matches the model (green)

much uncertainty is associated with each gold standard label. In our case, the richer information comes at a lower cost. Over the course of a five-year period that included development of the infrastructure, 17 undergraduates who annotated the 116 MASC words were paid an estimated total of \$80,000 for 116 words $\times$ 1000 sentences per word, which comes to a unit cost of \$0.70 per ground truth label. In a 12 month period with 6 months devoted to infrastructure and trial runs, we paid 228 Turkers a total of \$15,000 for 45 words $\times$ 1000 sentences per word, for a unit cost of \$0.33 per ground truth label. In short, the AMT data cost less than half the trained annotator data.

For annotation tasks such as this one, where each candidate word has multiple class labels, the comparison between the two methods of data collection shows that the model-based estimates from crowdsourced data have at least the same quality, if not higher, for less cost. The fact that each label has an associated confidence makes them more valuable because the end user can choose how to handle labels with lower certainty: for example, to assign them less weight in evaluating word sense disambiguation systems, or to eliminate them from training for statistical approaches to building such systems. Each word here has a distinct set of classes, and the results from both the trained annotators and model indicate that some sets of sense labels led to greater agreement or a higher proportion of high confidence labels. In many cases, results for the words with fewer high confidence labels could be improved by revising the sense inventories, as suggested by the examples with *meet (verb)* and *date (noun)*.

6 Related Work

Alternative metrics to measure association of raters on binary data have been proposed to overcome deficiencies in κ when there is data skew. The G-index (Holley and Guildford, 1964; Vegelius, 1981), for example, is argued to improve over the Matthews Correlation Coefficient (Matthews, 1975). Feinstein and Cicchetti (1990) outline the undesirable behavior that κ-like metrics will have lower values when there is high agreement on highly skewed data. κ assumes that chance agreement on the more prevalent class becomes high. Gwet (2008) presents a metric that estimates the likelihood of chance agreement based on the assumption that chance agreement occurs only when annotators assign labels randomly, which is estimated from the data. Klebanov and Beigman (2009) make a related assumption that annotators agree on easy cases and behave randomly on hard cases, and propose a model to estimate the proportion of hard cases.

Model-based gold-standard estimation such as (Dawid and Skene, 1979) has long been the standard in epidemiology, and has been applied to disease prevalence estimation (Albert and Dodd, 2008) and also to many other problems such as human annotation of craters in images of Venus (Smyth et al., 1995). Smyth et al. (1995), Rogers et al. (2010), and Raykar et al. (2010) all discuss the advantages of learning and evaluation with probabilistically annotated corpora. Rzhetsky et al. (2009) and Whitehill et al. (2009) estimate annotation models without gold-standard supervision, but neither models annotator biases, which are critical for estimating true labels.

Perhaps the first application of Dawid and Skene's model to NLP data was the Bruce and Wiebe (1999) investigation of word sense. Much later, Snow et al. (2008) used the same model to show that combining noisy crowdsourced annotations produced data of equal quality to five distinct published gold standards, including an example of word sense. Both works estimate the Dawid and Skene model using supervised gold-standard category data, which allows direct estimation of annotator accuracy and bias. Hovy et al. (2013) recently presented a much

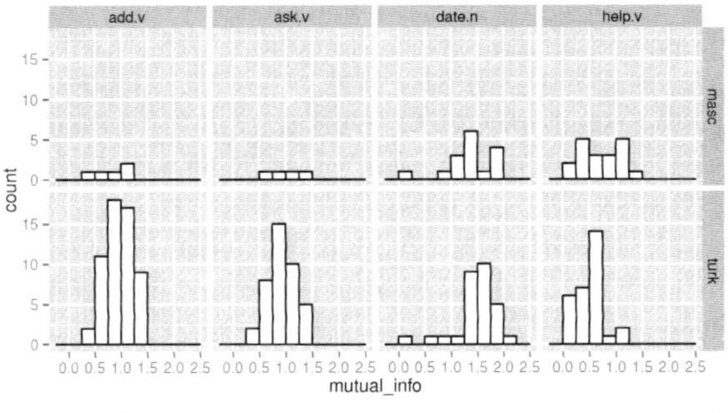

Figure 8: Histograms of mutual information estimates for the four example words; trained annotators are in the top row and Turkers in the bottom.

simpler model to filter out spam annotators. Crowdsourcing is now so widespread that NAACL 2010 sponsored a workshop on "Creating Speech and Language Data with Amazon's Mechanical Turk" and in 2011, TREC added a crowdsourcing track.

Active learning is an alternative method to annotate corpora, thus the Troia project (Ipeirotis et al., 2010) is a web service implementation of a maximum a posteriori estimator for the Dawid and Skene model, with a decision-theoretic module for active learning to select the next item to label. They draw on the Sheng et al. (2008) model to actively select the next label to elicit, which provides a very simple estimate of expected accuracy for a given number of labels. This essentially provides a statistical power calculation for annotation tasks. Because it is explicitly designed to measure reduction in uncertainty, mutual information should be the ideal choice for guiding such active labeling (MacKay, 1992). Such a strategy of selecting features with maximal mutual information has proven effective in greedy feature-selection strategies for classifiers, despite the fact that the objective function was classification accuracy, not entropy (Yang and Pedersen, 1997; Forman, 2003).

7 Conclusion

Interannotator agreement applies to a set of annotations, and provides no information about individual instances. When two or more annotators have very high interannotator agreement on a task, unless they have perfect accuracy, there will be instances where they agreed incorrectly, and no way to predict which instances these are. Moreover, for many semantic annotation tasks, high κ is impractical. In addition, there is often a pragmatic dimension where labels represent community-established conventions of usage. In such cases, no one individual can reliably assign labels because the ground truth derives from consensus among the community of language users. Word sense annotation is such a task.

An annotation model applied to the type of crowdsourced labels collected here provides more knowledge and higher quality gold standard labels at lower cost than the conventional method used in the MASC project. Those who would use the corpus for training benefit because they can differentiate high from low confidence labels. Those who would use such a corpus for cross-site evaluations of word sense disambiguation systems benefit because there are more evaluation options. Where the most probable label is relatively uncertain, systems can be penalized less for an incorrect but close response. Crowdsourcing has already made it possible to annotate corpora more cheaply, and wider use of annotation models in NLP should lead to more confidence from users in the corpora we create.

Acknowledgments

The first author was supported by NSF CRI-0708952 and CRI-1059312. The second author was supported by NSF CNS-1205516 and DoE DE-SC0002099. We thank Shreya Prasad for work on the data collection, Mizi Morris and Boyi Xie for results munging and feedback on the paper, and Marilyn Walker for advice on collaborating with turkers on the design of HITs through message boards.

References

Paul S. Albert and Lori E. Dodd. 2008. On estimating diagnostic accuracy from studies with multiple raters and partial gold standard evaluation. *Journal of the American Statistical Association*, 103(481):61–73.

Ron Artstein and Massimo Poesio. 2008. Inter-coder agreement for computational linguistics. *Computational Linguistics*, 34(4):555–596.

Rebecca F. Bruce and Janyce M. Wiebe. 1998. Word-sense distinguishability and inter-coder agreement. In *Proceedings of Empirical Methods in Natural Language Processing*, pages 53–60.

Rebecca F. Bruce and Janyce M. Wiebe. 1999. Recognizing subjectivity: a case study of manual tagging. *Natural Language Engineering*, 1(1):1–16.

Chris Callison-Burch and Mark Dredze. 2010. Creating speech and language data with Amazon's Mechanical Turk. In *Proceedings of the NAACL HLT 2010 Workshop on Creating Speech and Language Data with Amazon's Mechanical Turk*, pages 1–12.

Bob Carpenter. 2008. Multilevel Bayesian models of categorical data annotation. Technical report, Alias-i, Inc.

Jacob Cohen. 1960. A coefficient of agreement for nominal scales. *Educational and Psychological Measurement*, 20:37–46.

Thomas M. Cover and Joy A. Thomas. 1991. *Elements of Information Theory*. Wiley-Interscience, New York, NY, USA.

A. P. Dawid and A. M. Skene. 1979. Maximum likelihood estimation of observer error-rates using the EM algorithm. *Journal of the Royal Statistical Society. Series C (Applied Statistics)*, 28(1):20–28.

Barbara di Eugenio and Michael Glass. 2004. The Kappa statistic: A second look. *Computational Linguistics*, 30(1):95–101.

Barbara di Eugenio. 2000. On the usage of Kappa to evaluate agreement on coding tasks. In *Proceedings of the Second International Conference on Language Resources and Evaluation (LREC)*.

B. Efron and R. Tibshirani. 1986. Bootstrap methods for standard errors, confidence intervals, and other measures of statistical accuracy. *Statistical Science*, 1(1):54–77.

Alvan R. Feinstein and Domenic V. Cicchetti. 1990. High agreement but low Kappa: I. The problems of two paradoxes. *Journal of Clinical Epidemiology*, 43(6):543 – 549.

George Forman. 2003. An extensive empirical study of feature selection metrics for text classification. *Journal of Machine Learning Research*, 3:1289–1305.

Kilem Li Gwet. 2008. Computing inter-rater reliability and its variance in the presence of high agreement. *British Journal of Mathematical and Statistical Psychology*, 61(1):29–48.

J. W. Holley and J. P. Guildford. 1964. A note on the G index of agreement. *Educational and Psychological Measurement*, 24:749–753.

Dirk Hovy, Tayler Berg-Kirkpatrick, Ashish Vaswani, and Eduard Hovy. 2013. Learning whom to trust with MACE. In *Proceedings of the 2013 Conference of the North American Chapter of the Association for Computational Linguistics: Human Language Technologies*, pages 1120–1130, Atlanta, Georgia, June. Association for Computational Linguistics.

Panagiotis G. Ipeirotis, Foster Provost, and Jing Wang. 2010. Quality management on Amazon Mechanical Turk. In *Proceedings of the ACM SIGKDD Workshop on Human Computation*, HCOMP 2010, pages 64–67, New York, NY, USA. ACM.

Beata Beigman Klebanov and Eyal Beigman. 2009. From annotator agreement to noise models. *Computational Linguistics*, 35(4):495–503.

Klaus Krippendorff. 1980. *Content analysis: An introduction to its methodology*. Sage Publications, Beverly Hills, CA.

David J. C. MacKay. 1992. Information-based objective functions for active data selection. *Neural Computation*, 4:590–604.

B. W. Matthews. 1975. Comparison of the predicted and observed secondary structure of t4 phage lysozyme. *Biochimica et Biophysica Acta (BBA) - Protein Structure*, 405(2):442–451.

George A. Miller. 1995. A lexical database for English. *Communications of the ACM*, 38(11):39–41.

Rebecca J. Passonneau, Collin F. Baker, Christiane Fellbaum, and Nancy Ide. 2012a. The MASC word sense corpus. In *Proceedings of the Eighth International Conference on Language Resources and Evaluation (LREC'12)*, pages 3025–3030, Istanbul, Turkey. European Language Resources Association (ELRA).

Rebecca J. Passonneau, Vikas Bhardwaj, Ansaf Salleb-Aouissi, and Nancy Ide. 2012b. Multiplicity and word sense: Evaluating and learning from multiply labeled word sense annotations. *Language Resources and Evaluation*, 46(2):219–252.

Vikas C. Raykar, Shipeng Yu, Linda H. Zhao, Gerardo Hermosillo Valadez, Charles Florin, Luca Bogoni, and Linda Moy. 2010. Learning from crowds. *Journal of Machine Learning Research*, 11:1297–1322.

Simon Rogers, Mark Girolami, and Tamara Polajnar. 2010. Semi-parametric analysis of multi-rater data. *Statistical Computing*, 20:317–334.

Andrey Rzhetsky, Hagit Shatkay, and W. John Wilbur. 2009. How to get the most out of your curation effort. *PLoS Computational Biology.*, 5(5):1–13.

Victor S. Sheng, Foster Provost, and Panagiotis G. Ipeirotis. 2008. Get another label? Improving data quality and data mining using multiple, noisy labelers. In *Proceedings of the Fourteenth ACM International Conference on Knowledge Discovery and Data Mining (KDD)*.

Padhraic Smyth, Usama Fayyad, Michael Burl, Pietro Perona, and Pierre Baldi. 1995. Inferring ground truth from subjectively-labeled images of Venus. In *Advances in Neural Information Processing Systems 7*, pages 1085–1092. MIT Press.

Rion Snow, Brendan O'Connor, Daniel Jurafsky, and Andrew Y. Ng. 2008. Cheap and fast - but is it good? Evaluating non-expert annotations for natural language tasks. In *Proceedings of Empirical Methods in Natural Language Processing (EMNLP)*, pages 254–263, Honolulu.

Jan Vegelius. 1981. Significance tests for the G-index. *Educational and Psychological Measurement*, 41:99–108.

Jacob Whitehill, Paul Ruvolo, Tingfan Wu, Jacob Bergsma, and Javier Movellan. 2009. Whose vote should count more: Optimal integration of labels from labelers of unknown expertise. In Y. Bengio, D. Schuurmans, J. Lafferty, C. K. I. Williams, and A. Culotta, editors, *Advances in Neural Information Processing Systems 22*, pages 2035–2043, December.

Yiming Yang and Jan O. Pedersen. 1997. A comparative study on feature selection in text categorization. In *Proceedings of the Fourteenth International Conference on Machine Learning*, ICML '97, pages 412–420, San Francisco, CA, USA. Morgan Kaufmann Publishers Inc.

Improved CCG Parsing with Semi-supervised Supertagging

Mike Lewis
School of Informatics
University of Edinburgh
Edinburgh, EH8 9AB, UK
mike.lewis@ed.ac.uk

Mark Steedman
School of Informatics
University of Edinburgh
Edinburgh, EH8 9AB, UK
steedman@inf.ed.ac.uk

Abstract

Current supervised parsers are limited by the size of their labelled training data, making improving them with unlabelled data an important goal. We show how a state-of-the-art CCG parser can be enhanced, by predicting lexical categories using unsupervised vector-space embeddings of words. The use of word embeddings enables our model to better generalize from the labelled data, and allows us to accurately assign lexical categories without depending on a POS-tagger. Our approach leads to substantial improvements in dependency parsing results over the standard supervised CCG parser when evaluated on Wall Street Journal (0.8%), Wikipedia (1.8%) and biomedical (3.4%) text. We compare the performance of two recently proposed approaches for classification using a wide variety of word embeddings. We also give a detailed error analysis demonstrating where using embeddings outperforms traditional feature sets, and showing how including POS features can decrease accuracy.

1 Introduction

Combinatory Categorial Grammar (CCG) is widely used in natural language semantics (Bos, 2008; Kwiatkowski et al., 2010; Krishnamurthy and Mitchell, 2012; Lewis and Steedman, 2013a; Lewis and Steedman, 2013b; Kwiatkowski et al., 2013), largely because of its direct linkage of syntax and semantics. However, this connection means that performance on semantic applications is highly dependent on the quality of the syntactic parse. Although CCG parsers perform at state-of-the-art levels (Rimell et al., 2009; Nivre et al., 2010), full-sentence accuracy is just 25.6% on Wikipedia text, which gives a low upper bound on logical inference approaches to question-answering and textual entailment.

Supertags are rich lexical categories that go beyond POS tags by encoding information about predicate-argument structure. Supertagging is "almost parsing", and is used by parsers based on strongly lexicalized formalisms such as CCG and TAG to improve accuracy and efficiency, by delegating many of the parsing decisions to finite-state models (Bangalore and Joshi, 1999). A disadvantage of this approach is that larger sets of lexical categories mean increased sparsity, decreasing tagging accuracy. As large amounts of labelled data are unlikely to be made available, recent work has explored using unlabelled data to improve parser lexicons (Thomforde and Steedman, 2011; Deoskar et al., 2011; Deoskar et al., 2014). However, existing work has failed to improve the overall accuracy of state-of-the-art supervised parsers in-domain.

Another strand of recent work has explored using unsupervised word embeddings as features in supervised models (Turian et al., 2010; Collobert et al., 2011b), largely motivated as a simpler and more general alternative to standard feature sets. We apply similar techniques to CCG supertagging, hypothesising that words which are close in the embedding space will have similar supertags. Most existing work has focused on flat tagging tasks, and has not produced state-of-the-art results on structured prediction tasks like parsing (Collobert, 2011; Andreas and Klein, 2014). CCG's lexicalized nature provides a simple and elegant solution to treating parsing as a flat tagging task, as the lexical categories encode information about hierarchical structure.

Transactions of the Association for Computational Linguistics, 2 (2014) 327–338. Action Editor: Ryan McDonald.
Submitted 4/2014; Revised 6/2014; Published 10/2014.

As well as improving parsing accuracy, our model has a number of advantages over current CCG parsing work. Our supertagger does not make use of a POS-tagger, a fact which simplifies the model architecture, reduces the number of parameters, and eliminates errors caused by a pipeline approach. Also, learning word embeddings is an active area of research, and future developments may directly lead to better parsing accuracy, with no change required to our model.

2 Background

2.1 CCG Parsing

The widely-used C&C parser (Clark and Curran, 2007) for CCG takes a pipeline approach, where first sentences are POS-tagged, then supertagged, and then parsed. The supertagger outputs a distribution over tags for each word, and a beam is used to aggressively prune supertags to reduce the parser search space. If the parser is unable to find a parse with a given set of supertags, the beam is relaxed. This approach is known as *adaptive supertagging*.

The pipeline approach has two major drawbacks. Firstly, the use of a POS-tagger can overly prune the search space for the supertagger. Whilst POS-taggers have an accuracy of around 97% in domain, this drops to just 93.4% on biomedical text (Rimell and Clark, 2009), meaning that most sentences will contain an erroneous POS-tag. The supertagger model is overly dependent on POS-features—in Section 4.6 we show that supertagger performance drops dramatically on words which have been assigned an incorrect POS-tag.

Secondly, both the POS-tagger and supertagger are highly reliant on lexical features, meaning that performance drops both on unknown words, and words used differently from the training data. Many common words do not appear at all in the training data of the Penn Treebank, such as *ten*, *militants*, *insight*, and *teenager*. Many others are not seen with all their possible uses—for example *European* only occurs as an adjective, never a noun, meaning that the C&C parser is unable to analyse simple sentences like *The director of the IMF is traditionally a European*. These problems are particularly acute when parsing other domains (Rimell and Clark, 2009).

2.2 Semi Supervised NLP using Word Embeddings

Recent work has explored using vector space embeddings for words as features in supervised models for a variety of tasks, such as POS-tagging, chunking, named-entity recognition, semantic role labelling, and phrase structure parsing (Turian et al., 2010; Collobert et al., 2011b; Collobert, 2011; Socher et al., 2013). The major motivation for using these techniques has been to minimize the level of task-specific feature engineering required, as the same feature set can lead to good results on a variety of tasks. Performance varies between tasks, but any gains over state-of-the-art traditional features have been small. A variety of techniques have been used for learning such embeddings from large unlabelled corpora, such as neural-network language models.

3 Models

We introduce models for predicting CCG lexical categories based on vector-space embeddings. The models can then be used to replace the POS-tagging and supertagging stages used by existing CCG parsers. We experiment with the neural network model proposed by Collobert et al. (2011b), and conditional random field (CRF) model used by Turian et al. (2010). We only use features that can be expected to work well out-of-domain—in particular, we use no lexical or POS features.

3.1 Features

Our features are similar to those used by Collobert et al. (2011b) for POS-tagging. For every word in a context window, we add features for the embedding of the word, its 2-character suffix, and whether or not it is capitalised. We expect such features to generalize well to other domains—and in Section 4.5 we show that adding traditional POS-tag and lexical features does not help.

To further reduce sparsity, we apply some simple preprocessing techniques. Words are lower-cased[1], and all digits are replaced with *0*. If an unknown word is hyphenated, we first try backing-off to the substring after the hyphen.

[1]For embeddings that include separate entries for the same word with different capitalization, we take the most frequently occurring version in the unlabelled corpus.

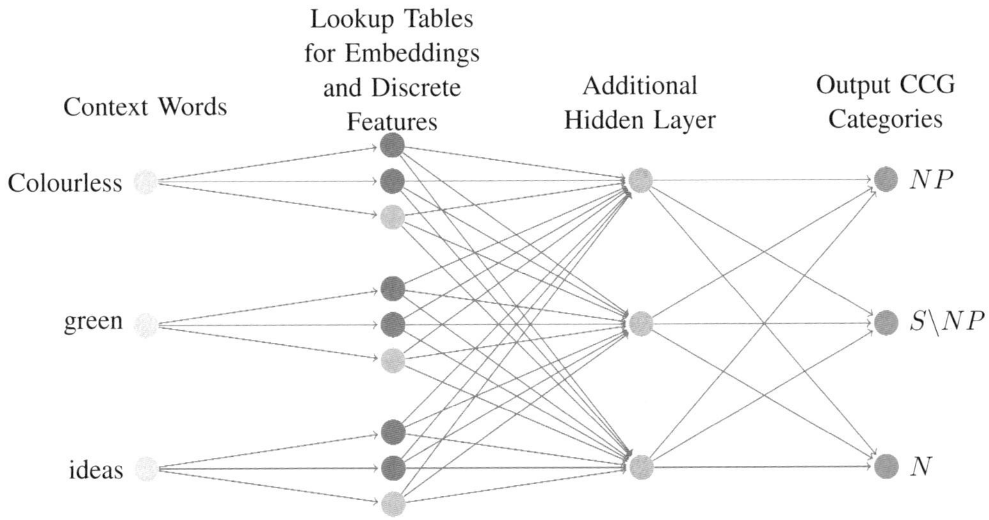

Figure 1: Collobert et al. (2011b)'s *Window approach network*, applied to CCG supertagging. Each context word C_i is connected to one hidden node per dimension of the embedding E_{ij} with weight W_{ij}, and additional hidden nodes representing capitalization and suffix features. The weights W_{ij} are initialized using pre-trained word embeddings, but can be modified during supervised training. The additional hidden layer uses a *hard-tanh* activation function, and the output layer uses a *softmax* activation function.

Words which do not have an entry in the word embeddings share an 'unknown' embedding. Different 'unknown' vectors are used for capitalized and uncapitalized words, and non-alphabetic symbols. We also add entries for context words which are before the start and after the end of the sentence. All of these were initialized to the 'unknown' vector in the pre-trained embeddings (or with Gaussian noise if not available).

3.2 Neural Network Model

We predict word supertags with the neural network classifier used by Collobert et al. (2011b) for POS-tagging, as shown in Figure 1. Each feature is implemented as a lookup table, which maps context words onto vectors. The same lookup table parameters are used wherever a word appears in the context window.

Word embeddings are implemented with a lookup table $W \in R^{V \times D}$, where V is the size of the vocabulary, and D is the dimension of the word embeddings. The parameters of the lookup table are initialized using unsupervised embeddings, but are modified during supervised training.

As in Collobert et al. (2011b), non-embedding features (2-character suffixes and capitalization) are also each represented with lookup tables, which map each feature onto a K dimensional vector (as in Collobert et al. (2011b), we use $K = 5$). Lookup table parameters for non-embeddings features are initialized with Gaussian noise.

The first hidden layer therefore contains $C \times (D + KF)$ nodes, where F is the number of discrete features and C is the size of the context window. We also experimented adding an additional hidden layer, with a *hard-tanh* activation function, which makes the classifier non-linear. Finally, a *logistic softmax* layer is used for classifying output categories.

The model is trained using stochastic gradient descent, with a learning rate of 0.01, optimizing for cross-entropy. We use early-stopping as an alternative to regularization—after each iteration the model is evaluated for accuracy on held-out data, and we use the best performing model. Training was run until performance decreased on held-out data.

3.3 CRF Model

The neural network model treats the probability of each supertag as being conditionally independent. However, conditioning on surrounding supertags

Embeddings	Model	Dimensionality	Training Words	Training Domain
Collobert&Weston	NNLM	50	660M	Wikipedia
Skip-Gram	Skip Gram	300	100B	Google News
Turian	NNLM	25, 50, 100, 200	37M	Newswire
HLBL	HLBL	50, 100	37M	Newswire
Mikolov	RNNLM	80, 640	320M	Broadcast News

Table 1: Embeddings used in our experiments. Dimensionality is the set of dimensions of the word embedding space that we experimented with, and Training Words refers to the size of the unlabelled corpus the embeddings were trained on.

may be very useful—for example, a noun is much more likely to follow an adjective than a verb. Curran et al. (2006) report a large improvement using a maximum-entropy Markov model for supertagging, conditioned on the surrounding supertags.

We follow Turian et al. (2010) in using a linear chain CRF model for sequence classification using embeddings as features. This model does not allow supervised training to fine-tune the embeddings, though it would be possible to build a CRF/NN hybrid that enabled this. We use the same feature set as with the neural network model—so the probability of a category depends on embeddings, capitalization and suffix features—as well as the previous category. The model is trained using the averaged-perceptron algorithm (Collins, 2002), again using early-stopping based on development data accuracy.

4 Experiments

4.1 Domains

We experiment with three domains:

- CCGBank (Hockenmaier and Steedman, 2007), which is a conversion of the Penn Treebank (Marcus et al., 1993) to CCG. Section 23 is used for evaluation.
- Wikipedia, using the corpus of 200 sentences annotated with CCG derivations by Honnibal et al. (2009). As the text is out-of-domain, parsing accuracy drops substantially on this corpus.
- Biomedical text, which is even less related to the newswire text than Wikipedia, due to large numbers of unseen words and different writing styles, causing low parsing accuracy. For parsing experiments, we use the Bioinfer corpus (Pyysalo et al., 2007) as a test set. For measuring supertagging accuracy, we use the CCG annotation produced by Rimell and Clark (2008).

4.2 Neural Network Model Parameters

In this section, we explore how adjusting the parameters of our neural network model[2] affects 1-best lexical category accuracy on the Section 00 of CCG-Bank (all development was done on this data). The C&C supertagger achieves 91.5% accuracy on this task. The models were trained on Sections 02-21 of CCGBank, and the reported numbers are the best accuracy achieved on Section 00. As in Clark and Curran (2007), all models use only the 425 most frequent categories in CCGBank.

4.2.1 Embeddings

A number of word embeddings have recently been released, aiming to capture a variety of syntactic and semantic phenomena, based on neural network language models (NNLMs) (Turian et al., 2010; Collobert et al., 2011b), recurrent neural network language models (Mikolov, 2012), the hierarchical log bilinear model (HLBL) (Mnih and Hinton, 2008), and Mikolov et al. (2013)'s Skip Gram model. However, there has been a lack of experiments comparing which embeddings provide the most effective features for downstream tasks.

First, we investigated the performance of several publicly available embeddings, to find which was most effective for supertagging. The embeddings we used are summarized in Table 1. For efficiency, we used our simplest architecture, with no additional

[2]Implemented using the Torch7 library (Collobert et al., 2011a)

Embeddings	Category Accuracy (window=5)	Category Accuracy (window=7)
Collobert&Weston	90.0%	89.6%
Skip Gram	90.9%	91.0%
Turian-25	91.0%	91.1%
Turian-50	**91.1%**	**91.3%**
Turian-100	91.0%	91.1%
Turian-200	90.8%	90.7%
HLBL-50	90.9%	91.2%
HLBL-100	**91.1%**	**91.3%**
Mikolov-80	87.2%	88.1%
Mikolov-640	87.9%	88.4%

Table 2: Comparison of different embeddings and context windows on Section 00 of CCGBank. Abbreviations such as Turian-50 refer to the Turian embeddings with a 50-dimensional embedding space.

hidden layer. We also investigate which size context window is most effective.

Results are shown in Table 2, and show that the choice of embeddings is crucial to performance on this task. The performance of the Turian and HLBL embeddings is surprisingly high given the relatively small amount of unlabelled data, suggesting that parameters other than the size of the corpus are more important. Of course, we have not performed a grid-search of the parameter space, and it is possible that other embeddings would perform better with different training data, dimensionality, or model architectures. The Mikolov embeddings may suffer from being trained on broadcast news, which has no punctuation and different language use. Using a context window of 7 words generally outperformed using a window of 5 words (we also experimented with a 9 word window, but found performance decreased slightly to 91.2% for the Turian-50 embeddings). There is no clear trend on the optimal dimension of the embedding space, and it is likely to vary with training methods and corpus size.

Next, we experimented with the size of the additional hidden layer—for efficiency, using the Turian-50 embeddings with a 5-word context window. Results are shown in Table 3, and suggest that a hidden layer is not useful for this task—possibly due to over-fitting.

Embeddings	Additional Hidden Layer Size	Accuracy
Turian-50	0	91.1%
Turian-50	100	90.9%
Turian-50	300	90.6%
Turian-50	500	90.9%
Turian-50	1000	90.5%

Table 3: Comparison of different model architectures, using the Turian embeddings and a 5-word context window. A size of 0 means no additional hidden layer was used.

In all subsequent experiments we used a context window of 7 words, no additional hidden layer, and the Turian-50 embeddings.

4.3 CRF Model

We also experimented with the CRF model for supertagging[3]. Training these models took far longer than our neural-network model, due to the need to use the forward-backward algorithm with a 425×425-dimensional transition matrix during training (rather than considering each word's category independently). Consequently, we only experimented with the Turian-50 embeddings with a 7-word context window, which attained the best performance using the neural network.

We found that using the Turian-50 embeddings gave a surprisingly weak performance of just 90.3% (compared to 91.3% for the neural network model). We hypothesised that one reason for this result could be that the model is unable to modify the embeddings during supervised training (in contrast to the neural-network model). Consequently, we built a new set of embeddings, using the weight-matrix learned by our best neural network model. A new CRF model was then trained using the tuned embeddings. Performance then improved dramatically to 91.5%, and slightly outperformed the neural network—showing that while there is a small advantage to using sequence information, it is crucial to allow supervised training to modify the embeddings. These results help explain why Collobert et al. (2011b)'s neural network models outperform Turian et al. (2010)'s sequence models—but greater

[3]Implemented using CRFSuite (Okazaki,)

improvements may be possible with the combined approach we introduce here, which allows the model to both tune the embeddings and exploit sequence information. However, tagging with this model was considerably slower than the neural network (again, due to the cost of decoding), so we used the neural network architecture in the remaining experiments.

4.4 Multitagging Accuracy

The C&C parser takes a set of supertags per word as input, which is used to prune the search space. If no parse is found, the sentence is supertagged again with a wider beam. The effectiveness of the pruning therefore depends on the accuracy of the supertagger at a given level of ambiguity.

We experimented with the accuracy of different supertaggers at different levels of ambiguity. For the C&C supertagger, we vary the number of categories per word using the same back-off beam settings reported in Clark and Curran (2007). For our supertagger, we vary recall by adjusting the a variable-width beam, which removes tags whose probability is less than β times that of the most likely tag.

Results are shown in Figure 2. The supertaggers based on embeddings consistently match or outperform the C&C supertagger at all levels of recall across all domains. While performance is similar with a small number of tags per word, our supertaggers perform better with a more relaxed beam—perhaps representing cases which are challenging for the C&C model, such as POS-tag errors.

4.5 Parsing Accuracy

We investigate whether our supertagger improves the performance of the C&C parser, by replacing the standard C&C supertagger with our model. This evaluation is somewhat indirect, as the parser does not make use of the supertagger probabilities for categories, but instead simply uses it to prune the search space. However, we show that better pruning leads directly to better parsing accuracies.

C&C parser results on CCGBank and Wikipedia are reported using Clark and Curran (2007)'s best performing *hybrid* model[4] (trained on Sections 02-21), with automatic POS-tags, and the parameters

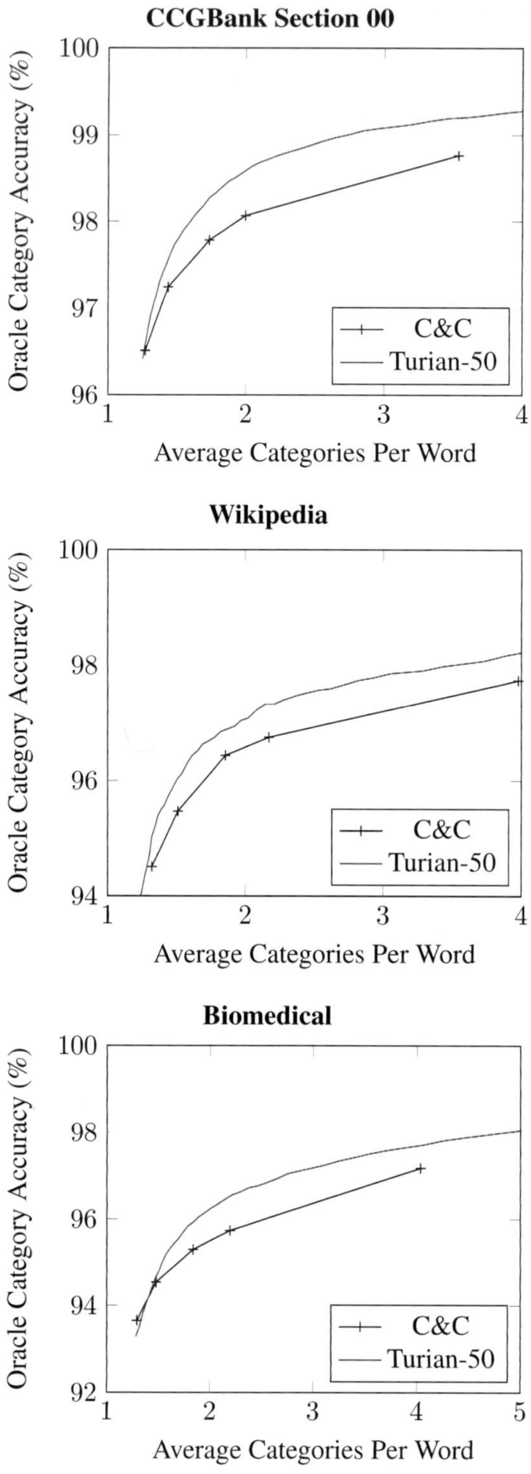

Figure 2: Ambiguity vs. Accuracy for different supertaggers across different domains. Datapoints for the C&C parser use its standard back-off parameters.

[4]This model is not publicly available, so we re-trained it following the instructions at `http://aclweb.org/aclwiki/index.php?title=Training_the_C&C_Parser`

Supertagger	CCGBank			Wikipedia			Bioinfer		
	F1 (cov)	COV	F1 (all)	F1 (cov)	COV	F1 (all)	F1 (cov)	COV	F1 (all)
C&C	85.47	99.6	85.30	81.19	99.0	80.64	76.08	97.2	74.88
Honnibal et al. (2009)	85.19	99.8	-	81.75	99.4	-	-	-	-
Brown Clusters	85.27	99.9	85.21	80.89	**100.0**	80.89	76.06	**100.0**	76.06
Turian-50 Embeddings	**86.11**	**100.0**	**86.11**	82.30	**100.0**	82.30	**78.41**	99.8	**78.28**
Turian-50 + POS tags	85.62	99.9	85.55	81.77	**100.0**	81.77	77.05	**100.0**	77.05
Turian-50 + Frequent words	86.04	**100.0**	86.04	**82.44**	**100.0**	**82.44**	78.10	**100.0**	78.10

Table 4: Parsing F1-scores for labelled dependencies across a range of domains, using the C&C parser with different supertaggers. Embeddings models used a context window of 7 words, and no additional hidden layer. Following previous CCG parsing work, we report F1-scores on the subset of sentences where the parser is able to produce a parse (F1-cov), and the parser's coverage (COV). Where available we also report overall scores (F1-all), including parser failures, which we believe gives a more realistic assessment.

used in the published results. Biomedical results use the publicly available parsing model, setting the 'parser beam ratio' parameter to 10^{-4}, which improved results on development data. To achieve full coverage on the Wikipedia corpus, we increased the 'max supercats' parameter to 10^7. C&C accuracies differ very slightly from previously reported results, due to differences in the retrained models.

As in Clark and Curran (2007), we use a variable-width beam β that prunes categories whose probability is less than β times that of the most likely category. For simplicity, our supertaggers use the same β back-off parameters as are used by the C&C parser, though it is possible that further improvements could be gained by carefully tuning these parameters.[5] In contrast to the C&C supertaggers, we do not make use a tag-dictionaries.

Results are shown in Table 4, and our supertaggers consistently lead to improvements over the baseline parser across all domains, with larger improvements out-of-domain. Our best model also outperforms Honnibal et al. (2009)'s self-training approach to domain adaptation on Wikipedia (which lowers performance on CCGBank).

Our results show that word embeddings are an effective way of adding distributional information into CCG supertagging. A popular alternative approach for semi-supervised learning is to use Brown clusters (Brown et al., 1992). To ensure a fair comparison with the Turian embeddings, we use clusters trained on the same corpus, and use a comparable feature set (clusters, capitalization, and 2-character suffixes—all implemented as sparse binary features). Brown clusters are hierarchical, and following Koo et al. (2008), we incorporate Brown clusters features at multiple levels of granularity—using 64 coarse clusters (loosely analogous to POS-tags) and 1000 fine-grained clusters. Results show slightly lower performance than C&C in domain, but higher performance out of domain. However, they are substantially lower than results using the Turian-50 embeddings.

We also experimented with adding traditional word and POS features, which were implemented as sparse vectors for each word in the context window. We found that including POS features (derived from the C&C POS-tagger) reduced accuracy across all domains. One reason is that POS tags are highly discriminative features, therefore errors can be hard to recover from. Adding lexical features for the most frequent 250 words had little impact on results, showing that the embeddings already represent this information.

For infrequent words, the C&C parser uses a hard constraint that only certain POS-tag/supertag combinations are allowed. This constraint means that the parser may be particularly vulnerable to POS-

[5]We briefly experimented setting the β parameters to match the ambiguity of the C&C supertagger on Section 00 of CCGBank, which caused the F1-score using the Turian-50 embeddings to drop slightly from 86.11 to 85.95.

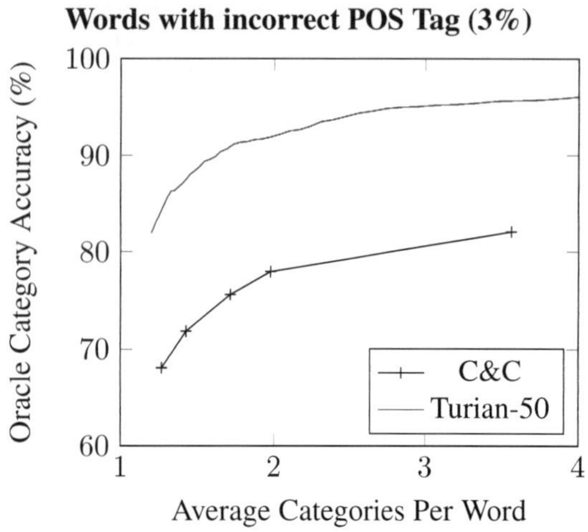

Figure 3: Ambiguity vs. Accuracy for different supertaggers, on words with incorrect POS tags.

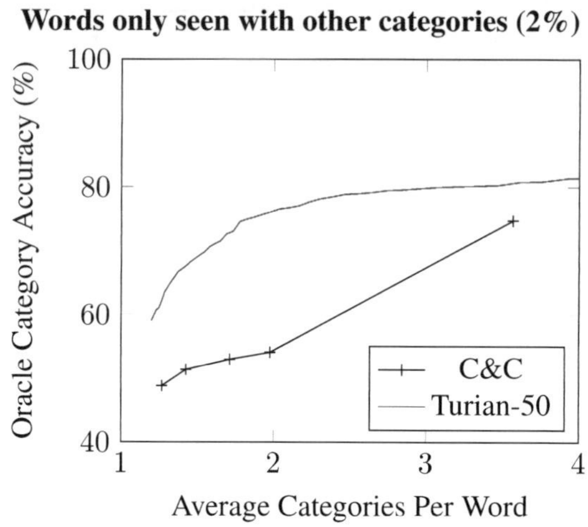

Figure 4: Ambiguity vs. Accuracy for different supertaggers, on words that do occur in the training data, but not with the category required in the test data.

tag errors, as the model cannot override the hard-constraint. We therefore also ran the model allowing any POS-tag/supertag combination. We found that parsing accuracy was 0.02 higher on development data (and much slower), suggesting that the model itself is overly reliant on POS-features.

4.6 Error Analysis

We have demonstrated that word embeddings are highly effective for CCG supertagging. In this section, we investigate several cases in which they are particularly helpful—by measuring supertagger performance when the POS tagger made mistakes, when words were unseen in the labelled data, and when the labelled data only contains the word with a different category. Our supertaggers show substantial improvements over more complex existing models.

Figure 3 shows performance when the POS-tagger assigns the wrong tag to a word. Both systems show dramatically lower performance on these cases—the embeddings supertagger does not use POS features, but POS errors are likely to represent generally difficult examples. However, the embeddings supertagger is almost 15% more accurate on this subset than the C&C supertagger, and with a relaxed beam reaches 96% accuracy, showing the advantages of avoiding a pipeline approach. In contrast, the C&C tagger is not robust to POS tagger errors, and asymptotes at just 82% accuracy. An alternative way of mitigating POS errors is to use a distribution over POS tags as features in the supertagger—Curran et al. (2006) show that this technique improves supertagging accuracy by 0.4% over the C&C baseline, but do not report the impact on parsing.

Figure 4 shows performance when the a word has been seen in the training data, but only with a different category from the instance in the test data (for example, *European* only occurs as a adjective in the training data, but it may occur as a noun in the test data). Performance is even worse on these cases, which appear to be extremely difficult for existing models. The accuracy of the embeddings supertagger converges at just 80%, suggesting that our model has overfit the labelled data. However, it still outperforms the C&C supertagger by 22% with a beam allowing 2 tags per word. The large jump in C&C supertagger performance for the final back-off level is due to a change in the word frequency threshold at which the C&C parser only considers word/category pairs that occur in the labelled data.

Figure 5 gives results for cases where the word is unseen in the labelled data. The C&C supertagger performance is surprisingly good on such cases, suggesting that the morphological and context used

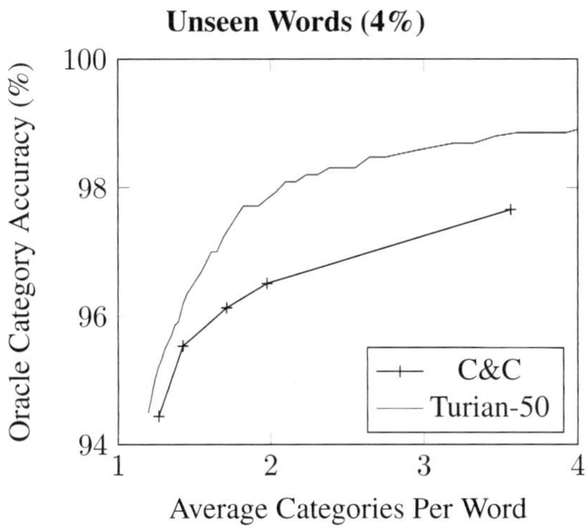

Figure 5: Ambiguity vs. Accuracy for different supertaggers, on words which are unseen in the labelled data.

is normally sufficient for inferring categories for unseen words. However, our supertagger still clearly outperforms the C&C supertagger, suggesting that the large vocabulary of the unsupervised embeddings helps it to generalize from the labelled data.

We also investigated supertagging accuracy on different types of word—Table 5 shows several interesting cases. While performance on nouns is similar, our supertagger is substantially better on verbs. Verbs can have many different CCG categories, depending on the number of arguments and tense, and not all valid word/category combinations will be seen in the labelled data. Our embeddings allow the supertagger to learn generalizations, such as that transitive verbs can also often have intransitive uses. Similarly, wh-words can have many possible categories in complex constructions like relative clauses and pied-piping—and our embeddings may help the model generalize from having seen a category for *which* to one for *whom*. On the other hand, the C&C supertagger performs much better on prepositions. Prepositions have different categories when appearing as arguments or adjuncts, and the distinction in the gold-standard was made using somewhat arbitrary heuristics (Hockenmaier and Steedman, 2007). It seems our embeddings have failed to capture these subtleties. Future work should explore methods for combining the strengths of each model.

Word Type	C&C Accuracy	Turian-50 Embeddings Accuracy
Verbs	93.9%	94.8%
Nouns	97.7%	97.3%
WH-words	90.1%	93.4%
Prepositions	94.8%	91.2%

Table 5: Supertagging accuracy on different types of words, with an ambiguity of 1.27 tags per word (corresponding to the C&C's initial beam setting). Overall performance with this beam is almost identical. Words types were identified using gold POS tags, using *IN* for prepositions.

4.7 Discussion

With a narrow supertagger beam, our method gives similar results to the C&C supertagger. However, it gains by being more accurate on difficult cases, due to not relying on lexical or POS features. These improvements lead directly to parser improvements. We identify two cases where our supertagger greatly outperforms the C&C parser: where the POS-tag is incorrect, and where the word-category pair is unseen in the labelled data. Our approach achieves larger improvements out-of-domain than in-domain, suggesting that the large vocabulary of embeddings built by the unsupervised pre-training allows it to better generalize from the labelled data.

Interestingly, the best-performing Turian-50 embeddings were trained on just 37M words of text (compared to 100B words for the Skip-gram embeddings), suggesting that further improvements may well be possible using larger unlabelled corpora. Future work should investigate whether the models and embeddings that work well for supertagging generalize to other tasks.

5 Related Work

Many methods have recently been proposed for improving supervised parsers with unlabelled data. Most of these are orthogonal to our work, and larger improvements may be possible by combining them.

Thomforde and Steedman (2011) extends a CCG lexicon by inferring categories for unseen words, based on the likely categories of surrounding words. Unlike our method, this approach is able to learn categories which were unseen in the labelled data, which is shown to be useful for parsing a corpus of questions. Deoskar et al. (2011) and Deoskar et al. (2014) use Viterbi-EM to learn new lexical entries by running a generative parser over a large unlabelled corpus. They show good improvements in accuracy on unseen words, but not overall parsing improvements in-domain. Their parsing model aims to capture non-local information about word usage, which would not be possible for the local context windows used to learn our embeddings.

Self-training is another popular method for domain adaptation, and was used successfully by Honnibal et al. (2009) to improve CCG parser performance on Wikipedia. However, it caused a decrease in performance on the in-domain data, and our method achieves better performance across all domains. McClosky et al. (2006) improve a Penn Treebank parser in-domain using self-training, but other work has failed to improve performance out-of-domain using self training (Dredze et al., 2007). In a similar spirit to our work, Koo et al. (2008) improve parsing accuracy using unsupervised word cluster features—we have shown that word-embeddings outperform Brown clusters for CCG supertagging.

An alternative approach to domain adaptation is to annotate a small corpus of out-of-domain text. Rimell and Clark (2008) argue that this annotation is simpler for lexicalized formalisms such as CCG, as large improvements can be gained from annotating lexical categories, rather than full syntax trees. They achieve higher parsing accuracies than us on biomedical text, but our unsupervised method requires no annotation. It seems likely that our method could be further improved by incorporating out-of-domain labelled data (where available).

The best reported CCG parsing results have been achieved with a model that integrates supertagging and parsing (Auli and Lopez, 2011a; Auli and Lopez, 2011b). This work still uses the same feature set as the C&C parser, suggesting further improvements may be possible by using our embeddings features. Auli and Lopez POS-tag the sentence before parsing, but using our features would allow us to fully eliminate the current pipeline approach to CCG parsing.

Our work also builds on approaches to semi-supervised NLP using neural embeddings (Turian et al., 2010; Collobert et al., 2011b). Existing work has mainly focused on 'flat' tagging problems, without hierarchical structure. Collobert (2011) gives a model for parsing using embeddings features, by treating each level of the parse tree as a sequence classification problem. Socher et al. (2013) introduce a model in which context-free grammar parses are reranked based on compositional distributional representations for each node. Andreas and Klein (2014) experiment with a number of approaches to improving the Berkeley parser with word embeddings. Such work has not improved over state-of-the-art existing feature sets for constituency parsing—although Bansal et al. (2014) achieve good results for dependency parsing using embeddings. CCG categories contain much of the hierarchical structure needed for parsing, giving a simpler way to improve a parser using embeddings.

6 Conclusions

We have shown that CCG parsing can be significantly improved by predicting lexical categories based on unsupervised word embeddings. The resulting parsing pipeline is simpler, and has improved performance both in and out of domain. We expect further improvements to follow as better word embeddings are developed, without other changes to our model. Our approach reduces the problem of sparsity caused by the large number of CCG categories, suggesting that finer-grained categories could be created for CCGBank (in the spirit of Honnibal et al. (2010)), which lead to improved performance in downstream semantic parsers. Future work should also explore domain-adaptation, either using unsupervised embeddings trained on out-of-domain text, or using supervised training on out-of-domain corpora. Our results also have implications for other NLP tasks—suggesting that using word embeddings features may be particularly useful out-of-domain, in pipelines that currently rely on POS taggers, and in tasks which suffer from sparsity in the labelled data.

Code for our supertagger is released as part of the EASYCCG parser (Lewis and Steedman, 2014), available from: `https://github.com/mikelewis0/easyccg`

Acknowledgments

We would like to thank Tejaswini Deoskar, Bharat Ram Ambati, Michael Roth and the anonymous reviewers for helpful feedback on an earlier version of this paper. We also thank Rahul Jha for sharing his re-implementation of Collobert et al. (2011b)'s model, and Stephen Clark, Laura Rimell and Matthew Honnibal for making their out-of-domain CCG corpora available.

References

Jacob Andreas and Dan Klein. 2014. How much do word embeddings encode about syntax. In *Proceedings of ACL*.

Michael Auli and Adam Lopez. 2011a. A comparison of loopy belief propagation and dual decomposition for integrated CCG supertagging and parsing. In *Proceedings of the 49th Annual Meeting of the Association for Computational Linguistics: Human Language Technologies-Volume 1*, pages 470–480. Association for Computational Linguistics.

Michael Auli and Adam Lopez. 2011b. Training a log-linear parser with loss functions via softmax-margin. In *Proceedings of the Conference on Empirical Methods in Natural Language Processing*, pages 333–343. Association for Computational Linguistics.

Srinivas Bangalore and Aravind K Joshi. 1999. Supertagging: An approach to almost parsing. *Computational Linguistics*, 25(2):237–265.

Mohit Bansal, Kevin Gimpel, and Karen Livescu. 2014. Tailoring continuous word representations for dependency parsing. In *Proceedings of the Annual Meeting of the Association for Computational Linguistics*.

Johan Bos. 2008. Wide-coverage semantic analysis with boxer. In Johan Bos and Rodolfo Delmonte, editors, *Semantics in Text Processing. STEP 2008 Conference Proceedings*, Research in Computational Semantics, pages 277–286. College Publications.

P.F. Brown, P.V. Desouza, R.L. Mercer, V.J.D. Pietra, and J.C. Lai. 1992. Class-based n-gram models of natural language. *Computational Linguistics*, 18(4):467–479.

Stephen Clark and James R Curran. 2007. Wide-coverage efficient statistical parsing with CCG and log-linear models. *Computational Linguistics*, 33(4):493–552.

Michael Collins. 2002. Discriminative training methods for hidden markov models: Theory and experiments with perceptron algorithms. In *Proceedings of the ACL-02 conference on Empirical methods in natural language processing-Volume 10*, pages 1–8. Association for Computational Linguistics.

Ronan Collobert, Koray Kavukcuoglu, and Clément Farabet. 2011a. Torch7: A Matlab-like environment for machine learning. In *BigLearn, NIPS Workshop*.

Ronan Collobert, Jason Weston, Léon Bottou, Michael Karlen, Koray Kavukcuoglu, and Pavel Kuksa. 2011b. Natural language processing (almost) from scratch. *The Journal of Machine Learning Research*, 12:2493–2537.

Ronan Collobert. 2011. Deep learning for efficient discriminative parsing. In Geoffrey J. Gordon, David B. Dunson, and Miroslav Dudk, editors, *AISTATS*, volume 15 of *JMLR Proceedings*, pages 224–232. JMLR.org.

James R Curran, Stephen Clark, and David Vadas. 2006. Multi-tagging for lexicalized-grammar parsing. In *Proceedings of the 21st International Conference on Computational Linguistics and the 44th annual meeting of the Association for Computational Linguistics*, pages 697–704. Association for Computational Linguistics.

Tejaswini Deoskar, Markos Mylonakis, and Khalil Sima'an. 2011. Learning structural dependencies of words in the zipfian tail. In *Proceedings of the 12th International Conference on Parsing Technologies*, pages 80–91. Association for Computational Linguistics.

Tejaswini Deoskar, Christos Christodoulopoulos, Alexandra Birch, and Mark Steedman. 2014. Generalizing a Strongly Lexicalized Parser using Unlabeled Data. In *Proceedings of the 14th Conference of the European Chapter of the Association for Computational Linguistics*. Association for Computational Linguistics.

Mark Dredze, John Blitzer, Partha Pratim Talukdar, Kuzman Ganchev, Joao Graca, and Fernando Pereira. 2007. Frustratingly hard domain adaptation for dependency parsing. In *EMNLP-CoNLL*, pages 1051–1055.

Julia Hockenmaier and Mark Steedman. 2007. CCGbank: a corpus of CCG derivations and dependency structures extracted from the Penn Treebank. *Computational Linguistics*, 33(3):355–396.

Matthew Honnibal, Joel Nothman, and James R Curran. 2009. Evaluating a statistical CCG parser on Wikipedia. In *Proceedings of the 2009 Workshop on The People's Web Meets NLP: Collaboratively Constructed Semantic Resources*, pages 38–41. Association for Computational Linguistics.

M. Honnibal, J.R. Curran, and J. Bos. 2010. Rebanking CCGbank for improved NP interpretation. In *Proceedings of the 48th Annual Meeting of the Association for Computational Linguistics*, pages 207–215. Association for Computational Linguistics.

Terry Koo, Xavier Carreras, and Michael Collins. 2008. Simple semi-supervised dependency parsing.

Jayant Krishnamurthy and Tom M. Mitchell. 2012. Weakly supervised training of semantic parsers. In *Proceedings of the 2012 Joint Conference on Empirical Methods in Natural Language Processing and Computational Natural Language Learning*, EMNLP-CoNLL '12, pages 754–765. Association for Computational Linguistics.

Tom Kwiatkowski, Luke Zettlemoyer, Sharon Goldwater, and Mark Steedman. 2010. Inducing probabilistic CCG grammars from logical form with higher-order unification. In *Proceedings of the 2010 Conference on Empirical Methods in Natural Language Processing*, EMNLP '10, pages 1223–1233. Association for Computational Linguistics.

Tom Kwiatkowski, Eunsol Choi, Yoav Artzi, and Luke Zettlemoyer. 2013. Scaling semantic parsers with on-the-fly ontology matching. In *Proceedings of the 2013 Conference on Empirical Methods in Natural Language Processing*, pages 1545–1556, Seattle, Washington, USA, October. Association for Computational Linguistics.

Mike Lewis and Mark Steedman. 2013a. Combined Distributional and Logical Semantics. *Transactions of the Association for Computational Linguistics*, 1:179–192.

Mike Lewis and Mark Steedman. 2013b. Unsupervised induction of cross-lingual semantic relations. In *Proceedings of the 2013 Conference on Empirical Methods in Natural Language Processing*, pages 681–692, Seattle, Washington, USA, October. Association for Computational Linguistics.

Mike Lewis and Mark Steedman. 2014. A* CCG Parsing with a Supertag-factored Model. In *Proceedings of the 2014 Conference on Empirical Methods in Natural Language Processing (EMNLP)*, Doha, Qatar, October.

Mitchell P Marcus, Mary Ann Marcinkiewicz, and Beatrice Santorini. 1993. Building a large annotated corpus of English: The Penn Treebank. *Computational Linguistics*, 19(2):313–330.

David McClosky, Eugene Charniak, and Mark Johnson. 2006. Effective self-training for parsing. In *Proceedings of the main conference on human language technology conference of the North American Chapter of the Association of Computational Linguistics*, pages 152–159. Association for Computational Linguistics.

Tomas Mikolov, Kai Chen, Greg Corrado, and Jeffrey Dean. 2013. Efficient estimation of word representations in vector space. *arXiv preprint arXiv:1301.3781*.

Tomáš Mikolov. 2012. *Statistical language models based on neural networks*. Ph.D. thesis, Ph. D. thesis, Brno University of Technology.

Andriy Mnih and Geoffrey E Hinton. 2008. A scalable hierarchical distributed language model. In *NIPS*, pages 1081–1088.

Joakim Nivre, Laura Rimell, Ryan McDonald, and Carlos Gómez Rodríguez. 2010. Evaluation of dependency parsers on unbounded dependencies. In *Proceedings of the 23rd International Conference on Computational Linguistics (Coling 2010)*, pages 833–841, Beijing, China, August. Coling 2010 Organizing Committee.

Naoaki Okazaki. CRFsuite: a fast implementation of conditional random fields (CRFs).

Sampo Pyysalo, Filip Ginter, Juho Heimonen, Jari Björne, Jorma Boberg, Jouni Järvinen, and Tapio Salakoski. 2007. Bioinfer: a corpus for information extraction in the biomedical domain. *BMC bioinformatics*, 8(1):50.

Laura Rimell and Stephen Clark. 2008. Adapting a lexicalized-grammar parser to contrasting domains. In *Proceedings of the Conference on Empirical Methods in Natural Language Processing*, pages 475–484. Association for Computational Linguistics.

Laura Rimell and Stephen Clark. 2009. Porting a lexicalized-grammar parser to the biomedical domain. *Journal of Biomedical Informatics*, 42(5):852–865.

Laura Rimell, Stephen Clark, and Mark Steedman. 2009. Unbounded dependency recovery for parser evaluation. In *Proceedings of the 2009 Conference on Empirical Methods in Natural Language Processing: Volume 2-Volume 2*, pages 813–821. Association for Computational Linguistics.

Richard Socher, John Bauer, Christopher D Manning, and Andrew Y Ng. 2013. Parsing with compositional vector grammars. In *In Proceedings of the ACL conference*. Citeseer.

Emily Thomforde and Mark Steedman. 2011. Semi-supervised CCG lexicon extension. In *Proceedings of the Conference on Empirical Methods in Natural Language Processing*, pages 1246–1256. Association for Computational Linguistics.

Joseph Turian, Lev Ratinov, and Yoshua Bengio. 2010. Word representations: a simple and general method for semi-supervised learning. In *Proceedings of the 48th Annual Meeting of the Association for Computational Linguistics*, pages 384–394. Association for Computational Linguistics.

2-Slave Dual Decomposition for Generalized Higher Order CRFs

Xian Qian and **Yang Liu**
Computer Science Department
The University of Texas at Dallas
{qx,yangl}@hlt.utdallas.edu

Abstract

We show that the decoding problem in generalized Higher Order Conditional Random Fields (CRFs) can be decomposed into two parts: one is a tree labeling problem that can be solved in linear time using dynamic programming; the other is a supermodular quadratic pseudo-Boolean maximization problem, which can be solved in cubic time using a minimum cut algorithm. We use dual decomposition to force their agreement. Experimental results on Twitter named entity recognition and sentence dependency tagging tasks show that our method outperforms spanning tree based dual decomposition.

1 Introduction

Conditional Random Fields (Lafferty et al., 2001) (CRFs) are popular models for many NLP tasks. In particular, the linear chain CRFs explore local structure information for sequence labeling tasks, such as part-of-speech (POS) tagging, named entity recognition (NER), and shallow parsing. Recent studies have shown that the predictive power of CRFs can be strengthened by breaking the locality assumption. They either add long distance dependencies and patterns to linear chains for improved sequence labeling (Galley, 2006; Finkel et al., 2005; Kazama and Torisawa, 2007), or directly use the 4-connected neighborhood lattice (Ding et al., 2008). The resulting non-local models generally suffer from exponential time complexity of inference except some special cases (Sarawagi and Cohen, 2004; Takhanov and Kolmogorov, 2013; Kolmogorov and Zabih, 2004).

Approximate decoding algorithms have been proposed in the past decade, such as reranking (Collins, 2002b), loopy belief propagation (Sutton and Mccallum, 2006), tree reweighted belief propagation (Kolmogorov, 2006). In this paper, we focus on dual decomposition (DD), which has attracted much attention recently due to its simplicity and effectiveness (Rush and Collins, 2012). In short, it decomposes the decoding problem into several sub-problems. For each sub-problem, an efficient decoding algorithm is deployed as a slave solver. Finally a simple method forces agreement among different slaves. A popular choice is the sub-gradient algorithm. Martins et al. (2011b) showed that the success of the sub-gradient algorithm is strongly tied to the ability of finding a good decomposition, i.e., one involving few overlapping slaves. However, for generalized higher order graphical models, a lightweight decomposition is not at hand and many overlapping slaves may be involved. Martins et al. (2011b) showed that the sub-gradient algorithm exhibits extremely slow convergence in such cases, and they proposed the alternating directions method (DD-ADMM) to tackle these.

In this paper, we propose a 2-slave dual decomposition approach for efficient decoding in higher order CRFs. One slave is a tree labeling model that can be solved in linear time using dynamic programming. The other is a supermodular quadratic pseudo-Boolean maximization problem, which can be solved in cubic time via minimum

Transactions of the Association for Computational Linguistics, 2 (2014) 339–350. Action Editor: Kristina Toutanova.
Submitted 11/2013; Revised 6/2014; Published 10/2014.

cut. Experimental results on Twitter NER and sentence dependency tagging tasks demonstrate the effectiveness of our technique.

2 Background

2.1 Generalized Higher Order CRFs

Given an undirected graph $G = (V, E)$ with N vertices, let $\mathbf{x} = x_1, x_2, \ldots, x_N$ denote the observations of the vertices, and each observation x_v is asked to assign one state (or label) in the state set $s \in \mathcal{S}$. The assignment of the graph can be represented by a binary matrix $Y_{N\times|\mathcal{S}|}$, where $|\mathcal{S}|$ is the cardinality of $\mathcal{S}$, and the element $Y_{v,s}$ indicates if x_v is assigned state s. In the rest of the paper, we use $Y_{v[s]}$ instead, and $v[s]$ to denote the vertex v with state s. The constraint

$$\sum_s Y_{v[s]} = 1 \tag{1}$$

is required so that each vertex has exactly one state. In this paper, we use $\mathcal{Y}$ to denote the space of state assignments.

The decoding problem is to search the optimal assignment that maximizes the scoring function

$$Y^* = \arg\max_{Y\in\mathcal{Y}(\mathbf{x})}\phi(\mathbf{x}, Y)$$

where $\phi(\mathbf{x}, Y)$ is a given scoring function. As $\mathbf{x}$ is constant in this maximization problem, we omit $\mathbf{x}$ for simplicity in the remainder of the paper. The decoding problem becomes

$$\max_{Y\in\mathcal{Y}} \phi(Y). \tag{2}$$

The scoring function $\phi(Y)$ is usually decomposed into small parts

$$\phi(Y) = \sum_{\mathbf{c}}\sum_{\mathbf{s}\in\mathbf{c}[\cdot]} \phi_{\mathbf{c}[\mathbf{s}]} \prod_{v[s]\in\mathbf{c}[\mathbf{s}]} Y_{v[s]}$$

where $\mathbf{c}$ is a subset of vertices, called a **factor**. $\mathbf{c}[\cdot]$ is the set of all possible assignments of $\mathbf{c}$. For example, factor $\mathbf{c} = \{u, v\}$ denotes the edge (u, v) in the graph, and $\mathbf{c}[\cdot] = \mathcal{S}^2$ is the set of the $|\mathcal{S}|^2$ transitions. A factor $\mathbf{c}$ with a specific state assignment $\mathbf{s}$ is called a **pattern**, denoted as $\mathbf{c}[\mathbf{s}]$. For example, $v[s]$ is a pattern of vertex v, and $uv[st]$ is a pattern of edge (u, v) as shown in Figure 1. Note that our definition extends of the work of Takhanov and Kolmogorov where patterns are restricted to the state sequences of consecutive vertices (Takhanov and Kolmogorov, 2013). $\prod_{v[s]\in\mathbf{c}[\mathbf{s}]} Y_{v[s]}$ means a pattern $\mathbf{c}[\mathbf{s}]$ is selected in the assignment only if all its members $v[s]$ are selected. For simplicity, in this paper we use

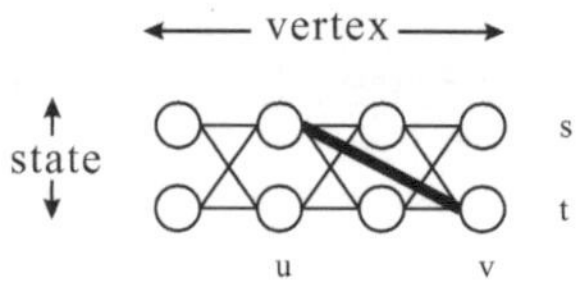

Figure 1: Pattern $\mathbf{c}[\mathbf{s}] = uv[st]$ is shown in bold.

$$Y_{\mathbf{c}[\mathbf{s}]} = \prod_{v[s]\in\mathbf{c}[\mathbf{s}]} Y_{v[s]}$$

to denote whether pattern $\mathbf{c}[\mathbf{s}]$ appears in the assignment. Then the scoring function becomes

$$\phi(Y) = \sum_{\mathbf{c}}\sum_{\mathbf{s}\in\mathbf{c}[\cdot]} \phi_{\mathbf{c}[\mathbf{s}]} Y_{\mathbf{c}[\mathbf{s}]}. \tag{3}$$

Many existing CRFs can be represented using Eq (3). For example, the popular linear chain CRFs consider two types of patterns: vertices and edges connecting adjacent vertices, resulting in the following scoring function

$$\phi(Y) = \sum_v\sum_s \phi_{v[s]}Y_{v[s]} + \sum_v\sum_{st\in\mathcal{S}^2} \phi_{v(v+1)[st]}Y_{v(v+1)[st]}$$

The optimal Y can be found in linear time using the Viterbi algorithm.

Another example is the skip-chain CRFs, which consider the interactions between similar vertices

$$\begin{aligned}\phi(Y) &= \sum_v\sum_s \phi_{v[s]}Y_{v[s]} \\ &+ \sum_v\sum_{st\in\mathcal{S}^2} \phi_{v(v+1)[st]}Y_{v(v+1)[st]} \\ &+ \sum_{u,v \text{ are similar}}\sum_{s\in\mathcal{S}} \phi_{uv[ss]}Y_{uv[ss]}.\end{aligned}$$

With positive $\phi_{uv[ss]}$, the model encourages similar vertices u and v to have identical state s, and thus it yields a more consistent labeling result compared with linear chain CRFs. Empirically, the use of complex patterns achieves better performance but suffers from high computational complexity of inference, which is generally NP-hard. Hence an efficient approximate inference algorithm is required to balance the trade-off.

2.2 Dual Decomposition

Dual decomposition is a popular approach due to its simplicity and effectiveness, and has been successfully applied to many tasks such as machine translation, cross sentential POS tagging, joint POS tagging and parsing.

Briefly, dual decomposition attempts to solve problems of the following form

$$\max_{Y} \sum_{i=1}^{M} \phi_i(Y)$$

The objective function is the sum of several small components that are tractable in isolation but whose combination is not. These components are called slaves. Rather than solving the problem directly, dual decomposition considers the equivalent problem

$$\begin{aligned} \max_{Y, Z_1 \ldots Z_M} \quad & \sum_{i=1}^{M} \phi_i(Z_i) \\ \text{s.t.} \quad & Z_i = Y \quad \forall i \end{aligned}$$

Using Lagrangian relaxation to eliminate the constraint, we get

$$\min_{\lambda} \max_{Y, Z_1 \ldots Z_M} \sum_{i=1}^{M} \phi_i(Z_i) + \sum_{i} \lambda_i^T (Y - Z_i) \quad (4)$$

which provides the upper bound of the original problem. λ is the Lagrange multiplier, which is typically optimized via sub-gradient algorithms.

Martins et al. (2011b) showed that the success of sub-gradient algorithms is strongly tied to the ability of finding a good decomposition, i.e., one involving few slaves. Finding a concise decomposition is usually task dependent. For example, Koo et al. (2010) introduced dual decomposition for parsing with non-projective head automata. They used only two slaves: one is the arc-factored model, and the other is head automata which involves adjacent siblings and can be solved using dynamic programming in linear time.

Dual decomposition is especially efficient for joint learning tasks because a concise decomposition can be derived naturally where each slave solves one subtask. For example, Rush et al. (2010) used two slaves for integrated phrase-structure parsing and trigram POS tagging task.

However, for generalized higher order CRFs, a lightweight decomposition may be not at hand. Martins et al. (2011a) showed that the sub-gradient algorithms exhibited extremely slow convergence when handling many slaves. For fast convergence, they employed alternating directions dual decomposition (AD^3), which relaxes the agreement constraint via augmented Lagrangian Relaxation, where an additional quadratic penalty term was added into the Lagrangian (Eq (4)). Similarly, Jojic et al. (2010) added a strongly concave term to the Lagrangian to make it differentiable, resulting in fast convergence.

The work most closely related to ours is the work by Komodakis (2011), where dual decomposition was used for decoding general higher order CRFs. Komodakis achieved great empirical success even with the naive decomposition where each slave processes a single higher order factor. His result demonstrates the effectiveness of the dual decomposition framework. Our work improves Komodakis' by using a concise decomposition with only two slaves.

2.3 Graph Representable Pseudo-Boolean Optimization

One slave in our approach is a graph representable pseudo-Boolean maximization problem, which can be reduced to a supermodular quadratic pseudo-Boolean maximization problem and solved efficiently using an algorithm for finding a minimal cut.

A pseudo-Boolean function (PBF) (Boros and Hammer, 2002) is a multilinear function of binary variables, that is

$$f(\mathbf{x}) = \sum_{i} a_i x_i + \sum_{i<j} a_{ij} x_i x_j + \sum_{i<j<k} a_{ijk} x_i x_j x_k + \ldots$$

where $x_i \in \{0, 1\}$. 'Maximizing a PBF is usually NP-hard, such as the maximum cut problem (Boros and Hammer, 1991).

A pseudo-Boolean function is said to be supermodular iff

$$f(\mathbf{x}) + f(\mathbf{y}) \le f(\mathbf{x} \wedge \mathbf{y}) + f(\mathbf{x} \vee \mathbf{y})$$

where $\mathbf{x} \wedge \mathbf{y}$, $\mathbf{x} \vee \mathbf{y}$ are the element-wise AND and OR operator of the two vectors respectively. This is an important concept, because a supermodular pseudo-Boolean function (SPBF) can be maximized in $O(n^6)$ running time (Orlin, 2009). A necessary and sufficient condition for identifying a SPBF is that all of its second order derivatives are non-negative (Nemhauser et al., 1978), i.e., for all $i < j$,

$$\frac{\partial f}{\partial x_i \partial x_j} \geq 0$$

For example a quadratic PBF is supermodular if its coefficients of all quadratic terms are non-negative.

Though the general supermodular maximization algorithm can be used for any SPBF, the special features of some specific problems allow more efficient algorithms to be used. For example, it is well known that the supermodular quadratic pseudo-Boolean maximization problem can be solved in cubic time using min-cut (Billionnet and Minoux, 1985; Kolmogorov and Zabih, 2004).

In fact, a subset of SPBFs can be maximized using a min-cut algorithm. A pseudo-Boolean function $f(\mathbf{x})$ is called **graph representable** or graph expressible if there exists a graph $G = (V, E)$ with terminals s and t and a subset of vertices $V_0 = V - \{s, t\} = \{v_1, \ldots, v_n, u_1, \ldots, u_m\}$ such that, for any configuration $x_1, \ldots, x_n$, the value of the function $f(\mathbf{x})$ is equal to a constant plus the cost of the minimum s-t cut among all cuts, in which v_i is connected with s if $x_i = 0$ and connected with t if $x_i = 1$.

Our definition extends the work of Kolmogorov and Zabih (2004) that focused on quadratic and cubic functions. Vertices $u_1, \ldots u_m$ correspond to the extra binary variables that are introduced to reduce the graph representable PBFs to equivalent quadratic forms. For example, the positive-negative PBFs where all terms of degree 2 or more have positive coefficients are graph representable, and each non-linear term requires one extra binary variable to obtain the equivalent quadratic form (Rhys, 1970).

3 The Tree-Cut Decomposition for Generalized Higher Order CRFs

We decompose the decoding problem, i.e., maximization of Eq (3), into two parts, a tree labeling problem and a PBF maximization problem. We show that the PBF can be graph representable by reparameterizing the scoring function in Eq (3). Then we reduce these pseudo-Boolean functions to quadratic forms based on the recent work of Živný and Jeavons (2010), and finally solve the slave problem via graph cuts.

3.1 Fully Connected Pairwise CRFs

We first describe our idea for a simple case, the fully connected pairwise CRFs (Krähenbühl and Koltun, 2011), which are generalizations of linear-chain CRFs and skip-chain CRFs. Formally, the decoding problem in fully connected pairwise CRFs can be formulated as follows:

$$\begin{aligned} \max_{Y} \quad & \sum_{v}\sum_{s} \phi_{v[s]} Y_{v[s]} + \sum_{u,v} \sum_{st \in \mathcal{S}^2} \phi_{uv[st]} Y_{uv[st]} \\ \text{s.t.} \quad & Y \in \mathcal{Y} \end{aligned} \tag{5}$$

Note that for any edge (u, v), adding a constant ψ_{uv} to all of its related patterns will not change the optimal solution of the problem. In other words, the optimal Y for the following problem is irrelevant to ψ_{uv}

$$\begin{aligned} \max_{Y} \quad & \sum_{v}\sum_{s} \phi_{v[s]} Y_{v[s]} \\ & + \sum_{u,v} \sum_{st \in \mathcal{S}^2} (\psi_{uv} + \phi_{uv[st]}) Y_{uv[st]} \\ \text{s.t.} \quad & Y \in \mathcal{Y} \end{aligned}$$

The reparameterization keeps the optimality of the problem and plays an important role for graph representation, as we will show later.

By introducing a new variable $Z = Y$ for the quadratic terms and relaxing the constraint $Z = Y$ using Lagrangian relaxation, we get the relaxed problem

$$\begin{aligned} \min_{\lambda} \max_{Y,Z} \quad & \sum_{v}\sum_{s} \phi_{v[s]} Y_{v[s]} \\ & + \sum_{u,v} \sum_{st \in \mathcal{S}^2} (\psi_{uv} + \phi_{uv[st]}) Z_{uv[st]} \\ & + \sum_{v}\sum_{s} \lambda_{v[s]} \left(Z_{v[s]} - Y_{v[s]}\right) \\ \text{s.t.} \quad & Y \in \mathcal{Y} \\ & Z_{v[s]} \in \{0, 1\}, \quad \forall v, s \end{aligned}$$

We split the inner $\max_{Y,Z}$ into two subproblems, and a minimal λ is found using sub-gradient descent algorithms which repeatedly find a maximizing assignment for the subproblems individually.

Let

$$f_\lambda(Y) = \sum_{v,s} \phi_{v[s]} Y_{v[s]} - \sum_{v,s} \lambda_{v[s]} Y_{v[s]}$$

$$g_\lambda(Z) = \sum_{u,v} \sum_{st \in \mathcal{S}^2} (\psi_{uv} + \phi_{uv[st]}) Z_{uv[st]} + \sum_{v,s} \lambda_{v[s]} Z_{v[s]}$$

The two subproblems are

$$\max_Y \quad f_\lambda(Y) \qquad \text{s.t.} \quad Y \in \mathcal{Y}$$

and

$$\max_Z \quad g_\lambda(Z) \qquad Z_{v[s]} \in \{0,1\}, \quad \forall v, s$$

The first subproblem can be solved in linear time since all vertices are independent. The second problem is a binary quadratic programming problem. As discussed in Section 2.3, $g_\lambda(Z)$ can be solved using min-cut if the coefficients of the quadratic terms are non-negative, i.e.

$$\psi_{uv} + \phi_{uv[st]} \geq 0, \quad \forall u, v, s, t$$

Hence, we can set

$$\psi_{uv} = -\min_{st \in uv[\cdot]} \{\phi_{uv[st]}\}$$

to guarantee the non-negativity. This supermodular binary quadratic programming problem can be solved via the push-relabel algorithm (Goldberg, 2008) in $O(|\mathcal{S}|N)^3$ running time.

Though Z may not satisfy the constraint $Z \in \mathcal{Y}$ after sub-gradient descent based optimization, Y must satisfy $Y \in \mathcal{Y}$, hence we could use Y as the final solution if Z and Y disagree.

3.2 Generalized Higher Order CRFs

Now we consider the general case, maximizing Eq (3). Similar with the pairwise case, we use two slaves. One is a set of independent vertices, and the other is a pseudo-Boolean optimization problem. That is, we can redefine $g_\lambda(Z)$ as

$$g_\lambda(Z) = \sum_{\mathbf{c}} \sum_{\mathbf{s} \in \mathbf{c}[\cdot]} \left(\psi_{\mathbf{c}} + \phi_{\mathbf{c}[\mathbf{s}]}\right) Z_{\mathbf{c}[\mathbf{s}]} + \sum_{v,s} \lambda_{v[s]} Z_{v[s]}$$

A sufficient condition for $g_\lambda(Z)$ to be graph representable is that coefficients of all non-linear terms are non-negative (Freedman and Drineas, 2005). Hence, we can set

$$\psi_{\mathbf{c}} = -\min_{\mathbf{s} \in \mathbf{c}[\cdot]} \{\phi_{\mathbf{c}[\mathbf{s}]}\}$$

to guarantee the non-negativity.

In real applications, higher order patterns are sparse, i.e., $\left|\{\mathbf{s} \in \mathbf{c}[\cdot] \mid \phi_{\mathbf{c}[\mathbf{s}] \neq 0}\}\right| \ll |\mathcal{S}|^{|\mathbf{c}|}$ (Qian et al., 2009; Ye et al., 2009). Hence we could skip the patterns with zero weights ($\phi_{\mathbf{c}[\mathbf{s}]} = 0$) when calculating $\sum_{\mathbf{s} \in \mathbf{c}[\cdot]} \phi_{\mathbf{c}[\mathbf{s}]} Z_{\mathbf{c}[\mathbf{s}]}$ for fast inference. However, the reparameterization described above may introduce many non-zero terms which destroy the sparsity. For example, in the NER task, a binary feature is defined as true if a word subsequence matches a location name in a gazetteer. Suppose $\mathbf{c}$ =*Little York village* is such a word subsequence, then among $|\mathcal{S}|^3$ possible assignments of $\mathbf{c}$, only the one that labels $\mathbf{c}$ =*Little York village* as a location name has non-zero weight. However, the reparameterization may add $\psi_{\mathbf{c}}$ to the other $|\mathcal{S}|^3 - 1$ assignments, yielding many new patterns.

Therefore, we use another reparameterization strategy that exploits the sparsity for efficient decomposition. We only reparameterize the weights of edges, i.e., quadratic terms. Let

$$g_\lambda(Z) = \sum_{\substack{\mathbf{c} \\ |\mathbf{c}|=2}} \sum_{\mathbf{s} \in \mathbf{c}[\cdot]} \left(\psi_{\mathbf{c}} + \phi_{\mathbf{c}[\mathbf{s}]}\right) Z_{\mathbf{c}[\mathbf{s}]} + \sum_{\substack{\mathbf{c} \\ |\mathbf{c}|\geq 3}} \sum_{\mathbf{s} \in \mathbf{c}[\cdot]} \phi_{\mathbf{c}[\mathbf{s}]} Z_{\mathbf{c}[\mathbf{s}]} + \sum_{v,s} \lambda_{v[s]} Z_{v[s]}$$

The optimal solution is unchanged for any ψ.

In Appendix A, we show that by setting a sufficiently large ψ, $g_\lambda(Z)$ is graph representable. Such reparameterization method requires at most $N^2|\mathcal{S}|^2$ new patterns $\psi_{\mathbf{c},|\mathbf{c}|=2}$ to make $g_\lambda(Z)$ graph representable. It preserves the sparsity of higher order patterns, hence is more efficient than the naive approach.

3.3 Tree-Cut Decomposition

In some cases, the graph is built by adding sparse global patterns to local models like trees, resulting in nearly tree-structured CRFs. For example, Sutton and Mccallum (2006) used skip-chain CRFs for NER, where skip-edges connecting identical words were added to linear chain CRFs. Since the skip-edges are sparse, the resulting graphical models are nearly linear chains. To handle the edges in local models efficiently, we reformulate the decomposition. Let $\mathcal{T}$ be a spanning tree of the graph, if edge $(u,v)\in\mathcal{T}$, we put its related patterns into the first slave, otherwise we put its related patterns into the second slave.

For clarity, we formulate the tree-cut decomposition for generalized higher order CRFs. The first slave involves the patterns covered by the spanning tree $\mathcal{T}$, and its scoring function is

$$f_\lambda(Y)=\sum_v\sum_s \phi_{v[s]}Y_{v[s]}-\sum_{v,s}\lambda_{v[s]}Y_{v[s]}$$
$$+\sum_{\substack{\mathbf{c}\in\mathcal{T}\\|\mathbf{c}|=2}}\sum_{\mathbf{s}\in\mathbf{c}[\cdot]}\left(\psi_{\mathbf{c}}+\phi_{\mathbf{c}[\mathbf{s}]}+\sum_{\substack{\mathbf{c}'[\mathbf{s}']\supseteq\mathbf{c}[\mathbf{s}]\\|\mathbf{c}'|\geq 3,\phi_{\mathbf{c}'[\mathbf{s}']}<0}}\phi_{\mathbf{c}'[\mathbf{s}']}\right)Y_{\mathbf{c}[\mathbf{s}]}.$$

The second slave involves the rest patterns. To get its quadratic form, for each pattern $\mathbf{c}[\mathbf{s}], |\mathbf{c}|=3$, we introduce one extra binary variable $u_{\mathbf{c}[\mathbf{s}]}$, and for each pattern $\mathbf{c}[\mathbf{s}], |\mathbf{c}|\geq 4$, we introduce $|\mathbf{c}|-3$ extra binary variables $u^k_{\mathbf{c}[\mathbf{s}]}, k=0,\dots,|\mathbf{c}|-4$. Let $\mathbf{u}$ denote the vector of all the introduced extra binary variables. For each pattern $\mathbf{c}[\mathbf{s}]$, denote

$$\overline{Z_{\mathbf{c}[\mathbf{s}]}}=\sum_{v[s]\in\mathbf{c}[\mathbf{s}]}Z_{v[s]}.$$

The scoring function of the second slave is

$$h(Z,\mathbf{u})=h_1(Z)+h_2(Z,\mathbf{u})+h_3(Z,\mathbf{u})+h_4(Z,\mathbf{u})$$

where

$$h_1(Z)=\sum_{v,s}\lambda_{v[s]}Z_{v[s]}$$
$$+\sum_{\substack{\mathbf{c}\notin\mathcal{T}\\|\mathbf{c}|=2}}\sum_{\mathbf{s}\in\mathbf{c}[\cdot]}\left(\psi_{\mathbf{c}}+\phi_{\mathbf{c}[\mathbf{s}]}+\sum_{\substack{\mathbf{c}'[\mathbf{s}']\supseteq\mathbf{c}[\mathbf{s}]\\|\mathbf{c}'|\geq 3,\phi_{\mathbf{c}'[\mathbf{s}']}<0}}\phi_{\mathbf{c}'[\mathbf{s}']}\right)Z_{\mathbf{c}[\mathbf{s}]}$$

$$h_2(Z,\mathbf{u})=\sum_{\substack{\mathbf{c}\\|\mathbf{c}|\geq 3}}\sum_{\substack{\mathbf{s}\in\mathbf{c}[\cdot]\\\phi_{\mathbf{c}[\mathbf{s}]}\geq 0}}\phi_{\mathbf{c}[\mathbf{s}]}\left(\overline{Z_{\mathbf{c}[\mathbf{s}]}}-|\mathbf{c}|+1\right)u_{\mathbf{c}[\mathbf{s}]}$$

$$h_3(Z,\mathbf{u})=\sum_{\substack{\mathbf{c}\\|\mathbf{c}|=3}}\sum_{\substack{\mathbf{s}\in\mathbf{c}[\cdot]\\\phi_{\mathbf{c}[\mathbf{s}]}<0}}\left|\phi_{\mathbf{c}[\mathbf{s}]}\right|u_{\mathbf{c}[\mathbf{s}]}\left(\overline{Z_{\mathbf{c}[\mathbf{s}]}}-1\right)$$

$$h_4(Z,\mathbf{u})=\sum_{\substack{\mathbf{c}\\|\mathbf{c}|\geq 4}}\sum_{\substack{\mathbf{s}\in\mathbf{c}[\cdot]\\\phi_{\mathbf{c}[\mathbf{s}]}<0}}\left|\phi_{\mathbf{c}[\mathbf{s}]}\right|\left(u^0_{\mathbf{c}[\mathbf{s}]}(2\overline{Z_{\mathbf{c}[\mathbf{s}]}}-3)\right.$$
$$\left.+\sum_{j=1}^{|\mathbf{c}|-4}u^j_{\mathbf{c}[\mathbf{s}]}(\overline{Z_{\mathbf{c}[\mathbf{s}]}}-j-2)\right).$$

Term	*Number of Variables*
$h_1(Z)$	$N^2\|\mathcal{S}\|^2$
$h_2(Z,\mathbf{u})$	$\sum_{\substack{\mathbf{c}\\\|\mathbf{c}\|\geq 3}}\sum_{\substack{\mathbf{s}\in\mathbf{c}[\cdot]\\\phi_{\mathbf{c}[\mathbf{s}]}\geq 0}}(1+\|\mathbf{c}\|)$
$h_3(Z,\mathbf{u})$	$\sum_{\substack{\mathbf{c}\\\|\mathbf{c}\|=3}}\sum_{\substack{\mathbf{s}\in\mathbf{c}[\cdot]\\\phi_{\mathbf{c}[\mathbf{s}]}<0}}(1+\|\mathbf{c}\|)$
$h_4(Z,\mathbf{u})$	$\sum_{\substack{\mathbf{c}\\\|\mathbf{c}\|\geq 4}}\sum_{\substack{\mathbf{s}\in\mathbf{c}[\cdot]\\\phi_{\mathbf{c}[\mathbf{s}]}<0}}(2\|\mathbf{c}\|-3)$

Table 1: Number of variables in each part of $h(Z,\mathbf{u})$

h_1 involves the edges that are not in $\mathcal{T}$, h_2 involves positive terms of degree 3 or more. h_3 involves negative cubic terms, h_4 involves negative terms of degree 4 or more.

The relaxed problem for generalized higher order CRFs, i.e., Problem (2) is

$$\begin{aligned}\min_{\lambda}\max_{Y,Z,\mathbf{u}}\quad & f_\lambda(Y)+h(Z,\mathbf{u})\\ \text{s.t.}\quad & Y\in\mathcal{Y}\\ & Z,\mathbf{u}\text{ are binary}\end{aligned}\tag{6}$$

3.4 Complexity Analysis

In this section, we theoretically analyze the time complexity for each iteration in dual decomposition. Running time for $\max_{Y\in\mathcal{Y}}f_\lambda(Y)$ is linear in the size of the graph, i.e., $N\times|\mathcal{S}|^2$. Running time for $\max_{Z,\mathbf{u}}h(Z,\mathbf{u})$ is cubic in the number of variables, which is the sum of variables in function h_1 to h_4. $h_1(Z)$ has at most $N^2|\mathcal{S}|^2$ variables; each pattern in $h_2(Z,\mathbf{u})$ requires one extra variable, hence $h_2(Z,\mathbf{u})$ has $\sum_{\substack{\mathbf{c}\\|\mathbf{c}|\geq 3}}\sum_{\substack{\mathbf{s}\in\mathbf{c}[\cdot]\\\phi_{\mathbf{c}[\mathbf{s}]}\geq 0}}(1+|\mathbf{c}|)$ variables. Similarly, we could count the number of variables in h_3 and h_4, as shown in Table 1.

In summary, each pattern in $h(Z,\mathbf{u})$ requires at most $2|\mathbf{c}|-2$ variables, so $h(Z,\mathbf{u})$ has no more than $\sum_{\mathbf{c}}\sum_{\mathbf{s}\in\mathbf{c}[\cdot]}(2|\mathbf{c}|-2)$ variables.

Finally, the time complexity for each iteration in dual decomposition is

$$O\left(N|\mathcal{S}|^2+\left(\sum_{\mathbf{c}}\sum_{\mathbf{s}\in\mathbf{c}[\cdot]}(2|\mathbf{c}|-2)\right)^3\right)$$

which is cubic in the total length of patterns.

4 Experimental Results

4.1 Named Entity Recognition in Tweets

4.1.1 Data Sets

Our first experiment is named entity recognition in tweets. Recently, information extraction on Twitter or Facebook data is attracting much attention (Ritter et al., 2011). Different from traditional information extraction for news articles, messages posted on these social media websites are short and noisy, making the task more challenging. In this paper, we use generalized higher order CRFs for Twitter NER with discriminative training, and compare our 2-slave dual decomposition approach with spanning tree based dual decomposition approach and other decoding algorithms.

So far as we know, there are two publicly available data sets for Twitter NER. One is the Ritter's (Ritter et al., 2011), the other is from MSM2013 Concept Extraction Challenge (Basave et al., 2013)[1]. Note that in Ritter's work (Ritter et al., 2011), all of the data are used for evaluating named entity type classification, and not used during training. However, our approach requires discriminative training, which makes our method not comparable with their results. Therefore we choose the MSM2013 dataset in our experiment and compare our system with the MSM2013 official runs.

The MSM2013 corpus has 4 types of named entities, person (PER), location (LOC), organization (ORG), and miscellaneous (MISC). The name entities are about film/movie, entertainment award event, political event, programming language, sporting event and TV show. The data is separated into a training set containing 2815 tweets, and a test set containing 1526 tweets.

4.1.2 Local Features

We cast the NER task as a structured classification problem, and adopt BIESO labeling, where for each multi-word entity of class *C*, the first word is labeled as *B-C*, the words in the entity are labeled as *I-C*, and the last word is labeled as *E-C*, a single word entity of class *C* is labeled as *S-C*, and other words are labeled as *O*.

[1]http://oak.dcs.shef.ac.uk/msm2013/challenge.html

Our baseline NER is a linear chain CRF. As the MSM2013 competition allows to use extra resources, we use several additional datasets to generate rich features. Specifically, we trained two POS taggers and two NER taggers using extra datasets. All the 4 taggers are trained using linear chain CRFs with perceptron training. One POS tagger is trained on Brown and Wall Street Journal corpora in Penn Tree Bank 3, and the other is trained on ARK Twitter NLP corpus (Gimpel et al., 2011) with slight modification. One of the NER taggers is trained on CoNLL 2003 English dataset[2], and the other is trained on Ritter's dataset.

We used dictionaries in Ark Twitter NLP toolkit[3], Ritter's Twitter NLP toolkit[4] and Moby Words project[5] to generate dictionary features. We also collected film names and TV shows from IMDB website and musician groups from wikipedia. These dictionaries are used to detect candidate named entities in the training and testing datasets using string matching. Those matched words are assigned with BIESO style labels which are used as features.

We also used the unsupervised word cluster features provided by Ark Twitter NLP toolkit, which has significantly improved the Twitter POS tagging accuracy (Owoputi et al., 2013). Similar with previous work, we used prefixes of the cluster bit strings with lengths $\in \{2, 4, \ldots, 16\}$ as features.

4.1.3 Global Features

Previous studies showed that the document level consistency features (same phrases in a document tend to have the same entity class) are effective for NER (Kazama and Torisawa, 2007; Finkel et al., 2005). However, unlike news articles, tweets are not organized in documents. To use these document level consistency features, we grouped the tweets in MSM2013 dataset using single linkage clustering algorithm where similarity between two tweets is the number of their overlapped words. If the similarity is greater than 4, then we put the two tweets into one group. Unlike standard document clustering, we did not normalize the length of tweets since all the tweets are limited to 140 characters. Then we

[2]www.cnts.ua.ac.be/conll2003/

[3]https://code.google.com/p/ark-tweet-nlp/

[4]http://github.com/aritter/Twitter_nlp

[5]http://icon.shef.ac.uk/Moby/mwords.html

extracted the group level features as follows. For any two identical phrases $x_i \dots x_{i+k}$, $x_j \dots x_{j+k}$ in a group, a binary feature is true if they have the same label subsequences. The pattern set of this feature is $\mathbf{c} = \{i, \dots, i+k, j, \dots, j+k\}$ and $\mathbf{c}[\cdot] = \{\mathbf{s} | s_i = s_j, \dots, s_{i+k} = s_{j+k}\}$.

4.1.4 Results

We use two evaluation metrics. One is the micro averaged F score, which is used in CoNLL2003 shared task. The other is macro averaged F score, which is used in MSM2013 official evaluation (Basave et al., 2013).

We compare our approach with two baselines, integer linear programming (ILP)[6] and a naive dual decomposition method. In naive dual decomposition, we use three types of slaves: a linear chain captures unigrams and bigrams, and the spanning trees cover the skip edges linking identical words. Identical multi-word phrases yield larger factors with more than 4 vertices. They could not be handled efficiently by belief propagation for spanning trees. Therefore, we create multiple slaves, each of which covers a pair of identical multi-word phrases.

To reduce the number of slaves, we use a greedy algorithm to choose the spanning trees. Each time we select the spanning tree that covers the most uncovered edges. This can be done by performing the maximum spanning tree algorithm on the graph where each uncovered edge has unit weight. Let x^* denote the most frequent word in a tweet cluster, and F^* is its frequency, then at least $(F^*-1)/2$ spanning trees are required to cover the complete subgraph spanned by x^*.

For both dual decomposition systems, averaged perceptron (Collins, 2002a) with 10 iterations is used for parameter estimation. We follow the work of Rush et al. (2010) to choose the step size in the sub-gradient algorithm.

Table 2 shows the comparison results, including two F scores and total running time (seconds) for training and testing. Performances of the top 4 official runs are also listed. Different from our approach, the top performing systems mainly benefit from rich open resources, such as DBpedia Gazetteer, ANNIE Gazetteer, Yago, Microsoft N-grams, and external NER system combination, such as ANNIE, OpenNLP, LingPipe, OpenCalais (Basave et al., 2013). We can see that general CRFs with global features are competitive with these top systems. Our 2-slave DD outperforms naive DD and achieves competitive performance with exact inference based on ILP, while is much faster than ILP.

[6]we use Gurobi as the ILP solver, http://www.gurobi.com/

System	F_{macro}	F_{micro}	Sec.
Linear chain CRFs	0.657	0.815	98
General CRFs (2-slave DD)	**0.680**	**0.827**	214
General CRFs (naive DD)	0.672	0.824	490
General CRFs (ILP)	**0.680**	**0.828**	8640
Official 1st	0.670	N/A	N/A
Official 2nd	0.662	N/A	N/A
Official 3rd	0.658	N/A	N/A
Official 4th	0.610	N/A	N/A

Table 2: Comparison results on MSM2013 Twitter NER task.

To compare the convergence speed and optimality of 2-slave DD and naive DD algorithms, we use the model trained by ILP, and record the F_{micro} scores, averaged dual objectives per instance (the lower the tighter), decoding time, and fraction of optimality certificates across iterations of the two DD algorithms on test data. Figure 2 shows the performances of the two algorithms relative to decoding time. Our method requires 0.0064 seconds for each iteration on average, about four times slower than the naive DD. However, our approach achieves a tighter upper bound and larger fraction of optimality certificates.

4.2 Sentence Dependency Tagging

Our second experiment is sentence dependency tagging in Question Answering forums task studied in Qu and Liu's work (Qu and Liu, 2012). The goal is to extract the dependency relationships between sentences for automatic question answering. For example, from the posts below, we would need to know that sentence $S4$ is a comment about sentence $S1$ and $S2$, not an answer to $S3$.

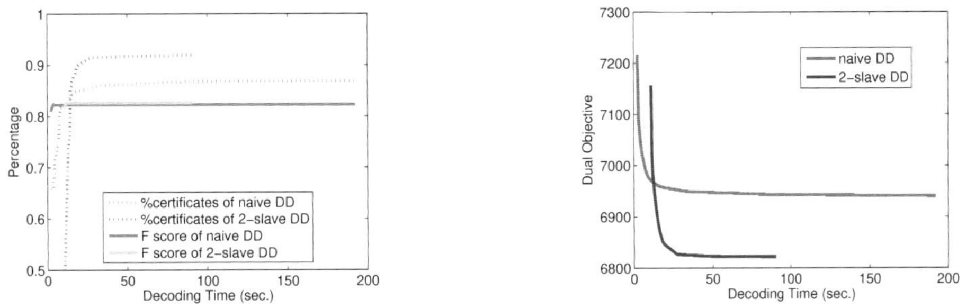

Figure 2: Twitter NER: The F_{micro} scores, dual objectives, and fraction of optimality certificates relative to decoding time.

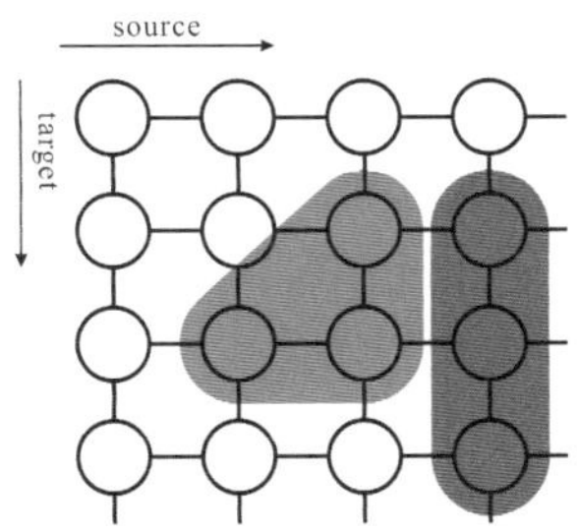

Figure 3: 3-wise CRF for QA sentence dependency tagging. Order-3 factors (e.g., red and blue) connects the 3 vertices in adjacent edge pairs.

System	F	Sec.
2D CRFs (naive)	0.564	9.2
2D CRFs (2-slave)	0.565	16.4
3-wise CRFs (naive)	0.572	18.7
3-wise CRFs (2-slave)	0.584	17.33
(Qu and Liu, 2012)	0.561	N/A

Table 3: Comparison results on QA sentence dependency tagging task.

A: [S1]I'm having trouble installing my DVB Card.
[S2]dmesg prints: ...
[S3]What could I do to resolve this problem?
B: [S4] I'm having similar problems with Ubuntu

For a pair of sentences, the depending sentence is called the source sentence, and the depended sentence the target sentence. One source sentence can potentially depend on many different target sentences, and one target sentence can also correspond to multiple sources. Qu and Liu (2012) casted the task as a binary classification problem, i.e., whether or not there exists a dependency relation between a pair of sentences. Formally, in this task, Y is a $N^2 \times 2$ matrix, where N is the number of sentences, $Y_{i*N+j[1]} = 1$ if the ith sentence depends on the jth sentence, otherwise, $Y_{i*N+j[0]} = 1$. We use the corpus in Qu and Liu's work (Qu and Liu, 2012), where dependencies between $3,483$ sentences in 200 threads were annotated. Following their settings we randomly split annotated threads into three disjoint sets, and run a three-fold cross validation. F score is used as the evaluation metric.

Qu and Liu (2012) used the pairwise CRF with a 4-connected neighborhood system (2D CRF) as their graphical model, where each vertex in the graph represents a sentence pair, and each edge connects adjacent source sentences or target sentences. The key observation is that given a source/target sentence, there is strong dependency between adjacent target/source sentences. In this paper, we extend their work by connecting the 3 vertices in adjacent edge pairs, resulting in 3-wise CRFs, as shown in Figure 3. We use the same vertex features and edge features as in Qu and Liu's work. For a 3-tuple of vertices, we use the following features: combination of the sentence types within the tuple, whether the related sentences are in one post or belong to the same author. Again, we use perceptron to train the model, and the max iteration number for dual decomposition is 200. The spanning tree in our decomposition is the concatenation of all the rows in the graph.

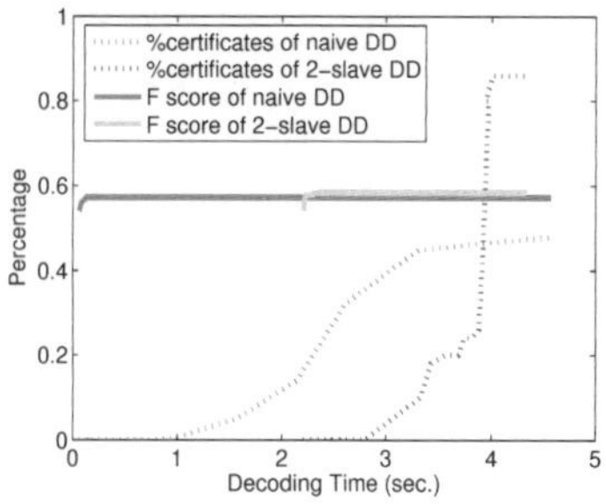

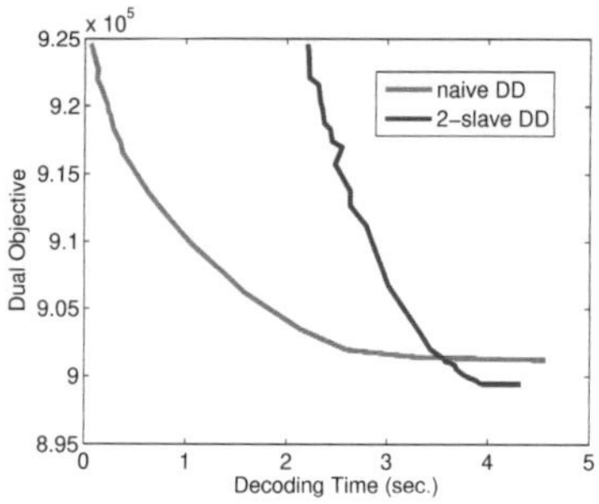

Figure 4: QA sentence dependency tagging using 3-wise CRFs: The F scores, dual objectives, and fraction of optimality certificates relative to decoding time.

Table 3 shows the experimental results. For 2D CRFs, the edges can be covered by 2 spanning trees (one covers all vertical edges and the other covers all horizontal edges), hence the naive dual decomposition has only two slaves. Compared with naive DD, our 2-slave DD achieved competitive performance while two times slower. This is because naive DD adopts dynamic programming that runs in linear time. However, for 3-wise CRFs, the naive dual decomposition requires many small slaves to cover the order-3 factors. Therefore our 2-slave method is more effective. The fraction of optimality certificates and dual objectives of 3-wise CRFs relative to decoding time during testing are shown in Figure 4. For each iteration, our method requires 0.0049 seconds and the naive DD requires 0.00054 seconds, about 10 times faster than ours, but our method converges to a lower lower bound.

5 Conclusion

We proposed a new decomposition approach for generalized higher order CRFs using only two slaves. Both permit polynomial decoding time. We evaluated our method on two different tasks: Twitter named entity recognition and forum sentence dependency detection. Experimental results show that though the compact decomposition requires more running time for each iteration, it achieves consistently tighter bounds and outperforms the naive dual decomposition. The two experiments demonstrate that our method works for general graphs, even if the graph can not be decomposed into a few spanning trees (for example, if the graph has large complete subgraphs or large factors).

Our code is available at https://github.com/qxred/higher-order-crf

Appendix A

We show that by setting a sufficiently large ψ, $g_\lambda(Z)$ in Section 3.2 is graph representable.

Let

$$g_\lambda(Z) = g_1(Z) + g_2(Z) + g_3(Z) + g_4(Z)$$

where

$$\begin{aligned} g_1(Z) &= \sum_{\substack{\mathbf{c} \\ |\mathbf{c}|=2}} \sum_{\mathbf{s}\in\mathbf{c}[\cdot]} \left(\psi_{\mathbf{c}} + \phi_{\mathbf{c}[\mathbf{s}]}\right) Z_{\mathbf{c}[\mathbf{s}]} + \sum_{v,s} \lambda_{v[s]} Z_{v[s]} \\ g_2(Z) &= \sum_{\substack{\mathbf{c} \\ |\mathbf{c}|\geq 3}} \sum_{\substack{\mathbf{s}\in\mathbf{c}[\cdot] \\ \phi_{\mathbf{c}[\mathbf{s}]}\geq 0}} \phi_{\mathbf{c}[\mathbf{s}]} Z_{\mathbf{c}[\mathbf{s}]} \\ g_3(Z) &= \sum_{\substack{\mathbf{c} \\ |\mathbf{c}|=3}} \sum_{\substack{\mathbf{s}\in\mathbf{c}[\cdot] \\ \phi_{\mathbf{c}[\mathbf{s}]}<0}} \phi_{\mathbf{c}[\mathbf{s}]} Z_{\mathbf{c}[\mathbf{s}]} \\ g_4(Z) &= \sum_{\substack{\mathbf{c} \\ |\mathbf{c}|\geq 4}} \sum_{\substack{\mathbf{s}\in\mathbf{c}[\cdot] \\ \phi_{\mathbf{c}[\mathbf{s}]}<0}} \phi_{\mathbf{c}[\mathbf{s}]} Z_{\mathbf{c}[\mathbf{s}]} \end{aligned}$$

For $g_2(Z)$, since coefficients of all terms are non-negative, we can use the fact

$$\prod_{\substack{i \\ a_i\in\{0,1\}}} a_i = \max_{b\in\{0,1\}} \left(\sum_i a_i - |\mathbf{a}| + 1\right) b \qquad (7)$$

to reduce $g_2(Z)$ into an equivalent quadratic form (Freedman and Drineas, 2005). That is, $\max_Z g_2(Z)$ is equivalent to

$$\max_{Z,\mathbf{u}} \sum_{\substack{\mathbf{c},|\mathbf{c}|\geq 3 \\ \phi_{\mathbf{c}[\mathbf{s}]}\geq 0}} \sum_{\mathbf{s}\in\mathbf{c}[\cdot]} \phi_{\mathbf{c}[\mathbf{s}]} \left(\sum_{v[s]\in\mathbf{c}[\mathbf{s}]} Z_{v[s]} - |\mathbf{c}| + 1\right) u_{\mathbf{c}[\mathbf{s}]}$$

which is graph representable because coefficients of all the quadratic terms are non-negative.

Coefficients of terms in $g_3(Z)$ and $g_4(Z)$ are negative, therefore $g_3(Z)$ and $g_4(Z)$ are not supermodular. To make them graph representable, we use the following fact

Proposition 1 *(Živný and Jeavons, 2010) The pseudo-Boolean function* $p(\mathbf{x}) = \sum_{1\le i<j\le K} x_i x_j - \prod_{i=1}^{K} x_i$ *is graph representable and can be reduced to the quadratic forms: if* $K = 3$*, then*

$$p(\mathbf{x}) = \max_{y\in\{0,1\}} (x_1 + x_2 + x_3 - 1)y \quad (8)$$

otherwise $K > 3$*,*

$$\begin{aligned} p(\mathbf{x}) &= \max_{y_0\in\{0,1\}} y_0(2\sum_{i=1}^{K} x_i - 3) \\ &+ \max_{\text{binary } \mathbf{y}} \sum_{j=1}^{K-4} y_j(\sum_{i=1}^{K} x_i - j - 2) \quad (9) \end{aligned}$$

According to Eq (8), for each cubic term in $g_3(Z)$, we have

$$\begin{aligned} &\phi_{\mathbf{c}[\mathbf{s}]} \prod_{v[s]\in\mathbf{c}[\mathbf{s}]} Z_{v[s]} \\ = &\left|\phi_{\mathbf{c}[\mathbf{s}]}\right| \left(\sum_{u[s],v[t]\in\mathbf{c}[\mathbf{s}]} Z_{u[s]}Z_{v[t]} - \prod_{v[s]\in\mathbf{c}[\mathbf{s}]} Z_{v[s]} \right) \\ &- \left|\phi_{\mathbf{c}[\mathbf{s}]}\right| \sum_{u[s],v[t]\in\mathbf{c}[\mathbf{s}]} Z_{u[s]}Z_{v[t]} \\ = &\left|\phi_{\mathbf{c}[\mathbf{s}]}\right| \max_{u_{\mathbf{c}[\mathbf{s}]}\in\{0,1\}} u_{\mathbf{c}[\mathbf{s}]} \left(\sum_{v[s]\in\mathbf{c}[\mathbf{s}]} Z_{v[s]} - 1 \right) \\ &- \left|\phi_{\mathbf{c}[\mathbf{s}]}\right| \sum_{u[s],v[t]\in\mathbf{c}[\mathbf{s}]} Z_{u[s]}Z_{v[t]} \end{aligned}$$

The first part on the right hand side is graph representable since all quadratic terms are non-negative. The second part is a quadratic function of Z, and it can be merged into $g_1(Z)$. With sufficiently large $\psi_{\mathbf{c}}$ in $g_1(Z)$, we could guarantee the non-negativity of all quadratic terms.

Similarly, we could apply Eq (9) to reduce $g_4(Z)$ to graph representable quadratic forms.

Acknowledgments

We thank three anonymous reviewers for their valuable comments. This work is partly supported by DARPA under Contract No. FA8750-13-2-0041. Any opinions expressed in this material are those of the authors and do not necessarily reflect the views of DARPA.

References

Amparo Elizabeth Cano Basave, Andrea Varga, Matthew Rowe, Milan Stankovic, and Aba-Sah Dadzie. 2013. Making sense of microposts (msm2013) concept extraction challenge (challenge report). In *Proceedings of the Concept Extraction Challenge at the Workshop on 'Making Sense of Microposts'*, pages 1–15.

A. Billionnet and M. Minoux. 1985. Maximizing a supermodular pseudoboolean function: A polynomial algorithm for supermodular cubic functions. *Discrete Applied Mathematics*, 12(1):1 – 11.

Endre Boros and PeterL. Hammer. 1991. The max-cut problem and quadratic 0-1 optimization; polyhedral aspects, relaxations and bounds. *Annals of Operations Research*, 33(3):151–180.

Endre Boros and Peter L. Hammer. 2002. Pseudo-boolean optimization. *Discrete Applied Mathematics*, 123(1C3):155 – 225.

Michael Collins. 2002a. Discriminative training methods for hidden markov models: Theory and experiments with perceptron algorithms. In *Proceedings of EMNLP*, pages 1–8.

Michael Collins. 2002b. Ranking algorithms for named entity extraction: Boosting and the votedperceptron. In *Proceedings of ACL*, pages 489–496, July.

Shilin Ding, Gao Cong, Chin-Yew Lin, and Xiaoyan Zhu. 2008. Using conditional random fields to extract contexts and answers of questions from online forums. In *Proceedings of ACL-08: HLT*, pages 710–718, June.

Jenny Rose Finkel, Trond Grenager, and Christopher Manning. 2005. Incorporating non-local information into information extraction systems by gibbs sampling. In *Proceedings of ACL*, pages 363–370, June.

Daniel Freedman and Petros Drineas. 2005. Energy minimization via graph cuts: Settling what is possible. In *Proceedings of CVPR*, pages 939–946. IEEE Computer Society.

Michel Galley. 2006. A skip-chain conditional random field for ranking meeting utterances by importance. In *Proceedings of EMNLP*, pages 364–372.

Kevin Gimpel, Nathan Schneider, Brendan O'Connor, Dipanjan Das, Daniel Mills, Jacob Eisenstein, Michael Heilman, Dani Yogatama, Jeffrey Flanigan, and Noah A. Smith. 2011. Part-of-speech tagging for twitter: annotation, features, and experiments. In *Proceedings of ACL-HLT*, HLT '11, pages 42–47.

AndrewV. Goldberg. 2008. The partial augmentcrelabel algorithm for the maximum flow problem. In Dan Halperin and Kurt Mehlhorn, editors, *Algorithms - ESA 2008*, volume 5193 of *Lecture Notes in Computer Science*, pages 466–477. Springer Berlin Heidelberg.

Vladimir Jojic, Stephen Gould, and Daphne Koller. 2010. Accelerated dual decomposition for map inference. In *Proceedings of ICML*, pages 503–510. Omnipress.

Jun'ichi Kazama and Kentaro Torisawa. 2007. A new perceptron algorithm for sequence labeling with non-local features. In *Proceedings of EMNLP-CoNLL*, pages 315–324, June.

Vladimir Kolmogorov and Ramin Zabih. 2004. What energy functions can be minimized via graph cuts? *IEEE Trans. Pattern Anal. Mach. Intell.*, 26(2):147–159.

Vladimir Kolmogorov. 2006. Convergent tree-reweighted message passing for energy minimization. *IEEE Trans. Pattern Anal. Mach. Intell.*, 28(10):1568–1583, October.

Nikos Komodakis. 2011. Efficient training for pairwise or higher order CRFs via dual decomposition. In *Proceedings of CVPR*, pages 1841–1848. IEEE Computer Society.

Terry Koo, Alexander M. Rush, Michael Collins, Tommi Jaakkola, and David Sontag. 2010. Dual decomposition for parsing with non-projective head automata. In *Proceedings of EMNLP*, pages 1288–1298, Cambridge, MA, October.

Philipp Krähenbühl and Vladlen Koltun. 2011. Efficient inference in fully connected crfs with gaussian edge potentials. In *Proceedings of NIPS*, pages 109–117.

John Lafferty, Andrew McCallum, and Fernando Pereira. 2001. Conditional random fields: Probabilistic models for segmenting and labeling sequence data. In *Proceedings of ICML*, pages 282–289.

Andre Martins, Mario Figueiredo, Pedro Aguiar, Noah Smith, and Eric Xing. 2011a. An augmented lagrangian approach to constrained map inference. In *Proceedings of ICML*, pages 169–176. ACM, June.

Andre Martins, Noah Smith, Mario Figueiredo, and Pedro Aguiar. 2011b. Dual decomposition with many overlapping components. In *Proceedings of the EMNLP*, pages 238–249, July.

G.L. Nemhauser, L.A. Wolsey, and M.L. Fisher. 1978. An analysis of approximations for maximizing submodular set functions-I. *Mathematical Programming*, 14(1):265–294.

James B. Orlin. 2009. A faster strongly polynomial time algorithm for submodular function minimization. *Math. Program.*, 118(2):237–251.

Olutobi Owoputi, Brendan O'Connor, Chris Dyer, Kevin Gimpel, Nathan Schneider, and Noah A. Smith. 2013. Improved part-of-speech tagging for online conversational text with word clusters. In *Proceedings of NAACL-HLT*, pages 380–390, June.

Xian Qian, Xiaoqian Jiang, Qi Zhang, Xuanjing Huang, and Lide Wu. 2009. Sparse higher order conditional random fields for improved sequence labeling. In *Proceedings of ICML*, volume 382, page 107. ACM.

Zhonghua Qu and Yang Liu. 2012. Sentence dependency tagging in online question answering forums. In *Proceedings of ACL*, pages 554–562, July.

J. M. W. Rhys. 1970. A selection problem of shared fixed costs and network flows. *Management Science*, 17(3):200–207.

Alan Ritter, Sam Clark, Mausam, and Oren Etzioni. 2011. Named entity recognition in tweets: An experimental study. In *Proceedings of EMNLP*, pages 1524–1534, July.

Alexander M. Rush and Michael Collins. 2012. A tutorial on dual decomposition and lagrangian relaxation for inference in natural language processing. *J. Artif. Int. Res.*, 45(1):305–362, September.

Alexander M Rush, David Sontag, Michael Collins, and Tommi Jaakkola. 2010. On dual decomposition and linear programming relaxations for natural language processing. In *Proceedings of EMNLP 2010*, pages 1–11, Cambridge, MA, October.

Sunita Sarawagi and William W. Cohen. 2004. Semi-markov conditional random fields for information extraction. In *Proceedings of NIPS*.

Charles Sutton and Andrew Mccallum, 2006. *Introduction to Conditional Random Fields for Relational Learning*. MIT Press.

Rustem Takhanov and Vladimir Kolmogorov. 2013. Inference algorithms for pattern-based CRFs on sequence data. In *Proceedings of ICML*, pages 145–153.

Stanislav Živný and Peter G. Jeavons. 2010. Classes of submodular constraints expressible by graph cuts. *Constraints*, 15(3):430–452, July.

Nan Ye, Wee Sun Lee, Hai Leong Chieu, and Dan Wu. 2009. Conditional random fields with high-order features for sequence labeling. In *Proceedings of NIPS*, pages 2196–2204.

TREETALK: Composition and Compression of Trees for Image Descriptions

Polina Kuznetsova[†] **Vicente Ordonez**[‡] **Tamara L. Berg**[‡] **Yejin Choi**[††]

† Stony Brook University
Stony Brook, NY
pkuznetsova
@cs.stonybrook.edu

‡ UNC Chapel Hill
Chapel Hill, NC
{vicente,tlberg}
@cs.unc.edu

††University of Washington
Seattle, WA
yejin@cs.washington.edu

Abstract

We present a new tree based approach to composing expressive image descriptions that makes use of naturally occuring web images with captions. We investigate two related tasks: image caption *generalization* and *generation*, where the former is an optional subtask of the latter. The high-level idea of our approach is to harvest expressive phrases (as tree fragments) from existing image descriptions, then to compose a new description by selectively combining the extracted (and optionally pruned) tree fragments. Key algorithmic components are *tree composition* and *compression*, both integrating tree structure with sequence structure. Our proposed system attains significantly better performance than previous approaches for both image caption *generalization* and *generation*. In addition, our work is the first to show the empirical benefit of automatically generalized captions for composing natural image descriptions.

1 Introduction

The web is increasingly visual, with hundreds of billions of user contributed photographs hosted online. A substantial portion of these images have some sort of accompanying text, ranging from keywords, to free text on web pages, to textual descriptions directly describing depicted image content (i.e. captions). We tap into the last kind of text, using naturally occuring pairs of images with natural language descriptions to compose *expressive* descriptions for query images via tree composition and compression.

Such automatic image captioning efforts could potentially be useful for many applications: from automatic organization of photo collections, to facilitating image search with complex natural language queries, to enhancing web accessibility for the visually impaired. On the intellectual side, by learning to describe the visual world from naturally existing web data, our study extends the domains of language grounding to the highly expressive language that people use in their everyday online activities.

There has been a recent spike in efforts to automatically describe visual content in natural language (Yang et al., 2011; Kulkarni et al., 2011; Li et al., 2011; Farhadi et al., 2010; Krishnamoorthy et al., 2013; Elliott and Keller, 2013; Yu and Siskind, 2013; Socher et al., 2014). This reflects the long standing understanding that encoding the complexities and subtleties of image content often requires more expressive language constructs than a set of tags. Now that visual recognition algorithms are beginning to produce reliable estimates of image content (Perronnin et al., 2012; Deng et al., 2012a; Deng et al., 2010; Krizhevsky et al., 2012), the time seems ripe to begin exploring higher level semantic tasks.

There have been two main complementary directions explored for automatic image captioning. The first focuses on describing exactly those items (e.g., objects, attributes) that are detected by vision recognition, which subsequently confines *what* should be described and *how* (Yao et al., 2010; Kulkarni et al., 2011; Kojima et al., 2002). Approaches in this direction could be ideal for various practical applications such as image description for the visually impaired. However, it is not clear whether the semantic expressiveness of these approaches can eventually scale up to the casual, but highly expressive language peo-

Transactions of the Association for Computational Linguistics, 2 (2014) 351–362. Action Editor: Hal Daume III.
Submitted 2/2014; Revised 5/2014; Published 10/2014.

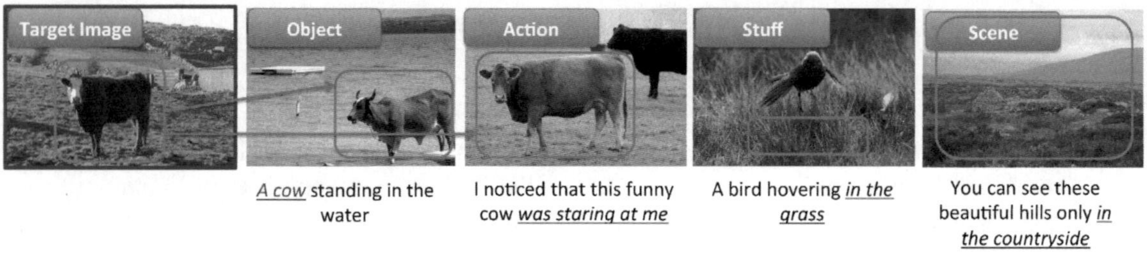

Figure 1: Harvesting phrases (as tree fragments) for the target image based on (partial) visual match.

ple naturally use in their online activities. In Figure 1, for example, it would be hard to compose *"I noticed that this funny cow was staring at me"* or *"You can see these beautiful hills only in the countryside"* in a purely bottom-up manner based on the exact content detected. The key technical bottleneck is that the range of describable content (i.e., objects, attributes, actions) is ultimately confined by the set of items that can be reliably recognized by state-of-the-art vision techniques.

The second direction, in a complementary avenue to the first, has explored ways to make use of the rich spectrum of visual descriptions contributed by online citizens (Kuznetsova et al., 2012; Feng and Lapata, 2013; Mason, 2013; Ordonez et al., 2011). In these approaches, *the set of what can be described* can be substantially larger than *the set of what can be recognized*, where the former is shaped and defined by the data, rather than by humans. This allows the resulting descriptions to be substantially more expressive, elaborate, and interesting than what would be possible in a purely bottom-up manner. Our work contributes to this second line of research.

One challenge in utilizing naturally existing multimodal data, however, is the noisy semantic alignment between images and text (Dodge et al., 2012; Berg et al., 2010). Therefore, we also investigate a related task of image caption *generalization* (Kuznetsova et al., 2013), which aims to improve the semantic image-text alignment by removing bits of text from existing captions that are less likely to be transferable to other images.

The high-level idea of our system is to harvest useful bits of text (as tree fragments) from existing image descriptions using detected visual content similarity, and then to compose a new description by selectively combining these extracted (and optionally pruned) tree fragments. This overall idea of *composition based on extracted phrases* is not new in itself (Kuznetsova et al., 2012), however, we make several technical and empirical contributions.

First, we propose a novel stochastic *tree composition* algorithm based on extracted tree fragments that integrates both tree structure and sequence cohesion into structural inference. Our algorithm permits a substantially higher level of linguistic expressiveness, flexibility, and creativity than those based on rules or templates (Kulkarni et al., 2011; Yang et al., 2011; Mitchell et al., 2012), while also addressing long-distance grammatical relations in a more principled way than those based on hand-coded constraints (Kuznetsova et al., 2012).

Second, we address image caption *generalization* as an optional subtask of image caption *generation*, and propose a *tree compression* algorithm that performs a light-weight parsing to search for the optimal set of tree branches to prune. Our work is the first to report empirical benefits of automatically compressed captions for image captioning.

The proposed approaches attain significantly better performance for both image caption *generalization* and *generation* tasks over competitive baselines and previous approaches. Our work results in an improved image caption corpus with automatic generalization, which is publicly available.[1]

2 Harvesting Tree Fragments

Given a query image, we retrieve images that are visually similar to the query image, then extract potentially useful segments (i.e., phrases) from their corresponding image descriptions. We then compose a new image description using these retrieved text fragments (§3). Extraction of useful phrases is guided by both visual similarity and the syntactic parse of the corresponding textual descrip-

[1]http://ilp-cky.appspot.com/

tion. This extraction strategy, originally proposed by Kuznetsova et al. (2012), attempts to make the best use of linguistic regularities with respect to objects, actions, and scenes, making it possible to obtain richer textual descriptions than what current state-of-the-art vision techniques can provide in isolation. In all of our experiments we use the captioned image corpus of Ordonez et al. (2011), first pre-processing the corpus for relevant content by running deformable part model object detectors (Felzenszwalb et al., 2010). For our study, we run detectors for 89 object classes set a high confidence threshold for detection.

As illustrated in Figure 1, for a query image detection, we extract four types of phrases (as tree fragments). First, we retrieve relevant noun phrases from images with visually similar object detections. We use color, texture (Leung and Malik, 1999), and shape (Dalal and Triggs, 2005; Lowe, 2004) based features encoded in a histogram of vector quantized responses to measure visual similarity. Second, we extract verb phrases for which the corresponding noun phrase takes the subject role. Third, from those images with *"stuff"* detections, e.g. *"water"*, or *"sky"* (typically mass nouns), we extract prepositional phrases based on similarity of both visual appearance and relative spatial relationships between detected objects and "stuff". Finally, we use global *"scene"* similarity[2] to extract prepositional phrases referring to the overall scene, e.g., *"at the conference,"* or *"in the market"*.

We perform this phrase retrieval process for each detected object in the query image and generate one sentence for each object. All sentences are then combined together to produce the final description. Optionally, we apply image caption generalization (via compression) (§4) to all captions in the corpus prior to the phrase extraction and composition.

3 Tree Composition

We model tree composition as constraint optimization. The input to our algorithm is the set of retrieved phrases (i.e., tree fragments), as illustrated in §2. Let $P = \{p_0, ..., p_{L-1}\}$ be the set of *all* phrases across the four phrase types (objects, actions, stuff and scene). We assume a mapping function $pt : [0, L) \rightarrow T$, where T is the set of phrase *types*, so that the phrase type of p_i is $pt(i)$. In addition, let R be the set of PCFG production rules and NT be the set of nonterminal symbols of the PCFG. The goal is to find and combine a good sequence of phrases G, $|G| \leq |T| = N = 4$, drawn from P, into a final sentence. More concretely, we want to select and order a subset of phrases (at most one phrase of each phrase type) while considering both the parse structure and n-gram cohesion across phrasal boundaries.

Figure 2 shows a simplified example of a composed sentence with its corresponding parse structure. For brevity, the figure shows only one phrase for each phrase type, but in actuality there would be a set of candidate phrases for each type. Figure 3 shows the CKY-style representation of the internal mechanics of constraint optimization for the example composition from Figure 2. Each cell ij of the CKY matrix corresponds to G_{ij}, a subsequence of G starting at position i and ending at position j. If a cell in the CKY matrix is labeled with a nonterminal symbol s, it means that the corresponding tree of G_{ij} has s as its root.

Although we visualize the operation using a CKY-style representation in Figure 3, note that composition requires more complex combinatorial decisions than CKY parsing due to two additional considerations. We are: (1) *selecting* a subset of candidate phrases, and (2) *re-ordering* the selected phrases (hence making the problem NP-hard). Therefore, we encode our problem using Integer Linear Programming (ILP) (Roth and tau Yih, 2004; Clarke and Lapata, 2008) and use the CPLEX (ILOG, Inc, 2006) solver.

3.1 ILP Variables

Variables for Sequence Structure: Variables α encode phrase selection and ordering:

$$\alpha_{ik} = 1 \quad \text{iff} \quad \text{phrase } i \in P \text{ is selected for position } k \in [0, N) \tag{1}$$

Where k is one of the N=4 positions in a sentence.[3] Additionally, we define variables for each pair of adjacent phrases to capture sequence cohesion:

[2] L2 distance between classification score vectors (Xiao et al., 2010)

[3] The number of positions is equal to the number of phrase types, since we select *at most* one from each type.

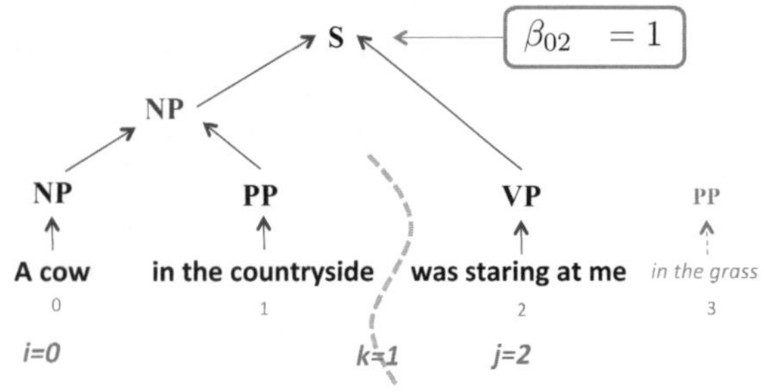

Figure 2: An example scenario of tree composition. Only the first three phrases are chosen for the composition.

$$\alpha_{ijk} = 1 \quad \text{iff} \quad \alpha_{ik} = \alpha_{j(k+1)} = 1 \tag{2}$$

Variables for Tree Structure: Variables β encode the parse structure:

$$\beta_{ijs} = 1 \quad \text{iff} \quad \text{the phrase sequence } G_{ij} \text{ maps to the nonterminal symbol } s \in NT \tag{3}$$

Where $i \in [0, N)$ and $j \in [i, N)$ index rows and columns of the CKY-style matrix in Figure 3. A corresponding example tree is shown in Figure 2, where the phrase sequence G_{02} corresponds to the cell labeled with S. We also define variables to indicate selected PCFG rules in the resulting parse:

$$\beta_{ijkr} = 1 \quad \text{iff} \quad \beta_{ijh} = \beta_{ikp} = \beta_{(k+1)jq} = 1, \tag{4}$$

Where $r = h \rightarrow pq \in R$ and $k \in [i, j)$. Index k points to the boundary of split between two children as shown in Figure 2 for the sequence G_{02}.

Auxiliary Variables: For notational convenience, we also include:

$$\gamma_{ijk} = 1 \quad \text{iff} \quad \sum_{s \in NT} \beta_{ijs} = \sum_{s \in NT} \beta_{iks} = \sum_{s \in NT} \beta_{(k+1)js} = 1 \tag{5}$$

3.2 ILP Objective Function

We model tree composition as maximization of the following objective function:

$$F = \sum_i F_i \times \sum_{k=0}^{N-1} \alpha_{ik} + \sum_{ij} F_{ij} \times \sum_{k=0}^{N-2} \alpha_{ijk} + \sum_{ij} \sum_{k=i}^{j-1} \sum_{r \in R} F_r \times \beta_{ijkr} \tag{6}$$

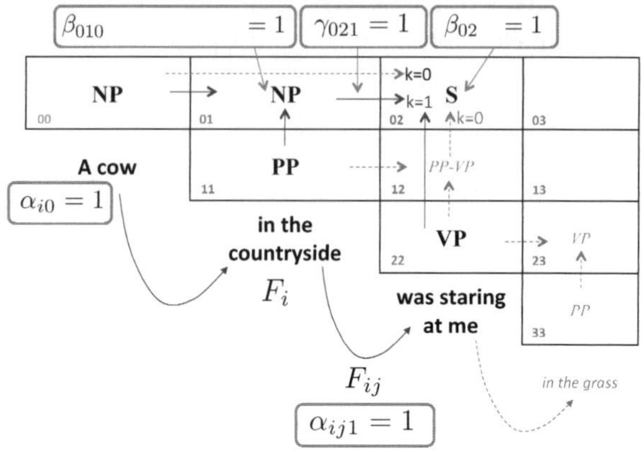

Figure 3: CKY-style representation of decision variables as defined in §3.1 for the tree example in Fig 2. Nonterminal symbols in boldface (in blue) and solid arrows (also in blue) represent the chosen PCFG rules to combine the selected set of phrases. Nonterminal symbols in smaller font (in red) and dotted arrows (also in red) represent possible other choices that are not selected.

This objective is comprised of three types of weights (confidence scores): F_i, F_{ij}, F_r.[4] F_i represents the phrase selection score based on visual similarity, described in §2. F_{ij} quantifies the sequence cohesion across phrase boundaries. For this, we use n-gram scores ($n \in [2, 5]$) between adjacent phrases computed using the Google Web 1-T corpus (Brants and Franz., 2006). Finally, F_r quantifies PCFG rule scores (log probabilities) estimated from the 1M image caption corpus (Ordonez et al., 2011) parsed using the Stanford parser (Klein and Manning, 2003).

One can view F_i as a *content selection* score, while F_{ij} and F_r correspond to *linguistic fluency* scores capturing sequence and tree structure respectively. If we set positive values for all of these weights, the optimization function would be biased toward verbose production, since selecting an additional phrase will increase the objective function. To control for verbosity, we set scores corresponding to linguistic fluency, i.e., F_{ij} and F_r using negative values (smaller absolute values for higher fluency), to balance dynamics between content selection and linguistic fluency.

3.3 ILP Constraints

Soundness Constraints: We need constraints to enforce consistency between different types of vari-

[4]All weights are normalized using z-score.

ables (Equations 2, 4, 5). Constraints for a product of two variables have been discussed by Clarke and Lapata (2008). For Equation 2, we add the following constraints (similar constraints are also added for Equations 4,5).

$$\forall_{ijk},\ \alpha_{ijk} \leq \alpha_{ik} \tag{7}$$
$$\alpha_{ijk} \leq \alpha_{j(k+1)}$$
$$\alpha_{ijk} + (1 - \alpha_{ik}) + (1 - \alpha_{j(k+1)}) \geq 1$$

Consistency between Tree Leafs and Sequences: The ordering of phrases implied by α_{ijk} must be consistent with the ordering of phrases implied by the β variables. This can be achieved by aligning the leaf cells (i.e., β_{kks}) in the CKY-style matrix with α variables as follows:

$$\forall_{ik}, \alpha_{ik} \leq \sum_{s \in NT^i} \beta_{kks} \tag{8}$$

$$\forall_k, \sum_i \alpha_{ik} = \sum_{s \in NT} \beta_{kks} \tag{9}$$

Where NT^i refers to the set of PCFG nonterminals that are compatible with a phrase type $pt(i)$ of p_i. For example, $NT^i = \{$NN,NP, ...$\}$ if p_i corresponds to an "object" (noun-phrase). Thus, Equation 8 enforces the correspondence between phrase types and nonterminal symbols at the tree leafs. Equation 9 enforces the constraint that the number of selected phrases and instantiated tree leafs must be the same.

Tree Congruence Constraints: To ensure that each CKY cell has at most one symbol we require

$$\forall_{ij}, \sum_{s \in NT} \beta_{ijs} \leq 1 \tag{10}$$

We also require that

$$\forall_{i,j>i,h}, \ \beta_{ijh} = \sum_{k=i}^{j-1} \sum_{r \in R_h} \beta_{ijkr} \tag{11}$$

Where $R_h = \{r \in R : r = h \rightarrow pq\}$. We enforce these constraints only for non-leafs. This constraint forbids instantiations where a nonterminal symbol h is selected for cell ij without selecting a corresponding PCFG rule.

We also ensure that we produce a valid tree structure. For instance, if we select 3 phrases as shown in Figure 3, we must have the root of the tree at the corresponding cell 02.

$$\forall_{k \in [1,N)}, \sum_{s \in NT} \beta_{kks} \leq \sum_{t=k}^{N-1} \sum_{s \in NT} \beta_{0ts} \tag{12}$$

We also require cells that are not selected for the resulting parse structure to be empty:

$$\forall ij \sum_k \gamma_{ijk} \leq 1 \tag{13}$$

Additionally, we penalize solutions without the S tag at the parse root as a soft-constraint.

Miscellaneous Constraints: Finally, we include several constraints to avoid degenerate solutions or to otherwise enhance the composed output. We: (1) enforce that a noun-phrase is selected (to ensure semantic relevance to the image content), (2) allow at most one phrase of each type, (3) do not allow multiple phrases with identical headwords (to avoid redundancy), (4) allow at most one scene phrase for all sentences in the description. We find that handling of sentence boundaries is important if the ILP formulation is based only on sequence structure, but with the integration of tree-based structure, we do not need to specifically handle sentence boundaries.

3.4 Discussion

An interesting aspect of description generation explored in this paper is using tree fragments as the building blocks of composition rather than individual words. There are three practical benefits: (1) *syntactic and semantic expressiveness*, (2) *correctness*, and (3) *computational efficiency*. Because we extract phrases from human written captions, we are able to use expressive language, and less likely to make syntactic or semantic errors. Our phrase extraction process can be viewed at a high level as visually-grounded or visually-situated paraphrasing. Also, because the unit of operation is tree fragments, the ILP formulation encoded in this work is computationally lightweight. If the unit of composition was words, the ILP instances would be significantly more computationally intensive, and more likely to suffer from grammatical and semantic errors.

4 Tree Compression

As noted by recent studies (Mason and Charniak, 2013; Kuznetsova et al., 2013; Jamieson et al., 2010), naturally existing image captions often include contextual information that does not directly describe visual content, which ultimately hinders their usefulness for describing other images. Therefore, to improve the fidelity of the generated descriptions, we explore image caption generalization as an

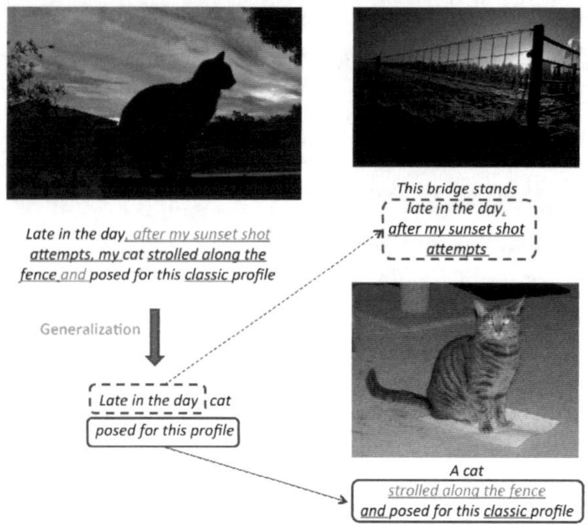

Figure 4: Compressed captions (on the left) are more applicable for describing new images (on the right).

optional pre-processing step. Figure 4 illustrates a concrete example of image caption generalization in the context of image caption generation.

We cast caption generalization as sentence compression. We encode the problem as tree pruning via lightweight CKY parsing, while also incorporating several other considerations such as leaf-level ngram cohesion scores and visually informed content selection. Figure 5 shows an example compression, and Figure 6 shows the corresponding CKY matrix.

At a high level, the compression operation resembles bottom-up CKY parsing, but in addition to parsing, we also consider deletion of parts of the trees. When deleting parts of the original tree, we might need to re-parse the remainder of the tree. Note that we consider re-parsing only with respect to the original parse tree produced by a state-of-the-art parser, hence it is only a *light-weight* parsing.[5]

4.1 Dynamic Programming

Input to the algorithm is a sentence, represented as a vector $\mathbf{x} = x_0 ... x_{n-1} = x[0 : n-1]$, and its PCFG parse $\pi(\mathbf{x})$ obtained from the Stanford parser. For simplicity of notation, we assume that both the parse tree and the word sequence are encoded in $\mathbf{x}$. Then, the compression can be formalized as:

$$\hat{\mathbf{y}} = \arg\max_{\mathbf{y}} \prod_i \phi_i(\mathbf{x}, \mathbf{y}) \tag{14}$$

Where each ϕ_i is a potential function, corresponding to a criteria of the desired compression:

$$\phi_i(\mathbf{x}, \mathbf{y}) = \exp(\theta_i \cdot f_i(\mathbf{x}, \mathbf{y})) \tag{15}$$

Where θ_i is the weight for a particular criteria (described in §4.2), whose scoring function is f_i.

We solve the decoding problem (Equation 14) using dynamic programming. For this, we need to solve the compression sub-problems for sequences $x[i : j]$, which can be viewed as branches $\hat{y}[i, j]$ of the final tree $\hat{y}[0 : n-1]$. For example, in Figure 5, the final solution is $\hat{y}[0 : 7]$, while a sub-solution of $x[4 : 7]$ corresponds to a tree branch PP. Notice that sub-solution $\hat{y}[3 : 7]$ represents the same branch as $\hat{y}[4 : 7]$ due to branch deletion. Some computed sub-solutions, e.g., $\hat{y}[1 : 4]$, get dropped from the final compressed tree.

We define a matrix of scores $D[i, j, h]$ (Equation 17), where h is one of the nonterminal symbols being considered for a cell indexed by i, j, i.e. a candidate for the root symbol of a branch $\hat{y}[i : j]$. When all values $D[i, j, h]$ are computed, we take

$$\hat{h} = \arg\max_{h} D[0, n-1, h] \tag{16}$$

and backtrack to reconstruct the final compression (the exact solution to equation 14).

$$D[i, j, h] = \max_{\substack{k \in [i, j) \\ r \in R_h}} \begin{cases} (1) & D[i, k, p] + D[k+1, j, q] \\ & \quad + \Delta\phi[r, ij] \\ (2) & D[i, k, p] + \Delta\phi[r, ij] \\ (3) & D[k+1, j, p] + \Delta\phi[r, ij] \end{cases} \tag{17}$$

Where $R_h = \{r \in R : r = h \to pq \vee r = h \to p\}$. Index k determines a split point for child branches of a subtree $\hat{y}[i : j]$. For example, in the Figure 5 the split point for children of the subtree $\hat{y}[0 : 7]$ is $k = 2$. The three cases ((1) – (3)) of the above equation correspond to the following tree pruning cases:

Pruning Case (1): None of the children of the current node is deleted. For example, in Figures 5 and 6, the PCFG rule $PP \to IN\ PP$, corresponding to the sequence *"in black and white"*, is retained. Another situation that can be encountered is tree re-parsing.

[5] Integrating full parsing into the original sentence would be a straightforward extension conceptually, but may not be an empirically better choice when parsing for compression is based on vanilla unlexicalized parsing.

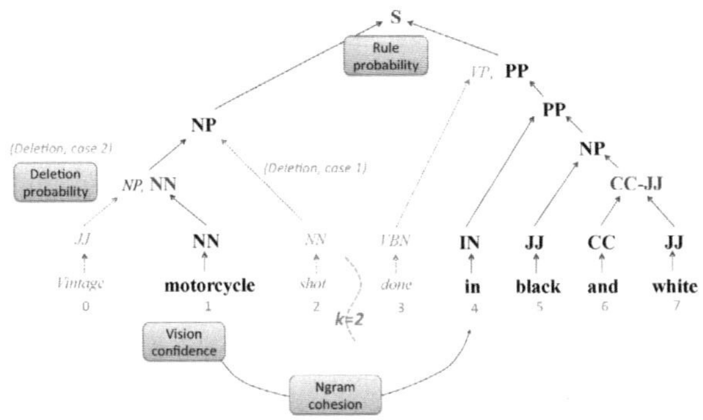

Figure 5: CKY compression. Both the chosen rules and phrases (blue bold font and blue solid arrows) and not chosen rules and phrases (red italic smaller font and red dashed lines) are shown.

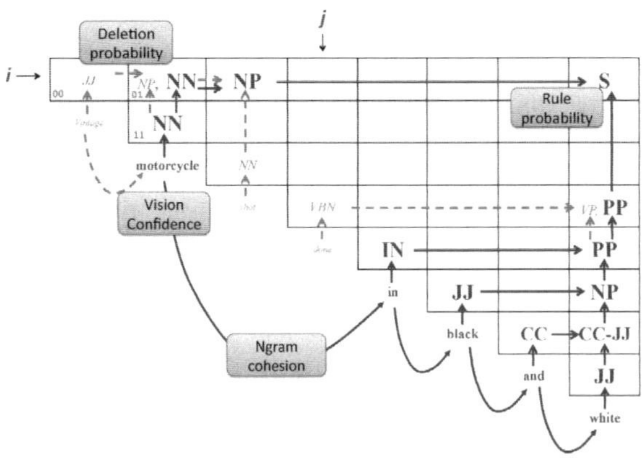

Figure 6: CKY compression. Both the chosen rules and phrases (blue bold font and blue solid arrows) and not chosen rules and phrases (red italic smaller font and red dashed lines) are shown.

Pruning Case (2)/(3): Deletion of the left/right child respectively. There are two types of deletion, as illustrated in Figures 5 and 6. The first corresponds to deletion of a child node. For example, the second child NN of rule $NP \rightarrow NP\, NN$ is deleted, which yields deletion of *"shot"*. The second type is a special case of propagating a node to a higher-level of the tree. In Figure 6, this situation occurs when deleting JJ "Vintage", which causes the propagation of NN from cell 11 to cell 01. For this purpose, we expand the set of rules R with additional special rules of the form $h \rightarrow h$, e.g., $NN \rightarrow NN$, which allows propagation of tree nodes to higher levels of the compressed tree.[6]

4.2 Modeling Compression Criteria

The $\Delta\phi$ term[7] in Equation 17 denotes the sum of log of potential functions for each criteria q:

$$\Delta\phi[r, ij] = \sum_q \theta \cdot \Delta f_q(r, ij) \tag{18}$$

Note that $\Delta\phi$ depends on the current rule r, along with the historical information before the current step ij, such as the original rule r_{ij}, and ngrams on the border between left and right child branches of rule r_{ij}. We use the following four criteria f_q in our model, which are demonstrated in Figures 5 and 6.

I. Tree Structure: We capture PCFG rule probabilities estimated from the corpus as $\Delta f_{pcfg} = \log P_{pcfg}(r)$.

II. Sequence Structure: We incorporate ngram cohesion scores only across the border between two branches of a subtree.

III. Branch Deletion Probabilities: We compute probabilities of deletion for children as:

$$\Delta f_{del} = \log P(r_t | r_{ij}) = \log \frac{count(r_t, r_{ij})}{count(r_{ij})} \tag{19}$$

Where $count(r_t, r_{ij})$ is the frequency in which r_{ij} is transformed to r_t by deletion of one of the children. We estimate this probability from a training corpus, described in §4.3. $count(r_{ij})$ is the count of r_{ij} in uncompressed sentences.

IV. Vision Detection (Content Selection): We want to keep words referring to actual objects in the image. Thus, we use $V(x_j)$, a visual similarity score, as our confidence of an object corresponding to word x_j. This similarity is obtained from the visual recognition predictions of (Deng et al., 2012b).

Note that some test instances include rules that we have not observed during training. We default to the original caption in those cases. The weights θ_i are set using a tuning dataset. We control over-compression by setting the weight for f_{del} to a small value relative to the other weights.

4.3 Human Compressed Captions

Although we model image caption generalization as sentence compression, in practical applications we may want the outputs of these two tasks to be different. For example, there may be differences in what should be deleted (named entities in newswire summaries could be important to keep, while they may

[6]We assign probabilities of these special propagation rules to 1 so that they will not affect the final parse tree score. Turner and Charniak (2005) handled propagation cases similarly.

[7]We use Δ to distinguish the potential value for the whole sentence from the gain of the potential during a single step of the algorithm.

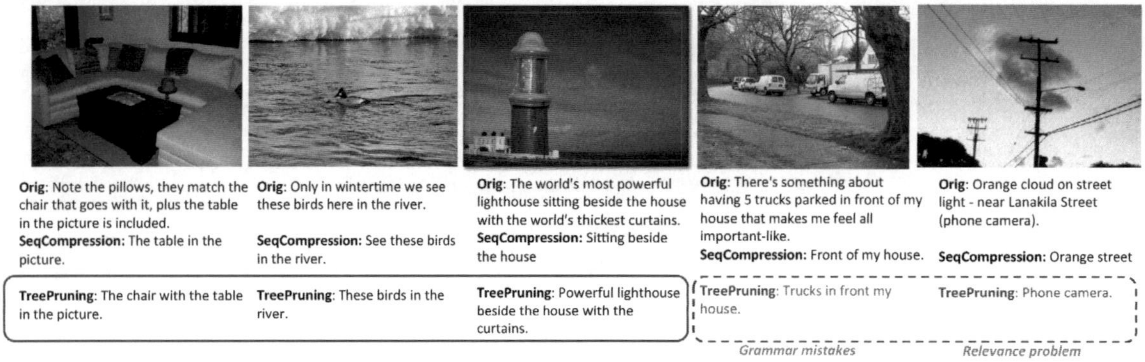

Figure 7: Caption generalization: good/bad examples.

be extraneous for image caption generalization). To learn the syntactic patterns for caption generalization, we collect a small set of example compressed captions (380 in total) using Amazon Mechanical Turk (AMT) (Snow et al., 2008). For each image, we asked 3 turkers to first list all visible objects in an image and then to write a compressed caption by removing not visually verifiable bits of text. We then align the original and compressed captions to measure rule deletion probabilities, excluding misalignments, similar to Knight and Marcu (2000). Note that we remove this dataset from the 1M caption corpus when we perform description generation.

5 Experiments

We use the 1M captioned image corpus of Ordonez et al. (2011). We reserve 1K images as a test set, and use the rest of the corpus for phrase extraction. We experiment with the following approaches:

Proposed Approaches:

- TREEPRUNING: Our tree compression approach as described in §4.
- SEQ+TREE: Our tree composition approach as described in §3.
- SEQ+TREE+PRUNING: SEQ+TREE using compressed captions of TREEPRUNING as building blocks.

Baselines for Composition:

- SEQ+LINGRULE: The most equivalent to the older sequence-driven system (Kuznetsova et al., 2012). Uses a few minor enhancements, such as sentence-boundary statistics, to improve grammaticality.
- SEQ: The §3 system without tree models and mentioned enhancements of SEQ+LINGRULE.

Method	Bleu w/ (w/o) penalty	Meteor P	Meteor R	Meteor M
SEQ+LINGRULE	0.152 (0.152)	0.13	0.17	0.095
SEQ	0.138 (0.138)	0.12	**0.18**	0.094
SEQ+TREE	0.149 (0.149)	0.13	0.14	0.082
SEQ+PRUNING	**0.177** (0.177)	0.15	0.16	**0.101**
SEQ+TREE+PRUNING	0.140 (**0.189**)	**0.16**	0.12	0.088

Table 1: Automatic Evaluation

- SEQ+PRUNING: SEQ using compressed captions of TREEPRUNING as building blocks.

We also experiment with the compression of human written captions, which are used to generate image descriptions for the new target images.

Baselines for Compression:

- SEQCOMPRESSION (Kuznetsova et al., 2013): Inference operates over the sequence structure. Although optimization is subject to constraints derived from dependency parse, parsing is not an explicit part of the inference structure. Example outputs are shown in Figure 7.

5.1 Automatic Evaluation

We perform automatic evaluation using two measures widely used in machine translation: BLEU (Papineni et al., 2002)[8] and METEOR (Denkowski and Lavie, 2011).[9] We remove all punctuation and convert captions to lower case. We use 1K test images from the captioned image corpus,[10] and assume the original captions as the gold standard captions to compare against. The results in Table 1

[8] We use the unigram NIST implementation: ftp://jaguar.ncsl.nist.gov/mt/resources/mteval-v13a-20091001.tar.gz

[9] With equal weight between precision and recall in Table 1.

[10] Except for those for which image URLs are broken, or CPLEX did not return a solution.

Method-1	Method-2	Criteria	Method-1 preferred over Method-2 (%)		
			all turkers	turkers w/ $\kappa > 0.55$	turkers w/ $\kappa > 0.6$
Image Description Generation					
SEQ+TREE	SEQ	Rel	72	72	72
SEQ+TREE	SEQ	Gmar	83	83	83
SEQ+TREE	SEQ	All	68	69	66
SEQ+TREE+PRUNING	SEQ+TREE	Rel	68	72	72
SEQ+TREE+PRUNING	SEQ+TREE	Gmar	41	38	41
SEQ+TREE+PRUNING	SEQ+TREE	All	63	64	66
SEQ+TREE	SEQ+LINGRULE	All	62	64	62
SEQ+TREE+PRUNING	SEQ+LINGRULE	All	67	75	77
SEQ+TREE+PRUNING	SEQ+PRUNING	All	73	75	75
SEQ+TREE+PRUNING	HUMAN	All	24	19	19
Image Caption Generalization					
TREEPRUNING	SEQCOMPRESSION*	Rel	65	65	66

Table 2: Human Evaluation: posed as a binary question *"which of the two options is better?"* with respect to *Relevance* (Rel), *Grammar* (Gmar), and *Overall* (All). According to Pearson's χ^2 test, all results are statistically significant.

show that both the integration of the tree structure (+TREE) and the generalization of captions using tree compression (+PRUNING) improve the BLEU score without brevity penalty significantly,[11] while improving METEOR only moderately (due to an improvement on precision with a decrease in recall.)

5.2 Human Evaluation

Neither BLEU nor METEOR directly measure grammatical correctness over long distances and may not correspond perfectly to human judgments. Therefore, we supplement automatic evaluation with human evaluation. For human evaluations, we present two options generated from two competing systems, and ask turkers to choose the one that is better with respect to: *relevance, grammar*, and *overall*. Results are shown in Table 2 with 3 turker ratings per image. We filter out turkers based on a control question. We then compute the selection rate (%) of preferring method-1 over method-2. The agreement among turkers is a frequent concern. Therefore, we vary the set of dependable users based on their Cohen's kappa score (κ) against other users. It turns out, filtering users based on κ does not make a big difference in determining the winning method.

As expected, tree-based systems significantly outperform sequence-based counterparts. For example,

[11]While 4-gram BLEU with brevity penalty is found to correlate better with human judges by recent studies (Elliott and Keller, 2014), we found that this is not the case for our task. This may be due to the differences in the gold standard captions. We use naturally existing ones, which include a wider range of content and style than crowd-sourced captions.

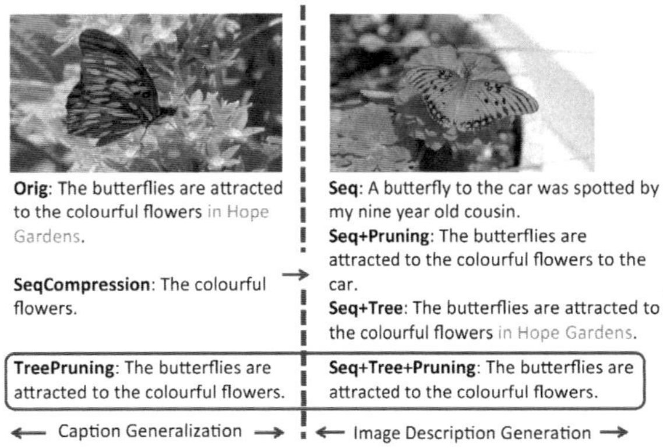

Figure 8: An example of a description preferred over human gold standard. Image description is improved due to caption generalization.

SEQ+TREE is strongly preferred over SEQ, with a selection rate of 83%. Somewhat surprisingly, improved grammaticality also seems to improve relevance scores (72%), possibly because it is harder to appreciate the semantic relevance of automatic captions when they are less comprehensible. Also as expected, compositions based on pruned tree fragments significantly improve relevance (68–72%), while slightly deteriorating grammar (38–41%).

Notably, the captions generated by our system are preferred over the original (owner generated) captions 19–24% of the time. One such example is included in Figure 8: *"The butterflies are attracted to the colorful flowers."*

Additional examples (good and bad) are provided in Figures 9 and 10. Many of these captions are highly expressive while remaining semantically

Figure 9: Description generation: good examples. Description preferred over human gold standard are highlighted.

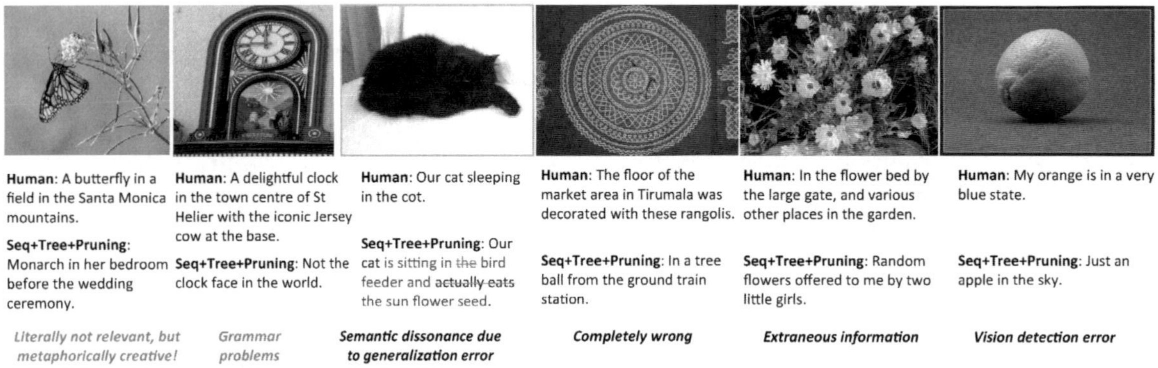

Figure 10: Description generation: bad examples.

plausible, thanks to the expressive, but somewhat predictable descriptions online users write about their photos. Even among the bad examples (Figure 10) one can find highly creative captions with not literal but metaphorical relevance: *"Monarch in her bedroom before the wedding ceremony"*.[12] The complete system captions and the original captions are available at `http://ilp-cky.appspot.com/`

6 Related Work

Sentence Fusion Sentence fusion has been studied mostly for multi-document summarization (Barzilay and McKeown, 2005), where redundancy across multiple sentences serves as a guideline for syntactic and semantic validity of generation. In contrast, we do not have the natural redundancy to rely upon in our task, therefore requiring the composition algorithm to be intrinsically better constrained for correct sentence structures.

[12]"Monarch" can be a type of butterfly.

Sentence Compression At the core of the image caption generalization task is sentence compression. Much work has considered deletion-only edits like ours (Knight and Marcu, 2000; Turner and Charniak, 2005; Cohn and Lapata, 2007; Filippova and Altun, 2013), while recent ones explore more complex edits, such as substitutions, insertions and reordering (Cohn and Lapata, 2008). The latter generally requires a larger training corpus. We leave more expressive compression as a future research work.

7 Conclusion

In this paper, we have presented a novel tree composition approach for generating expressive image descriptions. As an optional preprocessing step, we also presented a tree compression approach and reported the empirical benefit of using automatically compressed captions to improve image description generation. By integrating both the tree structure and the sequence structure, we have significantly improved the quality of composed image captions over several competitive baselines.

References

Regina Barzilay and Kathleen McKeown. 2005. Sentence fusion for multidocument news summarization. *Computational Linguistics*, 31(3):297–328.

Tamara L. Berg, Alexander C. Berg, and Jonathan Shih. 2010. Automatic attribute discovery and characterization from noisy web data. In *Proceedings of the 11th European Conference on Computer Vision: Part I*, ECCV'10, pages 663–676, Berlin, Heidelberg. Springer-Verlag.

Thorsten Brants and Alex Franz. 2006. Web 1t 5-gram version 1. In *Linguistic Data Consortium*.

James Clarke and Mirella Lapata. 2008. Global inference for sentence compression an integer linear programming approach. *Journal of Artificial Intelligence Research*, 31:399–429.

Trevor Cohn and Mirella Lapata. 2007. Large margin synchronous generation and its application to sentence compression. In *Proceedings of the 2007 Joint Conference on Empirical Methods in Natural Language Processing and Computational Natural Language Learning (EMNLP-CoNLL)*, pages 73–82, Prague, Czech Republic, June. Association for Computational Linguistics.

Trevor Cohn and Mirella Lapata. 2008. Sentence compression beyond word deletion. In *Proceedings of the 22nd International Conference on Computational Linguistics (Coling 2008)*, pages 137–144, Manchester, UK, August. Coling 2008 Organizing Committee.

Navneet Dalal and Bill Triggs. 2005. Histograms of oriented gradients for human detection. In *Proceedings of the 2005 IEEE Computer Society Conference on Computer Vision and Pattern Recognition (CVPR'05) - Volume 1 - Volume 01*, CVPR '05, pages 886–893, Washington, DC, USA. IEEE Computer Society.

Jia Deng, Alexander C. Berg, Kai Li, and Fei-Fei Li. 2010. What does classifying more than 10,000 image categories tell us? In *ECCV*.

Jia Deng, Alexander C. Berg, Sanjeev Satheesh, Hao Su, Aditya Khosla, and Fei-Fei Li. 2012a. Large scale visual recognition challenge. In *http://www.image-net.org/challenges/LSVRC/2012/index*.

Jia Deng, Jonathan Krause, Alexander C. Berg, and L. Fei-Fei. 2012b. Hedging your bets: Optimizing accuracy-specificity trade-offs in large scale visual recognition. In *Conference on Computer Vision and Pattern Recognition*.

Michael Denkowski and Alon Lavie. 2011. Meteor 1.3: Automatic Metric for Reliable Optimization and Evaluation of Machine Translation Systems. In *Proceedings of the EMNLP 2011 Workshop on Statistical Machine Translation*.

Jesse Dodge, Amit Goyal, Xufeng Han, Alyssa Mensch, Margaret Mitchell, Karl Stratos, Kota Yamaguchi, Yejin Choi, Hal Daume III, Alexander C. Berg, and Tamara L. Berg. 2012. Detecting visual text. In *Proceedings of the 2012 Conference of the North American Chapter of the Association for Computational Linguistics: Human Language Technologies*, pages 762–772, Montréal, Canada, June. Association for Computational Linguistics.

Desmond Elliott and Frank Keller. 2013. Image description using visual dependency representations. In *EMNLP*, pages 1292–1302.

Desmond Elliott and Frank Keller. 2014. Comparing automatic evaluation measures for image description. In *ACL (2)*, pages 452–457.

Ali Farhadi, Mohsen Hejrati, Mohammad Amin Sadeghi, Peter Young1, Cyrus Rashtchian, Julia Hockenmaier, and David Forsyth. 2010. Every picture tells a story: generating sentences for images. In *European Conference on Computer Vision*.

Pedro F. Felzenszwalb, Ross B. Girshick, David McAllester, and Deva Ramanan. 2010. Object detection with discriminatively trained part based models. *IEEE Transactions on Pattern Analysis and Machine Intelligence*, 32(9):1627–1645.

Yansong Feng and Mirella Lapata. 2013. Automatic caption generation for news images. *IEEE Transactions on Pattern Analysis and Machine Intelligence*, 35(4):797–812.

Katja Filippova and Yasemin Altun. 2013. Overcoming the lack of parallel data in sentence compression. In *EMNLP*, pages 1481–1491.

ILOG, Inc. 2006. ILOG CPLEX: High-performance software for mathematical programming and optimization. See `http://www.ilog.com/products/cplex/`.

Michael Jamieson, Afsaneh Fazly, Suzanne Stevenson, Sven J. Dickinson, and Sven Wachsmuth. 2010. Using language to learn structured appearance models for image annotation. *IEEE Trans. Pattern Anal. Mach. Intell.*, 32(1):148–164.

Dan Klein and Christopher D. Manning. 2003. Accurate unlexicalized parsing. In *Proceedings of the 41st Annual Meeting on Association for Computational Linguistics*, pages 423–430. Association for Computational Linguistics.

Kevin Knight and Daniel Marcu. 2000. Statistics-based summarization - step one: Sentence compression. In *AAAI/IAAI*, pages 703–710.

Atsuhiro Kojima, Takeshi Tamura, and Kunio Fukunaga. 2002. Natural language description of human activities from video images based on concept hierarchy of actions. *IJCV*, 50.

Niveda Krishnamoorthy, Girish Malkarnenkar, Raymond J. Mooney, Kate Saenko, and Sergio Guadarrama. 2013. Generating natural-language video descriptions using text-mined knowledge. In *AAAI*.

Alex Krizhevsky, Ilya Sutskever, and Geoffrey Hinton. 2012. Imagenet classification with deep convolutional neural networks. In *NIPS*.

Girish Kulkarni, Visruth Premraj, Sagnik Dhar, Siming Li, Yejin Choi, Alexander C. Berg, and Tamara L. Berg. 2011. BabyTalk: Understanding and generating simple image descriptions. In *Conference on Computer Vision and Pattern Recognition*.

Polina Kuznetsova, Vicente Ordonez, Alexander C. Berg, Tamara L. Berg, and Yejin Choi. 2012. Collective generation of natural image descriptions. In *Proceedings of the 50th Annual Meeting of the Association for Computational Linguistics (Volume 1: Long Papers)*, pages 359–368, Jeju Island, Korea, July. Association for Computational Linguistics.

Polina Kuznetsova, Vicente Ordonez, Alexander C. Berg, Tamara L. Berg, and Yejin Choi. 2013. Generalizing image captions for image-text parallel corpus. In *The 51st Annual Meeting of the Association for Computational Linguistics - Short Papers*, Sofia, Bulgaria, August. Association for Computational Linguistics.

Thomas K. Leung and Jitendra Malik. 1999. Recognizing surfaces using three-dimensional textons. In *ICCV*, pages 1010–1017.

Siming Li, Girish Kulkarni, Tamara L. Berg, Alexander C. Berg, and Yejin Choi. 2011. Composing simple image descriptions using web-scale n-grams. In *Proceedings of the Fifteenth Conference on Computational Natural Language Learning*, pages 220–228, Portland, Oregon, USA, June. Association for Computational Linguistics.

David G. Lowe. 2004. Distinctive image features from scale-invariant keypoints. *Int. J. Comput. Vision*, 60:91–110, November.

Rebecca Mason and Eugene Charniak. 2013. Annotation of online shopping images without labeled training examples. In *Proceedings of Workshop on Vision and Language*, Atlanta, Georgia, June. Association for Computational Linguistics.

Rebecca Mason. 2013. Domain-independent captioning of domain-specific images. In *Proceedings of the 2013 NAACL HLT Student Research Workshop*, pages 69–76, Atlanta, Georgia, June. Association for Computational Linguistics.

Margaret Mitchell, Jesse Dodge, Amit Goyal, Kota Yamaguchi, Karl Stratos, Xufeng Han, Alyssa Mensch, Alexander C. Berg, Tamara L. Berg, and Hal Daumé III. 2012. Midge: Generating image descriptions from computer vision detections. In *EACL*, pages 747–756.

Vicente Ordonez, Girish Kulkarni, and Tamara L. Berg. 2011. Im2text: Describing images using 1 million captioned photographs. In *Neural Information Processing Systems (NIPS)*.

Kishore Papineni, Salim Roukos, Todd Ward, and Wei jing Zhu. 2002. Bleu: a method for automatic evaluation of machine translation. In *ACL*.

Florent Perronnin, Zeynep Akata, Zaid Harchaoui, and Cordelia Schmid. 2012. Towards good practice in large-scale learning for image classification. In *CVPR*.

Dan Roth and Wen tau Yih. 2004. A linear programming formulation for global inference in natural language tasks. In *Proc. of the Annual Conference on Computational Natural Language Learning (CoNLL)*.

Rion Snow, Brendan O'Connor, Daniel Jurafsky, and Andrew Y. Ng. 2008. Cheap and fast—but is it good?: Evaluating non-expert annotations for natural language tasks. In *Proceedings of the Conference on Empirical Methods in Natural Language Processing*, EMNLP '08, pages 254–263, Stroudsburg, PA, USA. Association for Computational Linguistics.

Richard Socher, Andrej Karpathy, Quoc V. Le, Christopher D. Manning, and Andrew Y. Ng. 2014. Grounded compositional semantics for finding and describing images with sentences. In *Transactions of the Association for Computational Linguistics*, pages 207 – 218, April.

Jenine Turner and Eugene Charniak. 2005. Supervised and unsupervised learning for sentence compression. In *Proceedings of the 43rd Annual Meeting of the Association for Computational Linguistics (ACL'05)*, pages 290–297, Ann Arbor, Michigan, June. Association for Computational Linguistics.

Jianxiong Xiao, James Hays, Krista A. Ehinger, Aude Oliva, and Antonio Torralba. 2010. Sun database: Large-scale scene recognition from abbey to zoo. In *CVPR*.

Yezhou Yang, Ching Teo, Hal Daume III, and Yiannis Aloimonos. 2011. Corpus-guided sentence generation of natural images. In *Proceedings of the 2011 Conference on Empirical Methods in Natural Language Processing*, pages 444–454, Edinburgh, Scotland, UK., July. Association for Computational Linguistics.

Benjamin Z. Yao, Xiong Yang, Liang Lin, Mun Wai Lee, and Song-Chun Zhu. 2010. I2T: Image parsing to text description. *Proc. IEEE*, 98(8).

Haonan Yu and Jeffrey Mark Siskind. 2013. Grounded language learning from video described with sentences. In *Proceedings of the 51st Annual Meeting of the Association for Computational Linguistics (Volume 1: Long Papers)*, pages 53–63, Sofia, Bulgaria, August. Association for Computational Linguistics.

Unsupervised Discovery of Biographical Structure from Text

David Bamman
School of Computer Science
Carnegie Mellon University
Pittsburgh, PA 15213, USA
dbamman@cs.cmu.edu

Noah A. Smith
School of Computer Science
Carnegie Mellon University
Pittsburgh, PA 15213, USA
nasmith@cs.cmu.edu

Abstract

We present a method for discovering abstract event classes in biographies, based on a probabilistic latent-variable model. Taking as input timestamped text, we exploit latent correlations among events to learn a set of event classes (such as BORN, GRADUATES HIGH SCHOOL, and BECOMES CITIZEN), along with the typical times in a person's life when those events occur. In a quantitative evaluation at the task of predicting a person's age for a given event, we find that our generative model outperforms a strong linear regression baseline, along with simpler variants of the model that ablate some features. The abstract event classes that we learn allow us to perform a large-scale analysis of 242,970 Wikipedia biographies. Though it is known that women are greatly underrepresented on Wikipedia—not only as editors (Wikipedia, 2011) but also as subjects of articles (Reagle and Rhue, 2011)—we find that there is a bias in their *characterization* as well, with biographies of women containing significantly more emphasis on events of marriage and divorce than biographies of men.

1 Introduction

The written text that we interact with on an everyday basis—news articles, emails, social media, books—contains a vast amount of information centered on people: news (including common NLP corpora such as the *New York Times* and the *Wall Street Journal*) details the roles of actors in current events, social media (including Twitter and Facebook) documents the actions and attitudes of friends, and books chronicle the stories of fictional characters and real people alike. This focus on people gives us an abundance of information on how the lives of those portrayed unfold; for corpora that include historically deep biographical information (such as Wikipedia, book-length biographies and autobiographies, and even newspaper obituaries) this data includes the actors involved in particular historical events and the times and places in which they occur. The life events described in these texts have natural structure: event classes exhibit correlations with each other (e.g., those who DIVORCE must have been MARRIED), can occur at roughly similar times in the lives of different individuals (MARRIAGE is more likely to occur earlier in one's life than later), and can be bound to historical moments as well (FIGHTS IN WORLD WAR II peaks in the early 1940s).

Social scientists have long been interested in the structure of these events in investigating the role that individual agency and larger social forces play in shaping the course of an individual's life. Life stages marking "transitions to adulthood" (such as LEAVING SCHOOL, ENTERING THE WORKFORCE and MARRIAGE) have important correlates with demographic variables (Modell et al., 1976; Hogan and Astone, 1986; Shanahan, 2000); and researchers study the interactional effects that life events have on each other, such as the relationship between divorce and pre-marital cohabitation (Lillard et al., 1995; Reinhold, 2010) or having children (Lillard and Waite, 1993).

The data on which these studies draw, however, has largely been restricted to categorical surveys and observational data; we present here a latent-variable model that exploits the correlations of event descriptions in text to learn the structure of abstract events, grounded in time, from text alone. While our

Transactions of the Association for Computational Linguistics, 2 (2014) 363–376. Action Editor: Jian Su.
Submitted 6/2014; Published 10/2014.

model can be estimated on any set of texts where the birth dates of a set of mentioned entities are known, we illustrate our method on a large-scale dataset of 242,970 biographies extracted from Wikipedia.

This paper makes two contributions: first, we present a general unsupervised model for learning life event classes from biographical text, along with the structure that binds them; second, in using this method to learn event classes from Wikipedia, we uncover evidence of systematic bias in the presentation of male and female biographies (with biographies of women containing significantly disproportionate emphasis on the personal events of marriage and divorce). In addition to these contributions, we also present a range of other analyses that uncovering life events in text can make possible. Data and code to support this work can be found at `http://www.ark.cs.cmu.edu/bio/`.

2 Data

The data for this analysis originates in the January 2, 2014 dump of English-language Wikipedia.[1] We extract biographies by identifying all articles with `persondata` metadata[2] in which the `DATE OF BIRTH` field is known. This results in a set of 927,403 biographies.

For each biography, we perform part-of-speech tagging using the Stanford POS tagger (Toutanova et al., 2003) and named entity recognition using the Stanford named entity recognizer (Finkel et al., 2005), cluster all mentions of co-referring proper names (Davis et al., 2003; Elson et al., 2010) and resolve pronominal co-reference (Bamman et al., 2014), aided by gender inference for each entity as the gender corresponding to the maximum number of gendered pronouns (i.e., *he* and *she*) mentioned in the article, as also used by Reagle and Rhue (2011). In a random test set of 500 articles, this method of gender inference is overwhelmingly accurate, achieving 100% precision with 97.6% recall (12 articles had no pronominal mentions and so gender is not assigned).

As further preprocessing, we identify multiword expressions in all texts as maximal sequences of adjective + noun part of speech tags (yielding, for example, *New York*, *United States*, *early life* and *high school*), as first described in Justeson and Katz (1995). For each biographical article, we then extract all sentences in which the subject of the article is mentioned along with a single date and retain only the terms in each sentence that are among the most frequent 10,000 unigrams and multiword expressions in all documents, excluding stopwords such as *the* and all numbers (including dates). An "event" is the bag of these unigrams and multiword expressions extracted from one such sentence, along with a corresponding timestamp measured as the difference between the observed date in the sentence and the date of birth of the entity.

Table 1 illustrates the actual form of the data with a sample of extracted sentences from the biography of Frank Lloyd Wright, along with the data as input to the model. In the terminology of the model described below, each sentence constitutes one "event" in the subject's life.

For the final dataset we retain all biographies where the subject of the article is born after the year 1800 and for which there exist at least 5 events (242,970 people). The complete data consists of 2,313,867 events across these 242,970 people.

3 Model

The quantities of interest that we want to learn from the data are: 1.) a broad set of major life events recorded in Wikipedia biographies that people experience at similar stages in their lives (such as BEING BORN, GRADUATING HIGH SCHOOL, SERVING IN THE ARMY, GETTING MARRIED, and so on); 2.) correlations among those life events (e.g., knowing that if an individual WINS A NOBEL PRIZE that they're more likely to RECEIVE AN HONORARY DOCTORATE); and 3.) an attribution of those classes of events to particular moments in a specific individual's life (e.g., John Nash RECEIVED AN HONORARY DOCTORATE in 1999).

We cast this problem as an unsupervised learning one; given no labeled instances, can we infer these quantities from text alone? One possible alternative approach would be to leverage the categorical

[1] `http://dumps.wikimedia.org/enwiki/20140102/enwiki-20140102-pages-articles.xml.bz2`

[2] "`Persondata` is a special set of metadata that can and should be added to biographical articles only" (`http://en.wikipedia.org/wiki/Wikipedia:Persondata`).

Original sentence	Data as input to model	
	Terms (w)	Time (t)
He was admitted to the University of Wisconsin–Madison as a special student in 1886.	admitted university wisconsin madison special student	19
Wright first traveled to Japan in 1905, where he bought hundreds of prints.	wright first traveled japan bought hundreds prints	38
After Wright's return to the United States in October 1910, Wright persuaded his mother to buy land for him in Spring Green, Wisconsin.	wright return united_states wright persuaded mother buy land spring green wisconsin	43
This philosophy was best exemplified by his design for Fallingwater (1935), which has been called "the best all-time work of American architecture".	philosophy best design called best all-time work american architecture	68
Already well known during his lifetime, Wright was recognized in 1991 by the American Institute of Architects as " the greatest American architect of all time."	already well known lifetime wright recognized american institute architects greatest american architect time	124

Table 1: A sample of 5 of the 64 sentences (original and converted) that constitute the data for Frank Lloyd Wright (born 1867). Each event is defined as one such temporally-scoped sentence.

information contained in Wikipedia biographies (or its derivatives, such as Freebase; Google, 2014) as a form of supervision (e.g., George Washington is a member of the categories *Presidents of the United States* and *American cartographers*, among others). These manual categories, however, are often sporadically annotated and have a long tail (with most categories appearing very few times); in learning event structure directly from text, we avoid relying on categories' accuracy and being constrained by a fixed ontology. One advantage of an unsupervised approach is that we eliminate the need to define a pre-determined set of event classes *a priori*, allowing application across a variety of different domains and time periods, such as full-text books from the Internet Archive or Hathi Trust, or historical works like the *Oxford Dictionary of National Biography* (Matthew and Harrison, 2004).

Figure 1a illustrates the graphical form of our hierarchical Bayesian model, which articulates the relationship between an entity's set of *events* (where each event is an observation defined as the bag of terms in text and the difference between the year it was recorded as happening and the birth year), an abstract set of *event classes*, correlations among those abstract classes, and the distribution of vocabulary terms that defines each one. To capture correlations among different classes, we place a logistic normal prior on each biography's distribution over event classes (Blei and Lafferty, 2006a; Blei and Lafferty, 2007; Mimno et al., 2008); unlike a Dirichlet, a logistic normal is able to capture arbitrary correlations between elements through the structure of the covariance matrix of its underlying multivariate normal. We take a Bayesian approach to estimating the mean μ_η and covariance Σ_η, drawing them from a conjugate Normal-Inverse Wishart prior.

The generative story for the model runs as follows: let K be the number of latent event classes, P be the number of biographies, and E_p be the number of events in biography p.

- Draw event class means and covariances $\mu_\eta \in \mathbb{R}^K, \Sigma_\eta \in \mathbb{R}^{K \times K} \sim$ Normal-Inverse Wishart$(\mu_0, \lambda, \Psi, \nu)$
- For each event class $i \in \{1, \ldots, K\}$:
  - Draw event-term distribution $\phi_k \sim$ Dir(γ)
- For each biography p:
  - Draw $\eta_p \sim \mathcal{N}(\mu_\eta, \Sigma_\eta)$
  - Convert η_p into biography-event proportions β_p through the softmax function: $\beta_{p,i} = \frac{\exp(\eta_{p,i})}{\sum_{k=1}^{K} \exp(\eta_{p,k})}$
  - For each event e in biography p:
    - Draw event class index $z \sim$ Mult(β_p)
    - Draw timestamp $t \sim \mathcal{N}(\mu_z, \sigma_z^2)$
    - For each token in event e:
      - Draw term $w \sim$ Mult(ϕ_z)

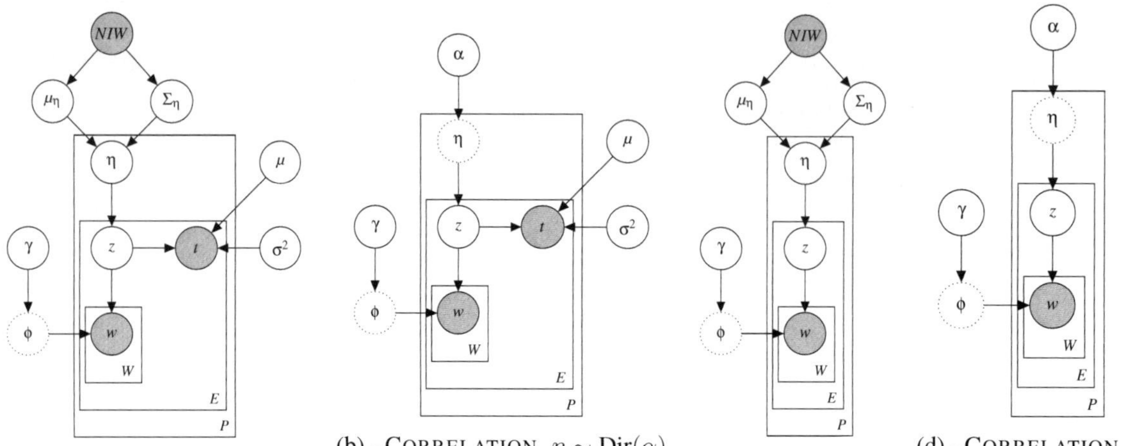

(a) FULL. (b) –CORRELATION. $\eta \sim \text{Dir}(\alpha)$ (c) –TIME (d) –CORRELATION, –TIME. $\eta \sim \text{Dir}(\alpha)$

Figure 1: Graphical form of the full model (described in §3) and models with ablations (described in §4).

Inference proceeds via stochastic EM: after initializing all variables to random values, we alternate between collapsed Gibbs sampling for the latent class indicators followed by maximization steps over all other parameters:

1. Sample all z using collapsed Gibbs sampling conditioned on current values for η and all other z.
2. For each biography p, maximize likelihood with respect to η_p via gradient ascent given the current samples of z and priors μ_η and Σ_η.
3. Assign MAP estimates of μ_η and Σ_η given current values of η and the Normal-Inverse Wishart prior. Update μ and σ^2 according to its maximum likelihood estimate given z.

We describe the technical details of each step below.

Sampling z. Given fixed biography-event class proportions η, observed tokens w, timestamp t, and current samples z^- for all other events, the probability of a given event belonging to event class k is as follows:

$$
\begin{aligned}
P(z = k \mid z^-, w, t, \eta, \gamma, \mu, \sigma^2) &\propto \exp(\eta_k) \\
&\times \sigma_k^{-1} \exp\left(-\frac{(t-\mu_k)^2}{2\sigma_k^2}\right) \\
&\times \frac{\prod_{v=1}^{V} \prod_{i=1}^{\mathbf{e}(v)} (\gamma + \mathbf{c}^-(k,v) + i - 1)}{\prod_{n=1}^{N_e} (V\gamma + \mathbf{c}^-(k,\star) + n - 1)}
\end{aligned}
\quad (1)
$$

Here $\mathbf{c}^-(k,v)$ is the count of the number of times vocabulary term v shows up in all events whose current sample $z = k$ (excepting the current one being sampled), $\mathbf{c}^-(k,\star)$ is the total count of all terms in all events whose current $z = k$ (again excepting the current one), N_e is the number of terms in event e, and $\mathbf{e}(v)$ is the count of vocabulary term v in the current event. (Note the complexity of the last term is due to drawing multiple observations from a single collapsed multinomial; Carpenter, 2010.)

Maximizing η. Under our model, the terms in the likelihood function that involve η include the likelihood of the samples drawn from it and its own probability given the multivariate Normal prior:

$$L(\eta) \propto \prod_{n=1}^{N} \frac{\exp(\eta_{z_n})}{\sum_{k=1}^{K} \exp(\eta_k)} \times \mathcal{N}(\eta \mid \mu_\eta, \Sigma_\eta) \quad (2)$$

The log likelihood is proportional to:

$$
\begin{aligned}
\ell(\eta) \propto & \sum_{n=1}^{N} \eta_{z_n} - \sum_{n=1}^{N} \sum_{k=1}^{K} \exp(\eta_k) \\
& - \frac{1}{2} (\eta - \mu_\eta)^\top \Sigma_\eta^{-1} (\eta - \mu_\eta)
\end{aligned}
\quad (3)
$$

Given samples of the latent event class z for all events in biography p, we maximize the value of η_p using gradient ascent. We can think of this as maximizing the likelihood of the observations z subject to ℓ_2 (Gaussian) regularization, where the covariance matrix in the regularizer encourages correlations in η: if a document contains many examples of $z = k$ and z_k is highly correlated with z_j, then the optimal η is encouraged to contain high weights at both η_k and η_j rather than simply η_k alone.

Maximizing $\mu_\eta, \Sigma_\eta, \mu, \sigma^2$. Given values for η, we then find maximum *a posteriori* estimates of μ_η and Σ_η conditioned on the Normal-Inverse Wishart (NIW) prior. The NIW is a conjugate prior to a multivariate Gaussian, parameterized by dimensionality K, initial mean μ_0, positive-definite scale matrix Ψ, and scalars $\nu > K - 1$ and $\lambda > 0$. The prior parameters Ψ and ν have an intuitive interpretation as the scatter matrix $\sum_{i=1}^{\nu} (x_i - \bar{x})(x_i - \bar{x})^\top$ for ν pseudo-observations.

The expected value of the covariance matrix drawn from a NIW distribution parameterized by Ψ and ν is $\frac{\Psi}{\nu - K - 1}$. To disprefer correlations among topics in the absence of strong evidence, we fix $\mu_0 = 0$ and set Ψ so that this prior expectation over Σ_η is the product of a scalar value ρ and the identity matrix $\mathbf{I}$: $\Psi = (\nu - K - 1)\rho\mathbf{I}$; ρ defines the expected variance, and the higher the value of ν, the more strongly the prior dominates the posterior estimate of the covariance matrix (i.e., the more the covariance matrix is shrunk toward $\rho\mathbf{I}$). λ likewise has an intuitive understanding as a dampening parameter: the higher its value, the more the posterior estimate of the mean $\hat{\mu}$ shrinks toward 0. For n data points, we set $\lambda = n/10$, $\nu = K + 2$, and $\rho = 1$.

Since the NIW is conjugate with the multivariate normal, posterior updates to μ_η and Σ_η have closed-form expressions given values of η (here, $\bar{\eta}$ denotes the mean value of η over all biographies).

$$\hat{\mu}_\eta = \frac{n}{\lambda + n}\bar{\eta} \tag{4}$$

$$\hat{\Sigma}_\eta = \frac{\Psi + \sum_{i=1}^{N} (\eta_i - \bar{\eta})(\eta_i - \bar{\eta})^\top + \frac{\lambda n}{\lambda + n}\bar{\eta}\bar{\eta}^\top}{\nu + n + K + 1} \tag{5}$$

Since we have no meaningful prior information on the values of μ and σ^2, we calculate their maximum likelihood estimate given current samples $\mathbf{z}$.

4 Evaluation

While the goal of this work is to learn qualitative categories of life events from text, we can quantitatively evaluate the performance of our model on the empirical task of predicting the age in a person's life when an event occurs.

For this task, we compare the full model described above with a strong baseline of ℓ_2-regularized linear regression and also with comparable models with feature ablations, in order to quantify the extent to which various aspects of the full model are contributing to its empirical performance. The comparable ablated models include the following:

- –CORRELATION, figure 1b. Rather than a logistic normal prior on the entity-specific distribution over event types (η), we draw η from a symmetric Dirichlet distribution parameterized by a global α. In a Dirichlet distribution, arbitrary correlations cannot be captured.
- –TIME, figure 1c. In the full model, the timestamps of the observed events influence the event classes we learn by encouraging them to be internally coherent and time-sensitive. To test this design choice, we ablate time as a feature during inference.
- –CORRELATION,–TIME, figure 1d. We also test a model that ablates both the correlation structure in the prior and the influence of time; this model corresponds to smoothed, unsupervised naïve Bayes.

As during inference, we define an event to be the set of terms, excluding stopwords and numbers, that are present in the vocabulary of the 10,000 most frequent words and multiword expressions in the data overall. Each event is accompanied by the year of its occurrence, from which we calculate the gold target prediction (the age of the person at the time of the event) as the year minus the entity's year of birth. For all of the four models described above (the full model and three ablations), we train the model on 4/5 of the biographies (194,376 entities, on average 1,851,094 events); we split the remaining 1/5 of the biographies into development data (where t is observed) and test data (where t is predicted). The details of inference for each model are as follows:

1. FULL. Inference as above for a burn-in period of 100 iterations, using slice sampling (Neal, 2003) to optimize the value of the Dirichlet hyperparameter γ every 10 iterations; after inference, the parameters $\mu_\eta, \Sigma_\eta, \mu, \sigma^2$ and ϕ are es-

timated from samples drawn at the final iteration and held fixed. For test entities, we infer the MAP value of η using development data, and predict the age of each test event as the mean time marginalizing over the event type indicator z. $\hat{t} = \mathbb{E}_z[\mu_z]$.

2. –CORRELATION. Here we perform collapsed Gibbs sampling for 100 iterations, using slice sampling to optimize the value of α and γ every 10 iterations; after inference, the parameters μ, σ^2 and ϕ are estimated from single final samples and held fixed. For development and test data, we run Gibbs sampling on event indicators z for 10 iterations and predict the age of each test event as the mean time marginalizing over the event type indicator z. $\hat{t} = \mathbb{E}_z[\mu_z]$.
3. –TIME. Inference as above for 100 iterations, using slice sampling to optimize the value of γ every 10 iterations; after inference, the parameters μ_η, Σ_η and ϕ are estimated from single final samples and held fixed. Since time is not known to this model during inference, we create post hoc estimates of $\hat{\mu}_z$ as the empirical mean age of events sampled to event class z using single samples for each event in the training data from the final sampling iteration. For test entities, we infer the MAP value of η using development data, and predict the age of each test event as the average empirical age marginalizing over the event type indicator z. $\hat{t} = \mathbb{E}_z[\hat{\mu}_z]$.
4. –CORRELATION,–TIME. We perform inference as above for the –CORRELATION model, and time prediction as in the –TIME model. $\hat{t} = \mathbb{E}_z[\hat{\mu}_z]$.

To compare against a potentially more powerful discriminative model, we also evaluate linear regression with ℓ_2 (ridge) regularization, using binary indicators of the same unigrams and multiword expressions available to the models above.

5. LINEAR REGRESSION. Train on training and development data, optimizing the regularization coefficient λ in three-fold cross-validation.

During training, linear regression learns that the terms most indicative of events that take place later in life are *stamp, descendant, commemorated, died, plaque, grandson*, and *lifetime achievement award*, while those that denote early events are *born, baptised, apprenticed*, and *acting debut*.

We evaluate all models on identical splits using 5-fold cross validation. For an interpretable error score, we use mean absolute error, which corresponds to the number of years, on average, by which each model is incorrect.

$$\text{MAE} = \frac{1}{N}\sum_{i=1}^{N}\left|\hat{t} - t_i\right| \qquad (6)$$

Figure 2 presents the results of this evaluation for all models and different choices of the number of latent event classes $K \in \{10, 25, 50, 100, 250, 500\}$. Linear regression represents a powerful model, achieving a mean absolute error of 11.87 years across all folds, but is eclipsed by the latent variable model at $K \geq 50$. The correlations captured by the logistic normal prior make a clear difference, uniformly yielding improvements over otherwise equivalent Dirichlet models across all K. As expected, models trained without knowledge of time during inference perform less well than models that contain that information.

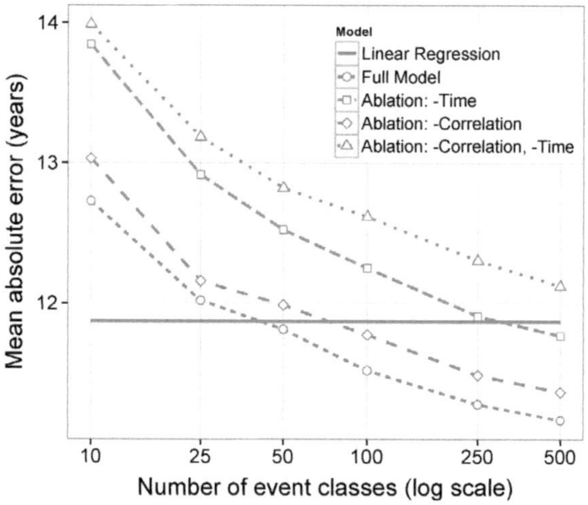

Figure 2: Mean average error (in years) for time prediction.

5 Analysis

To analyze the latent event classes in Wikipedia biographies, we train our full model (with a logistic normal prior and time as an observable variable) on the full dataset of 242,970 biographies with

Age μ	Age σ	% Fem.	Most probable terms in class
18.00	0.67	15.6%	high school, graduated, attended, graduating, school, born, early life, class, grew
21.89	1.83	0.2%	drafted, nfl draft, round, professional career, draft, overall, selected
22.27	1.19	17.6%	graduated, bachelor, degree, university, received, college, attended, earned, b. a.
22.67	4.33	3.6%	joined, enlisted, army, served, world war ii, united states army, years, corps
25.81	3.47	11.1%	law, university, graduated, received, school, law school, degree, law degree
32.32	8.19	12.0%	thesis, received, university, phd, dissertation, doctorate, degree, ph. d., completed
38.24	15.29	17.0%	citizen, became, citizenship, united states, american, u. s., british, granted, since
39.33	12.53	39.4%	divorce, marriage, divorced, married, filed, wife, separated, years, ended, later
42.57	13.78	16.3%	university, teaching, professor, college, taught, faculty, school, department, joined
43.79	15.54	13.8%	trial, murder, case, court, charges, guilty, jury, judge, death, convicted
45.89	18.71	13.3%	died, accident, killed, death, near, crash, car, involved, car accident, injured
46.22	16.30	11.2%	prison, released, years, sentence, sentenced, months, parole, federal, serving
49.81	10.28	7.0%	governor, candidate, unsuccessful candidate, congress, ran, reelection
51.41	11.23	1.2%	bishop, appointed, archbishop, diocese, pope, consecrated, named, cathedral
54.91	12.04	7.9%	chairman, board, president, ceo, became, company, directors, appointed, position
59.06	14.17	16.9%	awarded, university, received, honorary doctorate, honorary degree, degree, doctor
62.81	24.16	11.1%	fame, inducted, hall, sports hall, elected, national, football hall, international
72.52	13.69	12.4%	died, hospital, age, death, complications, cancer, home, heart attack, washington
92.39	46.06	13.0%	national, historic, park, state, house, named, memorial, home, honor, museum
95.29	42.65	12.1%	statue, unveiled, memorial, plaque, anniversary, erected, monument, death, bronze

Table 2: Salient event classes learned from 242,970 Wikipedia biographies. All 500 event classes can be viewed at `http://www.ark.cs.cmu.edu/bio`.

$K = 500$ event classes; as above, we run inference for a burn-in period of 100 iterations and collect 50 samples from the posterior distributions for z (the event class indicator for each event).

Table 2 illustrates a sample of 20 event classes along with the mean time μ and standard deviation σ, the gender distribution (calculated from the posterior distribution over z for all entities whose gender is known[3]) and the most probable terms in the class.

The latent classes that we learn span a mix of major life events of Wikipedia notable figures (including events that we might characterize as GRADUATING HIGH SCHOOL, BECOMING A CITIZEN, DIVORCE, BEING CONVICTED OF A CRIME, and DYING) and more fine-grained events (such as BEING DRAFTED BY A SPORTS TEAM and BEING INDUCTED INTO THE HALL OF FAME).

Emerging immediately from this summary is an imbalance in the gender distribution for many of these event classes. Among the 242,858 biographies whose gender is known, 14.8% are of women; we would therefore expect around 14.8% of the participants in most event classes to be female. Figures 3 and 4 illustrate five of the most highly skewed classes in both directions, ranked according to the z score of a two-tailed binomial proportion test ($H_0 = 14.8$).

While some of these classes reflect a biased world in which more men are drafted into sports teams, serve in the armed forces, and are ordained as priests, one latent class that calls out for explanation is that surrounding DIVORCE (*divorce, marriage, divorced, filed, married, wife, separated, years, ended, later*), whose female proportion of 39.4% is nearly triple that of the data overall (and whose z-score reveals it to be strongly statistically different [$p \ll 0.0001$] from the H_0 mean, even accounting for the Bonferroni correction we must make when considering the $K = 500$ tests we implicitly perform when ranking). While we did not approach this analysis with any *a priori* hypotheses to test, our unsupervised model reveals an interesting hypothesis to pursue with confirmatory analysis: biographies of women on Wikipedia disproportionately focus on marriage and divorce compared to those of men.

To test this hypothesis with more traditional

[3]Using our method of gender inference described in §2, we are able to infer gender for 99.95% of biographies (242,858).

z	%Fem.	Most frequent terms
60.46	76.9%	miss, pageant, title, usa, miss universe, beauty, held, teen, crowned, competed
57.21	49.9%	birth, gave, daughter, son, born, first child, named, wife, announced, baby
55.63	59.8%	fashion, model, show, campaign, week, appeared, face, career, became, modeling
37.89	39.4%	divorce, marriage, divorced, married, filed, wife, separated, years, ended, later
36.70	36.5%	summer olympics, competed, olympics, team, finished, event, final, world championships

Table 3: Female-skewed event classes, ranked by z-score in a two-tailed binomial proportion test.

z	%Fem.	Most frequent terms
-31.64	0.2%	drafted, nfl draft, round, professional career, draft, overall, selected, major league baseball
-23.81	2.1%	promoted, rank, captain, retired, army, lieutenant, colonel, major, brigadier general
-20.93	3.7%	bar, admitted, law, practice, called, commenced, studied, began, career, practiced
-20.48	1.0%	infantry, civil war, regiment, army, enlisted, served, company, colonel, captain
-20.30	1.7%	ordained, priest, seminary, priesthood, theology, theological, college, studies, rome

Table 4: Male-skewed event classes, ranked by z-score in a two-tailed binomial proportion test.

means, we estimated the empirical gender proportions of biographies containing terms explicitly denoting divorce (*divorced, divorce, divorces* and *divorcing*). The result of this analysis confirms that of the model. Of the 4,608 biographies in which at least one of these terms appears, 38.8% are those of a woman, far more than the 14.8% we would expect (in a two-tailed binomial proportion test against $H_0 = 14.8$, this difference is significant at $p < 0.0001$); this corresponds to divorce being mentioned in 5.0% of all 35,932 women's biographies, and 1.4% of all 206,926 men's; on average, a woman's biography is 3.66 times more likely to mention divorce than a man's.

We repeat the gender proportion experiment with terms denoting marriage (*married, marry, marries, marrying* and *marriage*) and find a similar trend: of the 39,142 biographies where at least one of these terms is mentioned, 23.6% belong to women; again, in a two-tailed proportion test, this difference is significant at $p < 0.0001$. This corresponds to marriage appearing in 25.7% of all women's biographies, and 14.5% of men's; a woman's biography is 1.78 times more likely to mention marriage than a man's.

6 Additional Analyses

The analysis above represents one substantive result that mining life events from biographical data makes possible. To illustrate the range of other analyses that this method can occasion, we briefly present two other directions that can be pursued: investigating correlations among event classes and the distribution of event classes over historical time.

6.1 Correlations among events

In our full model with a logistic normal prior over a document's set of events, correlations among latent event classes are learned during inference. From the covariance matrix Σ_η, we can directly read off correlations among events; for other models (such as those with a Dirichlet prior), we can infer correlations using the posterior estimates for η.

Table 5 illustrates the event classes that have the highest correlations to the event class defined by *family, boss, murder, crime, mafia, became, arrested, john, gang, chicago*. The structure that we learn here neatly corresponds to a CRIMINAL ACTION frame, with common events for KILLING, BEING SUBJECT TO FEDERAL INVESTIGATION, BEING ARRESTED and BEING BROUGHT TO TRIAL.

6.2 Historical distribution of events

Figure 3 likewise illustrates the distribution over time for a set of learned event classes. While the only notion of time that our model has access to during inference is that of time relative to a person's birth, we can estimate the empirical distribution of event classes in historical time by charting the density plot of their observed absolute dates. Several historically relevant event classes are legible, including SERVING IN THE ARMY (with peaks dur-

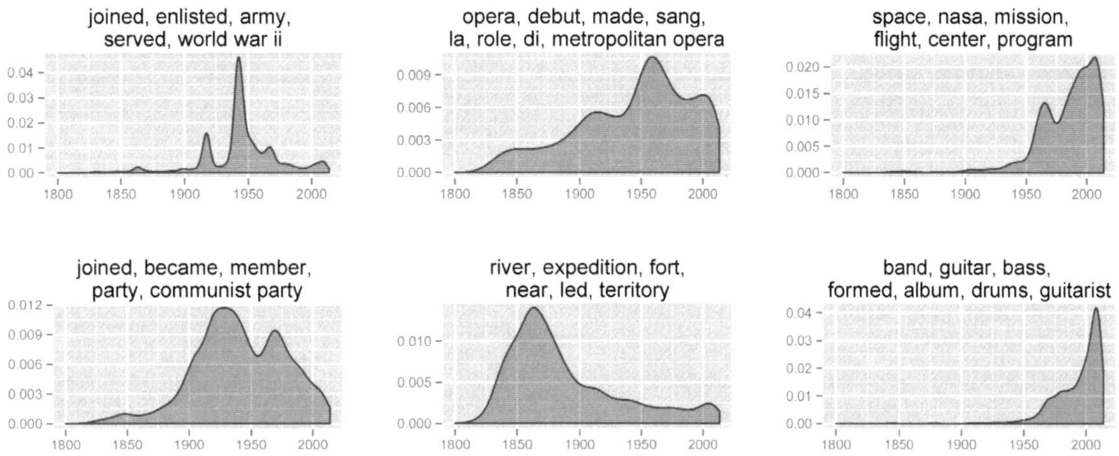

Figure 3: Historical distributions of event classes.

r	Event class
1.000	family, boss, murder, crime, mafia, became, arrested, john, gang, chicago
0.031	killed, shot, police, home, two, car, arrested, murder, death, -year-old
0.028	trial, murder, case, guilty, court, jury, charges, convicted, death, judge
0.021	investigation, federal, charges, office, fraud, campaign, state, commission, former, corruption
0.019	arrested, sentenced, years, prison, trial, death, court, convicted, military, months

Table 5: Highest correlations between the *family, boss, murder, crime, mafia* class and other events.

ing World War I and II, Vietnam and the later Iraq wars), OPERA DEBUT (with peaks in the 1950s), NASA (with peaks in 1960s and the turn of the millenium), JOINING THE COMMUNIST PARTY (with a rise in the early 20th century), LEADING AN EXPEDITION (with a slow historical decline) and JOINING A BAND (with increasing historical presence). Grounding specific life events in history has the potential to enable analysis of how historical time affects the life histories of individuals—including both the influence of the general passage of time, as on transitions to adulthood (Modell et al., 1976; Hogan, 1981; Modell, 1980), and the influence of specific historical moments like the Great Depression (Elder, 1974) or World War II (Mayer, 1988; Elder, 1991).

7 Related Work

In learning general classes of events from text, our work draws on a rich background spanning several research traditions. By considering the structure that exists between event classes, we draw on the original work on procedural scripts and schemas (Minsky, 1974; Schank and Abelson, 1977) and narrative chains (Chambers and Jurafsky, 2008; Chambers and Jurafsky, 2009), including more recent advances in the unsupervised learning of frame semantic representations (Modi et al., 2012; O'Connor, 2013; Cheung et al., 2013; Chambers, 2013).

In learning latent classes from text, our work is also clearly related to research on topic modeling (Blei et al., 2003; Griffiths and Steyvers, 2004). This work differs from that tradition by scoping our data only over text that we have reason to believe describes events (by including absolute dates). While other topic models have leveraged temporal information in the learning of latent topics, such as the dynamic topic model (Blei and Lafferty, 2006b; Wang et al., 2012) and "topics over time" (Wang and McCallum, 2006), our model is the first to infer classes of events whose contours are shaped by the time in a person's life that they take place.

While the information extraction tasks of template filling (Hobbs et al., 1993) and relation detection (Banko et al., 2007; Fader et al., 2011; Carlson et al., 2010) generally fall into a paradigm of classifying text segments into a predetermined ontology, they too have been informed by unsupervised approaches to learning relation classes (Yao et al., 2011) and events (Ritter et al., 2012). Our work here differs from this past work in leveraging explicit absolute temporal information in the unsupervised learning of event classes (and their structure). Reasoning about the temporal ordering of events likewise has a long tradition of its own, both in NLP (Pustejovsky et al., 2003; Mani et al., 2006; Verhagen et al., 2007; Chambers et al., 2007) and information extraction (Talukdar et al., 2012). Rather than attempting to model the ordering of events relative to each other, we focus instead on their occurrence relative to the beginning of a person's life.

Wikipedia likewise has been used extensively in NLP; Wikipedia biographies in particular have been used for the task of training summarization models (Biadsy et al., 2008), recognizing biographical sentences (Conway, 2010), learning correlates of "success" (Ng, 2012), and disambiguating named entities (Bunescu and Pasca, 2006; Cucerzan, 2007). In our work in mining biographical structure from it, we draw on previous research into automatically uncovering latent structure in resumés (Mimno and McCallum, 2007a) and approaches to learning life path trajectories from categorical survey data (Massoni et al., 2009; Ritschard et al., 2013).

In using Wikipedia as a dataset for analysis, we must note that the subjects of biographies are not a representative sample of the population, nor are their contents unbiased representations. Nearly all encyclopedias necessarily prefer the historically notorious (if due to nothing else than inherent biases in the preservation of historical records); many, like Wikipedia, also have disproportionately low coverage of women, minorities, and other demographic groups, in part because of biases in community membership. Estimates of the percentage of female editors on Wikipedia, for example, ranges from 9% to 16.1% (Collier and Bear, 2012; Reagle and Rhue, 2011; Cassell, 2011; Hill and Shaw, 2013; Wikipedia, 2011). Different language editions of Wikipedia have a natural geographic bias in article selection (Hecht and Gergle, 2009), with each emphasizing their own "local heroes" (Kolbitsch and Maurer, 2006), and also differ in the kind of information they present (Pfeil et al., 2006; Callahan and Herring, 2011). This extends to selection of biographies as well, with one study finding approximately 16% of 1000 sampled biographies being those of women (Reagle and Rhue, 2011), a figure very close to the 14.8% we observe in our analysis here.

8 Conclusion

We present a method for mining life events from biographies, leveraging the correlation structure of event descriptions. Unlike prior work that has focused on inferring "life trajectories" from categorical survey data, we learn relevant structure in an unsupervised manner directly from text, opening the door to applying this method to a broad set of biographies beyond Wikipedia (including full-text books from the Internet Archive or Hathi Trust, and other encyclopedic biographies as well). In a quantitative analysis, the model we present outperforms a strong baseline at the task of event time prediction, and surfaces a substantive qualitative distinction in the *content* of the biographies of men and women on Wikipedia: in contrast to previous work that uses computational methods to measure a difference in coverage, we show that such methods are able to tease apart differences in characterization as well.

While the task of event time prediction provides a quantitative means to compare different models, we expect the real application of this work will lie in the latent event classes themselves, and the information they provide both about the subjects and authors of biographies. Latent topics have provided one way of organizing large document collections in the past (Mimno and McCallum, 2007b); in addition to occasioning data analysis of the kind we describe here, we expect that personal event classes can have a practical application in helping to organize data describing people as well. Data and code to support this work, including an interface to explore event classes in Wikipedia, can be found at `http://www.ark.cs.cmu.edu/bio/`.

9 Acknowledgments

We thank the anonymous reviewers, along with Dallas Card, Brendan O'Connor, Bryan Routledge, Yanchuan Sim and Ted Underwood, for their helpful comments. The research reported in this article was supported by U.S. National Science Foundation grant CAREER IIS-1054319 to N.A.S. and Google's support of the Reading is Believing project at CMU. This work was made possible through the use of computing resources made available by the Open Science Data Cloud (OSDC), an Open Cloud Consortium (OCC)-sponsored project.

References

David Bamman, Ted Underwood, and Noah A. Smith. 2014. A Bayesian mixed effects model of literary character. In *ACL*.

Michele Banko, Michael J Cafarella, Stephen Soderland, Matthew Broadhead, and Oren Etzioni. 2007. Open information extraction for the web. In *IJCAI*, volume 7, pages 2670–2676.

Fadi Biadsy, Julia Hirschberg, and Elena Filatova. 2008. An unsupervised approach to biography production using Wikipedia. In *ACL '08*, pages 807–815.

David M. Blei and John D. Lafferty. 2006a. Correlated topic models. In *NIPS '06*.

David M. Blei and John D. Lafferty. 2006b. Dynamic topic models. In *ICML '06*, pages 113–120.

David M. Blei and John D. Lafferty. 2007. A correlated topic model of Science. *AAS*, 1(1):17–35.

David M. Blei, Andrew Ng, and Michael Jordan. 2003. Latent dirichlet allocation. *JMLR*, 3:993–1022.

Razvan Bunescu and Marius Pasca. 2006. Using encyclopedic knowledge for named entity disambiguation. In *EACL '06*, pages 9–16, Trento, Italy.

Ewa S. Callahan and Susan C. Herring. 2011. Cultural bias in Wikipedia content on famous persons. *J. Am. Soc. Inf. Sci. Technol.*, 62(10):1899–1915, October.

Andrew Carlson, Justin Betteridge, Bryan Kisiel, Burr Settles, Estevam R. Hruschka Jr., and Tom M. Mitchell. 2010. Toward an architecture for never-ending language learning. In *AAAI '10*.

Bob Carpenter. 2010. Integrating Out Multinomial Parameters in Latent Dirichlet Allocation and Naive Bayes for Collapsed Gibbs Sampling. Technical report, LingPipe.

Justine Cassell. 2011. Editing wars behind the scenes. *New York Times*, February 4.

Nathanael Chambers and Dan Jurafsky. 2008. Unsupervised learning of narrative event chains. In *ACL '08*.

Nathanael Chambers and Dan Jurafsky. 2009. Unsupervised learning of narrative schemas and their participants. In *ACL '09*, pages 602–610.

Nathanael Chambers, Shan Wang, and Dan Jurafsky. 2007. Classifying temporal relations between events. In *Proceedings of the 45th Annual Meeting of the ACL on Interactive Poster and Demonstration Sessions*, ACL '07, pages 173–176, Stroudsburg, PA, USA. Association for Computational Linguistics.

Nathanael Chambers. 2013. Event schema induction with a probabilistic entity-driven model. In *EMNLP '13*, pages 1797–1807, Seattle, Washington, USA, October. Association for Computational Linguistics.

Jackie Chi Kit Cheung, Hoifung Poon, and Lucy Vanderwende. 2013. Probabilistic frame induction. In *NAACL '13*, pages 837–846, Atlanta, Georgia, June. Association for Computational Linguistics.

Benjamin Collier and Julia Bear. 2012. Conflict, criticism, or confidence: An empirical examination of the gender gap in Wikipedia contributions. In *CSCW '12*.

Mike Conway. 2010. Mining a corpus of biographical texts using keywords. *Literary and Linguistic Computing*, 25(1):23–35.

Silviu Cucerzan. 2007. Large-scale named entity disambiguation based on wikipedia data. In *EMNLP-CoNLL*, volume 7, pages 708–716.

Peter T. Davis, David K. Elson, and Judith L. Klavans. 2003. Methods for precise named entity matching in digital collections. In *JCDL '03*.

Glen Elder. 1974. *Children of the Great Depression*. University of Chicago Press.

Glen Elder. 1991. Talent, history, and the fulfillment of promise. *Psychiatry*, 54(3):251–267.

David K. Elson, Nicholas Dames, and Kathleen R. McKeown. 2010. Extracting social networks from literary fiction. In *ACL '10*, pages 138–147.

Anthony Fader, Stephen Soderland, and Oren Etzioni. 2011. Identifying relations for open information extraction. In *EMNLP '11*, EMNLP '11, pages 1535–1545, Stroudsburg, PA, USA. Association for Computational Linguistics.

Jenny Rose Finkel, Trond Grenager, and Christopher Manning. 2005. Incorporating non-local information into information extraction systems by Gibbs sampling. In *ACL '05*, pages 363–370.

Google. 2014. Freebase data dumps. `https://developers.google.com/freebase/data`.

Thomas L Griffiths and Mark Steyvers. 2004. Finding scientific topics. *Proceedings of the National Academy of Sciences of the United States of America*, 101(Suppl 1):5228–5235.

Brent Hecht and Darren Gergle. 2009. Measuring self-focus bias in community-maintained knowledge repositories. In *C&T '09*, pages 11–20.

Benjamin Mako Hill and Aaron Shaw. 2013. The Wikipedia gender gap revisited: Characterizing survey response bias with propensity score estimation. *PLoS ONE*, 8(6).

Jerry R Hobbs, Douglas Appelt, John Bear, David Israel, Megumi Kameyama, and Mabry Tyson. 1993. Fastus: A system for extracting information from text.

In *Proceedings of the workshop on Human Language Technology*, pages 133–137. Association for Computational Linguistics.

Dennis P. Hogan and Nan Marie Astone. 1986. The transition to adulthood. *Annual Review of Sociology*, 12(1):109–130.

Dennis Hogan. 1981. *Transitions and Social Change: The Early Lives of American Men*. Academic, New York.

John S Justeson and Slava M Katz. 1995. Technical terminology: some linguistic properties and an algorithm for identification in text. *Natural Language Engineering*, 1(1):9–27.

Josef Kolbitsch and Hermann A. Maurer. 2006. The transformation of the web: How emerging communities shape the information we consume. *J. UCS*, 12(2):187–213.

Lee A. Lillard and Linda J. Waite. 1993. A joint model of marital childbearing and marital disruption. *Demography*, 30(4):pp. 653–681.

Lee A. Lillard, Michael J. Brien, and Linda J. Waite. 1995. Premarital cohabitation and subsequent marital dissolution: A matter of self-selection? *Demography*, 32(3):pp. 437–457.

Inderjeet Mani, Marc Verhagen, Ben Wellner, Chong Min Lee, and James Pustejovsky. 2006. Machine learning of temporal relations. In *Proceedings of the 21st International Conference on Computational Linguistics and the 44th Annual Meeting of the Association for Computational Linguistics*, ACL-44, pages 753–760, Stroudsburg, PA, USA. Association for Computational Linguistics.

Sébastien Massoni, Madalina Olteanu, and Patrick Rousset. 2009. Career-path analysis using optimal matching and self-organizing maps. In *WSOM '09*.

Henry Colin Gray Matthew and Brian Harrison. 2004. *The Oxford dictionary of national biography*. Oxford University Press.

Karl Ulrich Mayer. 1988. German survivors of World War II: The impact on the life course of the collective experience of birth cohorts. In *Social Structure and Human Lives*, Newbury Park. Sage.

David Mimno and Andrew McCallum. 2007a. Modeling career path trajectories. Technical Report 2007-69, University of Massachusetts, Amherst.

David Mimno and Andrew McCallum. 2007b. Organizing the OCA: Learning faceted subjects from a library of digital books. In *JCDL '07*, pages 376–385, New York, NY, USA. ACM.

David Mimno, Hanna M. Wallach, and Andrew McCallum. 2008. Gibbs sampling for logistic normal topic models with graph-based priors. In *NIPS Workshop on Analyzing Graphs*.

Marvin Minsky. 1974. A framework for representing knowledge. Technical report, MIT-AI Laboratory.

John Modell, Frank F. Furstenberg Jr., and Theodore Hershberg. 1976. Social change and transitions to adulthood in historical perspective. *Journal of Family History*, 1(1):7–32.

John Modell. 1980. Normative aspects of american marriage timing since World War II. *Journal of Family History*, 5(2):210–234.

Ashutosh Modi, Ivan Titov, and Alexandre Klementiev. 2012. Unsupervised induction of frame-semantic representations. In *Proceedings of the NAACL-HLT Workshop on the Induction of Linguistic Structure*, WILS '12, pages 1–7, Stroudsburg, PA, USA. Association for Computational Linguistics.

Radford M Neal. 2003. Slice sampling. *Annals of Statistics*, pages 705–741.

Pauline Ng. 2012. What Kobe Bryant and Britney Spears have in common: Mining Wikipedia for characteristics of notable individuals. In *ICWSM '12*.

Brendan O'Connor. 2013. Learning frames from text with an unsupervised latent variable model. *ArXiv*, abs/1307.7382.

Ulrike Pfeil, Panayiotis Zaphiris, and Chee Siang Ang. 2006. Cultural differences in collaborative authoring of Wikipedia. *Journal of Computer-Mediated Communication*, 12(1):88–113.

James Pustejovsky, Patrick Hanks, Roser Sauri, Andrew See, Robert Gaizauskas, Andrea Setzer, Dragomir Radev, Beth Sundheim, David Day, Lisa Ferro, et al. 2003. The timebank corpus. In *Corpus linguistics*, volume 2003, page 40.

Joseph Reagle and Lauren Rhue. 2011. Gender bias in Wikipedia and Britannica. *International Journal of Communication*, 5(0).

Steffen Reinhold. 2010. Reassessing the link between premarital cohabitation and marital instability. *Demography*, 47(3):719–733.

Gilbert Ritschard, Reto Bürgin, and Matthias Studer. 2013. Exploratory mining of life event histories. In J. J. McArdle and G. Ritschard, editors, *Contemporary Issues in Exploratory Data Mining in the Behavioral Sciences*, pages 221–253. Routledge, New York.

Alan Ritter, Mausam, Oren Etzioni, and Sam Clark. 2012. Open domain event extraction from Twitter. In *KDD '12*, pages 1104–1112, New York, NY, USA. ACM.

Roger C. Schank and Robert P. Abelson. 1977. *Scripts, plans, goals, and understanding: An inquiry into human knowledge structures*. Lawrence Erlbaum, Hillsdale, NJ.

Michael J. Shanahan. 2000. Pathways to adulthood in changing societies: Variability and mechanisms in life course perspective. *Annual Review of Sociology*, 26(1):667–692.

Partha Pratim Talukdar, Derry Wijaya, and Tom Mitchell. 2012. Acquiring temporal constraints between relations. In *CIKM '12*, pages 992–1001, New York, NY, USA. ACM.

Kristina Toutanova, Dan Klein, Christopher D. Manning, and Yoram Singer. 2003. Feature-rich part-of-speech tagging with a cyclic dependency network. In *NAACL '03*, pages 173–180.

Marc Verhagen, Robert Gaizauskas, Frank Schilder, Mark Hepple, Graham Katz, and James Pustejovsky. 2007. Semeval-2007 task 15: Tempeval temporal relation identification. In *Proceedings of the 4th International Workshop on Semantic Evaluations*, pages 75–80. Association for Computational Linguistics.

Xuerui Wang and Andrew McCallum. 2006. Topics over time: a non-markov continuous-time model of topical trends. In *KDD '06*, pages 424–433.

Chong Wang, David M. Blei, and David Heckerman. 2012. Continuous time dynamic topic models. *ArXiv*.

Wikipedia. 2011. Wikipedia editors study: Results from the editor survey.

Limin Yao, Aria Haghighi, Sebastian Riedel, and Andrew McCallum. 2011. Structured relation discovery using generative models. In *EMNLP '11*, pages 1456–1466, Stroudsburg, PA, USA. Association for Computational Linguistics.

Large-scale Semantic Parsing without Question-Answer Pairs

Siva Reddy, Mirella Lapata, Mark Steedman
School of Informatics, University of Edinburgh
10 Crichton Street, Edinburgh EH8 9AB
siva.reddy@ed.ac.uk, mlap@inf.ed.ac.uk, steedman@inf.ed.ac.uk

Abstract

In this paper we introduce a novel semantic parsing approach to query Freebase in natural language without requiring manual annotations or question-answer pairs. Our key insight is to represent natural language via semantic graphs whose topology shares many commonalities with Freebase. Given this representation, we conceptualize semantic parsing as a graph matching problem. Our model converts sentences to semantic graphs using CCG and subsequently grounds them to Freebase guided by denotations as a form of weak supervision. Evaluation experiments on a subset of the FREE917 and WEBQUESTIONS benchmark datasets show our semantic parser improves over the state of the art.

1 Introduction

Querying a database to retrieve an answer, telling a robot to perform an action, or teaching a computer to play a game are tasks requiring communication with machines in a language interpretable by them. *Semantic parsing* addresses the specific task of learning to map natural language (NL) to machine interpretable formal meaning representations. Traditionally, sentences are converted into logical form grounded in the symbols of some fixed ontology or relational database.

Approaches for learning semantic parsers have been for the most part supervised, using annotated training data consisting of sentences and their corresponding logical forms (Zelle and Mooney, 1996; Zettlemoyer and Collins, 2005; Wong and Mooney, 2007; Kwiatkowski et al., 2010). More recently, alternative forms of supervision have been proposed to alleviate the annotation burden, e.g., by learning from conversational logs (Artzi and Zettlemoyer, 2011), from sentences paired with system behavior (Chen and Mooney, 2011; Goldwasser and Roth, 2011; Artzi and Zettlemoyer, 2013), via distant supervision (Krishnamurthy and Mitchell, 2012; Cai and Yates, 2013), from questions (Goldwasser et al., 2011; Poon, 2013; Fader et al., 2013), and question-answer pairs (Clarke et al., 2010; Liang et al., 2011). Indeed, methods which learn from question-answer pairs have been gaining momentum as a means of scaling semantic parsers to large, open-domain problems (Kwiatkowski et al., 2013; Berant et al., 2013; Berant and Liang, 2014; Yao and Van Durme, 2014). Figure 1 shows an example of a question, its annotated logical form, and answer (or denotation).

Question	What is the capital of Texas?
Logical Form	$\lambda x.\ \text{city}(x) \wedge \text{capital}(x, \text{Texas})$
Answer	$\{\text{Austin}\}$

Figure 1: An example question with annotated logical query, and its answer.

In this paper, we build a semantic parser that does not require example annotations or question-answer pairs but instead learns from a large knowledge base (KB) and web-scale corpora. Specifically, we exploit Freebase, a large community-authored knowledge base that spans many sub-domains and stores real world facts in graphical format, and parsed sentences from a large corpus. We formulate semantic parsing as a graph matching problem. We convert the output of an open-domain combinatory categorial grammar (CCG) parser (Clark and Curran, 2007) into a graphical representation and subsequently map it onto Freebase. The parser's graphs (also called *ungrounded* graphs) are mapped to all possible Freebase subgraphs (also called *grounded* graphs) by replacing edges and nodes with relations and types in Freebase. Each grounded graph corresponds to a unique grounded logical query. During learning, our semantic parser is trained to identify which KB subgraph best corresponds to the NL graph. Problem-

Transactions of the Association for Computational Linguistics, 2 (2014) 377–392. Action Editor: Noah Smith.
Submitted 3/2014; Revised 6/2014; Published 10/2014.

$$\text{capital}(\text{Austin}) \wedge \textsc{unique}(\text{Austin}) \wedge \text{capital.of.arg1}(e, \text{Austin}) \wedge \text{capital.of.arg2}(e, \text{Texas})$$

(a) Semantic parse of the sentence *Austin is the capital of Texas.*

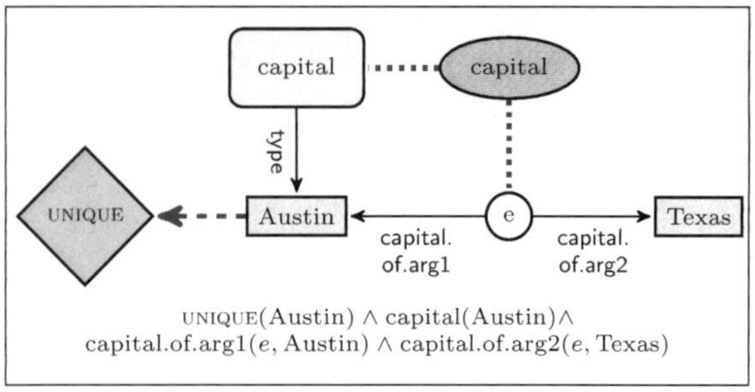

(b) Ungrounded graph for semantic parse (a); UNIQUE means that *Austin* is the only capital of *Texas*.

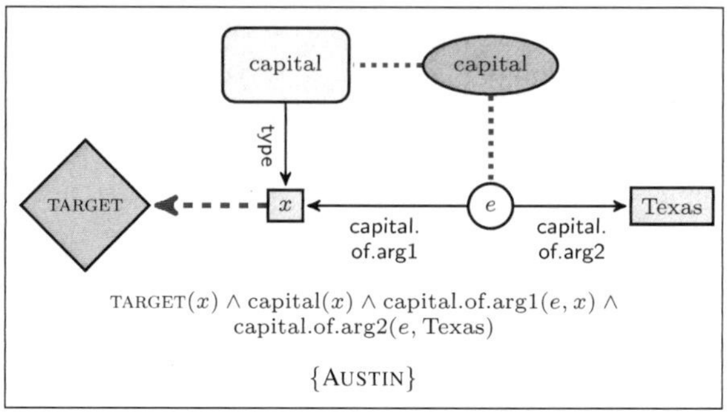

(c) Query graph after removing *Austin* from graph (b) and its denotation.

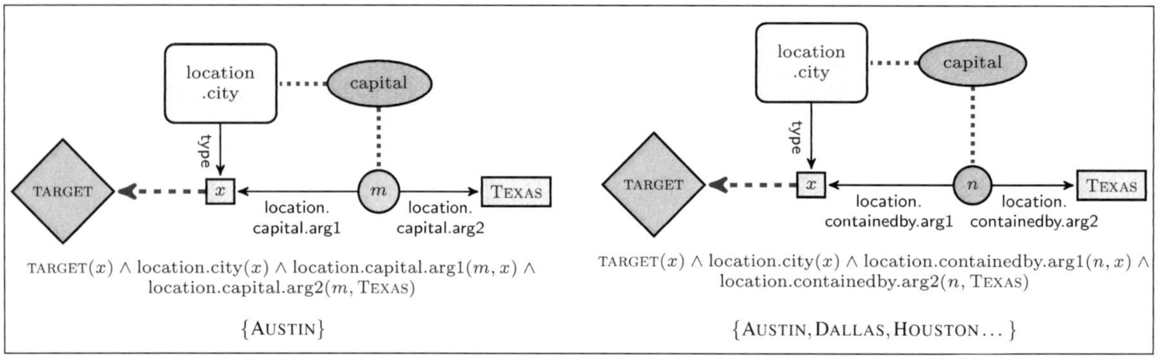

(d) Freebase graphs for NL graph (c) and their denotations.

Figure 2: Steps involved in converting a natural language sentence to a Freebase grounded graph.

atically, ungrounded graphs may give rise to many grounded graphs. Since we do not make use of manual annotations of sentences or question-answer pairs, we do not know which grounded graphs are correct. To overcome this, we rely on comparisons between denotations of natural language queries and related Freebase queries as a form of *weak supervision* in order to learn the mapping between NL and KB graphs.

Figure 2 illustrates our approach for the sentence *Austin is the capital of Texas.* From the CCG syntactic derivation (which we omit here for the sake of brevity) we obtain a semantic parse (Figure 2a) and convert it to an ungrounded graph (Figure 2b). Next, we select an entity from the graph and replace it with a variable x, creating a graph corresponding to the query *What is the capital of Texas?* (Figure 2c). The math function UNIQUE on *Austin* in Figure 2b indicates *Austin* is the only value of x which can satisfy the query graph in Figure 2c. Therefore, the denotation[1] of the NL query graph is {AUSTIN}. Figure 2d shows two different groundings of the query graph in the Freebase KB. We obtain these by replacing edges and nodes in the query graph with Freebase relations and types. We use the denotation of the NL query as a form of weak supervision to select the best grounded graph. Under the constraint that the denotation of a Freebase query should be the same as the denotation of the NL query, the graph on the left hand-side of Figure 2d is chosen as the correct grounding.

Experimental results on two benchmark datasets consisting of questions to Freebase — FREE917 (Cai and Yates, 2013) and WEBQUESTIONS (Berant

[1]The denotation of a graph is the set of feasible values for the nodes marked with TARGET.

et al., 2013) — show that our semantic parser improves over state-of-the-art approaches. Our contributions include: a novel graph-based method to convert natural language sentences to grounded semantic parses which exploits the similarities in the topology of knowledge graphs and linguistic structure, together with the ability to train using a wide range of features; a proposal to learn from a large scale web corpus, without question-answer pairs, based on denotations of queries from natural language statements as weak supervision; and the development of a scalable semantic parser which besides Freebase uses CLUEWEB09 for training, a corpus of 503.9 million webpages. Our semantic parser can be downloaded from `http://sivareddy.in/downloads`.

2 Framework

Our goal is to build a semantic parser which maps a natural language sentence to a logical form that can be executed against Freebase. We begin with CLUEWEB09, a web-scale corpus automatically annotated with Freebase entities (Gabrilovich et al., 2013). We extract the sentences containing at least two entities linked by a relation in Freebase. We parse these sentences using a CCG syntactic parser, and build semantic parses from the syntactic output. Semantic parses are then converted to semantic graphs which are subsequently grounded to Freebase. Grounded graphs can be easily converted to a KB query deterministically. During training we learn which grounded graphs correspond best to the natural language input. In the following, we provide a brief introduction to Freebase and its graph structure. Next, we explain how we obtain semantic parses from CCG (Section 2.2), how we convert them to graphs (Section 2.3), and ground them in Freebase (Section 2.4). Section 3 presents our learning algorithm.

2.1 The Freebase Knowledge Graph

Freebase consists of 42 million entities and 2.5 billion facts. A fact is defined by a triple containing two entities and a relation between them. Entities represent real world concepts, and edges represent relations, thus forming a graph-like structure.

A Freebase subgraph is shown in Figure 3 with

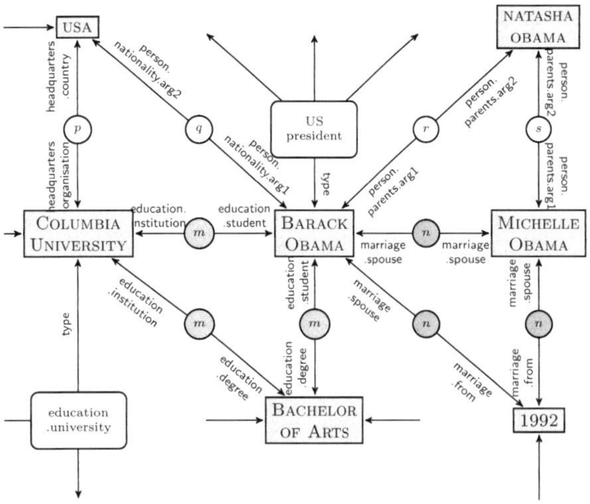

Figure 3: Freebase knowledge graph. Entities are represented by rectangles, relations between entities by edges, mediator nodes by circles, types by rounded rectangles.

rectangles denoting entities. In addition to simple facts, Freebase encodes complex facts, represented by multiple edges (e.g., the edges connecting BARACK OBAMA, COLUMBIA UNIVERSITY and BACHELOR OF ARTS). Complex facts have intermediate nodes called mediator nodes (circles in Figure 3 with the same identifiers e.g., m and n). For reasons of uniformity, we assume that simple facts are also represented via mediator nodes and split single edges into two with each subedge going from the mediator node to the target node (see person.nationality.arg1 and person.nationality.arg2 in Figure 3). Finally, Freebase also has entity types defining is-a relations. In Figure 3 types are represented by rounded rectangles (e.g., BARACK OBAMA is of type US president, and COLUMBIA UNIVERSITY is of type education.university).

2.2 Combinatory Categorial Grammar

The graph like structure of Freebase inspires us to create a graph like structure for natural language, and learn a mapping between them. To do this we take advantage of the representational power of Combinatory Categorial Grammar (Steedman, 2000). CCG is a linguistic formalism that tightly couples syntax and semantics, and can be used to model a wide range of language phenom-

Cameron	directed	*Titanic*
NP	$(S\backslash NP)/NP$	NP
Cameron	$\lambda y \lambda x.$ directed.arg1(e,x) $\wedge$ directed.arg2(e,y)	Titanic

$$\frac{(S\backslash NP)/NP \quad NP}{S\backslash NP} >$$

$\lambda x.$ directed.arg1(e,x) $\wedge$ directed.arg2$(e,$ Titanic$)$

$$\frac{NP \quad S\backslash NP}{S} <$$

directed.arg1$(e,$ Cameron$)$ $\wedge$ directed.arg2$(e,$ Titanic$)$

Figure 4: CCG derivation containing both syntactic and semantic parse construction.

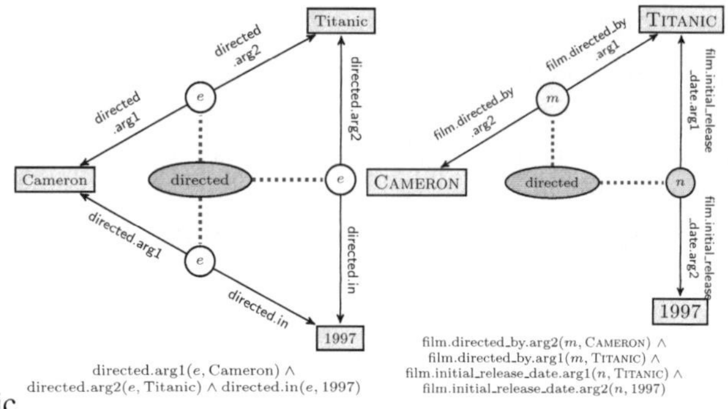

(a) Ungrounded graph (b) Grounded graph

Figure 5: Graph representations for the sentence *Cameron directed Titanic in 1997.*

ena. CCG is well known for capturing long-range dependencies inherent in constructions such as coordination, extraction, raising and control, as well as standard local predicate-argument dependencies (Clark et al., 2002), thus supporting wide-coverage semantic analysis. Moreover, due to the transparent interface between syntax and semantics, it is relatively straightforward to built a semantic parse for a sentence from its corresponding syntactic derivation tree (Bos et al., 2004).

In our case, the choice of syntactic parser is motivated by the scale of our problem; the parser must be broad-coverage and robust enough to handle a web-sized corpus. For these reasons, we rely on the C&C parser (Clark and Curran, 2004), a general-purpose CCG parser, to obtain syntactic derivations. To our knowledge, we present the first attempt to use a CCG parser trained on treebanks for grounded semantic parsing. Most previous work has induced task-specific CCG grammars (Zettlemoyer and Collins, 2005, 2007; Kwiatkowski et al., 2010). An example CCG derivation is shown in Figure 4.

Semantic parses are constructed from syntactic CCG parses, with semantic composition being guided by the CCG syntactic derivation.[2] We use a neo-Davidsonian (Parsons, 1990) semantics to represent semantic parses.[3] Each word has a semantic category based on its syntactic category and part of speech. For example, the syntactic category for *directed* is $(S\backslash NP)/NP$, i.e., it takes two argument NPs and becomes S. To represent its semantic category, we use a lambda term $\lambda y \lambda x.$ directed.arg1$(e,x) \wedge$ directed.arg2(e,y), where e identifies the event of *directed*, and x and y are arguments corresponding to the NPs in the syntactic category.

We obtain semantic categories automatically using the indexed syntactic categories provided by the C&C parser. The latter reveal the bindings of basic constituent categories in more complex categories. For example, in order to convert $((S\backslash NP)\backslash(S\backslash NP))/NP$ to its semantic category, we must know whether all NPs have the same referent and thus use the same variable name. The indexed category $((S_e\backslash NP_x)\backslash(S_e\backslash NP_x))/NP_y$ reveals that there are only two different NPs, x and y, and that one of them (i.e., x) is shared across two subcategories. We discuss the details of semantic category construction in the Appendix.

Apart from n-ary predicates representing events (mostly verbs), we also use unary predicates representing types in language (mostly common nouns and noun modifiers). For example, capital(Austin) indicates *Austin* is of type capital. Prepositions, adjectives and adverbs are represented by predicates lexicalized with their head words to provide more information (see capital.of.arg1 instead of of.arg1 in Figure 2a).

2.3 Ungrounded Semantic Graphs

We will now illustrate how we create ungrounded semantic graphs from CCG-derived semantic parses. Figure 5a displays the ungrounded graph for the sen-

[2]See Bos et al. (2004) for a detailed introduction to semantic representation using CCG.

[3]Neo-Davidsonian semantics is a form of first-order logic that uses event identifiers (e) to connect verb predicates and their subcategorized arguments through conjunctions.

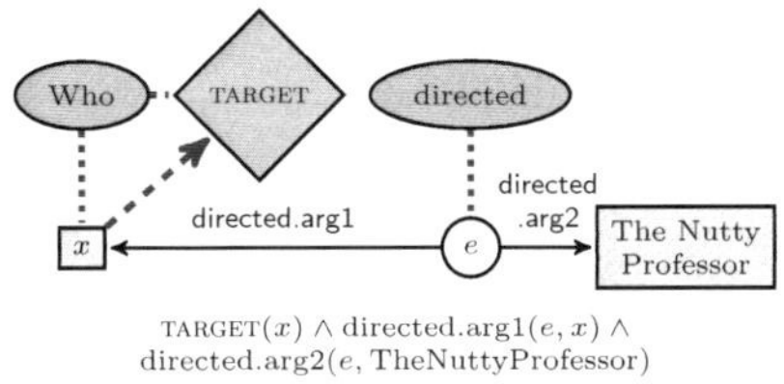

(a) Who directed The Nutty Professor?

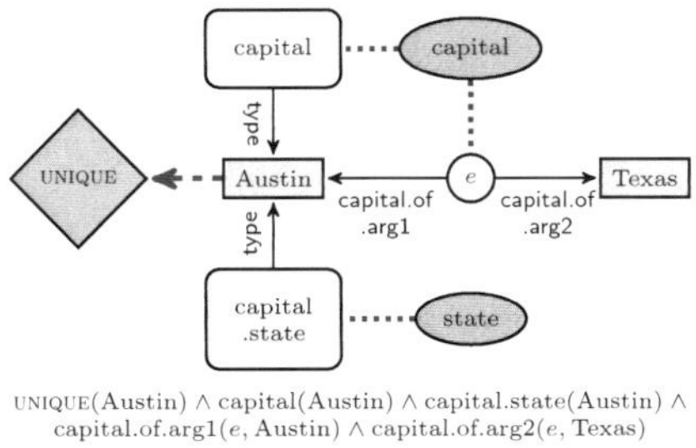

(b) Austin is the state capital of Texas.

Figure 6: Ungrounded graphs with math functions TARGET and UNIQUE.

tence *Cameron directed Titanic in 1997.* In order to construct ungrounded graphs topologically similar to Freebase, we define five types of nodes:

Word Nodes (Ovals) Word nodes are denoted by ovals. They represent natural language words (e.g., *directed* in Figure 5a, *capital* and *state* in Figure 6b). Word nodes are connected to other word nodes via syntactic dependencies. For readability, we do not show inter-word dependencies.

Entity Nodes (Rectangles) Entity nodes are denoted by rectangles and represent entities e.g., *Cameron* in Figure 5a. In cases where an entity is not known, we use variables e.g., x in Figure 6a. Entity variables are connected to their corresponding word nodes from which they originate by dotted links e.g., x in Figure 6a is connected to the word node *who.*

Mediator Nodes (Circles) Mediator nodes are denoted by circles and represent events in language. They connect pairs of entities which participate in an event forming a clique (see the entities *Cameron*, *Titanic* and *1997* in Figure 5a). We define an *edge* as a link that connects any two entities via a mediator. The *subedge* of an edge i.e., the link between a mediator and an entity, corresponds to the predicate denoting the event and taking the entity as its argument (e.g. directed.arg1 links e and *Cameron* in Figure 5a). Mediator nodes are connected to their corresponding word nodes from which they originate by dotted links e.g. mediators in Figure 5a are connected to word node *directed.*

Type nodes (Rounded rectangles) Type nodes are denoted by rounded rectangles. They represent unary predicates in natural language. In Figure 6b type nodes capital and capital.state are attached to *Austin* denoting *Austin* is of type capital and capital.state. Type nodes are also connected to their corresponding word nodes from which they originate by dotted links e.g. type node capital.state and word node *state* in Figure 6b.

Math nodes (Diamonds) Math nodes are denoted by diamonds. They describe functions to be applied on the nodes/subgraphs they attach to. The function TARGET attaches to the entity variable of interest. For example, the graph in Figure 6a represents the question *Who directed The Nutty Professor?.* Here, TARGET attaches to x representing the word *who.* UNIQUE attaches to the entity variable modified by the definite article *the.* In Figure 6b, UNIQUE attaches to *Austin* implying that only *Austin* satisfies the graph. Finally, COUNT attaches to entity nodes which have to be counted. For the sentence *Julie Andrews has appeared in 40 movies* in Figure 7, the KB could either link *Julie Andrews* and *40*, with type node *movies* matching the grounded type *integer*, or it could link *Julie Andrews* to each movie she acted in and the count of these different movies add to 40. In anticipation of this ambiguity, we generate two semantic parses resulting in two ungrounded graphs (see Figures 7a and 7b). We generate all possible grounded graphs corresponding to each ungrounded graph, and leave it up to the learning to decide which ones the KB prefers.

2.4 Grounded Semantic Graphs

We ground semantic graphs in Freebase by mapping edge labels to relations, type nodes to entity types, and entity nodes to Freebase entities. Math nodes remain unchanged. Though word nodes are not present in Freebase, we retain them in our grounded graphs to extract sophisticated features based on words and grounded predicates.

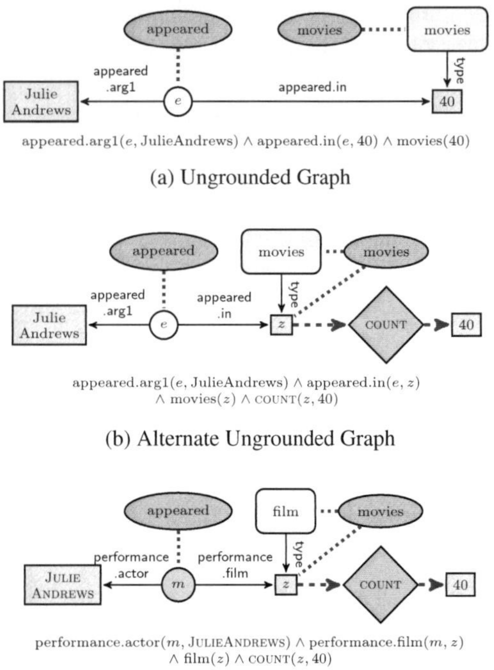

(a) Ungrounded Graph

(b) Alternate Ungrounded Graph

(c) Grounded graph

Figure 7: Graph representations for the sentence *Julie Andrews has appeared in 40 movies.* Ungrounded graph (a) directly connects *Julie Andrews* and *40*, whereas graph (b) uses the math function COUNT. Ungrounded graph (b) and grounded graph (c) have similar topology.

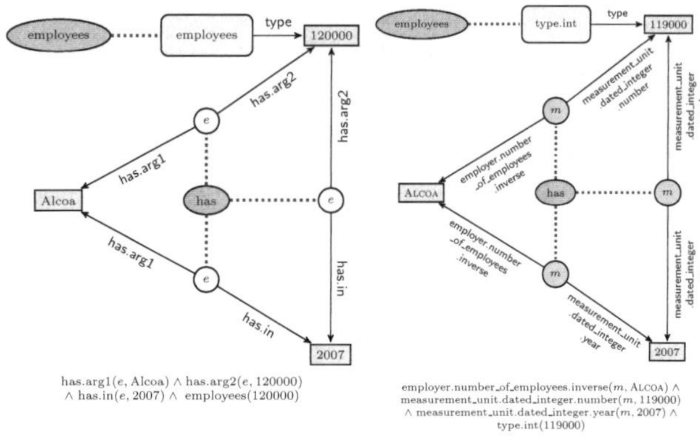

(a) Ungrounded Graph (b) Grounded Graph

Figure 8: Graph representations for *Alcoa has 120000 employees in 2007.*

Entity nodes Previous approaches (Cai and Yates, 2013; Berant et al., 2013; Kwiatkowski et al., 2013) use a manual lexicon or heuristics to ground named entities to Freebase entities. Fortunately, CLUEWEB09 sentences have been automatically annotated with Freebase entities, so we use these annotations to ground proper names to Freebase entities (denoted by uppercase words) e.g., *Cameron* in Figure 5a is grounded to Freebase entity CAMERON in Figure 5b. Common nouns like *movies* (see Figure 7b) are left as variables to be instantiated by the entities satisfying the graph.

Type nodes Type nodes are grounded to Freebase entity types. Type nodes capital and capital.state in Figure 6b are grounded to all possible types of Austin (e.g., location.city, location.capital_city, book.book_subject, broadcast.genre). In cases where entity nodes are not grounded, (e.g., z in Figure 7b), we use an automatically constructed lexicon which maps ungrounded types to grounded ones (see Section 4.2 for details).

Edges An edge between two entities is grounded using all edges linking the two entities in the knowledge graph. For example, to ground the edge between *Titanic* and *Cameron* in Figure 5, we use the following edges linking TITANIC and CAMERON in Freebase: (film.directed_by.arg1, film.directed_by.arg2), (film.produced_by.arg1, film.produced_by.arg2). If only one entity is grounded, we use all possible edges from this grounded entity. If no entity is grounded, we use a mapping lexicon which is automatically created as described in Section 4.2. Given an ungrounded graph with n edges, there are $O((k+1)^n)$ possible grounded graphs, with k being the grounded edges in the knowledge graph for each ungrounded edge together with an additional empty (no) edge.

Mediator nodes In an ungrounded graph, mediator nodes represent semantic event identifiers. In the grounded graph, they represent Freebase fact identifiers. Fact identifiers help distinguish if neighboring edges belong to a single complex fact, which may or may not be coextensive with an ungrounded event. In Figure 8a, the edges corresponding to the event identifier e are grounded to a single complex fact in Figure 8b, with the fact identifier m. However, in Figure 5a, the edges of the ungrounded event e are grounded to different Freebase facts, distinguished in Figure 5b by the identifiers m and n. Furthermore, the edge in 5a between CAMERON and 1997 is not grounded in 5b, since no Freebase edge exists between the two entities.

We convert grounded graphs to SPARQL queries, but for readability we only show logical expressions. The conversion is deterministic and is exactly the inverse of the semantic parse to graph conversion (Section 2.3). Wherever a node/edge is instantiated with a grounded entity/type/relation in Freebase, we use them in the grounded parse (e.g., type node capital.state in Figure 6b becomes location.capital_city). Math function TARGET is useful in retrieving instantiations of entity variables of interest (see Figure 6a).

3 Learning

A natural language sentence may give rise to several grounded graphs. But only one (or a few) of them will be a faithful representation of the sentence in Freebase. We next describe our algorithm for finding the best Freebase graph for a given sentence, our learning model, and the features it uses.

3.1 Algorithm

Freebase has a large number of relations and entities, and as a result there are many possible grounded graphs g for each ungrounded graph u. We construct and score graphs incrementally, traversing each node in the ungrounded graph and matching its edges and types in Freebase. Given a NL sentence s, we construct from its CCG syntactic derivation all corresponding ungrounded graphs u. Using a beam search procedure (described in Section 4.2), we find the best scoring graphs $(\hat{g}, \hat{u})$, maximizing over different graph configurations (g, u) of s:

$$(\hat{g}, \hat{u}) = \arg\max_{g,u} \Phi(g, u, s, \mathcal{KB}) \cdot \theta \quad (1)$$

We define the score of $(\hat{g}, \hat{u})$ as the dot product between a high dimensional feature representation $\Phi = (\Phi_1, \ldots \Phi_m)$ and a weight vector θ (see Section 3.3 for details on the features we employ).

We estimate the weights θ using the averaged structured perceptron algorithm (Collins, 2002). As shown in Algorithm 1, the perceptron makes several passes over sentences, and in each iteration it computes the best scoring $(\hat{g}, \hat{u})$ among the candidate graphs for a given sentence. In line 6, the algorithm updates θ with the difference (if any) between the feature representations of the best scoring graph $(\hat{g}, \hat{u})$ and the *gold standard* graph (g^+, u^+). The goal of the algorithm is to rank gold standard graphs higher than the any other graphs. The final weight vector θ is the average of weight vectors over T iterations and N sentences. This averaging procedure avoids overfitting and produces more stable results (Collins, 2002).

Algorithm 1: Averaged Structured Perceptron

Input: Training sentences: $\{s_i\}_{i=1}^N$

1 $\theta \leftarrow 0$

2 **for** $t \leftarrow 1 \ldots T$ **do**

3   **for** $i \leftarrow 1 \ldots N$ **do**

4     $(\hat{g}_i, \hat{u}_i) = \arg\max_{g_i,u_i} \Phi(g_i, u_i, s_i, \mathcal{KB}) \cdot \theta$

5   **if** $(u_i^+, g_i^+) \neq (\hat{u}_i, \hat{g}_i)$ **then**

6       $\theta \leftarrow \theta + \Phi(g_i^+, u_i^+, s_i, \mathcal{KB}) - \Phi(\hat{g}_i, \hat{u}_i, s_i, \mathcal{KB})$

7 **return** $\frac{1}{T} \sum_{t=i}^{T} \frac{1}{N} \sum_{i=1}^{N} \theta^i{}_t$

As we do not make use of question-answer pairs or manual annotations of sentences, gold standard graphs (g^+, u^+) are not available. In the following, we explain how we approximate them by relying on graph denotations as a form of weak supervision.

3.2 Selecting Surrogate Gold Graphs

Let u be an ungrounded semantic graph of s. We select an entity E in u, replace it with a variable x, and make it a target node. Let u^+ represent the resulting ungrounded graph. Next, we obtain all grounded graphs g^+ which correspond to u^+ such that the denotations $[\![u^+]\!]_{\mathcal{KB}} = [\![g^+]\!]_{\mathcal{NL}}$. We use these *surrogate* graphs g^+as gold standard, and the pairs (u^+, g^+) for model training. There is considerable latitude in choosing which entity E to replace. This can be done randomly, according to entity frequency, or some other criterion. We found that substituting the entity with the most connections to other entities in the sentence works well in practice. All the entities that can replace x in u^+ to constitute a valid fact in Freebase will be the denotation of u^+, $[\![u^+]\!]_{\mathcal{NL}}$. While it is straightforward to compute $[\![g^+]\!]_{\mathcal{KB}}$, it is hard to compute $[\![u^+]\!]_{\mathcal{NL}}$ because of the mismatch between our natural language semantic language and the Freebase query language. To ensure that graphs u^+ and g^+ have the same denotations, we impose the following constraints:

Constraint 1 If the math function UNIQUE is attached to the entity being replaced in the ungrounded graph, we assume the denotation of u^+ contains only that entity. For example, in Figure 2b, we replace *Austin* by x, and thus assume $[\![u^+]\!]_{\mathcal{NL}} = \{\text{AUSTIN}\}$.[4] Any grounded graph which results in $[\![g^+]\!]_{\mathcal{KB}} = \{\text{AUSTIN}\}$ will be considered a surrogate gold graph. This allows us to learn entailment relations, e.g., *capital.of* should be grounded to location.capital (left hand-side graph in Figure 2d) and not to location.containedby which results in all locations in *Texas* (right hand-side graph in Figure 2d).

Constraint 2 If the target entity node is a number, we select the Freebase graphs with denotation close to this number. For example, in Figure 8a if 120,000 is replaced by x, and we assume $[\![u^+]\!]_{\mathcal{NL}} = \{120{,}000\}$. However, the grounded graph 8b retrieves $[\![g^+]\!]_{\mathcal{KB}} = \{119{,}000\}$. We treat this as correct if $\frac{\beta}{\gamma} \in [0.9, 1.1]$ where $\beta \in [\![u^+]\!]_{\mathcal{NL}}$ and $\gamma \in [\![g^+]\!]_{\mathcal{KB}}$. Integers can either occur directly in relation with an entity as in Figure 8b, or must be enumerated as in Figure 7c.

Constraint 3 If the target entity node is a date, we select the grounded graph which results in the smallest set containing the date based on the intuition that most sentences in the data describe specific rather than general events.

Constraint 4 If none of the above constraints apply to the target entity E, we know $E \in [\![u^+]\!]_{\mathcal{NL}}$, and hence we select the grounded graphs which satisfy $E \in [\![g^+]\!]_{\mathcal{KB}}$ as surrogate gold graphs.

3.3 Features

Our feature vector $\Phi(g, u, s, \mathcal{KB})$ denotes the features extracted from a sentence s and its corresponding graphs u and g with respect to a knowledge base $\mathcal{KB}$. The elements of the vector $(\phi_1, \phi_2, \ldots)$ take integer values denoting the number of times a feature appeared. We devised the following broad feature classes:

Lexical alignments Since ungrounded graphs are similar in topology to grounded graphs, we extract ungrounded and grounded edge and type alignments. So, from graphs 5a and 5b, we obtain the edge alignment ϕ_{edge}(directed.arg1, directed.arg2, film.directed_by.arg2, film.directed_by.arg1) and the subedge alignments ϕ_{edge}(directed.arg1, film.directed_by.arg2) and ϕ_{edge}(directed.arg2, film.directed_by.arg1). In a similar fashion we extract type alignments (e.g., ϕ_{type}(capital, location.city)).

Contextual features In addition to lexical alignments, we also use contextual features which essentially record words or word combinations surrounding grounded edge labels. Feature ϕ_{event} records an event word and its grounded predicates (e.g., in Figure 7c we extract features ϕ_{event}(appear, performance.film) and ϕ_{event}(appear, performance.actor). Feature ϕ_{arg} records a predicate and its argument words (e.g., ϕ_{arg}(performance.film, movie) in Figure 7c). Word combination features are extracted from the parser's dependency output. The feature ϕ_{dep} records a predicate and the dependencies of its event word (e.g., from the grounded version of Figure 6b we extract features ϕ_{dep}(location.state.capital.arg1, capital, state) and ϕ_{dep}(location.state.capital.arg2, capital, state)). Using such features, we are able to handle multiword predicates.

Lexical similarity We count the number of word stems[5] shared by grounded and ungrounded edge labels e.g., in Figure 5 directed.arg1 and film.directed_by.arg2 have one stem overlap (ignoring the argument labels arg1 and arg2). For a grounded graph, we compute ϕ_{stem}, the aggregate stem overlap count over all its grounded and ungrounded edge labels. We did not incorporate WordNet/Wiktionary-based lexical similarity features but these were found fruitful in Kwiatkowski et al. (2013). We also have a feature for stem overlap count between the grounded edge labels and the context words.

Graph connectivity features These features penalize graphs with non-standard topologies. For example, we do not want a final graph with no edges. The feature value $\phi_{hasEdge}$ is one if there exists at least one edge in the graph. We also have a feature $\phi_{nodeCount}$ for counting the number of connected

[4] We also remove UNIQUE attached to x to exactly mimic the test time setting.

[5] We use the Porter stemmer.

Domain	#Rels	#Types	#Triples	#Train	#Free917	#WebQ
`business`	226	102	23m	30k	46	49
`film`	113	75	42m	13k	49	91
`people`	85	59	68m	56k	29	430
`all*`	411	210	120m	99k	124	570

Table 1: Domain-specific Freebase statistics (*some relations/types/triples are shared across domains); number of training CLUEWEB09 sentences; number of test questions in FREE917 and WEBQUESTIONS.

nodes in the graph. Finally, feature ϕ_{colloc} captures the collocation of grounded edges (e.g., edges belonging to a single complex fact are likely to cooccur; see Figure 8b).

4 Experimental Setup

In this section we present our experimental set-up for assessing the performance of the semantic parser described above. We present the datasets on which our model was trained and tested, discuss implementation details, and briefly introduce the models used for comparison with our approach.

4.1 Data

We evaluated our approach on the FREE917 (Cai and Yates, 2013) and WEBQUESTIONS (Berant et al., 2013) datasets. FREE917 consists of 917 questions and their meaning representations (written in a variant of lambda calculus) which we, however, do not use. The dataset represents 81 domains covering 635 Freebase relations, with most domains containing fewer than 10 questions. We report results on three domains, namely `film`, `business`, and `people` as these are relatively large in both FREE917 and Freebase. WEBQUESTIONS consists of 5,810 question-answer pairs, 2,780 of which are reserved for testing. Our experiments used a subset of WEBQUESTIONS representing the three target domains. We extracted domain-specific queries semi-automatically by identifying question-answer pairs with entities in target domain relations. In both datasets, named entities were disambiguated to Freebase entities with a named entity lexicon.[6]

Table 1 presents descriptive statistics for each domain. Evaluating on all domains in Freebase would generate a very large number of queries for which denotations would have to be computed (the number of queries is linear in the number of domains and the size of training data). Our system loads Freebase using Virtuoso[7] and queries it with SPARQL. Virtuoso is slow in dealing with millions of queries indexed on the entire Freebase, and is the only reason we did not work with the complete Freebase.

4.2 Implementation

To train our model, we extracted sentences from CLUEWEB09 which contain at least two entities associated with a relation in Freebase, and have an edge between them in the ungrounded graph. These were further filtered so as to remove sentences which do not yield at least one semantic parse without an uninstantiated entity variable. For example, the sentence *Avatar is directed by Cameron* would be used for training, whereas *Avatar directed by Cameron received a critical review* wouldn't. In the latter case, any semantic parse will have an uninstantiated entity variable for *review*. Table 1 (Train) shows the number of sentences we obtained.

In order to train our semantic parser, we initialized the alignment and type features (ϕ_{edge} and ϕ_{type}, respectively) with the alignment lexicon weights. These weights are computed as follows. Let $count(r', r)$ denote the number of pairs of entities which are linked with edge r' in Freebase and edge r in CLUEWEB09 sentences. We then estimate the probability distribution $P(r'/r) = \frac{count(r', r)}{\sum_i count(r'_i, r)}$. Analogously, we created a type alignment lexicon. The counts were collected from CLUEWEB09 sentences containing pairs of entities linked with an edge in Freebase (`business` 390k, `film` 130k, and `people` 490k). Contextual features were initialized to -1 since most word contexts and grounded predicates/types do not appear together. All other features were set to 0.

We used a beam-search algorithm to convert ungrounded graphs to grounded ones. The edges and types of each ungrounded graph are placed in a priority queue. Priority is based on edge/type tf-idf scores collected over CLUEWEB09. At each step, we pop an element from the queue and ground it in Freebase. We rank the resulting grounded graphs us-

[6]FREE917 comes with a named entity lexicon. For WEBQUESTIONS we hand-coded this lexicon.

[7]`http://virtuoso.openlinksw.com`

ing the perceptron model, and pick the n-best ones, where n is the beam size. We continue until the queue is empty. In our experiments we used a beam size of 100. We trained a single model for all the domains combined together. We ran the perceptron for 20 iterations (around 5–10 million queries). At each training iteration we used 6,000 randomly selected sentences from the training corpus.

4.3 Comparison Systems

We compared our graph-based semantic parser (henceforth GRAPHPARSER) against two state-of-the-art systems both of which are open-domain and work with Freebase. The semantic parser developed by Kwiatkowski et al. (2013) (henceforth KCAZ13) is learned from question-answer pairs and follows a two-stage procedure: first, a natural language sentence is converted to a domain-independent semantic parse and then grounded onto Freebase using a set of logical-type equivalent operators. The operators explore possible ways sentential meaning could be expressed in Freebase and essentially transform logical form to match the target ontology. Our approach also has two steps (i.e., we first generate multiple ungrounded graphs and then ground them to different Freebase graphs). We do not use operators to perform structure matching, rather we create multiple graphs and leave it up to the learner to find an appropriate grounding using a rich feature space. To give a specific example, their operator *literal to constant* is equivalent to having named entities for larger text chunks in our case. Their operator *split literal* explores different edge possibilities in an event whereas we start with a clique and remove unwanted edges. Our approach has (almost) similar expressive power but is conceptually simpler.

Our second comparison system was the semantic parser of Berant and Liang (2014) (henceforth PARASEMPRE) which also uses QA pairs for training and makes use of paraphrasing. Given an input NL sentence, they first construct a set of logical forms based on hand-coded rules, and then generate sentences from each logical form (using generation templates and a lexicon). Pairs of logical forms and natural language are finally scored using a paraphrase model consisting of two components. An association model determines whether they contain phrase pairs likely to be paraphrases and a vector space model assigns a vector representation for each sentence, and learns a scoring function that ranks paraphrase candidates. Our semantic parser employs a graph-based representation as a means of handling the mismatch between natural language, whereas PARASEMPRE opts for a text-based one through paraphrasing.

System	Prec	Rec	F1
MWG	52.6	49.1	50.8
KCAZ13	72.6	66.1	69.2
GRAPHPARSER	81.9	76.6	79.2

Table 2: Experimental results on FREE917.

Finally, we compared our semantic parser against a baseline which is based on graphs but employs no learning. The baseline converts an ungrounded graph to a grounded one by replacing each ungrounded edge/type with the highest weighted grounded label creating a *maximum weighted graph*, henceforth MWG. Both GRAPHPARSER and the baseline use the same alignment lexicon (a weighted mapping from ungrounded to grounded labels).

5 Results

Table 2 summarizes our results on FREE917. As described earlier, we evaluated GRAPHPARSER on a subset of the dataset representing three domains (business, film, and people). Since this subset contains a relatively small number of instances (124 in total), we performed 10-fold cross validation with 9 folds as development data[8], and one fold as test data. We report results averaged over all test folds. With respect to KCAZ13, we present results with their cross-domain trained models, where training data from multiple domains is used to test foreign domains.[9] KCAZ13 used generic features like string similarity and knowledge base features which apply across domains and do not require in-domain training data. We do not report results with PARASEMPRE as the small number of training instances would put their method at a disadvantage. We treat a predicted query as correct if its denota-

[8] The development data is only used for model selection and for determining the optimal training iteration.

[9] We are grateful to Tom Kwiatkowski for supplying us with the output of their system.

Features	FREE917	WEBQ
All	79.2	41.4
−Contextual	73.3	42.6
−Alignment	66.7	34.8
−Connectivity	65.0	36.6
−Similarity	62.5	35.0

Table 3: GRAPHPARSER ablation results on FREE917 and WEBQUESTIONS development set.

System	Prec	Rec	F1
MWG	39.4	34.0	36.5
PARASEMPRE	37.5	37.5	37.5
GRAPHPARSER	41.9	37.0	39.3
GRAPHPARSER + PARA	44.7	38.4	41.3

Table 4: Experimental results on WEBQUESTIONS.

tion is exactly equal to the denotation of the manually annotated gold query.

As can be seen, GRAPHPARSER outperforms KCAZ13 and the MWG baseline by a wide margin. This is an encouraging result bearing in mind that our model does not use question-answer pairs. We should also point out that our domain relation set is larger compared to KCAZ13. We do not prune any of the relations in Freebase, whereas KCAZ13 use only 112 relations and 83 types from our three domains (see Table 1). We further performed a feature ablation study to examine the contribution of different feature classes. As shown in Table 3, the most important features are those based on lexical similarity, as also observed in KCAZ13. Graph connectivity and lexical alignments are equally important (these features are absent from KCAZ13). Contextual features are not very helpful over and above alignment features which also encode contextual information. Overall, generic features like lexical similarity are helpful only to a certain extent; the performance of GRAPHPARSER improves considerably when additional graph-related features are taken into account.

We also analyzed the errors GRAPHPARSER makes. 25% of these are caused by the C&C parser and are cases where it either returns no syntactic analysis or a wrong one. 19% of the errors are due to Freebase inconsistencies. For example, our system answered the question *How many stores are in Nittany mall?* with 65 using the relation shopping_center.number_of_stores whereas the gold standard provides the answer 25 counting all stores using the relation shopping_center.store. Around 15% of errors include structural mismatches between natural language and Freebase; for the question *Who is the president of Gap Inc?*, our method grounds *president* to a grounded type whereas in Freebase it is represented as a relation employment.job.title. The remaining errors are miscellaneous. For example, the question *What are some films on Antarctica?* receives two interpretations, i.e., movies filmed in Antarctica or movies with Antarctica as their subject.

We next discuss our results on WEBQUESTIONS. PARASEMPRE was trained with 1,115 QA pairs (corresponding to our target domains) together with question paraphrases obtained from the PARALEX corpus (Fader et al., 2013).[10] While training PARASEMPRE, out-of-domain Freebase relations and types were removed. Both GRAPHPARSER and PARASEMPRE were tested on the same set of 570 in-domain QA pairs with exact answer match as the evaluation criterion. For development purposes, GRAPHPARSER uses 200 QA pairs. Table 4 displays our results. We observe that GRAPHPARSER obtains a higher F1 against MWG and PARASEMPRE. Differences in performance among these systems are less pronounced compared to FREE917. This is for a good reason. WEBQUESTIONS is a challenging dataset, created by non-experts. The questions are not tailored to Freebase in any way, they are more varied and display a wider vocabulary. As a result the mismatch between natural language and Freebase is greater and the semantic parsing task harder.

Error analysis further revealed that parsing errors are responsible for 13% of the questions GRAPHPARSER fails to answer. Another cause of errors is mismatches between natural language and Freebase. Around 7% of the questions are of the type *Where did X come from?*, and our model answers with the individual's nationality, whereas annotators provide the birthplace (city/town/village) as the right answer. Moreover, 8% of the questions are of the type *What does X do?*, which the annotators answer with the individual's profession. In natural language, we rarely attest constructions

[10] We used the SEMPRE package (http://www-nlp.stanford.edu/software/sempre/) which does not use any hand-coded entity disambiguation lexicon.

like *X does dentist/researcher/actor*. The proposed framework assumes that Freebase and natural language are somewhat isomorphic, which is not always true. An obvious future direction would be to paraphrase the questions so as to increase the number of grounded and ungrounded graphs. As an illustration, we rewrote questions like *Where did X come from* to *What is X's birth place*, and *What did X do* to *What is X's profession* and evaluated our model GRAPHPARSER + PARA. As shown in Table 4, even simple paraphrasing can boost performance.

Finally, Table 3 (third column) examines the contribution of different features on the WEBQUESTIONS development dataset. Interestingly, we observe that contextual features are not useful and in fact slightly harm performance. We hypothesize that this is due to the higher degree of mismatch between natural language and Freebase in this dataset. Features based on similarity, graph connectivity, and lexical alignments are more robust and generally useful across datasets.

6 Discussion

In this paper, we introduce a new semantic parsing approach for Freebase. A key idea in our work is to exploit the structural and conceptual similarities between natural language and Freebase through a common graph-based representation. We formalize semantic parsing as a graph matching problem and learn a semantic parser without using annotated question-answer pairs. We have shown how to obtain graph representations from the output of a CCG parser and subsequently learn their correspondence to Freebase using a rich feature set and their denotations as a form of weak supervision. Our parser yields state-of-the art performance on three large Freebase domains and is not limited to question answering. We can create semantic parses for any type of NL sentences.

Our work brings together several strands of research. Graph-based representations of sentential meaning have recently gained some attention in the literature (Banarescu et al., 2013), and attempts to map sentences to semantic graphs have met with good inter-annotator agreement. Our work is also closely related to Kwiatkowski et al. (2013) and Berant and Liang (2014) who present open-domain semantic parsers based on Freebase and trained on QA pairs. Despite differences in formulation and model structure, both approaches have explicit mechanisms for handling the mismatch between natural language and the KB (e.g., using logical-type equivalent operators or paraphrases). The mismatch is handled implicitly in our case via our graphical representation which allows for the incorporation of all manner of powerful features. More generally, our method is based on the assumption that linguistic structure has a correspondence to Freebase structure which does not always hold (e.g., in *Who is the grandmother of Prince William?*, *grandmother* is not directly expressed as a relation in Freebase). Additionally, our model fails when questions are too short without any lexical clues (e.g., *What did Charles Darwin do?*). Supervision from annotated data or paraphrasing could improve performance in such cases. In the future, we plan to explore cluster-based semantics (Lewis and Steedman, 2013) to increase the robustness on unseen NL predicates.

Our work joins others in exploiting the connections between natural language and open-domain knowledge bases. Recent approaches in relation extraction use distant supervision from a knowledge base to predict grounded relations between two target entities (Mintz et al., 2009; Hoffmann et al., 2011; Riedel et al., 2013). During learning, they aggregate sentences containing the target entities, ignoring richer contextual information. In contrast, we learn from each individual sentence taking into account all entities present, their relations, and how they interact. Krishnamurthy and Mitchell (2012) formalize semantic parsing as a distantly supervised relation extraction problem combined with a manually specified grammar to guide semantic parse composition.

Finally, our approach learns a model of semantics guided by denotations as a form of weak supervision. Beyond semantic parsing (Artzi and Zettlemoyer, 2013; Liang et al., 2011; Clarke et al., 2010), feedback-based learning has been previously used for interpreting and following NL instructions (Branavan et al., 2009; Chen and Mooney, 2011), playing computer games (Branavan et al., 2012), and grounding language in the physical world (Krishnamurthy and Kollar, 2013; Matuszek et al., 2012).

Lemma	POS	Semantic Class	Semantic Category
*	VB*, IN, TO, POS	EVENT	directed : $(S_e\backslash NP_x{<}1{>})/NP_y{<}2{>}$: $\lambda Q\lambda P\lambda e.\exists x\exists y.$ directed.arg1$(e,x) \wedge$ directed.arg2$(e,y) \wedge P(x) \wedge Q(y)$
*	NN, NNS	TYPE	movie : NP : $\lambda x.$movie(x)
*	NNP*, PRP*	ENTITY	Obama : NP : $\lambda x.equal(x,$ Obama$)$
*	RB*	EVENTMOD	annually : $S_e\backslash S_e$: $\lambda P\lambda e.lex_e.$annually$(e) \wedge P(e)$
*	JJ*	TYPEMOD	state : NP_x/NP_x : $\lambda P\lambda x.lex_x.$state$(x) \wedge P(x)$
be	*	COPULA	be: $(S_y\backslash NP_x)/NP_y$: $\lambda Q\lambda P\lambda y.\exists x.lex_y(x) \wedge P(x) \wedge Q(y)$
the	*	UNIQUE	the : NP_x/NP_x : $\lambda P\lambda x.$UNIQUE$(x) \wedge P(x)$
*	CD	COUNT	twenty : N_x/N_x : $\lambda P\lambda x.$COUNT$(x,20) \wedge P(x)$ twenty : N_x/N_x : $\lambda P\lambda x.equal(x,20) \wedge P(x)$
not, n't	*	NEGATION	not : $(S_e\backslash NP_x)/(S_e\backslash NP_x)$: $\lambda P\lambda Q\lambda e.\exists x.$NEGATION$(e) \wedge P(x,e) \wedge Q(x)$
no	*	COMPLEMENT	no : NP_x/N_x : $\lambda P\lambda x.$COMPLEMENT$(x) \wedge P(x)$
*	WDT, WP*, WRB	QUESTION	what : $S[wq]_e/(S[dcl]_e\backslash NP_x)$: $\lambda P\lambda e.\exists x.$TARGET$(x) \wedge P(x,e)$
*	WDT, WP*, WRB	CLOSED	which : $(NP_x\backslash NP_x)/(S[dcl]_e\backslash NP_x)$: $\lambda P\lambda Q\lambda x.\exists e.P(x,e) \wedge Q(x)$

Table 5: Rules used to classify words into semantic classes. * represents a wild card expression which matches anything. lex_x denotes the lexicalised form of x e.g., when $state : NP_x/NP_x : \lambda P\lambda x.lex_x.state(x) \wedge P(x)$ is applied to $capital : NP : \lambda y.capital(y)$, the lexicalised form of x becomes *capital*, and therefore the predicate $lex_x.state$ becomes $capital.state$. The resulting semantic parse after application is $\lambda x.capital.state(x) \wedge capital(x)$.

Appendix

We use a handful of rules to divide words into semantic classes. Based on a word's semantic class and indexed syntactic category, we construct its semantic category automatically. For example, *directed* is a member of the EVENT class, and its indexed syntactic category is $((S_e\backslash NP_x{<}1{>})/NP_y{<}2{>})$ (here, $<1>$ and $<2>$ indicate that x and y are the first and second arguments of e). We then generate its semantic category as $\lambda Q\lambda P\lambda e.\exists x\exists y.directed.arg1(e,x) \wedge directed.arg2(e,y) \wedge P(x) \wedge Q(y)$. Please refer to Appendix B of Clark and Curran (2007) for a list of their indexed syntactic categories.

The rules are described in Table 5. Syntactic categories are not shown for the sake of brevity. Most rules will match any syntactic category. Exceptions are copula-related rules (see *be* in the sixth row) which apply only to the syntactic category $(S\backslash NP)/NP$, and rules pertaining to *wh*-words (see the last two rows in the table). When more than one rule apply, we end up with multiple semantic parses. There are a few cases like passives, question words, and prepositional phrases where we modified the original indexed categories for better interpretation of the semantics (these are not displayed here). We also handle non-standard CCG operators involving unary and binary rules as described in Appendix A of Clark and Curran (2007).

Acknowledgements

We are grateful to the anonymous reviewers for their valuable feedback on an earlier version of this paper. Thanks to Mike Lewis and the members of ILCC for helpful discussions and comments. We acknowledge the support of EU ERC Advanced Fellowship 249520 GRAMPLUS and EU IST Cognitive Systems IP EC-FP7-270273 “Xperience”.

References

Artzi, Yoav and Luke Zettlemoyer. 2011. Bootstrapping semantic parsers from conversations. In *Proceedings of the 2011 Conference on Empirical*

Methods in Natural Language Processing. Edinburgh, Scotland, pages 421–432.

Artzi, Yoav and Luke Zettlemoyer. 2013. Weakly supervised learning of semantic parsers for mapping instructions to actions. *Transations of the Association for Computational Linguistics* 1(1):49–62.

Banarescu, Laura, Claire Bonial, Shu Cai, Madalina Georgescu, Kira Griffitt, Ulf Hermjakob, Kevin Knight, Philipp Koehn, Martha Palmer, and Nathan Schneider. 2013. Abstract meaning representation for sembanking. In *Proceedings of the 7th Linguistic Annotation Workshop and Interoperability with Discourse*. Sofia, Bulgaria, pages 178–186.

Berant, Jonathan, Andrew Chou, Roy Frostig, and Percy Liang. 2013. Semantic parsing on Freebase from question-answer pairs. In *Proceedings of the 2013 Conference on Empirical Methods in Natural Language Processing*. Seattle, Washington, USA, pages 1533–1544.

Berant, Jonathan and Percy Liang. 2014. Semantic parsing via paraphrasing. In *Proceedings of the 52nd Annual Meeting of the Association for Computational Linguistics*. Baltimore, Maryland, USA, pages 1415–1425.

Bos, Johan, Stephen Clark, Mark Steedman, James R. Curran, and Julia Hockenmaier. 2004. Wide-coverage semantic representations from a ccg parser. In *Proceedings of Coling 2004*. Geneva, Switzerland, pages 1240–1246.

Branavan, S.R.K., Harr Chen, Luke Zettlemoyer, and Regina Barzilay. 2009. Reinforcement learning for mapping instructions to actions. In *Proceedings of the Joint Conference of the 47th Annual Meeting of the ACL and the 4th International Joint Conference on Natural Language Processing of the AFNLP*. Suntec, Singapore, pages 82–90.

Branavan, S.R.K., Nate Kushman, Tao Lei, and Regina Barzilay. 2012. Learning high-level planning from text. In *Proceedings of the 50th Annual Meeting of the Association for Computational Linguistics*. Jeju Island, Korea, pages 126–135.

Cai, Qingqing and Alexander Yates. 2013. Large-scale semantic parsing via schema matching and lexicon extension. In *Proceedings of the 51st Annual Meeting of the Association for Computational Linguistics*. Sofia, Bulgaria, pages 423–433.

Chen, David L. and Raymond J. Mooney. 2011. Learning to interpret natural language navigation instructions from observations. In *Proceedings of the 25th AAAI Conference on Artificial Intelligence*. San Francisco, California, pages 859–865.

Clark, Stephen and James R Curran. 2004. Parsing the wsj using CCG and log-linear models. In *Proceedings of the 42nd Annual Meeting on Association for Computational Linguistics*. Barcelona, Spain, pages 103–111.

Clark, Stephen and James R Curran. 2007. Wide-coverage efficient statistical parsing with CCG and log-linear models. *Computational Linguistics* 33(4):493–552.

Clark, Stephen, Julia Hockenmaier, and Mark Steedman. 2002. Building deep dependency structures with a wide-coverage CCG parser. In *Proceedings of the 40th Annual Meeting on Association for Computational Linguistics*. pages 327–334.

Clarke, James, Dan Goldwasser, Ming-Wei Chang, and Dan Roth. 2010. Driving semantic parsing from the world's response. In *Proceedings of the 14th Conference on Natural Language Learning*. Uppsala, Sweden, pages 18–27.

Collins, Michael. 2002. Discriminative training methods for Hidden Markov models: Theory and experiments with perceptron algorithms. In *Proceedings of the 2002 Conference on Empirical Methods in Natural Language Processing*. Philadelphia, Pennsylvania, pages 1–8.

Fader, Anthony, Luke Zettlemoyer, and Oren Etzioni. 2013. Paraphrase-driven learning for open question answering. In *Proceedings of the 51st Annual Meeting of the Association for Computational Linguistics*. Sofia, Bulgaria, pages 1608–1618.

Gabrilovich, Evgeniy, Michael Ringgaard, and Amarnag Subramanya. 2013. FACC1: Freebase annotation of ClueWeb corpora, Version 1 (Release date 2013-06-26, Format version 1, Correction level 0).

Goldwasser, Dan, Roi Reichart, James Clarke, and Dan Roth. 2011. Confidence driven unsupervised semantic parsing. In *Proceedings of the 49th Annual Meeting of the Association for Computational Linguistics: Human Language Technologies*. Portland, Oregon, USA, pages 1486–1495.

Goldwasser, Dan and Dan Roth. 2011. Learning from natural instructions. In *Proceedings of the 22nd International Joint Conference on Artificial Intelligence*. Barcelona, Spain, pages 1794–1800.

Hoffmann, Raphael, Congle Zhang, Xiao Ling, Luke S Zettlemoyer, and Daniel S Weld. 2011. Knowledge-based weak supervision for information extraction of overlapping relations. In *Proceedings of the 49th Annual Meeting of the Association for Computational Linguistics: Human Language Technologies*. Portland, Oregon, USA, pages 541–550.

Krishnamurthy, Jayant and Thomas Kollar. 2013. Jointly learning to parse and perceive: Connecting natural language to the physical world. *Transations of the Association for Computational Linguistics* 1(1):193–206.

Krishnamurthy, Jayant and Tom Mitchell. 2012. Weakly supervised training of semantic parsers. In *Proceedings of the 2012 Joint Conference on Empirical Methods in Natural Language Processing and Computational Natural Language Learning*. Jeju Island, Korea, pages 754–765.

Kwiatkowski, Tom, Eunsol Choi, Yoav Artzi, and Luke Zettlemoyer. 2013. Scaling semantic parsers with on-the-fly ontology matching. In *Proceedings of the 2013 Conference on Empirical Methods in Natural Language Processing*. Seattle, Washington, USA, pages 1545–1556.

Kwiatkowski, Tom, Luke Zettlemoyer, Sharon Goldwater, and Mark Steedman. 2010. Inducing probabilistic CCG grammars from logical form with higher-order unification. In *Proceedings of the 2010 Conference on Empirical Methods in Natural Language Processing*. pages 1223–1233.

Lewis, Mike and Mark Steedman. 2013. Combined distributional and logical semantics. *Transactions of the Association for Computational Linguistics* 1:179–192.

Liang, Percy, Michael Jordan, and Dan Klein. 2011. Learning dependency-based compositional semantics. In *Proceedings of the 49th Annual Meeting of the Association for Computational Linguistics: Human Language Technologies*. Portland, Oregon, USA, pages 590–599.

Matuszek, Cynthia, Nicholas FitzGerald, Luke Zettlemoyer, Liefeng Bo, and Dieter Fox. 2012. A joint model of language and perception for grounded attribute learning. In *Proceedings of the 29th International Conference on Machine Learning*. Edinburgh, Scotland, pages 1671–1678.

Mintz, Mike, Steven Bills, Rion Snow, and Dan Jurafsky. 2009. Distant supervision for relation extraction without labeled data. In *Proceedings of the Joint conference of the 47th Annual Meeting of the Association for Computational Linguistics and the 4th International Joint Conference on Natural Language Processing of the Asian Federation of Natural Language Processing*. pages 1003–1011.

Parsons, Terence. 1990. *Events in the Semantics of English*. MIT Press, Cambridge, MA.

Poon, Hoifung. 2013. Grounded unsupervised semantic parsing. In *Proceedings of the 51st Annual Meeting of the Association for Computational Linguistics*. Sofia, Bulgaria, pages 933–943.

Riedel, Sebastian, Limin Yao, Andrew McCallum, and Benjamin M Marlin. 2013. Relation extraction with matrix factorization and universal schemas. In *Proceedings of the 2013 Conference of the North American Chapter of the Association for Computational Linguistics: Human Language Technologies*. Atlanta, Georgia, pages 74–84.

Steedman, Mark. 2000. *The Syntactic Process*. The MIT Press.

Wong, Yuk Wah and Raymond Mooney. 2007. Learning synchronous grammars for semantic parsing with lambda calculus. In *Proceedings of the 45th Annual Meeting of the Association of Computational Linguistics*. Prague, Czech Republic, pages 960–967.

Yao, Xuchen and Benjamin Van Durme. 2014. Information extraction over structured data: Question answering with freebase. In *Proceedings of the 52nd Annual Meeting of the Association for Computational Linguistics*. Baltimore, Maryland, USA, pages 956–966.

Zelle, John M and Raymond J Mooney. 1996. Learning to parse database queries using inductive logic programming. In *Proceedings of the National Conference on Artificial Intelligence*. Portland, Oregon, pages 1050–1055.

Zettlemoyer, Luke and Michael Collins. 2007. Online learning of relaxed CCG grammars for parsing to logical form. In *Proceedings of the 2007 Joint Conference on Empirical Methods in Natural Language Processing and Computational Natural Language Learning*. Prague, Czech Republic, pages 678–687.

Zettlemoyer, Luke S. and Michael Collins. 2005. Learning to map sentences to logical form: Structured classification with probabilistic categorial grammars. In *Proceedings of 21st Conference in Uncertainilty in Artificial Intelligence*. Edinburgh, Scotland, pages 658–666.

Locally Non-Linear Learning for Statistical Machine Translation via Discretization and Structured Regularization

Jonathan H. Clark* **Chris Dyer†** **Alon Lavie†**

*Microsoft Research
Redmond, WA 98052, USA
jonathan.clark@microsoft.com

†Carnegie Mellon University
Pittsburgh, PA 15213, USA
{cdyer,alavie}@cs.cmu.edu

Abstract

Linear models, which support efficient learning and inference, are the workhorses of statistical machine translation; however, linear decision rules are less attractive from a modeling perspective. In this work, we introduce a technique for learning arbitrary, rule-local, non-linear feature transforms that improve model expressivity, but do not sacrifice the efficient inference and learning associated with linear models. To demonstrate the value of our technique, we discard the customary log transform of lexical probabilities and drop the phrasal translation probability in favor of raw counts. We observe that our algorithm learns a variation of a log transform that leads to better translation quality compared to the explicit log transform. We conclude that non-linear responses play an important role in SMT, an observation that we hope will inform the efforts of feature engineers.

1 Introduction

Linear models using `log`-transformed probabilities as features have emerged as the dominant model in MT systems. This practice can be traced back to the IBM noisy channel models (Brown et al., 1993), which decompose decoding into the product of a translation model (TM) and a language model (LM), motivated by Bayes' Rule. When Och and Ney (2002) introduced a `log`-linear model for translation (a linear sum of `log`-space features), they noted that the noisy channel model was a special case of their model using `log` probabilities. This same formulation persisted even after the introduction of MERT (Och, 2003), which optimizes a linear model; again, using two `log` probability features (TM and LM) with equal weight recovered the noisy channel model. Yet systems now use many more features, some of which are not even probabilities. We no longer believe that equal weights between the TM and LM provides optimal translation quality; the probabilities in the TM do not obey the chain rule nor Bayes' rule, nullifying several theoretical mathematical justifications for multiplying probabilities. The story of multiplying probabilities may just amount to heavily penalizing small values.

The community has abandoned the original motivations for a linear interpolation of two `log`-transformed features. Is there empirical evidence that we should continue using this particular transformation? Do we have any reason to believe it is better than other non-linear transformations? To answer these, we explore the issue of non-linearity in models for MT. In the process, we will discuss the impact of linearity on feature engineering and develop a general mechanism for learning a class of non-linear transformations of real-valued features.

Applying a non-linear transformation such as `log` to features is one way of achieving a non-linear response function, even if those features are aggregated in a linear model. Alternatively, we could achieve a non-linear response using a natively non-linear model such as a SVM (Wang et al., 2007) or RankBoost (Sokolov et al., 2012). However, MT is a structured prediction problem, in which a full hypothesis is composed of partial hypotheses. MT decoders take advantage of the fact that the model

*This work was conducted as part of the first author's Ph.D. work at Carnegie Mellon University.

Transactions of the Association for Computational Linguistics, 2 (2014) 393–404. Action Editor: Robert C. Moore.
Submitted 2/2014; Revised 6/2014; Published 10/2014.

score decomposes as a linear sum over both local features and partial hypotheses to efficiently perform inference in these structured spaces (§2) – currently, there are no scalable solutions to integrating the hypothesis-level non-linear feature transforms typically associated with kernel methods while still maintaining polynomial time search. Another alternative is incorporating a recurrent neural network (Schwenk, 2012; Auli et al., 2013; Kalchbrenner and Blunsom, 2013) or an additive neural network (Liu et al., 2013a). While these models have shown promise as methods of augmenting existing models, they have not yet offered a path for replacing or transforming existing real-valued features.

In this article, we discuss background (§2), describe local discretization, our approach to learning non-linear transformations of individual features, compare it with globally non-linear models (§3), present our experimental setup (§5), empirically verify the importance of non-linear feature transformations in MT and demonstrate that discretization can be used to recover non-linear transformations (§6), discuss related work (§7), and conclude (§8).

2 Background and Definitions

2.1 Feature Locality & Structured Hypotheses

Decoding a given source sentence $\mathbf{f}$ can be expressed as search over target hypotheses $\mathbf{e}$, each with an associated complete derivation D. To find the best-scoring hypothesis $\hat{\mathbf{e}}(\mathbf{f})$, a linear model applies a set of weights $\mathbf{w}$ to a complete hypothesis' feature vector $\mathbf{H}$:

$$\hat{\mathbf{e}}(\mathbf{f}) = \arg\max_{\mathbf{e},D} \sum_{i=0}^{|\mathbf{H}|} w_i H_i(\mathbf{f}, \mathbf{e}, D) \quad (1)$$

However, this hides many of the realities of performing inference in modern decoders. Traditional inference would be intractable if every feature were allowed access to the entire derivation D and its associated target hypothesis $\mathbf{e}$. Decoders take advantage of the fact that features decompose over partial derivations d. For a complete derivation D, the global features $H(D)$ are an efficient summation over local features $h(d)$:

$$\hat{\mathbf{e}}(\mathbf{f}) = \arg\max_{\mathbf{e},D} \sum_{i=0}^{|\mathbf{H}|} w_i \underbrace{\sum_{d \in D} h_i(d)}_{H_i(D)} \quad (2)$$

This contrasts with non-local features such as the language model (LM), which cannot be exactly calculated given an arbitrary partial hypothesis, which may lack both left and right context.[1] Such features require special handling including future cost estimation. In this study, we limit ourselves to local features, leaving the traditional non-local LM feature unchanged. In general, feature locality is relative to a particular **structured hypothesis space**, and is unrelated to the structured features described in Section 4.2.

2.2 Feature Non-Linearity and Separability

Unlike models that rely primarily on a large number of sparse indicator features, state-of-the-art machine translation systems rely heavily on a small number of dense real-valued features. However, unlike indicator features, real-valued features may benefit from non-linear transformations to allow a linear model to better fit the data.

Decoders use a linear model to rank hypotheses, selecting the highest-*ranked* derivation. Since the absolute score of the model is irrelevant, non-linear responses are useful only in cases where they elicit novel rankings. In this section, we will discuss these cases in terms of separability. Here, we are separating the correctly ranked pairs of hypotheses from the incorrect in the implicit pairwise rankings defined by the total ordering on hypotheses provided by our model.

When the local feature vectors h of each oracle-best[2] hypothesis (or hypotheses) are distinct from those of all other competing hypotheses, we say that the inputs are **oracle separable** given the feature set. If there exists a weight vector that distinguishes the oracle-best ranking from all other rankings under a linear model, we say that the inputs are **linearly separable** given the feature set. If the inputs are oracle separable but not linearly separable, we say that there are **non-linearities** that are unexplained by the feature set. For example, this can happen if a feature is positively related to quality in some regions but negatively related in other regions.

As we add more sentences to our corpus, separability becomes increasingly difficult. For a given

[1] This is especially problematic for chart-based decoders.

[2] We define the oracle-best hypothesis in terms of some external quality measure such as BLEU

corpus, if all hypotheses are oracle separable, we can always produce the oracle translation – assuming an optimal (and potentially very complex) model and weight vector. If our hypothesis space also contains all reference translations, we can always recover the reference. In practice, both of these conditions are typically violated to a certain degree. However, if we modify our feature set such that some lower-ranked higher-quality hypothesis can be separated from all higher-ranked lower-quality hypotheses, then we can improve translation quality. For this reason, we believe that separability remains an informative tool for thinking about modeling in MT.

Currently, non-linearities in novel real-valued features are typically addressed via manual feature engineering involving a good deal of trial and error (Gimpel and Smith, 2009)[3] or by manually discretizing features (e.g. indicator features for count=N). We will explore one technique for automatically avoiding non-linearities in Section 3.

2.3 Learning with Large Feature Sets

While MERT has proven to be a strong baseline, it does not scale to larger feature sets in terms of both inefficiency and overfitting. While MIRA (Chiang et al., 2008), Rampion (Gimpel and Smith, 2012), and HOLS (Flanigan et al., 2013) have been shown to be effective over larger feature sets, they are difficult to explicitly regularize – this will become important in Section 4.2. Therefore, we use the PRO optimizer (Hopkins and May, 2011) as our baseline learner since it has been shown to perform comparably to MERT for a small number of features, and to significantly outperform MERT for a large number of features (Hopkins and May, 2011; Ganitkevitch et al., 2012). Other very recent MT optimizers such as the linear structured SVM (Cherry and Foster, 2012), AROW (Chiang, 2012) and regularized MERT (Galley et al., 2013) are also compatible with the discretization and structured regularization techniques described in this article.[4]

[3]Gimpel et al. eventually used raw probabilities in their model rather than log-probabilities.

[4]Since we dispense with nearly all of the original dense features and our structured regularizer is scale sensitive, one would need to use the ℓ_1-renormalized variant of regularized MERT.

3 Discretization and Feature Induction

In this section, we propose a feature induction technique based on discretization that produces a feature set that is less prone to non-linearities (see §2.2).

We define feature induction as a function $\Phi(y)$ that takes the result of the feature function $y = h(x) \in \mathbb{R}$ and returns a tuple $\langle y', j \rangle$ where $y' \in \mathbb{R}$ is a transformed feature value and j is the transformed feature index.[5] Building on equation 2, we can apply feature induction as follows:

$$\hat{\mathbf{e}}(\mathbf{f}) = \arg\max_{\mathbf{e},\mathbf{D}} \underbrace{\sum_{\mathbf{d} \in \mathbf{D}} \sum_{\substack{i=0 \\ \langle y',j\rangle = \Phi_i(h_i(d))}}^{|\mathbf{H}|} w'_j y'}_{\mathbf{H}'(\mathbf{f},\mathbf{e},\mathbf{D})} \quad (3)$$

At first glance, one might be tempted to simply choose some non-linear function for Φ (e.g. $\log(x), \exp(x), \sin(x), x^n$). However, even if we were to restrict ourselves to some "standard" set of non-linear functions, many of these functions have hyperparameters that are not directly tunable by conventional optimizers (e.g.period and amplitude for sin, n in x^n).

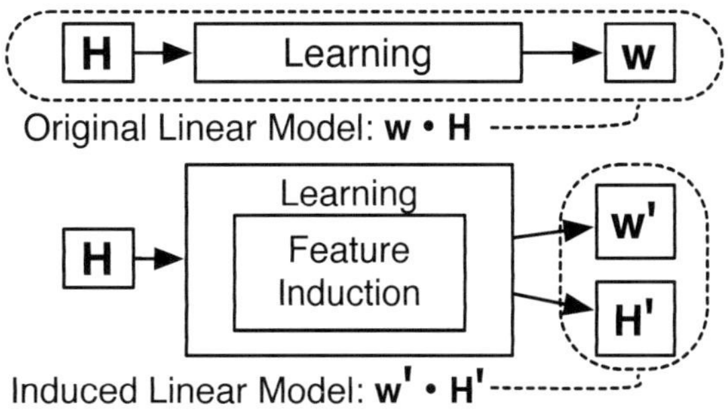

Figure 1: **Top:** A traditional learning procedure, assigning a set of weights to a fixed feature set. **Bottom:** Discretization, our feature induction technique, expands the feature set as part of learning, while still producing a linear model for inference, albeit with more features.

Discretization allows us to avoid many non-linearities (§2.2) while preserving the fast inference provided by feature locality (§2.1). We first discretize real-valued features into a set of indicator

[5]One could also imagine a feature transformation function Φ that returns a vector of bins for a single value returned by a feature function h or a transformation that has access to values from multiple feature functions at once.

features and then use a conventional optimizer to learn a weight for each indicator feature (Figure 1). This technique is sometimes referred to as binning and is closely related to quantization. Effectively, discretization allows us to re-shape a feature function (Figure 2). In fact, given an infinite number of bins, we can perform any non-linear transformation of the original function.

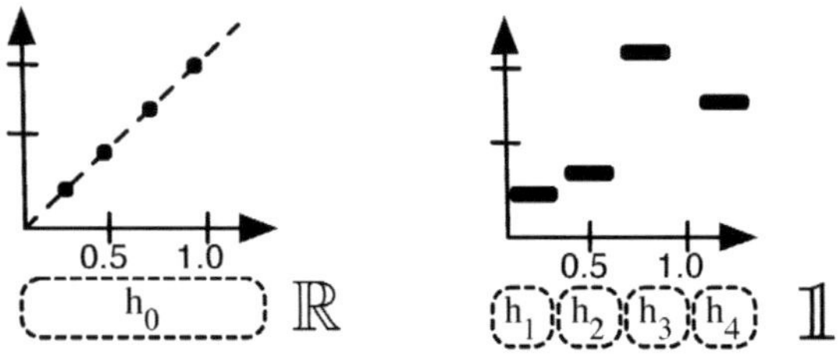

Figure 2: **Left:** A real-valued feature. Bold dots represent points where we could imagine bins being placed. However, since we may only adjust w_0, these "bins" will be rigidly fixed along the feature function's value. **Right:** After discretizing the feature into 4 bins, we may now adjust 4 weights independently, to achieve a non-linear re-shaping of the function.

For indicator discretization, we define Φ_i in terms of a binning function $\textsc{Bin}_i(x) \in \mathbb{R} \rightarrow \mathbb{N}$:

$$\Phi_i(x) = \langle 1, i \frown \textsc{Bin}_i(x) \rangle \quad (4)$$

where the $\frown$ operator indicates concatenation of a feature identifier with a bin identifier to form a new, unique feature identifier.

3.1 Local Discretization

Unlike other approaches to non-linear learning in MT, we perform non-linear transformation on *partial* hypotheses as in equation 3 where discretization is applied as $\Phi_i(h_i(d))$, which allows **locally non-linear** transformations, instead of applying Φ to complete hypotheses as in $\Phi_i(H_i(D))$, which would allow **globally non-linear** transformations. This enables our transformed model to produce non-linear responses with regard to the initial feature set $\mathbf{H}$ while inference remains linear with regard to the optimized parameters $\mathbf{w}'$. Importantly, our transformed feature set requires no additional non-local information for inference.

By performing transformations within a local context, we effectively reinterpret the feature set. For example, the familiar target word count feature found in many modern MT systems is often conceptualized as "what is the count of target words in the complete hypothesis?" A hypothesis-level view of discretization would view this as "Did this hypothesis have 5 target words?". Only one such feature will fire for each hypothesis. However, local discretization reinterprets this feature as "How many phrases in the complete hypothesis have 1 target word?" Many such features are likely to fire for each hypothesis. We provide a further example of this technique in Figure 3.

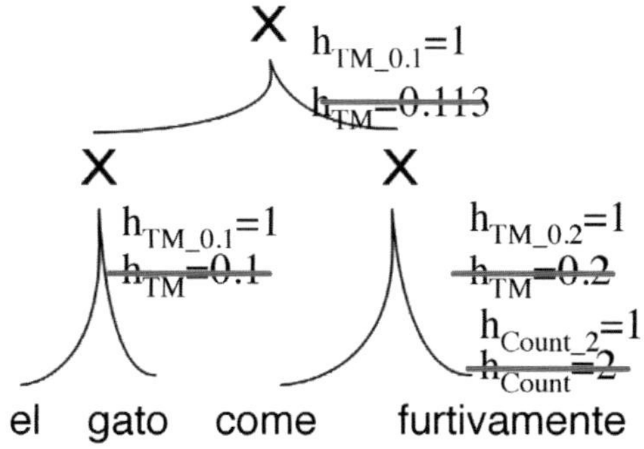

Figure 3: We perform discretization *locally* on each grammar rule or phrase pair, operating on the local feature vectors $\mathbf{h}$. In this example, the original real-valued features are crossed out with a solid gray line and their discretized indicator features are written above. When forming a complete hypothesis from partial hypotheses, we sum the counts of these indicator features to obtain the complete feature vector $\mathbf{H}$. In this example, $\mathbf{H} = \{H_{\text{TM\_0.1}} : 2, H_{\text{TM\_0.2}} : 1, H_{\text{Count\_2}} : 1\}$

In terms of predictive power, this transformation can provide the learned model with increased ability to discriminate between hypotheses. This is primarily a result of moving to a higher-dimensional feature space. As we introduce new parameters, we expect that some hypotheses that were previously indistinguishable under $\mathbf{H}$ become separable under $\mathbf{H}'$ (§2.2). We show specific examples comparing linear, locally non-linear, and globally non-linear models in Figures 4 - 6. As seen in these examples, locally non-linear models (Eq. 3, 4) are not an approximation nor a subset of globally non-linear models, but rather a different class of models.

3.2 Binning Algorithm

To initialize the learning procedure, we construct the binning function $\textsc{Bin}$ used by the indicator di-

	Linear	Globally Non-Linear	Locally Non-Linear
Ranking	$^*S_3^1$ he says h:1.0 h:1.0 = {H:2.0} S_3^2 she said h:2.0 h:2.0 = {H:4.0} S_4^1 small kitten h:2.0 h:2.0 = {H:4.0} $^*S_4^2$ big lion h:3.0 h:3.0 = {H:6.0}	$^*S_3^1$ he says h:1.0 h:1.0 = {H_2:1} S_3^2 she said h:2.0 h:2.0 = {H_4:1} S_4^1 small kitten h:2.0 h:2.0 = {H_4:1} $^*S_4^2$ big lion h:3.0 h:3.0 = {H_6:1}	$^*S_3^1$ he says h_1:1 h_1:1 = {H_1:2} S_3^2 she said h_2:1 h_2:1 = {H_2:2} S_4^1 small kitten h_2:1 h_2:1 = {H_2:2} $^*S_4^2$ big lion h_3:1 h_3:1 = {H_3:2}
Pairs	(S_3^1, S_3^2) {ΔH:-2.0} ⊕ (S_3^2, S_3^1) {ΔH:2.0} ⊖ (S_4^2, S_4^1) {ΔH:-2.0} ⊖ (S_4^1, S_4^2) {ΔH:2.0} ⊕	(S_3^1, S_3^2) {ΔH_2:1, ΔH_4:-1} ⊕ (S_3^2, S_3^1) {ΔH_2:-1, ΔH_4:1} ⊖ (S_4^2, S_4^1) {ΔH_4:1, ΔH_6:-1} ⊖ (S_4^1, S_4^2) {ΔH_4:-1, ΔH_6:1} ⊕	(S_3^1, S_3^2) {ΔH_1:2, ΔH_2:-2} ⊕ (S_3^2, S_3^1) {ΔH_1:-2, ΔH_2:2} ⊖ (S_4^2, S_4^1) {ΔH_2:2, ΔH_3:-2} ⊖ (S_4^1, S_4^2) {ΔH_2:-2, ΔH_3:2} ⊕
Pairwise Ranking	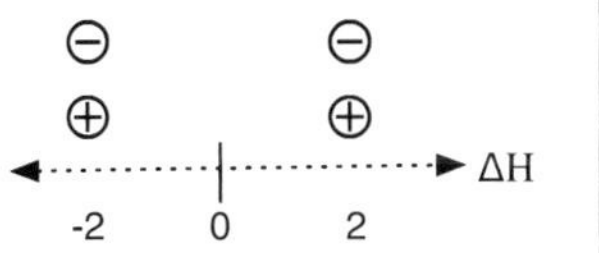 **Inseparable**	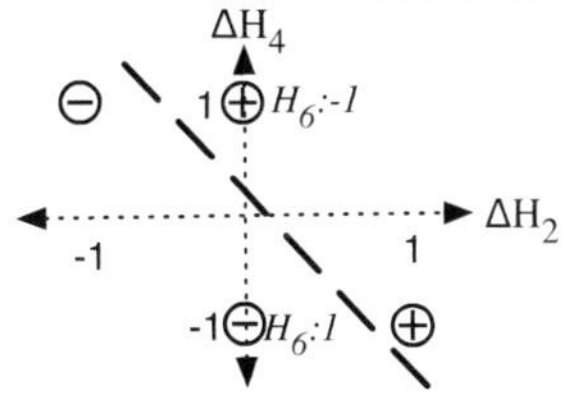 **Separable**	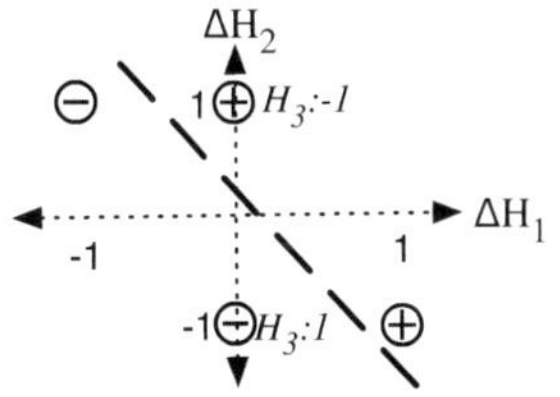 **Separable**

Figure 4: An example showing a **collinearity** over multiple input sentences S_3, S_4 in which the oracle-best hypothesis is "trapped" along a line with other lower quality hypotheses in the linear model's output space. **Ranking** shows how the hypotheses would appear in a k-best list with each partial derivation having its partial feature vector h under it; the complete feature vector H is shown to the right of each hypothesis and the oracle-best hypothesis is notated with a $*$. **Pairs** explicates the implicit pairwise rankings. **Pairwise Ranking** graphs those pairs in order to visualize whether or not the hypotheses are separable. (⊕ indicates that the pair of hypotheses is ranked correctly according to the extrinsic metric and ⊖ indicates the pair is ranked incorrectly. In the pairwise ranking row, some ⊕ and ⊖ points are annotated with their positions along the third axis H_3 (omitted for clarity). Collinearity can also occur with a single input having at least 3 hypotheses.

	Linear	Globally Non-Linear	Locally Non-Linear
Ranking	$^*S_2^1$ some things h:2.0 h:2.0 = {H:4.0} S_2^2 something h:4.0 = {H:4.0}	$^*S_2^1$ some things h:2.0 h:2.0 = {H_4:1} S_2^2 something h:4.0 = {H_4:1}	$^*S_2^1$ some things h_2:1 h_2:1 = {H_2:2} S_2^2 something h_4:1 = {H_4:1}
Pairs	(S_2^1, S_2^2) {ΔH:0.0} ⊕ (S_2^2, S_2^1) {ΔH:0.0} ⊖	(S_2^1, S_2^2) {ΔH_4:0} ⊕ (S_2^2, S_2^1) {ΔH_4:0} ⊖	(S_2^1, S_2^2) {ΔH_2:2, ΔH_4:-1} ⊕ (S_2^2, S_2^1) {ΔH_2:-2, ΔH_4:1} ⊖
Pairwise Ranking	**Inseparable**	**Inseparable**	**Separable**

Figure 5: An example showing a trivial "collision" in which two hypotheses of differing quality receive the same model score until local discretization is applied. The two hypotheses are indistinguishable under a linear model with the feature set H, as shown by the zero-difference in the "pairs" row. While a globally non-linear transformation does not yield any improvement, local discretization allows the hypotheses to be properly ranked due to the higher-dimensional feature space H_2, H_4. See Figure 4 for an explanation of notation.

	Linear	Locally Non-Linear
Ranking	$^*\mathrm{h}^B{:}1.0 = \{\mathrm{H}^B{:}1.0\}$ $\mathrm{h}^A{:}1.0\ \mathrm{h}^A{:}1.0 = \{\mathrm{H}^A{:}2.0\}$	$^*\mathrm{h}^B_1{:}1 = \{\mathrm{H}^B_1{:}1\}$ $\mathrm{h}^A_1{:}1\ \mathrm{h}^A_1{:}1 = \{\mathrm{H}^A_1{:}2\}$
	$^*\mathrm{h}^A{:}1.0\ \mathrm{h}^A{:}1.0\ \mathrm{h}^B{:}1.0 = \{\mathrm{H}^A{:}2.0, \mathrm{H}^B{:}1.0\}$ $\mathrm{h}^A{:}0.0 = \{\}$	$^*\mathrm{h}^A_1{:}1\ \mathrm{h}^A_1{:}1\ \mathrm{h}^B_1{:}1 = \{\mathrm{H}^A_1{:}2, \mathrm{H}^B_1{:}1\}$ $\mathrm{h}^A_1{:}0 = \{\}$
	$^*\ \mathrm{h}^B{:}\text{-}4.0\ \mathrm{h}^B{:}1.0\ \mathrm{h}^B{:}1.0\ \mathrm{h}^B{:}1.0 = \{\mathrm{H}^B{:}\text{-}1.0\}$ $\mathrm{h}^A{:}1.0 = \{\mathrm{H}^A{:}1.0\}$	$^*\mathrm{h}^B_{-4}{:}1\ \mathrm{h}^B_1{:}1\ \mathrm{h}^B_1{:}1\ \mathrm{h}^B_1{:}1 = \{\mathrm{H}^B_{-4}{:}1, \mathrm{H}^B_1{:}3\}$ $\mathrm{h}^A_1{:}1 = \{\mathrm{H}^A_1{:}1\}$
	$^*\mathrm{h}^B{:}\text{-}4.0\ \mathrm{h}^A{:}1.0 = \{\mathrm{H}^A{:}1.0, \mathrm{H}^B{:}\text{-}4.0\}$ $\mathrm{h}^B{:}1.0\ \mathrm{h}^B{:}1.0 = \{\mathrm{H}^B{:}2.0\}$	$^*\mathrm{h}^B_{-4}{:}1\ \mathrm{h}^A_1{:}1 = \{\mathrm{H}^A_1{:}1, \mathrm{H}^B_{-4}{:}1\}$ $\mathrm{h}^B_1{:}1\ \mathrm{h}^B_1{:}1 = \{\mathrm{H}^B_1{:}2\}$
Pairwise Ranking	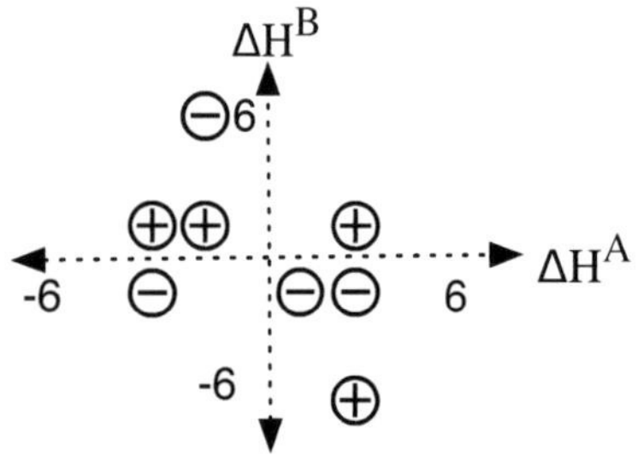 **Inseparable**	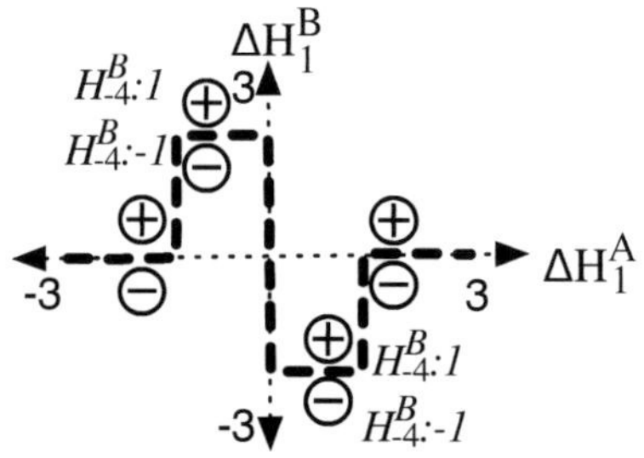 **Separable**

Figure 6: An example demonstrating a non-linear decision boundary induced by discretization. The non-linear nature of the decision boundary can be seen clearly when the induced feature set H_1^A, H_1^B, H_{-4}^B (right) is considered in the original feature space H^A, H^B (left). In the **pairwise ranking** row, two axes (H_1^A, H_1^B) are plotted while the third axis H_{-4}^B is indicated only as stand-off annotations for clarity . Given a larger number of hypotheses, such situations could also arise within a single sentence. See Figure 4 for an explanation of notation.

cretizer Φ. We have two desiderata: (1) any monotonic transformation of a feature should not affect the induced binning since we should not require feature engineers to determine the optimal feature transformation and (2) no bin's data should be so sparse that the optimizer cannot reliably estimate a weight for each bin. Therefore, we construct bins that are (i) populated uniformly subject to (ii) each bin containing no more than one feature value. We call this approach **uniform population feature binning**. While one could consider the predictive power of the features when determining bin boundaries, this would suggest that we should jointly optimize and determine bin boundaries, which is beyond the scope of this work. This problem has recently been considered for NLP by Suzuki and Nagata (2013) and for MT by Liu et al. (2013b), though the latter involves decoding the entire training data.

Let $\mathcal{X}$ be the list of feature values to bin where i indexes feature values $x_i \in \mathcal{X}$ and their associated frequencies f_i. We want each bin to have a uniform size u. For the sake of simplifying our final algorithm, we first create adjusted frequencies f_i' so that very frequent feature values will not occupy more than 100% of a bin via the following algorithm, which iterates over k:

$$u^k = \frac{1}{|\mathcal{X}|} \sum_{i=1}^{|\mathcal{X}|} f_i^k \tag{5}$$

$$f_i^{k+1} = \min(f_i^k, u^k) \tag{6}$$

which returns $u' = u^k$ when $f_i^k < u^k \ \forall i$. Next, we solve for a binning B of N bins where $\overline{\overline{b_j}}$ is the population of each bin:

$$\arg\min_B \frac{1}{N} \sum_{j=1}^{N} |\overline{\overline{b_j}} - u'| \tag{7}$$

We use Algorithm 1 to produce this binning. In our experiments, we construct a translation model for each sentence in our tuning corpus; we then add a feature value instances to $\mathcal{X}$ for each rule instance.

Algorithm 1 POPULATEBINSUNIFORMLY($\mathcal{X}, N$)

▷ Remaining values for b_j, s.t. $\overline{\overline{b_k}} > 0 \, \forall k$
def $R(j) = |\mathcal{X}| - (N - j - 1)$
▷ Remaining frequency mass within ideal bound
def $C(j) = j \cdot u' - \sum_k^j \overline{\overline{b_k}}$
$i \leftarrow 1$ ▷ Current feature value
for $j \in [1, N]$ **do**
  while $i \le R(j)$ **and** $f_i \le C(j)$ **do**
    $b_j \leftarrow b_j \cup \{x_i\}$
    $i \leftarrow i + 1$
  end while
  ▷ Handle value that straddles ideal boundaries by minimizing its violation of the ideal
  if $i \le R(j)$ **and** $\frac{f_i - C(j)}{f_i} < 0.5$ **then**
    $b_j \leftarrow b_j \cup \{x_i\}$
    $i \leftarrow i + 1$
  end if
end for
return B

4 Structured Regularization

Unfortunately, choosing the right number of bins can have important effects on the model, including:
Fidelity. If we choose too few bins, we risk degrading the model's performance by discarding important distinctions encoded in fine differences between the feature values. In the extreme, we could reduce a real-valued feature to a single indicator feature.
Sparsity. If we choose too many bins, we risk making each indicator feature too sparse, which is likely to result in the optimizer overfitting such that we generalize poorly to unseen data.

While one may be tempted to simply throw more data or millions of sparse features at the problem, we elect to more strategically use existing data, since (1) large in-domain tuning data is not always available, and (2) when it is available, it can add considerable computational expense. In this section, we explore methods for mitigating data sparsity by embedding more knowledge into the learning procedure.

4.1 Overlapping Bins

One very simplistic way we could combat sparsity is to extend the edges of each bin such that they cover their neighbors' values (see Equation 4):

$$\Phi_i'(x) = \langle 1, i \frown \text{BIN}_i(x) \rangle \text{ if } x \in \cup_{k=i-1}^{i+1} \text{BIN}_k \quad (8)$$

This way, each bin will have more data points to estimate its weight, reducing data sparsity, and the bins will mutually constrain each other, reducing the ability to overfit. We include this technique as a contrastive baseline for structured regularization.

4.2 Linear Neighbor Regularization

Regularization has long been used to discourage optimization solutions that give too much weight to any one feature. This encodes our prior knowledge that such solutions are unlikely to generalize. Regularization terms such as the ℓ_p norm are frequently used in gradient-based optimizers including our baseline implementation of PRO.

Unregularized discretization is potentially brittle with regard to the number of bins chosen. Primarily, it suffers from sparsity. At the same time, we note that we know much more about discretized features than initial features since we control how they are formed. These features make up a **structured feature space**. With these things in mind, we propose linear neighbor regularization, a structured regularizer that embeds a small amount of knowledge into the objective function: that the indicator features resulting from the discretization of a single real-valued feature are spatially related. We expect similar weights to be given to the indicator features that represent neighboring values of the original real-valued feature such that the resulting transformation appears somewhat smooth.

To incorporate this knowledge of nearby bins, the linear neighbor regularizer $\mathcal{R}_{\text{LNR}}$ penalizes each feature's weight by the squared amount it differs from its neighbors' midpoint:

$$\mathcal{R}_{\text{LNR}}(\mathbf{w}, j) = \left(\frac{1}{2}(w_{j-1} + w_{j+1}) - w_j \right)^2 \quad (9)$$

$$\mathcal{R}_{\text{LNR}}(\mathbf{w}) = \beta \sum_{j=2}^{|\mathbf{h}|-1} \mathcal{R}_{\text{LNR}}(\mathbf{w}, j) \quad (10)$$

This is a special case of the feature network regularizer of Sandler (2010). Unlike traditional regularizers, we do not hope to reduce the active feature count. With the PRO loss l and a ℓ_2 regularizater $\mathcal{R}_2$, our final loss function internal to each iteration of PRO is:

$$\mathcal{L}(\mathbf{w}) = l(\mathbf{x}, \mathbf{y}; \mathbf{w}) + \mathcal{R}_2(\mathbf{w}) + \mathcal{R}_{\text{LNR}}(\mathbf{w}) \quad (11)$$

4.3 Monotone Neighbor Regularization

However, as $\beta \to \infty$, the linear neighbor regularizer $\mathcal{R}_{\text{LNR}}$ forces a linear arrangement of weights – this violates our premise that we should be agnostic to non-linear transformations. We now describe a structured regularizer $\mathcal{R}_{\text{MNR}}$ whose limiting solution is any monotone arrangement of weights. We augment $\mathcal{R}_{\text{LNR}}$ with a smooth damping term $\mathcal{D}(\mathbf{w}, j)$, which has the shape of a bathtub curve with steepness γ:

$$\mathcal{D}(\mathbf{w}, j) = \tanh^{2\gamma} \frac{\frac{1}{2}(w_{j-1} + w_{j+1}) - w_j}{\frac{1}{2}(w_{j-1} - w_{j+1})} \quad (12)$$

$$\mathcal{R}_{\text{MNR}}(\mathbf{w}) = \beta \sum_{j=2}^{|\mathbf{h}|-1} \mathcal{D}(\mathbf{w}, j) \mathcal{R}_{\text{LNR}}(\mathbf{w}, j) \quad (13)$$

$\mathcal{D}$ is nearly zero while $w_j \in [w_{j-1}, w_{j+1}]$ and nearly one otherwise. Briefly, the numerator measures how far w_j is from the midpoint of w_{j-1} and w_{j+1} while the denominator scales that distance by the radius from the midpoint to the neighboring weight.

5 Experimental Setup[6]

Formalism: In our experiments, we use a hierarchical phrase-based translation model (Chiang, 2007). A corpus of parallel sentences is first word-aligned, and then phrase translations are extracted heuristically. In addition, hierarchical grammar rules are extracted where phrases are nested. In general, our choice of formalism is rather unimportant – our techniques should apply to most common phrase-based and chart-based paradigms including Hiero and syntactic systems.

Decoder: For decoding, we will use cdec (Dyer et al., 2010), a multi-pass decoder that supports syntactic translation models and sparse features.

Optimizer: Optimization is performed using PRO (Hopkins and May, 2011) as implemented by the cdec decoder. We run PRO for 30 iterations as suggested by Hopkins and May (2011). The PRO optimizer internally uses a L-BFGS optimizer with the default ℓ_2 regularization implemented in cdec. Any additional regularization is explicitly noted.

Baseline Features: We use the baseline features produced by Lopez' suffix array grammar extractor (Lopez, 2008), which is distributed with cdec. Bidirectional lexical log-probabilities, the coherent phrasal translation log-probability, target word count, glue rule count, source OOV count, target OOV count, and target language model log-probability. Note that these features may be simplified or removed as specified in each experimental condition.

	Zh→En	**Ar→En**	**Cz→En**
Train	303K	5.4M	1M
WeightTune	1664	1797	3000
HyperTune	1085	1056	2000
Test	1357	1313	2000

Table 1: Corpus statistics: number of parallel sentences.

Chinese Resources: For the Chinese→English experiments, including the completed work presented in this proposal, we train on the Foreign Broadcast Information Service (FBIS) corpus of approximately 300,000 sentence pairs with about 9.4 million English words. We tune weights on the NIST MT 2006 dataset, tune hyperparameters on NIST MT05, and test on NIST MT 2008.

Arabic Resources: We build an Arabic→English system, training on the large NIST MT 2009 constrained training corpus of approximately 5 million sentence pairs with about 181 million English words. We tune weights on the NIST MT 2006 dataset, tune hyperparameters on NIST MT 2005, and test on NIST MT 2008.

Czech resources: We also construct a Czech→English system based on the CzEng 1.0 data (Bojar et al., 2012). First, we lowercased and performed sentence-level deduplication of the data.[7] Then, we uniformly sampled a training set of 1M sentences (sections 1 – 97) along with a weight-tuning set (section 98), hyperparameter-tuning (section 99), and test set (section 99) from the paraweb domain contained of CzEng.[8] Sentences less than 5 words were discarded due to noise.

Evaluation: We quantify increases in translation quality using case-insensitive BLEU (Papineni et al., 2002). We control for test set variation and optimizer instability by averaging over multiple optimizer replicas (Clark et al., 2011).[9]

[6] All code at http://github.com/jhclark/cdec

[7] CzEng is distributed deduplicated at the document level, leading to very high sentence-level overlap.

[8] The section splits recommended by Bojar et al. (2012).

[9] MultEval 0.5.1: github.com/jhclark/multeval

Bits	4	8	12
Features	101	1302	12,910
Test BLEU	36.4	36.6	36.8

Table 2: Translation quality for Cz→En system with varying bits for discretization. For all other experiments, we tune the number of bits on held-out data.

Condition	Zh→En	Ar→En	Cz→En
P	$20.8^{\star}$ (-2.7)	$44.3^{\star}$ (-3.6)	$36.5^{\star}$ (-1.1)
log P	$23.5^{\dagger}$	$47.9^{\dagger}$	$37.6^{\dagger}$
Disc P	$23.4^{\dagger}$ (-0.1)	$47.2^{\dagger}$ (-0.7)	$36.8^{\star}$ (-0.8)
Over. P	$20.7^{\star}$ (-2.8)	$44.6^{\star}$ (-3.3)	$36.6^{\star}$ (-1.0)
LNR P	$23.1^{\star\dagger}$ (-0.4)	$48.0^{\dagger}$ (+0.1)	37.3 (-0.3)
MNR P	$23.8^{\dagger}$ (+0.3)	$48.7^{\star\dagger}$ (+0.8)	$37.6^{\dagger}$ (±)
MNR C	$23.6^{\dagger}$ (±)	$48.7^{\star\dagger}$ (+0.8)	$37.4^{\dagger}$ (-0.2)

Table 3: **Top:** Translation quality for systems with and without the typical log transform. **Bottom:** Translation quality for systems using discretization and structured regularization with probabilities P or counts C as the input of discretization. MNR P consistently recovers or outperforms a state-of-the-art system, but without any assumptions about how to transform the initial features. All scores are averaged over 3 end-to-end optimizer replications. * denotes significantly different than log probs (row2) with $p(\text{CHANCE}) < 0.01$ under Clark et al. (2011) and † is likewise used with regard to P (row 1).

6 Results

6.1 Does Non-Linearity Matter?

In our first set of experiments, we seek to answer "Does non-linearity matter?" by starting with our baseline system of 7 typical features (the log Probability system) and we then remove the log transform from all of the log probability features in our grammar (the Probs. system). The results are shown in Table 3 (rows 1, 2). If a naïve feature engineer were to remove the non-linear log transform, the systems would degrade between 1.1 BLEU and 3.6 BLEU. From this, we conclude that non-linearity does affect translation quality. This is a potential pitfall for any real-valued feature including probability features, count features, similarity measures, etc.

6.2 Learning Non-Linear Transformations

Next, we evaluate the effects of discretization (Disc), overlapping bins (Over.), linear neighbor regularization (LNR), and monotone neighbor regularization (MNR) on three language pairs: a small Zh→En system, a large Ar→En system and a large Cz→En system. In the first row of Table 3, we use raw probabilities rather than log probabilities for $p_{\text{coherent}}(t|s)$, $p_{\text{lex}}(t|s)$, and $p_{\text{lex}}(s|t)$. In rows 3 – 7, all translation model features (without the log-transformed features) are then discretized into indicator features.[10] The number of bins and the structured regularization strength were tuned on the hyperparameter tuning set.

Discretization alone does not consistently recover the performance of the log transformed features (row 3). The naïve overlap strategy in fact degrades performance (row 4). Linear neighbor regularization (row 5) behaves more consistently than discretization alone, but is consistently outperformed by the monotone neighbor regularizer (row 6), which is able to meet or significantly exceed the performance of the log transformed system. Importantly, this is done without any knowledge of the correct non-linear transformation. In the final row, we go a step further by removing $p_{\text{coherent}}(t|s)$ altogether and replacing it with simple count features: $c(s)$ and $c(s,t)$, with slight to no degradation in quality.[11] We take this as evidence that a feature engineer developing a new real-valued feature may find discretization and monotone neighbor regularization useful.

We also observe that different data sets benefit from non-linear feature transformation in to different degrees (Table 3, rows 1, 2). We noticed that discretization with monotone neighbor regularization is able to improve over a log transform (rows 2, 6) in proportion to the improvement of a log transform over probability-based features (rows 1, 2).

To provide insight into how translation quality can be affected by the number of bits for discretization, we offer Table 2.

In Figure 7, we present the weights learned by the Ar→En system for probability-based features. We see that even without a bias toward a log transform, a log-like shape still emerges for many SMT features based only on the criteria of optimizing BLEU and a preference for monotonicity. However, the optimizer chooses some important variations on the log curve, especially for low probabilities, that lead to

[10] We also keep a real-valued copy of the word penalty to help normalize the language model.

[11] These features can single-out rules with $c(s) = 1, c(s,t) = 1$, subsuming separate low-count features

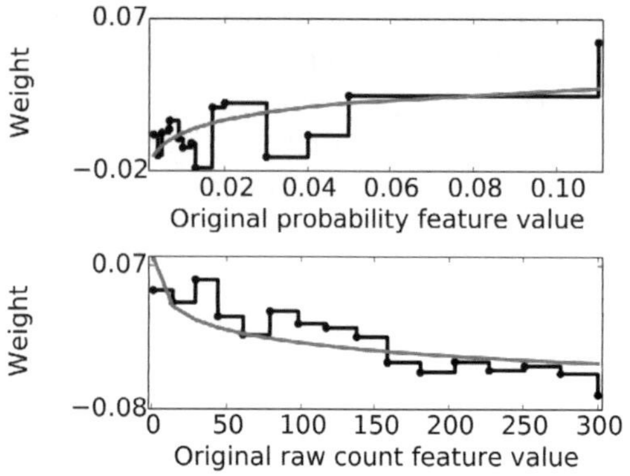

Figure 7: Plots of weights learned for the discretized $p_{\text{coherent}}(e|f)$ (top) and $c(f)$ (bottom) for the Ar→En system with 4 bits and monotone neighbor regularization. $p(e|f) > 0.11$ is omitted for exposition as values were constant after this point. The gray line fits a log curve to the weights. The system learns a shape that deviates from the log in several regions. Each non-monotonic segment represents the learner choosing to better fit the data while paying a strong regularization penalty.

7 Related Work

Previous work on feature discretization in machine learning has focused on the conversion of real-valued features into discrete values for learners that are either incapable of handling real-valued inputs or perform suboptimally given real-valued inputs (Dougherty et al., 1995; Kotsiantis and Kanellopoulos, 2006). Decision trees and random forests have been successfully used in language modeling (Jelinek et al., 1994; Xu and Jelinek, 2004) and parsing (Charniak, 2010; Magerman, 1995).

Kernel methods such as support vector machines (SVMs) are often considered when non-linear interactions between features are desired since they allow for easy usage of non-linear kernels. Wu et al. (2004) showed improvements using non-linear kernel PCA for word sense disambiguation. Taskar et al. (2003) describes a method for incorporating kernels into structured Markov networks. Tsochantaridis et al. (2004) then proposed a structured SVM for grammar learning, named-entity recognition, text classification, and sequence alignment. This was followed by a structured SVM with inexact inference (Finley and Joachims, 2008) and the latent structured SVM (Yu and Joachims, 2009). Even within kernel methods, learning non-linear mappings with kernels remains an open area of research; For example, Cortes et al. (2009) investigated learning non-linear combinations of kernels. In MT, Giménez and Màrquez (2007) used a SVM to annotate a phrase table with binary features indicating whether or not a phrase translation was appropriate in context. Nguyen et al. (2007) also applied non-linear features for SMT n-best reranking.

Toutanova and Ahn (2013) use a form of regression decision trees to induce locally non-linear features in a n-best reranking framework. He and Deng (2012) directly optimize the lexical and phrasal features using expected BLEU. Nelakanti et al. (2013) use tree-structured ℓ_p regularizers to train language models and improve perplexity over Kneser-Ney.

Learning parameters under weak order restrictions has also been studied for regression. Isotonic regression (Barlow et al., 1972; Robertson et al., 1988; Silvapulle and Sen, 2005) fits a curve to a set of data points such that each point in the fitted curve is greater than or equal to the previous point in the curve. Nearly isotonic regression allows violations in monotonicity (Tibshirani et al., 2011).

8 Conclusion

In the absence of highly refined knowledge about a feature, discretization with structured regularization enables higher quality impact of new feature sets that contain non-linearities. In our experiments, we observed that discretization out-performed naïve features lacking a good non-linear transformation by up to 4.4 BLEU and that it can outperform a baseline by up to 0.8 BLEU while dropping the log transform of the lexical probabilities and removing the phrasal probabilities in favor of counts. Looking beyond this basic feature set, non-linear transformations could be the difference between showing quality improvements or not for novel features. As researchers include more real-valued features including counts, similarity measures, and separately-trained models with millions of features, we suspect this will become an increasingly relevant issue. We conclude that non-linear responses play an important role in SMT, even for a commonly-used feature set, an observation that we hope will inform feature engineers.

Acknowledgments

This work was supported by Google Faculty Research grants 2011_R2_705 and 2012_R2_10 and by the NSF-sponsored XSEDE computing resources program under grant TG-CCR110017.

References

Michael Auli, Michel Galley, Chris Quirk, and Geoffrey Zweig. 2013. Joint Language and Translation Modeling with Recurrent Neural Networks. In *Empirical Methods in Natural Language Processing*, number October, pages 1044–1054.

R. E. Barlow, D. Bartholomew, J. M. Bremner, and H. D. Brunk. 1972. *Statistical inference under order restrictions; the theory and application of isotonic regression*. Wiley.

Ondej Bojar, Zdeněk Žabokrtský, Ondej Dušek, Petra Galuščáková, Martin Majliš, David Mareček, Jií Maršík, Michal Novák, Martin Popel, and Aleš Tamchyna. 2012. The Joy of Parallelism with CzEng 1 .0. In *Proceedings of LREC2012*, Istanbul, Turkey. European Language Resources Association.

Peter E Brown, Stephen A Della Pietra, Vincent J Della Pietra, and Robert L Mercer. 1993. The Mathematics of Statistical Machine Translation : Parameter Estimation. *Computational Linguistics*, 10598.

Eugene Charniak. 2010. Top-Down Nearly-Context-Sensitive Parsing. In *Empirical Methods in Natural Language Processing*, number October, pages 674–683.

Colin Cherry and George Foster. 2012. Batch Tuning Strategies for Statistical Machine Translation. In *Proceedings of the North American Association for Computational Linguistics*, pages 427–436.

David Chiang, Yuval Marton, and Philip Resnik. 2008. Online large-margin training of syntactic and structural translation features. In *Proceedings of the Conference on Empirical Methods in Natural Language Processing - EMNLP '08*, pages 224–233, Morristown, NJ, USA. Association for Computational Linguistics.

David Chiang. 2007. Hierarchical Phrase-Based Translation. *Computational Linguistics*, 33(2):201–228, June.

David Chiang. 2012. Hope and fear for discriminative training of statistical translation models. *Journal of Machine Learning Research*, 13:1159–1187.

Jonathan H Clark, Chris Dyer, Alon Lavie, and Noah A Smith. 2011. Better Hypothesis Testing for Statistical Machine Translation: Controlling for Optimizer Instability. In *Association for Computational Linguistics*.

Corinna Cortes, Mehryar Mohri, and Afshin Rostamizadeh. 2009. Learning Non-Linear Combinations of Kernels. In *Advances in Neural Information Processing Systems (NIPS 2009)*, pages 1–9, Vancouver, Canada.

James Dougherty, Ron Kohavi, and Mehran Sahami. 1995. Supervised and Unsupervised Discretization of Continuous Features. In *Proceedings of the Twelfth International Conference on Machine Learning*, pages 194–202, San Francisco, CA.

Chris Dyer, Jonathan Weese, Adam Lopez, Vladimir Eidelman, Phil Blunsom, and Philip Resnik. 2010. cdec: A Decoder, Alignment, and Learning Framework for Finite-State and Context-Free Translation Models. In *Association for Computational Linguistics*, number July, pages 7–12.

Thomas Finley and Thorsten Joachims. 2008. Training structural SVMs when exact inference is intractable. In *Proceedings of the International Conference on Machine Learning*, pages 304–311, New York, New York, USA. ACM Press.

Jeffrey Flanigan, Chris Dyer, and Jaime Carbonell. 2013. Large-Scale Discriminative Training for Statistical Machine Translation Using Held-Out Line Search. In *North American Association for Computational Linguistics*, number June, pages 248–258.

Michel Galley, Chris Quirk, Colin Cherry, and Kristina Toutanova. 2013. Regularized Minimum Error Rate Training. In *Empirical Methods in Natural Language Processing*.

Juri Ganitkevitch, Yuan Cao, Jonathan Weese, Matt Post, and Chris Callison-Burch. 2012. Joshua 4.0: Packing, PRO, and Paraphrases. In *Workshop on Statistical Machine Translation*, pages 283–291.

Jesús Giménez and Lluís Màrquez. 2007. Context-aware Discriminative Phrase Selection for Statistical Machine Translation. In *Workshop on Statistical Machine Translation*, number June, pages 159–166.

Kevin Gimpel and Noah A Smith. 2009. Feature-Rich Translation by Quasi-Synchronous Lattice Parsing. In *Empirical Methods in Natural Language Processing*.

Kevin Gimpel and Noah A Smith. 2012. Structured Ramp Loss Minimization for Machine Translation. In *North American Association for Computational Linguistics*.

Xiaodong He and Li Deng. 2012. Maximum Expected BLEU Training of Phrase and Lexicon Translation Models. In *Proceedings of the Association for Computational Linguistics*, Jeju Island, Korea. Microsoft Research.

Mark Hopkins and Jonathan May. 2011. Tuning as Ranking. *Computational Linguistics*, pages 1352–1362.

Frederick Jelinek, John Lafferty, David Magerman, Robert Mercer, Adwait Ratnaparkhi, and Salim Roukos. 1994. Decision Tree Parsing using a Hidden Derivation Model. In *Workshop on Human Language Technologies (HLT)*.

Nal Kalchbrenner and Phil Blunsom. 2013. Recurrent Continuous Translation Models. In *Empirical Methods in Natural Language Processing*.

Sotiris Kotsiantis and Dimitris Kanellopoulos. 2006. Discretization Techniques : A recent survey. In *GESTS International Transactions on Computer Science and Engineering*, volume 32, pages 47–58.

Lemao Liu, Taro Watanabe, Eiichiro Sumita, and Tiejun Zhao. 2013a. Additive Neural Networks for Statistical Machine Translation. In *Proceedings of the Association for Computational Linguistics*.

Lemao Liu, Tiejun Zhao, Taro Watanabe, and Eiichiro Sumita. 2013b. Tuning SMT with A Large Number of Features via Online Feature Grouping. In *Proceedings of the International Joint Conference on Natural Language Processing*.

Adam Lopez. 2008. Tera-Scale Translation Models via Pattern Matching. In *Association for Computational Linguistics Computational Linguistics*, number August, pages 505–512.

David M Magerman. 1995. Statistical Decision-Tree Models for Parsing. In *Association for Computational Linguistics*, pages 276–283.

Anil Nelakanti, Cedric Archambeau, Julien Mairal, Francis Bach, and Guillaume Bouchard. 2013. Structured Penalties for Log-linear Language Models. In *Empirical Methods in Natural Language Processing*, Seattle, WA.

Patrick Nguyen, Milind Mahajan, Xiaodong He, and Microsoft Way. 2007. Training Non-Parametric Features for Statistical Machine Translation. In *Association for Computational Linguistics*.

Franz Josef Och and Hermann Ney. 2002. Discriminative training and maximum entropy models for statistical machine translation. In *Proceedings of the Association for Computational Linguistics*, number July, page 295, Morristown, NJ, USA. Association for Computational Linguistics.

Franz J Och. 2003. Minimum Error Rate Training in Statistical Machine Translation. In *Association for Computational Linguistics*, number July, pages 160–167.

Kishore Papineni, Salim Roukos, Todd Ward, and Wei-jing Zhu. 2002. BLEU : a Method for Automatic Evaluation of Machine Translation. In *Computational Linguistics*, number July, pages 311–318.

Tim Robertson, F. T. Wright, and R. L. Dykstra. 1988. *Order Restricted Statistical Inference*. Wiley.

S Ted Sandler. 2010. *Regularized Learning with Feature Networks*. Ph.D. thesis, University of Pennsylvania.

Holger Schwenk. 2012. Continuous Space Translation Models for Phrase-Based Statistical Machine Translation. In *International Conference on Computational Linguistics (COLING)*, number December 2012, pages 1071–1080, Mumbai, India.

Mervyn J. Silvapulle and Pranab K. Sen. 2005. *Constrained Statistical Inference: Order, Inequality, and Shape Constraints*. Wiley.

Artem Sokolov, Guillaume Wisniewski, and François Yvon. 2012. Non-linear N-best List Reranking with Few Features. In *Association for Machine Translation in the Americas*.

Jun Suzuki and Masaaki Nagata. 2013. Supervised Model Learning with Feature Grouping based on a Discrete Constraint. In *Proceedings of the Association for Computational Linguistics*, pages 18–23.

Ben Taskar, Carlos Guestrin, and Daphne Koller. 2003. Max-Margin Markov Networks. In *Neural Information Processing Systems*.

Ryan J Tibshirani, Holger Hoefling, and Robert Tibshirani. 2011. Nearly-Isotonic Regression. *Technometrics*, 53(1):54–61.

Kristina Toutanova and Byung-Gyu Ahn. 2013. Learning Non-linear Features for Machine Translation Using Gradient Boosting Machines. In *Proceedings of the Association for Computational Linguistics*.

Ioannis Tsochantaridis, Thomas Hofmann, Thorsten Joachims, and Yasemin Altun. 2004. Support Vector Machine Learning for Interdependent and Structured Output Spaces. In *International Conference on Machine Learning (ICML)*.

Zhuoran Wang, John Shawe-Taylor, and Sandor Szedmak. 2007. Kernel Regression Based Machine Translation. In *North American Association for Computational Linguistics*, number April, pages 185–188, Rochester, N.

Dekai Wu, Weifeng Su, and Marine Carpuat. 2004. A Kernel PCA Method for Superior Word Sense Disambiguation. In *Association for Computational Linguistics*, Barcelona.

Peng Xu and Frederick Jelinek. 2004. Random Forests in Language Modeling. In *Empirical Methods in Natural Language Processing*.

Chun-Nam John Yu and Thorsten Joachims. 2009. Learning structural SVMs with latent variables. In *Proceedings of the 26th Annual International Conference on Machine Learning - ICML '09*, pages 1–8, New York, New York, USA. ACM Press.

A New Parsing Algorithm for Combinatory Categorial Grammar

Marco Kuhlmann
Department of
Computer and Information Science
Linköping University, Sweden
marco.kuhlmann@liu.se

Giorgio Satta
Department of
Information Engineering
University of Padua, Italy
satta@dei.unipd.it

Abstract

We present a polynomial-time parsing algorithm for CCG, based on a new decomposition of derivations into small, shareable parts. Our algorithm has the same asymptotic complexity, $\mathcal{O}(n^6)$, as a previous algorithm by Vijay-Shanker and Weir (1993), but is easier to understand, implement, and prove correct.

1 Introduction

Combinatory Categorial Grammar (CCG; Steedman and Baldridge (2011)) is a lexicalized grammar formalism that belongs to the class of so-called mildly context-sensitive formalisms, as characterized by Joshi (1985). CCG has been successfully used for a wide range of practical tasks including data-driven parsing (Clark and Curran, 2007), wide-coverage semantic construction (Bos et al., 2004; Kwiatkowski et al., 2010; Lewis and Steedman, 2013) and machine translation (Weese et al., 2012).

Several parsing algorithms for CCG have been presented in the literature. Earlier proposals show running time exponential in the length of the input string (Pareschi and Steedman, 1987; Tomita, 1988). A breakthrough came with the work of Vijay-Shanker and Weir (1990) and Vijay-Shanker and Weir (1993) who report the first polynomial-time algorithm for CCG parsing. Until this day, this algorithm, which we shall refer to as the V&W algorithm, remains the *only* published polynomial-time parsing algorithm for CCG. However, we are not aware of any practical parser for CCG that actually uses it. We speculate that this has two main reasons: First, some authors have argued that linguistic resources available for CCG can be covered with context-free fragments of the formalism (Fowler and Penn, 2010), for which more efficient parsing algorithms can be given. Second, the V&W algorithm is considerably more complex than parsing algorithms for equivalent mildly context-sensitive formalisms, such as Tree-Adjoining Grammar (Joshi and Schabes, 1997), and is quite hard to understand, implement, and prove correct.

The V&W algorithm is based on a special decomposition of CCG derivations into smaller parts that can then be shared among different derivations. This sharing is the key to the polynomial runtime. In this article we build on the same idea, but develop an alternative polynomial-time algorithm for CCG parsing. The new algorithm is based on a different decomposition of CCG derivations, and is arguably simpler than the V&W algorithm in at least two respects: First, the new algorithm uses only three basic steps, against the nine basic steps of the V&W parser. Second, the correctness proof of the new algorithm is simpler than the one reported by Vijay-Shanker and Weir (1993). The new algorithm runs in time $\mathcal{O}(n^6)$ where n is the length of the input string, the same as the V&W parser.

We organize our presentation as follows. In Section 2 we introduce CCG and the central notion of derivation trees. In Section 3 we start with a simple but exponential-time parser for CCG, from which we derive our polynomial-time parser in Section 4. Section 5 further simplifies the algorithm and proves its correctness. We then provide a discussion of our algorithm and possible extensions in Section 6. Section 7 concludes the article.

Transactions of the Association for Computational Linguistics, 2 (2014) 405–418. Action Editor: Mark Steedman.
Submitted 4/2014; Revised 8/2014; Published 10/2014.

2 Combinatory Categorial Grammar

We assume basic familiarity with CCG in general and the formalism of Weir and Joshi (1988) in particular. In this section we set up our terminology and notation. A CCG has two main parts: a *lexicon* that associates words with categories, and *rules* that specify how categories can be combined into other categories. Together, these components give rise to *derivations* such as the one shown in Figure 1.

2.1 Lexicon

The CCG lexicon is a finite set of word–category pairs $w := X$.[1] Categories are built from a finite set of *atomic categories* and two binary operators: forward slash (/) and backward slash (\). Atomic categories represent the syntactic types of complete constituents; they include a distinguished category S for complete sentences. A constituent with the complex category X/Y represents a function that seeks a constituent of category Y immediately to its right and returns a constituent of category X; similarly, $X\backslash Y$ represents a function that seeks a Y to its left. We treat slashes as left-associative operators and omit unnecessary parentheses. By this convention, every category X can be written as

$$X = A|_m X_m \cdots |_1 X_1$$

where $m \geq 0$, A is an atomic category called the *target* of X and the $|_i X_i$ are slash–category pairs called the *arguments* of X. We view these arguments as being arranged in a stack with $|_1 X_1$ at the top and $|_m X_m$ at the bottom. Thus another way of writing the category X above is as $X = A\alpha$, where α is a (possibly empty) stack of m arguments. The number m is called the *arity* of X; we denote it by $ar(X)$.

2.2 Rules

The rules of CCG are directed versions of (generalized) functional composition. There are two forms, *forward rules* and *backward rules*:

$$X/Y \quad Y|_d Y_d \cdots |_1 Y_1 \Rightarrow X|_d Y_d \cdots |_1 Y_1 \quad (>^d)$$
$$Y|_d Y_d \cdots |_1 Y_1 \quad X\backslash Y \Rightarrow X|_d Y_d \cdots |_1 Y_1 \quad (<^d)$$

[1]The formalism of Weir and Joshi (1988) also allows lexicon entries for the empty string, a feature that we ignore here.

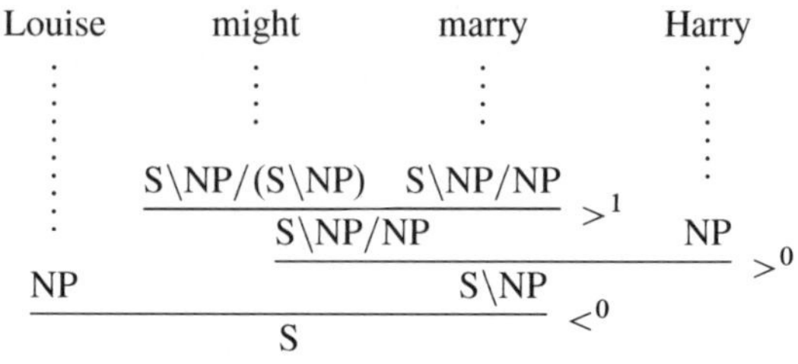

Figure 1: A sample derivation tree.

Every rule is obtained by choosing a specific *degree* $d \geq 0$ and specific directions (forward or backward) for each of the slashes $|_i$, while X, Y and the Y_i are variables ranging over categories. Thus for every degree $d \geq 0$ there are 2^d forward rules and 2^d backward rules. The rules of degree 0 are called *application* rules. In contexts where we refer to both application and composition, we use the latter term for "proper" composition rules of degree $d > 0$. Note that in most of this article we ignore additional rules required for linguistic analysis with CCG, in particular type-raising and substitution. We briefly discuss these rules in Section 6.

Every CCG grammar restricts itself to a finite set of rules, but each such rule may give rise to infinitely many *rule instances*. A rule is instantiated by substituting concrete categories for the variables. For example, the derivation in Figure 1 contains the following instance of forward composition ($>^1$):

$$S\backslash NP/(S\backslash NP) \; S\backslash NP/NP \Rightarrow S\backslash NP/NP$$

Note that we overload the double arrow to denote not only rules but also rule instances. Given a rule instance, the category that instantiates the pattern X/Y (forward) or $X\backslash Y$ (backward) is called the *primary input*, and the category that instantiates the pattern $Y|_d Y_d \cdots |_1 Y_1$ is called the *secondary input*. Adopting our stack-based view, each rule can be understood as an operation on argument stacks: pop $|Y$ off the stack of the primary input; pop the $|_i Y_i$ off the stack of the secondary input and push them to the stack of the primary input (preserving their order).

The formalism of Weir and Joshi (1988) allows to restrict the valid instances of individual rules. Similar to our treatment of additional combinatory rules, in most of this article we ignore these rule restrictions; but see the discussion in Section 6.

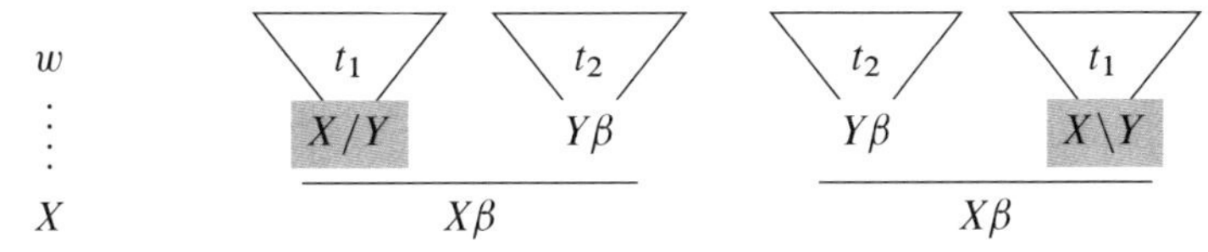

iff $w := X$ iff $X/Y \; Y\beta \Rightarrow X\beta$ iff $Y\beta \; X\backslash Y \Rightarrow X\beta$

Figure 2: Recursive definition of derivation trees. Nodes labeled with primary input categories are shaded.

2.3 Derivation Trees

The set of *derivation trees* of a CCG can be formally defined as in Figure 2. There and in the remainder of this article we use β and other symbols from the beginning of the Greek alphabet to denote a (possibly empty) stack of arguments. Derivation trees consist of unary branchings and binary branchings: unary branchings (drawn with dotted lines) correspond to lexicon entries; binary branchings correspond to (valid instances of) composition rules. The *yield* of a derivation tree is the left-to-right sequence of its leaves. The *type* of a derivation tree is the category at its root.

3 CKY-Style Parsing Algorithm

As the point of departure for our own work, we now introduce a straightforward, CKY-style parsing algorithm for CCGs. It is a simple generalization of the algorithm presented by Shieber et al. (1995), which is restricted to grammars with rules of degree 0 or 1. As in that article, we specify our algorithm in terms of a *grammatical deduction system*.

3.1 Deduction System

We are given a CCG and a string $w = w_1 \cdots w_n$ to be parsed, where each w_i is a lexical token. As a general notation, for integers i, j with $0 \leq i \leq j \leq n$ we write $w[i, j]$ to denote the substring $w_{i+1} \cdots w_j$ of w. As usual, we take $w[i, i]$ to be the empty string.

Items The CKY-style algorithm uses a logic with items of the form $[X, i, j]$ where X is a category and i, j are fencepost positions in w. The intended interpretation of such an item is to assert that we can build a derivation tree with yield $w[i, j]$ and type X. The goal of the algorithm is the construction of the item $[S, 0, n]$, which asserts the existence of a derivation tree for the entire input string. (Recall that S is the distinguished category for sentences.)

Axioms and Inference Rules The steps of the algorithm are specified by means of inference rules over items. These rules implement the recursive definition of derivation trees given in Figure 2. The construction starts with axioms of the form $[X, i, i+1]$ where $w_{i+1} := X$ is a lexicon entry; these items assert the existence of a unary-branching derivation tree of the form shown in the left of Figure 2 for each lexical token w_{i+1}. There is one inference rule for every forward rule (application or composition):

$$\frac{[X/Y, i, j] \quad [Y\beta, j, k]}{[X\beta, i, k]} \quad X/Y \; Y\beta \Rightarrow X\beta \qquad (1)$$

A symmetrical rule is used for backward application and composition. However, here and in the remainder of the article we only specify the forward version of each rule and leave the backward version implicit.

3.2 Correctness and Runtime

The soundness and completeness of the CKY-style algorithm can be proved by induction on the number of inferences and the number of nodes in a derivation tree, respectively.

It is not hard to see that, in the general case, the algorithm uses an amount of time and space exponential with respect to the length of the input string, n. This is because rule (1) may be used to grow the arity of primary input categories up to some linear function of n, resulting in exponentially many categories.[2] Note that this is only possible if there are rules with degree 2 or more. For grammars restricted to rules with degree 0 or 1, such as those considered by Shieber et al. (1995), the runtime of the algorithm is cubic in n. This restricted class of grammars only holds context-free generative power, while the power of general CCG is beyond that of context-free grammars (Vijay-Shanker and Weir, 1994).

[2]Categories whose arity is not bounded by a linear function of n are not useful, in the sense that they cannot occur in complete derivations.

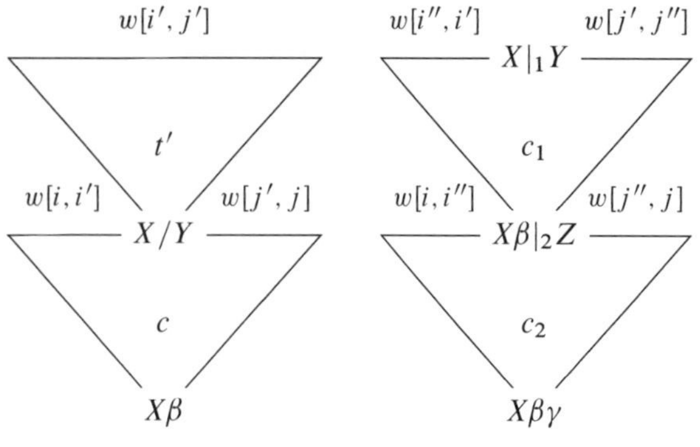

(a) tree t (b) context c

Figure 3: Decomposition of derivations.

4 A Polynomial-Time Algorithm

We now introduce our polynomial-time algorithm. This algorithm uses the same axioms and the same goal item as the CKY-style algorithm, but features new items and new inference rules.

4.1 New Items

In a first step, in order to avoid runtime exponential in n we restrict our item set to categories whose arity is bounded by some grammar constant c_G:

$$[X,i,j] \quad \text{where} \quad ar(X) \leq c_G$$

The exact choice of the constant will be discussed in Section 5. With the restricted item set, the new algorithm behaves like the old one as long as the arity of categories does not exceed c_G. However, rule (1) alone is no longer complete: Derivations with categories whose arity exceeds c_G cannot be simulated anymore. To remedy this deficiency, we introduce a new type of item to implement a specific decomposition of long derivations into smaller pieces.

Consider a derivation t of the form shown in Figure 3(a). Note that the yield of t is $w[i,j]$. The derivation consists of two parts, named t' and c; these share a common node with a category of the form X/Y. Now assume that c has the special property that none of the combinatory rules that it uses pops the argument stack of the category X. This means that c, after popping the argument $/Y$, may push new arguments and pop them again, but may never "touch" X. We call a fragment with this special property a *derivation context*. (A formal definition will be given in Section 5.2.)

The special property of c is useful because it implies that c can be carried out for any choice of X. To be more specific, let us write β for the (possibly empty) sequence of arguments that c pushes to the argument stack of X in place of $/Y$. We shall refer to $/Y$ as the *bridging argument* and to the sequence β as the *excess* of c. Suppose now that we replace t' by a derivation tree with the same yield but with a type X'/Y where $X' \neq X$. Then because c does not touch X' we obtain another valid derivation tree with the same yield as t; the type of this tree will be $X'\beta$.

For the combination with c, the internal structure of t' is of no importance; the only important information is the extent of the yield of t' and the identity of the bridging argument $/Y$. In terms of our deduction system, this can be expressed as follows: The derivation context c can be combined with any tree t' that is associated with an item of the form $[X/Y,i',j']$, where X is any category. Similarly, the internal structure of c is of no importance either, as long as the argument stack of the category X remains untouched. It suffices to record the following:

- the extent of the yield of t, specified in terms of the positions i and j;
- the extent of the yield of t', specified in terms of the positions i' and j';
- the bridging argument $/Y$; and
- the excess β.

We represent these pieces of information in a new type of item of the form $[/Y,\beta,i,i',j',j]$. The intended interpretation of these items is to assert that, for any choice of X, if we can build a derivation tree t' with yield $w[i',j']$ and type X/Y, then we can also build a derivation tree t' with yield $w[i,j]$ and type $X\beta$. We also use items $[\backslash Y,\beta,i,i',j',j]$ with a backward slash, with a similar meaning. Like items that represent derivation trees, our items for derivation contexts are arity-restricted:

$$[|Y,\beta,i,i',j',j] \quad \text{where} \quad ar(Y\beta) \leq c_G$$

As we will see in Section 5, these restricted items suffice to simulate all derivations of a CCG. Furthermore, this can be done in time polynomial in n, because our encoding allows sharing of the same items among several derivations.

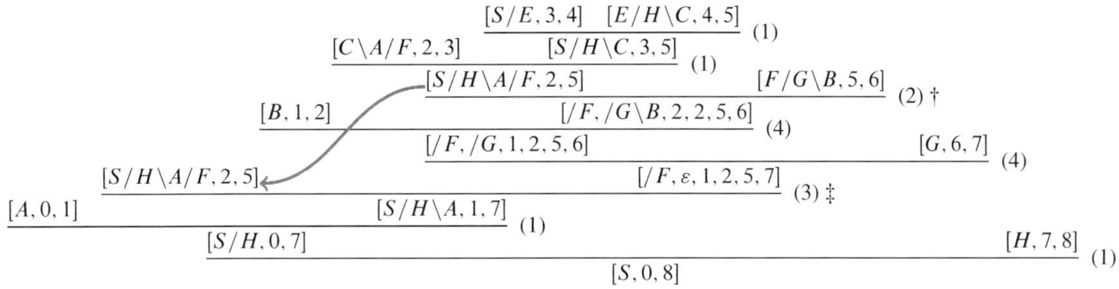

Figure 4: A sample derivation of the grammatical deduction system of Section 4. Inference † triggers a new context item from a tree item; inference ‡ reuses the tree item (as indicated by the arrow), recombining it with the (modified) context item.

4.2 New Inference Rules

In our parsing algorithm, context items are introduced whenever the composition of two categories whose arities are bounded by c_G would result in a category whose arity exceeds this bound:

$$\frac{[X/Y, i, j] \quad [Y\beta, j, k]}{[/Y, \beta, i, i, j, k]} \quad \begin{cases} X/Y \ Y\beta \Rightarrow X\beta \\ ar(X\beta) > c_G \end{cases} \tag{2}$$

The new rule has the same antecedents as rule (1), but rather than extending the derivation asserted by the first antecedent $[X/Y, i, j]$, which is not possible because of the arity bound, it triggers a new derivation context, asserted by the item $[/Y, \beta, i, i, j, k]$. Further applications and compositions will extend the new context, and only when the excess of this context has become sufficiently small will it be recombined with the derivation that originally triggered it. This is done by the following rule:

$$\frac{[X|Y, i', j'] \quad [|Y, \beta, i, i', j', j]}{[X\beta, i, j]} \tag{3}$$

Note that this rule (like all rules in the deduction system) is only defined on valid items; in particular it only fires if the arity of the category $X\beta$ is bounded by c_G.

The remaining rules of the algorithm parallel the three rules that we have introduced so far but take items that represent derivation contexts rather than derivation trees as their first antecedents. First out, rule (4) extends a derivation context in the same way as rule (1) extends a derivation tree.

$$\frac{[|Y, \beta/Z, i, i', j', j] \quad [Z\gamma, j, k]}{[|Y, \beta\gamma, i, i', j', k]} \quad \begin{cases} X/Z \ Z\gamma \Rightarrow X\gamma \\ ar(Y\beta\gamma) \le c_G \end{cases} \tag{4}$$

Rule (5) is the obvious correspondent of rule (2): It triggers a new context when the antecedent context cannot be extended because of the arity bound.

$$\frac{[|Y, \beta/Z, i, i', j', j] \quad [Z\gamma, j, k]}{[/Z, \gamma, i, i, j, k]} \quad \begin{cases} X/Z \ Z\gamma \Rightarrow X\gamma \\ ar(Y\beta\gamma) > c_G \end{cases} \tag{5}$$

Finally, and parallel to rule (3), we need a rule to recombine a context with the context that originally triggered it. As it will turn out, we only need this in cases where the triggered context has no excess.

$$\frac{[|_1Y, \beta|_2Z, i'', i', j', j''] \quad [|_2Z, \varepsilon, i, i'', j'', j]}{[|_1Y, \beta, i, i', j', j]} \tag{6}$$

4.3 Sample Derivation

We now illustrate our algorithm on a toy grammar. The grammar has the following lexicon:

$w_1 := A$	$w_5 := E/H\backslash C$
$w_2 := B$	$w_6 := F/G\backslash B$
$w_3 := C\backslash A/F$	$w_7 := G$
$w_4 := S/E$	$w_8 := H$

The start symbol is S. The grammar allows all instances of application and all instances of composition with degree bounded by 2. We let $c_G = 3$ (as explained later in Section 5.2).

A derivation of our deduction system on the input string $w_1 \cdots w_8$ is given in Figure 4. We start by applying rule (1) twice (once forward, once backward) to obtain the item $[S/H\backslash A/F, 2, 5]$. Combining this item with the axiom $[F/G\backslash B, 5, 6]$ is not possible using rule (1), as this would result in a category with arity 4, exceeding the arity bound. We therefore use rule (2) to trigger the context item $[/F, /G\backslash B, 2, 2, 5, 6]$ (†). Successively, we use rule (4) twice to obtain the item $[/F, \varepsilon, 1, 2, 5, 7]$. At this point we use rule (3) (with $\beta = \varepsilon$) to recombine the context item with the tree item that originally triggered it (‡); this yields the item $[S/H\backslash A, 1, 7]$. Note that the recombination effectively retrieves the portion of the stack that was below the argument $/F$ when the context item was triggered in †. Double application of rule (1) produces the goal item $[S, 0, 8]$.

4.4 Runtime Analysis

We now turn to an analysis of the runtime complexity of our algorithm. We first consider runtime complexity with respect to the length of the input string, n. The runtime is dominated by the number of instantiations of rule (6) which involves two context items as antecedents. By inspection of this rule, we see that the number of possible instantiations is bounded by n^6. Therefore we conclude that the algorithm runs in time $\mathcal{O}(n^6)$.

We now consider runtime complexity with respect to the size of the input grammar. Here the runtime is dominated by the number of instantiations of rules (1)–(5). For example, rule (5) combines items

$$[|Y, \beta/Z, i, i', j', j] \quad \text{and} \quad [Z\gamma, j, k]\,.$$

By our restrictions on items, both the arity of $Y\beta/Z$ and the arity of $Z\gamma$ are upper-bounded by the constant c_G. Now recall that every category X can be written as $X = A\alpha$ for some atomic category A and stack of arguments α. Let $\mathcal{A}$ be the set of atomic categories in the input grammar, and let $\mathcal{L}$ be the set of all arguments occurring in any category of the lexicon. By a result of Vijay-Shanker and Weir (1994, Lemma 3.1), every argument that may occur in a derived category occurs in $\mathcal{L}$. Then the number of possible instantiations of rule (5) as well as rules (1)–(4), and hence the runtime of the algorithm, is in

$$\mathcal{O}(|\mathcal{A}|\,|\mathcal{L}|^{c_G} \cdot |\mathcal{L}|^{c_G}) = \mathcal{O}(|\mathcal{A}|\,|\mathcal{L}|^{2c_G})\,.$$

Note that both $\mathcal{A}$ and $\mathcal{L}$ may grow with the grammar size. As we will see in Section 5.2, the constant c_G also depends on the grammar size. This means that the worst-case runtime complexity of our parser is exponential in the size of the input grammar. We will return to this point in Section 7.

5 Correctness

In this section we prove the correctness of our parsing algorithm. In order to simplify the proofs, we start by simplifying our algorithm, at the cost of making it less efficient:

- We remove the rules for extending trees and contexts, rule (1) and rule (4).
- We conflate the rules for triggering contexts, rule (2) and rule (5), into the single rule

$$\frac{[Y\beta, j, k]}{[/Y, \beta, i, i, j, k]} \qquad X/Y \;\; Y\beta \Rightarrow X\beta \qquad (7)$$

  This rule blindly guesses the extension of the triggering tree or context (specified by positions i and j), rather than waiting for a corresponding item to be derived.

The simplified algorithm is specified in Figure 5. We now argue that this algorithm and the algorithm from Section 4 parse exactly the same derivation trees, although they use different parsing strategies. First, we observe that rule (1) in the old algorithm can be simulated by a combination of other rules in the simplified algorithm, as follows:

$$\cfrac{[X/Y, i, j] \qquad \cfrac{[Y\beta, j, k]}{[/Y, \beta, i, i, j, k]}\,(7)}{[X\beta, i, k]}\,(3)$$

Furthermore, the simplified algorithm does no longer need rule (4), whose role is now taken over by rule (7). To see this, recall that rule (4) extends an existing context whenever the composition of two categories results in a new category whose arity does not exceed c_G. In contrast, rule (7) *always* triggers a new context c, even if the result of the composition of c with some existing context satisfies the above arity restriction. Despite the difference in the adopted strategy, these two rules are equivalent in terms of stack content, leading to the same derivation trees.

5.1 Definitions

We introduce some additional terminology and notation that we will use in the proofs. For a derivation tree t and a node u of t, we write $t[u]$ to denote the category at u, and we write $t|_u$ to denote the subtree of t at u. Formally, $t|_u$ is the restriction of t to node u and all of its descendants. Each subtree of a derivation tree is another derivation tree.

Items of type 1: $[X, i, j],\ ar(X) \leq c_G$ **Items of type 2:** $[|Y, \beta, i, i', j', j],\ ar(Y\beta) \leq c_G$

Axioms: $[X, i, i+1],\ w_{i+1} := X$ **Goal:** $[S, 0, n]$

Inference rules: $$\frac{[Y\beta, j, k]}{[/Y, \beta, i, i, j, k]}\ X/Y\ Y\beta \Rightarrow X\beta \quad (7)$$

$$\frac{[X/Y, i', j']\quad [/Y, \beta, i, i', j', j]}{[X\beta, i, j]} \quad (3) \qquad \frac{[|_1 Y, \beta|_2 Z, i'', i', j', j'']\quad [|_2 Z, \varepsilon, i, i'', j'', j]}{[|_1 Y, \beta, i, i', j', j]} \quad (6)$$

Figure 5: Items and inference rules of the simplified algorithm for an input string $w_1 \cdots w_n$.

Definition 1 Let t be a derivation tree with root r. Then t has *signature* $[X, i, j]$ if

1. the yield of t is $w[i, j]$ and
2. the type of t is X, that is, $t[r] = X$.

Note that while we use the same notation for signatures as for items, the signature of a derivation tree is a purely structural concept, whereas an item is an object in the algorithm.

A central concept in our proof is the notion of *spine*. Recall that a derivation tree consists of unary branchings and binary branchings. In each binary branching, we refer to the two children of the branching's root node as the *primary child* and the *secondary child*, depending on which of the two is labeled with the primary and secondary input category of the corresponding rule instance. In Figure 2, the primary children of the root node are shaded.

Definition 2 For a derivation tree t, the *spine* of t is the unique path that starts at the root node of t and at each node u continues to the primary child of u.

The spine of a derivation tree always ends at a node that is labeled with a category from the lexicon.

Definition 3 Let t be a derivation tree with root r. A *derivation context* c is obtained by removing all proper descendants of some node $f \neq r$ on the spine of t, under the restriction that $ar(t[u]) > ar(t[r])$ for every node u on the spine properly between f and r.

The node f is called the *foot node* of c. The *yield* of c is the pair whose first component is the yield of t to the left of f and whose second component is the yield of t to the right of f. For a derivation context c and a node u of c, we write $c[u]$ to denote the category at u.

Definition 3 formalizes the concept of derivation contexts that we introduced in Section 4.1. First, because f is on the spine and $f \neq r$, the category $c[f]$ takes the form X/Y. The arity restriction implies that the category of every node u on the spine properly between f and r takes the form $X\beta_u$, $|\beta_u| > 0$, and that the category at the root takes the form $X\beta$, $|\beta| \geq 0$. Thus the category X is never exposed in c, except perhaps at r. As we will see in Section 5.4, this property, together with a careful selection of "split nodes", will allow us to decompose derivations into smaller, shareable parts. The basic idea is the same as in the tabulation of pushdown automata (Lang, 1974; Nederhof and Satta, 2004), where the pushdown in our case is the argument stack of the primary input categories along a spine.

The concepts of signature and spine are generalized to derivation contexts as follows:

Definition 4 Let c be a derivation context with root node r and foot node f. Then c has *signature* $[|Y, \beta, i, i', j', j]$ if

1. the yield of c is $(w[i, i'], w[j', j])$;
2. for some X, $c[f] = X|Y$ and $c[r] = X\beta$.

Definition 5 For a derivation context c, the *spine* of c is the path from its root node to its foot node.

5.2 Grammar Constant

Before we start with the proof as such, we turn to the choice of the grammar constant c_G, which was left pending in previous sections. Recall that we are using c_G as a bound on the arity of X in type 1 items $[X, i, j]$. Since these items are produced by our axioms from the set of categories in the lexicon, c_G must not be smaller than the maximum arity ℓ of a category in this finite set.

We also use c_G as a bound on the arity of the category $Y\beta$ in type 2 items $[|Y, \beta, i, i', j', j]$. These items are produced by inference rule (7) to simulate instances of composition of the form $X/Y \;\; Y\beta \Rightarrow X\beta$. Here the length of β is bounded by the maximum degree d of a composition rule in the grammar, and $ar(Y)$ is bounded by the maximum arity a of an argument from the (finite) set $\mathcal{L}$ of arguments in the lexicon (recall Section 4.4). Therefore c_G cannot be smaller than $a + d$. Putting everything together, we obtain the condition

$$c_G \;\geq\; \max\{\ell, a + d\}. \tag{8}$$

The next lemma will be used in several places later.

Lemma 1 *Let c be a derivation context with signature $[|Y, \beta, i, i', j', j]$. Then $ar(Y\beta) \leq c_G$.*

Proof. Let r and f be the root and the foot node, respectively, of c. From the definition of signature, there must be some X such that $c[r] = X\beta$ and $c[f] = X|Y$. Now let p be the parent node of f, and assume that the rule used at p is instantiated as $X/Y \;\; Y\beta' \Rightarrow X\beta'$, so that $c[p] = X\beta'$. If $p = r$ then $\beta' = \beta$; otherwise, because of the arity restriction in the definition of derivation contexts (Definition 3) we have $|\beta'| > |\beta|$. Then

$$ar(Y\beta) \leq ar(Y\beta') \leq c_G,$$

where the right inequality follows from the assumption that $X/Y \;\; Y\beta' \Rightarrow X\beta'$ is a rule instance of the grammar, and from inequality (8).

5.3 Soundness

We start the correctness proof by arguing for the soundness of the deduction system in Figure 5. More specifically, we show that for every item of type 1 there exists a derivation tree with the same signature, and that for every item of type 2 there exists a derivation context with the same signature.

The soundness of the axioms is obvious.

Rule (7) states that, if we have built a derivation tree t with signature $[Y\beta, j, k]$ then we can build a derivation context c with signature $[/Y, \beta, i, i, j, k]$. Under the condition that the grammar admits the rule instance $X/Y \;\; Y\beta \Rightarrow X\beta$, this inference is sound; the context can be built as shown in Figure 6.

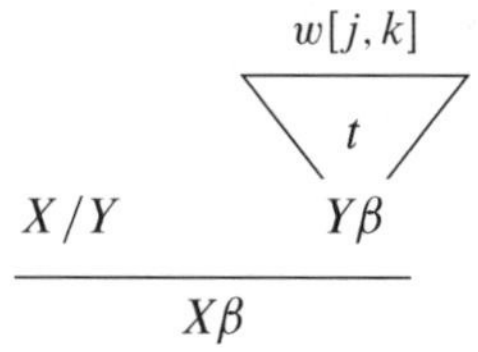

Figure 6: Soundness of rule (7).

Rule (3) states that, if we have built a derivation tree t' with signature $[X/Y, i', j']$ and a context c with signature $[/Y, \beta, i, i', j', j]$, then we can build a new tree t with signature $[X\beta, i, j]$. We obtain t by substituting t' for the foot node of c (see Figure 3(a)).

Rule (6) states that, if we have built a derivation context c_1 with signature $[|_1 Y, \beta |_2 Z, i'', i', j', j'']$ and another context c_2 with signature $[|_2 Z, \varepsilon, i, i'', j'', j]$, then we can build a derivation context c with signature $[|_1 Y, \beta, i, i', j', j]$. We obtain c by substituting c_1 for the foot node of c_2; this is illustrated by Figure 3(b) if we assume $\gamma = \varepsilon$.

5.4 Completeness

In the final part of our correctness proof we now prove the completeness of the deduction system in Figure 5. Specifically we show the following stronger statement: For every derivation tree and for every derivation context with a signature I satisfying the arity bounds for items of Figure 5, the deduction system infers the corresponding item I. From this statement we can immediately conclude that the system constructs the goal item whenever there exists a derivation tree whose yield is the complete input string and whose type is the distinguished category S.

Our proof is by induction on a measure that we call *rank*. The rank of a derivation tree or context is the number of its non-leaf nodes. Note that this definition implies that the foot node of a context is not counted against its rank. The rank of a tree or context is always at least 1, with rank 1 only realized for derivation trees consisting of a single node.

5.4.1 Base Case

Consider a derivation tree t with signature $[X, i, j]$ and $rank(t) = 1$. The tree t takes the form shown in the left of Figure 2, and we have $j = i + 1$ and $w_j := X$. The item $[X, i, j]$ is then produced by one of the axioms of our deduction system.

5.4.2 Inductive Case

The general idea underlying the inductive case can be stated as follows. We consider a derivation tree or context φ with signature I satisfying the bounds stated in Figure 5 for items of type 1 or 2. We then identify a special node s in φ's spine, which we call the *split* node. We use s to "split" φ into two parts that are either derivation trees or contexts, that both satisfy the bounds for items of type 1 or 2, and that both have rank smaller than the rank of φ. We then apply the induction hypothesis to obtain two items that can be combined by one of the inference rules of our algorithm, resulting in the desired item I for φ. We first consider the case in which φ is a tree, and later the case in which φ is a context.

5.4.3 Splitting Trees

Consider a derivation tree t with signature $[X', i, j]$, root node r, and $rank(t) > 1$. Then the spine of t consists of at least 2 nodes. Now assume that $ar(X') \leq c_G$, that is, $[X', i, j]$ is a valid item.

Choose the split node s to be the highest (closest to the root) non-root node on the spine for which $ar(t[s]) \leq c_G$. Node s always exists, as the arity constraint is satisfied at least for the lowest (farthest from the root) node on the spine, which is labeled with a category from the lexicon.

Consider the subtree $t' = t|_s$; thus s is the root node of t'. Because s is a primary node in t, the category at s has at least one argument. We deal here with the case where this category takes the form $t[s] = X/Y$; the case $t[s] = X\backslash Y$ is symmetrical. Thus the signature of t' takes the form $[X/Y, i', j']$ where i', j' are integers with $i \leq i' < j' \leq j$. By our choice of s, $ar(X/Y) \leq c_G$, and therefore $[X/Y, i', j']$ is a valid item. Furthermore, $rank(t|_s) < rank(t)$, as r does not belong to $t|_s$. We may then use the induction hypothesis to deduce that our algorithm constructs the item $[X/Y, i', j']$.

Now consider the context c that is obtained from t by removing all proper descendants of s; thus r is the root node of c and s is its foot node. To see that c is well-defined, note that our choice of s guarantees that $ar(t[u]) > ar(t[r])$ for every node u that is properly between s and r: If there was a node u such that $ar(t[u]) \leq ar(t[r])$ then because of $t[r] = X'$ and our assumption that $ar(X') \leq c_G$ we would have chosen u instead of s.

Now let β be the excess of c; then $X' = t[r] = t[s]\beta = X\beta$. Thus the signature of c takes the form $[/Y, \beta, i, i', j', j]$. Applying Lemma 1 to c, we get $ar(Y\beta) \leq c_G$, and therefore $[/Y, \beta, i, i', j', j]$ is also a valid item. Furthermore, $rank(c) < rank(t)$, since node s is counted in $rank(t)$ but not in $rank(c)$. By the induction hypothesis, we conclude that our algorithm constructs the item $[/Y, \alpha, i, i', j', j]$.

Finally, we apply the inference rule (3) to the previously constructed items $[X/Y, i', j']$ and $[/Y, \beta, i, i', j', j]$. This yields the item $[X\beta, i, j] = [X', i, j]$ for t, as desired.

5.4.4 Splitting Contexts

Consider a derivation context c with signature $[/Y, \beta, i, i', j', j]$, root r, and foot f. (The case where we have $\backslash Y$ instead of $/Y$ can be covered with a symmetrical argument.) From Definition 4 we know that there is a category X such that $c[f] = X/Y$ and $c[r] = X\beta$, and from the definition of context we know that for every spinal node u that is properly between f and r it holds that $ar(c[u]) > ar(c[r])$. Now assume that $ar(Y\beta) \leq c_G$, that is, $[/Y, \beta, i, i', j', j]$ is a valid item. We distinguish two cases below.

Case 1 Suppose that the spine of c consists of exactly 2 nodes. In this case the foot f is the left child of the root r and $i = i'$. Let f' be the right sibling of f and consider the subtree $t' = t|_{f'}$; thus f' is the root node of t'. The signature of t' takes the form $[Y\beta, j', j]$. By our assumption, $ar(Y\beta) \leq c_G$, and then $[Y\beta, j', j]$ is a valid item. Furthermore, $rank(t') < rank(c)$ since the root node r is counted in $rank(c)$ but not in $rank(t')$. Then, by the induction hypothesis, the item $[Y\beta, j', j]$ is constructed by our algorithm. We now apply inference rule (7) to this item; this yields the item $[/Y, \beta, i, i', j', j]$ for c, as required.

Case 2 Suppose that the spine of c consists of more than 2 nodes. This means that there is at least one spinal node that is properly between f and r.

Choose the split node s to be the deepest (farthest from the root) node properly between f and r for which $ar(c[s]) = ar(c[r]) + 1$. Node s always exists, as the arity constraint is satisfied at least for the primary child of r. This is because the definition of context states that $ar(c[u]) > ar(c[r])$ for every node u in the spine, and at the same time, no combinatory rule can reduce the arity of its primary input category by more than one unit.

Consider the context c_1 that is obtained by restricting c to node s and all of its descendants; thus s is the root node of c_1 and f is the foot node. To see that c_1 is well-defined, note that our choice of s guarantees that $ar(c[u]) > ar(c[s])$ for every node u that is properly between f and s. To see this, suppose that there was a node $u \neq s$ such that $ar(c[u]) \leq ar(c[s])$. Since $ar(c[s]) = ar(c[r]) + 1$ and $ar(c[u]) \neq ar(c[s])$, by our definition of s, we would have $ar(c[u]) \leq ar(c[r])$, which cannot be because in c, every node u properly between f and s has arity $ar(c[u]) > ar(c[r])$.

Because f is a primary node in c, the category at f has at least one argument; call it $|_1 Y$. The node s is a primary node in c as well, so the excess of c_1 takes the form $\beta|_2 Z$, where $|_2 Z$ is the topmost argument of the category at s. Thus the signature of c_1 takes the form $[|_1 Y, \beta|_2 Z, i'', i', j', j'']$ where i'', j'' are integers with $i \leq i'' \leq i'$ and $j' \leq j'' \leq j$. Applying Lemma 1 to c_1, we get $ar(Y\beta|_2 Z) \leq c_G$, and therefore $[|_1 Y, \beta|_2 Z, i'', i', j', j'']$ is a valid item. Finally, we note that $rank(c_1) < rank(c)$, since the root node r is counted in c but not in c_1. By the induction hypothesis we conclude that our algorithm constructs the item $[|_1 Y, \beta|_2 Z, i'', i', j', j'']$.

Now consider the context c_2 that is obtained from c by removing all proper descendants of the node s; thus r is the root node of c_2 and s is the foot node. To see that c_2 is well-defined, note that $ar(c[u]) > ar(c[r])$ for every node u that is properly between s and r simply because every such node is also properly between f and r. The excess of c_2 is the empty stack ε by our choice of s. Thus the signature of c_2 is $[|_2 Z, \varepsilon, i, i'', j'', j]$. We apply Lemma 1 once more, this time to c_2, to show that $ar(Z) \leq c_G$, and conclude that $[|_2 Z, \varepsilon, i, i'', j'', j]$ is also a valid item. Finally we note that $rank(c_2) < rank(c)$, as the node s is counted in c but not in c_2. By the induction hypothesis we conclude that our algorithm constructs the item $[|_2 Z, \varepsilon, i, i'', j'', j]$.

We now apply inference rule (6) to the previously constructed items $[|_1 Y, \beta|_2 Z, i'', i', j', j'']$ and $[|_2 Z, \varepsilon, i, i'', j'', j]$. This yields the item $[|_1 Y, \beta, i, i', j', j]$ as desired.

6 Discussion

We round off the article with a discussion of our algorithm and possible extensions.

6.1 Support for Rule Restrictions

As we mentioned in Section 2, the CCG formalism of Weir and Joshi (1988) allows a grammar to impose certain restrictions on valid rule instances. More specifically, for every rule a grammar may restrict
(a) the target of the primary input category and/or
(b) parts of or the entire secondary input category.[3]

The algorithm in Figure 5 can be extended to support such rule restrictions. Note that already in its present form, the algorithm only allows inferences that are licensed by valid instances of a given rule. Supporting restrictions on the secondary input category (restrictions of type b) is straightforward—assuming that these restrictions can be efficiently tested. To also support restrictions on the target of the primary input category (restrictions of type a) the items can be extended by an additional component that keeps track of that target category for the corresponding derivation subtree or context. With this information, rule (7) can perform a check against the restrictions specified for the composition rule, and rules (3) and (6) merely need to test whether the target categories of their two antecedents match, and propagate the common target category to the conclusion. This is essentially the same solution as the one adopted in the V&W algorithm.

6.2 Support for Multi-Modal CCG

The modern version of CCG has abandoned rule restrictions in favor of a new, lexicalized control mechanism in the form of *modalities* or *slash types* (Steedman and Baldridge, 2011). However, as shown by Baldridge and Kruijff (2003), every multi-modal CCG can be translated into an equivalent CCG with rule restrictions. The basic idea is to specialize the target of each category and argument for a slash type, and to reformulate the multi-modal rules as rules with restrictions that reference this information. With this simulation, our parsing algorithm can also be used as a parsing algorithm for multi-modal CCG.

[3] Such restrictions can be used, for example, to impose the linguistically relevant distinction between *harmonic* and *crossed* forms of composition.

6.3 Comparison with the V&W Algorithm

As already mentioned in Section 1, apart from the algorithm presented in this article, the only other algorithm known to run in polynomial time in the length of the input string is the one presented by Vijay-Shanker and Weir (1993). At an abstract level, the two algorithms are based on the same basic idea of decomposing CCG derivations into pieces of two different types, one of which spans a portion of the input string that includes a gap. This idea actually underlies several parsing algorithms for equivalent mildly context-sensitive formalisms, such as Tree-Adjoining Grammar (Joshi and Schabes, 1997).

The main difference between the V&W algorithm and the one presented in this article is the use of different decompositions for CCG derivations. In our algorithm we allow the excess of a derivation context to be the empty list of arguments, something that is not possible in the V&W algorithm. There, when an application operation empties the excess β of some context, one is forced to retrieve, in the same elementary step, the portion of the stack placed right below β. This requires the distinction of several possible cases, resulting in four different realizations of the application rule (Vijay-Shanker and Weir, 1993, p. 616). As a consequence, the V&W algorithm uses nine (forward) inference rules, against our algorithm in Figure 5 which uses only three. Furthermore, some of the inference rules in the V&W algorithm use three antecedent items, while our use a maximum of two. This results in a runtime complexity of $\mathcal{O}(n^7)$ for the V&W algorithm, n the length of the input string; however, Vijay-Shanker and Weir (1993) show how their algorithm can be implemented in time $\mathcal{O}(n^6)$ at the cost of some extra bookkeeping. In contrast, our algorithm directly runs in time $\mathcal{O}(n^6)$.

The relative proliferation of inference rules, combined with the increase in their complexity, makes, in our own opinion, the specification of the V&W parser more difficult to understand and implement, and calls for a more articulated correctness proof.

6.4 Support for Additional Types of Rules

Like the V&W algorithm, our algorithm currently only supports (generalized) composition but no other combinatory rules required for linguistic analysis, in particular type-raising and substitution.

Type-raising is a unary rule of the (forward) form $X \Rightarrow T/(T\backslash X)$ where T is a variable over categories. Under the standard assumption that $T\backslash X$ is limited to a finite set of categories (Steedman, 2000), this rule can be implemented in our algorithm by introducing a new unary inference rule and choosing the constant c_G large enough to accomodate all instances of $T\backslash X$.

Substitution is a binary rule of the (forward) form $X/Y|Z \; Y|Z \Rightarrow X/Z$. This rule is easy to implement if both $/Y$ and $|Z$ are stored in the same item. Otherwise, we need to pass $|Z$ to any item storing the $/Y$. This can be done by changing the second antecedent of rule (6) to allow a single argument $|Z$ instead of the empty excess ε. The price of this change is spurious ambiguity in the derivations of the grammatical deduction system.

7 Conclusion

Recently, there has been a surge of interest in the mathematical properties of CCG; see for instance Hockenmaier and Young (2008), Koller and Kuhlmann (2009), Fowler and Penn (2010) and Kuhlmann et al. (2010). Following this line, this article has revisited the parsing problem for CCG.

Our work, like the polynomial-time parsing algorithm previously discovered by Vijay-Shanker and Weir (1993), is based on the idea of decomposing large CCG derivations into smaller, shareable pieces. Here we have proposed a derivation decomposition different from the one adopted by Vijay-Shanker and Weir (1993). This results in an algorithm which, in our own opinion, is simpler and easier to understand.

Although we have specified only a recognition version of the algorithm, standard techniques can be applied to obtain a derivation forest from our parsing table. This consists in saving backpointers at each inference rule, linking newly inferred items to their antecedent items.

As observed in Section 4.4, the worst case runtime of our algorithm is exponential in the size of the grammar. The same holds true for the algorithm of Vijay-Shanker and Weir (1993). We are not aware of any published discussion on this issue, and we therefore leave as an open problem the question whether CCG parsing can be done in polynomial time when the grammar is considered as part of the input.

Acknowledgments

We thank the Action Editor and the reviewers for their detailed and insightful feedback on the first version of this article. GS has been partially supported by MIUR under project PRIN No. 2010LYA9RH_006.

References

Jason Baldridge and Geert-Jan M. Kruijff. 2003. Multimodal combinatory categorial grammar. In *Tenth Conference of the European Chapter of the Association for Computational Linguistics (EACL)*, pages 211–218, Budapest, Hungary.

Johan Bos, Stephen Clark, Mark Steedman, James R. Curran, and Julia Hockenmaier. 2004. Wide-coverage semantic representations from a CCG parser. In *Proceedings of the 20th International Conference on Computational Linguistics (COLING)*, pages 1240–1246, Geneva, Switzerland.

Stephen Clark and James R. Curran. 2007. Wide-coverage efficient statistical parsing with CCG and log-linear models. *Computational Linguistics*, 33(4):493–552.

Timothy Fowler and Gerald Penn. 2010. Accurate context-free parsing with combinatory categorial grammar. In *Proceedings of the 48th Annual Meeting of the Association for Computational Linguistics (ACL)*, pages 335–344, Uppsala, Sweden.

Julia Hockenmaier and Peter Young. 2008. Non-local scrambling: The equivalence of TAG and CCG revisited. In *Ninth International Workshop on Tree Adjoining Grammars and Related Formalisms (TAG+)*, Tübingen, Germany.

Aravind K. Joshi and Yves Schabes. 1997. Tree-Adjoining Grammars. In Grzegorz Rozenberg and Arto Salomaa, editors, *Handbook of Formal Languages*, volume 3, pages 69–123. Springer.

Aravind K. Joshi. 1985. Tree Adjoining Grammars: How much context-sensitivity is required to provide reasonable structural descriptions? In David R. Dowty, Lauri Karttunen, and Arnold M. Zwicky, editors, *Natural Language Parsing*, pages 206–250. Cambridge University Press.

Alexander Koller and Marco Kuhlmann. 2009. Dependency trees and the strong generative capacity of CCG. In *Proceedings of the 12th Conference of the European Chapter of the Association for Computational Linguistics (EACL)*, pages 460–468, Athens, Greece.

Marco Kuhlmann, Alexander Koller, and Giorgio Satta. 2010. The importance of rule restrictions in CCG. In *Proceedings of the 48th Annual Meeting of the Association for Computational Linguistics (ACL)*, pages 534–543, Uppsala, Sweden.

Tom Kwiatkowski, Luke Zettlemoyer, Sharon Goldwater, and Mark Steedman. 2010. Inducing probabilistic CCG grammars from logical form with higher-order unification. In *Proceedings of the 2010 Conference on Empirical Methods in Natural Language Processing (EMNLP)*, pages 1223–1233, Cambridge, MA, USA.

Bernard Lang. 1974. Deterministic techniques for efficient non-deterministic parsers. In Jacques Loecx, editor, *Automata, Languages and Programming, 2nd Colloquium, University of Saarbrücken, July 29–August 2, 1974*, number 14 in Lecture Notes in Computer Science, pages 255–269. Springer.

Mike Lewis and Mark Steedman. 2013. Combined distributional and logical semantics. *Transactions of the Association for Computational Linguistics*, 1(May):179–192.

Mark-Jan Nederhof and Giorgio Satta. 2004. Tabular parsing. In Carlos Martín-Vide, Victor Mitrana, and Gheorghe Păun, editors, *Formal Languages and Applications*, volume 148 of *Studies in Fuzziness and Soft Computing*, pages 529–549. Springer.

Remo Pareschi and Mark Steedman. 1987. A lazy way to chart-parse with categorial grammars. In *Proceedings of the 25th Annual Meeting of the Association for Computational Linguistics (ACL)*, pages 81–88, Stanford, CA, USA.

Stuart M. Shieber, Yves Schabes, and Fernando Pereira. 1995. Principles and implementation of deductive parsing. *Journal of Logic Programming*, 24(1–2):3–36.

Mark Steedman and Jason Baldridge. 2011. Combinatory categorial grammar. In Robert D. Borsley and Kersti Börjars, editors, *Non-Transformational Syntax: Formal and Explicit Models of Grammar*, chapter 5, pages 181–224. Blackwell.

Mark Steedman. 2000. *The Syntactic Process*. MIT Press.

Masaru Tomita. 1988. Graph-structured stack and natural language parsing. In *Proceedings of the 26th Annual Meeting of the Association for Computational Linguistics (ACL)*, pages 249–257, Buffalo, USA.

K. Vijay-Shanker and David J. Weir. 1990. Polynomial time parsing of combinatory categorial grammars. In *Proceedings of the 28th Annual Meeting of the Association for Computational Linguistics (ACL)*, pages 1–8, Pittsburgh, USA.

K. Vijay-Shanker and David J. Weir. 1993. Parsing some constrained grammar formalisms. *Computational Linguistics*, 19(4):591–636.

K. Vijay-Shanker and David J. Weir. 1994. The equivalence of four extensions of context-free grammars. *Mathematical Systems Theory*, 27(6):511–546.

Jonathan Weese, Chris Callison-Burch, and Adam Lopez. 2012. Using categorial grammar to label translation rules. In *Proceedings of the Seventh Workshop on Statistical Machine Translation*, pages 222–231, Montréal, Canada.

David J. Weir and Aravind K. Joshi. 1988. Combinatory categorial grammars: Generative power and relationship to linear context-free rewriting systems. In *Proceedings of the 26th Annual Meeting of the Association for Computational Linguistics (ACL)*, pages 278–285, Buffalo, USA.

Building a State-of-the-Art Grammatical Error Correction System

Alla Rozovskaya
Center for Computational Learning Systems
Columbia University
New York, NY 10115
alla@ccls.columbia.edu

Dan Roth
Department of Computer Science
University of Illinois
Urbana, IL 61801
danr@illinois.edu

Abstract

This paper identifies and examines the key principles underlying building a state-of-the-art grammatical error correction system. We do this by analyzing the Illinois system that placed first among seventeen teams in the recent CoNLL-2013 shared task on grammatical error correction.

The system focuses on five different types of errors common among non-native English writers. We describe four design principles that are relevant for correcting all of these errors, analyze the system along these dimensions, and show how each of these dimensions contributes to the performance.

1 Introduction

The field of text correction has seen an increased interest in the past several years, with a focus on correcting grammatical errors made by English as a Second Language (ESL) learners. Three competitions devoted to error correction for non-native writers took place recently: HOO-2011 (Dale and Kilgarriff, 2011), HOO-2012 (Dale et al., 2012), and the CoNLL-2013 shared task (Ng et al., 2013). The most recent and most prominent among these, the CoNLL-2013 shared task, covers several common ESL errors, including article and preposition usage mistakes, mistakes in noun number, and various verb errors, as illustrated in Fig. 1.[1] Seventeen teams that

Nowadays **phone/phones* **has/have* many functionalities, **included/including* *∅*/a* camera and *∅/a Wi-Fi receiver.

Figure 1: Examples of representative ESL errors.

participated in the task developed a wide array of approaches that include discriminative classifiers, language models, statistical machine-translation systems, and rule-based modules. Many of the systems also made use of linguistic resources such as additional annotated learner corpora, and defined high-level features that take into account syntactic and semantic knowledge.

Even though the systems incorporated similar resources, the scores varied widely. The top system, from the University of Illinois, obtained an F1 score of 31.20[2], while the second team scored 25.01 and the median result was 8.48 points.[3] These results suggest that there is not enough understanding of what works best and what elements are essential for building a state-of-the-art error correction system.

In this paper, we identify key principles for building a robust grammatical error correction system and show their importance in the context of the shared task. We do this by analyzing the Illinois system and evaluating it along several dimensions: choice

[1]The CoNLL-2014 shared task that completed at the time of writing this paper was an extension of the CoNLL-2013 competition (Ng et al., 2014) but addressed all types of errors. The Illinois-Columbia submission, a slightly extended version of the Illinois CoNLL-2013 system, ranked at the top. For a description of the Illinois-Columbia submission, we refer the reader to Rozovskaya et al. (2014a).

[2]The state-of-the-art performance of the Illinois system discussed here is with respect to individual components for different errors. Improvements in Rozovskaya and Roth (2013) over the Illinois system that are due to joint learning and inference are orthogonal, and the analysis in this paper still applies there.

[3]F1 might not be the ideal metric for this task but this was the one chosen in the evaluation. See more in Sec. 6.

Transactions of the Association for Computational Linguistics, 2 (2014) 419–434. Action Editor: Alexander Koller.
Submitted 10/2013; Revised 6/2014; Published 10/2014.

of learning algorithm; choice of training data (native or annotated learner data); model adaptation to the mistakes made by the writers; and the use of linguistic knowledge. For each dimension, several implementations are compared, including, when possible, approaches chosen by other teams. We also validate the obtained results on another learner corpus. Overall, this paper makes two contributions: (1) we explain the success of the Illinois system, and (2) we provide an understanding and qualitative analysis of different dimensions that are essential for success in this task, with the goal of aiding future research on it. Given that the Illinois system has been the top system in four competitive evaluations over the last few years (HOO and CoNLL), we believe that the analysis we propose will be useful for researchers in this area.

In the next section, we present the CoNLL-2013 competition. Sec. 3 gives an overview of the approaches adopted by the top five teams. Sec. 4 describes the Illinois system. In Sec. 5, the analysis of the Illinois system is presented. Sec. 6 offers a brief discussion, and Sec. 7 concludes the paper.

2 Task Description

The CoNLL-2013 shared task focuses on five common mistakes made by ESL writers: *article/determiner*, *preposition*, *noun number*, *verb agreement*, *verb form*. The training data of the shared task is the NUCLE corpus (Dahlmeier et al., 2013), which contains essays written by learners of English (we also refer to it as *learner data* or *shared task training data*). The test data consists of 50 essays by students from the same linguistic background. The training and the test data contain 1.2M and 29K words, respectively.

Table 1 shows the number of errors by type and the error rates. Determiner errors are the most common and account for 42.1% of all errors in training. Note that the test data contains a much larger proportion of annotated mistakes; e.g. determiner errors occur four times more often in the test data than in the training data (only 2.4% of noun phrases in the training data have determiner errors, versus 10% in the test data). The differences might be attributed to differences in annotation standards, annotators, or writers, as the test data was annotated at a later time. The shared task provided two sets of test annotations: the original annotated data and a set with additional revisions that also includes alternative annotations proposed by participants. Clearly, having alternative answers is the right approach as there are typically multiple ways to correct an error. However, because the alternatives are based on the error analysis of the participating systems, the revised set may be biased (Ng et al., 2013). Consequently, we report results on the original set.

Error	**Number of errors and error rates**	
	Train	**Test**
Art.	6658 (2.4%)	690 (10.0%)
Prep.	2404 (2.0%)	311 (10.7%)
Noun	3779 (1.6%)	396 (6.0%)
Verb agr.	1527 (2.0%)	124 (5.2%)
Verb form	1453 (0.8%)	122 (2.5%)

Table 1: **Statistics on annotated errors in the CoNLL-2013 shared task data.** Percentage denotes the error rates, i.e. the number of erroneous instances with respect to the total number of relevant instances in the data.

3 Model Dimensions

Table 2 summarizes approaches and methodologies of the top five systems. The prevailing approach consists in building a statistical model either on learner data or on a much larger corpus of native English data. For native data, several teams make use of the Web 1T 5-gram corpus (henceforth Web1T, (Brants and Franz, 2006)). NARA employs a statistical machine translation model for two error types; two systems have rule-based components for selected errors. Based on the analysis of the Illinois system, we identify the following, inter-dependent, dimensions that will be examined in this work:

1. Learning algorithm: Most of the teams, including Illinois, built statistical models. We show that the choice of the learning algorithm is very important and affects the performance of the system.

2. Adaptation to learner errors: Previous studies, e.g. (Rozovskaya and Roth, 2011) showed that adaptation, i.e. developing models that utilize knowledge about error patterns of the non-native writers, is extremely important. We summarize adaptation techniques proposed earlier and examine their impact on the performance of the system.

3. Linguistic knowledge: It is essential to use some linguistic knowledge when developing error correction modules, e.g., to identify which type of verb

System	Error	Approach
Illinois (Rozovskaya et al., 2013)	Art.	AP model on NUCLE with word, POS, shallow parse features
	Prep.	NB model trained on Web1T and adapted to learner errors
	Noun/Agr./Form	NB model trained on Web1T
NTHU (Kao et al., 2013)	All	Count model with backoff trained on Web1T
HIT (Xiang et al., 2013)	Art./Prep./Noun	ME on NUCLE with word, POS, dependency features
	Agr./Form	Rule-based
NARA (Yoshimoto et al., 2013)	Art./Prep.	SMT model trained on learner data from Lang-8 corpus
	Noun	ME model on NUCLE with word, POS and dependency features
	Agr./Form	Treelet LM on Gigaword and Penn TreeBank corpora
UMC (Xing et al., 2013)	Art./Prep.	Two LMs – on NUCLE and Web1T corpus – with voting
	Noun	Rules and ME model on NUCLE + LM trained on Web1T
	Agr./Form	ME model on NUCLE (agr.) and rules (form)

Table 2: **Top systems in the CoNLL-2013 shared task.** The second column indicates the error type; the third column describes the approach adopted by the system. *ME* stands for Maximum Entropy; *LM* stands for language model; *SMT* stands for Statistical Machine Translation; *AP* stands for Averaged Perceptron; *NB* stands for Naïve Bayes.

	Classifier				
	Art.	**Prep.**	**Noun**	**Agr.**	**Form**
Train	254K	103K	240K	75K	175K
Test	6K	2.5K	2.6K	2.4K	4.8K

Table 3: **Number of candidate words by classifier type.**

error occurs in a given context, before the appropriate correction module is employed. We describe and evaluate the contribution of these elements.

4. Training data: We discuss the advantages of training on learner data or native English data in the context of the shared task and in broader context.

4 The Illinois System

The Illinois system consists of five machine-learning models, each specializing in correcting one of the errors described above. The words that are selected as input to a classifier are called *candidates* (Table 3). In the preposition system, for example, candidates are determined by surface forms. In other systems, determining the candidates might be more involved.

All modules take as input the corpus documents pre-processed with a part-of-speech tagger[4] (Even-Zohar and Roth, 2001) and shallow parser[5] (Punyakanok and Roth, 2001). In the Illinois submission, some modules are trained on native data, others on learner data. The modules trained on learner data make use of a discriminative algorithm, while native-trained modules make use of the Naïve Bayes (NB) algorithm. The Illinois system has an option for a post-processing step where corrections that always result in a false positive in training are ignored but this option is not used here.

4.1 Determiner Errors

The majority of determiner errors involve articles, although some errors also involve pronouns. The Illinois system addresses only article errors. Candidates include articles ("a","an","the")[6] and omissions, by considering noun-phrase-initial contexts where an article is likely to be omitted. The *confusion set* for articles is thus $\{a, the, \varnothing\}$. The article classifier is the same as the one in the HOO shared tasks (Rozovskaya et al., 2012; Rozovskaya et al., 2011), where it demonstrated superior performance. It is a discriminative model that makes use of the Averaged Perceptron algorithm (AP, (Freund and Schapire, 1996)) implemented with LBJava (Rizzolo and Roth, 2010) and is trained on learner data with rich features and adaptation to learner errors. See Sec. 5.2 and Sec. 5.3.

4.2 Preposition Errors

Similar to determiners, we distinguish three types of preposition mistakes: choosing an incorrect preposition, using a superfluous preposition, and omitting a preposition. In contrast to determiners, for learners of many first language backgrounds, most of the preposition errors are replacements, i.e., where the

[4]http://cogcomp.cs.illinois.edu/page/software_view/POS

[5]http://cogcomp.cs.illinois.edu/page/software_view/Chunker

[6]The variants "a" and "an" are collapsed to one class.

“Hence, the environmental factors also ***contributes/ contribute** to various difficulties, ***giving/given** problems in nuclear technology.”	
Error	**Confusion set**
Agr.	{INF=contribute, S=contributes}
Form	{INF=give, ED=given, ING=giving, S=gives }

Table 4: **Confusion sets for agreement and form.** For irregular verbs, the second candidate in the confusion set for *Verb form* is the past participle.

Dimension	Systems used in the comparison
Learn. alg. (Sec. 5.1)	NTHU, UMC
Adaptation (Sec. 5.2)	Error inflation: HIT
Ling. knowledge (Sec. 5.3)	Cand. identification: NTHU, HIT Verb finiteness: NTHU
Train. data (Sec. 5.4)	HIT, NARA

Table 5: **System comparisons.** Column 1 indicates the dimension, and column 2 lists systems whose approaches provide a relevant point of comparison.

author correctly recognized the need for a preposition, but chose the wrong one (Leacock et al., 2010). However, learner errors depend on the first language; in NUCLE, spurious prepositions occur more frequently: 29% versus 18% of all preposition mistakes in other learner corpora (Rozovskaya and Roth, 2010a; Yannakoudakis et al., 2011).

The Illinois preposition classifier is a NB model trained on Web1T that uses word n-gram features in the 4-word window around the preposition. The 4-word window refers to the four words before and the four words after the preposition, e.g. “problem as the search *of* alternative resources to the” for the preposition “of”. Features consist of word n-grams of various lengths spanning the target preposition. For example, “the search of” is a 3-gram feature. The model is adapted to likely preposition confusions using the priors method (see Sec. 5.2). The Illinois model targets replacement errors of the 12 most common English prepositions. Here we augment it to identify spurious prepositions. The *confusion set* for prepositions is as follows: {*in, of, on, for, to, at, about, with, from, by, into, during*, ∅}.

4.3 Agreement and Form Errors

The Illinois system implements two verb modules – agreement and form – that consist of the following components: (1) candidate identification; (2) determining the relevant module for each candidate based on *verb finiteness*; (3) correction modules for each error type. The *confusion set* for verbs depends on the target word and includes its morphological variants (Table 4). For irregular verbs, the past participle form is included, while the past tense form is not (i.e. “given” is included but “gave” is not), since tense errors are not part of the task. To generate morphological variants, the system makes use of a morphological analyzer *verbMorph*; it assumes (1) a list of valid verb lemmas (compiled using a POS-tagged version of the NYT section of the Gigaword corpus) and (2) a list of irregular English verbs.[7]

Candidate Identification stage selects the set of words that are presented as input to the classifier. This is a crucial step: errors missed at this stage will not be detected by the later stages. See Sec. 5.3.

Verb Finiteness is used in the Illinois system to separately process verbs that fulfill different grammatical functions and thus are marked for different grammatical properties. See Sec. 5.3.

Correction Modules The agreement module is a binary classifier. The form module is a 4-class system. Both classifiers are trained on the Web1T corpus.

4.4 Noun Errors

Noun number errors involve confusing singular and plural noun forms (e.g. “phone” instead of “phones” in Fig. 1) and are the second most common error type in the NUCLE corpus after determiner mistakes (Table 1). The Illinois noun module is trained on the Web1T corpus using NB. Similar to verbs, *candidate identification* is an important step in the noun classifier. See Sec. 5.3.

5 System Analysis

In this section, we evaluate the Illinois system along the four dimensions identified in Sec. 3, compare its components to alternative configurations implemented by other teams, and present additional experiments that further analyze each dimension. While a direct comparison with other systems is not always possible due to other differences between the systems, we believe that these results are still useful. Table 5 lists systems used for comparion. It is important to note that the dimensions are not independent. For instance, there is a correlation between algorithm choice and training data.

[7]The tool and more detail about it can be found at http://cogcomp.cs.illinois.edu/page/publication_view/743

Results are reported on the test data using F1 computed with the CoNLL scorer (Dahlmeier and Ng, 2012). Error-specific results are generated based on the output of individual modules. Note that these are not directly comparable to error-specific results in the CoNLL overview paper: the latter are approximate as the organizers did not have the error type information for corrections in the output. The complete system includes the union of corrections made by each of these modules, where the corrections are applied in order. Ordering overlapping candidates[8] might potentially affect the final output, when modules correctly identify an error but propose different corrections, but this does not happen in practice. Modules that are part of the Illinois submission are marked with an asterisk in all tables.

To demonstrate that our findings are not specific to CoNLL, we also show results on the FCE dataset. It is produced by learners from seventeen first language backgrounds and contains 500,000 words from the Cambridge Learner Corpus (CLC) (Yannakoudakis et al., 2011). We split the corpus into two equal parts – training and test. The statistics are shown in Appendix Tables A.16 and A.17.

5.1 Dim. 1: Learning Algorithm

Rozovskaya and Roth (2011, Sec. 3) discuss the relations between the amount of training data, learning algorithms, and the resulting performance. They show that on training sets of similar sizes, discriminative classifiers outperform other machine learning methods on this task. Following these results, the Illinois article module that is trained on the NUCLE corpus uses the discriminative approach AP. Most of the other teams that train on the NUCLE corpus also use a discriminative method.

However, when a very large native training set such as the Web1T corpus is available, it is often advantageous to use it. The Web1T corpus is a collection of n-gram counts of length one to five over a corpus of 10^{12} words. Since the corpus does not come with complete sentences, it is not straightforward to make use of a discriminative classifier because of the limited window provided around each example: training a discriminative model would limit the surrounding context features to a 2-word window. Because we wish to make use of the context features that extend beyond the 2-word window, it is only possible to use count-based methods, such as NB or LM. Several teams make use of the Web1T corpus: UMC uses a count-based LM for article, preposition, and noun number errors; NTHU addresses all errors with a count-based model with backoff, which is essentially a variation of a language model with backoff. The Illinois system employs the Web1T corpus for all errors, except articles, using NB.

Training Naïve Bayes for Deletions and Insertions The reason for not using the Web1T corpus for article errors is that training NB on Web1T for deletions and insertions presents a problem, and the majority of article errors are of this type. Recall that Web1T contains only n-gram counts, which makes it difficult to estimate the prior count for the $\varnothing$ candidate. (With access to complete sentences, the prior of $\varnothing$ is estimated by counting the total number of $\varnothing$ candidates; e.g., in case of articles, the number of NPs with $\varnothing$ article is computed.) We solve this problem by treating the article and the word following it as one target. For instance, to estimate prior counts for the article candidates in front of the word "camera" in "including camera", we obtain counts for "camera", "a camera", "the camera". In the case of the $\varnothing$ candidate, the word "camera" acts as the target. Thus, the confusion set for the article classifier is modified as follows: instead of the three articles (as shown in Sec. 4.1), each member of the confusion set is a concatenation of the article and the word that follows it, e.g. {a_camera, the_camera, camera}. The counts for contextual features are obtained similarly, e.g. a feature that includes a preceding word would correspond to the count of "including x", where x can take any value from the confusion set. The above solution allows us to train NB for article errors and to extend the preposition classifier to handle extraneous preposition errors (Table 6).

Rozovskaya and Roth (2011) study several algorithms trained on the Web1T corpus and observe that, when evaluated with the same context window size, NB performs better than other count-based methods. In order to show the impact of the algorithm choice, in Table 6, we compare LM and NB models. Both models use word n-grams spanning the target word in the 4-word window. We train LMs

[8]Overlapping candidates are included in more than one module: if "work" is tagged as *NN*, it is included in the noun module, but also in the form module (as a valid verb lemma).

Error	Model	F1	
		CoNLL	FCE
Art.	LM	21.11	24.15
	NB	**32.45**	**30.78**
Prep.	LM	12.09	**30.01**
	NB	**14.04**	29.40
Noun	LM	40.72	32.41
	NB*	**42.60**	**34.40**
Agr.	LM	20.65	33.53
	NB*	**26.46**	**36.42**
Form	LM	13.40	08.46
	NB*	**14.50**	**12.16**

Table 6: **Comparison of learning models.** Web1T corpus. Modules that are part of the Illinois submission are marked with an asterisk.

Source	Candidates			
	ED	INF	ING	S
ED	0.99675	0.00192	0.00103	0.00030
INF	0.00177	0.99630	0.00168	0.00025
ING	0.00124	0.00447	0.99407	0.00022
S	0.00054	0.00544	0.00132	0.99269

Table 7: **Priors confusion matrix used for adapting NB.** Each entry shows Prob(candidate|source), where source corresponds to the verb form chosen by the author.

with SRILM (Stolcke, 2002) using Jelinek-Mercer linear interpolation as a smoothing method (Chen and Goodman, 1996). On the CoNLL test data, NB outperforms LM on all errors; on the FCE corpus, NB is superior on all errors, except preposition errors, where LM outperforms NB only very slightly. We attribute this to the fact that the preposition problem has more labels; when there is a big confusion set, more features have default smooth weights, so there is no advantage to running NB. We found that with fewer classes (6 rather than 12 prepositions), NB outperforms LM. It is also possible that when we have a lot of labels, the theoretical difference between the algorithms disappears. Note that NB can be improved via adaptation (next section) and then it outperforms the LM also for preposition errors.

5.2 Dim. 2: Adaptation to Learner Errors

In the previous section, the models were trained on native data. These models have no notion of the error patterns of the learners. Here we discuss *model adaptation to learner errors*, i.e. developing models that utilize the knowledge about the types of mistakes learners make. Adaptation is based on the fact that learners make mistakes in a systematic manner, e.g. errors are influenced by the writer's first language (Gass and Selinker, 1992; Ionin et al., 2008).

There are different ways to adapt a model that depend on the type of training data (learner or native) and the algorithm choice. The key application of adaptation is for models trained on native English data, because the learned models do not know anything about the errors learners make. With adaptation, models trained on native data can use the author's word (the source word) as a feature and thus propose a correction based on what the author originally wrote. This is crucial, as the source word is an important piece of information (Rozovskaya and Roth, 2010b). Below, several adaptation techniques are summarized and evaluated. The Illinois system makes use of adaptation in the article model via the inflation method and adapts its NB preposition classifier trained on Web1T with the priors method.

Adapting NB The *priors method* (Rozovskaya and Roth, 2011, Sec. 4) is an adaptation technique for a NB model trained on native English data; it is based on changing the distribution of priors over the correction candidates. Candidate prior is a special parameter in NB; when NB is trained on native data, candidate priors correspond to the relative frequencies of the candidates in the native corpus and do not provide any information on the real distribution of mistakes and the dependence of the correction on the word used by the author.

In the priors method, candidate priors are changed using an error confusion matrix based on learner data that specifies how likely each confusion pair is. Table 7 shows the confusion matrix for verb form errors, computed on the NUCLE data. Adapted priors are dependent on the author's original verb form used: let s be a form of the verb appearing in the source text, and c a correction candidate. Then the adapted prior of c given s is:

$$prior(c|s) = \frac{C(s,c)}{C(s)}$$

where $C(s)$ denotes the number of times s appeared in the learner data, and $C(s,c)$ denotes the number of times c was the correct form when s was used by a writer. The adapted priors differ by the source: the probability of candidate *INF* when the source form is *S*, is more than twice than when the source form is

Error	Model	F1		
		CoNLL		FCE
		Train	Test	
Art.	NB	18.28	32.45	30.78
	NB-adapted	**19.18**	**34.49**	**31.76**
Prep.	NB	09.03	**14.04**	29.40
	NB-adapted*	**10.94**	12.14	**32.22**
Noun	NB*	**23.06**	**42.60**	**34.40**
	NB-adapted	22.89	42.31	32.38
Agr.	NB*	16.72	**26.46**	36.42
	NB-adapted	**17.62**	23.46	**38.57**
Form	NB*	11.93	14.50	12.16
	NB-adapted	**14.63**	**18.35**	**16.67**

Table 8: **Adapting NB with the priors method.** All models are trained on the Web1T corpus. Modules that are part of the Illinois submission are marked with an asterisk.

ED; the probability that S is the correct form is very high, which reflects the low error rates.

Table 8 compares NB and NB-adapted models. Because of the dichotomy in the error rates in CoNLL training and test data, we also show experiments using 5-fold cross-validation on the training data. Adaptation always helps on the CoNLL training data and the FCE data (except noun errors), but on the test data it only helps on article and verb form errors. This is due to discrepancies in the error rates, as adaptation exploits the property that learner errors are systematic. Indeed, when priors are estimated on the test data (in 5-fold cross-validation), the performance improves, e.g. the preposition module attains an F1 of 18.05 instead of 12.14.

Concerning lack of improvement on noun number errors, we hypothesize that these errors differ from the other mistakes in that the appropriate form strongly depends on the surface form of the noun, which would, in turn, suggest that the dependency of the label on the grammatical form of the source that the adaptation is trying to discover is weak. Indeed, the prior distribution of {singular, plural} label space does not change much when the source feature is taken into account. The unadapted priors for "singular" and "plural" are 0.75 and 0.25, respectively. Similarly, the adapted priors (singular|plural) and (plural|singular) are 0.034 and 0.016, respectively. In other words, the unadapted prior probability for "plural" is three times lower than for "singular", which does not change much with adaptation. This is different for other errors. For instance, in case of verb agreement, the unadapted prior for "plural" is 0.617, more than three times than the "singular" prior of 0.20. With adaptation, these priors become almost the same (0.016 and 0.012).

Adapting AP The AP is a discriminative learning algorithm and does not use priors on the set of candidates. In order to reflect our estimate of the error distribution, the AP algorithm is adapted differently, by introducing into the native data artificial errors, in a rate that reflects the errors made by the ESL writers (Rozovskaya and Roth, 2010b). The idea is to simulate learner errors in training, through artificial mistakes (also produced using an error confusion matrix).[9] The original method was proposed for models trained on native data. This technique can be further enhanced using *the error inflation method* (Rozovskaya et al., 2012, Sec. 6) applied to models trained on native or learner data.

The Illinois system uses error inflation in its article classifier. Because this classifier is trained on learner data, the *source* article can be used as a feature. However, since learner errors are sparse, the *source* feature encourages the model to abstain from flagging a mistake, which results in low recall. The error inflation technique addresses this problem by boosting the proportion of errors in the training data. It does this by generating additional artificial errors using the error distribution from the training set.

Table 9 shows the results of adapting the AP classifier using error inflation. (We omit noun results, since the noun AP model performs better without the source feature, which is similar to the noun NB model, as discussed above.) The inflation method improves recall and, consequently, F1. It should be noted that although inflation also decreases precision it is still helpful. In fact, because of the low error rates, performance on the CoNLL dataset with natural errors is very poor, often resulting in F1 being equal to 0 due to no errors being detected.

Inflation vs. Sampling To demonstrate the impact of error inflation, we compare it against sampling, an approach used by other teams – e.g. HIT – that improves recall by removing correct examples in training. The HIT article model is similar to the

[9] The idea of using artificial errors goes back to Izumi et al. (2003) and was also used in Foster and Andersen (2009). The approach discussed here refers to the *adaptation* method in Rozovskaya and Roth (2010b) that generates artificial errors using the distribution of naturally-occurring errors.

Error	Model	F1	
		CoNLL	FCE
Art.	AP (natural errors)	07.06	27.65
	AP (infl. const. 0.9)*	24.61	30.96
Prep.	AP (natural errors)	0.0	14.69
	AP (infl. const. 0.7)	07.37	34.77
Agr.	AP (natural errors)	0.0	08.05
	AP (infl. const. 0.8)	17.06	31.03
Form	AP (natural errors)	0.0	01.56
	AP (infl. const. 0.9)	10.53	09.43

Table 9: **Adapting AP using error inflation.** Models are trained on learner data with word n-gram features and the source feature. *Inflation constant* shows how many correct instances remain (e.g. 0.9 indicates that 90% of correct examples are unchanged, while 10% are converted to mistakes.) Modules that are part of the Illinois submission are marked with an asterisk.

Infl. constant	F1	
	Sampling	Inflation
0.90	23.22	24.61
0.85	27.75	29.29
0.80	30.04	33.47
0.70	33.02	35.52
0.60	32.78	35.03

Table 10: **Comparison of the inflation and sampling methods on article errors (CoNLL).** The proportion of errors in training in each row is identical.

Illinois model but scored three points below. Table 10 shows that sampling falls behind the inflation method, since it considerably reduces the training size to achieve similar error rates. The proportion of errors in training in each row is identical: sampling achieves the error rates by removing correct examples, whereas the inflation method converts some positive examples to artificial mistakes. *Inflation constant* shows how many correct instances remain; smaller inflation values correspond to more erroneous instances in training; the sampling approach, correspondingly, removes more positive examples.

To summarize, we have demonstrated the impact of error inflation by comparing it to a similar method used by another team; we have also shown that further improvements can be obtained by adapting NB to learner errors using the priors method, when training and test data exhibit similar error patterns.

5.3 Dim. 3: Linguistic Knowledge

The use of linguistic knowledge is important in several components of the error correction system: feature engineering, candidate identification, and special techniques for correcting verb errors.

Error	Features	F1	
		CoNLL	FCE
Art.	n-gram	24.61	30.96
	n-gram+POS+chunk*	**33.50**	**35.66**
Agr.	n-gram	17.06	31.03
	n-gram+POS	24.14	35.29
	n-gram+POS+syntax	**27.93**	**41.23**

Table 11: **Feature evaluation.** Models are trained on learner data, use the source word and error inflation. Modules that are part of the Illinois submission are marked with an asterisk.

Features It is known from many NLP tasks that feature engineering is important, and this is the case here. Note that this is relevant only when training on learner data, as models trained on Web1T can make use of n-gram features only but for the NUCLE corpus we have several layers of linguistic annotation.[10] We found that for article and agreement errors, using deeper linguistic knowledge is especially beneficial. The article features in the Illinois module, in addition to the surface form of the context, encode POS and shallow parse properties. These features are presented in Rozovskaya et al. (2013, Table 3) and Appendix Table A.19. The Illinois agreement module is trained on Web1T but further analysis reveals that it is better to train on learner data with rich features. The word n-gram and POS agreement features are the same as those in the article module. Syntactic features encode properties of the subject of the verb and are presented in Rozovskaya et al. (2014b, Table 7) and Appendix Table A.18; these are based on the syntactic parser (Klein and Manning, 2003) and the dependency converter (Marneffe et al., 2006).

Table 11 shows that adding rich features is helpful. Notably, adding deeper syntactic knowledge to the agreement module is useful, although parse features are likely to contain more noise.[11] Foster (2007) and Lee and Seneff (2008) observe a degrade in performance on syntactic parsers due to grammatical noise that also includes agreement errors. For articles, we chose to add syntactic knowledge from shallow parse as it is likely to be sufficient for articles and more accurate than full-parse features.

Candidate Identification for errors on open-class

[10]Feature engineering will also be relevant when training on a native corpus that has linguistic annotation.

[11]Parse features have also been found useful in preposition error correction (Tetreault et al., 2010).

words is rarely discussed but is a crucial step: it is not possible to identify the relevant candidates using a closed list of words, and the procedure needs to rely on pre-processing tools, whose performance on learner data is suboptimal.[12] Rozovskaya et al. (2014b, Sec. 5.1) describe and evaluate several candidate selection methods for verbs. The Illinois system implements their best method that addresses pre-processing errors, by selecting words tagged as verbs as well as words tagged as *NN*, whose lemma is on the list of valid verb lemmas (Sec. 4.3).

Following descriptions provided by several teams, we evaluate several candidate selection methods for nouns. The first method includes words tagged as *NN* or *NNS* that head an NP. NTHU and HIT use this method; NTHU obtained the second best noun score, after the Illinois system; its model is also trained on Web1T. The second method includes all words tagged as *NN* and *NNS* and is used in several other systems, e.g. SZEG, (Berend et al., 2013).

The above procedures suffer from pre-processing errors. The Illinois method addresses this problem by adding words that end in common noun suffixes, e.g. "ment", "ments", and "ist". The percentage of noun errors selected as candidates by each method and the impact of each method on the performance are shown in Table 12. The Illinois method has the best result on both datasets; on CoNLL, it improves F1 score by 2 points and recovers 43% of the candidates that are missed by the first approach. On FCE, the second method is able to recover more erroneous candidates, but it does not perform as well as the last method, possibly, due to the number of noisy candidates it generates. To conclude, pre-processing mistakes should be taken into consideration, when correcting errors, especially on open-class words.

Using Verb Finiteness to Correct Verb Errors As shown in Table 4, the surface realizations that correspond to the agreement candidates are a subset of the possible surface realizations of the form classifier. One natural approach, thus, is to train one classifier to predict the correct surface form of the verb. However, the same surface realization may correspond to multiple grammatical properties. This observation motivates the approach that corrects agreement and form errors separately (Rozovskaya et al., 2014b). It uses the linguistic notion of *verb finiteness* (Radford, 1988) that distinguishes between finite and non-finite verbs, each of which fulfill different grammatical functions and thus are marked for different grammatical properties.

[12]Candidate selection is also difficult for closed-class errors in the case of omissions, e.g. articles, but article errors have been studied rather extensively, e.g. (Han et al., 2006), and we have no room to elaborate on it here.

Candidate ident. method	Error recall (%)		F1	
	CoNLL	FCE	CoNLL	FCE
NP heads	87.72	92.32	40.47	34.16
All nouns	89.50	95.29	41.08	33.16
Nouns+heuristics*	92.84	94.86	**42.60**	**34.40**

Table 12: **Nouns: effect of candidate identification methods on the correction performance.** Models are trained using NB. *Error recall* denotes the percentage of nouns containing number errors that are selected as candidates. Modules that are part of the Illinois submission are marked with an asterisk.

Training method	F1	
	CoNLL	FCE
One classifier	16.43	21.14
Finiteness-based training (I)	18.59	27.72
Finiteness-based training (II)	**21.08**	**29.98**

Table 13: **Improvement due to separate training for verb errors.** Models are trained using the AP algorithm.

Verb finiteness is used to direct each verb to the appropriate classifier. The candidates for the agreement module are verbs that take agreement markers: the finite surface forms of the be-verbs ("is", "are", "was", and "were"), auxiliaries "have" and "has", and finite verbs tagged as *VB* and *VBZ* that have explicit subjects (identified with the parser). The form candidates are non-finite verbs and some of the verbs whose finiteness is ambiguous.

Table 13 compares the two approaches: when all verbs are handled together; and when verbs are processed separately. All of the classifiers use surface form and POS features of the words in the 4-word window around the verb. Several subsets of these features were tried; the single classifier uses the best combination, which is the same word and POS features shown in Appendix Table A.19. Finiteness-based classifier (I) uses the same features for agreement and form as the single classifier.

When training separately, we can also explore whether different errors benefit from different features; finiteness-based classifier (II) optimizes features for each classifier. The differences in the feature sets are minor and consist of removing several unigram word and POS features of tokens that do not appear immediately next to the verb. Recall from the discussion on features that the agreement module can be further improved by adding syntactic knowledge. In the next section, it is shown that an even better approach is to train on learner data for agreement mistakes and on native data for form errors. The results in Table 13 are for AP models but similar improvements due to separate training are observed for NB models trained on Web1T. Note that the NTHU system also corrects all verb errors using a model trained on Web1T but handles all these errors together; its verb module scored 8 F1 points below the Illinois one. While there are other differences between the two systems, the results suggest that part of the improvement within the Illinois system is indeed due to handling the two errors separately.

5.4 Dim. 4: Training Data

NUCLE is a large corpus produced by learners of the same language background as the test data. Because of its large size, training on this corpus is a natural choice. Indeed, many teams follow this approach. On the other hand, an important issue in the CoNLL task is the difference between the training and test sets, which has impact on the selection of the training set – the large Web1T has more coverage and allows for better generalization. We show that for some errors it is especially advantageous to train on a larger corpus of native data. It should be noted that while we refer to the Web1T corpus as "native", it certainly contains data from language learners; we assume that the noise can be neglected.

Table 14 compares models trained on native and learner data in their best configurations based on the training data. Overall, we find that Web1T is clearly preferable for noun errors. We attribute this to the observation that noun number usage strongly depends on the surface form of the noun, and not just the contextual cues and syntactic structure. For example, certain nouns in English tend to be used exclusively in singular or plural form. Thus, considerably more data compared to other error types is required to learn model parameters.

On article and preposition errors, native-trained models perform slightly better on CoNLL, while learner-trained models are better on FCE. We conjecture that the FCE training set is more similar to the respective test data and thus provides an advantage over training on native data.

Error	Train. data	Learning algorithm	Features	F1	
				CoNLL	FCE
Art.	Native	NB-adapt.	n-gram	**34.49**	31.76
	Learner	AP-infl.*	+POS+chunk	33.50	**35.66**
Prep.	Native	LM; NB-adapt.	n-gram	**12.09**	32.22
	Learner	AP-infl.	n-gram	10.26	**33.93**
Noun	Native	NB*	n-gram	**42.60**	**32.38**
	Learner	AP-infl.	+POS	19.22	17.28
Agr.	Native	NB-adapt.	n-gram	23.46	38.57
	Learner	AP-infl.	+POS+syntax	**27.93**	**41.23**
Form	Native	NB-adapt.	n-gram	**18.35**	**16.67**
	Learner	AP-infl.	+POS	12.32	12.02

Table 14: **Choice of training data: learner vs. native (Web1T).** For prepositions, LM is chosen for CoNLL, and NB-adapted for FCE. Modules that are part of the Illinois submission are marked with an asterisk.

On verb agreement errors, native-trained models perform better than those trained on learner data, when the same n-gram features are used. However, when we add POS and syntactic knowledge, training on learner data is advantageous. Finally, for verb form errors, there is an advantage when training on a lot of native data, although the difference is not as substantial as for noun errors. This suggests that unlike agreement mistakes that are better addressed using syntax, form errors, similarly to nouns, benefit from training on a lot of data with n-gram features.

To summarize, choice of the training data is an important consideration for building a robust system. Researchers compared native- and learner-trained models for prepositions (Han et al., 2010; Cahill et al., 2013), while the analysis in this work addresses five error types – showing that errors behave differently – and evaluates on two corpora.[13]

6 Discussion

In Table 15, we show the results of the system, where the best modules are selected based on the performance on the training data. We also show the Illinois modules (without post-processing). The following changes are made with respect to the Illinois submission: the preposition system is based on an LM and enhanced to handle spurious preposition errors (thus the Illinois result of 7.10 shown here is

[13]For studies that directly combine native and learner data in training, see Gamon (2010) and Dahlmeier and Ng (2011).

Error	Illinois submission		This work	
	Model	**F1**	**Model**	**F1**
Art.	AP-infl.	33.50	AP-infl.	33.50
Prep.	NB-adapt.	07.10	LM	**12.09**
Noun	NB	42.60	NB	42.60
Agr.	NB	26.14	AP-infl.	**27.93**
Form	NB	14.50	NB-adapt.	**18.35**
All		31.43		**31.75**

Table 15: **Results on CoNLL of the Illinois system (without post-processing) and this work.** NB and LM models are trained on Web1T; AP models are trained on NUCLE. Modules different from the Illinois submission are in bold.

different from the 12.14 in Table 8); the agreement classifier is trained on the learner data using AP with rich features and error inflation; the form classifier is adapted to learner mistakes, whereas the Illinois submission trains NB without adaptation. The key improvements are observed with respect to least frequent errors, so the overall improvement is small. Importantly, the Illinois system already takes into account the four dimensions analyzed in this paper.

In CoNLL-2013, systems were compared using F1. Practical systems, however, should be tuned for good precision to guarantee that the overall quality of the text does not go down. Clearly, optimizing for F1 does not ensure that the system improves the quality of the text (see Appendix B). A different evaluation metric based on the *accuracy* of the data is proposed in Rozovskaya and Roth (2010b). For further discussion of evaluation metrics, see also Wagner (2012) and Chodorow et al. (2012).

It is also worth noting that the obtained results underestimate the performance because the agreement on what constitutes a mistake can be quite low (Madnani et al., 2011), so providing alternative corrections is important. The revised annotations address this problem. The Illinois system improves its F1 from 31.20 to 42.14 on revised annotations. However, these numbers are still an underestimation because the analysis typically eliminates precision errors but not recall errors. This is not specific to CoNLL: an error analysis of the false positives in CLC that includes the FCE showed an increase in precision from 33% to 85% and 33% to 75% for preposition and article errors (Gamon, 2010).

An error analysis of the training data also allows us to determine prominent groups of system errors and identify areas for potential improvement, which we outline below. **Cascading NLP errors:** In the example below, the Illinois system incorrectly changes "need" to "needs" as it considers "victim" to be the subject of that verb: "*Also, not only the kidnappers and the victim* ***needs*** *to be tracked down, but also jailbreakers.*" **Errors in interacting linguistic structures:** The Illinois system considers every word independently and thus cannot handle interacting phenomena. In the example below, the article and the noun number classifiers propose corrections that result in an ungrammatical structure "such a situations": "*In* ***such situation****, individuals will lose their basic privacy.*" This problem is addressed via global models (Rozovskaya and Roth, 2013) and results in an improvement over the Illinois system. **Errors due to limited context:** The Illinois system does not consider context beyond sentence level. In the example below, the system incorrectly proposes to delete "the" but the wider context indicates that the definite article is more appropriate here: "*We have to admit that how to prevent* ***the*** *abuse and how to use it reasonably depend on a sound legal system, and it means surveillance has its own restriction.*"

7 Conclusion

We identified key design principles in developing a state-of-the-art error correction system. We did this through analysis of the top system in the CoNLL-2013 shared task along several dimensions. The key dimensions that we identified and analyzed concern the choice of a learning algorithm, adaptation to learner mistakes, linguistic knowledge, and the choice of the training data. We showed that the decisions in each case depend both on the type of a mistake and the specific setting, e.g. how much annotated learner data is available. Furthermore, we provided points of comparison with other systems along these four dimensions.

Acknowledgments

We thank Peter Chew and the anonymous reviewers for the feedback. Most of this work was done while the first author was at the University of Illinois. This material is based on research sponsored by DARPA under agreement number FA8750-13-2-0008 and by the Army Research Laboratory (ARL) under agreement W911NF-09-2-0053. Any opinions, findings, conclusions or recommendations are those of the authors and do not necessarily reflect the view of the agencies.

References

G. Berend, V. Vincze, S. Zarrieß, and R. Farkas. 2013. Lfg-based features for noun number and article grammatical errors. In *Proceedings of CoNLL: Shared Task*.

T. Brants and A. Franz. 2006. *Web 1T 5-gram Version 1*. Linguistic Data Consortium.

A. Cahill, N. Madnani, J. Tetreault, and D. Napolitano. 2013. Robust systems for preposition error correction using wikipedia revisions. In *Proceedings of NAACL*.

S. Chen and J. Goodman. 1996. An empirical study of smoothing techniques for language modeling. In *Proceedings of ACL*.

M. Chodorow, M. Dickinson, R. Israel, and J. Tetreault. 2012. Problems in evaluating grammatical error detection systems. In *Proceedings of COLING*.

D. Dahlmeier and H. T. Ng. 2011. Grammatical error correction with alternating structure optimization. In *Proceedings of ACL*.

D. Dahlmeier and H.T Ng. 2012. A beam-search decoder for grammatical error correction. In *Proceedings of EMNLP-CoNLL*.

D. Dahlmeier, H.T. Ng, and S.M. Wu. 2013. Building a large annotated corpus of learner English: The NUS corpus of learner English. In *Proceedings of the NAACL Workshop on Innovative Use of NLP for Building Educational Applications*.

R. Dale and A. Kilgarriff. 2011. Helping Our Own: The HOO 2011 pilot shared task. In *Proceedings of the 13th European Workshop on Natural Language Generation*.

R. Dale, I. Anisimoff, and G. Narroway. 2012. A report on the preposition and determiner error correction shared task. In *Proceedings of the NAACL Workshop on Innovative Use of NLP for Building Educational Applications*.

Y. Even-Zohar and D. Roth. 2001. A sequential model for multi class classification. In *Proceedings of EMNLP*.

J. Foster and Ø. Andersen. 2009. Generrate: Generating errors for use in grammatical error detection. In *Proceedings of the NAACL Workshop on Innovative Use of NLP for Building Educational Applications*.

J. Foster. 2007. Treebanks gone bad: Generating a treebank of ungrammatical english. In *Proceedings of the IJCAI Workshop on Analytics for Noisy Unstructures Data*.

Y. Freund and R. E. Schapire. 1996. Experiments with a new boosting algorithm. In *Proceedings of the 13th International Conference on Machine Learning*.

M. Gamon. 2010. Using mostly native data to correct errors in learners' writing. In *Proceedings of NAACL*.

S. Gass and L. Selinker. 1992. *Language transfer in language learning*. John Benjamins.

N. Han, M. Chodorow, and C. Leacock. 2006. Detecting errors in English article usage by non-native speakers. *Journal of Natural Language Engineering*, 12(2):115–129.

N. Han, J. Tetreault, S. Lee, and J. Ha. 2010. Using an error-annotated learner corpus to develop and ESL/EFL error correction system. In *Proceedings of LREC*.

T. Ionin, M.L. Zubizarreta, and S. Bautista. 2008. Sources of linguistic knowledge in the second language acquisition of English articles. *Lingua*, 118:554–576.

E. Izumi, K. Uchimoto, T. Saiga, T. Supnithi, and H. Isahara. 2003. Automatic error detection in the Japanese learners' English spoken data. In *Proceedings of ACL*.

T.-H. Kao, Y.-W. Chang, H.-W. Chiu, T-.H. Yen, J. Boisson, J.-C. Wu, and J.S. Chang. 2013. CoNLL-2013 shared task: Grammatical error correction NTHU system description. In *Proceedings of CoNLL: Shared Task*.

D. Klein and C. D. Manning. 2003. Fast exact inference with a factored model for natural language parsing. In *Proceedings of NIPS*.

C. Leacock, M. Chodorow, M. Gamon, and J. Tetreault. 2010. *Automated Grammatical Error Detection for Language Learners*. Morgan and Claypool Publishers.

J. Lee and S. Seneff. 2008. Correcting misuse of verb forms. In *Proceedings of ACL*.

N. Madnani, M. Chodorow, J. Tetreault, and A. Rozovskaya. 2011. They can help: Using crowdsourcing to improve the evaluation of grammatical error detection systems. In *Proceedings of ACL*.

M. Marneffe, B. MacCartney, and Ch. Manning. 2006. Generating typed dependency parses from phrase structure parses. In *Proceedings of LREC*.

H. T. Ng, S. M. Wu, Y. Wu, Ch. Hadiwinoto, and J. Tetreault. 2013. The CoNLL-2013 shared task on grammatical error correction. In *Proceedings of CoNLL: Shared Task*.

H. T. Ng, S. M. Wu, T. Briscoe, C. Hadiwinoto, R. H. Susanto, and C. Bryant. 2014. The CoNLL-2014 shared task on grammatical error correction. In *Proceedings of CoNLL: Shared Task*.

V. Punyakanok and D. Roth. 2001. The use of classifiers in sequential inference. In *Proceedings of NIPS*.

A. Radford. 1988. *Transformational Grammar*. Cambridge University Press.

N. Rizzolo and D. Roth. 2010. Learning Based Java for Rapid Development of NLP Systems. In *Proceedings of LREC*.

A. Rozovskaya and D. Roth. 2010a. Annotating ESL errors: Challenges and rewards. In *Proceedings of the NAACL Workshop on Innovative Use of NLP for Building Educational Applications*.

A. Rozovskaya and D. Roth. 2010b. Training paradigms for correcting errors in grammar and usage. In *Proceedings of NAACL*.

A. Rozovskaya and D. Roth. 2011. Algorithm selection and model adaptation for ESL correction tasks. In *Proceedings of ACL*.

A. Rozovskaya and D. Roth. 2013. Joint learning and inference for grammatical error correction. In *Proceedings of EMNLP*.

A. Rozovskaya, M. Sammons, J. Gioja, and D. Roth. 2011. University of Illinois system in HOO text correction shared task. In *Proceedings of the European Workshop on Natural Language Generation (ENLG)*.

A. Rozovskaya, M. Sammons, and D. Roth. 2012. The UI system in the HOO 2012 shared task on error correction. In *Proceedings of the NAACL Workshop on Innovative Use of NLP for Building Educational Applications*.

A. Rozovskaya, K.-W. Chang, M. Sammons, and D. Roth. 2013. The University of Illinois system in the CoNLL-2013 shared task. In *Proceedings of CoNLL Shared Task*.

A. Rozovskaya, K.-W. Chang, M. Sammons, D. Roth, and N. Habash. 2014a. The University of Illinois and Columbia system in the CoNLL-2014 shared task. In *Proceedings of CoNLL Shared Task*.

A. Rozovskaya, D. Roth, and V. Srikumar. 2014b. Correcting grammatical verb errors. In *Proceedings of EACL*.

A. Stolcke. 2002. Srilm-an extensible language modeling toolkit. In *Proceedings of International Conference on Spoken Language Processing*.

J. Tetreault, J. Foster, and M. Chodorow. 2010. Using parse features for preposition selection and error detection. In *Proceedings of ACL*.

J. Wagner. 2012. *Detecting Grammatical Errors with Treebank-Induced, Probabilistic Parsers*. Ph.D. thesis.

Y. Xiang, B. Yuan, Y. Zhang, X. Wang, W. Zheng, and C. Wei. 2013. A hybrid model for grammatical error correction. In *Proceedings of CoNLL: Shared Task*.

J. Xing, L. Wang, D.F. Wong, L.S. Chao, and X. Zeng. 2013. UM-Checker: A hybrid system for English grammatical error correction. In *Proceedings of CoNLL: Shared Task*.

H. Yannakoudakis, T. Briscoe, and B. Medlock. 2011. A new dataset and method for automatically grading ESOL texts. In *Proceedings of ACL*.

I. Yoshimoto, T. Kose, K. Mitsuzawa, K. Sakaguchi, T. Mizumoto, Y. Hayashibe, M. Komachi, and Y. Matsumoto. 2013. NAIST at 2013 CoNLL grammatical error correction shared task. In *Proceedings of CoNLL: Shared Task*.

Appendix A Features and Additional Information about the Data

	Classifier				
	Art.	**Prep.**	**Noun**	**Agr.**	**Form**
Train	43K	20K	39K	22K	37K
Test	43K	20K	39K	22K	37K

Table A.16: **Number of candidate words by classifier type in training and test data (FCE).**

Error	**Number of errors and error rate**	
	Train	**Test**
Art.	2336 (5.4%)	2290 (5.3%)
Prep.	1263 (6.4%)	1205 (6.1%)
Noun	858 (2.2%)	805 (2.0%)
Verb agr.	319 (1.5%)	330 (1.4%)
Verb form	104 (0.3%)	127 (0.3%)

Table A.17: **Statistics on annotated errors in the FCE corpus.** Percentage denotes the error rates, i.e. the number of erroneous instances with respect to the total number of relevant instances in the data.

	Features	**Description**
(1)	subjHead, subjPOS	the surface form and the POS tag of the subject head
(2)	subjDet	determiner of the subject NP
(3)	subjDistance	distance between the verb and the subject head
(4)	subjNumber	*Sing* – singular pronouns and nouns; *Pl* – plural pronouns and nouns
(5)	subjPerson	*3rdSing* – "she", "he", "it", singular nouns; *Not3rdSing* – "we", "you", "they", plural nouns; *1stSing* – "I"
(6)	conjunctions	(1)&(3); (4)&(5)

Table A.18: **Verb agreement features that use syntactic knowledge.**

Appendix B Evaluation Metrics

Here, we discuss the CoNLL-2013 shared task evaluation metric and provide a little bit more detail on

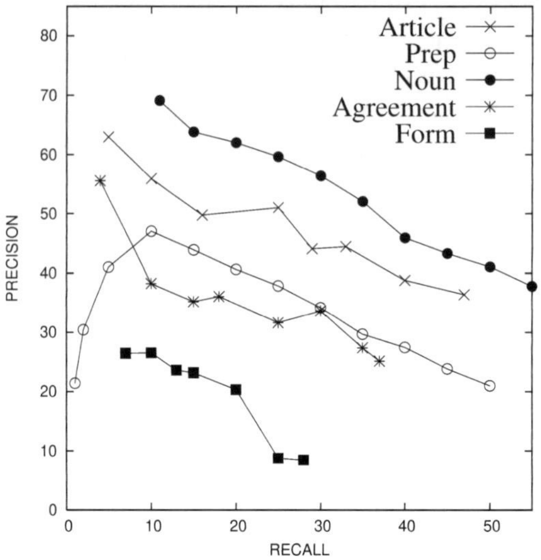

Figure 2: **Precision/Recall curves by error type.**

the performance of the Illinois modules in this context. As shown in Table 1 in Sec. 2, over 90% of words (about 98% in training) are used correctly. The low error rates are the key reason the error correction task is so difficult: it is quite challenging for a system to improve over a writer that already performs at the level of over 90%. Indeed, very few NLP tasks already have systems that perform at that level. The error sparsity makes it very challenging to identify mistakes accurately. In fact, the highest precision of 46.45%, as calculated by the shared task evaluation metric, is achieved by the Illinois system. However, once the precision drops below 50%, the system introduces more mistakes than it identifies.

We can look at individual modules and see whether for any type of mistake the system improves the quality of the text. Fig. 2 shows Precision/Recall curves for the system in Table 15. It is interesting to note that performance varies widely by error type. The easiest are noun and article usage errors: for nouns, we can do pretty well at the recall point 20% (with the corresponding precision of over 60%); for articles, the precision is around 50% at the recall value of 20%. For agreement errors, we can get a precision of 55% with a very high threshold (identifying only 5% of mistakes). Finally, on two mistakes – preposition and verb form – the system never achieves a precision over 50%.

Feature type	Feature group	Features
Word n-gram		*wB*, *w_2B*, *w_3B*, *wA*, *w_2A*, *w_3A*, *wBwA*, *w_2BwB*, *wAw_2A*, *w_3Bw_2BwB*, *w_2BwBwA*, *$wBwAw_2A$*, *wAw_2Aw_3A*, *$w_4Bw_3Bw_2BwB$*, *w_3Bw_2BwBwA*, *$w_2BwBwAw_2A$*, *$wBwAw_2Aw_3A$*, *$wAw_2Aw_3w_4A$*
POS		*pB*, *p_2B*, *p_3B*, *pA*, *p_2A*, *p_3A*, *pBpA*, *p_2BpB*, *pAp_2A*, *pBwB*, *pAwA*, *p_2Bw_2B*, *p_2Aw_2A*, *p_2BpBpA*, *$pBpAp_2A$*, *pAp_2Ap_3A*
Chunk	NP_1	*headWord*, *npWords*, *NC*, *adj&headWord*, *adjTag&headWord*, *adj&NC*, *adjTag&NC*, *npTags&headWord*, *npTags&NC*
	NP_2	*headWord&headPOS*, *headNumber*
	wordsAfterNP	*headWord&wordAfterNP*, *npWords&wordAfterNP*, *headWord&2wordsAfterNP*, *npWords&2wordsAfterNP*, *headWord&3wordsAfterNP*, *npWords&3wordsAfterNP*
	wordBeforeNP	$wB\&f_i\ \forall i \in NP_1$
	Verb	*verb*, $verb\&f_i\ \forall i \in NP_1$
	Preposition	$prep\&f_i\ \forall i \in NP_1$

Table A.19: **Features used in the article error correction system.** wB and wA denote the word immediately before and after the target, respectively; and pB and pA denote the POS tag before and after the target. *headWord* denotes the head of the NP complement. NC stands for noun compound and is active if second to last word in the NP is tagged as a noun. *Verb* features are active if the NP is the direct object of a verb. *Preposition* features are active if the NP is immediately preceded by a preposition. *Adj* feature is active if the first word (or the second word preceded by an adverb) in the NP is an adjective. *NpWords* and *npTags* denote all words (POS tags) in the NP.

Extracting Lexically Divergent Paraphrases from Twitter

Wei Xu[1], Alan Ritter[2], Chris Callison-Burch[1], William B. Dolan[3] and Yangfeng Ji[4]

[1] University of Pennsylvania, Philadelphia, PA, USA
{xwe, ccb}@cis.upenn.edu
[2] The Ohio State University, Columbus, OH, USA
ritter.1492@osu.edu
[3] Microsoft Research, Redmond, WA, USA
billdol@microsoft.com
[4] Georgia Institute of Technology, Atlanta, GA, USA
jiyfeng@gatech.edu

Abstract

We present MULTIP (Multi-instance Learning Paraphrase Model), a new model suited to identify paraphrases within the short messages on Twitter. We jointly model paraphrase relations between word and sentence pairs and assume only sentence-level annotations during learning. Using this principled latent variable model alone, we achieve the performance competitive with a state-of-the-art method which combines a latent space model with a feature-based supervised classifier. Our model also captures lexically divergent paraphrases that differ from yet complement previous methods; combining our model with previous work significantly outperforms the state-of-the-art. In addition, we present a novel annotation methodology that has allowed us to crowdsource a paraphrase corpus from Twitter. We make this new dataset available to the research community.

1 Introduction

Paraphrases are alternative linguistic expressions of the same or similar meaning (Bhagat and Hovy, 2013). Twitter engages millions of users, who naturally talk about the same topics simultaneously and frequently convey similar meaning using diverse linguistic expressions. The unique characteristics of this user-generated text presents new challenges and opportunities for paraphrase research (Xu et al., 2013b; Wang et al., 2013). For many applications, like automatic summarization, first story detection (Petrović et al., 2012) and search (Zanzotto et al., 2011), it is crucial to resolve redundancy in tweets (e.g. *oscar nom'd doc* ↔ *Oscar-nominated documentary*).

In this paper, we investigate the task of determining whether two tweets are paraphrases. Previous work has exploited a pair of shared named entities to locate semantically equivalent patterns from related news articles (Shinyama et al., 2002; Sekine, 2005; Zhang and Weld, 2013). But short sentences in Twitter do not often mention two named entities (Ritter et al., 2012) and require nontrivial generalization from named entities to other words. For example, consider the following two sentences about basketball player *Brook Lopez* from Twitter:

- *That boy* ***Brook Lopez*** *with a deep* <u>*3*</u>
- ***brook lopez*** *hit a* <u>*3*</u> *and i missed it*

Although these sentences do not have many words in common, the identical word *"3"* is a strong indicator that the two sentences are paraphrases.

We therefore propose a novel joint word-sentence approach, incorporating a multi-instance learning assumption (Dietterich et al., 1997) that two sentences under the same **topic** (we highlight topics in bold) are paraphrases if they contain at least one word pair (we call it an <u>anchor</u> and highlight with underscores; the words in the anchor pair need not be identical) that is indicative of sentential paraphrase. This *at-least-one-anchor* assumption might be ineffective for long or randomly paired sentences, but holds up better for short sentences that are temporally and topically related on Twitter. Moreover, our model design (see Figure 1) allows exploitation of arbitrary features and linguistic resources, such as part-of-speech features and a normalization lex-

Transactions of the Association for Computational Linguistics, 2 (2014) 435–448. Action Editor: Sharon Goldwater.
Submitted 8/2014; Revised 10/2014; Published 10/2014.

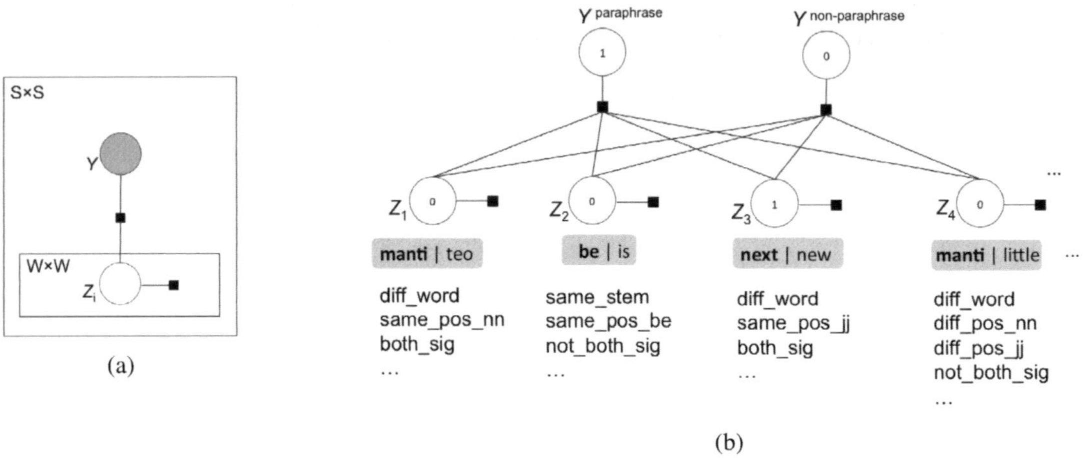

Figure 1: (a) a plate representation of the MULTIP model (b) an example instantiation of MULTIP for the pair of sentences "*Manti bout to be the* <u>*next*</u> ***Junior Seau***" and "*Teo is the little* <u>*new*</u> ***Junior Seau***", in which a new American football player *Manti Te'o* was being compared to a famous former player *Junior Seau*. Only 4 out of the total 6×5 word pairs, z_1 - z_{30}, are shown here.

icon, to discriminatively determine word pairs as paraphrastic anchors or not.

Our graphical model is a major departure from popular surface- or latent- similarity methods (Wan et al., 2006; Guo and Diab, 2012; Ji and Eisenstein, 2013, and others). Our approach to extract paraphrases from Twitter is general and can be combined with various topic detecting solutions. As a demonstration, we use Twitter's own trending topic service[1] to collect data and conduct experiments. While having a principled and extensible design, our model alone achieves performance on par with a state-of-the-art ensemble approach that involves both latent semantic modeling and supervised classification. The proposed model also captures radically different paraphrases from previous approaches; a combined system shows significant improvement over the state-of-the-art.

This paper makes the following contributions:

1) We present a novel latent variable model for paraphrase identification, that specifically accommodates the very short context and divergent wording in Twitter data. We experimentally compare several representative approaches and show that our proposed method yields state-of-the-art results and identifies paraphrases that are complementary to previous methods.

2) We develop an efficient crowdsourcing method and construct a Twitter Paraphrase Corpus of about 18,000 sentence pairs, as a first common testbed for the development and comparison of paraphrase identification and semantic similarity systems. We make this dataset available to the research community.[2]

2 Joint Word-Sentence Paraphrase Model

We present a new latent variable model that jointly captures paraphrase relations between sentence pairs and word pairs. It is very different from previous approaches in that its primary design goal and motivation is targeted towards short, lexically diverse text on the social web.

2.1 At-least-one-anchor Assumption

Much previous work on paraphrase identification has been developed and evaluated on a specific benchmark dataset, the Microsoft Research Paraphrase Corpus (Dolan et al., 2004), which is de-

[1] More information about Twitter's trends: `https://support.twitter.com/articles/101125-faqs-about-twitter-s-trends`

[2] The dataset and code are made available at: SemEval-2015 shared task `http://alt.qcri.org/semeval2015/task1/` and `https://github.com/cocoxu/twitterparaphrase/`

Corpus	Examples
News (Dolan and Brockett, 2005)	◦ Revenue in the first quarter of the year dropped 15 percent from the same period a year earlier. ◦ With the scandal hanging over Stewart's company, revenue in the first quarter of the year dropped 15 percent from the same period a year earlier.
	◦ The Senate Select Committee on Intelligence is preparing a blistering report on prewar intelligence on Iraq. ◦ American intelligence leading up to the war on Iraq will be criticized by a powerful US Congressional committee due to report soon, officials said today.
Twitter (This Work)	◦ Can Klay Thompson wake up ◦ Cmon Klay need u to get it going
	◦ Ezekiel Ansah wearing 3D glasses wout the lens ◦ Wait Ezekiel ansah is wearing 3d movie glasses with the lenses knocked out
	◦ Marriage equality law passed in Rhode Island ◦ Congrats to Rhode Island becoming the 10th state to enact marriage equality

Table 1: Representative examples from paraphrase corpora. The average sentence length is 11.9 words in Twitter vs. 18.6 in the news corpus.

rived from news articles. Twitter data is very different, as shown in Table 1. We observe that among tweets posted around the same time about the same topic (e.g. a named entity), sentential paraphrases are short and can often be *"anchored"* by lexical paraphrases. This intuition leads to the *at-least-one-anchor* assumption we stated in the introduction.

The anchor could be a word the two sentences share in common. It also could be a pair of different words. For example, the word pair *"next || new"* in two tweets about a new player *Manti Te'o* to a famous former American football player *Junior Seau*:

◦ *Manti bout to be the <u>next</u>* ***Junior Seau***
◦ *Teo is the little <u>new</u>* ***Junior Seau***

Further note that not every word pair of similar meaning indicates sentence-level paraphrase. For example, the word *"3"*, shared by two sentences about movie *"Iron Man"* that refers to the 3rd sequel of the movie, is **not** a paraphrastic anchor:

◦ ***Iron Man*** *<u>3</u> was brilliant fun*
◦ ***Iron Man*** *<u>3</u> tonight see what this is like*

Therefore, we use a discriminative model at the word-level to incorporate various features, such as part-of-speech features, to determine how probable a word pair is a paraphrase anchor.

2.2 Multi-instance Learning Paraphrase Model (MULTIP)

The *at-least-one-anchor* assumption naturally leads to a multi-instance learning problem (Dietterich et al., 1997), where the learner only observes labels on bags of instances (i.e. sentence-level paraphrases in this case) instead of labels on each individual instance (i.e. word pair).

We formally define an undirected graphical model of multi-instance learning for paraphrase identification – MULTIP. Figure 1 shows the proposed model in plate form and gives an example instantiation. The model has two layers, which allows joint reasoning between sentence-level and word-level components.

For each pair of sentences $s_i = (s_{i_1}, s_{i_2})$, there is *an aggregate binary variable* y_i that represents whether they are paraphrases, and which is observed in the labeled training data. Let $W(s_{i_k})$ be the set of words in the sentence s_{i_k}, excluding the topic names. For each word pair $w_j = (w_{j_1}, w_{j_2}) \in W(s_{i_1}) \times W(s_{i_2})$, there exists *a latent variable* z_j which denotes whether the word pair is a paraphrase anchor. In total there are $m = |W(s_{i_1})| \times |W(s_{i_2})|$ word pairs, and thus $\mathbf{z}_i = z_1, z_2, ..., z_j, ..., z_m$. Our *at-least-one-anchor* assumption is realized by a deterministic-or function; that is, if there exists at least one j such that $z_j = 1$, then the sentence pair is a paraphrase.

Our conditional paraphrase identification model is defined as follows:

$$\begin{aligned} P(\mathbf{z}_i, y_i|\mathbf{w}_i;\theta) &= \prod_{j=1}^{m} \phi(z_j, w_j;\theta) \times \sigma(\mathbf{z}_i, y_i) \\ &= \prod_{j=1}^{m} \exp(\theta \cdot f(z_j, w_j)) \times \sigma(\mathbf{z}_i, y_i) \end{aligned} \quad (1)$$

where $f(z_j, w_j)$ is a vector of features extracted for the word pair w_j, θ is the parameter vector, and σ is the factor that corresponds to the deterministic-or constraint:

$$\sigma(\mathbf{z}_i, y_i) = \begin{cases} 1 & \text{if } y_i = true \wedge \exists j : z_j = 1 \\ 1 & \text{if } y_i = false \wedge \forall j : z_j = 0 \\ 0 & \text{otherwise} \end{cases} \quad (2)$$

2.3 Learning

To learn the parameters of the word-level paraphrase anchor classifier, θ, we maximize likelihood over the sentence-level annotations in our paraphrase corpus:

$$\begin{aligned} \theta^* &= \arg\max_{\theta} P(\mathbf{y}|\mathbf{w};\theta) \\ &= \arg\max_{\theta} \prod_{i} \sum_{\mathbf{z}_i} P(\mathbf{z}_i, y_i|\mathbf{w}_i;\theta) \end{aligned} \quad (3)$$

An iterative gradient-ascent approach is used to estimate θ using perceptron-style additive updates (Collins, 2002; Liang et al., 2006; Zettlemoyer and Collins, 2007; Hoffmann et al., 2011). We define an update based on the gradient of the conditional log likelihood using Viterbi approximation, as follows:

$$\begin{aligned} \frac{\partial \log P(\mathbf{y}|\mathbf{w};\theta)}{\partial \theta} &= \mathbf{E}_{P(\mathbf{z}|\mathbf{w},\mathbf{y};\theta)}(\sum_i f(\mathbf{z}_i, \mathbf{w}_i)) \\ &\quad - \mathbf{E}_{P(\mathbf{z},\mathbf{y}|\mathbf{w};\theta)}(\sum_i f(\mathbf{z}_i, \mathbf{w}_i)) \quad (4) \\ &\approx \sum_i f(\mathbf{z}_i^*, \mathbf{w}_i) - \sum_i f(\mathbf{z}_i', \mathbf{w}_i) \end{aligned}$$

where we define the feature sum for each sentence $f(\mathbf{z}_i, \mathbf{w}_i) = \sum_j f(z_j, w_j)$ over all word pairs.

These two above expectations are approximated by solving two simple inference problems as maximizations:

$$\begin{aligned} \mathbf{z}^* &= \arg\max_{\mathbf{z}} P(\mathbf{z}|\mathbf{w}, \mathbf{y};\theta) \\ \mathbf{y}', \mathbf{z}' &= \arg\max_{\mathbf{y},\mathbf{z}} P(\mathbf{z}, \mathbf{y}|\mathbf{w};\theta) \end{aligned} \quad (5)$$

Input: a training set $\{(\mathbf{s}_i, y_i)|i = 1...n\}$, where i is an index corresponding to a particular sentence pair $\mathbf{s}_i$, and y_i is the training label.

initialize parameter vector $\theta \leftarrow \mathbf{0}$
for $i \leftarrow 1$ **to** n **do**
  extract all possible word pairs $\mathbf{w}_i = w_1, w_2, ..., w_m$ and their features from the sentence pair $\mathbf{s}_i$
end for
for $l \leftarrow 1$ **to** maximum iterations **do**
  for $i \leftarrow 1$ **to** n **do**
    $(y_i', \mathbf{z}_i') \leftarrow \arg\max_{y_i, \mathbf{z}_i} P(\mathbf{z}_i, y_i|\mathbf{w}_i;\theta)$
    if $y_i' \neq y_i$ **then**
      $\mathbf{z}_i^* \leftarrow \arg\max_{\mathbf{z}_i} P(\mathbf{z}_i|\mathbf{w}_i, y_i;\theta)$
      $\theta \leftarrow \theta + f(\mathbf{z}_i^*, \mathbf{w}_i) - f(\mathbf{z}_i', \mathbf{w}_i)$
    end if
  end for
end for
return model parameters θ

Figure 2: MULTIP Learning Algorithm

Computing both $\mathbf{z}'$ and $\mathbf{z}^*$ are rather straightforward under the structure of our model and can be solved in time linear in the number of word pairs. The dependencies between $\mathbf{z}$ and $\mathbf{y}$ are defined as deterministic-or factors $\sigma(\mathbf{z}_i, y_i)$, which when satisfied do not affect the overall probability of the solution. Each sentence pair is independent conditioned on the parameters. For $\mathbf{z}'$, it is sufficient to independently compute the most likely assignment $\mathbf{z}_i'$ for each word pair, ignoring the deterministic dependencies. $\mathbf{y}_i'$ is then set by aggregating all $\mathbf{z}_i'$ through the deterministic-or operation. Similarly, we can find the exact solution for $\mathbf{z}^*$, the most likely assignment that respects the sentence-level training label $\mathbf{y}$. For a positive training instance, we simply find its highest scored word pair w_τ by the word-level classifier, then set $z_\tau^* = 1$ and $z_j^* = \arg\max_{x \in 0,1} \phi(x, w_j;\theta)$ for all $j \neq \tau$; for a negative example, we set $\mathbf{z}_i^* = \mathbf{0}$. The time complexity of both inferences for one sentence pair is $O(|W(s)|^2)$, where $|W(s)|^2$ is the number of word pairs.

In practice, we use online learning instead of optimizing the full objective. The detailed learning algorithm is presented in Figure 2. Following Hoffmann et al. (2011), we use 50 iterations in the experiments.

2.4 Feature Design

At the word-level, our discriminative model allows use of arbitrary features that are similar to those in monolingual word alignment models (MacCartney et al., 2008; Thadani and McKeown, 2011; Yao et al., 2013a,b). But unlike discriminative monolingual word alignment, we only use sentence-level training labels instead of word-level alignment annotation. For every word pair, we extract the following features:

String Features that indicate whether the two words, their stemmed forms and their normalized forms are the same, similar or dissimilar. We used the Morpha stemmer (Minnen et al., 2001),[3] Jaro-Winkler string similarity (Winkler, 1999) and the Twitter normalization lexicon by Han et al. (2012).

POS Features that are based on the part-of-speech tags of the two words in the pair, specifying whether the two words have same or different POS tags and what the specific tags are. We use the Twitter Part-Of-Speech tagger developed by Derczynski et al. (2013). We add new fine-grained tags for variations of the eight words: "a", "be", "do", "have", "get", "go", "follow" and "please". For example, we use a tag *HA* for words "have", "has" and "had".

Topical Features that relate to the strength of a word's association to the topic. This feature identifies the popular words in each topic, e.g. *"3"* in tweets about basketball game, *"RIP"* in tweets about a celebrity's death. We use G^2 log-likelihood-ratio statistic, which has been frequently used in NLP, as a measure of word associations (Dunning, 1993; Moore, 2004). The significant scores are computed for each trend on an average of about 1500 sentences and converted to binary features for every word pair, indicating whether the two words are both significant or not.

Our topical features are novel and were not used in previous work. Following Riedel et al. (2010) and Hoffmann et al. (2011), we also incorporate conjunction features into our system for better accuracy, namely Word+POS, Word+Topical and Word+POS+Topical features.

[3] `https://github.com/knowitall/morpha`

3 Experiments

3.1 Data

It is nontrivial to gather a gold-standard dataset of naturally occurring paraphrases and non-paraphrases efficiently from Twitter, since this requires pairwise comparison of tweets and faces a very large search space. To make this annotation task tractable, we design a novel and efficient crowdsourcing method using Amazon Mechanical Turk. Our entire data collection process is detailed in Section §4, with several experiments that demonstrate annotation quality and efficiency.

In total, we constructed a Twitter Paraphrase Corpus of 18,762 sentence pairs and 19,946 unique sentences. The training and development set consists of 17,790 sentence pairs posted between April 24th and May 3rd, 2014 from 500+ trending topics (excluding hashtags). Our paraphrase model and data collection approach is general and can be combined with various Twitter topic detecting solutions (Diao et al., 2012; Ritter et al., 2012). As a demonstration, we use Twitter's own trends service since it is easily available. Twitter trending topics are determined by an unpublished algorithm, which finds words, phrases and hashtags that have had a sharp increase in popularity, as opposed to overall volume. We use case-insensitive exact matching to locate topic names in the sentences.

Each sentence pair was annotated by 5 different crowdsourcing workers. For the test set, we obtained both crowdsourced and expert labels on 972 sentence pairs from 20 randomly sampled Twitter trending topics between May 13th and June 10th. Our dataset is more realistic and balanced, containing 79% non-paraphrases vs. 34% in the benchmark Microsoft Paraphrase Corpus of news data. As noted in (Das and Smith, 2009), the lack of natural non-paraphrases in the MSR corpus creates bias towards certain models.

3.2 Baselines

We use four baselines to compare with our proposed approach for the sentential paraphrase identification task. For the first baseline, we choose a supervised logistic regression (LR) baseline used by Das and Smith (2009). It uses simple n-gram (also in stemmed form) overlapping features but shows very

Method	F1	Precision	Recall
Random	0.294	0.208	0.500
WTMF (Guo and Diab, 2012)*	0.583	0.525	0.655
LR (Das and Smith, 2009)**	0.630	0.629	0.632
LEXLATENT	0.641	0.663	0.621
LEXDISCRIM (Ji and Eisenstein, 2013)	0.645	0.664	0.628
MULTIP	0.724	0.722	0.726
Human Upperbound	0.823	0.752	0.908

Table 2: Performance of different paraphrase identification approaches on Twitter data. *An enhanced version that uses additional 1.6 million sentences from Twitter. ** Reimplementation of a strong baseline used by Das and Smith (2009).

competitive performance on the MSR corpus.

The second baseline is a state-of-the-art unsupervised method, Weighted Textual Matrix Factorization (WTMF),[4] which is specially developed for short sentences by modeling the semantic space of both words that are present in and absent from the sentences (Guo and Diab, 2012). The original model was learned from WordNet (Fellbaum, 2010), OntoNotes (Hovy et al., 2006), Wiktionary, the Brown corpus (Francis and Kucera, 1979). We enhance the model with 1.6 million sentences from Twitter as suggested by Guo et al. (2013).

Ji and Eisenstein (2013) presented a state-of-the-art ensemble system, which we call LEXDISCRIM.[5] It directly combines both discriminatively-tuned latent features and surface lexical features into a SVM classifier. Specifically, the latent representation of a pair of sentences $\vec{v_1}$ and $\vec{v_2}$ is converted into a feature vector, $[\vec{v_1}+\vec{v_2}, |\vec{v_1}-\vec{v_2}|]$, by concatenating the element-wise sum $\vec{v_1}+\vec{v_2}$ and absolute different $|\vec{v_1}-\vec{v_2}|$.

We also introduce a new baseline, LEXLATENT, which is a simplified version of LEXDISCRIM and easy to reproduce. It uses the same method to combine latent features and surface features, but combines the open-sourced WTMF latent space model and the logistic regression model from above instead. It achieves similar performance as LEXDISCRIM on our dataset (Table 2).

[4]The source code and data for WTMF is available at: `http://www.cs.columbia.edu/~weiwei/code.html`

[5]The parsing feature was removed because it was not helpful on our Twitter dataset.

3.3 System Performance

For evaluation of different systems, we compute precision-recall curves and report the highest F1 measure of any point on the curve, on the test dataset of 972 sentence pairs against the expert labels. Table 2 shows the performance of different systems. Our proposed MULTIP, a principled latent variable model alone, achieves competitive results with the state-of-the-art system that combines discriminative training and latent semantics.

In Table 2, we also show the agreement levels of labels derived from 5 non-expert annotations on Mechanical Turk, which can be considered as an upperbound for automatic paraphrase recognition task performed on this data set. The annotation quality of our corpus is surprisingly good given the fact that the definition of paraphrase is rather inexact (Bhagat and Hovy, 2013); the inter-rater agreement between expert annotators on news data is only 0.83 as reported by Dolan et al. (2004).

	F1	Prec	Recall
MULTIP	0.724	0.722	0.726
- String features	0.509	0.448	0.589
- POS features	0.496	0.350	0.851
- Topical features	0.715	0.694	0.737

Table 3: Feature ablation by removing each individual feature group from the full set.

To assess the impact of different features on the model's performance, we conduct feature ablation experiments, removing one group of features at a time. The results are shown in Table 3. Both string

Para?	Sentence Pair from Twitter	MULTIP	LEXLATENT
YES	○ The new **Ciroc** flavor has arrived ○ **Ciroc** got a new flavor comin out	rank=12	rank=266
YES	○ **Roberto Mancini** gets the boot from Man City ○ **Roberto Mancini** has been sacked by Manchester City with the Blues saying	rank=64	rank=452
YES	○ I want to watch **the purge** tonight ○ I want to go see **The Purge** who wants to come with	rank=136	rank=11
NO	○ Somebody took the **Marlins** to 20 innings ○ Anyone who stayed 20 innings for the **marlins**	rank= 8	rank=54
NO	○ **WORLD OF JENKS** IS ON AT 11 ○ **World of Jenks** is my favorite show on tv	rank=167	rank=9

Table 4: Example system outputs; *rank* is the position in the list of all candidate paraphrase pairs in the test set ordered by model score. MULTIP discovers lexically divergent paraphrases while LEXLATENT prefers more overall sentence similarity. Underline marks the word pair(s) with highest estimated probability as paraphrastic anchor(s) for each sentence pair.

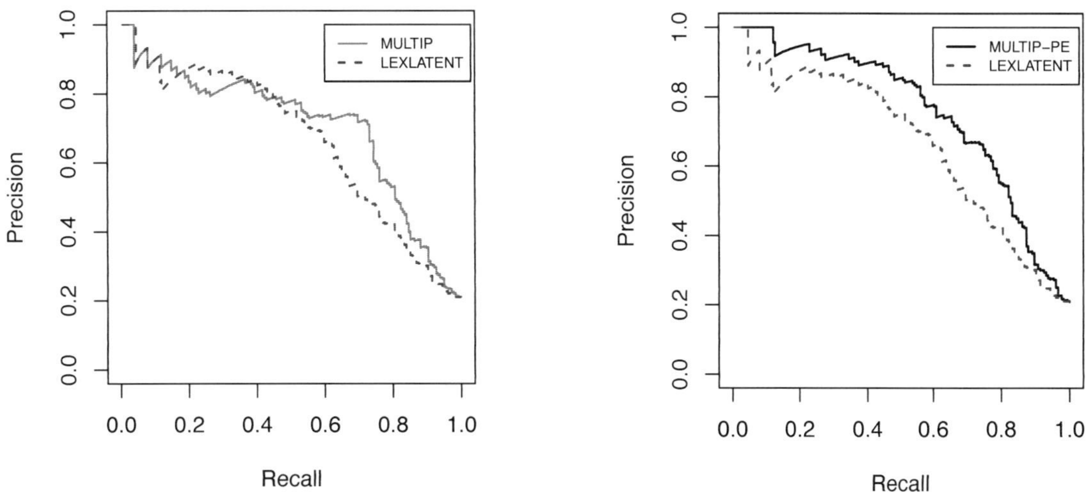

Figure 3: Precision and recall curves. Our MULTIP model alone achieves competitive performance with the LEXLATENT system that combines latent space model and feature-based supervised classifier. The two approaches have complementary strengths, and achieves significant improvement when combined together (MULTIP-PE).

and POS features are essential for system performance, while topical features are helpful but not as crucial.

Figure 3 presents precision-recall curves and shows the sensitivity and specificity of each model in comparison. In the first half of the curve (recall < 0.5), MULTIP model makes bolder and less accurate decisions than LEXLATENT. However, the curve for MULTIP model is more flat and shows consistently better precision at the second half (recall > 0.5) as well as a higher maximum F1 score. This result reflects our design concept of MULTIP, which is intended to pick up sentential paraphrases with more divergent wordings aggressively. LEXLATENT, as a combined system, considers sentence features in both surface and latent space and is more conservative. Table 4 further illustrates this difference with some example system outputs.

3.4 Product of Experts (MULTIP-PE)

Our MULTIP model and previous similarity-based approaches have complementary strengths, so we experiment with combining MULTIP (P_m) and LEXLATENT (P_l) through a product of experts (Hinton, 2002):

$$P(\mathbf{y}|s_1, s_2) = \frac{P_m(\mathbf{y}|s_1, s_2) \times P_l(\mathbf{y}|s_1, s_2)}{\sum_{\mathbf{y}} P_m(\mathbf{y}|s_1, s_2) \times P_l(\mathbf{y}|s_1, s_2)} \tag{6}$$

The resulting system MULTIP-PE provides consistently better precision and recall over the LEXLATENT model, as shown on the right in Figure 3. The MULTIP-PE system outperforms LEXLATENT significantly according to a paired t-test with ρ less than 0.05. Our proposed MULTIP takes advantage of Twitter's specific properties and provides complementary information to previous approaches. Previously, Das and Smith (2009) has also used a product of experts to combine a lexical and a syntax-based model together.

4 Constructing Twitter Paraphrase Corpus

We now turn to describing our data collection and annotation methodology. Our goal is to construct a high quality dataset that contains representative examples of paraphrases and non-paraphrases in Twitter. Since Twitter users are free to talk about anything regarding any topic, a random pair of sentences about the same topic has a low chance (less than 8%) of expressing the same meaning. This causes two problems: a) it is expensive to obtain paraphrases via manual annotation; b) non-expert annotators tend to loosen the criteria and are more likely to make false positive errors. To address these challenges, we design a simple annotation task and introduce two selection mechanisms to select sentences which are more likely to be paraphrases, while preserving diversity and representativeness.

4.1 Raw Data from Twitter

We crawl Twitter's trending topics and their associated tweets using public APIs.[6] According to Twitter, trends are determined by an algorithm which identifies topics that are immediately popular, rather than those that have been popular for longer periods of time or which trend on a daily basis. We tokenize and split each tweet into sentences.[7]

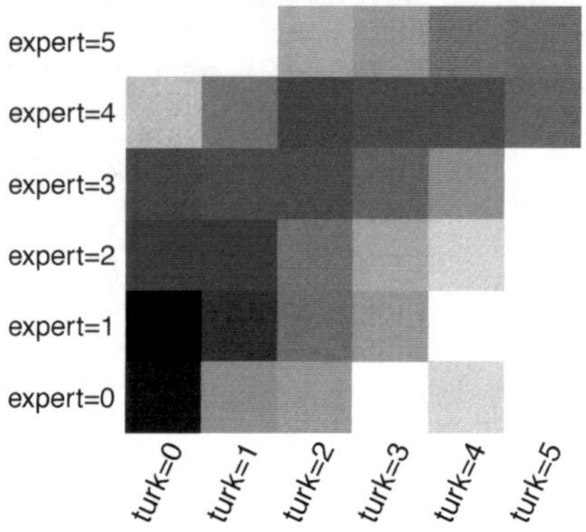

Figure 4: A heat-map showing overlap between expert and crowdsourcing annotation. The intensity along the diagonal indicates good reliability of crowdsourcing workers for this particular task; and the shift above the diagonal reflects the difference between the two annotation schemas. For crowdsourcing (turk), the numbers indicate how many annotators out of 5 picked the sentence pair as paraphrases; 0,1 are considered non-paraphrases; 3,4,5 are paraphrases. For expert annotation, all 0,1,2 are non-paraphrases; 4,5 are paraphrases. Medium-scored cases are discarded in training and testing in our experiments.

4.2 Task Design on Mechanical Turk

We show the annotator an **original** sentence, then ask them to pick sentences with the same meaning from 10 **candidate** sentences. The original and candidate sentences are randomly sampled from the same topic. For each such 1 vs. 10 question, we obtain binary judgements from 5 different annotators, paying each annotator $0.02 per question. On average, each question takes one annotator about 30 $\sim$ 45 seconds to answer.

4.3 Annotation Quality

We remove problematic annotators by checking their Cohen's Kappa agreement (Artstein and Poe-

[6] More information about Twitter's APIs: `https://dev.twitter.com/docs/api/1.1/overview`

[7] We use the toolkit developed by O'Connor et al. (2010): `https://github.com/brendano/tweetmotif`

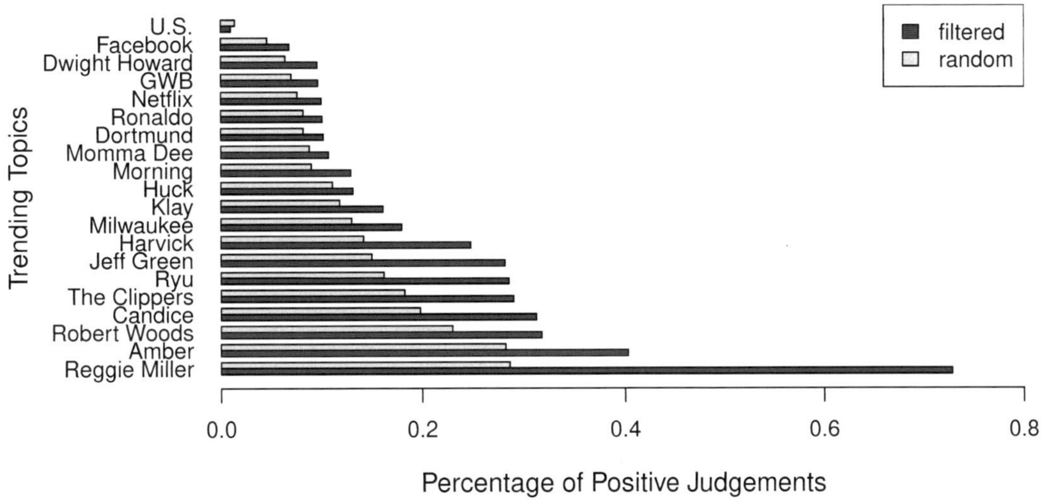

Figure 5: The proportion of paraphrases (percentage of positive votes from annotators) vary greatly across different topics. Automatic filtering in Section 4.4 roughly doubles the paraphrase yield.

sio, 2008) with other annotators. We also compute inter-annotator agreement with an expert annotator on 971 sentence pairs. In the expert annotation, we adopt a 5-point Likert scale to measure the degree of semantic similarity between sentences, which is defined by Agirre et al. (2012) as follows:

5: Completely equivalent, as they mean the same thing;
4: Mostly equivalent, but some unimportant details differ;
3: Roughly equivalent, but some important information differs/missing.
2: Not equivalent, but share some details;
1: Not equivalent, but are on the same topic;
0: On different topics.

Although the two scales of expert and crowdsourcing annotation are defined differently, their Pearson correlation coefficient reaches 0.735 (two-tailed significance 0.001). Figure 4 shows a heatmap representing the detailed overlap between the two annotations. It suggests that the graded similarity annotation task could be reduced to a binary choice in a crowdsourcing setup.

4.4 Automatic Summarization Inspired Sentence Filtering

We filter the sentences within each topic to select more probable paraphrases for annotation. Our method is inspired by a typical problem in extractive summarization, that the salient sentences are likely redundant (paraphrases) and need to be removed in the output summaries. We employ the scoring method used in SumBasic (Nenkova and Vanderwende, 2005; Vanderwende et al., 2007), a simple but powerful summarization system, to find salient sentences. For each topic, we compute the probability of each word $P(w_i)$ by simply dividing its frequency by the total number of all words in all sentences. Each sentence s is scored as the average of the probabilities of the words in it, i.e.

$$Salience(s) = \sum_{w_i \in s} \frac{P(w_i)}{|\{w_i | w_i \in s\}|} \qquad (7)$$

We then rank the sentences and pick the **original** sentence randomly from top 10% salient sentences and **candidate** sentences from top 50% to present to the annotators.

In a trial experiment of 20 topics, the filtering technique double the yield of paraphrases from 152 to 329 out of 2000 sentence pairs over naïve random sampling (Figure 5 and Figure 6). We also use PINC (Chen and Dolan, 2011) to measure the quality of paraphrases collected (Figure 7). PINC was designed to measure n-gram dissimilarity between two sentences, and in essence it is the inverse of BLEU. In general, the cases with high PINC scores include more complex and interesting rephrasings.

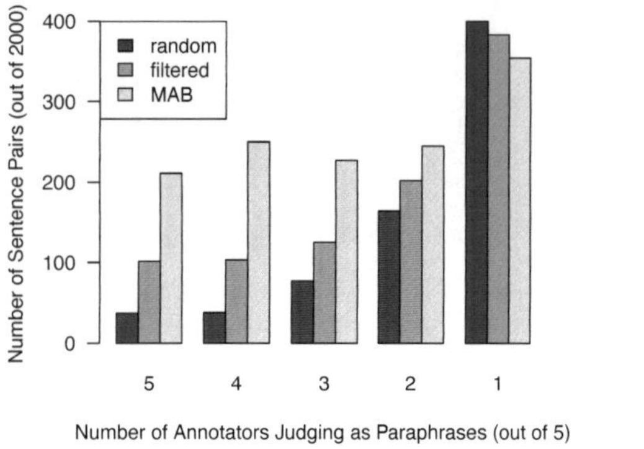

Figure 6: Numbers of paraphrases collected by different methods. The annotation efficiency (3,4,5 are regarded as paraphrases) is significantly improved by the sentence filtering and Multi-Armed Bandits (MAB) based topic selection.

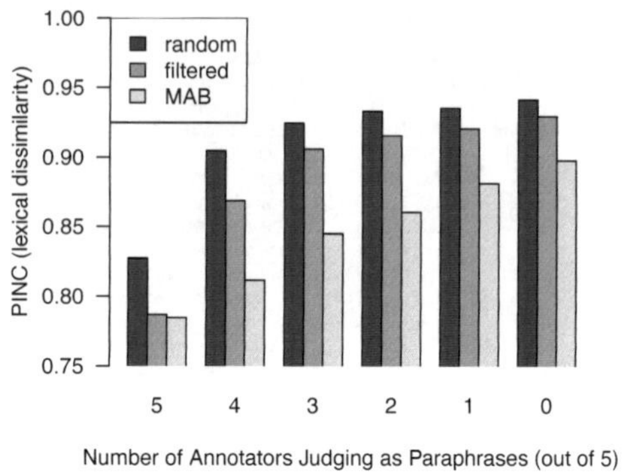

Figure 7: PINC scores of paraphrases collected. The higher the PINC, the more significant the rewording. Our proposed annotation strategy quadruples paraphrase yield, while not greatly reducing diversity as measured by PINC.

4.5 Topic Selection using Multi-Armed Bandits (MAB) Algorithm

Another approach to increasing paraphrase yield is to choose more appropriate topics. This is particularly important because the number of paraphrases varies greatly from topic to topic and thus the chance to encounter paraphrases during annotation (Figure 5). We treat this topic selection problem as a variation of the Multi-Armed Bandit (MAB) problem (Robbins, 1985) and adapt a greedy algorithm, the bounded ϵ-first algorithm, of Tran-Thanh et al. (2012) to accelerate our corpus construction.

Our strategy consists of two phases. In the first exploration phase, we dedicate a fraction of the total budget, ϵ, to explore randomly chosen arms of each slot machine (trending topic on Twitter), each m times. In the second exploitation phase, we sort all topics according to their estimated proportion of paraphrases, and sequentially annotate $\lceil\frac{(1-\epsilon)B}{l-m}\rceil$ arms that have the highest estimated reward until reaching the maximum $l = 10$ annotations for any topic to insure data diversity.

We tune the parameters m to be 1 and ϵ to be between $0.35 \sim 0.55$ through simulation experiments, by artificially duplicating a small amount of real annotation data. We then apply this MAB algorithm in the real-world. We explore 500 random topics and then exploited 100 of them. The yield of paraphrases rises to 688 out of 2000 sentence pairs by using MAB and sentence filtering, a 4-fold increase compared to only using random selection (Figure 6).

5 Related Work

Automatic Paraphrase Identification has been widely studied (Androutsopoulos and Malakasiotis, 2010; Madnani and Dorr, 2010). The ACL Wiki gives an excellent summary of various techniques.[8] Many recent high-performance approaches use system combination (Das and Smith, 2009; Madnani et al., 2012; Ji and Eisenstein, 2013). For example, Madnani et al. (2012) combines multiple sophisticated machine translation metrics using a meta-classifier. An earlier attempt on Twitter data is that of Xu et al. (2013b). They limited the search space to only the tweets that explicitly mention a same date and a same named entity, however there remain a considerable amount of mislabels in their data.[9] Zanzotto et al. (2011) also experimented with SVM tree kernel methods on Twitter data.

Departing from the previous work, we propose a latent variable model to jointly infer the correspondence between words and sentences. It is related to discriminative monolingual word alignment (MacCartney et al., 2008; Thadani and McKeown,

[8] `http://aclweb.org/aclwiki/index.php?title=Paraphrase_Identification_(State_of_the_art)`

[9] The data is released by Xu et al. (2013b) at: `https://github.com/cocoxu/twitterparaphrase/`

2011; Yao et al., 2013a,b), but different in that the paraphrase task requires additional sentence alignment modeling with no word alignment data. Our approach is also inspired by Fung and Cheung's (2004a; 2004b) work on bootstrapping bilingual parallel sentence and word translations from comparable corpora.

Multiple Instance Learning (Dietterich et al., 1997) has been used by different research groups in the field of information extraction (Riedel et al., 2010; Hoffmann et al., 2011; Surdeanu et al., 2012; Ritter et al., 2013; Xu et al., 2013a). The idea is to leverage structured data as weak supervision for tasks such as relation extraction. This is done, for example, by making the assumption that at least one sentence in the corpus which mentions a pair of entities (e_1, e_2) participating in a relation (r) expresses the proposition: $r(e_1, e_2)$.

Crowdsourcing Paraphrase Acquisition: Buzek et al. (2010) and Denkowski et al. (2010) focused specifically on collecting paraphrases of text to be translated to improve machine translation quality. Chen and Dolan (2011) gathered a large-scale paraphrase corpus by asking Mechanical Turk workers to caption the action in short video segments. Similarly, Burrows et al. (2012) asked crowdsourcing workers to rewrite selected excerpts from books. Ling et al. (2014) crowdsourced bilingual parallel text using Twitter as the source of data.

In contrast, we design a simple crowdsourcing task requiring only binary judgements on sentences collected from Twitter. There are several advantages as compared to existing work: a) the corpus also covers a very diverse range of topics and linguistic expressions, especially colloquial language, which is different from and thus complements previous paraphrase corpora; b) the paraphrase corpus collected contains a representative proportion of both negative and positive instances, while lack of good negative examples was an issue in the previous research (Das and Smith, 2009); c) this method is scalable and sustainable due to the simplicity of the task and real-time, virtually unlimited text supply from Twitter.

6 Conclusions

This paper introduced MULTIP, a joint word-sentence model to learn paraphrases from temporally and topically grouped messages in Twitter. While simple and principled, our model achieves performance competitive with a state-of-the-art ensemble system combining latent semantic representations and surface similarity. By combining our method with previous work as a product-of-experts we outperform the state-of-the-art. Our latent-variable approach is capable of learning word-level paraphrase anchors given only sentence annotations. Because our graphical model is modular and extensible (for example it should be possible to replace the deterministic-or with other aggregators), we are optimistic this work might provide a path towards weakly supervised word alignment models using only sentence-level annotations.

In addition, we presented a novel and efficient annotation methodology which was used to crowdsource a unique corpus of paraphrases harvested from Twitter. We make this resource available to the research community.

Acknowledgments

The author would like to thank editor Sharon Goldwater and three anonymous reviewers for their thoughtful comments, which substantially improved this paper. We also thank Ralph Grishman, Sameer Singh, Yoav Artzi, Mark Yatskar, Chris Quirk, Ani Nenkova and Mitch Marcus for their feedback.

This material is based in part on research sponsored by the NSF under grant IIS-1430651, DARPA under agreement number FA8750-13-2-0017 (the DEFT program) and through a Google Faculty Research Award to Chris Callison-Burch. The U.S. Government is authorized to reproduce and distribute reprints for governmental purposes. The views and conclusions contained in this publication are those of the authors and should not be interpreted as representing official policies or endorsements of DARPA or the U.S. Government. Yangfeng Ji is supported by a Google Faculty Research Award awarded to Jacob Eisenstein.

References

Agirre, E., Diab, M., Cer, D., and Gonzalez-Agirre, A. (2012). Semeval-2012 task 6: A pilot on semantic textual similarity. In *Proceedings of the First Joint Conference on Lexical and Computational Semantics (*SEM)*.

Androutsopoulos, I. and Malakasiotis, P. (2010). A survey of paraphrasing and textual entailment methods. *Journal of Artificial Intelligence Research*, 38.

Artstein, R. and Poesio, M. (2008). Inter-coder agreement for computational linguistics. *Computational Linguistics*, 34(4).

Bhagat, R. and Hovy, E. (2013). What is a paraphrase? *Computational Linguistics*, 39(3).

Burrows, S., Potthast, M., and Stein, B. (2012). Paraphrase acquisition via crowdsourcing and machine learning. *Transactions on Intelligent Systems and Technology (ACM TIST)*.

Buzek, O., Resnik, P., and Bederson, B. B. (2010). Error driven paraphrase annotation using Mechanical Turk. In *Proceedings of the Workshop on Creating Speech and Language Data with Amazon's Mechanical Turk*.

Chen, D. L. and Dolan, W. B. (2011). Collecting highly parallel data for paraphrase evaluation. In *Proceedings of the 49th Annual Meeting of the Association for Computational Linguistics (ACL)*.

Collins, M. (2002). Discriminative training methods for hidden Markov models: Theory and experiments with perceptron algorithms. In *Proceedings of the Conference on Empirical Methods on Natural Language Processing (EMNLP)*.

Das, D. and Smith, N. A. (2009). Paraphrase identification as probabilistic quasi-synchronous recognition. In *Proceedings of the Joint Conference of the 47th Annual Meeting of the Association for Computational Linguistics and the 4th International Joint Conference on Natural Language Processing of the Asian Federation of Natural Language Processing (ACL-IJCNLP)*.

Denkowski, M., Al-Haj, H., and Lavie, A. (2010). Turker-assisted paraphrasing for English-Arabic machine translation. In *Proceedings of the Workshop on Creating Speech and Language Data with Amazon's Mechanical Turk*.

Derczynski, L., Ritter, A., Clark, S., and Bontcheva, K. (2013). Twitter part-of-speech tagging for all: Overcoming sparse and noisy data. In *Proceedings of the Recent Advances in Natural Language Processing (RANLP)*.

Diao, Q., Jiang, J., Zhu, F., and Lim, E.-P. (2012). Finding bursty topics from microblogs. In *Proceedings of the 50th Annual Meeting of the Association for Computational Linguistics (ACL)*.

Dietterich, T. G., Lathrop, R. H., and Lozano-Pérez, T. (1997). Solving the multiple instance problem with axis-parallel rectangles. *Artificial Intelligence*, 89(1).

Dolan, B., Quirk, C., and Brockett, C. (2004). Unsupervised construction of large paraphrase corpora: Exploiting massively parallel news sources. In *Proceedings of the 20th International Conference on Computational Linguistics (COLING)*.

Dolan, W. and Brockett, C. (2005). Automatically constructing a corpus of sentential paraphrases. In *Proceedings of the 3rd International Workshop on Paraphrasing*.

Dunning, T. (1993). Accurate methods for the statistics of surprise and coincidence. *Computational Linguistics*, 19(1).

Fellbaum, C. (2010). WordNet. In *Theory and Applications of Ontology: Computer Applications*. Springer.

Francis, W. N. and Kucera, H. (1979). *Brown corpus manual*. Brown University.

Fung, P. and Cheung, P. (2004a). Mining very-non-parallel corpora: Parallel sentence and lexicon extraction via bootstrapping and EM. In *Proceedings of the Conference on Empirical Methods in Natural Language Processing (EMNLP)*.

Fung, P. and Cheung, P. (2004b). Multi-level bootstrapping for extracting parallel sentences from a quasi-comparable corpus. In *Proceedings of the International Conference on Computational Linguistics (COLING)*.

Guo, W. and Diab, M. (2012). Modeling sentences in the latent space. In *Proceedings of the 50th*

Annual Meeting of the Association for Computational Linguistics (ACL).

Guo, W., Li, H., Ji, H., and Diab, M. (2013). Linking tweets to news: A framework to enrich short text data in social media. In *Proceedings of the 51th Annual Meeting of the Association for Computational Linguistics (ACL)*.

Han, B., Cook, P., and Baldwin, T. (2012). Automatically constructing a normalisation dictionary for microblogs. In *Proceedings of the Conference on Empirical Methods on Natural Language Processing and Computational Natural Language Learning (EMNLP-CoNLL)*.

Hinton, G. E. (2002). Training products of experts by minimizing contrastive divergence. *Neural Computation*, 14(8).

Hoffmann, R., Zhang, C., Ling, X., Zettlemoyer, L. S., and Weld, D. S. (2011). Knowledge-based weak supervision for information extraction of overlapping relations. In *Proceedings of the 49th Annual Meeting of the Association for Computational Linguistics (ACL)*.

Hovy, E., Marcus, M., Palmer, M., Ramshaw, L., and Weischedel, R. (2006). OntoNotes: the 90% solution. In *Proceedings of the Human Language Technology Conference - North American Chapter of the Association for Computational Linguistics Annual Meeting (HLT-NAACL)*.

Ji, Y. and Eisenstein, J. (2013). Discriminative improvements to distributional sentence similarity. In *Proceedings of the Conference on Empirical Methods in Natural Language Processing (EMNLP)*.

Liang, P., Bouchard-Côté, A., Klein, D., and Taskar, B. (2006). An end-to-end discriminative approach to machine translation. In *Proceedings of the 21st International Conference on Computational Linguistics and the 44th annual meeting of the Association for Computational Linguistics (COLING-ACL)*.

Ling, W., Marujo, L., Dyer, C., Alan, B., and Isabel, T. (2014). Crowdsourcing high-quality parallel data extraction from Twitter. In *Proceedings of the Ninth Workshop on Statistical Machine Translation (WMT)*.

MacCartney, B., Galley, M., and Manning, C. (2008). A phrase-based alignment model for natural language inference. In *Proceedings of the Conference on Empirical Methods in Natural Language Processing (EMNLP)*.

Madnani, N. and Dorr, B. J. (2010). Generating phrasal and sentential paraphrases: A survey of data-driven methods. *Computational Linguistics*, 36(3).

Madnani, N., Tetreault, J., and Chodorow, M. (2012). Re-examining machine translation metrics for paraphrase identification. In *Proceedings of the Conference of the North American Chapter of the Association for Computational Linguistics - Human Language Technologies (NAACL-HLT)*.

Minnen, G., Carroll, J., and Pearce, D. (2001). Applied morphological processing of english. *Natural Language Engineering*, 7(03).

Moore, R. C. (2004). On log-likelihood-ratios and the significance of rare events. In *Proceedings of the Conference on Empirical Methods in Natural Language Processing (EMNLP)*.

Nenkova, A. and Vanderwende, L. (2005). The impact of frequency on summarization. Technical report, Microsoft Research. MSR-TR-2005-101.

O'Connor, B., Krieger, M., and Ahn, D. (2010). Tweetmotif: Exploratory search and topic summarization for Twitter. In *Proceedings of the 4th International AAAI Conference on Weblogs and Social Media (ICWSM)*.

Petrović, S., Osborne, M., and Lavrenko, V. (2012). Using paraphrases for improving first story detection in news and Twitter. In *Proceedings of the Conference of the North American Chapter of the Association for Computational Linguistics - Human Language Technologies (NAACL-HLT)*.

Riedel, S., Yao, L., and McCallum, A. (2010). Modeling relations and their mentions without labeled text. In *Proceedigns of the European Conference on Machine Learning and Principles and Practice of Knowledge Discovery in Databases (ECML-PKDD)*.

Ritter, A., Mausam, Etzioni, O., and Clark, S. (2012). Open domain event extraction from Twitter. In *Proceedings of the 18th International Con-*

ference on Knowledge Discovery and Data Mining (SIGKDD).

Ritter, A., Zettlemoyer, L., Mausam, and Etzioni, O. (2013). Modeling missing data in distant supervision for information extraction. *Transactions of the Association for Computational Linguistics (TACL).*

Robbins, H. (1985). Some aspects of the sequential design of experiments. In *Herbert Robbins Selected Papers*. Springer.

Sekine, S. (2005). Automatic paraphrase discovery based on context and keywords between NE pairs. In *Proceedings of the 3rd International Workshop on Paraphrasing.*

Shinyama, Y., Sekine, S., and Sudo, K. (2002). Automatic paraphrase acquisition from news articles. In *Proceedings of the 2nd International Conference on Human Language Technology Research (HLT).*

Surdeanu, M., Tibshirani, J., Nallapati, R., and Manning, C. D. (2012). Multi-instance multi-label learning for relation extraction. In *Proceedings of the 50th Annual Meeting of the Association for Computational Linguistics (ACL).*

Thadani, K. and McKeown, K. (2011). Optimal and syntactically-informed decoding for monolingual phrase-based alignment. In *Proceedings of the 49th Annual Meeting of the Association for Computational Linguistics - Human Language Technologies (ACL-HLT).*

Tran-Thanh, L., Stein, S., Rogers, A., and Jennings, N. R. (2012). Efficient crowdsourcing of unknown experts using multi-armed bandits. In *Proceedings of the European Conference on Artificial Intelligence (ECAI).*

Vanderwende, L., Suzuki, H., Brockett, C., and Nenkova, A. (2007). Beyond SumBasic: Task-focused summarization with sentence simplification and lexical expansion. *Information Processing & Management*, 43.

Wan, S., Dras, M., Dale, R., and Paris, C. (2006). Using dependency-based features to take the "para-farce" out of paraphrase. In *Proceedings of the Australasian Language Technology Workshop.*

Wang, L., Dyer, C., Black, A. W., and Trancoso, I. (2013). Paraphrasing 4 microblog normalization. In *Proceedings of the Conference on Empirical Methods on Natural Language Processing (EMNLP).*

Winkler, W. E. (1999). The state of record linkage and current research problems. Technical report, Statistical Research Division, U.S. Census Bureau.

Xu, W., Hoffmann, R., Zhao, L., and Grishman, R. (2013a). Filling knowledge base gaps for distant supervision of relation extraction. In *Proceedings of the 51st Annual Meeting of the Association for Computational Linguistics (ACL).*

Xu, W., Ritter, A., and Grishman, R. (2013b). Gathering and generating paraphrases from Twitter with application to normalization. In *Proceedings of the Sixth Workshop on Building and Using Comparable Corpora (BUCC).*

Yao, X., Van Durme, B., Callison-Burch, C., and Clark, P. (2013a). A lightweight and high performance monolingual word aligner. In *Proceedings of the 49th Annual Meeting of the Association for Computational Linguistics (ACL).*

Yao, X., Van Durme, B., and Clark, P. (2013b). Semi-markov phrase-based monolingual alignment. In *Proceedings of the Conference on Empirical Methods on Natural Language Processing (EMNLP).*

Zanzotto, F. M., Pennacchiotti, M., and Tsioutsiouliklis, K. (2011). Linguistic redundancy in Twitter. In *Proceedings of the Conference on Empirical Methods in Natural Language Processing (EMNLP).*

Zettlemoyer, L. S. and Collins, M. (2007). Online learning of relaxed CCG grammars for parsing to logical form. In *Proceedings of the 2007 Joint Conference on Empirical Methods in Natural Language Processing and Computational Natural Language Learning (EMNLP-CoNLL).*

Zhang, C. and Weld, D. S. (2013). Harvesting parallel news streams to generate paraphrases of event relations. In *Proceedings of the Conference on Empirical Methods in Natural Language Processing (EMNLP).*

It's All Fun and Games until Someone Annotates: Video Games with a Purpose for Linguistic Annotation

David Jurgens and **Roberto Navigli**
Department of Computer Science
Sapienza University of Rome
{jurgens,navigli}@di.uniroma1.it

Abstract

Annotated data is prerequisite for many NLP applications. Acquiring large-scale annotated corpora is a major bottleneck, requiring significant time and resources. Recent work has proposed turning annotation into a game to increase its appeal and lower its cost; however, current games are largely text-based and closely resemble traditional annotation tasks. We propose a new linguistic annotation paradigm that produces annotations from playing graphical video games. The effectiveness of this design is demonstrated using two video games: one to create a mapping from WordNet senses to images, and a second game that performs Word Sense Disambiguation. Both games produce accurate results. The first game yields annotation quality equal to that of experts and a cost reduction of 73% over equivalent crowdsourcing; the second game provides a 16.3% improvement in accuracy over current state-of-the-art sense disambiguation games with WordNet.

1 Introduction

Nearly all of Natural Language Processing (NLP) depends on annotated examples, either for training systems or for evaluating their quality. Typically, annotations are created by linguistic experts or trained annotators. However, such effort is often very time- and cost-intensive, and as a result creating large-scale annotated datasets remains a long-standing bottleneck for many areas of NLP.

As an alternative to requiring expert-based annotations, many studies used untrained, online workers, commonly known as crowdsourcing. When successful, crowdsourcing enables gathering annotations at scale; however, its performance is still limited by (1) the difficulty of expressing the annotation task as a simply-understood task suitable for the layman, (2) the cost of collecting many annotations, and (3) the tediousness of the task, which can fail to attract workers. Therefore, several groups have proposed an alternate annotation method using games: an annotation task is converted into a game which, as a result of game play, produces annotations (Pe-Than et al., 2012; Chamberlain et al., 2013). Turning an annotation task into a Game with a Purpose (GWAP) has been shown to lead to better quality results and higher worker engagement (Lee et al., 2013), thanks to the annotators being stimulated by the playful component. Furthermore, because games may appeal to a different group of people than crowdsourcing, they provide a complementary channel for attracting new annotators.

Within NLP, gamified annotation tasks include anaphora resolution (Hladká et al., 2009; Poesio et al., 2013), paraphrasing (Chklovski and Gil, 2005), term associations (Artignan et al., 2009) and disambiguation (Seemakurty et al., 2010; Venhuizen et al., 2013). The games' interfaces typically incorporate common game elements such as scores, leaderboards, or difficulty levels. However, the game itself remains largely text-based, with a strong resemblance to a traditional annotation task, and little resemblance to games most people actively play.

In the current work, we propose a radical shift in NLP-focused GWAP design, building *graphical*, dynamic games that achieve the same result as traditional annotation. Rather than embellish an annota-

Transactions of the Association for Computational Linguistics, 2 (2014) 449–463. Action Editor: Mirella Lapata.
Submitted 10/2013; Revised 03/2014; Revised 08/2014; Published 10/2014.

tion task with game elements, we start from a video game that is playable alone and build the task into the game as a central component. By focusing on the game aspect, players are presented with a more familiar task, which leads to higher engagement. Furthermore, the video game interface can potentially attract more interest from the large percentage of the populace who play video games.

In two video games, we demonstrate how certain linguistic annotation tasks can be effectively represented as video games. The first video game, Puzzle Racer, produces a mapping between images and WordNet senses (Fellbaum, 1998), thereby creating a large-scale library of visual analogs of concepts. While resources such as ImageNet (Deng et al., 2009) provide a partial sense-image mapping, they are limited to only a few thousand concrete noun senses, whereas Puzzle Racer annotates all parts of speech and both concrete and abstract senses. Furthermore, Puzzle Racer's output enables new visual games for tasks using word senses such as Word Sense Disambiguation, frame detection, and selectional preference acquisition. The second game, Ka-boom!, performs Word Sense Disambiguation (WSD) to identify the meaning of a word in context by players interacting with pictures. Sense annotation is regarded to be one of the most challenging NLP annotation tasks (Fellbaum et al., 1998; Edmonds and Kilgarriff, 2002; Palmer et al., 2007; Artstein and Poesio, 2008), so we view it as a challenging application for testing the limits of visual NLP games.

Our work provides the following four contributions. First, we present a new game-centric design methodology for NLP games with a purpose. Second, we demonstrate with the first game that video games can produce linguistic annotations equal in quality to those of experts and at a cost reduction from gathering the same annotations via crowdsourcing; with the second game we show that video games provide a statistically significant performance improvement over a current state-of-the-art non-video game with a purpose for sense annotation. Third, we release both games as a platform for other researchers to use in building new games and for annotating new data. Fourth, we provide multiple resources produced by the games: (1) an image library mapped to noun, verb, and adjective WordNet senses, consisting of 19,073 images across 443 senses, (2) a set of associated word labels for most images, (3) sense annotations as a distribution over images and senses, and (4) mappings between word senses and related Web queries.

2 Related Work

Games with a Purpose Multiple works have proposed linguistic annotation-based games with a purpose for tasks such as anaphora resolution (Hladká et al., 2009; Poesio et al., 2013), paraphrasing (Chklovski and Gil, 2005), term associations (Artignan et al., 2009; Lafourcade and Joubert, 2010; Vannella et al., 2014), acquiring common sense knowledge (Kuo et al., 2009; Herdağdelen and Baroni, 2012), and WSD (Chklovski and Mihalcea, 2002; Seemakurty et al., 2010; Venhuizen et al., 2013). Notably, all of these linguistic games have players primarily interacting with text, in contrast to other highly successful games with a purpose such as Foldit (Cooper et al., 2010), in which players fold protein sequences, and the ESP game (von Ahn and Dabbish, 2004), where players label images with words.

Most similar to our games are Wordrobe (Venhuizen et al., 2013) and Jinx (Seemakurty et al., 2010), which perform WSD, and The Knowledge Towers (Vannella et al., 2014), which associates images with senses. Wordrobe asks players to disambiguate nouns and verbs using multiple choice questions where options are sense definitions and disambiguation is limited to terms with at most five senses, a limitation that does not exist in our games. Jinx uses two players who both have to independently provide lexical substitutes of an ambiguous word and are then scored on the basis of their shared substitutes. While Jinx has a more game-like feel, producing annotations from the substitutes is non-trivial and requires looking for locality of the substitutes in the WordNet graph.

In contrast to Wordrobe and Jinx, we provide a game-centric design methodology for the seamless integration of the annotation task into a video game with dynamic, graphical elements.

The Knowledge Towers (TKT) is a video game for validating the associations between images and word senses in BabelNet (Navigli and Ponzetto, 2012) and associating each of the senses with new images acquired from a Web query of one of the sense's lemmas. To perform the annotation, players are shown a word and its definition and then asked to retrieve pictures matching that definition during game play.

In contrast, our Puzzle Racer game is purely visual and does not require players to read definitions, instead showing picture examples, increasing its video game-like quality. Furthermore, Puzzle Racer is tested on nouns, verbs, and adjectives whereas TKT is only applicable to annotate nouns since it relies on the BabelNet knowledge base to acquire its initial set of image-sense associations, which contains images only for nouns.

Image Libraries Associating images with conceptual entities is a long-standing goal in Computer Vision (Barnard et al., 2003) and two approaches have built large-scale image libraries based on the WordNet hypernym ontology. The data set of Torralba et al. (2008) contains over 80M images across all 75,062 non-abstract WordNet noun synsets. However, to support the size of the data set, images are down-scaled to 32x32 pixels; furthermore, their image-sense mapping error rates vary between 25-80% with more general concepts having higher error rates. The second significant image library comes from ImageNet (Deng et al., 2009), which contains 3.2M high-resolution images for 5,247 non-abstract WordNet noun synsets. Notably, both libraries focus only on concrete nouns. In contrast, the present work provides a methodology for generating image-sense associations for all parts of speech and for both abstract and concrete concepts. Within NLP resources, BabelNet (Navigli and Ponzetto, 2012) merges Wikipedia and WordNet sense inventories and contains mappings from WordNet senses to the pictures present on the corresponding Wikipedia page. However, since images come from an encyclopedia, the associations are inherently limited to only nouns and, due to inherently partial mapping, only 38.6% of the WordNet senses have images, with an average of 3.01 images for those senses. The present work also varies from previous approaches in that image-sense pairs are rated according to the strength of association between the image and sense, rather than having a binary ungraded association.

Crowdsourced WSD Many NLP areas have applied crowdsourcing (Wang et al., 2013); of these areas, the most related to this work is crowdsourcing word sense annotations. Despite initial success in performing WSD using crowdsourcing (Snow et al., 2008), many approaches noted the difficulty of performing WSD with untrained annotators, especially as the degree of polysemy increases or when word senses are related. Several approaches have attempted to make the task more suitable for untrained annotators by (1) using the crowd itself to define the sense inventory (Biemann and Nygaard, 2010), thereby ensuring the crowd understands the sense distinctions, (2) modifying the questions to explicitly model annotator uncertainty (Hong and Baker, 2011; Jurgens, 2013), or (3) using sophisticated methods to aggregate multiple annotations (Passonneau et al., 2012; Passonneau and Carpenter, 2013). In all cases, annotation was purely text based, in contrast to our work.

3 Game 1: Puzzle Racer

The first game was designed to fill an important need for enabling engaging NLP games: image representations of concepts, specifically WordNet senses. Our goals are two-fold: (1) to overcome the limits of current sense-image libraries, which have focused largely on concrete nouns and (2) to provide a general game platform for annotation tasks that need to associate lexical items with images. Following, we first describe the design, annotation process, and extensibility of the game, and then discuss how its input data is generated. A live demonstration of the game is available online.[1]

3.1 Design and Game Play

Puzzle Racer was designed to be as "video game-like" as possible, with no mentioning of linguistic terminology. Because the game is targeted for the layperson, we view this a fundamental design objective to make the game more engaging and long-lasting. Therefore, Puzzle Racer is modeled after popular games such as Temple Run and Subway Surfers, but with the twist of combining two game genres: racing and puzzle solving. Racing provides the core of game play, while the annotation is embedded as puzzle solving during and after the race.

[1]http://www.knowledgeforge.org

Following, we describe the game play and then detail how playing produces annotations.

Racing To race, players navigate a race car along a linear track filled with obstacles and enemy pieces. During play, players collect coins, which can be used to obtain non-annotation achievements and to increase their score. Enemies were added to introduce variety into the game and increase the strategy required to keep playing. Players begin the race with 2–4 health points, depending on the racer chosen, which are decreased when touching enemies. During game play, players may collect power-ups with familiar actions such as restoring lost health, doubling their speed, or acting as a magnet to collect coins. To bring a sense of familiarity, the game was designed using a combination of sprites, sound effects, and music from Super Mario World, Mario Kart 64, and custom assets created by us. Races initially last for 90 seconds, but may last longer if players collect specific power-ups that add time.

Puzzle Solving Prior to racing, players are shown three images, described as "puzzle clues," and instructions asking them to find the common theme in the three pictures (Fig. 1a). Then, during racing, players encounter obstacles, referred to as *puzzle gates*, that show a series of images. To stay alive, players must navigate their racer through the one picture in the series with the same theme as the puzzle clues. Players activate a gate after touching one of its images; a gate may only be activated once and racer movement over other pictures has no effect. Puzzle gates appear at random intervals during game play.

Two types of gate appear. In the first, the gate shows pictures where one picture is known to be related to the puzzle clues. We refer to these as golden gates. Racing over an unrelated image in a golden gate causes the player to lose one health point, which causes the race to end if their health reaches zero. The second type of gate, referred to as a mystery gate, shows three images that are *potentially* related to the clue. Moving over an image in a mystery gate has no effect on health. Prior to activating a gate, there is no visual difference between the two gates.

Figure 1b shows a racer approaching a puzzle gate. Upon first moving their racer on one of the gate's images, the player receives visual and auditory feedback based on the type of gate. In the case of a golden gate, the borders around all pictures change colors showing which picture should have been selected, a feedback icon appears on the chosen picture (shown in Figure 1c), and an appropriate sound effect plays. For mystery gates, borders become blue, indicating the gate has no effect.

Finally, when the race ends, players are asked to solve the race's puzzle by entering a single word that describes the race's puzzle theme. For example, in the race shown in Figure 1, an answer of "paper" would solve the puzzle. Correctly answering the puzzle doubles the points accumulated by the player during the race. The initial question motivates players to pay attention to picture content shown during the race; the longer the player stays alive, the more clues they can observe to help solve the puzzle.

Annotation Image-sense annotation takes place by means of the puzzle gates. Each race's puzzle theme is based on a specific WordNet sense. Initially, each sense is associated with a small set of gold standard images, G, and a much larger set of potentially-associated images, U, whose quality is unknown. At the start of a race, three gold standard images are randomly selected from G to serve as puzzle clues. The details of gold standard image selection are described later in Sec. 3.2. We note that not all gold standard images are shown initially as puzzle clues, helping mask potential differences between golden and mystery gates.

Mystery gates annotate the images in U. The images in a mystery gate are chosen by selecting the least-rated image in U and then pairing it with n-1 random images from U, where n is the number of pictures shown per gate. By always including the least-rated image, we guarantee that, given sufficient plays, all images for a sense will eventually be rated. When a player chooses an image in the mystery gate, that image receives n-1 positive votes for it being a good depiction of the sense; the remaining unselected images receive one negative vote. Thus, an image's *rating* is the cumulative sum of the positive and negative votes it receives. This rating scheme is zero-sum so image ratings cannot become inflated such that all images have a positive rating. However, we do note that if U includes many related images, due to the voting, some good images may have

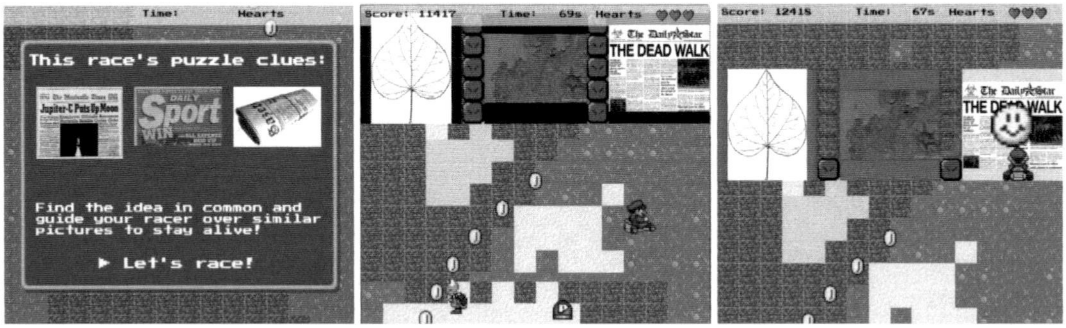

(a) Puzzle clues (b) A puzzle gate prior to activation (c) An activated puzzle gate

Figure 1: Screenshots of the key elements of the Puzzle Racer game

negative ratings if even-better images become higher ranked.

Golden gates are used to measure how well a player understands the race's puzzle concept (i.e., the sense being annotated). The first three puzzle gates in a race are always golden gates. We denote the percentage of golden gates correctly answered thus far as α. After the three initial golden gates are shown, the type of new puzzle gates is metered by α: golden gates are generated with probability $0.3 + 0.7(1 - \alpha)$ and mystery gates are generated for the remainder. In essence, accurate players with high α are more likely to be shown mystery gates that annotate pictures from U, whereas completely inaccurate players are prevented from adding new annotations. This mechanism adjusts the number of new annotations a player can produce in real-time based on their current accuracy at recognizing the target concept, which is not currently possible in common crowdsourcing platforms. Last, we note that puzzle answering also provides labels for the race's images, data that might prove valuable for tasks such as image labeling (Mensink et al., 2013) and image caption generation (Feng and Lapata, 2013; Kulkarni et al., 2013).

Additional Game Elements Puzzle Racer incorporates a number of standard Game with a Purpose design elements (von Ahn and Dabbish, 2008), with two notable features: unlockable achievements and a leaderboard. Players initially start out with a single racer and power-up available. Players can then unlock new racers and power-ups through various game play actions of varying difficulty, e.g., correctly answering three puzzle questions in a row. This feature proved highly popular and provided an extrinsic motivation for continued playing. Second, players were ranked according to level, which was determined by the number of correct puzzle answers, correct golden gates, and their total score. The top-ranking players were shown at the end of every round and via a special screen in-game. A full, live-updated leaderboard was added halfway through the study and proved an important feature for new players to use in competing for the top ranks.

Extensibility At its core, Puzzle Racer provides three central annotation-related mechanics: (1) an initial set of instructions on how players are to interact with images, (2) multiple series of images shown during game play, and (3) an open-ended question at the end of the game. These mechanics can be easily extended to other types of annotation where players must choose between several concepts shown as options in the puzzle gates. For example, the instructions could show players a phrase such as "a bowl of *" and ask players to race over images of things that might fit the "*" argument in order to obtain selectional preference annotations of the phrase (à la Flati and Navigli (2013)); the lemmas or senses associated with the selected images can be aggregated to identify the types of arguments preferred by players for the game's provided phrase. Similarly, the instructions could be changed to provide a set of keywords or phrases (instead of images associated with a sense) and ask players to navigate over images of the words in order to perform image labeling.

Nouns	argument, arm, atmosphere, bank, difficulty, disc, interest, paper, party, shelter
Verbs	activate, add, climb, eat, encounter expect, rule, smell, suspend, win
Adjectives	different, important, simple

Table 1: Lemmas for Puzzle Racer and Ka-boom!

disc_n^4: a flat circular plate		
circular plate	dish plate	plate
paper_n^3: a daily or weekly publication on folded sheets		
news paper	daily newspaper	newspaper headline
simple_a^2: elementary, simple, uncomplicated		
simple problem	1+1=2	elementary equation
win_v^1: be the winner in a contest or competition		
olympic winner	lottery winner	world cup victory

Table 2: Examples of queries used to gather images

3.2 Image Data

Puzzle Racer requires sets of images G and U as input. Both were constructed using image queries via the Yahoo! Boss API as follows. Three annotators were asked to each produce three queries for each sense of a target word and, for each query, to select three images as gold standard images. Queries were checked for uniqueness and to ensure that at least a few of its image results were related to the sense. Each query was used to retrieve one result set of 35 images. Two additional annotators then validated the queries and gold standard images produced by the first three annotators. Validation ensured that each sense had at least three queries and $|G| \geq 6$ for all senses. After validation, the gold standard images were added to G and all non-gold images in the result set were added to U, discarding duplicates.

During game play, puzzle clues are sampled across queries, rather than sampling directly from G. Query-based sampling ensures that players are not biased towards images for a single visual representation of the sense.

While the construction of G and U is manual, we note that alternate methods of constructing the sets could be considered, including automatic approaches such as those used by ImageNet (Deng et al., 2009). However, as the focus of this game is on ranking images, a manual process was used to ensure high-quality images in G.

Importantly, we stress that the images in G alone are often insufficient due to two reasons. First, most senses – especially those denoting abstract concepts – can be depicted in many ways. Relying on a small set of images for a sense can omit common visualizations, which may limit downstream applications that require general representations. Second, many games rely on a sense of novelty, i.e., not seeing the same pictures repeatedly; however, limiting the images to those in G can create issues where too few images exist to keep player interest high. While additional manual annotation could be used to select more gold standard images, such a process is time-intensive; hence, one of our game's purposes is to eventually move high-quality images from U to G.

4 Puzzle Racer Annotation Analysis

Puzzle Racer is intended to produce a sense-image mapping comparable to what would be produced by crowdsourcing. Therefore, we performed a large-scale study involving over 100 players and 16,000 images. Two experiments were performed. First, we directly compared the quality of the game-based annotations with those of crowdsourcing. Second, we compared the difference in quality between expert-based gold standard images and the highest-ranked images rated by players.

4.1 Experimental Setup

To test the potential of our approach, we selected a range of 23 polysemous noun, verb, and adjective lemmas, shown in Table 1. Lemmas had 4-10 senses each, for a total of 132 senses. Many lemmas have both abstract and concrete senses and some are known to have highly-related senses (Erk and McCarthy, 2009). Hence, given their potential annotation difficulty, we view performance on these lemmas as a *lower* bound.

For all lemmas, during the image generation process (Sec. 3.2) annotators were able to produce queries for all but one sense, $expect_v^2$;[2] this produced 1356 gold images in G and 16,656 unrated images

[2]The sense $expect_v^2$ has the definition, "consider obligatory; request and expect." Annotators were able to formulate many queries that could have potentially shown images of this definition, but the images results of such queries were consistently unrelated to the meaning.

interest_n^1: a sense of concern with and curiosity about someone or something	eat_v^1: take in solid food	different_a^1: unlike in nature or quality or form or degree

party_n^2: a group of people gathered together for pleasure	expect_v^6: be pregnant with	shelter_n^5: temporary housing for homeless or displaced persons
	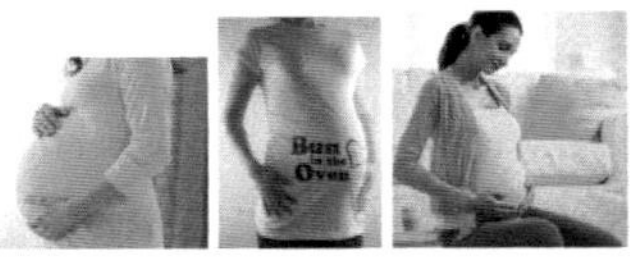	

Table 3: Examples of gold standard images

in U. Tables 2 and 3 show examples of the queries and gold standard images, respectively.

The game play study was conducted over two weeks using a pool of undergraduate students, who were allowed to recruit other students. After an email announcement, 126 players participated. Players were ranked according to their character's level and provided with an incentive that the four top-ranking players at the end of the study would be provided with gift cards ranging from \$15-25USD, with a total compensation of \$70USD.

4.2 Experiment 1: Crowdsourcing Comparison

The first experiment directly compares the image rankings produced by the game with those from an analogous crowdsourcing task. Tasks were created on the CrowdFlower platform using the identical set of examples and annotation questions encountered by players. In each task, workers were shown three example gold standard images (sampled from those configurations seen by players) and asked to identify the common theme among the three examples. Then, five annotation questions were shown in which workers were asked to choose which of three images was most related to the theme. Questions were created after the Puzzle Racer study finished in order to use the identical set of questions seen by players as mystery gates. Workers were paid \$0.03USD per task.

To compare the quality of the Puzzle Racer image rankings with those from CrowdFlower, the three highest-rated images of each sense from both rankings were compared. Two annotators were shown a sense's definition and example uses, and then asked to compare the quality of three image pairs, selecting whether (a) the left image was a better depiction of the sense, (b) the right image was better, or (c) the images were approximately equal in quality. In the case of disagreements, a third annotator was asked to compare the images; the majority answer was used when present or, in the case of all three ratings, images were treated as equal, the latter of which occurred for only 17% of the questions. For all 396 questions, the method used to rank the image was hidden and the order in which images appeared was randomized.

Results During the study period, players completed 7199 races, generating 20,253 ratings across 16,479 images. Ratings were balanced across senses, with a minimum and maximum of 231 and 329 ratings per sense. Players accurately identified each race's theme, selecting the correct image in 83% of all golden puzzle gates shown. Table 4 shows example top-rated images from Puzzle Racer.

Experiment 1 measures differences in the quality of the three top-ranked images produced by Puzzle Racer and CrowdFlower for each sense. Puzzle Racer and CrowdFlower produced similar ratings, with at least one image appearing in the top-three positions of both ranks for 55% of the senses.

Both annotators agreed in 72% of cases in selecting the best sense depiction, finding that in 88% of the agreed cases both images were approximately equal representations of the sense. In the remaining, the Puzzle Racer image was better in 4% and

activate^4_v: aerate (sewage) so as to favor the growth of organisms that decompose organic matter	argument^2_n: a contentious speech act; a dispute where there is strong disagreement	atmosphere^4_n: the weather or climate at some place
		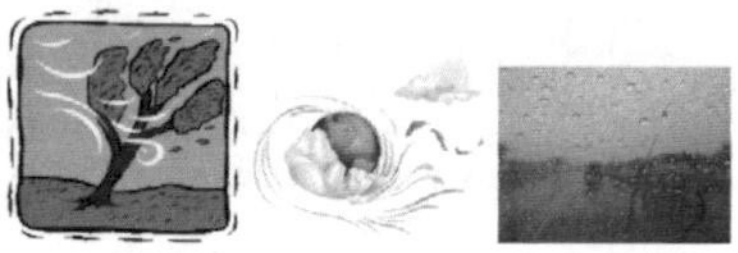
climb^1_v: go upward with gradual or continuous progress	important^1_a: of great significance or value	rule^2_v: decide with authority
	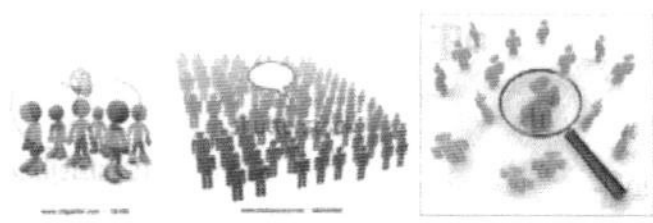	

Table 4: Examples of the three highest-rated images for six senses

CrowdFlower image better in 8%. When resolutions from a third annotator were included, a similar trend emerges: both images were equivalent in 79% of all cases, Puzzle Racer images were preferred in 7% and Crowflower images in 14%. These results show that, as a video game, Puzzle Racer produces very similar results to what would be expected under equivalent conditions with crowdsourcing.

4.3 Experiment 2: Image Quality

The second experiment evaluates the ability of the games to produce high-quality images by measuring the difference in quality between gold standard images and top-rated images in the game. CrowdFlower workers were shown a question with a sense's definition and example uses and then asked to choose which of two images was a better visual representation of the gloss. Questions were created for each of the three highest-rated images for each sense, pairing each with a randomly-selected gold standard image for that sense. Image order was randomized between questions. Five questions were shown per task and workers were paid $0.05USD per task.[3] The 2670 worker responses were aggregated by selecting each question's most frequent answer.

Results For senses within each part of speech, workers preferred the gold standard image to the top-rated image for nouns, verbs, and adjectives 57.4%, 53.1%, and 56.2% of the time, respectively. This preference is not significant at $p < 0.05$, indicating that the top-ranked images produced through Puzzle Racer game play are approximately equivalent in quality to images manually chosen by experts with full knowledge of the sense inventory.

4.4 Cost Comparison

Puzzle Racer annotations cost $70, or $0.0034USD per rating. In comparison, the analogous CrowdFlower annotations cost $256.60, or $0.0126USD per annotation. Because the game's costs are fixed, the cost per annotation is driven down as players compete. As a result, Puzzle Racer reduces the annotation cost to ≤27% of that required by crowdsourcing. We note that other factors could have contributed to the cost reduction over crowdsourcing beyond the video game itself. However, as we demonstrate in Vannella et al. (2014), players will play a video game with a purpose without compensation just as much as they do when compensated using a similar setup as was performed in this experiment. Hence, the video game itself is likely the largest motivating factor for the cost reduction.

Video game-based annotation does come with indirect costs due to game development. For example, Poesio et al. (2013) report spending £60,000 over a two-year period to develop their linguistic game with a purpose. In contrast, Puzzle Racer was created using open source software in just over a month and developed in the context of a Java programming class, removing any professional development costs.

[3] Workers were paid more for the second task to adjust for the time required to read each question's sense definition and example uses; thus, hourly compensation rates in the two experiments were approximately equivalent.

Furthermore, Puzzle Racer is easily extensible for other text-image annotation tasks, enabling the platform to be re-used with minimal effort.

The decreased cost does come with an increase in the time per annotation. All tasks on the CrowdFlower platform required only a few hours to complete, whereas the Puzzle Racer data was gathered over the two-week contest period. The difference in collection time reflects an important difference in the current resources: while crowdsourcing has established platforms with on-demand workers, no central platforms exist for games with a purpose with an analogous pool of game players. However, although the current games were released in a limited fashion, later game releases to larger venues such as Facebook may attract more players and significantly decrease both collection times and overall annotation cost.

5 Game 2: Ka-boom!

Building large-scale sense-annotated corpora is a long-standing objective (see (Pilehvar and Navigli, 2014)) and has sparked significant interest in developing effective crowdsourcing annotation and GWAP strategies (cf. Sec. 2). Therefore, we propose a second video game, *Ka-boom!*, that produces sense annotations from game play. A live demonstration of the game is available online.[4]

Design and Game Play Ka-boom! is an action game in the style of the popular Fruit Ninja game: pictures are tossed on screen from the boundaries of the screen, which the player must then selectively destroy in order to score points. The game's challenge stems from rapidly identifying which pictures should be destroyed or not destroyed as they appear.

Prior to the start of a round, players are shown a sentence with a word in bold (Fig. 2a) and asked to envision pictures related to that word's meaning in the context. Players are then instructed to destroy pictures that do *not* remind them of the bolded word's meaning and let live pictures showing something reminiscent. Once finished reading the instructions, players begin a round of game play that shows (1) images for each sense of the word and (2) images for unrelated lemmas, referred to as distractor images.

[4]http://www.knowledgeforge.org/

Players destroy pictures by clicking or touching them, depending on their device's input (Fig. 2b). Players are penalized for failing to destroy the distractor images. Rounds begin with a limit of at most three pictures on screen at once, which increases as the round progresses. The additional images provide two important benefits: (1) an increasing degree of challenge to keep the player's interest, (2) more image interactions to use in producing the annotation. Additionally, the increasing picture rate enables us to measure the interaction between game play speed and annotation quality in order to help tune the speeds of future games. The round ends when players fail to destroy five or more distractor images or 60 seconds elapses. Ending the game early after players fail to destroy distractor images provides Ka-boom! a mechanism for limiting the impact of inaccurate or adversarial players on annotation quality. After game play finishes, players are shown their score and all the lemma-related pictures they spared (Fig. 2c), proving a positive feedback loop where players can evaluate their choices.

Annotation Traditionally, sense annotation is performed by having an annotator examine a word in context and then chose the word's sense from a list of definitions. Ka-boom! replaces the sense definitions with image examples of that sense. A sense annotation is built from the senses associated with the images that the player spared. Images are presented to players based on a sequence of flights. Each flight contains one randomly-selected picture for each of a word's n senses and n distractor images. Images within a flight are randomly ordered. The structure of a flight's images ensures that, as the game progresses, players see the same number of images for each sense; otherwise, the player's annotation may become biased simply due to one sense's images appearing more often.

Once the game ends, the senses associated with the spared images are aggregated to produce a sense distribution. For simplicity, the sense with the highest probability is selected as the player's answer; in the case of ties, multiple senses are reported, though, we note that the game's annotation method could also produce a weighted distribution over senses (Erk et al., 2012), revealing different meanings that a player considered valid in the context.

(a) The context and target word (b) Players destroying images (c) The round-over summary

Figure 2: Screenshots of the three key elements of the Ka-boom! game

The highest probability of a sense from this distribution is then multiplied by the duration of the game to produce the player's score for the round. Players maximize their score when they consistently choose images associated with a single sense, which encourages precise game play.

The annotation design of having players destroy unrelated images was motivated by two factors. First, the mechanism of destroying unrelated images does not introduce noise into the annotation when a player mistakenly destroys an image; because only retained images count towards the sense annotation, players may be highly selective in which images they retain – even destroying some images that are associated with the correct sense – while still producing a correct annotation. Second, our internal testing showed the objective of destroying unrelated pictures keeps players more actively engaged. In the inverse type of play where players destroy only related pictures, players often had to wait for a single picture to destroy, causing them to lose interest.

Extensibility Ka-boom! contains two core mechanics: (1) instructions on which pictures should be destroyed and which should be spared, and (2) series of images shown to the player during game play. As with Puzzle Racer, the Ka-boom! mechanics can be modified to extend the game to new types of annotation. For example, instructions could display picture examples and ask players to destroy either similar or opposite-meaning ideas in order to annotate synonyms or antonyms. In another setting, images can be associated with semantic frames (e.g., from FrameNet (Baker et al., 1998)) and players must spare images showing the frame of the game's sentence in order to provide frame annotations.

6 Ka-boom! Annotation Analysis

Ka-boom! is intended to provide a complementary and more-enjoyable method for sense annotation using only pictures. To test its effectiveness, we perform a direct comparison with the state-of-the-art GWAP for sense annotation, Wordrobe (Venhuizen et al., 2013), which is not a video game.

6.1 Experimental Setup

Organizers of the Wordrobe project (Venhuizen et al., 2013) provided a data set of 111 recently-annotated contexts having between one and nine games played for each (mean 3.2 games). This data was distinct from the contexts used to evaluate Wordrobe in Venhuizen et al. (2013) in which case all contexts had six games played each. Contexts were for 74 noun and 16 verb lemmas with a total of 310 senses (mean 3.4 senses per word). Contexts were assigned the most-selected sense label from the Wordrobe games.

To gather the images for each lemma used with Ka-boom!, we repeated a similar image-gathering process as done for the gold standard images in Puzzle Racer. Annotators generated at least three queries for each sense, selecting three images for each query as gold standard examples of the sense. During annotation, four senses could not be associated with any queries that produced high-quality images. In total, 2594 images were gathered, with an average of 8.36 images per sense. The query data and unrated images are included in the data set, but were not used further in Ka-boom! experiments.

Game players were drawn from a small group of

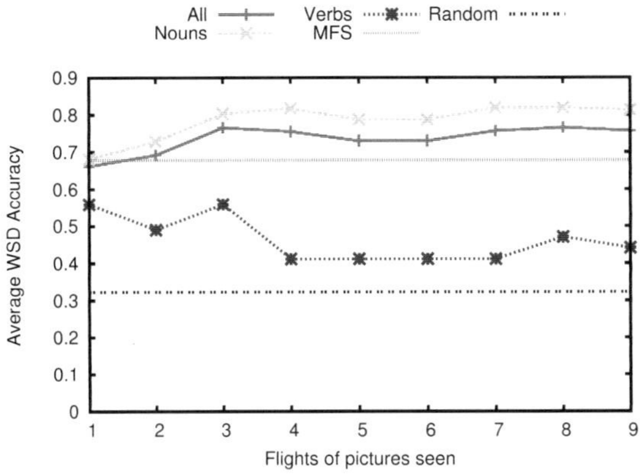

Figure 3: Players' average WSD accuracy within a single game relative to the number of flights seen

	Accuracy		
Method	All	Noun	Verb
Ka-boom!	**0.766**	**0.803**	0.559
Wordrobe	0.603	0.659	0.313
MFS	0.678	0.702	**0.588**
Random	0.322	0.325	0.312

Table 5: Sense disambiguation accuracies

fluent English speakers and were free to recruit other players. A total of 19 players participated. Unlike Puzzle Racer, players were not compensated. Each context was seen in at least six games.

WSD performance is measured using the traditional precision and recall definitions and the F1 measure of the two (Navigli, 2009); because all items are annotated, precision and recall are equivalent and we report performance as accuracy. Performance is measured relative to two baselines: (1) a baseline that picks the sense of the lemma that is most frequent in SemCor (Miller et al., 1993), denoted as MFS, and (2) a baseline equivalent to performance if players had randomly clicked on images, denoted as Random.[5]

6.2 Results

Two analyses were performed. Because Ka-boom! continuously revises the annotation during gameplay based on which pictures players spare, the first analysis assesses how the accuracy changes with respect to the length of one Ka-boom! game. The second analysis measures the accuracy with respect to the number of games played per context.

In the first analysis, each context's annotation was evaluated using the most-probable sense after each flight of gameplay. Figure 3 shows results after six games were played. Players were highly accurate at playing, surpassing the MFS baseline after seeing two flights of pictures (i.e., two pictures for each sense). Accuracy remained approximately equivalent after three rounds for noun lemmas, while verb lemmas showed a small drop-off in performance. We believe that the increased rate at which images occur on screen likely caused lower performance, where players were unable to react quickly enough. Many noun lemmas had easily-recognizable associated images, so higher-speed game play may still be accurate. In contrast, verbs were more general (e.g., "decide," "concern," and "include"), which required more abstract thinking in order to recognize an associated picture; as the game speed increased, players were not able to identify these associated pictures as easily, causing slightly decreased performance.

Table 5 shows the players' disambiguation accuracy after three flights in comparison to the players' accuracy with Wordrobe and the two baselines. Ka-boom! provides an increased performance over Wordrobe that is statistically significant at $p < 0.01$.[6] Ka-boom! also provides a performance increase over the MFS baseline, though it is statistically significant only at $p = 0.14$. The time required to gather annotations after three flights varied based on the number of senses, but was under a minute in all cases, which puts the rate of annotation on par with that of expert-based annotation (Krishnamurthy and Nicholls, 2000).

In the second analysis, disambiguation accuracy was measured based on the number of games played for a context.[7] Because the provided Wordrobe data set has 3.2 games played per context on average, results are reported only for the subset of contexts played in at least four Wordrobe games in order to obtain consistent performance estimates. Ka-

[5]This baseline is similar to random sense selection but takes into account differences in the number of pictures per sense.

[6]We note that, although Venhuizen et al. (2013) report a higher accuracy for Wordrobe in their original experiments (85.7 F1), that performance was measured on a different data set and used six games per context.

[7]In all cases, players played at most one game per context.

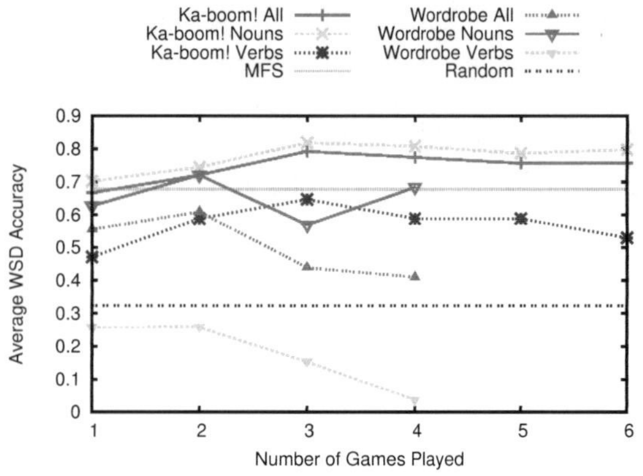

Figure 4: Average WSD accuracy as a function of the number of games played for a context

boom! annotations are recorded after three flights were seen in each game. Figure 4 shows the performance relative to the number of annotators for both Ka-boom! and Wordrobe, i.e., the number of games played for that context by different players.

For nouns, Ka-boom! is able to exceed the MFS baseline after only two games are played. For both nouns and verbs, multiple rounds of Ka-boom! game play improve performance. In contrast to Ka-Boom!, Wordrobe accuracy declines as the number of players increases; when multiple players disagree on the sense, no clear majority emerges in Wordrobe, lowering the accuracy of the resulting annotation. In contrast, a single player in Ka-boom! produces multiple sense judgments for a context in a single game via interacting with each flight of images. These interactions provide a robust distributional annotation over senses that can be easily aggregated with other players' judgments to produce a higher-quality single sense annotation. This analysis suggests that Ka-boom! can produce accurate annotations with just a few games per context, removing the need for many redundant annotations and improving the overall annotation throughput.

7 Conclusion and Future Work

In this work we have presented a new model of linguistic Games with a Purpose focused on annotation using *video games*. Our contributions show that designing linguistic annotation tasks as video games can produce high-quality annotations. In the first game, Puzzle Racer, we demonstrated that game play can produce a high-quality library of images associated with WordNet senses, equivalent to those produced by expert annotators. Moreover, Puzzle Racer reduces the cost of producing an equivalent resource via crowdsourcing by at least 73% while providing similar-quality image ratings. In the second game, Ka-boom!, we demonstrated that a video game could be used to perform accurate word sense annotation with a large improvement over the MFS baseline and a statistically significant improvement over current game-based WSD.

While not all linguistic annotations tasks are easily representable as video games, our two games provide an important starting point for building new types of NLP games with a purpose based on video games mechanics. Software for both games will be open-sourced, providing a new resource for future game development and extensions of our work. Furthermore, the multiple data sets produced by this work are available at `http://lcl.uniroma1.it/videogames`, providing (1) a sense-image mapping from hundreds of senses to tens of thousands of images, (2) word labels for most images in our dataset, (3) Web queries associated with all senses, and (4) image-based word sense annotations.

Based on our results, three directions for future work are planned. The two games presented here focus on concepts that can be represented visually and thus lend themselves to annotations for lexical semantics. However, the fact that the games are graphical does not prevent them from showing textual items (see Vannella et al. (2014)) and more apt video games could be developed for text-based annotations such as PP-attachment or pronoun resolution. Therefore, in our first future work, we plan to develop new types of video games for textual items as well as extend the current games for new semantic tasks such as selectional preferences and frame annotation. Second, we plan to scale up both games to a broader audience such as Facebook, creating a larger sense-image library and a standard platform for releasing video games with a purpose. Third, we plan to build multilingual games using the images from Puzzle Racer, which provide a language-independent concept representation, and could therefore be used to enable the annotation and validation of automatically-created knowledge resources (Hovy et al., 2013).

Acknowledgments

The authors gratefully acknowledge the support of the ERC Starting Grant MultiJEDI No. 259234.

We thank the many game players whose collective passion for video games made this work possible.

References

Guillaume Artignan, Mountaz Hascoët, and Mathieu Lafourcade. 2009. Multiscale visual analysis of lexical networks. In *Proceedings of the International Conference on Information Visualisation*, pages 685–690.

Ron Artstein and Massimo Poesio. 2008. Inter-coder agreement for computational linguistics. *Computational Linguistics*, 34(4):555–596.

Collin F. Baker, Charles J. Fillmore, and John B. Lowe. 1998. The Berkeley FrameNet project. In *Proceedings of the 17th International Conference on Computational Linguistics and 36th Annual Meeting of the Association for Computational Linguistics,* Montréal, Québec, Canada, 10–14 August 1998, Montreal, Canada.

Kobus Barnard, Pinar Duygulu, David Forsyth, Nando De Freitas, David M. Blei, and Michael I. Jordan. 2003. Matching words and pictures. *The Journal of Machine Learning Research*, 3:1107–1135.

Chris Biemann and Valerie Nygaard. 2010. Crowdsourcing WordNet. In *The 5th International Conference of the Global WordNet Association (GWC-2010).*

Jon Chamberlain, Karën Fort, Udo Kruschwitz, Mathieu Lafourcade, and Massimo Poesio. 2013. Using games to create language resources: Successes and limitations of the approach. In Iryna Gurevych and Jungi Kim, editors, *The People's Web Meets NLP*, Theory and Applications of Natural Language Processing, pages 3–44. Springer.

Tim Chklovski and Yolanda Gil. 2005. Improving the design of intelligent acquisition interfaces for collecting world knowledge from web contributors. In *Proceedings of the International Conference on Knowledge Capture*, pages 35–42. ACM.

Tim Chklovski and Rada Mihalcea. 2002. Building a Sense Tagged Corpus with Open Mind Word Expert. In *Proceedings of ACL 2002 Workshop on WSD: Recent Successes and Future Directions*, Philadelphia, PA, USA.

Seth Cooper, Firas Khatib, Adrien Treuille, Janos Barbero, Jeehyung Lee, Michael Beenen, Andrew Leaver-Fay, David Baker, Zoran Popović, and Foldit players. 2010. Predicting protein structures with a multiplayer online game. *Nature*, 466(7307):756–760.

Jia Deng, Wei Dong, Richard Socher, Li-Jia Li, Kai Li, and Li Fei-Fei. 2009. ImageNet: A large-scale hierarchical image database. In *Proceedings of the Conference on Computer Vision and Pattern Recognition (CVPR)*, pages 248–255.

Philip Edmonds and Adam Kilgarriff. 2002. Introduction to the special issue on evaluating word sense disambiguation systems. *Natural Language Engineering*, 8(4):279–291.

Katrin Erk and Diana McCarthy. 2009. Graded word sense assignment. In *Proceedings of the 2009 Conference on Empirical Methods in Natural Language Processing (EMNLP)*, pages 440–449, Singapore.

Katrin Erk, Diana McCarthy, and Nicholas Gaylord. 2012. Measuring word meaning in context. *Computational Linguistics*, 39(3):511–554.

Christiane Fellbaum, Joachim Grabowski, and Shari Landes. 1998. Performance and confidence in a semantic annotation task. In Christiane Fellbaum, editor, *WordNet: An electronic lexical database*, pages 217–237. MIT Press.

Christiane Fellbaum, editor. 1998. *WordNet: An Electronic Database.* MIT Press, Cambridge, MA.

Yansong Feng and Mirella Lapata. 2013. Automatic caption generation for news images. *IEEE Transactions on Pattern Analysis and Machine Intelligence*, 35(4):797–812.

Tiziano Flati and Roberto Navigli. 2013. SPred: Large-scale Harvesting of Semantic Predicates. In *Proceedings of the 51st Annual Meeting of the Association for Computational Linguistics (ACL)*, pages 1222–1232, Sofia, Bulgaria.

Amaç Herdağdelen and Marco Baroni. 2012. Bootstrapping a game with a purpose for common sense collection. *ACM Transactions on Intelligent Systems and Technology*, 3(4):1–24.

Barbora Hladká, Jiří Mírovský, and Pavel Schlesinger. 2009. Play the language: Play coreference. In *Proceedings of the Joint Conference of the Association for Computational Linguistics and International Joint Conference of the Asian Federation of Natural Language Processing (ACL-IJCNLP)*, pages 209–212. Association for Computational Linguistics.

Jisup Hong and Collin F. Baker. 2011. How Good is the Crowd at "real" WSD? In *Proceedings of the Fifth Linguistic Annotation Workshop (LAW V)*, pages 30–37. ACL.

Eduard H. Hovy, Roberto Navigli, and Simone Paolo Ponzetto. 2013. Collaboratively built semi-structured content and Artificial Intelligence: The story so far. *Artificial Intelligence*, 194:2–27.

David Jurgens. 2013. Embracing ambiguity: A comparison of annotation methodologies for crowdsourcing word sense labels. In *Proceedings of the Conference of the North American Chapter of the Association of Computational Linguistics (NAACL)*, pages 556–562.

Ramesh Krishnamurthy and Diane Nicholls. 2000. Peeling an onion: The lexicographer's experience of manual sense-tagging. *Computers and the Humanities*, 34(1-2):85–97.

Girish Kulkarni, Visruth Premraj, Vicente Ordonez, Sagnik Dhar, Siming Li, Yejin Choi, Alexander C. Berg, and Tamara L. Berg. 2013. Babytalk: Understanding and generating simple image descriptions. *IEEE Transactions on Pattern Analysis and Machine Intelligence*, 35(12):2891–2903.

Yen-ling Kuo, Jong-Chuan Lee, Kai-yang Chiang, Rex Wang, Edward Shen, Cheng-wei Chan, and Jane Yung-jen Hsu. 2009. Community-based game design: experiments on social games for commonsense data collection. In *Proceedings of the ACM SIGKDD Workshop on Human Computation*, pages 15–22.

Mathieu Lafourcade and Alain Joubert. 2010. Computing trees of named word usages from a crowdsourced lexical network. In *Proceedings of the International Multiconference on Computer Science and Information Technology (IMCSIT)*, pages 439–446, Wisla, Poland.

Tak Yeon Lee, Casey Dugan, Werner Geyer, Tristan Ratchford, Jamie Rasmussen, N. Sadat Shami, and Stela Lupushor. 2013. Experiments on motivational feedback for crowdsourced workers. In *Seventh International AAAI Conference on Weblogs and Social Media (ICWSM)*, pages 341–350.

Thomas Mensink, Jakob J. Verbeek, and Gabriela Csurka. 2013. Tree-structured crf models for interactive image labeling. *IEEE Transactions on Pattern Analysis and Machine Intelligence*, 35(2):476–489.

George A. Miller, Claudia Leacock, Randee Tengi, and Ross Bunker. 1993. A semantic concordance. In *Proceedings of the 3rd DARPA Workshop on Human Language Technology*, pages 303–308, Plainsboro, N.J.

Roberto Navigli and Simone Paolo Ponzetto. 2012. BabelNet: The automatic construction, evaluation and application of a wide-coverage multilingual semantic network. *Artificial Intelligence*, 193:217–250.

Roberto Navigli. 2009. Word Sense Disambiguation: A survey. *ACM Computing Surveys (CSUR)*, 41(2):1–69.

Martha Palmer, Hoa Dang, and Christiane Fellbaum. 2007. Making fine-grained and coarse-grained sense distinctions, both manually and automatically. *Natural Language Engineering*, 13(2):137–163.

Rebecca J. Passonneau and Bob Carpenter. 2013. The benefits of a model of annotation. In *7th Linguistic Annotation Workshop and Interoperability with Discourse*, August 8–9.

Rebecca J. Passonneau, Vikas Bhardwaj, Ansaf Salleb-Aouissi, and Nancy Ide. 2012. Multiplicity and word sense: evaluating and learning from multiply labeled word sense annotations. *Language Resources and Evaluation*, 46(2):209–252.

Ei Pa Pa Pe-Than, DH-L Goh, and Chei Sian Lee. 2012. A survey and typology of human computation games. In *Information Technology: New Generations (ITNG), 2012 Ninth International Conference on*, pages 720–725. IEEE.

Mohammad Taher Pilehvar and Roberto Navigli. 2014. A Large-scale Pseudoword-based Evaluation Framework for State-of-the-Art Word Sense Disambiguation. *Computational Linguistics*, 40(4).

Massimo Poesio, Jon Chamberlain, Udo Kruschwitz, Livio Robaldo, and Luca Ducceschi. 2013. Phrase detectives: Utilizing collective intelligence for internet-scale language resource creation. *ACM Transactions on Interactive Intelligent Systems*, 3(1):3:1–3:44, April.

Nitin Seemakurty, Jonathan Chu, Luis Von Ahn, and Anthony Tomasic. 2010. Word sense disambiguation via human computation. In *Proceedings of the ACM SIGKDD Workshop on Human Computation*, pages 60–63. ACM.

Rion Snow, Brendan O'Connor, Daniel Jurafsky, and Andrew Ng. 2008. Cheap and fast – but is it good? evaluating non-expert annotations for natural language tasks. In *Proceedings of the 2008 Conference on Empirical Methods in Natural Language Processing,* Waikiki, Honolulu, Hawaii, 25-27 October, pages 254–263.

Antonio Torralba, Robert Fergus, and William T Freeman. 2008. 80 million tiny images: A large data set for nonparametric object and scene recognition. *IEEE Transactions on Pattern Analysis and Machine Intelligence*, 30(11):1958–1970.

Daniele Vannella, David Jurgens, Daniele Scarfini, Domenico Toscani, and Roberto Navigli. 2014. Validating and extending semantic knowledge bases using video games with a purpose. In *Proceedings of the 52nd Annual Meeting of the Association for Computational Linguistics (ACL)*, pages 1294–1304.

Noortje J. Venhuizen, Valerio Basile, Kilian Evang, and Johan Bos. 2013. Gamification for word sense labeling. In *Proceedings of the International Conference on Computational Semantics (IWCS)*, pages 397–403.

Luis von Ahn and Laura Dabbish. 2004. Labeling images with a computer game. In *Proceedings of the Conference on Human Factors in Computing Systems (CHI)*, pages 319–326.

Luis von Ahn and Laura Dabbish. 2008. Designing games with a purpose. *Communications of the ACM*, 51(8):58–67.

Aobo Wang, Cong Duy Vu Hoang, and Min-Yen Kan. 2013. Perspectives on crowdsourcing annotations for natural language processing. *Language Resources and Evaluation*, 47(1):9–31.

Online Adaptor Grammars with Hybrid Inference

Ke Zhai
Computer Science and UMIACS
University of Maryland
College Park, MD USA
zhaike@cs.umd.edu

Jordan Boyd-Graber
Computer Science
University of Colorado
Boulder, CO USA
jordan.boyd.graber@colorado.edu

Shay B. Cohen
School of Informatics
University of Edinburgh
Edinburgh, Scotland, UK
scohen@inf.ed.ac.uk

Abstract

Adaptor grammars are a flexible, powerful formalism for defining nonparametric, unsupervised models of grammar productions. This flexibility comes at the cost of expensive inference. We address the difficulty of inference through an online algorithm which uses a hybrid of Markov chain Monte Carlo and variational inference. We show that this inference strategy improves scalability without sacrificing performance on unsupervised word segmentation and topic modeling tasks.

1 Introduction

Nonparametric Bayesian models are effective tools to discover latent structure in data (Müller and Quintana, 2004). These models have had great success in text analysis, especially syntax (Shindo et al., 2012). Nonparametric distributions provide support over a countably infinite long-tailed distributions common in natural language (Goldwater et al., 2011).

We focus on adaptor grammars (Johnson et al., 2006), syntactic nonparametric models based on probabilistic context-free grammars. Adaptor grammars weaken the strong statistical independence assumptions PCFGs make (Section 2).

The weaker statistical independence assumptions that adaptor grammars make come at the cost of expensive inference. Adaptor grammars are not alone in this trade-off. For example, nonparametric extensions of topic models (Teh et al., 2006) have substantially more expensive inference than their parametric counterparts (Yao et al., 2009).

A common approach to address this computational bottleneck is through variational inference (Wainwright and Jordan, 2008). One of the advantages of variational inference is that it can be easily parallelized (Nallapati et al., 2007) or transformed into an online algorithm (Hoffman et al., 2010), which often converges in fewer iterations than batch variational inference.

Past variational inference techniques for adaptor grammars assume a preprocessing step that looks at *all available data* to establish the support of these nonparametric distributions (Cohen et al., 2010). Thus, these past approaches are not directly amenable to online inference.

Markov chain Monte Carlo (MCMC) inference, an alternative to variational inference, does not have this disadvantage. MCMC is easier to implement, and it *discovers* the support of nonparametric models during inference rather than assuming it *a priori*.

We apply stochastic hybrid inference (Mimno et al., 2012) to adaptor grammars to get the best of both worlds. We interleave MCMC inference *inside* variational inference. This preserves the scalability of variational inference while adding the sparse statistics and improved exploration MCMC provides.

Our inference algorithm for adaptor grammars starts with a variational algorithm similar to Cohen et al. (2010) and adds hybrid sampling within variational inference (Section 3). This obviates the need for expensive preprocessing and is a necessary step to create an online algorithm for adaptor grammars.

Our online extension (Section 4) processes examples in small batches taken from a stream of data. As data arrive, the algorithm dynamically extends the underlying approximate posterior distributions as more data are observed. This makes the algorithm flexible, scalable, and amenable to datasets that cannot be examined exhaustively because of their size—e.g., terabytes of social media data appear every second—or their nature—e.g., speech acquisition, where a language learner is limited to the bandwidth of the human perceptual system and cannot acquire data in a monolithic batch (Börschinger and Johnson, 2012).

We show our approach's scalability and effective-

Transactions of the Association for Computational Linguistics, 2 (2014) 465–476. Action Editor: Kristina Toutanova.
Submitted 11/2013; Revised 5/2014; Revised 9/2014; Published 10/2014.

ness by applying our inference framework in Section 5 on two tasks: unsupervised word segmentation and infinite-vocabulary topic modeling.

2 Background

In this section, we review probabilistic context-free grammars and adaptor grammars.

2.1 Probabilistic Context-free Grammars

Probabilistic context-free grammars (PCFG) define probability distributions over derivations of a context-free grammar. We define a PCFG $\boldsymbol{\mathcal{G}}$ to be a tuple $\langle \boldsymbol{W}, \boldsymbol{N}, \boldsymbol{R}, S, \boldsymbol{\theta} \rangle$: a set of terminals $\boldsymbol{W}$, a set of nonterminals $\boldsymbol{N}$, productions $\boldsymbol{R}$, start symbol $S \in \boldsymbol{N}$ and a vector of rule probabilities $\boldsymbol{\theta}$. The rules that rewrite nonterminal c is $\boldsymbol{R}(c)$. For a more complete description of PCFGs, see Manning and Schütze (1999).

PCFGs typically use nonterminals with a syntactic interpretation. A sequence of terminals (the **yield**) is generated by recursively rewriting nonterminals as sequences of child symbols (either a nonterminal or a symbol). This builds a hierarchical **phrase-tree structure** for every yield.

For example, a nonterminal VP represents a verb phrase, which probabilistically rewrites into a sequence of nonterminals V, N (corresponding to verb and noun) using the production rule VP $\rightarrow$ V N. Both nonterminals can be further rewritten. Each nonterminal has a multinomial distribution over expansions; for example, a multinomial for nonterminal N would rewrite as "cake", with probability $\theta_{\mathrm{N}\rightarrow\mathrm{cake}} = 0.03$. Rewriting terminates when the derivation has reached a terminal symbol such as "cake" (which does not rewrite).

While PCFGs are used both in the supervised setting and in the unsupervised setting, in this paper we assume an unsupervised setting, in which only terminals are observed. Our goal is to predict the underlying phrase-structure tree.

2.2 Adaptor Grammars

PCFGs assume that the rewriting operations are independent given the nonterminal. This context-freeness assumption often is too strong for modeling natural language.

Adaptor grammars break this independence assumption by transforming a PCFG's distribution over trees G_c rooted at nonterminal c into a richer distribution H_c over the trees headed by a nonterminal c, which is often referred to as the *grammaton*.

Algorithm 1 Generative Process

1: For nonterminals $c \in \boldsymbol{N}$, draw rule probabilities $\boldsymbol{\theta}_c \sim \mathrm{Dir}(\boldsymbol{\alpha}_c)$ for PCFG $\boldsymbol{\mathcal{G}}$.
2: **for** adapted nonterminal c in $c_1, \ldots, c_{|\boldsymbol{M}|}$ **do**
3: Draw grammaton $H_c \sim \mathrm{PYGEM}(a_c, b_c, G_c)$ according to Equation 1, where G_c is defined by the PCFG rules $\boldsymbol{R}$.
4: For $i \in \{1, \ldots, D\}$, generate a phrase-structure tree $t_{S,i}$ using the PCFG rules $\boldsymbol{R}(e)$ at non-adapted nonterminal e and the grammatons H_c at adapted nonterminals c.
5: The yields of trees $t_1, \ldots, t_D$ are observations $x_1, \ldots, x_D$.

A *Pitman-Yor Adaptor grammar* (PYAG) forms the adapted tree distributions H_c using a *Pitman-Yor process* (Pitman and Yor, 1997, PY), a generalization of the Dirichlet process (Ferguson, 1973, DP).[1] A draw $H_c \equiv (\boldsymbol{\pi}_c, \boldsymbol{z}_c)$ is formed by the stick breaking process (Sudderth and Jordan, 2008, PYGEM) parametrized by scale parameter a, discount factor b, and base distribution G_c:

$$\begin{aligned} \pi'_k &\sim \mathrm{Beta}(1-b, a+kb), & z_k &\sim G_c, \\ \pi_k &\equiv \pi'_k \textstyle\prod_{j=1}^{k-1}(1-\pi'_j), & H &\equiv \textstyle\sum_k \pi_k \delta_{z_k}. \end{aligned} \quad (1)$$

Intuitively, the distribution H_c is a discrete reconstruction of the atoms sampled from G_c—hence, reweights G_c. Grammaton H_c assigns non-zero stick-breaking weights $\boldsymbol{\pi}$ to a countably infinite number of parse trees $\boldsymbol{z}$. We describe learning these grammatons in Section 3.

More formally, a PYAG is a quintuple $\boldsymbol{\mathcal{A}} = \langle \boldsymbol{\mathcal{G}}, \boldsymbol{M}, \boldsymbol{a}, \boldsymbol{b}, \boldsymbol{\alpha} \rangle$ with: a PCFG $\boldsymbol{\mathcal{G}}$; a set of adapted nonterminals $\boldsymbol{M} \subseteq \boldsymbol{N}$; Pitman-Yor process parameters a_c, b_c at each adaptor $c \in \boldsymbol{M}$ and Dirichlet parameters $\boldsymbol{\alpha}_c$ for each nonterminal $c \in \boldsymbol{N}$. We also assume an order on the adapted nonterminals, $c_1, \ldots, c_{|\boldsymbol{M}|}$ such that c_j is not reachable from c_i in a derivation if $j > i$.[2]

Algorithm 1 describes the generative process of an adaptor grammar on a set of D observed sentences $x_1, \ldots, x_D$.

[1] Adaptor grammars, in their general form, do not have to use the Pitman-Yor process but have only been used with the Pitman-Yor process.

[2] This is possible because we assume that recursive nonterminals are not adapted.

Given a PYAG $\mathcal{A}$, the joint probability for a set of sentences $\boldsymbol{X}$ and its collection of trees $\boldsymbol{T}$ is

$$p(\boldsymbol{X}, \boldsymbol{T}, \boldsymbol{\pi}, \boldsymbol{\theta}, \boldsymbol{z}|\mathcal{A}) = \prod_{c \in \boldsymbol{M}} p(\boldsymbol{\pi}_c|a_c, b_c) p(\boldsymbol{z}_c|G_c) \cdot \prod_{c \in \boldsymbol{N}} p(\boldsymbol{\theta}_c|\alpha_c) \prod_{x_d \in \boldsymbol{X}} p(x_d, t_d|\boldsymbol{\theta}, \boldsymbol{\pi}, \boldsymbol{z}),$$

where x_d and t_d represent the dth observed string and its corresponding parse. The multinomial PCFG parameter $\boldsymbol{\theta}_c$ is drawn from a Dirichlet distribution at nonterminal $c \in \boldsymbol{N}$. At each adapted nonterminal $c \in \boldsymbol{M}$, the stick-breaking weights $\boldsymbol{\pi}_c$ are drawn from a PYGEM (Equation 1). Each weight has an associated atom $z_{c,i}$ from base distribution G_c, a subtree rooted at c. The probability $p(x_d, t_d \mid \boldsymbol{\theta}, \boldsymbol{\pi}, \boldsymbol{z})$ is the PCFG likelihood of yield x_d with parse tree t_d.

Adaptor grammars require a base PCFG such that it does not have recursive adapted nonterminals, i.e., there cannot be a path in a derivation from a given adapted nonterminal to a second appearance of that adapted nonterminal.

3 Hybrid Variational-MCMC Inference

Discovering the latent variables of the model—trees, adapted probabilities, and PCFG rules—is a problem of posterior inference given observed data. Previous approaches use MCMC (Johnson et al., 2006) or variational inference (Cohen et al., 2010).

MCMC discovers the support of nonparametric models during the inference, but does not scale to larger datasets (due to tight coupling of variables). Variational inference, however, is inherently parallel and easily amendable to online inference, but requires preprocessing to discover the adapted productions. We combine the best of both worlds and propose a hybrid variational-MCMC inference algorithm for adaptor grammars.

Variational inference posits a variational distribution over the latent variables in the model; this in turn induces an "evidence lower bound" (ELBO, $\mathcal{L}$) as a function of a variational distribution q, a lower bound on the marginal log-likelihood. Variational inference optimizes this objective function with respect to the parameters that define q.

In this section, we derive coordinate-ascent updates for these variational parameters. A key mathematical component is taking expectations with respect to the variational distribution q. We strategically use MCMC sampling to compute the expectation of q *over parse trees* z. Instead of explicitly computing the variational distribution for all parameters, one can sample from it. This produces a sparse approximation of the variational distribution, which improves both scalability and performance. Sparse distributions are easier to store and transmit in implementations, which improves scalability. Mimno et al. (2012) also show that sparse representations improve performance. Moreover, because it can flexibly adjust its support, it is a necessary prerequisite to online inference (Section 4).

3.1 Variational Lower Bound

We posit a mean-field variational distribution:

$$q(\boldsymbol{\pi}, \boldsymbol{\theta}, \boldsymbol{T}|\gamma, \boldsymbol{\nu}, \boldsymbol{\phi}) = \prod_{c \in \boldsymbol{M}} \prod_{i=1}^{\infty} q(\pi'_{c,i}|\nu^1_{c,i}, \nu^2_{c,i}) \cdot \prod_{c \in \boldsymbol{N}} q(\boldsymbol{\theta}_c|\gamma_c) \prod_{x_d \in \boldsymbol{X}} q(t_d|\boldsymbol{\phi}_d), \tag{2}$$

where $\pi'_{c,i}$ is drawn from a variational Beta distribution parameterized by $\nu^1_{c,i}, \nu^2_{c,i}$; and $\boldsymbol{\theta}_c$ is from a variational Dirichlet prior $\boldsymbol{\gamma}_c \in \mathbb{R}_+^{|\boldsymbol{R}(c)|}$. Index i ranges over a possibly infinite number of adapted rules. The parse for the dth observation, t_d is modeled by a multinomial $\boldsymbol{\phi}_d$, where $\phi_{d,i}$ is the probability generating the ith phrase-structure tree $t_{d,i}$.

The variational distribution over latent variables induces the following ELBO on the likelihood:

$$\begin{aligned}\mathcal{L}(\boldsymbol{z}, \boldsymbol{\pi}, \boldsymbol{\theta}, \boldsymbol{T}, \boldsymbol{D}; \boldsymbol{a}, \boldsymbol{b}, \boldsymbol{\alpha}) &= H[q(\boldsymbol{\theta}, \boldsymbol{\pi}, \boldsymbol{T})] \\ &+ \textstyle\sum_{c \in \boldsymbol{N}} \mathbb{E}_q[\log p(\boldsymbol{\theta}_c|\boldsymbol{\alpha}_c)] \qquad (3) \\ &+ \textstyle\sum_{c \in \boldsymbol{M}} \sum_{i=1}^{\infty} \mathbb{E}_q[\log p(\pi'_{c,i}|a_c, b_c)] \\ &+ \textstyle\sum_{c \in \boldsymbol{M}} \sum_{i=1}^{\infty} \mathbb{E}_q[\log p(z_{c,i} \mid \boldsymbol{\pi}, \boldsymbol{\theta})] \\ &+ \textstyle\sum_{x_d \in \boldsymbol{X}} \mathbb{E}_q[\log p(x_d, t_d \mid \boldsymbol{\pi}, \boldsymbol{\theta}, \boldsymbol{z})],\end{aligned}$$

where $H[\bullet]$ is the entropy function.

To make this lower bound tractable, we truncate the distribution over π to a finite set (Blei and Jordan, 2005) for each adapted nonterminal $c \in \boldsymbol{M}$, i.e., $\pi'_{c,K_c} \equiv 1$ for some index K_c. Because the atom weights π_k are deterministically defined by Equation 1, this implies that $\pi_{c,i}$ is zero beyond index K_c. Each weight $\pi_{c,i}$ is associated with an atom $z_{c,i}$, a subtree rooted at c. We call the ordered set of $z_{c,i}$ the *truncated nonterminal grammaton* (TNG). Each adapted nonterminal $c \in \boldsymbol{M}$ has its own TNG_c. The ith subtree in TNG_c is denoted $\text{TNG}_c(i)$.

In the rest of this section, we describe approximate inference to maximize $\mathcal{L}$. The most important update is $\phi_{d,i}$, which we update using stochastic MCMC inference (Section 3.2). Past variational approaches for adaptor grammars (Cohen et al., 2010) rely on a preprocessing step and heuristics to define a *static* TNG. In contrast, our model dynamically discovers trees. The TNG grows as the model sees more data, allowing online updates (Section 4).

The remaining variational parameters are optimized using expected counts of adaptor grammar rules. These expected counts are described in Section 3.3, and the variational updates for the variational parameters excluding $\phi_{d,i}$ are described in Section 3.4.

3.2 Stochastic MCMC Inference

Each observation x_d has an associated variational multinomial distribution $\boldsymbol{\phi}_d$ over trees $\boldsymbol{t}_d$ that can yield observation x_d with probability $\phi_{d,i}$. Holding all other variational parameters fixed, the coordinate-ascent update (Mimno et al., 2012; Bishop, 2006) for $\phi_{d,i}$ is

$$\phi_{d,i} \propto \exp\{\mathbb{E}_q^{\neg\phi_d}[\log p(t_{d,i}|x_d, \boldsymbol{\pi}, \boldsymbol{\theta}, \boldsymbol{z})]\}, \quad (4)$$

where $\phi_{d,i}$ is the probability generating the ith phrase-structure tree $t_{d,i}$ and $\mathbb{E}_q^{\neg\phi_d}[\bullet]$ is the expectation with respect to the variational distribution q, excluding the value of $\boldsymbol{\phi}_d$.

Instead of computing this expectation explicitly, we turn to stochastic variational inference (Mimno et al., 2012; Hoffman et al., 2013) to sample from this distribution. This produces a set of sampled trees $\boldsymbol{\sigma}_d \equiv \{\sigma_{d,1}, \ldots, \sigma_{d,k}\}$. From this set of trees we can approximate our variational distribution over trees $\boldsymbol{\phi}$ using the empirical distribution $\boldsymbol{\sigma}_d$, i.e.,

$$\phi_{d,i} \propto \mathbb{I}[\sigma_{d,j} = t_{d,i}, \forall \sigma_{d,j} \in \boldsymbol{\sigma}_d]. \quad (5)$$

This leads to a sparse approximation of variational distribution $\boldsymbol{\phi}$.[3]

Previous inference strategies (Johnson et al., 2006; Börschinger and Johnson, 2012) for adaptor grammars have used sampling. The adaptor grammar inference methods use an approximate PCFG to emulate the marginalized Pitman-Yor distributions at each nonterminal. Given this approximate PCFG, we can then sample a derivation z for string x from the possible trees (Johnson et al., 2007).

Sampling requires a derived PCFG $\boldsymbol{\mathcal{G}'}$ that approximates the distribution over tree derivations conditioned on a yield. It includes the original PCFG rules $\boldsymbol{R} = \{c \rightarrow \beta\}$ that define the base distribution and the new adapted productions $\boldsymbol{R'} = \{c \Rightarrow z, z \in \text{TNG}_c\}$. Under $\boldsymbol{\mathcal{G}'}$, the probability θ' of adapted production $c \Rightarrow z$ is

$$\log \theta'_{c\Rightarrow z} = \begin{cases} \mathbb{E}_q[\log \pi_{c,i}], & \text{if } \text{TNG}_c(i) = z \\ \mathbb{E}_q[\log \pi_{c,K_c}] + \mathbb{E}_q[\log \theta_{c\Rightarrow z}], & \\ \quad \text{otherwise} & \end{cases} \quad (6)$$

where K_c is the truncation level of TNG_c and π_{c,K_c} represents the left-over stick weights in the stick-breaking process for adaptor $c \in \boldsymbol{M}$. $\theta_{c\Rightarrow z}$ represents the probability of generating tree $c \Rightarrow z$ under the base distribution. See also Cohen (2011).

The expectation of the Pitman-Yor multinomial $\pi_{c,i}$ under the truncated variational stick-breaking distribution is

$$\begin{aligned} \mathbb{E}_q[\log \pi_{a,i}] &= \Psi(\nu^1_{a,i}) - \Psi(\nu^1_{a,i} + \nu^2_{a,i}) \quad (7) \\ &+ \textstyle\sum_{j=1}^{i-1}(\Psi(\nu^2_{a,j}) - \Psi(\nu^1_{a,j} + \nu^2_{a,j})), \end{aligned}$$

and the expectation of generating the phrase-structure tree $a \Rightarrow z$ based on PCFG productions under the variational Dirichlet distribution is

$$\begin{aligned} \mathbb{E}_q[\log \theta_{a\Rightarrow z}] = \textstyle\sum_{c\rightarrow\beta\in a\Rightarrow z} \big(\Psi(\gamma_{c\rightarrow\beta}) \quad (8) \\ - \Psi(\textstyle\sum_{c\rightarrow\beta'\in \boldsymbol{R}_c} \gamma_{c\rightarrow\beta'})\big) \end{aligned}$$

where $\Psi(\bullet)$ is the digamma function, and $c \rightarrow \beta \in a \Rightarrow z$ represents all PCFG productions in the phrase-structure tree $a \Rightarrow z$.

This PCFG can compose arbitrary subtrees and thus discover new trees that better describe the data, even if those trees are not part of the TNG. This is equivalent to creating a "new table" in MCMC inference and provides *truncation-free* variational updates (Wang and Blei, 2012) by sampling a unseen subtree with adapted nonterminal $c \in \boldsymbol{M}$ at the root. This frees our model from preprocessing to initialize truncated grammatons in Cohen et al. (2010). This stochastic approach has the advantage of creating sparse distributions (Wang and Blei, 2012): few unique trees will be represented.

[3] In our experiments, we use ten samples.

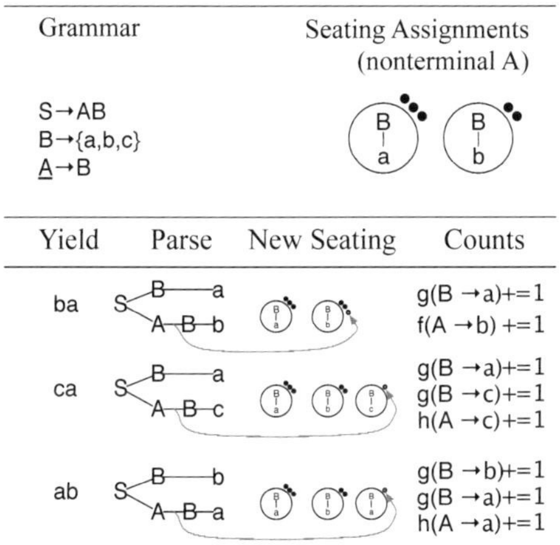

Figure 1: Given an adaptor grammar, we sample derivations given an approximate PCFG and show how these affect counts. The sampled derivations can be understood via the Chinese restaurant metaphor (Johnson et al., 2006). Existing cached rules (elements in the TNG) can be thought of as occupied tables; this happens in the case of the yield "ba", which increases counts for unadapted rules g and for entries in TNG_A, f. For the yield "ca", there is no appropriate entry in the TNG, so it must use the base distribution, which corresponds to sitting at a new table. This generates counts for g, as it uses the unadapted rule and for h, which represents entries that could be included in the TNG in the future. The final yield, "ab", shows that even when compatible entries are in the TNG, it might still create a new table, changing the underlying base distribution.

Parallelization As noted in Cohen et al. (2010), the *inside-outside* algorithm dominates the runtime of every iteration, both for sampling and variational inference. However, unlike MCMC, variational inference is highly parallelizable and requires fewer synchronizations per iteration (Zhai et al., 2012). In our approach, both inside algorithms and sampling process can be distributed, and those counts can be aggregated afterwards. In our implementation, we use multiple threads to parallelize tree sampling.

3.3 Calculating Expected Rule Counts

For every observation x_d, the hybrid approach produces a set of sampled trees, each of which contains three types of productions: adapted rules, original PCFG rules, and potentially adapted rules. The last set is most important, as these are new rules discovered by the sampler. These are explained using the Chinese restaurant metaphor in Figure 1. The multiset of all adapted productions is $M(t_{d,i})$ and the multiset of non-adapted productions that generate tree $t_{d,i}$ is $N(t_{d,i})$. We compute three counts:

1: f is the expected number of productions within the TNG. It is the sum over the probability of a tree $t_{d,k}$ times the number of times an *adapted* production appeared in $t_{d,k}$, $f_d(a \Rightarrow z_{a,i}) =$

$$\sum_k \big(\phi_{d,k} \underbrace{|a \Rightarrow z_{a,i} : a \Rightarrow z_{a,i} \in M(t_{d,k})|}_{\text{count of rule } a \Rightarrow z_{a,i} \text{ in tree } t_{d,k}}\big).$$

2: g is the expected counts of PCFG productions $\boldsymbol{R}$ that defines the *base* distribution of the adaptor grammar, $g_d(a \to \beta) =$

$$\sum_k \left(\phi_{d,k} \, |a \to \beta : a \to \beta \in N(t_{d,k})|\right).$$

3: Finally, a third set of productions are newly discovered by the sampler and not in the TNG. These subtrees are rules that *could be adapted*, with expected counts $h_d(c \Rightarrow z_{c,i}) =$

$$\sum_k \left(\phi_{d,k} \, |c \Rightarrow z_{c,i} : c \Rightarrow z_{c,i} \notin M(t_{d,k})|\right).$$

These subtrees—lists of PCFG rules sampled from Equation 6—correspond to adapted productions not yet present in the TNG.

3.4 Variational Updates

Given the sparse vectors ϕ sampled from the hybrid MCMC step, we update all variational parameters as

$$\begin{aligned}
\gamma_{a\to\beta} =& \alpha_{a\to\beta} + \textstyle\sum_{x_d \in \boldsymbol{X}} g_d(a \to \beta) \\
&+ \textstyle\sum_{b \in \boldsymbol{M}} \sum_{i=1}^{K_b} n(a \to \beta, z_{b,i}), \\
\nu^1_{a,i} =& 1 - b_a + \textstyle\sum_{x_d \in \boldsymbol{X}} f_d(a \Rightarrow z_{a,i}) \\
&+ \textstyle\sum_{b \in \boldsymbol{M}} \sum_{k=1}^{K_b} n(a \Rightarrow z_{a,i}, z_{b,k}), \\
\nu^2_{a,i} =& a_a + i b_a + \textstyle\sum_{x_d \in \boldsymbol{X}} \sum_{j=1}^{K_a} f_d(a \Rightarrow z_{a,j}) \\
&+ \textstyle\sum_{b \in \boldsymbol{M}} \sum_{k=1}^{K_b} \sum_{j=1}^{K_a} n(a \Rightarrow z_{a,j}, z_{b,k}),
\end{aligned}$$

where $n(r, t)$ is the expected number of times production r is in tree t, estimated during sampling.

Hyperparameter Update We update our PCFG hyperparameter $\boldsymbol{\alpha}$, PYGEM hyperparameters $\boldsymbol{a}$ and $\boldsymbol{b}$ as in Cohen et al. (2010).

4 Online Variational Inference

Online inference for probabilistic models requires us to update our posterior distribution as new observations arrive. Unlike batch inference algorithms, we do not assume we always have access to the entire dataset. Instead, we assume that observations arrive in small groups called *minibatches*. The advantage of online inference is threefold: a) it does not require retaining the whole dataset in memory; b) each online update is fast; and c) the model usually converges faster. All of these make adaptor grammars scalable to larger datasets.

Our approach is based on the stochastic variational inference for topic models (Hoffman et al., 2013). This inference strategy uses a form of stochastic gradient descent (Bottou, 1998): using the gradient of the ELBO, it finds the sufficient statistics necessary to update variational parameters (which are mostly expected counts calculated using the inside-outside algorithm), and interpolates the result with the current model.

We assume data arrive in minibatches $\boldsymbol{B}$ (a set of sentences). We accumulate expected counts

$$\begin{aligned}\tilde{f}^{(l)}(a \Rightarrow z_{a,i}) =& (1-\epsilon)\cdot \tilde{f}^{(l-1)}(a \Rightarrow z_{a,i}) \quad (9)\\ &+ \epsilon \cdot \tfrac{|\boldsymbol{X}|}{|\boldsymbol{B}_l|} \textstyle\sum_{x_d \in \boldsymbol{B}_l} f_d(a \Rightarrow z_{a,i}),\\ \tilde{g}^{(l)}(a \rightarrow \beta) =& (1-\epsilon)\cdot \tilde{g}^{(l-1)}(a \rightarrow \beta) \quad (10)\\ &+ \epsilon \cdot \tfrac{|\boldsymbol{X}|}{|\boldsymbol{B}_l|} \textstyle\sum_{x_d \in \boldsymbol{B}_l} g_d(a \rightarrow \beta),\end{aligned}$$

with *decay factor* $\epsilon \in (0,1)$ to guarantee convergence. We set it to $\epsilon = (\tau + l)^{-\kappa}$, where l is the minibatch counter. The *decay inertia* τ prevents premature convergence, and *decay rate* κ controls the speed of change in sufficient statistics (Hoffman et al., 2010). We recover batch variational approach when $\boldsymbol{B} = \boldsymbol{D}$ and $\kappa = 0$.

The variables $\tilde{f}^{(l)}$ and $\tilde{g}^{(l)}$ are accumulated sufficient statistics of adapted and unadapted productions after processing minibatch $\boldsymbol{B}_l$. They update the approximate gradient. The updates for variational parameters become

$$\begin{aligned}\gamma_{a\rightarrow\beta} =& \alpha_{a\rightarrow\beta} + \tilde{g}^{(l)}(a \rightarrow \beta) \quad (11)\\ &+ \textstyle\sum_{b\in \boldsymbol{M}} \sum_{i=1}^{K_b} n(a \rightarrow \beta, z_{b,i}),\\ \nu^1_{a,i} =& 1 - b_a + \tilde{f}^{(l)}(a \Rightarrow z_{a,i}) \quad (12)\\ &+ \textstyle\sum_{b\in \boldsymbol{M}} \sum_{k=1}^{K_b} n(a \Rightarrow z_{a,i}, z_{b,k}),\\ \nu^2_{a,i} =& a_a + ib_a + \textstyle\sum_{j=1}^{K_a} \tilde{f}^{(l)}(a \Rightarrow z_{a,j}) \quad (13)\\ &+ \textstyle\sum_{b\in \boldsymbol{M}} \sum_{k=1}^{K_b} \sum_{j=1}^{K_a} n(a \Rightarrow z_{a,j}, z_{b,k}),\end{aligned}$$

where K_a is the size of the TNG at adaptor $a \in \boldsymbol{M}$.

4.1 Refining the Truncation

As we observe more data during inference, our TNGs need to change. New rules should be added, useless rules should be removed, and derivations for existing rules should be updated. In this section, we describe heuristics for performing each of these operations.

Adding Productions Sampling can identify productions that are not adapted but were instead drawn from the base distribution. These are candidates for the TNG. For every nonterminal a, we add these potentially adapted productions to TNG$_a$ after each minibatch. The count associated with candidate productions is now associated with an adapted production, i.e., the h count contributes to the relevant f count. This mechanism dynamically expands TNG$_a$.

Sorting and Removing Productions Our model does not require a preprocessing step to initialize the TNGs, rather, it constructs and expands all TNGs on the fly. To prevent the TNG from growing unwieldy, we prune TNG after every u minibatches. As a result, we need to impose an ordering over all the parse trees in the TNG. The underlying PYGEM distribution implicitly places an ranking over all the atoms according to their corresponding sufficient statistics (Kurihara et al., 2007), as shown in Equation 9. It measures the "usefulness" of every adapted production throughout inference process.

In addition to accumulated sufficient statistics, Cohen et al. (2010) add a secondary term to discourage short constituents (Mochihashi et al., 2009). We impose a reward term for longer phrases in addition to $\tilde{f}$ and sort all adapted productions in TNG$_a$ using the ranking score

$$\Lambda(a \Rightarrow z_{a,i}) = \tilde{f}^{(l)}(a \Rightarrow z_{a,i}) \cdot \log(\epsilon \cdot |s| + 1),$$

where $|s|$ is the number of yields in production $a \Rightarrow z_{a,i}$. Because ϵ decreases each minibatch, the reward for long phrases diminishes. This is similar to an annealed version of Cohen et al. (2010)—where the reward for long phrases is fixed, see also Mochihashi et al. (2009). After sorting, we remove all but the top K_a adapted productions.

Rederiving Adapted Productions For MCMC inference, Johnson and Goldwater (2009) observe that atoms already associated with a yield may have trees

Algorithm 2 Online inference for adaptor grammars

Random initialize all variational parameters.
for minibatch of $l = 1, 2, \ldots$ **do**
  Construct approximate PCFG $\boldsymbol{\theta}'$ of $\boldsymbol{\mathcal{A}}$ (Equation 6).
  for input sentence $d = 1, 2, \ldots, D_l$ **do**
    Accumulate inside probabilities from approximate PCFG $\boldsymbol{\theta}'$.
    Sample phrase-structure trees $\boldsymbol{\sigma}$ and update the tree distribution $\boldsymbol{\phi}$ (Equation 5).
  For every adapted nonterminal c, append adapted productions to TNG_c.
  Accumulate sufficient statistics (Equations 9 and 10).
  Update $\boldsymbol{\gamma}$, $\boldsymbol{\nu}^1$, and $\boldsymbol{\nu}^2$ (Equations 11-13).
Refine and prune the truncation every u minibatches.

that do not explain their yield well. They propose *table label resampling* to rederive yields.

In our approach this is equivalent to "mutating" some derivations in a TNG. After pruning rules every u minibatches, we perform table label resampling for adapted nonterminals from general to specific (i.e., a topological sort). This provides better expected counts $n(r, \bullet)$ for rules used in phrase-structure subtrees. Empirically, we find table label resampling only marginally improves the word-segmentation result.

Initialization Our inference begins with random variational Dirichlets and empty TNGs, which obviates the preprocessing step in Cohen et al. (2010). Our model constructs and expands all TNGs on the fly. It mimics the *incremental initialization* of Johnson and Goldwater (2009). Algorithm 2 summarizes the pseudo-code of our online approach.

4.2 Complexity

Inside and outside calls dominate execution time for adaptor grammar inference. Variational approaches compute inside-outside algorithms and estimate the expected counts for every possible tree derivation (Cohen et al., 2010). For a dataset with D observations, variational inference requires $O(DI)$ calls to *inside-outside* algorithm, where I is the number of iterations, typically in the tens.

In contrast, MCMC only needs to accumulate inside probabilities, and then sample a tree derivation (Chappelier and Rajman, 2000). The sampling step is negligible in processing time compared to the inside algorithm. MCMC inference requires $O(DI)$ calls to the *inside* algorithm—hence every iteration

collocation		SENT ↦ COLLOC	*InfVoc LDA*	SENT ↦ DOC_j
		SENT ↦ COLLOC SENT		j=1, 2, ...D
		COLLOC ↦ WORDS		$\text{DOC}_j \mapsto {}_{-j}\ \text{TOPIC}_i$
	unigram	WORDS ↦ WORD		i=1, 2, ...K
		WORDS ↦ WORD WORDS		TOPIC_i ↦ WORD
		WORD ↦ CHARS		WORD ↦ CHARS
		CHARS ↦ CHAR		CHARS ↦ CHAR
		CHARS ↦ CHAR CHARS		CHARS ↦ CHAR CHARS
		CHAR ↦ ⋆		CHAR ↦ ⋆

Table 1: Grammars used in our experiments. The nonterminal CHAR is a non-adapted rule that expands to all characters used in the data, sometimes called *pre-terminals*. Adapted nonterminals are underlined. For the *unigram* grammar, only nonterminal WORD is adapted; whereas for the *collocation* grammar, both nonterminals WORD and COLLOC are adapted. For the INFVOC LDA grammar, D is the total number of documents and K is the number of topics. Therefore, j ranges over $\{1, \ldots, D\}$ and i ranges over $\{1, \ldots, K\}$.

is much faster than variational approach—but I is usually on the order of thousands.

Likewise, our hybrid approach also only needs the less expensive inside algorithm to sample trees. And while each iteration is less expensive, our approach can achieve reasonable results with only a single pass through the data. And thus only requires $O(D)$ calls to the *inside* algorithm.

Because the inside-outside algorithm is fundamental to each of these algorithms, we use it as a common basis for comparison across different implementations. This is over-generous to variational approaches, as the full inside-outside computation is more expensive than the inside algorithm required for sampling in MCMC and our hybrid approach.

5 Experiments and Discussion

We implement our online adaptor grammar model (ONLINE) in Python[4] and compare it against both MCMC (Johnson and Goldwater, 2009, MCMC) and the variational inference (Cohen et al., 2010, VARIATIONAL). We use the latest implementation of MCMC sampler for adaptor grammars[5] and simulate the variational approach using our implementation. For MCMC approach, we use the best settings reported in Johnson and Goldwater (2009) with *incremental initialization* and *table label resampling*.

[4]Available at http://www.umiacs.umd.edu/~zhaike/.

[5]http://web.science.mq.edu.au/~mjohnson/code/py-cfg-2013-02-25.tgz

Model and Settings			*ctb7*		*pku*		*cityu*	
			unigram	*collocation*	*unigram*	*collocation*	*unigram*	*collocation*
MCMC	500 iter		72.70 (2.81)	50.53 (2.82)	72.01 (2.82)	49.06 (2.81)	74.19 (3.55)	63.14 (3.53)
MCMC	1000 iter		72.65 (2.83)	62.27 (2.79)	71.81 (2.81)	62.47 (2.77)	74.37 (3.54)	70.62 (3.51)
MCMC	1500 iter		72.17 (2.80)	69.65 (2.77)	71.46 (2.80)	70.20 (2.73)	74.22 (3.54)	72.33 (3.50)
MCMC	2000 iter		71.75 (2.79)	71.66 (2.76)	71.04 (2.79)	72.55 (2.70)	74.01 (3.53)	73.15 (3.48)
ONLINE	κ	τ	$K_{\text{Word}} = 30k$	$K_{\text{Colloc}} = 100k$	$K_{\text{Word}} = 40k$	$K_{\text{Colloc}} = 120k$	$K_{\text{Word}} = 50k$	$K_{\text{Colloc}} = 150K$
ONLINE	0.6	32	70.17 (2.84)	68.43 (2.77)	69.93 (2.89)	68.09 (2.71)	72.59 (3.62)	69.27 (3.61)
ONLINE	0.6	128	72.98 (2.72)	65.20 (2.81)	72.26 (2.63)	65.57 (2.83)	74.73 (3.40)	64.83 (3.62)
ONLINE	0.6	512	72.76 (2.78)	56.05 (2.85)	71.99 (2.74)	58.94 (2.94)	73.68 (3.60)	60.40 (3.70)
ONLINE	0.8	32	71.10 (2.77)	70.84 (2.76)	70.31 (2.78)	70.91 (2.71)	73.12 (3.60)	71.89 (3.50)
ONLINE	0.8	128	72.79 (2.64)	70.93 (2.63)	72.08 (2.62)	72.02 (2.63)	74.62 (3.45)	72.28 (3.51)
ONLINE	0.8	512	72.82 (2.58)	68.53 (2.76)	72.14 (2.58)	70.07 (2.69)	74.71 (3.37)	72.58 (3.49)
ONLINE	1.0	32	69.98 (2.87)	70.71 (2.63)	69.42 (2.84)	71.45 (2.67)	73.18 (3.59)	72.42 (3.45)
ONLINE	1.0	128	71.84 (2.72)	71.29 (2.58)	71.29 (2.67)	72.56 (2.61)	73.23 (3.39)	72.61 (3.41)
ONLINE	1.0	512	72.68 (2.62)	70.67 (2.60)	71.86 (2.63)	71.39 (2.66)	74.45 (3.41)	72.88 (3.38)
VARIATIONAL			69.83 (2.85)	67.78 (2.75)	67.82 (2.80)	66.97 (2.75)	70.47 (3.72)	69.06 (3.69)

Table 2: Word segmentation accuracy measured by word token F_1 scores and negative log-likelihood on held-out test dataset in the brackets (lower the better, on the scale of 10^6) for our ONLINE model against MCMC approach (Johnson et al., 2006) on various dataset using the *unigram* and *collocation* grammar.[7]

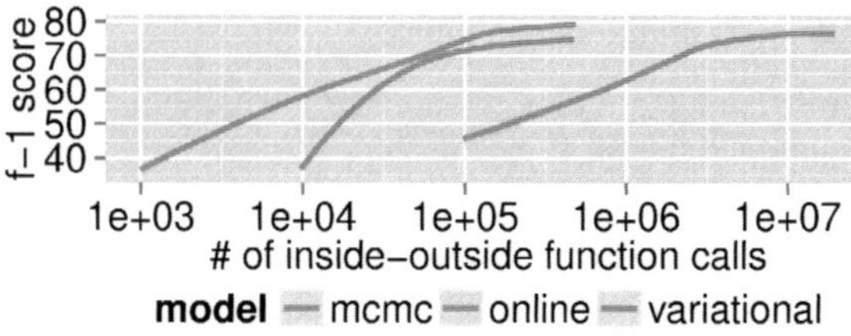

(a) *unigram* grammar.

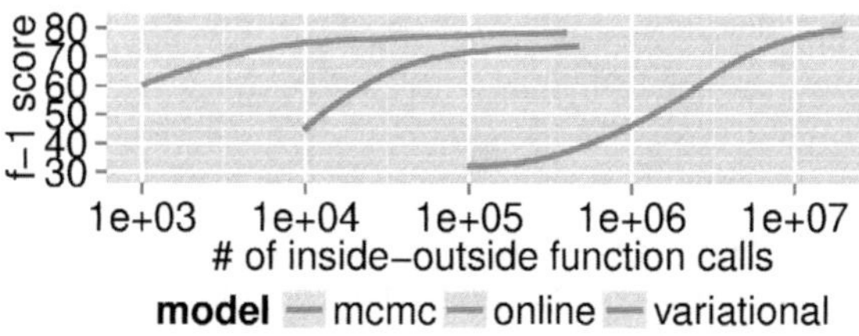

(b) *collocation* grammar.

Figure 2: Word segmentation accuracy measured by word token F_1 scores on *brent* corpus of three approaches against number of inside-outside function call using *unigram* (upper) and *collocation* (lower) grammars in Table 1.[6]

[6]Our ONLINE settings are batch size $B = 20$, decay inertia $\tau = 128$, decay rate $\kappa = 0.6$ for *unigram* grammar; and minibatch size $B = 5$, decay inertia $\tau = 256$, decay rate $\kappa = 0.8$ for *collocation* grammar. TNGs are refined at interval $u = 50$. Truncation size is set to $K_{\text{Word}} = 1.5k$ and $K_{\text{Colloc}} = 3k$. The settings are chosen from cross validation. We observe similar behavior under $\kappa = \{0.7, 0.9, 1.0\}$, $\tau = \{32, 64, 512\}$, $B = \{10, 50\}$ and $u = \{10, 20, 100\}$.

[7]For ONLINE inference, we parallelize each minibatch with four threads with settings: batch size $B = 100$ and TNG refinement interval $u = 100$. ONLINE approach runns for two passes over datasets. VARIATIONAL runs fifty iterations, with the same truncation level as in ONLINE. For negative log-likelihood evaluation, we train the model on a random 70% of the data, and hold out the rest for testing. We observe similar behavior for our model under $\kappa = \{0.7, 0.9\}$ and $\tau = \{64, 256\}$.

5.1 Word Segmentation

We evaluate our online adaptor grammar on the task of word segmentation, which focuses on identifying word boundaries from a sequence of characters. This is especially the case for Chinese, since characters are written in sequence without word boundaries.

We first evaluate all three models on the standard Brent version of the Bernstein-Ratner corpus (Bernstein-Ratner, 1987; Brent and Cartwright, 1996, *brent*). The dataset contains $10k$ sentences, $1.3k$ distinct words, and 72 distinct characters. We compare the results on both *unigram* and *collocation* grammars introduced in Johnson and Goldwater (2009) as listed in Table 1.

Figure 2 illustrates the word segmentation accuracy in terms of word token F_1-scores on *brent* against the number of inside-outside function calls for all three approaches using *unigram* and *collocation* grammars. In both cases, our ONLINE approach converges faster than MCMC and VARIATIONAL approaches, yet yields comparable or better performance when seeing more data.

In addition to the *brent* corpus, we also evaluate three approaches on three other Chinese datasets compiled by Xue et al. (2005) and Emerson (2005):[8]

- Chinese Treebank 7.0 (*ctb7*): $162k$ sentences, $57k$ distinct words, $4.5k$ distinct characters;

[8]We use all punctuation as natural delimiters (i.e., words cannot cross punctuation).

- Peking University (*pku*): $183k$ sentences, $53k$ distinct words, $4.6k$ distinct characters; and
- City University of Hong Kong (*cityu*): $207k$ sentences, $64k$ distinct words, and $5k$ distinct characters.

We compare our inference method against other approaches on F_1 score. While other unsupervised word segmentation systems are available (Mochihashi et al. (2009), inter alia),[9] our focus is on a direct comparison of inference techniques for adaptor grammar, which achieve competitive (if not state-of-the-art) performance.

Table 2 shows the word token F_1-scores and negative likelihood on held-out test dataset of our model against MCMC and VARIATIONAL. We randomly sample 30% of the data for testing and the rest for training. We compute the held-out likelihood of the most likely sampled parse trees out of each model.[10] Our ONLINE approach consistently better segments words than VARIATIONAL and achieves comparable or better results than MCMC.

For MCMC, Johnson and Goldwater (2009) show that *incremental initialization*—or online updates in general—results in more accurate word segmentation, even though the trees have lower posterior probability. Similarly, our ONLINE approach initializes and learns them on the fly, instead of initializing the grammatons and parse trees for all data upfront as for VARIATIONAL. This uniformly outperforms batch initialization on the word segmentation tasks.

5.2 Infinite Vocabulary Topic Modeling

Topic models often can be replicated using a carefully crafted PCFG (Johnson, 2010). These powerful extensions can capture topical collocations and sticky topics; these embelishments could further improve NLP applications of simple unigram topic models such as word sense disambiguation (Boyd-Graber and Blei, 2007), part of speech tagging (Toutanova and Johnson, 2008) or dialogue modeling (Zhai and Williams, 2014). However, expressing topic models in adaptor grammars is much slower than traditional topic models, for which fast online inference (Hoffman et al., 2010) is available.

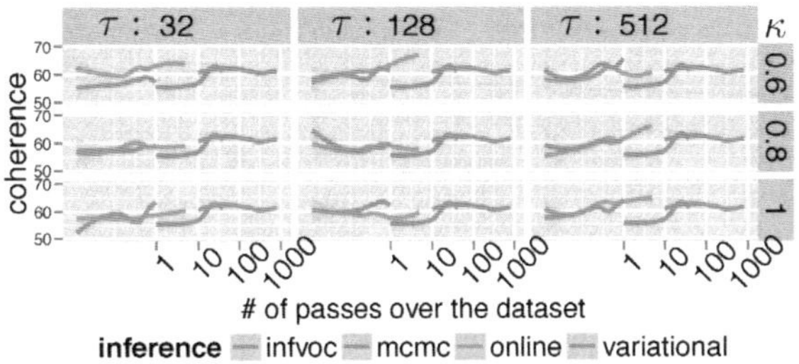

Figure 3: The average coherence score of topics on *de-news* datasets against INFVOC approach and other inference techniques (MCMC, VARIATIONAL) under different settings of decay rate κ and decay inertia τ using the *InfVoc LDA* grammar in Table 1. The horizontal axis shows the number of passes over the entire dataset.[11]

Zhai and Boyd-Graber (2013) argue that online inference and topic models violate a fundamental assumption in online algorithms: new words are introduced as more data are streamed to the algorithm. Zhai and Boyd-Graber (2013) then introduce an inference framework, INFVOC, to discover words from a Dirichlet process with a character n-gram base distribution.

We show that their complicated model and online inference can be captured and extended via an appropriate PCFG grammar and our online adaptor grammar inference algorithm. Our extension to INFVOC generalizes their static character n-gram model, learning the base distribution (i.e., how words are composed from characters) from data. In contrast, their base distribution was learned from a dictionary as a preprocessing step and held fixed.

This is an attractive testbed for our online inference. Within a topic, we can verify that the words we discover are relevant to the topic and that new words rise in importance in the topic over time if they are relevant. For these experiments, we treat each token (with its associated document pseudo-word $_{-j}$) as a single sentence, and each minibatch contains only one sentence (token).

[9]Their results are not directly comparable: they use different subsets and assume different preprocessing.

[10]Note that this is only an approximation to the true held-out likelihood, since it is impossible to enumerate all the possible parse trees and hence compute the likelihood for a given sentence under the model.

[11]We train all models with 5 topics with settings: TNG refinement interval $u = 100$, truncation size $K_{\text{Topic}} = 3k$, and the mini-batch size $B = 50$. We observe a similar behavior under $\kappa \in \{0.7, 0.9\}$ and $\tau \in \{64, 256\}$.

[12]The plot is generated with truncation size $K_{\text{Topic}} = 2k$, mini-batch size $B = 1$, truncation pruning interval $u = 50$, decay inertia $\tau = 256$, and decay rate $\kappa = 0.8$. All PY hyperparameters are optimized.

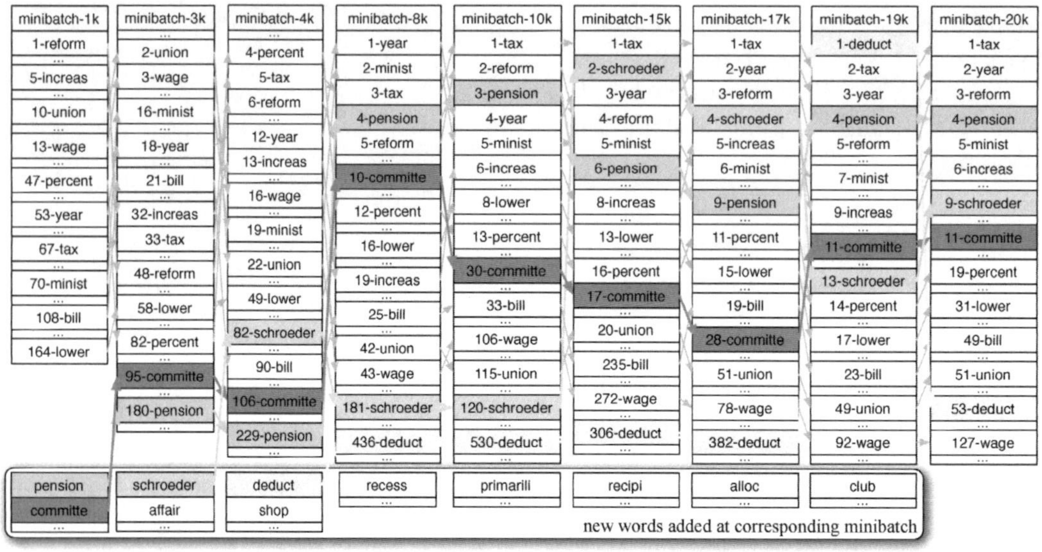

Figure 4: The evolution of one topic—concerning tax policy—out of five topics learned using online adaptor grammar inference on the *de-news* dataset. Each minibatch represents a word processed by this online algorithm; time progresses from left to right. As the algorithm encounters new words (bottom) they can make their way into the topic. The numbers next to words represent their overall rank in the topic. For example, the word "pension" first appeared in mini-batch 100, was ranked at 229 after minibatch 400 and became one of the top 10 words in this topic after 2000 minibatches (tokens).[12]

Quantitatively, we evaluate three different inference schemes and the INFVOC approach[13] on a collection of English daily news snippets (*de-news*).[14] We used the *InfVoc LDA* grammar (Table 1). For all approaches, we train the model with five topics, and evaluate topic coherence (Newman et al., 2009), which correlates well with human ratings of topic interpretability (Chang et al., 2009). We collect the co-occurrence counts from Wikipedia and compute the average pairwise *pointwise mutual information* (PMI) score between the top 10 ranked words of every topic. Figure 3 illustrates the PMI score, and our approach yields comparable or better results against all other approaches under most conditions.

Qualitatively, Figure 4 shows an example of a topic evolution using online adaptor grammar for the *de-news* dataset. The topic is about "tax policy". The topic improves over time; words like "year", "tax" and "minist(er)" become more prominent. More importantly, the online approach discovers new words and incorporates them into the topic. For example, "schroeder" (former German chancellor) first appeared in minibatch 300, was successfully picked up by our model, and became one of the top ranked words in the topic.

[13]Available at `http://www.umiacs.umd.edu/~zhaike/`.

[14]The *de-news* dataset is randomly selected subset of $2.2k$ English documents from `http://homepages.inf.ed.ac.uk/pkoehn/publications/de-news/`. It contains $6.5k$ unique types and over $200k$ word tokens. Tokenization and stemming provided by NLTK (Bird et al., 2009).

6 Conclusion

Probabilistic modeling is a useful tool in understanding unstructured data or data where the structure is latent, like language. However, developing these models is often a difficult process, requiring significant machine learning expertise.

Adaptor grammars offer a flexible and quick way to prototype and test new models. Despite expensive inference, they have been used for topic modeling (Johnson, 2010), discovering perspective (Hardisty et al., 2010), segmentation (Johnson and Goldwater, 2009), and grammar induction (Cohen et al., 2010).

We have presented a new online, hybrid inference scheme for adaptor grammars. Unlike previous approaches, it does not require extensive preprocessing. It is also able to faster discover useful structure in text; with further development, these algorithms could further speed the development and application of new nonparametric models to large datasets.

Acknowledgments

We would like to thank the anonymous reviewers, Kristina Toutanova, Mark Johnson, and Ke Wu for insightful discussions. This work was supported by NSF Grant CCF-1018625. Boyd-Graber is also supported by NSF Grant IIS-1320538. Any opinions, findings, conclusions, or recommendations expressed here are those of the authors and do not necessarily reflect the view of the sponsor.

References

Nan Bernstein-Ratner. 1987. The phonology of parent child speech. *Children's language*, 6:159–174.

Steven Bird, Ewan Klein, and Edward Loper. 2009. *Natural Language Processing with Python*. O'Reilly Media.

Christopher M. Bishop. 2006. *Pattern Recognition and Machine Learning*. Springer-Verlag New York, Inc., Secaucus, NJ, USA.

David M. Blei and Michael I. Jordan. 2005. Variational inference for Dirichlet process mixtures. *Journal of Bayesian Analysis*, 1(1):121–144.

Benjamin Börschinger and Mark Johnson. 2012. Using rejuvenation to improve particle filtering for bayesian word segmentation. In *Proceedings of the Association for Computational Linguistics*.

Léon Bottou. 1998. Online algorithms and stochastic approximations. In *Online Learning and Neural Networks*. Cambridge University Press, Cambridge, UK.

Jordan Boyd-Graber and David M. Blei. 2007. PUTOP: Turning predominant senses into a topic model for WSD. In *4th International Workshop on Semantic Evaluations*.

Michael R. Brent and Timothy A. Cartwright. 1996. Distributional regularity and phonotactic constraints are useful for segmentation. volume 61, pages 93–125.

Jonathan Chang, Jordan Boyd-Graber, and David M. Blei. 2009. Connections between the lines: Augmenting social networks with text. In *Knowledge Discovery and Data Mining*.

Jean-Cédric Chappelier and Martin Rajman. 2000. Monte-Carlo sampling for NP-hard maximization problems in the framework of weighted parsing. In *Natural Language Processing*, pages 106–117.

Shay B. Cohen, David M. Blei, and Noah A. Smith. 2010. Variational inference for adaptor grammars. In *Conference of the North American Chapter of the Association for Computational Linguistics*.

Shay B. Cohen. 2011. *Computational Learning of Probabilistic Grammars in the Unsupervised Setting*. Ph.D. thesis, Carnegie Mellon University.

Thomas Emerson. 2005. The second international chinese word segmentation bakeoff. In *Fourth SIGHAN Workshop on Chinese Language*, Jeju, Korea.

Thomas S. Ferguson. 1973. A Bayesian analysis of some nonparametric problems. *The Annals of Statistics*, 1(2).

Sharon Goldwater, Thomas L. Griffiths, and Mark Johnson. 2011. Producing power-law distributions and damping word frequencies with two-stage language models. *Journal of Machine Learning Research*, pages 2335–2382, July.

Eric Hardisty, Jordan Boyd-Graber, and Philip Resnik. 2010. Modeling perspective using adaptor grammars. In *Proceedings of Emperical Methods in Natural Language Processing*.

Matthew Hoffman, David M. Blei, and Francis Bach. 2010. Online learning for latent Dirichlet allocation. In *Proceedings of Advances in Neural Information Processing Systems*.

Matthew Hoffman, David M. Blei, Chong Wang, and John Paisley. 2013. Stochastic variational inference. In *Journal of Machine Learning Research*.

Mark Johnson and Sharon Goldwater. 2009. Improving nonparameteric Bayesian inference: experiments on unsupervised word segmentation with adaptor grammars. In *Conference of the North American Chapter of the Association for Computational Linguistics*.

Mark Johnson, Thomas L. Griffiths, and Sharon Goldwater. 2006. Adaptor grammars: A framework for specifying compositional nonparametric Bayesian models. In *Proceedings of Advances in Neural Information Processing Systems*.

Mark Johnson, Thomas L. Griffiths, and Sharon Goldwater. 2007. Bayesian inference for PCFGs via Markov chain Monte Carlo. In *Conference of the North American Chapter of the Association for Computational Linguistics*.

Mark Johnson. 2010. PCFGs, topic models, adaptor grammars and learning topical collocations and the structure of proper names. In *Proceedings of the Association for Computational Linguistics*.

Kenichi Kurihara, Max Welling, and Yee Whye Teh. 2007. Collapsed variational Dirichlet process mixture models. In *International Joint Conference on Artificial Intelligence*.

Christopher D. Manning and Hinrich Schütze. 1999. *Foundations of Statistical Natural Language Processing*. The MIT Press, Cambridge, MA.

David Mimno, Matthew Hoffman, and David Blei. 2012. Sparse stochastic inference for latent Dirichlet allocation. In *Proceedings of the International Conference of Machine Learning*.

Daichi Mochihashi, Takeshi Yamada, and Naonori Ueda. 2009. Bayesian unsupervised word segmentation with nested pitman-yor language modeling. In *Proceedings of the Association for Computational Linguistics*.

Peter Müller and Fernando A. Quintana. 2004. Nonparametric Bayesian data analysis. *Statistical Science*, 19(1).

Ramesh Nallapati, William Cohen, and John Lafferty. 2007. Parallelized variational EM for latent Dirichlet allocation: An experimental evaluation of speed and scalability. In *ICDMW*.

David Newman, Sarvnaz Karimi, and Lawrence Cavedon. 2009. External evaluation of topic models. In *Proceedings of the Aurstralasian Document Computing Symposium*.

J. Pitman and M. Yor. 1997. The two-parameter Poisson-Dirichlet distribution derived from a stable subordinator. *Annals of Probability*, 25(2):855–900.

Hiroyuki Shindo, Yusuke Miyao, Akinori Fujino, and Masaaki Nagata. 2012. Bayesian symbol-refined tree substitution grammars for syntactic parsing. In *Proceedings of the Association for Computational Linguistics*.

Erik B. Sudderth and Michael I. Jordan. 2008. Shared segmentation of natural scenes using dependent Pitman-Yor processes. In *Proceedings of Advances in Neural Information Processing Systems*.

Yee Whye Teh, Michael I. Jordan, Matthew J. Beal, and David M. Blei. 2006. Hierarchical Dirichlet processes. *Journal of the American Statistical Association*, 101(476):1566–1581.

Kristina Toutanova and Mark Johnson. 2008. A Bayesian LDA-based model for semi-supervised part-of-speech tagging. In *Proceedings of Advances in Neural Information Processing Systems*, pages 1521–1528.

Martin J. Wainwright and Michael I. Jordan. 2008. Graphical models, exponential families, and variational inference. *Foundations and Trends in Machine Learning*, 1(1–2):1–305.

Chong Wang and David M. Blei. 2012. Truncation-free online variational inference for Bayesian nonparametric models. In *Proceedings of Advances in Neural Information Processing Systems*.

Naiwen Xue, Fei Xia, Fu-dong Chiou, and Marta Palmer. 2005. The Penn Chinese TreeBank: Phrase structure annotation of a large corpus. *Natural Language Engineering*.

Limin Yao, David Mimno, and Andrew McCallum. 2009. Efficient methods for topic model inference on streaming document collections. In *Knowledge Discovery and Data Mining*.

Ke Zhai and Jordan Boyd-Graber. 2013. Online latent Dirichlet allocation with infinite vocabulary. In *Proceedings of the International Conference of Machine Learning*.

Ke Zhai and Jason D. Williams. 2014. Discovering latent structure in task-oriented dialogues. In *Proceedings of the Association for Computational Linguistics*.

Ke Zhai, Jordan Boyd-Graber, Nima Asadi, and Mohamad Alkhouja. 2012. Mr. LDA: A flexible large scale topic modeling package using variational inference in mapreduce. In *Proceedings of World Wide Web Conference*.

A Joint Model for Entity Analysis: Coreference, Typing, and Linking

Greg Durrett and **Dan Klein**
Computer Science Division
University of California, Berkeley
{gdurrett,klein}@cs.berkeley.edu

Abstract

We present a joint model of three core tasks in the entity analysis stack: coreference resolution (within-document clustering), named entity recognition (coarse semantic typing), and entity linking (matching to Wikipedia entities). Our model is formally a structured conditional random field. Unary factors encode local features from strong baselines for each task. We then add binary and ternary factors to capture cross-task interactions, such as the constraint that coreferent mentions have the same semantic type. On the ACE 2005 and OntoNotes datasets, we achieve state-of-the-art results for all three tasks. Moreover, joint modeling improves performance on each task over strong independent baselines.[1]

1 Introduction

How do we characterize the collection of entities present in a document? Two broad threads exist in the literature. The first is coreference resolution (Soon et al., 2001; Ng, 2010; Pradhan et al., 2011), which identifies clusters of mentions in a document referring to the same entity. This process gives us access to useful information about the referents of pronouns and nominal expressions, but because clusters are local to each document, it is often hard to situate document entities in a broader context. A separate line of work has considered the problem of entity linking or "Wikification" (Cucerzan, 2007; Milne and Witten, 2008; Ji and Grishman, 2011), where mentions are linked to entries in a given knowledge base. This is useful for grounding proper entities, but in the absence of coreference gives an incomplete picture of document content itself, in that nominal expressions and pronouns are left unresolved.

In this paper, we describe a joint model of coreference, entity linking, and semantic typing (named entity recognition) using a structured conditional random field. Variables in the model capture decisions about antecedence, semantic type, and entity links for each mention. Unary factors on these variables incorporate features that are commonly employed when solving each task in isolation. Binary and higher-order factors capture interactions between pairs of tasks. For entity linking and NER, factors capture a mapping between NER's semantic types and Wikipedia's semantics as described by infoboxes, categories, and article text. Coreference interacts with the other tasks in a more complex way, via factors that softly encourage consistency of semantic types and entity links across coreference arcs, similar to the method of Durrett et al. (2013). Figure 1 shows an example of the effects such factors can capture. The non-locality of coreference factors make exact inference intractable, but we find that belief propagation is a suitable approximation technique and performs well.

Our joint modeling of these three tasks is motivated by their heavy interdependencies, which have been noted in previous work (discussed more in Section 7). Entity linking has been employed for coreference resolution (Ponzetto and Strube, 2006; Rahman and Ng, 2011; Ratinov and Roth, 2012) and coreference for entity linking (Cheng and Roth, 2013) as part of pipelined systems. Past work has

[1] System available at http://nlp.cs.berkeley.edu

Transactions of the Association for Computational Linguistics, vol. 2, pp. 477–490, 2014. Action Editor: Jason Eisner.
Submitted 8/2014; Revised 10/2014; Published November 1, 2014.

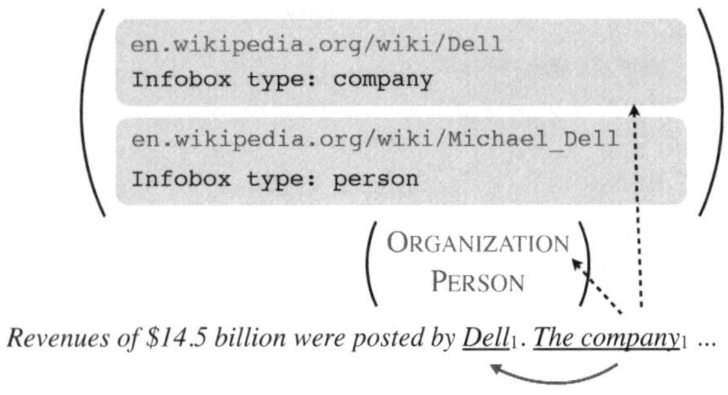

Figure 1: Coreference can help resolve ambiguous cases of semantic types or entity links: propagating information across coreference arcs can inform us that, in this context, *Dell* is an organization and should therefore link to the article on `Dell` in Wikipedia.

shown that tighter integration of coreference and entity linking is promising (Hajishirzi et al., 2013; Zheng et al., 2013); we extend these approaches and model the entire process more holistically. Named entity recognition is improved by simple coreference (Finkel et al., 2005; Ratinov and Roth, 2009) and knowledge from Wikipedia (Kazama and Torisawa, 2007; Ratinov and Roth, 2009; Nothman et al., 2013; Sil and Yates, 2013). Joint models of coreference and NER have been proposed in Haghighi and Klein (2010) and Durrett et al. (2013), but in neither case was supervised data used for both tasks. Technically, our model is most closely related to that of Singh et al. (2013), who handle coreference, named entity recognition, and relation extraction.[2] Our system is novel in three ways: the choice of tasks to model jointly, the fact that we maintain uncertainty about all decisions throughout inference (rather than using a greedy approach), and the feature sets we deploy for cross-task interactions.

In designing a joint model, we would like to preserve the modularity, efficiency, and structural simplicity of pipelined approaches. Our model's feature-based structure permits improvement of features specific to a particular task or to a pair of tasks. By pruning variable domains with a coarse model and using approximate inference via belief propagation, we maintain efficiency and our model is only a factor of two slower than the union of the individual models. Finally, as a structured CRF, it is conceptually no more complex than its component models and its behavior can be understood using the same intuition.

We apply our model to two datasets, ACE 2005 and OntoNotes, with different mention standards and layers of annotation. In both settings, our joint model outperforms our independent baseline models. On ACE, we achieve state-of-the-art entity linking results, matching the performance of the system of Fahrni and Strube (2014). On OntoNotes, we match the performance of the best published coreference system (Björkelund and Kuhn, 2014) and outperform two strong NER systems (Ratinov and Roth, 2009; Passos et al., 2014).

2 Motivating Examples

We first present two examples to motivate our approach. Figure 1 shows an example of a case where coreference is beneficial for named entity recognition and entity linking. *The company* is clearly coreferent to *Dell* by virtue of the lack of other possible antecedents; this in turn indicates that *Dell* refers to the corporation rather than to Michael Dell. This effect can be captured for entity linking by a feature tying the lexical item *company* to the fact that COMPANY is in the Wikipedia infobox for `Dell`,[3] thereby helping the linker make the correct decision. This would also be important for recovering the fact that the mention *the company* links to `Dell`; however, in the version of the task we consider, a mention like *the company* actually links to the Wikipedia article for `Company`.[4]

Figure 2 shows a different example, one where the coreference is now ambiguous but entity linking is transparent. In this case, an NER system based on surface statistics alone would likely predict that *Freddie Mac* is a PERSON. However, the Wikipedia article for Freddie Mac is unambiguous, which allows us to fix this error. The pronoun *his* can then be correctly resolved.

These examples justify why these tasks should be handled jointly: there is no obvious pipeline order for a system designer who cares about the perfor-

[2]Our model could potentially be extended to handle relation extraction or mention detection, which has also been addressed in past joint modeling efforts (Daumé and Marcu, 2005; Li and Ji, 2014), but that is outside the scope of the current work.

[3]Monospaced fonts indicate titles of Wikipedia articles.

[4]This decision was largely driven by a need to match the ACE linking annotations provided by Bentivogli et al. (2010).

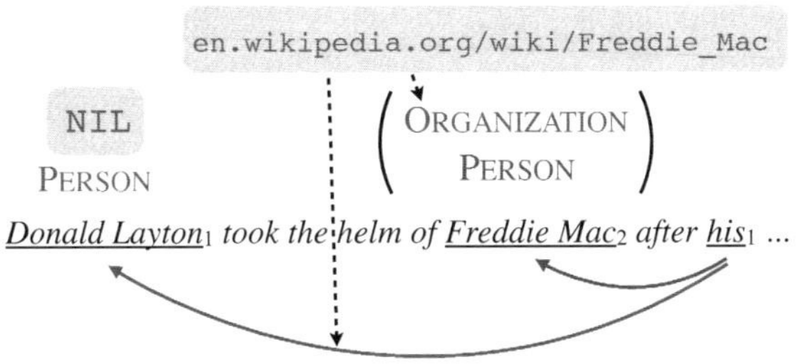

Figure 2: Entity links can help resolve ambiguous cases of coreference and entity types. Standard NER and coreference systems might fail to handle *Freddie Mac* correctly, but incorporating semantic information from Wikipedia makes this decision easier.

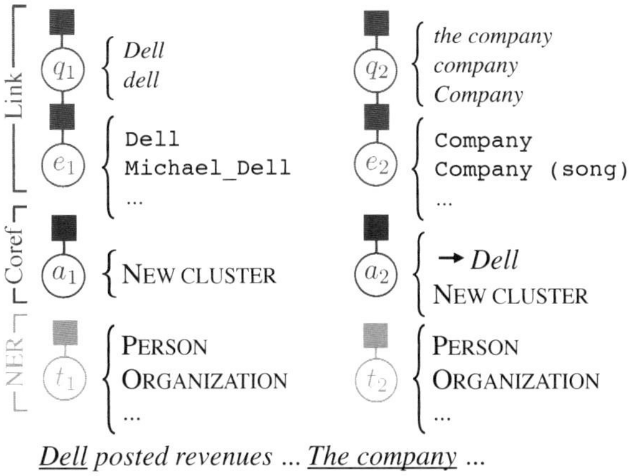

Figure 3: Random variables and task-specific factors present in our model. The a_i model coreference antecedents, the t_i model semantic types, the e_i model entity links, and the q_i are latent Wikipedia queries. Factors shown for each task integrate baseline features used when that task is handled in isolation. Coreference factors are described in Section 3.1.1, NER factors are described in Section 3.1.2, and entity linking factors are described in Section 3.1.3.

mance of the model on all three tasks.

3 Model

Our model is a structured conditional random field (Lafferty et al., 2001). The input (conditioning context) is the text of a document, automatic parses, and a set of pre-extracted mentions (spans of text). Mentions are allowed to overlap or nest: our model makes no structural assumptions here, and in fact we will show results on datasets with two different mention annotation standards (see Section 6.1 and Section 6.3).

Figure 3 shows the random variables in our model. We are trying to predict three distinct types of annotation, so we naturally have one variable per annotation type per mention (of which there are n):

- Coreference variables $\mathbf{a} = (a_1, \ldots, a_n)$ which indicate antecedents: $a_i \in \{1, \ldots, i-1, \text{NEW}\}$, indicating that the mention refers to some previous mention or that it begins a new cluster.
- Named entity type variables $\mathbf{t} = (t_1, \ldots, t_n)$ which take values in a fixed inventory of semantic types.[5]
- Entity link variables $\mathbf{e} = (e_1, \ldots, e_n)$ which take values in the set of all Wikipedia titles.

In addition we have variables $\mathbf{q} = (q_1, \ldots, q_n)$ which represent queries to Wikipedia. These are explained further in Section 3.1.3; for now, it suffices to remark that they are unobserved during both training and testing.

We place a log-linear probability distribution over these variables as follows:

$$p(\mathbf{a}, \mathbf{t}, \mathbf{e}|x; \theta) \propto \sum_{\mathbf{q}} \exp\left(\theta^\top f(\mathbf{a}, \mathbf{t}, \mathbf{e}, \mathbf{q}, x)\right)$$

where θ is a weight vector, f is a feature function, and x indicates the document text, automatic parses, and mention boundaries.

We represent the features in this model with standard factor graph notation; features over a particular set of output variables (and x) are associated with factors connected to those variables. Figure 3 shows the task-specific factors in the model, discussed next in Section 3.1. Higher-order factors coupling variables between tasks are discussed in Section 3.2.

3.1 Independent Model

Figure 3 shows a version of the model with only task-specific factors. Though this framework is structurally simple, it is nevertheless powerful enough for us to implement high-performing models for each task. State-of-the-art approaches to coreference (Durrett and Klein, 2013) and entity linking (Ratinov et al., 2011) already have this independent

[5]For the next few sections, we assume a fixed-mention version of the NER task, which looks like multi-way classification of semantic types. In Section 6.3.1, we adapt the model to the standard non-fixed-mention setting for OntoNotes.

structure and Ratinov and Roth (2009) note that it is a reasonable assumption to make for NER as well.[6] In this section, we describe the features present in the task-specific factors of each type (which also serve as our three separate baseline systems).

3.1.1 Coreference

Our modeling of the coreference output space (as antecedents chosen for each mention) follows the mention-ranking approach to coreference (Denis and Baldridge, 2008; Durrett and Klein, 2013). Our feature set is that of Durrett and Klein, targeting surface properties of mentions: for each mention, we examine the first word, head word, last word, context words, the mention's length, and whether the mention is nominal, proper or pronominal. Anaphoricity features examine each of these properties in turn; coreference features conjoin various properties between mention pairs and also use properties of the mention pair itself, such as the distance between the mentions and whether their heads match. Note that this baseline does not rely on having access to named entity chunks.

3.1.2 Named Entity Recognition

Our NER model places a distribution over possible semantic types for each mention, which corresponds to a fixed span of the input text. We define the features of a span to be the concatenation of standard NER surface features associated with each token in that chunk. We use surface token features similar to those from previous work (Zhang and Johnson, 2003; Ratinov and Roth, 2009; Passos et al., 2014): for tokens at offsets of $\{-2,-1,0,1,2\}$ from the current token, we fire features based on 1) word identity, 2) POS tag, 3) word class (based on capitalization, presence of numbers, suffixes, etc.), 4) word shape (based on the pattern of uppercase and lowercase letters, digits, and punctuation), 5) Brown cluster prefixes of length 4, 6, 10, 20 using the clusters from Koo et al. (2008), and 6) common bigrams of word shape and word identity.

[6] Pairwise potentials in sequence-based NER are useful for producing coherent output (e.g. prohibiting configurations like O I-PER), but since we have so far defined the task as operating over fixed mentions, this structural constraint does not come into play for our system.

3.1.3 Entity Linking

Our entity linking system diverges more substantially from past work than the coreference or NER systems. Most entity linking systems operate in two distinct phases (Cucerzan, 2007; Milne and Witten, 2008; Dredze et al., 2010; Ratinov et al., 2011). First, in the candidate generation phase, a system generates a ranked set of possible candidates for a given mention by querying Wikipedia. The standard approach for doing so is to collect all hyperlinks in Wikipedia and associate each hyperlinked span of text (e.g. *Michael Jordan*) with a distribution over titles of Wikipedia articles it is observed to link to (`Michael_Jordan`, `Michael_I._Jordan`, etc.). Second, in the disambiguation phase, a learned model selects the correct candidate from the set of possibilities.

As noted by Hachey et al. (2013) and Guo et al. (2013), candidate generation is often overlooked and yet accounts for large gaps in performance between different systems. It is not always clear how to best turn the text of a mention into a query for our set of hyperlinks. For example, the phrase *Chief Executive Michael Dell* has never been hyperlinked on Wikipedia. If we query the substring *Michael Dell*, the highest-ranked title is correct; however, querying the substring *Dell* returns the article on the company.

Our model for entity linking therefore includes both predictions of final Wikipedia titles e_i as well as latent query variables q_i that model the choice of query. Given a mention, possible queries are all prefixes of the mention containing the head with optional truecasing or lemmatization applied. Unary factors on the q_i model the appropriateness of a query based on surface text of the mention, investigating the following properties: whether the mention is proper or nominal, whether the query employed truecasing or lemmatization, the query's length, the POS tag sequence within the query and the tag immediately preceding it, and whether the query is the longest query to yield a nonempty set of candidates for the mention. This part of the model can learn, for example, that queries based on lemmatized proper names are bad, whereas queries based on lemmatized common nouns are good.

Our set of candidates links for a mention is the set of all titles produced by some query. The bi-

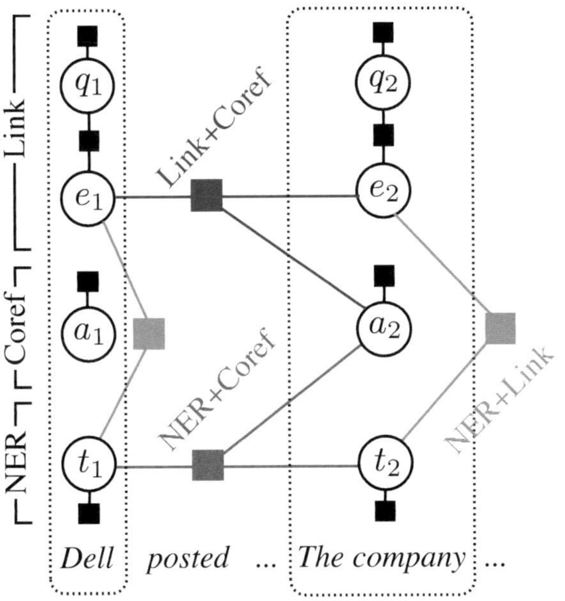

Figure 4: Factors that tie predictions between variables across tasks. Joint NER and entity linking factors (Section 3.2.1) tie semantic information from Wikipedia articles to semantic type predictions. Joint coreference and NER factors (Section 3.2.2) couple type decisions between mentions, encouraging consistent type assignments within an entity. Joint coreference and entity linking factors (Section 3.2.3) encourage relatedness between articles linked from coreferent mentions.

nary factors connecting q_i and e_i then decide which title a given query should yield. These include: the rank of the article title among all possible titles returned by that query (sorted by relative frequency count), whether the title is a close string match of the query, and whether the title matches the query up to a parenthetical (e.g. *Paul Allen* and `Paul_Allen_(editor)`).

We could also at this point add factors between pairs of variables (e_i, e_j) to capture coherence between choices of linked entities. Integration with the rest of the model, learning, and inference would remain unchanged. However, while such features have been employed in past entity linking systems (Ratinov et al., 2011; Hoffart et al., 2011), Ratinov et al. found them to be of limited utility, so we omit them from the present work.

3.2 Cross-task Interaction Factors

We now add factors that tie the predictions of multiple output variables in a feature-based way. Figure 4 shows the general structure of these factors. Each couples variables from one pair of tasks.

3.2.1 Entity Linking and NER

We want to exploit the semantic information in Wikipedia for better semantic typing of mentions. We also want to use semantic types to disambiguate tricky Wikipedia links. We use three sources of semantics from Wikipedia (Kazama and Torisawa, 2007; Nothman et al., 2013):

- Categories (e.g. `American financiers`); used by Ponzetto and Strube (2006; Kazama and Torisawa (2007; Ratinov and Roth (2012)
- Infobox type (e.g. `Person`, `Company`)
- Copula in the first sentence (*is a British politician*); used for coreference previously in Haghighi and Klein (2009)

We fire features that conjoin the information from the selected Wikipedia article with the selected NER type. Because these types of information from Wikipedia are of a moderate granularity, we should be able to learn a mapping between them and NER types and exploit Wikipedia as a soft gazetteer.

3.2.2 Coreference and NER

Coreference can improve NER by ensuring consistent semantic type predictions across coreferent mentions; likewise, NER can help coreference by encouraging the system to link up mentions of the same type. The factors we implement for these purposes closely resemble the factors employed for latent semantic clusters in Durrett et al. (2013). That structure is as follows:

$$\log F_{i-j}(a_i, t_i, t_j) = \begin{cases} 0 & \text{if } a_i \neq j \\ f(i, j, t_i, t_j) & \text{otherwise} \end{cases}$$

That is, the features between the type variables for mentions i and j does not come into play unless i and j are coreferent. Note that there are quadratically many such factors in the graph (before pruning; see Section 5), one for each ordered pair of mentions (j, i) with $j < i$. When scoring a particular configuration of variables, only a small subset of the factors is active, but during inference when we marginalize over all settings of variables, each of the factors comes into play for some configuration.

This model structure allows us to maintain uncertainty about coreference decisions but still propagate information along coreference arcs in a soft way.

Given this factor definition, we define features that should fire over *coreferent* pairs of entity types. Our features target:

- The pair of semantic types for the current and antecedent mention
- The semantic type of the current mention and the head of the antecedent mention, and the type of the antecedent and head of the current

We found such monolexical features to improve over just type pairs and while not suffering from the sparsity problems of bilexical features.

3.2.3 Coreference and Entity Linking

As we said in Section 2, coreferent mentions can actually have different entity links (e.g. `Dell` and `Company`), so encouraging equality alone is less effective for entity linking than it is for NER. Our factors have the same structure as those for coreference-NER, but features now target overall semantic relatedness of Wikipedia articles using the structure of Wikipedia by computing whether the articles have the same title, share any out links, or link to each other. More complex relatedness schemes such as those described in Ratinov et al. (2011) can be implemented in this framework. Nevertheless, these basic features still promise to help identify related articles as well as name variations by exploiting the abundance of entity mentions on Wikipedia.

4 Learning

Our training data consists of d documents, where a given document consists of a tuple $(x, C^*, \mathbf{t}^*, \mathbf{e}^*)$. Gold-standard labels for types $(\mathbf{t}^*)$ and entity links $(\mathbf{e}^*)$ are provided directly, while supervision for coreference is provided in the form of a clustering C^*. Regardless, we can simply marginalize over the uncertainty about $\mathbf{a}^*$ and form the conditional log-likelihood of the training labels as follows:

$$\mathcal{L}(\theta) = \sum_{i=1}^{d} \log \sum_{\mathbf{a}^* \in \mathcal{A}(C_i^*)} p(\mathbf{a}^*, \mathbf{t}_i^*, \mathbf{e}_i^* | x; \theta)$$

where $\mathcal{A}(C^*)$ is the set of antecedent structures consistent with the gold annotation: the first mention in a cluster must pick the NEW label and subsequent mentions must pick an antecedent from the set of those preceding them in the cluster. This marginalization over latent structure has been employed in prior work as well (Fernandes et al., 2012; Durrett and Klein, 2013).

We adapt this objective to exploit parameterized loss functions for each task by modifying the distribution as follows:

$$p'(\mathbf{a}, \mathbf{t}, \mathbf{e} | x; \theta) \propto p(\mathbf{a}, \mathbf{t}, \mathbf{e}, x) \exp\left[\alpha_c \ell_c(\mathbf{a}, C^*) + \alpha_t \ell_t(\mathbf{t}, \mathbf{t}^*) + \alpha_e \ell_e(\mathbf{e}, \mathbf{e}^*)\right]$$

where ℓ_c, ℓ_t, and ℓ_e are task-specific loss functions with weight parameters α. This technique, softmax-margin, allows us to shape the distribution learned by the model and encourage the model to move probability mass away from outputs that are bad according to our loss functions (Gimpel and Smith, 2010). As in Durrett and Klein (2013), we take $\alpha_c = 1$ and use ℓ_c as defined there, penalizing the model by $\alpha_{c,\text{FA}} = 0.1$ for linking up a mention that should have been nonanaphoric, by $\alpha_{c,\text{FN}} = 3$ for calling nonanaphoric a mention that should have an antecedent, and by $\alpha_{c,\text{WL}} = 1$ for picking the wrong antecedent for an anaphoric mention. ℓ_t and ℓ_e are simply Hamming distance, with $\alpha_t = 3$ and $\alpha_e = 0$ for all experiments. We found that the outcome of learning was not particularly sensitive to these parameters.[7]

We optimize our objective using AdaGrad (Duchi et al., 2011) with L_1 regularization and $\lambda = 0.001$. Our final objective is

$$\mathcal{L}(\theta) = \sum_{i=1}^{d} \log \sum_{\mathbf{a}^* \in \mathcal{A}(C_i^*)} p'(\mathbf{a}^*, \mathbf{t}_i^*, \mathbf{e}_i^* | x; \theta) + \lambda \|\theta\|_1$$

This objective is nonconvex, but in practice we have found that it is very stable. One reason is that for any mention that has fewer than two antecedents in its cluster, all elements of $\mathcal{A}(C^*)$ only contain one possibility for that mention, and even for mentions with ambiguity, the parameters that the model ends up learning tend to place almost all of the probability mass consistently on one antecedent.

[7]These parameters allow us to trade off contributions to the objective from the different tasks, addressing Singh et al. (2013)'s objection to single objectives for joint models.

	Dev						Test					
	MUC	B^3	CEAF$_e$	Avg.	NER	Link	MUC	B^3	CEAF$_e$	Avg.	NER	Link
INDEP.	77.95	74.81	71.84	74.87	83.04	73.07	81.03	74.89	72.56	76.16	82.35	74.71
JOINT	**79.41**	**75.56**	**73.34**	**76.10**	**85.94**	**75.69**	81.41	74.70	72.93	76.35	**85.60**	**76.78**
Δ	+1.46	+0.75	+1.50	+1.23	+2.90	+2.62	+0.42	−0.19	+0.37	+0.19	+3.25	+2.07

Table 1: Results on the ACE 2005 dev and test sets for the INDEP. (task-specific factors only) and JOINT models. Coreference metrics are computed using their reference implementations (Pradhan et al., 2014). We report accuracy on NER because the set of mentions is fixed and all mentions have named entity types. Coreference and NER are compared to prior work in a more standard setting in Section 6.3. Finally, we also report accuracy of our entity linker (including links to NIL); entity linking is analyzed more thoroughly in Table 2. Bolded values represent statistically significant improvements with $p < 0.05$ according to a bootstrap resampling test.

5 Inference

For both learning and decoding, inference consists of computing marginals for individual variables or for sets of variables adjacent to a factor. Exact inference is intractabile due to our factor graph's loopiness; however, we can still perform efficient inference using belief propagation, which has been successfully employed for a similar model (Durrett et al., 2013) as well as for other NLP tasks (Smith and Eisner, 2008; Burkett and Klein, 2012). Marginals typically converge in 3-5 iterations of belief propagation; we use 5 iterations for all experiments.

However, belief propagation would still be quite computationally expensive if run on the full factor graph as described in Section 3. In particular, the factors in Section 3.2.2 and Section 3.2.3 are costly to sum over due to their ternary structure and the fact that there are quadratically many of them in the number of mentions. The solution to this is to prune the domains of the coreference variables using a coarse model consisting of the coreference factors trained in isolation. Given marginals $p_0(a_i|x)$, we prune values a_i such that $\log p_0(a_i|x) < \log p_0(a_i^*|x) - k$ for a threshold parameter k, which we set to 5 for our experiments; this is sufficient to prune over 90% of possible coreference arcs while leaving at least one possible gold link for 98% of mentions.[8] With this optimization, our full joint model could be trained for 20 iterations on the ACE 2005 corpus in around an hour.

We use minimum Bayes risk (MBR) decoding, where we compute marginals for each variable under the full model and independently return the most likely setting of each variable. Note that for coreference, this implies that we produce the MBR antecedent structure rather than the MBR clustering; the latter is much more computationally difficult to find and would be largely the same, since the posterior distributions of the a_i are quite peaked.

[8]In addition to inferential benefits, pruning an arc allows us to prune entire joint coreference factors and avoid instantiating their associated features, which reduces the memory footprint and time needed to build a factor graph.

6 Experiments

We present results on two corpora. First, we use the ACE 2005 corpus (NIST, 2005): this corpus annotates mentions complete with coreference, semantic types (per mention), and entity links (also per mention) later added by Bentivogli et al. (2010). We evaluate on gold mentions in this setting for comparability with prior work on entity linking; we lift this restriction in Section 6.3.

Second, we evaluate on the OntoNotes 5 corpus (Hovy et al., 2006) as used in the CoNLL 2012 coreference shared task (Pradhan et al., 2012). This corpus does not contain gold-standard entity links, so we cannot evaluate this portion of our model, though the model still exploits the information from Wikipedia to make coreference and named entity decisions. We will compare to prior coreference and named entity work in the system mentions setting.

6.1 ACE Evaluation

We tokenize and sentence-split the ACE dataset using the tools bundled with Reconcile (Stoyanov et al., 2010) and parse it using the Berkeley Parser (Petrov et al., 2006). We use the train/test split from Stoyanov et al. (2009), Haghighi and Klein (2010), and Bansal and Klein (2012).

	Non-NILS			NILS			
	Prec.	Rec.	F_1	Prec.	Rec.	F_1	Accuracy
FAHRNI	81.15	78.10	79.60	41.25	61.10	49.25	76.87
INDEP.	80.26	76.30	78.23	33.39	54.47	41.40	74.71
JOINT	83.26	77.67	80.37	35.19	65.42	45.77	76.78
Δ over INDEP.	+3.00	+1.37	+2.14	+1.80	+10.95	+3.37	+2.07

Table 2: Detailed entity linking results on the ACE 2005 test set. We evaluate both our INDEP. (task-specific factors only) and JOINT models and compare to the results of the FAHRNI model, a state-of-the-art entity linking system. We compare overall accuracy as well as performance at predicting NILS (mentions not in the knowledge base) and non-NILS. The JOINT model roughly matches the performance of FAHRNI and gives strong gains over the INDEP. system.

Table 1 shows our results. Coreference results are reported using MUC (Vilain et al., 1995), B^3 (Bagga and Baldwin, 1998), and CEAF$_e$ (Luo, 2005), as well as their average, the CoNLL metric, all computed from the reference implementation of the CoNLL scorer (Pradhan et al., 2014). We see that the joint model improves all three tasks compared to the individual task models in the baseline.

More in-depth entity linking results are shown in Table 2. We both evaluate on overall accuracy (how many mentions are correctly linked) as well as two more specific criteria: precision/recall/F_1 of non-NIL[9] predictions, and precision/recall/F_1 of NIL predictions. This latter measure may be important if a system designer is trying to identify new entities in a document. We compare to the results of the best model from Fahrni and Strube (2014), which is a sophisticated discriminative model incorporating a latent model of mention scope.[10]

Our performance is similar to that of Fahrni and Strube (2014), though the results are not exactly comparable for two reasons. First, our models are trained on different datasets: Fahrni and Strube (2014) train on Wikipedia data whereas we train on the ACE training set. Second, they make use of the annotated head spans in ACE whereas we only use detected heads based on automatic parses. Note that this information is particularly beneficial for locating the right query because "heads" may be multiword expressions such as *West Bank* as part of the phrase *southern West Bank*.

[9] NIL is a placeholder for mentions which do not link to an article in Wikipedia.

[10] On the TAC datasets, this FAHRNI model substantially outperforms Ratinov et al. (2011) and has comparable performance to Cheng and Roth (2013), hence it is quite competitive.

	Coref	NER	Link
INDEP.	74.87	83.04	73.07
INDEP+LINKNER		+1.85	+2.41
INDEP+COREFNER	+0.56	+1.15	
INDEP+COREFLINK	+0.48		−0.16
JOINT−LINKNER	+0.79	+1.28	−0.06
JOINT−COREFNER	+0.56	+1.94	+2.07
JOINT−COREFLINK	+0.85	+2.68	+2.57
JOINT	+1.23	+2.90	+2.62
JOINT/LATENTLINK	+1.26	+3.47	−18.8

Table 3: Results of model ablations on the ACE development set. We hold out each type of factor in turn from the JOINT model and add each in turn over the INDEP. model. We evaluate the coreference performance using the CoNLL metric, NER accuracy, and entity linking accuracy.

6.2 Model Ablations

To evaluate the importance of the different parts of the model, we perform a series of ablations on the model interaction factors. Table 3 shows the results of adding each interaction factor in turn to the baseline and removing each of the three interaction factors from the full joint model (see Figure 4).

Link–NER interactions. These joint factors are the strongest out of any considered here and give large improvements to entity linking and NER. Their utility is unsurprising: effectively, they give NER access to a gazetteer that it did not have in the baseline model. Moreover, our relatively rich featurization of the semantic information on Wikipedia allows the model to make effective use of it.

Coref–NER interactions. These are moderately beneficial to both coreference and NER. Having reliable semantic types allows the coreference system to be bolder about linking up mention pairs that do not exhibit direct head matches. Part of this is due to our use of monolexical features, which are fine-grained enough to avoid the problems with coarse semantic type matching (Durrett and Klein, 2013) but still effectively learnable.

Coref–Link interactions. These are the least useful of any of the major factors, providing only a small benefit to coreference. This is likely a result of the ACE entity linking annotation standard: a mention like *the company* is not linked to the specific company it refers to, but instead the Wikipedia article `Company`. Determining the relatedness of `Company` to an article like `Dell` is surprisingly difficult: many related articles share almost no out-links and may not explicitly link to one another. Further feature engineering could likely improve the utility of these factors.

The last line of Table 3 shows the results of an experiment where the entity links were not observed during training, i.e. they were left latent. Unsurprisingly, the system is not good at entity linking; however, the model is still able to do as well or even slightly better on coreference and named entity recognition. A possible explanation for this is that even the wrong Wikipedia link can in many cases provide correct semantic information: for example, not knowing which *Donald Layton* is being referred to is irrelevant for the question of determining that he is a PERSON and may also have little impact on coreference performance. This result indicates that the joint modeling approach is not necessarily dependent on having all tasks annotated. The model can make use of cross-task information even when that information comes via latent variables.

6.3 OntoNotes Evaluation

The second part of our evaluation uses the datasets from the CoNLL 2012 Shared Task (Pradhan et al., 2012), specifically the coreference and NER annotations. All experiments use the standard automatic parses from the shared task and mentions detected according to the method of Durrett and Klein (2013).

Evaluating on OntoNotes carries with it a few complications. First, gold-standard entity linking annotations are not available; we can handle this by

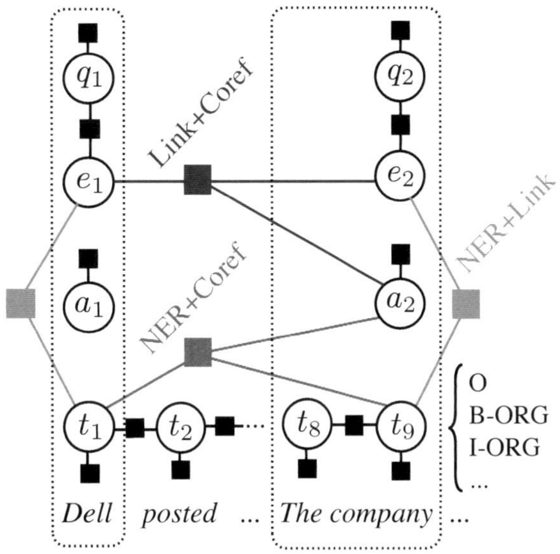

Figure 5: Modified factor graph for OntoNotes-style annotations, where NER chunks can now diverge from mentions for the other two tasks. NER is now modeled with token-synchronous random variables taking values in a BIO tagset. Factors coupling NER and the other tasks now interact with the NER chain via the NER nodes associated with the heads of mentions.

leaving the e_i variables in our model latent. Second, and more seriously, NER chunks are no longer the same as coreference mentions, so our assumption of fixed NER spans no longer holds.

6.3.1 Divergent Coreference and NER

Our model can be adapted to handle NER chunks that diverge from mentions for the other two tasks, as shown in Figure 5. We have kept the coreference and entity linking portions of our model the same, now defined over system predicted mentions. However, we have replaced mention-synchronous type variables with standard token-synchronous BIO-valued variables. The unary NER features developed in Section 3.1.2 are now applied in the standard way, namely they are conjoined with the BIO labels at each token position. Binary factors between adjacent NER nodes enforce appropriate structural constraints and fire indicator features on transitions. In order to maintain tractability in the face of a larger number of variables and factors in the NER portion of our model, we prune the NER variables' domains using the NER model trained in isolation, similar to the procedure that we described for pruning coreference arcs in Section 5.

	MUC			B^3			CEAF$_e$			Avg.
	Prec.	Rec.	F_1	Prec.	Rec.	F_1	Prec.	Rec.	F_1	F_1
BERKELEY	72.85	65.87	69.18	63.55	52.47	57.48	54.31	54.36	54.34	60.33
FERNANDES	–	–	70.51	–	–	57.58	–	–	53.86	60.65
BJORKELUND	74.30	67.46	70.72	62.71	54.96	58.58	59.40	52.27	**55.61**	61.63
INDEP.	72.25	69.30	70.75	60.92	55.73	58.21	55.33	54.14	54.73	61.23
JOINT	72.61	69.91	**71.24**	61.18	56.43	**58.71**	56.17	54.23	55.18	**61.71**

Table 4: CoNLL metric scores for our systems on the CoNLL 2012 blind test set, compared to Durrett and Klein (2013) (the Berkeley system), Fernandes et al. (2012) (the winner of the CoNLL shared task), and Björkelund and Kuhn (2014) (the best reported results on the dataset to date). INDEP. and JOINT are the contributions of this work; JOINT improves substantially over INDEP. (these improvements are statistically significant with $p < 0.05$ according to a bootstrap resampling test) and achieves state-of-the-art results.

Cross-task factors that previously would have fired features based on the NE type for a whole mention now instead consult the NE type of that mention's head.[11] In Figure 5, this can be seen with factors involving e_2 and a_2 touching t_9 (*company*), the head of the second mention. Since the chain structure enforces consistency between adjacent labels, features that strongly prefer a particular label on one node of a mention will implicitly affect other nodes in that mention and beyond.

Training and inference proceed as before, with a slight modification: instead of computing the MBR setting of every variable in isolation, we instead compute the MBR sequence of labeled NER chunks to avoid the problem of producing inconsistent tag sequences, e.g. O I-PER or B-PER I-ORG.

6.3.2 Results

Table 4 shows coreference results from our INDEP. and JOINT models compared to three strong systems: Durrett and Klein (2013), Fernandes et al. (2012) (the winner of the CoNLL shared task), and Björkelund and Kuhn (2014) (the best reported results on the dataset). Our JOINT method outperforms all three as well as the INDEP. system.[12]

Next, we report results on named entity recognition. We use the same OntoNotes splits as for the coreference data; however, the New Testament (NT) portion of the CoNLL 2012 test set does not have gold-standard named entity annotations, so we omit it from our evaluation. This leaves us with exactly the CoNLL 2011 test set. We compare to two existing baselines from the literature: the Illinois NER system of Ratinov and Roth (2009) and the results of Passos et al. (2014). Table 5 shows that we outperform both prior systems in terms of F_1, though the ILLINOIS system features higher recall while our system features higher precision.

	Prec.	Rec.	F_1
ILLINOIS	82.00	**84.95**	83.45
PASSOS	–	–	82.24
INDEP.	83.79	81.53	82.64
JOINT	**85.22**	82.89	**84.04**
Δ over INDEP.	+1.43	+1.36	+1.40

Table 5: Results for NER tagging on the OntoNotes 5.0 / CoNLL 2011 test set. We compare our systems to the Illinois system (Ratinov and Roth, 2009) and the system of Passos et al. (2014). Our model outperforms both other systems in terms of F_1, and once again joint modeling gives substantial improvements over our baseline system.

7 Related Work

There are two closely related threads of prior work: those that address the tasks we consider in a different way and those that propose joint models for other related sets of tasks. In the first category, Hajishirzi et al. (2013) integrate entity linking into a sieve-based coreference system (Raghunathan et al., 2010), the aim being to propagate link decisions throughout coreference chains, block corefer-

[11] The NER-coreference portion of the model now resembles the skip-chain CRF from Finkel et al. (2005), though with soft coreference.

[12] The systems of Chang et al. (2013) and Webster and Curran (2014) perform similarly to the FERNANDES system; changes in the reference implementation of the metrics make exact comparison to printed numbers difficult.

ence links between different entities, and use semantic information to make additional coreference links. Zheng et al. (2013) build coreference clusters greedily left-to-right and maintain entity link information for each cluster, namely a list of possible targets in the knowledge base as well as a current best link target that is used to extract features (though that might not be the target that is chosen by the end of inference). Cheng and Roth (2013) use coreference as a preprocessing step for entity linking and then solve an ILP to determine the optimal entity link assignments for each mention based on surface properties of that mention, other mentions in its cluster, and other mentions that it is related to. Compared to these systems, our approach maintains greater uncertainty about all random variables throughout inference and uses features to capture cross-task interactions as opposed to rules or hard constraints, which can be less effective for incorporating semantic knowledge (Lee et al., 2011).

The joint model most closely related to ours is that of Singh et al. (2013), modeling coreference, named entity recognition, and relation extraction. Their techniques differ from ours in a few notable ways: they choose a different objective function than we do and also opt to freeze the values of certain variables during the belief propagation process rather than pruning with a coarse pass. Sil and Yates (2013) jointly model NER and entity linking in such a way that they maintain uncertainty over mention boundaries, allowing information from Wikipedia to inform segmentation choices. We could strengthen our model by integrating this capability; however, the primary cause of errors for mention detection on OntoNotes is parsing ambiguities rather than named entity ambiguities, so we would be unlikely to see improvements in the experiments presented here. Beyond maintaining uncertainty over mention boundaries, we might also consider maintaining uncertainty over the entire parse structure, as in Finkel and Manning (2009), who consider parsing and named entity recognition together with a PCFG.

8 Conclusion

We return to our initial motivation for joint modeling, namely that the three tasks we address have the potential to influence one another. Table 3 shows that failing to exploit any of the pairwise interactions between the tasks causes lower performance on at least one of them. Therefore, any pipelined system would necessarily underperform a joint model on whatever task came first in the pipeline, which is undesirable given the importance of these tasks. The trend towards broader and deeper NLP pipelines will only exacerbate this problem and make it more difficult to find a suitable pipeline ordering. In addition to showing that joint modeling is high-performing, we have also shown that it can be implemented with relatively low overhead, requiring no fundamentally new learning or inference techniques, and that it is extensible, due to its modular structure and natural partitioning of features. Taken together, these aspects make a compelling case that joint models can provide a way to integrate deeper levels of processing, particularly for semantic layers of annotation, and that this modeling power does not need to come at the expense of computational efficiency, structural simplicity, or modularity.

The Berkeley Entity Resolution System is available at `http://nlp.cs.berkeley.edu`.

Acknowledgments

This work was partially supported by BBN under DARPA contract HR0011-12-C-0014, by an NSF fellowship for the first author, and by a Google Faculty Research Award to the second author. Thanks to Angela Fahrni for helpful discussions about entity linking and for providing system output, to the anonymous reviewers for their insightful comments, and to our action editor Jason Eisner.

References

Amit Bagga and Breck Baldwin. 1998. Algorithms for Scoring Coreference Chains. In *Proceedings of the Conference on Language Resources and Evaluation Workshop on Linguistics Coreference*.

Mohit Bansal and Dan Klein. 2012. Coreference Semantics from Web Features. In *Proceedings of the Association for Computational Linguistics*.

Luisa Bentivogli, Pamela Forner, Claudio Giuliano, Alessandro Marchetti, Emanuele Pianta, and Kateryna Tymoshenko. 2010. Extending English ACE 2005 Corpus Annotation with Ground-truth Links to Wikipedia. In *Proceedings of the Workshop on*

The People's Web Meets NLP: Collaboratively Constructed Semantic Resources.

Anders Björkelund and Jonas Kuhn. 2014. Learning Structured Perceptrons for Coreference Resolution with Latent Antecedents and Non-local Features. In *Proceedings of the Association for Computational Linguistics.*

David Burkett and Dan Klein. 2012. Fast Inference in Phrase Extraction Models with Belief Propagation. In *Proceedings of the North American Chapter of the Association for Computational Linguistics.*

Kai-Wei Chang, Rajhans Samdani, and Dan Roth. 2013. A Constrained Latent Variable Model for Coreference Resolution. In *Proceedings of the Conference on Empirical Methods in Natural Language Processing.*

Xiao Cheng and Dan Roth. 2013. Relational Inference for Wikification. In *Proceedings of the Conference on Empirical Methods in Natural Language Processing.*

Silviu Cucerzan. 2007. Large-Scale Named Entity Disambiguation Based on Wikipedia Data. In *Proceedings of the Joint Conference on Empirical Methods in Natural Language Processing and Computational Natural Language Learning (EMNLP-CoNLL).*

Hal Daumé, III and Daniel Marcu. 2005. A Large-scale Exploration of Effective Global Features for a Joint Entity Detection and Tracking Model. In *Proceedings of the Conference on Empirical Methods in Natural Language Processing.*

Pascal Denis and Jason Baldridge. 2008. Specialized Models and Ranking for Coreference Resolution. In *Proceedings of the Conference on Empirical Methods in Natural Language Processing.*

Mark Dredze, Paul McNamee, Delip Rao, Adam Gerber, and Tim Finin. 2010. Entity Disambiguation for Knowledge Base Population. In *Proceedings of the International Conference on Computational Linguistics.*

John Duchi, Elad Hazan, and Yoram Singer. 2011. Adaptive Subgradient Methods for Online Learning and Stochastic Optimization. *Journal of Machine Learning Research*, 12:2121–2159, July.

Greg Durrett and Dan Klein. 2013. Easy Victories and Uphill Battles in Coreference Resolution. In *Proceedings of the Conference on Empirical Methods in Natural Language Processing*, October.

Greg Durrett, David Hall, and Dan Klein. 2013. Decentralized Entity-Level Modeling for Coreference Resolution. In *Proceedings of the Association for Computational Linguistics.*

Angela Fahrni and Michael Strube. 2014. A Latent Variable Model for Discourse-aware Concept and Entity Disambiguation. In *Proceedings of the European Chapter of the Association for Computational Linguistics.*

Eraldo Rezende Fernandes, Cícero Nogueira dos Santos, and Ruy Luiz Milidiú. 2012. Latent Structure Perceptron with Feature Induction for Unrestricted Coreference Resolution. In *Proceedings of the Joint Conference on Empirical Methods in Natural Language Proceedings and Conference on Computational Natural Language Learning - Shared Task.*

Jenny Rose Finkel and Christopher D. Manning. 2009. Joint Parsing and Named Entity Recognition. In *Proceedings of the North American Chapter for the Association for Computational Linguistics.*

Jenny Rose Finkel, Trond Grenager, and Christopher Manning. 2005. Incorporating Non-local Information into Information Extraction Systems by Gibbs Sampling. In *Proceedings of the Association for Computational Linguistics.*

Kevin Gimpel and Noah A. Smith. 2010. Softmax-Margin CRFs: Training Log-Linear Models with Cost Functions. In *Proceedings of the North American Chapter for the Association for Computational Linguistics.*

Yuhang Guo, Bing Qin, Yuqin Li, Ting Liu, and Sheng Li Li. 2013. Improving Candidate Generation for Entity Linking. In *Natural Language Processing and Information Systems.*

Ben Hachey, Will Radford, Joel Nothman, Matthew Honnibal, and James R. Curran. 2013. Evaluating Entity Linking with Wikipedia. *Artificial Intelligence*, 194:130–150, January.

Aria Haghighi and Dan Klein. 2009. Simple Coreference Resolution with Rich Syntactic and Semantic Features. In *Proceedings of the Conference on Empirical Methods in Natural Language Processing.*

Aria Haghighi and Dan Klein. 2010. Coreference Resolution in a Modular, Entity-Centered Model. In *Proceedings of the North American Chapter of the Association for Computational Linguistics.*

Hannaneh Hajishirzi, Leila Zilles, Daniel S. Weld, and Luke Zettlemoyer. 2013. Joint Coreference Resolution and Named-Entity Linking with Multi-Pass Sieves. In *Proceedings of the Conference on Empirical Methods in Natural Language Processing.*

Johannes Hoffart, Mohamed Amir Yosef, Ilaria Bordino, Hagen Fürstenau, Manfred Pinkal, Marc Spaniol, Bilyana Taneva, Stefan Thater, and Gerhard Weikum. 2011. Robust Disambiguation of Named Entities in Text. In *Proceedings of the Conference on Empirical Methods in Natural Language Processing.*

Eduard Hovy, Mitchell Marcus, Martha Palmer, Lance Ramshaw, and Ralph Weischedel. 2006. OntoNotes: The 90% Solution. In *Proceedings of the North American Chapter of the Association for Computational Linguistics: Short Papers.*

Heng Ji and Ralph Grishman. 2011. Knowledge Base Population: Successful Approaches and Challenges. In *Proceedings of the Association for Computational Linguistics*.

Jun'ichi Kazama and Kentaro Torisawa. 2007. Exploiting Wikipedia as External Knowledge for Named Entity Recognition. In *Proceedings of the Joint Conference on Empirical Methods in Natural Language Processing and Computational Natural Language Learning*.

Terry Koo, Xavier Carreras, and Michael Collins. 2008. Simple Semi-supervised Dependency Parsing. In *Proceedings of the Association for Computational Linguistics*.

John D. Lafferty, Andrew McCallum, and Fernando C. N. Pereira. 2001. Conditional Random Fields: Probabilistic Models for Segmenting and Labeling Sequence Data. In *Proceedings of the International Conference on Machine Learning*.

Heeyoung Lee, Yves Peirsman, Angel Chang, Nathanael Chambers, Mihai Surdeanu, and Dan Jurafsky. 2011. Stanford's Multi-Pass Sieve Coreference Resolution System at the CoNLL-2011 Shared Task. In *Proceedings of the Conference on Computational Natural Language Learning: Shared Task*.

Qi Li and Heng Ji. 2014. Incremental Joint Extraction of Entity Mentions and Relations. In *Proceedings of the Association for Computational Linguistics*.

Xiaoqiang Luo. 2005. On Coreference Resolution Performance Metrics. In *Proceedings of the Conference on Empirical Methods in Natural Language Processing*.

David Milne and Ian H. Witten. 2008. Learning to Link with Wikipedia. In *Proceedings of the Conference on Information and Knowledge Management*.

Vincent Ng. 2010. Supervised Noun Phrase Coreference Research: The First Fifteen Years. In *Proceedings of the Association for Computational Linguistics*.

NIST. 2005. The ACE 2005 Evaluation Plan. In *NIST*.

Joel Nothman, Nicky Ringland, Will Radford, Tara Murphy, and James R. Curran. 2013. Learning Multilingual Named Entity Recognition from Wikipedia. *Artificial Intelligence*, 194:151–175, January.

Alexandre Passos, Vineet Kumar, and Andrew McCallum. 2014. Lexicon Infused Phrase Embeddings for Named Entity Resolution. In *Proceedings of the Conference on Computational Natural Language Learning*.

Slav Petrov, Leon Barrett, Romain Thibaux, and Dan Klein. 2006. Learning Accurate, Compact, and Interpretable Tree Annotation. In *Proceedings of the Conference on Computational Linguistics and the Association for Computational Linguistics*.

Simone Paolo Ponzetto and Michael Strube. 2006. Exploiting Semantic Role Labeling, WordNet and Wikipedia for Coreference Resolution. In *Proceedings of the North American Chapter of the Association of Computational Linguistics*.

Sameer Pradhan, Lance Ramshaw, Mitchell Marcus, Martha Palmer, Ralph Weischedel, and Nianwen Xue. 2011. CoNLL-2011 Shared Task: Modeling Unrestricted Coreference in OntoNotes. In *Proceedings of the Conference on Computational Natural Language Learning: Shared Task*.

Sameer Pradhan, Alessandro Moschitti, Nianwen Xue, Olga Uryupina, and Yuchen Zhang. 2012. CoNLL-2012 Shared Task: Modeling Multilingual Unrestricted Coreference in OntoNotes. In *Joint Conference on EMNLP and CoNLL - Shared Task*.

Sameer Pradhan, Xiaoqiang Luo, Marta Recasens, Eduard Hovy, Vincent Ng, and Michael Strube. 2014. Scoring Coreference Partitions of Predicted Mentions: A Reference Implementation. In *Proceedings of the Association for Computational Linguistics*.

Karthik Raghunathan, Heeyoung Lee, Sudarshan Rangarajan, Nathanael Chambers, Mihai Surdeanu, Dan Jurafsky, and Christopher Manning. 2010. A Multi-Pass Sieve for Coreference Resolution. In *Proceedings of the Conference on Empirical Methods in Natural Language Processing*.

Altaf Rahman and Vincent Ng. 2011. Coreference Resolution with World Knowledge. In *Proceedings of the Association for Computational Linguistics: Human Language Technologies*.

Lev Ratinov and Dan Roth. 2009. Design Challenges and Misconceptions in Named Entity Recognition. In *Proceedings of the Conference on Computational Natural Language Learning*.

Lev Ratinov and Dan Roth. 2012. Learning-based Multi-sieve Co-reference Resolution with Knowledge. In *Proceedings of the Joint Conference on Empirical Methods in Natural Language Processing and Computational Natural Language Learning*.

Lev Ratinov, Dan Roth, Doug Downey, and Mike Anderson. 2011. Local and Global Algorithms for Disambiguation to Wikipedia. In *Proceedings of the Association for Computational Linguistics*.

Avirup Sil and Alexander Yates. 2013. Re-ranking for Joint Named-Entity Recognition and Linking. In *Proceedings of the International Conference on Information and Knowledge Management*.

Sameer Singh, Sebastian Riedel, Brian Martin, Jiaping Zheng, and Andrew McCallum. 2013. Joint Inference of Entities, Relations, and Coreference. In *Proceedings of the 2013 Workshop on Automated Knowledge Base Construction*.

David A. Smith and Jason Eisner. 2008. Dependency Parsing by Belief Propagation. In *Proceedings of the Conference on Empirical Methods in Natural Language Processing*.

Wee Meng Soon, Hwee Tou Ng, and Daniel Chung Yong Lim. 2001. A Machine Learning Approach to Coreference Resolution of Noun Phrases. *Computational Linguistics*, 27(4):521–544, December.

Veselin Stoyanov, Nathan Gilbert, Claire Cardie, and Ellen Riloff. 2009. Conundrums in Noun Phrase Coreference Resolution: Making Sense of the State-of-the-Art. In *Proceedings of the Association for Computational Linguistics*.

Veselin Stoyanov, Claire Cardie, Nathan Gilbert, Ellen Riloff, David Buttler, and David Hysom. 2010. Coreference Resolution with Reconcile. In *Proceedings of the Association for Computational Linguistics: Short Papers*.

Marc Vilain, John Burger, John Aberdeen, Dennis Connolly, and Lynette Hirschman. 1995. A Model-Theoretic Coreference Scoring Scheme. In *Proceedings of the Conference on Message Understanding*.

Kellie Webster and James R. Curran. 2014. Limited Memory Incremental Coreference Resolution. In *Proceedings of the Conference on Computational Linguistics*.

Tong Zhang and David Johnson. 2003. A Robust Risk Minimization Based Named Entity Recognition System. In *Proceedings of the Conference on Natural Language Learning*.

Jiaping Zheng, Luke Vilnis, Sameer Singh, Jinho D. Choi, and Andrew McCallum. 2013. Dynamic Knowledge-Base Alignment for Coreference Resolution. In *Proceedings of the Conference on Computational Natural Language Learning*.

Learning Strictly Local Subsequential Functions

Jane Chandlee
University of Delaware
Department of Linguistics
and Cognitive Science
125 East Main Street
Newark, DE 19716
janemc@udel.edu

Rémi Eyraud
QARMA team
Laboratoire d'Informatique
Fondamentale
Marseille, France
remi.eyraud@
lif.univ-mrs.fr

Jeffrey Heinz
University of Delaware
Department of Linguistics
and Cognitive Science
125 East Main Street
Newark, DE 19716
heinz@udel.edu

Abstract

We define two proper subclasses of subsequential functions based on the concept of Strict Locality (McNaughton and Papert, 1971; Rogers and Pullum, 2011; Rogers et al., 2013) for formal languages. They are called Input and Output Strictly Local (ISL and OSL). We provide an automata-theoretic characterization of the ISL class and theorems establishing how the classes are related to each other and to Strictly Local languages. We give evidence that local phonological and morphological processes belong to these classes. Finally we provide a learning algorithm which provably identifies the class of ISL functions in the limit from positive data in polynomial time and data. We demonstrate this learning result on appropriately synthesized artificial corpora. We leave a similar learning result for OSL functions for future work and suggest future directions for addressing non-local phonological processes.

1 Introduction

In this paper we define two proper subclasses of subsequential functions based on the properties of the well-studied Strictly Local formal languages (McNaughton and Papert, 1971; Rogers and Pullum, 2011; Rogers et al., 2013). These are languages that can be defined with grammars of substrings of length k (called k-factors), such that a string is in the language only if its own k-factors are a subset of the grammar. These languages have also been characterized by Rogers and Pullum (2011) as those that have the property expressed in the following theorem (which can be taken as a defining property):

Theorem 1 (Suffix Substitution Closure). *L is Strictly Local iff for all strings u_1, v_1, u_2, v_2, there exists $k \in \mathbb{N}$ such that for any string x of length $k-1$, if $u_1xv_1, u_2xv_2 \in L$, then $u_1xv_2 \in L$.*

These languages can model natural language phonotactic constraints which pick out contiguous substrings bounded by some length k (Heinz, 2007; Heinz, 2010). We define Input Strictly Local (ISL) and Output Strictly Local (OSL) functions which model phonological *processes* for which the target and triggering context are a bounded contiguous substring. Here our use of 'process' is not specific to rule-based grammatical formalisms (such as SPE (Chomsky and Halle, 1968)). ISL and OSL functions model *mappings* from underlying forms to surface forms, which are also the bedrock of constraint-based frameworks like Optimality Theory (Prince and Smolensky, 1993).

By showing that local phonological processes can be modeled with ISL (and OSL) functions, we provide the strongest computational characterization of the input-output mappings these processes represent. While it has been shown that phonological mappings describable with rules of the form A $\rightarrow$ B / C __ D (where A, B, C, and D are regular languages) are regular (Johnson, 1972; Kaplan and Kay, 1994), and even subsequential (Chandlee and Heinz, 2012; Heinz and Lai, 2013), many logically possible regular and subsequential mappings are not plausible phonological mappings. Since these implausible mappings cannot be modeled with ISL or OSL functions, we provide a more precise notion of

Transactions of the Association for Computational Linguistics, vol. 2, pp. 491–503, 2014. Action Editor: Alexander Clark.
Submitted 4/2014; Revised 8/2014; Published November 1, 2014.

what constitues plausible phonological mappings.

In addition, we present the Input SL Function Learning Algorithm (ISLFLA) and prove that it identifies this class in the limit (Gold, 1967) in polynomial time and data (de la Higuera, 1997). Our approach follows previous work on learning subsequential transductions, namely Oncina et al. (1993), Oncina and Varò (1996), Castellanos et al. (1998), and Gildea and Jurafsky (1996). Oncina et al. (1993) present OSTIA (Onward Subsequential Transducer Inference Algorithm), an algorithm that learns the class of subsequential functions in the limit from positive data. OSTIA is only guaranteed to identify total functions exactly, but Oncina and Varò (1996) and Castellanos et al. (1998) present the modifications OSTIA-N, OSTIA-D, and OSTIA-R, which learn partial functions using negative data, domain information, and range information, respectively.

In terms of linguistic applications, Gildea and Jurafsky (1996) show that OSTIA fails to learn the phonological mapping of English flapping when given natural language data. The authors modified OSTIA with three learning heuristics (context, community, and faithfulness) and showed that the modified learner successfully learns flapping and several other phonological rules. *Context* encodes the idea that phonological changes depend on the context of the segment undergoing the change. *Community* gives the learner the ability to deduce that segments belonging to a natural class are likely to behave similarly. Lastly, *faithfulness*, by which underlying segments are assumed to be realized similarly on the surface, was encoded with a forced alignment between the input-output strings in the data set.[1] We believe this alignment removes OSTIA's guarantee that all subsequential functions are learned.

Similar to the approach of Gildea and Jurafsky (1996), our learner employs a context bias because it knows its target is an ISL function and therefore the transduction only involves bounded contiguous substrings. And similar to OSTIA-D (Oncina and Varò, 1996; Castellanos et al., 1998), the ISLFLA makes use of domain information, because it makes decisions based on the input strings of the data set. It also employs a faithfulness bias in terms of the property *onwardness* (see §2). The ISLFLA is supported by a theoretical result like Oncina et al. (1993), but learns a more restrictive class of mappings. We believe the theoretical results for this class will lead to new algorithms which include something akin to the community bias and that will succeed on natural language data while keeping strong theoretical results.

The proposed learner also builds on earlier work by Chandlee and Koirala (2014) and Chandlee and Jardine (2014) which also used strict locality to learn phonological processes but with weaker theoretical results. The former did not precisely identify the class of functions the learner could learn, and the latter could only guarantee learnability of the ISL functions with a closed learning sample.

The paper is organized as follows. §2 presents the mathematical notations to be used. §3 defines ISL and OSL functions, provides an automata-theoretic characterization for ISL, and establishes some properties of these classes. §4 demonstrates how these functions can model local phonological processes, including substitution, insertion, and deletion. §5 presents the ISLFLA, proves that it efficiently learns the class of ISL functions, and provides demonstrations. §6 concludes.

2 Preliminaries

The set of all possible finite strings of symbols from a finite alphabet Σ and the set of strings of length $\leq n$ are Σ^* and $\Sigma^{\leq n}$, respectively. The unique empty string is represented with λ. The length of a string w is $|w|$, so $|\lambda| = 0$. The set of prefixes of w, $\texttt{Pref}(w)$, is $\{p \in \Sigma^* \mid (\exists s \in \Sigma^*)[w = ps]\}$, and the set of suffixes of w, $\texttt{Suff}(w)$, is $\{s \in \Sigma^* \mid (\exists p \in \Sigma^*)[w = ps]\}$. For all $w \in \Sigma^*$ and $n \in \mathbb{N}$, $\texttt{Suff}^n(w)$ is the single suffix of w of length n if $|w| \geq n$; otherwise $\texttt{Suff}^n(w) = w$. If $w = ps$, then $ws^{-1} = p$ and $p^{-1}w = s$. The longest common prefix of a set of strings S, $\texttt{lcp}(S)$, is $p \in \cap_{w \in S}\texttt{Pref}(w)$ such that $\forall p' \in \cap_{w \in S}\texttt{Pref}(w), |p'| < |p|$.

A function f with domain A and co-domain B is written $f : A \rightarrow B$. We sometimes write $x \mapsto_f y$ for $f(x) = y$. When A and B are free monoids (like Σ^*), the input and output languages of a function f are the stringsets $\texttt{dom}(f) = \{x \mid (\exists y)[x \mapsto_f y]\}$ and $\texttt{image}(f) = \{y \mid (\exists x)[x \mapsto_f y]\}$, respectively.

Following Oncina et al. (1993), a *subsequen-*

[1] The alignment was similar to the string-edit distance mehod used in Hulden et al. (2011).

tial finite state transducer (SFST) is a 6-tuple $(Q, q_0, \Sigma, \Gamma, \delta, \sigma)$, where Q is a finite set of states, Σ and Γ are finite alphabets, $q_0 \in Q$ is the initial state, $\delta \subseteq Q \times \Sigma \times \Gamma^* \times Q$ is a set of edges, and $\sigma : Q \to \Gamma^*$ is the final output function that maps states to strings that are appended to the output if the input ends in that state. δ recursively defines a mapping δ^*: $(q, \lambda, \lambda, q) \in \delta^*$; if $(q, u, v, q') \in \delta^*$ and $(q', \sigma, w, q'') \in \delta$ then $(q, u\sigma, vw, q'') \in \delta^*$. SFSTs are deterministic, which means their edges have the following property: $[(q, a, u, r), (q, a, v, s) \in \delta \Rightarrow u = v \wedge r = s]$. Hence, we also refer to δ as the transition *function*, and $\forall (q, a, u, r) \in \delta$, we let $\delta_1(q, a) = u$ and $\delta_2(q, a) = r$.

The relation that a SFST $\mathcal{T}$ recognizes/accepts/generates is

$$R(\mathcal{T}) = \Big\{ (x, yz) \in \Sigma^* \times \Gamma^* \mid (\exists q \in Q) \\ \big[(q_0, x, y, q) \in \delta^* \wedge z = \sigma(q)\big] \Big\} .$$

Since SFSTs are deterministic, the relations they recognize are functions. *Subsequential functions* are defined as those describable with SFSTs.

For any function $f : \Sigma^* \to \Gamma^*$ and $x \in \Sigma^*$, let the *tails* of x with respect to f be defined as

$$\texttt{tails}_f(x) = \big\{ (y, v) \mid f(xy) = uv \wedge \\ u = \texttt{lcp}(f(x\Sigma^*)) \big\} .$$

If strings $x_1, x_2 \in \Sigma^*$ have the same set of tails with respect to a function f, they are *tail-equivalent* with respect to f and we write $x_1 \sim_f x_2$. Clearly, $\sim_f$ is an equivalence relation which partitions Σ^*.

Theorem 2 (Oncina and Garcia, 1991). *A function f is* subsequential *iff $\sim_f$ partitions Σ^* into* finitely *many blocks.*

The above theorem can be seen as the functional analogue to the MyHill-Nerode theorem for regular languages. Recall that for any stringset L, the tails of a word w w.r.t. L is defined as $\texttt{tails}_L(w) = \{u \mid wu \in L\}$. These tails can be used to partition Σ^* into a finite set of equivalence classes iff L is regular. Furthermore, these equivalence classes are the basis for constructing the (unique up to isomorphism) smallest deterministic acceptor for a regular language. Likewise, Oncina and Garcia's proof of Theorem 2 shows how to construct the (unique up to isomorphism) smallest SFST for a subsequential function f. We refer to this transducer as the canonical transducer for f and denote it with $\mathcal{T}_f^{\mathsf{C}}$. The states of $\mathcal{T}_f^{\mathsf{C}}$ are in one-to-one correspondence with $\texttt{tails}_f(x)$ for all $x \in \Sigma^*$ (Oncina and García, 1991). To construct $\mathcal{T}_f^{\mathsf{C}}$ first let, for all $x \in \Sigma^*$ and $a \in \Sigma$, the contribution of a w.r.t. x be $\texttt{cont}_f(a, x) = \texttt{lcp}(f(x\Sigma^*)^{-1}\texttt{lcp}(f(xa\Sigma^*))$. Then,

- $Q = \{\texttt{tails}_f(x) \mid x \in \Sigma^*\}$,
- $q_0 = \texttt{tails}_f(\lambda)$,
- $\forall \texttt{tails}_f(x) \in Q$, $\sigma(\texttt{tails}_f(x)) = \texttt{lcp}(f(x\Sigma^*))^{-1} f(x)$ if $x \in \texttt{dom}(f)$ and is undefined otherwise,
- $\delta = \big\{(\texttt{tails}_f(x), a, \texttt{cont}_f(a, x), \texttt{tails}_f(xa))\big\}$.

$\mathcal{T}_f^{\mathsf{C}}$ has an important property called *onwardness*.

Definition 1 (onwardness). *For all $q \in Q$ let the outputs of the edges out of q be $\texttt{outs}(q) = \big\{u \mid (\exists a \in \Sigma)(\exists r \in Q)[(q, a, u, r) \in \delta]\big\}$. A SFST $\mathcal{T}$ is* onward *if for all $q \in Q \setminus \{q_0\}$, $\texttt{lcp}(\texttt{outs}(q)) = \lambda$.*

Informally, this means that the writing of output is never delayed. Readers are referred to Oncina and García (1991), Oncina et al. (1993), and Mohri (1997) for more on SFSTs.

3 Strictly Local Functions

In this section we define Input and Output Strictly Local functions and provide properties of these classes. These definitions are analogous to the language-theoretic definition of Strictly Local languages (Theorem 1) (Rogers and Pullum, 2011; Rogers et al., 2013).

Definition 2 (Input Strictly Local Function). *A function f is Input Strictly Local (ISL) if there is a k such that for all $u_1, u_2 \in \Sigma^*$, if $\texttt{Suff}^{k-1}(u_1) = \texttt{Suff}^{k-1}(u_2)$ then $\texttt{tails}_f(u_1) = \texttt{tails}_f(u_2)$.*

The theorem below establishes an automata-theoretic characterization of ISL functions.

Theorem 3. *A function f is ISL iff there is some k such that f can be described with a SFST for which*

1. *$Q = \Sigma^{\leq k-1}$ and $q_0 = \lambda$*
2. *$(\forall q \in Q, \forall a \in \Sigma, \forall u \in \Gamma^*)$ $\big[(q, a, u, q') \in \delta \Rightarrow q' = \texttt{Suff}^{k-1}(qa)\big]$.*

This theorem helps make clear how ISL functions are Markovian: the output for input symbol a depends on the last $(k-1)$ input symbols. Also, since the transducer defined in Theorem 3 is deterministic, it is unique and we refer to it as $\mathcal{T}_f^{\texttt{ISL}}$. $\mathcal{T}_f^{\texttt{ISL}}$ may not be isomorphic to $\mathcal{T}_f^{\texttt{C}}$. Figure 1 shows $\mathcal{T}_f^{\texttt{ISL}}$ (with $k=2$) and $\mathcal{T}_f^{\texttt{C}}$ for the identity function.[2]

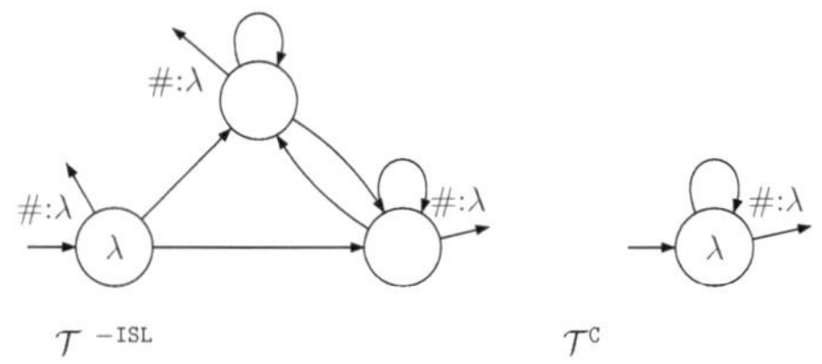

Figure 1: Non-isomorphic $\mathcal{T}_f^{\texttt{ISL}}$ (left) and $\mathcal{T}_f^{\texttt{C}}$ (right)

Before we present the proof of Theorem 3, we make the following remarks, and then prove a lemma.

Remark 1. *For all $n, m \in \mathbb{N}$ with $n \leq m$, and for all $w \in \Sigma^*$, $\texttt{Suff}^n(\texttt{Suff}^m(w)) = \texttt{Suff}^n(w)$ since both w and $\texttt{Suff}^m(w)$ share the same n-long suffix.*

Remark 2. *For all $w, v \in \Sigma^*, k \in \mathbb{N}$, $\texttt{Suff}^{k-1}\big(\texttt{Suff}^{k-1}(w)v\big) = \texttt{Suff}^{k-1}(wv)$. This is a direct consequence of Remark 1.*

Lemma 1. *Let $\mathcal{T}$ be a SFST constructed as in Theorem 3. If (λ, w, u, q) in δ^* then $q = \texttt{Suff}^{k-1}(w)$.*

Proof. The proof is by induction on δ^*. The base case follows from the facts that $(\lambda,\lambda,\lambda,\lambda) \in \delta^*$ (by definition of δ^*), and that $\lambda = \texttt{Suff}^{k-1}(\lambda)$.

Next assume the inductive hypothesis (IH) that there exists $w \in \Sigma^*, u \in \Gamma^*$, such that $(\lambda, w, u, q) \in \delta^*$ implies $q = \texttt{Suff}^{k-1}(w)$. We show $\forall a \in \Sigma$, $\forall x \in \Gamma^*$ that $(\lambda, wa, ux, q') \in \delta^*$ implies $q' = \texttt{Suff}^{k-1}(wa)$. Now $(\lambda, w, u, \texttt{Suff}^{k-1}(w)) \in \delta^*$ (by IH) so $(\texttt{Suff}^{k-1}(w), a, x, q') \in \delta$. By construction of $\mathcal{T}$, $q' = \texttt{Suff}^{k-1}(\texttt{Suff}^{k-1}(w)a)$, which by Remark 2, equals $\texttt{Suff}^{k-1}(wa)$. □

Proof of Theorem 3. ($\Leftarrow$) Fix $k \in \mathbb{N}$ and let f be a function described by $\mathcal{T} = \{Q, q_0, \Sigma, \Gamma, \delta, \sigma\}$ constructed as in Theorem 3. Let $w_1, w_2 \in \Sigma^*$ such that $\texttt{Suff}^{k-1}(w_1) = \texttt{Suff}^{k-1}(w_2)$. By Lemma 1, both w_1 and w_2 lead to the same state and therefore $\texttt{tails}_f(w_1) = \texttt{tails}_f(w_2)$. Thus f is k-ISL.

($\Rightarrow$) Consider any ISL function f. Then there is a k such that $(\forall w_1, w_2 \in \Sigma^*)[\texttt{Suff}^{k-1}(w_1) = \texttt{Suff}^{k-1}(w_2) \Rightarrow \texttt{tails}_f(w_1) = \texttt{tails}_f(w_2)]$. We show that $\mathcal{T}_f^{\texttt{ISL}}$ exists. Since $\Sigma^{\leq k-1}$ is a finite set, the equivalence relation $\sim_f$ partitions Σ^* into at most $|\Sigma^{\leq k-1}|$ blocks. Hence by Theorem 2, f is subsequential and a canonical subsequential transducer $\mathcal{T}_f^{\texttt{C}} = \{Q_c, q_{0c}, \Sigma, \Gamma, \delta_c, \sigma_c\}$ exists.

Construct $\mathcal{T} = \{Q, q_0, \Sigma, \Gamma, \delta, \sigma\}$ as follows:

- $Q = \Sigma^{\leq k-1}$ and $q_0 = \lambda$
- $\forall q \in Q, \sigma(q) = \sigma_c\big(\texttt{tails}_f(q)\big)$ if $f(q)$ is defined, else $\sigma(q)$ is undefined.
- $\forall q \in Q$, $\forall a \in \Sigma$, $\forall u \in \Gamma^*$, $\big(q, a, u, \texttt{Suff}^{k-1}(qa)\big) \in \delta$ iff $\big(\texttt{tails}_f(q), a, u, \texttt{tails}_f(qa)\big) \in \delta_c$.

First, by its construction, the states and transitions of $\mathcal{T}$ meet requirements (1) and (2) of Theorem 3.

Next, we show that $\mathcal{T}$ computes the same function as $\mathcal{T}_f^{\texttt{C}}$. We first establish by induction on δ^* the following ($\star$): $\forall w \in \Sigma^*$, $\forall u \in \Gamma^*$, $\big(q_0, w, u, \texttt{Suff}^{k-1}(w)\big) \in \delta^*$ iff $\big(\texttt{tails}_f(\lambda), w, u, \texttt{tails}_f(w)\big) \in \delta_c^*$.

Clearly $\big(\texttt{tails}_f(\lambda), \lambda, \lambda, \texttt{tails}_f(\lambda)\big) \in \delta_c^*$ and $\big(\lambda,\lambda,\lambda,\lambda\big) \in \delta^*$ by definition of the extended transition function. Thus the base case is satisfied.

Next assume the inductive hypothesis (IH) for $w \in \Sigma^*$ and $u \in \Gamma^*$. We show $\forall a \in \Sigma$ and $\forall x \in \Gamma^*$ that $\big(\lambda, wa, ux, \texttt{Suff}^{k-1}(wa)\big) \in \delta^*$ iff $\big(\texttt{tails}_f(\lambda), wa, ux, \texttt{tails}_f(wa)\big) \in \delta_c^*$.

Suppose $\big(\texttt{tails}_f(\lambda), wa, ux, \texttt{tails}_f(wa)\big) \in \delta_c^*$. By IH, $\big(\texttt{tails}_f(\lambda), w, u, \texttt{tails}_f(w)\big) \in \delta_c^*$; hence $\big(\texttt{tails}_f(w), a, x, \texttt{tails}_f(wa)\big) \in \delta_c$.

Let $q = \texttt{Suff}^{k-1}(w)$. Observe that $\texttt{Suff}^{k-1}(w) = \texttt{Suff}^{k-1}(q)$ by Remark 1. Consequently, since f is k-ISL, $\texttt{tails}_f(w) = \texttt{tails}_f(q)$. Similarly, $\texttt{Suff}^{k-1}(wa) = \texttt{Suff}^{k-1}(qa)$ and thus $\texttt{tails}_f(wa) = \texttt{tails}_f(qa)$. By substitution then, we have $\big(\texttt{tails}_f(\lambda), w, u, \texttt{tails}_f(q)\big) \in \delta_c^*$ and $\big(\texttt{tails}_f(q), a, x, \texttt{tails}_f(qa)\big) \in \delta_c$.

By construction of $\mathcal{T}$, $\big(q, a, x, \texttt{Suff}^{k-1}(qa)\big) \in \delta$. By IH, $\big(\lambda, w, u, \texttt{Suff}^{k-1}(w)\big) = \big(\lambda, w, u, q\big) \in \delta^*$. Thus, $\big(\lambda, wa, ux, \texttt{Suff}^{k-1}(qa)\big) \in \delta^*$ which is the same as saying $\big(\lambda, wa, ux, \texttt{Suff}^{k-1}(wa)\big) \in \delta^*$.

Conversely, consider any $a \in \Sigma$ and $x \in \Gamma^*$ and suppose $\big(\lambda, wa, ux, \texttt{Suff}^{k-1}(wa)\big) \in \delta^*$.

[2]In all figures, single-symbol transition labels indicate that the input and output are identical, and the final output function is represented as a transition on the end-of-word symbol #.

By IH, $(\lambda, w, u, \mathtt{Suff}^{k-1}(w)) \in \delta^*$; hence $(\mathtt{Suff}^{k-1}(w), a, x, \mathtt{Suff}^{k-1}(wa)) \in \delta$. As before, letting $q = \mathtt{Suff}^{k-1}(w)$, it follows that $\mathtt{Suff}^{k-1}(w) = \mathtt{Suff}^{k-1}(q)$ so $\mathtt{tails}_f(w) = \mathtt{tails}_f(q)$, and $\mathtt{Suff}^{k-1}(wa) = \mathtt{Suff}^{k-1}(qa)$ so $\mathtt{tails}_f(wa) = \mathtt{tails}_f(qa)$. Therefore, $(q, a, x, \mathtt{Suff}^{k-1}(qa)) \in \delta$.

By construction of $\mathcal{T}$, this means $(\mathtt{tails}_f(w), a, x, \mathtt{tails}_f(wa)) \in \delta_c$. By IH, $(\mathtt{tails}_f(\lambda), w, u, \mathtt{tails}_f(w)) \in \delta_c^*$. By the definition of the extended transition function, it follows that $(\mathtt{tails}_f(\lambda), wa, ux, \mathtt{tails}_f(wa)) \in \delta_c^*$. This completes the induction, establishing ($\star$).

Let $w \in \Sigma^*$. If $f(w)$ is defined then $f(w) = uv$ where $(\mathtt{tails}_f(\lambda), w, u, \mathtt{tails}_f(w)) \in \delta_c^*$ and $\sigma_c(\mathtt{tails}_f(w)) = v$. From ($\star$), we know $(\lambda, w, u, \mathtt{Suff}^{k-1}(w)) \in \delta^*$. Also, $\sigma(\mathtt{Suff}^{k-1}(w)) = \sigma_c(\mathtt{tails}_f(\mathtt{Suff}^{k-1}(w)))$. Since f is k-ISL, $\mathtt{tails}_f(w) = \mathtt{tails}_f(\mathtt{Suff}^{k-1}(w))$ (cf. Remark 1). Thus $\sigma(\mathtt{Suff}^{k-1}(w)) = \sigma_c(\mathtt{tails}_f(w)) = v$. Therefore $\mathcal{T}(w) = uv$ also.

If $f(w)$ is not defined then there are two cases. Case 1: $(\mathtt{tails}_f(\lambda), w, u, \mathtt{tails}_f(w)) \notin \delta_c^*$. By the above lemma, it follows $(\lambda, w, u, \mathtt{Suff}^{k-1}(w)) \notin \delta^*$ and so $\mathcal{T}(w)$ is also defined. Case 2: $(\mathtt{tails}_f(\lambda), w, u, \mathtt{tails}_f(w)) \in \delta_c^*$ but $\sigma_c(\mathtt{tails}_f(w))$ is undefined. By construction of $\mathcal{T}$, $\sigma(\mathtt{Suff}^{k-1}(w))$ is also undefined. □

Similar to Definition 2 above, the following definition of OSL functions says that if the outputs of two input strings share the same suffix of length $(k-1)$, then those inputs have the same tails.

Definition 3 (Output Strictly Local Function). *A function f is Output Strictly Local (OSL) if there is a k such that for all $u_1, u_2 \in \Sigma^*$, if $\mathtt{Suff}^{k-1}(f(u_1)) = \mathtt{Suff}^{k-1}(f(u_2))$ then $\mathtt{tails}_f(u_1) = \mathtt{tails}_f(u_2)$.*

The automata-theoretic characterization of this class is left as future work.

Next, some properties of ISL and OSL functions are identified. The proofs of the following theorems will refer to the example SFSTs in Figure 2.

First we establish that ISL and OSL functions are proper subclasses of the subsequential functions. (They are subclasses by definition.)

Theorem 4. *There are subsequential functions which are neither ISL nor OSL.*

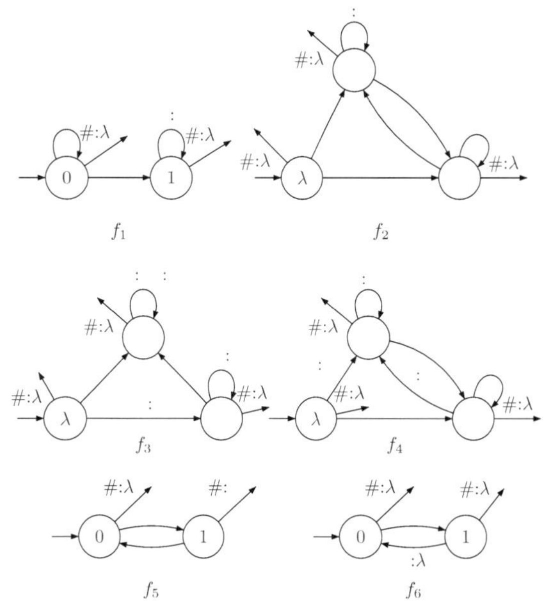

Figure 2: Examples for proofs of Theorems 4-7

Proof. Consider the subsequential function f_1 in Figure 2 and choose any $k \in \mathbb{N}$. Since $f_1(bc^kb) = bc^kb$ and $f_1(ac^kb) = ac^ka$ it follows that $\mathtt{tails}_{f_1}(bc^k) \neq \mathtt{tails}_{f_1}(ac^k)$ even though inputs bc^k and ac^k share a common suffix of length $(k-1)$. Likewise, the outputs of these inputs $f_1(bc^k) = bc^k$ and $f_1(ac^k) = ac^k$ share a common suffix of length $(k-1)$, but the tails of these inputs, as mentioned, are distinct. Hence by Definitions 2 and 3, there is no k for which f_1 is ISL or OSL. □

Theorem 5. *The class of ISL functions is incomparable to the class of OSL functions.*

Proof. Consider f_2 in Figure 2. This function is ISL by Theorem 3. However it is not OSL. Consider any $k \in \mathbb{N}$. Observe that $f_2(aa^k) = f_2(ab^k) = ab^k$ and so the outputs share the same suffix of length $(k-1)$. However, $\mathtt{tails}_{f_2}(aa^k) \neq \mathtt{tails}_{f_2}(ab^k)$ since $(a, b) \in \mathtt{tails}_{f_2}(aa^k)$ but $(a, a) \in \mathtt{tails}_{f_2}(ab^k)$.

Similarly, consider f_3 in Figure 2. This function is 2-OSL because inputs mapped to outputs which end in a have the same tails (i.e., they all lead to state a), and inputs mapped to outputs ending in b have the same tails.

However, f_3 is not ISL. Consider any $k \in \mathbb{N}$. The inputs cb^k and ab^k share the same suffix of length $(k-1)$. However, $\mathtt{tails}_{f_3}(cb^k) \neq$

$\mathtt{tails}_{f3}(ab^k)$ since $(b, b) \in \mathtt{tails}_{f3}(cb^k)$ but $(b, a) \in \mathtt{tails}_{f3}(ab^k)$.

Finally, the two classes are obviously not disjoint, since the identity function is both ISL and OSL. □

Theorem 6. *The output language of an ISL or OSL function is not necessarily a Strictly Local language.*

Proof. Consider f_4 in Figure 2. By Theorem 3, it is ISL. It is also 2-OSL since inputs mapped to outputs which end in a have the same tails (i.e., they all lead to state a). Similarly, inputs mapped to outputs ending in b have the same tails.

Let $k \in \mathbb{N}$. Observe that $f_4(a^k) = a^{2k}$ and further that there is no input x and k such that $f_4(x) = a^{2k+1}$. Since $a^{2k} = a^{k-1}a^k a = a^{k-2}a^k aa$, if the output language of f_4 were SL it would follow, by Theorem 1, that $a^{k-1}a^k aa = a^{2k+1}$ also belongs to the output language. But there is no input in Σ^* which f_4 maps to an odd sequence of a's. □

Theorem 7. *If either the output or input language of a subsequential function f is Strictly Local then it does not follow that f belongs to either ISL or OSL.*

Proof. Let $\Sigma = \Gamma = \{a\}$ and consider the function f_5 which, for all $n \in \mathbb{N}$, maps a^n to a^n if n is even and a^n to $a^n a$ if n is odd. f_5 is subsequential, as shown in Figure 2, and its domain, a^*, is a Strictly Local language. However, f_5 is neither ISL nor OSL for any k since the $\mathtt{tails}$ of a^{2k} includes (λ, λ) but the $\mathtt{tails}$ of aa^{2k} includes (λ, a).

Next consider f_6, which for all $n \in \mathbb{N}$ maps a^n to a^m where m = (n div 2) if n is even and m = (n div 2)+1 if n is odd. f_6 is subsequential, as shown in Figure 2, and the $\mathtt{image}(f) = a^*$ is Strictly Local. However, f is neither ISL nor OSL for any k since the $\mathtt{tails}$ of a^{2k} includes (a, a) but the $\mathtt{tails}$ of aa^{2k} includes (a, λ). □

4 Relevance to Phonology

This section will briefly discuss the range of phonological processes that can be modeled with ISL and/or OSL functions by providing illustrative examples for three common, representative processes. These are shown in (1) with SPE-style rules.

(1) a. Devoicing: D → T / __ #
b. Epenthesis: ∅ → ə / {l, r} __ [-coronal]
c. Deletion: {θ, ð} → ∅ / __ {θ, s}

See Chandlee (2014) for more details.

First, consider the process of final obstruent devoicing (1-a), attested in German and other languages. This process causes an underlying voiced obstruent in word-final position to surface as its voiceless counterpart. In (1-a), D abbreviates the set of voiced obstruents and T the voiceless obstruents.[3]

The mapping from underlying form to surface form that this process describes is represented with the 2-ISL function in Figure 3 (note N represents any sonorant).

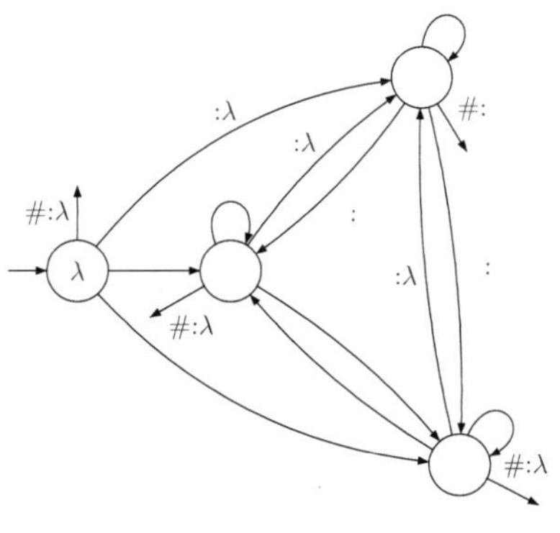

Figure 3: $\mathcal{T}_f^{\mathtt{ISL}}$ for (1-a) with $k = 2$ and $\Sigma = \{$T, D, N$\}$

In addition to substitution processes like (1-a), another common type of process is insertion of a segment, such as the ə-epenthesis process attested in Dutch (Warner et al., 2001). This process inserts a schwa between a liquid and a non-coronal consonant, as specified by (1-b). Using L to represent the liquids {l, r} and K to represent any non-coronal consonant, Figure 4 presents $\mathcal{T}_f^{\mathtt{ISL}}$ for this process. Following Beesley and Karttunen (2003), the symbol '?' represents any segment of the alphabet other than the ones for which transitions are defined.[4]

Lastly, an example deletion process from Greek (Joseph and Philippaki-Warburton, 1987) deletes interdental fricatives before /θ/ or /s/, as in (1-c). Figure 5 presents $\mathcal{T}_f^{\mathtt{ISL}}$ for this process.

[3]These abbreviations serve to improve the readability of the FST - it is assumed that the transduction replaces a given voiced obstruent with its voiceless counterpart (not with any voiceless obstruent).

[4]This means Figure 4 is actually a shorthand for $\mathcal{T}_f^{\mathtt{ISL}}$, which would otherwise have a distinct state for each symbol now represented with '?'.

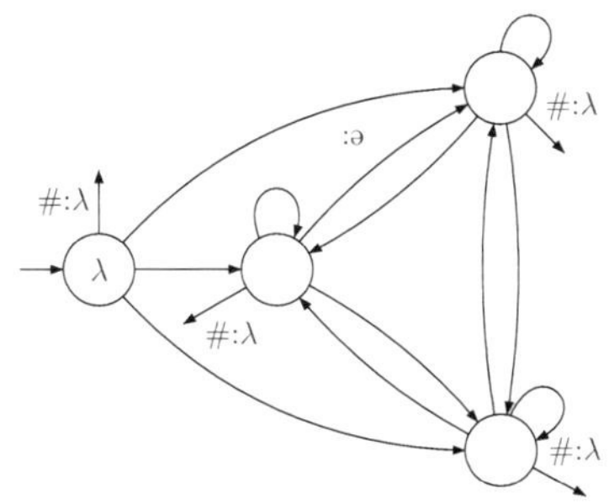

Figure 4: $\mathcal{T}_f^{\mathrm{ISL}}$ for (1-b) with $k = 2$ and $\Sigma = \{$L, K, ?$\}$

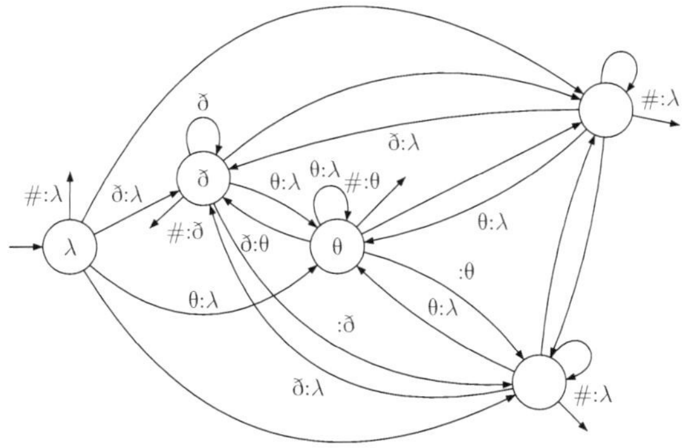

Figure 5: $\mathcal{T}_f^{\mathrm{ISL}}$ for (1-c) with $k = 2$ and $\Sigma = \{$θ, ð, s, ?$\}$

The German, Dutch, and Greek examples demonstrate how ISL functions can be used to model the input-output mapping of a phonological rule. Beyond substitution, insertion, and deletion, it is shown in Chandlee (2014) that ISL and/or OSL functions can also model many metathesis patterns, specifically those for which there is an upper bound on the amount of material that intervenes between a segment's original and surface positions (this appears to include all synchronic patterns). In addition, morpho-phonological processes such as local partial reduplication (i.e., in which the reduplicant is affixed adjacent to the portion of the base it was copied from) and general affixation are also shown to be ISL or OSL. More generally, we currently conjecture that a SPE-style rewrite rule of the form A → B/ C__ D which applies simultaneously (left-to-right) describes an Input (Output) Strictly Local function iff there is a k such that for all $w \in CAD$ it is the case that $|w| \leq k$. We refer readers to Kaplan and Kay (1994) and Hulden (2009) for more on how SPE rules and application modes determine mappings.

In contrast, non-local (long-distance) processes such as vowel harmony with transparent vowels (Gainor et al., 2012; Heinz and Lai, 2013), long distance consonant harmony (Hansson, 2001; Rose and Walker, 2004; Luo, 2013) and dissimilation (Suzuki, 1998; Bennett, 2013; Payne, 2013), unbounded displacement/metathesis (Chandlee et al., 2012; Chandlee and Heinz, 2012), non-local partial reduplication (Riggle, 2003), and some tonal patterns (Jardine, 2013) cannot be modeled with ISL or OSL functions. In §6 we comment on the potential for adapting the current analysis to non-local mappings.

The next section presents a learning algorithm for ISL functions, the ISLFLA. The development of a corresponding algorithm for OSL functions is the subject of ongoing work, but see §6 for comments.

5 Learning Input Strictly Local Functions

We now present a learning algorithm for the class of ISL functions that uses its defining property as an inductive principle to generalize from a finite amount of data to a possibly infinite function. This learner begins with a prefix tree representation of this data and then generalizes by merging states.[5] Its state merging criterion is based on the defining property of ISL functions: two input strings with the same suffix of length $(k-1)$ have the same tails. The next section explains in detail how the algorithm works.

5.1 The Algorithm: ISLFLA

Given a finite dataset D of input-output string pairs (w, w') such that $f(w) = w'$, where f is the target function, the learner tries to build $\mathcal{T}_f^{\mathrm{ISL}}$. The dataset is submitted to the learner in the form of a prefix tree transducer (PTT), which is defined in Definition 4.

Definition 4 (Prefix Tree Transducer)**.** *A prefix tree transducer for finite set* $D = \{(w, w') \mid f(w) = w'\}$ *for some* f *is* $PTT(D) = (Q, q_0, \Sigma, \Gamma, \delta, \sigma)$*, where*

- $Q = \bigcup\{\texttt{Pref}(w) | (w, w') \in D\}$ *and* $q_0 = \lambda$
- $\delta = \{(u, a, \lambda, ua) \mid u, ua \in Q\}$
- $\sigma(w) = w'$ *for all* $(w, w') \in D$

[5]This general strategy is common in grammatical inference. See Angluin (1982), Heinz (2009), and de la Higuera (2010).

As an example, the sample of data in (2) exemplifies the final devoicing rule in (1-a). Figure 6 gives the PTT for this data.

(2) {(D, T), (DD, DT), (DNT, DNT), (NND, NNT), (TDN, TDN)}

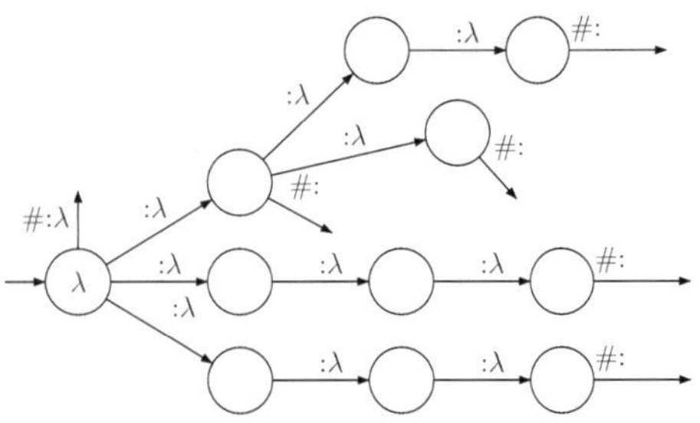

Figure 6: PTT for the data in (2)

Given such a PTT, the learner's first step is to make it *onward*. In the PTT, the output string is withheld until the end of the input (i.e., #) is reached. In the onward version (shown in Figure 7), output is advanced as close to the root as possible. This involves determining the `lcp` of all the output strings of all outgoing transitions of a state (starting from the leaves) and suffixing that `lcp` to the output of the single incoming transition of the state.

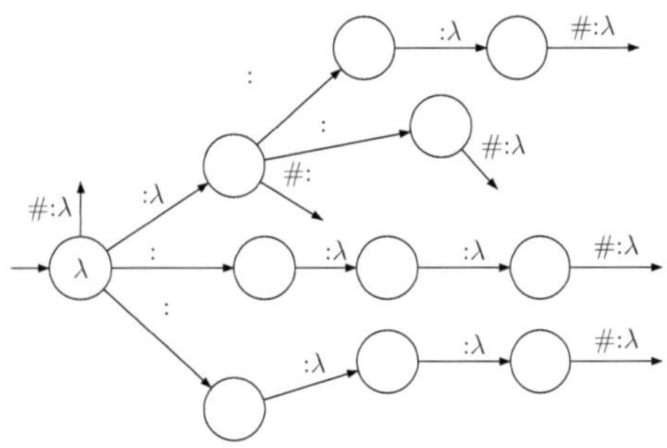

Figure 7: Onward version of the PTT in Figure 6

Once the learner has constructed this onward representation of the data, it begins to merge states, using two nested loops. The outer loop proceeds through the entire state set (ordered lexicographically) and merges each state with the state that corresponds to its $(k-1)$-length suffix. For example, for final devoicing $k = 2$, so each state will be merged with the state that represents its final symbol. This merging may introduce non-determinism, which must be removed since by definition $\mathcal{T}_f^{\text{ISL}}$ is deterministic. Non-determinism is removed in the inner loop with additional state merges.

Consider the situation depicted on the lefthand side of Figure 8, which resulted from a previous merge. The non-determinism could be resolved by

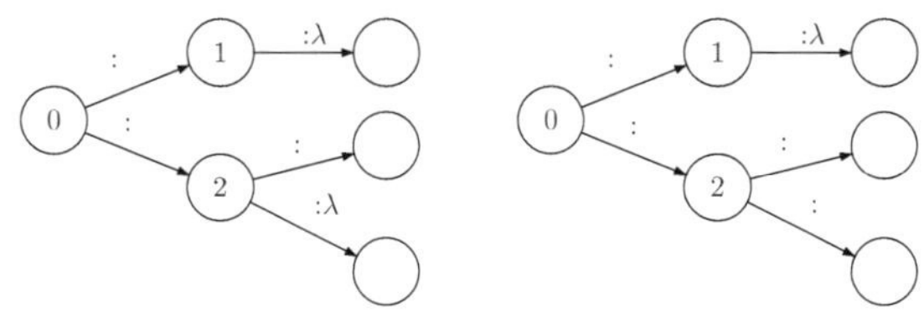

Figure 8: Before (left) and after (right) `pushback`

merging states 1 and 2, except for the fact that the output strings of the two transitions differ. Before merging 1 and 2, therefore, the learner performs an operation called `pushback` that retains the `lcp` of the two output strings and prefixes what's left to all output strings of all outgoing transitions from the respective destination states.

Definition 5 (`pushback` (Oncina et al., 1993)). *For SFST* $\mathcal{T} = (Q, q_0, \Sigma, \Gamma, \delta, \sigma)$, $v \in \Sigma^*$, *and* $e = (q, a, w, q') \in \delta$, $\texttt{pushback}(\mathcal{T}, v, e) = (Q, q_0, \Sigma, \Gamma, \delta', \sigma)$ *where* $\delta' = (\delta \cup \{q, a, wv^{-1}, q')\} \cup \{(q', b, vz, q'')|(q', b, z, q'') \in \delta\}) \setminus (\{(q', b, z, q'')\} \cup \{e\})$.

In the example in Figure 8, `pushback` is applied to the edges $(0, T, DT, 1)$ and $(0, T, DTN, 2)$. Only the `lcp` of the output strings, which is DT, is retained as the output string of both edges. The remainder (which is λ and N, respectively) is prefixed to the output string of all transitions leaving the respective destination state. The result is shown on the righthand side of Figure 8. Essentially, `pushback` 'undoes' onwardness when needed.

After `pushback`, states 1 and 2 can be merged. This removes the initial non-determinism but creates new non-determinism. The inner loop iterates until all non-determinism is resolved, after which the outer loop continues with the next state in the order. If the inner loop encounters non-determinism that cannot be removed, the ISLFLA exits with a message indicating that the data sample is insufficient.

Non-removable non-determinism occurs if and only if the situation depicted on the left in Figure 9 obtains. The normal procedure for removing non-

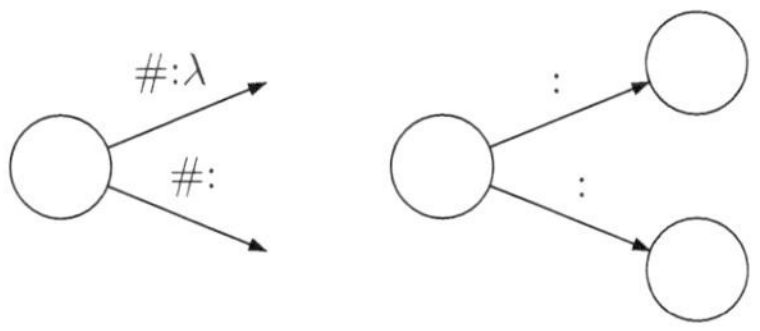

Figure 9: Irreparable non-determinism (left) and non-determinism from an outer loop merge (right).

determinism cannot be applied in this case. Assuming $z \neq \lambda$, all of z would have to be pushed back, but since this transition has no destination state there is nowhere for z to go. OSTIA handles this situation by rejecting the outer loop merge that led to it, restoring the FST to its state before that merge and moving on to the next possible merge. But the ISLFLA cannot reject merges. If it could, the possibility would arise that two states with the same $(k-1)$-length suffix would remain distinct in the final FST the learner outputs. Such a FST would not (by definition) be ISL. Therefore, the algorithm is at an impasse: rejecting a merge can lead to a non-ISL FST, while allowing it can lead to a non-subsequential (hence non-ISL) FST. It therefore terminates. Below is pseudo-code for the ISLFLA.

Data: $PTT(D)$
Result: $\mathcal{T}_f^{\mathtt{ISL}}$
$\tau = \mathtt{onward}(PTT)$
$q = \mathtt{next}(Q_\tau, \mathtt{first}(Q_\tau))$
while $q < \mathtt{last}(Q_\tau)$ **do**
  $\mathtt{merge}(q, \mathtt{Suff}^{k-1}(q))$
  while $\exists (q, a, x, q_1), (q, a, y, q_2) \in \delta_\tau$ **do**
    if $a = \#$ *and* $x \neq y$ **then**
      exit 'Insufficient data'
    else
      $\mathtt{pushback}(\tau, (q, a, x, q_1), \mathtt{lcp}(x, y))$
      $\mathtt{pushback}(\tau, (q, a, y, q_2), \mathtt{lcp}(x, y))$
      $\mathtt{merge}(q_1, q_2)$
  $q = \mathtt{next}(Q_\tau, q)$
return τ

Algorithm 1: Pseudo-code for the ISLFLA

5.2 Learning Results

Here, we present a proof that the ISLFLA identifies the class of ISL functions in the limit from positive data, in the sense of Gold (1967), with polynomial bounds on time and data (de la Higuera, 1997). First, we establish the notion of characteristic sample.

Definition 6 (Characteristic sample). *A sample CS is characteristic of a function f for an algorithm $\mathfrak{A}$ if for all samples S s.t. $CS \subseteq S$, $\mathfrak{A}$ returns a representation τ such that for all $x \in \mathtt{dom}(f)$, $\tau(x) = f(x)$, and for all $x \notin \mathtt{dom}(f)$, $\tau(x)$ is not defined.*

We can now define the learning criteria.

Definition 7 (Identification in polynomial time and data (de la Higuera, 1997)). *A class $\mathbb{F}$ of functions is identifiable in polynomial time and data using a class $\mathbb{T}$ of representations iff there exist an algorithm $\mathfrak{A}$ and two polynomials $p()$ and $q()$ such that:*

1. *Given a sample S of size m for $f \in \mathbb{F}$, $\mathfrak{A}$ returns a hypothesis in $\mathcal{O}(p(m))$ time;*
2. *For each representation τ of size k of a function $f \in \mathbb{F}$, there exists a characteristic sample CS of f for $\mathfrak{A}$ of size at most $\mathcal{O}(q(k))$.*

Essentially the proof for convergence follows from the fact that given a sufficient sample the algorithm merges *all* and *only* states with the same $(k-1)$-length suffix.

Clearly, merges in the outer loop only involve states with the same $(k-1)$-length suffix. This is also the case for inner loop merges. Consider the scenario depicted on the right in Figure 9, in which q is a state created by an outer loop merge.

After pushback, states s and t will be merged. If $x = \mathtt{Suff}^{k-1}(q)$, then both s and t must have xa as a suffix. Since $|xa| = k$, it follows that $\mathtt{Suff}^{k-1}(s) = \mathtt{Suff}^{k-1}(t)$. It also follows that additional states merged to remove non-determinism resulting from the merge of s and t will have the same suffix of length $(k-1)$. To show that all states with the same $(k-1)$-length suffix will be merged, it is shown that the ISLFLA will *never* encounter the situation in Figure 9, provided the data set includes a *seed* defined as follows.

Definition 8 (ISLFLA seed). *Given a k-ISL function f and $\mathcal{T}_f^{\mathtt{ISL}}$, let $Q' = \{q \in Q \mid \delta_1(q, \#) \neq \lambda\}$. A* seed *for f is $S = S' \cup S''$, where*

- $S' = \{(w, w') \mid [w \in \Sigma^{\leq k} \wedge f(w) = w']\}$
- $S'' = \{(wa, w'') \mid a \in \Sigma, [w \in \Sigma^k \wedge \mathtt{Suff}^{k-1}(w) \in Q' \wedge f(wa) = w'']\}$.

Lemma 2 (Convergence)**.** *A seed for an ISL function f is a characteristic sample for ISLFLA.*

Proof. We show that for any ISL function f and a dataset D that contains a seed S the output of the ISLFLA is $\mathcal{T}_f^{\mathtt{ISL}}$.

Let $PTT(D) = (Q_{PTT}, q_{0_{PTT}}, \Sigma, \Gamma, \delta_{PTT}, \sigma_{PTT})$ be the input to the ISLFLA and $\mathcal{T} = (Q_{\mathcal{T}}, q_{0_{\mathcal{T}}}, \Sigma, \Gamma, \delta_{\mathcal{T}}, \sigma_{\mathcal{T}})$ be its output. First we show that $Q_{\mathcal{T}} = \Sigma^{\leq k-1}$. By Definitions 4 and 8, $\Sigma^{\leq k-1} \subseteq Q_{PTT}$. Since the ISLFLA only merges states with the same $(k-1)$-length suffix, $\Sigma^{\leq k-1} \subseteq Q_{\mathcal{T}}$. Since it does not exit until all states q have been merged with $\mathtt{Suff}^{k-1}(q)$, $Q_{\mathcal{T}} = \Sigma^{\leq k-1}$.

Next we show that given S, the algorithm will never need to merge two states q_1 and q_2 such that $\delta_1(q_1, \#) \neq \delta_1(q_2, \#)$. Let $\delta_1(q_1, \#) = z$, and $\delta_1(q_2, \#) = x$ with $z \neq x$ and $q_1 = \mathtt{Suff}^{k-1}(q_2)$. By Definition 2, $\mathtt{tails}_f(q_1) = \mathtt{tails}_f(q_2)$, so if $z \neq x$ it must be the case that q_2 does not have transitions for all $a \in \Sigma$. This is because the only way for the output strings of the outgoing transitions of q_2 to differ from those of q_1 is if fewer transitions were present on q_2 when the PTT was made onward. (By definition of S we know q_1 has transitions for all $a \in \Sigma$.) But since $\mathtt{tails}_f(q_1) = \mathtt{tails}_f(q_2)$, we also know that $z = ux$ for some $u \in \Gamma^*$.

By Definition 8, all states up to length k have transitions for all $a \in \Sigma$; therefore, $|q_2| \geq k+1$. This means $\exists q' \in \Sigma^k$ between q_1 and q_2, which will be merged with some other state before q_2 will. This merge will cause non-determinism, which in turn will trigger $\mathtt{pushback}$ and cause u to move further down the branch toward q_2. By extension there will be $|q_2| - k$ states between q_1 and q_2, each of which will be merged, triggering $\mathtt{pushback}$ of u, so that by the time q_1 and q_2 are merged, $\delta_1(q_2, \#) = ux = z = \delta_1(q_2, \#)$. Thus, all non-determinism can be removed, and so $\mathcal{T}$ is subsequential.

It remains to show that $\forall q \in Q_{\mathcal{T}}, a \in \Sigma$, $\delta_2(q, a) = \mathtt{Suff}^{k-1}(qa)$. Since state merging preserves transitions, this follows from the construction of $PTT(D)$. By Theorem 3, $\mathcal{T} = \mathcal{T}_f^{\mathtt{ISL}}$. □

Next we establish complexity bounds on the runtime of the ISLFLA and the size of the characteristic sample for ISL functions. We observe that both of these bounds improve the bounds of OSTIA. While not surprising, since ISL functions are less general than subsequential functions, the result is important since it is an example of greater *a priori* knowledge enabling learning with less time and data.

Let m be the length of the longest output string in the sample and let n denote the number of states of the PTT; n is at most the sum of the lengths of the input strings of the pairs in the sample.

Lemma 3 (Polynomial time)**.** *The time complexity of the ISLFLA is in $\mathcal{O}(n \cdot m \cdot k \cdot |\Sigma|)$.*

Proof. First, making the PTT onward can be done in $\mathcal{O}(m \cdot n)$: it consists of a depth-first parsing of the PTT from its root, with a computation at each state of the $\mathtt{lcp}$ of the outgoing transition outputs after the recursive computation of the function (see de la Higuera (2010), Chap. 18, for details). As the computation of the $\mathtt{lcp}$ takes at most m steps, and as it has to be done for each state, the complexity of this step is effectively in $\mathcal{O}(m \cdot n)$.

For the two loops, we need to find a bound on the number of merges that can occur. States q such that $|q| < k$ do not yield any merges in the outer loop. All other states q' are merged with $\mathtt{Suff}^{k-1}(q)$, in the outer loop or in the inner one. The number of merges is thus bounded by n. Computing the suffix of length $(k-1)$ of any word can be done in $\mathcal{O}(k)$ with a correct implementation of strings of characters. The test of the inner loop can be done in constant time and so can the $\mathtt{merge}$ and $\mathtt{pushback}$ procedures. After each merge, the test of the inner loop needs to be done at most $|\Sigma|$ times. As computing the $\mathtt{lcp}$ has a complexity in $\mathcal{O}(m)$, the overall complexity of the two loops is in $\mathcal{O}(n \cdot m \cdot k \cdot |\Sigma|)$.

The overall complexity of the algorithm is thus $\mathcal{O}(m \cdot n + n \cdot m \cdot k \cdot |\Sigma|) = \mathcal{O}(n \cdot m \cdot k \cdot |\Sigma|)$. □

Let $\mathcal{T}_f^{\mathtt{ISL}} = (Q, q_0, \Sigma, \Gamma, \delta, \sigma)$ be a target transducer. We define $m = \mathtt{max}\{|u| \mid (q, a, u, q') \in \delta\}$, $n = |Q|$, and $p = \mathtt{max}\ \{|v| \mid (q, \#, v) \in \sigma\}$.

Lemma 4 (Polynomial data)**.** *The size of the characteristic sample is in $\mathcal{O}(n \cdot |\Sigma| \cdot k \cdot m + n^2 \cdot m + n \cdot |\Sigma| \cdot p)$.*

Proof. The first item of the seed, S', covers all and only the states of the target: the left projection of these pairs is thus linear in n and every right projection is at most $n \cdot m + p$. Thus the size of S' is at most $n \cdot (n + n \cdot m + p) = \mathcal{O}(n^2 \cdot m + n \cdot p)$.

Concerning the second part, S'', its cardinality is at most $n \cdot |\Sigma|$ (in the rare case where $Q' = Q$).

Each element of the left projection of S'' is of length $(k+1)$ and each element of its right projection is at most of length $(k+1) \cdot m+p$. The size of S'' is thus in $\mathcal{O}(n \cdot |\Sigma| \cdot (k \cdot m+p))$.

Therefore, the size of the characteristic sample is in $\mathcal{O}(n \cdot |\Sigma| \cdot k \cdot m+n^2 \cdot m+n \cdot |\Sigma| \cdot p)$, which is clearly polynomial in the size of the target transducer. □

Theorem 8. *The ISLFLA identifies the class of ISL functions in polynomial time and data.*

Proof. Immediate from Lemmas 2, 3, and 4. □

5.3 Demonstrations

We tested the ISLFLA with the three examples in §4, as well as the English flapping process (t → ɾ / V́ __ V). For each case, a data set was constructed according to Definition 8 using the alphabets presented in §4. The alphabet for English flapping was {V́, V, t, ?}. The value of k is 2 for final devoicing, ə-epenthesis, and fricative deletion and 3 for English flapping. A few additional data points of length 5 or 6 were also added to make the data set a superset of the seed. In all four cases, the learner returned the correct $\mathcal{T}_f^{\text{ISL}}$.

The decision to use artificial corpora in these demonstrations was motivated by the fact that the sample in Definition 8 will not be present in a natural language corpus. That sample includes all possible sequences of symbols from the alphabet of a given length, whereas a natural language corpus will reflect the language-particular restrictions against certain segment sequences (i.e., phonotactics).

As discussed in the introduction, Gildea and Jurafsky (1996) address this issue with natural language data by equipping OSTIA with a community bias, whereby segments belonging to a natural class (i.e., stops, fricatives, sonorants) are expected to behave similarly, and a faithfulness bias, whereby segments are assumed to be realized similarly on the surface. In our demonstrations we put aside the issue of the behavior of segments in a natural class by using abbreviated alphabets (e.g., T for all voiceless stops). But if in fact knowledge of natural classes precedes the learning of phonological processes, the use of such an alphabet is appropriate.

In future developments of the ISLFLA we likewise aim to accommodate natural language data, but in a way that maintains the theoretical result of identification in the limit. The restrictions on segment sequences represented in natural language data amount to 'missing' transitions in the initial prefix tree transducer that is built from that data. In other words, the transducer represents a partial, not a total function. Thus it seems the approach of Oncina and Varò (1996) and Castellanos et al. (1998) could be very instructive, as their use of domain information enabled OSTIA to learn partial functions. In our case, the fact that the domain of an ISL function is an SL language could provide a means of 'filling in' the missing transitions. The details of such an approach are, however, being left for future work.

6 Conclusion

This paper has defined Input and Output Strictly Local functions, which synthesize the properties of subsequential transduction and Strictly Local formal languages. It has provided language-theoretic characterizations of these functions and argued that they can model many phonological and morphological processes. Lastly, an automata-theoretic characterization of ISL functions was presented, along with a learning algorithm that efficiently learn this class in the limit from positive data.

Current work includes developing a comparable automata characterization and learning algorithm for OSL functions, as well as defining additional functional classes to model those phonological processes that cannot be modeled with ISL or OSL functions. The SL languages are just one region of a subregular hierarchy of formal languages (McNaughton and Papert, 1971; Rogers and Pullum, 2011; Rogers et al., 2013). The ISL and OSL functions defined here are the first step in developing a corresponding hierarchy of subregular functions. Of immediate interest to phonology are functional counterparts for the Tier-Based Strictly Local and Strictly Piecewise language classes, which have been shown to model long-distance phonotactics (Heinz, 2010; Heinz et al., 2011). Such functions might be useful for modeling the long-distance processes that repair violations of these phonotactic constraints.

Acknowledgements

We thank Adam Jardine, Jim Rogers, and the three anonymous reviewers for helpful comments. This research was supported by NSF CPS#1035577.

References

Dana Angluin. 1982. Inference of reversible languages. *Journal for the Association of Computing Machinery*, 29(3):741–765.

Kenneth R. Beesley and Lauri Karttunen. 2003. *Finite State Morphology*. Center for the Study of Language and Information.

William Bennett. 2013. *Dissimilation, Consonant Harmony, and Surface Correspondence*. Ph.D. thesis, Rutgers University.

Antonio Castellanos, Enrique Vidal, Miguel A. Varó, and José Oncina. 1998. Language understanding and subsequential transducer learning. *Computer Speech and Language*, 12:193–228.

Jane Chandlee and Jeffrey Heinz. 2012. Bounded copying is subsequential: implications for metathesis and reduplication. In *Proceedings of SIGMORPHON 12*.

Jane Chandlee and Adam Jardine. 2014. Learning phonological mappings by learning Strictly Local functions. In John Kingston, Claire Moore-Cantwell, Joe Pater, and Robert Staubs, editors, *Proceedings of the 2013 Meeting on Phonology*. LSA.

Jane Chandlee and Cesar Koirala. 2014. Learning local phonological rules. In *Proceedings of the 37th Penn Linguistics Conference*.

Jane Chandlee, Angeliki Athanasopoulou, and Jeffrey Heinz. 2012. Evidence for classifying metathesis patterns as subsequential. In *The Proceedings of the 29th West Coast Conference on Formal Linguistics*, Somerville, MA. Cascadilla.

Jane Chandlee. 2014. *Strictly Local Phonological Processes*. Ph.D. thesis, University of Delaware.

Noam Chomsky and Morris Halle. 1968. *The Sound Pattern of English*. Harper & Row, New York.

Colin de la Higuera. 1997. Characteristic sets for polynomial grammatical inference. *Machine Learning*, 27(2):125–138.

Colin de la Higuera. 2010. *Grammatical Inference: Learning Automata and Grammars*. Cambridge University Press.

Brian Gainor, Regine Lai, and Jeffrey Heinz. 2012. Computational characterizations of vowel harmony patterns and pathologies. In *The Proceedings of the 29th West Coast Conference on Formal Linguistics*, pages 63–71, Somerville, MA. Cascadilla.

Daniel Gildea and Daniel Jurafsky. 1996. Learning bias and phonological-rule induction. *Computational Linguistics*, 22(4):497–530.

E. Mark Gold. 1967. Language identification in the limit. *Information and Control*, 10:447–474.

Gunnar Hansson. 2001. *Theoretical and Typological Issues in Consonant Harmony*. Ph.D. thesis, University of California, Berkeley.

Jeffrey Heinz and Regine Lai. 2013. Vowel harmony and subsequentiality. In Andras Kornai and Marco Kuhlmann, editors, *Proceedings of the 13th Meeting on the Mathematics of Language (MoL 13)*, pages 52–63.

Jeffrey Heinz, Chetan Rawal, and Herbert G. Tanner. 2011. Tier-based Strictly Local constraints for phonology. In *Proceedings of the 49th Annual Meeting of the Association for Computational Linguistics*, pages 58–64. Association for Computational Linguistics.

Jeffrey Heinz. 2007. *The Inductive Learning of Phonotactic Patterns*. Ph.D. thesis, University of California, Los Angeles.

Jeffrey Heinz. 2009. On the role of locality in learning stress patterns. *Phonology*, 26:303–351.

Jeffrey Heinz. 2010. Learning long-distance phonotactics. *Linguistic Inquiry*, 41:623–661.

Mans Hulden, Iñaki Alegria, Izaskun Etxeberria, and Montse Maritxalar. 2011. Learning word-level dialectal variation as phonological replacement rules using a limited parallel corpus. In *Proceedings of the First Workshop on Algorithms and Resources for Modelling of Dialects and Language Varieties*, DIALECTS '11, pages 39–48. Association for Computational Linguistics.

Mans Hulden. 2009. *Finite-State Machine Construction Methods and Algorithms for Phonology and Morphology*. Ph.D. thesis, University of Arizona.

Adam Jardine. 2013. Tone is (computationally) different. Unpublished manuscript, University of Delaware.

C. Douglas Johnson. 1972. *Formal Aspects of Phonological Description*. The Hague, Mouton.

Brian D. Joseph and Irene Philippaki-Warburton. 1987. *Modern Greek*. Croom Helm, Wolfeboro, NH.

Ronald M. Kaplan and Martin Kay. 1994. Regular models of phonological rule systems. *Computational Linguistics*, 20:371–387.

Huan Luo. 2013. Long-distance consonant harmony and subsequentiality. Unpublished manuscript, University of Delaware.

Robert McNaughton and Seymour A. Papert. 1971. *Counter-Free Automata*. MIT Press.

Mehryar Mohri. 1997. Finite-state transducers in language and speech processing. *Computational Linguistics*, 23:269–311.

José Oncina and Pedro García. 1991. Inductive learning of subsequential functions. Technical Report DSIC II-34, University Politécnia de Valencia.

José Oncina and Miguel A. Varò. 1996. Using domain information during the learning of a subsequential transducer. *Lecture Notes in Computer Science - Lecture Notes in Artificial Intelligence*, pages 313–325.

José Oncina, Pedro García, and Enrique Vidal. 1993. Learning subsequential transducers for pattern recognition interpretation tasks. *IEEE Transactions on Pattern Analysis and Machine Intelligence*, 15(5):448–457.

Amanda Payne. 2013. Dissimilation as a subsequential process. Unpublished manuscript, University of Delaware.

Alan Prince and Paul Smolensky. 1993. Optimality Theory: Constraint interaction in generative grammar. Technical Report 2, Rutgers University Center for Cognitive Science.

Jason Riggle. 2003. Non-local reduplication. In *Proceedings of the 34th Annual Meeting of the North Eastern Linguistic Society*.

James Rogers and Geoffrey K. Pullum. 2011. Aural pattern recognition experiments and the subregular hierarchy. *Journal of Logic, Language and Information*, 20:329–342.

James Rogers, Jeffrey Heinz, Margaret Fero, Jeremy Hurst, Dakotah Lambert, and Sean Wibel. 2013. Cognitive and sub-regular complexity. In Glyn Morrill and Mark-Jan Nederhof, editors, *Formal Grammar, Lecture Notes in Computer Science*, volume 8036, pages 90–108. Springer.

Sharon Rose and Rachel Walker. 2004. A typology of consonant agreement as correspondence. *Language*, 80:475–531.

Keiichiro Suzuki. 1998. *A Typological Investigation of Dissimilation*. Ph.D. thesis, University of Arizona.

Natasha Warner, Allard Jongman, Anne Cutler, and Doris Mücke. 2001. The phonological status of Dutch epenthetic schwa. *Phonology*, 18:387–420.

Joint Modeling of Opinion Expression Extraction and Attribute Classification

Bishan Yang
Department of Computer Science
Cornell University
bishan@cs.cornell.edu

Claire Cardie
Department of Computer Science
Cornell University
cardie@cs.cornell.edu

Abstract

In this paper, we study the problems of opinion expression extraction and expression-level polarity and intensity classification. Traditional fine-grained opinion analysis systems address these problems in isolation and thus cannot capture interactions among the textual spans of opinion expressions and their opinion-related properties. We present two types of joint approaches that can account for such interactions during 1) both learning and inference or 2) only during inference. Extensive experiments on a standard dataset demonstrate that our approaches provide substantial improvements over previously published results. By analyzing the results, we gain some insight into the advantages of different joint models.

1 Introduction

Automatic extraction of opinions from text has attracted considerable attention in recent years. In particular, significant research has focused on extracting detailed information for opinions at the fine-grained level, e.g. identifying opinion expressions within a sentence and predicting phrase-level polarity and intensity. The ability to extract fine-grained opinion information is crucial in supporting many opinion-mining applications such as opinion summarization, opinion-oriented question answering and opinion retrieval.

In this paper, we focus on the problem of identifying opinion expressions and classifying their attributes. We consider as an opinion expression any subjective expression that explicitly or implicitly conveys emotions, sentiment, beliefs, opinions (i.e. private states) (Wiebe et al., 2005), and consider two key attributes — polarity and intensity — for characterizing the opinions. Consider the sentence in Figure 1, for example. The phrases "a bias in favor of" and "being severely criticized" are opinion expressions containing positive sentiment with medium intensity and negative sentiment with high intensity, respectively.

Most existing approaches tackle the tasks of opinion expression extraction and attribute classification in isolation. The first task is typically formulated as a sequence labeling problem, where the goal is to label the boundaries of text spans that correspond to opinion expressions (Breck et al., 2007; Yang and Cardie, 2012). The second task is usually treated as a binary or multi-class classification problem (Wilson et al., 2005; Choi and Cardie, 2008; Yessenalina and Cardie, 2011), where the goal is to assign a class label to a text fragment (e.g. a phrase or a sentence). Solutions to the two tasks can be applied in a pipeline architecture to extract opinion expressions and their attributes. However, pipeline systems suffer from error propagation: opinion expression errors propagate and lead to unrecoverable errors in attribute classification.

Limited work has been done on the joint modeling of opinion expression extraction and attribute classification. Choi and Cardie (2010) first proposed a joint sequence labeling approach to extract opinion expressions and label them with polarity and intensity. Their approach treats both expression extraction and attribute classification as token-level se-

Transactions of the Association for Computational Linguistics, vol. 2, pp. 505–516, 2014. Action Editor: Janyce Wiebe.
Submitted 4/2014; Revised 8/2014; Published November 1, 2014.

He demonstrated a bias in favor of $_{medium}$ the rebels despite being severely criticized $_{high}$.

Figure 1: An example sentence annotated with opinion expressions and their polarity and intensity. We use colored boxes to mark the textual spans of opinion expressions where green (red) denotes positive (negative) polarity, and use subscripts to denote intensity.

quence labeling tasks, and thus cannot model the label distribution over expressions even though the annotations are given at the expression level. Johansson and Moschitti (2011) considered a pipeline of opinion extraction followed by polarity classification and propose re-ranking its k-best outputs using global features. One key issue, however, is that the approach enumerates the k-best output in a pipeline manner and thus they do not necessarily correspond to the k-best global decisions. Moreover, as the number of opinion attributes grows, it is not clear how to identify the best k for each attribute.

In contrast to existing approaches, we formulate opinion expression extraction as a segmentation problem and attribute classification as segment-level attribute labeling. To capture their interactions, we present two types of joint approaches: (1) *joint learning* approaches, which combine opinion segment detection and attribute labeling into a single probabilistic model, and estimate parameters for this joint model; and (2) *joint inference* approaches, which build separate models for opinion segment detection and attribute labeling at training time, and jointly apply these (via a single objective function) only at test time to identify the best "combined" decision of the two models.

To investigate the effectiveness of our approaches, we conducted extensive experiments on a standard corpus for fine-grained opinion analysis (the MPQA corpus (Wiebe et al., 2005)). We found that all of our proposed approaches provide substantial improvements over the previously published results. We also compared our approaches to a strong pipeline baseline and observed that joint learning results in a significant boost in precision while joint inference, with an appropriate objective, can significantly boost both precision and recall and obtain the best overall performance. Error analysis provides additional understanding of the differences between the joint learning and joint inference approaches, and suggests that joint inference can be more effective and more efficient for the task in practice.

2 Related Work

Significant research effort has been invested in the task of fine-grained opinion analysis in recent years (Wiebe et al., 2005; Wilson et al., 2009). Wilson et al. (2005) first motivated and studied phrase-level polarity classification on an open-domain corpus. Choi and Cardie (2008) developed inference rules to capture compositional effects at the lexical level on phrase-level polarity classification. Yessenalina and Cardie (2011) and Socher et al. (2013) learn continuous-valued phrase representations by combining the representations of words within an opinion expression and using them as features for classifying polarity and intensity. All of these approaches assume the opinion expressions are available before training the classifiers. However, in real-world settings, the spans of opinion expressions within the sentence are not available. In fact, Choi and Cardie (2008) demonstrated that the performance of expression-level polarity classification degrades as more surrounding (but irrelevant) context is considered. This motivates the additional task of identifying the spans of opinion expressions.

Opinion expression extraction has been successfully tackled via sequence tagging methods. Breck et al. (2007) applied conditional random fields to assign each token a label indicating whether it belongs to an opinion expression or not. Yang and Cardie (2012) employed a segment-level sequence labeler based on semi-CRFs with rich phrase-level syntactic features. In this work, we also utilize semi-CRFs to model opinion expression extraction.

There has been limited work on the joint modeling of opinion expression extraction and attribute classification. Choi and Cardie (2010) first developed a joint sequence labeler that jointly tags opinions, polarity and intensity by training CRFs with hierarchical features (Zhao et al., 2008). One major drawback of their approach is that it models both opinion extraction and attribute labeling as tasks in token-level sequence labeling, and thus cannot model their interactions at the expression-level. Johansson and Moschitti (2011) and Johansson and Moschitti (2013) propose a joint approach to opinion expression extraction and polarity classification by re-ranking its k-best output using global features. One major issue with their approach is that the k-best candidates were obtained without global reasoning about the relative uncertainty in the individual stages. As the number of considered attributes grows, it also becomes harder to decide how many predictions to select from each attribute classifier.

Compared to the existing approaches, our joint models have the advantage of modeling opinion expression extraction and attribute classification at the segment-level, and more importantly, they provide a principled way of combining the segmentation and classification components.

Our work follows a long line of joint modeling research that has demonstrated great success for various NLP tasks (Roth and Yih, 2004; Punyakanok et al., 2004; Finkel and Manning, 2010; Rush et al., 2010; Choi et al., 2006; Yang and Cardie, 2013). Methods tend to fall into one of two joint modeling frameworks: the first learns a joint model that captures global dependencies; the other uses independently-learned models and considers global dependencies only during inference. In this work, we study both types of joint approaches for opinion expression extraction and opinion attribute classification.

3 Approach

In this section, we present our approaches for the joint modeling of opinion expression extraction and attribute classification. Specifically, given a sentence, our goal is to identify the spans of opinion expressions, and simultaneously assign their polarity and intensity. Training data consists of a collection of sentences with manually annotated opinion expression spans, each associated with a polarity label that takes values from {*positive, negative, neutral*}, and an intensity label, taking values from {*high, medium, low*}.

In the following, we first describe how we model opinion expression extraction as a segment-level sequence labeling problem and model attribute prediction as a classification problem. Then we propose our joint models for combining opinion segmentation and attribute classification.

3.1 Opinion Expression Extraction

The problem of opinion expression extraction assumes tokenized sentences as input and outputs the spans of the opinion expressions in each sentence. Previous work has tackled this problem using token-based sequence labeling methods such as CRFs (e.g. Breck et al. (2007), Yang and Cardie (2012)). However, semi-Markov CRFs (Sarawagi and Cohen, 2004) (henceforth *semi-CRF*) have been shown more appropriate for the task than CRFs since they allow contiguous spans in the input sequence (e.g. a noun phrase) to be treated as a group rather than as distinct tokens. Thus, they can easily capture segment-level information like syntactic constituent structure (Yang and Cardie, 2012). Therefore we adopt the semi-CRF model for opinion expression extraction here.

Given a sentence $\mathbf{x}$, denote an opinion segmentation as $\mathbf{y_s} = \langle(s_0, b_0), ..., (s_k, b_k)\rangle$, where the $s_{0:k}$ are consecutive segments that form a segmentation of $\mathbf{x}$; each segment $s_i = (t_i, u_i)$ consists of the positions of the start token t_i and an end token u_i; and each s_i is associated with a binary variable $b_i \in \{I, O\}$, which indicates whether it is an opinion expression (I) or not (O). Take the sentence in Figure 1, for example. The corresponding opinion segmentation is $\mathbf{y_s} = \langle((0,0),O),((1,1),O),((2,6),I),((7,8),O),((9,9),O),((10,12),I),((13,13),O)\rangle$, where each segment corresponds to an opinion expression or to a phrase unit that does not express any opinion.

Using a semi-Markov CRF, we model the conditional distribution over all possible opinion segmentations given the input $\mathbf{x}$:

$$P(\mathbf{y_s}|\mathbf{x}) = \frac{\exp\{\sum_{i=1}^{|\mathbf{y_s}|} \theta \cdot f(y_{s_i}, y_{s_{i-1}}, \mathbf{x})\}}{\sum_{\mathbf{y'_s}\in\mathcal{Y}} \exp\{\sum_{i=1}^{|\mathbf{y'_s}|} \theta \cdot f(y'_{s_i}, y'_{s_{i-1}}, \mathbf{x})\}} \quad (1)$$

where θ denotes the model parameters, $y_{s_i} = (s_i, b_i)$ and f denotes a feature function that encodes the potentials of the boundaries for opinion segments and the potentials of transitions between two consecutive labeled segments.

Note that the probability is normalized over all possible opinion segmentations. To reduce the training complexity, we adopted the method described in Yang and Cardie (2012), which only normalizes over segment candidates that are plausible according to the parsing structure of the sentence. Figure 2 shows some candidate segmentations generated for an example sentence. Such a technique results in a large reduction in training time and was shown to be effective for identifying opinion expressions.

The standard training objective of a semi-CRF, is to minimize the log loss

$$L(\theta) = \arg\min_{\theta} - \sum_{i=1}^{N} \log P(\mathbf{y_s^{(i)}} | \mathbf{x}^{(i)}) \quad (2)$$

It penalizes any predicted opinion expression whose boundaries do not exactly align with the boundaries of the correct opinion expressions using 0-1 loss. Unfortunately, exact boundary matching is often not used as an evaluation metric for opinion expression extraction since it is hard for human annotators to agree on the exact boundaries of opinion expressions.[1] Most previous work used *proportional matching* (Johansson and Moschitti, 2013) as it takes into account the overlapping proportion of the predicted and the correct opinion expressions to compute precision and recall. To incorporate this evaluation metric into training, we use softmax-margin (Gimpel and Smith, 2010) that replace $P(\mathbf{y_s^{(i)}}|\mathbf{x}^{(i)})$ in (2) with $P_{cost}(\mathbf{y_s^{(i)}}|\mathbf{x}^{(i)})$, which equals

$$\frac{\exp\{\sum_{i=1}^{|\mathbf{y_s}|} \theta \cdot f(y_{s_i}, y_{s_{i-1}}, \mathbf{x})\}}{\sum_{\mathbf{y'_s} \in \mathcal{Y}} \exp\{\sum_{i=1}^{|\mathbf{y'_s}|} \theta \cdot f(y'_{s_i}, y'_{s_{i-1}}, \mathbf{x}) + l(\mathbf{y'_s}, \mathbf{y_s})\}}$$

and we define the loss function $l(\mathbf{y'_s}, \mathbf{y_s})$ as

$$\sum_{i=1}^{|\mathbf{y'_s}|} \sum_{j=1}^{|\mathbf{y_s}|} (\mathbb{1}\{b'_i \neq b_j \wedge b'_i \neq O\} \frac{|s_j \cap s'_i|}{|s'_i|} + \mathbb{1}\{b'_i \neq b_j \wedge b_j \neq O\} \frac{|s_j \cap s'_i|}{|s_j|})$$

which is the sum of the precision and recall errors of segment labeling using proportional matching. The loss-augmented probability is only computed during training. The more the proposed labeled segmentation overlaps with the true labeled segmentation for $\mathbf{x}$, the less it will be penalized.

[1]The inter-annotator agreement on boundaries of opinion expressions is not stressed in MPQA (Wiebe et al., 2005).

```
We hope to eradicate the eternal scourge of corruption .
[  ][    ][ ][       ][                  ][ ][         ][]
[  ][    ][ ][       ][                  ][            ][]
[  ][    ][ ][                           ][            ][]
[  ][    ][ ][                                         ][]
```

Figure 2: Examples of Segmentation Candidates

During inference, we can obtain the best labeled segmentation by solving

$$\underset{\mathbf{y_s}}{\text{argmax}} P(\mathbf{y_s}|\mathbf{x}) = \underset{\mathbf{y_s}}{\text{argmax}} \sum_{i=1}^{|\mathbf{y_s}|} \theta \cdot f(y_{s_i}, y_{s_{i-1}}, \mathbf{x})$$

This can be done efficiently via dynamic programming:

$$V(t) = \underset{s=(u,t) \in s_{:t}, y=(s,b), y'}{\text{argmax}} G(y, y') + V(u-1) \quad (3)$$

where $s_{:t}$ denotes all candidate segments ending at position t and $G(y, y') = \theta \cdot f(y, y', \mathbf{x})$. The optimal $\mathbf{y_s}^*$ can be obtained by computing $V(n)$, where n is the length of the sentence.

3.2 Opinion Attribute Classification

We consider two types of opinion attributes: *polarity* and *intensity*. For each attribute, we model the multinomial distribution of an attribute class given a text segment Denoting the class variable for each attribute as a^j, we have

$$P(a^j | \mathbf{x}_s) = \frac{\exp\{\phi_j \cdot g_j(a^j, \mathbf{x}_s)\}}{\sum_{a' \in \mathcal{A}_j} \exp\{\phi_j \cdot g_j(a', \mathbf{x}_s)\}} \quad (4)$$

where x_s denotes a text segment, ϕ_j is a parameter vector and g_j denotes feature functions for attribute a^j. The label space for polarity classification is $\{positive, negative, neutral, \varnothing\}$ and the label space for intensity classification is $\{high, medium, low, \varnothing\}$. We include an empty value $\varnothing$ to denote assigning no attribute value to those text segments that are not opinion expressions.

In the following description of our joint models, we omit the superscript on the attribute variable and derive our models with one single opinion attribute for simplicity. The derivations can be carried through with more than one opinion attribute by assuming the independence of different attributes.

3.3 The Joint Models

We propose two types of joint models for opinion segmentation and attribute classification: (1) *joint learning* models, which train a single sequence labeling model that maximizes a joint probability distribution over segmentation and attribute labeling, and infers the most probable labeled segmentations according to the joint probability; and (2) *joint inference* models, which train a sequence labeling model for opinion segmentation and separately train classification models for attribute labeling, and combine the segmentation and classification models during inference to make global decisions. In the following, we first present the joint learning models and then introduce the joint inference models.

3.3.1 Joint Sequence Labeling

We can formulate joint opinion segmentation and classification as a sequence labeling problem on the label space $\mathcal{Y} = \{\mathbf{y}|\mathbf{y} = \langle(s_0, \tilde{b}_0), ..., (s_k, \tilde{b}_k)\rangle\}$ where $\tilde{b}_i = (b_i, a_i) \in \{I, O\} \times \mathcal{A}$, where b_i is a binary variable as described before and a_i is an attribute class variable associated with segment s_i. Since only opinion expressions should be assigned opinion attributes, we consider the following labeling constraints: $a_i = \varnothing$ if and only if $b_i = O$.

We can apply the same training and inference procedure described in Section 3.1 by replacing the label space $\mathbf{y_s}$ with the joint label space $\mathbf{y}$. Note that the feature functions are shared over the joint label space. For the loss function in the loss-augmented objective, the opinion segment label b is also replaced with the augmented label $\tilde{b}$.

3.3.2 Hierarchical Joint Sequence Labeling

The above joint sequence labeling model does not explicitly model the dependencies between opinion segmentation and attribute labeling. The two subtasks share the same set of features and parameters. In the following, we introduce an alternative approach that explicitly models the conditional dependency between opinion segmentation and attribute labeling, and allows segmentation- and attribute-specific parameters to be jointly learned in one single model.

Note that the joint label space naturally forms a hierarchical structure: the probability of choosing a sequence label $\mathbf{y}$ can be interpreted as the probability of first choosing an opinion segmentation $\mathbf{y_s} = \langle(s_0, b_0), ..., (s_k, b_k)\rangle$ given the input $\mathbf{x}$, and then choose a sequence of attribute labels $\mathbf{y_a} = \langle a_0, ..., a_k\rangle$ given the chosen segment sequence. Following this intuition, the joint probability can be decomposed as

$$P(\mathbf{y}|\mathbf{x}) = P(\mathbf{y_s}|\mathbf{x})P(\mathbf{y_a}|\mathbf{y_s}, \mathbf{x})$$

where $P(\mathbf{y_s}|\mathbf{x})$ is modeled as Equation (1) and

$$\begin{aligned} P(\mathbf{y_a}|\mathbf{y_s}, \mathbf{x}) &= \prod_{i=1}^{|\mathbf{y_s}|} P(a_i|y_{s_i}, \mathbf{x}) \\ &\propto \exp\{\sum_{i=1}^{|\mathbf{y_s}|} \phi \cdot g(a_i, y_{s_i}, \mathbf{x})\} \end{aligned}$$

where g denotes a feature function that encodes attribute-specific information for discriminating different attribute classes for each segment.

For training, we can also apply a softmax-margin by adding a loss function $l(\mathbf{y}', \mathbf{y})$ to the denominator of $P(\mathbf{y}|\mathbf{x})$ (as in the basic joint sequence labeling model described in Section 3.3.1).

With the estimated parameters, we can infer the optimal opinion segmentation and attribute labeling by solving

$$\underset{\mathbf{y_s}, \mathbf{y_a}}{\operatorname{argmax}} P(\mathbf{y_s}|\mathbf{x})P(\mathbf{y_a}|\mathbf{y_s}, \mathbf{x})$$

We can apply a similar dynamic programming procedure by replaceing y in Equation (3) with $y = (s, b, a)$ and $G(y, y')$ with $\theta \cdot f(y, y', \mathbf{x}) + \phi \cdot g(y, \mathbf{x})$.

Our decomposition of labels and features is similar to the hierarchical construction of CRF features in Choi and Cardie (2010). The difference is that our model is based on semi-CRFs and the decomposition is based on a joint probability. We will show that this results in better performance than the methods in Choi and Cardie (2010) in our experiments.

3.3.3 Joint Inference

Modeling the joint probability of opinion segmentation and attribute labeling is arguably elegant. However, training can be expensive as the computation involves normalizing over all possible segmentations and all possible attribute labelings for each segment. Thus, we also investigate joint inference approaches which combine the separately-trained models during inference without computing the normalization term.

For opinion segmentation, we train a semi-CRF-based model using the approach described in Section 1. For attribute classification, we train a MaxEnt model by maximizing $P(a^j|\mathbf{x}_s)$ in Equation (4). As we only need to estimate the probability of an attribute label given individual text segments, the training data can be constructed by collecting a list of text segments labeled with correct attribute labels. The text segments do not need to form all possible sentence segmentations. To construct such training examples, we collected from each sentence all opinion expressions labeled with their corresponding attributes and use the remaining text segments as examples for the empty attribute value. The training of the MaxEnt model is much more efficient than the training of the segmentation model.

Joint Inference with Probability-based Estimates To combine the separately-trained models at inference time, a natural inference objective is to jointly maximize the probability of opinion segmentation and the probability of attribute labeling given the chosen segmentation

$$\underset{\mathbf{y_s},\mathbf{y_a}}{\text{argmax}} P(\mathbf{y_s}|\mathbf{x})P'(\mathbf{y_a}|\mathbf{y_s},\mathbf{x}) \tag{5}$$

We approximate the conditional probability as

$$P'(\mathbf{y_a}|\mathbf{y_s},\mathbf{x}) = \prod_{i=1}^{|\mathbf{y_s}|} P(a_i|\mathbf{x}_{s_i})^{\alpha} \tag{6}$$

where $\alpha \in (0,1]$. We found that $\alpha < 1$ provides better performance than $\alpha = 1$ empirically. This is an approximation since the distribution of attribute labeling is estimated independently from the opinion segmentation during training.

Joint Inference with Loss-based Estimates Instead of directly using the output probabilities of the attribute classifiers, we explore an alternative that estimates $P'(\mathbf{y_a}|\mathbf{y_s},\mathbf{x})$ based on the prediction uncertainty:

$$P'(\mathbf{y_a}|\mathbf{y_s},\mathbf{x}) \propto \exp(-\alpha \sum_{i=1}^{|\mathbf{y_s}|} U(a_i|\mathbf{x}_{s_i})) \tag{7}$$

where $U(a_i|\mathbf{x}_{s_i})$ is a uncertainty function that measures the classification model's uncertainty in its assignment of attribute class a_i to segment $\mathbf{x}_{s_i}$. Intuitively, we want to penalize attribute assignments that are uncertain or favor attribute assignments with low uncertainty. The prediction uncertainty is measured using the expected loss. The expected loss for a predicted label a' can be written as

$$E_{a|\mathbf{x}_{s_i}}[l(a,a')] = \sum_a P(a|\mathbf{x}_{s_i})l(a,a')$$

where $l(a,a')$ is a loss function over a' and the true label a. We used the standard 0-1 loss function in our experiments[2] and set $U(a_i|\mathbf{x}_{s_i}) = \log(E_{a|\mathbf{x}_{s_i}}[l(a,a_i)])$.

Both joint inference objectives can be solved efficiently via dynamic programming.

4 Features

We consider a set of basic features as well as task-specific features for opinion segmentation and attribute labeling, respectively.

4.1 Basic Features

Unigrams: word unigrams and POS tag unigrams for all tokens in the segment candidate.
Bigrams: word bigrams and POS bigrams within the segment candidate.
Phrase embeddings: for each segment candidate, we associate with it a 300-dimensional phrase embedding as a dense feature representation for the segment. We make use of the recently published word embeddings trained on Google News (Mikolov et al., 2013). For each segment, we compute the average of the word embedding vectors that comprise the phrase. We omit words that are not found in the vocabulary. If no words are found in the text segment, we assign a feature vector of zeros.
Opinion lexicon: For each word in the segment candidate, we include its polarity and intensity as indicated in an existing Subjectivity Lexicon (Wilson et al., 2005).

[2]The loss function can be tuned to better tradeoff precision and recall according to the applications at hand. We did not explore this option in this paper.

4.2 Segmentation-specific Features

Boundary words and POS tags: word-level features (words, POS, lexicon) before and after the segment candidate.

Phrase structure: the syntactic categories of the deepest constituents that cover the segment in the parse tree, e.g. NP, VP, TO_VB.

VP patterns: VP-related syntactic patterns described in Yang and Cardie (2012), e.g. VPsubj, VParg, which have been shown useful for opinion expression extraction.

4.3 Polarity-specific Features

Polarity count: counts of positive, negative and neutral words within the segment candidate according to the opinion lexicon.

Negation: indicator for negators within the segment candidate.

4.4 Intensity-specific Features

Intensity count: counts of words with strong and weak intensity within the segment candidate according to the opinion lexicon.

Intensity dictionary: As suggested in Choi and Cardie (2010), we include features indicating whether the segment contains an intensifier (e.g. highly, really), a diminisher (e.g. little, less), a strong modal verb (e.g. must, will), and a weak modal verb (e.g. may, could).

5 Experiments

All our experiments were conducted on the MPQA corpus (Wiebe et al., 2005), a widely used corpus for fine-grained opinion analysis. We used the same evaluation setting as in Choi and Cardie (2010), where 135 documents were used for development and 10-fold cross-validation was performed on a different set of 400 documents. Each training fold consists of sentences labeled with opinion expression boundaries and each expression is labeled with polarity and intensity. Table 1 shows some statistics of the evaluation data.

We used precision, recall and F1 as evaluation metrics for opinion extraction and computed them using both *proportional matching* and *binary matching* criteria. *Proportional matching* considers the overlapping proportion of a predicted expression s and a gold standard expression s^*, and computes precision as $\sum_{s\in S}\sum_{s^*\in S^*}\frac{|s\cap s^*|}{|s|}/|S|$ and recall as $\sum_{s\in S}\sum_{s^*\in S^*}\frac{|s\cap s^*|}{|s^*|}/|S^*|$, where S and S^* denote the set of predicted opinion expressions and the set of correct opinion expressions, respectively. *Binary matching* is a more relaxed metric that considers a predicted opinion expression to be correct if it overlaps with a correct opinion expression.

We experimented with the following models:

(1) PIPELINE: first extracts the spans of opinion expressions using the semi-CRF model in Section 3.1, and then assigns polarity and intensity to the extracted opinion expressions using MaxEnt models in Section 3.2. Note that the label space of the MaxEnt models does not include $\varnothing$ since they assume that all the opinion expressions extracted by the previous stage are correct.

(2) JSL: the joint sequence labeling method described in Section 3.3.1.

(3) HJSL: the hierarchical joint sequence labeling method described in Section 3.3.2.

(4) JI-PROB: the joint inference method using probability-based estimates (Equation 6).

(5) JI-LOSS: the joint inference method using loss-based estimates (Equation 7).

We also compare our results with previously published results from Choi and Cardie (2010) on the same task.

All our models are log linear models. We use L-BFGS with L2 regularization for training and set the regularization parameter to 1.0. We set the scaling parameter α in JI-PROB and JI-LOSS via grid search over values between 0.1 and 1 with increments of 0.1 using the development set.

We consider the same set of features described in Section 4 in all the models. For the pipeline and joint inference models where the opinion segmentator and attribute classifiers are separately trained, we employ basic features plus segmentation-specific features in the opinion segmentator; and employ basic features plus attribute-specific features in the attribute classifiers.

5.1 Results

We would like to first investigate how much we can gain from using the loss-augmented training compared to using the standard training objective. Loss-

Number of Opinion Expressions		
Positive	Negative	Neutral
2170	4863	6368
High	Medium	Low
2805	5721	4875

Number of Documents	400
Number of Sentences	8241
Average Length of Opinion Expressions	2.86 words

Table 1: Statistics of the evaluation corpus

augmented training can be applied to the training of the opinion segmentation model used in the pipeline method and the joint inference methods, or be applied to the training of the joint sequence labeling approaches, JSL and HJSL (the loss function takes into account both the span overlap and the matching of attribute values). We evaluate two versions of each method: one uses loss-augmented training and one uses standard log-loss training. Table 2 shows the results of opinion expression detection without evaluating their attributes. Similar trends can be observed in the results of opinion expression detection with respect to each attribute. We can see that incorporating the evaluation-metric-based loss function during training consistently improves the performance for all models in terms of F1 measure. This confirms the effectiveness of loss-augmented training of our sequence models for opinion extraction. As a result, all following results are based on the loss-augmented version of our models.

Comparing the results of different models in Table 2, we can see that PIPELINE provides a strong baseline. In comparison, JSL and HJSL significantly improve precision but fail in recall, which indicates that joint sequence labeling is more conservative and precision-biased for extracting opinion expressions. HJSL significantly outperforms JSL, and this confirms the benefit of modeling the conditional dependency between opinion segmentation and attribute classification. In addition, we see that combining opinion segmentation and attribute classification without joint training (JI-PROB and JI-LOSS) hurt precision but improves recall (vs. JSL and HJSL). JI-LOSS presents the best F1 performance and significantly outperforms the PIPELINE baseline in all evaluation metrics. This suggests that JI-LOSS provides an effective joint inference objective and is able to provide more balanced precision and recall than other joint approaches.

Table 3 shows the performance on opinion extraction with respect to polarity and intensity attributes. Similarly, we can see that JI-LOSS outperforms all other baselines in F1; HJSL outperforms JSL but is slightly worse than PIPELINE in F1; JI-PROB is recall-oriented and less effective than JI-LOSS.

We hypothesize that the worse performance of joint sequence labeling is due to its strong assumption on the dependencies between opinion segmentation and attribute labeling in the training data. For example, the expression "fundamentally unfair and unjust" as a whole is labeled as an opinion expression with negative polarity. However, the subexpression "unjust" can be also viewed as a negative expression but it is not annotated as an opinion expression in this example (as MPQA does not consider nested opinion expressions). As a result, the model would wrongly prefer an empty attribute to the expression "unjust". However, in our joint inference approaches, the attribute classification models are trained independently from the segmentation model, and the training examples for the classifiers only consist of correctly labeled expressions ("unjust" as a nested opinion expression in this example would not be considered in the training data for the attribute classifier). Therefore, the joint inference approaches do not suffer from this issue. Although joint inference does not account for task dependencies during training, the promising performance of JI-LOSS demonstrates that modeling label dependencies during inference can be more effective than the PIPELINE baseline.

In Table 3, we can see that the improvement of JI-LOSS is less significant in the *positive* class and the *high* class. This is due to the lack of training data in these classes. The improvement in the *medium* class is also less significant. This may be because it is inherently harder to disambiguate *medium* from *low*. In general, we observe that extracting opinion expressions with correct intensity is a harder task than extracting opinion expressions with correct polarity.

Table 4 presents the F1 scores (due to space limit only F1 scores are reported) for all subtasks using the binary matching metric. We include the previously published results of Choi and Cardie (2010) for the same task using the same fold split and eval-

	Loss-augmented Training			Standard Training		
	P	R	F1	P	R	F1
PIPELINE	60.96	63.29	62.10	60.05	60.59	60.32
JSL	64.98†	54.60	59.29	67.09†	50.56	57.62
HJSL	**66.16***	56.77	61.05	**67.98†**	50.81	58.11
JI-PROB	50.95	**77.44***	61.32	50.06	**76.98***	60.54
JI-LOSS	63.77†	64.51†	**64.04***	64.97†	61.55†	**63.12***

Table 2: Opinion Expression Extraction (Proportional Matching). In all tables, we use **bold** to indicate the highest score among all the methods; use $*$ to indicate statistically significant improvements ($p < 0.05$) over all the other methods under the paired-t test; use † to denote statistically significance ($p < 0.05$) over the pipeline baseline.

	Positive			Negative			Neutral		
	P	R	F1	P	R	F1	P	R	F1
PIPELINE	45.26	43.07	44.04	50.59	47.91	49.11	40.98	49.30	44.57
JSL	**50.58†**	32.34	39.37	50.22	44.01	46.81	46.83†	39.81	42.85
HJSL	50.34†	37.06	42.59	53.29†	43.98	48.07	**47.29†**	43.27	45.03
JI-PROB	36.47	**47.81***	41.24	40.83	**54.40***	46.51	33.59	**59.22***	42.66
JI-LOSS	46.44†	44.58†	**45.40***	**54.88***	48.50	**51.40***	43.42†	52.02†	**47.09***
	High			Medium			Low		
	P	R	F1	P	R	F1	P	R	F1
PIPELINE	40.98	28.10	33.25	35.44	44.72	39.36	31.19	34.46	32.63
JSL	37.91	30.83†	**33.88**	**39.07†**	37.31	38.05	**40.95†**	26.71	32.24
HJSL	41.05	28.80	33.63	39.06†	39.71	39.17	40.01†	29.88	34.12
JI-PROB	34.82	**30.94†**	32.54	29.16	**50.89***	36.89	25.06	**42.99***	31.53
JI-LOSS	**46.11***	26.36	33.39	37.58†	43.58	**40.15***	33.85†	40.92†	**36.93***

Table 3: Opinion Extraction with Correct Attributes (Proportional Matching)

uation metric. CRF-JSL and CRF-HJSL are both joint sequence labeling methods based on CRFs. Different from JSL and HJSL, they perform sequence labeling at the token level instead of the segment level, and in HJSL, the decomposition of labels are not based on the decomposition of the joint probability of opinion segmentation and attribute labeling. We can see that both the pipeline and joint methods clearly outperform previous results in all evaluation criteria.[3] We can also see that JI-LOSS provides the best performance among all baselines.

5.1.1 Error Analysis

Joint vs. Pipeline We found that many errors made by the pipeline system are due to error propagation. Table 5 lists three examples, representing three types of the propagated errors:(1) the attribute classifiers miss the prediction since the opinion expression extractor fails to identify the opinion expression; (2) the attribute classifiers assign attributes to a non-opinionated expression since it was mistakenly extracted; (3) the attribute classifiers misclassify the attributes since the boundaries of opinion expressions are not correctly determined by the opinion expression extractor. Our joint models are able to correct many of these errors, such as the examples in Table 5, due to the modeling of the dependency between opinion expression extraction and attribute classification.

Joint Learning vs. Joint Inference Note that JSL and HJSL both employ joint learning while JI-PROB and JI-LOSS employ joint inference. To investigate the difference between these two types of joint models, we look into the errors made by HJSL and JI-LOSS. In general, we observed that HJSL extracts many fewer opinion expressions compared to JI-LOSS, and as a result, it presents high precision but low recall. The first two examples in Table 6

[3]Significance test was not conducted over the results in Choi and Cardie (2010) as we do not have their 10 fold results.

	Extraction	Positive	Negative	Neutral	High	Medium	Low
PIPELINE	73.30	51.50	58.45	52.45	39.34	47.08	39.05
JSL	69.76	45.24	57.11	50.25	41.48†	45.88	36.49
HJSL	71.43	49.08	58.38	52.25	41.06†	46.82	38.45
JI-PROB	74.37†	50.93	58.20	54.03†	39.80	46.65	40.73†
JI-LOSS	**75.11***	**53.02***	**62.01***	**54.33†**	**41.79†**	**47.38**	**42.53***
Previous work (Choi and Cardie (2010))							
CRF-JSL	60.5	41.9	50.3	41.2	38.4	37.6	28.0
CRF-HJSL	62.0	43.1	52.8	43.1	36.3	40.9	30.7

Table 4: Opinion Extraction Results (Binary Matching)

Example Sentences	**Pipeline**	**Joint Models**
It is the victim of an explosive situation $_{high}$ at the economic, ...	No opinions ×	✓
A white farmer who was shot dead Monday was the 10th to be killed.	the 10th to be killed $_{medium}$ ×	✓
They would " fall below minimum standards $_{medium}$ for humane $_{medium}$ treatment".	minimum standards for humane treatment $_{medium}$ ×	✓

Table 5: Examples of mistakes made by the pipeline baseline that are corrected by the joint models

are cases where HJSL gains in precision and loses in recall, respectively. The last example in Table 6 shows an error made by HJSL but corrected by JI-LOSS. Theoretically, joint learning is more powerful than joint inference as it models the task dependencies during training. However, we only observe improvements on precision and see drops in recall. As discussed before, we hypothesize that this is due to the mismatch of dependency assumptions between the model and the jointly annotated data. We found that joint inference can be superior to both pipeline and joint learning, and it is also much more efficient in training. In our experiments on an Amazon EC2 instance with 64-bit processor, 4 CPUs and 15GB memory, training for the joint learning approaches took one hour for each training fold, but only 5 minutes for the joint inference approaches.

5.2 Additional Experiments

5.2.1 Evaluation with Reranking

Previous work (Johansson and Moschitti, 2011) showed that reranking is effective in improving the pipeline of opinion expression extraction and polarity classification. We extended their approach to handle both polarity and intensity and investigated the effect of reranking on both the pipeline and joint models. For the pipeline model, we generated 64-best (distinct) output with 4-best labeling at each pipeline stage; for the joint models, we generated 50-best (distinct) output using Viterbi-like dynamic programming. We trained the reranker using the online PassiveAggressive algorithm (Crammer et al., 2006) as in Johansson and Moschitti (2013) with 100 iterations and a regularization constant $C = 0.01$. For features, we included the probability output by the base models, the polarity and intensity of each pair of extracted opinion expressions, and the word sequence and the POS sequence between the adjacent pairs of extracted opinion expressions.

Table 7 shows the reranking performance (F1) for all subtasks. We can see that after reranking, JI-LOSS still provides the best performance and HJSL achieves comparable performance to PIPELINE. We also found that reranking leads to less performance gain for the joint inference approaches than for the joint learning approaches. This is because the k-best output of JI-PROB and JI-LOSS present less diversity than JSL and HJSL. A similar issue for reranking has also been discussed in Finkel et al. (2006).

5.2.2 Evaluation on Sentence-level Tasks

As an additional experiment, we consider a supervised sentence-level sentiment classification task using features derived from the prediction output of different opinion extraction models. As a stan-

Example Sentences	JointLearn	JointInfer
The expression is undoubtedly strong and well thought out $_{high}$.	✓	well thought out $_{medium}$ ×
But the Sadc Ministerial Task Force said the election was free and fair $_{medium}$.	No opinions ×	✓
The president branded $_{high}$ as the "axis of evil" $_{high}$ in his statement ...	of evil $_{high}$ ×	✓

Table 6: Examples of mistakes that are made by the joint learning model but are corrected by the joint inference model and vice versa. We use the same colored box notation as before, and use yellow color to denote neutral sentiment.

	Extraction	Positive	Negative	Neutral	High	Medium	Low
PIPELINE + reranking	73.72	51.45	60.51	53.24	40.07	47.65	40.47
JSL + reranking	72.02	47.52	59.81	52.84	41.04†	46.58	39.40
HJSL + reranking	72.60	50.78	60.85	53.45	41.04†	47.75	40.08
JI-PROB + reranking	74.81†	51.45	59.59	53.98	40.66	46.87	40.80
JI-LOSS + reranking	**75.59**†	**53.29***	**62.50***	**54.94***	**41.79***	**47.67**	**42.66***

Table 7: Opinion Extraction with Reranking (Binary Matching)

Features	Acc	Positive	Negative	Neutral
BOW	65.26	51.90	77.47	36.41
PIPELINE-OP	67.41	55.49	79.42	39.48
JSL-OP	65.86	55.97	77.68	36.46
HJSL-OP	66.79	55.12	79.29	37.56
JI-PROB-OP	67.13	56.49	79.30	38.49
JI-LOSS-OP	**68.23***	**57.32***	**80.12***	**40.45***

Table 8: Sentence-level Sentiment Classification

dard baseline, we train a MaxEnt classifier using unigrams, bigrams and opinion lexicon features extracted from the sentence. Using the prediction output of an opinion extraction model, we construct features by using only words from the extracted opinion expressions, and include the predicted opinion attributes as additional features. We hypothesize that the more informative the extracted opinion expressions are, the more they can contribute to sentence-level sentiment classification as features. Table 8 shows the results in terms of classification accuracy and F1 score in each sentiment category. BOW is the standard MaxEnt baseline. We can see that using features constructed from the opinion expressions *always* improved the performance. This confirms the informativeness of the extracted opinion expressions. In particular, using the opinion expressions extracted by JI-LOSS gives the best performance among all the baselines in all evaluation criteria. This is consistent with its superior performance in our previous experiments.

6 Conclusion

We address the problem of opinion expression extraction and opinion attribute classification by presenting two types of joint models: joint learning, which optimizes the parameters of different subtasks in a joint probabilistic framework; joint inference, which optimizes the separately-trained models jointly during inference time. We show that our models achieve substantially better performance than the previously published results, and demonstrate that joint inference with an appropriate objective can be more effective and efficient than joint learning for the task. We also demonstrate the usefulness of output of our systems for sentence-level sentiment analysis tasks. For future work, we plan to improve joint modeling for the task by capturing semantic relations among different opinion expressions.

Acknowledgement

This work was supported in part by DARPA-BAA-12-47 DEFT grant #12475008 and NSF grant BCS-0904822. We thank the anonymous reviewers, Igor Labutov and the Cornell NLP Group for helpful suggestions.

References

E. Breck, Y. Choi, and C. Cardie. 2007. Identifying expressions of opinion in context. In *Proceedings of the international joint conference on Artifical intelligence*.

Yejin Choi and Claire Cardie. 2008. Learning with compositional semantics as structural inference for subsentential sentiment analysis. In *Proceedings of the Conference on Empirical Methods in Natural Language Processing*.

Yejin Choi and Claire Cardie. 2010. Hierarchical sequential learning for extracting opinions and their attributes. In *Proceedings of the Annual Meeting of the Association for Computational Linguistics - Short Papers*.

Yejin Choi, Eric Breck, and Claire Cardie. 2006. Joint extraction of entities and relations for opinion recognition. In *Proceedings of the Conference on Empirical Methods in Natural Language Processing*.

Koby Crammer, Ofer Dekel, Joseph Keshet, Shai Shalev-Shwartz, and Yoram Singer. 2006. Online passive-aggressive algorithms. *The Journal of Machine Learning Research*, 7:551–585.

Jenny Rose Finkel and Christopher D Manning. 2010. Hierarchical joint learning: Improving joint parsing and named entity recognition with non-jointly labeled data. In *Proceedings of the Annual Meeting of the Association for Computational Linguistics*.

Jenny Rose Finkel, Christopher D Manning, and Andrew Y Ng. 2006. Solving the problem of cascading errors: Approximate bayesian inference for linguistic annotation pipelines. In *Proceedings of the Conference on Empirical Methods in Natural Language Processing*.

Kevin Gimpel and Noah A Smith. 2010. Softmax-margin crfs: Training log-linear models with cost functions. In *Human Language Technologies: Conference of the North American Chapter of the Association for Computational Linguistics*.

Richard Johansson and Alessandro Moschitti. 2011. Extracting opinion expressions and their polarities: exploration of pipelines and joint models. In *Proceedings of the Association for Computational Linguistics: Human Language Technologies: short papers*.

Richard Johansson and Alessandro Moschitti. 2013. Relational features in fine-grained opinion analysis. *Computational Linguistics*, 39(3):473–509.

Tomas Mikolov, Ilya Sutskever, Kai Chen, Greg S Corrado, and Jeff Dean. 2013. Distributed representations of words and phrases and their compositionality. In *Advances in Neural Information Processing Systems*.

V. Punyakanok, D. Roth, W. Yih, and D. Zimak. 2004. Semantic role labeling via integer linear programming inference. In *Proceedings of the international conference on Computational Linguistics*.

D. Roth and W. Yih. 2004. *A linear programming formulation for global inference in natural language tasks*.

Alexander M Rush, David Sontag, Michael Collins, and Tommi Jaakkola. 2010. On dual decomposition and linear programming relaxations for natural language processing. In *Proceedings of the Conference on Empirical Methods in Natural Language Processing*.

Sunita Sarawagi and William W Cohen. 2004. Semi-markov conditional random fields for information extraction. In *Advances in Neural Information Processing Systems*.

Richard Socher, Alex Perelygin, Jean Y Wu, Jason Chuang, Christopher D Manning, Andrew Y Ng, and Christopher Potts. 2013. Recursive deep models for semantic compositionality over a sentiment treebank. In *Proceedings of the Conference on Empirical Methods in Natural Language Processing*.

J. Wiebe, T. Wilson, and C. Cardie. 2005. Annotating expressions of opinions and emotions in language. *Language Resources and Evaluation*, 39(2):165–210.

Theresa Wilson, Janyce Wiebe, and Paul Hoffmann. 2005. Recognizing contextual polarity in phrase-level sentiment analysis. In *Proceedings of the conference on human language technology and empirical methods in natural language processing*.

Theresa Wilson, Janyce Wiebe, and Paul Hoffmann. 2009. Recognizing contextual polarity: An exploration of features for phrase-level sentiment analysis. *Computational linguistics*, 35(3):399–433.

Bishan Yang and Claire Cardie. 2012. Extracting opinion expressions with semi-markov conditional random fields. In *Proceedings of the Joint Conference on Empirical Methods in Natural Language Processing and Computational Natural Language Learning*.

Bishan Yang and Claire Cardie. 2013. Joint inference for fine-grained opinion extraction. In *Proceedings of the Annual Meeting of the Association for Computational Linguistics*.

Ainur Yessenalina and Claire Cardie. 2011. Compositional matrix-space models for sentiment analysis. In *Proceedings of the Conference on Empirical Methods in Natural Language Processing*.

Jun Zhao, Kang Liu, and Gen Wang. 2008. Adding redundant features for crfs-based sentence sentiment classification. In *Proceedings of the conference on empirical methods in natural language processing*.

AUTHOR INDEX

AUTHOR INDEX